The Slavery Reader

The Slavery Reader brings together the most recent and essential writings on slavery. The focus is on Atlantic slavery – the enforced movement of millions of Africans from their homelands into the Americas, and the complex historical story of slavery in the Americas. Spanning almost five centuries – from the late fifteenth until the mid-nineteenth – the articles trace the range and impact of slavery on the modern Western world. Key themes include:

- The origins and development of American slavery
- Work
- Family, gender and community
- Slave culture
- Slave economy and material culture
- Resistance
- Race and social structure
- Africans in the Atlantic world

Together with the editors' clear and authoritative commentaries and substantial introductions to each part, this volume will become central to the study of slavery.

Contributors to this collection include: Hilary McD. Beckles, Ira Berlin, Edward Kamau Brathwaite, Cheryll Ann Cody, Michael Craton, Philip D. Curtin, David Eltis, Sylvia R. Frey, Herbert Gutman, Gad Heuman, Winthrop D. Jordan, Robin Law, Roderick A. McDonald, Kristin Mann, Patrick Manning, Woodville K. Marshall, Joseph C. Miller, Sidney W. Mintz, Philip D. Morgan, David Northrup, Edward A. Pearson, Richard Price, David Richardson, Stuart B. Schwartz, Verene Shepherd, Simon Smith, Daniel L. Schafer, Arnold A. Sio, John Thornton, Shane White, Graham White, Betty Wood and Peter H. Wood

Gad Heuman is Professor of History at the University of Warwick. His publications include *Between Black and White* and *The Killing Time*. He is editor of the journal *Slavery & Abolition*.
James Walvin is Professor of History at the University of York. His publications include *Black Ivory* and *Questioning Slavery*.

The
Slavery
Reader

Edited by

Gad Heuman and James Walvin

Routledge
Taylor & Francis Group

LONDON AND NEW YORK

First published 2003
by Routledge
2 Park Square, Milton Park, Abingdon, Oxon, OX14 4RN

Simultaneously published in the USA and Canada
by Routledge
711 Third Avenue, New York, NY 10017, USA

Routledge is an imprint of the Taylor & Francis Group, an informa business

© 2003 Selection and editorial material Gad Heuman and James Walvin;
individual chapters to their authors

Typeset in Bell Gothic and Perpetua by
Florence Production Ltd, Stoodleigh, Devon

All rights reserved. No part of this book may be reprinted or
reproduced or utilised in any form or by any electronic, mechanical,
or other means, now known or hereafter invented, including
photocopying and recording, or in any information storage or
retrieval system, without permission in writing from the
publishers.

British Library Cataloguing in Publication Data
A catalogue record for this book is available from the British Library

Library of Congress Cataloging in Publication Data
Heuman, Gad J.
    The slavery reader/Gad Heuman and James Walvin.
        p. cm.
    Includes bibliographical references and index.
    1. Slavery – United States – History.   2. Slavery – America – History.
    I. Walvin, James.   II. Title.
    E441 .H48 2003
    306.3′62′097–dc21   2002153075

ISBN 9780415213035 (hbk)
ISBN 9780415213042 (pbk)

Contents

Sources

S & A = Slavery & Abolition – publisher: Frank Cass
William & Mary Quarterly – publisher: Omohundro Institute of Early American History, Williamsburg, Virginia

Part One

1 Philip D. Curtin, 'Epidemiology and the Slave Trade' (1968), *Political Science Quarterly*, vol. 83 (The Academy of Political Science)
2 Patrick Manning, 'Why Africans? The Rise of the Slave Trade to 1700' (1990), in Patrick Manning, *Slavery and African Life: Occidental, Oriental, and African Slave Trades* (Cambridge University Press)
3 David Eltis and David Richardson, 'West Africa and the Transatlantic Slave Trade: New Evidence of Long-Run Trends' (1997), *S & A*, vol. 18, no. 1, April
4 David Eltis, 'Labour and Coercion in the English Atlantic World from the Seventeenth to the Early Twentieth Century' (1993), *S & A*, vol. 14, no. 1, April

Part Two

5 Stuart B. Schwartz, 'First Slavery: From Indian to African' (1985), in Stuart B. Schwartz, *Sugar Plantations in the Formation of Brazilian Society, Bahia, 1550–1834* (Cambridge University Press)
6 Michael Craton, 'Slavery and Slave Society in the British Caribbean' (1997), in Michael Craton, *Empire, Enslavement and Freedom in the Caribbean* (Ian Randle Publishers)
7 Winthrop D. Jordan, 'Modern Tensions and the Origins of American Slavery' (1962), *Journal of Southern History*, vol. 28 (The Southern Historical Association)
8 Ira Berlin, 'Time, Space, and the Evolution of Afro-American Society on British Mainland North America' (1980), *American Historical Review*, vol. 85, no. 1 (The American Historical Association)

Part Three

Part Four

Part Five

Part Six

Part Seven

Part Eight

Part Nine

Acknowledgements

The authors and publishers wish to thank the following for their permission to reproduce copyright material:

'Epidemiology and the Slave Trade' by Philip D. Curtin from *Political Science Quarterly*, vol. 83, no. 2 (1968), pp. 190–216 by permission of The Academy of Political Science; 'Why Africans? The Rise of the Slave Trade to 1700' from *Slavery and African Life: Occidental, Oriental, and African Slave Trades* (1990) by permission of Cambridge University Press and Patrick Manning; 'First Slavery, from Indian to African' from *Sugar Plantations in the Formation of Brazilian Society, Bahia, 1550–1834* by Stuart B. Schwartz by permission of Cambridge University Press and the author; 'Modern Tensions and the Origins of American Slavery' from *Journal of Southern History* vol. 28 by permission of The Southern Historical Association and Winthrop Jordan; 'Time, Space and the Evolution of Afro-American Society on British Mainland North America' from *American Historical Review*, vol. 85, no. 1 (1980) by permission of Ira Berlin; 'Work and Culture: The Task System and the World of Lowcountry Blacks 1700–1880', 'From Creole to African: Atlantic Creoles and the Origins of African-American Society in Mainland North America,' 'American Chiaroscuro: The Status and Definition of Mulattoes in the British Colonies', 'West Africa in the Atlantic Community: The Case of the Slave Coast' and 'The African Experience of the "20. and Odd Negroes" Arriving in Virginia in 1619' from *William & Mary Quarterly* by permission of the Omohundro Institute of Early American History and Culture; 'Black Labour – White Rice' from Peter H. Wood, *Black Majority: Negroes in Colonial South Carolina from 1670 through the Stono Rebellion* by permission of Alfred A. Knopf, a division of Random House Inc.; 'There Was No "Absalom" on the Ball Plantations: Slave-Naming Practices in the South Carolina Low Country, 1720–1865' by permission of Cheryll Ann Cody; 'The Significance of Kin' from Philip D. Morgan, *Slave Counterpoint: Black Culture in the Eighteenth-Century Chesapeake & Lowcountry* (1998) and 'The Americas: The Survival of African Religions' from Sylvia R. Frey and Betty Wood, *Come Shouting to Zion: African American Protestantism in the American South and British Caribbean to 1830* (1998) by permission of University of North Carolina Press; 'The Origins of the Jamaican Market System' from Sidney W. Mintz, *Caribbean Transformations* (1974) by permission of the author; Stuart B. Schwartz, 'Resistance and Accommodation in

Eighteenth-Century Brazil: The Slaves' View of Slavery', from *Hispanic American Historical Review*, vol. 57, no. 1, pp. 69–81 (1977) by permission of Duke University Press (all rights reserved); 'The Free Coloreds in Jamaican Slave Society' from Gad Heuman, *Between Black and White: Race, Politics, and the Free Coloreds in Jamaica, 1792–1865*, pp. 3–19, copyright 1981 Greenwood Publishing Group, Inc., Westport, CT.

Every effort has been made to obtain permission to reproduce copyright material. If any proper acknowledgement has not been made, we would invite copyright holders to inform us of the oversight.

Unfortunately, due to constraints of space it has proved impossible to reproduce in full the notes of several chapters. Readers anxious to consult such notes should refer to the original articles.

General Introduction

THERE ARE FEW AREAS of historical scholarship which have undergone so dramatic an expansion, in so short a period, as the study of slavery. So rapid and voluminous is the growth of historical literature in the field that even the specialist has trouble keeping up with the scholarly output. Each year the major scholarly journal devoted to slave studies, *Slavery & Abolition*, publishes a substantial bibliography devoted solely to scholarship published on slavery in the previous year. In addition, there has been an expanding public awareness of slavery, prompted in part by a number of popular books, television and movies. The subject has recently gained even greater prominence (and political attention) by the wide-ranging debate about reparations for slavery. There is, then, no doubt that slavery is very much in the public eye, and we hope that this volume will prove a timely addition to the continuing debate about the subject.

We need to explain what the book seeks to do. It is concerned with Atlantic slavery; with that extraordinary enforced movement of millions of Africans from their homelands to the Americas, and the complex historical story of slavery in the Americas. The story of black slavery is not, of course, the *only* slave experience. There are any number of societies, from the classical world to the modern, which command scholarly and political attention. This book, however, has a more specific focus and concentrates on African slavery in the Atlantic world between the late fifteenth and mid-nineteenth centuries. Yet even that provides a daunting undertaking.

Atlantic slavery is so complex a historical issue because of its range and impact, across both time and space. It involved three continents – Africa, the Americas and Europe – though it also had economic consequences much further afield. It spanned the best part of four centuries and had major ramifications on myriad different cultures, notably among the peoples of Africa and the native peoples of the Americas. We are still in the process of comprehending the extent of those consequences. In order to develop their tropical and semi-tropical colonies in the Americas, Europeans tried a number of labour systems: free, indentured, European, local Indian and a mix of all of them. But the development of the early sugar industry, first in Brazil, later in the Caribbean, with its labour-intensive plantation system of production, forced Europeans to look elsewhere for labour. They turned to Africa. And they quickly acquired an appetite for Africans as *slave* labourers. In retrospect, it seems an odd decision. Why transport Africans across the Atlantic to work in Brazil or the Caribbean, to produce luxury goods (sugar, initially) which Europeans had managed perfectly well without previously? Why African labour? Why slave labour? And why tropical produce?

Once established in its sugar enclaves, black slavery soon seeped into all corners of economic and social life throughout the settled Americas. Slaves came to be viewed as the natural and obvious means of labour for a host of different crops (tobacco and rice, for example) and were available, in time, to undertake any form of manual labour required by the slave-owning classes. As local societies and economies matured across the Americas, slaves could be found in all corners of local life, from highly skilled artisans to cowboys on the advancing frontiers, from nurses on plantations to sailors in the Atlantic merchant marine and navies. The number of Africans involved was vast, and though the great majority of those shipped across the Atlantic were destined to work in the sugar fields, others were quickly scattered around the extended lines of Atlantic commercial and migratory development. Africans and their descendants were to be found around the rim of the Atlantic, from Nova Scotia to Buenos Aires, from Liverpool to Luanda.

Black slavery was, then, an inescapable feature of life in the pre-modern Atlantic economy. Yet it is a curious fact that the importance of slavery (its size, its economic consequences and its cultural impact) has only been fully recognised in recent years. Even in those societies most obviously and directly influenced by slavery, notably the American societies transformed by the settlement of millions of Africans, slavery remained an oddly marginal topic for local historians. That changed, however, in the second half of the twentieth century, partly because of changing patterns of historical interests, but largely because of the related upheavals in contemporary black life throughout the Americas. The independence of former colonies in the Caribbean, the development of the civil rights movement in the United States, and the influence of African independence movements all encouraged a reappraisal of black history. There were also a number of seminal writers and political activists whose work served to remind us of a black past which needed to be addressed. The rise of modern slave studies was therefore a complex and tortuous process, not wholly explained by the fluctuations in scholarly interests. But, in time, scholarship responded by undergoing a quite dramatic revolution in its engagement with slavery.

What follows is an attempt to provide readers with a guide to the recent history of slavery, through a sample of some of the more important scholarly contributions to slave studies. Yet, to describe many of the pieces in this way is to do them a disservice. Like all important scholarship, the best work on the history of slavery often has a significance which transcends its chosen field, offering instead an example of historical craftsmanship at its best. For that reason, we have included essays in this collection which were pioneering, revisionary, or remain, despite more recent critiques of their arguments, model examples of historical approaches to slavery. The book is divided into what we consider to be the major themes in the recent historiography of slavery. Each section is introduced by an editors' essay which seeks to explore that theme in its broader setting.

PART ONE

The Atlantic Slave Trade

THE HISTORY OF the Atlantic slave trade has attracted some of the finest and most innovative historical research. It was led above all by Philip D. Curtin, whose major work, *The Atlantic Slave Trade: A Census* (1969), prompted a dramatic reassessment of the slave trade and provided for the first time a carefully calibrated assessment of the numbers of Africans shipped across the Atlantic. The consequences of Curtin's work were far-reaching (and continue to reverberate to this day). Here we have chosen to include Curtin's seminal essay on disease and the slave trade (1968). It was, again, a crucial element in persuading historians to think more deeply about factors in the history of human migrations (enforced or free) which had previously been neglected. Curtin's essay was, in effect, a starting point for a historical investigation of the role and impact of disease in the peopling of the Americas.

The waves of enforced African migrations westwards to the slave colonies formed an unprecedented drain of population. While most historians have been interested in the impact of African arrivals in the Americas, Patrick Manning's study from 1990 provides an important assessment of the impact on Africa itself. It is an investigation which touches on the economic and cultural origins of slaving, far from the European eye on the African coastline. Manning seeks to explore why Africa yielded up such vast numbers of people to traders on the coast.

Before Curtin's work, historians had simply guessed about the numbers of Africans involved. In the past generation, however, a group of primarily economic historians have followed Curtin's lead to rework the data and have uncovered previously unknown or unused materials. Among those historians of the Atlantic slave is David Eltis, who, with David Richardson (1997), assessed the broad patterns of population flows across the Atlantic. Their conclusion was that the slave trade was a complex economic system rather than the preconceived image of an exercise in raw brutality.

Precisely why Europeans should turn to slave labour – rather than other forms of coerced labour – is the topic of Eltis's important essay of 1993. He suggests that the drift towards African slavery was more complex and less easily explained than we might initially imagine. The decision to use African slave labour was more problematic than many historians have argued.

———•◆•———

INTRODUCTION TO PART ONE

THE OCEANIC TRANSPORTATION across the Atlantic was a critical
experience in the shaping of slavery throughout the Americas. The Atlantic
slave trade was crucial in the history of three continents. First, and most obviously,
Africa was dramatically affected by the regular haemorrhage of its peoples over
four centuries. Second, Europe – or rather its successive maritime powers – waxed
powerful and rich in proportion to its involvement with Atlantic slavery. And finally,
the Americas were utterly transformed by the importation of millions of Africans.

The number of Africans involved is stunning. Though the history of the Atlantic
crossing is remarkably varied and changed across time and from place to place,
the evidence remains astounding. Something like 12 million Africans were forced
into the Atlantic slave ships, and perhaps 10.5 million Africans survived the
ordeal to make landfall in the Americas. Although it would be wrong to concentrate solely on the simple data and to be sidetracked into the statistics of the
problem, it is nevertheless vital to get the figures right and to come to as accurate a conclusion as possible about the volume and scale of this enforced human
migration. The figures cannot speak for themselves, of course, and must be teased
apart to reveal the human experience which lurks behind them. Fortunately, the
research of the past thirty years now allows us to make some straightforward
assertions about the Atlantic slave trade.

Europeans were aware of African slavery long before they settled their pioneering colonies in the Americas. Traditional overland slave routes to North Africa had
brought Africans to southern Europe. Though the initial European maritime contacts
with West Africa were not forged with an eye to gathering slaves (gold and other
commercial commodities were more important), African labour soon proved its
value both to the Portuguese and Spaniards. The early European development of the
Atlantic islands and the islands off West Africa (São Tomé and Principe) used
African slave labour, notably when sugar was transplanted there from earlier sites in
the Mediterranean. African slaves also became common sights in both Spain and
Portugal. Europeans had thus bought and traded in Africans, shipping them back
and forth (admittedly on a relatively small scale) *before* the opening of the Americas.
But this early European use of African slaves, often for domestic use, was utterly
transformed by events in the Americas.

It was the Portuguese settlements in Brazil, and the creation of the local sugar
industry (small scale and experimental though it was) after 1560 which revealed
the value of African labour. Africans were shipped to Brazil for their muscle
power. Despite experiments with local Indian labour, by the end of the sixteenth
century, the formative link had been forged between African slave labour and sugar

cultivation on plantations. Thereafter, Europeans and local-born planters consistently preferred Africans as labourers on sugar plantations. Later planters came to think that African slaves and their descendants were the only appropriate form of labour for work on plantations, whatever the crop.

From these small beginnings, growing numbers of Africans were shipped to Brazil. Perhaps 15,000 African slaves lived there in 1600. But over the next fifty years some 200,000 were shipped across the Atlantic to Brazil.[1] They were able to rely on a relatively secure Portuguese trading presence in Africa, especially in central and south-west Africa. By about 1600 roughly 10,000 Africans a year were leaving Angola as slaves for Brazil and for Spanish colonies in the Americas. It was, of course, a more protracted and complex process than this may suggest. Moreover, in the process, the planter class in Brazil – and later throughout the Americas – devised self-serving ideologies of race to justify their slave systems. Thus, from rather simple beginnings – Portuguese settlers in Brazil casting around for ways of producing sugar in a region plagued by the decline of the indigenous population – were laid the foundations of the Atlantic slave trade and the transformation of the fortunes of three continents.

The Spanish experience took a broadly similar trajectory. Like the Portuguese, the Spanish impact on the Caribbean and Central Americas brought about a series of epidemiological disasters for local native peoples. Again, after a series of labour experiments, the Spanish settlers turned to enslaved African labour to fill the labour vacuum in their settlements. In their case, however, the Spanish used a series of treaties (*asiento*) with other European suppliers of slaves. Thus it was first the Portuguese and later the English who ferried Africans into the Spanish American colonies. The numbers were small initially (perhaps 36,000 in the forty years to 1595) but rose rapidly thereafter, totalling as many as 268,000 between 1595 and 1640.[2]

Demand for labour in the Americas was then the engine which dictated the rise and direction of the Atlantic slave trade. Events in the Americas determined the growing European presence in West Africa in search of slaves. The initial European piratical raids for slaves matured, in time, into a series of complex and sophisticated trading systems along a coast of 3,000 miles. In time the slave systems drew on a catchment area which stretched deep into the African interior. Inevitably, it embraced a host of African cultures and societies. Whatever the slave holders of the Americas *expected* from the slave ships – and whatever the ideal sought by traders and sailors alike on the African coast – increasingly the nature of the African slaves brought from the interior to the coast was a function of internal African factors. It is also important to remember that Africans travelled great distances, often through a series of enslavements, before reaching the Atlantic and having their first sight of Europeans and their sailing ships.

The Portuguese were the first to establish an effective slave-trading presence on the coast. It seemed so obviously lucrative that privateering incursions by other nations (notably the French and English) soon made an impact on the coast. But it was the Dutch, by the mid-1590s, who became an increasingly powerful trading force in the Atlantic, their power confirmed by their seizure of Brazil (briefly) in 1630. Dutch maritime and commercial power rose as the Portuguese declined – part and parcel of the emergence of the Dutch 'Golden Age'. Between 1630 and 1651, the Dutch were transporting 2,500 Africans a year to Brazil.

The English were drawn to West Africa by the Portuguese and Spanish successes. Their initial efforts were mainly privateering raids, but by the early seventeenth century the English began to trade seriously in the region, thanks in part to the acquisition of colonies in the Americas. The English slave trade was organised first through state-backed monopoly companies. But from the beginning, interlopers sought to penetrate those trading restrictions. Like others nations before them, the English found that the key to the expansion of their slave trading was to be found in the Americas. The settlement of West Indian islands, notably Barbados and Jamaica, and the development of the Chesapeake colonies, laid the foundations for British colonial demand for imported labour. After experiments with different forms of labour, local settlers in all those places turned to African slaves. In Barbados between 1650 and 1680, the slaves increased from 50 per cent to 70 per cent of the population. In Jamaica the 9,500 slaves of 1673 grew to 100,000 by 1740.[3] The numbers in the Chesapeake were smaller, but still significant. The handful of Africans landed at Jamestown in 1619 had increased, but only to 1,700 by 1660, to 4,000 in 1680, with perhaps an extra 3,000 arriving in the last years of the century. This changed dramatically in the next century, however, when 100,000 Africans were landed in the region.[4]

So expansive was this demand in the Americas that English monopolists were never able fully to satisfy it. Yet by 1670 the British had become the dominant force in the Atlantic trade. Indeed, in the 150 years to 1807 (when the British abolished their slave trade) they carried as many Africans across the Atlantic as all other slave-trading nations combined.[5] They shipped some 3.5 million Africans in those years, at a rate of about 6,700 a year in 1670 and perhaps 42,000 a year a century later.

Three British ports – London, then Bristol and, from about 1750 onwards, Liverpool – dominated the British slave trade. By 1728–1729 half of the British tonnage clearing for Africa came from Bristol, and by the early 1730s Bristol merchants were investing up to £60,000 a year into the slave trade, rising to £150,000 a year at mid-century.[6] But a host of small ports joined in, although often it is true on a very small scale. These included, remarkably enough, Lyme Regis, Whitehaven and Lancaster. Throughout, however, London remained the dominant financial force within the British slave trade. Though ports drew on local backers and skills, London financed most slave-trading investments until the early eighteenth century. From about 1750 onwards that role fell to Liverpool, although London was always vital to the Atlantic trade, accepting bills of exchange used by West Indians, Americans and Britons. From a total of some 11,000 slave voyages made by British ships, about one-half sailed from Liverpool.

At first sight the Atlantic slave trade looks relatively straightforward, itself perhaps a function of an oversimplified view of the trade as 'triangular'. It was, in fact, a hugely complex trading system which was genuinely global in reach and consequences. European states were heavily involved, from the outset, in encouraging and shaping their own involvement in Atlantic slave trading. Joint stock companies also proved critical, but so voracious was American demand that a more open trade eventually became the norm by the eighteenth century. A typical slave voyage and slave ship represented an investment by a large group of backers, often from the home port. It was costly to fit-out and load a slave ship, notably because of the range of goods African middlemen expected in return for their slaves. Moreover, much of the cargo shipped to the slave coast had already been imported and was therefore expensive, notably Asian textiles (the largest single export for slaves) and cowrie shells, in addition to metal goods, armaments, French wines, rum and tobacco from the Americas. In all these cases, the European slave traders had to buy many of their goods from outside their own nation's trading area, that is in return for hard currency.

African slaves were bought from different coastal regions. The British, for example, bought Africans from Senegambia, Sierra Leone, the Gold Coast, the Bight of Benin, West Central Africa and, most important of all, from the Bight of Biafra. They trawled for slaves in those regions at different periods, shifting from one to the other depending on the nature or paucity of supplies arriving from the interior. In some regions slaves were acquired quickly; elsewhere more slowly. Throughout, however, the British and their European competitors for African slaves, notably the French and Portuguese, were dependent on African middlemen and dealers bringing slaves to the coast. We need to remember that it was Africans who controlled the slaves until the moment they were sold and handed over to the European slave traders on the coast.

It is clear enough that even though forms of slavery existed in Africa before the maritime arrival of the Europeans and long before the emergence of American slave systems, the European appetite for African slaves had a transforming impact on a range of African societies. Europeans imported a vast range of European and Asian manufactured goods to barter for slaves, creating a demand which could only be satisfied by still more Africans. Warfare between African states and aggressive, predatory attacks on neighbouring peoples yielded prisoners who were fed into the internal slaving system, then to Europeans on the coast.

The impact of this new and greedy appetite for humanity had enormous consequences for Africa. First, and obviously, Africa lost huge numbers of people. While the slave trade may therefore have retarded population growth in parts of the continent, the political consequences were equally disastrous. Three major West African states collapsed, though others (notably the Asante and Dahomey) rose to power because of the slave trade. Overall, the Atlantic slave trade had an enormous impact on the course of African history.

It also seems clear that European demand stimulated the expansion and growth of slavery within Africa, especially for female slaves. But it was not Europeans who determined the gender and age of the slaves sent across the Atlantic. Although it is clear that slave owners in the Americas preferred youths and young adults, and males over females, David Eltis has shown that '. . . the major force shaping the age and sex of Africans entering the trade must be sought in Africa'.[7]

Africans were driven or purchased onwards, from their initial point of enslavement, towards the Europeans on the coast. For their part, Europeans were generally restricted to the coast by the physical dangers of life in Africa, notably disease. The best-remembered (but most unusual) trading posts were those slave forts which survive to this day. More commonly, however, Europeans traded from their ships, haggling with local traders on board, or on shore, before the deal was struck. In return for the agreed exchange of goods (often after protracted dining and exchanges of gifts), the latest batch of Africans passed into European hands and into the holds of the slave ships, where decks and platforms had converted the open holds into slave accommodation segregated by sex and age.

So far, it had been relatively cheap to acquire African slaves and to move them to the coast. Often African slaves had already paid their way by carrying other goods – that is, acting as porters (for ivory, for instance). But slaves arrived on the coast or riverside in small groups, which meant that European slave traders had to linger there – or cruise up and down – until they acquired a sufficiently large number of Africans to depart for the Americas. It was in this period of 'coasting' that mortality for slaves and Europeans alike was at its worst. Elsewhere, however, there were highly organised trading posts (Elmina, Luanda, for example) where ships could anchor and conduct the whole of the slave-trading business. The ships also stocked up with water and local foodstuffs for the Atlantic crossing.

The Middle Passage – the oceanic transit to the Americas – is perhaps the best-known feature of the slave trade because its ghastly images have loomed large in public memory and have been actively promoted in the popular media. But films and novels are hard pressed to match the reality of that experience.

The Atlantic voyage normally took a month to Brazil and two months to the West Indies or North America (most slaves had already been enslaved six to twelve months in Africa). African slaves were packed tighter than any other contemporary group, such as migrants or soldiers; for example, the infamous Brookes slave ship provided an average of about seven square feet per slave. However, this 'packing' seems not to have affected slave mortality. Not surprisingly, though, the death rates on the slave ships were higher than for other long-distance oceanic travellers. But, slave mortality on slave ships declined by one-half over the history of the slave trade, and it varied greatly, depending on which region of Africa the slaves had embarked from. Curiously, the time spent at sea seems to have made little impact on slave seaborne mortality, though improvements in slave ship design speeded the voyages over time. Slave traders of all nationalities clearly made greater efforts to safeguard their cargoes by improved provisioning for their Africans; the post-1700 rule of thumb was to carry twice the volume of provisions normally expected for the length of voyage. Over the years, slavers decided on the ideal size and shape of slave ships, which tended to be smaller than other vessels and better suited to trading and cruising West African coastal and riverine waters, thence for a fast Atlantic crossing.

The end result of these factors – all minutely examined in recent years by historians – was an average mortality rate of 7.5 per cent for a voyage of thirty to fifty days in the later stages of the slave trade. Although traders managed to reduce their losses over the course of the slave trade, the levels remained high; much higher than comparable land-based rates, or of other comparable seaborne groups. But what did slaves succumb to on the boats? About half of all deaths were from stomach complaints (notably dysentery) and fevers brought on board from Africa, and made worse by the ships' conditions. A substantial proportion of slave deaths took place on the African coast, in the period when the captain was trying to fill his ship's holds with other slaves. The white crews of the slave ships also suffered unusually high death rates (again, worst on the African coast), though that too declined with time. In addition, there were always the unpredictable attacks of diseases and ailments which could cause havoc at sea, in the filth of the slave quarters.

There had undoubtedly been a number of slave deaths before reaching the African coast – on the protracted movement of slaves within Africa – though the evidence for this is sparse. We also know that a considerable number of slaves died after landfall in the Americas, not surprising perhaps given the levels of sickness on board the Atlantic vessels. What is clear is that European and American slave traders generally sought to preserve the lives and health of their African slaves. They were, after all – and however crude it may seem – a valuable investment. Moreover, many slave traders tried to improve the shipboard conditions, with the result that slave mortality fell on all European and American ships over time. Yet there remains the unavoidable fact that slaves continued to die at a rate which would have horrified shippers of military or emigrant Europeans. And they died 'not only from disease and accident, but from rebellion, suicide, and natural disasters'. We know of rebellions on more than 300 voyages, and of violent incidents on the African coast. There were some 443 shipwrecks of slave ships, while more than 800 vessels were seized by privateers. In the nineteenth century 1,871 slave ships were impounded by anti-slave-trade patrols.[8] Yet the great majority of slaves packed into the slave ships on the African coast arrived, whatever their condition, for sale to the slave owners of the Americas.

Landfall brought relief to the crew but almost certainly more fears and uncertainties among the Africans. They were sold as soon as was possible, having been prepared on board ship to look fit for sale and work. They were sold either on the ship or at a local market. Sicker slaves, of course, took longer to sell. The slave traders usually accepted a percentage of the agreed price, the rest to be paid later, normally in local produce. Contrary to popular belief, the slave ships returned to Europe not loaded with colonial produce but often in ballast (normal cargo vessels shipped colonial produce back to Europe), and with a greatly reduced crew, many of whom were shabbily treated and simply paid off in the Americas. On return to Britain (or elsewhere), the slave captain's main task was securing repayment on his outlay, and, over the next few years, selling goods arriving from the Americas from people who had bought his slave cargo. It was a protracted business that might last up to six years. And yet there seems to have been no reluctance among shippers and investors to involve themselves in the Atlantic slave trade. They clearly thought that it had profitable potential.

Despite some highly inflated estimates, the slave trade yielded profits averaging about 10 per cent. And there seem to have been important linkages between the African trade and early European industry. The slave trade made use of and expanded complex systems of international finance and credit, and became central to a genuinely global economy which linked the trades of Asia to those of Africa, Europe and the Americas. At the heart of this Atlantic slave system was a consumer revolution which saw Europeans consuming the crops from the slave colonies of the Americas in enormous volumes. All this was made possible by the imported Africans. In the words of Herbert Klein, 'Until European immigrants replaced them in the late nineteenth century, it was African slaves who enabled this consumption revolution to occur. Without that labor most of America would never have developed at the pace it did.'[9]

Thus, what appears to be a relatively simple historical story – the enforced migration of Africans into the Americas – lies at the heart of the transformation and the emergence of the modern Western world.

Notes

1   Robin Blackburn, *The Making of New World Slavery: From the Baroque to the Modern, 1492–1800*, London, 1997, p. 168.

2   *Ibid.*, pp. 142–144.

3   Michael Craton, 'Property and Propriety: Land Tenure and Slave Property in the Creation of a British West Indian Plantocracy, 1712–1740', in *Empire, Enslavement and Freedom in the Caribbean*, Kingston, 1997.

4   Alan Kulikoff, *Tobacco and Slaves: The Development of Southern Cultures in the Chesapeake, 1680–1800*, Chapel Hill, 1986, pp. 40–44.

5   David Richardson, 'The British Empire and the Atlantic Slave Trade, 1660–1807', in P.J. Marshall, ed., *The Oxford History of the British Empire*, vol. II, *The Eighteenth Century*, Oxford, 1998.

6   David Richardson, ed., *Bristol, Africa and the Eighteenth-Century Slave Trade to America* (Bristol Record Society), 4 vols, 1986–1996; vol. I, (1986), pp. vii–xxviii.

7   David Eltis, 'Fluctuations in the Age and Sex Ratios of Slaves in the Nineteenth-Century Transatlantic Slave Traffic', *Slavery and Abolition*, vol. VII, 1986, p. 269. See also his important book, *Economic Growth and the Ending of the Transatlantic Slave Trade*, New York, 1987.

8   Herbert S. Klein, *The Atlantic Slave Trade*, Cambridge, 1999, p. 159.

9   *Ibid.*, p. 102.

Chapter 1

Philip D. Curtin

EPIDEMIOLOGY AND THE SLAVE TRADE

HISTORIANS HAVE BEGUN to show a new interest in the slave trade. Recent developments in historical demography, economic history, and the history of Africa have solved some of the old problems and posed new ones. The mere passage of time makes it possible to go beyond the largely humanitarian concerns of the nineteenth-century writers, concerns that arose out of the great debate over slavery as a question of policy. We can now accept the trade as an evil and move on to the problem of why and how it took place for so many centuries and on such a scale.

The recent trend toward a world-historical perspective and away from parochial national history also calls for a new approach to the broad patterns of Atlantic history. Social and economic development on the tropical shores of the Atlantic was a single process, regardless of the theoretically self-contained empires of mercantilist Europe. From the late sixteenth century to the early nineteenth, the central institution was the plantation, located in tropical America, worked by slave labor from tropical Africa, but directed by Europeans and producing tropical staples for European consumption. The broader patterns of society and economy were much the same in all the plantation colonies, regardless of metropolitan control. These patterns were not only different from those of Europe; they were also different from those of European settlements in temperate North America, the Indian Ocean trading posts, and territorial empires in New Spain and Peru. Yet the commercial influence of the plantations stretched far and wide—to the English settlements of North America, to mainland Spanish America, and even beyond the Atlantic world to the textile markets of India. The whole complex of commerce and production was an entity which can be called the South Atlantic System.

I

The slave trade was a key institution in this system, as it was in the history of the United States; but in the broad view North America was only marginal to the system as a whole. The "cotton kingdom" of the nineteenth century was a late flowering of the slave plantation. The thirteen colonies imported very few slaves before the eighteenth century; even then, they received only about twenty per cent of the British slave trade between 1700 and the American Revolution. Through the whole course of the slave trade, the present territory of the United States imported less than five per cent of all slaves brought to the New World.[1] Important as slavery and its aftermath have been for the history of the United States, the fundamental development of plantation slavery in the Americas took place elsewhere—in tropical America.

The first territory to achieve a full-blown model of the South Atlantic System was Brazil in the late sixteenth century. From these beginnings it spread to the Caribbean, where it reached a kind of apogee in the late eighteenth century, just before the Democratic Revolutions. As a pre-industrial economic order, the system had some remarkable features at the very beginning. Nothing in earlier European economic experience could compare with its dependence on long-distance transportation. Not only was virtually all of output of the plantations consumed in Europe; timber, cattle, and even food were often imported from North America or Ireland. Most remarkable of all, the system apparently required a continuous and growing stream of workers from tropical Africa, a trade in human beings that became the most massive intercontinental migration before the industrial era.

A full explanation of the demographic, economic, and social forces that set this trade in motion is not yet available. It is clear, however, that they included both a European demand and an African supply. On the supply side in particular we still know far too little about the sources of slaves within Africa, about the commercial institutions through which they were delivered to the coast, and about the technological and economic conditions that made it possible for African societies to sell slaves on terms of trade that were extremely favorable to European buyers. The demand side is far better documented, but many difficulties remain. One of these is a location problem which has bothered students of the slave trade since the early eighteenth century: given a European demand for tropical staples, why satisfy that demand by placing the plantations several thousand miles away from the principal source of labor?

One form of answer can be found in the chronological sequence through which the South Atlantic System grew out of its Mediterranean origins. Long before the discovery of the Americas, Europeans had created an embryo of the later South Atlantic System. Venetians, Genoese, Catalans, and others had sugar grown in overseas "colonies" like Crete and Cyprus and Sicily. These early plantations were often worked by slave labor supplied through the existing Mediterranean slave trade, some of it from the Mediterranean basin itself and some of it imported from the slave-trade posts of the northern and eastern Black Sea coasts. In the late Middle Ages, sugar planting migrated westward, first to southern Iberia, then to the Atlantic islands like Madeira and the Canaries.[2] With the great sixteenth-century maritime out-burst into the Atlantic, newer and greater opportunities presented themselves.

The Europeans experimented with a number of alternative locations and forms of development between about 1500 and the middle of the seventeenth century. In the early sixteenth century, plantations were established on São Thomé in the Gulf of Guinea, convenient to a source of slave labor in tropical Africa. Another alternative was to offer technical assistance to an African state, which might then produce goods for the European market. This was tried most intensively by the Portuguese in the kingdom of Kongo at the same period.[3] On the American shore, plantations were also established using varying sources of labor. Indian slave labor served the Portuguese in sixteenth-century Brazil and the Spanish in sixteenth-century Hispaniola.[4] European labor, most of it either forced convict labor or contract labor, was used extensively by the French and British in the Lesser Antilles, especially during the middle third of the seventeenth century.[5] But the combination that appeared to work best, and which spread most widely, was the plantation located in tropical America, staffed by European managers, and worked by slaves from Africa. The solution of the early planners was thus empirical; trial and error showed that the expedient of importing labor from Africa to the American plantations succeeded, while other alternatives failed.

II

Though the full explanation must wait for further research into supply and demand conditions on both sides of the Atlantic, one aspect worth exploring is the epidemiology of migration. Europeans discovered at a very early date that they experienced high mortality rates overseas. The Portuguese failure in Kongo is largely accountable to the high mortality rate among missionary and agents sent to Africa. On the American side of the ocean, planters soon found that both the local Indians and imported European workers tended to die out, while Africans apparently worked better and lived longer in the "climate" of tropical America.

Their first explanations were overwhelmingly racial. Europeans in tropical America believed that Negroes were peculiarly immune to the effects of a hot climate, just as Europeans seemed peculiarly liable to death in the climate of the West Indies or the "white man's grave" on the Gulf of Guinea.[6] The same racial theories could be used to explain that American Indians were not useful, since they were a "weak race" that died out on contact with "white civilization." The general conclusion, that certain races had inborn qualities of strength and weakness fitting them for specific "climates," became an accepted "fact" and a cornerstone of pseudo-scientific racism.[7]

This racist explanation has, of course, been contradicted long since, not merely by the general fall of pseudo-scientific racism, but also by the genuine fact that people of European descent now live as successfully as anyone else in tropical environments—those of Cuba, Costa Rica, Puerto Rico, and Queensland, among others. Yet we are left with the judgment of generations of planters in the Caribbean and Brazil that Negroes were somehow much better workers than any other group.

This opinion might be written off as a social or race prejudice—no one wants to work in the hot sun if he can find someone else to work for him—but epidemiology suggests another answer.[8] People die from disease, not from climate, and the world contains many different disease environments, each with a range of viruses and bacteria that differ in varying degrees from those found elsewhere. Physical environment and climate obviously play a role, but epidemiological differences exist even where physical environment is the same. In the United States, for example, measurable differences in the incidence of disease are found in a single region, even between an urban area and the surrounding countryside.

One cause of this diversity is relative isolation. Diseases themselves change radically over short periods; new strains of virus or bacteria appear, and old strains die out. These changes are not merely random; they are often a response to the immunities of the host population. (A recent and striking example is the appearance within the past two decades of a new strain of the malarial parasite, *Plasmodium falciparum*. This strain is resistant to the chloraquin preparations, which earlier varieties of *P. falciparum* were not, yet the new anti-malarials came into use only at the end of the Second World War.) At the same time, the host population itself develops immunities to the endemic diseases of its environment. Thus, each disease environment has a constantly changing equilibrium between the host population's pattern of immunity and its range of endemic disease. The more isolated a human community, the more specialized and individual its disease environment is likely to become.[9]

In the longer sweep of history over the past two or three millennia, increasing intercommunication has made disease environments more nearly alike, not more diverse; but each breach of previous isolation has brought higher death rates, as unfamiliar diseases attacked populations whose environment provided no source of immunity.[10] The Atlantic basin on the eve of the great European discoveries was especially open to this pattern of high death rates from new diseases. All the shores of the Atlantic were relatively isolated from one another. As men moved across the ocean from one disease environment to another, their death rates rose—the increased mortality of human migration. As diseases moved with them from one previously isolated environment to another, they spread to non-immune host populations, who then experienced the increased mortality of disease migration.[11]

This interchange of diseases and peoples was extremely complex, and the data are far from complete. The historical process will not be fully understood until comparative statistical and medical studies have been made of the many isolated peoples who were brought into contact with the ecumenical range of disease between the sixteenth century and the present. This would include many different American Indian groups, the Maori and other Polynesians, the Australian aborigines, and the Koisan-speaking peoples of southern Africa.

Present medical knowledge, however, can outline certain theoretical limits and some of the conditions to be expected when a non-immune population meets a range of new diseases. Some theoretical expectations can be based on the process of immunization itself. The most significant immunities are acquired, not inherited. The ordinary procedures for artificial immunization are based on the fact that people can create antibodies which will oppose specific forms of infection. The individual can be immunized either by giving him antibodies directly, or else by inducing a light infection so that his own organism will produce the required antibodies. Similar immunities are, of course, produced by the attack of a disease, but the form of immunity and its duration will vary greatly. It may last only a few weeks after a common cold, or a lifetime after yellow fever. It may be partial, making recurrent attacks less harmful, or it may be a total immunity to all future infection from that source.

Childhood disease environment is the crucial factor in determining the immunities of a given adult population. Not only will the weakest members of society be removed, leaving a more resistant population of survivors; childhood and infancy are also a period of life when many infections are relatively benign. This is so of yellow fever—a disease of special importance to the tropical Atlantic—which is rarely fatal to children but frequently fatal to adults. In addition, children often experience infection in such a mild form they are not even aware of it, yet they acquire an immunity that protects them in later life just as effectively as a severe attack would have done.[12] (Before the widespread use of poliomyelitis vaccines, tests showed that, for every recognized case, one hundred to one thousand persons were infected without being conscious of the fact and developed the characteristic immunity.) In general, then, the individual will be safest if he stays in the disease environment of his childhood; if he migrates, a fully effective set of immunities to match a new disease environment could not be expected to appear in his generation.

But immunities are also inherited. These are less important than the acquired immunities, but they raise special problems. First of all, medical science has so far discovered most of these inherited immunities only by statistical inference. We are, therefore, in an area of uncertainty. Second, the very fact that some immunities are heritable raises again the old and discarded racist hypothesis that Negroes could easily work in the tropical climates, simply because they were Negroes. It is, therefore, important to consider the present state of medical knowledge.

One kind of heritable immunity is universal: all children inherit antibodies transmitted by the mother to the fetus, and these protect the child during the first months of life, before its own ability to generate antibodies is fully developed. People of differing blood groups also appear to have differing degrees of immunity to some diseases. These are nothing like the perfect immunity given by an attack of yellow fever, but they are statistically detectable. Family histories also indicate statistical tendencies of susceptibility (or relative immunity) to particular diseases.

In addition, whole populations exposed to early and constant infection may undergo genetic change. Those individuals whose genetic inheritance predisposes them to serious illness from a particular disease may die in childhood, leaving no descendants. Other individuals, whose genetic tendency allows them to escape with a milder illness from the same cause, are likely to live and reproduce. As a result, the genetic make-up of each succeeding generation will shift slightly toward a tendency to mild infection rather than fatal infection. Genetic changes of this sort, however, do not appear to alter the *incidence* of infection; people will still be attacked by the disease in the same proportion, but more will experience a mild illness and fewer will die. Recent studies indicate that this type of genetic influence is important to the epidemiology of poliomyelitis, rheumatic fever, and tuberculosis.[13]

Malaria is another disease which can be influenced by heredity—and one of considerably greater importance in the tropical Atlantic. The important factor in this instance is an inherited hemoglobin characteristic known as the sickle-cell trait, from the characteristic shape of some blood cells under the microscope. This trait is a balanced polymorphism—the circumstance where a particular organic weakness, which would be expected to disappear through natural selection, recurs generation after generation because it also has balancing "good" qualities. Sickle-cell trait is the best known of all balanced polymorphisms, and it can serve to illustrate the process in general. It is found in certain malarial areas, and particularly in Africa. Where it is present, three types of people can be distinguished—those with normal hemoglobin, those with the inherited sickle-cell trait, and those with both the sickle-cell trait and the anemia that often accompanies it. Since sickle-cell anemia is usually fatal in childhood, many of this third group would be expected to die before reproducing; and known laws of genetics suggest that the sickle-cell trait itself should die out over a period of time. But the sickle-cell has another characteristic which permits it to survive. It provides some protection against *P. falciparum*, the dominant form of malaria in tropical Africa and an important cause of infant mortality. Thus, in that environment, malaria tends to cut off those without the sickle-cell trait, while anemia cuts off those with the trait plus anemia. The two causes of early death balance each other, and the trait persists.[14]

It is important to distinguish between these epidemiological characteristics, which are genetic or heritable, and race, which is also heritable. The crucial distinction is that genetic immunities are a variable independent of physical appearance. In addition, the immunities of great historical significance are relatively short-lived. A balanced polymorphism such as sickle-cell trait, for example, tends to disappear from a population once *falciparum* malaria is no longer present. In addition, it is not a "Negro" trait. Even though it is found in tropical Africa, where many Negroes live, it is also found among some white populations in the Mediterranean basin, and it is absent among certain Negro groups in West Africa. Finally, the scientific interest of the balanced polymorphism to genetic studies can obscure the possible historical role of the sickle-cell trait. Statistical studies of Puerto Rican deaths from malaria by race indicate that, between 1937 and 1944, 4.29 per cent of "white" deaths were from malaria, as against 4.19 per cent of "colored" deaths from the same cause. Whatever the differential immunities of the modern Puerto Ricans' ancestors in Africa and Europe, their twentieth-century differences are quantitatively insignificant.[15]

III

On the shores of the pre-Columbian Atlantic, different immunities to disease were caused by different disease environments. These disease environments fell into three separate groups, each created by different circumstances of physical environment and isolation. Europe and North Africa were in the belt of intense inter-communication stretching from the north Atlantic to China. Most diseases of the temperate Afro-Eurasian land mass were already endemic there, and the Europeans had a wide range of immunities to match. They lacked, however, the diseases and the immunities of the Old World tropics.

In tropical Africa, intercommunication was less intense, and disease environments would have been more diverse than those of Europe. Even though Africa had most of the full range of Old World temperate diseases—and its own assortment of tropical diseases, including *falciparum* malaria, yellow fever, sleeping sickness, yaws, and bilharzia—each African community was relatively isolated from its neighbors. It would, therefore, have been unlikely that any single African people would have an endemic assortment that covered the whole range of diseases and strains of disease available in the Sub-Saharan region. As a result, Africans had a wide range of immunities, but travel, even within Africa, would be likely to increase the death rate.

In the Americas, a third set of disease environments had been isolated from the Old World for a very long time. Little is known about them, but the lack of frequent communication between one region and another was even greater than in tropical Africa. Each region would, therefore, be expected to have little protection from the diseases of its neighbors, and virtually none against the strange diseases that were to come from across the Atlantic.

When, in the sixteenth century and later, the Africans and Europeans crossed the ocean, they infected the American Indians. Europeans encountered new diseases from the African tropics, and Africans met new strains of Afro-Eurasian diseases. The possible role of New World diseases is not clear in the medical records of the period. (Even the former belief in a New World origin for syphilis is now in serious doubt.)[16] The basic pattern is nevertheless clear enough: everyone in the Americas, or who came to the Americas, paid a price in increased death rates for his entry into this newly created disease environment.

Even though we lack statistical data for sixteenth-century American populations, the quantitative impact on the Indians is known in outline. Especially in the tropical lowlands, many groups died out as a people before they had an opportunity to build immunities against the joint assault of African and European disease. The mortality was most striking and drastic with the densely settled population of the Greater Antilles where the Spanish first landed—and to which they brought the first Africans. Indians on the South and North American mainlands fared somewhat better, and so did the Caribs of the Lesser Antilles, though they, too, almost disappeared. In this case, isolation seems to have protected them from simultaneous attack by the full range of Old World diseases. With the highland peoples of Middle America, Colombia, and the Andes, a cooler environment prevented the spread of malaria and yellow fever, both of African origin. Thus, though these peoples sustained steep declines of population over the sixteenth and part of the seventeenth century, they were able to maintain themselves and ultimately to recover, once new immunities had been acquired.[17]

Epidemiological factors were thus responsible for depopulating some of the best agricultural land in the tropical world. The most obvious reason for locating the productive centers of the South Atlantic System in the American tropics was simply that land was there for the taking, and it was far better land for intensive agriculture than any available in tropical Africa. But land without people has no economic value. Labor had to come from somewhere else, even though bringing people into this disease environment was bound to exact a price from the increased mortality of human migration.

It is impossible to know precisely the size of this mortality rate in the sixteenth or seventeenth centuries, but some data are available for the late eighteenth and early nineteenth centuries. It is justifiable to accept these as suggestive of earlier mortality rates among migrants to the American tropics. While it is possible, and even probable, that diseases had changed somewhat during three centuries of adjustment to new host populations, it is unlikely that early nineteenty-century mortality rates were higher than those of earlier centuries. Indeed, the growing intensity of communication in the Atlantic over these centuries suggests that they should have been somewhat lower. Improving medical care may also have lowered mortality rates over time; but even the use of chinchona against malaria was irregular, and death rates from the more important diseases could hardly have been altered before about the eighteen-forties.[18]

Statistics on military mortality are the most useful source for the mortality of migration, since they make it possible to isolate groups moving from one disease environment to another. In 1835, the British government became concerned about the death rates of British troops overseas and ordered a series of statistical studies by Major Alexander Tulloch.[19] These reports, based on the medical transactions of the British Army (begun in 1816) were carried out with a scientific care that was only then beginning to be applied to statistics. Among other things, they show quantitative levels for the mortality of migration from Britain to either the West Indies or West Africa, and from West Africa to the West Indies. (See Tables 1.1–3.) Tulloch's data are also useful for comparative purposes, since he took the two decades 1817–36 as a common base period, and his samples normally contained significant bodies of men of common background and subject to a common epidemiological experience. They are by far the best data we now have, or are likely to discover.

To study the movement of British troops, Tulloch began with the expected civilian mortality rate among men of military age in the United Kingdom. Deaths from all causes among this group, calculated from actuarial tables and census data, were at the rate of 11.5 per thousand per annum. Once men from this group were recruited into the army, however, the death rate (based on 1830–36) rose to 15.3 per thousand—a predictable increase from the relatively crowded and unsanitary conditions of barracks life.[20] Movement overseas, however, produced far more substantial changes as the men entered new disease environments. (See Table 1.1.) Service in the Mediterranean, the temperate climate of South Africa, or North America produced a range of mortality that was not drastically different from that of the United Kingdom itself—between 12 and 20 per thousand per annum. (Two Mediterranean exceptions, Gibraltar and the Ionian Islands, were unusually high because of severe epidemics within the period of the survey.)

The tropical world, however, produced a strikingly different result, and it can be separated into three broad regions of increasing mortality. Around the tropical

Table 1.1 Death rates per thousand mean strength per annum, among British military personnel recruited in the United Kingdom and serving overseas, from all causes, 1817–36, unless otherwise noted

Eastern Frontier District, South Africa (1818–36)	12.0
Nova Scotia and New Brunswick	14.7
Cape District, South Africa (1818–36)	15.5
Malta	18.7
Canada (Quebec and Ontario)	20.0
Gibraltar (1818–36)	22.0
Ionian Islands	28.3
Mauritius (1818–36)	30.5
Tenasserim (1827–36)	44.7
Ceylon	75.0
Windward and Leeward Command, West Indies	85.0
Jamaica Command (1803–17, War Office data)	127.0
Jamaica Command (1817–36)	130.0
Windward and Leeward Command (1803–16, War Office data)	138.0
Sierra Leone Command, deaths from disease only	483.0
Cape Coast Command, Gold Coast (1823–26)	668.3

Sources: Parliamentary Papers, 1837–38, XL [138], 5–7, 44–45; 1839, XVI [166], 4–7, 6a, 15b, 22a, 25b, 39a; 1840, XXX [228], 4b, 7, 19, 19b; 1842, XXVII [358], 5–7, 44–45.

Indian Ocean, mortality rates ranged from 30 to 75 per thousand. In the American tropics, the rate rose to a level between 85 and 138 per thousand. Finally, West Africa showed a disastrous mortality range from 483 to 668 per thousand mean strength per annum. This level is confirmed by the qualitative impressions of early visitors to the African coast, and by a variety of other statistical data for the early nineteenth century.[21] Even if the Europeans had not had the better agricultural possibilities of tropical America at their disposal, their reluctance to locate plantations in tropical Africa would be explained by these figures. Whatever the possibility of European residence in West Africa (once the migrants had acquired the proper immunities), the mortality rate of each entering group was simply too high to allow more intensive occupation than that of a few thinly-manned posts for the slave trade.

One of the often neglected inefficiencies of the slave trade is, indeed, the loss of life in the African posts and aboard the slave ships. A study of the slave trade of Nantes between 1715 and 1774 shows, for example, that crew mortality from disease alone varied between about 150 and 250 per thousand per voyage, though it was usually higher than 200 per thousand. During the same period, Nantes slave traders lost only 145 slaves per thousand from disease in transit.[22] Another and smaller sample of 116 slave ships sailing from English ports in the seventeen-eighties shows a crew death-rate from disease of 210 per thousand per voyage, and a further loss of 263 per thousand from desertion or discharge overseas.[23] At least in the eighteenth century, the maritime slave trade took proportionately more lives of crewmen than of slaves, in spite of the notoriously bad conditions of the "middle passage."

African migrants to the New World by way of the slave trade also experienced increased mortality rates after their arrival. Tulloch's sample of African soldiers serving in the West Indies was made up of men recruited mainly from among the slaves recaptured at sea by the British Navy as part of its anti-slavery blockade. They were not, therefore, from any particular region, but from the whole of West Africa with a special concentration from western Nigeria and Dahomey and only a few from either the Congo basin or East Africa.[24] This was an excellent sample of the kind of men who were sent to America as slaves—they *were* part of the slave trade before they joined the army.

When these men served as soldiers even in Sierra Leone, they had death rates markedly higher than other non-European troops serving in their respective countries of origin. (See Table 1.2.) Mortality among African troops in the Sierra Leone Command between 1819 and 1836 was 31.1 per thousand per annum from disease

Table 1.2   Mortality per thousand mean strength per annum among non-European British troops serving in their region or country of origin

Maltese Fencible corps	9
Hottentot Cape Corps	11
Bengal Native Troops	11
Madras Native Troops	13
Royal African Corps, West Africa	32

Source: PP, 1840, XXX [228], 15–16.

Table 1.3   Death rates from disease, per thousand mean strength per annum among British troops recruited in Africa and serving in the West Indies

Jamaica Command, 1803–17	49
Bahama Islands, 1817–36	41
Windward and Leeward Command, 1817–36*	40
Jamaica Command, 1817–36	30
Slave population of Jamaica, 3 years of age and over, 1803–17	25

Note: * The statistics for this command can be taken as most trustworthy. Not only is the mortality figure an approximate median; the sample force had an average mean strength of 2,047 over these decades, while the Bahama Islands had a smaller sample of only 355 men and the Jamaica command had only a force of labor troops with a mean strength of 286 men.

Source: PP, 1827–28, XL [138], 11, 50, 73.

—double the death rate of British troops serving in England.[25] Tulloch was puzzled by this high figure, but a probable explanation is possible. These men were not, in fact, serving in their country of origin. They had already moved from one African disease environment to another. Even without hard data for a comparable sample of men who were able to stay home, a reasonable estimate would put their mortality from disease alone within the range of 15 to 20 per thousand per annum. The soldiers' mortality rate thus increased by more than 50 per cent, simply as a result of movement *within* tropical Africa—an indication of the price exacted by the diversity of African disease environments.[26]

When men recruited in the same way were moved from Africa to the West Indies, a second increase in mortality would be expected, and it occurred. (See Table 1.3.) The death rate rose from about 30 per thousand to 40 per thousand. The price of movement to America was thus a further 30 per cent increase in mortality, and the death rate of these new arrivals in the American tropics was markedly higher than that of 25 per thousand per annum, calculated for the Jamaican slave population over three years of age during the period 1803–17.[27]

High as this rate was, it was lower than that of European troops serving in the same command. Tulloch's sample of European troops in the Windward and Leeward command can be set aside because the usual yellow fever epidemics missed these islands during the survey period. (Table 1.1.) The other three samples closely bracket their mean at 131 per thousand per annum. The rate of 40 per thousand for African troops in the Windward and Leeward Command is not only the mean of the four samples; that command also had the largest and probably the most representative sample. (In this case, the non-occurrence of yellow fever would not be significant, since fever was not an important cause of death among the African troops.) One finding of Tulloch's survey is that these African migrants to the New World outlived a comparable group of European migrants by a ratio of 3.2 to one. This difference is in line with the expectations of epidemiological theory. Africans, even with a combined background of Old World temperate diseases and Old World tropical diseases, would be expected to die at somewhat increased rates on migration to the New World; but Europeans who lacked the relative immunity to malaria and yellow fever, would be expected to die at still higher rates.

Other data from the eighteenth century confirm this pattern, though they cannot be taken to be as reliable as Tulloch's survey. A sample of white and black troops serving Great Britain in the West Indies between 1796 and 1807—hence in wartime conditions—showed an annual average mortality of 244 per thousand effectives per annum among the Europeans and an annual average of only 59.2 per thousand among those of African descent. These statistics are weak, partly because it is only probable—not certain—that these African troops were recruited by purchase in Africa, rather than by purchase from among the West Indian slaves. Nevertheless, the ratio of differential mortality was 4.1 to one in favor of the Africans. Another survey of French troops serving on Martinique and Guadeloupe between 1802 and 1807 shows an annual average death rate of 302 per thousand.[28] If these earlier surveys are at all reliable, Tulloch's rate of 130 per thousand may well lie at the low side of the range of death rates among European immigrants.

IV

The planters' belief in the superiority of African labor, therefore, had a basis in fact. They merely mistook the outward and visible sign of color for the independent variable of disease environment. This error is curiously like their other error of writing about the horrors of a tropical "climate." As every visitor to the West Indies will recognize, the climate, measured by any standard of human comfort, is more pleasant in summer than that of the eastern or central United States, and the winter climate is one of the greatest economic assets of the Carribbean. But the planters saw only that newly arrived Europeans died, and they attached this fact to the most obvious difference from the environment they had known in Europe—the tropical climate.

From an economic point of view, the price paid for a slave or an indentured white worker was a claim to future labor. Assuming that the cost of maintaining each was about equal, the slave was preferable at anything up to three times the price of the European. (The fact that indentures were limited in time, while slavery was not, would make little difference. A death rate of 130 per thousand per annum would practically use up a draft of seven-year indentures before their time had expired.) On the demand side, at least, here was sufficient reason for the slave trade from Africa as the preferred alternative to labor recruitment in Europe.

Tulloch was also concerned with the cause of death, and this aspect of his survey throws further light on the epidemiology of migration. Statistics on the cause of death are obviously weaker than those for gross mortality. (Even today, it is easier to establish the fact of death than to know its cause.) Nineteenth-century disease classifications and methods of diagnoses were far from accurate by modern standards. "Fevers" as a category covered yellow fever, malaria, typhoid, and a great deal more—not merely because they were grouped together for purposes of classification, but also because medical men could not always make valid distinctions between them. "Eruptive fevers" in the same way covered smallpox, syphilis, yaws, typhus, and measles, at the very least. "Diseases of the lungs" can be taken to mean principally pneumonia and tuberculosis, but it might include influenza as well. Intestinal diseases were clearly dysentery, but without further distinction.

Even so, Tulloch's data made it clear that Europeans died in the West Indies principally from "fevers." (See Tables 1.4 and 1.5.) These fevers were mainly yellow fever and malaria, both of them Old World diseases brought by earlier African immigrants.[29] Diagnostic distinctions between the two major tropical fevers were notoriously bad at the time, but a rough division is possible. Yellow fever occurred only in periodic epidemics. In Jamaica, for example, where "fevers" accounted for

Table 1.4   Principal causes of death among British troops recruited in Britain (in deaths per thousand mean strength per annum)

Disease	(1) Among Dragoons Serving in Britain 1830–36	(2) White Troops — Windward and Leeward Command 1817–36	(3) White Troops — Jamaica Command 1817–36
Fevers	1.4	36.9	101.9
Diseases of the Lung	7.7	10.4	7.5
Epidemic Cholera	1.2	–	–
Violent Deaths	1.3	–	–
Diseases of the Liver	–	1.8	1.0
Intestinal Diseases	–	20.7	5.1
Diseases of the Brain	–	3.7	1.2
Dropsies	–	2.1	–
Other (with mortality rates less than 1 per 1,000 per annum)	4.2	2.9	2.0
Total	15.8	78.5	121.3

Sources: PP, 1837–38, XL [138], 7, 44; 1839, XVI [166], 4.

Table 1.5   Principal cause of death among British troops recruited in Africa (in deaths per thousand mean strength per annum)

Disease	Sierra Leone Command (1819–36)	Windward and Leeward Command (West Indies) (1817–36)	Difference Between Cols. 1 and 2
Fevers	2.4	4.6	+2.2
Eruptive Fevers	6.9	2.5	–4.4
Diseases of the Lungs	6.3	16.5	+10.2
Diseases of the Liver	1.9	.9	–1.0
Intestinal Diseases	5.3	7.4	+2.1
Diseases of the Brain	1.6	2.2	+.6
Wounds	1.4	–	–1.4
Dropsies	–	2.1	+2.1
Other	6.2	3.8	
Total	32.0	40.0	

Sources: PP, 1837–38, XL [138], 11; 1840, XXX [228], 16.

more than 100 deaths per thousand per annum over the whole period of the survey, yellow fever epidemics occurred in 1819, 1822, 1825, and 1827. "Fever" mortality thus varied from only 67 per thousand in the best year to 259 per thousand in the worst. If the figure 67 per thousand represents a death rate mainly from malaria, then about 60 per cent of the fever deaths were from this cause, and 40 per cent from yellow fever.

The pattern in the Windward and Leeward Command was somewhat different. Barbados, where many of the troops were stationed, was unusually free of malaria. In addition, the Lesser Antilles passed through a period without serious yellow fever epidemics during the decades of the survey,[30] an indication that the fever mortality—36.9 per thousand per annum—was mainly malaria. Compared to Jamaica, white troops in the Lesser Antilles died at a higher rate from dysentery, but this difference is probably accountable to differences in water supply.

Among African troops, "diseases of the lungs" accounted for most of the increased deaths, though pneumonia and tuberculosis, the principal killers, were also found in the African homeland.[31] Part of the increased mortality was undoubtedly the result of crowded conditions in barracks or slave quarters, and even more may have come from lack of immunity to certain strains of disease not present in Africa. But it may be that genetic susceptibility played some role. Early epidemiologists believed that Negroes were particularly susceptible to lung disease if they moved from Africa to either Europe or North America.[32] Even today, Negro Americans are slightly more susceptible than white Americans to certain forms of tubercular infection. While the differences today are far less than those suggested by Tulloch's figures, it is likely that African environmental conditions over many generations have produced a genetic susceptibility that is still detectable.

The experience of Tulloch's African sample with "fevers" illustrates the point that immunities from one disease environment are not necessarily valid against all possible strains and varieties of a particular disease encountered in another. The West African "fever" environment was probably the most dangerous in the world to outsiders. Fever death rates of European soldiers were 382.6 per thousand per annum in the Cape Coast Command and 410.2 per thousand in Sierra Leone,[33] while African troops in Sierra Leone died from fevers at the rate of only 2.5 per thousand per annum. Once they migrated to America, however, Africans of the same origin sustained nearly twice that rate in the Lesser Antilles, and a rate of 8.2 per thousand per annum in Jamaica.[34] The probable explanation is that the West African pattern of apparent immunity to *falciparum* malaria was not effective against other varieties of malaria, nor against other strains of *P. falciparum*.

Once in America, both Europeans and Africans should have begun to acquire new immunities from the new disease environment. The medical mythology of Europeans involved in the South Atlantic System on either shore of the ocean always included a belief in the "seasoning sickness"—the first attack of tropical disease, which left survivors with the expectation of better health. The planters also thought of slaves as passing through the same seasoning process, and seasoned slaves commanded higher prices than newcomers. Military planning was also occasionally based on the concept of seasoning; European troops were given periods of residence in the West Indies before being sent into combat.

Tulloch was understandably concerned with the quantitative aspects of seasoning. His data were weak, however, since his samples had only two dimensions—

place of recruitment and annual mean strength. Some of the soldiers in a particular unit might be twenty-year veterans of the tropics, while others were fresh from England. He therefore took pains to trace the medical history of a series of drafts of European troops sent to Jamaica, and he found that the death rates rose during each successive year of service, rather than falling as the common belief in seasoning would suggest. One sample moved from 77 deaths per thousand per annum in the first year, to 87 in the second and third years, and then to 93 per thousand from the fourth year onward. The same tendency was also found in other data from the Windward and Leeward Command.[35] If the samples were representative, seasoning was a longer process than many believed it to be.

In Africa, however, he discovered another seasoning pattern. By chance, the non-commissioned officers serving with African troops were easily divisible into two groups. In the years 1819–24, the British non-coms were freshly arrived from Europe, and they died at a predictable West African rate of 397 per thousand per annum. After 1830, the main body of British troops was withdrawn, leaving behind a group of non-commissioned officers who were already veterans of the African environment. Between 1830 and 1836, these men died at the rate of 72 per thousand per annum, only 18 per cent of the initial rate.[36] The survivors had clearly been seasoned, though their death rate was still more than double that of the African troops under their command. Tulloch's findings therefore suggest a rather slow seasoning process in the American tropics, as against a rapid and costly one in tropical Africa.

The difference can be partly explained by differing patterns of malaria on the two sides of the ocean. West Africa is a hyperendemic area for *falciparum* malaria; new arrivals could hardly escape infection for as long as a year. Once permanently infested with the parasite, the survivors would experience few clinical symptoms —but only if they were regularly reinfected, as they would have been in West Africa. In addition, Sierra Leone was struck by an especially serious epidemic of yellow fever in 1829. Thus the veteran non-coms in Sierra Leone after 1830 can be counted as having survived the two most dangerous diseases of that region. In the West Indies, on the other hand, *Anopheles gambiae*, the most deadly of the African malarial vectors, was missing. Many American forms of malarial parasite were less deadly than the virtually universal *P. falciparum* of the African coast. A European arriving in the West Indies would almost certainly have malaria sooner or later; but its onset was not likely to be so rapid as in West Africa, nor was death so likely. In addition, yellow fever epidemics were less frequent in the West Indies.[37] An individual island might escape for as long as thirty years at a time, just as the Lesser Antilles did during the survey period.

V

Whatever the seasoning process among the immigrants themselves, a new generation born and raised in the American tropics should have been relatively immune to the American disease environment. One would, therefore, expect the early slave trade and a trickle of European migrants to produce a tropical American population capable of growth by natural increase—if not immediately, at least within a century or so after the trade began. If this had happened, the high mortality of migration would have been limited to the sixteenth and part of the seventeenth century. In fact, this did not happen. The most striking demographic peculiarity of the South Atlantic System was its failure to produce a self-sustaining slave population in tropical America.[38] As a result, the slave trade was necessary not merely to increase the American production of tropical staples, but even to maintain the population level. The final result was an increasing flow of slaves from Africa to America, far into the nineteenth century.

An overall figure for the excess of deaths over births among American slave populations cannot be established, but the general picture for tropical America is clear. Eighteenth-century commentators on the slave trade gave estimates of net natural decrease that varied between about 20 and 50 per thousand per annum for the Caribbean.[39] Similar estimates put the population loss among Brazilian slaves at 50 per thousand per annum for the period 1772–1873 and at 30 to 40 per thousand for the late period of slavery, 1872–85.[40] More recent calculations show a natural decrease in Jamaica from nearly 40 per thousand per annum over the period 1703–34, down to a little less than 20 per thousand per annum in the years 1734–39.[41] Barbados' slave population experienced a natural decrease of 43 per thousand per annum between 1712 and 1762.[42] The fact of natural decrease, if not a solidly established rate, is confirmed for other islands in the Caribbean as well.[43]

One cause, perhaps the chief cause, of this excess of deaths over births is to be found on the supply side of the Atlantic slave trade. Slaves were cheap in Africa, whether measured in terms of their marginal productivity on the plantation, or by the replacement cost of breeding and raising a slave to working age in the tropical Americans. Planters therefore preferred to buy more men than women, and they rarely followed a policy of encouraging a high birth rate in order to produce a self-perpetuating slave gang. The preference for male workers in turn reflected on supply, and the slave trade carried a remarkably consistent proportion of about two men for every woman. Other things being equal, this in itself would be expected to produce a birth rate per capita 33 per cent lower than that of a balanced population. In addition, birth rates were low even in proportion to female slaves – a reflection of the planters' common decision not to encourage breeding. The evidence from Jamaica indicates that female slaves themselves avoided having children in the conditions of slavery, and they knew about abortives and techniques for contraception in Africa.[44]

Since newly arrived slaves had very high mortality rates for people in the prime of life, we can assume that morbidity rates were correspondingly high. This had a large (if unmeasurable) influence on per-capita birth rates among migrants. One result was a curious paradox in the relation of the slave trade to demographic patterns in the Americas. Where economic growth was most rapid, and slave imports were greatest, population decrease from an excess of deaths over births tended to be most severe. Since the African-born part of the population was the portion with the marked sexual imbalance, the higher morbidity rates, and the higher mortality rates, it was they who pulled down the growth rate of the population as a whole. On the other hand, colonies without notable economic growth over a few decades began to import fewer slaves. They could then begin to achieve more favorable rates of population growth.

The comparative position of the various British West Indian colonies after the end of the British slave trade in 1808 is an interesting illustration of this demographic peculiarity. Barbados, which had virtually ceased importing slaves before the official abolition of the trade, achieved a self-sustaining population shortly after 1808.[45] Jamaica, however, had substantial slave imports up to the end of the trade. As a result, its slave population still had an excess of deaths over births at 5 per thousand per annum in the period 1817–29. British Guiana, on the other hand, passed through its period of rapid development just before the ending of the slave trade. As a result, it was left in 1817 with a slave population 65 per cent African-born and a rate of natural decrease at 11 per thousand between 1817 and 1829. As the African-born died in each territory, the population decline stopped, as it did in Jamaica by the early eighteen-forties.[46] Meanwhile, Cuba and Brazil had the most rapidly developing planting economies in tropical America, with continued (if illegal) slave imports to the mid-century and beyond. As a result, the pattern of a naturally decreasing slave population persisted there into the second half of the nineteenth century.[47]

Epidemiological factors by themselves cannot explain the origins and development of the South Atlantic System, but they clearly impinged on the system in extremely important ways. They influenced economic decisions and economic patterns, the demography of tropical America, and the planters' preference for Africans over other workers. Nothing that has been said here, however, should be extended to slavery or the slave trade outside the core area of tropical plantations. North America was certainly different, as was highland South America. The role of epidemiological factors in the core area nevertheless suggests that North American slavery might well be re-examined in the light of comparative studies from tropical America. In the same sense, American Indian history would profit from a broad and comparative look at the history of similarly isolated peoples on other continents. In Africa itself, the relative isolation of many human communities suggests that epidemiological factors *must* have been of great importance throughout the history of the continent—and especially at the moment when isolation was broken in the early colonial period. The role of epidemiological factors in the history of the slave trade is, therefore, only one instance among many where the role of disease in history has not yet been fully explored.

Notes

1   The most careful and probably the most reliable recent estimates of the British slave trade between 1701 and 1775 are those of K. W. Stetson, "A Quantitative Approach to Britain's American Slave Trade" (unpublished M.S. thesis, University of Wisconsin, 1967). An authoritative estimate of the total slave imports into the United States indicates that total imports were probably less than 400,000 and certainly not more than 500,000. (J. Potter, "The Growth of Population in America, 1700–1860," in D. V. Glass and D. E. Eversley [eds.], *Population in History: Essays in Historical Demography* [Chicago, 1965].) The size of the total Atlantic slave trade is considerably reduced by recent monographic research from the earlier estimates of fifteen or twenty millions, or even more. Until more research is published, however, a round number of ten million seems a reasonable guess.

2   For this development see the work of Charles Verlinden, particularly: *Précédents médiévaux de la colonie en Amérique* (Mexico, D. F., 1954); "Les origines coloniales de la civilisation atlantique. Antécédents et types de structure," *Journal of World History*, 1 (1954), 378–98; "La colonie vénitienne de Tana, centre de la traite des esclaves au xive et au début du xve siècles," *Studi in onore di Gino Luzzato*, 2 Vols. (Milano, 1950), II, 1–25; *L'esclavage dans l'Europe médiévale. Peninsule Ibérique-France* (Bruges, 1955).

3   J. Vansina, *Kingdoms of the Savanna* (Madison, 1966), 41–64.

4   M. Ratekin, "The Early Sugar Industry in Española," *Hispanic American Historical Review*, XXIII (1954), 1–19.

5   F. W. Pitman, *The Development of the British West Indies* (New Haven, 1917); Léon Vignols, "L'institution des engagés, 1624–1774," *Revue d'histoire économique et sociale*, I (1928), 24–45; G. Devien, *Les engagés pour les Antilles, 1634–1713* (Paris, 1952).

6   See P. D. Curtin, "'The White Man's Grave': Image and Reality, 1780–1850," *Journal of British Studies*, I (1961), 94–110.

7   P. D. Curtin, *The Image of Africa* (Madison, 1964), 227–43, 363–87; R. H. Pearce, *The Savages of America* (Baltimore, 1952), 42–49; P. M. Ashburn, *The Ranks of Death* (New York, 1947), *passim*.

8   The standard general work on epidemiology is Maxcy-Rosenau, *Preventive Medicine and Public Health* (New York, 9th ed., 1965), edited by Philip E. Sartwell. But the most convenient recent and brief summary is Ian Taylor and John Knowleden, *Principles of Epidemiology* (London, 1964). I should like to express my appreciation to Dr. Alfred S. Evans, professor of epidemiology, Yale University, for his kindness in introducing me to this field.

9   See T. Dublin and B. S. Blumberg, "Inherited Disease Susceptibility," *Public Health Reports*, LXXVI (1961), especially 499, 502.

10   William H. McNeill, in *The Rise of the West* (Chicago, 1963), has traced this pattern in world history.

11   In spite of its age, August Hirsch, *Handbook of Geographical and Historical Pathology*, 3 Vols. (London, 1883), continues to be the most convenient reference work for historical epidemiology.

12   Taylor and Knowleden, 162–64.

13   *Ibid.*, 159–60, 221–24; personal communication from Professor Alfred S. Evans.

14   For balanced polymorphisms in general, see Dublin and Blumberg, *passim*.

15   See W. Zelinsky, "The Historical Geography of the Negro Population of Latin America," *Journal of Negro History*, XXXIV (1949), 203.

16   The most extensive study of the medical records of the sixteenth century Americas is Ashburn; see 176–90, 238–44. See also, Maxcy-Rosenau, 274.

17   Ashburn, *passim*; S. F. Cook and W. Borah, "The Rate of Population Change in Central Mexico, 1550–1570," *Hispanic American Historical Review*, XXXVII (1957), 463–70; W. Borah and S. F. Cook, *The Aboriginal Population of Mexico on the Eve of the Spanish Conquest* (Berkeley, 1963); J. H. Steward (ed.), *Handbook of the South American Indians*, 5 Vols. (Washington, 1946–49).

18   Curtin, *Image of Africa*, 58–87, 177–97, 343–62.

19   Great Britain, *Parliamentary Papers* (hereafter, *PP*), 1837–38, XL (*Accounts and Papers*, V) [138], "Statistical Account of Sickness, Mortality and Invaliding among Troops in the West Indies"; 1839, XVI (*Reports from Commissioners*, III) [166], "Statistical Report of the Sickness, Mortality and Invaliding among the Troops in the United Kingdom, Mediterranean and British North America"; 1840, XXX (*Accounts and Papers*, II) [228], "Statistical Report of the Sickness, Mortality and Invaliding among Troops in Western Africa, St. Helena, Cape of Good Hope and Mauritius"; 1842, XXVII (*Accounts and Papers*, II) [358], "Statistical Report of the Sickness, Mortality and Invaliding among Her Majesty's Troops Serving in Ceylon, the Tenasserim Provinces, and the Burmese Empire."

20   *PP*, 1839 [166], 4–7.

21   The early nineteenth-century mortality of newly arrived Europeans varied between about 350 and 800 per thousand. See Curtin, *Image of Africa*, 483–87, for a collection of sample data.

22   Gaston Martin, *L'ère des négriers (1714–1774)* (Paris, 1931), 43, 115.

23   Thomas Clarkson to Lords of Trade and Plantations, July 27, 1788, in Great Britain, Privy Council, *Report of the Lords of the Committee of Council for . . . Trade and Foreign Plantations . . . Concerning the Present State of Trade to Africa, and Particularly the Trade in Slaves . . .* (London, 1789).

24   For a statistical study of the origins of Sierra Leone recaptives, see P. D. Curtin and Jan Vansina, "Sources of the Nineteenth Century Atlantic Slave Trade" *Journal of African History*, V (1964), 185 208.

25   *PP*, 1840, XXX [228], 15–16.

26   This level of increased mortality following movement within Africa is relatively low compared with the experience of some drafts of forced labor at railroad building and other projects during the colonial period. It is estimated, for example, that 10–15 per cent of all the workers died in the construction of the Pointe Noire-Brazzaville line in Moyen Congo, and annual mortality rates ran as high as 452 per thousand in 1927 and 172 per thousand in 1929. V. Thompson and R. Adloff, *The Emerging States of French Equatorial Africa* (Stanford, 1960), 142; Lord Hailey, *An African Survey* (London, 1938), 1590.

27   *PP*, 1837–38, XL [138], 49. See, also, G. W. Roberts, *The Population of Jamaica* (New Haven, 1957), 171–72.

28   F. Guerra, "The Influence of Disease on Race, Logistics and Colonization in the Antilles," *Journal of Tropical Medicine and Hygiene*, LXIX (1966), 23–35.

29   For the Afro-Eurasian origin of these diseases, see Ashburn, 102–40.

30   Yellow fever epidemics occurred in Grenada, St. Kitts, Barbados, and Antigua in 1816, but these were largely over by February of 1817, the first year of Tulloch's sample. The disease appeared in St. Vincent in 1822, but otherwise only the French islands of Martinique and Guadeloupe among the Lesser Antilles were attacked during the remainder of the period; though a very serious epidemic affecting all the Lesser Antilles reappeared in 1852–53 (Hirsch, I, 322–25).

31   The death rate from "diseases of the lungs" among African troops in Jamaica, however, was only 7.5 per thousand per annum, a figure reasonably in line with that of African troops in Sierra Leone itself. (*PP*, 1837–38, XL [138], 50.) The Windward and Leeward Command's figure has been accepted as more reliable, however, largely on account of the larger size of the sample.

32   Hirsch, III, 151–52, 225–28.

33   *PP*, 1840, XXX [228], 7, 19.

34   *PP*, 1837–38, XL [138], 50.

35   *PP*, 1837–38, XL [138], 89, 92.

36   *PP*, 1840, XXX [228], 7.

37   Hirsch, J, 328–29, 335.

38   Population data concerning the immigration and emigration of white populations in the West Indies and Brazil are extremely scarce, but it appears more than likely that the white populations of the South Atlantic plantation colonies also failed to become self-sustaining during the period of the slave trade. The sex ratios of white populations in the French and English Caribbean colonies were very heavily overbalanced with men. Estimates for the French Caribbean about 1700 put the sex ratio at three thousand to four thousand white men per thousand women. (Gaston Martin, *Histoire de l'esclavage dans les colonies françaises* [Paris, 1948], 26.) This pattern developed from the fact that most white immigrants were either indented servants or else part of the group of merchants, officials, or planters who came to the New World as young men hoping to make their fortunes and return home. Given the fact of an initial mortality of migration at more than ten times the European mortality rate, as Tulloch's data show, the pattern of short-term immigration must have exacted a very high price indeed. E. Revert states bluntly for Martinique that the white population could only be maintained by continuous immigration, at least up to 1848. (*Géographie de la Martinique* [Fort-de-France, 1947], 19.) Yet the European populations of these West Indian colonies grew throughout the eighteenth century. In other territories, such as Cuba and Brazil, however, a self-sustaining and even a naturally growing white population may well have emerged at an earlier date. In Cuba, for example, the white sex ratio in 1827 was 1,185 males per thousand females, as compared with a white Jamaican sex ratio of 1,432 as late as 1844. (R. Guerra y Sanchez *et al.* [eds.], *Historia de la nación cubana*, 10 Vols. [Havana, 1952], III, 348; Roberts, 73.)

39   For samples of eighteenth-century estimates, see L. Peytraud, *L'esclavage aux Antilles françaises avant 1789* (Paris, 1897).

40   A. Gomes, "Achegas para a história do tráfico africano no Brasil—Aspectos numericos," *IV Congresso de História Nacional, 21–28 Abril de 1949* (Rio de Janeiro, 1950), 65–66 (volume 5 of *Anais* of the *Instituto Histórico e Geográfico Brasileiro*).

41   Roberts, 36–37.

42   D. Lowenthal, "The Population of Barbados," *Social and Economic Studies*, VI (1957), 452.

43   See Pitman, *passim*; Martin, *Histoire de l'esclavage dans les colonies françaises*, 125; E. V. Goveia, *Slave Society in the British Leeward Islands at the End of the Eighteenth Century* (New Haven, 1965), 234; L. M. Díaz Soler, *Historia de la esclavitud en Puerto Rico, 1493–1890* (Madrid, 1953), 117; Julio J. Brusone, in Guerra y Sanchez *et al.*, IV, 188. The United States, however, was a striking exception to this pattern of natural decrease among the slave population. R. R. Kuczynski pointed out the remarkable contrast between the North American colonies and Jamaica more than thirty years ago, in *Population Movements* (London, 1936), 15–17. Net slave imports into the territory of the later United States were probably no more than 500,000 in all, but Negro population at the time of emancipation was more than 4.5 millions. In Jamaica, by contrast, net imports during the whole period of the slave trade have been estimated at more than 700,000, while the Negro population at the time of emancipation was only 350,000.

44   For discussions of planters' policies on slave breeding or replacement from Africa, see B. Edwards, *The History, Civil and Commercial of the British Colonies in the West Indies*, 2 Vols. (London, 1794), II, 147–54; R. Pares, *West India Fortune* (London, 1950), 123–24; Roberts, 219–47; G. Debien, *Plantations et esclaves à Saint-Domingue* (Dakar, 1962), 44–51.

45   Lowenthal, 453.

46   Roberts, 39–41.

47   Julio J. Brusone, in Guerra y Sanchez *et al.*, IV, 167–81; Gomes, 65–66.

Chapter 2

Patrick Manning

WHY AFRICANS? THE RISE OF THE SLAVE TRADE TO 1700

WHY WERE AFRICANS ENSLAVED in such large numbers, and over such a wide area, that there grew up in western thought an almost automatic connection between black people and slave status? Why did the European conquerors of the New World need to import so much labor? Why did it have to be African labor? And why, finally, did the laborers have to be in slave status?

In fact, the connection that has been made between Africans and slavery is often overdrawn. Slavery has been an institution common to many – perhaps most – societies in recorded history. What distinguishes Africa and Africans with regard to slavery, however, is *modernity*. The enslavement of Africans increased in the modern period, a time when enslavement of most other peoples was dying out. This was true in the Occidental and Oriental areas which imported African slaves; it was also true in Africa, where slavery expanded from a somewhat marginal institution to one of central importance during the modern period.

Orlando Patterson, in his cross-cultural, transhistorical study of slavery, demonstrates the near-universality of the slave condition, touching on ancient Mesopotamia, classical Greece, medieval Korea, the Vikings of Europe, and Native North Americans, to name but a few of the societies he discusses.[1] Let us investigate this universality of slavery a bit further, in order to set African slavery in a broader context.

Slavery in the ancient, medieval, and modern worlds

In ancient times, slavery is best documented for the Mediterranean societies of Greece and Rome, though it is known in some detail for ancient Mesopotamia as well. Greek slavery was dominantly urban and artisanal. Slaves were mostly non-Greeks, captured in war or purchased, and they came to represent as much as one-third of the population in the leading Greek states. In Rome, such urban slave artisans, while of great importance in the economy, were outnumbered by a much larger rural population of slave agricultural laborers, so that as much as one-third of the entire population of Roman Italy was in slave status.[2] The slave population did not reproduce itself – both because of manumission and a low rate of reproduction – so that slavery could only be sustained by the continual capture of new slaves. If slave production was not especially efficient, the exploitation of slaves nonetheless produced a substantial surplus which, concentrated in the hands of a small elite, helped significantly to bring about the brilliant achievements of the ancient Mediterranean.

Slavery is also documented for ancient China and the civilizations of India, although the place of slaves in these economies seems to have been lesser than in Rome. In China, the presence of a large agricultural population under the administration of a strong central government (since the days of the Han dynasty beginning in the first millennium BC if not before) meant that there was no great shortage of servile labor, and little need for slaves. Slaves were but a small proportion of the population, probably under 5 percent, and they were owned mainly by the state.[3] Slavery in ancient India was likewise limited in its extent; conquest to obtain slaves and agricultural exploitation of slaves appeared there as well.[4]

With the medieval period (the period from roughly 400 to 1500 AD), slavery can be documented for a wider range of societies. Slavery in India and China continued for the medieval period, the institution expanded in medieval Korea, and debt-servitude came to be of significance in South East Asia.[5] For portions of India and China this slavery came under Islamic regulation. The Mongol conquests of the thirteenth century resulted in the enslavement of a great number of people, and in the extension of large-scale slavery to new areas, notably to Russia. Two of the Mongol successor states, the Il-Khanids of Persia and the Khanate of the Golden Horde in Central Asia, adopted Islam, and in those areas as well slavery came under Muslim regulation.[6]

In the Mediterranean slavery survived the fall of Rome, though its extent diminished and it was eventually replaced, in many areas of Europe, with serfdom. Slavery in the Mediterranean, however, came to be dominated by a new order: that of the rapidly expanding Islamic world. A controversy has long raged as to whether Islam served more to spread slavery or to restrict it. Did the institutions of Islam have the effect of expanding slavery by recognizing and codifying it, or did Islam limit the extent of slavery by legislating against the abuse of the slave?[7] The answer seems to vary with the time and the place. The latter argument is convincing for the case of the Arabian peninsula and, to a lesser degree, for the whole area of the Umayyad Caliphate: slavery had existed since the most ancient times in what became the Islamic heartland, so that the Qur'ān and religious law served to limit the abuses of slaves with such injunctions as the encouragement of slave owners to manumit their slaves at death. But with the passage of time and the extension of Islam into further areas, Islam seems to have done more to protect and expand slavery than the reverse. In an early example of this influence, the Muslim conquerors of Egypt levied an annual tribute on the Christian kingdom of Dongola in the middle Nile valley: this tribute, known as the *baqt*, was paid by the rulers of Dongola to the rulers of Egypt from about 650 AD until the fourteenth century, and required Dongola to furnish some 400 slaves each year. Throughout the medieval period, much larger numbers of slaves were drawn into the Islamic heartland from Africa, the Caucasus, the Black Sea, and other areas.[8]

In the medieval era, Islam spread to significant areas of sub-Saharan Africa. These areas must therefore be viewed as part of the Islamic world and not, as is too often the case, as irrelevant appendages to it. While it is known that Mali and Borno exported slaves across the Sahara, it may also be the case that slavery expanded within those societies by the same logic that sustained the institution else-where in the Islamic world.[9]

Slavery in most of Europe declined in the medieval era, as the Roman heritage of slavery was gradually transformed into medieval serfdom. But European slavery went beyond the heritage of Rome: the Vikings, especially during the period of their emigration, conquests, and long-distance trade, held slaves in fairly large numbers.[10]

During the Crusades – the Mediterranean religious wars of the eleventh through fifteenth centuries – Christians enslaved Muslims and Muslims enslaved Christians. These Crusades continued longest in the west, where the long Christian *reconquista* of the Iberian peninsula, along with wars in North Africa and piracy in the Mediterranean, served to keep slavery alive and well. Indeed, the Spanish and Portuguese voyages of discovery may be seen, in part, as extensions of the Crusades.

Meanwhile, the association between sugar and slavery took form in the medieval Mediterranean, and spread slowly from east to west. The Belgian histo-rian Charles Verlinden has provided magnificent documentation of the early days of sugar production in Syria and Palestine, of its adoption by European Crusaders, of the use of slaves to perform the heavy labor of planting, cutting, and refining, and of the concentration of sugar production on islands, beginning with Cyprus, and then moving to Malta, the Balearic Islands and later, with the early Atlantic voyages, to the Canaries, the Madeiras, and particularly to São Thomé.[11]

With the modern period, after 1500, slavery contracted in some areas of the world, in Europe, in China, and in parts of the Islamic world. One outstanding exception to this regression of slavery was Russia. Russian slavery was unusual in several respects: the slaves were Russian slaves of Russian masters, and they were often self-enslaved. That is, persons without land and unable to gain an existence sold themselves into slavery as a last resort. This system expanded greatly in the sixteenth and seventeenth centuries, and was replaced by the 'second serfdom' of Russian peasants.[12] Another case of modern expansion of slavery was in the Dutch East Indies, where Dutch planters enslaved Indonesians for work on sugar and coffee plantations. Slavery, however, was gradually replaced with other forms of servile labor as the Dutch regime proceeded.[13] The demand for slaves in the Islamic heartland of the Middle East and North Africa remained at much the same level as the medieval era shaded into the modern, but the points of origin of the slaves moved southward: Black Sea slaves tended to be replaced by African slaves. In the New World, Spanish and Portuguese conquerors enslaved Indians as well as Africans in Central and South America during the sixteenth century, but by the seventeenth century almost all slaves in the Americas were of African origin.

The net result of all these transformations in the extent of slavery can be summarized by saying that, in 1500, Africans and persons of African descent were a clear minority of the world's slave population, but that by 1700 Africans and persons of African descent had become the majority of the world's slave popula-tion. African slavery is a phenomenon of the modern world.

To explain why African slavery grew to such an extent in the modern period, and why it lasted so long, we will turn first to a narrative of its expansion, and then draw from the narrative some specific consideration of the demand for and the supply of African slaves.

The Occidental demand for African slaves

As the Portuguese first worked their way along the African coast from around 1440, they captured and purchased slaves which they took to Portugal and to such Atlantic islands as the Azores, the Madeira Islands, the Cape Verde Islands, the Canaries, and São Thomé. The slaves in Portugal were surprisingly numerous, but they were only part of a larger slave labor force including Arab and Andalusian (or Spanish Muslim) captives. The islands, on the other hand, which had been generally unpopulated, became miniature models of what was to develop in the New World.[14]

It is only with the New World that one can explain the European demand for large numbers of slaves. As the Spanish and Portuguese *conquistadores* strode across the Americas, they expropriated wealth and shipped it home until there was little left to seize. Soon enough, they found that they would have to satisfy their thirst for wealth by going beyond expropriation: they would have to *produce* wealth. But since these *conquistadores* had no intention of performing the work themselves, their desire to produce entailed the creation of a labor force under their control. Such a labor force would have to be both productive and cheap, for otherwise the cost of production and transportation would prevent the resulting goods from being sold on the distant markets of Europe, and no profit would be realized. The first impulse of the Spanish was to enslave the Native Americans, but their high mortality and their continuing hope of escape made them unsatisfactory slaves.[15]

Epidemiology is one major factor which pointed toward a demand for African labor. The introduction of Old World diseases to the isolated New World populations decimated them. Smallpox, plague, typhus, yellow fever, and influenza carried away large numbers. While one may doubt the very high estimates of pre-Columbian population proposed by Dobyns and Borah (they estimate as many as 100 million inhabitants of the New World in 1492), their estimated low point of some 5 million Native Americans in the early seventeenth century can be accepted as plausible.[16] With such a rate of extinction, it is remarkable that the cultures and societies of the New World survived.

Of the Old World populations, the Africans had the misfortune and the advantage of living in the most disease-ridden area.[17] Malarial mortality rates for African children took a very heavy toll, but those who survived to maturity had near immunity from malaria, from other African diseases, and also from many of the diseases known in Europe. For European adults not previously exposed to African malaria, on the other hand, the death-rate in the first year of exposure ranged from 30 per cent to 50 per cent; death-rates from New World malaria were slightly lower. So it was that Africans, all other things being equal, had the lowest mortality rate of any population in the New World.

All other things were not equal, of course. The full picture of the Occidental demand for slaves must include not only this epidemiological factor, but other aspects of demography, institutional factors, and such economic factors as labor cost and the demand for slave produce, especially sugar. Since the slaves were given the heaviest work, a minimum of physical care, and poor social conditions, they died in large numbers and failed to bear enough children to reproduce themselves.

This leads us to consider the nature of the work as a cause for the demand for African labor and the demand for slaves in particular. Much of the work done by slaves was on sugar plantations and in mines, though they also provided a great deal of domestic service. We have already seen for the Mediterranean how the particular intensity of labor in sugar production always seemed to point to slavery. For mines as well, a coerced labor force presented great advantages for the owners. Africans mined gold in Brazil and various minerals in lowland Spanish territories.[18] (In one important exception, the silver mines of the *altiplano*, the Spanish relied on a work-force drawn from the local population – miners whose descendants are now the tin miners of Bolivia.)

Slaves did more than cut cane and mine gold: there was always a range of agricultural, domestic, and artisanal tasks to be performed. This range of tasks is one of the reasons for the remarkable stability in the age and sex composition of slaves purchased by Europeans from the fifteenth through the nineteenth century. For example sixteenth-century Spanish settlers in the Canary Islands bought slaves ranging widely in age but averaging just over 20 years of age, of whom just over 60 per cent were male; prices of male slaves averaged 5 per cent higher than those of females.[19] These figures were similar to those for African slave exports over two centuries later. While the range of slave tasks was wide, the slaves were often prevented from becoming skilled artisans. But from manumitted slaves and free mulattos in sixteenth-century Peru and Mexico, for instance, there grew up classes of artisans whose ambitions and competitiveness brought down upon them wrath and restrictions from their Spanish competitors. This ethnic competition among whites, mulattos, and free blacks for artisanal work was to show up repeatedly in New World colonies.[20]

African disease resistance, the economic advantages of slavery in sugar and mine work, and the need to replenish lost slaves with new ones set the pattern for the demand for slaves. But new developments were required for the amplitude of this demand to increase. Among these was the entry of the northern European powers into competition for power on the oceans. Early in the seventeenth century the Dutch, followed by the English, French, as well as the Danes, Swedes, and Brandenburgers, scoured the oceans for treasure, trade, and colonies.[21] When the Dutch took much of Brazil in 1630, they showed little interest in European settlement and instead got right to work on extending Brazilian sugar plantations, implementing a number of significant and cost-saving technical improvements as they did so. They also began to seek out new sources of African slaves. The Dutch experience in Brazil, while it ended with their expulsion at the hands of the Portuguese in 1654, was the harbinger of the new order. British and French colonies in the West Indian islands began with the settlement of Europeans but within a generation sugar showed itself to be the most remunerative crop and a slave population progressively crowded out the white settlers.[22]

One may ask why the European demand for sugar increased so rapidly at this time. Part of it was the reduction of the cost in sugar brought by improved technology and perhaps cheaper shipping. More importantly, European consumption habits were changing, with the advance of urbanization. With changes in the countryside, bee-keeping had been undercut and production of honey reduced.[23]

With these factors now in place, sugar plantations expanded steadily, and with them increased their need for slave labor. The flow of slaves to the New World, which came to exceed the number going to the Orient in about 1650, continued to increase for a century at a rate of about 2 percent per year.

The supply of African slaves

This continuing upward spiral of slave purchases was possible, however, only because of the relatively low prices at which African slaves could be bought. Transportation costs for moving Africans to the New World were lower than for Europeans, but this was not a major factor. So the explanation for the concentration of modern slavery on Africans is not complete until it accounts for the supply of slaves from Africa.

Could it be, as some have argued, that Africa was simply burdened with a surplus population? Was Africa overpopulated in relation to its resources? Were thousands – ultimately millions – of Africans incapable of making valuable contributions to their societies? Or, to put it more gently, is it possible that the captives were removed from Africa without significantly reducing African levels of production?[24] The error in such approaches becomes apparent immediately when one considers Africa's relative abundance of land and labor, the two great factors of production in agricultural societies. For most parts of precolonial Africa, land, rather than labor, was abundant. African patterns of shifting cultivation, preserved well into the twentieth century, demonstrate the ready availability of land. Farmers typically opened up new fields every second year, and left their previous fields in fallow for ten years or more. Labor, in comparison to land, was relatively scarce, and its utilization involved difficult choices. The opening of new fields was limited not so much by the shortage of land as by the shortage of labor. And if labor was not initially in short supply, it certainly should have become so in the wake of the disorientation and depopulation that was to come in the eighteenth and nineteenth centuries.[25]

To argue in this way, however, is to propose a paradox: if labor was the limiting resource in Africa, why did Africans agree to sell so many million able-bodied persons to be carried away from their homes? A clue to the solution is suggested in a cynical old saw: "Every man has his price." Or, to update the language a little, European slave buyers were able to make African merchants an offer they could not refuse.

The resolution of this paradox relies on an insight offered by Jack Goody in one of his wide-ranging, cross-cultural studies. Goody divided the peoples of the world acording to their technology, into peoples of the plow and peoples of the hoe. Peoples of the plow – in Europe, North Africa, and the Middle East – were able, thanks to an efficient technology, to produce a relatively large amount of agricultural output and to support relatively large urban populations. Peoples of the hoe, regardless of their individual levels of energy and initiative, were doomed by their technology to produce smaller amounts of agricultural output. The reasons for the technical inferiority of African agriculture, in turn, were technical rather than social – the difficulty of using draft animals because of tsetse fly and sleeping sickness, and lateritic tropical soils, easily leached, which generally respond poorly to plowing.[26]

Thus, to the degree that a person is valued in terms of the value of goods he or she can produce, the value of an African in African society – even where labor was the limiting resource – was less than that of a European in European society. Since agricultural labor was the primary producer of value in early modern society (in Africa, Europe, and elsewhere) the value of an agricultural worker's productivity set the value of labor in general in a given society.[27]

The logic of African supply of slaves depends, therefore, on the notion that slaves in the New World were more productive than free producers in Africa, with a margin large enough that New World slave owners could pay for the costs of transportation, mortality, and seasoning of their slaves. As long as African agricultural technology, constricted by the limits of the hoe, was trapped at a level of productivity below that of Europeans, European buyers were able to pay consistently more than the value of an African person's produce at home.[28]

So far I have argued that the value of a person (in this case the price of a slave) is determined most fundamentally by his or her productivity: the additional value that person can produce. But every price is a compromise, accepted provisionally by buyer and seller, and prices of slaves were influenced by many more factors than productivity. These additional factors in price determination can generally be classified either as market factors or as institutional factors.

Normally a key element in the price of a commodity is the cost of its production. The problem here is that slaves were "produced" by their families, but were then carried off without the family ever gaining compensation. That is, the economics of slave capture, as Philip Curtin has noted, are the economics of theft.[29] To the captors, the "cost" of a captive was the cost of turning a free person into a captive (that is the cost of capturing, transporting, and sustaining the captive), rather than the much higher cost of "producing" the captive (that is, the cost of raising and educating a person, borne by his or her family). The initial captors sold their captives at low prices precisely because of their low costs of acquiring slaves. This was a market factor, in the sense that these captives were sold at prices well below the normal value of a laborer because they were stolen. But it was also an institutional factor, in the sense that the institutions of enslavement – the structures permitting the theft of humans from their families – made labor appear cheap.[30]

Prices of slaves in Africa were also held down by the limited demand for slave labor or for slave-produced produce: while monarchs relied on slaves to produce for the palace entourage, few other Africans had the wealth to sustain many slaves, nor could they find purchasers for goods the slaves might produce. Yet another type of market factor was the relative preference of European buyers for male slaves, and the preference of African buyers for female slaves.

One key institutional factor keeping African slave prices low was the political fragmentation of the continent. For even given the attractive prices slave purchasers might offer African merchants, there can be no doubt that many Africans, arguing on the basis of personal and societal welfare, opposed the enslavement and export of slaves. Such reactions are reflected in the policy statements and the actions of sixteenth-century kings in Jolof, Benin, and Kongo.[31] Yet they were insufficient. One way or another, European slave buyers could always find an African who would supply them with slaves. It only required a few greedy or opportunistic persons, who felt they should enrich themselves rather than resist the inexorable pressures of supply and demand, to keep the slave trade alive. Those suppliers, in turn, rapidly became wealthy enough to become a focus of power to whom others had to accommodate.

On the other hand, big men, slave merchants, warlords, all had, through their own greed, inspired feelings of cupidity and revenge in their allies and enemies. So the fortunes built up by slave exporters, while impressive, were often short-lived, as their allies or enemies expropriated them. In yet another reversal, however, the leaders of a successful movement of revenge against African slavers found themselves in control of captives, and then found it to their advantage to sell these captives as slaves for export.[32]

There are, however, records of efforts – some successful – to restrict the scope of enslavement. The rise of the kingdom of Asante in the Gold Coast region, for instance, brought a virtual end to the export of slaves from the area it governed. On the other hand, the state was active in buying and capturing slaves from surrounding areas, with the result that the total volume of Gold Coast slave exports grew in the decades following the rise of Asante. Similarly, the Oyo empire of the Bight of Benin was able to prevent the export of slaves from within its borders as long as it remained strong. However, with the nineteenth-century decline and collapse of Oyo, exports of Yoruba slaves skyrocketed. The nearby but smaller kingdom of Danhomè expanded dramatically at the beginning of the eighteenth century, and at least discussed the policy of attempting to halt slave exports – a policy that was certainly relevant for a region whose population was declining as a result of slave exports. But Danhomè itself was rendered tributary by Oyo and prevented from conquering its whole region, so that the situation was frozen for a century with implacable enemies within easy reach of one another, and the toll in warfare and slave exports continued to be inordinately high.[33]

These examples of the relentless growth of slave exports show that slave exports in many ways fit the model of primary exports from Third World countries in recent years: as prices rose, so did the quantity of slaves supplied. But slaves were unlike exports of rice or palm oil, in that the "producers" of slaves could not simply plant more of their resource to meet increases in demand. The expansion of the slave trade can more accurately be compared to the case of overfishing, where the resource is ultimately unable to renew itself, especially given the long time required to bring a human to adulthood. Those who harvested the slaves were motivated by the higher prices, but the real producers – the families of those to be enslaved – received nothing in reward.[34]

If African agricultural productivity had been as high as that in the Occident, prices for African labor would have been bid up until only a trickling stream of laborers flowed across the Atlantic, rather than the great rush of laborers who crossed the ocean in the holds of slave ships. But the low level of African productivity did not in itself make the slave trade inevitable. Indeed, it is at least an interesting thought experiment – a counterfactual – to consider what would have happened if Europeans had engaged Africans as wage or contract laborers, i.e. if African political fragmentation had not been a factor. African workers would still have been cheaper than Europeans and might have emigrated if offered a sufficiently high remuneration. The Europeans engaging this labor, in paying a higher remuneration, would have earned lower profit levels, which would have reduced the growth rate and the extent of the New World economic system to that degree. African merchants would not have received the earnings from the sale of slaves. On the other hand, after a time, African families would have received remittances from the migrants to the New World (much as European families of the nineteenth and twentieth centuries received remittances from sons and daughters in the Americas). Further, most of the mortality and disorder accompanying enslavement might have been avoided; more generally, Africa would have experienced in much less severe form the contradiction between the grasping for private gain and the achievement of public social welfare. The great private gains to be won through slavery, however, meant that this contract-labor alternative was passed by.

Yet perhaps (the reader may argue) it was not economic logic that brought Africans to sell slaves, but rather social tradition. After all, had not Africans sold slaves across the Sahara for centuries? Was not African participation in the Occidental trade but the continuation of an established pattern? Indeed, Paul Lovejoy has emphasized the Islamic links in the earliest Portuguese slave trade along the West Coast of Africa.[35] This set of facts might encourage us to treat the slave trade not as an economically or socially rational (if inhuman) activity, but as an addiction or as a contagion, a behavior based on non-rational motivation. In such a view slavery, once begun, continues to replicate itself until it runs out its course, regardless of economic or social consequences [. . .] While it does help to explain the propagation of slavery, it cannot explain slavery's origins. The motivation of revenge and the logic of contagion served to catalyze the spread of enslavement, but did not cause it.

Instead, of course, we may seek to explain the reasons for the African export of slaves to the Orient. The explanation of the Oriental slave trade breaks down into two parts: in medieval times, the reasons for the movement of African slaves to the Orient before the Atlantic trade became significant; and in modern times, the reasons why the slave trade to the Orient increased after the expansion of the Atlantic slave trade. I shall sketch an explanation of the medieval Oriental trade here [. . .]

The medieval Oriental demand for slaves was based in large part on the desire for domestic servants, though the demand also included demand for soldiers, laborers, and eunuchs. As long as there were alternative sources of supply, African slaves joined slaves of other origins in the Orient. The differential in productivity provides some explanatory power for the movement of slaves to the Orient; most of the slaves were women who were involved in domestic services in the Orient, but many of them had come from agricultural work in Africa. Market forces appear to be more important in this case: the development of market forces in general and a market for slaves in particular caused slaves to move toward the Islamic heartland even when productivity differences were not great.[36]

We have considered the causes of the slave trade, particularly that linking Africa and the Occident. This combination of forces for the European demand for slave labor and African willingness to supply slaves at a relatively low price set in place, by the end of the seventeenth century, a powerful mechanism for large-scale slave migration [. . .] Let us . . . consider one remarkable and well-hidden effect of the slave trade in the Americas. The New World demographic results of this migration, after three centuries, are striking, particularly when it is remembered that Africans had an epidemiological advantage over Europeans. By 1820, some 10 million Africans had migrated to the New World as compared to some 2 million Europeans. But in 1820, the New World white population of some 12 million was roughly twice as great as the black population.[37] The relative rates of survival and reproduction of whites and blacks in the Americas were sharply different.

Notes

1   Orlando Patterson, *Slavery and Social Death: A Comparative Study* (Cambridge, Mass., 1982).
2   Ibid., 30, 179; M. I. Finley, ed., *Slavery in Classical Antiquity* (Cambridge, 1960); *Ancient Slavery and Modern Ideology* (London, 1980). On Mesopotamia see, for instance, Bernard J. Siegel, *Slavery during the Third Dynasty of Ur* (Memoirs of the American Anthropological Association, 66, 1947).
3   Martin C. Wilbur, *Slavery in China During the Former Han Dynasty, 206 BC–AD 25* (Chicago, 1943); E. G. Pulleyblank, "The origins and nature of chattel slavery in China," *Journal of the Economic and Social History of the Orient*, 1 (1958), 204–11.
4   Dev Raj Chanana, *Slavery in Ancient India* (New Delhi, 1960).
5   Mark Elvin, *The Pattern of the Chinese Past* (Stanford, 1973), 30–2, 73–4; Olga Lang, *Chinese Family and Society* (New Haven, 1946); Amal Kumar Chattopadhyay, *Slavery in India* (Calcutta, 1959); Ellen S. Unruh, "Slavery in medieval Korea" (Ph.D. dissertation, Columbia University, 1978); Bruno Lasker, *Human Bondage in Southeast Asia* (Chapel Hill, 1950).
6   Berthold Spüler, *History of the Mongols* (Berkeley, 1972), 22–3, 86–7; Richard Hellie, *Slavery in Russia, 1450–1725* (Chicago, 1982).
7   Marc Bloch, *Slavery and Serfdom in the Middle Ages: Selected Essays*, trans. William R. Baer (Berkeley,1975); H. A. R. Gibb, *Mohammedanism*, 2nd ed. (London, 1953); Ali Abd Elwahed, *Contribution à une théorie sociologique de l'esclavage* (Paris, 1931). An analogous debate rages on the impact of Islam on the status of women: see Lois Beck and Nikki Keddie, eds., *Women in the Muslim World* (Cambridge, Mass., 1978).
8   Harold A. McMichael, *A History of the Arabs in the Sudan*, 2 vols. (Cambridge, 1922); Patterson, *Slavery and Social Death*, 148–59; Andrew Ehrenkreutz, "Strategic implications of the slave trade between Genoa and Mamluk Egypt in the second half of the thirteenth century" in A. L. Udovitch, ed., *The Islamic Middle East, 700–1900: Studies in Economic and Social History* (Princeton, 1981), 335–45; I. M. Lewis, ed., *Islam in Tropical Africa* (London, 1966).
9   Austen, "Trans-Saharan slave trade," 58–65; Jean-Pierre Oliver de Sardan, "Captifs ruraux et esclaves impériaux du Songhay," in Meillassoux, *L'Eslavage en Afrique précoloniale*, 99–134; Lovejoy, *Transformations in Slavery*, 15–18, 28–35.
10 Bloch, *Slavery and Serfdom*; Peter Foote and David. M. Wilson, *The Viking Achievement* (London, 1970), 65–78.
11 Charles Verlinden, *L'Esclavage dans l'Europe médiévale* (Bruges, 1955, vol. 1), (Ghent, 1977), vol. 2). In contrast, William D. Phillips has more recently emphasized the Mediterranean tradition of small-scale slavery (in contrast to the large-scale or gang slavery of New World plantations), and has expressed skepticism about the importance of slave labor in the sugar plantations of the medieval Mediterranean: Phillips, *Slavery from Roman Times to the Early Transatlantic Trade* (Minneapolis, 1985).
12 Hellie, *Slavery in Russia*.
13 H. J. Nieboer, *Slavery as an Industrial System* (The Hague, 1910).
14 Charles Verlinden, *Les origines de la civilisation atlantique. De la Renaissance à l'Age des Lumières* (Neuchatel, 1966); Lobo Cabrera, *La Esclavitud en las Canarias Orientales*; A. C. de M. Saunders, *A Social History of Black Slaves and Freedmen in Portugal, 1441–1555* (Cambridge, 1982).
15 Frederick Bowser, *The African Slave in Colonial Peru, 1524–1650* (Stanford, 1973); Colin Palmer, *Slaves of the White God: Blacks in Mexico, 1570–1650* (Cambridge, Mass., 1976); Klein, *African Slavery in Latin America*.
    An influential economic model of the demand for slaves is that of Evsey Domar, who focuses on the relative shortage of labor (in comparison to land) as the principal cause of demand for slaves; Domar acknowledged his debt to Nieboer's earlier statement of this view. Domar, "The causes of slavery or serfdom: a hypothesis," *Journal of Economic History*, 30, 1 (1970), 18–32; Nieboer, *Slavery as an Industrial System*; see also Pryor, "Comparative study of slave societies."
16 Sherburne F. Cook and Woodrow Wilson Borah, *Essays in Population History: Mexico and the Caribbean*, 3 vols. (Berkeley, 1971, 1974, 1979); Henry F. Dobyns, "Estimating

aboriginal American population: an appraisal of techniques with a new hemispheric esti-mate," *Current Anthropology*, 7 (1966), 395–416; William N. Deneven, ed., *The Native Population of the Americas in 1492* (Madison, 1976); Noble David Cook, *Demographic Collapse: Indian Peru, 1520–1620* (Cambridge, 1981); Alfred W. Crosby, *The Columbian Exchange: Biological and Cultural Consequences of 1492* (Westport, Conn., 1972).

17 Philip D. Curtin, "Epidemiology and the slave trade," *Political Science Quarterly*, 83 (1968), 190–216; Kenneth F. Kiple and Virginia Himmelsteib King, *Another Dimension to the Black Diaspora: Diet, Disease, and Racism* (Cambridge, 1981).

18 A. J. R. Russell-Wood, "Technology and society: the impact of gold mining on the insti-tution of slavery in Portuguese America," *Journal of Economic History* 37, 1 (1977), 59–86.

19 Lobo Cabrera, *La Esclavitud en las Canarias Orientales*, 141–78.

20 Bowser, *The African Slave in Colonial Peru*; Palmer, *Slaves of the White God*; Edmund Morgan, *American Slavery, American Freedom: The Ordeal of Colonial Virginia* (New York, 1975).

21 J. H. Parry, *The Age of Reconnaissance* (London, 1963); C. R. Boxer, *the Dutch in Brazil, 1624–1654* (Oxford, 1957); *The Portuguese Seaborne Empire 1415–1825* (New York, 1969).

22 Richard N. Bean and Robert P. Thomas, "The adoption of slave labor in British America" in Gemery and Hogendorn, *The Uncommon Market*, 377–98; Richard S. Dunn, *Sugar and Slaves: The Rise of the Planter Class in the English West Indies, 1624–1713* (Chapel Hill, 1972); David Galenson, *White Servitude in Colonial America, An Economic Analysis* (Cambridge, 1981); Richard B. Sheridan, *Sugar and Slavery: An Economic History of the British West Indies* (Bridgetown, Barbados, 1974).
      For a detailed description of Portuguese trading practices of the seventeenth century in Africa, see Joseph C. Miller, "Capitalism and slaving: the financial and commercial organi-zation of the Angolan slave trade, according to the accounts of Antonio Coelho Guerreiro (1684–1692)," *International Journal of African Historical Studies*, 17, 1 (1984), 1–56.

23 Sidney Mintz, *Sweetness and Power: The Place of Sugar in Modern History* (Harmondsworth, 1985); J.-L. Vellut, "Diversification de l'économie de cueillette: miel et cire dans les sociétés de la forêt claire d'Afrique centrale (c. 1750–1950)," *African Economic History*, 7 (1979), 93–112.

24 Some defenders of the slave trade argued that Africa had a population surplus. John D. Fage comes close to the same conclusion in his argument that, for West Africa, "the effect may have been no more than to cream-off surplus population" (Fage, "Effect of the export slave trade," 20). Henery Gemery and Jan Hogendorn developed a well-known model of slave supply based on the vent-for-surplus model popularized by the development economist Hla Myint. See H. A. Gemery and J. S. Hogendorn, "The Atlantic slave trade: a tentative economic model," *Journal of African History*, 15, 2 (1974), 233–46; and Hla Myint, *The Economies of the Developing Countries* (New York, 1964). The model does not actually require a labor surplus, but only requires that labor be underutilized. Gemery and Hogendorn do, however, use the term "surplus capacity available for export" (for instance on pages 237–9, 246). E. Phillip LeVeen labelled his analogous model an "excess supply" model: LeVeen, *British Slave Trade Suppression Policies, 1821–1865* (New York, 1977).

25 For a classic study of shifting cultivation, see Pierre de Schlippe, *Shifting Cultivation in Africa: the Zande System of Agriculture* (London, 1956).

26 Jack Goody, *Technology, Tradition and the State in Africa* (Cambridge, 1971), 25.

27 Jan de Vries has demonstrated this principle nicely for Holland in the early modern period, where the high productivity of agricultural labor (which resulted from capital improve-ments in the land) raised the general level of wages so high that industrial firms chose to locate in other areas, with the result that Dutch industry never became as brilliant as Dutch commerce: De Vries, *The Dutch Rural Economy in the Golden Age, 1500–1700* (New Haven, 1974), 182–6, 238–40; "Labor in the Dutch golden age" (unpublished paper, Berkeley, 1980), 14–15.
      Asian producers of rice, it may be noted, occupied a level of technical efficiency inter-mediate between those of Europe and Africa. This factor, in addition to the extra distance from Asia to the New World colonies, tented to isolate Asians from being drawn into European-dominated plantation work. There were, nevertheless, important cases of enslavement and plantation work in Asia, notably Dutch slave plantations in Indonesia and

Dutch importation of Malaysian slaves into South Africa. Further, as African slave exports came to an end in the nineteenth century, millions of Indian and Chinese workers were recruited as cheap contract laborers for plantations and mines in the Caribbean, the Indian Ocean, Pacific islands, and elsewhere: A. J. H. Latham, *The International Economy and the Undeveloped World 1865–1914* (London, 1978), 105–16.

28 Stefano Fenoaltea has constructed an alternative explanation for slave exports on the assumption that African productivity equalled that in Europe. His model is driven by price differences resulting from African demand for imports. While his assumption on productivity is probably ill-founded, his observations on the relative costs of transporting gold, slaves, and agricultural goods are of importance in explaining the changing nature of African exports in the seventeenth, eighteenth, and nineteenth centuries: Fenoaltea, "Europe in the African mirror: the slave trade and the rise of feudalism" (unpublished paper, Princeton University, 1988).

29 Philip D. Curtin, "The African diaspora" in Michael Craton, ed., *Roots and Branches: Current Directions in Slave Studies* (Toronto, 1979), 15–16.

30 This reasoning has some analogies to Marx's discussion of cost and productivity in wage labor, in which he argued that employers pay workers the cost of their reproduction but keep the difference between that and the value of their output. For the American South, there are numerous studies of the value of slaves: these are based both on the value of goods produced by slaves, and on the cost of raising a slave (in a situation where, in contrast to the case of African captives, slaves were born into the master's household): Robert William Fogel and Stanley L. Engerman, *Time on the Cross*, 2 vols. (Boston, 1974).

31 Philip D. Curtin, Stephen Feierman, Leonard M. Thompson, and Jan Vansina, *African History* (Boston, 1978), 188–9; Davidson, *Black Mother*, 120–52, 224–37.

32 Fenoaltea has implicitly demonstrated the importance of African political and social fragmentation in sustaining slave exports by asking why more slaves were not ransomed by their families or by their own efforts: Fenoaltea, "Europe in the African mirror."

33 Christopher Udry, "The Akan transitional zone" (unpublished paper, Yale University, 1985); Robin Law, *The Oyo Empire c. 1600–c. 1836* (Oxford, 1977), 158–61; Manning, *Slavery, Colonialism and Economic Growth*, 27–46.

34 Thomas and Bean have used the image of fishing on the high seas to emphasize the competitiveness of the African slave trade; here I offer instead the image of fishing in a river or lake to emphasize the limits on renewing resources. Robert Paul Thomas and Richard Bean, "The fishers of men – the profits of the slave trade," *Journal of Economic History*, 34, 4 (1974), 885–914.

35 Lovejoy, *Transformations in Slavery*, 35–40.

36 The main work on the medieval market for slaves is that of Charles Verlinden. See, for example, "La Traite des esclaves: un grand commerce international au Xe siècle" in *Etudes de civilisation médiévale, IXe–XIIe siècles: mélanges offertes à Edmond René Labande à l'occasion de son départ à la retraite* (Poitiers, 1974), 721–30.

37 David Eltis, "Free and coerced transatlantic migrations: some comparisons," *American Historical Review*, 88, 2 (1983), 251–80.

Chapter 3

David Eltis and David Richardson

WEST AFRICA AND THE TRANSATLANTIC SLAVE TRADE
New evidence of long-run trends

THE TRANSATLANTIC SLAVE TRADE was the largest long-distance coerced migration in history. On the African side, three regions – the Gold Coast, the Bight of Benin and Bight of Biafra – dominate the historiography. These areas tend to be seen as the centre of gravity of the traffic not just from West Africa but from the whole of sub-Saharan Africa, a situation captured by the description of a section of the Bight of Benin as 'the Slave Coast' on most maps printed before 1820. With the possible exception of Senegambia, the history of these regions is better known than the rest of sub-Saharan Africa. These regions also contained the largest population densities on the subcontinent, and, consistent with this, contained the greatest urban development and, in the cases of the Gold Coast and Bight of Benin, the most sophisticated state structures, All three regions tended to draw on largely exclusive provenance zones, and indeed there is a reasonably exclusive ethno-linguistic homogeneity within their hinterlands. Yet it is still useful to treat these areas together. African slave traders were always likely to view embarkation points in the east of the Bight of Benin and the west of the Bight of Biafra as alternate routes – particularly after Lagos began its rise to major outlet status in the late eighteenth century – and European traders often ensured that ties existed between ports in the eastern Gold Coast and western Slave Coast.[1]

In both the popular and scholarly worlds these heartland regions of West Africa – defined here as the west coast of Africa from Cape Apollonia to Cape Lopez inclusive – have a higher profile than do other regions. They are seen as the major source of slaves entering the Americas; they contain most of the sites and monuments to the slave trade on the western African littoral; and at the same time they are the subject of the majority of the monographs on the trade. The Du Bois Institute's transatlantic slave trade database permits the reassessment of the role of this region in the slave trade and uncovers many new detailed patterns in the movement of its peoples into the Atlantic trade. No long-run overview of slaving activity in any of these regions has been undertaken since the late 1970s.[2] It should be noted that the data currently available are still incomplete as far as distinguishing actual places of trade in Africa and America are concerned. Where such data are not available, we have used intended ports of embarkation and disembarkation of slaves instead. Further, for about 15 per cent of the voyages, we lack data on numbers of slaves carried. In these cases we have estimated the numbers of slaves on board from means computed from very large numbers of observations.

The database suggests that, overall, West Africa probably played a larger role in the transatlantic traffic than non-specialists have appreciated. Curtin's work and the research that his 1969 book triggered suggested that about two out of five slaves entering the transatlantic traffic did so in one of the two Bights between 1700 and 1867 (no breakdown of African origins before 1700 existing in the current literature). The new data set suggests a somewhat higher ratio – perhaps 48 per cent of all slaves – for the period 1595–1867, though much of the higher ratio comes at the expense of Senegambia, rather than regions south of the equator. West-Central Africa in other words sites near the mouth of the Zaire river and from Luanda, Benguela and the adjacent regions – is still the dominant regional supplier of slaves in the eighteenth and nineteenth centuries as a result of this reassessment. This large region south of the equator supplied 40 per cent of the slaves entering the Atlantic slave trade. However, while West-Central Africa was far more important than any of the three individual West African regions examined here, the size of the three regions together is comparable to the West-Central African slave provenance zone as a whole. A West African/West-Central African comparison may thus be more appropriate than a strictly regional comparison.

Within West Africa as defined here, the new data suggest an increased importance for the Gold Coast and the Bight of Benin relative to other West African regions. Whereas earlier estimates gave the Gold Coast six per cent of the total trade and the Bight of Benin about 17 per cent, the distribution made possible by the new data set almost doubles the importance of the Gold Coast and increases the Bight of Benin share to 22 per cent. The Bight of Biafra's share, by contrast, falls slightly to 15 per cent.[3] In sum, the data set currently contains records of 7,085 voyages to these three regions and implies that just under 2.5 million left Africa for the Americas from points between Cape Apollonia and Cape Lopez. All but one of these voyages began between 1662 and 1863. There is no way of estimating with any precision the proportion of all voyages to these regions that the current set represents, but given the range of sources and the coverage of the major national traders, we would be surprised if the current estimates comprised less than half the Africans entering the traffic after the mid-seventeenth century from the area between Cape Apollonia and Cape Lopez. With few signs that gaps in the present data are 'clumped' by region or period, the trends suggested here are likely to be reliable, whatever opinions might be on the volume of the traffic – and therefore the share of the total represented by the present data.

The temporal distribution of these departures is shown in Figure 3.1, which presents estimates of slave departures grouped in broad 25-year bands. Keeping in mind that the Du Bois Institute data set is a sample only, and not a population, it is likely that departures from the Bight of Benin exceeded 10,000 per year over a period of 125 years from 1687 to 1811. Indeed, if we allow for bias in the declarations of Bahian slave ship captains in the period after the British took suppressive action against the trade after 1815, this high volume era probably extended over a century and a half to 1830. The two peaks in the traffic from this region came at the very beginning – 1687–1711 – and near the end – 1787–1811 – of these 125 years, with a rather lower, but still high and steady volume of departures in between. More refined analysis, not shown here, does little to change

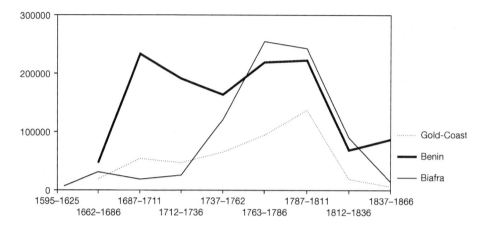

Figure 3.1   Slaves leaving West Africa, 1595–1866

Source: All diagrams and tables in this study have been compiled from information in the Du Bois Institute slave ship data set.

this picture of a large and sustained trade in people in the sense that annual fluctuations in the volume of departures were relatively small. European wars and conflicts within the African supply networks might interrupt business at particular ports and for short periods, but not until the 1830s were these disruptions anything more than temporary.

A quite different pattern emerges from the Bight of Biafra, the second most important West African region for slave departures. Here, ships and numbers carried per ship were somewhat smaller than in the Bight of Benin, 313 slaves per ship compared to 387, and ship size averaging some 122 tons in the Bight of Biafra and 192 in the Bight of Benin.[4] While slave trading began early in the Niger delta, the traffic approached Slave Coast levels only toward the mid-eighteenth century. Moreover, for a time in the late seventeenth century, slave departures from the Bight of Biafra appear to have lagged behind those from the Gold Coast. For fifty years after the 1760s, however, slave departures from the Bight of Biafra exceeded those from both the Gold Coast and the Bight of Benin, though they also subsequently fell off far more rapidly than in the Bight of Benin in the era of suppression after 1815. This rapid decline of slave shipments from Niger delta ports is well documented, with most of the few thousand leaving after the early 1840s passing through points closer to Cape Lopez.[5] As the British were always by far the most important slave traders in Biafran ports, and as British records are particularly well represented in the data, it seems unlikely that further improvements in the data set will change the shape of the time profile for the region shown in Figure 3.1.

The Gold Coast was the least important of the three West African regions examined here, with total departures running at half or less of those in the other two regions. This finding is entirely consistent with recent estimates of regional departures from Africa.[6] However, the temporal distribution of this Gold Coast total is at odds with some recent estimates. Figure 3.1 shows departures gradually doubling in the course of the eighteenth century, as opposed to the currently accepted profile of a strong increase into 1730s followed by a gradual decrease through to the 1780s. Further contributions to the data set may yet clarify this discrepancy.

Slave traders from all parts of the Atlantic world traded in West Africa. Yet there is little doubt that the trading community was much more cosmopolitan on the Slave Coast than on the Gold Coast or the Bight of Biafra. In brief, Portuguese based in Brazil dominated trade in the Bight of Benin, with 55 per cent of all voyages recorded there setting out from Bahia. On the Gold Coast and in the Bight of Biafra, however, the British were even more dominant, sending out 81 per cent of the voyages recorded as trading (or intending to trade) on the Gold Coast and 78 per cent of those trading or intending to trade between the main outlets of the Niger River and Cape Lopez. It might he noted that one quarter of the British voyages to the Gold Coast is accounted for by voyages from the British Americas, the Gold Coast being the African mecca for the small rum-carrying ships from New England and the Caribbean. Within these British-dominated regions, an interesting specialization by port emerges, with the vast majority of slavers in the Bight of Biafra at the peak of the region's slave trade being from Liverpool, while ships from Bristol and London dominated trade with the Gold Coast. After the British, Dutch ports were responsible for the second largest number of voyages to the Gold Coast, accounting for 10 per cent of voyages to the region, while French ports played a similar role in the Bight of Biafra, accounting for 12 per cent of voyages there. After Liverpool merchants switched from slaves to palm oil in 1808, Cuban-based Spanish slave traders became the largest group in the Bight of Biafra. On the Slave Coast, French ships from a wide range of French ports were the second largest group of traders after the Portuguese, accounting for 20 per cent of voyages, but Dutch, English, and, later, Spanish (mainly Cuban) ships were also well represented.

Where did the slaves carried on these ships go after leaving West Africa? The first point to note is that many did not reach the Americas. Mortality data exist for 2,317 of the slaving voyages leaving West Africas. Of those leaving the Gold Coast (n = 1,008), 14.3 per cent died on board. The equivalent figure for Slave Coast ships (n = 760) was 14.6 per cent and for Bight of Biafra ships (n = 496) 19.2 per cent. Mortality on ships leaving all three regions was above the average for all regions in the data set and was well above the 8.4 per cent observed for the 1,916 voyages recorded as leaving West-Central Africa. However, as always with slave ship mortality, the high variances observed – typically approaching the size of the mean itself – makes firm conclusions on interregional mortality variations difficult.[7]

The pattern of West African arrivals in the Americas was far from random. The major single destination of Gold Coast slaves was Jamaica which accounted for 36 per cent of arrivals, but as many again went to other parts of the British Americas. Thus, well over two-thirds of all slaves leaving the Gold Coast went to the English-speaking New World, Barbados being the major seventeenth-century destination and Jamaica dominating the eighteenth century. Akan cultural prominence in Jamaica (including Ahanta, Fanti, Akim and Asante peoples among others) is well rooted in the slave trade according to this data set. Spanish America, the second most important destination for Gold Coast slaves after Jamaica, accounted for 15 per cent of departures.

By comparison with the British American dominance of slave shipments from the Gold Coast, six out of every ten slaves leaving the Bight of Benin went to Bahia in Brazil, two out of ten went to the French Americas, notably St Domingue, and one out of ten went to the British Caribbean. This broad breakdown disguises, however, major shifts in time in the pattern of destinations in the Americas of slaves shipped from the Bight of Benin. In the late seventeenth century, the English Americas took the majority of slaves leaving the Slave Coast. After 1700 the Reconcavo of Bahia in Brazil and the French Caribbean replaced the English, with the former predominating until the quarter century before 1791 when the French share came closer to matching that of Bahia. From 1791 to 1830, however, Bahia took 75 per cent of deportees from the Bight of Benin. Thereafter, Cuba became more important as a market for slaves from the region, and for fifteen years after 1851 was, indeed, the only market available to shippers of slaves from the Bight of Benin. Compared to Bahia, Cuba's links with the Bight of Benin were relatively short-lived. It is, nevertheless, striking that the strong Yoruba presence in Cuba noted by some historians should be based on such limited exposure to the region – at least compared to Cuban ties to other African regions.

In the Bight of Biafra, a much simpler pattern emerges. In the Niger delta ports, which supplied over 90 per cent of the slaves leaving the Bight of Biafra, the first English ship is recorded as shipping slaves from Calabar in 1662 and from this point to 1807, the British took perhaps 80 per cent of all slaves from the region. Igbo and Ibibio peoples, who dominated slave shipments from the region, went to all parts of the British Americas, with Jamaica and the Leewards taking no less than three out of every five, and Barbados and the British American mainlands playing a smaller role. This region also supplied those non-British regions with which the British traded, notably the Spanish Americas. The French Americas received about 10 per cent of Biafran slaves. After the British ended their direct involvement in the traffic, the Spanish Americas, particularly Cuba, continued to draw on the Niger delta. For a decade and a half between 1814 and 1830 the revived and largely illicit French slave trade also drew on these outlets, delivering the slaves mostly to Martinique and Guadeloupe. The absence of Portuguese traders and the slight presence of the Dutch and the pre-1800 French in this area is striking.[8]

The major contribution of the Du Bois Institute data set, however, is to provide more refined geographic and temporal analyses of the slave trade. At this point in the project it is possible to identify the specific points of embarkation (as opposed to regions of departure) of 28 per cent of those leaving the Gold Coast, 37 per cent of those leaving the Bight of Benin, and 69 per cent of those leaving the Bight of Biafra. The relatively low identification rate for the Gold Coast is accounted for by the limited range of the coastline that comprises the region, or at least from which slaves could be expected. The same phenomenon in the Bight of Benin has a different origin. A large part of this region's data is drawn from passes for ships leaving Bahia de Todos os Santos for Africa. These are held at the Arquivo Publico da Bahia. Most of these ships simply declared their destinations to be the 'Mina Coast', which, following an agreement with the Dutch – the effective controllers of Portuguese access to this part of Africa – meant the four ports of Grand Popo, Whydah, Jaquin and Apa. Unhappily, the Brazilian passes do not allow breakdowns among these ports, although Whydah was certainly the most important of the four ports to the Portuguese from the 1680s, when the records begin, until the second quarter of the nineteenth century, when Lagos emerged as a serious rival. From the last third of the eighteenth century, the designation 'Mina' came to include additional ports, all east of Whydah – namely, Porto Novo, Badagry and Lagos (also commonly known as Onim).[9] After 1810, British records of the

Portuguese slave trade allow a more precise identification of African embarkation points. A crude assumption that 75 per cent of those ships designated for Mina in fact took in their slaves at Whydah would perhaps not do too much violence to the historical reality, although it should be noted that in some years departures from Whydah were very low.

Table 3.1 presents a breakdown of departures from individual sites as far as these can be identified in the Du Bois Institute set. Most of these are shown on the accompanying map which dates from the last years of the transatlantic traffic. The concentration of departures from a handful of sites is particularly marked in the two Bight regions, but even on the Gold Coast two embarkation points – Cape Coast Castle and Anomabu – account for 76 per cent of departures.[10] On the Slave Coast, if we allow that at least 75 per cent of slaves leaving from 'Costa da Mina' were taken from Whydah, then the latter port by itself accounts for no less 695,000 slaves, or a little over two-thirds of recorded departures from the Bight of Benin. Indeed, as the current data set is clearly less than the total trade, probably well over one million slaves left from Whydah, making it perhaps the single most important oceanic outlet for slaves in sub-Saharan Africa. Lagos, the second most important Slave Coast port, lagged far behind, though in the closing years of the trade it was probably the most important embarkation point in either of the Bights, a fact accounting for the intense attention it was by then receiving from the British – at this time seeking to end the traffic rather than encourage it.[11]

In the Bight of Biafra, the concentration of departures was almost as severe, with almost 80 per cent of all slaves leaving from just two outlets, Bonny and Calabar, and a further 8 per cent leaving from a third port, New Calabar. The Cameroons and, further south, Gabon, were by comparison of only minor importance, accounting together for only one in ten of departures from the region. There is no doubt that Whydah, Bonny and Calabar were key trading sites not only in Africa, but in the whole Atlantic slave trading system. By this we mean that overall each perhaps imported more goods to be exchanged for slaves than, with the possible exception of Liverpool, any single port in Europe exported into the traffic, and Whydah may have sent more slaves into the trade than any single port in the Americas attracted in the way of arrivals.

An examination of the temporal distribution of departures at these major ports is presented in Table 3.2. Gold Coast ports are excluded because none of them rivalled the Bights ports listed in this table. Whydah's greatest relative importance came in the quarter century from 1712 to 1736. As a result, peak departures from Whydah fall outside the periods for peak departures from the Bight of Benin as a whole shown in Figure 3.1. Given the attention Dahomey has received in the historiography, Figure 3.2 provides annual totals for Whydah as well. Interestingly, the peak of departures corresponds with the era of internal instability in Whydah and its conquest by Dahomey in 1727. It also includes most of the 1730s. Conquest by Dahomey did bring about an immediate decline in departures, but this was very short-lived, and while departures in the 1730s were below those of earlier decades, they were still running at over 1,000 per year – higher than the 1740s and much higher than, say, the twenty years from 1791 to 1810. Cumulatively, more slaves left Whydah after the conquest than before, and close inspection suggests that the decline in the 1730s may have been due more to weakness in the Brazilian markets than to supply constraints. One possible explanation for the quarter-century peak

Table 3.1   Slave departures (thousands) from outlets in the Gold Coast, Bight of Benin and Bight of Biafra, 1662–1863 (listed from west to east)

	Slaves	*Ships*
Gold Coast		
Assinie	0.3	1
Axim	0.1	1
Quaqua	6.7	17
Kormantine	3.0	11
Elmina	2.4	9
Cape Coast Castle	38.9	191
Anomabu	53.9	196
Apam	1.2	5
Tantumquerry	0.4	1
Wiamba	0.2	1
Accra	7.1	24
Christiansborg	4.7	14
Alampo	2.0	6
Total identified	120.9	477
Bight of Benin		
Keta	4.0	14
Little Popo	6.1	18
Grand Popo	0.4	1
Popo (Unspecified)	11.3	36
Whydah	260.2	696
Jaquin (Offra) (Ardrah)	38.8	106
Apa (Epe)	9.3	25
Porto Novo	31.8	77
Badagry	21.0	57
Lagos	63.5	162
Costa da Mina	579.5	1,497
Benin	29.5	84
Total identified	1,055.5	2,773
Bight of Biafra		
Rio Nun	2.2	9
Formosa	0.2	1
Rio Brass	5.0	16
New Calabar	46.3	150
Bonny	240.4	678
Andony	0.8	3
Calabar (or Old Calabar)	196.5	633
Bimbia	1.1	4
Cameroons	22.7	63
Cameroons River	4.8	16
Corisco	0.3	2
Gabon	25.3	84
Cape Lopez	6.6	26
Total identified	552.2	1,686

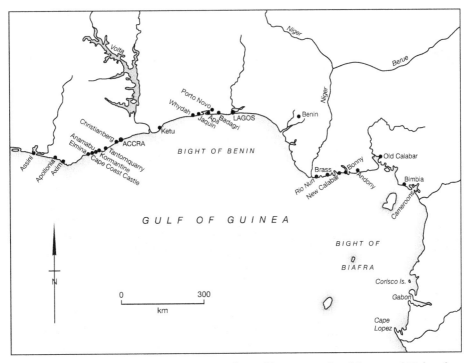

Map 3.1   Ports of embarkation of slaves at the Gold Coast, Bight of Benin and Bight of Biafra, 1662–1863

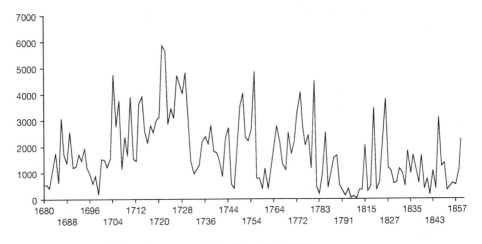

Figure 3.2   Annual slave departures, Whydah, 1680–1863

Table 3.2   Slave departures (thousands) from the Bights of Benin and Biafra: major outlets for slaves by twenty-five-year intervals, 1662–1863

	Slaves (thousands)	Ships
Whydah		
1662–1686	7.9	23
1687–1711	44.2	102
1712–1736	75.6	223
1737–1761	40.8	108
1762–1786	41.7	107
1787–1811	5.8	21
1812–1836	24.2	70
1837–1866	19.9	42
Eastern Bight of Benina[a]		
1712–1736	0.4	1
1737–1761	5.3	14
1762–1786	28.8	65
1787–1811	16.5	39
1812–1836	26.7	83
1837–1866	39.3	94
Bonny		
1712–1736	7.3	27
1737–1761	63.6	176
1762–1786	96.8	253
1787–1811	22.4	66
1812–1836	47.8	149
1837–1866	2.5	7
Calabar		
1662–1686	14.0	55
1687–1711	12.3	47
1712–1736	15.3	66
1737–1761	34.2	98
1762–1786	77.2	218
1787–1811	21.9	74
1812–1836	20.4	71
1837–1866	1.1	3
South-East Bight of Biafra[b]		
1712–1736	0.5	1
1737–1762	6.5	18
1762–1786	30.9	90
1787–1811	4.7	24
1812–1836	11.6	42
1837–1863	6.6	20

Notes: [a] includes Porto Novo, Badagry and Lagos combined. [b] includes Gabon, Bimbia, Cameroons, Corisco, Cape Lopez

in the Whydah trade was the fact that the period from 1712 to 1736 saw the least disruption from European wars of any of the quarter centuries listed. The troughs in departures in 1756–62, 1779–84 and 1790–1814 are clearly associated with European conflict. Moreover, the decline of the slave trade of Dahomey in the 1760s and 1770s suggested by Akinjogbin turns out scarcely to have existed – except in comparison with the pre-1727 era.[12]

Apart from European wars, fluctuations in departures from Whydah at the end of the eighteenth century and thereafter are best explained by increased competition from other outlets in the Bight of Benin. The shift eastwards in the main flow of departures is very marked in the annual breakdowns of departures. Badagry was most important in the late 1770s, and Porto Novo in the following decade. Lagos became of major importance at the end of the Napoleonic Wars and, as already noted, from 1837 down to the British take-over, sent more slaves each year into the Atlantic trade than did Whydah. It is important to note here that the key to understanding this situation lies in Africa rather than Europe. The collapse of the Oyo Empire and the flow of slaves associated with this event was probably the major impulse behind the emergence of these eastern outlets.[13] Table 3.2 shows departures from the three ports grouped together. Yet the most easterly of all, Benin, appears to have followed a path independent of these events. It is at least clear that with nearly 30,000 departures in the seventy years after 1721, Benin was not sealed off from the slave trade to quite the extent that earlier interpretations would have us believe.[14] Outlets between Whydah and Porto Novo – Jaquin and Apa – supplied slaves only in the middle quarters of the eighteenth century, according to these data, which capture nothing of slaving activity there before 1700. Likewise, the western ports are underrepresented here. These were clearly more important before 1750 than after, but so far the Du Bois Institute set has provided a disappointingly small amount of detail on Keta, the Popos and Awey.

In the Bight of Biafra, it was the ports due east of the Niger delta which entered the trade first. The first record of a departure at Calabar in the present data set is for 1625, and from the early 1660s down to the late 1830s (with the exception of the 1690s) departures were rarely far short of a thousand a year. Figure 3.3 gives the annual trend line far this embarkation point. By the 1780s and 1790s shipments from

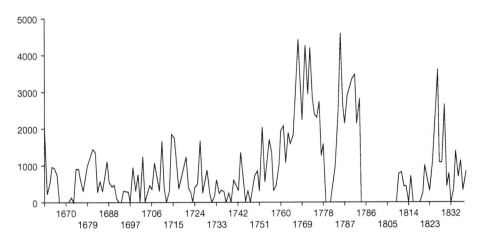

Figure 3.3   Annual slave departures, Calabar, 1662–1838

Calabar were three or four times earlier levels, yet they still lagged behind the flow of slaves from the River Bonny at this time. Bonny entered the trade as early as the 1660s, one of the Efik chiefs being named after an English slave captain of the period. However, Bonny does not show up in the present data set until 1712, but by the 1770s and 1780s was sending more people into the trade than Whydah at its peak. This time profile also holds for the other major Niger delta outlet of New Calabar as well as the less important outlets of Bimbia and Cameroon to the east of Calabar and Gabon to the south. The most southerly outlets, Corisco and Cape Lopez were significant only in the nineteenth century. Unlike the Slave Coast ports which tended to take turns in stepping up trading volumes, swings in departures at Biafran ports north of Corisco tended to coincide with each other. During the years from the 1760s to the 1790s, all these ports contributed to the record stream of departures from the Bight of Biafra. It is much more difficult to link these trends with African political and economic developments than it is in the Bight of Benin. But perhaps there is a significant point here. The massive number of departures through the eastern rivers of the Niger delta and the Cross River was neither the product nor the cause of the rise and fall of major new political structures. The Kings of Bonny and Dukes of Calabar remained rulers of what were essentially still trading enclaves at the end of the eighteenth century and continued to be enclaves throughout, first, the slave trading and palm oil era, and then after 1839, the palm oil era proper. Indeed, beyond the growth of Duke Town at the expense of Old Town in the Cross River, the rise of *Ekpe*, and the consolidation of the Aro trading network, it is difficult to see how political structures and the distribution of power at Bonny and Calabar differed in 1830 from what they had been in the 1660s when slave trade volumes were very low or non-existent.[15]

Some additional insights are possible if we take into account the age and sex characteristics of the coerced migrants. It is now clear that over the last two centuries of the slave trade the proportion of males and especially the proportion of children in the traffic both increased. In addition, it is also now clear that substantial variations existed in the sex and age profiles of slaves from the different African coastal regions supplying the trade. Generally, the Gold Coast, the Bight of Benin, and the Bight of Biafra shared in the general increase in male and child ratios over two centuries, but all three regions typically sent fewer males and fewer children into the traffic than did other areas at any given period. Indeed, a larger proportion of women was always to be observed among those leaving the Bight of Biafra than from any other major embarkation zone in sub-Saharan Africa.[16] Table 3.3 provides additional detail to this broad picture by presenting age and sex ratios among those leaving the major ports within the Bights broken down by century – the data not yet being sufficiently abundant to allow working with the quarter-century intervals used earlier. The table focuses once more on the three leading outlets in the regions – Whydah, Bonny, and Calabar – and two composite categories comprising the three most important embarkation points in eastern Bight of Benin – Badagry, Porto Novo and Lagos – and the outlets south of Calabar – Gabon, Bimbia, Cameroon, Corisco and Cape Lopez. Data for the Gold Coast as a whole are added for comparative purposes. Recorded observations are rather small for the grouped ports, but we expect to be able to increase these in the near future.

Generally the extra detail provided by these more localised breakdowns simply confirms the larger picture. All outlets shared in the trend toward more males, fewer women, and more children through time. These broad similarities across embarkation points should not be allowed to obscure significant differences, however. In the Bight of Benin, a smaller proportion of deportees from the eastern ports than from Whydah were boys and girls, although the gap did narrow in the nineteenth century and for boys, at least, becomes statistically insignificant. In addition, while shares of women leaving Whydah on the one hand, and ports further east on the other, do not seem markedly different after controlling for time, the 40 per cent fall in the proportion of women leaving the eastern Slave Coast between the eighteenth and nineteenth centuries is rather larger than the 27 per cent fall among those leaving Whydah. The more than threefold increase in the share of children among slave departures from Whydah, albeit over two centuries, is also worthy of note. The major political and military event in the hinterland of the Bight of Benin outlets in the late eighteenth and early nineteenth centuries was the collapse of Oyo. The resulting disturbances can plausibly explain why relatively more slaves left the eastern ports over time, but it is harder to make a link between the collapse of the Oyo empire and a surge in the number of children entering the slave trade. Interestingly, the pattern on the Gold Coast is closer to that displayed at Whydah – the point on the Slave Coast in Table 3.3 most adjacent to the Gold Coast – than to that at any other West African port. Nevertheless, the high ratio of women in the seventeenth century, the subject of frequent comment by contemporaries, is reminiscent of the Bight of Biafra.[17]

In the Bight of Biafra, the minor ports south and east of Calabar had smaller shares of women and more children among their deportees than did either of the major ports, though the differences are less marked in the nineteenth century than earlier. The principal points of note in the Bight of Biafra, however, relate to changes at the major ports through time. At Bonny, the decline in the proportion of women entering the trade – from 40 to 14 per cent – is the largest observed for any outlet. The fourfold increase in the ratio of children at both Calabar and Bonny, apparently confined to the period from the eighteenth to the nineteenth century, is also dramatic. Both the decline in the share of women and the rise in proportion of children carried from east and south of the Bight of Biafra were much less than among the slaves leaving the main ports of Bonny and Calabar, though we should take note of what is at present a relatively small number of observations here.

To what extent can the regional trends he explained by shifts in the flow of slaves from outlets located *within* the regions themselves-in other words by shifts in the relative importance of individual embarkation points? The short answer supplied by Table 3.3 is very little. In the Bight of Benin, the minor parts increased significantly in importance so that a major impact on the overall ratios is possible. However, some elementary interactive analysis suggests that this was not the case. This involves two steps. First, we recalculate Table 3.2 so that the time periods correspond with those in Table 3.3 (century-long instead of quarter-century), and in addition compute the proportion of the total departures from the region accounted for by each outlet (or grouping of outlets) in each century. We then select the age/sex ratios for which change over time appears to be greatest – the proportion of women and the proportion of children – and ask the question how would the ratios in the nineteenth century have been different from what they were if the distribution of departures among ports had changed, but the demographic

Table 3.3   Mean percentages of African males, women, men, girls and boys carried to the Americas from major outlets in the Bights, 1662–1863 (number of observations in thousands in parentheses)

	Males	*Women*	*Men*	*Girls*	*Boys*	
Gold Coast						
1662–1700	56.0	41.0	49.4	3.0	6.5	(12.8)
1701–1809	66.6	28.3	54.6	5.5	11.7	(57.3)
1810–1863	–	–	–	–	–	
Whydah						
1662–1700	58.1	37.1	49.3	4.8	8.8	(11.5)
1701–1809	62.0	30.0	48.6	7.9	13.5	(42.6)
1810–1863	63.2	21.3	37.5	16.2	25.0	(7.4)
Eastern B. of Benin[a]						
1662–1700	–	–	–	–	–	
1701–1809	63.4	33.8	57.5	2.6	6.0	(6.6)
1810–1863	67.4	20.2	44.0	12.4	23.3	(13.6)
Bonny						
1662–1700	–	–	–	–	–	
1701–1809	56.2	40.3	52.7	3.5	3.4	(20.0)
1810–1863	68.2	14.3	51.3	17.1	17.3	(12.2)
Calabar						
1662–1700	49.5	47.3	39.0	3.4	10.3	(5.5)
1701–1809	57.4	38.6	50.9	5.9	4.6	(12.2)
1810–1863	64.7	16.6	42.8	18.8	21.9	(7.3)
South-East Bight of Biafra[b]						
1662–1700	–	–	–	–	–	
1701–1809	62.0	29.8	48.6	8.7	12.4	(2.0)
1810–1863	62.5	18.3	38.3	18.9	24.5	(4.9)

Notes: [a] includes Porto Novo, Badagry and Lagos combined. [b] includes Gabon, Bimbia, Cameroons, Corisco, Cape Lopez

profile from each outlet had remained constant between the eighteenth and nineteenth centuries. For the Bight of Benin, the women ratio would have increased slightly rather than declined, and the child ratio would have fallen by 17 per cent rather than increased. The same question posed in the Bight of Biafra results in about 10 per cent of the observed rise in child ratios being explained by shifts in the distribution of departures between ports, but the women's ratio stays constant. It is thus clear that the key factor influencing trends in the demographic structure of the slave trade was not shifts between one strongly differentiated African region and another. Differences between ports certainly existed, but these do not explain the major changes through time – shared by all ports – that emerge from the historical record.

It is obviously easier to highlight these large changes than account for them – whether we look within or without Africa. Why, over time, would fewer women, more men, and more children of both sexes leave *all* ports? These trends were as strong when the trade was expanding between the seventeenth and eighteenth centuries as they were between the eighteenth and nineteenth centuries, when the volume of departures declined. European wars, indeed events in the Atlantic World generally, might have had temporary effects, but it is difficult to pinpoint any developments in Europe or the Americas that could account for these secular trends. Plantation crop type, for example – a factor that might be construed, potentially, as a major influence on the demographic profile of peoples entering the slave trade – remained largely constant throughout most of the two centuries of the trade covered here. From the seventeenth century to the 1820s, it was sugar production, and sugar production alone, that absorbed 90 per cent of those carried across the Atlantic. Thereafter, coffee became important, but the pattern of more children, fewer women, and more men held for all branches of the traffic – the one that led to Cuban and Bahian sugar plantations as well as the one that fed their coffee counterparts in southern Brazil. In effect, the demographic characteristics of the coerced migrant flow from Africa changed from one of rough balance between males and females and the presence of some children in the seventeenth century, to one in which males and children predominated by the nineteenth century. Such a pattern, observed across a wide range of African cultures, political and social structures, and economic activities, should pose something of a challenge for specialists in African history.

To the extent that the age and sex of the forced migrants reflect African patterns of slave supply as well as the requirements of European planters in the Americas (and behind them European consumers of plantation produce), the three West African regions examined here exhibit interesting similarities. They provide evidence which, taken together with other cultural traits as diverse as language structure, religion, and even musical instruments, provides grounds for treating the three regions as a unit when pursuing the topic of cross-Atlantic influences – at least for some purposes.[18] For example, in parts of Jamaica today, 'Igbo' is a term for a nation or sub-group within a religion that is called 'Akan' by all adherents and has clear Akan origins. We are on the threshold of acquiring much more precise knowledge of the direction and composition of the slave trade from West Africa to the Americas. Full recognition of the traits shared by West African peoples will permit more effective use of the new Du Bois Institute data set in nailing down what it was Africans carried with them and what it was that they developed after their arrival. Clearly, the forced migration from West Africa to the Americas was no more random and chaotic than was its free European counterpart.

Notes

Research for this paper was supported by funding from the National Endowment of the Humanities. Fur comments on an earlier draft of this study, we wish to thank Stanley L. Engerman and participants of the York University (Canada) conference, 'The African Diaspora and the Nigerian Hinterland', held in February 1996.

1   Aboh, a major slave market at the head of Niger delta supplied slaves to both Bight of Benin and Bight of Biafra outlets. Also see the comments in 'Extracts from Mr Lyall's Journal', in Macgregor Laird to Malmesbury, 14 March 1859, Public Record Office FO 84/1095, on slaves destined for the Atlantic slave trade being carried down the Niger River. These slaves could only have been embarked via the lagoons of the Slave Coast. More generally see Mahdi Adamu, 'The Delivery of Slaves from the Central Sudan to the Bight of Benin in the Eighteenth and Nineteenth Centuries', in Henry A. Gemery and Jan S. Hogendorn (eds.), *The Uncommon Market: Essays in the Economic History of the Atlantic Slave Trade* (New York. 1979), pp. 172–8.

2   Apart from the syntheses an the Atlantic slave trade published by Paul Lovejoy ('The Volume of the Atlantic Slave Trade: A Synthesis', *Journal of African History*, 23 [1982], pp. 473–501 and 'The Impact of the Atlantic Slave Trade on Africa: A Review of the Literature', ibid., 30 [1989], pp. 365–94), which evaluate the relative importance of African regions, the last full assessment of either region was Patrick Manning, 'The Slave Trade in the Bight of Benin, 1640–1890', in Gemery and Hogendorn (eds.), *The Uncommon Market*, pp. 107–40. For studies on parts of the period covered here see Robin Law, *The Slave Coast of West Africa, 1550–1750: The Impact of the Atlantic Slave Trade on an African Society* (Oxford, 1991), and David Northrup, *Trade Without Rulers: Pre-Colonial Economic Development in South-Eastern Nigeria* (Oxford, 1978).

3   For assessments of earlier quantitative work on the slave state and comparisons between this and findings based on the Du Bois Institute set, see David Eltis, David Richardson and Stephen D. Behrendt, 'The Structure of the Transatlantic Slave Trade, 1595–1867', in Henry Louis Gores Jr., Carl Pedersen and Maria Diedrich (eds.), *Transatlantic Passages* (forthcoming). For the modern starting point of this work see Philip D. Curtin, *The Atlantic Slave Trade: A Census* (Madison, Wisconsin, 1969).

4   For tonnage, numbers are 181 ships with a standard deviation of 59.5 in the Bight of Biafra. and for the Bight of Benin 332 ships were used to calculate the mean, the standard deviation being 91.3. Definitions of tonnage varied over time and between countries. These data were calculated after attempts to standardize the data; see the appendix to David Eltis and David Richardson, 'Productivity in the Transatlantic Slave Trade', *Explorations in Economic History*, 32 (1995), pp. 465–84 for the procedures used.

5   For the ending of the traffic in the Rights see David Eltis, *Economic Growth and the Ending of the Transatlantic Slave Trade* (New York, 1987), pp. 168–73, and more recently, Robin Law, 'An African Response to Abolition: Anglo-Dahomian Negotiations on the Ending of the Slave Trade', *Slavery and Abolition*, 16 (1995), pp. 281–311.

6   David Richardson, 'Slave Exports from West and West-Central Africa, 1700–1810: New Estimates of Volume and Distribution', *Journal of African History*, 30 (1989), pp. 1–22.

7   For a fuller discussion of the inter-regional differentials see the article by Herbert S. Klein and Stanley L. Engerman in this volume.

8   See Eltis, Richardson and Behrendt, 'The Structure of the Transatlantic Slave Trade, 1595–1867', Table 7 for a more precise breakdown of destinations in the Americas within the major African regions of provenance.

9   Much of this is based on Pierre Verger, *Flux et Réflux de la Traite des Nègres entre Le Golfe de Benin et Bahia de Todos os Santos du XVIIe au XIXe siècle* (Paris, 1968), pp. 3–5. For the relative importance of Whydah see Law, *Slave Coast of West Africa*, pp. 118–48.

10   Before 1740, Dutch slave ships from the Gold Coast obtained almost all their slaves at the Dutch castle of Elmina, even though they enter the Postma data set with designation 'Gold Coast'. A recoding of this embarkation point yields the result that these three ports supplied 82 per cent of Gold Coast slaves from known destinations (36 per cent from Anomabu, 26 per cent from Cape Coast Castle, and 21 per cent from Elmina).

11   Lagos, of course, was also far more accessible to the mid-nineteenth century British navy than was Whydah. The town of Whydah was located beyond the range of British guns and the Admiralty recognized that it could not be taken without a massive commitment of resources. See Admiralty to Malmesbury, 9 February 1858, enclosure, Commander Wise, 21 December 1857, Public Record Office FO 84/1068.

12 I.A. Akinjogbin, *Dahomey and its Neighbours, 1708–1818* (Cambridge, 1967), pp. 76–7, 141–51; cf. Law, *Slave Coast of West Africa*, pp. 103–4, 284–6.

13 Akinjogbin, *Dahomey and its Neighbours*, pp. 169–71; Robin Law, *The Oyo Empire c. 1600–c. 1836: A West African Imperialism in the Era of the Atlantic Slave Trade* (Oxford, 1977); idem, 'Dahomey and the Slave Trade; Reflections on the Historiography of the Rise of Dahomey'. *Journal of African History*, 27 (1986), pp. 237–67.

14 Ryder's account of slaving activity in Benin is broadly consistent with the pattern displayed by the data set. Alan Ryder, *Benin and the Europeans, 1485–1897* (New York, 1969), pp. 196–238.

15 For a convenient description of the 'ritual trading' networks supplying Bonny, the Cross River and Cameroon (the Aro, Ekpe and Bilaba), see Ralph Austen, *African Economic History* (London, 1987), pp. 94–5. For Gabon and its slave supply networks, see Henry Bucher, 'The Atlantic Slave Trade and the Gabon Estuary', in Paul E. Lovejoy (ed.), *Africans in Bondage: Studies in Slavery and the Slave Trade* (Madison, Wisconsin, 1986), pp. 136–54.

16 Eltis, Richardson and Behrendt, 'Structure of the Transatlantic Slave Trade'; David Eltis and Stanley L. Engerman, 'Fluctuations in Sex and Age Ratios in the Transatlantic Slave Trade, 1663–1864', *Economic History Review*, 46 (1993), pp. 308–23.

17 See, for example, Stede & Gescoigne, Barbados, 4 April 1683, Public Record Office, T 70/16, f.50: Stede & Skutt, Barbados, to Royal African Company, 22 August 1688, T 70/12, p. 31; Royal African Company to Petley Wyborne and Henry Stronghill, 8 August 1688, T 70/50, f.70; Royal African Company to Browne, Peck, and Hicks at Cape Coast Castle, 23 July 1702. T 70/51, f.131.

18 See John Thornton, *Africa and Africans in the Making of the Atlantic World. 1400–1680* (Cambridge, 1992), pp. 184–92, 235–71 for a discussion of the language and religious commonalities.

Chapter 4

David Eltis

LABOUR AND COERCION IN THE ENGLISH ATLANTIC WORLD FROM THE SEVENTEENTH TO THE EARLY TWENTIETH CENTURY

MAINSTREAM WESTERN CULTURE HAS viewed slave labour on the one hand and free or wage labour on the other as polar opposites since at least the eighteenth century, from the time that abolitionism became a major political force. If the legal distinction between slave and non-slave status has usually been clear, differences in the day-to-day experiences of workers under different labour regimes are often less obvious. Indeed, for some any distinction between slave and waged labour is spurious in that industrialisation brought wage slavery to the developed world. For others the ending of slavery in the West Indies may not have brought industrialization, but it certainly saw the continuation of restrictions on labour. From these standpoints emancipation was something less than a water-shed.[1] It is, however, possible to get a different view of the slave-free polarity and where English and West Indian societies lie in relationship to it, if we focus on attitudes to labour in the seventeenth century, both elite and non-elite, colonial and domestic.

Briefly, the argument here is that differences in relations between propertied classes and their potential workers in Britain and the British Americas were much less pronounced in the seventeenth century than they were to become even though chattel slavery was always seen as something separate. As earlier studies make clear slave labour was not as totally powerless as an earlier historiographical tradition believed. Likewise labour in seventeenth-century England was not 'free' in the sense it was to become. It is more useful to regard slave and non-slave labour as part of a continuum than as polar opposites. The issue to be addressed is the nature of the distinction between slave and non-slave labour and why transatlantic differentials increased over time. Equally important are the implications of these distinctions for the timing and nature of Caribbean settlement, as well as the larger picture of transatlantic migration in general and the development of the North Atlantic economy.

To derive a return from their land, propertied classes in most historical societies have needed to create a supply of labour. In the English case this need was common to both colonial and domestic economies, and the propertied classes were willing to employ coercion, albeit with the sanction of the law, to satisfy it despite massive differences in the resource mix and the social structure of the two regions, and the supposed rights of the English compared to the rightlessness of African captives in the Americas. If slavery is the most extreme form of domination, there is an element of the latter in all arrangements between employer and employed, in that they include specific performance and payment expectations backed by law. The systemic violence and dishonouring of the subordinate – if not the natal alienation – that Patterson sees as distinguishing slavery from other forms of domination may be found in many non-slave systems.[2] What has changed over time is the stress on voluntary recruitment and the relative power that the law has accorded the two parties.

Both slavery and serfdom were part of the social fabric of early medieval England, with nine per cent of the population classified as slaves in 1086.[3] Even as these institutions died new forms of compulsion evolved. The Statute of Labourers (1350–51) forced all persons not in a recognized occupation to serve in husbandry, and the only change before its repeal in the nineteenth century was the addition of a lower age limit of 12 in the Elizabethan Statute of Artificers. A major goal of these laws was the control of wages as well as exaction of labour, and there are many examples of implementation in the seventeenth century.[4] A servant was normally bound to the master for a year, and indeed the transatlantic indentured servitude arrangement was a direct outgrowth of this English institution. Like slave-owners, masters habitually complained of servant insubordination, but they nevertheless held rather large powers. Physical punishment was unexceptional and, more important, the law required that servants carry with them evidence of good behaviour to new masters. Such testimonials, explored more fully below, were a potential route to renewed serfdom. There were also restrictions on marriage and pregnancy during service. If we accept Gregory King's taxonomy, 40 per cent of the English population lived in service to others, and others, not fortunate enough to attain such status, were vagrants. From 1572 the definition of a vagabond was simply 'anyone refusing to work for reasonable wages'.[5]

Vagrants were, by definition, not subject to the direct power of employers, though it is worth noting that Scottish colliery owners were for a time permitted by law to kidnap vagabonds and set them to work.[6] For those who avoided kidnapping, the law was even more draconian than for their servant counterparts. According to a well-known guide (for constables, churchwardens, and overseers), appropriately referenced to the statutes, and reprinted frequently after its first appearance in the 1660s, vagrants were subject to compulsory labour on pain of whipping and imprisonment.[7]

Children in this group were forcibly separated from their parents and put out to masters. Elizabethan poor law permitted overseers to bind out destitute children until the age of 24 (21 for females), 'to any man, whom the Officers . . . think fit to receive them in the same parish, or elsewhere in other Parishes in the same Hundred, either with or without mony'.[8] By the end of the seventeenth century, 'with mony' was standard for pre-teenage children, and overseers of London parishes usually attempted to place such children in other parishes, often well outside the city. In the following century the overseers sent cartloads of children across England to the highest bidder, often northern textile mills. Only chimney sweeps were prepared to pay a positive price for the young, and their needs were confined to the particularly undersized.[9] The parish paid £5 to a master when apprenticing a young teenager. Part of the fee (conceptually a negative price) derived from the anticipation that the apprentice would be taught a skill, though in practice parish apprenticeship was for labour, not for education. Moreover, there were instances of compulsory binding, where two JPs could force parish children on to a household, again with an accompanying fee, but clearly not one sufficient to induce a voluntary transaction. The aged poor were likewise compelled to labour for as long as they were capable of doing anything useful. In return they, and indeed all inmates of workhouses, received the rudiments of food, clothing and shelter, but no wages.[10]

Outright enslavement for the destitute was certainly contemplated by property owners. Statute law provided enslavement as a penalty for vagabonds in 1547. This provision survived only two years before being repealed as too extreme to be enforced.[11] But even the relatively egalitarian levellers were advocating a return to such laws a century later. At the base of their plan of society in the early 1650s was a class of slaves comprising idlers who might try to 'feed and cloth themselves' on other men's labours. These were to be whipped into working for others for extended terms until they saw the error of their ways, and if this did not happen they were to be permanent slaves.[12]

In Scotland, serfdom among salters and colliers was not a relic from medieval times. On the contrary, the last claim of nefyship or serfdom proved in a Scottish court was in 1364,[13] and Scotland may have been the first country in Europe to abandon the institution. Salter and collier serfdom was *sui generis* originating in an Act of the Scottish Parliament in 1606 that did no more than make it an offence for anyone to hire a salter or a collier without a testimonial from the current employer. In a time of expanding coal production it was aimed simply at cutting back on the poaching of workers. The Elizabethan Poor Law contains a similar clause. In the course of the seventeenth century, the power of the mineowner to withhold the testimonial became the basis of binding the collier for life to a particular mine. Nor was this a purely Scottish phenomenon. On Tyneside also contracts and character notes came close to generating serfdom at the coal-face, and Germans were working mines in Derbyshire under similar conditions during Queen Elizabeth's reign.[14]

In 1661 further Scottish legislation increased the range of occupations within mining to which the 1606 Act applied – a recognition of the specialization of task in the mining industry. The colliers were sold along with collieries, and valuations for the former were provided separately and with as full appreciation for the discounted present value of future labour as any sale of a West Indian plantation and slaves ever demonstrated. The system had a similar life-span to slavery in the British Americas. The first Emancipation Act, passed in Westminster in 1775, freed Scottish miners, not West Indian slaves, and the refusal of the masters to co-operate was such that further legislation was required in 1799.[15] These anticipated the 1833 and 1838 Acts aimed at the colonies by about as much as the 1606 Act had preceded the establishment of chattel slavery in Barbados.

These elements of coercion in 'free' societies are rather obvious. Less obvious are aspects of slave societies that might be construed as reducing the slave-free polarity. The Hegelian need of the master to achieve the recognition of the slave has preoccupied several scholars. This has provided a philosophical and psychological base on which some historians have built an interpretation of slave culture or at least space between master and slave. Others see a similar outcome resulting from self-interest of masters and the enormous potential for profit that slave labour offered.[16] There are documented instances of slaves on a collective basis being able to change an overseer or protect rights to provision grounds.[17]

A related issue arising from the powerful economic performance of slave societies in the Americas is the relative material well-being of slaves. In the last two decades evidence of the material advantages of New World slavery for the slave has become too strong to ignore. Modern political theorists increasingly stress not only the positive rights of individuals but also negative rights, among which is counted freedom from extreme material deprivation.[18] While slavery constitutes the total destruction of some negative rights, it might actually enhance others – relative at least to some forms of freedom. Measured by such standards the dichotomy between freedom and slavery becomes much less sharp. Most English vagrants were probably less nutritionally secure than their slave counterparts.

Even setting aside these considerations, there was the fundamental issue of power over life and death. One of the most enduring justifications of slavery, especially as practised on war captives, was that if a master spared a captive's life, then the former henceforward had total control over the enslaved person. In fact, it was not only the master that had choice. People in both Africa and in early medieval Europe on occasion voluntarily enslaved themselves, and while the occasion was often deprivation so extreme that the alternative was probable death from starvation, the phenomenon does point to a potential source of accommodation in the master-slave relationship not much explored in the literature.[19] The slave could and did choose between enslavement and death, in this case the death of him- or herself. Suicide was rare, even on slave ships. Similarly, the slaughtering of war captives when a market for slaves was available was rather unusual.[20] But if the master–slave power was severely maldistributed, it was never totally one-sided.

Yet despite factors that appear to reduce the distance between seventeenth-century freedom and slavery, and despite the thrust of other essays in the present collection, essential differences remained, not least in the minds of those who were chattels and those who were not. For slaves, 'wage slavery' was no doubt preferable to their own situation. For the seventeenth-century English, the distinction was sufficiently clear that, as discussed below, they never imposed such status on members of their own community. The fact that slaves might be materially better off than free persons in the Americas, Africa or Europe was irrelevant. Historical evidence of the English poor lining up to become slaves on the sugar plantations of the Caribbean is as scarce as that of similar behaviour by their African counterparts. Control over one's life was generally more important than material benefits beyond the absolute minimum.

In theory there may be little difference between 'fear of the lash' and the 'fear of hunger' which some abolitionists argued would replace the whip in the aftermath of slavery. Such a proposition is basic to the analysis of those who stress the lack of distinction between 'chattel slavery' and 'wage slavery'. In practice, however, chattel slavery did provide fewer options. A slave could rarely change masters, and his or her ability to avoid tasks assigned was generally less than for free labour. For non-slaves, whether they were vagrants, indentured servants or starving wage labourers, there were simply more alternatives, either present or future. For the 'wage-slave', refusal to work for a specific employer was more likely to mean poor relief than death from starvation. The ability to choose masters, albeit only once a year (or once in four years for indentured servants) and in an intensively competitive labour market with many unemployed, was never within the provenance of any slave. Much less could he or she participate in the amazing mobility of much of the vagrant class of seventeenth-century England. There are thus two propositions to be drawn from the discussion so far: first, that the coercive element in labour loomed large on both sides of the Atlantic in the seventeenth century and, second, that despite this chattel slavery was always perceived as different.

Between the seventeenth and nineteenth centuries, it seems probable that both workers in England and slaves in the Americas were able to improve their positions relative to their employers or masters. As a general proposition the ability of both servant and slave to create space and acquire control over aspects of life (and ultimately, perhaps, room for resistance to the system) increased with productivity. Both slave and free worker were producing far more per person in 1850 than in 1650; the value of both was thus increased over time as was the ability of both to harm the employer-master, either by collective action, maronage, or *in extremis* via suicide. Indeed, some have argued that it was pressure from the dominated that put an end to the worst systems of exploitation because those systems had become too expensive to maintain.[21] Given rising labour productivity in the nineteenth century this seems unlikely, but it is not without relevance that the 'proto-peasant' phenomenon as well as instances of slaves being able to influence their own working conditions occurred late in the era of slavery, when slave values had increased markedly. Nor is it accidental that many of the leaders of revolts were slaves with skills or responsibilities. Similarly, the first unions in Britain to make wage gains were organized around crafts.

But if the distribution of power between master and servant became less unbalanced over two centuries, the process went much further in England than in the English slave colonies. The attitude of the slave master to the slave in the nineteenth century was still one presaged on the seventeenth-century mercantilist assumption that individuals would not work unless they were forced to do so. There is abundant evidence of positive incentives in plantation records, but the basic underpinning of the system by physical coercion had not changed. By the late eighteenth century, England, on the other hand, had seen the emergence of a free labour ideology. While corporal punishment was still common enough, it was supplemented by fining and dismissal. The role of force was much less than in earlier centuries and payment by results and other positive incentives were the norm.[22] Both the law and the custom governing free labour relations had, from the worker standpoint, eased over time. For slaves, this process was much less apparent.

One indication of the gap that had opened up between domestic and colonial society lies in the state's reaction to challenges to its authority. In 1685, in the wake of the Monmouth rebellion, 350 English were executed and dismembered.[23] The ferocity is comparable to the reaction to the 1831 rebellion in Jamaica or the later Morant Bay disturbances under a free labour regime. The sharp distinction is with reactions to equivalent threats to the state in nineteenth-century Britain. Trials of conspirators in the 1790–1820 period, suppression of the Irish under Wolf Tone in 1798, the Peterloo massacre of 1819, the Captain Swing movement ten years later, all occurred when the British state was more threatened than at any point in the last three centuries, yet mass executions and torture – the norm in nineteenth-century Jamaica – were not part of the outcome. But before examining some of the factors that might account for a widening gap, we should first lay out the pattern of seventeenth-century Caribbean settlement.

The British Americas were settled and carried firmly into the plantation export sector of the Atlantic economy with the aid of a mainly British, rather than African or Amerindian labour force. Yet well before the end of the seventeenth century Africans had largely replaced British plantation workers. What is there in the first two sections of this paper that can illuminate this dramatic shift? The relative availability of labour – or the familiar land-labour ratio argument – provides the background to a partial answer. In the English context, propertied classes could initially gain abundant supplies of labour without the draconian measures applied in the tropical colonies. The English ruling class had no need to coerce English servants more than they did. In the tropical colonies the master–slave relationship became the norm because of the scarcity of labour. Without coercion there would have been little production for export in a land-abundant environment. The slave was highly valued not just because of the future value of the slave's work, but because any worker in the tropical and sub-tropical Americas could produce more in a given time period than could servant counterparts in Britain. But it was not just the ethnic base of the labour force that changed; it was also the nature of the master–servant relationship. All English workers arrived in the Americas under terms of indentured servitude. In other words, their servitude was entered into voluntarily, on the whole, and that servitude was temporary. Almost all Africans came to the Americas involuntarily and faced servitude for life. There was no question of a 'negative price' for African children in, for example, Barbados to parallel that for wards of the parish in London.[24]

Why then did England not ship people from home, where labour was low valued, to the colonies, where it was clearly more productive? It was not just in product types and natural resources that the colonies complemented the mother country, but also in human resources. To a degree the English did export the latter. The first major shipment of poor children from London went not to northern mills but to Virginia shortly after its foundation and the last was as recent as the twentieth century when Dr Barnardo's children were sent to Canada.[25] Most social commentators before 1650 saw the colonies as a desirable outlet for England's surplus population and, before the Barbadian tobacco era, the best prospects for this were seen as temperate regions such as Newfoundland. Colonies in warmer climes were initially targets for trade rather than settlement.[26] Yet after 1660 there was more concern with preventing departures (and indeed, encouraging immigration into England) than getting rid of excess population, and the English Americas were peopled by Africans rather than English. Moreover, it was the semi-tropical regions that received most migrants, both black and white, before 1700.

Two salient characteristics of the seventeenth-century economy are relevant here. One was the propertied classes' perceptions of the non-propertied response to wage incentives, the other, the link the former group made between wages and exports, and the perceived importance of manufactured exports to the English economy. On the first of these, mercantilistic attitudes to labour are well known. In short, no seventeenth-century commentator believed that labour could be fully mobilized by wages alone. Richard Haines's evocation of the backward-bending supply curve for labour in 1678 is typical:

> Is it not true [he asked] that the Poor rarely endeavour to lay up anything
> for Sickness and Old age, and will work by their good wills onely for
> Necessity? Which is the reason that our Manufactures are generally more
> plenty, and as cheap, when provisions are dearest. Most of them, if they
> can but get Victuals, will play away half their time.[27]

Stanley Engerman has drawn attention to similarities between this and slaveowners'
approach to creating a supply of labour, a similarity that has led many scholars to
see slavery as a pre-modern, or certainly pre-industrial solution to the labour
problem.[28] As noted above this attitude largely disappeared in England during the
eighteenth century – a development significant to the emergence of anti-slavery –
but re-emerged later to dominate European views of labour in what became known
as the Third World.[29]

A second key economic preoccupation of seventeenth-century social commentators was concern with manufactured exports – mainly cloth – and the associated
need to ensure a cheap supply of labour to the domestic economy. Europe was by
far the largest market for English exports, and woollen cloths by far the most
important category of merchandise exported there. In 1640, 80 to 90 per cent of
London's exports comprised woollen cloth.[30] Europe was also a highly competitive market, not least because of tariffs on finished goods, and for these the level
of wages was a critical cost factor. When continental markets for English cloth
periodically collapsed, the distress in England was widespread especially before
1650. As noted below, much of the drive later in the century to put the poor to
work was fuelled by an expectation of cheap labour and increased exports that
would result from this.[31]

These concerns were constants in the period before 1700, but beginning in the
mid-seventeenth century they interacted with some new demographic and colonial
factors, the result of which was fundamentally to reshape the relationship between
labour markets in England, the Americas, and Africa. The first partial switch to
slaves in an English colony occurred during the 1640s. This was probably less
dramatic than has been portrayed. First, sugar production was still very modest at
this stage. Even in the mid-1660s, when the first reliable data become available,
West Indian sugar products comprised only seven per cent of total imports into
London, and, with the much smaller tobacco component, still amounted to much
less than East India Company imports, for example. Fifteen years earlier, at the
end of the 1640s, it would be surprising if the sugar 'boom' in Barbados generated sugar imports of £100,000, a minuscule share of the London's imports. This
could not represent more than a few hundred tons of sugar. The major expansion
of English plantation agriculture came between 1650 and 1700. By the latter year
tobacco and sugar comprised 15 per cent of English imports, and London imported
nearly 20,000 tons of muscovado sugar.[32] Second, servants were probably still
important in the 1640s. We know little of the Barbados population in this decade
nor the number and composition of the island's immigrants. However, we do know
that more people (in excess of 100,000) left England in these years than had ever
done so before. With Ireland in rebellion, Jamaica yet to be acquired, the population of Virginia about the same size as that of Barbados at the beginning of the
decade, and a new demand for labour triggered by sugar, it seems likely that many
of them went to Barbados.[33]

The labour for the post-1650 expansion might have come from England, as indeed much of it had in the 1640s. In the 1650s English emigration was nearly 20 per cent larger than in the 1640s, but by now there was much stronger competition for migrants from elsewhere in the British Empire, noticeably Ireland. Here and, increasingly as the century wore on, in the Chesapeake too, mortality rates for migrants were less severe than in the West Indies and lower, too, than in the very earliest days of settlement. It is also likely that the availability of land in mainland North America drew people away from Barbados, though the prevalence of white migration from the West Indies to the mainland might suggest that land availability has been given too much emphasis in the literature.

Yet the most fundamental drag on English migration was the fall in the natural rate of population increase in England. After a century of annual rates of growth approaching an average of one per cent, the rate of natural increase fell to less than one-tenth of one per cent per year in the half-century after 1650.[34] For the three decades, 1651 to 1680, the mean rate of natural increase was actually negative. Allowing for the effects of migration, the estimated population of 1656 was not again attained until 1721. In the 1680s it was perhaps eight per cent smaller than it had been a quarter of a century earlier. Estimated age and sex distributions suggest that the labour force was not affected as much as the population as a whole, but in an era of expanding trade, few signs of declining production for domestic consumption and moderate productivity gains, labour could only have been less available after say 1660 than before.

The English acquired their plantation colonies in two major steps; Ireland, Barbados, Jamaica, and the base of the mainland North American possessions in the 1600 to 1655 period, with most of the balance in the Western Hemisphere coming after 1750. More specifically, English control of Ireland, limited to Derry and Dublin in 1649, extended two years later to most of the island. The overriding English concern was how to people it and at the same time make it secure. In the sub-tropics, the new lands meant not only an increase in settlement opportunities, but also new labour-intensive crops. It is striking that these developments coincided with the most enduring check to English population growth in four centuries. More people left England in the 25 years after 1640 than in any other quarter-century before 1820. In the last quarter of the seventeenth century, the total in both absolute and relative terms was the second lowest of any quarter from the mid-sixteenth century to the present day.[35]

There were thus new pressures on both colonial and domestic labour markets after 1650. In England, wages of building craftsmen rose much faster in the second half of the century than in the first. If this was indicative of wages in general and the supply curve for labour really was backward-bending, then the impact on output would have been severe, though we have no way of establishing whether this was in fact the case. We might also note that this was a period of increasing mercantilist restrictions on English goods in Europe – France in particular. Productivity gains at this time were certainly insufficient to absorb these higher cost pressures without there being some impact on the final selling price of the goods. Higher wages would have meant lost European markets for English cloth.[36] In the Caribbean, rising prices for indentured servants occurred with the transition to sugar and persisted even after sugar prices declined. In the Chesapeake the early evidence is scarce, but the high price of servants in the later seventeenth century encouraged planters to look for alternative sources of labour.[37]

Was Africa the only possible solution? The labour options for colonial investors were limited. Payment of wages high enough to attract free labour to the colonies was not one of them. As Adam Smith pointed out in the following century, these wages would have to have been very high. Colliers escaped from servitude in Scottish mines to take wages of less than half what they could earn at the coalface, simply to avoid the disamenities of servitude.[38] To pay enough to attract voluntary labour in the even more restrictive (and higher mortality) West Indian environment was clearly impossible in a competitive market. Coerced labour in some form was essential. But why did it have to be African? The tightening labour market in Britain after 1650 is an argument for more coercion, but not for more Africans.

Ireland, as George Frederickson has pointed out, was one possible source of coerced workers.[39] The Irish not only did not share in the nascent tradition of 'English liberties', they were perceived as different, not least in religion. There was at least one suggestion to ship Irish children aged between seven and fourteen to England and Virginia as part of the 'pacification' process, but no slave trade in this or any other age group ever developed.[40] Perhaps the conquest of Ireland was difficult enough without creating resistance to a trade in coerced labour as well, but the hundreds of Irish prisoners of war sent across the Atlantic could have become full chattel slaves.

As for the English option, we should note that several European countries, particularly England and Portugal, sent convicts overseas for extended terms of unrecompensed labour in the three centuries before 1900. The English investor could surely exercise and extend the existing coercive structures and send English convicts, if not the poor, into the colonies. Again there was no suggestion of this except under terms of temporary servitude. The parallels between the 1601 English and 1606 Scottish Acts, as well as the 1547 English and the 1672 Scottish Laws on vagrants, are obvious. English property owners were more sympathetic to coercion after 1650 but in the end they did not go down the Scottish road, either domestically or, as far as non-Africans were concerned, in the colonies. Just as Scottish colliery-owners were being licensed to kidnap vagrants, in England, Edward Chamberlayne could comment that testimonials (the avenue to collier serfdom) were rarely used.[41]

In the colonies the process was aided by developments on the African side. A trade in coerced labour, including supply networks and well-organized markets, already existed, thanks to the Portuguese and Dutch. Moreover, in the 40 years after 1645 or so the price of Africans newly arrived in the Americas decreased. Indeed, by the 1680s, slave prices in Barbados had probably reached an all-time low for any market in the Caribbean.[42] The reasons for this were partly very low sugar prices, partly the temporary absence of competing national producers in the Americas, and partly productivity gains in the English slave-shipping sector. Yet however low prices of African slaves fell they cannot possibly have matched the cost of sending a convict or a prisoner of war direct from Europe to the Carribbean. There is simply no purely economic explanation as to why European prisoners were never sentenced to a lifetime of servitude in the plantations.

At home, the propertied classes coped differently. In the first place there was a response to changing wages. The large emigration from England in the quarter-century after 1640 coupled with a declining population after 1650 were undoubted factors in driving up domestic wage rates, which in turn slowed down the trans-atlantic movement of English people. But this was not enough to meet the labour needs of the domestic propertied classes. Because of the tightening situation in England, the second half of the seventeenth century saw not only a large slave trade to the colonies, but also an increased interest in obtaining labour through coercion within England. The rapid expansion of slavery in the English colonies in the second half of the seventeenth century coincided with revisions of the Poor Laws at home in 1662, 1683 and 1697. These encouraged local authorities to establish perma-nent physical facilities for the poor. They also facilitated a shift from the concept of the poorhouse as an aid to social control dominant earlier in the century, to that of a workhouse with its emphasis on using the poor as an economic resource.[43] This shift also coincided with a marked change of thrust in the pamphlet literature. All these may be interpreted as the reaction of property holders faced with a labour shortage and a conviction that, for the poor at least, higher wages might elicit less rather than more labour.[44]

The post-1650 English fascination with the potential of the poor as a produc-tive resource has been noted by Joyce Appleby, among others. If we take this into account with demographic and trade data, it is possible to argue that the first half of the seventeenth century in England saw labour in such abundance that land-owners were less interested in coercion. After 1650 a careful reading suggests that property owners were more interested in increasing the hours of labour available, or the participation rate, as well as the work intensity beyond what they would be in the absence of coercion. Children and the old were to be set to work at as early and as late an age as possible, in the former case in the hope of encouraging 'habits of industry' in later life.[45] Several pamphleteers advocated the use of machines in special workhouses to increase the pace of work in a striking parallel to the gang-labour system on Caribbean sugar plantations. Schools for the poor – and almost everyone who addressed the issue advocated these – were aimed at both targets – increasing hours of work as well as work intensity during those hours. But all this stopped well short of advocating or introducing chattel slavery in England.

How much exploitation of the poor actually increased after 1650 is hard to assess. There are relatively few known cases where the grandiose plans for extract-ing labour progressed beyond planning (for example, the odd linen-producing workhouse in London). One reason was no doubt administrative weakness. Local government in England, as the Shakespearean comedies testify, was not very efficient. And the capital required to establish such work centres appears hopelessly large in the light of the effective tax base. But, perhaps in the end, for English employers such centres of coercion were unnecessary because, unlike the sugar colonies, significant output was possible without full coercion. Factory production, with its greater work intensities where slaves would have been particularly useful, had to wait for a later technology, and by then, significantly, social commentators were much more likely to be arguing for the benefits of a high-wage economy. The implications of an English willingness to enslave their own are explored below, but one possibility is that perhaps the industrial revolution would have occurred in England a century before it did and the relationship between capitalism and slavery would be beyond debate.

We turn finally to an expansion of the broader implications of the distinctions between slavery and freedom explored above. The failure of the English to enslave their own has implications for the debate over the relationship between slavery and racism. The refusal or inability of the English to take the least cost option for plantation labour (in other words, using convict labour and prisoners-of-war as chattel slaves) suggests that the switch to African labour was not as purely economic as some have suggested. This argument will be pursued more fully elsewhere, but it seems at least that the cost of plantation produce could have been lower than it was. For transatlantic migration, the ramifications are enormous. Much English migration, indeed the movement of Europeans generally, occurred before the slave trade developed fully. The peak years of the slave trade, say 1680 to 1830, come as an interlude in the European shift to the Americas, sandwiched between early Spanish then English emigration on one side, and the mass migration emanating from first Northern and then Southern Europe on the other. African participation was always much larger than European involvement before the nineteenth century, but for a century and a half it was very much a substitute for it. Without an English, or more generally a European, aversion to enslaving Europeans, it is hard to see how there would have been any Africans in the New World before the twentieth century.

A second set of implications relate to British economic growth. Did Africa significantly hold down English labour costs in the period 1650 to 1750? Some rough assessment of magnitude is possible. Rather more than 300,000 English came to the Americas in the second half of the seventeenth century, and about the same number of Africans (allowing for mortality) arrived in English territory in the Americas. All the migration to the sugar islands could have been English before 1700. Three hundred thousand extra emigrants, 1650 to 1700, or about 6,000 per year constitutes about a quarter of one per cent of the English labour force in this period. The impact of this could not have been very great.

Another important, though still not overly significant, way in which the Americas and Africa affected the English labour market was through demand for labour-intensive manufactured goods. Both the Americas and Africa helped create markets separate from Europe and with fewer restrictions. International trade was certainly more important to the English in 1800 than in 1660. But most of the growth between these two dates was in trade with long-distance markets, Asia and the Americas, and in re-exports of the products of these regions to the continent of Europe. Most long-distance markets afforded some protection for English goods. Transportation costs certainly acted like a tariff barrier, but at least it was a tariff barrier not susceptible to sudden changes and tending to fall over the long term. Similarly, the other taxes and impediments in long-distance British markets were altogether moderate or non-existent compared to European markets.[46] These latter, the traditional, highly competitive markets for English products, grew slowly, lagging behind both total trade and national income in growth, though Europe continued to comprise the largest single market for manufactured exports. In 1640 close to 90 per cent of exports from London comprised manufactured goods to Europe; in the mid-1660s, the equivalent ratio was 76 per cent, and in 1700, 69 per cent. The major decline came after 1700. By 1785, if we take exports from Great Britain as the base instead of exports from London, manufactured goods to Europe accounted for just 28 per cent of the total. Relative to national income, the figures are equally suggestive. In 1700 European purchases of English manufactured goods may be estimated at 5.2 per cent of English national income; in 1785, only 2.3 per cent, though of course the growth in absolute terms of all these markets was considerable.[47]

The importance of this for English wages is that as long as the continent of Europe was the market for English manufacturers, low wages were essential. As this market became less important, so would the preoccupation with a low-wage economy. The slave system of the Americas provided a much more secure and less competitive market for English manufactures than did continental Europe. Thus the strong growth of the slave-based Atlantic system after the Restoration removed some of the urgent need to keep domestic wages as low as those in mainland Europe. Many scholars have noted the changing ideal in eighteenth-century pamphlets from a low- to a high-wage economy. This has been attributed to a change in leisure preferences among English workers and improved productivity. This, and the growth of a large English domestic market formed the backdrop to more rapid economic growth conventionally measured. But an additional stimulus to this acceptance of a 'high'-wage economy was the gradual change in the direction of English exports – from exclusive dependence on highly competitive European continental markets to the more protected environment of the British Americas and British East India markets. This helped relieve some of the pressure for low wages, though the impact of this should not be exaggerated. Given the relatively small importance of overseas trade when measured against the domestic economy, we might conclude that it was a supplementary influence rather than a prime mover.

Likewise, we should not exaggerate the impact of Africa on the development of the Americas. Much recent literature on the early modern Atlantic world has implied that without the African slave trade there would have been no, or at least very few, plantations operating in the Americas, and a greatly reduced level of transatlantic commerce. Indeed for some, beginning with Eric Williams, there would have been no industrial revolution either in England or in North America. Malachy Postlethwaite on the importance of the slave system is often cited. Of the superior efficiency of African slave labour in the Americas there can be no doubt. Yet to assume that in its absence there would have been nothing but subsistence agriculture in the Americas is unrealistic. As we have seen, the dichotomy between free and slave labour was not as sharp for the seventeenth-century English as it became later. Coerced labour came in many forms, and while there are no instances of modern Western individuals reducing their own race to outright chattel slavery, some form of coerced labour, either of their own people or of others would have been possible in the absence of Africans. The sixteenth-century Iberians exported many commodities from the Americas, including sugar, using forced, but not initially African labour. The absence of Africans in the seventeenth-century English Americas may have increased prices for sugar, tobacco, cotton and indigo. Any estimate of the impact of this on consumption or, more widely, the general development of the English economy, hinges on technical considerations that cannot be addressed here. But only some rather improbable assumptions would support an assessment of no production of these commodities in the Americas.

Finally, we should note the most important implication of the race-based slave system on seventeenth-century England may not have been economic at all – in the sense that substitute forms of coerced labour are not inconceivable – but rather ideological. In effect, the growth of the slave system in the second half of the seventeenth century well outside England (if not outside English jurisdiction) allowed the full celebration of English liberties. English ideologues did not have to cope with the dilemma of free labour in land-abundant environments until the nineteenth century. Perhaps this is why the ideological tensions between slavery and freedom in Revolutionary America have received more attention than the same phenomenon in late seventeenth-century England. The oft-cited case of John Locke writing a constitution for the Carolinas that incorporated a slave code, while at the same time laying out the theoretical basis for the Glorious Revolution in England, is nevertheless striking.[48]

Notes

The research for this paper was funded by the Canadian Social Science and Humanities Research Council and the Queen's University Advisory Research Committee. I would like to thank Stanley Engerman, Farley Grubb and Mary Turner for comments on an earlier draft.

1   For example, Nigel Bolland, 'Systems of Domination after Slavery: The Control of Land and Labour in the British West Indies after 1838', *Comparative Studies in Society and History*, 23 (1981), pp. 591–619; Hugh Tinker, *A New System of Slavery: The Export of Indian Labour Overseas, 1830–1920* (Oxford, 1974).

2   Orlando Patterson, *Slavery and Social Death: A Comparative Study* (Cambridge, MA., 1982), pp. 1–14.

3   Edward J. Mitchell, 'Servitude in Early England: Alternative Economic Explanations' (unpublished manuscript, 1969).

4   Ann Kussmaul, *Servants in Husbandry in Early Modern England* (Cambridge, 1981), pp. 166–7.

5   C.S.L. Davies, 'Slavery and Protector Somerset: The Vagrancy Act of 1847', *Economic History Review*, 19 (1966), p. 535. For a modern revision of King, see Peter H. Lindert and Jeffrey G. Williamson, 'Revising England's Social Tables, 1688–1913', *Explorations in Economic History*, 19 (1982), pp. 385–408.

6   A 1672 Act allowed 'coal-masters, salt-masters, and others, who have manufactories in this kingdom, to seize upon any vagabonds or beggars wherever they can find them, and put them to work in the coal-heughs or other manufactories, who are to have the same power of correcting them and the benefit of their work as the masters of correction houses.' Cited in James Barrowman, 'Slavery in the Coal-Mines of Scotland', *Transactions of the Mining Institute of Scotland*, 19 (1897–8), p. 119.

7   George Meriton, *A Guide for constables, churchwardens, overseers of the poor* . . . (London, 1669). There is of course the issue familiar to students of slavery on the frequency with which these extreme measures were invoked. According to the widely read Josiah Child, in London vagrants could beg undisturbed for many months, and the whipping and expulsion of the poor from a parish was rarely carried out 'not one justice of twenty (through pity or other cause) will do it . . .', *A New Discourse of Trade* (London, 1679), Ch. 2. Those meeting the legal definition of vagrants, and therefore liable to whipping and forcible relocation, probably comprised only a very small fraction of the mobile poor. The definition varied over time and place, not least because parish officials and JPs had considerable latitude in interpreting the law (Paul A. Slack, 'Vagrants and Vagrancy in England, 1598–1664', *Economic History Review*, 27 [1974], pp. 362–8). Moreover, recent research has not disturbed Dorothy Marshall's assessment that 'the number of persons moved was not large enough to have much effect on the mobility of labour. The number of removal orders obtained and enforced never seems to have exceeded a few tens of thousands per year for the whole 15,000 parishes and townships involved' ('The Old Poor Law, 1662–1795', *Economic History Review*, 8 [1937], p. 39).

8 *Statutes at Large*, 43 Eliz c. 2. The sex differential may have stemmed from the perception that women were less threatening than men as vagrants, and could be discharged
   sooner (see M. Dorothy George, *London Life in the Eighteenth Century* [London, 1925],
   pp. 232–3). The quote is from Meriton, *A Guide for constables, churchwardens, overseers of the
   poor*, p. 169.
9 George, *London Life*, pp. 215–67. In fact the incidence of child employment during the
   industrial revolution was regionally specific and nowhere extensive. See Hugh Cunningham,
   'The Employment and Unemployment of Children in England c. 1680–1851', *Past and
   Present*, 126 (1990), pp. 115–50.
10 *Laws Concerning the Poor*, p. 86; George, *London Life*, pp. 226, 259.
11 Winthrop D. Jordan, *White Over Black: American Attitudes Toward the Negro, 1550–1812*
   (Chapel Hill, 1968), p. 51; Davies, 'Slavery and Protector Somerset', pp. 533–49.
12 Gerrard Winstanley, *The law of freedom in a platform . . . Wherein is declared, what is kingly
   government and what is commonwealth's government* (London, 1652).
13 Barrowman, 'Slavery in the Coal-Mines of Scotland', p. 129; I.S. Leadham, 'The Last Days
   of Bondage in England', *Law Quarterly Review*, 36 (1893), pp. 348–65.
14 Sidney Pollard, *The Genesis of Modern Management* (London, 1965), p. 188.
15 For details and different interpretations, see Alan B. Campbell, *The Lanarkshire Miners:
   A Social History of their Trade Unions, 1775–1874* (Edinburgh, 1979), and T. Dickson, *Scottish
   Capitalism: Class, State and Nation from Before the Union to the Present* (London, 1980).
16 For the former, see Eugene Genovese, *The World the Slaveholders Made* (New York, 1971),
   pp. 5–8; David Brion Davis, *The Problem of Slavery in the Age of Revolution, 1770–1823*
   (Ithaca, 1975), pp. 561–4. For the latter, Robert W. Fogel, *Without Consent or Contract:
   The Rise and Fall of American Slavery* (New York and London, 1989), pp. 154–98. Cf.
   Patterson, *Slavery and Social Death*, pp. 97–101.
17 Mary Turner, 'Chattel Slaves into Wage Slaves: A Jamaican Case Study', in Malcolm Cross
   and Gad Heuman (eds.), *Labour in the Caribbean: From Emancipation to Independence* (London,
   1988), pp. 14–31.
18 See the literature cited in Amartya Sen, 'Individual Freedom as a Social Commitment',
   New York Review of Books, 14 June, 1990, pp. 49–54; Carol Gould, *Rethinking Democracy:
   Freedom and Social Cooperation in Politics, Economy and Society* (New York, 1988). There are
   parallels between this and recent critiques of freedom in post-emancipation societies. See,
   for example, Thomas C. Holt, *The Problem of Freedom: Race, Labor and Politics in Jamaica and
   Britain, 1832–1938* (Baltimore, 1992), pp. 4–7.
19 Jill R. Dias, 'Famine and Disease in the History of Angola, c. 1830–1930', *Journal of African
   History*, 22 (1981), p. 357. These were usually the times when slave traders were least
   willing to accept such a 'gift', because it was at such times that their own food supplies
   were so restricted. For England, see Mitchell, 'Servitude in Early England'.
20 For data showing the low incidence of suicide on slave ships – the phase of African slaves'
   life when self-destruction was most likely – see Richard H. Steckel and Richard A. Jensen,
   'New Evidence on the Causes of Slave and Crew Mortality in the Atlantic Slave Trade',
   Journal of Economic History, 46 (1986), pp. 57–78. For a different view, see William D.
   Piersen, 'White Cannibals, Black Martyrs: Fear, Depression, and Religious Faith as Causes
   of Suicide among New Slaves', *Journal of Negro History*, 62 (1977), pp. 147–60.
21 Christopher Whatley has argued that the serfs in the Scottish coal-mining industry improved
   their position considerably through collective action ('"The fettering bonds of brotherhood": combination and labour relations in the Scottish coal-mining industry c. 1690–
   1775', *Social History*, 12 [1987], pp. 139–54). Both he and A.B. Campbell see the Acts of
   1775 and 1799 that ended serfdom being in reality aimed at destroying collier combinations that had increased labour costs for the colliery owners (ibid; Campbell, *The Lanarkshire
   Miners*, Ch. 1).
22 Stanley L. Engerman, 'Coerced and Free Labor: Property Rights and the Development of
   the Labor Force', *Explorations in Economic History*, 29 (1992), pp. 1–29; Pollard, *Genesis of
   Modern Management*, pp. 181–92.
23 Peter Earle, *Monmouth's Rebels: The Road to Sedgemoor 1685* (London, 1977), pp. 174–5.

24 Such comparisons are difficult because of differences in life expectancy, health and, most important, period of servitude. Slaves were bound for life, London poor children until the age of 24. A more direct comparison of transatlantic coerced labour costs is possible between colliers and slaves. In 1771 a Lanarkshire colliery with 23 years remaining on the lease had 40 colliers attached to it, the present value of whom, including their wives and children was £32.50 each. In other words, each family unit was valued at £32.50 (calculated from Barrowman, 'Slavery in the Coal-Mines of Scotland', pp. 125–6). This would not have purchased an adult male in any colony in the Americas at this time, let alone a family, though without the limit on the lease Scottish values would presumably have been slightly higher.

25 R.C. Johnson, 'The Transportation of Vagrant Children from London to Virginia, 1618–22', in H.S. Reinmuth (ed.), *Early Stuart Studies in Honor of D.G. Willson* (Minneapolis, 1970), pp. 137–51; Great Britain, Public Record Office, *Calendar of State Papers. Colonial Series: America and the West Indies* (London, 1860), Vol. 1, p. 28, 28 Jan. 1620.

26 See, for example, Richard Eburne, *Plaine pathway to plantations: that is, A discourse in generall concerning the plantation of our English People in other countries . . .* (London, 1624).

27 *Provision for the Poor: or Reasons for the erecting of a working-hospital in every county . . . Linnen Manufactory* (London, 1678), p. 3. 'Typical' does not mean that many writers did not dissent from this view even in the late seventeenth century. See Joyce Oldham Appleby, *Economic Thought and Ideology in Seventeenth Century England* (Princeton, N.J., 1978), pp. 129–57.

28 Stanley L. Engerman, 'Some Considerations Relating to Property Rights in Man; *Journal of Economic History*, 33 (1973), pp. 43–66. On the association between slavery and mercantilism, see most recently Elizabeth Fox-Genovese, *Within the Plantation Household: Women in the Slave South* (New York, 1988), pp. 37–99.

29 See, for example, the views of the geographer James McQueen in the early nineteenth century, and in the present century (though presented in an altogether more sympathetic context) Marshall Sahlins, *Stone Age Economics* (New York, 1974), pp. 1–39. Compare with the comment of the southern US defender of slavery, Edmund Ruffin, 'the greater the demand, and the higher the rewards, for labor, the less will be performed' (cited in Engerman, 'Some Consideration Relating to Property Rights' p. 52).

30 F.J. Fisher, 'London's Export Trade in the Early Seventeenth Century', *Economic History Review*, 3 (1950), pp. 151–61; Ralph Davis, 'English Foreign Trade, 1660–1700', *Economic History Review*, 7 (1954), pp. 163–6.

31 D.C. Coleman, 'Labour in the English Economy of the Seventeenth Century', *Economic History Review*, 8 (1956), pp. 280–1; A.W. Coats, 'Changing Attitudes to Labour in the mid-eighteenth Century', *Economic History Review*, 11 (1958–59), pp. 35–51.

32 Davis, 'English Foreign Trade, 1660–1700, pp. 150–66; John James McCusker, *Rum and the American Revolution: The Rum Trade and the Balance of Payments of the Thirteen Continental Colonies, 1650–1775* (New York, 1989), p. 891.

33 Richard S. Dunn, *Sugar and Slaves: The Rise of the Planter Class in the English West Indies, 1624–1713* (Norton, 1972), p. 55. The widely cited compilation of London passenger registers for 1635 predated the sugar boom in Barbados whereas data on destinations of indentured servants begin only in the 1650s, *after* the switch to African labour began.

34 This paragraph and part of the next are based on E.A. Wrigley and R.S. Schofield, *The Population History of England, 1541–1871* (Cambridge, 1981), pp. 207–9, 227, 441–9.

35 Henry A. Gemery, 'Emigration from the British Isles to the New World, 1630–1700: Inferences from Colonial Populations', *Research in Economic History*, 5 (1980), pp. 179–231.

36 Wrigley and Schofield, *Population History of England*, pp. 420, 638–44; David Galenson, *White Servitude in Colonial America: An Economic Analysis* (Cambridge, 1981), p. 151–5; Russell Menard, 'From Servants to Slaves: The Transformation of the Chesapeake Labor System', *Southern Studies*, 16 (1971), pp. 355–90; William A. Green, 'Race and Slavery: Consideration of the Williams Thesis', in Barbara L. Solow and Stanley L. Engerman (eds.), *British Capitalism and Caribbean Slavery: The Legacy of Eric Williams* (New York, 1987), pp. 35–42.

37 Another possible source noted below was coerced labour from the aboriginal Americas. Both Spanish and Portuguese had used this extensively and the Portuguese organized an extensive long-distance slave trade along the coast of South America.

38 Adam Smith, 'Report dated 1766', in R.L. Meek, D.D. Raphael and P. Stein (eds.), *Lectures on Jurisprudence* (Oxford, 1978), p. 453. I am indebted to Stanley L. Engerman for drawing my attention to this reference.

39 George M. Fredrickson, *White Supremacy: A Comparative Study in American and South African History* (New York, 1981), p. 15; for a review of the literature on the population of Ireland in the pre-famine era. see Joel Mokyr and Cormac O Grada, 'New Developments in Irish Population History, 1700–1850', *Economic History Review*, 37 (1984), pp. 473–88.

40 Anon, *The Present Posture and Condition of Ireland* (London, 1652).

41 Edward Chamberlayne, *Angliae Notitia or the Present State of England: Together with Divers Reflections on the Antient State thereof* (London, 1672), 6th edn., p. 383.

42 David Galenson, *Traders, Planters and Slaves: Market Behaviour in Early English America* (Cambridge, 1986), pp. 64–9; Richard N. Bean, *The British Trans-Atlantic Slave Trade* (New York, 1975), p. 211.

43 Appleby, *Economic Thought and Ideology*, pp. 129–57.

44 A further contrast might be drawn with the nineteenth century, where after 1834 the function of workhouses was to provide a goad to participation in the labour market; in the late seventeenth century the workhouses were seen as a direct way to organize the poor and force them to produce.

45 Spinning flax was widely advocated for this group 'who cannot see to wind silk, nor yet stitch bodies, or work with a needle' (T. Firmin, *Some Proposals for the imploying of the poor especially in and about the city of London* [London, 1678], p. 8).

46 Anon, *Popery and Tyranny; or, the present state of France in relation to its government, trade, manners of the people, and nature of the country* (London, 1679), complained at the various subsidies and state aid to business provided by the French king. The latter was endeavouring 'to make his subjects sole merchants of all Trades, as well imported as exported, and not only by the Priviledges already mentioned . . . but also by putting all manner of Discouragements upon all Foreign Factories and Merchants by Difficulty in their Dispatches, delayes in point of Justice, subjecting them to Foreign Duties and Seizures, not suffering them to be factors to the French or any other Nation but their own, and in case of Death to have their Estates seized as Aliens, and the countenance and conceiving the French have as to all Duty when employ'd in the service of Foreigners' (p. 13). For the importance of protected transatlantic markets to English manufacturers, see Davis, 'English Foreign Trade, 1660–1700', p. 153.

47 London exports calculated from Fisher, 'London's Export Trade', and Davis, 'English Foreign Trade, 1660–1700', pp. 163–6; London and English manufactured exports to Europe for 1699–1701 are calculated from Davis. For 1784–86, see idem, *The Industrial Revolution and British Overseas Trade* (Leicester, 1979), Table 38. Re-exports are excluded as are all trade data for the 1790s and early 1800s on account of the distorting effect of war. National income data for 1700 and 1785 was interpolated from the Gregory King and Joseph Massie estimates as revised in Lindert and Williamson, 'Revising England's Social Tables, 1688–1913'. For 1785 the Lindert and Williamson estimate for 1801–3 was adjusted using the rate of growth estimates for 1780–1801 in N.F.R. Crafts, *British Economic Growth During the Industrial Revolution* (Oxford, 1985), pp. 9–47.

48 For the recent discussion of Locke in this context, see Robin Blackburn, *The Overthrow of Colonial Slavery, 1776–1848* (London, 1988), pp. 39–42.

PART TWO

Origins and Development of Slavery in the Americas

THE ORIGINS OF THE SLAVE systems of the Americas lie in the complex story of sugar. Europeans had long cultivated sugar on plantations in various Mediterranean societies *before* they embarked on expansion into the Atlantic islands and the Americas. The process whereby sugar and plantation cultivation was transposed from the Mediterranean into the wider Atlantic world had a protracted, uncertain and uneven history. Once established in the Americas, sugar became the engine of economic growth, and the rationale for the creation and consolidation of African slave communities, both in Brazil (Stuart Schwartz, 1985) and the Caribbean. Though the British came relatively late to sugar cultivation, once they had adopted it, primarily in Barbados and then Jamaica, sugar transformed the British islands and greatly enhanced British material well-being.

The communities which developed and thrived in the slave islands were more varied and complex than might first be imagined. Their economic activities (and therefore their importance to Britain) went far beyond the production of sugar, their social structure was more variegated than a mere divide between white slave owners and black slaves, and their cultures became an intriguing (through sometimes confusing) blend of European and African. Michael Craton's essay of 1997 provides an overall analysis of Caribbean slavery, and the society it brought into being. It might be tempting to think that slaves (always numerically dominant in the Caribbean) were kept in place by the raw power and violence of the slave-owning class.

It was by no means clear to many white settlers in the pioneering American settlements that Africans were necessary to their endeavours. The origin of slavery in North America is the subject of Winthrop Jordan's classic essay of 1962. Once tobacco proved a lucrative export crop, the Chesapeake region was transformed. As tobacco became ever more important, so too did slave labour. But slavery in the Americas differed enormously, across time and place. These differences were even marked within what we now regard as a single, unitary society, and Ira Berlin's article of 1980 explores the differing patterns of Afro-American life in North America, revealing a diversity of black experience.

———•◆•———

INTRODUCTION TO PART TWO

S LAVERY HAD BEEN A COMMONPLACE institution long before the
Europeans began to enslave Africans. Slavery had characterised the ancient
civilisations of Greece and Rome, it had been ubiquitous in medieval Europe, and
it existed throughout Africa on the eve of European maritime incursions. Slaves
undertook all forms of domestic and agricultural labour, and were generally treated
as different peoples, as outsiders, by slave owners. Slaves were people who were
rootless and who could be shifted around at their owner's will to whatever task
was required or could be sold to other slave owners. Other groups (notably serfs)
shared some of the slaves' characteristics, but slaves were distinct in their isolation
from kin, family or community and were utterly dependent on their owners.[1] Slaves
generally formed only a small numerical position in society. That was to change,
however, with the emergence of the Atlantic economy and the labour needs of the
Americas. The nearest historical comparison we have to American slavery[2] is that
of the Roman Empire of *c.* 200 BC, with its vast dominance over the Middle
East, North Africa and Europe. The enslaved population of classical Italy, roughly
2–3 million people, formed perhaps 35–40 per cent of the overall population.[3] It
was a slave system which needed an empire for its supply of slaves. Moreover,
it was the law and custom of this Roman slave system which proved important in
the shaping of slavery in the Americas in the sixteenth century.[4]

Forms of slavery continued throughout the medieval and early modern periods,
often fed by warfare and by the accumulation of alien captives who formed the
basis for the slave class. One particular association which was to be critical for
the later history of the Americas was the link forged between slavery and sugar
on plantations in the Mediterranean. In time, sugar plantations (and their slaves)
developed across the Mediterranean: from Palestine, to Cyprus, Crete, Sicily, later
to Spain and Portugal.[5] Yet by the time European maritime explorers and traders
began to make contact with West Africa, later with the Americas, slavery in Europe
itself was a marginal and declining force.

The slave systems which developed in the Americas were based on Africans
transported vast distances from a great variety of regions. The systems were themselves very different one from another; they varied across time and place, from
crop to crop and between town and country. But they were linked, whatever the
distinctions, by the colour of their victims. Slavery in the Americas became a black
institution. Yet this was not always so. There are examples of Indian peoples of
the Americas being enslaved (quite apart from whatever indigenous slave systems
those Indian societies may have employed). White indentured labour was also
important in certain of the American settlements. But these (and mixes of all of

them) were quite different from the slave systems based on imported Africans which came to dominate key sectors of the economy in Brazil, the Caribbean and British North America.

Slavery in the Americas became so enormous, so important in a string of societies, that there is a temptation to regard it as typical. Yet quite apart from the fact that it took varied forms, black slavery was, in many respects, unusual. It was grounded in racial (or rather ethnic) difference, and appears in many respects to be quite unlike other forms of slavery. How did slavery in the Americas develop as, when and where it did? And why was it uniquely black? What, in brief, were its origins?

African slavery existed when Europeans made their first maritime contacts with West Africa. African slaves had, for centuries, been transported overland to the Mediterranean, and with the rising influence of Islam between the eighth and fifteenth centuries, slave trades from Africa expanded to the Red Sea and from East Africa. Though figures are virtually impossible to compute, most African societies sustained local forms of slavery, and though some accorded slaves a major role, on the whole most slavery was domestic. Inevitably, there were slave-trading systems within Africa, and slaves were recruited by a wide range of methods.[6] The emergence of a European maritime trading presence on the African west coast would change that fundamentally.

The pioneering Portuguese were not looking for slaves, but rather for other valuable commodities Africa was known to offer, most notably gold, hoping to divert the flow of gold which traditionally moved overland to Morocco into their own floating coffers. From 1441 onwards, the Portuguese encountered local African slave-trading practices. From first to last, Europeans on the coast had to buy slaves from Africans. The Portuguese bought slaves at Arguin from Moors long accustomed to selling in the Saharan slave trade. Further south, the Portuguese similarly found slave traders willing to sell Africans to them as they had to the overland trade. There were, however, African societies which refused to be involved and which had no interest in what the Europeans offered. By the time the Portuguese reached the Akan peoples of the Gold Coast, about 1471, they gained direct access to gold supplies, which they bought with firearms, and with African slaves acquired from further north. Thus far, the Portuguese had intruded themselves into existing Islamic trading and slaving systems. Moreover, the number of slaves involved was small: perhaps 800 a year in the 1450s and some 2,000 a year by the 1480s and 1490s.[7] This changed from 1500 onwards when, moving further south, the Portuguese established trading relations with the King of Kongo (whom they Christianised), acquiring slaves from him for use on the new sugar plantations on São Tomé. By 1526 Kongo was exporting between two and three thousand slaves a year.[8] The Portuguese consolidated their dealings with Kongo in the very period they settled Brazil, and the Spanish established their own settlements in the West Indies.

The first African slaves had been taken to Portugal, then to Madeira and finally to São Tomé. After 1523, however, African slaves began to move in a westerly flow – to the Americas. Once sugar had been firmly established in Brazil in the 1540s, the future direction of the slave trade was sealed. The first blacks shipped to the Americas were those already accustomed to Spain or Portugal or the Atlantic islands. Henceforth, Africans were shipped directly across the Atlantic. By the end of the sixteenth century, about 80 per cent of slaves exported from West Africa went to the Americas. This was confirmed in 1576 by the Portuguese settlement of Luanda, which quickly became their main African slave-trading base. Thereafter, Africans were shipped from a region 'that was to provide America with the most slaves of any area of Africa over the next three centuries'.[9]

There is a temptation to imagine that this development was natural, even inevitable. Yet closer scrutiny illustrates a puzzling issue. Why should Europeans, settling colonies in the Americas, turn to Africa for labour? And why did they require that labour to be enslaved? The answers to these questions lie not so much in Africa, but in what was happening elsewhere in the Atlantic world.

What evolved in the early Iberian settlements in the Americas had been pioneered intitially in the Atlantic islands: the Azores, Madeira, Cape Verde, the Canaries and São Tomé. The most important innovation was the establishment of sugar plantations (similar to those already in operation in a number of Mediterranean sites) in Madeira, the Canaries and São Tomé. European markets emerged for this island-grown sugar, which was cultivated by a mix of imported African slaves and free labour.[10] Those islands' sugar industries waxed and waned; first Maderia, then the Canaries, then São Tomé. On São Tomé by the mid-sixteenth century the industry thrived on the backs of between five and six thousand African slaves. São Tomé was also to become important as a transit point, transporting Africans onwards to the slave markets of the Americas.[11]

By the mid-sixteenth century, a substantial number of African slaves had been transported to the Atlantic islands, as well as to Europe. Though Europeans had made tentative explorations and settlements at a number of points around the Atlantic litoral, the number of Europeans involved was very small. The risks and dangers of oceanic travel and settlement deterred all but the most desperate, brave or foolhardy. There was, from the first, a shortage of labour throughout the European settlements of the Americas. Moreover, Indian labour, though tried in a variety of different contexts, proved itself notoriously reluctant or unable to work at what white settlers required. In the Caribbean, the invading Spaniards had a devastating demographic impact on local Indian peoples, made worse by harsh treatment in experimental agricultural and gold ventures. The fate of the native peoples in the islands helped persuade the Spaniards (urged by Las Casas) not to enslave Indian peoples, but the savage conquests of Mesoamerica saw enslavement and transportation of local peoples to other parts of the region (for urban building, transport and gold-panning) on a massive and violent scale. After the early years, however, the Spanish came to appreciate that they might secure better returns from native Indians by not enslaving them, a point reinforced by a number of decrees. By about 1558, enslavement of Native Americans was effectively ended, though it survived in frontier regions where settlers could in effect operate outside the law.[12]

In Brazil, the enslavement of native people began more slowly and lasted longer, but never proved satisfactory, especially for work in the sugar industry. Indians died, drifted away or simply failed to work as the Portuguese settlers required. But both the Spaniards and the Portuguese knew that other peoples – Africans – had already proved their worth as slaves in the sugar industry of the Atlantic islands. Though some regions of Brazil saw a survival of enslavement of native peoples, it was Africans who, in time, came to dominate the sugar industry. Africans and sugar cultivation were thus wedded together, as were slavery and Africans.

Parts of the American settlement did not require labour on such a scale, but sugar did. Whatever the legal or moral objections to slavery, both the Portuguese and the Spanish turned towards African slavery. This was especially true of the Portuguese in their Brazilian sugar industry. European immigrant labour was non-existent; they would not, or could not, uproot and migrate to the uncertainties and dangers of the Americas, and local Indian labour was inadequate for a variety of reasons. Africans, however, were readily available, courtesy of the Portuguese slaving presence on the African coast, and at what contemporaries regarded as an acceptable price.

The wealth disgorged by Spanish America (often on a fabulous scale) provided the money to buy African slaves, who poured into Mexico and Peru, where they were used in a wide range of urban occupations, such as in mining, agriculture and ranching. By the mid-seventeenth century the slave population of Mexico was 35,000 (less than 2 per cent of the population) but in Peru it stood at 100,000 (between 10 and 15 per cent of the population). However, it was in Brazil and the Caribbean that demand for African slaves took off in spectacular fashion. The sugar plantations and mills of Brazil and later the West Indies devoured Africans. By the early seventeenth century, some 170,000 Africans had been imported to Brazil and Brazilian sugar now dominated the European market. In this the Dutch were crucial, capturing key slave-trading posts from the Portuguese in Africa, gaining a temporary toehold in Brazil itself, but also providing money, financial expertise and markets.[13]

When the Dutch were finally pushed out of Brazil, they sought new areas to develop the sugar craved by the markets served by Amsterdam. Thus, Dutch money, expertise, technology and slaves moved from Brazil to the West Indies. Dutch finance and know-how (especially their sophisticated credit arrangements) enabled British and other settlers in the islands to buy the Africans needed to work in their fledgling settlements. With this invaluable Dutch help, the English in particular were able to brush aside the fading power of Spain in the Caribbean. They were uncertain, at first, how best to develop their newly secured lands, trying a range of agricultural crops and labour systems – notably tobacco. Barbados offers the best example of what happened.

The initial settlement was on smallholdings, worked by white indentured servants from Britain. But the arrival of sugar saw the emergence of large-scale sugar plantations (the landscape was dotted with windmills used for crushing the cane) and the widespread use of African slaves.[14] By the end of the seventeenth century, Barbados, a small island, no larger than the Isle of Wight, was home to 50,000 slaves. A similar pattern unfolded close by on the French islands of Martinique and Guadeloupe. Altogether, the Caribbean islands had, in a relatively short period, absorbed more than 450,000 Africans, Brazil 500,000 to 600,000, and Spanish America between 350,000 and 400,000.[15]

But even these figures began to pale with the development, in the late seventeenth and early eighteenth centuries, of the two islands which came to dominate the Atlantic sugar industry and consequently the slave trade: Jamaica and St Domingue (later Haiti). The English seized Jamaica in 1655 from the Spanish and, like their neighbours on the smaller islands, the pioneering settlers created a string of small-scale agricultural settlements. When the settlers turned to sugar (aided by migrants from Barbados), they developed a society characterised by large-scale plantations and large slave holdings. Much the same pattern evolved in St Domingue. Africans soon came to dominate the islands' populations, outnumbering local whites to such an extent that whites and colonial governments began to fear for social and racial tranquillity (i.e., white dominance and control). Moreover, Jamaica produced sugar on a phenomenal scale: the 500 tons of 1669 rose to 6,056 tons by 1704.[16] St Domingue's rapid expansion was even more impressive. By 1780 its sugar industry was the best in the world and the slave population stood at almost half a million. Exports from the island formed a substantial slice of France's trading wealth, but it was built at a terrible price and exploded in revolutionary and racial fury in the 1790s.

The Dutch had been vital in the early English and French settlements in the Caribbean, but the commercial and military rise of those two nations (enemies from first to last) effectively displaced the Dutch in the Atlantic. The Atlantic slave trade was now dominated by English and French slave ships. Between them, in the eighteenth century, they shipped more than 4 million Africans into the Americas, the very great majority destined to work in sugar. By then, slaves were employed everywhere throughout the Atlantic economy, from the myriad domestic chores in the homes of local whites through to sailor's tasks on the Atlantic ships, but sugar dominated – in Brazil and the Caribbean – and therefore the Atlantic slave trade. It was all made possible not solely by African slave labour, but by the use of plantations. The plantation had become a critical institution in developing the Americas; it made it possible for Europeans, through their African slaves, to bring profitable cultivation to vast reaches of the Americas. What happened in North America was, however, slightly different.

The English settlement of the colonies in the Chesapeake saw slaves introduced from the earliest days, but, as in Barbados, slaves did not become vital until much later. Tobacco transformed everything. Though labour was organised initially around imported European indentured labour, by the end of the seventeenth century tobacco had been effectively taken over by slaves. As tobacco exports boomed, the number of African slaves increased. In South Carolina, the introduction of rice cultivation (like sugar, hard, unpleasant work in difficult conditions) saw a similar drift to African slave labour. By the mid-century, there were about 145,000 slaves in the Chesapeake and 40,000 working in the rice fields. Shortly after Independence, there were 698,000 slaves scattered throughout North America. Though concentrated mainly in the old South, slavery had slipped into all corners of North American life.[17] Slavery in North America was a remarkable institution. It differed greatly between colonies, between town and country, and especially between crops. The slave experience was, then, much more complex than we might initially imagine.

Of course, North American slavery is most popularly associated with the cotton states of the nineteenth century. On the eve of the Civil War, cotton was the most valuable US export, flooding world markets. It was cultivated overwhelmingly by slaves. By then, American cotton planters, unlike their sugar, rice or tobacco forebears, had no need of a transatlantic slave trade for their supplies of slaves. The

United States developed its own internal slave trade, with slaves moving from the eastern slave states towards the south and the advancing western frontier. One million slaves were moved in this way, to work and live on the new cotton plantations. Though it may have lacked the oceanic horrors of crossing the Atlantic, this migration had its own pains and sufferings (notably family break-up and separations).[18]

The slave population of the United States was quite different from most other societies. It was, most crucially, a population which expanded. Though half a million Africans had been imported into North America, by the 1860s there was a slave population of almost 4 million.

Slavery had taken root throughout the hemisphere: in Argentina and Peru, throughout Spanish possessions in Central America and the West Indies, each time in response to new economic initiatives, such as gold-mining, cacao or sugar cultivation. The resurgence of slavery in new locations throughout the region was accentuated by the seismic impact of the slave revolt in St Domingue (Haiti) after 1791. Whatever the causes and inspiration behind that upheaval, the former French colony collapsed. The world's leading sugar producer (30 per cent of world sugar came from St Domingue on the eve of the revolution) left a huge and tempting void, which other American planters rushed to fill.[19] Planters from Brazil to Cuba hastened to produce more sugar (and coffee), all using slaves. Cuba especially boomed in this early nineteenth-century expansion. By 1862, slaves formed about 27 per cent of the island's population (368,550 out of a total of 1,359,238).[20] Both there and in Brazil, there was a determined effort to capitalise on the collapse of Haitian coffee. Since Brazilian coffee was slave-grown, planters relied on a continuing supply of imported Africans (despite the Atlantic anti-slave patrols of the British and Americans). As late as the 1870s, a quarter of a million slaves toiled in Brazilian coffee plantations.[21]

While such buoyant demand existed in the Americas, slave traders could be found to ship Africans 'illegally' across the Atlantic. In the years after the abolition of the slave trade (1807), 1.1 million Africans were shipped into Brazil, 600,000 into Cuba; that is, into the two societies with a voracious appetite for slave labour for their sugar, coffee and tobacco plantations. In roughly the same period, the cotton plantations of the United States absorbed a similar number of slaves, but that demand could be satisfied by internal US migrations.

The history of Atlantic slavery is, then, peculiarly complex. Though the origins of that slave system may seem, at first glance, to lie in the initial European dealings with Africans on the West African coast in the fifteenth century, that episode provides only one piece of a historical jigsaw puzzle. A fuller explanation lies in the story of the rise and fall of European slave systems and of European expansion. It also lies in the internal history of Africa, and the varied reactions of African societies to the incursions of European influence inland from the coast and rivers. But it needs to be placed in the context of the post-Columbus settlement and economic development of particular regions of the Americas. Even then the origins of slavery offer a varied and confusing story. But if there is one overriding factor which changed both the direction and velocity of Atlantic slavery, it was surely the coming of the sugar plantation and the remarkable profits (and tastes) generated by the produce of those plantations for Europe itself. With sugar and the plantation securely in place, both African slave labour and the plantation proved their importance and value. From its critical role on the sugar plantation, black slavery thereafter drifted into nearly every corner of American life: from the roughest of frontier cowboys, to the hardiest of Atlantic sailors, through to the domestic skills of enslaved nurses and cooks. Moreover, slavery had slipped its moorings in the Americas and could be found throughout the Atlantic world, from Lima to London, from Luanda to Boston.

Notes

1   For recent definitions of, and discussion about, the institution of slavery, see Junius P. Rodriguez, ed., *The Historical Encyclopedia of World Slavery*, 2 vols, Oxford, 1997; Seymour Drescher and Stanley L. Engerman, eds, *A Historical Guide to World Slavery*, Oxford, New York, 1998.

2   By American slavery, we mean slavery throughout the Americas, not simply (as common usage often suggests) slavery in North America.

3   Herbert S. Klein, *The Atlantic Slave Trade*, Cambridge, 1999, ch. 1.

4   See 'Ancient World', in Drescher and Engerman, eds, *Historical Guide*, pp. 192–197

5   Philip D. Curtin, *The Rise and Fall of the Plantation Complex*, Cambridge, 1990.

6   See John K. Thornton, 'Overview', in Drescher and Engerman, eds, *Historical Guide*, pp. 27–32.

7   Klein, *Slave Trade*, p. 10.

8   John Iliffe, *Africans: The History of a Continent*, Cambridge, 1995, pp. 127–130.

9   Klein, *Slave Trade*, p. 11.

10 Curtin, *Plantation Complex*, ch. 2.

11 Klein, *Slave Trade*, p. 14.

12 See Murdo J. MacLeod, 'Native Americans', in Drescher and Engerman, eds, *Historical Guide*, pp. 293–296.

13 Jonathan I. Israel, *The Dutch Republic: Its Rise, Greatness, and Fall, 1477–1806*, Oxford, 1995, ch. 14.

14 Hilary Beckles, *A History of Barbados*, Cambridge, 1990, ch. 2 and 3.

15 Klein, *Slave Trade*, pp. 30–31.

16 R.S. Dunn, *Sugar and Slaves*, London, 1973, p. 203.

17 Klein, *Slave Trade*, p. 43.

18 Michael Tadman, *Speculators and Slaves*, Madison, 1996 edn.

19 See David Geggus, *Slavery, War and Revolution*, Oxford, 1982, and David Barry Gaspar and David Patrick Geggus, eds, *A Turbulent Time in the Caribbean: The French Revolution and the Greater Caribbean*, Bloomington, 1997.

20 Rebecca J. Scott, *Slave Emancipation in Cuba: The Transition to Free Labor, 1860–1899*, Princeton, 1985, p. 7.

21 Klein, *Slave Trade*, p. 42.

Chapter 5

Stuart B. Schwartz

FIRST SLAVERY
From Indian to African

Since the gentiles of Brazil unlike those of the African coast do not have the custom of daily labor and farm only when in need, relaxing when they have enough to eat; they thus greatly suffer the new life, working by obligation rather than out of desire, as they had in the state of freedom; and in its loss and in their repugnance to, and thought of, captivity so many die that even at the lowest price they are expensive.

Sebastião da Rocha Pitta (1720)

The Brazilian sugar-plantation colony began with the extensive use of Indian labor. From the vantage point of the present, Indian slavery appears to have been a passing moment in this history of colonial export agriculture in Northeast Brazil – and so it was. But to leave this formative stage with only a systemic account of its position within the process of European expansion, or to see it as simply a preview of what was to follow, is to tell only a part of the story. To the people who lived in these times, the inevitability of the transition was far less apparent. The Indians who underwent this experience inhabited a world whose perimeters were often defined by others, and the Indians were forced to accommodate themselves to new modes of behavior. From the viewpoint of the Portuguese, the period of Indian slavery was one in which the system of labor relations was worked out in detail. It was also a time when the contact between Europeans and Indians began to create social and racial categories and definitions that would continually mark the colonial experience. Finally, in the transition from Indian to African labor we can see reflected attitudes, perceptions, and realities that eventually underlay the engenho regime throughout its subsequent history.

Although the stage of Indian slavery has been recognized by other historians in the past, they have rarely been able to examine the actual conditions of life and labor on the engenhos during this period. Indians left no written records in Brazil, and Jesuit observers generally commented on abuses rather than the specific conditions of plantation labor. Extant but little-used plantation records and parish registers offer another option.[1] Using them, this chapter will examine the forms, usages, and structures of Indian labor on the Bahian engenhos during a period when slave labor became essential to this tropical-plantation economy.

Indian labor: terminology, acquisition, and types

The terminology of Indian labor is in itself revealing of its position within the plans and perceptions of the Portuguese. I must emphasize here two points. First, there was a European tendency to reduce all Indians, and to some extent Africans, to a common terminology, which tended to obscure individual cultural distinctions. The Portuguese did recognize differences between Congos and Minas or between Tamoio and Tupinambá but these were secondary to more general classifications. These less precise terms like *negro de Guiné* (black from Guinea), *índio* (Indian), *gentio da terra* (gentile of the land) were, after all, expressions of European perceptions. Second, the categories of social definition and of social structure in Brazil were created to a great extent by the nature of the agricultural enterprise and by the previous continental and overseas experience of the Portuguese. Whatever the philosophical and theological problems provoked in Europe by the discovery of a new "race" of men, the Portuguese on the scene in Brazil tended to draw upon familiar models, especially the recent past of African contacts and Atlantic plantations.

This is made clear by the term *negro da terra*, used often by both Jesuits and colonists to describe Indians. "Negros da terra" was a phrase parallel to the description of Africans as "negros de Guiné." The word "negro" itself had in medieval Portugal become almost a synonym for slave, and certainly by the sixteenth century it carried implications of servility. Its use to describe Indians is revealing of Portuguese perceptions of both Africans and Indians, not so much as to skin color, as to relative social and cultural position vis-à-vis the Portuguese. Over the course of the sixteenth century, "negro da terra" slowly disappeared from common usage as more and more Africans were introduced into the colony. It disappeared, in fact, as Indian slavery itself disappeared.[2]

For those Indians not enslaved but still under Portuguese control and direction, a variety of terms were used. Such people were called *índios aldeados* (village Indians), *índios sob a administração* (Indians under the control of . . .) or, most commonly, *forros*. This last term is somewhat confusing since it was also used to describe a slave who had gained his freedom through manumission (*alforria*), but in sixteenth-century Brazil it was not used exclusively in this way. Instead, índios forros were not only freedmen, but also Indians who were not enslaved but under Portuguese control, especially, though not exclusively, that of the Jesuits. The engenhos of Bahia made use of all three categories of Indians during the sixteenth century.

The engenhos of the Recôncavo acquired Indian labor by three principal methods – enslavement, barter, and wages. The law of 1570 had prohibited the illegal enslavement of indigenous people but allowed the acquisition of captives by ransoming them through trade with their captors. This trade, called *resgate*, was theoretically designed to save those already destined for a cruel death at the hands of their traditional enemies. Thus rescue was a favor, which the captive was then required to repay with labor. The practice was open to many abuses, but it was decided in 1574 to proceed with caution in limiting resgate "because of the necessity that the estates have for Indians."[3] A special junta of civil administrators, the senior judge, and the Jesuits decided on this course of moderation because "in Brazil there would be no estates or commerce without the Indians." Thus resgate continued, along with "just wars" carried out against those who refused to accept

Portuguese sovereignty or to receive Catholic missionaries. In 1574, Engenho Sergipe had over fifty Indians recently brought in by a resgate expedition, and an inventory of the property made at about that time contained references to axes, cloth, and knives intended for the resgate trade.[4] Resgate enabled the Portuguese settlers to obtain Indian slaves without having to call them slaves, and it permitted the continuance of a type of coerced labor.

Indians already enslaved might be passed from one owner to another and, following traditional practice, the children of slave mothers remained slaves. Natural increase was another element in the acquisition of Indian labor, but it was more than offset by population losses due to intermittent warfare and epidemic disease. In 1582, a plague struck Ilhéus and caused so many deaths that for five months the mills did not operate. Combined with attacks by the Aimoré, depopulation caused a considerable disruption of the sugar economy in that region.[5]

As labor and disease decimated the engenho populations, natural disaster and Portuguese pressure brought in new workers from the interior. In 1599, a group of Tapuyas driven by hunger appeared at Engenho Santana in Ilhéus and were put to work.[6] In 1603, with labor again in short supply, a group of eighteen Indians were brought in from the sertão, and it was during these years that Potiguar from Pernambuco were brought to Ilhéus.[7]

By the 1580s, royal legislation and the increasing effectiveness of the Jesuits had begun to create problems for those who had wished to obtain Indian labor by resgate and "just war." After a visit to the captaincy of Bahia in 1588–9, the Jesuit Cristóvão de Gouvea recommended that the sacrament of confession be refused to anyone involved in the resgate of Indians.[8] Moreover, Jesuit effectiveness in overseeing the activities of free Indians within the Portuguese sphere of influence began to create difficulties for the colonists. In 1589, Ruy Teixeira, administrator of Engenho Sergipe, complained to his absentee employer, the count of Linhares, that new legislation had made the Jesuits "masters of the land and of the Indians who with the title of 'forros' serve them, being in reality more captive than the Guiné slaves." He lamented that no Indians remained for resgate, but he realized that nothing could be done. "I will speak no more of this for these are matters that have no remedy – may God grant us His mercy."[9]

Faced with increasing difficulties in obtaining unencumbered Indian labor, the count of Linhares and others began to seek royal permission to establish Indian villages in the vicinity of the engenhos. A few of these grants were awarded, usually in exceptional cases when the petitioners were powerful nobles with much political leverage at court. Thus the success of the count of Linhares in being allowed to bring Indians from the sertão and place them in villages under his protection makes the situation at Engenhos Santana and Sergipe somewhat a typical. Still, other engenhos made use of aldeia Indians under Jesuit tutelage or hired Indians directly, so that the use of free or forro Indians was not strange to the sugar planters of the Recôncavo. In fact, one is struck in reading the records of the Inquisition in Bahia in 1591–2 by the presence of Indians in the everyday life of the captaincy, of their participation in expeditions into the sertão, and of their role in the Recôncavo.[10]

Free Indians were employed at specific tasks on the plantations. At Engenho Sergipe, they were used primarily as an auxiliary workforce and put to tasks of maintenance or service peripheral to the business of sugar production. They were used to clean and repair the water system, work in the boats, fish, hunt, and cut firewood.[11] Access to aldeia Indians allowed the engenho owners to concentrate their slaves on the central tasks of sugar making, where the returns on investment were highest. The owner of Engenho Sergipe paid the tithe for the aldeia on its boundary and probably felt that the expense was worthwhile.[12] Other free Indians were also employed. In the sixteenth century, the principal labor arrangement was an exchange of trade goods for the completion of a specific task: thus the inventory entries of a corral built at Engenho Sergipe in return for some knife blades, or of a canefield cut by a group of Tupiniquins at Engenho Santana who were then paid with iron hatchets.[13] Similar references are found in the account books of the seventeenth century.[14] By that time, however, Indians worked for wages (although under certain limitations). Slavery, aldeia labor, barter, and the wage system all existed simultaneously on the Bahian engenhos. The relative importance of predominance of each form varied from place to place and time to time, although the general trend was from enslavement to forms of remunerated voluntary labor. Access to free Indian labor allowed the planters to concentrate the capital invested in slaves in those aspects of production that were crucial and where the continuous labor justified the fixed capital that slaves represented.

The ethnic composition of the Indian slave force

The listing by name of Indian slaves in engenho inventories allows us to draw some tentative conclusions about the composition of the Indian slave force of Bahia in the late sixteenth century. As expected, many people recorded in the Sergipe and Santana inventories of 1572–4 were Tupinambá, native to the coastal area of Bahia. Some were further identified by location references such as *taparique* (Itaparica Island), Tamamaripe, *tapecuru* (Itapicuru River) and *Peroaçu* (Paraguaçu River), or by common Tupí-guaraní descriptive terms such as *açu* (big) or *merim* (small). Other names seem to be clearly of Tupinambá origin. Table 5.1 presents some of the more obvious Tupí names.

Table 5.1   Etymology of selected Tupí personal names, Engenho Sergipe, 1572–4

Name	Probable derivation
Pejuira	peju = to blow; ira = to detach (interrogative)
Pedro rari	rari = to be born
Iraoca	Ita = stone; oka = house
Ocaparnna	Oka = house; parana = sea
Mandionaem	Mandio = manioc; nhaẽ = pan
Antonio Jaguare	Jaguare = iâguara = jaguar
Francisco Tapira	Tapira = tapiira = ox
Birapipo	Bira = ybyra = wood; pipó is an interrogative
Cunhamocumarava	kunhãmuku = a girl of marriageable age; marava = marabá = child of an Indian and a stranger
Ubatiba	Uba = port, thighs, fish roe; tyba is a plural ending

Source: Documentos para a história do açucar, 3 vols. (Rio de Janeiro, 1954–63) III, 89–103.

Etymological analysis is made uncertain by a variety of problems, some of which are themselves revealing of engenho life. Aside from the usual difficulty of parallel words in more than one language, the Portuguese who recorded these names transformed them into sounds and an orthography suitable to a Romance language. What remains is what a Portuguese heard, not what an Indian said. The Portuguese were themselves sometimes puzzled by the Indian languages and were not always sure of the tribal origins of their slaves. Phrases such as *"pela lingua que não he cristão"* (by his language not a Christian) indicate that the Portuguese were unsure of the linguistic stock of some slaves.[15] At Engenho Sergipe, one of the field observers, Tristão Pacheco, also served as translator (*lingoa do gentio*).[16] Portuguese and mestiços, lay people and clerics, who spoke Indian languages were usually proud of this accomplishment and never failed to point it out to the crown or other authorities since it was a necessary and valuable skill in the sixteenth and early seventeenth centuries.[17]

Locational and ethnographic identification make clear that the plantations drew their Indian slaves from a wide range of geographical and cultural backgrounds. Engenho Sergipe counted among its slaves not only local Tupinambá, but peoples brought from Sergipe de El-Rey to the north, Rio das Contas to the south, and the sertão of the São Francisco River to the west, as well as a large contingent brought from Pernambuco. Also listed are Carijó, Tamoio, and Cayté, all of them Tupí speakers and all from regions hundreds of miles from Bahia.[18] Although the large number of southern Indians on the Sergipe do Conde and Santana plantations may have been extraordinary, Indian laborers were not. The Nossa Senhora da Purificação Church at Engenho Sergipe listed over twenty-five holders of Indian slaves or forros in the period 1595–1626. Indians were the primary element of the Bahian labor force during this period.[19]

Not all the engenho Indians were Tupians. Tapuya names are often encountered in the Engenhos Sergipe and Santana registers of the 1570s and 1591. Here and there, other ethnic references are made. For example, a few Nãmbipiras appear. Also, both inventories of the 1570s contain many identifications that appear to be of ethnic or tribal origins, although they cannot be positively identified (Tingua, Tarabe, Taipe). The conclusion that must be drawn is that Engenhos Sergipe and Santana in particular, and probably all the Bahian mills that depended on Indian labor, made use of a heterogeneous Indian labor force. Whether this policy was intentional – designed, as it was later to be for African slaves, to prevent their close cooperation and forestall rebellion – or was simply a response to the shortage of local laborers is a moot question. Planters seemed to realize the advantage of having slaves who were "strangers" because this made flight more difficult. Although some Indian captives from the South could be found on the Bahian plantations, the interior of the Northeast seems to have been a more common source.[20]

At Engenho Sergipe, the Indians and African slaves lived in separate buildings. There is reason to believe that the over two hundred Indian slaves did not live in a row-house arrangement (*senzala*) so common on the seventeenth-century engenhos, but rather in Tupinambá-style long houses. The inventory mentions "two great houses of straw in which the negros [Indians] are kept."[21] Tupinambá multifamily long houses could hold, according to some observers, over two hundred people, so that it is quite possible that similar arrangements were made at the engenhos.[22]

Table 5.2   Sex distribution, Engenhos Sergipe and Santana, 1572–91

Engenho	Married males	Unmarried males	(% male)	Married females	Unmarried females	(% female)
Sergipe, 1572	51	41	(61%)	51	8	(39%)
Santana, 1572	18	47	(60%)	18	26	(40%)
Sergipe, 1591	17	19	(58%)	17	9	(42%)

The sex distribution of the Indian slave force was remarkably similar to that encountered later among black slaves. Usually, about 60 percent of the slaves were male, and naturally there was a tendency for the men to be young adults. The marital status of Indian slaves and their ability to maintain family ties is difficult to determine from the Engenho Sergipe and Santana inventories because these offer conflicting pictures (see Table 5.2). At Engenho Santana, only 18 married men were listed in an adult population of 109 (65 men, 44 women). At Engenho Sergipe, closer to Salvador and perhaps to ecclesiastical observation, the number of married men was much higher. There, of the 92 men, 51 were married. Whether this difference is explained by variant notarial procedures of recording slave conjugal units or by a different composition of the slave force is impossible to establish. Perhaps more revealing is that among Engenho Sergipe's regular work force there were only 8 unmarried women, and of these 3 were widows and 2 were relatives of other slaves at the mill. This figure underlines the expected preference of slave-owners for young males.

Despite this preference, the nature of Indian slavery resulted in the presence of family units on the plantation. Men were often accompanied into slavery by wife, children, siblings, or other relatives. This pattern placed many people on or near the sugar mills and cane farms whose contribution to the process of sugar making was only marginal. The great Schetz engenho in São Vicente had in 1548 130 slaves, half of whom were children or old people and thus of little use to the owners. Nevertheless, a contemporary observer called this slave force the best in the region.[23] The lists of Engenhos Sergipe and Santana also suggest a high ratio of semi- or unproductive slaves. At Engenho Santana, some 25 percent of the total work force was too old, too young, or too sick to contribute very much to the mill's activity. Obviously, this percentage greatly increased in the years of epidemic disease.

Women [. . .] made up a significant part of the Indian labor force, but they were not as a rule considered to have skills that contributed directly to sugar making. Female slaves in the sixteenth-century inventories are invariably listed without occupation, and their values result from Combinations of age and health more than anything else. Surely, the susceptibility of Indians to disease diminished their reproductive value. Thus women appear as an omnipresent but not particularly skilled sector of an engenho's primary operations. There is some evidence from Engenho Sergipe that suggests recognition of the traditional role of Indian women in subsistence agriculture: A separate *roça* (farm) was maintained to supply the engenho's food needs, and a group of fifty slaves was assigned there. Two-thirds of these slaves were women – a proportion quite unlike the general sex ratio of the total population of the engenho. This implies a recognition of Indian women's roles in certain kinds of agriculture.[24]

Even when epidemic disease was not important, mortality rates were high. In 1572, a relatively plague-free year, five slaves died at Engenho Santana – a crude mortality rate of forty-three per thousand. In 1606, the chapel of Engenho Sergipe recorded thirty-two Indian deaths and only thirty-five baptisms. Because in this period accurate statistics for compiling general mortality rates are unavailable, there is some advantage in comparing figures with data from other regions of a similar social or economic composition. The crude mortality rate in Pernambuco in 1774 was almost thirty-three per thousand, and it remained at about that level until the late nineteenth century.[25] In Maranhão, the crude mortality rate for Indians in 1798 was close to twenty-two per thousand, whereas that for black slaves was just over twenty-seven per thousand.[26] Thus, the figure from Engenho Santana seems high, although it does not approach the rate of seventy per thousand experienced by African slaves in Jamaica and Barbados in the late seventeenth century.[27]

Acculturation and interaction

For those Indians who survived and for their Portuguese masters and employers, the major problems that remained were introduction to the regime of large-scale export agriculture and adoption of cultural patterns acceptable to Portuguese religious and social sensitivities. The rate and intensity of acculturation are difficult if not impossible to estimate. Indians were not able to select those aspects of European culture that they found best suited to their needs; instead, they were often forced to adopt or accommodate material and mental elements of culture on which the Portuguese placed a high priority. The increasing use of wages to secure Indian labor in the early seventeenth century was to some extent a symbol of their integration into Portuguese society. The fact that even at the end of this period such payments were often made in kind or were a mixture of money and goods should caution us about the completeness of the process. [. . .]

When possible, the Portuguese employed Indians in activities with which they were already familiar, but some had to be "seasoned" to sugar production. At Engenho Sergipe, the manioc garden seems to have served this purpose. Among the Indian slaves assigned to this activity were a large number of people from other regions of Brazil as well as non-Tupinambá.[28] This diversity of backgrounds suggests that the manioc farm served as an introduction to the engenho regime, a place where new slaves could acquire a knowledge of the rules and expectations of plantation slavery.

The first superficial sign of acculturation was the adoption of a Portuguese name. The inventories of 1572–4 list many Indians who were still using their indigenous names exclusively, even though the tendency of the Portuguese was to assign easily recognizable and, for them, pronounceable names. Of the 191 Indians at Engenho Sergipe, 50 still used only their original names. The inventory of Engenho Santana demonstrates that a period of transition existed during which the Portuguese used one name and the Indians another. This situation is demonstrated by entries such as "by her tongue Capea and by ours, Domingas," or "Salvador, by his tongue Itacaraiba."[29] The assignment of Portuguese names and their eventual recognition and acceptance constituted steps toward integration into the engenho community. When possible, this process was formalized by baptism of the formerly pagan Indians. The assumption of new names had been an important part in Tupí life and had marked changes in social status. Indians could easily comprehend the importance and significance of the baptismal ceremony and the relationship between a new name and a new status.

The trend if not the rate of acculturation is suggested by a comparison of the Engenho Sergipe inventories of 1572–4 and 1591. Whereas the former contained some fifty slaves using only their Indian name, the latter had none. This comparison probably documents the fact that Indians were conforming to Portuguese patterns and that newly captured peoples were relatively rare on the Bahian engenhos by the end of the century.[30] Instead, their places were being filled by Indians born in captivity and baptized at that time, by free Indians, and by increasing numbers of African slaves.

Religion, of course, provided a major avenue of acculturation. The willingness of slaves to participate in church ritual or to accept the sacraments of the Catholic religion is a rough measure of their integration into the framework of Portuguese society. For this reason, the chapel register of Engenho Sergipe is a valuable document despite its incomplete and fragmentary condition. In its record of marriages (1600–26), burials (1598–1627), and especially baptisms (1595–1608), the basic patterns of sexual interaction and ritually defined responsibilities among the three principal racial groups are apparent.[31] The period covered is interesting because between 1570 and 1630 the Bahian plantations crystallized into the distinctive social structure that characterized the area for the next two hundred years.

The chapel register contains 234 complete adolescent baptisms for the period 1595 to 1608, or about 75 percent of the total baptismal entries. Of the 234 baptized, 171 (74 percent) were the children of slave mothers and, therefore, slaves. The racial origins of the 234 mothers (for whom a racial designation has been determined) can be used as a rough gauge of the ethnic proportions of the population. It results in the following distribution: whites, 32 percent; Indians, 40 percent; Afro-Brazilians, 28 percent. Given the predominance of men in the Atlantic slave trade, the sex ratio of Afro-Brazilians would be distorted, and thus these figures probably underestimate this segment of the population. Still, it would appear that Indians continued to be an important part of the plantations' population at the beginning of the seventeenth century, equaling if not outnumbering the Africans and their descendants. Each register of baptism followed a formula such as: "5 August Joana young daughter of Thome de Sousa, single, and of Luiza, an Indian of Domingos Ribeiro; godparents, Bras Dias and Antonia [slaves] of the same Domingos Ribeiro." This formula allows us to examine the relationships between five individuals – the baptized, father, mother, godfather, and godmother. The pattern of these relationships reveals additional information about social organization and contact. Table 5.3 presents a distribution by racial/ethnic group of the four categories.

It is clear that baptism for slaves was a somewhat less formal matter than it was for free people and especially for whites. Whereas a godmother and godfather were always present when the child of a white couple was baptized, this was not always the case for slave children. There were some twenty-five instances (13%) when the godmother or godfather or both were omitted (or unregistered) at the ceremony. On one occasion, a group of slaves served as padrinhos (godparents), and on another there were two godfathers and no godmother. Such asymmetry and

Table 5.3   Racial/ethnic designations of parents and godparents, Engenho Sergipe, 1595–1608

	White	Indian	African	Negro/crioulo	Mulatto	Unknown[a]
Father	61	42	27	6	0	98
Mother	43	54	33	8	3	93
Godfather	132	9	6	7	0	70
Godmother	59	21	8	7	7	114

Note: [a] The many unknowns (98) in the case of the fathers result from illegitimate unions and no father present at baptism. In the cases of mothers, godfathers, and godmothers, unknowns are due to failure to report this information or gaps in the documentation.

irregularity were never found among the Portuguese baptisms of Engenho Sergipe. When adult pagans received baptism, they usually did so in small groups of three or four at a time. On these occasions, one set of godparents might sponsor all the baptized individuals.

Among the three principal racial groups, there was a strong tendency toward endogamy, at least in formal, church-sanctioned unions. Between 1601 and 1626 in thirty slave marriages in which the origins of the partners could be determined, all were between individuals of the same racial category, although not of the same ethnic or linguistic group.[32]

Despite this tendency toward endogamy, sexual interaction across the color lines did take place. White males were most easily able to take advantage of their dominant role to select sexual partners from among the slave and free populations. White men fathered over 11 percent of all children born to Indian mothers and 8 percent of those born to African women registered at Engenho Sergipe. If these figures are adjusted to include those cases in which no father was reported, a sign of illegitimacy and unstable or secret relationship, then the percentages rise sharply to 18.5 percent for Indians and almost 30 percent for Afro-Brazilian women.

Opportunities for contact between Africans and Indians also existed in the slave quarters. The Engenho Sergipe inventories list a number of cases in which Africans and Indians had formed permanent family units. Such was the case of Domingos Valente, a sugar master who had married Luiza, *gentio da terra*, and fathered two children, or of Marcos, a Guiné slave who married Martha, an Indian.[33] More impressive, however, is the relative lack of such unions in the chapel register. Only two cases were recorded of children born to such couples, and both of these, unlike those just mentioned, were between Indian men and African women. It appears, therefore, that in the period of transition from Indian to African slavery, the majority of Indians married or had sexual relations with other Indians and maintained themselves to a large extent sexually separate from others. The miscegenation that did take place occurred most frequently between whites and Indians or whites and Africans.[34] It is interesting to note that in sixteenth-century Bahia no distinctive descriptive term was used for the offspring of Indians and Africans. The term *mameluco* was used for any person of mixed parentage in which one parent was an Indian.[35] It was not until the eighteenth century that *cafuso* or *curiboca* was used to describe the children of Indian–African unions.

According to Roman Catholic doctrine and practice, the roles of godfather and godmother were vital to the child's guidance. 'The relationship between godchild (*afilhado*) and godparents (*padrinhos*) was as binding as that between child and parents. The parallel set of ties between the parents and godparents established a set of mutual obligations and dependencies. By examining these, we can observe some of the ways in which slaves and masters interacted.

The padrinho or godfather exercised an important function as baptismal sponsor and possible eventual guardian and protector of the child. The role of godfather placed very real obligations on those holding it, and it was not uncommon for godchildren eventually to depend on their padrinhos for economic assistance or protection. Also, at the time of the baptism the godfather usually assumed the expenses. The position of the godfather, therefore, was one of status and prestige. It is not surprising to find a very high percentage of whites in the godfather role in the baptisms examined. Not only did white parents always choose a white godfather, but Indians and Africans also sought out whites to assume this role. In more than 80 percent of the baptisms of the children of Indian mothers, white men served as godfather. Indian men served as godfathers in only nine cases, and in the six in which the ethnic origins of the parents can be identified, all were Indian couples. African men were in a somewhat similar position and like the Indians continually looked to whites (or had to accept them) as godfathers for their children. The predominance of whites can be seen in Table 5.4.

The most pronounced pattern to emerge from data concerning godparents is a marked difference between the godfathers and godmothers: The selection of godmother seems to have been based on different criteria than that of godfather, because it was much more common to find Indians and Afro-Brazilians in the female sponsorship role. White women rarely presented slave children for baptism. Instead, Indian mothers sought Indian godmothers. The godfather could be white, for as protector and benefactor whites were best equipped to aid the child, but the godmother was considered an auxiliary to the child's upbringing and a surrogate parent in the case of the death of the biological mother. Although there were a few instances in which Indian women served as godmothers for children born to African women or of mulatto women who were godmothers to the children of Indian mothers, the vast majority of the cases indicate that Indians, Africans, and whites selected women of the same racial category as *comadres* (co-mothers). Usually, the *madrinha* (godmother) was a slave of the same master as either or both of the parents.

A few statistics make this situation clear. Whereas male slaves comprised fewer than 12 percent of all godfathers registered, female slaves were more than 30 percent

Table 5.4   Index of godparentage prestige

	Parents	Godparents	Ratio
Whites	104	191	1.84
Indians	96	30	.31
Afro-Brazilians	64	13	.20

Source: Archivo da Curia, Metro politana do Salvador, Conceição da Praia (Engenho Sergipe) bautismos.

of the godmothers. If only slave and forro baptisms are considered, then the percentage of slave and forro madrinhas rises to more than 80 percent of the total. The ties among the Indians were strong, and in more than 60 percent of the baptisms of children born to Indians, Indian women were in the godmother's role. When both parents were Indians, this figure rose to 90 percent.

Only on rare occasions did a slaveowner or his close relative serve as a baptismal sponsor for the child of his slave. In these early baptisms, a case such as that of Antônio Gonçalves and his daughter, who stood for the child of their Indian slaves in 1604, does appear from time to time.[36] But in truth such occasions were rare, and in fewer than 4 percent of the slave baptisms did the owner, or more frequently his relative, serve as godparent for his own slaves. Even so, such sponsorship seems to have been more characteristic of the period of Indian slavery. [. . .] By the eighteenth century masters never sponsored their black and mulatto slaves. Paternalism did not commonly find expression through godparent ties. Instead, what appears to be the dominant pattern was the selection of a white man who might intercede with the master in case of some future difficulty.

Finally, the use of materials such as a parish register is perhaps somewhat misleading, underlining the process of acculturation because it is set in the framework of Portuguese institutions and culture. There was always a reverse side in this story. The santidade cult demonstrated that acculturation was often shallow or incomplete and that sentiments of resistance often lay close to the surface of life.[37] Indian resistance to enslavement was constant, and runaways from the plantations were a chronic problem, although the Portuguese often turned to free or aldeia Indians to hunt down the fugitives.[38] Moreover, acculturation always had a potential to move in the other direction. Indian cultures offered, or seemed to offer, to some Europeans or to mestiços certain freedoms of thought and behavior.[39] The farther they were from the densely colonized areas or the coastal cities, the more likely were colonists and their descendants to adapt Indian ways. This was especially true in the period before 1600, when the matrix of social norms and structures was still relatively fluid. The interaction of port, engenhos, and sertão and the mixing of populations created geographical and human conditions in Bahia that contributed to the adoption of many features of Indian culture and life.

In this connection, the depositions of a number of mamelucos before the Inquisition in 1591–2 are most revealing. Many admitted that while in the sertão in search of Indians for the fazendas, they had joined the Indians in dances, smoking, drinking the "sacred herb," and generally comporting themselves like pagans.[40] Some painted their bodies like the Indians, and a number admitted to having undergone scarification or tattooing of their arms, legs, and buttocks. Such was the case with Manoel Bronco, Thomas Ferreira, Francisco Afonso Capara, and Antônio Dias, a mestre de açúcar.[41] In a number of instances, mamelucos and Portuguese adolescents were converted to santidade. Gonçalo Fernandes, a mameluco subsistence farmer from Paripe, underwent such a conversion brought about by an Indian who had preached to him in an Indian language that "he understood very well."[42] Luisa Barbosa, a Portuguese woman, admitted to such a conversion in 1566 when she was a young girl of twelve and easily misled, she claimed, by the Indians with whom she spoke.[43]

The pattern is perhaps summarized in the epic of Domingos Fernandes Nobre, called Tomacauna. The son of a Portuguese man and an Indian woman, himself married to a white woman, he nevertheless lived from age eighteen to thirty-six more like an Indian than a Portuguese. He abandoned Catholicism and confessed only when necessary to avoid detection. He went often into the sertão and on expeditions to Pernambuco, Porto Seguro, and Paraíba. He lived with the Indians, taking many wives, tattooing his body, putting feathers in his hair, and generally living like an Indian. It was he who was sent to make contact with the main village of santidade in the 1580s, and while there he paid homage to an idol and to the leaders of the religion. Eventually, he brought a number of these people to the plantation of Fernão Cabral de Atayde. The case of Tomacauna is surely exceptional, but it does indicate that the interchange between Europeans and Indians in Northeast Brazil could move in both directions.

From Indian to African

The transition from a predominantly indigenous slave force to one composed mainly of Africans occurred gradually over the course of approximately half a century. As individual engenho owners acquired sufficient financial resources, they bought a few African slaves, and they added more as capital and credit became available. By the end of the sixteenth century, engenho labor forces were racially mixed, and the proportion increasingly changed in favor of imported Africans and their offspring. In the 1550s and 1560s, there were virtually no African slaves at the Northeast sugar mills.[44] By the mid-1580s, Pernambuco had sixty-six engenhos and a reported 2,000 African slaves. If we estimate an average of 100 slaves per engenho, then Africans composed one-third of the captaincy's slaves. In 1577, Engenho São Panteleão do Monteiro near Olinda had 40 slaves, of whom two-thirds were Indians and the rest Africans. This was apparently an average distribution.[45]

In Bahia, the change can be observed in the transformation of a single engenho's population over time. In 1572, Engenho Sergipe had 280 adult slaves, of whom only 20 (7 percent) were African. In 1591, the engenho had a slave population of 103, of whom 38 (37%) came from Africa. When, in 1638, Engenho Sergipe was rented to Pedro Gonçalves de Mattos, it had 81 slaves, all of whom were African or Afro-Brazilian.[46] The transition to an African labor force was made in the first two decades of the seventeenth century at a time when the sugar industry experienced rapid expansion and considerable internal growth arising from high international sugar prices, a growing European market, and, perhaps, the peaceful maritime conditions brought about by the twelve-year truce between Spain and the Netherlands (1609–21). A comparison of the positions and roles of Indian and African slaves should help explain why the transition to African labor took place.

The shift to African labor depended in part on Portuguese perceptions of the relative abilities of Africans and Indians. With a long history of black slavery in Iberia, which had intensified during the expansion of the sugar industry in the Atlantic, the Portuguese were well acquainted with Africans and their skills. By the end of the sixteenth century, Africans had already impressed the Portuguese with their ability to master the techniques of sugar production on Madeira and São Tomé. The Portuguese in Brazil, long familiar with the use of blacks as servants, urban artisans, and skilled slaves in Portugal and the Atlantic islands, began to look toward Africa as a logical source for these skills. The first black slaves in Brazil came as body servants or skilled laborers, not as field hands. The three extant engenho slave lists from the sixteenth century indicate a high percentage of Africans with various skills, and invariably the most complicated tasks assigned to slaves were given to Africans. In 1548, Engenho São Jorge dos Erasmos in São Vicente had 130 slaves "of the land" as well as seven or eight Africans. All the Africans were *oficiais*, that is, skilled at various tasks, and one was sugar master, the most important managerial position on any engenho. The director of Engenho São Jorge's operations proudly wrote to the absentee owners, the Schetz family of Antwerp, that sugar masters on Madeira usually received $30 a year, a sum that their engenho now saved by using this skilled black slave.[47] Three other Africans were employed in positions requiring skilled judgment, one as purger (*purgador*) and two as kettleman (*caldereiro*).

A similar situation is found in the inventory lists of Engenhos Sergipe and Santana of the late sixteenth century. At Engenho Sergipe, Indians and Africans were used in different ways during the period of transition. Because the engenho could afford Portuguese technicians and managers, the occupational pyramid of the slaves was truncated. The work force was heavily indigenous; of 134 male slaves, 115 were Indians. The same proportions of Africans and Indians were listed with a specific occupation; but, when certain jobs such as fishermen, hunters, and boatmen are not included, the proportion of Indians with special occupations drops considerably. Table 5.5 shows these differences.

The inventory of 1572 – taken when Indians were still plentiful and relatively inexpensive to obtain, when Africans were still not available in large numbers, and when the legislation against Indian slavery was not yet effectively in force – represents a specific period in the history of Indian slavery. Twenty years later, the situation had changed considerably. By 1591, the sugar economy of the Northeast was expanding rapidly to supply a growing European demand. The Atlantic slave trade had been regularized to the extent that the supply, though not yet great, was at least dependable. The majority of Engenho Sergipe's slave force was still Indian, but Africans and Afro-Brazilians now filled almost all the skilled occupations on the estate. Angolan and Guinean men were employed as sugar master, purger, assistant purger, blacksmith, kettleman, and sugar crater. Others were employed in the milling operations of the engenho and a few as cowhands. The Indian occupations were far more rudimentary, and aside from one sugar crater, only three were listed with occupations, one woodcutter and two herdsmen. In other words, when possible, the Portuguese turned to Africans to provide skilled slave labor. [. . .]

This policy, like the relative price of Indians and Africans, is to some extent explained by demographic and cultural features of both peoples. Many West Africans came from cultures where ironworking, cattle herding, and other activities of value to sugar agriculture were practiced.[48] These skills and a familiarity with long-term agriculture made them more valuable to the Portuguese for the specific slavery of sugar. Africans were certainly no more "predisposed" to slavery than were Indians, Portuguese, Englishmen, or any other people taken from their homes and bent to the will of others by force, but the similiarity of their cultural heritage to European traditions made them more valuable in European eyes. The Indian susceptibility to European disease at all ages made riskier the investment of time and capital in training them as artisans or managers. Africans, of course, also

Table 5.5   Occupational structure, Engenho Sergipe, 1572, 1591

	1572		1591	
	Africans	*Indians*	*Africans*	*Indians*
Sugar-making skills				
Mestre de açúcar (sugar master)			1	
Ajuda do mestre (assistant sugar master)			1	
Purgador (purger)			2	1
Ajuda do purgador (assistant purger)	1	2	1	
Tacherio (small kettleman)	1	2	3	
Escumeiro (skimmer)	1			
Ajuda do escumeiro (assistant skimmer)		3		
Caldereiro (kettleman)		6		
Moedor (mill tender)		3	2	
Premseiro (presser)	1	1		
Virador de bagaço (bagasse feeder)		1	1	
Caixeiro (crater)		2	1	1
Dos melles (molasses maker)	1	1		
Artisan skills				
Carapina (carpenter)		1		
Ferreiro (blacksmith)			1	
Calafate (boat caulker)		1		
Falleiro (?)	1	1		
Auxiliary skills				
Vaqueiro (cowboy)	1	1	2	1
Carreiro (carter)	1	1		
Boieiro (herdsman)				3
Pescador (fisherman)		11		
Serrador (sawyer)		7		
Lenadeiro (firewood cutter)				1
Porqueiro/ovelheiro (pig/sheep tender)		2		
"Barcas" (boatman)	1	4		
Management				
Feitor (overseer)		1		
Totals	9 (19)[a]	51 (115)	15 (30)	7 (65)

Note: [a] Number in parentheses is total number of that ethnic category.

suffered in the environment of Brazil, but the highest rate of black mortality was always found among the newly arrived (*boçal*) and among infants. Thus, once a slave was "seasoned" and had passed through infancy and childhood, the chances of survival and therefore of safe investment in skill were very good.

African health and skill, as well as lack of resistance, may explain the reluctance of planters to invest in the training of Indian slaves, but it does not respond to the question why, even in cases where Indians were free workers earning a wage, the value of their labor was considered unequal to that of whites, mulattoes, and free blacks. At Engenho Sergipe, an Indian carpenter received only 20 percent of the wages paid to whites for the same task. During the seventeenth century, Indian workers received only 20 réis a day, and skilled artisans averaged 30 réis. In the 1630s, the municipal council of Salvador paid Indian laborers a daily wage of 30 réis, and Paraíba Indians could be paid in manioc and cloth a daily wage of about 15 réis. Black slaves, by contrast, could earn an average of 240 réis per day.[49]

The wage-labor system, therefore, constantly proposed as the ideal way to integrate the Indian into colonial society, was a failure. Indians were often reluctant to participate in the labor market; and the Portuguese, furthermore, did not really allow that market to operate freely: The wages paid to Indians were always below existing rates.[50] The colonists placed Indian wage earners on a scale of reward and labor different from that of other workers. At Engenho Sergipe, they were usually paid by the month rather than by the day, or even more commonly by the task. Their work did not usually require completion at a specific time, and often they received payment in kind rather than in cash. Manioc flour, trade cloth (*pano*), and alcohol were the common "wages" for Indians from Maranhão to São Paulo.[51] Obviously, the Portuguese seemed to believe, for whatever reasons, that Indian workers could not be treated like others.

There was, in fact, a remarkable similarity among all the colonial regimes in the New World in the low value placed on Indian laborers in comparison with Africans. In times and places as widely different as sixteenth-century Mexico, seventeenth-century Brazil, and eighteenth-century Carolina, Spaniards, Portuguese, and Englishmen held similar opinions of Indian and African laborers. The colonists in each situation usually valued Africans three to five times higher than the Indians.[52] Certainly, market availability, demographic patterns, opportunities for flight or resistance (management costs), and European prejudices entered into these calculations. Still, despite the racist implications of arguments about the relative adaptability to tropical labor of one people over another, the similarity of opinion among all the New World slaveholding regimes suggests that there was a comparative advantage, especially in the formative period of slaveholding, in the use of African rather than Indian slaves and that this advantage was based on productivity in terms of return on investment. The statement of one observer in the Carolinas in 1740 that "with them [Indians] one cannot accomplish as much as with Negroes" was echoed everywhere in the Americas.[53]

In Brazil, the relative position of Indian and African slaves within the sugar labor force can be seen in its simplest and crudest form in the comparative prices of the two peoples. The average price of an African slave listed with occupation in 1572 was $25, whereas Indians with the same skills averaged only $9. The only skilled Indians whose prices equaled, or even approached, those of African slaves were those who were truly practicing skilled crafts – carpenters, sugar craters, and boat caulkers, for example, or those engaged in the specialized positions of a sugar mill. The vast majority of Indians listed with some occupation, but not an artisan skill, were priced far below the average value of unskilled Africans. The price differ-ence between skilled and unskilled Indians was greater, moreover, than that among Africans.

There is evidence that these values represent real differences in the produc-tivity of Indian and African labor. Production figures from Bahia at the close of the sixteenth century support this interpretation. Although there is some discrepancy in the reported total of engenhos, a number of accounts list fifty mills operating in the captaincy of Bahia by 1590.[54] For 1589, Father Francisco Soares reported that there were fifty engenhos, eighteen thousand slaves, and thirty-six thousand aldeia Indians.[55] If we assume that two-thirds of the slave force was involved in sugar agriculture, then the ratio of slaves to engenhos was 240 to 1. This figure – which does not include any of the settled Indians that also provided labor to the engenhos – is extremely high. It represents not only slaves owned directly by the mills, but those owned by tenants, sharecroppers, and others as well. Father Soares estimated an annual production per mill of four thousand arrobas or fifty-eight tons. Thus, each slave produced at the time almost seventeen arrobas (over five hundred pounds) a year – a very low level of productivity, since the later calcula-tion in Brazil based on black slaves was forty to seventy arrobas annually.[56] Even allowing for technological changes and inexact information, the only conclu-sion that can be drawn from such figures is that Indian labor was characterized by low productivity.[57]

At the time Father Soares mode his estimates, Bahia had between three and four thousand African slaves; thus, three-fourths of its slave force was still Indian in the last decade of the sixteenth century.[58] With the low level of Indian produc-tivity, the price differential between African and Indian slaves becomes readily understandable. In the inventories of 1572–4, African slaves were valued at an average price of $20, whereas adult Indians averaged about $7.[59] This ratio of roughly three to one is also the ratio between the estimates of African and Indian productivity in sugar agriculture. It would appear that the Portuguese made a reasonable economic calculation of the comparative profitability of their two alter-nate work forces. Africans surely cost more to obtain, but in the long run they were a more profitable investment.

We can speculate that the early presence of large numbers of Indians allowed the mills to begin production with a small original outlay in slaves. The expansion of the sugar economy in the 1550s and 1560s depended on the availability of this source of "cheap" labor. During the 1570s, however, resistance, plague, and antienslavement legislation reduced the availability – and profitability – of Indians. Plantation owners now found that the cost differential between Indian and African laborers no longer outweighed differences in productivity between the two labor forces. This disparity in overall productivity also helps to explain why the Portu-guese preferred imported Africans to coerced but "free" Indians. Although there were occasional proponents of the Spanish-American-style grants of Indian labor (encomienda), or of peonage in Brazil, the colonists believed that, given the high mortality and low productivity of Indians, Africans were a better investment. The Bahian historian and planter Sebastião da Rocha Pitta probably summarized majority opinion when he observed that Indians suffered from "working by obligation rather than out of desire, as they had in the state of freedom; and in its loss and in their repugnance to, and thought of, captivity so many die that even at the lowest price they are expensive."[60]

A discussion of profitability in strictly neoclassical economic terms will not suffice as an explanation of the transition of the labor force. There were always cultural and political determinants as well. Not everyone in Brazil was convinced of the wisdom of the shift. Portuguese colonists were generally unwilling to surrender control of Indians, especially when they could be obtained for nothing. The colonists demonstrated their reluctance by political remonstrance and demonstration – most notably in 1609 and 1640. Gaspar da Cunha, overseer of Engenho Sergipe, wrote to the count of Linhares in 1585 that Africans "cost too much and are prejudicial to the plantation and to the neighborhood; they are neither as necessary nor as beneficial as the Indians of this land."[61] He then petitioned for more free Indians to be brought to the engenho. By the early seventeenth century, such requests and sentiments were far less frequent.[62] The shift to African labor was well on its way, especially in the Northeast sugar region, where capital had accumulated and the patterns of international commerce were securely established. Colonial slavery had emerged as the dominant mode of production, and the process of its emergence was not dictated by the market so much as by the organization of production. The system of labor and the nature of the labor force were determined not only in the court at Lisbon or in the countinghouses of Amsterdam and London but also in the forests and canefields of America.

Notes

1   Historians of sixteenth-century Brazil depended to a large extent on Jesuit letters and reports and on governmental correspondence and legislation. The account books of Engenhos Sergipe do Conde and Santana from 1572–4, 1591, and 1638, along with other supporting documentation, are, for that reason, particularly valuable. These materials reveal a great deal about the labor force in that period. Moreover, the chapel of Engenhos Sergipe served as the parish church, and its fragmentary register that survives for the period 1595–1626 is another valuable source on various social relationships. These materials, limited as the admittedly are, at least provide a glimpse of life on the Bahian engenhos in their early, formative period. Engenhos Sergipe and Santana were originally built by Governor Mem de Sá and later became the property of the Jesuits.

2   The term negro de terra seems to have persisted in São Paulo well into the seventeenth century. In Bahia, although it was occasionally employed in the period after 1600, it was gradually replaced. Cf. Zenha, *Mamelucos*, 52–72 passim.

3   The inventories of engenhos Sergipe and Santana made between 1572 and 1574 are printed, along with the will and testament of Mem de Sá and other relevant materials, in *DHA*, III; Inventário Engenho Sergipe (1572), *DHA*, III, 65; Livro de contas do procurador (1574), *DHA*, III, 406.

4   ANTT, CSJ, maço 15, doc. 9.

5   Ibid.

6   *Feitor* (overseer) of Engenho Santana to count of Linhares (15 Aug. 1599), ANTT, CSJ, maço 8, doc. 105. The feitor called them "gentio do sertão tapuyas do catingua" (gentiles of the backlands, savages of the forest).

7   Domingos Fernandes da Cunha to count of Linhares (Ilhéus, 16 March 1603), ANTT, CSJ, maço 8, doc. 125. Fernandes da Cunha was sent by the count of Linhares to rebuild Engenho Santana sometime in 1601. It was he who in concert with Alvaro de Carvalho brought in the Potiguares, and at one point he went to the Recôncavo to bring settled Indians back to Ilhéus. See ANTT, CSJ, maço 8, doc. 108.

8   Biblioteca Nazionale di Roma, Fondo Gesuitico 1367, "O que pareceo ao Padre Visitador Cristóvão de Gouvea ordernar na visita deste Collegio da Bahia (1 Jan. 1589).

9   Bahia (1 March 1589), ANTT, CSJ, maço 8, doc. 136.

10 *PVCB*, 1591–2, J. Capistrano de Abreu, ed. (Rio de Janeiro, 1935). Although Indians did not come in to make depositions, except in one instance, many who appeared before the inquisitors spoke of their relations with Indians, of the aldeias, of *entradas* (expeditions) to the sertão to bring more Indians down to the coast, and of considerable interaction. A number of mestiços also admitted to practicing Indian customs and speaking Indian languages. See, e.g., 34, 36–7, 64–5, 93–5, 96–7, 104–5, 123–4, 164–5, 167–72.

11 Sebastião Vaz to Dingo Cardim, provincial of the College of Santo Antão (Bahia, 5 June 1629), ANTT, CSJ, maço 69, doc. 74. This letter is most revealing of the history of the Indians in the village near Sergipe do Conde. They had been brought in at great expense by the count of Linhares, but by the time his wife and heir had died there were few left. When the Jesuits had assumed control of the engenho, these Indians were incorporated with those of the Jesuit aldeia called São Sebastião located nearby. When, however, the village was moved elsewhere, the engenho Indians went along. This situation moved Vaz to petition for their return.

12 Safra 1611–12, ANTT, CSJ, maço 14, doc. 4, 24. The *dizimos* (tithe) for the aldeia was 10$400 for 2 years.

13 *DHA*, III, 406, 102.

14 *DHA*, III, 298, 311.

15 *DHA*, III, 92.

16 *DHA*, III, 392–4.

17 *PVCB*, 1591–2, 87, 104–5, 167–72. See also the petition of Luís de Aguiar. AGS, *Guerra antigua*, legajo 906.

18 Carijó was the name sometimes given to the Guaraní of Paraguay and southern Brazil. The Tamoio inhabited the area near Rio de Janeiro, whereas the Cayté had lived near the mouth of the São Francisco River. A war of extermination and enslavement had been declared against them for killing the first bishop of Brazil and eating him. The presence of Carijó and, Tamoio at Engenhos Sergipe and Santana may have been atypical. Mem de Sá's expeditions in the south probably gave him access to the Indians of that area that other planters in Bahia did not have. Moreover, his son, Estácio de Sá, had left a group of slaves on these estates that were the result of his exploits in the Rio de Janeiro area.

19 The chapel register of Engenho Sergipe was mistakenly bound together with materials from another parish. It is presently located in the ACMS, Conceição da Praia, Baptismos 1649–76. It will he cited hereafter as chapel register 1595–1628.

20 Alfredo Eills, Júnior, "O bandeirismo na economia do século xvii," in *Curso de bandeirologia* (São Paulo, 1956), 55–76. For the opposite opinion, see Zenha, *Mamelucos*, 193–6.

21 *DHA*, III, 58.

22 Fernandes, *Organização*, 64–74.

23 Stols, "Um dos primeiros," 407–20.

24 *DHA*, III, 348–9.

25 These figures are my calculations based on the census of Pernambuco (1774) in *ABNR*, 40 (1918), 21–111. Undoubtedly, they reflect underreporting of infant mortality. For the nineteenth century, see Peter Eisenberg, *The Sugar Industry of Pernambuco* (Berkeley, 1974), 148–51; Brainbridge Cowell, "Cityward Migration in the Nineteenth Century: The Case of Recife, Brazil," *Journal of Interamerican Studies and World Affairs* 17, no. 1 (Feb. 1975): 43–63.

26 *BNL*, Fundo geral, Codice 6936.

27 Michael Craton, *Sinews of Empire* (New York, 1974), 194–5.

28 *DHA*, III, 348–9.

29 Ibid., 93.

30 Inventory of 1591, ANTT, CSJ, maço 13, n. 4.

31 The chapel register is presently located in the Arquivo da Curia Metropolitana of Salvador. It is bound and erroneously titled Book I of Conceição da Praia. I consulted it in 1968 and realized that it was mislabeled, but not until David Smith called it to my attention again

in 1973 did I realize what it was. The chapel, dedicated to Nossa Senhora da Purificação, served as the parish church for the region until a new parish church was erected in Santo Amaro in 1722. The register contains information, therefore, about the population of the whole surrounding parish and not solely Engenho Sergipe. Unfortunately, there are also drawbacks that limit the utility of the register for historical analysis. First, its present physical state is poor. Many entries are illegible because pieces of the pages are missing, and, in fact, most of the pages covering the sixteenth century have been lost, as have most of the marriage entries. There are also problems created by imprecision in registry. The term negro was used to describe both Indians and Afro-Brazilians; thus it is impossible to distinguish between them on this basis alone. Whites were never identified as such in the chapel register, and thus when an individual has both Christian name and family name and no other ethnic or color designation, I have assumed him or her to be white. This method probably results in a slight inflation of the white category at the expense of mulattoes and mestiços, but since my major concern here is with Indians and Africans this is not a serious distortion. Also, many individuals are simply described as *escravo* (slave) with no more specific identification as to color or origin. These problems complicate any analysis, and therefore the results presented here are tentative at best.

32   Slave marriages at Engenho Sergipe, 1601–26, were as follows: Indian–Indian, 6; same nation–African, 7; mixed nation–African, 6; crioulo–crioulo, 1; unidentified origins, 9.

33   Inventory, Engenho Sergipe, 1591.

34   This pattern continued throughout the colonial period in Bahia. In the parish of Inhambupe between 1750 and 1800, 80 percent of the 1,294 registered marriages were between couples of the same racial category. See Consuelo Pondé de Sena, "Relações interétnicas através de casamentos realizados na freguesia do Inhambupe, na segunda metade do século xviii" (unpublished paper, Salvador, 1974).

35   Cristóvão de Bulhões, who appeared before the Inquisition in 1591, called himself a mameluco despite the fact that this father was not a Portuguese but a mulatto. See *PVCB*, 104–5.

36   Chapel register, Engenho Sergipe, 1595–1628, f. 75v.

37   Inventory, Engenho Sergipe, 1572–4, *DHA*, III, 65; see the discussion in Stuart B. Schwartz, "The Mocambo: Slave Resistance in Colonial Bahia," *Journal of Social History* 3, no. 4 (summer 1970): 318–19.

38   Cf. Sergio Buarque de Holanda, *Caminhos e fronteiras* (Rio de Janeiro, 1957), 15–180.

39   Confessions of Rodrigo Martins, Paulo Adorno, Cristóvão de Bulhões, *PVCB*, 94–5, 104–5, 164–5.

40   Ibid., 96–8. The confession of João Gonçalves, a tailor from Ilhéus, is interesting because it reveals a number of mameluco artisans like himself who also went in search of Indians.

41   Ibid., 79–87.

42   Ibid., 64–5.

43   Ibid., 167–72. The deposition of Tomacauna, described in the next paragraph, on the santidade cult is the most complete eyewitness account that remains in the historical record. He and other mamelucos with him all claimed that they practiced the rites to deceive the Indians and that Christ never left their hearts. The fact that these statements were made during the proceedings of the Inquisition makes their claims somewhat suspect.

44   Mauro, *Portugal et l'Atlantique*, 192–4. The Jesuits of Bahia asked for two dozen Africans in 1558, "and these can come together with these the King may send to the [Royal] engenho because often he sends ships here loaded with them." Leite, *Cartas Nóbrega* (Bahia, 8 May 1558), 288.

45   Pereira da Costa, *Anais pernambucanos*, 1, 455.

46   Inventário de Mem de Sá in *DHA*, III, 1–22, 73–6. Engenho Santana had the same distribution, with 7 Africans in a slave force of 107, or 6.5 percent; ANTT, CSJ, maço 13, n. 4; "Treslado do inventário do Engenho Sergipe," ANTT, CSJ, maço 30, f. 1040.

47   Stols, "Um dos primeiros," 418–20.

48   The Portuguese slave trade in the sixteenth century was concentrated in the Senegambia. On the cultural and agricultural traditions of the peoples in that region, see Philip D. Curtin, *Economic Change in Precolonial Africa: Senegambia in the Era of the Slave Trade*, 2 vols.

(Madison, Wis., 1975), 1, 3–58; and Walter Rodney, *A History of the Upper Guinea Coast,*
1545–1800 (Oxford, 1970), 1–38.

49   Paul Silberstein, "Wage Earners in a Slave Economy," BNM, Codice 2436, fs. 105–9.

50   See Antonio Garcia, "Regimenes indigenas de salariado: El salariado natural y el salariado
capitalista en la historia de América," *América Indigena* 8 (1948): 250–87.

51   Silberstein, "Wage Earners," based on *DHA*, II, passim; and Leite, *HCJB*, II, 63. Also see
Adrien van der Dussen, *Relatório sobre as capitanias conquistados no Brasil pelos holandeses*, ed.
José Antônio Gonçalves de Mello (Rio de Janeiro, 1947), 88–9.

52   Almon Wheeler Lauber, *Indian Slavery in Colonial Times within the Present Limits of the United*
States, Columbia University Studies in History (New York, 1913), 298–300, presents scattered references to relative prices from New England, New York, and the Carolinas.
Verner Crane, *The Southern Frontier, 1670–1732,* (Ann Arbor, Mich., 1929), 113–15,
provides data showing that Indians were valued at one-half to one-third the price of black
slaves, Peter H. Wood, *Black Majority* (New York, 1974), 38–40, reviews the literature
on Indian slavery in Carolina but is silent on this point. Instead see John Donald Duncan,
"Servitude and Slavery in Colonial South Carolina, 1670–1776," 2 vols. (Ph.D. thesis,
Emory University, 1972). On French Canada, see Marcel Trudel, *L'esclavage au Canada*
Français: Histoire et condition de l'esclavage (Quebec, 1960); and Guy Fregault, *La civilisation*
de la Nouvelle-France (Montreal, 1944), 83–4. Colin Palmer, *Slaves of the White God: Blacks*
in Mexico, 1570–1650 (Cambridge, Mass., 1976), 34, provides considerable evidence from
the 1520s in Mexico, as does Silvio Zavala, *Los indios esclavos en Nueva España* (Mexico City,
1968). Most important is Gonzalo Aguirre Beltrán, "El trabajo del indio comparado con
el del negro en Nueva España," *México Agrario* 4 (1942): 203–7.

53   As quoted in Duncan, "Servitude and Slavery in Colonial South Carolina, 1670–1776," 36.
For the traditional racist arguments of the nineteenth century, *see* Herman Merivale, *Lectures*
on Colonialism and Colonies [1861] (London, 1967), 283.

54   Gabriel Soares de Sousa's account of 1587 lists 36 engenhos for Bahia, but he also speaks
of 8 *casas de melles* (molasses-producing units), He gives an annual production of 120,000
arrobas for the captaincy, or somewhat less than 4,000 arrobas per mill. Fernão Cardim
also speaks of 36 engenhos in Bahia, but José de Anchieta lists 46. I have taken Father
Soares's figure of 50 – because it yields the lowest ratio of slaves to engenhos – as a control
on my argument that the ratio is extraordinarily high. Using the estimates of Soares de
Sousa or Cardim yields over 333 slaves for each mill; see Mauro, *Le Portugal et l'Atlantique*,
193; and Mauricio Goulart, *Escravidão africana no Brasil* (São Paulo, 1950), 100.

55   Soares, *Coisas notáveis*, 11.

56   See Barrett and Schwartz, "Comparación entre dos economías azucareras coloniales,"
550–5. Also see Ward Barrett, *The Sugar Hacienda of the Marqueses del Valle* (Minneapolis,
1970), 98–9.

57   Gandavo, *Histories of Brazil*, 153.

58   M. Goulart, *Escravidão africana no Brasil*, 100.

59   Buescu, *300 anos da inflação*, 44–5.

60   Sebastião da Rocha Pitta, *História da America portugueza*, 2d ed. (Lisbon 1880), 196–7.

61   Gaspar da Cunha to the count of Linhares (Bahia, 28 Aug. 1585), ANTT, CSJ, maço 8,
no. 9. For a similar opinion, see Martim Leitão's *Parecer*, in which he valued 1 Indian equal
to 4 Guiné slaves. BA, 44-XIV-6, fs. 185–93v.

62   These requests reappeared from time to time. It was suggested in 1653 that the Tapuyas
of Maranhão could be used to develop sugar engenhos in that captaincy, thereby "advancing
[them] by removing them from the misery in which they hive and teaching them in this
way to get along by agriculture." Duarte Ribeiro de Macedo to a friend (Paris, 20 Jan.
1653), LC/Port. Mss. P-271.

Chapter 6

Michael Craton

SLAVERY AND SLAVE SOCIETY IN THE BRITISH CARIBBEAN

Introduction

WRITTEN FOR A GENERAL ENCYCLOPEDIA of slavery edited by Seymour Drescher and Stanley Engerman published in 1998, this essay can be regarded both as an up-to-date introductory overview and as a glossary of the concepts currently regarded as of salient importance by the author. Distinguishing the slavery of the British West Indies from other forms, it stresses the distinctions between true slave colonies and mere slaveowning colonies, between the slave systems of sugar plantation, non-sugar plantation and non-plantation colonies, between types of slaves, and between slaves as economic units and as human beings. Besides defining such key current terms and concepts as slave society, plantocracy, creolisation, proto-peasants and proto-proletarians, the essay introduces such hotly debated issues as slave resistance versus accommodation, the reasons for abolition, amelioration, apprenticeship and emancipation, and even the fact of the ex-slaves once nominally freed. It includes a short selective bibliography up-to-date in 1996.

Africans were enslaved in all the English colonies of the Caribbean region virtually from the beginning, and black slavery became the predominant system of labour from the time it superseded the use of Amerindians and white indentured 'servants' in the mid-seventeenth century, until emancipation was enforced in 1834–38. The slave labour system involved a trade in blacks from West Africa that suddenly surged with the introduction of large-scale sugar cultivation and increased along with the expansion of plantations to reach an annual peak of around 38,000 before the abolition of the trade in 1807. Because of the deadly climate and diseased environment as much as the harsh work regime and overt cruelty, a traffic totalling some 2 million over 180 years left a population of no more than 670,000 slaves in 1834 (compared with a slave population of 3 million in the USA in 1865 from some 400,000 imported), but these still outnumbered resident whites by nearly ten to one, and the intermediate class of non-white free persons in similar proportion.

The English colonies of the Caribbean region were not only scattered but extremely diverse. Largely as a consequence, their slavery systems (as well as differing from those of the other imperial powers) also varied in important ways;

broadly according to the type and intensity of the economic system, but more subtly according to the time when, and the circumstances under which, each colony was acquired, its relative stage and pace of development, and the form of its government. The majority were plantation colonies, and sugar (with its by-products, molasses and rum) was much and most important crop, accounting for as much as 80 per cent of exports by value. But geographical factors such as mountains, low rainfall or sparse soils determined a degree of diversification (cotton, coffee, spices, stock animals, provisions), and some of the colonies acquired later, despite their fertility, had not fully developed plantations before the slave trade or slavery ended. Besides this, there were non-plantation or marginal colonies, dedicated to maritime activity (Bermuda, Bahamas), logwood cutting (Belize), salt production (Turks & Caicos) and turtling (Caymans).

Politically, all English Caribbean colonies can be termed 'plantocracies' in that the white slave-owners ruled, although there were subtle variations between colonies that were English from the beginning and those acquired later from the French or Dutch, and the fact that planters made their own laws in most colonies led to subtle legal variations within a broad general pattern. Towards the end of slavery an important distinction also occurred between the original self-legislating colonies and those acquired during the Napoleonic Wars which were directly ruled as Crown Colonies, and thus came more under the influence of an increasingly liberal Colonial Office.

Sociologically, however, just as all were true slave rather than mere 'slave-owning' colonies, all English Caribbean colonies were 'slave societies' in the sense defined by Elsa Goveia; that despite the whites' pretensions to be a socially distinct elite, the entire social fabric was shaped by the slavery system, encompassing whites and free non-whites as well as the slaves themselves. Slave society, though, was by no means static, and the over-arching process was that termed creolisation, in both its demographic and cultural aspects. Confusingly, the adjective creole has often been applied narrowly either to local whites or to persons of mixed race; but more conveniently it describes all persons (or even animals) not indigenously native but born and bred in the region, as well as aspects of the creoles' locally shaped and essentially syncretic culture. As a process, the term creolisation is used both for the gradual increase in the proportion of creoles in the population (blacks and whites who were no longer true Africans or Europeans, as well as persons of mixed race), and for the equally gradual evolution of their distinct regional culture. In its limited and covert way, racial miscegenation was the most extreme, but by no means a necessary feature of creolisation. The most general notable aspect of cultural creolisation – which can stand as a paradigm for all other aspects – was the evolution out of the slavetraders' pidgin of a genuine creole language (or rather languages, for every colony had its own); a *lingua franca* in which, as befitted the origins of masters and slaves, the lexicon was predominantly European, while much of the grammar, sentence structure and intonation was generically, and some of the vocabulary specifically, African in derivation.

The slave codes which the plantocrats constructed could derive little except general concepts of property, punishment and the control of labour out of an English legal system from which the ideas of chattel slavery and serfdom had long since faded. Instead, the slave laws of the English colonies (which, unlike those of the other imperial powers, were not codified until the last years of the eighteenth century, when each self-legislating colony passed its own Consolidated Slave Act) reflected the planters' pragmatic needs and prejudices as well as borrowing from Roman Law principles found in the Spanish *siete partidas* and the French *code noir*. The general purposes of these laws were simple: to define slaves as chattel, to restrict their mobility, to control their lives and work, and to punish them for infractions. In many islands, slaves were defined as real estate so that they could be tied to their owners' other goods, chattels and land. Everywhere, manumission was made almost impossible; the uterine law that children inherited their mother's status was generally adopted; and strict pass laws and savage punishments were enacted for running away, as well as for acts of sabotage, insubordination and overt resistance.

Until the late eighteenth century laws remained on the books decreeing or permitting mutilation, and execution by slow burning or starving to death in gibbets for the worst offenses. However, the inequity and impracticality of the laws (punishing runaways with lashes but their harbourers with death, slave insolence with death but white slave-murderers with fines; never quite determining whether a slave as a chattel could actually commit a crime like theft) meant that usage and custom were always more important, and generally more lenient, than enacted slave laws, and that when 'ameliorative' laws were introduced under metropolitan pressure from the 1780s they were mostly dead letters, simply enacted what had long been customary, or endorsed changes – such as the wholesale adoption and adaptation of Christianity by the slaves – that were occurring independently.

In the age of the buccaneers, slaves were acquired from foreign plantations or ships, but as English plantations developed, the West African trade was formalised through a series of chartered monopoly companies of which the Royal African Company (1672–1750) was the most important. In contrast to the continuing protection afforded sugar and other plantation products (thanks to a powerful lobby of merchants and planters), slave-trading was deregulated and thrown open to free trade by 1712 – partly explaining, perhaps, why the slave trade lost its imperial support and was abolished a quarter of a century before the institution of slavery itself.

The lethal process of acclimatisation called seasoning (which carried off nearly half of all new slaves within three years), as well as the steady expansion of plantations throughout the slavery era, ensured the vigorous continuation of the slave trade until 1807 and the consequently continuous cultural links with Mother Africa. Yet the wealth of African retentions and degree of creolisation varied greatly at any given time. Barbados and the marginal colonies, having become economically fully developed or static and demographically self-sustaining, no longer needed African imports, and as many as 90 per cent of their slaves were creoles when the African slave trade ended. On the other hand, 37 per cent of Jamaican slaves were still African-born as late as 1817, and those of Trinidad and Guyana (where the labour demand was exacerbated by a natural decrease in the slave population of around 15 per thousand a year) no more than 45 per cent were colony-born.

The slaves' lives were shaped by the dominant economy and their culture reshaped by the creolisation process, but within the variations of their Caribbean environment and assigned functions, the slaves preserved what they could of their existential identity, and in fact increased their own contribution to the English Caribbean economy and culture as the institution of slavery ran its course.

Domestic and town slaves lived in smaller groups in closer proximity to their white masters, and tended to experience a more intimate intercourse with them, than did the majority of slaves who lived on large plantations. Mariner and wood-cutting crews also enjoyed to a degree the essential freemasonry of the sea and interior forests – their relative freedom being a transactional equation based on the comparative ease with which they could abscond or arm themselves. Yet such a large proportion of English Caribbean slaves lived their whole lives within the size-able community and closely guarded cellular bounds of a single plantation, that the plantation may be taken as the quintessential form of their existence.

At the apex of the plantation hierarchy, the owner, known by the slaves as Massa, was often an absentee (most commonly in Jamaica, least in Barbados) and could therefore exercise aristocratic luxuries, even noblesse oblige. When resi-dent, he occupied a so-called Great House, proprietarily overlooking his land, slaves and factory. The harsher realities, however, were handled by subordinate whites; attorney-managers (generally resident in the colonial capital), overseers and under-managers called bookkeepers. Those whites set in immediate authority were an isolated and beleaguered minority, non-gentlemen of limited education, dissolute and shiftless for the most part, outnumbered fifty to one by their charges, tied by contract and the requirement to make a profit, with only the parlous rewards of power to offset unpleasant work in a harsh climate, the ever-present threat of lethal or crippling disease, and the perils of insurrection.

As far as the plantation management was concerned, slaves were graded according to their usefulness, which was roughly equivalent to their monetary valuation. The able-bodied labourers were divided into three or more gangs by age and strength with little regard to gender, with only the roughly 10 per cent who were hopelessly diseased, senile or under six years of age regarded as unproduc-tive. Yet even within the managers' own formulation there was a complex implied hierarchy which separated out the domestics and those of mixed race from the labourers, the factory workers and artisans from the field workers, and gave at least some delegated, if reversible, authority to trusted slave headmen. Africans were regarded as inferior to creoles only to the degree that they were less accul-turated, with fewer useful skills or amenable attitudes. That field headmen were often Africans rather than creoles, however, suggested that there was an under-lying hierarchy among the slaves that owed more to traditional canons of reputation than to the simple economic imperatives of the plantation. In that fraction of the day, week and year that the slaves had to themselves, and within their own quar-ters and grounds, they fashioned a social, economic and cultural life of which the masters were largely ignorant or dismissive, but which came to have a critical effect on plantation life and culture as a whole before slavery ended.

Much of this influence went unnoticed not just because it was so gradual but because it was syncretic and thus more easily accepted by the whites, or even assim-ilated by them. Besides strongly influencing the development of creole languages, Africans introduced new foods and methods of cooking, and new music and modes of dancing that employed European as well as African instruments and adapted European measures and rhythms. African festivals and festival forms such as Crop-over and Junkanoo were melded to European celebrations like Harvest Home, Carnival or Christmas mumming. African games, folklore, proverbs and even beliefs also found their way into the creole culture.

Even more significant was the way that the English Caribbean slaves adopted and adapted Christianity. Unlike the slaves of the Catholic imperial powers, the English slaves were not actively proselytised from the beginning, and the established Anglican Church was regarded as mainly for whites, as well, as in England, as having a secular role in local government and society. The Anglican Church had considerable success in attracting slaves in Barbados and Antigua, and there were many nominally Catholic slaves in the colonies acquired from France and Spain after 1763. But when nonconformist missionaries – the first invited by planters in the expectation that they would have a socialising or 'civilising' function – became widely active from the 1780s onwards, the great majority of English Caribbean slaves became baptised Christians. As the more perceptive (mainly Anglican) planters recognised, however, the majority of slaves were attracted to theologies and liturgies that were mostly consonant with African beliefs and practices, as well as to the more participatory churches. Most popular of all were the Baptists of Jamaica and the Bahamas, whose first congregations were formed by evangelical slave preachers who had come from the mainland with their Loyalist owners after 1783, a whole generation before white Baptist missionaries appeared on the scene from England.

Most important of all, however, was the influence that the slaves themselves had on English Caribbean socioeconomic patterns both during and after slavery. Despite the intentional jumbling of Africans by the traders and slave-owners, Afro-Caribbean slaves quickly reconstituted kinship networks, beginning as early as the 'shipmate bond' yet soon reinforced by more or less inevitable endogamy and the sense of belonging to a localised plantation community. Contrary to the arguments of some scholars that slave sales inevitably broke up families and that family dysfunction was increased by sexual relations between slave women and whites that were tantamount to prostitution and rape, English Caribbean slaves had a strong commitment to the immediate family, in which the roles of father and mother owed more to African traditions of domestic economy than to any concern on the masters' part.

Of fundamental importance in this respect were the ways in which slave mothers dominated in the domestic economy in and around the family house, and that slave families were able to control and exploit the provision grounds they were allotted by their owners. Slaves cultivated gardens and raised small stock around their hutments, and on some plantations there were 'shell blow' grounds near the canefields where slaves were set to grow provision crops during the mid-day breaks. But slave family heads were assigned more extensive grounds wherever there was sufficient and sufficiently cultivable land on the margins of the areas most suitable for planting export crops. It was clearly in the owners' interest for the slaves to be as self-supporting in food as possible, but many slaves went much further. Working as families in the evenings and one and a half days at weekends when they were released from plantation labour (and surely working with greater enthusiasm than ever for their owners), they raised small stock, fruits and surplus ground provisions, collected wild produce and made simple craft items. These goods were marketed, particularly by the slave women who carried them for sale to the Sunday markets in town, to informal markets at plantation intersections, or even to their own owners. The money received was used to purchase small semi-luxuries (such as crockery, cutlery, glassware, mirrors and combs), or fancier items of clothing than were issued by their owners, from itinerant peddlers or market stall-holders. So prevalent did the system of informal slave production and marketing become (most notably in Jamaica) that scholars, following the lead of Sidney Mintz, commonly refer to slaves in the late slave period as proto-peasants. One Marxist, Ciro Cardoso, has even referred to 'the peasant breach in the slave mode of production'.

Other scholars, like Mary Turner, Nigel Bolland and Howard Johnson, bearing in mind that the fate (if not the ideal) of ex-slaves was to fill the ranks of that peculiarly Caribbean hybrid class of 'part-peasant, part-proletarian', have stressed the ways in which slaves organised themselves to challenge and mitigate the terms under which they worked and to receive fixed rewards, even cash for work beyond the normal call, to the degree that we may call them proto-proletarians. Considering what slaves did with the money they earned to ease the poverty of their material life – and thus contribute in a small way to the incorporation of the plantation periphery into the industrialising world – one might even go as far as to term them proto-consumers. In all three ways of anticipating later trends slaves probably contributed almost as much to the transition out of slavery as did any external actors or forces, quite apart from what they did to discredit and bring down slavery by manifold more aggressive forms of resistance.

The simplest, earliest and least effective way to work slaves was to form them into gangs and force them to labour under duress as long as was physically possible. The general substitution for pure gang labour of fixed daily tasks – after which slaves would be free, to rest or labour for themselves as they willed – was an early recognition that slaves worked better under some form of incentive. As time went on, slaves showed great enterprise in reducing the size of tasks that could reasonably be expected, and in raising the level of incentives by playing upon their managers' need to maximise their labour. At one extreme, slaves in Bermuda and the Bahamas helped to crew privateers during wartime, but would only fight with a will if they received a seaman's share of the booty. In all colonies, surplus and skilled slaves were often hired out, and were usually able to command a share of their hire in return for performing satisfactorily. Some were even allowed to hire themselves out and simply pay their owner for the privilege. Even on the strictest plantations, the levels of tasks and rewards (including more time to work the grounds) became so customary that managers risked virtual strikes, or even a sacking from the attorney or owner, if they attempted to extract more than was practicable from their charges.

Beyond the transactional calculus of such primitive industrial relations was the fearsome threat of escalating forms of slave resistance: from malingering, recalcitrance and running away, to arson, cattle-maiming and other acts of sabotage; through individual acts of violence against the whites (including poisoning and the casting of African spells), to widening plots, and the ultimate horror of a general slave uprising. Although there was never a completely successful slave revolt in the English Caribbean like that in Haiti (1791–1804), it is clear that English slaves, like those everywhere, perennially resisted their enslavement however they could; that they rose up 'whenever they could or had to' (for example, when the forces of control were weakened or distracted by war, or when the slaves were driven intolerably); and that their resistance, ultimately, drove home the impracticality of slavery as a labour system compared with its alternatives.

Overt slave resistance in the English Caribbean, as elsewhere in plantation America, went through several distinct phases. The earliest manifestations involved mass running away and the forming of obdurate maroon communities in the forested and mountainous interior, sometimes cooperating with Amerindian survivors. Fighting when they had to, maroons forced the planters into making treaties, although these were not permanently honoured by the whites. The fierce Black Caribs of St Vincent and the maroons of Dominica were not finally subdued until the 1790s, while the Bush Negroes and maroons of the Guianese and Belizean riverine hinterlands were able to survive permanently beyond the reach of planter imperialism. The fate of the most famous maroons of the English Caribbean, those of Jamaica, was rather more equivocal. They fought a successful guerrilla war against the colonial regime in the 1730s, but were divided by the subsequent treaties of accommodation. The more troublesome Leeward maroons were expelled to Nova Scotia and Sierra Leone after a second war in the 1790s, but the remaining maroons retained a nominal independence as the planters' allies to the end of slavery and beyond, keeping a distinct if fading cultural identity right up to the present day.

While African-born slaves remained the majority, African-led revolts were the worst threat to plantocratic hegemony, particularly when Akan-speaking 'Coromantine' slaves from the warrior culture of Ghana were involved. The most serious such crisis was the islandwide Coromantine-led rebellion of 1760 in Jamaica, which occurred when British forces were heavily engaged in the Seven Years' War. Subsequent plots and localised uprisings were weakened by divisions in aims and leadership between African and creole slaves, and the worldwide ferment that included the American, French and Haitian revolutions did not lead to a general slave uprising throughout the English Caribbean, both because British naval and military forces were heavily mobilised, and because a majority of English slaves were persuaded to stay neutral or actually to fight for the regime by promises, largely unfulfilled, or ameliorated conditions of manumission.

To the consternation of the English planters, however, the progressive creolisation of their slaves did not lessen the incidence of overt rebellion, but rather the reverse. As the creole slaves became gradually more aware of philanthropic allies in Britain, and of a changing climate of opinion about slavery in the British Parliament, the three most serious slave revolts occurred in the three most important sugar plantation colonies of the British Caribbean: in Barbados in 1816; in Demerara (British Guiana) in 1823; and in Jamaica in 1831–2. These involved tens of thousands of slaves, led by the most creolised and trusted slave headmen, who in the latter two cases included black Christian deacons. What the rebels wanted above all, of course, was freedom from chattel slavery. But there is overwhelming evidence that they did not seek violence, retribution or the destruction of the plantation system. Rather, they wanted the freedom of choice to live either as free townsfolk, or more like free peasants, retaining the option of working for wages how, when and only for as long as it suited them.

All three rebellions were suppressed with bloody savagery. Planters and imperial conservatives alike were convinced that slavery must continue and that less rather than more leniency was called for. Yet in the British parliamentary debates rising to a climax even as the Jamaican insurrection occurred, the philanthropic minority was joined by two types of realists: those economic liberals who believed with Adam Smith that a system of competitive wage labour was superior to the coercion of slavery, and those who were convinced that if freedom of this kind were not granted from above, it would be seized from below, and the very existence of the colonial empire in the Caribbean jeopardised. In these respects, therefore, the slaves of the British Caribbean can be said to have contributed to their own emancipation.

Emancipation for all slaves in the British Caribbean (as well as South Africa, Mauritius and Ceylon) was decreed by the imperial Parliament a year in advance, to come into effect at midnight on July 31, 1834. It was endorsed by the colonial legislatures with a promptitude spurred by the fear of losing the monetary compensation voted for the owners (not, of course, for the slaves), and the right to impose a transitional period of compulsory labour called apprenticeship. Apprenticeship was designed to last six years but in the event was terminated after four. This was partly because it proved unworkable and provoked scandal, but mainly because it was deemed unnecessary. The legislators of Bermuda and Antigua, where there was no spare land and ex-slaves had no option but to work for their former owners, even chose to forgo apprenticeship altogether. As the disciples of Adam Smith predicted, labour relations fell into a natural pattern without regulation or physical coercion, although only in colonies with a surplus of land and a shortage of workers were these conditions even remotely favourable to the ex-slaves.

With their numbers for the first time increasing everywhere, the ex-slaves of the British Caribbean and their descendants were faced with a rapidly declining economy, an increasingly indifferent imperial government, and a local ruling class able to sustain its hegemony through the control of land and commerce, if not also, absolutely, the structure of local politics. Although still proudly struggling to construct a life of their own and intermittently continuing the fight against oppression, in an age driven by *laissez-faire* ideas as well as the racist distortions of Social Darwinism, formal slavery's black legatees were condemned to a century or more of a different, and scarcely preferable, form of involuntary servitude, while the racism that stemmed from the correlation between functional, class and ethnic divisions was an even longer-lived legacy.

Bibliography

Hilary Beckles, *Natural Rebels: A Social History of Enslaved Black Women in Barbados*, New Brunswick, NJ, 1989; *White Servitude and Black Slavery in Barbados, 1627–1715*, Knoxville, TN, 1989.

Hilary Beckles and Verene Shepherd, *Caribbean Slave Society and Economy: A Student Reader*, Kingston, 1993.

Nigel Bolland, 'Systems of Domination after Slavery: The Control of Land and Labor in the British West Indies after 1838', *Comparative Studies in Society and History*, 23, 4, 1981, 591–619.

Edward K. Brathwaite, *The Development of Creole Society in Jamaica, 1770–1820*, Oxford, 1971.

Barbara Bush, *Slave Women in Caribbean Society, 1650–1838*, Bloomington, IN, 1990.

Ciro F. S. Cardoso, 'The Peasant Breach in the Slave System: New Developments in Brazil', *Luso-Brazilian Review*, 25, 1988, 49–57.

Frederic G. Cassidy, *Jamaica Talk: Three Hundred Years of the English Language in Jamaica*, Kingston, 1961.

Michael Craton, *Sinews of Empire: A Short History of British Slavery*, New York, 1974; *Searching for the Invisible Man: Slaves and Plantation Life in Jamaica*, Cambridge, MA, 1978; *Testing the Chains: Resistance to Slavery in the British West Indies*, Ithaca, 1982; 'Reshuffling the Pack:

The Transition from Slavery to Other Forms of Labour in the British Caribbean, c. 1790–1890', *Nieuwe Westindische Gids*, 1995.

Philip D. Curtin, *The Atlantic Slave Trade: A Census*, Madison, 1969.

Richard S. Dunn, *Sugar and Slaves: The Rise of the Planter Class in the English West Indies, 1624–1713*, Chapel Hill, NC, 1972.

Barry Gaspar, *Bondmen and Rebels: A Study of Master-Slave Relations in Antigua*, Baltimore, MD, 1985.

Elsa Goveia, *Slave Society in the British Leeward Islands at the End of the Eighteenth Century*, New Haven CT, 1965.

Douglas Hall, *In Miserable Slavery: Thomas Thistlewood in Jamaica, 1750–86*, Basingstoke, 1989.

Barry W. Higman, *Slave Populations of the British Caribbean, 1807–1834*, Baltimore, MD, 1984.

Howard Johnson, *The Bahamas in Slavery and Freedom*, Kingston, 1991.

Kenneth Kiple, *The Caribbean Slave: A Biological History*, Cambridge, 1984.

Roderick McDonald, *The Economy and Material Culture of Slaves: Goods and Chattels on the Sugar Plantations of Jamaica and Louisiana*, Baton Rouge, 1993.

Sidney Mintz, *Caribbean Transformations*, Chicago, 1974.

Richard Pares, *A West Indian Fortune*, London, 1936.

Orlando H. Patterson, *The Sociology of Slavery: An Analysis of the Origins, Development and Structure of Negro Slave Society in Jamaica*, London, 1967.

Frank W. Pitman, *The Development of the British West Indies, 1700–1763*, New Haven, CT, 1917.

Lowell J. Ragatz, *The Fall of the Planter Class in the British West Indies, 1763–1833*, New York, 1928.

Richard B. Sheridan, *Sugar and Slavery: An Economic History of the British West Indies, 1623–1775*, Baltimore, MD, 1974; *Doctors and Slaves: A Medical and Demographic History of Slavery in the British West Indies, 1680–1834*, New York, 1985.

Mary Turner, *Slaves and Missionaries: The Disintegration of Jamaican Slave Society, 1787–1834*, Urbana, IL, 1982.

John R Ward, *British West Indian Slavery, 1750–1834: The Process of Amelioration*, Oxford, 1988.

Eric E. Williams, *Capitalism and Slavery*, London, 1944.

Chapter 7

Winthrop D. Jordan

MODERN TENSIONS AND THE ORIGINS OF AMERICAN SLAVERY

THANKS TO JOHN SMITH we know that negroes first came to the British continental colonies in 1619.[1] What we do not know is exactly when Negroes were first enslaved there. This question has been debated by historians for the past seventy years, the critical point being whether Negroes were enslaved almost from their first importation or whether they were at first simply servants and only later reduced to the status of slaves. The long duration and vigor of the controversy suggest that more than a simple question of dating has been involved. In fact certain current tensions in American society have complicated the historical problem and greatly heightened its significance. Dating the origins of slavery has taken on a striking modern relevance.

During the nineteenth century historians assumed almost universally that the first Negroes came to Virginia as slaves. So close was their acquaintance with the problem of racial slavery that it did not occur to them that Negroes could ever have been anything but slaves. Philip A. Bruce, the first man to probe with some thoroughness into the early years of American slavery, adopted this view in 1896, although he emphasized that the original difference in treatment between white servants and Negroes was merely that Negroes served for life. Just six years later, however, came a challenge from a younger, professionally trained historian, James C. Ballagh. His *A History of Slavery in Virginia* appeared in the *Johns Hopkins University Studies in Historical and Political Science*, an aptly named series which was to usher in the new era of scholarly detachment in the writing of institutional history. Ballagh offered a new and different interpretation; he took the position that the first Negroes served merely as servants and that enslavement did not begin until around 1660, when statutes bearing on slavery were passed for the first time.[2]

There has since been agreement on dating the statutory establishment of slavery, and differences of opinion have centered on when enslavement began in actual practice. Fortunately there has also been general agreement on slavery's distinguishing characteristics: service for life and inheritance of like obligation by any offspring. Writing on the free Negro in Virginia for the Johns Hopkins series, John H. Russell in 1913 tackled the central question and showed that some Negroes were indeed servants but concluded that "between 1640 and 1660 slavery was fast becoming an established fact. In this twenty years the colored population was divided, part being servants and part being slaves, and some who were servants defended themselves with increasing difficulty from the encroachments of slavery."[3] Ulrich B. Phillips, though little interested in the matter, in 1918 accepted Russell's conclusion of early servitude and transition toward slavery after 1640. Helen T. Catterall took much the same position in 1926. On the other hand, in 1921 James M. Wright, discussing the free Negro in Maryland, implied that Negroes were slaves almost from the beginning, and in 1940 Susie M. Ames reviewed several cases in Virginia which seemed to indicate that genuine slavery had existed well before Ballagh's date of 1660.[4]

All this was a very small academic gale, well insulated from the outside world. Yet despite disagreement on dating enslavement, the earlier writers—Bruce, Ballagh, and Russell—shared a common assumption which, though at the time seemingly irrelevant to the main question, has since proved of considerable importance. They assumed that prejudice against the Negro was natural and almost innate in the white man. It would be surprising if they had felt otherwise in this period of segregation statutes, overseas imperialism, immigration restriction, and full-throated Anglo-Saxonism. By the 1920s, however, with the easing of these tensions, the assumption of natural prejudice was dropped unnoticed. Yet only one historian explicitly contradicted that assumption: Ulrich Phillips of Georgia, impressed with the geniality of both slavery and twentieth-century race relations, found no natural prejudice in the white man and expressed his "conviction that Southern racial asperities are mainly superficial, and that the two great elements are fundamentally in accord."[5]

Only when tensions over race relations intensified once more did the older assumption of natural prejudice crop up again. After World War II American Negroes found themselves beneficiaries of New Deal politics and reforms, wartime need for manpower, world-wide repulsion at racist excesses in Nazi Germany, and growingly successful colored anticolonialism. With new militancy Negroes mounted an attack on the citadel of separate but equal, and soon it became clear that America was in for a period of self-conscious reappraisal of its racial arrangements. Writing in this period of heightened tension (1949) a practiced and careful scholar, Wesley F. Craven, raised the old question of the Negro's original status, suggesting that Negroes had been enslaved at an early date. Craven also cautiously resuscitated the idea that white men may have had natural distaste for the Negro, an idea which fitted neatly with the suggestion of early enslavement. Original antipathy would mean rapid debasement.[6]

In the next year (1950) came a sophisticated counterstatement, which contradicted both Craven's dating and implicitly any suggestion of early prejudice. Oscar and Mary F. Handlin in "Origins of the Southern Labor System" offered a case for late enslavement, with servitude as the status of Negroes before about 1660. Originally the status of both Negroes and white servants was far short of freedom, the Handlins maintained, but Negroes failed to benefit from increased freedom for servants in mid-century and became less free rather than more.[7] Embedded in this description of diverging status were broader implications: Late and gradual enslavement undercut the possibility of natural, deep-seated antipathy toward Negroes. On the contrary, if whites and Negroes could share the same status of half freedom for forty years in the seventeenth century, why could they not share full freedom in the twentieth?

The same implications were rendered more explicit by Kenneth M. Stampp in a major reassessment of Southern slavery published two years after the Supreme Court's 1954 school decision. Reading physiology with the eye of faith, Stampp frankly stated his assumption "that innately Negroes *are*, after all, only white men with black skins, nothing more, nothing less."[8] Closely following the Handlins' article on the origins of slavery itself, he almost directly denied any pattern of early and inherent racial antipathy: ". . . Negro and white servants of the seventeenth century seemed to be remarkably unconcerned about their visible physical differences." As for "the trend toward special treatment" of the Negro, "physical and cultural differences provided handy excuses to justify it."[9] Distaste for the Negro, then, was in the beginning scarcely more than an appurtenance of slavery.

These views squared nicely with the hopes of those even more directly concerned with the problem of contemporary race relations, sociologists and social psychologists. Liberal on the race question almost to a man, they tended to see slavery as the initial cause of the Negro's current degradation. The modern Negro was the unhappy victim of long association with base status. Sociologists, though uninterested in tired questions of historical evidence, could not easily assume a natural prejudice in the white man as the cause of slavery. Natural or innate prejudice would not only violate their basic assumptions concerning the dominance of culture but would undermine the power of their new Baconian science. For if prejudice was natural there would be little one could do to wipe it out. Prejudice must have followed enslavement, not vice versa, else any liberal program of action would be badly compromised. One prominent social scientist suggested in a UNESCO pamphlet that racial prejudice in the United States commenced with the cotton gin![10]

Just how closely the question of dating had become tied to the practical matter of action against racial prejudice was made apparent by the suggestions of still another historian. Carl N. Degler grappled with the dating problem in an article frankly entitled "Slavery and the Genesis of American Race Prejudice."[11] The article appeared in 1959, a time when Southern resistance to school desegregation seemed more adamant than ever and the North's hands none too clean, a period of discouragement for those hoping to end racial discrimination. Prejudice against the Negro now appeared firm and deep-seated, less easily eradicated than had been supposed in, say, 1954. It was Degler's view that enslavement began early, as a result of white settlers' prejudice or antipathy toward the first Negroes. Thus not only were the sociologists contradicted but the dating problem was now overtly and consciously tied to the broader question of whether slavery caused prejudice or prejudice caused slavery. A new self-consciousness over the American racial dilemma had snatched an arid historical controversy from the hands of an unsuspecting earlier generation and had tossed it into the arena of current debate.

Ironically there might have been no historical controversy at all if every historian dealing with the subject had exercised greater care with facts and greater restraint in interpretation. Too often the debate entered the realm of inference and assumption. For the crucial early years after 1619 there is simply not enough evidence to indicate with any certainty whether Negroes were treated like white servants or not. No historian has found anything resembling proof one way or the other. The first Negroes were sold to the English settlers, yet so were other Englishmen. It can be said, however, that Negroes were set apart from white men by the word *Negroes*, and a distinct name is not attached to a group unless it is seen as different. The earliest Virginia census reports plainly distinguished Negroes from white men, sometimes giving Negroes no personal name; and in 1629 every commander of the several plantations was ordered to "take a generall muster of all the inhabitants men woemen and Children as well *Englishe* as Negroes."[12] Difference, however, might or might not involve inferiority.

The first evidence as to the actual status of Negroes does not appear until about 1640. Then it becomes clear that *some* Negroes were serving for life and some children inheriting the same obligation. Here it is necessary to suggest with some candor that the Handlins' statement to the contrary rests on unsatisfactory documentation.[13] That some Negroes were held as slaves after about 1640 is no indication, however, that American slavery popped into the world fully developed at that time. Many historians, most cogently the Handlins, have shown slavery to have been a gradual development, a process not completed until the eighteenth century. The complete deprivation of civil and personal rights, the legal conversion of the Negro into a chattel, in short slavery as Americans came to know it, was not accomplished overnight. Yet these developments practically and logically depended on the practice of hereditary lifetime service, and it is certainly possible to find in the 1640's and 1650's traces of slavery's most essential feature.[14]

The first definite trace appears in 1640 when the Virginia General Court pronounced sentence on three servants who had been retaken after running away to Maryland. Two of them, a Dutchman and a Scot, were ordered to serve their masters for one additional year and then the colony for three more, but "the third being a negro named John Punch shall serve his said master or his assigns for the time of his natural life here or else where." No white servant in America, so far as is known, ever received a like sentence.[15] Later the same month a Negro was again singled out from a group of recaptured runaways; six of the seven were assigned additional time while the Negro was given none, presumably because he was already serving for life.[16] After 1640, too, county court records began to mention Negroes, in part because there were more of them than previously—about two per cent of the Virginia population in 1649.[17] Sales for life, often including any future progeny, were recorded in unmistakable language. In 1646 Francis Pott sold a Negro woman and boy to Stephen Charlton "to the use of him . . . forever." Similarly, six years later William Whittington sold to John Pott "one Negro girle named Jowan; aged about Ten years and with her Issue and produce duringe her (or either of them) for their Life tyme. And their Successors forever"; and a Maryland man in 1649 deeded two Negro men and a woman "and all their issue both male and Female." The executors of a York County estate in 1647 disposed of eight Negroes—four men, two women, and two children—to Captain John Chisman "to have hold occupy posesse and inioy and every one of the afforementioned Negroes forever[.]"[18] The will of Rowland Burnham of "Rapahanocke," made in 1657, dispensed his considerable number of Negroes and white servants in language which clearly differentiated between the two by specifying that the whites were to serve for their "full terme of tyme" and the Negroes "for ever."[19] Nor did anything in the will indicate that this distinction was exceptional or novel.

In addition to these clear indications that some Negroes were owned for life, there were cases of Negroes held for terms far longer than the normal five or seven years.[20] On the other hand, some Negroes served only the term usual for white servants, and others were completely free.[21] One Negro freeman, Anthony Johnson, himself owned a Negro.[22] Obviously the enslavement of some Negroes did not mean the immediate enslavement of all.

Further evidence of Negroes serving for life lies in the prices paid for them. In many instances the valuations placed on Negroes (in estate inventories and bills of sale) were far higher than for white servants, even those servants with full terms yet to serve. Since there was ordinarily no preference for Negroes as such, higher prices must have meant that Negroes were more highly valued because of their greater length of service. Negro women may have been especially prized, moreover, because their progeny could also be held perpetually. In 1645, for example, two Negro women and a boy were sold for 5,500 pounds of tobacco. Two years earlier William Burdett's inventory listed eight servants (with the time each had still to serve) at valuations ranging from 400 to 1,100 pounds, while a "very anntient" Negro was valued at 3,000 and an eight-year-old Negro girl at 2,000 pounds, with no time-remaining indicated for either. In the late 1650s an inventory of Thomas Ludlow's large estate evaluated a white servant with six years to serve at less than an elderly Negro man and only one half of a Negro woman.[23] The labor owned by James Stone in 1648 was evaluated as follows:

	lb tobo
Thomas Groves, 4 yeares to serve	1300
Francis Bomley for 6 yeares	1500
John Thackstone for 3 yeares	1300
Susan Davis for 3 yeares	1000
Emaniell a Negro man	2000
Roger Stone 3 yeares	1300
Mingo a Negro man	2000[24]

Besides setting a higher value on the two Negroes, Stone's inventory, like Burdett's, failed to indicate the number of years they had still to serve. It would seem safe to assume that the time remaining was omitted in this and similar documents simply because the Negroes were regarded as serving for an unlimited time.

The situation in Maryland was apparently the same. In 1643 Governor Leonard Calvert agreed with John Skinner, "mariner," to exchange certain estates for seventeen sound Negro "slaves," fourteen men and three women between sixteen and twenty-six years old. The total value of these was placed at 24,000 pounds of tobacco, which would work out to 1,000 pounds for the women and 1,500 for the men, prices considerably higher than those paid for white servants at the time.[25]

Wherever Negro women were involved, however, higher valuations may have reflected the fact that they could be used for field work while white women generally were not. This discrimination between Negro and white women, of course, fell short of actual enslavement. It meant merely that Negroes were set apart in a way clearly not to their advantage. Yet this is not the only evidence that Negroes were subjected to degrading distinctions not directly related to slavery. In several ways Negroes were singled out for special treatment which suggested a generalized debasing of Negroes as a group. Significantly, the first indications of debasement appeared at about the same time as the first indications of actual enslavement.

The distinction concerning field work is a case in point. It first appeared on the written record in 1643, when Virginia pointedly recognized it in her taxation policy. Previously tithable persons had been defined (1629) as "all those that worke in the ground of what qualitie or condition soever." Now the law stated that all adult men and *Negro* women were to be tithable, and this distinction was made twice again before 1660. Maryland followed a similar course, beginning in 1654.[26] John Hammond, in a 1656 tract defending the tobacco colonies, wrote that servant women were not put to work in the fields but in domestic employments, "yet som wenches that are nasty, and beastly and not fit to be so imployed are put into the ground."[27] Since all Negro women were taxed as working in the fields, it would seem logical to conclude that Virginians found them "nasty" and "beastly." The essentially racial nature of this discrimination was bared by a 1668 law at the time slavery was crystallizing on the statute books:

> Whereas some doubts, have arisen whether negro women set free were still to be accompted tithable according to a former act, *It is declared by this grand assembly* that negro women, though permitted to enjoy their free-dome yet ought not in all respects to be admitted to a full fruition of the exemptions and impunities of the English, and are still lyable to payment of taxes.[28]

Virginia law set Negroes apart in a second way by denying them the important right and obligation to bear arms. Few restraints could indicate more clearly the denial to Negroes of membership in the white community. This action, in a sense the first foreshadowing of the slave codes, came in 1640, at just the time when other indications first appear that Negroes were subject to special treatment.[29]

Finally, an even more compelling sense of the separateness of Negroes was revealed in early distress concerning sexual union between the races. In 1630 a Virginia court pronounced a now famous sentence: "Hugh Davis to be soundly whipped, before an assembly of Negroes and others for abusing himself to the dishonor of God and shame of Christians, by defiling his body in lying with a negro."[30] While there were other instances of punishment for interracial union in the ensuing years, fornication rather than miscegenation may well have been the primary offense, though in 1651 a Maryland man sued someone who he claimed had said "that he had a black bastard in Virginia."[31] There may have been nothing racial about the 1640 case by which Robert Sweet was compelled "to do penance in church according to laws of England, for getting a negroe woman with child and the woman whipt."[32] About 1650 a white man and a Negro woman were required to stand clad in white sheets before a congregation in Lower Norfolk County for having had relations, but this punishment was sometimes used in ordinary cases of fornication between two whites.[33]

It is certain, however, that in the early 1660s when slavery was gaining statutory recognition, the colonial assemblies legislated with feeling against miscegenation. Nor was this merely a matter of avoiding confusion of status, as was suggested by the Handlins. In 1662 Virginia declared that "if any christian shall committ ffornication with a negro man or woman, hee or shee soe offending" should pay double the usual fine. Two years later Maryland prohibited interracial marriages:

> forasmuch as divers freeborne English women forgettfull of their free
> Condicōn and to the disgrace of our Nation doe intermarry with Negro
> Slaves by which alsoe divers suites may arise touching the Issue of such
> woemen and a great damage doth befall the Masters of such Negros for
> prevention whereof for deterring such freeborne women from such shame-
> full Matches . . .

strong language indeed if the problem had only been confusion of status. A Maryland
act of 1681 described marriages of white women with Negroes as, among other
things, "always to the Satisfaccōn of theire Lascivious & Lustfull desires, & to the
disgrace not only of the English butt allso of many other Christian Nations." When
Virginia finally prohibited all interracial liaisons in 1691, the assembly vigorously
denounced miscegenation and its fruits as "that abominable mixture and spurious
issue."[34]

One is confronted, then, with the fact that the first evidences of enslavement
and of other forms of debasement appeared at about the same time. Such coincidence comports poorly with both views on the causation of prejudice and slavery.
If slavery caused prejudice, then invidious distinctions concerning working in the
fields, bearing arms, and sexual union should have appeared only after slavery's
firm establishment. If prejudice caused slavery, then one would expect to find
such lesser discriminations preceding the greater discrimination of outright
enslavement.

Perhaps a third explanation of the relationship between slavery and prejudice
may be offered, one that might fit the pattern of events as revealed by existing
evidence. Both current views share a common starting point: They predicate two
factors, prejudice and slavery, and demand a distinct order of causality. No matter
how qualified by recognition that the effect may in turn react upon the cause, each
approach inevitably tends to deny the validity of its opposite. But what if one
were to regard both slavery and prejudice as species of a general debasement of
the Negro? Both may have been equally cause and effect, constantly reacting
upon each other, dynamically joining hands to hustle the Negro down the road to
complete degradation. Mutual causation is, of course, a highly useful concept for
describing social situations in the modern world.[35] Indeed it has been widely
applied in only slightly altered fashion to the current racial situation: Racial
prejudice and the Negro's lowly position are widely accepted as constantly reinforcing each other.

This way of looking at the facts might well fit better with what we know of
slavery itself. Slavery was an organized pattern of human relationships. No matter
what the law might say, it was of different character than cattle ownership. No
matter how degrading, slavery involved human beings. No one seriously pretended
otherwise. Slavery was not an isolated economic or institutional phenomenon; it
was the practical facet of a general debasement without which slavery could have
no rationality. (Prejudice, too, was a form of debasement, a kind of slavery in the
mind.) Certainly the urgent need for labor in a virgin country guided the direction which debasement took, molded it, in fact, into an institutional framework.
That economic practicalities shaped the external form of debasement should not
tempt one to forget, however, that slavery was at bottom a social arrangement, a
way of society's ordering its members in its own mind.

Notes

1   "About the last of August came in a dutch man of warre that sold us twenty Negars." Smith was quoting John Rolfe's account. Edward Arber and A. G. Bradley (eds.), *Travels and Works of Captain John Smith* . . . (2 vols., Edinburgh, 1910), II, 541.

2   Philip A. Bruce, *Economic History of Virginia in the Seventeenth Century* (2 vols., New York, 1896), II, 57–130; James C. Ballagh, *A History of Slavery in Virginia* (Baltimore, 1902), 28–35.

3   John H. Russell, *The Free Negro in Virginia, 1619–1865* (Baltimore, 1913), 29.

4   *Ibid.*, 23–39; Ulrich B. Phillips, *American Negro Slavery* (New York, 1918), 75–77, and *Life and Labor in the Old South* (Boston, 1929), 170; Helen T. Catterall (ed.), *Judicial Cases Concerning American Slavery and the Negro* (5 vols., Washington, 1926–1937), I, 54–55, 57–63; James M. Wright, *The Free Negro in Maryland, 1634–1860* (New York, 1921), 21–23; Susie M. Ames, *Studies of the Virginia Eastern Shore in the Seventeenth Century* (Richmond, 1940), 100–106. See also T. R. Davis, "Negro Servitude in the United States," *Journal of Negro History*, VIII (July 1923), 247–83, and Edgar T. Thompson, "The Natural History of Agricultural Labor in the South" in David K. Jackson (ed.), *American Studies in Honor of William Kenneth Boyd* (Durham, N. C., 1940), 127–46.

5   Phillips, *American Negro Slavery*, viii.

6   Wesley F. Craven, *The Southern Colonies in the Seventeenth Century, 1607–1689* (Baton Rouge, 1949), 217–19, 402–403.

7   *William and Mary Quarterly*, s. 3, VII (April 1950), 199–222.

8   Kenneth M. Stampp, *The Peculiar Institution: Slavery in the Ante-Bellum South* (New York, 1956), vii–viii, 3–33.

9   *Ibid.*, 21–22.

10   Arnold Rose, "The Roots of Prejudice" in UNESCO, *The Race Question in Modern Science* (New York, 1956), 224. For examples of the more general view see Frederick G. Detweiler, "The Rise of Modern Race Antagonisms," *American Journal of Sociology*, XXXVII (March 1932), 743; M. F. Ashley Montagu, *Man's Most Dangerous Myth: The Fallacy of Race* (New York, 1945), 10–11, 19–20; Gunnar Myrdal, *An American Dilemma: The Negro Problem and Modern Democracy* (New York, 1944), 83–89, 97; Paul Kecskemeti, "The Psychological Theory of Prejudice: Does it Underrate the Role of Social History?" *Commentary*, XVIII (October 1954), 364–66.

11   *Comparative Studies in Society and History*, II (October 1959), 49–66. See also Degler, *Out of Our Past: The Forces that Shaped Modern America* (New York, 1959), 26–39.

12   H. R. McIlwaine (ed.), *Minutes of the Council and General Court of Colonial Virginia, 1622–1632, 1670–1676* (Richmond, 1924), 196. See the lists and musters of 1624 and 1625 in John C. Hotten (ed.), *The Original Lists of Persons of Quality* . . . (New York, 1880), 169–265.

13   "The status of Negroes was that of servants; and so they were identified and treated down to the 1660's." ("Origins," 203). The footnote to this statement reads, "For disciplinary and revenue laws in Virginia that did not discriminate Negroes from other servants, see Hening, *Statutes*, I, 174, 198, 200, 243, 306 (1631–1645)." But pp. 200 and 243 of William Waller Hening (ed.), *The Statutes at Large; Being a Collection of All the Laws of Virginia* . . . (2nd ed. of vols. 1–4, New York, 1823), I, in fact contain nothing about either servants or Negroes, while a tax provision on p. 242 specifically discriminates against Negro women. The revenue act on p. 306 lists the number of pounds of tobacco levied on land, cattle, sheep, horses, etc., and on tithable persons, and provides for collection of lists of the above so that the colony can compute its tax program; nothing else is said of servants and tithables. To say, as the Handlins did in the same note, that Negroes, English servants, and horses, etc., were listed all together in some early Virginia wills, with the implication that Negroes and English servants were regarded as alike in status, is hardly correct unless one is to assume that the horses were sharing this status as well. (For complete bibliographical information on Hening [ed.], *Statutes*, see E. G. Swem, *Virginia Historical Index* [2 vols., Roanoke, Va., 1934–1936], I, xv–xvi.)

14 Latin-American Negroes did not lose all civil and personal rights, did not become mere chattels, yet we speak of "slavery" in Latin America without hesitation. See Frank Tannenbaum, *Slave and Citizen: The Negro in the Americas* (New York, 1947), and Gilberto Freyre, *The Masters and the Slaves: A Study in the Development of Brazilian Civilization* (New York, 1946).

15 "Decisions of the General Court," *Virginia Magazine of History and Biography*, V (January 1898), 236. Abbot Emerson Smith in the standard work on servitude in America, *Colonists in Bondage: White Servitude and Convict Labor in America, 1607–1776* (Chapel Hill, 1947), 171, says that "there was never any such thing as perpetual slavery for any white man in any English colony." There were instances in the seventeenth century of white men sold into "slavery," but this was when the meaning of the term was still indefinite and often equated with servitude.

16 "Decisions of the General Court," 236–37.

17 *A Perfect Description of Virginia* . . . (London, 1649), reprinted in Peter Force (ed.), *Tracts* . . . (4 vols., Washington, 1836–1846), II.

18 These four cases may be found in Northampton County Deeds, Wills &c. (Virginia State Library, Richmond), No. 4 (1651–1654), 28 (misnumbered 29), 124; *Archives of Maryland* (69 vols., Baltimore, 1883–1961), XLI, 261–62; York County Records (Virginia State Library), No. 2 (transcribed Wills & Deeds, 1645–1649), 256–57.

19 Lancaster County Loose Papers (Virginia State Library), Box of Wills, 1650–1719, Folder 1656–1659.

20 For examples running for as long as thirty-five years, see *William and Mary Quarterly*, s. 1, XX (October 1911), 148; Russell, *Free Negro in Virginia*, 26–27; Ames, *Eastern Shore*, 105. Compare the cases of a Negro and an Irish servant in *Calendar of Virginia State Papers* . . . (11 vols., Richmond, 1875–1893), I, 9–10, and *Maryland Archives*, XLI, 476–78; XLIX, 123–24.

21 Russell, *Free Negro in Virginia*, 24–41. See especially the cases in *Virginia Magazine of History and Biography*, V (July 1897), 40; York County Deeds, Wills, Orders, etc. (Virginia State Library), No. 1 (1633–1657, 1691–1694), 338–39.

22 John H. Russell, "Colored Freemen As Slave Owners in Virginia," *Journal of Negro History*, I (July 1916), 234–37.

23 York County Records, No. 2, 63; Northampton County Orders, Deeds, Wills, &c., No. 2 (1640–1645), 224; York County Deeds, Orders, Wills, &c. (1657–1662), 108–109.

24 York County Records, No. 2, 390.

25 Apparently Calvert's deal with Skinner was never consummated. *Maryland Archives*, IV, vii, 189, 320–21. For prices of white servants see *ibid.*, IV, 31, 47–48, 74, 78–79, 81, 83, 92, 98, 108–109, 184, 200, 319.

26 Hening (ed.), *Statutes*, I, 144, 242, 292, 454. The Handlins erroneously placed the "first sign of discrimination" in this matter at 1668 ("Origins," 217*n*). For Maryland, see *Maryland Archives*, I, 342; II, 136, 399, 538–39; XIII, 538–39.

27 John Hammond, *Leah and Rachel, or, the Two Fruitfull Sisters Virginia, and Mary-land: Their Present Condition, Impartially Stated and Related* . . . (London, 1656), reprinted in Force (ed.), *Tracts*, II.

28 Hening (ed.), *Statutes*, II, 267. The distinction between white and colored women was neatly described at the turn of the century by Robert Beverley, *The History and Present State of Virginia*, Louis B. Wright, ed. (Chapel Hill, 1947), 271–72.

29 Hening (ed.), *Statutes*, I, 226, and for the same act in more detail see *William and Mary Quarterly*, s. 2, IV (July 1924), 147. The Handlins discounted this law: "Until the 1660's the statutes on the Negroes were not at all unique. Nor did they add up to a decided trend." ("Origins," 209.) The note added to this statement reads, "That there was no trend is evident from the fluctuations in naming Negroes slaves or servants and in their right to bear arms. See Hening, *Statutes*, I, 226, 258, 292, 540; Bruce, *Institutional History*, II, 5 ff., 199 ff. For similar fluctuations with regard to Indians, see Hening, *Statutes*, I, 391, 518." But since the terms "servants" and "slaves" did not have precise meaning, as the Handlins themselves asserted, fluctuations in naming Negroes one or the other cannot be taken to mean that their status itself was fluctuating. Of the pages cited in Hening, p. 258

is an act encouraging Dutch traders and contains nothing about Negroes, servants, slaves, or arms. Page 292 is an act providing that fifteen tithable persons should support one soldier; Negroes were among those tithable, but nothing was said of allowing them to arm. Page 540 refers to "any negro slaves" and "said negro," but mentions nothing about servants or arms. In the pages dealing with Indians, p. 391 provides that no one is to employ Indian servants with guns, and p. 518 that Indians (not "Indian servants") are to be allowed to use their own guns; the two provisions are not contradictory. Philip A. Bruce, *Institutional History of Virginia in the Seventeenth Century* (2 vols., New York, 1910), II, 5 ff., indicates that Negroes were barred from arming in 1639 and offers no suggestion that there was any later fluctuation in this practice.

30 Hening (ed.), *Statutes*, I, 146. "Christianity" appears instead of "Christians" in McIlwaine (ed.), *Minutes of the Council*, 479.

31 *Maryland Archives*, X, 114–15.

32 Hening (ed.), *Statutes*, I, 552; McIlwaine, *Minutes of the Council*, 477.

33 Bruce, *Economic History of Virginia*, II, 110.

34 Hening (ed.), *Statutes*, II, 170; III, 86–87; *Maryland Archives*, I, 533–34; VII, 204. Opinion on this matter apparently was not unanimous, for a petition of several citizens to the Council in 1699 asked repeal of the intermarriage prohibition. H. R. McIlwaine (ed.), *Legislative Journals of the Council of Colonial Virginia* (3 vols., Richmond, 1918–1919), I, 262. The Handlins wrote ("Origins," 215), "Mixed marriages of free men and servants were particularly frowned upon as complicating status and therefore limited by law." Their citation for this, Hening (ed.), *Statutes*, II, 114 (1661/62), and Marcus W. Jernegan, *Laboring and Dependent Classes in Colonial America, 1607–1783* (Chicago, 1931), 55, 180, gives little backing to the statement. In Virginia secret marriage or bastardy between whites of different status got the same punishment as such between whites of the same status. A white servant might marry any white if his master consented. See Hening (ed.), *Statutes*, I, 252–53, 438–39; II, 114–15, 167; III, 71–75, 137–40. See also James C. Ballagh, *White Servitude in the Colony of Virginia* (Baltimore, 1895), 50. For Maryland, see *Maryland Archives*, I, 73, 373–74, 441–42; II, 396–97; XIII, 501–502. The Handlins also suggested that in the 1691 Virginia law, "spurious" meant simply "illegitimate," and they cited Arthur W. Calhoun, *A Social History of the American Family from Colonial Times to the Present* (3 vols., Cleveland, O., 1917–1919), I, 42, which turns out to be one quotation from John Milton. However, "spurious" was used in colonial laws with reference only to unions between white and black, and never in bastardy laws involving whites only. Mulattoes were often labeled "spurious" offspring.

35 For example, George C. Homans, *The Human Group* (New York, 1950).

Chapter 8

Ira Berlin

TIME, SPACE, AND THE EVOLUTION OF AFRO-AMERICAN SOCIETY ON BRITISH MAINLAND NORTH AMERICA

TIME AND SPACE ARE the usual boundaries of historical inquiry. The last generation of slavery studies in the United States has largely ignored these critical dimensions but has, instead, been preoccupied with defining the nature of American slavery, especially as compared with racial bondage elsewhere in the Americas. These studies have been extraordinarily valuable not only in revealing much about slave society but also in telling a good deal about free society. They have been essential to the development of a new understanding of American life centered on social transformation: the emergence of bourgeois society in the North with an upward-striving middle class and an increasingly self-conscious working class and the development of a plantocracy in the South with a segmented social order and ideals of interdependence, stability, and hierarchy. But viewing Southern slavery from the point of maturity, dissecting it into component parts, comparing it to other slave societies, and juxtaposing it to free society have produced an essentially static vision of slave culture. This has been especially evident in the studies of Afro-American life. From Stanley M. Elkins's Sambo to John W. Blassingame's Nat-Sambo-Jack typology, scholars of all persuasions have held time constant and ignored the influence of place. Even the most comprehensive recent interpretation of slave life, Eugene D. Genovese's *Roll, Jordan, Roll*, has been more concerned with explicating the dynamic of the patriarchal ideal in the making of Afro-American culture than in explaining its development in time and space. None of the histories written since World War II has equaled the temporal and spatial specificity of U. B. Phillips's *American Negro Slavery*.[1]

Recent interest in the beginnings of slavery on the mainland of British North America, however, has revealed a striking diversity in Afro-American life. During the seventeenth and eighteenth centuries, three distinct slave systems evolved: a Northern nonplantation system and two Southern plantation systems, one around Chesapeake Bay and the other in the Carolina and Georgia lowcountry. Slavery took shape differently in each with important consequences for the growth of black culture and society. The development of these slave societies depended upon the nature of the slave trade and the demographic configurations of blacks and whites as well as upon the diverse character of colonial economy. Thus, while cultural differences between newly arrived Africans and second and third generation Afro-Americans or creoles[2] everywhere provided the basis for social stratification within black society, African-creole differences emerged at different times with different force and even different meaning in the North, the Chesapeake region, and the lowcountry.[3] A careful examination of the diverse development of Afro-American culture in the colonial era yields important clues for an understanding of the full complexity of black society in the centuries that followed.

The nature of slavery and the demographic balance of whites and blacks during the seventeenth and first decades of the eighteenth centuries tended to incorporate Northern blacks into the emerging Euro-American culture, even as whites denied them a place in Northern society.[4] But changes in the character of the slave trade during the middle third of the eighteenth century gave new impetus to African culture and institutions in the Northern colonies. By the American Revolution, Afro-American culture had been integrated into the larger Euro-American one, but black people remained acutely conscious of their African inheritance and freely drew on it in shaping their lives.

Throughout the colonial years, blacks composed a small fraction of the population of New England and the Middle Colonies. Only in New York and Rhode Island did they reach 15 percent of the population. In most Northern colonies the proportion was considerably smaller. At its height, the black population totaled 8 percent of the population of New Jersey and less than 4 percent in Massachusetts and Connecticut. But these colony-wide enumerations dilute the presence of blacks and underestimate the importance of slave labor. In some of the most productive agricultural regions and in the cities, blacks composed a larger share of the population, sometimes constituting as much as one-third of the whole and perhaps one-half of the work force.[5] Although many Northern whites never saw a black slave, others had daily, intimate contact with them. And, although some blacks found it difficult to join together with their former countrymen, others lived in close contact.

The vast majority of Northern blacks lived and worked in the countryside. A few labored in highly capitalized rural industries—tanneries, salt works, and iron furnaces—where they often composed the bulk of the work force, skilled and unskilled. Iron masters, the largest employers of industrial slaves, also were often the largest slaveholders in the North. Pennsylvania iron masters manifested their dependence on slave labor when, in 1727, they petitioned for a reduction in the tariff on slaves so they might keep their furnaces in operation. Bloomeries and forges in other colonies similarly relied on slave labor.[6] But in an overwhelmingly agrarian society only a small proportion of the slave population engaged in industrial labor.

Like most rural whites, most rural blacks toiled as agricultural workers. In southern New England, on Long Island, and in northern New Jersey, which contained the North's densest black populations, slaves tended stock and raised crops for export to the sugar islands. Farmers engaged in provisioning the West Indies with draft animals and foodstuffs were familiar with slavery and had easy access to slaves. Some, like the Barbadian émigrés in northern New Jersey, had migrated from the sugar islands. Others, particularly those around Narragansett Bay, styled themselves planters in the West Indian manner. They built great houses, bred race horses, and accumulated slaves, sometimes holding twenty or more bondsmen. But, whatever the aspirations of this commercial gentry, the provisioning trade could not support a plantation regime. Most slaves lived on farms (not plantations), worked at a variety of tasks, and never labored in large gangs. No one in the North suggested that agricultural labor could be done only by black people, a common assertion in the sugar islands and the Carolina lowcountry. In northern New England, the Hudson Valley, and Pennsylvania, the seasonal demands of cereal farming undermined the viability of slavery. For most wheat farmers, as Peter Kalm shrewdly observed, "a Negro or black slave requires too much money at one time," and they relied instead on white indentured servants and free workers to supplement their own labor. Throughout the North's bread basket, even those members of the gentry who could afford the larger capital investment and the concomitant risk that slave ownership entailed generally depended on the labor of indentured servants more than on that of slaves. Fully two-thirds of the bond servants held by the wealthiest farmers in Lancaster and Chester counties, Pennsylvania, were indentured whites rather than chattel blacks. These farmers tended to view their slaves more as status symbols than as agricultural workers. While slaves labored in the fields part of the year, as did nearly everyone, they also spent a large portion of their time working in and around their masters' houses as domestic servants, stable keepers, and gardeners. Significantly, the wills and inventories of Northern slaveholders listed their slaves with other high status objects like clocks and carriages rather than with land or agricultural implements.[7]

The distinct demands of Northern agriculture shaped black life in the countryside. Where the provisioning trade predominated, black men worked as stock minders and herdsmen while black women labored as dairy maids as well as domestics of various kinds. The large number of slaves demanded by the provisioning trade and the ready access to horses and mules it allowed placed black companionship within easy reach of most bondsmen. Such was not always true in the cereal region. Living scattered throughout the countryside on the largest farms and working in the house as often as in the field, blacks enjoyed neither the mobility nor the autonomy of slaves employed in the provisioning trade. But, if the demands of Northern agriculture affected black life in different ways, almost all rural blacks lived and worked in close proximity to whites. Slaves quickly learned the rudiments of the English language, the Christian religion, the white man's ways. In the North, few rural blacks remained untouched by the larger forces of Euro-American life.

Northern slaves were also disproportionately urban. During the eighteenth century, a fifth to a quarter of the blacks in New York lived in New York City. Portsmouth and Boston contained fully a third of the blacks in New Hampshire and Massachusetts, and nearly half of Rhode Island's black population resided in Newport. Ownership of slaves was almost universal among the urban elite and commonplace among the middling classes as well. On the eve of the Revolution, nearly three-fourths of Boston's wealthiest quartile of propertyholders ranked in the slaveholding class. Fragmentary evidence from earlier in the century suggests that urban slave-ownership had been even more widespread but contracted with the growth of a free working class. Viewed from the top of colonial society, the observation of one visitor that there was "not a house in Boston" that did "not have one or two" slaves might be applied to every Northern city with but slight exaggeration.[8]

Urban slaves generally worked as house servants—cooking, cleaning, tending gardens and stables, and running errands. They lived in back rooms, lofts, closets, and, occasionally, makeshift alley shacks. Under these cramped conditions, few masters held more than one or two slaves. However they might cherish a large retinue of retainers, urban slaveholders rarely had the room to lodge them. Because of the general shortage of space, masters discouraged their slaves from establishing families in the cities. Women with reputations for fecundity found few buyers, and some slaveholders sold their domestics at the first sign of pregnancy. A New York master candidly announced the sale of his cook "because she breeds too fast for her owners to put up with such inconvenience," and others gave away children because they were an unwarranted expense. As a result, black women had few children, and their fertility ratio was generally lower than that of whites. The inability or unwillingness of urban masters to support large households placed a severe strain on black family life.[9] But it also encouraged masters to allow their slaves to live out, hire their own time, and thereby gain a measure of independence and freedom.

Slave hirelings along with those bondsmen owned by merchants, warehouse keepers, and ship chandlers kept Northern cities moving. Working outside their masters' houses, these bondsmen found employment as teamsters, wagoners, and stockmen on the docks and drays and in the warehouses and shops that composed the essential core of the mercantile economy. In addition, many slaves labored in the maritime trades not only as sailors on coasting vessels, but also in the rope walks, shipyards, and sail factories that supported the colonial maritime industry. Generally, the importance of these slaves to the growth of Northern cities increased during the eighteenth century. Urban slavery moved steadily away from the household to the docks, warehouses, and shops, as demonstrated by the growing disproportion of slave men in the urban North. Aside from those skills associated with the maritime trades, however, few slaves entered artisan work. Only a handful could be found in the carriage trades that enjoyed higher status and that offered greater opportunity for an independent livelihood and perhaps the chance to buy freedom.[10]

In the cities as in the countryside, blacks tended to live and work in close proximity to whites. Northern slaves not only gained first-hand knowledge of their masters' world, but they also rubbed elbows with lower-class whites in taverns, cock fights, and fairs where poor people of varying status mingled.[11] If urban life allowed slaves to meet more frequently and enjoy a larger degree of social autonomy than did slavery in the countryside, the cosmopolitan nature of cities speeded the transformation of Africans to Afro-Americans. Acculturation in the cities of the North was a matter of years, not generations.

For many blacks, the process of cultural transformation was well under way before they stepped off the boat. During the first century of American settlement, few blacks arrived in the North directly from Africa. Although American slavers generally originated in the North, few gave priority to Northern ports. The markets to the south were simply too large and too lucrative. Slaves dribbled into the Northern colonies from the West Indies or the mainland South singly, in twos and threes, or by the score but rarely by the boatload. Some came on special order from merchants or farmers with connections to the West Indian trade. Others arrived on consignment, since few Northern merchants specialized in selling slaves. Many of these were the unsalable "refuse" (as traders contemptuously called them) of larger shipments. Northern slaveholders generally disliked these scourings of the transatlantic trade who, the governor of Massachusetts observed, were "usually the worst servants they have"; they feared that the West Indian re-exports had records of recalcitrance and criminality as well as physical defects. In time, some masters may have come to prefer seasoned slaves because of their knowledge of English, familiarity with work routines, or resistance to New World diseases. But, whatever their preference, Northern colonies could not compete with the wealthier staple-producing colonies for prime African field hands. Before the 1740s, Africans appear to have arrived in the North only when a temporary glut made sale impossible in the West Indies and the mainland South. Even then they did not always remain in the North. When conditions in the plantation colonies changed, merchants re-exported them for a quick profit. The absence of direct importation during the early years and the slow, random, haphazard entry of West Indian creoles shaped the development of black culture in the Northern colonies.[12] While the nature of the slave trade prevented the survival of tribal or even shipboard ties that figured so prominently in Afro-American life in the West Indies and the Lower South, it better prepared blacks to take advantage of the special circumstances of their captivity.

Newly arrived blacks, most already experienced in the New World and familiar with their proscribed status, turned Northern bondage to their advantage where they could. They quickly established a stable family life and, unlike newly imported Africans elsewhere on the continent, increased their numbers by natural means during the first generation. By 1708, the governor of Rhode Island observed that the colony's slaves were "supplied by the offspring of those they have already, which increase daily. . . ." The transplanted creoles also seized the opportunities provided by the complex Northern economy, the relatively close ties of master and slave, and, for many, the independence afforded by urban life. In New Amsterdam, for example, the diverse needs of the Dutch mercantile economy induced the West India Company, the largest slaveholder in the colony, to allow its slaves to live out and work on their own in return for a stipulated amount of labor and an annual tribute. "Half-freedom," as this system came to be called, enlarged black opportunities and allowed for the development of a strong black community. When the West India Company refused to make these privileges hereditary, "half-free" slaves organized and protested, demanding that they be allowed to pass their rights to their children. Failing that, New Amsterdam slaves pressed their masters in other ways to elevate their children's status. Some, hearing rumors that baptism meant freedom, tried to gain church membership. A Dutch prelate complained that these blacks "wanted nothing else than to deliver their children from bodily slavery, without striving for piety and Christian virtues." Even after the conquering English abolished "half-freedom" and instituted a more rigorous system of racial servitude, blacks continued to use the leverage gained by their prominent role in the city's economy to set standards of treatment well above those in the plantation colonies. Into the eighteenth century, New York slaves informally enjoyed the rights of an earlier era, including the right to hold property of their own. "The Custome of this Country," bristled a frustrated New York master to a West Indian friend, "will not allow us to use our Negroes as you doe in Barbados."[13]

Throughout the North, the same factors that mitigated the harshest features of bondage in New York strengthened the position of slaves in dealing with their masters. Small holdings, close living conditions, and the absence of gang labor drew masters and slaves together. A visitor to Connecticut noted in disgust that slaveowners were "too Indulgent (especially the farmers) to their Slaves, suffering too great a familiarity from them, permitting them to sit at Table and eat with them (as they say to save time) and into the dish goes the black hoof as freely as the white hand." Slaves used knowledge gained at their masters' tables to press for additional privileges: the right to visit friends, live with their families, or hire their own time. One slaveholder reluctantly cancelled the sale of his slaves because of "an invariable indulgence here to permit Slaves of any kind of worth or Character who must change Masters, to choose those Masters," and he could not persuade his slaves "to leave their Country (if I may call it so), their acquaintances & friends."[14] Such indulgences originated not only in the ability of slaves to manipulate their masters to their own benefit, but also from the confidence of slaveholders in their own hegemony. Surety of white dominance, derived from white numerical superiority, complemented the blacks' understanding of how best to bend bondage to their own advantage and to maximize black opportunities within slavery.

During the middle decades of the eighteenth century, the nature of Northern slavery changed dramatically. Growing demand for labor, especially when European wars limited the supply of white indentured servants and when depression sent free workers west in search of new opportunities, increased the importance of slaves in the work force. Between 1732 and 1754, blacks composed fully a third of the immigrants (forced and voluntary) arriving in New York. The new importance of slave labor changed the nature of the slave trade. Merchants who previously took black slaves only on consignment now began to import them directly from Africa, often in large numbers. Before 1741, for example, 70 percent of the slaves arriving in New York originated in the West Indies and other mainland sources and only 30 percent came directly from Africa. After that date, the proportions were reversed. Specializing in the slave trade, African slavers carried many times more slaves than did West Indian traders. Whereas slaves had earlier arrived in small parcels rarely numbering more than a half-dozen, direct shipments from Africa at times now totaled over a hundred and, occasionally, several times that. Slaves increasingly replaced white indentured servants as the chief source of unfree labor not only in the areas that had produced for the provisioning trade, where their preeminence had been established earlier in the century, but in the cities as well. In the 1760s, when slave importation into Pennsylvania peaked, blacks composed more than three-quarters of Philadelphia's servant population.[15]

Northern whites generally viewed this new wave of slaves as substitutes for indentured labor. White indentured servants had come as young men without families, and slaves were now imported in much the same way. "For this market they must be young, the younger the better if not quite children," declared a New York merchant. "Males are best." As a result, the sex ratio of the black population, which earlier in the century had been roughly balanced, suddenly swung heavily in favor of men. In Massachusetts, black men outnumbered black women nearly two to one. Elsewhere sex ratios of 130 or more became commonplace.[16] Such sexual imbalance and the proscription of interracial marriage made it increasingly difficult for blacks to enjoy normal family lives. As the birth rate slipped, mortality rates soared, especially in the cities where newly arrived blacks appeared to be concentrated. Since most slaves came without any previous exposure to New World diseases, the harsh Northern winters took an ever higher toll. Blacks died by the score; the crude death rate of Philadelphia and Boston blacks in the 1750s and 1760s was well over sixty per thousand, almost double that of whites.[17] In its demographic outline, Northern slavery at mid-century often bore a closer resemblance to the horrors of the West Indies during the height of a sugar boom than to the relatively benign bondage of the earlier years.

Whites easily recovered from this demographic disaster by again switching to European indentured servants and then to free labor as supplies became available, and, as the influx of slaves subsided, black life also regained its balance. But the transformation of Northern slavery had a lasting influence on the development of Afro-American culture. Although the Northern black population remained predominantly Afro-American after nearly a century of slow importation from the West Indies and steady natural increase, the direct entry of Africans into Northern society reoriented black culture.

Even before the redirection of the Northern slave trade, those few Africans in the Northern colonies often stood apart from the creole majority. While Afro-American slaves established precedents and customs, which they then drew upon to improve their condition, Africans tended to stake all to recapture the world they had lost. Significantly, Africans, many of whom did not yet speak English and still carried tribal names, composed the majority of the participants in the New York slave insurrection of 1712, even though most of the city's blacks were creoles.[18] The division between Africans and Afro-Americans became more visible as the number of Africans increased after mid-century. Not only did creoles and Africans evince different aspirations, but their life-chances—as reflected in their resistance to disease and their likelihood of establishing a family—also diverged sharply. Greater visibility may have sharpened differences between creoles and Africans, but Africans were too few in number to stand apart for long. Whatever conflicts different life-chances and beliefs created, whites paid such distinctions little heed in incorporating the African minority into their slaveholdings. The propensity of Northern whites to lump blacks together mitigated intraracial differences. Rather than permanently dividing blacks, the entry of Africans into Northern society gave a new direction to Afro-American culture.[19]

Newly arrived Africans reawakened Afro-Americans to their African past by providing direct knowledge of West African society. Creole blacks began to combine their African inheritance into their own evolving culture. In some measure, the easy confidence of Northern whites in their own dominance speeded the syncretization of African and creole culture by allowing blacks to act far more openly than slaves in the plantation colonies. Northern blacks incorporated African culture into their own Afro-American culture not only in the common-place and unconscious way that generally characterizes the transit of culture but also with a high degree of consciousness and deliberateness. They designated their churches "African," and they called themselves "Sons of Africa."[20] They adopted African forms to maximize their freedom, to choose their leaders, and, in general, to give shape to their lives. This new African influence was manifested most fully in Negro election day, a ritual festival of role reversal common throughout West Africa and celebrated openly by blacks in New England and a scattering of places in the Middle Colonies.

The celebration of Negro election day took a variety of forms, but everywhere it was a day of great merrymaking that drew blacks from all over the countryside.

"All the various languages of Africa, mixed with broken and ludicrous English, filled the air, accompanied with the music of the fiddle, tambourine, the banjo, [and] drum," recalled an observer of the festival in Newport. Negro election day culminated with the selection of black kings, governors, and judges. These officials sometimes held symbolic power over the whole community and real power over the black community. While the black governors held court, adjudicating minor disputes, the blacks paraded and partied, dressed in their masters' clothes and mounted on their masters' horses. Such role reversal, like similar status inversions in Africa and elsewhere, confirmed rather than challenged the existing order, but it also gave blacks an opportunity to express themselves more fully than the narrow boundaries of slavery ordinarily allowed. Negro election day permitted a seeming release from bondage, and it also provided a mechanism for blacks to recognize and honor their own notables. Most important, it established a framework for the development of black politics. In the places where Negro election day survived into the nineteenth century, its politics shaped the politics within the black community and merged with partisan divisions of American society. Slaves elsewhere in the New World also celebrated this holiday, but whites in the plantation colonies found the implications of role reversal too frightening to allow even symbolically. Northern whites, on the other hand, not only aided election day materially but sometimes joined in themselves. Still, white cooperation was an important but not the crucial element in the rise of Negro election day. Its origin in the 1740s and 1750s suggests how the entry of Africans reoriented Afro-American culture at a formative point in its development.[21]

African acculturation in the Northern colonies at once incorporated blacks into American society and sharpened the memory of their African past and their desire to preserve it. While small numbers and close proximity to whites forced blacks to conform to the forms of the dominant Euro-American culture, the confidence of whites in their own hegemony allowed black slaves a good measure of autonomy. In this context it is not surprising that a black New England sea captain established the first back-to-Africa movement in mainland North America.[22]

Unlike African acculturation in the Northern colonies, the transformation of Africans into Afro-Americans in the Carolina and Georgia lowcountry was a slow, halting process whose effects resonated differently within black society. While creolization created a unified Afro-American population in the North, it left lowcountry blacks deeply divided. A minority lived and worked in close proximity to whites in the cities that lined the rice coast, fully conversant with the most cosmopolitan sector of lowland society. A portion of this urban elite, increasingly light-skinned, pressed for further incorporation into white society, confident they could compete as equals. The mass of black people, however, remained physically separated and psychologically estranged from the Anglo-American world and culturally closer to Africa than any other blacks on continental North America.

The sharp division was not immediately apparent. At first it seemed that African acculturation in the Lower South would follow the Northern pattern. The first blacks arrived in the lowcountry in small groups from the West Indies. Often they accompanied their owners and, like them, frequently immigrated in small family groups. Many had already spent considerable time on the sugar islands, and some had doubtless been born there. Most spoke English, understood European customs and manners, and, as their language skills and family ties suggest, had made the difficult adjustment to the conditions of black life in the New World.

As in the Northern colonies, whites dominated the population of the pioneer Carolina settlement. Until the end of the seventeenth century, they composed better than two-thirds of the settlers. During this period and into the first years of the eighteenth century, most white slaveholders engaged in mixed farming and stock raising for export to the West Indian islands where they had originated. Generally, they lived on small farms, held few slaves, and worked closely with their bond servants. Even when they hated and feared blacks and yearned for the prerogatives of West Indian slave masters, the demands of the primitive, labor-scarce economy frequently placed master and slave face-to-face on opposite sides of a sawbuck.[23] Such direct, equalitarian confrontations tempered white domination and curbed slavery's harshest features.

White dependence on blacks to defend their valuable lowland beachhead reinforced this "sawbuck equality." The threat of invasion by the Spanish and French to the south and Indians to the west hung ominously over the lowcountry during its formative years. To bolster colonial defenses, officials not only drafted slaves in time of war but also regularly enlisted them into the militia. In 1710 Thomas Nairne, a knowledgeable Carolina Indian agent, observed that "enrolled in our Militia [are] a considerable Number of active, able, Negro Slaves; and Law gives every one of those his freedom, who in Time of an Invasion kills an Enemy." Between the settlement of the Carolinas and the conclusion of the Yamasee War almost fifty years later, black soldiers helped fend off every military threat to the colony. Although only a handful of slaves won their freedom through military service, the continued presence of armed, militarily experienced slaves weighed heavily on whites. During the Yamasee War, when the governor of Virginia demanded one Negro woman in return for each Virginia soldier sent to defend South Carolina, the beleaguered Carolinians rejected the offer, observing that it was "impracticable to Send Negro Women in their Roomes by reason of the Discontent such Usage would have given their husbands to have their wives taken from them which might have occasioned a Revolt."[24]

The unsettled conditions that made the lowcountry vulnerable to external enemies strengthened the slave's hand in other ways. Confronted by an over-bearing master or a particularly onerous assignment, many blacks took to the woods. Truancy was an easy alternative in the thinly settled, heavily forested lowcountry. Forest dangers generally sent truant slaves back to their owners, but the possibility of another flight induced slaveholders to accept them with few questions asked. Some bondsmen, however, took advantage of these circumstances to escape permanently. Maroon colonies existed throughout the lowland swamps and into the backcountry. Maroons lived a hard life, perhaps more difficult than slaves, and few blacks chose to join these outlaw bands. But the ease of escape and the existence of a maroon alternative made masters chary about abusing their slaves.[25]

The transplanted African's intimate knowledge of the subtropical lowland environment—especially when compared to the Englishman's dense ignorance—magnified white dependence on blacks and enlarged black opportunities within the slave regime. Since the geography, climate, and topography of the lowcountry more closely resembled the West African than the English countryside, African not European technology and agronomy often guided lowland development. From the first, whites depended on blacks to identify useful flora and fauna and to define the appropriate methods of production. Blacks, adapting African techniques to the circumstances of the Carolina wilderness, shaped the lowland cattle industry and played a central role in the introduction and development of the region's leading staple. In short, transplanted Englishmen learned as much or more from transplanted Africans as did the former Africans from them.[26] While whites eventually appropriated this knowledge and turned it against black people to rivet tighter the bonds of servitude, white dependence on African know-how operated during those first years to place blacks in managerial as well as menial positions and thereby permitted blacks to gain a larger share of the fruits of the new land than whites might otherwise allow. In such circumstances, white domination made itself felt, but both whites and blacks incorporated much of West African culture into their new way of life.

The structure of the fledgling lowland economy and the demands of stock raising, with deerskins as the dominant "crop" during the initial years of settlement, allowed blacks to stretch white military and economic dependence into generous grants of autonomy. On the small farms and isolated cowpens (hardly plantations by even the most latitudinous definition), rude frontier conditions permitted only perfunctory supervision and the most elementary division of labor. Most units were simply too small to employ overseers, single out specialists, or benefit from the economies of gang labor. White, red, and black laborers of varying legal status worked shoulder to shoulder, participating in the dullest drudgery as well as the most sophisticated undertakings. Rather than skilled artisans or prime field hands, most blacks could best be characterized as jacks-of-all-trades. Since cattle roamed freely through the woods until fattened for market, moreover, black cowboys—suggestively called "cattle chasers"—moved with equal freedom through the countryside, gaining full familiarity with the terrain.[27] The autonomy of the isolated cowpen and the freedom of movement stock raising allowed made a mockery of the total dominance that chattel bondage implied. Slaves set the pace of work, defined standards of workmanship, and divided labor among themselves, doubtless leaving a good measure of time for their own use. The insistence of many hard-pressed frontier slaveowners that their slaves raise their own provisions legitimated this autonomy. By law, slaves had Sunday to themselves. Time allowed for gardening, hunting, and fishing both affirmed slave independence and supplemented the slave diet. It also enabled some industrious blacks to produce a small surplus and to participate in the colony's internal economy, establishing an important precedent for black life in the lowcountry.[28]

Such independence burdened whites. They complained bitterly and frequently about blacks traveling unsupervised through the countryside, congregating in the woods, and visiting Charles Town to carouse, conspire, or worse. Yet knowledge of the countryside and a willingness to take the initiative in hunting down cattle or standing up to Spaniards were precisely the characteristics that whites valued in their slaves. They complained but they accepted. Indeed, to resolve internal disputes within their own community, whites sometimes promoted black participation in the affairs of the colony far beyond the bounds later permitted slaves or even black freemen. "For this last election," grumbled several petitioners in 1706, "Jews, Strangers, Sailors, Servants, Negroes, & almost every French Man in Craven & Berkly County came down to elect, & their votes were taken."[29] Such breaches of what became an iron law of Southern racial policy suggest how the circumstances of the pioneer lowcountry life shrank the social as well as the cultural distance between transplanted Africans and the mélange of European settlers. During the first generations of settlement, Afro-American and Anglo-American culture and society developed along parallel lines with a large degree of overlap.

If the distinction between white and black culture remained small in the lowcountry, so too did differences within black society. The absence of direct importation of African slaves prevented the emergence of African–creole differences; and, since few blacks gained their liberty during those years, differences in status within the black community were almost nonexistent. The small radius of settlement and the ease of water transportation, moreover, placed most blacks within easy reach of Charles Town. A "city" of several dozen rude buildings where the colonial legislature met in a tavern could hardly have impressed slaves as radically different from their own primitive quarters. Town slaves, for their part, doubtless had first-hand familiarity with farm work as few masters could afford the luxury of placing their slaves in livery.[30]

Thus, during the first years of settlement, black life in the lowcountry, like black life in the North, evolved toward a unified Afro-American culture. Although their numbers combined with other circumstances to allow Carolina blacks a larger role in shaping their culture than that enjoyed by blacks in the North, there remained striking similarities in the early development of Afro-American life in both regions. During the last few years of the seventeenth century, however, changes in economy and society undermined these commonalities and set the development of lowcountry Afro-American life on a distinctive course.

The discovery of exportable staples, first naval stores and then rice and indigo, transformed the lowcountry as surely as the sugar revolution transformed the West Indies. Under the pressure of the riches that staple production provided, planters banished the white yeomanry to the hinterland, consolidated small farms into large plantations, and carved new plantations out of the malaria-ridden swamps. Before long, black slaves began pouring into the region and, sometime during the first decade of the eighteenth century, white numerical superiority gave way to the lowcountry's distinguishing demographic characteristic: the black majority.

Black numerical dominance grew rapidly during the eighteenth century. By the 1720s, blacks outnumbered whites by more than two to one in South Carolina. In the heavily settled plantation parishes surrounding Charles Town, blacks enjoyed a three to one majority. That margin grew steadily until the disruptions of the Revolutionary era, but it again increased thereafter. Georgia, where metropolitan policies reined planter ambition, remained slaveless until mid-century. Once restrictions on slavery were removed, planters imported blacks in large numbers, giving lowland Georgia counties considerable black majorities.[31]

Direct importation of slaves from Africa provided the impetus to the growth of the black majority. Some West Indian Afro-Americans continued to enter the lowcountry, but they shrank to a small fraction of the whole.[32] As African importation increased, Charles Town took its place as the largest mainland slave mart and the center of the lowland slave trade. Almost all of the slaves in Carolina and later in Georgia—indeed, fully 40 percent of all pre-Revolutionary black arrivals in mainland North America—entered at Charles Town. The enormous number of slaves allowed slave masters a wide range of choices. Lowcountry planters developed preferences far beyond the usual demands for healthy adult and adolescent males and concerned themselves with the regional and tribal origins of their purchases. Some planters may have based their choices on long experience and a considered understanding of the physical and social character of various African nations. But, for the most part, these preferences were shallow ethnic stereotypes. Coromantees revolted; Angolans ran away; Iboes destroyed themselves. At other times, lowland planters apparently preferred just those slaves they did not get, perhaps because all Africans made unsatisfactory slaves and the unobtainable ones looked better at a distance. Although lowcountry slave masters desired Gambian people above all others, Angolans composed a far larger proportion of the African arrivals. But, however confused or mistaken in their beliefs, planters held them firmly and, in some measure, put them into practice. "Gold Coast and Gambia's are the best, next to them the Windward Coast are prefer'd to Angola's," observed a Charles Town merchant in describing the most salable mixture. "There must not be a Callabar amongst them."[33] Planter preferences informed lowcountry slave traders and, to a considerable degree, determined the tribal origins of lowland blacks.

Whatever their origins, rice cultivation shaped the destiny of African people arriving at Charles Town. Although the production of pitch and tar played a pivotal role in the early development of the staple-based economy in South Carolina, rice quickly became the dominant plantation crop. Rice cultivation evolved slowly during the late seventeenth and early eighteenth centuries as planters, aided by knowledgeable blacks, mastered the complex techniques necessary for commercial production. During the first half of the eighteenth century, rice culture was limited to the inland swamps, where slave-built dikes controlled the irrigation of low-lying rice fields. But by mid-century planters had discovered how to regulate the tidal floods to irrigate and drain their fields. Rice production moved to the tidal swamps that lined the region's many rivers and expanded greatly. By the beginning of the nineteenth century, the rice coast stretched from Cape Fear in North Carolina to the Satilla River in Georgia.[34] Throughout the lowcountry, rice was king.

The relatively mild slave regime of the pioneer years disappeared as rice cultivation expanded. Slaves increasingly lived in large units, and they worked in field gangs rather than at a variety of tasks. The strict requirements of rice production set the course of their work. And rice was a hard master. For a large portion of the year, slaves labored knee deep in brackish muck under the hot tropical sun; and, even after the fields were drained, the crops laid-by, and the grain threshed, there were canals to clear and dams to repair. By mid-century planters had also begun to grow indigo on the upland sections of their estates. Indigo complemented rice in its seasonal requirements, and it made even heavier labor demands.[35] The ready availability of African imports compounded the new harsh realities of plantation slavery by cheapening black life in the eyes of many masters. As long as the slave trade remained open, they skimped on food, clothing, and medical attention for their slaves, knowing full well that substitutes could be easily had. With the planters' reliance on male African imports, slaves found it increasingly difficult to establish and maintain a normal family life. Brutal working conditions, the disease-ridden, lowland environment, and the open slave trade made for a deadly combination. Slave birth rates fell steadily during the middle years of the eighteenth century and mortality rates rose sharply. Between 1730 and 1760, deaths out-numbered births among blacks and only African importation allowed for continued population growth. Not until the eve of the Revolution did the black population begin again to reproduce naturally.[36]

As the lowcountry plantation system took shape, the great slave masters retreated to the cities of the region; their evacuation of the countryside was but another manifestation of the growing social and cultural distance between them and their slaves. The streets of Charles Town, and, later, of Beaufort, Georgetown, Savannah, Darien, and Wilmington sprouted great new mansions as planters fled the malarial lowlands and the black majority. By the 1740s, urban life in the lowcountry had become attractive enough that men who made their fortunes in rice and slaves no longer returned home to England in the West Indian tradition. Instead, through intermarriage and business connections, they began to weave their disparate social relations into a close-knit ruling class, whose self-consciousness and pride of place became legendary. Charles Town, as the capital of this new elite, grew rapidly. Between 1720 and 1740 its population doubled, and it nearly doubled again by the eve of the Revolution to stand at about twelve thousand. With its many fine houses, its great churches, its shops packed with luxury goods, Charles Town's prosperity bespoke the maturation of the lowland plantation system and the rise of the planter class.[37]

Planters, ensconced in their new urban mansions, their pockets lined with the riches rice produced, ruled their lowcountry domains through a long chain of command: stewards located in the smaller rice ports, overseers stationed near or on their plantations, and plantation-based black drivers. But their removal from the plantation did not breed the callous indifference of West Indian absenteeism. For one thing, they were no more than a day's boat ride away from their estates. Generally, they resided on their plantations during the non-malarial season. Their physical removal from the direct supervision of slave labor and the leisure their urban residences afforded appear to have sharpened their concern for "their people" and bred a paternalist ideology that at once legitimated their rule and informed all social relations.[38]

The lowcountry plantation system with its urban centers, its black majority, its dependence on "salt-water" slaves transformed black culture and society just as it reshaped the white world. The unified Afro-American culture and society that had evolved during the pioneer years disappeared as rice cultivation spread. In its place a sharp division developed between an increasingly urban creole and a plan-tation-based African population. The growth of plantation slavery not only set blacks further apart from whites, it also sharply divided blacks.

One branch of black society took shape within the bounds of the region's cities and towns. If planters lived removed from most slaves, they maintained close, inti-mate relations with some. The masters' great wealth, transient life, and seasonal urban residence placed them in close contact with house servants who kept their estates, boatmen who carried messages and supplies back and forth to their plan-tations, and urban artisans who made city life not only possible but comfortable. In addition, coastal cities needed large numbers of workers to transport and process the plantation staples, to serve the hundreds of ships that annually visited the lowcountry, and to satisfy the planters' newly acquired taste for luxury goods. Blacks did most of this work. Throughout the eighteenth century they composed more than half the population of Charles Town and other lowcountry ports. Probably nothing arrived or left these cities without some black handling it. Black artisans also played a large role in urban life. Master craftsmen employed them in every variety of work. A visitor to Charles Town found that even barbers "are supported in idleness & ease by their negroes . . .; & in fact many of the mechaniks bear nothing more of their trade than the name." Although most black artisans labored along the waterfront as ship-wrights, ropemakers, and coopers, lowcounty blacks—unlike blacks in Northern cities—also entered the higher trades, working as gold beaters, silversmiths, and cabinetmakers. In addition, black women gained control over much of the marketing in the lowcountry ports, mediating between slave-grown produce in the countryside and urban consumption. White tradesmen and journeymen periodically protested against slave competition, but planters, master craftsmen, and urban consumers who benefited from black labor and services easily brushed aside these objections.[39]

Mobile, often skilled, and occasionally literate, urban slaves understood the white world. They used their knowledge to improve their position within lowcountry society even while the condition of the mass of black people deteriorated in the wake of the rice revolution. Many urban creoles not only retained the independence of the earlier years but enlarged upon it. They hired their own time, earned wages from "overwork;" kept market stalls, and sometimes even opened shops. Some lived apart from their masters and rented houses of their own, paying their owners a portion of their earnings in return for *de facto* freedom. Such liberty enabled a few black people to keep their families intact and perhaps even accumulate property for themselves. The small black communities that developed below the Bluff in Savannah and in Charles Town's Neck confirm the growing independence of urban creoles.[40]

The incongruous prosperity of urban bondsmen jarred whites. By hiring their own time, living apart from their masters, and controlling their own family life, these blacks forcibly and visibly claimed the white man's privileges. Perhaps no aspect of their behavior was as obvious and, hence, as galling as their elaborate dress. While plantation slaves—men and women—worked stripped to the waist wearing no more than loin cloths (thereby confirming the white man's image of savagery), urban slaves appropriated their masters' taste for fine clothes and often the clothes themselves. Lowcountry legislators enacted various sumptuary regulations to restrain the slaves' penchant for dressing above their station. The South Carolina Assembly once even considered prohibiting masters from giving their old clothes to their slaves. But hand-me-downs were clearly not the problem as long as slaves earned wages and had easy access to the urban marketplace. Frustrated by the realities of urban slavery, lawmakers passed and repassed the old regulations to little effect. On the eve of the Revolution, a Charles Town Grand Jury continued to bemoan the fact that the "Law for preventing the excessive and costly Apparel of Negroes and other Slaves in this province (especially in *Charles Town*) [was] not being put into Force."[41]

Most of these privileged bondsmen appear to have been creoles with long experience in the New World. Although some Africans entered urban society, the language skills and the mastery of the complex interpersonal relations needed in the cities gave creoles a clear advantage over Africans in securing elevated positions within the growing urban enclaves. To be sure, their special status was far from "equal." No matter how essential their function or intimate their interaction, their relations with whites no longer smacked of the earlier "sawbuck equality." Instead, these relations might better be characterized as paternal, sometimes literally so.

Increasingly during the eighteenth century, blacks gained privileged positions within lowcountry society as a result of intimate, usually sexual, relations with white slave masters. Like slaveholders everywhere, lowland planters assumed that sexual access to slave women was simply another of the master's prerogatives. Perhaps because their origin was West Indian or perhaps because their dual residence separated them from their white wives part of the year, white men established sexual liaisons with black women frequently and openly. Some white men and black women formed stable, long-lasting unions, legitimate in everything but law. More often than other slaveholders on continental British North America, lowcountry planters recognized and provided for their mulatto offspring, and, occasionally, extended legal freedom. South Carolina's small free Negro population, almost totally confined to Charles Town, was largely the product of such relations. Light-skinned people of color enjoyed special standing in the lowcountry ports, as they did in the West Indies, and whites occasionally looked the other way when such creoles passed into the dominant caste. But even when the planters did not grant legal freedom, they usually assured the elevated standing of their mulatto scions by training them for artisan trades or placing them in household positions. If the countryside was "blackened" by African imports, Charles Town and the other lowcountry ports exhibited a mélange of "colored" peoples.[42]

While one branch of black society stood so close to whites that its members sometimes disappeared into the white population, most plantation slaves remained alienated from the world of their masters, physically and culturally. Living in large units often numbering in the hundreds on plantations that they had carved out of the malarial swamps and working under the direction of black drivers, the black majority gained only fleeting knowledge of Anglo-American culture. What they knew did not encourage them to learn more. Instead, they strove to widen the distance between themselves and their captors. In doing so, they too built upon the large degree of autonomy black people had earlier enjoyed.

In the pioneer period, many masters required slaves to raise their own provisions. Slaves regularly kept small gardens and tended barnyard fowl to maintain themselves, and they often marketed their surplus. Blacks kept these prerogatives with the development of the plantation system. In fact, the growth of lowcountry towns, the increasing specialization in staple production, and the comparative absence of nonslaveholding whites enlarged the market for slave-grown produce. Planters, of course, disliked the independence truck gardening afforded plantation blacks and the tendency of slaves to confuse their owners' produce with their own, but the ease of water transportation and the absence of white supervision made it difficult to prevent.

To keep their slaves on the plantation, some planters traded directly with their bondsmen, bartering manufactured goods for slave produce. Henry Laurens, a planter who described himself as a "factor" for his slaves, exchanged some "very gay Wastcoats which some of the Negro Men may want" for grain at "10 Bushels per Wastcoat." Later, learning that a plantation under his supervision was short of provisions, he authorized the overseer "to purchase of your own Negroes all that you know Lawfully belongs to themselves at the lowest price they will sell it for."

As Laurens's notation suggests, planters found benefits in slave participation in the lowcountry's internal economy, but the small profits gained by bartering with their bondsmen only strengthened the slaves' customary right to their garden and barnyard fowl. Early in the nineteenth century, when Charles C. Pinckney decided to produce his own provisions, he purchased breeding stock from his slaves. By the Civil War, lowland slaves controlled considerable personal property—flocks of ducks, pigs, milch cows, and occasionally horses—often the product of stock that had been in their families for generations.[43] For the most part, slave property-holding remained small during the eighteenth century. But it helped insulate plantation blacks from the harsh conditions of primitive rice production and provided social distance from their masters' domination.

The task system, a mode of work organization peculiar to the lowcountry, further strengthened black autonomy. Under the task system, a slave's daily routine was sharply defined: so many rows of rice to be sowed, so much grain to be threshed, or so many lines of canal to be cleared. Such a precise definition of work suggests that city-bound planters found it almost impossible to keep their slaves in the fields from sunup to sundown. With little direct white supervision, slaves and their black foremen conspired to preserve a large portion of the day for their own use, while meeting their masters' minimum work requirements. Struggle over the definition of a task doubtless continued throughout the formative years of the lowcountry plantation system and after, but by the end of the century certain lines had been drawn. Slaves generally left the field sometime in the early afternoon, a practice that protected them from the harsh afternoon sun and allowed them time to tend their own gardens and stock.[44] Like participation in the lowcountry's internal economy, the task system provided slaves with a large measure of control over their own lives.

The autonomy generated by both the task system and truck gardening provided the material basis for lowland black culture. Within the confines of the overwhelmingly black countryside, African culture survived well. The continual arrival of Africans into the lowcountry renewed and refreshed slave knowledge of West African life. In such a setting blacks could hardly lose their past. The distinctive pattern of the lowland slave trade, moreover, heightened the impact of the newly arrived Africans on the evolution of black culture. While slaves dribbled into the North through a multiplicity of ports, they poured into the lowcountry through a single city. The large, unicentered slave trade and the large slaveholding units assured the survival not only of the common denominators of West African culture but also many of its particular tribal and national forms. Planter preferences or perhaps the chance ascendancy of one group sometimes allowed specific African cultures to reconstitute themselves within the plantation setting. To be sure, Africans changed in the lowcountry. Even where blacks enjoyed numerical superiority and a considerable degree of autonomy, they could no more transport their culture unchanged than could their masters. But lowcountry blacks incorporated more of West African culture—as reflected in their language, religion, work patterns, and much else—into their new lives than did other black Americans. Throughout the eighteenth century and into the nineteenth, lowcountry blacks continued to work the land, name their children, and communicate through word and song in a manner that openly combined African traditions with the circumstances of plantation life.[45]

The new pattern of creolization that developed following the rice revolution smashed the emerging homogeneity of black life in the first years of settlement and left lowcountry blacks deeply divided. One branch of black culture evolved in close proximity to whites. Urban, often skilled, well-traveled, and increasingly American-born, creoles knew white society well, and they used their knowledge to better themselves. Some, clearly a well-connected minority, pressed for incorporation into the white world. They urged missionary groups to admit their children to school and later petitioned lawmakers to allow their testimony in court, carefully adding that they did not expect full equality with whites.[46] Plantation slaves shared few of the assimilationist aspirations of urban creoles. By their dress, language, and work routine, they lived in a world apart. Rather than demand incorporation into white society, they yearned only to be left alone. Within the quarter, aided by their numerical dominance, their plantation-based social hierarchy, and their continued contact with Africa, they developed their own distinctive culture, different not only from that of whites but also from the cosmopolitan world of their Afro-American brethren. To be sure, there were connections between the black majority and the urban creoles. Many—market women, jobbing artisans, and boatmen—moved easily between these two worlds, and most blacks undoubtedly learned something of the other world through chance encounters, occasional visits, and word of mouth.[47] Common white oppression continually shrank the social distance that the distinctive experience created, but by the eve of the Revolution, deep cultural differences separated those blacks who sought to improve their lives through incorporation into the white world and those who determined to disregard the white man's ways. If the movement from African to creole obliterated cultural differences among Northern blacks, creolization fractured black society in the lowcountry.

Cultural distinctions between Africans and Afro-Americans developed in the Chesapeake as well, although the dimension of differences between African and creole tended to be time rather than space. Unlike in the lowcountry, white planters did not promote the creation of a distinctive group whose origins, function, and physical appearance distinguished them from the mass of plantation slaves and offered them hope, however faint, of eventual incorporation into white society. And, compared to the North, African immigration into the Chesapeake came relatively early in the process of cultural transformation. As a result, African-creole differences disappeared with time and a single, unified Afro-American culture slowly emerged in the Chesapeake.

As in the lowcountry, little distinguished black and white laborers during the early years of settlement. Most of the first blacks brought into the Chesapeake region were West Indian creoles who bore English or Spanish surnames and carried records of baptism. Along the James, as along the Cooper, the demands of pioneer life at times operated to strengthen the slaves' bargaining position. Some blacks set the condition of their labor, secured their family life, participated in the region's internal economy, and occasionally bartered for their liberty. This, of course, did not save most black people from the brutal exploitation that almost all propertyless men and women faced as planters squeezed the last pound of profit from the tobacco economy. The blacks' treatment at the hands of planters differed little from that of white bound labor in large measure because it was difficult to treat people more brutally.[48] While the advantages of this peculiar brand of equality may have been lost on its beneficiaries, those blacks who were able to complete their terms of servitude quickly joined whites in the mad scramble for land, servants, and status.

Many did well. During the seventeenth century, black freemen could be found throughout the region owning land, holding servants, and occasionally attaining minor offices. Like whites, they accumulated property, sued their neighbors, and passed their estates to their children. In 1651, Anthony Johnson, the best known of these early Negro freemen, received a two-hundred-and-fifty-acre headright for importing five persons into Virginia. John Johnson, a neighbor and probably a relative, did even better, earning five hundred and fifty acres for bringing eleven persons into the colony. Both men owned substantial farms on the Eastern Shore, held servants, and left their heirs sizable estates. As established members of their communities, they enjoyed the rights of citizens. When a servant claiming his freedom fled Anthony Johnson's plantation and took refuge with a nearby white farmer, Johnson took his neighbor to court and won the return of his servant along with damages against the white man.[49]

The class rather than racial basis of early Chesapeake society enabled many black men to compete successfully for that scarcest of all New World commodities: the affection of white women. Bastardy lists indicate that white female servants ignored the strictures against what white lawmakers labeled "shameful" and "unnatural" acts and joined together with men of their own condition regardless of color. Fragmentary evidence from various parts of seventeenth-century Virginia reveals that approximately one-quarter to one-third of the bastard children born to white women were mulattoes. The commonplace nature of these interracial unions might have been the reason why one justice legally sanctified the marriage of Hester, an English servant woman, to James Tate, a black slave. Some successful, property-owning whites and blacks also intermarried. In Virginia's Northampton county, Francis Payne, a Negro freeman, married a white woman, who later remarried a white man after Payne's death. William Greensted, a white attorney who represented Elizabeth Key, a mulatto woman, in her successful suit for her freedom, later married her. In 1691, when the Virginia General Assembly finally ruled against the practice, some propertied whites found the legislation novel and obnoxious enough to muster a protest.[50]

By the middle of the seventeenth century, Negro freemen sharing and fulfilling the same ideals and aspirations that whites held were no anomaly in the Chesapeake region. An Eastern Shore tax list of 1668 counted nearly a third of black tithables free. If most blacks did not escape the tightening noose of enslavement, they continued to live and work under conditions not much different from white servants. Throughout the seventeenth and into the first decades of the eighteenth century, black and white servants ran away together, slept together, and, upon occasion, stood shoulder to shoulder against the weighty champions of established authority. Thus viewed from the first years of settlement—the relatively small number of blacks, their creole origins, and the initial success of some in establishing a place in society—black acculturation in the Chesapeake appeared to be following the nonplantation pattern of the Northern colonies and the pioneer lowcountry.[51]

The emergence of a planter class and its consolidation of power during a series of political crises in the middle years of the seventeenth century transformed black life in the Chesapeake and threatened this pattern of cultural change. Following the legalization of slavery in the 1660s, black slaves slowly but steadily replaced white indentured servants as the main source of plantation labor. By 1700, blacks made up more than half the agricultural work force in Virginia and, since the great planters could best afford to purchase slaves, blacks composed an even larger share of the workers on the largest estates. Increased reliance on slave labor quickly outstripped West Indian supplies. Beginning in the 1680s, Africans entered the region in increasingly large numbers. The proportion of blacks born in Africa grew steadily throughout the waning years of the seventeenth century, so that by the first decade of the eighteenth century, Africans composed some three-quarters of the region's blacks.[52] Unlike the lowcountry, African imports never threatened the Chesapeake's overall white numerical superiority, but by the beginning of the eighteenth century they dominated black society. Some eighty years after the first blacks arrived at Jamestown and some forty years after the legalization of slavery, African importation profoundly transformed black life.

Slave conditions deteriorated as their numbers increased. With an eye for a quick profit, planters in the Chesapeake imported males disproportionately. Generally men outnumbered women more than two to one on Chesapeake slavers. Wildly imbalanced sex ratios undermined black family life. Physically spent and emotionally drained by the rigors of the Middle Passage, African women had few children. Thus, as in the North and the Carolina lowlands, the black birth rate fell and mortality rate surged upward with the commencement of direct African importation.[53]

The hard facts of life and death in the Chesapeake region distinguished creoles and Africans at the beginning of the eighteenth century. The demands of the tobacco economy enlarged these differences in several ways. Generally, planters placed little trust in newly arrived Africans with their strange tongues and alien customs. While they assigned creoles to artisanal duties on their plantations and to service within their households, they sent Africans to the distant, upland quarters where the slaves did the dull, backbreaking work of clearing the land and tending tobacco. The small size of these specialized upcountry units, their isolation from the mainstream of Chesapeake life, and their rude frontier conditions made these largely male compounds lonely, unhealthy places that narrowed men's vision. The dynamics of creole life, however, broadened black understanding of life in the New World. Traveling freely through the countryside as artisans, watermen, and domestic servants, creoles gained in confidence as they mastered the terrain, perfected their English, and learned about Christianity and other cultural modes that whites equated with civilization. Knowledge of the white world enabled black creoles to manipulate their masters to their own advantage. If Afro-Americans became increasingly knowledgeable about their circumstances and confident of their ability to deal with them, Africans remained provincials, limited by the narrow alternatives of plantation life.[54]

As in the lowcountry and the Northern colonies, Africans in the Chesapeake strove to escape whites, while creoles used their knowledge of white society for their own benefit. These cultural differences, which were reflected in all aspects of black life, can be seen most clearly in the diverse patterns of resistance. Africans ran away toward the back country and isolated swamps. They generally moved in groups that included women and children, despite the hazards such groups entailed for a successful escape. Their purpose was to recreate the only society they knew free from white domination. In 1727, Governor William Gooch of Virginia reported that about a dozen slaves had left a new plantation near the falls of the James River. They headed west and settled near Lexington, built houses, and planted a crop before being retaken. But Afro-Americans ran away alone, usually with the hope of escaping into American society. Moving toward the areas of heaviest settlement, they found refuge in the thick network of black kinship that covered the countryside and sold their labor to white yeomen with few questions asked. While the possibility of passing as free remained small in the years before the Revolution, the creoles' obvious confidence in their ability to integrate themselves into American society stands in stark contrast to that of Africans, who sought first to flee it.[55]

As reflected in the mode of resistance, place of residence, occupation, and much else, Africans and creoles developed distinctive patterns of behavior and belief. To a degree, whites recognized these differences. They stigmatized Africans as "outlandish" and noted how creoles "affect our language, habits, and customs." They played on African–creole differences to divide blacks from each other, and they utilized creole skills to maximize the benefits of slave labor. But this recognition did not elevate creoles over Africans in any lasting way. Over the course of the century following legal enslavement, it had precisely the opposite effect. Chesapeake planters consolidated their class position by asserting white racial unity. In this context, the entry of large numbers of African—as opposed to creole—blacks into the region enlarged racial differences and helped secure planter domination. Thus, as reliance on black labor increased, the opportunities for any black—no matter how fluent in English or conversant with the countryside—to escape bondage and join the scramble for land, servants, and status diminished steadily.

By the middle of the eighteenth century, the size and character of the free Negro population had been significantly altered. Instead of a large minority of the black population, Negro freemen now composed just a small proportion of all blacks, probably not more than 5 percent. Many were cripples and old folks whom planters discarded when they could no longer wring a profit from their labor. While most were of mixed racial origins, few of these free mulattoes of the Chesapeake, in contrast to those of the lowcountry, traced their ancestry to the planter class. Instead, they descended from white servants, frequently women. These impoverished people had little status to offer their children. Indeed, planter-inspired legislation further compromised their liberty by requiring that the offspring of white women and black men serve their mother's master for thirty-one years. Those who survived the term could scarcely hope for the opportunities an earlier generation of Negro freemen had enjoyed.[56] The transformation of the free Negro caste in the century between 1660 and 1760 measured the change in Chesapeake society as its organizing principle changed from class to race.

The free Negro's decline reveals how the racial imperatives of Chesapeake society operated to lump all black people together, free and slave, creole and African. In the Chesapeake, planters dared not grant creoles special status at the expense of Africans. Since the Africans would shortly be creoles and since creoles shared so much with whites, distinctions among blacks threatened the racial division that underlay planter domination. In the lowcountry, where geography, economy, and language separated white and black, those few blacks who spoke, dressed, acted, and looked like whites might be allowed some white prerogatives. But, if lowcountry planters could argue that no white man could do the work required to grow rice commercially, no one in the Chesapeake could reasonably deny that whites could grow tobacco. The fundamental unity of Chesapeake life and the long-term instability of African–creole differences pushed blacks together in the white mind and in fact.

During the middle years of the eighteenth century, changes in the Chesapeake economy and society further diminished differences within black society and created a unified Afro-American culture. The success of the tobacco economy enlarged the area of settlement and allowed planters to increase their holdings. The most successful planters, anxious to protect themselves from the rigors of the world marketplace, strove for plantation self-sufficiency. The great estates of the Chesapeake became self-contained enterprises with slaves taking positions as artisans, tradesmen, wagoners, and, sometimes, managers; the plantation was "like a Town," as a tutor on Robert Carter's estate observed, "but most of the Inhabitants are black." The increased sophistication of the Chesapeake economy propelled many more blacks into artisanal positions and the larger units of production, tighter pattern of settlement, and the greater mobility allowed by the growing network of roads ended the deadening isolation of the upcountry quarter. Bondsmen increasingly lived in large groups, and those who did not could generally find black companionship within a few miles' walk. Finally, better food, clothing, and shelter and, perhaps, the development of immunities to New World diseases enabled blacks to live longer, healthier lives.[57]

As part of their drive for self-sufficiency, Chesapeake slaveholders encouraged the development of an indigenous slave population. Spurred by the proven ability of Africans to survive and reproduce and pressed in the international slave market by the superior resources of West Indian sugar magnates and lowland rice growers, Chesapeake planters strove to correct the sexual imbalance within the black population, perhaps by importing a large proportion of women or lessening the burden of female slaves. Blacks quickly took advantage of this new circumstance and placed their family life on a firmer footing. Husbands and wives petitioned their owners to allow them to reside together on the same quarter and saw to it that their families were fed, beyond their masters' rations. Planters, for their part, were usually receptive to slaves' demands for a secure family life, both because it reflected their own values and because they profited mightily from the addition of slave children. Thomas Jefferson frankly considered "a woman who brings a child every two years as more profitable than the best man on the farm [for] what she produces is an addition to capital, while his labor disappears in mere consumption." Under these circumstances, the black population increased rapidly. Planters relied less and less on African importation and, by the 1740s, most of the growth of the black population came from natural increase. Within a generation, African importation was, for all practical purposes, no longer a significant source of slave labor. In the early 1770s, the period of the greatest importation into the lowcountry, only five hundred of the five thousand slaves added annually to the black population of Virginia derived directly from Africa.[58]

The establishment of the black family marked the re-emergence of Afro-American culture in the Chesapeake. Although Africans continued to enter the region, albeit at a slower pace, the nature of the slave trade minimized their impact on the development of black society in the region. Unlike those in the lowcountry, newly arrived Africans could rarely hope to remain together. Rather than funnel their cargo through a single port, Chesapeake slavers peddled it in small lots at the many tobacco landings that lined the bay's extensive perimeter. Planters rarely bought more than a few slaves at a time, and larger purchasers, usually the great planter-merchants, often acted as jobbers, quickly reselling these slaves to back-country freeholders.[59] The resulting fragmentation sent newly arrived Africans in all directions and prevented the maintenance of tribal or shipboard ties. Chesapeake slaveholders cared little about the origins of their slaves. In their eyes, newly arrived Africans were not Iboes, Coromantees, or Angolans, but "new Negroes." While the unicentered slave trade sustained and strengthened African culture in the lowcountry, the Chesapeake slave trade facilitated the absorption of Africans into the evolving creole society.

Differences between creoles and Africans did not disappear with the creation of a self-sustaining Afro-American population. The creoles' advantages—language skills, familiarity with the countryside, artisanal standing, and knowledge of the plantation routine—continued to propel them into positions of authority within the slave hierarchy. In some ways, the growing complexity of the Chesapeake economy widened the distance between Africans and creoles, at least at first. Most of the skilled and managerial positions within the region's expanding iron industry went to creole blacks as did the artisanal work in flour mills and weaving houses. On some plantations, moreover, artisan and house status became lodged in partic-ular families with parents passing privileged positions on to their children. Increasingly, skilled slaves entered the market economy by selling their own time and earning money from "overwork," thereby gaining a large measure of freedom. For the most part, Africans remained on rude, back-woods plantations tending the broad-leaf weed. Since creole slaves sold at a premium price and most great planters had already established self-sustaining slave forces, small planters purchased nearly all of the newly arrived Africans after mid-century. These upward-striving men generally owned the least developed, most distant farms. Their labor requirements remained primitive compared to the sophisticated division of labor on the self-contained plantation-towns.[60]

Over the long term, however, economic changes sped the integration of Africans into Afro-American society. Under the pressure of a world-wide food shortage, Chesapeake planters turned from the production of tobacco to that of food-stuff, especially wheat. The demands of wheat cultivation transformed the nature of labor in the region. Whereas tobacco farming required season-long labor, wheat farming employed workers steadily only during planting and harvesting. The remainder of the year, laborers had little to do with the crop. At the same time, however, wheat required a larger and more skilled labor force to transport the grain to market and to store it, mill it, and reship it as flour, bread, or bulk grain. Economic changes encouraged masters to teach their slaves skills and to hire them out during the slack season. At first, these opportunities went mostly to creoles, but as the wheat economy grew, spurring urbanization and manufacturing, the demands for artisans and hirelings outstripped the creole population.[61] An increasing number of Africans were placed in positions previously reserved for creoles. The process of cultural transformation that earlier in the eighteenth century had taken a generation or more was considerably shorter at mid-century. Africans became Afro-Americans with increasing rapidity as the century wore on, eliminating the differences within black society that African importation had created.

Chesapeake blacks enjoyed considerably less autonomy than their lowcountry counterparts. Resident planters, small units of production, and the presence of large numbers of whites meant that most blacks lived and worked in close proximity to whites. While lowcountry planters fled to coastal cities for a large part of the year, the resident planter was a fixture of Chesapeake life. Small free-holders labored alongside slaves, and great planters prided themselves on regulating all aspects of their far-flung estates through a combination of direct personal supervision and plantation-based overseers. The latter were usually white, drawn from the region's white majority. Those few blacks who achieved managerial positions, moreover, enjoyed considerably less authority than lowland drivers. The presence of numerous nonslaveholding whites circumscribed black opportunities in other ways as well. While Chesapeake slaves commonly kept gardens and flocks of barnyard animals, white competitors limited their market and created a variety of social tensions. If lowcountry masters sometimes encouraged their slaves to produce nonstaple garden crops, whites in the Chesapeake—slaveholders and nonslaveholders alike—complained that blacks stole more than they raised and worked to curb the practice. Thus, at every turn, economy and society conspired to constrain black autonomy.

The requirements of tobacco cultivation reinforced the planters' concern about daily work routine. Whereas the task system insulated lowcountry blacks against white intervention and maximized black control over their work, the constant attention demanded by tobacco impelled Chesapeake planters to oversee the tedious process of cultivating, topping, worming, suckering, and curing tobacco. The desire of Chesapeake masters to control their slaves went beyond the supervision of labor. Believing that slaves depended on them "for every necessity of life," they intervened in the most intimate aspects of black life. "I hope you will take care that the Negroes both men and women I sent you up last always go by the names we gave them," Robert "King" Carter reminded his steward. "I am sure we repeated them so often . . . that everyone knew their names & would readily answer to them." Chesapeake planters sought to shape domestic relations, cure physical maladies, and form personalities. However miserably they failed to ensure black domestic tranquility and reform slave drunkards, paternalism at close quarters in the Chesapeake had a far more potent influence on black life than the distant paternalism that developed in the lowcountry. Chesapeake blacks developed no distinct language and rarely utilized African day names for their children.[62] Afro-American culture in the Chesapeake evolved parallel with Anglo-American culture and with a considerable measure of congruence.

The diverse development of Afro-American culture during the seventeenth and eighteenth centuries reveals the importance of time and place in the study of American slavery. Black people in colonial America shared many things: a common African lineage, a common racial oppressor, a common desire to create the richest life possible for themselves and their posterity in the most difficult of circumstances.

But these commonalities took different shape and meaning within the diverse circumstances of the North American mainland. The nature of the slave trade, the various demographic configurations of whites and blacks, and the demands of particular staples—to name some of the factors influencing the development of slave society—created at least three distinctive patterns of Afro-American life. Perhaps a finer analysis will reveal still others.

This diversity did not end with the American Revolution. While African–creole differences slowly disappeared as the centerpole of black society with the closing of the slave trade and the steady growth of an Afro-American population, other sources of cohesion and division came to the fore.[63] Differences between freemen and bondsmen, urban and rural folk, skilled and unskilled workers, and browns and blacks united and divided black people, and made black society every bit as variable and diverse during the nineteenth century as in the eighteenth. Indeed the diversity of black life increased substantially during the antebellum years as political changes abolished slavery in some places and strengthened it in others, as demographic changes set in motion by the Great Migration across the Lower South took effect, as the introduction of new crops enlarged the South's repertoire of staples, and as the kaleidoscopic movement of the world market sent the American economy in all directions.

If slave society during the colonial era can be comprehended only through a careful delineation of temporal and spatial differences among Northern, Chesapeake, and lowcountry colonies, a similar division will be necessary for a full understanding of black life in nineteenth-century America. The actions of black people during the American Revolution, the Civil War, and the long years of bondage between these two cataclysmic events cannot be understood merely as a function of the dynamics of slavery or the possibilities of liberty, but must be viewed within the specific social circumstances and cultural traditions of black people. These varied from time to time and from place to place. Thus no matter how complete recent studies of black life appear, they are limited to the extent that they provide a static and singular vision of a dynamic and complex society.

Notes

Earlier versions of this essay were presented at the Conference on Comparative Perspectives on Slavery in the New World, held in New York, May 1976, at the Ninth World Congress of Sociology, held in Uppsala, Sweden, August 1978, and at the Symposium on the Slave Trade, held in Petersburg, Virginia, October 1979. In addition to the commentators at these conferences, I am grateful to Stanley Engerman, Eric Foner, Eugene D. Genovese, Herbert G. Gutman, Ronald Hoffman, Philip Morgan, Joseph P. Reidy, Leslie S. Rowland, and Armstead Robinson for their critical comments and suggestions. Much of the research for this essay was done while I was a fellow at the Davis Center for Historical Studies. I would especially like to thank the center's director, Lawrence Stone, for his support and intellectual comraderie.

1   Stanley Elkins, *Slavery: A Problem in American Institutional and Intellectual Life* (Chicago, 1959); John W. Blassingame, *The Slave Community: Plantation Life in the Antebellum South* (New York, 1972); Eugene D. Genovese, *Roll, Jordon, Roll: The World the Slaves Made* (New York, 1974); and Ulrich B. Phillips, *American Negro Slavery* (New York, 1918). For a historical perspective on post-World War II scholarship on slavery, see David Brion Davis, "Slavery and the Post-World War II Historians," *Daedalus*, 103 (1947): 1–16; and, on the importance of

temporal change, see Herbert G. Gutman, "Slave Culture and Slave Family and Kin Network: The Importance of Time," *South Atlantic Urban Studies*, 2 (1978): 73–88.

2   I have used these terms synonymously. Both are mined with difficulties. "Afro-American" has recently come into common usage as a synonym for "black" and "Negro" in referring to people of African descent in the United States. Although "creole" generally refers to native-born peoples, it has also been applied to people of partly European, but mixed racial and national, origins in various European colonies. In the United States, "creole" has also been specifically applied to people of mixed but usually non-African origins in Louisiana. Staying within the bounds of the broadest definition of "creole" and the literal definition of "Afro-American," I have used both terms to refer to black people of native American birth.

3   As used in this essay, the concept of acculturation or creolization does not mean the liquidation of a culture, only its transformation. African culture transported to the New World was not lost or destroyed but transformed. The transformation of Africans to Afro-Americans entailed the joining together of a variety of distinctive African cultures as well as the compounding of those cultures with various European and native American ones to create a new cultural type: the Afro-American. Scholars have only begun to study the making of Afro-American culture; therefore, any judgment about its nature and the process of its creation must be tentative and incomplete. I would emphasize that "Africans" and "creoles" as used here do not represent autonomous categories, if for no other reason than African and creole people were connected by ties of blood and kinship. Instead, these categories are used as two poles within a range of an historical experience that was varied and overlapping. The process of creolization was not always synchronized with generational change. Beginning with Melville J. Herskovits's *The Myth of the Negro Past* (New York, 1941), scholars have produced a wide-ranging theoretical literature on the question of cultural transformation of African people in the New World. For some that have been most useful for this essay, see Sidney W. Mintz and Richard Price, *An Anthropological Approach to the Caribbean Past* (Philadelphia, 1976); Melville J. Herskovits, "Problem, Method, and Theory in Afro-American Studies," *Phylon*, 7 (1946): 337–54; M. G. Smith, *The Plural Society in the British West Indies* (Berkeley and Los Angeles, 1965), and "The African Heritage in the Caribbean," in Vera Rubin, ed., *Caribbean Studies* (Seattle, 1960), 34–45; H. Orlando Patterson, "Slavery, Acculturation, and Social Change: The Jamaican Case," *British Journal of Sociology*, 17 (1966): 151–64; and Edward Brathwaite, *The Development of Creole Society in Jamaica, 1770–1820* (London, 1971), and "Caliban, Ariel, and Unprospero in the Conflict of Creolization: A Study of the Slave Revolt in Jamaica in 1831–32," in Vera Rubin and Arthur Tuden, eds., *Comparative Perspectives on Slavery in New World Plantation Societies*, Annals of the New York Academy of Sciences, no. 292, (New York, 1977), 41, 62.

4   In the discussion of the Chesapeake region and the lowcountry, scholars have employed the term "Anglo-American" to refer to the culture of white people. Because of the greater diversity of origins of white peoples in the Middle Colonies, the term "Euro-American" seems more applicable to white culture in the North.

5   For a collection of the relevant censuses, see William S. Rossiter, *A Century of Population Growth* (Washington, 1909), 149–84. Also see Robert V. Wells, *The Population of the British Colonies in American before 1776: A Survey of Census Data* (Princeton, 1975), 69–143, and Wells's correction of the 1731 enumeration, "The New York Census of 1731," *New York Historical Society Quarterly*, 57 (1973): 255–59. For estimates of the Northern black population predating these censuses, see U.S. Bureau of the Census, *Historical Statistics of the United States, Colonial Times to 1957* (Washington, 1960), 756.

6   Edgar J. McManus, *Black Bondage in the North* (Syracuse, N.Y., 1973), 42–43; Charles S. Boyer, *Early Forges and Furnaces in New Jersey* (Philadelphia, 1963), 30–31, 149, 166, 194–99, 239; Frances D. Pingeon, "Slavery in New Jersey on the Eve of the Revolution," in Williams C. Wright, ed., *New Jersey in the American Revolution* (rev. ed., Trenton, N.J., 1974), 51–52, 57; Darold D. Wax, "The Demand for Slave Labor in Colonial Pennsylvania," *Pennsylvania History*, 34 (1967): 334–35; and William Binning, *Pennsylvania Iron Manufacture in the Eighteenth Century* (Harrisburg, Pa., 1931), 122–25.

7 Kalm, *Peter Kalm's Travels in North America*, ed. and trans. A. B. Benson, 1 (New York, 1937): 205, as quoted in Alan Tully, "Patterns of Slaveholding in Colonial Pennsylvania: Chester and Lancaster Counties, 1729–1758," *Journal of Social History*, 6 (1973): 286; Lorenzo J. Greene, *The Negro in Colonial New England* (New York, 1942), 103–12; McManus, *Black Bondage in the North*, 40–41; Pingeon, "Slavery in New Jersey," 51; William D. Miller, "The Narragansett Planters," *American Antiquarian Society Proceedings*, 43 (1933): 67–71; Tully, "Patterns of Slaveholding in Colonial Pennsylvania," 284–303; Steven B. Frankt, "Patterns of Slave-Holding in Somerset County, N.J.," seminar paper, 1967, in Special Collections, Rutgers University Library, New Brunswick, N.J.: Wax, "The Demand for Slave Labor in Colonial Pennsylvania," 332–40; and Jerome H. Woods, Jr., "The Negro in Early Pennsylvania: The Lancaster Experience, 1730–1790," in Elinor Miller and Eugene D. Genovese, eds., *Plantation, Town, and County: Essays on the Local History of American Slave Society* (Urbana, Ill., 1974), 447–48.

8 N. B. Shurtleff *et al.*, eds., *Records of the Governor and Company of Massachusetts Bay in New England (1628–1698)*, 1 (Boston, 1853): 79, as quoted in Carl Bridenbaugh, *Cities in the Wilderness, 1625–1742* (New York, 1938), 49; Rossiter, *A Century of Population Growth*, 149–84; Greene, *The Negro in Colonial New England*, 78, 81–82, 84–88, 92–93; Gary B. Nash, "Slaves and Slaveowners in Colonial Philadelphia," *William and Mary Quarterly*, 3d ser., 30 (1973): 226–52; and Thomas Archdeacon, *New York City, 1664–1710: Conquest and Change* (Ithaca, N.Y., 1976), 46–47.

9 New York *Weekly Post-Boy*, May 17, 1756, as quoted in McManus, *Black Bondage in the North*, 38; Carl Bridenbaugh, *Cities in Revolt, 1743–1776* (New York, 1955), 88, 285–86, and *Cities in the Wilderness*, 163, 200–01; Nash, "Slaves and Slaveowners in Colonial Pennsylvania," 243–44; Archdeacon, *New York City*, 89–90; Rossiter, *A Century of Population Growth*, 170–80; Edgar J. McManus, *A History of Slavery in New York* (Syracuse, N.Y., 1966), 44–45, and *Black Bondage in the North*, 37–39; and Wells, *The Population in the British Colonies of America before 1776*, 116–23. The low ratio of women to children may have been the result of high child mortality as well as low fertility. In 1788, J. P. Brissot de Warville observed, "Married Negroes certainly have as many children as whites, but it has been observed that in the cities the death rate of Negro children is higher"; Brissot de Warville, *New Travels in the United States of America, 1788*, ed. Durand Echeverria (Cambridge, Mass., 1964), 232n.

10 Nash, "Slaves and Slaveowners in Colonial Philadelphia," 248–52; Archdeacon, *New York City*, 89–90, esp. 89 n. 16; Greene, *The Negro in Colonial New England*, 111–18; and Bridenbaugh, *Cities in Revolt*, 88, 274, 285–86.

11 Eric Foner, *Tom Paine and Revolutionary America* (New York, 1976), 48–56.

12 W. N. Sainsbury *et al.*, eds., *Calendar of State Papers, Colonial Series, 1708–1709*, 110, as quoted in Greene, *The Negro in Colonial New England*, 35; McManus, *Black Bondage in the North*, 18–25, and *Slavery in New York*, 23–39; James G. Lydon, "New York and the Slave Trade, 1700 to 1774," *William and Mary Quarterly*, 3d ser., 35 (1978): 275–79, 381–90; Greene, *The Negro in Colonial New England*, 15–45; and Darold D. Wax, "Negro Imports into Pennsylvania, 1720–1766," *Pennsylvania History*, 32 (1965): 254–87, and "Preferences for Slaves in Colonial America," *Journal of Negro History*, 58 (1973): 374–76, 379–87. So many of the slaves entering the North were re-exports from other parts of the Americas that Philip D. Curtin has not included the North in his calculation of the African population transported to the New World; see *The Atlantic Slave Trade: A Census* (Madison, Wisc., 1969), 143.

13 Governor Samuel Cranston to the Board of Trade, December 5, 1708, in J. R. Bartlett, ed., *Records of the Colony of Rhode Island and Providence Plantations*, 4 (1860): 55, as quoted in Miller, "Narragansett Planters," 68 n. 2; and Cadwallader Colden to Mr. Jordan, March 26, 1717, in *Letters and Papers of Cadwallader Colden*, 1 (New York, 1917): 39, as quoted in Arthur Zilversmit, *The First Emancipation: The Abolition of Negro Slavery in the North* (Chicago, 1967), 22. Joyce D. Goodfriend, "Burghers and Blacks: The Evolution of a Slave Society at New Amsterdam," *New York History*, 59 (1978): 125–44; McManus, *Slavery in New York*, 2–22; and Gerald F. DeJong, "The Dutch Reformed Church and Negro Slavery in Colonial America," *Church History*, 40 (1971): 430.

14   Sara Kemble Knight, as quoted in Ralph F. Weld, *Slavery in Connecticut* (New Haven, 1935), 8–9; John Watts, *Letterbook of John Watts*, New York Historical Society Collections, no. 61 (New York, 1938), 151; and McManus, *Black Bondage in the North, passim.*

15   Nash, "Slaves and Slaveowners in Colonial Philadelphia," 226–37; Lydon, "New York and the Slave Trade," 387–88; and Darold D. Wax, "Quaker Merchants and the Slave Trade in Colonial Pennsylvania," *Pennsylvania Magazine of History and Biography*, 86 (1962): 145, and "Negro Imports into Pennsylvania," 256–57, 280–87.

16   Watts, *Letterbook of John Watts*, 31; McManus, *Black Bondage in the North*, 38–39; Wax, "Preferences for Slaves in Colonial America," 400–01; Rossiter, *A Century of Population Growth*, 149–84; and Greene, *The Negro in Colonial New England*, 93–96.

17   Nash, "Slaves and Slaveowners in Colonial Philadelphia," 232–41, esp. n. 46.

18   Kenneth Scott, "The Slave Insurrection in New York in 1712," *New York Historical Society Quarterly*, 45 (1961): 43–74, esp. 62–67.

19   The shortage of African women and a sexual balance among Indians and, to a lesser extent, whites that favored women encouraged black men to marry Indian and, occasionally, white women, especially in New England; Winthrop D. Jordan, "American Chiaroscuro: The Status and Definition of Mulattoes in the British Colonies," *William and Mary Quarterly*, 3d ser., 19 (1962): 197–98, esp. n. 28.

20   For petitions by blacks, see Robert C. Twombly, "Black Resistance to Slavery in Massachusetts," in William L. O'Neill, ed., *Insights and Parallels* (Minneapolis, 1973), 13–16; and, for various association names, see Dorothy Porter, ed., *Early Negro Writings, 1760–1837* (Boston, 1971).

21   Henry Bull, "Memoir of Rhode Island," Newport *Rhode-Island Republican*, April 19, 1837, as quoted in William D. Pierson, "Afro-American Culture in Eighteenth-Century New England" (Ph.D. dissertation, Indiana University, 1975), 181; Joseph P. Reidy, "'Negro Election Day' and Black Community Life in New England, 1750–1860," *Marxist Perspectives*, 1 (1978): 102–17; Alice M. Earle, *Colonial Days in Old New York* (5th ed., New York, 1922); Woods, "The Negro in Early Pennsylvania," 451; and Pierson, "Afro-American Culture in Eighteenth-Century New England," 181–313.

22   Peter Williams, *A Discourse, Deliverd in the Death of Capt. Paul Cuffee* (New York, 1817).

23   Peter H. Wood, *Black Majority: Negroes in Colonial South Carolina from 1670 through the Stono Rebellion* (New York, 1974), 13–24, 94–97. The image is derived from an account of a French refugee living near the Santee River who reported in 1697 that "he worked many days with a Negro man at the Whip saw"; Alexander S. Salley, ed., "Journal of General Peter Horry," *South Carolina Historical Magazine*, 38 (1937): 51–52, as quoted in *ibid.*, 97.

24   Memorial of Joseph Boone and Richard Beresford to the Lord Commissioners of Trade and Plantations, December 6, 1716, Public Record Office, London, as quoted in Clarence L. Ver Steeg, *Origins of a Southern Mosaic: Studies of Early Carolina and Georgia* (Athens, Ga., 1975), 106; Wood, *Black Majority: Negroes in Colonial South Carolina*, 124–30; Ver Steeg, *Origins of a Southern Mosaic*, 105–07; and Verner W. Crane, *The Southern Frontier, 1670–1732* (Durham, N.C., 1928), 162–81.

25   John D. Duncan, "Servitude and Slavery in Colonial South Carolina, 1670–1776" (Ph.D. dissertation, Emory University, 1971), 587–601; and Herbert Aptheker, "Maroons within the Present Limits of the United States," *Journal of Negro History*, 24 (1939): 167–84.

26   Wood, *Black Majority: Negroes in Colonial South Carolina*, 35–62, 119–30.

27   *Ibid.*, 28–34; Converse D. Clowse, *Economic Beginnings of Colonial South Carolina, 1670–1730* (Columbia, S.C., 1971), 61; Crane, *The Southern Frontier, 1670–1732*, 91, 120, 163, 184–85; Ver Steeg *Origins of a Southern Mosaic*, 114–16; Gary S. Dunbar, "Colonial Carolina Cowpens," *Agricultural History*, 35 (1961): 125–30; and David L. Coon, "The Development of Market Agriculture in South Carolina, 1670–1785" (Ph.D. dissertation, University of Illinois, Urbana-Champaign, 1972), 113–14, 134–37. Georgia developed later than South Carolina; a description of an isolated cowpen in the Georgia countryside in 1765 may, therefore, suggest practices of an earlier era in South Carolina. See Harold E. Davis, *The Fledgling Province: Social and Cultural Life in Colonial Georgia, 1733–1776* (Chapel Hill, N.C., 1976), 67–68.

28   Frank J. Klingberg, *An Appraisal of the Negro in Colonial South Carolina* (Washington, 1941), 6–7; Klaus G. Leowald, Beverly Starika, and Paul S. Taylor, trans. and eds., "Johann Martin Bolzius Answers a Questionnaire on Carolina and Georgia," *William and Mary Quarterly*, 3d ser., 14 (1957): 235–36, 256; Thomas Cooper and David J. McCord, comps., *The Statutes at Large of South Carolina*, 10 vols. (Columbia, S.C., 1836–41), 7: 404; and Wood, *Black Majority: Negroes in Colonial South Carolina*, 62. For black participation in the internal economy of the sugar islands, see Sidney W. Mintz, *Caribbean Transformations* (Chicago, 1974), esp. chap. 7.

29   "The Representation and Address of Several Members of This Present Assembly," in William James Rivers, *A Sketch of the History of South Carolina* (Charleston, S.C., 1856), 459, as quoted in Ver Steeg, *Origins of a Southern Mosaic*, 38 (italics removed); and Wood, *Black Majority: Negroes in Colonial South Carolina*, 102–03.

30   Wood, *Black Majority: Negroes in Colonial South Carolina*, 99–103, 157, 159.

31   Peter H. Wood, "'More like a Negro Country': Demographic Patterns in Colonial South Carolina, 1670–1740," in Stanley L. Engerman and Eugene D. Genovese, eds., *Race and Slavery in the Western Hemisphere: Quantitative Studies* (Princeton, 1975), 131–45; Julian J. Petty, *The Growth and Distribution of Population in South Carolina* (Columbia, S.C., 1943), 15–58, 220–27; Bureau of the Census, *Historical Statistics of the United States*, 756; and *Returns of the Whole Number of Persons within the . . . United States [1790]* (Philadelphia, 1791).

32   W. Robert Higgins, "Charleston: Terminus and Entrepôt of the Colonial Slave Trade," in Martin L. Kilson and Robert I. Rotberg, eds., *The African Diaspora* (Cambridge, Mass., 1976), 115.

33   Wood, *Black Majority: Negroes in Colonial South Carolina*, xiv, and "'More like a Negro Country,'" 149–54; Higgins, "Charleston: Terminus and Entrepôt of the Colonial Slave Trade," 118–27; Wax, "Preferences for Slaves in Colonial America," 388–99; Curtin, *The Atlantic Slave Trade*, 143, 156–57; and Henry Laurens, *The Papers of Henry Laurens*, ed. Philip M. Hamer, George C. Rogers, Jr., and David R. Chesnutt, 7 vols. (Columbia, S.C., 1970–), 1: 294–95. For a continuing discussion of slave preferences in the lowcountry, see Laurens, *Papers of Henry Laurens*, esp. vols. 1–3.

34   Clowse, *Economic Beginnings of Colonial South Carolina*, 122–33, 167–71, 220–21, 231–35, 256–58; Wood, *Black Majority: Negroes in Colonial South Carolina*, 35–62; Lewis C. Gray, *History of Agriculture in the Southern United States to 1860*, 2 vols. (Washington, 1933), 1: 277–89; James M. Clifton, "Golden Grains of White; Rice Planting on the Lower Cape Fear," *North Carolina Historical Review*, 50 (1973): 368–78; Douglas C. Wilms, "The Development of Rice Culture in 18th-Century Georgia," *Southeastern Geographer*, 12 (1972): 45–57; and Coon, "Market Agriculture in South Carolina," 126–27, 168–69, 178–86, 215–68. For the importance of naval stores in the transformation, see Ver Steeg, *Origins of a Southern Mosaic*, 117–32.

35   For excellent descriptions of the process of rice growing and its changing technology, see David Doar, *Rice and Rice Planting in the Carolina Low Country* (Charleston, S.C., 1936), 7–41; and Gray, *Agriculture in the Southern United States*, 1: 290–97.

36   Wood, "'More like a Negro Country,'" 153–64; and Philip D. Morgan, "Afro-American Cultural Change: The Case of Colonial South Carolina Slaves," paper presented at the annual meeting of the Organization of American Historians, held in New Orleans, April 1979, 3–6, esp. tables 1, 4, 7. In the 1760s, as blacks began to increase naturally, slaveholders began to show some concern for their slaves' family life; see Laurens, *Papers of Henry Laurens*, 4: 595–96, 625, 5: 370.

37   George C. Rogers, Jr., *Charleston in the Age of the Pinckneys* (Norman, Okla., 1969); Carl Bridenbaugh, *Myths and Realities* (Baton Rouge, 1952), 59–60, 76–94, and *Cities in Revolt*, 216; and Frederick P. Bowes, *The Culture of Early Charleston* (Chapel Hill, N.C., 1942).

38   Eugene D. Genovese has not made either regional or temporal distinctions in the development of Southern ideology but has leaned heavily on South Carolina for his understanding of Southern paternalism; see his *Roll, Jordan, Roll*, 1–113. For the interplay of quasi-absenteeism and planter ideology in the nineteenth century, see William W. Freehling, *Prelude to Civil War: The Nullification Controversy in South Carolina, 1813–1836* (New York, 1966), 65–70; and Michael P. Johnson, "Planters and Patriarchy: A Family History of

Planter Ideology, Charleston, South Carolina," *Journal of Southern History* (forthcoming). The degree of absenteeism and its effect on social relations between planters and slaves has yet to be explored.

39   Joseph W. Barnwell, ed., "The Diary of Timothy Ford," *South Carolina Historical Magazine*, 13 (1914): 142; Alexander Hewatt, *An Historical Account of the Rise and Progress of the Colonies of South Carolina and Georgia*, 2 (London, 1779): 97; Alan Candler, ed., *The Colonial Records of the State of Georgia*, 18 (Atlanta, 1912): 277–82; Charles S. Henry, comp., *A Digest of All the Ordinances of Savannah* (Savannah, Ga., 1854), 94–97; Petition from Charleston Carpenters and Bricklayers, 1783, and Petition from Charleston Coopers, 1793, Legislative Papers, South Carolina Department of Archives and History, Columbia; Cooper and McCord, *Statutes at Large of South Carolina*, 2: 22–23, 7: 385–87, 9: 692–97; Donald R. Lennon and Ida B. Kellam, eds., *The Wilmington Town Book, 1743–1778* (Raleigh, N.C., 1973), 165–66; Petition from Newberne, 1785, North Carolina Legislative Papers, North Carolina State Archives, Raleigh; Carl Bridenbaugh, *Colonial Craftsmen* (New York, 1950) 139–41, and *Cities in Revolt*, 88–89, 244, 274, 285–86; Leila Sellers, *Charleston Business on the Eve of the American Revolution* (Chapel Hill, N.C., 1934), 99–108; Duncan, "Servitude and Slavery in Colonial South Carolina," 439–46; and Kenneth Coleman, *Colonial Georgia, A History* (New York, 1976), 229–30.

40   Candler, *Colonial Records of the State of Georgia*, 23–30, 252–62; Henry, *Ordinances of Savannah*, 95–97; Alexander Edwards, comp., *Ordinances of the City Council of Charleston* (Charleston, S.C., 1802), 65–68; Cooper and McCord, *Statutes at Large of South Carolina*, 7: 363, 380–81, 393; Lennon and Kellam, *The Wilmington Town Book*, xxx–xxxi, 165–68, 204–05; Duncan, "Servitude and Slavery in Colonial South Carolina," 467–69, 481–84; and Sellers, *Charleston Business on the Eve of the American Revolution*, 99–102, 106–08.

41   *South Carolina Gazette*, May 24, 1773, as quoted in Duncan, "Servitude and Slavery in Colonial South Carolina," 234; Leowald, *et al.*, "Bolzius Answers a Questionnaire on Carolina and Georgia," 236; Cooper and McCord, *Statutes at Large of South Carolina*, 7: 396–412; and Duncan, "Servitude and Slavery in Colonial South Carolina," 233–37.

42   Winthrop D. Jordan, *White over Black: American Attitudes toward the Negro* (Chapel Hill, N.C., 1968), 144–50, 167–78, and "American Chiaroscuro: The Status and Definition of Mulattoes in the British Colonies," 186–200; Wood, *Black Majority: Negroes in Colonial South Carolina*, 100–03; and General Tax, Receipts and Payments, 1761–69, Records of the Public Treasurers of South Carolina, South Carolina Department of Archives and History, Columbia (I am grateful to Peter H. Wood for telling me about these records). A sample of manumissions taken from the South Carolina records between 1729 and 1776 indicates that two-thirds of the slaves freed were female and one-third of the slaves freed were mulattoes at a time when the slave population of South Carolina was disproportionately male and black; Duncan, "Servitude and Slavery in Colonial South Carolina," 395–98.

43   Laurens, *Papers of Henry Laurens*, 4: 616, 5: 20, 41; C. C. Pinckney, Plantation Journal, 1812, and George Lucas to Charles Pinckney, January 30, 1745/46, Manuscript Division, Library of Congress, Washington, D.C.; Entries in Memo Book "per self" and "Negro Esquire per self," Cameron Family Papers, Southern Historical Collection, University of North Carolina, Chapel Hill; Charles Town Grand Jury Presentment, January 1772, South Carolina Department of Archives and History; and Depositions from Liberty County, Georgia, Southern Claims Commission, Third Auditor, General Accounting Office, RG 217, National Archives, Washington, D.C. A similar division of labor between master and slave has been found in various nineteenth-century African slave societies. Whether these similar patterns have a common root or are the product of independent development is a subject for future research. See Paul O. Lovejoy, "The Characteristics of Plantations in the Nineteenth-Century Sokoto Caliphate (Islamic West Africa)," *AHR*, 84 (1979): 1283–84. Also see note 19, above.

44   By the middle of the nineteenth century, the work required under the task system had been carefully defined. Indeed, for many lowcountry crops, the task had become so standardized that it was often used interchangably as a unit of land (the amount necessary to grow a task of peas) or even a unit of time (the amount of time it took to plant a task of peas). Nevertheless, the struggle over the definition of the task did not end. Following

emancipation, when planters attempted to eliminate the task system, freed people objected, often violently. In 1865, a Union soldier reported from Georgetown that the freedmen "have been accustomed to working by task, which has always given them leisure to cultivate land for themselves, tend their stock, and amuse themselves, and, therefore very correctly, I think, [believe] that with such a change in the march of labor all their privileges will go and their condition will be less to their taste than it was when they were slaves." Lt. Col. A. J. Willard to Capt. George H. Hooker, Georgetown, November 7, 1865, Letters Sent, vol. 156 DS, U.S. Army Commands, RG 393, pt. 2, National Archives, Washington, D.C. Also see Ulrich B. Phillips, ed., *Plantation and Frontier*, 1 (Cleveland, 1909): 115–19; and Frederick Law Olmsted, *The Cotton Kingdom*, ed. Arthur M. Schlesinger, 1 (New York, 1953): 190–94. The origins of the task system and the struggle over the definition of work in the eighteenth century has not yet been investigated, but, for the kinds of disputes that defined the measure of a task, see Josiah Smith to George Austin, July 22, 1773, Josiah Smith Letterbook, Southern Historical Collection, and Richard Hutson to Mr. Croll, "per Caser," August 22, 1767, Charles W. Hutson Papers, Southern Historical Collection, University of North Carolina, Chapel Hill.

45   Wood, *Black Majority: Negroes in Colonial South Carolina*, esp. chap. 6; Lorenzo D. Turner, *Africanisms in the Gullah Dialect* (Chicago, 1949); William R. Bascom, "Acculturation among the Gullah Negroes," *American Anthropologist*, 43 (1941): 43–50; Klingberg, *An Appraisal of the Negro in South Carolina*; and Hennig Cohen, "Slave Names in Colonial South Carolina," *American Speech*, 28 (1952): 102–07.

46   Klingberg, *An Appraisal of the Negro in Colonial South Carolina*, 116–17; and Petition of John and William Morriss, 1791, and Petition from Camden Negroes, 1793, South Carolina Legislative Papers, South Carolina Department of Archives and History, Columbia.

47   For one planter's attempt to keep boatmen from mixing with his plantation hands, see Laurens, *Papers of Henry Laurens*, 4: 319, 633; and Sellers, *Charleston Business on the Eve of the American Revolution*, 108.

48   Edmund S. Morgan, *American Slavery, American Freedom: The Ordeal of Colonial Virginia* (New York, 1975), 108–79, 215–49; and Wesley Frank Craven, *White, Red, and Black: The Seventeenth-Century Virginian* (Charlottesville, Va., 1971), 75–99.

49   Ross M. Kimmel, "Free Blacks in Seventeenth-Century Maryland," *Maryland Historical Magazine*, 71 (1976): 19–25; John H. Russell, *The Free Negro in Virginia, 1619–1865* (Baltimore, 1913), 24–38, 88, 116, 119–20, 136–37; James H. Brewer, "Negro Property Owners in Seventeenth-Century Virginia," *William and Mary Quarterly*, 3d ser., 12 (1955): 575–80; and Susie M. Ames, *Studies of the Virginia Eastern Shore in the Seventeenth Century* (Richmond, Va., 1940), 99–108.

50   Morgan, *American Slavery, American Freedom*, 329–37; Warren M. Billings, "The Cases of Ferna and Elizabeth Key: A Note on the Status of Blacks in the Seventeenth Century," *William and Mary Quarterly*, 3d ser., 30 (1973): 467–74; and Kimmel, "Free Blacks in Seventeenth-Century Maryland," 20–21.

51   Edmund S. Morgan, "Slavery and Freedom: The American Paradox," *Journal of American History*, 59 (1972): 17–18; and T. H. Breen, "A Changing Labor Force and Race Relations in Virginia, 1660–1710," *Journal of Social History*, 7 (1973): 3–25. The confused, uncertain status of black people generally and of free blacks in particular during the seventeenth century also indicates the unwillingness, inability, or, more probably, lack of interest on the part of whites in firmly fixing the status of blacks. For the farrago of legislation governing free blacks, see Ira Berlin, *Slaves without Masters: The Free Negro in the Antebellum South* (New York, 1974), 7–9; and Jordan, *White over Black*, 136–78. The status of blacks free or slave, has become something of a historical perennial, with scholars agreeing that before the 1660s at least some blacks were free and some were slave and the precise status of most is simply impossible to determine. For a review of the evidence, see Jordan, *White over Black*, chap. 2.

52   Allan Kulikoff, "A 'Prolifick' People: Black Population Growth in the Chesapeake Colonies, 1700–1790," *Southern Studies*, 16 (1977): 391–96, 403–05, and "The Origins of Afro-American Society in Tidewater Maryland and Virginia, 1700 to 1790," *William and Mary Quarterly*, 3d ser., 35 (1978): 229–31; Russell R. Menard, "The Maryland Slave Population,

1638 to 1730: A Demographic Profile of Blacks in Four Counties," *ibid.*, 32 (1975): 30–32; and Craven, *White, Red, and Black*, 89–103. Herbert S. Klein has maintained that West Indian re-exports remained the majority into the first two decades of the eighteenth century; see his "Slaves and Shipping in Eighteenth-Century Virginia," *Journal of Interdisciplinary History*, 5 (1975): 384–85.

53 Kulikoff, "A 'Prolifick' People: Black Population Growth," 392–406; Menard, "The Maryland Slave Population," 30–35, 38–49; and Craven, *White, Red, and Black*, 98–101.

54 Gerald W. Mullin, *Flight and Rebellion: Slave Resistance in Eighteenth-Century Virginia* (New York, 1972), esp. chaps. 2–3; Menard, "The Maryland Slave Population," 32–54; and Kulikoff, "Origins of Afro-American Society in Tidewater Maryland and Virginia," 236–49.

55 Mullin, *Flight and Rebellion: Slave Resistance in Eighteenth-Century Virginia*, 34–110, esp. table 3 (pp. 108–09); and Kulikoff, "Origins of Afro-American Society in Tidewater Maryland and Virginia," 253–54.

56 Hugh Jones, *The Present State of Virginia* (1724), ed. Richard L. Morton (Chapel Hill, N.C., 1956), 75; Berlin, *Slaves without Masters*, 3–6; Donald L. Horowitz, "Color Differentiation in the American Systems of Slavery," *Journal of Interdisciplinary History*, 3 (1973): 526–30; and George M. Fredrickson, "Toward a Social Interpretation of the Development of American Racism," in Nathan I. Huggins *et al.*, eds., *Key Issues in the Afro-American Experience*, 1 (New York, 1971): 246–47.

57 Philip V. Fithian, *The Journal and Letters of Philip Vickers Fithian, 1773–1774*, ed. Hunter D. Farish (Williamsburg, Va., 1943), 73; Mullin, *Flight and Resistance: Slave Resistance in Eighteenth-Century Virginia*, 19–32; Kulikoff, "Origins of Afro-American Society in Tidewater Maryland and Virginia," 240–42, 246–49; Louis Morton, *Robert Carter of Nomini Hall: A Virginia Tobacco Planter of the Eighteenth Century* (Charlottesville, Va., 1941); Michael Greenberg, "William Byrd II and the World of the Market," *Southern Studies*, 16 (1977): 429–56; and, especially, Landon Carter, *The Diary of Colonel Landon Carter of Sabine Hall, 1752–1778*, ed. Jack P. Greene, 2 vols (Charlottesville, Va., 1966), *passim*.

58 Allan Kulikoff, "The Beginnings of the Afro-American Family in Maryland," in Aubrey C. Land *et al.*, eds., *Law, Society, and Politics in Early Maryland* (Baltimore, 1977), 177–96, "A 'Prolifick' People: Black Population Growth," 401–03, 405–14, and "Origins of Afro-American Society in Tidewater Maryland and Virginia," 246–53; Daniel Dulany to Robert Carter, December 18, 1768, Colonial Papers, Maryland Historical Society, Baltimore; Robert Carter to John Pound, March 16, 1779, to Fleet Cox, January 2, 1788, and to George Newman, December 29, 1789, typescript, Robert Carter Papers, Duke University, Durham, N.C.; John C. Fitzpatrick, ed., *The Writings of George Washington*, 39 vols. (Washington, 1931–44), 2: 526, 29: 154, 398; and Edwin M. Betts, ed., *Thomas Jefferson's Farm Book* (New York, 1953), pt. 2: 46, 12–13, 21, 24–26, 42–46. Planters also found a relationship between family stability and social stability. A Maryland planter instructed his overseer about a returned fugitive: "While his wife continues at home, I suppose there will be no danger of his making a second attempt to get off. You may let him know, that his pardon depends upon his good future behavior, that if he behaves well, and endeavours to make amends for his past behavior I will when I return purchase his wife if her master will sell her at a reasonable price." Letter of John Hanson, January 29, 1782, John Hanson Papers, Maryland Historical Society, Baltimore.

59 Mullin, *Flight and Rebellion: Slave Resistance in Eighteenth-Century Virginia*, 14–16; Kulikoff, "Origins of Afro-American Society in Tidewater Maryland and Virginia," 230–35; Darold D. Wax, "Black Immigrants: The Slave Trade in Colonial Maryland," *Maryland Magazine of History*, 73 (1978): 30–45; and Winthrop D. Jordan, "Planter and Slave Identity Formation: Some Problems in the Comparative Approach," in Rubin and Tuden, *Comparative Perspectives on Slavery in New World Plantation Societies*, 38.

60 Kulikoff, "The Beginnings of the Afro-American Family in Maryland," 185–86; Jordan, *White over Black*, 405 n. 7; Mullin, *Flight and Rebellion: Slave Resistance in Eighteenth-Century Virginia*, 83–139; "Description of Servants, 1772," Northampton Furnace, Ridgely Account Books, Maryland Historical Society, Baltimore; and Ronald L. Lewis, *Coal, Iron, and Slaves: Industrial Slavery in Maryland and Virginia, 1715–1865* (Westport, Conn., 1979), 82–84, 162–63.

61   Carville Earle and Ronald Hoffman, "The Urban South: The First Two Centuries," *Perspectives in American History*, 10 (1976): 26–76; Mullin, *Flight and Rebellion: Slave Resistance in Eighteenth-Century Virginia*, 87–88, 124–27; and Gray, *Agriculture in the Southern United States*, 2: 602–17. Although the best study of slave hiring in the Chesapeake region focuses on the post-Revolution years, the forces promoting slave hire after the war suggest that the practice predates the Revolution. See Sarah S. Hughes, "Slaves for Hire: The Allocation of Black Labor in Elizabeth City County, Virginia, 1782 to 1810," *William and Mary Quarterly*, 3d ser., 35 (1978): 260–86. Also see Robert Carter to Warner Lewis, October 16, 1773, and October 20, 1774, to Mrs. Corbin, September 27, 1775, to Griffin Garland, September 29, 1775, and to John Ballantine, July 7, 1777, Carter Papers, typescript, Duke University, Durham, N.C. Allan Kulikoff has estimated that the proportion of blacks working as agricultural laborers dropped from 90 to 82 percent between 1733 and 1776; see his "Tobacco and Slaves: Population, Economy, and Society in Eighteenth-Century Prince George's County, Maryland" (Ph.D. dissertation, Brandeis University, 1976), 235–39.

62   Robert Carter to Robert Jones, Robert "King" Carter Letterbooks, Alderman Library, University of Virginia, Charlottesville (I am grateful to Emory Evans for alerting me to this letter); and Robert Carter to William Carr, March 15, 1785, Carter Papers, typescript, Duke University, Durham, N.C. Also see Carter, *Diary of Colonel London Carter of Sabine Hall, passim*; Robert Carter to his various stewards and overseers (Rubin Sanford, Clement Brooke, Newyear Branson), Carter Papers, typescript, Duke University, Durham, N.C.; Fitzpatrick, *The Writings of George Washington*, esp. vols. 32–34; Depositions of James Holland, William Ferguson, and Charles Gardiner, August 23, 1793, Lloyd Family Papers, Maryland Historical Society, Baltimore; and Betts, *Thomas Jefferson's Farm Book*, pt. 2: 16. For the striking difference in naming patterns of Chesapeake and lowcountry bondsmen, compare the slave lists in the Charles Carroll Account Book, Maryland Hall of Records, Annapolis, and the Charles C. Pinckney Plantation Journal, Manuscript Division, Library of Congress, Washington, D.C.

63   For the importance of African–creole differences in understanding black reactions to the revolutionary crises of the last quarter of the eighteenth century, see Michael Mullin, "British Caribbean and North American Slaves in an Era of War and Revolution, 1775–1807," in Jeffrey J. Crow and Larry E. Tise, eds., *The Southern Experience in the American Revolution* (Chapel Hill, N.C., 1978), 235–67.

PART THREE

Slaves at Work

AFRICANS WERE SHIPPED INTO the Americas to work. Their prime task was to tap the commercial bounty of the settled colonies, to work the land and to cultivate the primary export crops, which were first the lifeline and later the prosperity for colony and metropolis alike. Slaves worked in sugar, tobacco and rice. Later, of course, they made possible the rise and prosperity of the cotton industry in the US South (though the supply of slaves came, in that case, not across the Atlantic, but from established states in the Old South). Yet slave work involved much more than brutal field work. In time, there were few activities in the slave societies that were not undertaken by slaves.

Africans were first imported in significant numbers to work in the Brazilian sugar fields. The tentative experiments first with Indian labour were later transformed into a massive slave labour force, fed by an apparently inexhaustible appetite for Africans. But throughout the slave colonies, slaves found themselves undertaking a host of tasks. Even in communities apparently dominated by sugar, the plantations needed a varied economic infrastructure to provide their practical needs. Verene Shepherd's piece (1991) is an important analysis of the commercial and labouring diversity which lay at the heart of rural Jamaica, even when the island was dominated by sugar production. If sugar was the engine of local life, it was maintained by the lubricants of diverse slave labours in non-sugar industries. In their preoccupation with slavery in sugar, historians have often overlooked other key crops cultivated by imported African labour. Simon Smith's essay (1998) on the Jamaican coffee industry draws our attention, again, towards another area of slave labour. Yet coffee remained a volatile industry whose main benefits were not fully exploited until the nineteenth century in Brazil.

In all slave societies, slave owners preferred, above all, healthy young male slaves. It is now abundantly clear that, in practice, the sociology of slavery was very different. Slave women, for example, were critically important, both at work and in the slave community, in ways which earlier historians simply did not recognise. Everywhere slave women came to be valued for their reproductive potential. They were, in effect, doubly valuable (and exploited) as workers and as mothers to a new generation of slaves. In places, it took time for planters to accept the economic importance of slave motherhood.

Slaves in the Chesapeake and the Carolinas worked to a different labouring regime and pace than their contemporaries in sugar. Above all else, their lives were regulated not by the gang system common in the Caribbean, but by a task system. In his essay of 1982, Philip D. Morgan provides a seminal analysis of the nature of slave life and work under that task system. It is an essay which proved a turning point in historical assessments of slave life in the Americas. Peter Wood's (1975) account of slave labour in the rice fields of South Carolina is, similarly, a classic historical analysis which is, at once, a snapshot of the uniqueness of rice slavery and also a brilliant study of the sociology of a previously neglected form of slavery.

———•◆•———

INTRODUCTION TO PART THREE

AFRICANS WERE IMPORTED INTO the Americas to work. They were prized and valued, on arrival and throughout their lives, in proportion to their ability to undertake their allotted tasks. Age and strength, skills and experience all added to a slave's commercial value – but all hinged ultimately on the slave's working strength or skills. It was a crude economic analysis which ignored all other social and human attributes of the slave. But it goes some way to explain the nature of slavery in the Americas, and indeed the entire Atlantic slaving system. The whole purpose of the Atlantic slave trade was to deliver Africans to slave owners, mainly planters, across the Americas. What they wanted, ideally, were healthy young men, capable of undertaking strenuous labour in their fields. What they got, however, was often very different: Africans debilitated by prolonged migration within Africa and physically reduced by the agonies and squalor of the slave ships.

It was widely accepted that newly arrived Africans were incapable of heavy work on arrival. Too sick, too weak, too traumatised to do little more than survive (often not even that), slaves had first to be nursed back to something like normal health (i.e., so they could be worked profitably). Slave owners normally 'seasoned' their slaves, acclimatising them to local life, edging them back to fuller health, by less rigorous regimes and labour. Sooner or later, however, the Africans were turned over to the labours that would dominate their lives thereafter. The great majority of Africans were destined, initially at least, to work in the sugar fields. They were to be found, however, in practically every corner of the economy, in all sorts of employments, throughout the slave colonies. As those colonies matured from simple, rough pioneering settlements, slaves were dragooned to most forms of work, from the most demanding of physical labour through to the most unusual and valuable of skilled occupations. Moreover, slaves also worked extensively for themselves, notably on their plots and gardens and in improving their economic and social lives by their own efforts. But their greatest contribution was at the behest of their owners – in the sugar, tobacco and rice fields of colonial America.

In time, slave owners came to justify their use of African slaves on environmental grounds: that Africans were physically best suited to such labour in those regions. But initially whites (and Indians) had undertaken similar work. In truth, African slaves were used for economic reasons. They – and they alone – seemed to offer the most economic means of tapping the agricultural potential of the regions concerned. Yet there was a distinct problem built into the slave system: the reliance on imported Africans meant that a proportion of them (i.e., those recently arrived from Africa) were sick and needed time to recover from their ordeal before being turned over to heavy field work. In the early years of settlement, pioneering life was harsh and difficult for everyone. Black and white (and Indian) worked together at the difficult task of creating a viable habitat and winning over a resistant wilderness to manageable cultivation. In that initial phase, men outnumbered women, but as pioneer societies were transformed into settled communities, with viable export crops to Europe, new work patterns emerged. As ever more Africans were imported, a distinct divide began to emerge between what was thought appropriate for slaves and inappropriate for non-slaves. Increasingly, the heavy field work was thought best suited to slaves. This was most striking in the sugar colonies and, later, on the rice plantations of South Carolina. Where sugar dominated, there the African was in greatest demand and remained so (with some notable exceptions) until the abolition of the slave trade after 1807.

Slave work varied greatly from one region to another and, more especially, from one crop to another. At one level, this ought not to surprise us. Work, after all, varied hugely and the nature and quality of labouring life is largely determined by the kind of work undertaken. So it was among the slaves. In sugar, and as plantations grew in size, first in Barbados and later in Jamaica, slaves worked in gangs. The strongest slaves (men and women) worked at the heaviest field work, planting and harvesting, while other gangs of older or less able slaves undertook the less onerous tasks in the fields. Slaves moved in and out of the gangs, depending on their strengths, weaknesses or ages. It was a system which sought to use all sorts of slaves, from the very young (employed in simple tasks) through to the old, similarly used for less demanding work in and around the fields and yards.

Gangs proved an effective means of managing sugar plantations, and they were used wherever sugar dominated. But the gang system had consequences well beyond the world of work. They formed, in effect, a brutal working process (visitors were often struck by the military nature of the gang system) which had to be dragooned and controlled by a heavy-handed managerial presence, often via corporal punishment. It was a labouring system in which blacks greatly outnumbered whites in the fields and on the plantations at large. This raises the broader, more complex issue of social control. How was it possible for relatively small bands of white men to control large gangs of slaves who, in crop time, were equipped with a variety of dangerous agricultural tools?

Elsewhere, slave work was organised differently. In rice, for example, slaves were given tasks to complete, on their 'own' particular section of the rice fields. Their labours for their owner ended when those tasks were completed. Then they were able to turn to cultivation on their gardens and plots. It was a system which, of course, favoured the healthy and the nimble, who would complete their work early. Older slaves, however, would take longer over the same tasks.[1] Slave work on tobacco plantations was different again. Tobacco required careful scrutiny and monitoring, and labour was consequently divided into small units, gangs, which could themselves be monitored. This was done more easily than in sugar because the number of slaves on tobacco plantations was generally much smaller and the ratio of black to white lower than in the sugar fields. On the eve of the American Revolution, Virginian slaves were owned in groups of five or fewer, at a time when Caribbean planters averaged 240 slaves on their holdings.[2] Tobacco planters chose their best slaves (the quickest, nimblest, most experienced) to set the pace which others were expected to follow. Tobacco was an agricultural system which was unsuitable to the task system, yet its gang system, requiring finesse and expertise in testing and assessing the growth and condition of the tobacco leaf, was utterly different from the life of slaves working in sugar gangs. Thus in the three main staples of colonial slave cultivation (sugar, tobacco and rice), slave work differed greatly from one crop to another.

In all of these crops, of course, the planters' aim was to get the most from their slaves. Yet it was rarely possible to work slaves all the time. Their lives were shaped by the rhythms of the natural seasons and the agricultural cycle. Each crop afforded its workers breaks from the more strenuous periods of hectic activity. And, in time, the development of the Christian calendar granted slaves regular, weekly breaks from work. All this was in addition to the high-days and holidays allowed slaves by law and convention, though much depended inevitably on the whim and caprice of local slave owners. Yet only the most perverse of planters failed to realise the benefits (to themselves as well as to their slaves) of granting free time to their enslaved labour force.

Slave work involved much more than mere labouring in the fields. Indeed, slaves undertook the most varied of working tasks, from the simplest of labours through to the most skilled of crafts, everywhere in the Americas. Each of the major American export crops required its own particular skills, in cultivation, cropping, processing and transportion. And each slave settlement required that range of artisans whose abilities made possible the functioning of local economic and social life. Carpenters and masons, factory foremen, distillers, nurses and transport slaves all added their skills and working experiences to the well-being of local slave society. The domestic life of whites was dominated by slave domestics. Visitors, again, were struck by the huge numbers of black servants working in and around the homes of white people in the slave colonies. Nannies and nurses, cooks, and washers, gardeners and cleaners, each and every conceivable domestic role was undertaken by slaves. Overwhelmingly women, slave domestics faced different problems from their contemporaries in the fields. Though perhaps better-off materially, domestic slaves often had uncomfortable relations with their white owners. They faced all the potential aggravations of close proximity, from sexual threats through to white women's dissatisfaction and anger. But it is surely a sign of the domestic slaves' superior station that a standard threat and punishment was to dispatch troublesome domestics to field work. Female domestic slaves generally wanted their daughters to follow them, rather than be trained up for manual labour outside.

As colonial society matured, the number of skilled slaves increased, itself a reflection of enhanced social and economic sophistication. A sizeable proportion of slaves could be found in urban areas, notably in colonial ports, where they handled imports and exports from the ships (including, of course, newly arrived Africans), and where they catered for the domestic needs of local resident white people. 'Negro yards' consequently developed in all the major towns of the Americas, and it was inevitable that slaves working in those urban environments would experience a very different lifestyle from slaves living on rural, and often isolated, plantations. In the towns of colonial America we also find more skilled slaves (those employed in workshops, for example) plus the occupations and skills associated solely with urban or maritime life, from printing to sail-making. There were also large numbers of enslaved sailors, plying their trades along the river systems of the Chesapeake or the Low Country of the Carolinas, around and between the islands of the Caribbean, and even on the oceanic voyages of the Atlantic routes. Stated simply, the streets of the American colonies were thronged with working slaves; slaves from the boats, from the countryside or heading back to their plantations, buying and selling at street markets, all of them enjoying that degree of social freedom afforded by town life which their contemporaries in the country could only have envied. And this was true for women as much as men.

Slave women worked throughout the slave colonies. Despite the planters' frequently asserted demand for male slaves (and prices of males were always higher than comparable female slaves), slave owners everywhere made ample use of their females slaves. Even in the hardest of labours – the sugar fields – women toiled alongside men. The basic point remains, whatever planters claimed as a labouring ideal, they invariably used their slaves as best they could, moving slaves in and out of different jobs according to strength, age and skills. There were limits, however, to how far women could expect to climb through the local slave hierarchy (artisan jobs, for example, tended to go to the sons of skilled slaves). Yet it is clear enough that women were an economically vital part of the overall slave system. They serviced all corners of local life: washing, cleaning, cooking, nursing, rearing and nurturing the offspring of their owners (as well as their own). In addition, in their physical prime, slave women trudged out to the fields to work alongside their menfolk at the physically demanding tasks. In their prime, slave women were, of course, valuable as mothers of future slaves. In places it took time for planters to accept the benefits of a sympathetic policy towards pregnant women and mothers of young children. But as prices of imported Africans rose, the crude economic formula sank in: slave women were an asset over and above their labouring skills, for they held the key to subsequent generations of slaves. Doubtless there were many cases where a simple humanity took over, especially where local white women got to know female slave workers (this was more likely in smaller communities, notably in North America, where slaves were owned in smaller groups). But the real impulse behind 'amelioration' was the impersonal drive of economics: it made economic sense to treat slaves better, to relieve pregnant women of the most onerous tasks, to allow them time and facilities to nurture their babies and to reward them for successfully rearing healthy children. Through all this, it is important to remember the double burden of slave women, caught as they were between the demands of labouring for their owners, and also expected to bring forth future generations of slaves, again for the ultimate benefit of their owners.

In time, there were few jobs in the slave colonies which were denied to slaves, though that too changed in North America with the development of local white plebeian and semi-skilled groups, keen to distance and distinguish themselves from neighbouring blacks. Slaves everywhere found their lives shaped by the nature and rhythms of local agricultural life. Even in the towns and seaports, the pace of local labour reflected the ups and downs of the agricultural seasons, and the peaks and troughs of imports and exports. There were times of the year when life was harder than others for slaves. There were certain forms of work which were tougher than others. Again, if we need confirmation of this, we need only recall that slaves were often punished by being shifted from one form of work to another, more strenuous form of labour. The harsher the form of work, the tougher the local slave regime. The management of working slaves varied enormously, and sugar planters, for example, faced very different problems from those of tobacco planters. How to get the slaves to work, how to keep them at it throughout a hot, difficult day, how best to mix threats and punishments with incentives and inducements? All these factors tested the experience and the adaptability of slave owners and their slave drivers. It was rarely possible simply to dragoon slaves to work and to keep them working, by sheer physical coercion and cruelty (though there was plenty of both throughout the slave colonies). For all its physical violence, the successful management of slave labour involved an experienced mix of the carrot and the stick, and wiser slave owners recognised this.

Africans were shipped across the Atlantic primarily to work at the demands of local export crops, notably sugar, tobacco and, later, rice. Yet across the settled Americas, slavery quickly moved out of the major industries and infiltrated other areas of local life. Slaves were to be found everywhere, undertaking a huge range of chores and labours. There were slave cowboys on the American frontier, slave interpreters negotiating between arriving Africans and Europeans in the Americas. We find slave musicians in all corners of the Atlantic community. Slaves lived on isolated plantations on the very edge of settlement, and they lived and worked in towns and cities throughout the Americas. There was then a great variety of slave labour, and major differences within the slave experience, but slaves everywhere were treated and viewed merely as beasts of burden, to be used, as their owners saw fit, for purposes over which they had little control. They were the labouring task force which tamed and brought to profitable cultivation huge swathes of the Americas. It is true that they were able to secure for themselves a better life than we once imagined (thanks to their own efforts), but slavery was designed not for the benefit of the slaves, but for others. Their successes can be measured in those great areas of cultivable land which brought forth the wealth of the tropical and semi-tropical Americas, and which so quickly transformed the well-being and the cultural habits of the Western world. Slave labour caused that transformation in ways that have gone largely unrecognised.

Notes

1   Philip D. Morgan, *Slave Counterpoint*, Chapel Hill, 1998, pp. 179–187.
2   James Walvin, *Questioning Slavery*, London, 1996, p. 38.

Chapter 9

Verene A. Shepherd

TRADE AND EXCHANGE IN JAMAICA IN THE PERIOD OF SLAVERY

I

TRADITIONAL ACCOUNTS OF COMMERCIAL transactions in British Caribbean sugar plantation societies have been located within the context of external trading relations. Where domestic trade and exchange have been addressed, the focus has been on the marketing system of the slaves. Scholars have been less concerned with the other dimension of local trade – that which developed among the different rural agrarian units. Such inter-property relations were most evident in Jamaica among Britain's mercantilist empire in the Caribbean; for unlike in the classical plantation economies of the Eastern Caribbean, sugar monoculture was never a persistent feature of the island's colonial economy. Jamaica produced and exported, in addition to sugar, significant quantities of coffee, cotton, ginger, pimento, dyewoods and hardwood. The island also produced food and livestock. Most of these commodities were produced on properties geared towards the export market although some output was exchanged locally from the estates and 'minor' staple plantations. Indeed, Barry Higman indicated that towards the time of emancipation, the flow of goods and labour from one unit to another resulted in about 17% of the total production on sugar estates and coffee plantations remaining in Jamaica.[1] Unlike sugar estates, coffee plantations and other monocultural 'minor staple' units, however, the island's livestock farmers catered primarily to the domestic market. Livestock farmers were able to sustain a vibrant trade with other properties, but especially with the sugar estates which needed large numbers of working animals (as well as grass and pasturage facilities) for the production of sugar. Animals were especially vital where planters did not utilize wind, steam or water power. Even where alternative forms of power existed, 'standby' 'cattle' mills were often maintained.

This essay, using examples from the Accounts Produce,[2] illustrates another dimension of the domestic system of trade and exchange which developed during the period of slavery – the economic relations which developed between the locally based 'pens' (livestock farms) and the dominant sugar estates, arguably the best example of inter-property trade in the island. It examines the pens' transition from primarily export-based production in the seventeenth century to the dominant form of domestic trade and exchange by the nineteenth century. The essay, while intended as a contribution to the empirical base of knowledge on commercial relations in Caribbean plantation societies, has the potential to contribute to theoretical discussions on the nature and socio-economic implications of diversification of commodity production in colonial economies within a region characterized by sugar monoculture.

II The transition from export to a dominant local trade

The Accounts Produce show quite clearly that by the mid-nineteenth century Jamaica's livestock farms participated only minimally in the direct export trade. This was in contrast to their participation in the export trade in the preceding century. Indeed, the early history of the livestock industry in the sixteenth and seventeenth centuries indicates that the export dimension of trade was highly developed. In that period, these farms had an independent economic dynamic, exporting hides, lard and dried meat to the Spanish Indies and Spain. By 1740, the majority of the livestock farms disposed of their output on the domestic market, principally the sugar estates. Quantitative data on the disposal of pen output are not abundant, especially for those units owned by resident proprietors. The available trade statistics provided by the Accounts Produce from 1740 relate primarily to the properties of absentees; nevertheless, they can be used effectively to demonstrate some broad trends in the extent of pen participation in the export trade.

From the data available, it would seem that from the mid-eighteenth century, where pens produced goods for export, the value of such goods did not, in general, exceed the proceeds from local transaction. Before 1800, the commodities exported were ginger, pimento, cotton, dyewoods and hardwood (logwood, fustic, mahogany). These products could be related clearly to specific parishes. Ginger was sold from the pens in St. Andrew; pimento from St. Ann and Trelawny, but mostly from the former; dyewoods, fustic and cotton from St. Elizabeth with some cotton also from the pens in St. Catherine.

Two distinct patterns of trade seemed to have existed. One method was to ship the commodity to Britain, presumably to an agent who handled the sale there. The most frequently observed practice, however, and one which was in direct contract to the usual method of disposing of sugar, was to sell the product to merchants in Kingston, who then arranged the sale.

Evidence of the participation of pens in the export trade was most available from the 1770s. Accounts for the earlier period were scanty, perhaps because of the greater residency of the penkeepers then. In 1740, for example, whereas it was evident that estates were exporting minor staples in addition to sugar (such crops also being exported from plantations of minor staples), only two of the eighteen pens for which returns were seen exported any commodity, in this case, cotton. In this period, most of the pens were located on the southside, particularly St. Catherine, and supplied primarily grass and provisions to the urban markets.[3] Forty years later, of the 21 returns relating to livestock farms, only five participated in the export trade. From Dornoch, Riverhead and Gordon Valley pens in St. Ann were shipped 118 bags of pimento valued at £256 17s. Several other bags valued at £161 0s.4d. were sold in Kingston, presumably for later export. In all then, pimento sales totalled £417 17s.4d., but this represented only 11 per cent of the total earnings of the pen which amounted to £38,587 7s. 7d.[4]

Taking the period 1776–85 together, it is evident that the pens continued to export ginger, pimento, fustic, mahogany, logwood and cotton. A similar commodity-parish relationship existed as in 1740.[5] The just over 40 returns seen (representing 25 pens), showed a mere seven pens active in the export market. In all cases, the value of exports fell far below the receipts from internal transactions. The best example in this period is from Luana Pen in St. Elizabeth which had eight separate returns in the period under review. Between 1776 and 1785, Luana exported 58 tons of fustic (£340 16s. 9d.), 65 tons of logwood (£325) and 995 lbs of cotton (£87 1s. 3d.), totalling £1,083 10s. 6d; but over the same period, receipts from livestock sales and pen services totalled £3,156 12s. 0d. Exports thus represented 34% of total earnings of just over £4,240.[6] In the other accounts, the percentage represented by exports was lower. The receipts of Dornoch, Riverhead and Gordon Valley pens from exports together represented 11 per cent of all goods and services sold.

Accounts for 1800 and 1820, the other years sampled, also replicated these earlier trends with respect to commodities produced, parishes in which produced, patterns of trade and comparative receipts from sales – with one important exception, the addition of coffee to the list of exports. In 1800, coffee was shipped from pens in St. Ann, Clarendon and St. James. Cotton, logwood and fustic continued to be produced in St. Elizabeth and Westmoreland, by this time an important exporter of logwood. One pen in St. Dorothy shipped a quantity of lignum vitae wood, and pimento continued to be associated with the St. Ann pens.[7]

Unlike in the preceding period, the value of exports from the pens in 1800 and 1820 at times exceeded earnings from internal transactions. Two notable examples were firstly Bellemont Pen which in 1800 exported coffee valued at £1,117 6s. 8d., 67% of total receipts for that year. The second case was Patherton Pen whose coffee exports formed 82 per cent of total earnings. As not all the accounts contained the volume and value of the commodities and as it is not at all times safe to assign current prices to the crops (if sold in Jamaica, for example, commodities fetched a different price from those exported directly to Great Britain), it is impossible to ascertain the extent to which Patherton and Bellemont typified the situation with the pens in 1800 with respect to value of exports *vs* internal trade. A further complication limiting generalization about the trend is that it would seem that it is those pen/coffee combined units, mostly in Manchester, which showed an increase of exports over internal sales. Pens like Luana, which were primarily devoted to livestock rearing, continued to show an excess of internal transactions over exports. In 1800, Luana earned 32% from export sales, for example. Indeed, of the eight complete accounts seen for this year, six recorded that sales from internal transactions exceeded those from exports. It should also be added that of 73 returns of pens in 1800, 21 (29%) participated in the external trade – a significant enough improvement over previous years in numbers, though not necessarily in percentage. This improvement seemed attributable to the increase of pens producing and exporting coffee.

In 1820, 153 returns of pens were seen. Of this number 43 or 28% participated in the direct export trade. The products exported were coffee, pimento, fustic, lignum vitae, logwood and hides. One pen, Castille Fort, provided ballast for outgoing ships. Most pens exported only one commodity. Only a minority[8] exported two. The usual combination was pimento and coffee (four pens) or log-wood and fustic (two pens). One pen exported both pimento and fustic. St. Ann's pens continued to be overrepresented in the export of pimento. The combined pen/coffee units in Manchester most likely dominated the export of coffee, but because of the high residency among the coffee farmers, were underrepresented in the Accounts Produce. In the 1820 returns, it is the St. Ann pens which seemed to be exporting most of the coffee.

Most of the products were recorded as having been 'sent to Kingston'. Again, as not all commodity prices were included, only tentative statements can be made about the value of the products sold abroad. What seems clear is that of the 18 pens which had detailed information on prices and volume of goods, only three seemed to have earned more from exports than from internal transactions, the percentage from exports ranging from 59% to 71%. The others earned between 0.2% and 39% from external trade. The limited quantitative data, therefore, serve to reinforce the impression from qualitative sources that unlike the sugar estates, by the nineteenth century, pens catered essentially to the domestic market in the island.

III The domestic trade

In contrast to their relatively minimal involvement in the direct export trade, Jamaican pens participated actively in the domestic system of exchange. The pens conducted two levels of exchange locally. One was the domestic trade in provisions and livestock in which money was used as a medium of exchange. The other was a form of barter, an informal, non-monetary exchange of commodities among properties. A variety of goods were involved in the internal system of exchange among Jamaican properties. The primary product was livestock, comprising work-ing steers, spayed heifers, breeding cows, mules, horses, bulls, calves, asses, fat cattle, old, wornout estate cattle and small stock. Other goods included food provisions (mainly corn and plantains), grass, milk, bricks, white lime, shingles, fresh beef, fish, timber, staves, sugar, rum, coffee and miscellaneous items. Most of these goods were sold by the pens. Those sold or exchanged by estates were sugar, rum and old working cattle. Where pen/coffee units or monocultural coffee units were involved in the trade, they sold coffee and livestock in the case of the former.

Various services (including labour) were also provided. The principal services provided by pens were jobbing, pasturage and wainage (cartage). Sugar estates rented excess land, at times in exchange for more pastureland from nearby prop-erties. They also jobbed their tradesmen. Jobbing was, however, probably dominated by pens and specialized, independent jobbing gangs.

Of the goods listed above, the trade in livestock was the most lucrative for pens. According to Bryan Edwards, an eighteenth-century estate spent a minimum of £300 per annum to replace 'stock'.[9] The majority, indeed, spent far more. In 1783, Simon Taylor, the attorney for Golden Grove estate in St. Thomas-in-the-East, reported that that estate needed 100 working steers annually.[10] At around £30 each in 1820, this would cost this estate £3,000 per annum. As estates also bought mules and spayed heifers annually, pens stood to gain considerably from the trade in working stock, especially around 1820 when the price of a mule was

£40 and for a young, spayed heifer, £22 10s.–26 each. J. B. Moreton recorded that an estate with even 100 acres of cane needed to buy 40 mules annually and maintain 100 always on the estate in the late eighteenth century.[11] Horses, proof asses and fat stock sold to the butchers also fetched considerable sums.

Of the services provided by pens, jobbing was the most financially rewarding. Jobbing consisted chiefly of digging cane holes and planting the spring canes on estates. In 1834, the cost of digging cane holes was £8 per acre. In this and previous years, some pens profited considerably from this service provided by their hired slaves. Stoneyfield Pen in St. Ann, for example, earned £660 1s. 6d. in 1820 for jobbing done on Fellowship Hall estate. This represented 52.54% of its total earnings from internal transactions.[12]

Pasturage, particularly for St. Catherine's pens, was also quite lucrative. In the eighteenth century, the typical rates charged for this service were 15s. per month for each horse or mule, and 10s. per month for each head of cattle. If pastured in batches of 20, rates were slightly lower. For example, 7s. 6d. for each animal was charged where cattle were pastured in batches of 20 or more. Rates increased in the nineteenth century to a maximum of 20s. for each horse.[13]

For sugar estates, the sale of their old, meagre or fat cattle after the crop to pens or butchers gave them handsome returns on their initial investment in young working stock. James Stevenson, the attorney for the Scarlett's estates in Jamaica, noted in 1800 that fat cattle from the estates sold at around £40 each. He stressed that formerly, old, fat cattle sold at between £18 and £25 each, but now fetched almost as much as for young cattle. Even though estates then had to buy fresh beef from such stock, at 1s.–1s. 8d. a pound, he felt they still made a profit in the sale of fat stock.[14] The army used a substantial proportion of the fresh beef sold by pens, at times up to 425 head per annum.[15]

The internal sale of rum also provided estates with money to help with local contingencies. As most of this product would have eventually been re-exported by Kingston merchants, however, this was, perhaps, not a true part of the domestic trade. However, sugar estates still participated in local transactions by providing the sugar and rum needs of non-sugar producing units.

The availability of goods and services provided by Jamaican pens was made known to potential customers in one of three ways. First, the sale of livestock was advertised in various newspapers. One hundred and twenty pens advertised the sale of animals in various newspapers sampled between 1780 and the end of slavery.[16] Second, pen-keepers or overseers, utilizing the services of slave couriers, sent letters to sugar planters or their representatives and butchers indicating the availability of planters' stock and fat cattle respectively. Thomas Thistlewood, owner of Vineyard Pen, noted in 1751, for example, that he 'sent Julius to Mr. Markham [a butcher in Black River] with a letter to let him know what fat cattle we have . . .'.[17] Third, pen-keepers or pen overseers themselves visited estates to enquire about the availability of livestock for sale. Over time, estates developed a relationship with particular pens, getting to know their routine and approximate selling time for young steers, heifers and mules.

In the majority of cases, pen slaves supplied the orders sent in by estates for livestock. The driving of cattle and horsekind to and from estates provided the slaves involved with a great deal of mobility. On 27 July 1750, for example, Charles Guy and Julius left Vineyard Pen with 15 steers, two young horses, ten heifers and two mules for a property in Westmoreland. They did not all return until August 2. Their explanation was that they had been delayed unduly because several people asked them to collect and deliver letters.[18] Pen slaves often covered longer distances than were involved in the case of Vineyard Pen's labourers. Slaves from Agualta Vale Pen in St Mary, for example, drove animals to Spring Estate in St Andrew, approximately 34 miles away.[19] Slaves from other properties, or those belonging to individual butchers, also went to the pens to collect goods for their masters. Mr. Markham, for example, 'sent his negroes for one dozen crabs caught by Titus and a he-lamb'.[20] Markham similarly sent his slaves to purchase fat cattle from Vineyard Pen. According to Thistlewood, however, his 'hands' were inadequate to manage the nine cows and calves; so that Charles and Cuffie had to help with them as far as Black River.[21] In some cases, the butchers, or estate overseers, visited the pen personally to make arrangements for purchase.[22]

In addition to driving livestock to 'markets', pen slaves fetched animals bought for the pen or to be pastured on its lands. In 1807, for example, the overseer of Thetford Hall Pen in St John sent slaves from that property to Mile Gully in Clarendon for a bull purchased from that pen.[23] Similarly, Thistlewood sent the slaves Dick, Guy, Charles, Julius and Simon to Mr. Allen's pen to fetch the mares for pasturage.[24] When pen slaves themselves delivered livestock to markets, or fetched and returned animals for fattening or pasturage, an extra cost was added.

The method by which other pen products were disposed of seemed less systematic. On Vineyard and Breadnut Island pens, for example, no letters were exchanged respecting the sale of vegetables and food crops. Also, no advertisements appeared in the newspapers relating to the sale of products other than large stock and its by-products. Products such as capons, crabs, poultry,[25] eggs, fruits, sheep, goats and vegetables were sent to market in Westmoreland or Black River each week.[26] These were clearly not marketed by slaves on their own account as such sales were not usually made on Saturdays or Sundays. On some Saturdays, however, products were prepared for sale the following week.[27] In addition to these products, Phibbah, Thistlewood's 'house-keeper', frequently sold cloth (usually check) in Westmoreland.

Few pens returned in the Accounts Produce established butcheries in the period under review. Those that did also developed significant links with properties and individuals within and outside of the area of their location. The best example of the scale of transactions in fresh beef from a pen is provided by Batchelor's Hall Pen's accounts. In 1833, this pen earned £2,120 2s. 11d. from its sale of fresh beef to estates, individuals, the troops and ships. This represented 57.63% of its total earnings for that year.[28]

The participation of the various units in the internal commodity trade varied in extent, volume and value from year to year. In 1740, when the Accounts Produce returns begin, 175 accounts were sent in by overseers. These represented 85 sugar estates, 20 pens, five plantations of minor staples, 19 jobbing gangs, 19 multiple crop combinations and 27 returns relating to merchants' earnings or house rents collected. Eighteen of the 20 pens, 20 of the 85 estates and the plantations of minor staples participated in the internal trade. Unfortunately, there is no detailed accounts of the buyers involved, so that the extent of economic links for 1740 cannot be measured.

The returns for 1760 indicate that interproperty transactions remained essentially the same as for 1740 in terms of the total number of properties involved. Sugar estates had, however, improved their participation, moving from 23.52% in 1740 to 35.68% in 1760. Pens basically remained at the same level, but the participation by plantations had declined. By 1780, 120 properties of the 266 returned were involved in local transactions. The number of properties involved continued to increase along with the increase in the number of returns. These indications are for units owned by absentees, but resident proprietors also participated in the trade, though the extent of their involvement cannot be ascertained. In the post-slavery period, however, the nature of transactions underwent slight changes. While the sale of livestock continued between pens and estates, there was a drastic reduction in the jobbing of pen labourers on the estates. Indeed, only five such cases were noted in the 152 returns of pens in 1840, compared with 64 of the 145 such units in the 1820 return.

The extent of trade is clearer in the nineteenth-century returns. The majority of estates relied either on pens or local butchers to buy their old stock. Pens dominated this trade, however, as they were better placed than the butchers to fatten such animals prior to their being killed for fresh beef. Only five of the pens returned in 1820 had their own butcheries, and the supply of beef – a form of final demand linkage – was probably in the hands of urban butchers and independent pens not returned.

The volume of livestock being sold in the island can be partially ascertained from the Accounts Produce. In the first return when pens were not as numerous as later on, these units supplied only 34 head of working stock to estates. In that year, few pens were monocultural livestock units, and St. Catherine's units, in particular, sold more sheep and small stock than cattle and mules. By 1780, 21 of the 266 returns were pens. The latter were involved in the sale of livestock to the number of 942. This represented 50.7 per cent of the 1,881 sold by the 120 units involved in local trading. Table 9.1, showing the specific breakdown of the numbers traded, indicates the relative importance of each type of livestock in the eighteenth century. It is clear that in the late eighteenth century, heifers and mules were overrepresented in terms of working animals. The mule, indeed, was recognizedly unsurpassed in its hardiness as a work animal. The horses, on the other hand, and the 'steers' were underrepresented as work animals, the former being more important for transportation and the horse-racing industry. This was in contrast to the trend in England where by 1850, English farmers, with some regional variations, had virtually dispensed with the working of cattle in favour of the use of horses. This was because after the Napoleonic Wars, more favourable price conditions and the increasing efficiency of horses in farming caused the emphasis in cattle husbandry to shift to beef production.[29] In Jamaica, however, competition from horse-racing and the expensiveness of procuring and maintaining horses determined their unattractiveness as draught animals.

By the mid-nineteenth century, however, mules had largely been displaced by steers and spayed heifers. A partial indication of this shift is that by 1820, and in contrast to 1780, an estimated 3,162 steers, 1,162 spayed heifers and only 511 mules were sold or exchanged internally. By the post-slavery period, the number of mules sold by the pens represented in the Accounts Produce had fallen

Table 9.1 Breakdown of livestock sales by type and volume, 1780

All properties		Pens only	%
Working steers	278	137	49.28
Heifers	19	15	78.94
Cows	30	24	80.00
Calves	56	38	67.85
Horses	123*	91	73.98
Old/fat/cattle	1,039	407	39.17
Bulls	3	—	—
Sheep	140	95	67.85
Mules	181	131	72.37
Asses	12	4	33.33
	1,881	942	50.70

* Including six mill horses

Source: J.A., A.P., 1780, 18/11/4/9.

significantly. In 1840, for example, the 283 mules compared with 2,461 steers and 1,006 heifers were sold from the pens.[30]

Contemporary sources provide no explanations for this shift, but one can speculate that the dual income yielded by oxen was attractive to both planters and pen-keepers. Unlike the oxen, mules realized little of a return on initial investment at the end of their working life. Indeed, the table also reinforces qualitative statements about the lucrative nature of the sale of old stock from the estates and the dominance of pens in the trade in working stock.

By 1820, when the total number of livestock traded internally was 14,134 head, pens were responsible for 8,267 or 54.49%, an improvement over their 1780 level. In the former year, the returns included 145 pens and 470 sugar estates. As in previous years, sugar estates dominated the sale of old, meagre stock, while pens controlled the sale of working animals. Pens acted as 'middlemen' in the trade in old stock which could not be sold straight to the butcher. These were fattened on the pens' pastures prior to sale to urban butchers. This enabled them to make a profit on their purchases from the estates.

As a result of the trade in livestock, therefore, a significant degree of economic links developed among the island's main economic units. These links typified the relations between estates and pens throughout the island.

The Accounts Produce give some indication of the relative value of each type of good and service to properties involved in the internal trade, as is demonstrated by Table 9.2, based on examples drawn from the 1820 Accounts (which are far more detailed than previous samples returned). In 1740, for example, though 35 units indicated earnings from the domestic trade, the purchases of these goods and services were rarely given. Values were equally generally absent, making calculations based on known price rates virtually impossible. Table 9.2 indicates that 11 of the 16 pens involved earned most from the sale of livestock and its by-product, beef. It should be stressed that not all transactions involved money, but all could be reduced to monetary value. Where goods were exchanged for other goods or services, however, a money value was not given. Flamstead Estate in St. James,

Table 9.2   Sample of inter-property trade, 1820

Property	Type	Parish	Total earnings from the internal trade			Proportion earned from dealings with estates/pens			
			£	s.	d.	£	s.	d.	%
1 Golden Grove	Sugar estate	Hanover	2,405	2	0	84	2	0	3.5
2 Silver Grove	Sugar estate	Hanover	1,923	14	0	157	2	0	8.2
3 Steelfield	Sugar estate	Trelawny	1,318	10	6	135	0	0	10.2
4 Unity Hall	Sugar estate	St. James	2,300	16	6	179	0	0	7.8
5 Seven Rivers	Sugar estate	St. James	267	3	0	267	3	0	100
6 Old Montpelier	Sugar estate	St. James	3,896	18	0	219	0	0	5.6
7 Grange	Sugar estate	Hanover	1,540	15	8	115	0	0	7.5
8 Fontabelle	Sugar estate	Westmoreland	695	9	4	622	0	0	89.4
9 Frome	Sugar estate	Westmoreland	178	15	7	82	4	7	46.0
10 Spring Garden	Sugar estate	Westmoreland	186	0	0	128	0	0	56.06
11 Silver Grove	Sugar estate	Trelawny	169	10	0	136	0	0	80.2
12 Golden Grove	Sugar estate	Trelawny	134	10	0	119	10	0	88.8
13 Harding Hall	Sugar estate	Hanover	1,348	5	8	108	0	0	8.0
14 Old Shafston	Pen	Westmoreland	1,321	0	6	204	0	0	15.4
15 Carysfort	Pen	Westmoreland	3,998	19	3½	3,396	19	3½	84.9
16 Midgham	Pen	Westmoreland	1,451	12	11	1,251	15	0	86.2
17 Paradise	Pen	Westmoreland	790	6	8	218	18	0	27.6
18 Mount Edgercombe	Pen	Westmoreland	2,120	13	0½	1,350	8	10½	63.6
19 Hamstead	Pen	St. Mary	428	8	0	428	8	0	100

Source: J.A., A.P., 1B/11/4/54–6.

Table 9.3   The internal trade: relative value of goods and services from selected properties, 1820

Property	Livestock			Jobbing			Pasturage			Wainage			Provisions			Wood, staves shingles			Misc. rents, etc.		
	£	s.	d.	£	s.	d.	£	s.	d.	£	s.	d.	£	s.	d.	£	s.	d.	£	s.	d.
1 Forest Pen	4,027	16	8	75	0	0	—			—			—			—			—		
2 Maverly Estate	137	0	0	—			—			—			—			363	7	6	134	4	11
3 Lyndhurst Plan.	620	0	0	—			—			—			—			554	7	7	—		
4 Pindar's River Estate	124	0	0	—			—			20	0	0	—			—			150	0	0
5 Phantilland's Pen	356	13	4	746	16	8	45	6	8	—			—			—			122	4	5
6 Chudleigh Plan	1,326	10	0	—			—			—			—			—			—		
7 Brazellitta Est.	174	0	0	294	0	9½	—			40	0	0	—			—			37	3	4
8 Crescent Park Pen	787	0	0	20	0	0	—			—			—			—			—		
9 Batchelor's Hall Pen	1,304	0	0	—			—			84	0	0	2,272	3	9	—			—		
10 Petersville Est.	1,655	10	0	—			—			—			—			—			—		
11 Monymusk Estate	—			60	0	0	—			—			—			—			45	0	0
12 Spring Gdn. Pen	1,740	13	0	—			18	10	0	—			—			—			16	5	0
13 Worthy Part Est.	225	0	0	—			—			—			—			—			—		
14 Aboukir Plan.	72	10	0	—			—			97	0	0	38	1	3	70	16	0	—		
15 Paynestown Pen	640	0	0	1	5	0	—			3	0	0	—			—			—		
16 New Forest Pen	219	16	0	47	10	0	207	2	6	263	13	4	39	0	0	—			—		
17 Chesterfield Est.	220	0	0	—			—			10	0	0	32	8	4	—			25	0	0
18 Crawle Pen	2,379	0	8	211	7	9	446	5	10	393	3	8½	—			—			—		
19 Lower Works Pen	1049	0	0½	—			375	0	0½	—			—			—			—		

Table 9.3   (cont.)

Property	Livestock £	s.	d.	Jobbing £	s.	d.	Pasturage £	s.	d.	Wainage £	s.	d.	Provisions £	s.	d.	Wood, slaves shingles £	s.	d.	Misc. rents, etc. £	s.	d.
20 Palmyra Pen	167	6	8	662	0	0	—			50	18		9	—		—			—		
21 Rosehall Estate	148	0	0	50	10	0	—			5	6	8	—			—			—		
22 Cherry Gdns. Est	52	0	0	—			—			—			—			—			—		
23 Holland Estate	400	0	0	—			—			—			—			—			—		
24 Sevens Plan	300	0	0	—			—			—			88	5	0	—			—		
25 Santa Cruz Park Pen	924	0	0	72	0	0	—			—			—			10	0	0	—		
26 Ramble Pen	1,450	0	0	—			—			105	5	0	78	0	0	427	15	0	155	0	0
27 St. Fail's Pen	1,386	7	0	99	14	10½	6	18	4	—			—			403	1	6	—		
28 Ardoch Pen	574	10	0	190	9	7½	20	8	0	—			—			16	0	0	—		
29 Bryan's Pen	980	7	8	476	0	0	—			368	0	0	115	0	0	—			78	17	6
30 New Ground Est.	108	0	0	—			—			38	0	0	—			—			—		
31 Dunbarlon Est.	—			80	0	0	—			—			522	0	2	—			—		
32 Phoenix Park Pen	2,028	6	8	—			—			—			—			202	0	0	—		
33 Prospect Est.	368	8	0	—			—			—			88	8	0	—			47	0	0
35 Roaring River Est.	32	0	0	—			—			—			58	4	6	—			—		
35 Williamsfield Est.	12	10	0	85	0	0	—			—			—			—			—		

Source: J.A., A.P., 1B/11/4/54–6.

for example, bartered 110 gallons of rum for stock in 1780.[31] Unlike in other West Indian islands, however, the products of the island were not made legal tender after 1751, despite an attempt to get the Assembly to sanction this. Where it occurred, it was more custom than law. Indeed, Edward Long confirmed that 'money is the chief agent for carrying on any trade'.[32] Increased draining of money from the island by American and Spanish merchants, however, not only made bartering common, but according to Long, 'credit became a part of Commerce'.[33] Although pens diversified their activities to a greater extent after the abolition of slavery, up to 1840, earnings from the livestock trade still accounted for the largest share of their income. A sample of 24% of the pens returned in 1820 (representing 9–10% of the estimated island total) reveals earnings of £25,990 5s.8½d. from livestock sales to estates. These pens earned more from such sales (69%) than from other important income-generating activities such as jobbing, wainage, pasturage, the sale of food (ground provisions and fresh beef) and wood. These other sales and services combined yielded £11,974 19s. 0d. or 31 per cent of the total earnings of £37,965. Taken singly, jobbing represented 8%, pasturage 3%, wainage 4%, provisions 9% and miscellaneous items (rents, shingles, wood, staves) 7%. These percentages varied, of course, from pen to pen. Forest pen, for example, earned only 2% from non-livestock sources.

It should be pointed out that on the whole, estates and pens were unequal partners in the internal trade. In the majority of cases, as Table 9.3 illustrates, estates accumulated less from their internal transactions with pens than they did from other sources such as the sale of rum to Kingston merchants and fat cattle to butchers. On the other hand, pens relied on the estates for the greater portion of their earnings. Additionally, the estates' gains from the internal trade represented an insignificant part of their total earnings from the domestic export trade. For example, Prospect Estate in Hanover earned £12,650 18s. 0d. from the sale of sugar and rum and only £183 10s. 0d. from internal transactions. Of the money accumulated locally, £128 10s. 0d. resulted from trade with pens. Similarly, Mint Estate in Westmoreland earned £7,818 17s. 0d. from the export of sugar and rum and £420 14s. 0d. from the domestic trade.[34]

Conclusion

It should be clear from the foregoing analysis that commercial relations in eighteenth- and nineteenth-century Jamaica did not conform to the trade patterns in monocultural or classic plantation economies. The island's colonial economy was diversified and led not only to the availability of a wider range of export crops, but to the emergence of non-staple producers who traded their goods on the domestic market.

Despite the importance of this domestic trade in livestock, however, local producers were never able to supply the total livestock requirements of the island. The competition between estates and pens for land made the pens unable to maintain the required livestock density which would cater to the island's needs. Furthermore, the high cost of production of local livestock made pen-keepers unable to compete with external producers, notably Hispanic America. This lack of self-sufficiency in working animals encouraged the development and maintenance of a vibrant import trade with Spanish America. Between 1815 and 1825, for example, the Spanish Main and Islands supplied 57,704 of the total 59,182 mules, horses, asses and cattle imported into the island.[35] Nevertheless, the domestic trade in livestock reduced the island's dependence on foreign sources and supplied locally a larger share of Jamaica's total demand for plantation animals than did any other island in the British Caribbean.

Notes

1   B. W. Higman, 'Slave Population and Economy in Jamaica at the time of Emancipation' (Ph.D. diss., UWI, Mona, 1970), p. 313.
2   Accounts Produce contain returns of commodities produced, method of disposal and value of goods and services in some cases. These accounts related to the properties of absentees, but information pertaining to pens owned by residents is available where the latter traded with the former.
3   Jamaica Archives (J.A.), Accounts Produce (A.P.), 1B/11/4/1.
4   *Ibid.*, 1B/11/4/9.
5   *Ibid.*
6   *Ibid.*
7   *Ibid.*, 1B/11/4/27–28.
8   *Ibid.*, 1B/11/4/54–56.
9   B. Edwards, *The History of the West Indies*, 2 vols (London, 1793), I, p. 259.
10 Simon Taylor to Chaloner Arcedeckne, 29 October 1782, Jamaica Estate Paper, Vanneck Manuscripts, Box 2, Bundle 10.
11 J. B. Moreton, *Manners and Customs in the West Indian Islands* (London, 1790), p. 57.
12 A.P. 1B/11/4/56.
13 *St. Jago de la Vega Gazette*, 4–11 April 1801, p. 93.
14 James Stevenson to Mrs Scarlett, 8 April 1800. Scarlett Family Collection, DDCA/41/17, Hull University Library (Brynmor Jones).
15 *Jamaica House of Assembly Votes (J.H.A.V.)* 1795–6, p. 282.
16 *Royal Gazette*, 1780–1834; *St. Jago de la Vega Gazette*, 1791–1831; *Falmouth Post*, 1791–1836.
17 Thomas Thistlewood's Journal, Vineyard Pen, 15 January 1751, Monson 31/2 fol. 8, Lincolnshire Archives Office.
18 *Ibid.*, Monson 31/1, fols. 342, 348.
19 V. Shepherd, 'Problems in the Supply of Livestock to Sugar Estates in the Period of Slavery', UWI, Mona, 1987.
20 Thistlewood's Journal, 26 January 1751, Monson 31/2, fol. 14.
21 *Ibid.*, 10 April 1751, fol. 58.
22 *Ibid.*, 23 April 1751, fol. 59.
23 Thetford Hall Pen Accounts, 1807. D.M. 444, Special Collections. Bristol University Library.
24 Thistlewood's Journal, 11 April 1751, Monson 31/2, fol. 25.
25 *Ibid.*, 5 September 1750, Monson 31/1, fol. 374.
26 *Ibid.*, 1750–51, Monson 31/1–2.
27 *Ibid.*, 11 July 1750, Monson 31/1, fol. 355.
28 Accounts Produce, Batchelor's Hall Pen, January–December 1833, Vanneck MSS; Jamaica Estate Papers, Box 2, Bundle 60.
29 J.A. Perkins, 'The Ox, the Horse, and English Farming, 1750–1850', Working Papers in Economic History, 3/1975, University of New South Wales, Dept, of Economic History, School of Economics, pp. 2–15. (I am grateful to Prof. Barry Higman for this source.)
30 A.P. 1B/11/4/84–5, 1840.
31 *Ibid.*, 1B/11/4/9, 1780.

32 Add. MS 12,404, fols. 450–2, E. Long, *History of Jamaica*, 3 vols (London, 1774), 1, fols. 450–52.
33 *Ibid.*, fol. 450.
34 A.P. 1B/11/4/54–56.
35 V. Shepherd, 'Pens and Penkeepers in a Plantation Society', Ph.D., Cambridge, 1988, p. 163.

Chapter 10

Simon Smith

SUGAR'S POOR RELATION
Coffee planting in the British West Indies,
1720–1833

T HE DOMINANCE OF SUGAR in Britain's eighteenth-century West
India trade has long been recognized by historians, just as it was appreciated
by contemporaries who frequently referred to the colonies simply as the sugar
islands. Monoculture was a feature of all European territories in the Caribbean
during this period, but the preference for sugar was strongest in the British West
Indies (BWI). In 1770 no less than 80 per cent of merchandise exports from the
BWI consisted of sugar or the sugar-based products molasses and rum. In comparison, the share of sugar in the colony trade of France, Britain's most important
imperial rival, was only a little over one half.[1] The economic consequences of
dependence on sugar has been a favourite subject of research in Caribbean studies.
Of particular influence has been Eric Williams' plantation economy model, which
stresses the retarding effects of a prolonged exposure to export-orientated, large-
scale plantation agriculture epitomized by the sugar estate. Williams observed
that once sugar holdings attained a threshold size of approximately 1,000 acres (or
between 240 and 250 slaves), the owners characteristically appointed a manager
and retired to become absentee proprietors resident in Britain. The inclination of
estate owners to return home, Williams stressed, not only transferred surpluses
from the Caribbean to Great Britain, but also accentuated the tendency of the
planter elite to look to Britain for social, cultural and political leadership. In consequence, Williams argued, a system of navigation laws and political institutions grew
up around sugar which collectively served to reinforce British supremacy and West
Indian dependency to the detriment of long-term development.[2]

Though the market for sugar experienced fluctuation, typified by the so-called
golden and silver ages of the 1640s and the late 1760s, growth in cane production
was sustained over a long period of time by rising demand for sugar in the British
home market.[3] It must he emphasized, however, that while cane was the most
lucrative staple during the decades after the 1640s, alternatives to sugar existed and
slavery was never confined solely to sugar production.[4] Indeed, the very strength
of consumer demand for sugar also helped to raise up a potential rival and during the
early eighteenth century coffee established itself in several European colonies as
one of sugar's most significant competitors for the use of slave labour. Experiments
in coffee cultivation were undertaken in order to break the Mocha trade's monopoly of supply. Dutch merchants were in the vanguard of the movement to globalize

coffee production and introduced the crop into Java between 1696 and 1699. The effort met with a favourable outcome when, in 1711, the first non-Arabian coffee shipments were auctioned in Amsterdam. Encouraged by this success, between 1713 and 1723 French and Dutch planters introduced coffee to St. Domingue, Surinam and Martinique, and within a short period of time Caribbean and Javanese coffees began beating Mocha supplies out of the European market.[5] In view of these initiatives, it is striking that in the BWI coffee failed to pose a significant challenge to king sugar for most of the period of slavery. This failure was a key factor in the inability of the British colonies to create a more diversified export base and the limited progress of coffee, therefore, enhanced the influence of sugar on the form that slavery assumed. In this article, the difficulties of expanding coffee production in the BWI are analysed in order to explain why more colonists did not emulate their French and Dutch counterparts by growing coffee.

Britain's West India planters were not oblivious to the potential of coffee; indeed, the first trials took place at the same time as those carried out by Dutch and French pioneers, The earliest reference to coffee entering British colonial trade occurs in 1694, when it was included in a list of commodities imported into London from Jamaica.[6] These beans were almost certainly a reshipment of a cargo originating elsewhere, but the fact they passed through the West Indies at all is indicative of an interest in the crop. The first documented experiments in coffee colonisation date from the early 1720s. Interestingly, they took place on Barbados: the colony where developments in cane cultivation and rum distilling were also pioneered. A treatise by the physician and botanist James Douglas published in 1727 noted that in 1720 the first coffee plants were carried to Barbados by a certain Captain Young, though whether they originated from Arabia, botanical gardens in Europe, or other islands in the Caribbean is not made clear. Douglas adds that several seedlings grown from these trees were sent back from Barbados to England, including shipments made by the Governor of the island destined for the gardens of George I, the Prince of Wales, and the Duke of Chandos.[7] The Barbadian experiments assisted in the introduction of the coffee bush to England, where it could be studied by naturalists, but the island's almost total commitment to sugar prevented the development of a coffee exporting capacity and the early plantings came to nothing. It was to be on Jamaica, where land not suited to sugar was available in greater abundance, that coffee gained a permanent foothold. Yet despite Jamaica's potential as a coffee producer, it was not until 1728 that Sir Nicholas Lewes raised the first seven plants on his Townwell estate at Liguanea, in St. Andrew's parish.[8] Moreover, this experiment, like its Barbadian precursor, was also short-lived, Lewes dying in 1731 before the trees had even matured.

Coffee growing in the BWI failed to make lasting progress until private initiatives received state sponsorship. In the same year that Lewes died, a petition was raised by several Jamaican planters calling for the promotion of coffee. Cultivating coffee, the petition stated, was well suited to 'the poorer sort of people, whose stocks and plantations are small'.[9] This action was followed by a subscription campaign supported by 22 planters and merchants, which raised £220.10s towards a lobbying fund aimed at securing an act of parliament to promote coffee growing. The Commons responded by establishing a committee to examine the matter, whose membership both a former and future governor of Jamaica as well as Martin Bladen, a prominent spokesman for the West India interest. Notwithstanding such strong pro-West Indian representation, the committee was not merely packed with members sympathetic to the planters. It was headed by the merchants Micajah Perry and John Barnard, both of whom proved vocal opponents of the Molasses Act the following year. Nonetheless, on this occasion Perry and Bernard also aligned themselves with the West India lobby. It is probable that they saw the proposed preferential tariff as a means of counter-balancing the advance of the sugar interest and as an opportunity to take a snipe at the East India Company (EIC). The two aldermen carried fresh memories of an unsuccessful campaign, mounted in 1730, against the EIC's monopoly of Asian commerce and they may have welcomed an opportunity to challenge the Company's position as sole supplier of coffee to Britain.

During its proceedings the committee heard evidence from James Laws that Jamaica was 'at present very thinly inhabited by white people'. Laws suggested that coffee might prove 'a means to bring in the poorer sort of people there, which is very much wanted'.[10] The use of a demographic argument in support of coffee reflected the fact that the shift towards sugar during the later seventeenth century was accompanied by a decline in the white population as large-scale plantations based almost exclusively on slave labour became the norm. Whereas in 1650 the BWI was home to 44,000 white colonists comprising three-quarters of the population, by 1700 their numbers had fallen to 33,000, or just over one-fifth of all inhabitants. At the time the petition was presented to parliament, the numbers of whites had steadied at 37,000, but by this date the volume of slave imports had reduced the white share to a mere fourteen per cent of the total.[11] The dwindling numbers of white settlers provoked concerns that the security of British imperial possessions was being jeopardized and in response a number of measures were introduced during the 1730s and 1740s designed to slow down or reverse the trend. The policies included 'deficiency laws' (a requirement that there be a ratio of one white worker to every 30 black plantation labourers, on pain of a fine), land grants and a head-right system: the offer of free passage, and gifts of land and start-up capital.[12] The promotion of coffee as a secondary staple should, therefore, be placed in the wider context of what was perceived as a growing settlement problem. Laws' argument that planting coffee would be able to reverse the white population slide, however, was far from convincing; indeed, under cross-examination he was forced to concede that in the long term coffee might even boost the number of sugar estates 'by reason, as the poor people get money by the produce of coffee, they will be encouraged to erect sugar works'. Nevertheless, the committee's response to the petitioners was positive and 'An act towards the encouraging the growing of coffee in the British plantations' passed into law on 30 March 1732. This measure introduced the first preferential coffee tariff; by reducing the import duties on plantation coffee from 24d. to 18d. per lb, while making foreign imports and East India imports liable to the higher rate.[13]

After a five-year gestation period, coffee was exported from Jamaica for the first time, but for several years the level of shipments remained small despite the stimulus of tariff discrimination. A contemporary account states that between 1737 and 1744 only 266 casks per annum were shipped from the island, while between 1745 and 1751 yearly exports dropped to just 187 casks.[14] After 1751 there is evidence that coffee production on Jamaica increased. A modern study suggests that the volume of exports doubled between 1745–51 and 1752–56 to reach

73,940 lb. This statement receives support from the Jamaican naval officer's lists, which record that coffee exports rose from 50,367 lb, during the years 1744–47, to 102,526 lb between 1752 and 1754, and to 252,460 lb by 1764. Though indicative of expansion, however, these data must be set in context by comparing growth in exports with those of other European colonies. In the case of the French West Indies, Thibault de Chanvalon noted in 1753 that on Martinique 'le prix considerable du café depuis la derniere guerre a Presque fait renoncer à toute autre production'. He reports that several Martinique cotton and cocoa growers, and even a few sugar cultivators, switched towards coffee in consequence of the price movements. During the years 1733 to 1737 coffee exports to France from Martinique averaged 22,700 quintaux per annum, but they rose to reach 70,000 quintaux between 1739 and 1753. On Dominica there is also evidence of expansion. The number of coffee trees planted on Dominica grew from 685,000, in 1743, to reach 1.4 million by 1749, and 1.6 million by 1753. A similar process also took place in the Dutch colony of Surinam after coffee prices reached 17 stuivers per lb between 1745 and 1748, encouraging planters to shift from sugar to coffee. Though prices recorded in Amsterdam slipped back after 1748, they rose again in 1755 due to the threat of war. Coffee exports from Surinam to Holland responded to favourable market conditions by increasing from a level of 1.6 million lb, between 1730 and 1739, to 3.3 million lb during the years 1740 to 1749, and to 5.9 million lb in the decade 1750 to 1759.[15] These comparative statistics indicate that though Jamaica's export performance improved during the 1750s, its growth in coffee production lagged badly behind that of other European colonies, notwithstanding the stimulus of favourable prices. Even during the period 1752 to 1756 Jamaican exports were equivalent to just five per cent of Britain's total importation of coffee, nearly all of which originated from Arabia.[16]

In order to boost coffee output further an additional source of encouragement was required. The growth of coffee cultivation in the BWI, in consequence, was a discontinuous rather than a smooth process and was characterized by abrupt responses to specific stimuli. The first stimulus was provided by the Seven Years War (1756–63). During the conflict coffee supplies were initially augmented by the temporary occupation of Martinique and Guadeloupe during the war, then permanently enhanced by the retention of the ceded islands of Grenada, Dominica, and St Vincent under the terms of the Peace of Paris (1763). During the next two decades these colonies usurped Jamaica as the leading coffee producer in the British empire and accounted for 94 per cent of the 3.3 million lb of coffee imported on average from the West Indies between 1763 and 1774.[17] Though a stagnant trade had received a major boost, the British colonies' share of Caribbean output remained small and accounted for at most between five and six per cent of total production in this region, c. 1775.[18] There is evidence that in Jamaica coffee growing experienced stagnation in the aftermath of the Seven Years War. Stephen Fuller, the colonial agent for Jamaica, put on a brave face when he informed the Lords of the Treasury in 1774 that coffee 'being upon a more contracted scale than that of Sugar and Rum has till of late years employed and given bread to a very great number of White Inhabitants'. The truth of the matter was revealed in a report compiled the same year which valued sugar and rum exports from Jamaica to all markets at £1.4 million, but valued coffee shipments at a mere £13,100. On the eve of the American Revolution, no less than three-quarters of Jamaica's slaves were employed on sugar estates, which buoyed by the prosperity of the post-war years had increased their the scale of operation.[19]

Coffee growing in Jamaica remained circumscribed until the St Domingue revolution of 1791 provided the second stimulus. The revolution temporarily crippled the world's largest producer of coffee and, in consequence, raised European prices sharply. Circumstances were rendered more favourable still by the dissemination of cultivating techniques by French refugees. In response to events on St Domingue, coffee production increased on several Caribbean islands, but most rapidly on Jamaica. Between 1790 and 1815 coffee reached its apotheosis on Jamaica as exports rose abruptly from a level of 2.3 million lb to 13.4 million lb during the 1790s, to peak at 34 million lb in 1814. During this period output accounted for between 15 and 30 per cent of world coffee exports.[20] Moreover, Jamaican producers were successful in raising the quality of their coffees as well as the quantity. The limited expansion that occurred after 1750 was fuelled primarily by the demand of German-speaking consumers for cheap, low-quality coffees. No less than 80 per cent of coffee imported into Britain during the 1770s was re-exported to European ports, particularly Hamburg, and in consequence Jamaican producers were encouraged to harvest light green berries, which were subjected to rapid and often careless processing. German immigrants into Continental North America, particularly the Philadelphia and Lancaster regions of Pennsylvania and the Charleston district of South Carolina, also formed an important market for the Jamaican growers. Approximately forty per cent of Jamaica's export crop was shipped to North America during the years 1744 to 1747; moreover, as Jamaican exports expanded, the importance of the North American market also rose. Between 1752 and 1754, 67 per cent of the annual crop was despatched to the American mainland, while 58 per cent of the 1764 crop was sent to the same destination.[21] The rapid increase of production during the 1790s, however, was accompanied by a market shift as British home consumption temporarily increased, boosted by reduced taxation. The improvement in the quality of output is demonstrated by the rise in the premium best coffee was able to command over worst and an increase in the number of grades of Caribbean coffee recorded in the London prices current.[22]

The third and final stimulus to coffee growing within the BWI was provided by the Napoleonic Wars, which left Britain in territorial possession of five more coffee producing colonies: Trinidad (1797), St Lucia (1803), Demerara, Essequibo and Berbice (1803). Though Jamaica remained the single most important supplier of coffee, the new acquisitions encroached significantly on, her trade and their output was sufficient to supply approximately one-third of Britain's coffee imports. Moreover, the conflict also led to the British acquisition of additional imperial territories outside of the Caribbean capable of supplying tropical commodities, including Mauritius in 1810. Despite a revival of the West India coffee trade during the years immediately after 1815, as the nineteenth century progressed conditions for Caribbean producers became increasingly difficult. The importance of BWI coffee to Britain steadily declined as new plantations were established in Ceylon, adding to the number of cultivators able to claim access to the privileged imperial trading network. The benefits of the preferential tariffs themselves were reduced as the customs regime became progressively more liberal and plantation coffee lost the benefits of protection. Coffee growing was ultimately undermined by the adoption of policies which caused general problems for Caribbean plantation agriculture; namely, the abolition of the transatlantic slave trade in 1807, the abolition of slavery itself between 1834 and 1838, and the erosion of tariff protection during the 1840s.

Reviewing the course of coffee production in the BWI, it is evident that most of the growth in coffee planting over the eighteenth and early nineteenth centuries occurred in distinct surges in response to tariffs, warfare, or revolution. As a result, the expansion of cultivation was largely unplanned and imperial policy tended, in consequence, to be primarily reactive in nature after 1732. The stimulus to the growth of output within the BWI provided by the Seven Years War and the Napoleonic Wars caused particular problems for Jamaican producers, illustrating how the expansion of coffee production within imperial boundaries could have divisive consequences. Policy inconsistencies go a long way towards explaining why coffee failed to become a viable long-run alternative to sugar in the BWI. Perhaps the most serious impediment to the creation of a large, sustainable coffee sector was the limited size of the British home market, itself largely a function of a tax regime which discriminated heavily in favour of coffee's great caffeine-rich rival, tea. The British market was undermined further by the creation of free ports in Jamaica and Dominica in 1764 and 1766, which inadvertently enabled French colonial coffee producers to gain access to the British market by circumventing discriminatory tariffs. The Lieutenant Governor of Jamaica, John Dolling, reported to the Earl of Dartmouth, in April 1773 that 'The French, under colour of bringing Indigo here, have, amongst other things, introduced large quantities of Coffee, which has reduced the price of that article so much, that it has alarmed the whole body of Coffee Planters.'[23] Re-exports, in consequence, were a vital element in the expansion of the colonial coffee trade because they permitted Caribbean coffee to compete with tea on a level playing field in Europe,[24] yet Britain's navigation acts handicapped colonial producers in this market also. In 1764, coffee was placed on the list of enumerated goods, thereby compelling all coffee shipments to pass through British ports prior to re-export to their final destination. The measure served to aggravate a problem coffee growers were already facing, since even before the passage of the act coffee was usually consigned on ships carrying sugar and other enumerated produce headed for British ports. Both law and practice combined to ensure that coffee was despatched to Europe via the British mainland. The necessity of reshipment raised transport costs and prices reducing the quantity that could be profitably sold.[25] While coffee laboured under these difficulties, without much compensation from the British fiscal regime, sugar producers enjoyed the exclusive benefits of rapidly increasing British home consumption and protection from competitive foreign producers. The home market monopoly held by sugar may itself have burdened coffee producers further. As a result of restrictions placed on supply stemming from the effective exclusion of foreign sugar producers, British sugar prices consistently exceeded those recorded in European markets, encouraging an extension of sugar production in the BWI. A natural consequence of this was the bidding up of the prices of all inputs into plantation agriculture in less than perfectly elastic supply used by the producers of other staples.[26]

Naturally, not every policy measure adopted by the British government was detrimental to coffee. Indeed, several initiatives were mounted that attempted to improve prospects for the growers. In 1783, 1807 and again in 1825 tariffs levied on coffee entering the British home market were cut to boost colonial production.

The benefits flowing from these favourable adjustments to the tax regime, however, were transitory and the measures themselves were adopted more to assist the industry in times of depression than as part of a long-term strategy to promote coffee as an alternative to sugar.[27] Coffee, therefore, provides a good example of the shackles of dependency outlined by Williams. The crop benefited from imperial regulation of colonial trade less than the dominant sugar staple, while the fortunes of coffee planters were consistently undermined by high taxation, market distortion, and territorial expansion which favoured stronger imperial interests. In order to reach a definitive assessment of how coffee planters fared in the BWI an estimate of the profitability of the crop is required. An accurate calculation of the profitability of coffee planting, however, is difficult to perform because no complete set of plantation accounts has survived. The official records of production, the accounts current, are also unhelpful in this context. These documents were compiled by the managers of the properties of deceased planters and the small numbers of absentee coffee planters; though they provide a reasonable account of revenue earned, they are deficient in their reporting of costs incurred.[28] Nonetheless, it is possible to draw some conclusions about the circumstances of coffee planters within the BWI by analysing two sets of accounts prepared by contemporaries with first-hand knowledge of agricultural conditions. The first account refers to conditions in Dominica, c. 1772, and was compiled by the planter Joseph Senhouse for his personal use; the second relates to Jamaica and was published by Bryan Edwards in 1793. Details of each set of accounts are displayed in Table 10.1.[29]

Neither Senhouse's nor Edwards' account by itself is comprehensive or ideal: the Dominican estimate contains no allowance for the repair of mill equipment, while the Jamaican account does not state the cost of forest clearance. Moreover, neither set of costs allows for slave mortality or general depreciation.[30] Nevertheless, a comparison of the two documents is a useful exercise, despite these limitations. Each plantation covered approximately 300 acres, but the Jamaican unit was far more extensively cultivated with half of all available land planted in coffee, whereas the Dominican property had just 20 per cent of its acreage in crop.[31] This is a most significant difference, for without recourse to fertilizer the planting of a large proportion of the total area in coffee limited the scope for shifting cultivation and could, therefore, be expected to reduce a plantation's working life. The cultivation strategy suggested by Edwards is also out of line with the limited amount of material available documenting farming techniques on the larger Jamaican properties. A small sample of plantation surveys collected by Higman spanning the period 1780 to 1860, coupled with a general report of coffee acreage compiled in 1799, suggests that only between 12 and 14 per cent of the area of properties were normally planted in coffee. The assumption that coffee, like sugar, was grown on only a limited portion of the plantation may, however, need to be reviewed, since knowledge of practices on the majority of small plantations is limited. By way of comparison, it is notable that the 158 coffee monoculture properties recorded in a 1772 survey of Grenada had 58.2 per cent of their acreage planted in coffee, while the 23 largest properties over 200 acres also had no less than 45.7 per cent of land under coffee.[32] A strategy of boosting early plantation income in return for a shorter operating life would make sense if planters expected the booms that occurred in coffee prices during the early 1770s, and during the years following

Table 10.1   Comparative estimates of costs and revenues on coffee plantations in Dominica and Jamaica

Dominica, c. 1772		Jamaica, c. 1793	
(A) FIXED COSTS		(A) FIXED COSTS	
293 acres woodland		300 acres mountain land	643
(surveyed and fees paid)	985	100 slaves	5000
10 acres cleared and planted in coffee	121	20 mules	400
cost of clearing 50 acres using hired		buildings, processing equipment, and	
cutters	303	tools	1429
53 slaves (50 field hands, 2 carpenters,		provisions for a full year before slave	
1 mason)	1388	grounds established	357
provisions for a full year before slave		Total	7829
grounds established	1134		
buildings, barbecues and tools	363[a]	(B) ANNUAL EXPENSES	
Total	4294	overseer's salary	143
		assistant overseer's salary	50
(B) ANNUAL EXPENSES		medical costs	18
managerial salary	61	provisions and clothes for slaves	143
provisions end incidental expenses	91	mill repairs	71
tools and clothing for slaves	21	sacks and saddles	57
quit rents	8[b]	taxation	71
medical costs	6[b]	Total	553
Total	187		
		(C) ANNUAL REVENUE (after 5 years)	
(C) ANNUAL REVENUE (after 5 years)		112,000 lb coffee at £2.86 per cwt	
50,000 lb coffee at an average of		(of 100 lb)	3203
£1.82 per cwt (of 100 lb)	910		

Notes and Sources: Cumbria Record Office, D/Sen, 'Joseph Senhouse and the West Indies: Plantation Estimates'; Bryan Edwards, *The History, Civil and Commercial, of the British Colonies in the West Indies* (2 vols; Dublin, 1793), vol.ii, 286–8. The original sources give values in currency; the table converts to sterling at £165 Dominican and £140 Jamaican equals £100 sterling.

[a] The 10 acre plot purchased above included a dwelling house, a store and an unspecified number of slave houses, thereby reducing the value of this item of expenditure. [b] This item is based (on details of expenditure recorded in the plantation journal.

the crippling of St Domingue's capacity, to be temporary in nature. Intensive land use on Jamaican plantations would also help explain why damage from flood erosion early in the nineteenth century was so serious that many planters were unable to recover.[33] The cost schedules in Table 10.1 differ markedly from one another in other respects. Since the Jamaican plantation purchased nearly double the number of slaves as the Dominican, its accounts record higher set-up costs as well as higher annual provisioning and medical bills, plus the employment of an additional overseer. Moreover, according to Edwards, the Jamaican estimates refer to a mountainous property situated 14 miles from the sea requiring the use of mules for transportation. The Dominican property was, in contrast, situated upon Canary Bay in the parish of St Davids and its proximity to the point of shipment and the possibility of moving coffee by water resulted in much lower transportation costs, advantages which are reflected by the higher land prices cited in comparison with

Edwards' estimate. Most striking of all the differences, however, is that of the prices of slaves on the two colonies: Jamaican slave prices in 1793 averaged £50, whereas Dominican slave prices in 1773 averaged only £26.2. This is a highly significant differential, even allowing for the rise in the general price level between the two dates in the order of 15 to 20 per cent suggested by English and North American price indexes.[34] Allowing for differences in scale and situation, and harmonizing the tax levels, the annual running costs appear to have remained roughly constant between 1772 and 1793, but the Jamaican fixed costs are much higher owing to the hike in slave prices.

Edwards and Senhouse set out very different methods of establishing a new plantation. In Edwards' estimate the planter expends the full fixed outlay immediately and also assumes all the running costs in the first year. Returns appear only after four years of cultivation, when the 150 acres are predicted to yield 45,000 lb, before reaching full production of 112,000 lb in the fifth year.[35] Senhouse's account spreads the set-up costs over a lengthier time period. Only the carpenters and a mason, plus 20 additional slaves, arc purchased in the first year, followed by further purchases of 10 slaves in each of the three succeeding years. Had it not been for the ten acres of coffee land already cleared and in production that Senhouse was able to purchase at the same time as the rest of the property, it is likely that even fewer slaves would have been acquired in the first year. The plantation journal records the hire of three woodcutters who carried out land clearance at an average rate of £5.5 sterling per acre. The existence of the plot already in cultivation explains the projected crops of 2,000 lb in the first year and 5,000 lb in the second. Expected output thereafter rises to 20,000 lb in the third, 40,000 lb in the fourth, and 50,000 lb in the fifth year, when full capacity is attained. In Senhouse's example, payments for land are also spread out over a five-year period, with a deposit of 20 per cent followed by two annual instalments each of 10 per cent and three annual instalments of 20 per cent.[36] Although the task of setting up plantations on Dominica, therefore, appears to have been an easier business than in Jamaica 20 years later, the effort expended in clearing land and resources required to tide the plantation over before the appearance of the first crop remained considerable. High set up costs explain the differences between the valuations of a fully established Jamaican plantations and these estimates. An inventory of the estate of William Haldane of Westmoreland drawn up in 1812, for example, valued the plantation's 100 acres of coffee of different ages at £3,047 (currency), compared with values of £2,711 for 527 acres of pasture and woodland, £1,000 for the mill buildings and barbecues, and £5,775 for the slaves. Though a much smaller unit, the inventory of Robert Dalhouse, in 1815, valued the plantation's 16 acres of coffee land at £210, the 188 acres of provision grounds and woodland at £734, the coffee works at £100, and the slaves at £2,700.[37] The ratio of land values to total sunk capital in these inventories, of between 25 and 45 per cent, is much closer to the 33 per cent suggested by Senhouse than it is to the eight per cent in Edwards' schedule, indicating how forest clearance and the planting of coffee led to strong appreciation in the value of agricultural land.[38]

The revenue estimates presented in each account appear to have been founded on a solid basis at the time they were written, but the assumptions written into the accounts regarding the future were to prove less realistic. Edwards' account has each slave tending 1.5 acres with an average yield of 747 lb per acre, whereas

Senhouse's slaves cared for 1.2 acres with an average yield of 833 lb per acre. These figures are consistent with other sources detailing cultivation practices elsewhere in the Caribbean. In Essequibo-Demerara, for example, the normal ratio on coffee plantations at the beginning of the nineteenth century was two slaves for every three acres, while an early promotional tract written c. 1730 stated generally that 'after the land is cleared and planted, six or eight Negroes, who are incapable of any labourious Employment, are sufficient to manage ten or twelve Acres, and to raise Provisions sufficient for their own subsistence'.[39] Coffee was, therefore, a crop that featured a land and labour ratio similar to sugar and tobacco. If coffee could not quite match sugar's conventional formula of one slave per acre (or even three slaves to two acres in some areas), its land–labour ratio was comparable with the one or two slaves per acre characteristic of tobacco planting. In consequence, the density of labour on the parts of a plantation planted in coffee was high relative to cotton or rice.[40] Dominica's higher yield per acre undoubtedly reflected the fact that it was feasible to plant trees closer together, since the plantation was situated on lower lying ground, a circumstance which reduced the risk of erosion. If Senhouse had planted trees at seven feet intervals it would have resulted in 888 bushes per acre, whereas Edwards' account states that coffee was planted at eight feet intervals, giving 680 trees per acre. The amount of coffee a tree could bear depended primarily on the fertility of the soil and amount of shade given it. A coffee bush might quite easily be made to yield 6 or even 8 lb in an average season, but such a yield would quickly deplete soil nutrients unless fertilizer was applied. In the eighteenth-century Caribbean, fertilizer was usually only applied at the time of planting seedlings and supplies were largely restricted to animal dung, though coffee husks and soil deposits washed down hillsides and trapped in specially planted hedges and trees called 'pois-doux' in Dominica were also employed to replace nutrients.[41] Spreading fertilizer was considered too labour intensive and planters preferred to adopt extensive methods of cultivation, whereby smaller yields were compensated for by planting more seedlings. Shade-giving trees were planted in between the coffee rows and plantations established at attitude to make use of cloud cover in order to bring crop production into equilibrium with available soil nutrients. A yield of between 1 lb and 1 lb 8 oz was, in consequence, the norm in most coffee regions.

Turning to consider the revenue side of the accounts, it is not clear whether the prices realized for coffee in the two accounts are net of all charges, but they seem low enough to be treated as farm prices.[42] In deciding whether their respective enterprises were viable, Senhouse and Edwards took into account two considerations: the number of years before each project would show a return on the initial investment and the annual rate of return, once the plantation had attained full capacity, relative to the capital 'sunk' into the project at its outset. Senhouse envisaged that his Dominican plantation would show a return on investment after ten years, while Edwards envisaged that the Jamaican concern would move into profit after just seven years. The data sets also predict that on attaining maturity the properties would earn a return on capital of 17.0 per cent and 33.9 per cent respectively for Dominica and Jamaica, where profit is defined as revenue minus costs expressed as a rote of return on fixed capital invested, Edwards made an allowance of expenses and interest on capital foregone during the three years prior to the first crop, which reduces the expected Jamaican rate of return to 24.7 per cent. Senhouse and Edwards, as well as other contemporary commentators, also used the projected earnings per slave, or per acre, as a guide to the attractiveness of the investments. The Dominica plantation was expected to yield a net revenue of £13.6 per slave and £12.1 per acre planted in coffee; the Jamaica plantation £26.5 per slave and £17.7 per cultivated acre. These estimates of potential returns may be compared with both contemporary and modern accounts. Moseley noted that the net profits earned planting coffee in Jamaica, c. 1785, lay between £10 and £12 per acre, whereas Higman reports that in 1832 the coffee monoculture listed in the accounts produce earned £19.2 currency (£13.7 sterling) per slave.

According to the estimates, coffee cultivation was a very attractive investment during the 1770s and 1790s, particularly on Jamaica. The methodology of assessment adopted by Senhouse and Edwards, however, was flawed. To put the projected rates of return of 17 per cent and 24.7 per cent in context it should he noted that estimates of the profits earned on sugar estates in Jamaica and the ceded islands, calculated by Ward from a small sample of surviving accounts, averaged only 7.6 per cent and 11.4 per cent respectively between 1750 and 1832. Moreover, out of the 54 estates in Ward's sample there is only one instance of a property generating a rate of return in excess of 20 per cent.[43] In appraising an investment, modern accounting practice compares the discounted flow of costs and benefits over the whole life of a project in order to calculate the present value of the investment and the expected returns. Two measures are routinely calculated: the cost–benefit ratio and the net-present worth, defined as follows:

$$\text{cost–benefit ratio} = \frac{\sum_{t-1}^{n} R_n / (1+i)^n}{\sum_{t-1}^{n} C_n / (1+i)^n} \tag{1}$$

$$\text{net-present worth} = \sum_{t-1}^{n} \frac{R_n - C_n}{(1+i)^n} \tag{2}$$

In the above formulae, R_n is revenue each year, C_n cost each year, n the number of years the plantation operates, and i the interest or discount rate. In applying these formulae, important decisions must be taken concerning the life-span of the project and the appropriate discount rate. Once the ground was cleared and planted in coffee, a well-tended coffee tree was capable of yielding a commercial crop for up to 30 years. A plantation could, therefore, in theory be expected to have a long working life, provided that the mill equipment was regularly maintained and the slave labour force remained in good health. In view of this, the investment and returns set out by Senhouse and Edwards were discounted over a 25-year period.[44] Fixing the rate with which to discount revenues and costs is the next problem. During the later eighteenth century, the peacetime rate of return on secure, real estate mortgages in England averaged approximately 4.5 per cent. The average return from holding the almost risk-less government consols was 3.5 per cent. These rates are of relevance in discounting the social value of an investment return, but are too low for use in appraising a project financed for private gain where the risks are greater. A guide to business interest rates is provided by both the legal ceiling of six per cent that prevailed throughout British Colonial America and the

Table 10.2   Cost–benefit analysis of Senhouse's and Edwards' plantation proposals

	Dominica	Dominica	Jamaica I	Jamaica I	Jamaica II	Jamaica II
	(A) 5% discount rate	*(B) 10% discount rate*	*(A) 5% discount rate*	*(B) 10% discount rate*	*(A) 5% discount rate*	*(B) 10% discount rate*
Present value of gross costs	£6,422	£5,148	£15,250	£12,138	£17,012	£13,254
Present value of gross revenue	£10,633	£6,256	£34,853	£19,806	£46,202	£27,780
Cost–benefit ratio	1.66	1.22	2.29	1.63	2.72	2.10
Net present value	£4,210	£1,092	£19,601	£7,573	£29,395	£14,517
Years to achieve positive incremental benefits	11	15	9	11	7	8

Sources: see text.

Note: Jamaica I utilizes Edwards' data from Table 1; Jamaica II includes an estimate of slave mortality and substitutes market prices far Edwards' expected average annual price.

evidence of Benjamin Franklin that effective market rates in Philadelphia (the largest commercial centre in the colonies) during the second half of the eighteenth century ranged from six to ten per cent. These rates, and the profits of sugar planting reported by Ward, suggest plausible upper and lower bounds within which the appropriate discount rate should be located.[45] Accordingly, two estimates of the cost–benefit ratio and net-present worth were calculated, using discount rates of five and ten per cent respectively. The results are presented in Table 10.2.

In Table 10.2 the first four columns report the results of cost–benefit appraisal using the data provided by Senhouse and Edwards. The calculations reveal that both undertakings were viable on the basis of the data submitted by each author, but that conditions on Jamaica during the 1790s were far more favourable than they had been on Dominica 20 years earlier. In both cases, however, the gestation period before each plantation generated a positive return was higher than that anticipated by either Senhouse or Edwards. The assumption that normal growing conditions and attractive prices would prevail over a long run of years, therefore, exposed each project to risks. In practice, cultivators had to face both climatic variation and price volatility that could cripple production and saddle a plantation with debts. Drought, for example, was a major worry that could reduce the coffee harvest and also result in short provisions, obliging the overseer to purchase necessities for the support of the workforce from off the property. Spencer McKay described how droughts in Demerara, at the close of the eighteenth century, ruined the coffee blossom and wrecked the plantain harvest, obliging him to expend £2,500 on provisions for his two plantations. It could take several seasons for a property to recover from a setback like this.[46] Senhouse's failure to consider risks of this nature were to cost him dear. Lowther Hall Plantation proved a grave disappointment to its owner and by the end of 1777 Senhouse was reflecting that in view of 'the constant expense attending it, without any tolerable return, I am almost inclin'd to wish I could in any reasonable way get rid of the whole concern'.[47] Even before Senhouse had finished laying out his capital, a rise in European food prices, combined with the imposition of import restrictions in the single largest market of the German territories, plunged the coffee trade into depression. Apart from a brief interruption during the latter stages of the Seven Years War (1756–63), coffee prices had been generally favourable since the late 1740s. French coffee imported into Nantes from Martinique and St Domingue, for example, consistently fetched above 50 sols per lb between 1740 and 1765. During the later 1760s, the price rose above 60 sols and between 1770 and 1772 prices increased further and breached 75 sols. This peak, however, was succeeded by a precipitous decline. By the end of 1773, coffee had slipped to 45 sols, and prices kept on falling to record 35 sols in 1775. In the same year local conditions on Dominica proved diabolical: violent gales and torrential rain destroyed half of the island's coffee crop. Prices hit rock bottom at 31 sols per lb, in 1776, and failed to recover to above 50 sols until 1783. On top of these woes, Dominica was reoccupied by the French from 1778 until the end of the War of the American Revolution (1776–1783). The appraised value of Lowther Hall tumbled in step with these events. On 1 January 1776 the plantation was still valued at £4,500, but by 1782 its worth had more than halved to a mere £2,000.[48] Senhouse's bitter experiences were shared by other planters on the colony who had similarly miscalculated. A petition drawn up seeking government relief during the depression of the 1770s recounted how 'many of your subjects led by the most favourable accounts and opinions of the fertility of the soil were induced to become purchasers buoyed up with the flattering hopes that they were thereby laying a foundation for benefits to themselves and the commercial interest of their country'. This account goes on to emphasize how settlers underestimated the costs of clearing land and constructing roads, bid up land values to unprofitable levels in the expectation of continuing high coffee prices, and experienced further difficulties in cultivation that arose out of inadequate land surveys and a basic unfamiliarity with the crop itself. The hardship experienced by planters are reflected in the decline in coffee works and switch to sugar cultivation on the ceded islands in the aftermath of the Seven Years War and which became more marked during the 1770s.[49]

Edwards' estimate was also compiled in the anticipation of an especially favourable period for Jamaican coffee producers. In contrast to Senhouse, however, his predictions of a continuing boom were to prove better founded. The average London sale price of Jamaican ordinary coffee (exclusive of duty) rose from 142s. per cwt, 1790–94, to 239s., 1795–1800, and remained at or above 200s. for more than five years. After 1809, however, prices collapsed to average just 66s, 1810–14, as the Continental Blockade cut off European markets and caused a chronic glut of coffee. Though prices briefly revived between 1814 and 1823, the long-term trend was downwards because of competition from newly acquired colonial possessions. Jamaican producers, moreover, began to suffer from soil exhaustion and erosion and between 1805 and 1815 some 78 plantations were abandoned.[50] During periods of depression the coffee planters most likely to survive were those able to raise mortgages on their properties or to fall back on alternative sources of income. In the case of both Dominica and Jamaica, many small producers were driven out of the industry and their slaves redeployed on to sugar estates, with all the attendant upheavals for the slave population.[51] A planter who established his property in 1793, however, escaped the worst of these woes. The final two columns of Table 10.2 adjust the farm price supplied by Edwards by an index of London market prices in order to obtain a more realistic flow of discounted revenue during the period 1793 to 1818. The rest of the data is the same as in Table 10.1, except that the calculation has been modified to incorporate an estimate of the cost of replacing slaves under the assumption of an annual slave mortality rate of 2.5 per cent.[52] Table 10.2 reports a rise in both the cost–benefit ratio and net-present worth, as well as a reduction in the number of seasons required before the property generated a positive benefit. Though still an approximation of actual performance, these estimates reiterate how propitious a time the early nineteenth century was to establish a coffee plantation. Nonetheless, the review of prices above emphasizes that the window of opportunity was short-lived and after 1810 the Jamaican coffee industry moved from boom to bust with remarkable swiftness.

Coffee planting in the British West Indies during the period of slavery was an uncertain and quasi-permanent secondary activity that was capable of heaping riches or ruin upon its practitioners. Senhouse's plan was conceived on the eve of a calamitous slump; Edwards' at the start of a powerful upswing. The boom and bust nature of the industry reflected the fact that growth was largely the outcome of a response to opportunities generated by war and revolution within the Caribbean region as a whole. In the case of the ceded islands of Dominica, Grenada and St Vincent coffee growing attracted relatively few British white settlers. According to the Grenada census of 1772 and a map of Dominica produced in 1776 giving estate details, the coffee cultivators were for the most part made up of French settlers choosing to remain on the islands after they passed to Britain, many of whom held their land as small-holding tenants.[53] The acquisition of the ceded islands was rapidly accompanied by a shift in the composition of their exports away from coffee towards sugar, though the process was slower on Dominica where the knowledge that Dominica would be a key target in any future war held back heavy investment in sugar.[54] In Jamaica, following the revolution in St Domingue, the greater part of the coffee cultivators consisted of whites of lesser social standing, many of whom derived income from serving the sugar complex.[55] Coffee's relatively low set-up costs provided an opportunity for persons of modest means to establish plantations far more easily than was the case with sugar. In contrast to the ceded islands, a sample of planters' inventories reveals no instances of coffee growers with French surnames, indicating that the role played by refugees from St Domingue in building up Jamaican production was small.[56] A strong commitment by elements of the island's white population to the crop, however, was insufficient to sustain Jamaican coffee boom. In view of the tax system in place and the body of commercial laws that regulated imperial trade, the position of coffee as a British Caribbean staple was bound to remain precarious. The experiences of coffee planters in the BWI, therefore, lends support to William's sugar-orientated model of Caribbean development during the two centuries after 1640 and provides a graphic illustration of the extent to which the cultivators of a minor staple were heavily influenced by the system of navigation laws that grew up around the dominant staple.

Notes

Research for this article was carried out with the assistance of a British Academy Small Personal Research Grant (BA-AN 1392/APN 2170). An earlier version of the paper was presented to the LSE Business History Unit seminar and the XXIX Conference of the Association of Caribbean Historians, Martinique. The author acknowledges the comments of an anonymous referee, but accepts responsibility for any remaining errors.

1   Ralph Davis, *The Rise of the Atlantic Economics* (London, 1973), p. 261. Davis does not give his source, but the figures are similar to those reported in Edward Long, *The History of Jamaica* (3 vols; London, 1774), vol.i, p. 517.

2   Eric Williams, *Capitalism and Slavery* (London, 1964), pp. 85–97; Hilary McD. Beckles, '"The Williams Effect": Eric Williams' *Capitalism and Slavery* and the Growth of West Indian Political Economy' in Barbara L. Solow and Stanley L. Engerman (eds.), *British Capitalism and Caribbean Slavery: The Legacy of Eric Williams* (Cambridge, 1987), pp. 303–12; B.W. Higman, 'Economic and Social Development of the British West Indies, From Settlement to ca. 1850', in Stanley L. Engerman and Robert E. Gallman (eds.), *The Cambridge Economic History of the United Shares, volume 1, The Colonial Era* (Cambridge, 1996), pp. 300, 307, 310–15, 324–26.

3   The description of sugar enjoying a 'golden age' and 'silver age' was originally made in Richard Pares', 'Merchants and Planters', *Economic History Review*, Supplement No. 4 (Cambridge, 1960), p. 40. For an analysis of rising demand for sugar in eighteenth-century Britain, see David Richardson, 'The Slave Trade, Sugar and Economic Growth, 1748–1776', *Journal of Interdisciplinary History*, Vol.XXIV (1987).

4   The best general explanation of the rise of sugar remains Robert C. Batie, 'Why Sugar? Economic Cycles and the Changing of Staples in the English and French Antilles, 1624–54', *Journal of Caribbean History*, Vols.8–9 (1976). Jamaican historians have argued that linkages generated between sugar and other sectors, particularly livestock farming, may have been more extensive than Williams and others have suggested; see Verene Shepherd, 'Livestock and Sugar: Aspects of Jamaica's Agricultural Development from the Late Seventeenth to the Early Nineteenth Century', *Historical Journal*, Vol.34 (1991), pp. 631–3.

5   Jürgen Schneider, 'The Effects on European Markets of Imports of Overseas Agriculture: the Production, Trade and Consumption of Coffee (15th to 18th Century)', in José C. Pardo (ed.), *Economic Effects of the European Expansion* (Stuttgart, 1992), pp. 293–4.

6   House of Lords Record Office, Large Parchment Collection, 831–42, customs ledger for Christmas 1693 to Christmas 1694. This source records an isolated shipment of 28 lb.

7   James Douglas, *Arbor Yemensis fructum Cofe ferens, or; a Description and History of the Coffee Tree* (London, 1727), pp. 20, 22.

8   D.W. Rodriquez, *Coffee: a Short Economic History with Special Reference to Jamaica* (Ministry of Agriculture and Lands, Commodity Bulletin No.2; Kingston, Jamaica, 1961), p. 13. According to Rodriquez, the coffee seedlings originated from Martinique but Clinton V. Black gives their origin as Hispaniola in his *History of Jamaica* (London, 1965), p. 82.

9   'Petition of Several Planters . . . of Jamaica', 2 March, 1731, reprinted in F.R. Augier and Shirley C. Gordon, *Sources of West Indian History* (Longman; London, 1962), p. 62; Benjamin Moseley, *A Treatise Concerning the Properties and Effects of Coffee* (1785; 5th (ed.), J. Sewell, London, 1792), p. xv; Leo Francis Stock, (ed.), *Proceedings and Debates of the British Parliament Respecting North America*, 5 vols, (Carnegie Institution of Washington; Washington D.C., 1927–1937), Vol.iv, pp. 149–152, 166 Romney Sedgwick, *The House of Commons, 1715–1754* (HMSO, London, 1970), Vol.ii, p. 341; Jacob M. Price, *Parry of London: A Family and a Firm on the Chesapeake Frontier, 1615–1753* (Cambridge, Mass., 1992), pp. 75, 169.

10 Stock, *Proceedings and Debates*, pp. 151–2.

11 John J. McCusker *Rum and the American Revolution: The Rum Trade and the Balance of Payments of the Thirteen Continental Colonies* (New York, 1989), p. 712.

12 See Lawrence H. Gipson, *The British Isles and the American Colonies* (3 vols., New York, 1936), Vol.2, pp. 191–2.

13 5 Geo. 11. C.24. The act originally granted the preferential rate of duty for a period of four years, but the legislation was subsequently renewed and extended.

14 Patrick Browne, *The Civil and Natural History of Jamaica* (London, 1756), p. 14. Rodriguez, *Coffee*, p. 24, gives export figures of 53,225 lb, 1737–44, and 37,343 lb, 1745–1751, without specifying a source. Possibly his export figures are derived from Browne using a conversion rate of 200 lb to the cask.

15 Thibault de Chanvalon, *Voyage à la Martinique* (Paris, 1753), p. 17; Louis-Philippe May, *Histoire Économique de la Martinique, 1635–1763* (Paris, 1930), p. 22; Michel-Rolph *Trouillot, Peasants and Capital: Dominica at the World Economy* (Baltimore, 1988), p. 54; Cornelius Ch. Goslinga, *The Dutch in the Caribbean and in the Guianas, 1680–1791* (Maastricht, 1985), pp. 327–8; R.M.N. Pandy, *Agriculture in Surinam, 1650–1950: an Enquiry into the Causes of its Decline* (Amsterdam, 1959), pp, 19–20; Johannes Postma, 'The Fruits of Slave Labour: Tropical Commodities from Surinam to Holland, 1683–1794', in Maxine Berg (ed.), *Oceanic Trade, Colonial Wares and Industrial Development, 1600–1800, Eleventh International Economic History Conference* [n.p.] (mimeo, Milan, 1994). The Jamaican export figures are from Rodriquez, *Coffee*, p. 24 (where again no source is given), and PRO CO 142/15, 18, Jamaican naval officer's lists.

16 E.B. Schumpeter *English Overseas Trade Statistics, 1696–1808* (Oxford, 1960), p. 60.

17 L.J. Ragatz, *Statistics for the Study of British Caribbean Economic History, 1763–1833* (London, 1927), p. 14.

18 The Abbé Raynal [*A Philosophical and Political History of the Settlements and Trade of the Europeans in the East and West Indies* (4 vols; Dublin, 1776; originally published in French, Paris 1774) estimated Caribbean output c. 1775 at 88 million lb and exports from Jamaica and the Ceded Islands at 4.6 million lb. Raynel's estimates are conveniently tabulated in Peter B. Brown, *In Praise of Hot Liquors: The Study of Chocolate, Coffee and Tea–Drinking, 1600–1850* (York, 1995), p. 101. Shipments from British colonies, however, included an unknown amount of coffee that originated from the French Antilles and which passed through the free port system (see also next note). Raynal's data tellies with modern estimates of exports from Surinam, Martinique, St Domingue and with the British customs accounts.

19 PRO CO 137/69, 'Copy of a Memorial to the Lords of the Treasury'; Berkshire Record Office, Trumbull Add. MSS, 141, 'Present State of the British Colonies in America; Richard B. Sheridan, 'From Chattel to Wage Slavery in Jamaica, 1740–1860', *Slavery and Abolition*, Vol.14 (1993). pp. 14–15.

20 B.W. Higman, *Jamaica Surveyed: Plantation Maps and Plans of the Eighteenth and Nineteenth Centuries* (Institute of Jamaica Publications, 1988), pp. 159–91.

21 PRO CO 142/15, 18, Jamaican navel officer's lists. In comparison, North American demand accounted for a mere 7 per cent of Grenada's exports of 1.5 million lb between 1766 and 1767 (PRO CO 106/1, Grenadian navel officer's lists).

22 See S.D. Smith, 'Accounting for Taste: British Coffee Consumption in Historical Perspective', *Journal of Interdisciplinary History*, Vol.XXVII (1996), pp. 212–14.

23 House of Lords Record Office, Main Papers, fol.2493–2494.

24 The analogy of the 'level playing field' has a long history of use by lobbyists. Robert Nicol, for example, argued it was not until Huskisson's duty reduction of 1825, 'that Coffee was admitted in this country to the field of fair competition: that field which in Germany, France, and other parts of the Continent, it has held for more than a century', *A Treatise on Coffee* (London. 1831), p. 17.

25 This aspect of the navigation system has been intensively studied, mainly from the perspective of the tobacco trade. For a summary of the debate, see Larry Sawyers, 'The Navigation Acts revisited', *Economic History Review*, Vol.XLV (1992), pp. 262–84.

26 Phillip R.P. Coelho, 'The Profitability of Imperialism: the British Experience in the West Indies', *Explorations in Economic History*, Vol.X (1972), pp. 260–7; Smith, 'Accounting for Taste', pp. 203–5.

27 It is likely, however, that much of the rise in the price of sugar was capitalized into the price of cane fields which were not used to grow coffee, but any extension of sugar production on to marginal land suited to minor staples would have affected coffee. For further

elaboration of these themes see, Smith, 'Accounting for Taste', pp. 183–214. In addition to the lowering of duties by the British parliament, the Jamaica legislature experimented with bounties to encourage production in 1773 and 1776, Edward Braithwaite, *The Development of Creole Society in Jamaica, 1770–1820* (Oxford. 1971), pp. 80–1, 147.

28 Jamaica Archives, 1B/11/5, Accounts Current. As well as the problem of representativeness, these accounts record only contingencies (such as the purchase of provisions in times of scarcity) or certain regular payments (such as mortgages). Expenditure maintaining buildings and the works are excluded, as are costs incurred extending cultivation on to new grounds.

29 Bryan Edwards, *The History, Civil and Commercial, of the British Colonies in the West Indies* (2 volumes, Dublin, 1793), Vol.ii, pp. 286–8; Cumbria Record Office, Senhouse Muniments. D/Sen, Joseph Senhouse and the West Indies, 'Plantation Estimates'. Joseph Senhouse was appointed comptroller of customs at Roseau, in 1774, and customs collector at Barbados, in 1776. As a customs official Senhouse was barred from engaging in trade, but was permitted to ship produce from his own properties. Senhouse's plantation was named 'Lowther Hall' in honour of the family patron Sir James Lowther, for whom he acted as political agent on his return to England, in 1782. For further biographical details see, Edward Hughes. *North Country Life in the Eighteenth Century* (2 vols; 1952–1965), Vol.II, pp. 334–54; Richard B. Sheridan, 'Material Relating to the West Indies from the Senhouse Papers, 1762–1831', in W.E. Minchinton (ed.), *British Records Relating of America in Microform* (Wakefield, 1977); James C. Brandow, 'The Senhouse Papers', *The Journal of the Barbados Museum and Historical Society*, Vol.XXXVII (1985).

30 The overseer William Adlam wrote from Hermitage Plantation, in Apri 1820, that the works badly needed a new mill, mill house, kitchen and wash house: 'the old mill is in a very bad condition, scarcely able to take off the crop, and having no house over it; when it rains and some time after it, we cannot make use of it'. There appears to have been no general fund set aside to meet the task of rebuilding, however, for Adlam conceded that the tasks, 'must be done as the property can afford the means and time' (National Library of Jamaica, MS. 250, Hermitage Plantation Letter book [n.p.], Adlam to Wemys, 12 April 1820).

31 Financial constraints, rather than ecological considerations, may have prevented a greater proportion of the Dominica plantation from being planted in coffee, as Senhouse wrote in July 1772 that 'I intend cultivating as much of it as I possibly can, as far as my finances will go.' Later, in August, he noted that 50 acres were being cultivated, 'with this additional advantage that as I am able to settle the above with my own money, I can therefore send the produce to what market I please', Carlisle Record Office, D/Sen, Joseph Senhouse Letter and Memorandum Book, fols.12–13.

32 PRO CO 101/18, 'State of the Parishes in the Island of Grenada', April, 1772. The 158 monoculture covered a mean area of 114.5 acres and possessed a mean coffee acreage of 66.7 acres; the 23 largest properties covered a mean area of 302.5 acres and possessed a mean coffee acreage of 138.2 acres. Land not planted in coffee was mostly left in woodland or used for pasture.

33 B.W. Higman, *Slave Population and Economy in Jamaica, 1807–1834*, p. 224.

34 John J. McCusker, 'How Much is That in Real Money? A Historical Price Index for Use as a Deflator of Money Values in the Economy of the United States', *Proceedings of the American Antiquarian Society*, Vol.101 (1991), pp. 342–3.

35 Edwards also notes that bushes raised from old roots yielded on average 300 lb per acre in their second year, 500 lb in their second and between 600 and 700 lb in their fourth and subsequent years. Coffee raised from seedlings, however, yielded nothing in the first three years, 700 lb in the fourth and 750 lb in the fifth year, Edwards, *History, Civil and Commercial*, Vol.II, pp. 279–281; P.J. Laborie, *The Coffee Planter of Saint Domingo* (London, 1797), p. 152.

36 These were the standard payment terms set by the Crown Commissioners charged with disposing of lands by public sale, Thomas Atwood, *The History of the Island of Dominica* (1791; rpt. Frank Cass, 1971). pp. 2–3.

37 Jamaica Archives, 1B/11/4, Inventories, libers 119 fol.80, libers 126 fol.191.

38 Coffee land was reported to vary in value in 1807 from £20 per acre for best land to 6–8s. an acre for land lying distant from established roads, *House of Commons Sessional Papers*, III (1807), pp. 41–2.

39 Emilia Viotti da Costa, *Crowns of Glory, Tears of Blood: the Demerara Slave Rebellion of 1823* (Oxford, 1994), 47; Henry Bolingbroke, *A Voyage to Demerary, 1799–1806* (1807; rpt. Demerara, 1947), p. 177; John Lowndes, *The Coffee-Planter* (London, 1807), p. 70; Luborie. *Coffee Planter*, p. 152; Moseley, *Treatise*, pp. xvii–xviii; Browne, *Natural and Civil History*, p. 162; Edwards, *History, Civil and Commercial*, Vol.ii, pp. 279–281; Chetham's Library, Manchester, MS. 2,168 (bound with *A Narrative of Affairs Lately Received from His Majesty's Island of Jamaica*), 'A Letter on the Advantages of Cultivating Coffee and Cocoa on the British Sugar Islands' [n.d.]. The ratio in the latter tract is repeated in Moseley, *Treatise*, XVIII. Long states that, 'eight Negroes are equal to clean and gather from fifty to sixty acres, and upwards, according to the bearing of the trees . . . I have known a man, with two assistants, manage a walk of thirty acres, besides attending other work', *History of Jamaica*, p. 685. This estimate may not be far out of line with the others, given the small percentage of total acreage planted in coffee.

40 The data presented here question the placing of coffee (with cotton) between the limits set by sugar and rice in staples cultivation by Philip U. Morgan. 'Task and Gang Systems: The Organisation of Labour on New World Plantations', in Stephen Innes (ed.), *Work and Labour in Early America* (North Caroline, 1988), p. 205.

41 Lownes, *Coffee-Planter*, pp. 17–18. Another practical account of planting in the French Antilles, not based on Laborie, notes that, 'l'opinion général des lles de France et de Bourbon, est que l'on doit placer les plants de Café è sept pieds et demi de distance en tout sens; mais cette distance doit cependant être subornnée à la nature du sol et à la force qu'il donna à la végétation (M. Buc'hoz, *Dissertations sur l'Utilite et les Bons et Mauvais effects du Tabac, du Café, du Cacao, et du Thé* [Paris, 1788], p. 53).

42 Between 1770 and 1774 the free on board (fob) price of coffee imported into Great Britain was £3.4 per cwt of 112 lb, whereas in 1779 Dominican coffee was being sold in London exclusive of taxation, but inclusive of insurance and freight, at £3.06 per cwt of 112 lb. Over the period 1791–96 Jamaica ordinary coffee sold in London net of duty, inclusive of insurance and freight, for £7.62 per cwt of 112 lb, *The London Price Current*, Guildhall Library, London; A.D. Gayer, W.W. Rostow, A.J. Schwartz, *The Growth and Fluctuation of the British Economy, 1790–1850* (Oxford, 1953), microfilm supplement, p. 777; Thomas Tooke, *A History of Prices and of the State of the Circulalion* (2 vols; London, 1838), Vol.ii, p. 399.

43 Moseley, *Treatise*, p. xix; Higman, *Slave Population*, p. 217; J.R. Ward, 'The Profitability of suger Planting in the British West Indies', *Economic History Review*, Vol.XXXI (1978), pp. 210–13. The highest recorded rate of return was 28.4 per cent for Hillsborough, Dominica, and Cane Garden, St Vincent.

44 Laborie, *Coffee Planter*, p. 108. Senhouse took out a 40-year lease on his property, indicating a long time horizon.

45 R.P. Thomas, 'The Sugar Colonies of the Old Empire: Profit or Loss for Great Britain?', *Economic History Review*, Vol.XXI (1968), p. 34; Sidney Homer, *A History of Interest Rates* (New Brunswick, 1963), pp. 274–9. In 1775 Senhouse took out a mortgage of £700 on Lowther Hall at 6 per cent interest.

46 National Library of Jamaica, MS 250, Hermitage Plantation Letter book, William Adlam to John Wemys, 30 January 1822; Library of the University of the West Indies, Mona, Jamaica, Copybook of business letters written from Demerera–British Guiana, 1798–1800, McKay to Gordon and Hamilton August 1798, fols. 39, 42. Drought reduced the size of the Hermitage crop to just 40 casks, from its normal 80 to 100 casks, while McKay predicted that drought would reduce the coffee crop in Demerara to a quarter of its ordinary level.

47 Carlisle Record Office, D/Sen, Letter and Memorandum Book, fol.101.

48 Jean Tarrade, *Le Commerce Colonial de la France* (2 vols; Paris, 1972), Vol.II pp. 771–2; Carlisle Record Office, D/Sen, Waste Book, 1776–1778. The inventory values the estate at £11,607 15s. in 1776, but this figure includes Senhouse's salary as customs controller

of £500 sterling, capitalized at 25 years' purchase (£4,125 currency). In late December, 1775, 60 acres were planted in coffee, but only 10 seasoned slaves and a Malayan boy were living on the property. As noted earlier, by this time the estate was carrying a mortgage of £700 (sterling).

49 PRO, CO 71/6, 'The Address, Memorial and Humble Petition of the Representatives of the People of Dominica', fol.42. On the decline of coffee in the ceded islands, see Smith, 'Accounting for Taste' p. 204.

50 Gayer, Rostow and Schwartz, *Fluctuations*, pp. 777–8; Tooke, *History of Prices*, p. 399; B.W. Higman, 'Jamaican Coffee Plantations, 1780–1860: A Cartographic Analysis', *Caribbean Geography*, Vol.2 (1986), p. 74.

51 A few examples of coffee planters raising mortgages from London merchants are documented. William Mackintosh, owner of Digue and Richmond plantations on Grenada valued at £21,600, raised a montage of £4,000 from John Crawley in November, 1772 (Bedford County Record Office, Crawley Muniments, CI526). Absentee Jamaica proprietor Archibald Ingram raised £4,000 from John Mills and Sherland Swanson in 1776 by mortgaging two coffee plantations in St Patrick's of 90 and 53 acres, containing 53 slaves (Essex Record Office, D/DA/T575).

52 Price data are from Gayer, Rostow and Schwartz, *Fluctuations*, pp. 777–8; the estimate of slave mortality is taken from Higman, *Slave Population*, p. 123.

53 Patrick L. Baker, *Centring the Periphery: Chaos, Order and the Ethnohistory of Dominica* (University of the West Indies, 1994), pp. 62–5.

54 Dominica was occupied by French forces under the Marquis Duchillean during the American Revolutionary War.

55 S.D. Smith, 'Coffee and "the Poorer Sort of People" in Jamaica during the Period of Slavery', *Plantation Society in the Americas* (forthcoming).

56 This finding is consistent with the view that refugees setting permanently in Jamaica were few in number and mainly composed of the more affluent planters from the south coast who already had links with Jamaica. See David P. Geggus, *Slavery, War and Revolution: The British Occupation of Saint Domingue, 1793–1798* (Oxford, 1982), pp. 272–4.

Chapter 11

Philip D. Morgan

WORK AND CULTURE

The task system and the world of lowcountry
blacks, 1700 to 1800

Who built Thebes of the seven Gates?
In the books stand the names of Kings.
Did they then drag up the rock-slabs?
And Babylon so often destroyed,
Who kept rebuilding it?
In which houses did the builders live
In gold-glittering Lima?
Where did the brick-layers go
The evening the Great Wall of China was finished?
. . .

Even in legendary Atlantis
Didn't the drowning shout for their slaves
As the ocean engulfed it?
. . .

So many reports
So many questions.

Bertolt Brecht, 1939

WITHIN THE REALM OF SLAVERY STUDIES there has been a
pronounced preoccupation with the external or institutional aspects of the
slave system. Despite repeated clarion calls for investigations of life in the slave
quarters, little scholarly attention has been directed to the domestic economy of
the slaves, their work routines, their attitudes toward resource allocation, their
attempts to accumulate, and their patterns of consumption.[1] This academic short-
sightedness is more easily identified than remedied. Attitudes toward work and
patterns of work constitute an area of inquiry that sprawls awkwardly across academic demarcations: the subject is all too easily neglected.[2] In addition, the genre
to which this type of history is most akin, namely, labor history, often suffers from
its own myopia: studies that begin by aiming to uncover the experience of workers
can all too readily focus instead on management priorities.[3] Moreover, what has
been said with respect to the English farm laborer applies even more forcefully to

the Afro-American slave: "No one has written his signature more plainly across the countryside; but no one has left more scanty records of his achievements."[4]

Mindful of these difficulties and pitfalls, this article accepts the challenge posed by Brecht's questions: it attempts to bring history closer to the central concerns of ordinary people's lives—in this case, the lives of Afro-American slaves in the lowcountry region of South Carolina and Georgia. In this light, perhaps the most distinctive and central feature of lowcountry slave life was the task system. In Lewis Gray's words, "Under the task system the slave was assigned a certain amount of work for the day, and after completing the task he could use his time as he pleased," whereas under the gang system, prevalent in most Anglo-American plantation societies, "slaves were worked in groups under the control of a driver or leader . . . and the laborer was compelled to work the entire day."[5] While previous commentators have drawn attention to the task system, few have explored how this peculiarity arose and how it structured the world of those who labored under it. In order to shed light on the first matter, I shall open three windows onto different phases in the development of this labor arrangement: its origins in the first half of the eighteenth century, its routinization during the Revolutionary era, and its full flowering by the time of the Civil War. I shall also explore the ramifications of the task system for the slaves by analyzing its most distinctive feature so far as they were concerned: the opportunities it provided for working on their own behalf once the stipulated task had been completed.[6] I shall argue, then, that a particular mode of labor organization and a particular domestic economy evolved simultaneously in the colonial and antebellum lowcountry.[7]

This argument can best be secured by broadening our horizons to take in not only colonial and early national developments but also those of the antebellum and even postbellum years. On the one hand, such a strategy will show how colonial developments bore directly on nineteenth- and even twentieth-century realities. To take a minor example, the basic task unit still current in the minds of freedmen in the 1930s will be shown to have had a precise colonial origin. On the other hand, the opportunities that the task system presented slaves can be understood only in the light of mid-nineteenth-century experiences. To take a more significant example, the resemblance between the experiences of some lowcountry slaves and of the protopeasants found among the slaves of certain Caribbean plantation societies emerges most clearly from a glance at the behavior of slaves and freedmen in the years surrounding the Civil War.[8] In other words, to understand the evolution of the task system and its concomitant domestic economy, we shall need a telescope rather than a microscope.

I

If the Negroes are skilful and industrious, they
plant something for themselves after the day's work.
Johann Bolzius, 1751

The earliest, fragmentary descriptions of work practices in the lowcountry rice economy indicate that a prominent characteristic of the task system—a sharp division between the master's "time" and the slave's "time"—was already in place.

In the first decade of the eighteenth century the clergy of South Carolina complained that slaves were planting "for themselves as much as will cloath and subsist them and their famil[ies]." During the investigation of a suspected slave conspiracy in mid-century, a lowcountry planter readily acknowledged that one of his slaves had planted rice "in his own time" and could do with it as he wished.[9] The most acute observer of early work practices, Johann Bolzius, described how slaves, after "their required day's work," were "given as much land as they can handle" on which they planted corn, potatoes, tobacco, peanuts, sugar and water melons, and pumpkins and bottle pumpkins.[10] The opportunity to grow such a wide range of provisions on readily available land owed much to the early establishment and institutionalization of the daily work requirement. By mid-century the basic "task" unit had been set at a quarter of an acre. Moreover, other activities, outside of the rice field, were also tasked: in pounding the rice grain, slaves were "tasked at seven Mortars for one day," and in providing fences lowcountry slaves were expected to split 100 poles of about twelve feet in length (a daily "task" that remained unchanged throughout the slave era, as Table 11.1 indicates).[11] These tasks were not, of course, easily accomplished, and occasionally planters exacted even higher daily requirements; but, as Bolzius noted, the advantage to the slaves of having a daily goal was that they could, once it was met, "plant something for themselves."[12]

A tried and tested model of labor organization—the gang system practiced on both tobacco and sugar plantations—was available when lowcountry planters discovered their own plantation staple. In fact, many of the first immigrants were from Barbados, where they must have had direct experience of operating gangs of slaves.[13] Why did they and others decide to adopt a new system? U. B. Phillips claimed that temporary absenteeism was responsible: "The necessity of the master's moving away from his estate in the warm months, to escape the malaria, involved the adoption of some system of routine which would work with more or less automatic regularity without his own inspiring or impelling presence." However, while absenteeism may have contributed to the attractiveness of this system, it seems an insufficiently powerful agent to account for its inception. The example of Caribbean sugar production is pertinent here; if the withdrawal of an inspiring master encouraged the development of tasking, why did not sugar planters in the West Indies, where absenteeism began relatively early, adopt the system?[14]

The absence of masters may be an unconvincing explanation for the development of a task system, but perhaps the presence of particular slaves can serve in its place. Peter H. Wood and Daniel C. Littlefield have pointed out that some black immigrants to early South Carolina were already familiar with the techniques of rice cultivation.[15] These slaves' expertise, it might be argued, accounts for the evolution of a system that would operate more or less automatically. It has even been suggested, in this regard, that a work pattern of alternating bouts of intense labor and idleness tends to occur wherever men are to some degree in control of their own working lives (need one look any further than authors?).[16] By displaying their own understanding of the basic requirements of rice cultivation, lowcountry slaves might have gained a measure of control over their lives, at least to the extent of determining the length of their working days. While this is an attractive argument, it is not without problems. The coastal regions that seem to have supplied a majority of slaves to early South Carolina were not rice-producing areas; lowcountry whites have left no record of valuing the knowledge of rice planting

Table 11.1 Tasking requirements, *c.*1750 to *c.*1860

Representative tasks		*1750s*[1]	*1770s*[2]	*1820s*[3]	*1830s*[4]	*1840*[5]	*1850s–1860s*[6]
Rice	Turning up land	¼a		¼a	¼a	¼a–½a	¼a
	Trenching/covering	½a		¾a	¾a	¾a	½a
	First hoeing	¼a		¼a–½a	½a	½a	¼–½a
	Second hoeing				½a	½a	
	Third hoeing	½a			¾a	20c	
	Reaping					¾a	¾a
	Threshing			600s	600s	600s	600s
	Pounding	7m					
	Ditching			600sf	700sf	500sf	600sf
Cotton	Listing			¼a	¼a	½a	¼–½a
	Bedding			¼a	¼a	⅜a	¼–½a
	Hoeing			½a	½a	½a	½a
	Picking			90–100lbs	70–100lbs		
	Assorting			30–50lbs	60lbs		
	Ginning			20–30lbs	30lbs		20–30lbs
	Moting			30–50lbs	30lbs		
General	Splitting rails	100	100	100	100		100–125
	Squaring timber		100′	100′	100′		100′

Sources: [1] "Bolzius Answers a Questionnaire," trans. and ed. Loewald *et al.*, *WMQ*, 3d Ser., XIV (1957), 258; Garden to the Royal Society, Apr. 20, 1755, Guard Book 1, 36. [2] John Gerar William De Brahm, *Report of the General Survey in the Southern District of North America*, ed. Louis De Vorsey, Jr. (Columbia, S.C., 1971), 94. [3] "Estimate of the Daily Labour of Negroes," *American Farmer*, V (1823–1824), 319–320; [Edwin C. Holland], *A Refutation of the Calumnies Circulated against . . . Slavery . . .* (New York, 1969 [orig. publ. Charleston, S.C., 1822]), 53; Basil Hall, *Travels in North America in the Years 1827 and 1828*, III (London, 1829), 219–223. [4] "A Memorandum of Tasks," *Southern Agriculturalist*, VII (1834), 297–299; W. H. Capers, "On the Culture of Sea-Island Cotton," *ibid.*, VIII (1835), 402–411. [5] Edmund Ruffin, *Report of the Commencement and Progress of the Agricultural Survey of South-Carolina for 1843* (Columbia, S.C., 1843), 118; J. A. Turner, *The Cotton Planter's Manual* (New York, 1865), 285. [6] Frederick Law Olmsted, *A Journey in the Seabord Slave States . . .* (New York, 1968 [orig. publ. 1856]), 434–435; Francis S. Holmes, *Southern Farmer and Market Gardener* (Charleston, S.C., 1852), 234–236; Weehaw Plantation Book, 1855–1861, South Carolina Historical Society, Charleston; "Tasks for Negroes," *Southern Cultivator*, XVIII (1860), 247; Col. A. J. Willard to W. H. Smith, Nov. 13, 1865 (A7011); testimony of Harry McMillan, 1863 (K78) (see below, n. 81 for explanation of these notations); J. A. Turner, *The Cotton Planter's Manual*, 133–135. See also George P. Rawick, ed., *The American Slave: A Composite Autobiography* (Westport, Conn., 1972), II, Pt. ii, 302, III, Pt. iii, 92, Pt. iv, 117.

Notes: a = acre; s = sheaves; m = mortars; c = compasses; sf = square feet.

that some slaves might have displayed; and familiarity with rice planting is hardly the same as familiarity with irrigated rice culture, practiced in South Carolina from early days.[17] Slaves undoubtedly contributed a great deal to the development of South Carolina's rice economy; but, on present evidence, it would be rash to attribute the development of a task system to their prowess, especially when that prowess went largely unrecognized and may not have been significant.

A consideration of staple-crop requirements provides the most satisfactory, if not complete, answer to the question of the system's origins. The amount of direct supervision demanded by various crops offers at least one clue to the puzzle. Unlike tobacco, which involved scrupulous care in all phases of the production cycle and was therefore best cultivated by small gangs of closely attended laborers, rice was a hardy plant, requiring a few relatively straightforward operations for its successful cultivation.[18] The great expansion of rice culture in seventeenth-century Lombardy, for instance, was predicated not on a stable, sophisticated, and well-supervised labor force but on a pool of transient labor drawn from far afield.[19] Nor did rice production require the strict regimentation and "semi-industrialised" production techniques that attended the cultivation of sugar and necessitated gang labor.[20] However, the Caribbean plantation experience does offer parallels to the lowcountry rice economy: in the British West Indies, crops that required little supervision or regimentation—notably coffee and pimento—were, like rice, grown by a slave labor force organized by tasks rather than into gangs.[21]

In addition to the degree of direct supervision required by a crop, the facility with which the laborers' output could be measured also shaped different forms of labor organization. For example, the productivity of a single coffee and pimento worker could be measured accurately and cheaply, particularly in the harvesting cycle. It was easy to weigh an individual's baskets of coffee or pimento berries, and tasking may have first developed in this stage of the respective crop cycles before being extended to other operations. Conversely, the much larger volumes involved in the cane harvest would have proved far less easy and much more expensive to measure on an individual "task" basis; not surprisingly, gang labor was employed at this and other stages of the sugar cycle.[22] In the case of rice, it was less the harvesting and more the cultivation of the crop that lent itself to inexpensive and efficient measurement. As Phillips pointed out, drainage ditches, which were necessary in lowcountry rice cultivation, provided convenient units by which the performance of tasks could be measured.[23] The ubiquity and long-standing history of the quarter-acre task suggest that the planting and weeding stages of the rice cycle provided the initial rationale for the task system; once tasking became firmly established, it was extended to a whole host of plantation operations.

Thus various staple-crop requirements seem to have served as the most important catalysts for the development of particular modes of labor organization. Undoubtedly other imperatives contributed to the attractiveness of one or the other labor arrangement: absenteeism and the ease with which slaves took to rice cultivation may well have encouraged a more widespread and rapid diffusion of the task system in the lowcountry than might otherwise have been the case. Moreover, once a task system had been tried, tested, and not found wanting, it could be extended to crops that were produced elsewhere by means of gang labor. In other words, once tasking became a way of life, means were found to circumvent the otherwise powerful dictates of the various staple crops.[24]

Whatever the origins of the task system, its consequences soon became apparent. Indeed, the way in which slaves chose to spend their own "time" created unease among ruling South Carolinians. One of the earliest laws relating to slaves, enacted in 1686, prohibited the exchange of goods between slaves or between slaves and freemen without their masters' consent. A decade later, slaves were expressly forbidden from felling and carrying away timber on lands other than their masters'. In 1714 the legislature enacted its stiffest prohibition; slaves were no longer to "plant for themselves any corn, peas or rice."[25] While this stark ban appears definitive, later legislation suggests its ineffectiveness. In 1734, for example, an act for the better regulation of patrols allowed patrollers to confiscate "all fowls and other provisions" found in the possession of "stragling negroes." That slaves produced provisions independently is further implied in a 1738 act for the licensing of hawkers and pedlars, which aimed to stamp out the illicit traffic in rice and provisions between slaves and itinerant traders. By 1751 the legislators bowed to the inevitable. By outlawing the sale of slaves' rice and corn to anybody other than their masters, they were implicitly recognizing the right of slaves to cultivate such crops.[26] The law of 1714 had thus died a natural death.

From the evidence of plantation account books and estate records, the act of 1751 simply brought the law closer into line with social practice. In 1728 Abraham, a Ball family slave, was paid £1 10s. for providing his master with eighteen fowls, while a female slave received £8 for supplying hogs. In 1736 twenty-two Ball family slaves were paid more than £50 for supplying varying amounts of rice to their master.[27] The extent of this trade in provisions was occasionally impressive; over the course of two years, the slaves belonging to James Hartley's estate were paid £124 for supplying 290 bushels of their corn.[28] Henry Ravenel not only purchased his slaves' provision goods, consisting of corn, fowls, hogs, and catfish, but also their canoes, baskets, and myrtle wax.[29]

Masters undoubtedly benefited from these exchanges while displaying their benevolence, but we should not assume that there was no bargaining, however unequal, between the parties. Henry Laurens, for example, advised one of his newly appointed overseers to "purchase of your own Negroes all [the provisions] that you know Lawfully belongs to themselves at the lowest price that they will sell it for."[30] If a master refused to give slaves a fair price for their produce, they could take it elsewhere. One of the most persistent complaints of lowcountry planters and legislators concerned illicit trading across plantation boundaries.[31] A slave who produced rice "in his own time" also traveled more than fifteen miles up the Cooper River to sell a barrel of his crop to his brother, who resided on another plantation.[32] A white boatman, implicated in a slave conspiracy, openly acknowledged that he had exchanged his hog for a slave's deer skin.[33] The records of one lowcountry estate even register payments to a neighboring planter's slaves for their seed rice.[34] In other words, once slaves were allowed to produce provisions, they would always find ways to market them, be it to passing traders, neighboring whites, or fellow slaves.

Lowcountry slaves took the opportunity to raise a wide array of agricultural products, many of which reflected their African background. In the third decade of the eighteenth century Mark Catesby observed two African varieties of corn in the lowcountry but only among the "Plantations of *Negroes*." When William Bartram visited the lowcountry in the 1770s he noticed that the tania or tannier (a tuberous root found in the West Indies and tropical Africa) was "much cultivated and esteemed for food, particularly by the Negroes."[35] Bernard Romans claimed that slaves had introduced the groundnut into South Carolina; by the early nineteenth century, according to David Ramsay's informants on Edisto Island, groundnuts were "planted in small patches chiefly by the negroes, for market."[36] Romans also attributed the introduction of the "sesamen or oily grain" to lowcountry slaves; they used it, he maintained, "as a food either raw, toasted or boiled in their soups and are very fond of it, they call it *Benni*." Over one-and-a-half centuries later, a black sea islander was to be found planting what he called "bene." He used it in the same ways that his ancestors had done. Most significant, when asked where he acquired the seed, he said "his parents always had it and he was told 'Dey brung it fum Africa'."[37] Apparently peppers were also the preserve of slaves. Knowing that his slave old Tom "plants a good deal of pepper," Elias Ball desired him to send "sum Read pepper pounded and corked up in a pint Bottle." In 1742, when Eliza Lucas sent her friend some of the same product, she referred to it, in revealing fashion, as "negroe pepper."[38] The only tobacco grown in early eighteenth-century South Carolina belonged to the slaves.[39] Janet Schaw was so impressed by the way in which Carolina slaves used their "little piece[s] of land" to grow vegetables, "rear hogs and poultry, sow calabashes, etc." that she thought they cultivated them "much better than their Master[s]." Furthermore, she believed that "the Negroes are the only people that seem to pay any attention to the various uses that the wild vegetables may be put to."[40]

The cultivation and subsequent exchange of provisions allowed some slaves to claim more substantial items of property. In 1714 the South Carolina legislature denied the slaves' claim to "any stock of hogs, cattle or horses." This directive apparently fell on deaf ears, for in 1722 it became lawful to seize any hogs, boats, or canoes belonging to slaves. Moreover, this later act referred to the "great inconveniences [that] do arise from negroes and other slaves keeping and breeding of horses"; not only were these horses (and cattle) to be seized, but the proceeds of their sale were to be put to the support of the parish poor. The irony of slave property sustaining white paupers was presumably lost on South Carolina legislators but perhaps not on the slaves. Once again, legislative intentions seem to have been thwarted, for in 1740 more complaints were to be heard about those "several owners of slaves [who] have permitted them to keep canoes, and to breed and raise horses, neat cattle and hogs, and to traffic and barter in several parts of this Province, for the particular and peculiar benefit of such slaves."[41] The most dramatic example of property ownership by a lowcountry slave in the first half of the eighteenth century involved not horses or canoes, but men. According to a deed of manumission, a slave named Sampson "by his Industry and the Assistance of Friends" had purchased and "procured in his owne Right and property and for his owne Use" another Negro slave named Tom. Sampson then exchanged his slave Tom for "fifty years of his [that is, Sampson's] Life time and Servitude (to come)."[42] If the task system had created the opportunities for Sampson's "Industry" to manifest itself in this way, it truly was a potent force.

II

> Once a slave has completed his task, his
> master feels no right to call on him.
>   Daniel Turner, 1806

By the late eighteenth century the task system had taken deep root in the low-country. Tasks were set for almost all operations—from clearing new ground (one-eighth of an acre) to the weekly task of a pair of sawyers (600 feet of pine or 780 feet of cypress).[43] However, the basic unit, a quarter-acre, was still the yardstick for virtually all rice-planting operations.[44] In recognition of this reality, one Georgia absentee in 1786 sent a chain "for running out the Tasks" to his plantation manager. "It is 105 feet long," he noted, "and will save a great deal of time in Laying out the field, and do it with more exactness." Henry Ferguson, an East Floridian who had spent seventeen years in South Carolina and Georgia, was able to specify precisely how much land his slaves had cleared "from the Tasks which he set to his Negroes having measured the Ground frequently for that purpose." He added that "a Task was a quarter of an Acre to weed p. day."[45] Even opponents of the task system testify to its pervasiveness. William Butler, a keen observer of rice culture, argued in 1786 that slaves "should always be Kept in Gangs or parcels and not scattered over a field in Tasks as is too generally done, for while in gangs they are more immediately under the Superintendants Eyes, [and] of course may be much better and more immediately inspected."[46]

The extension of the task system to the cultivation of sea island cotton confirms the failure of Butler's advice. Since both the long- and short-staple varieties of cotton required close attention, especially in the tedious hoeing and thinning phases of their cultivation, they were ideal candidates for gang labor. Most upcountry South Carolina planters adopted this arrangement from the first, and sea island planters were encouraged to do the same: one lowcountry planter from Georgia advised his South Carolina colleagues that "there is no possibility of tasking Negroes" in cotton culture. However, his peers proved him wrong. By the early nineteenth century the tasking requirements of all sea island cotton operations were well established. They remained substantially unchanged throughout the nineteenth century (see Table 11.1).[47]

Perhaps the profits being generated under the existing task system discouraged lowcountry planters from adopting gang labor, for they were not likely to restructure an arrangement that was so patently successful. In 1751 James Glen reported that South Carolina planters expected a slave to pay for himself within four to five years. Dr. Alexander Garden calculated that in 1756 planters made between £15 to £30 sterling for every slave they employed in the field, which he noted was "indeed a great deal." At that rate, a slave would pay for himself in two to three years. In 1772 a visitor to South Carolina noted that indigo planters made from £35 to £45 sterling for every able Negro; in this case, a newly purchased slave paid for himself in less than two years.[48] The rate of return of a 200-acre rice plantation, employing forty slaves in the late colonial period, was estimated to be 25 percent, more than double the opportunity cost of capital.[49] And although the Revolutionary war was enormously disruptive of the lowcountry economy, the 1790s were boom years for planters, as they replaced one highly profitable secondary staple (indigo) with another (sea island cotton). So profitable was this second staple that planters on Edisto Island in 1808 averaged a return of between $170 and $260 for every field hand.[50]

Crucial to the continuing profitability of rice plantations was the wholesale transfer of production from inland to tidal swamps, a process that was well underway by the late eighteenth century. John Drayton, writing at the turn of the century, identified some of the advantages of this shift in location: "River swamp plantations, from the command of water, which at high tides can be introduced over the fields, have an undoubted preference to inland plantations; as the crop is more certain, and the work of the negroes less toilsome." Surely it was a tidewater rice plantation that a Virginian witnessed in 1780 when he observed that "after the ground is once well cleared little cultivation does the ground [need] being soft by continual moisture."[51] In short, the development of tidewater rice culture reduced the heavy hoeing formerly required of slaves in the summer months. As might be expected, the daily task unit expanded, and squares of 150 feet (approximately a half of an acre) appeared in tidewater rice fields.[52] The other side of this coin was the increase in heavy labor required of slaves in the winter months, for tidewater cultivation demanded an elaborate system of banks, dams, canals, and ditches. By the turn of the century, no doubt, lowcountry laborers were as familiar with the daily ditching requirement (about 600 to 700 square feet or ten compasses) as they had ever been with the quarter-acre task.[53]

Although the precise definition of daily tasks had advantages from the slaves' point of view, the potential conflict that stereotyped tasks and their careless assignment could engender should not be underestimated. Indeed, the evidence of conflict should alert us to a battle that undoubtedly was being waged but that rarely surfaces in the historical record; namely, the constant warring between taskmaster and laborer over what constituted a fair day's work. After one such altercation between a black driver and a group of slaves, the latter took their case to their master in Charleston. When he asked them "why they could not do their Tasks as well as the rest," they answered that "their Tasks were harder." The master was sympathetic, knowing that "there is sometimes a great difference in Tasks, and Paul told me he remembered that Jimmy had a bad Task that Day. I was sorry to see poor Caesar amongst them for I knew him to be an honest, inoffensive fellow and tho't if any will do without severity, he will. I inquired his fault, & Paul told me . . . he had been 2 days in a Task."[54] Hoeing was at issue in this dispute; on another plantation, threshing became a source of conflict. Three slaves belonging to George Austin—Liverpool, Moosa, and Dutay—"ran off early in December, for being a little chastis'd on Account of not finishing the Task of Thrashing in due time."[55] By the early nineteenth century, a *modus vivendi* had apparently been reached on most lowcountry plantations. One South Carolina planter reckoned that the "daily task does not vary according to the arbitrary will and caprice of their owners, and although [it] is not fixed by law, it is so well settled by long usage, that upon every plantation it is the *same*. Should any owner increase the work beyond what is customary, he subjects himself to the reproach of his neighbors, and to such discontent amongst his slaves as to make them of but little use to him."[56] The task system's requirements were hammered out just as much in conflicts with the work force as in the supposedly inevitable march of technological progress.

However onerous tasking could become for some slaves, the system at least had the virtue of allowing the slave a certain latitude to apportion his own day, to work intensively in his task and then have the balance of his time. With the institutionalization of the task system, the slave's "time" became sacrosanct. The right not to be called on once the task had been completed was duly acknowledged by lowcountry masters.[57] One of the advantages of such a right is neatly illustrated in an incident that befell a Methodist circuit rider, Joseph Pilmore. On March 18, 1773—a Thursday—he arrived at the banks of the Santee River in the Georgetown district of South Carolina. After waiting in vain for the appearance of the regular ferry, he was met by a few Negroes. Presumably they told him that they "had finished their task," for that is how he explained their availability in his journal. He then hired their "time" so that he could be ferried across the river. The actual time was about three o'clock in the afternoon.[58] Slaves could not only complete their work by mid-afternoon; they might then earn money on their own account.

In the same year that Pilmore visited the Georgetown district, another observer of lowcountry society, "Scotus Americanus," testified more fully to the advantages that a fully institutionalized task system presented to slaves:

> Their work is performed by a daily task, allotted by their master or overseer, which they have generally done by one or two o'clock in the afternoon, and have the rest of the day for themselves, which they spend in working in their own private fields, consisting of 5 or 6 acres of ground, allowed them by their masters, for planting of rice, corn, potatoes, tobacco, &c. for their own use and profit, of which the industrious among them make a great deal. In some plantations, they have also the liberty to raise hogs and poultry, which, with the former articles, they are to dispose of to none but their masters (this is done to prevent bad consequences) for which, in exchange, when they do not chuse money, their masters give Osnaburgs, negro cloths, caps, hats, handkerchiefs, pipes, and knives. They do not plant in their fields for subsistence, but for amusement, pleasure, and profit, their masters giving them clothes, and sufficient provisions from their granaries.[59]

As we shall see, planting for "amusement, pleasure, and profit" continued to be a prerogative of lowcountry slaves.

Pilmore and Scotus Americanus alert us to the ways in which lowcountry slaves continued to acquire money. It should hardly surprise us, then, that lowcountry bondmen still aspired to the ownership of more substantial items of property. In spite of the acts of 1714, 1722, and 1740, slaves remained singularly reluctant to relinquish their claims to horses. In 1772 the Charleston District Grand Jury was still objecting to "Negroes being allowed to keep horses . . . contrary to Law."[60] In a transaction that bore a remarkable similarity to the one effected by Sampson a half-century earlier, a slave named Will showed even less regard for the law by exchanging his horses for his freedom. A witness to the exchange heard Will's master, Lewis Dutarque, say to

> old fellow Will that he had been a faithful servant to him and if he had a mind to purchase his freedom he should obtain the same by paying him

three hundred pounds old currency and says he Will you have two Horses which will nearly pay me. I will allow you hundred pounds old currency for a Roan Gelding and forty five currency for your Gray for which the fellow Will readily consented to the proposals and Mr. Dutarque took possession of the Horses and the fellow Will was to pay the Balance as soon as he could make it up. Mr. Dutarque also borrowed of the fellow Will a small Black mare which he lost and he said she was worth six Guineas and would allow him that price for her.[61]

One begins to wonder how many horses Will possessed. Horse trading may even have been possible within the slave community, if a notice placed in a South Carolina newspaper in 1793 is any indication: "On Sunday last was apprehended by the patrol in St. George's parish, a certain negro man who calls himself *Titus* and his son about 10 year who is called *Tom*; he was trading with the negroes in that neighbourhood, and he had in his possession 2 horses . . . one poultry cart, and several articles of merchandise, consisting of stripes, linens, and handkerchiefs."[62] Given these examples, one lowcountry master was perhaps right to be sanguine about an unsuccessful hunt that he had launched for a group of seven absentees. He was "convinced these runaways would not go far, being connected at home, and having too much property to leave."[63]

III

Q. You think that they have a love for property?
A. Yes, Sir; Very strong; they delight in accumulating.
                    Testimony of Rufus Saxton, 1863

By the middle of the nineteenth century the task system dominated agricultural life in the lowcountry. Indeed, the term so pervaded the region's agricultural terminology that its varied meanings have to be disentangled. For example, a lowcountry planter might say that he had planted "seven tasks (within one task of two acres, as a planter well knows)." At this time, a slave was expected to be able to sow two acres of rice a day; this is presumably what this planter had in mind when referring to the single task of two acres. And yet, the early eighteenth-century definition of a task as measuring one-quarter of an acre was still very much current. It was possible, therefore, to speak of seven units, measuring one-quarter of an acre each, within a larger unit measuring two acres.[64] Similarly, a planter might say that he had penned "thirty head of cattle on a task for one week" (the "task" here refers to one-quarter of an acre); or he might mention setting a "task" of three rice barrels a day for his cooper.[65] In other words, in common usage the term "task" not only referred to a unit of labor (a fixed or specified quantity of labor exacted from a person is the dictionary definition) but also to a unit of land measurement (almost invariably one-quarter of an acre or 105 square feet).

Slaves were completely conversant with this terminology, as the recollections of ex-slaves attest. Testifying before Southern Claims Commissioners in 1873, Peter Way knew precisely what constituted a "task" as a unit of land measurement. "Five poles make a task," he noted authoritatively, "and there is twenty-one feet in a pole."[66] Using the term in this sense, former slaves might say that "Mr. Mallard's house was about four or five tasks from Mr. Busby's house" (about 420 or 525 feet distant), or that Sherman's troops were "about three tasks off in the woods. I could see [them] from [my] house" (about 315 feet away).[67] When Mason Crum interviewed an old Negro woman (a former slave) in the 1930s, she told him that she owned her land "and that she had in the tract t'ree acres and a tass'," by which she meant three-and-a-quarter acres.[68] When freedmen referred to the crops that they had produced for themselves in "slavery times," they used the units acres and "tasks" interchangeably (tasks here again refer to quarter-acre plots).[69] At the same time, ex-slaves used the term "task" to connote a unit of labor. A freedman, referring to the terms of the contract that he had signed with his employer, spoke of giving "five tasks, that is, I work five tasks for him and plant everything he has a mind to have it planted in for all the land myself and wife can cultivate."[70] The dual meaning of the term is nowhere better illustrated than in the words of one former slave, interviewed in the 1930s, who in one and the same breath recalled "de slave [having] but two taks ob land to cultivate for se'f" (by which he meant half an acre) and "in daytime [having] to do his task" (by which he meant a quantity of labor depending on the operation at hand).[71]

Tasking was so much a way of life in the antebellum lowcountry that virtually all crops and a whole host of plantation operations were subject to its dictates. The cultivation of corn was discussed in terms of the number of hills in a "task-row" and the number of "beds" in a task.[72] Sea island cotton had its own task-acre as distinct from the task-acre utilized in tidewater rice culture.[73] Even when lowcountry planters experimented with sugar cultivation in the 1820s and 1830s, they attempted to retain the notion of a task: a hundred plants, according to one authority, were to be put in a task-row and two hands could then both plant and cut a task a day.[74] On Hopeton plantation, where sugar was grown on a large scale, task work was "resorted to whenever the nature of the work admits of it; and working in gangs as is practiced in the West Indies and the upper country, is avoided. The advantages of this system are encouragement to the labourers, by equalizing the work of each agreeably to strength, and the avoidance of watchful superintendance and incessant driving."[75] Whether this attempt to adapt sugar cultivation to the task system contributed to the failure of lowcountry sugar production is difficult to say; but it is possible that sugar, unlike cotton, just could not be successfully grown without gang labor.

Tasking was ubiquitous in another sense: those slaves not able to benefit from the system's opportunities had to be compensated in other ways. The proposition that drivers, as a group, suffered discrimination is barely credible, but in the lowcountry, at least, such was the case. As one ex-slave recalled, "I suppose the Foreman had advantages in some respects and in others not, for he had no task-work and had no time of his own, while the other slaves had the Evenings to themselves." The son of a Georgia planter remembered that his father's driver was "obliged to oversee all day," whereas the field hands "were allowed to work in any way they chose for themselves after the tasks were done."[76] By way of compensation, lowcountry drivers were entitled to receive a certain amount of help in tending their own crops. Thomas Mallard's driver "had the privilege of having hands to work one acre of corn and one acre of rice" on his behalf; the driver on Raymond Cay's plantation had Cay's field hands plant one acre of corn and three to five "tasks" in rice on his account.[77] One ex-slave recalled that "drivers had the privilege of planting two or three acres of rice and some corn and having it worked by the slaves"; and, in order to dispel any misimpressions, he emphasized that "these hands worked for [the drivers] in the White people's time."[78] Other occupational groups received different forms of compensation. A former slave plowman recalled that he "didn't work by the task but at the end of the year [his master] gave [him] 6 bushels of corn" by way of redress. A former slave carpenter recollected that "when [he] worked carpentering [his] master allowed [him] every other saturday and when [he] worked farming [his master] gave him tasks."[79] In this man's mind, apparently, these "privileges" were about equal.

The central role of the task system in lowcountry life can best be gauged by investigating its fate immediately after emancipation. Throughout the postwar cotton South freedmen firmly rejected most of the elements of their old system of labor: from the first, gang labor was anathema.[80] At the same time, however, freedmen in the lowcountry were tenaciously striving to retain—and even extend —the fundamentals of their former system. A Freedmen's Bureau official, resident in lowcountry Georgia in 1867, identified a basic response of the former slaves to their new work environment when he observed that they "usually stipulate to work by the task."[81] Lowcountry freedmen even demonstrated their attachment to the task system when they rejected one element of their former slave past by refusing to do the ditching and draining so necessary in rice and sea island cotton cultivation.[82] This work was arduous and disagreeable, of course, and since ditching was more amenable to gang labor than any other operation in lowcountry agriculture, blacks appropriately sought to avoid it at all costs. But in an 1865 petition a group of planters from Georgetown district touched on an even more compelling reason for the freedmen's refusal to perform this familiar task. They pointed out that "it is a work which, as it does not pertain to the present crop, the negroes are unwilling to perform." The recipient of this petition, Colonel Willard, was a sympathetic and sensitive observer, and his elaboration of this rationale penetrates to the heart of the issue. The freedmen's real fear, he explained, was that having prepared the ditches for the forthcoming crop, the planters would "insist on having them by the month." This arrangement would be absolutely unacceptable, because the freedmen had "been accustomed to working by the task, which has always given them leisure to cultivate land for themselves, tend their stock, and amuse themselves." If they gave way on this issue, he continued, "their privileges will go and their condition will be less to their taste than it was when they were slaves."[83]

Precisely to avoid such a condition was the overriding imperative governing the actions of lowcountry freedmen. Once this is understood, the multifarious and fluid labor arrangements that characterized the postwar lowcountry become comprehensible. In 1865 and 1866 two basic forms of labor contract (with many individual variations) were employed in the lowlands of South Carolina and Georgia. Either the freedmen worked for a share of the crop (anywhere from one-half to three-quarters, a higher share than found elsewhere in the South), with the freedmen's share being divided among them on the basis of tasks performed, or they hired themselves for the year, with payment being made on the basis of the numbers of tasks completed (usually fifty cents a task, although payment was by no means always made in cash).[84] Whatever the mode of reimbursement, the task was central to most early contracts.

In 1866 a third labor arrangement arose that soon became general throughout the lowcountry. Known as the "two-day" or, less frequently, "three-day" system, it simply extended the concept of task labor, for it drew an even more rigid demarcation between the planters' "time" and the laborers' "time." The Freedmen's Bureau agent for eastern Liberty County, Georgia, observed as early as February 1867 that there were in his district no freedmen working by the month and only a few for wages. Some were working for a share of the crop, but most were employed by the "two-day" system, working a third of the time on the employers' crop and receiving land to work on their own account for the remainder of the time.[85] The agricultural census of 1880 reported that the "two-day" system was ubiquitous on the South Carolina sea islands. For ten months of the year, slaves worked two days in each week for their employers and received in return a house, fuel, and six acres of land for their own use, free of rent. Proprietors were said to dislike the system because their employees only cultivated about two acres in the owners' "time." However, the report continued, "the laborers themselves prefer this system, having four days out of the week for themselves." As a result, "they are more independent and can make any day they choose a holiday."[86]

The reasons for the slaves' (and the freedmen's) attachment to the task system should be readily apparent, but the subject is worth a moment's extra consideration because we are in the privileged and rare position of being able to listen to the participants themselves. The most obvious advantage of the task system was the flexibility it permitted slaves in determining the length of the working day. Working from sunup to sundown was the pervasive reality for most antebellum slaves; but ex-slaves from the lowcountry recall a different reality. Richard Cummings, a former field hand, recalled that "a good active industrious man would finish his task sometimes at 12, sometimes at 1 and 2 oclock and the rest of the time was his own to use as he pleased." Scipio King, another former field hand, reckoned, as he put it, that "I could save for myself sometimes a whole day if I could do 2 tasks in a day then I had the next day to myself. Some kind of work I could do 3 tasks in a day."[87] Exhausting as task labor undoubtedly was, its prime virtue was that it was not unremitting.

A second advantage concerned the relationship between the slaves' provisions and the planters' rations. Whatever slaves produced beyond the task was regarded as surplus to, not a substitute for, basic planter allocations of food and clothing. One former slave recalled that his master continued to dispense rations "no matter how much they [the slaves] made of their own . . . [which] they could sell . . . if they chose." July Roberts, another ex-slave, emphasized that "every week we drew our rations no matter what we raised." When one former slave claimed the loss of corn, rice, and clothing taken by Federal troops, an attempt was made to deny him his title because these represented rations and "so belonged to the master." The response of this freedman's attorneys no doubt reflected the prevailing attitude of former slaves: "It is obvious to remark that if these things had not been taken from the claimant by the army, he would have had them after 'freedom came' and were to all intents his property."[88] Not only did slaves plant in their own time for "amusement, pleasure, and profit," they claimed the master's rations as their own to do with as they wished.

In view of these advantages, we might expect the scale and range of property owning by slaves to have assumed significant dimensions by the middle of the nineteenth century. An analysis of the settled claims submitted by former slaves to the Southern Claims Commission for loss of property to Federal troops provides the best test of this hypothesis.[89] Taking the Liberty County, Georgia, claimants as a sample, former field hands outnumber all other occupational groups. While most were mature adults when their property was taken, 30 percent were under the age of thirty-five. In terms of occupation and age these claimants constitute a relatively broad cross section of the slave population. Moreover, whether field hands or artisans, young or old, virtually all of them had apparently been deprived of a number of hogs, and a substantial majority listed corn, rice, and fowls among their losses. In addition, a surprising number apparently possessed horses and cows, while buggies or wagons, beehives, peanuts, fodder, syrup, butter, sugar, and tea were, if these claims are to be believed, in the hands of at least some slaves. The average cash value (in 1864 dollars) claimed by Liberty County former slaves was $357.43, with the highest claim totaling $2,290 and the lowest $49.[90]

Some claims were spectacular. Paris James, a former slave driver, was described by a neighboring white planter as a "substantial man before the war [and] was more like a free man than any slave."[91] James claimed, among other things, a horse, eight cows, sixteen sheep, twenty-six hogs, and a wagon. Another slave driver, according to one of his black witnesses, lived "just like a white man except his color. His credit was just as good as a white man's because he had the property to back it." Although the claims commissioners were skeptical about his alleged loss of twenty cows—as they explained, "twenty cows would make a good large dairy for a Northern farmer"—his two white and three black witnesses supported him in his claim.[92] Other blacks were considered to be "more than usually prosperous," "pretty well off," and "hardworking and moneysaving"—unremarkable characterizations, perhaps, but surprising when the individuals were also slaves.[93] Alexander Steele, a carpenter by trade and a former house servant of Chatham County, Georgia, submitted a claim for $2,205 based on the loss of his four horses, mule, silver watch, two cows, wagon, and large quantities of fodder, hay, and corn. He had been able to acquire these possessions by "trading" for himself for some thirty years; he had had "much time of [his] own" because his master "always went north" in the summer months. He took "a fancy [to] fine horses," a whim he was able to indulge when he purchased "a blooded mare," from which he raised three colts. He was resourceful enough to hide his livestock on Onslow Island when Sherman's army drew near, but some of the Federal troops secured boats and took off his prize possessions. Three white planters supported Steele in his claim; indeed, one of them recollected making an unsuccessful offer of $300 for one of Steele's colts before the war. Lewis Dutarque's Will, a horse owner of note in the late eighteenth century, had found a worthy successor in Alexander Steele.[94]

The ownership of horses was not, however, confined to a privileged minority of slaves. Among the Liberty County claimants, almost as many ex-field hands as former drivers and skilled slaves claimed horses. This evidence supplies a context for the exchange recorded by Frederick Law Olmsted when he was being shown around the plantation of Richard J. Arnold in Bryan County, Georgia. Olsmsted noticed a horse drawing a wagon of "common fieldhand negroes" and asked his host

> "[Do you] usually let them have horses to go to Church?"
> "Oh no; that horse belongs to the old man."

"Belongs to him! Why, do they own horses?"

"Oh yes; William (the House Servant) owns two, and Robert, I believe, has three now; that was one of them he was riding."

"How do they get them?"

"Oh they buy them."[95]

Although a few freedmen recalled that former masters had either prohibited horse ownership or confined the practice to drivers, most placed the proportion of horse owners on any single plantation at between 15 and 20 percent.[96] A former slave of George Washington Walthour estimated that "in all my master's plantations there were over 30 horses owned by slaves. . . . I think come to count up there were as many as 45 that owned horses—he would let them own any thing they could if they only did his work."[97] Nedger Frazer, a former slave of the Reverend C. C. Jones, recalled that on one of his master's plantations (obviously Arcadia, from Frazer's description) there were forty working hands, of whom five owned horses; and on another (obviously Montevideo) another 'ten hands out of fifty owned horses.[98] This, in turn, supplies a context for an interesting incident that occurred within the Jones's "family" in 1857. After much soul-searching, Jones sold one of his slave families, headed by Cassius, a field hand. A man of integrity, Jones then forwarded Cassius the balance of his account, which amounted to $85, a sum that included the proceeds from the sale of Cassius's horse.[99] Perhaps one freedman was not exaggerating when he observed in 1873 that "there was more stock property owned by slaves before the war than are owned now by both white and black people together in this county."[100]

The spectacular claims and the widespread ownership of horses naturally catch the eye, but even the most humdrum claim has a story to tell. Each claim contains, for instance, a description of how property was accumulated. The narrative of John Bacon can stand as proxy for many such accounts: "I had a little crop to sell and bought some chickens and then I bought a fine large sow and gave $10.00 for her. This was about ten years before the war and then I raised hogs and sold them till I bought a horse. This was about eight years before freedom. This was a breeding mare and from this mare I raised this horse which the Yankees took from me."[101] This was not so much primitive as painstaking accumulation; no wonder one freedman referred to his former property as his "laborment."[102] And yet, occasionally, the mode of procurement assumed a slightly more sophisticated cast: some slaves recall purchasing horses by installment;[103] some hired additional labor to cultivate their crops;[104] two slaves (a mill engineer and a stockminder) went into partnership to raise livestock;[105] and a driver lent out money at interest.[106] Whatever the mode of accumulation, the ultimate source, as identified by virtually all the ex-slaves, was the task system. As Joseph James, a freedman, explained, "They all worked by tasks, and had a plenty of time to work for themselves and in that way all slaves who were industrious could get around them considerable property in a short time."[107]

By the middle of the nineteenth century, in sum, it is possible to speak of a significant internal economy operating within a more conventional lowcountry economy. According to the depositions of the freedmen, this internal economy rested on two major planks. The first concerns the degree to which some slaves engaged in stock raising. One white planter, testifying on behalf of a freedman, recalled that "a good many" slaves owned a number of animals; he then checked himself, perhaps realizing the impression that he was creating, and guardedly stated that "what I mean was they were not allowed to go generally into stock raising."[108] And yet some slaves seem to have been doing just that. One ex-slave spoke of raising "horses to sell"; another claimed to have raised fourteen horses over a twenty-five-to-thirty-year period, most of which he had sold; and one freedwoman named some of the purchasers, all of whom were slaves, of the nine horses that she had raised.[109] The other major foundation of this internal economy was the amount of crop production by slaves. Jeremiah Everts observed that the slaves in Chatham County, Georgia, had "as much land as they can till for their own use."[110] The freedmen's recollections from all over the lowcountry support this statement: a number of ex-slaves reckoned that they had more than ten acres under cultivation, while four or five acres was the norm.[111] The proprietorial attitude encouraged by this independent production is suggested in one freedman's passing comment that he worked in his "own field."[112] Through the raising of stock and the production of provisions (together with the sale of produce from woodworking, basketmaking, hunting, and fishing), slaves were able to attract money into their internal economy. Robert W. Gibbes knew of an individual slave who received $120 for his year's crop of corn and fodder; Richard Arnold owed his slaves $500 in 1853 when Olmsted visited him.[113] Thus, while produce and livestock were constantly being bartered by slaves—"swapping" was rife, according to the freedmen—one observer of the mid-nineteenth-century lowcountry was undoubtedly correct when he noted that "in a small way a good deal of money circulated among the negroes, both in the country and in the towns."[114]

The autonomy of this internal economy is further indicated by the development of a highly significant practice. By the middle of the nineteenth century, if not before, slave property was not only being produced and exchanged but also inherited. The father of Joseph Bacon bequeathed him a mare and all his other children $50 each.[115] Samuel Elliot claimed a more substantial legacy, for his father "had 20 head of cattle, about 70 head of hogs—Turkeys Geese Ducks and Chickens a Plenty—he was foreman for his master and had been raising such things for years. When he died the property was divided among his children and we continued to raise things just as he had been raising."[116] The role of less immediate kin was also not negligible. Two freedmen recalled receiving property from their grandfathers; another inherited a sow from his cousin; and William Drayton of Beaufort County, South Carolina, noted that when his father died he "left with his oldest brother, my uncle, the means or property he left for his children," and Drayton bought a mule "by the advice of my uncle who had the means belonging to me."[117] There were rules governing lines of descent. One female claimant emphasized that she had not inherited any of her first husband's property because she had borne him no children; rather, his son by a former marriage received the property.[118] The ability to bequeath wealth and to link patrimony to genealogy serves to indicate the extent to which slaves created a measure of autonomy.

The property rights of slaves were recognized across proprietorial boundaries as well as across generations. Slaves even employed guardians to facilitate the transfer of property from one plantation to another. Thus when Nancy Bacon, belonging to John Baker, inherited cattle from her deceased husband who belonged to Mr. Walthour, she employed her second cousin, Andrew Stacy, a slave on the

Walthour plantation, to take charge of the cattle and drive them over to her plantation. According to Stacy, Mr. Walthour "didn't object to my taking them [and] never claimed them."[119] The way in which slave couples took advantage of their divided ownership is suggested by Diana Cummings of Chatham County, Georgia. Her husband's master, she explained, "allowed him to sell but mine didn't," so Diana marketed her crops and stock through her husband and received a part of the proceeds. On her husband's death, she received all his property for, as she put it, her "entitle" (surname) was then the same as her husband's. She had since changed it, through remarriage to Sydney Cummings, but she noted that Cummings had "no interest in [the] property [being claimed]."[120]

By the middle of the nineteenth century the ownership of property by lowcountry slaves had become extensive and had assumed relatively sophisticated dimensions. This, in turn, gives rise to an obvious question. What significance was attached to the practice by the slaves? What was the *mentalité*, the moral economy, of this property-owning group? Certainly some freedmen spoke of "getting ahead" and of "accumulating" under slavery.[121] Jacob Monroe, a freedman, admitted that as a slave under the task system he "could go and come when [he] pleased, work and play after [his] task was done," but he pointedly emphasized that "he chose to work."[122] Competitiveness was also not alien to the slave quarters. One freedman recalled how the young adults on one plantation "were jealous of one another and tried to see which would get their days work done first."[123] William Gilmore referred to the disparities in property ownership that characterized Raymond Cay's slaves; he likened them to the "five wise and five foolish" and disparaged those who "slept and slumbered the time away."[124] Similar impressions are derived from those Northerners who came into contact with sea island blacks in the early 1860s. B. K. Lee observed that "they are very acquisitive indeed"; Henry Judd described their "passion for ownership of horses or some animal"; and Rufus Saxton was impressed to find that "they regard the rights of property among themselves. If a man has a claim upon a horse or sow he maintains his right and his neighbours recognize it."[125]

Acquisitiveness and respect for property had other overtones, as Rufus Saxton's resonant phrase—"they delight in accumulating"—suggests.[126] Display and ostentation, while not on any grand scale, of course, seem an accurate characterization of some slaves' behavior. The ownership of horses undoubtedly had practical purposes—one freedman explained that "some of the slaves had families a good ways off and they used their horses to visit them. The masters said it was for their interest to have us own horses so that we could get back home to work."[127] But the exhibition of status appears also to have been involved. William Golding's ownership of a horse and saddle was proved because "he was given to riding about on Sundays." Frederick Law Olmsted not only witnessed a head house-servant mount his horse after church service but, in true paternalistic fashion, slip a coin to the boy who had been holding its reins.[128] Ex-slaves commonly justified their ownership of a horse and wagon by their need to go to church on Sunday. This was not just a practical matter: Leah Wilson could not disguise the sense of status she derived from being able to drive "right along together with our master going to church."[129] A horse, as Edward Philbrick observed in 1862, was more than a means of transport; it was "a badge of power and caste." Sea island blacks had no respect for people who could not present themselves on a horse. "They will hardly lift their hats to a white man on foot," he noted, and viewed a "walking nigger" with contempt.[130]

Although we find elements of display, of accumulation for its own sake, and of "getting ahead," the *mentalité* of the slaves cannot be reduced to any one of these traits and was indeed much more. We can uncover better the meaning and limits of such behavior by exploring, once again, the slaves' immediate response to freedom. In terms of their attitude toward labor, the freedmen firmly resisted the overtures of northern reformers and proclaimed a resounding attachment to what may be resonantly characterized as a task-orientation. Employers and Freedmen's Bureau officials alike constantly bemoaned the impossibility of persuading the freedmen to "perform more than their allotted tasks."[131] In 1867 Frances Butler Leigh observed freedmen who begged "to be allowed to go back to the old task system" when the agent of the Freedmen's Bureau attempted to have them work by the day. "One man," she reported, "indignantly asked Major D—— what the use of being free was, if he had to work harder than when he was a slave."[132] Few freedmen would work a full day, a full week, "and very seldom a full month steady," complained one employer.[133] One Northerner advocated the confiscation of the freedmen's boats so that instead of continuing in their ways of "precarious living," they might develop "habits of steady industry."[134] The freedmen were said to work "when they please and do just as much as they please"; they then relied on hunting and fishing "to make up for what they lose in the field."[135]

This clash between the proponents of Northeastern business methods and a laboring population wedded to an alternative work ethic reverberated throughout the postwar lowcountry. The conflict is nearly illustrated in an exchange that occurred in 1865 between Colonel Willard, a man generally sympathetic to the freedmen's plight, and two ex-slaves who were sawmill workers. Willard was approached by the harassed owner of the mill, who was unable to impress his workers with the virtues of "steady" work: they claimed, for example, at least two hours of rest during their work day. From the standpoint of a Northern businessman, Willard's argument to the two representatives of the work force was impeccable: "Laborers at the North," he pointed out, "got less wages, and worked from sunrise to sunset, this season of the year, only having an hour at noon." The freedmen's reply was equally forceful: "We want," they emphasized, "to work just as we have always worked." Willard was left to expostulate that these former slaves "have no just sense of the importance of persistent labor."[136]

The freedmen's attitude toward the accumulation of property, much like their attitude toward work, was decisively shaped by their former experience under the task system. The argument that "the more they cultivate, the more they gain" had, as one Northern army officer discovered, no appeal. In 1868 Frances Butler Leigh made a similar discovery when she found that some freedmen refused wages and rations, preferring to "raise a little corn and sweet potatoes, and with their facilities for catching fish and oysters, and shooting wild game, they have as much to eat as they want, and now are quite satisfied with that."[137] In short, lowcountry freedmen apparently wished to avoid an unlimited involvement in the market, favoring production for sale only within the familiar context of an assured production for subsistence. This explains, in large measure, why the freedmen would not forego their hunting and fishing activities for a greater concentration on cash crops, why they aspired to the ownership or rental of land, and why they refused to work for wages.[138] The degree to which subsistence (in this case, hunting) formed the priorities of one freedman is captured in a brief anecdote. A special agent, who toured the lowcountry in 1878 investigating disputed claims, visited the home of Samuel Maxwell, a former slave. He was not impressed with this particular claimant's adaptation to freedom and advised him to participate more fully in the wider society. For a start, he suggested, why not raise hogs rather than dogs? To which Maxwell replied: "A pig won't help us catch coons and rabbits."[139]

The preferences and ambitions of the freedmen reflected, above all, a desire for autonomy not only from the impersonal marketplace but also from individual whites. As one would-be employer found out in 1866, the freedmen who rejected wages and wanted to supply their own seed were expressing a fundamental desire to "be free from personal constraint."[140] They sought, in other words, to build upon a foundation that the task system had laid, consisting of that part of a day, that plot of land, or those few animals that they, as slaves, had been able to call their own. Thus for many, if not most, lowcountry freedmen, the central priorities of subsistence and autonomy shaped whatever propensity for material accumulation and for "getting ahead" they may have had. And what these goals of subsistence and autonomy signally call to mind, of course, are nothing more than the central priorities of peasants throughout the world.[141]

The freedman's quest for a measure of autonomy from individual whites should not be construed, however, as a desire for total disengagement from whites, particularly in the immediate postemancipation years. The moral universe of lowcountry slaves apparently contained notions of social equity and of reciprocal obligations between blacks and whites that were not jettisoned when freedom came.[142] Henry Ravenel's slaves, for example, voluntarily presented themselves before their master in March 1865 and "said they would be willing to take a certain piece of land which they would cultivate for old Master—that they would not want a driver or overseer, but would work that faithfully for him—and that they would take another piece of land to work for their own use." Another set of plantation blacks dumbfounded their former owner in July 1865 when they told him that they now considered the land as their own; perhaps more striking, however, was their readiness to grant "Master" a portion of the crop as "a free gift from themselves."[143] When the promise of land dimmed, the freedmen could be expected to assume a more hostile posture. While evidence of such hostility exists, some sensitive observers were still aware of a basic and continuing paradox. Thus Joseph Le Conte, writing of Liberty County, Georgia, freedmen in the 1890s, noted their refusal to be tied to whites and their rejection of wage labor based, in his view, on their ability to "live almost without work on fish, crawfish, and oysters." At the same time, however, he referred to "the kindliest feelings" existing "among the blacks . . . toward their former masters." While Le Conte may have been guilty of some self-deception, similar observations from his fellow whites suggest the reality of this paradox.[144] Once again, this aspect of the freedmen's world view is strikingly reminiscent of a central feature of peasant life that, according to one authority, is permeated by the moral principle of reciprocity.[145]

The significance of the particular conjunction that this article set out to explore—the conjunction between a certain mode of labor organization and a particular domestic economy—can now be assessed. From the short-run perspective of masters, this conjunction had a number of benefits. They could escape their plan-tations in the summer months, they were supplied with additional provisions, and their slaves were *relatively* content, or so they believed. Oliver Bostick, a Beaufort County planter, explained that he "allowed [his] slaves to own and have their property and have little crops of their own for it Encouraged them to do well and be satisfied at home." Rufus King, another lowcountry master, was satisfied that "no Negro with a well-stocked poultry house, a small crop advancing, a canoe partly finished or a few tubs unsold, all of which he calculates soon to enjoy, will ever run away."[146] From the short-run perspective of the slaves, this conjunction increased their autonomy, allowed them to accumulate (and bequeath) wealth, fed individual initiative, sponsored collective discipline and esteem, and otherwise benefited them economically and socially.[147] In other words, on a much reduced scale, there were lowcountry slaves who resembled the protopeasants found among Caribbean slaves. This similarity was derived from very different origins: in the lowcountry, from a particular mode of labor organization; in the Caribbean, from the need for slaves to grow most of their own food and provision the free population. There was, in short, a much wider "peasant breach in the slave mode of production" in the Caribbean than in the lowcountry.[148]

Still, the parallel is suggestive, for in the same way that protopeasant adapta-tions had a comparable short-term significance for masters and slaves in both Caribbean and lowcountry, there were comparable long-term results. Wherever there were significant protopeasant activities among the slaves, there emerged after emancipation a class of people who had acquired the requisite skills that helped them escape, at least in part or temporarily, their dependence on the plantation.[149] In the lowcountry, the course of the war, the capital requirements of its major staple crop, and the development of phosphates production go some way toward explaining the particular shape of its postwar labor history.[150] But surely certain elements of this configuration had deeper roots, roots that without exaggeration can be traced all the way back to the early eighteenth century. The imperatives so dear to generations of lowcountry slaves achieved a measure of realization in the more distinctive features of the region's postwar labor arrangements. By 1880 the percentage of farms sharecropped in the coastal districts of South Carolina and Georgia ranked among the lowest in the South; the proportion of rural black landowners was one of the highest in the South; it is possible to speak of a "black yeomanry" in the late nineteenth-century lowcountry; and by 1880 one observer in coastal Georgia could describe how most of the Negroes in his county had "bought a small tract of land, ten acres or more [on which they made] enough rice . . . to be perfectly independent of the white man."[151] To paraphrase Sidney Mintz, nothing else during the history of lowcountry slavery was as important as the task system and its concomitant domestic economy in making possible the freed person's adaptation to freedom without the blessings of the former masters.[152]

Notes

1   Comparative studies of slavery have been especially prone to the institutional or external perspective. Even one of the best studies of slave life—Eugene D. Genovese's *Roll, Jordan, Roll: The World the Slaves Made* (New York, 1974)—devotes only a few pages to the domestic

economy of the slaves (pp. 535–540), although slave work routines (pp. 285–324) and aspects of consumption patterns (pp. 550–561) are explored sensitively and at length.

2 Anthropologists, for example, have been criticized for neglecting the subject. See the introduction to Sandra Wallman, ed., *Social Anthropology of Work*, Association of Social Anthropologists, Monograph 19 (London, 1979).

3 The labor history that is practiced in *History Workshop* and in the volumes published in the *History Workshop* series are the kind to which this article aspires. Also noteworthy is a recent trend in American labor history that treats the reality of work as the focus, or starting point, of investigation. See David Brody, "Labor History in the 1970s: Toward a History of the American Worker," in Michael Kammen, ed., *The Past before Us: Contemporary Historical Writing in the United States* (Ithaca, N.Y., 1980), 268.

4 Alan Everitt, "Farm Labourers," in Joan Thirsk, ed., *The Agrarian History of England and Wales*, IV (Cambridge, 1967), 396.

5 Lewis Cecil Gray, *History of Agriculture in the Southern United States to 1860* (Gloucester, Mass., 1958 [orig. publ. Washington, D.C., 1933]), I, 550–551.

6 Equally, we could investigate more fully than will be possible here the special role of the black driver, the marketing opportunities, or the occupational structure that a rice tasking system produced.

7 The word *particular* is important here because I do not intend to suggest that the independent production of goods and the accumulation of property by slaves was necessarily predicated on a task system. From situations as diverse as a sugar plantation in Jamaica to an iron foundry in the United States, slaves were often able to control the accumulation and disposal of sizable earnings and possessions. Rather, in the lowcountry, a particular conjunction arose that probably led—but this would need much greater space for comparative presentation—to a distinctive internal economy among the slaves.

8 In exploring these resemblances, I have found the work of Sidney W. Mintz to be particularly helpful. See "The Origins of Reconstituted Peasantries," in *Caribbean Transformations* (Chicago, 1974), 146–156, and "Slavery and the Rise of Peasantries," in Michael Craton, ed., *Roots and Branches: Current Directions in Slave Studies* (Toronto, 1979), 213–242.

9 The Instructions of the Clergy of South Carolina given to Mr. Johnston, 1712, A8/429, Society of the Propagation of the Gospel, London; testimony of Thomas Akin and Ammon, Feb. 7, 1749, Council Journal, No. 17, Pt. 1, 160, South Carolina Department of Archives and History, Columbia.

10 "Johann Martin Bolzius Answers a Questionnaire on Carolina and Georgia," trans. and ed. Klaus G. Loewald *et al.*, *William and Mary Quarterly*, 3d Ser., XIV (1957), 259.

11 Dr. Alexander Garden to the Royal Society, Apr. 20, 1755, Guard Book 1, 36, Royal Society of Arts, London; "Bolzius Answers a Questionnaire," trans. and ed. Loewald *et al.*, *WMQ*, 3d Ser., XIV (1957), 258.

12 "Bolzius Answers a Questionnaire," trans. and ed. Loewald *et al.*, *WMQ*, 3d Ser., XIV (1957), 256.

13 Richard S. Dunn, "The English Sugar Islands and the Founding of South Carolina," *South Carolina Historical Magazine*, LXXII (1971), 81–93; Richard Waterhouse, "England, the Caribbean, and the Settlement of Carolina," *Journal of American Studies*, IX (1975), 259–281.

14 Ulrich Bonnell Phillips, "The Slave Labor Problem in the Charleston District," in Elinor Miller and Eugene D. Genovese, eds., *Plantation, Town, and County: Essays on the Local History of American Slave Society* (Urbana, Ill., 1974), 9. For Caribbean absenteeism see Richard S. Dunn, *Sugar and Slaves: The Rise of the Planter Class in the English West Indies, 1624–1713* (Chapel Hill, N.C., 1972), 101–103, 161–163.

15 Wood, *Black Majority: Negroes in Colonial South Carolina from 1670 through the Stono Rebellion* (New York, 1974), 56–62; Littlefield, *Rice and Slaves: Ethnicity and the Slave Trade in Colonial South Carolina* (Baton Rouge, La., 1981), 74–114.

16 E. P. Thompson, "Time, Work-Discipline, and Industrial Capitalism," *Past and Present*, No. 38 (1967), 73.

17 Of those slaves imported into South Carolina before 1740 and for whom an African coastal region of origin is known, I calculate that 15% were from rice-producing areas. Unfortunately, we know little or nothing about the regional origins of the earliest slave vessels to

216 PHILIP D. MORGAN

South Carolina. The first association between an African region and the cultivation of rice that I have found comes late in the day and may have been no more than a mercantile gambit. In 1758 the merchant firm Austin and Laurens described the origins of the slave ship *Betsey* as the "Windward and Rice Coast" (*South-Carolina Gazette* [Charleston], Aug. 11, 1758). Whites in other areas of North America are on record as valuing the familiarity with rice planting that some Africans displayed (see Henry P. Dart, "The First Cargo of African Slaves for Louisiana, 1718," *Louisiana Historical Quarterly*, XIV [1931], 176–177, as referred to in Joe Gray Taylor, *Negro Slavery in Louisiana* [Baton Rouge, La., 1963], 14). For the West Africans' widespread unfamiliarity with irrigation see Littlefield, *Rice and Slaves*, 86, and the issue of *Africa*, LI, No. 2 (1981), devoted to "Rice and Yams in West Africa." A fuller discussion of all these matters will be presented in my "Slave Counterpoint: Black Culture in the Eighteenth-Century Chesapeake and Lowcountry" (unpubl. MS).

18 In 1830 one Cuban planter, with little historical sense, could even argue that the culture of the tobacco plant "properly belongs to a white population, for there are few plants requiring more attention and tender treatment than this does" (Joseph M. Hernandez, "On the Cultivation of the Cuba Tobacco Plant," *Southern Agriculturalist*, III [1830], 463).

19 Domenico Sella, *Crisis and Continuity: The Economy of Spanish Lombardy in the Seventeenth Century* (Cambridge, Mass., 1979), 121–122.

20 Dunn, *Sugar and Slaves*, 189–200. The connection between sugar cultivation and gang labor was not absolutely axiomatic, at least in the postemancipation era. See Douglas Hall, *Free Jamaica, 1838–1865: An Economic History* (New Haven, Conn., 1959), 44–45; Jerome Handler, "Some Aspects of Work Organization on Sugar Plantations in Barbados," *Ethnology*, IV (1965), 16–38; and James McNeill and Chimman Lal, *Report to the Government of India on the Conditions of Indian Immigrants in Four British Colonies and Surinam* in *British Parliamentary Papers*, 1915, Cd. 7744, 7745 (I am indebted to Stanley Engerman for the last reference).

21 B. W. Higman, *Slave Population and Economy in Jamaica, 1807–1834,* (Cambridge, 1976), 23–24, 220. A Jamaican bookkeeper reported that the only work on a coffee plantation *not* carried out by tasks was the drying of the berries, because "this required constant attention" (*ibid.*, 23).

22 Barry Higman suggested this to me in a personal communication.

23 Ulrich Bonnell Phillips, *American Negro Slavery: A Survey of the Supply, Employment and Control of Negro Labor As Determined by the Plantation Regime* (Baton Rouge, La., 1966 [orig. publ. New York, 1918]), 247.

24 See the relevant discussions, below, of how the task system was extended to the cultivation of cotton and even sugar in the late 18th- and early 19th-century lowcountry.

25 Thomas Cooper and David J. McCord, eds., *The Statutes at Large of South Carolina* (Columbia, S.C., 1836–1841), II, 22–23, VII, 11, 368.

26 *Ibid.*, III, 398, 489, VII, 423.

27 Ball Family Account Book, 174, 32, and unpaginated memorandum, Jan. 21, 1736, South Carolina Historical Society, Charleston.

28 Administration of James Hartley's estate, Aug. 1758–July 1760, Inventory Book V, 160–175, S.C. Archs., Columbia.

29 Henry Ravenel's Day Book, particularly for the years 1763–1767, S.C. Hist. Soc., Charleston.

30 George C. Rogers *et al.*, eds., *The Papers of Henry Laurens*, V (Columbia, S.C., 1976), 41.

31 Apart from the acts already mentioned, see Cooper and McCord, eds., *Statutes*, VII, 407–409, 434–435. See also Charlestown Grand Jury Presentments, *S.C. Gaz.*, Nov. 5, 1737.

32 Testimony of Thomas Akin and Ammon, Feb. 7, 1749, Council Journal, No. 17, Pt. 1, 160.

33 Testimony of Lawrence Kelly, Jan. 30, 1749, *ibid.*, 85.

34 Administration of David Caw's estate, Oct. 20, 1761, Inventory Book V, 12–19.

35 Mark Catesby, *The Natural History of Carolina, Florida and the Bahama Islands . . .*, II (London, 1743), xviii; Francis Harper, ed., *The Travels of William Bartram* (New Haven, Conn., 1958), 297.

36 Romans, *A Concise Natural History of East and West Florida . . .*, I (New York, 1775), 131;
    Ramsay, *The History of South Carolina*, II (Charleston, S.C., 1808), 289. The groundnut is
    a South American cultivated plant which was disseminated so widely and rapidly within
    Africa that some have postulated an African origin. This is not the case, but Africans appar-
    ently introduced the plant into North America (A. Krapovickas, "The Origin, Variability
    and Spread of the Groundnut," in Peter J. Ucko and G. W. Dimbleby, eds., *The
    Domestication and Exploitation of Plants and Animals* [London, 1969], 427–441).

37 Romans, *History of East and West Florida*, I, 130; Orrin Sage Wightman and Margaret Davis
    Cate, *Early Days of Coastal Georgia* (St. Simons Island, Ga., 1955), 163.

38 Elias Ball to Elias Ball, Feb. 26, 1786, Ball Family Papers, University of South Carolina,
    Columbia; Elise Pinckney, ed., *The Letterbook of Eliza Lucas Pinckney, 1739–1762* (Chapel
    Hill, N.C., 1972), 28.

39 "Bolzius Answers a Questionnaire," trans. and ed. Loewald *et al.*, *WMQ*, 3d Ser., XIV
    (1957), 236; John Glen to the Board of Trade, Mar. 1753, C.O. 5/374, 147, Public
    Record Office; Bernhard A. Uhlendorf, trans. and ed., *The Siege of Charleston: With an
    Account of the Province of South Carolina . . .* (Ann Arbor, Mich., 1938), 353. The cultiva-
    tion of tobacco spread rapidly through West Africa during the 17th century, so that
    18th-century black immigrants to South Carolina might well have been familiar with the
    crop. See, for example, Jack R. Harlan *et al.*, eds., *Origins of African Plant Domestication*
    (The Hague, 1976), 296, 302, and Philip D. Curtin, *Economic Change in Precolonial Africa:
    Senegambia in the Era of the Slave Trade* (Madison, Wis., 1975), 230.

40 Evangeline Walker Andrews and Charles McLean Andrews, eds., *Journal of a Lady of Quality*
    . . . (New Haven, Conn., 1923), 176–177.

41 Cooper and McCord, eds., *Statutes*, VII, 368, 382, 409.

42 Mr. Isaac Bodett's Release to a Negro for Fifty Years, Nov. 13, 1728, Records of the
    Secretary of the Province, Book H, 42–43, S.C. Archs.; Columbia.

43 John Gerar William De Brahm, *Report of the General Survey in the Southern District of North
    America*, ed. Louis De Vorsey, Jr. (Columbia, S.C., 1971), 94.

44 William Butler, "Observations on the Culture of Rice," 1786, S.C. Hist. Soc., Charleston.
    One plantation journal recorded completed daily tasks and acres planted: the quarter-acre
    task was uniformly applied throughout the planting season. See Plantation Journal, 1773,
    Wragg Papers, S.C. Hist. Soc.

45 J. Channing to Edward Telfair, Aug. 10, 1786, Telfair Papers, Duke University, Durham,
    N.C.; Wilbur H. Siebert, ed., *Loyalists in East Florida, 1774 to 1785*, II (DeLand, Fla.,
    1929), 67.

46 Butler, "Observations," 1786. There was a parallel debate in England at this time between
    the advocates of regularly employed wage-labor and the advocates of "taken-work." One
    of those who censured the recourse to taken-work made a similar point to that of Butler:
    people only agreed to tasking, this critic alleged, in order "to save themselves the trouble
    of watching their workmen" (Thompson, "Time, Work-Discipline," *Past and Present*, No.
    38 [1967], 78–79).

47 Letter to printers, *City Gazette* (Charleston), Mar. 14, 1796. The readiness with which sea
    island planters extended the task system to sea island cotton planting suggests prior famil-
    iarity which, in turn, suggests that indigo planting had been subject to tasking. No direct
    evidence of this connection is available, so far as I am aware. Few upland cotton planta-
    tions employed a thoroughgoing task system. One that did—the Silver Bluff plantation
    belonging to Christopher Fitzsimmons, subsequently owned by James Henry Hammond—
    was run as an absentee property and was more than likely populated by slaves already
    inured to tasking when resident on Fitzsimmons's tidewater plantation (Drew Gilpin Faust,
    personal communication).

48 James Glen to the Board of Trade, July 15, 1751, C.O. 5/373, 155–157, P.R.O.; Garden
    to the Royal Society, May 1, 1757, Guard Book III, 86; G. Moulton to [?], Dec. 20, 1772,
    Add. MSS 22677, 70, British Library.

49 John Gerar William De Brahm, *History of the Province of Georgia . . .* (Wormsloe, Ga., 1849),
    51; Ralph Gray and Betty Wood, "The Transition from Indentured to Involuntary Servitude
    in Colonial Georgia," *Explorations in Economic History*, XIII (1976), 361–364.

50 Ramsay, *History of South Carolina*, II, 278–280. High rates of profit continued to charac-
    terize the large rice plantations (see Dale Evans Swan, *The Structure and Profitability of the
    Antebellum Rice Industry, 1859* [New York, 1975]).

51 John Drayton, *A View of South-Carolina as Respects Her Natural and Civil Concerns* (Spartanburg,
    S.C., 1972 [orig. publ. Charleston, S.C., 1802]), 116; James Parker's Journal of the
    Charlestown Expedition, Feb. 5, 1780, Parker Family Papers, 920 PAR I 13/2, Liverpool
    City Libraries, Liverpool, England.

52 Timothy Ford speaks of half-acre tasks (Joseph W. Barnwell, ed., "Diary of Timothy Ford,
    1785–1786," *S.C. Hist. Mag.*, XIII [1912], 182). However, the first specific reference that
    I have so far found to the 150-square-feet task is in Edmund Ruffin, *Report of the
    Commencement and Progress of the Agricultural Survey of South-Carolina for 1843* (Columbia,
    S.C., 1843), 104.

53 See Table 11.1. Time and space do not permit an investigation of the effect of develop-
    ments in machinery on slave work routines. However, to give but one example, the
    pounding task of the early 18th century was, by the end of the century, redundant.
    Agricultural manuals in the 19th century do not set daily tasks for pounding.

54 Richard Hutson to Mr. Croll, Aug. 22, 1767, Charles Woodward Hutson Papers,
    University of North Carolina, Chapel Hill.

55 Josiah Smith to George Austin, Jan. 31, 1774, Josiah Smith Letterbook, Univ. N.C., Chapel
    Hill.

56 [Edwin C. Holland], *A Refutation of the Calumnies Circulated against . . . Slavery . . .* (New
    York, 1969 [orig. publ. Charleston, S.C., 1822]), 53. In the antebellum era, the role of
    the laborers continued to be significant in the evolution of the task system. For a partic-
    ularly good example of the difficulty in modifying a long-established task (in this case,
    threshing), see James M. Clifton, ed., *Life and Labor on Argyle Island: Letters and Documents
    of a Savannah River Rice Plantation, 1833–1867* (Savannah, Ga., 1978), 8–9. Frederick Law
    Olmsted also noted that "in all ordinary work custom has settled the extent of the task,
    and it is difficult to increase it." If these customs were systematically ignored, Olmsted
    continued, the planter simply increased the likelihood of "a general stampede to the
    'swamp'" (*A Journey in the Seabord Slave States* [New York, 1968 (orig. publ. 1856)],
    435–436). James Henry Hammond waged what appears to have been an unsuccessful battle
    with his laborers when he tried to impose gang labor in place of the task system much
    preferred by his slaves (Drew Gilpin Faust, "Culture, Conflict, and Community: The
    Meaning of Power on an Ante-bellum Plantation," *Journal of Social History*, XIV
    [1980], 86).

57 Daniel Turner to his parents, Aug. 13, 1806, Daniel Turner Papers, Library of Congress
    (microfilm). Equally sacrosanct, at least to some slaves, was the product of their "time."
    Thus, in 1781 a set of plantation slaves attempted to kill their overseer because he tried
    to appropriate the corn that they were apparently planning to market (*South-Carolina and
    American General Gazette* [Charleston], Jan. 20, 1781).

58 Frederick E. Maser and Howard T. Maag, eds., *The Journal of Joseph Pilmore, Methodist
    Itinerant: For the Years August 1, 1769 to January 2, 1774* (Philadelphia, 1969), 188.

59 ["Scotus Americanus"], *Information Concerning the Province of North Carolina, Addressed to
    Emigrants from the Highlands and Western Isles of Scotland* (Glasgow, 1773), in William K.
    Boyd, "Some North Carolina Tracts of the Eighteenth Century," *North Carolina Historical
    Review*, III (1926), 616. This account almost certainly refers to the Cape Fear region of
    North Carolina. For slightly less detailed accounts see François Alexandre Frédéric, duc
    de La Rochefoucauld-Liancourt, *Travels through the United States of North America . . .*, I
    (London, 1799), 599; Drayton, *View of South Carolina*, 145; and Edmund Botsford, *Sambo
    & Tony, a Dialogue in Three Parts* (Georgetown, S.C., 1808), 8, 13, 34.

60 Charlestown District Grand Jury Presentments, *S.C. Gaz.*, Jan. 25, 1772.

61 Declaration of John Blake, Apr. 25, 1788, Miscellaneous Record Book VV, 473, S.C.
    Archs., Columbia.

62 *State Gazette of South-Carolina* (Charleston), Oct. 26, 1793.

63 William Read to Jacob Read, Mar. 22, 1800, Read Family Papers, S.C. Hist. Soc.,
    Charleston. For another description of property owning by lowcountry slaves in the early

19th century, see Sidney Walter Martin, ed., "A New Englander's Impressions of Georgia in 1817–1818: Extracts from the Diary of Ebenezer Kellogg," *Journal of Southern History*, XII (1946), 259–260.

64 A Georgian, "Account of the Culture and Produce of the Bearded Rice," *South. Agric.*, III (1830), 292. For the evidence that about two acres was the sowing "task," see "A Memorandum of Tasks," *ibid.*, VII (1834), 297, and Ruffin, *Report*, 118.

65 A Plain Farmer, "On the Culture of Sweet Potatoes," *South. Agric.*, V (1832), 120; for the cooper's task see the sources cited for Table 11.1.

66 Testimony of Peter Way, claim of William Roberts, July 4, 1873, Liberty County, Georgia, Case Files, Southern Claims Commission, Records of the 3d Auditor, Record Group 217, Records of the U.S. General Accounting Office, National Archives. Hereafter, only the name and date—county and state will be added whenever a claim originates from an area other than Liberty Co., Ga.—will be given, followed by the abbreviation, SCC.

67 Testimony of Philip Campbell, claim of Windsor Stevens, July 12, 1873, SCC; claimant's deposition, claim of Diana Cummings, June 17, 1873, Chatham County, Ga.; see also testimony of Henry LeCount, claim of Marlborough Jones, July 30, 1873.

68 Mason Crum, *Gullah: Negro Life in the Carolina Sea Islands* (Durham, N.C., 1940), 51; for a similar use of the term, but by a son of former slave parents, see Wightman and Cate, *Early Days of Coastal Georgia*, 81.

69 For example, see the claim depositions of James Anderson, William Cassell, Prince Cumings, Hamlet Delegal, and Thomas Irving of Liberty Co., Ga., SCC.

70 Claimant's deposition, claim of Marlborough Jones, July 30, 1873, SCC; see also claimant's deposition, claim of Somerset Stewart, July 30, 1873.

71 George P. Rawick, ed., *The American Slave: A Composite Autobiography*, III (Westport, Conn., 1972), Pt. iii, 200–201. A black Edisto Islander, born in 1897, interviewed in 1970, was also conversant with the dual meaning of the term "task" (Nick Lindsay, transc., *An Oral History of Edisto Island: The Life and Times of Bubberson Brown* [Goshen, Ind., 1977], 27, 46–47, 50, 53).

72 "Memoranda of a Crop of Corn Grown in St. Andrew's Parish," *South. Agric.*, III (1830), 77; "Account of the Mode of Culture Pursued in Cultivating Corn and, Peas," *ibid.*, IV (1831), 236. An intensive application of tasking to operations that ranged from the construction of post and rail fences to the digging of groundnuts can be found in the Plantation Journal of Thomas W. Peyre, 1834–1851, esp. 259, 332, 365, S.C. Hist. Soc., Charleston. (I am grateful to Gene Waddell, Director of the Society, for bringing this to my attention.)

73 Even Lewis Gray and U. B. Phillips, the two standard authorities on the task system, are confused on this issue. The task-acre in tidewater rice cultivation ideally took the form of a field 300′ × 150′, divided into two half-acre "tasks" of 150′ square. The task-acre on inland rice and sea island cotton plantations was ideally a square of 210′, divided into four quarter-acre squares, each side 105′ in length. See R.F.W. Allston, "Sea-Coast Crops of the South," *De Bow's Review*, XVI (1854), 596, 609; cf. Phillips, *Negro Slavery*, 247, 259, and Gray, *History of Agriculture*, I, 553.

74 Jacob Wood, "Account of the Process of Cultivating, Harvesting and Manufacturing the Sugar Cane," *South. Agric.*, III (1830), 226.

75 The Editor, "Account of an Agricultural Excursion Made into the South of Georgia in the Winter of 1832," *ibid.*, VI (1833), 576.

76 Testimony of William Winn, claim of David Stevens, July 17, 1873, SCC; testimony of James Frazer, claim of John Bacon, July 7, 1873.

77 Claimant's deposition, claim of Joseph Bacon, Aug. 12, 1873, SCC; testimony of Peter Way, claim of Silvia Baker, Aug. 9, 1873.

78 Testimony of Tony Law, claim of Linda Roberts, July 19, 1873, SCC. See also D. E. Huger Smith, *A Charlestonian's Recollections, 1846–1913* (Charleston, S.C., 1950), 29.

79 Claimant's deposition, claim of John Crawford, Mar. 3, 1874, SCC; claimant's deposition, claim of Frank James, Mar. 14, 1874.

80 See, for example, Leon F. Litwack, *Been in the Storm So Long: The Aftermath of Slavery* (New York, 1980), 410.

81 Lt. Douglas G. Risley to Col. C. C. Sibley, June 2, 1867 (A123), Freedman and Southern Society, files of documents in the Natl. Archs., University of Maryland, College Park. (Hereafter reference to documents read at the Society will be given in parentheses.) But cf. Litwack, *Been in the Storm*, 410.

82 Bvt. Maj. Gen. Charles Devens to Bvt. Lt. Col. W.L.M. Burger, AAG, Oct. 29, 1865, and Nov. 13, 1865 (C1361, Pt. 1, C4160, Pt. 1); Brig. Gen. W. T. Bennett to Bvt. Lt. Col. W.L.M. Burger, AAG, Oct. 11, 1865 (C1361, Pt. 1).

83 Ben Allston *et al.*, to Col. Willard, Oct. 30, 1865 (C1602, Pt. 2); Lt. Col. A. J. Willard to Capt. G. W. Hooker, AAG, Nov. 7, 1865 (C1614, Pt. 2).

84 This information was derived from Lt. Col. A. J. Williard to Capt. G. W. Hooker, AAG, Nov. 7, 1865, and Dec. 6, 1865 (C1614, Pt. 2, C1503, Pt. 1); case #104, James Geddes v. William B. Seabrook, Feb. 11, 1867 (C1534, Pt. 1); contract between William H. Gibbons and 120 Freedmen, Chatham Co., Ga., Mar. 1, 1866 (A5798); Maj. Gen. James B. Steedman and Bvt. Brig. Gen. J. S. Fullerton to E. M. Stanton, June 4, 1866 (A5829); Capt. Henry C. Brandt to Lt. Col. A. W. Smith, Jan. 12, 1867 (A5395). See also John David Smith, "More than Slaves, Less than Freedmen: The 'Share Wages' Labor System During Reconstruction," *Civil War History*, XXVI (1980), 256–266, for the example of a contract, *not* the analysis that accompanies it. A detailed analysis of the labor contracts in operation in these years would undoubtedly enrich, and perhaps modify, this section.

85 A. M. McIver to Lt. J. M. Hogg (SAC), Feb. 28, 1867 (A5769); see also Lt. W. M. Wallace to Capt. E.W.H. Read, Jan. 8, 1867 (C1619); D. M. Burns to [?], Mar. 17, 1867 (A7188); and Joel Williamson, *After Slavery: The Negro in South Carolina during Reconstruction, 1861–1877* (Chapel Hill, N.C., 1965), 135–136.

86 Harry Hammond, "Report on the Cotton Production of the State of South Carolina," in U.S. Census Office, *Tenth Census, 1880* (Washington, D.C., 1884), VI, Pt. ii, 60–61.

87 Testimony of Richard Cummings, claim of Lafayette Delegal, July 11, 1873, SCC; claimant's deposition, claim of Scipio King, July 9, 1873. A number of lowcountry freedmen made similar statements. For the general recollections of ex-slaves see, obviously, George P. Rawick, *From Sundown to Sunup: The Making of the Black Community* (Westport, Conn., 1972), and Paul D. Escott, *Slavery Remembered: A Record of Twentieth-Century Slave Narratives* (Chapel Hill, N.C., 1979), 38.

88 Testimony of Peter Stevens, claim of Toney Elliott, Aug. 8, 1873, SCC; testimony of July Roberts, claim of Nedger Frazer, Feb. 27, 1874; report of R. B. Avery and testimony of Gilmore and Co., attorneys for claimant, claim of Jacob Dryer, Nov. 1, 1873.

89 The settled or allowed claims from ex-slaves for Liberty and Chatham counties, Ga., and Beaufort, Charleston, and Georgetown counties, S.C., were investigated. For a fuller presentation of my findings, see "The Ownership of Property by Slaves in the Mid-Nineteenth-Century Lowcountry," *Jour. So. Hist.* (forthcoming).

90 The Liberty Co., Ga., claims are the most numerous and most detailed. They contain few urban claimants and form the ideal sample for the purposes of this study. Eighty-nine former slaves from this county submitted claims that were settled: 50 of the 89 were field hands and 25 of 86 were under the age of 35 when their property was taken. For a fuller discussion of the reliability of these claims and an analysis of the claimed property, see my article cited in n. 89.

91 Testimony of Raymond Cay, Jr., claim of Paris James, June 2, 1874, SCC. Cay also said that he "looked upon [James] as one of the most thrifty slaves in Liberty County." His claim totaled $1,218.

92 Testimony of W. A. Golding, claim of Linda (and Caesar) Roberts, July 19, 1873, SCC. His claim totaled $1,519.

93 Report of R. B. Avery, claim of Jacob Quarterman, July 5, 1873, SCC; report of R. B. Avery, claim of Prince Stewart, July 29, 1873; report of the Commissioners of Claims, claim of James Stacy, Aug. 15, 1873.

94 Claimant's deposition and testimony of John Fish, claim of Alexander Steele, Aug. 17, 1872, Chatham Co., Ga., SCC.

95 Charles E. Beveridge *et al.*, eds., *The Papers of Frederick Law Olmsted*, II (Baltimore, 1981), 182. Twenty-four field hands, out of a total of 53 slaves, claimed horses.

 96 Two Liberty Co. freedmen testified to a ban on horse ownership on their plantations; three recalled that only drivers had horses; and fourteen supply the proportions mentioned here.

 97 Claimant's deposition, claim of Paris James, June 2, 1874, SCC.

 98 Claimant's deposition, claim of Nedger Frazer, Feb. 27, 1874, SCC. This is the same Niger, as he was known as a slave, who objected to being hired out in 1864 because he was unable, as he put it, to "make anything for himself," and who pretended to have yellow fever so that Sherman's troops would not deprive him of his property (see Robert Manson Myers, ed., *The Children of Pride: A True Story of Georgia and the Civil War* [New Haven, Conn., 1972], 1162, 1237).

 99 Myers, ed., *Children of Pride*, 244, 306.

100 Testimony of W. A. Golding, claim of Linda (and Caesar) Roberts, July 19, 1873, SCC.

101 Claimant's deposition, claim of John Bacon, July 7, 1873, SCC.

102 Report of R. B. Avery, claim of Robert Bryant, Oct. 6, 1877, Beaufort Co., S.C., SCC.

103 Claimant's deposition, claim of William Drayton, Feb. 20, 1874, Beaufort Co., S.C., SCC; testimony of Sterling Jones, claim of Sandy Austin, July 21, 1873.

104 James Miller, for example, recalled that "many times I would get some one to help me, and get along that way, I would pay them whatever they asked according to the time they worked" (report of R. B. Avery, claim of James Miller, July 29, 1873, SCC). See also claimant's deposition, claim of Pompey Bacon, Aug. 7, 1873–.

105 Claimant's deposition, claim of Edward Moddick and Jacob Hicks, Mar. 17, 1873, Chatham Co., Ga., SCC.

106 Report of J.P.M. Epping, claim of Pompey Smith, n.d., Beaufort Co., S.C., SCC.

107 Testimony of Joseph James, claim of Linda and Caesar Jones, Aug. 1, 1873, SCC.

108 Testimony of T. Fleming before R. B. Avery, claim of Prince Wilson, Jr., July 28, 1873, Chatham Co., Ga., SCC. The widespread ownership of animals is also indicated in the records of one lowcountry plantation. In 1859 almost 40 slaves, over half the adult males on the plantation, owned at least one cow, cow and calf, steer or heifer. Only about 10 of the 40 held skilled or privileged positions (Weehaw Plantation Book, 1855–1861, 87, S.C. Hist. Soc., Charleston).

109 Testimony of Fortune James, claim of Charles Warner, Aug. 6, 1873, SCC; claimant's deposition, claim of Prince Wilson, Jr., July 28, 1873, Chatham Co., Ga.; claimant's deposition, claim of Jane Holmes, July 21, 1873.

110 Jeremiah Evarts Diary, Apr. 5, 1822, Georgia Historical Society, Savannah, as quoted in Thomas F. Armstrong, "From Task Labor to Free Labor: The Transition along Georgia's Rice Coast, 1820–1880," *Georgia Historical Quarterly*, LXIV (1980), 436.

111 The Liberty Co. claimants who mention such acreages include Daniel Bryant, William Cassell, Prince Cumings, George Gould, Ned Quarterman, Paris James, and Richard LeCounte. The Chatham Co. claimants include Dennis Smith and Alfred Barnard. The Beaufort Co. claimants include John Morree, Andrew Riley, Pompey Smith, Moses Washington, and Benjamin Platts. When James Miller's brother, Lawrence, a student at Howard University, was asked whether the hundred bushels of rice claimed by his brother was not excessive, he replied, "I should not think so—not in his condition." James's "condition" was only that of a field hand, but he was the "director" of the family, and the family planted five acres (testimony of Lawrence Miller, claim of James Miller, July 29, 1873, SCC).

112 Claimant's deposition, claim of Adam LeCount, Feb. 26, 1874, SCC.

113 Gibbes, "Southern Slave Life," *De Bow's Review*, XXIV (1858), 324; Olmsted, *Journey*, 443. Fanny Kemble noted that two carpenters on the Butler estate sold a canoe to a neighboring planter for $60 and that slaves could earn large sums by collecting Spanish moss (Frances Anne Kemble, *Journal of a Residence on a Georgian Plantation in 1838–1839*, ed. John A. Scott [New York, 1961], 62, 364). Unfortunately, there are no estimates of the proportion of money circulating among the slaves. The handling of money certainly gave rise to some discernment: one freedman remembered paying $60 in "good money" for a horse. He continued, "I call silver money good money, I call confederate money

wasps' nests" (claimant's deposition, claim of Simon Middleton, June 2, 1873, Chatham Co., Ga., SCC).

114   Alice R. Huger Smith, *A Carolina Rice Plantation of the Fifties* (New York, 1936), 72.

115   Claimant's deposition, claim of Joseph Bacon, Aug. 12, 1873, SCC.

116   Claimant's deposition, claim of Samuel Elliott, July 17, 1873, SCC.

117   Claimant's deposition, claim of York Stevens, Mar. 2, 1874, SCC; claimant's deposition, claim of Edward Brown, Feb. 20, 1874, Beaufort Co., S.C.; claimant's deposition, claim of William Roberts, July 4, 1873; claimant's deposition, claim of William Drayton, Feb. 20, 1874, Beaufort Co., S.C.

118   Claimant's deposition, claim of Jane Holmes, July 21, 1873, SCC. Twenty-three Liberty Co. freedmen referred to inheriting property within the same plantation.

119   Claimant's deposition and testimony of Andrew Stacy, claim of Nancy Bacon, Mar. 14, 1874, SCC; Stacy performed the same service for Clarinda Porter (claimant's deposition, claim of Clarinda Porter, Feb. 18, 1874). Nine Liberty Co. freedmen referred to inheriting property across plantation boundaries.

120   Claimant's deposition, claim of Diana Cummings, June 17, 1873, Chatham Co., Ga., SCC.

121   See, for example, claimant's deposition, claim of Silvia Baker, Aug. 9, 1873, SCC; claimant's deposition, claim of Hamlet Delegal, Mar. 7, 1874; and claimant's deposition, claim of William Golding, May 16, 1874.

122   Claimant's deposition, claim of Jacob Monroe, July 18, 1873, SCC.

123   Testimony of Joshua Cassell, claim of George Gould, Aug. 11, 1873, SCC.

124   Testimony of William Gilmore, claim of York Stevens, Mar. 2, 1874, SCC.

125   Testimony of B. K. Lee, 1863 (K72); testimony of Henry G. Judd, 1863 (K74); testimony of Brig. Gen. Rufus Saxton, 1863 (K70).

126   Testimony of Saxton, 1863 (K70).

127   Testimony of Lafayette Delegal, claim of Richard Cummings, Feb. 28, 1874, SCC.

128   Report of R. B. Avery, claim of William Golding, May 16, 1874, SCC; Olmsted, *Journey*, 428.

129   Testimony of Leah Wilson, claim of Prince Wilson, Jr., July 28, 1873, Chatham Co., Ga., SCC. See also the claim depositions of William Gilmore and Hamlet Delegal, and the testimony of Simon Cassell, Henry Stephens, and Fortune James in the claims of Jacob Monroe, Clarinda Porter, and Charles Warner respectively.

130   Edward S. Philbrick to Pierce. Mar. 27, 1862 (Q12).

131   Bvt. Lt. Col. R. F. Smith report in Bvt. Maj. Gen. R. K. Scott to O. O. Howard, July 9, 1866 (C1428, Pt. 1). See also Bvt. Lt. Col. B. F. Smith to O. A. Hart, Apr. 25, 1866 (C1617).

132   Leigh, *Ten Years on a Georgia Plantation* (London, 1883), 55.

133   E. T. Wright to Lt. Col. H. B. Clitz, Oct. 6, 1865 (C1361, Pt. 1).

134   J. G. Foster to [?], Sept. 20, 1864 (C1334, Pt. 1).

135   Joseph D. Pope to Maj. Gen. Q. A. Gilmore, June 29, 1865 (C1472).

136   Lt. Col. A. J. Willard to W. H. Smith, Nov. 13, 1865 (A7011).

137   Smith report in Scott to Howard, July 9, 1866 (C1428, Pt. 1); Leigh, *Ten Years on a Georgia Plantation*, 124.

138   I have been influenced by Eric Foner, *Politics and Ideology in the Age of the Civil War* (New York, 1980), 97–127; Willie Lee Rose, *Rehearsal for Reconstruction: The Port Royal Experiment* (New York, 1976 [orig. publ. Indianapolis, Ind., 1964]), 226, 303, 406; and the works by Mintz cited in n. 8.

139   Report of R. B. Avery, claim of Samuel Maxwell, June 8, 1878, SCC.

140   J. R. Cheves to A. P. Ketchum, Jan. 21, 1866 (A7058).

141   Apart from the standard works on peasants by Wolf, Shanin, and Mintz, I found the general implications of James C. Scott, *The Moral Economy of the Peasant: Rebellion and Subsistence in Southeast Asia* (New Haven, Conn., 1976) particularly helpful.

142   For antebellum slaves, and on a general level, this is the argument of Genovese, *Roll, Jordan, Roll*, esp. 133–149.

143 Arney Robinson Childs, ed., *The Private Journal of Henry William Ravenel, 1859–1887* (Columbia, S.C., 1947), 216; Capt. H. A. Storey to C. B. Fillebrown, July 9, 1865 (C1468). Ravenel still considered his plantation hands to be slaves in Mar. 1865.

144 William Dallam Armes, ed., *The Autobiography of Joseph Le Conte* (New York, 1903), 234. Long after emancipation, when he had ceased to be a landowner, Daniel Huger Smith still shared in "the same interchange of small gifts of eggs or a chicken or two on the one side and perhaps an article of clothing on the other" that had characterized master–slave relations many years before (*Recollections*, 127).

145 Scott, *Moral Economy of the Peasant*, 157–192.

146 Testimony of Oliver P. Bostick, claim of Andrew Jackson, Mar. 10, 1874, Beaufort Co., S.C., SCC; Rufus King, Jr., to William Washington, Sept. 13, 1828, in *American Farmer*, X (1828), 346.

147 See Mintz, "Slavery and the Rise of Peasantries," in Craton, ed., *Roots and Branches*, 241.

148 The phrase was coined by Tadeusz Lepkowski, referred to by Sidney W. Mintz, "Was the Plantation Slave a Proletarian?" *Review*, II (1978), 94. I would also suggest that there was a significantly wider peasant breach in the slave mode of production in the lowcountry than elsewhere in North America where "incentives," in the forms of garden plots, opportunities to earn money, etc., were accorded slaves. More comparative work is obviously needed, but evidence from one area of the antebellum South supports my supposition (Roderick A. McDonald, "The Internal Economies of Slaves on Sugar Plantations in Jamaica and Louisiana" [unpubl. paper, Southern Historical Association Meeting, 1981]). In any case, I am reluctant to describe the task system as an incentive system; it was more a way of life.

149 Mintz, "Slavery and the Rise of Peasantries," in Craton, ed., *Roots and Branches*, esp. 226–233. In the same way that I consider there to have been a wider peasant breach in the slave mode of production in the lowcountry than elsewhere in North America (though it was certainly not absent elsewhere), I also believe—and this is almost a corollary—that the ability to escape the plantation, while not unique to the lowcountry, was more effectively secured here than elsewhere in North America.

150 As we might expect, lowcountry freedmen, particularly sea islanders, proved an unreliable source of labor for the phosphate mines. Their plots of land took precedence, and their earnings from mining formed only a welcome supplement to the income derived from farming (Tom W. Schick and Don H. Doyle, "Labor, Capital, and Politics in South Carolina: The Low Country Phosphate Industry, 1867–1920" [unpubl. paper], 11).

151 Roger L. Ransom and Richard Sutch, *One Kind of Freedom: The Economic Consequences of Emancipation* (Cambridge, 1977), 91–93; Williamson, *After Slavery*, 155; W. E. B. DuBois, "The Negro Landholder of Georgia," *Bulletin of the United States Department of Labor*, VI, 35 (1901), 647–677; T. J. Woofter, *Black Yeomanry* (New York, 1930); *Morning News* (Savannah), Jan. 30, 1880, quoted in Armstrong, "From Task Labor to Free Labor," *Ga. Hist. Qtly.*, LXIV (1980), 443. This last-mentioned article makes a similar argument to the one here.

152 Mintz, "Plantation Slave," *Review*, II (1978), 95.

Chapter 12

Peter H. Wood

BLACK LABOR—WHITE RICE

I

NO DEVELOPMENT HAD GREATER impact upon the course of South
Carolina history than the successful introduction of rice. The plant itself,
shallow-rooted and delicate, is now rare on the landscape it once dominated, but
its historical place in the expansion of the colony and state is deep-seated and secure,
hedged round by a tangle of tradition and lore almost as impenetrable as the wilderness swamps near which it was first grown for profit. Despite its eventual
prominence, the mastery of this grain took more than a generation, for rice was a
crop about which Englishmen, even those who had lived in the Caribbean, knew
nothing at all. White immigrants from elsewhere in northern Europe were equally
ignorant at first, and local Indians, who gathered small quantities of wild rice, had
little to teach them. But gradually, after discouraging initial efforts, rice emerged
as the mainstay of the lowland economy during the first fifty years of settlement,
and the cultivation of this grain for export came to dominate Carolina life during
the major part of the eighteenth century. "The only Commodity of Consequence
produced in South Carolina is Rice," commented James Glen in 1761, "and they
reckon it as much their staple Commodity, as Sugar is to Barbadoes and Jamaica,
or Tobacco to Virginia and Maryland."[1]

Throughout the eighteenth century white Carolinians marveled at their own
industry and good fortune in having conjured this impressive trade from a single
bushel of rice, and they debated which Englishman should wear the laurels for
introducing the first successful bag of seed. In 1726 a Swiss correspondent stated
that "it was by a woman that Rice was transplanted into Carolina,"[2] and occasional
mention was made of the idea that the first seeds came aboard a slaving ship from
Africa. "Opinions differ about the manner in which rice hath been naturalized in
Carolina," wrote the Abbé Raynal at the end of the eighteenth century. "But
whether the province may have acquired it by a shipwreck, or whether it may have
been carried there with slaves, or whether it be sent from England, it is certain
that the soil is favourable for it."[3]

Since rice cultivation had a halting beginning which stretched over several
decades, numerous bags of imported seed could have contributed to its growth.
Documentary evidence is scanty, and it therefore seems likely that minor issues of

individual precedence may never be fully resolved. One fact which can be clearly documented, however, and which may have considerably greater significance, is that during precisely those two decades after 1695 when rice production took permanent hold in South Carolina, the African portion of the population drew equal to, and then surpassed, the European portion. Black inhabitants probably did not actually outnumber whites until roughly 1708. But whatever the exact year in which a black majority was established, the development was unprecedented within England's North American colonies and was fully acknowledged long before the English crown took control of the proprietary settlement in 1720.

The fact that the mastery of rice paralleled closely in time the emergence of a black majority in the colony's population has not been lost upon scholars of the early South. But while few have failed to note it, none can be said to have explained it adequately. What could either be a mere coincidence on the one hand, or a crucial interrelation on the other, has been bypassed with short passages carefully phrased. One author observed that in 1700 "The transition from mixed farming and cattle raising to rice culture was just beginning, and with it the development of negro slavery."[4] Another stated that "South Carolina's especially heavy commitment to the use of Negro labor coincided closely with the development of rice as a new and profitable staple."[5] Similarly, a third scholar concluded that despite an earlier preference for Negro labor, white "South Carolinians did not import Negroes in large numbers until after the introduction of rice in the 1690's."[6] In short, there appears to be an ongoing consensus among the leading southernists that somehow "rice culture turned planters increasingly to slave labor,"[7] but the causal relationships suggested, or perhaps skirted, by such observations have received little analysis.

Were Negro slaves simply the cheapest and most numerous individuals available to a young colony in need of labor? Or were there other variables involved in determining the composition of the Carolina work force? In exploring such questions it is first necessary to examine the different sorts of potential labor—red, white, and black—which existed in the early years. It will then be possible, by focusing on the process of rice cultivation at the end of this chapter and on matters of health in the next, to suggest two separate factors which may have contributed far more than has been acknowledged in fostering the employment of African slaves.

II

Although persons from Africa had been enmeshed in New World colonization for more than a century and a half before the founding of Carolina, alternative sources of labor were very real possibilities during the early years of the lowland settlement. The option closest at hand was that presented by the numerous Indian tribes which had inhabited the area for centuries. Their interaction with white and black foreigners during the colonial era constitutes a separate story, but it is clear that they provided some much-needed support in the early years. English trade goods could be used to purchase their services cheaply, and no expensive importation costs were incurred. Difficulties in verbal communication were offset by the Indians' impressive knowledge of the land; they could provide ready food, suitable medicine, and safe passage in a semitropical wilderness environment which was unfamiliar to Europeans. Several neighboring tribes, with a pragmatic eye upon English firearms and woolens, were quick in coming forward to assist the new colonists, offering "to fish, and hunt their Game for a Trifle; to fell Tim[ber, to plant] Corn, and to gather in their Crop: as also to Pilot, and convey them from on[e place] to another."[8]

Settlers were greedy for involuntary as well as voluntary Indian labor, despite obvious disadvantages.[9] Acts of enslavement were risky, since any provocations in the earliest years contained the danger of retaliation.[10] In later decades, as the colony became slightly more secure, local slaving ventures presented a threat to the growing Indian trade. Moreover, women and children were more likely than men to be taken alive during intertribal wars and sold to the colonists. Even when white traders promoted intertribal conflicts to obtain cheap slaves, the likelihood of later escape by the captives reduced their value in the vicinity.[11]

But when Indians were sold to an unfamiliar region where they were less likely to run away, their value as slaves went up. Therefore a small commerce developed in exchanging Indian captives abroad for more tractable white or black labor,[12] or for additional livestock which would encroach further upon Indian land. During the late seventeenth century, in fact, Carolina was more active than any other English colony in the export of Indian slaves. In 1679, for example, the Carolina bark Mary carried "goods and slaves" to Virginia to exchange for several mares and a hold full of neat cattle.[13] At the Proprietors' insistence, a system of permits was established to regulate these deportations. It provided that no slave was to be exported "without his owne consent," but among the victims fear of their Indian captors and ignorance of their white purchasers seems to have made this consent readily obtainable.[14]

Although the Proprietors had few scruples about slavery as an institution, they protested strenuously against the "evill men" who "made a trade of enslaving & sending away the pore Indians."[15] In part they were fearful of prompting hostilities with local tribes or the nearby Spanish (fears realized when a combined force of Spaniards, Indians, and Negroes attacked the settlement in 1686), and in part they were anxious to protect their peaceful trade in deerskins, which provided the colony's first source of direct revenue to England.[16] With the opening up of this lucrative Indian trade to more people in the 1690s, the European settlers themselves became increasingly willing to curtail their limited reliance upon native American labor. Although enslavement of Indians continued on into the settlement's second generation, any thought of utilizing such laborers as the core of the colonial work force had dissipated well before the end of the seventeenth century.

The alternative of a white labor force presented a different set of variables. Simple reasons of custom, language, and religion naturally made Europeans prefer to have other Europeans working with and under them. But it was one thing to promote independent migration from Europe and another to contract serviceable labor from there. Some of the difficulties became apparent with the first fleet that paused at Kinsale in Ireland to obtain several dozen servants. The attempt failed totally, and Robert Southwell wrote to Lord Ashley that the Irish there had been so "terrified with the ill practice" of being shipped to the Caribbean islands "where they were sold as slaves that as yet they will hardly give credence to any other usage."[17] Not even offers of brief service and generous land grants could offset this negative publicity entirely.[18]

BLACK LABOR—WHITE RICE 227

For the overall availability of white labor in the colony, the number of Europeans recruited was less important than the terms of indenture under which they came. Individual contracts varied widely. Some whites may have signed on as servants for the outward passage in order to help someone else obtain land through the headlight system, only to be released upon arrival to take up lands of their own.[19] Others worked until the cost of their passage was paid. It was not unheard-of for elderly people to indent themselves for life, but generally a specific term of service was set. Among colonies competing for European labor such terms of service had to be roughly comparable, and they tended to decrease through time. The usual term in Barbados dropped from five to seven years before the Restoration to three to five years after, with bargains for as little as one year's labor being struck in certain instances.[20] Carolina contracts diminished similarly: in an indenture surviving from 1682 a London sawyer promised to serve for two years in the Charlestown settlement.[21]

Such brief contracts resulted in a rapid turnover in the dependent white work force, and Gov. Archdale, addressing the commons in 1695, was not the first to complain of the "Servants that Dayley become free."[22] More important, even a steady flow of indentured servants failed to increase the available pool of unfree manpower beyond a certain fixed point; it merely replenished the small supply of persons serving work-terms, while the overall population continued to grow.[23] To maintain even this supply it was necessary for the colony to avoid the risk of adverse rumors about extended servitude. In 1687, therefore, a statute was passed which set maximum limits upon terms of service for new white arrivals according to their age. The same act imposed a further expense upon the employer by requiring him to provide each servant at the end of his term with "one suite of Apparell, one barrel of Indian Corne, one Axe and one Hoe."[24]

Even before their terms expired, English servants who sensed their value in a labor-scarce economy could often better their lot. One man appealed successfully to the grand council for a change of household, since his current master "could not at present maintaine him with convenient & necessary provisions, and clothes."[25] And many who could not bargain for their well-being must have stolen instead, for "Servants purloyning their masters goods" became an early topic of concern.[26] Occasional disappearances and acts of flagrant disobedience were other matters of common anxiety. Severe penalties deterred most, though by no means all, white servants from attempting to flee the colony altogether, but many shared the disposition of Philip Orrill, who was sentenced to twenty-one lashes for threatening his mistress, tossing his rations to the dogs, "and divers other Gross abuses and destructive practices."[27]

General lethargy and laziness constituted one further vice which seemed prevalent among whites (and which was by no means confined to servants). Whether the Europeans were simply diverted from their Protestant ethic of work by the mild climate or instead actually sacrificed some measure of their physical health is debatable, but the observation was commonplace. "Inhabitants toil not in summer to accommodate themselves with Winter's Provision," wrote Gascoyne, and Archdale observed bluntly that the "natural Fertility and easy Manurement, is apt to make the People incline to Sloth."[28] Thus in quality, as well as in quantity, white indentured labor clearly left something to be desired.

III

The alternative of African labor was a plausible one from the outset. It appeared natural to colonizers from the West Indies and intriguing to those from western Europe, and it afforded certain advantages to both. Since Africans came from a distance, their exploitation did not present the serious diplomatic and strategic questions posed by Indian labor, yet their Caribbean sources were closer and their transportation costs lower than those of white workers. Unlike white servants, Negroes could be held for unlimited terms, and there was no means by which word of harsh or arbitrary treatment could reach their homelands or affect the further flow of slaves. Moreover, Africans had long had the reputation of being able to fend for themselves more readily than Europeans in the subtropical southern Atlantic climate—a valuable asset when provisions were scarce.[29]

The barriers posed by language were scarcely more formidable for Africans than for other non-English-speakers and had often been reduced through time spent in the West Indies. The useful effects of this Caribbean "seasoning" are noted in a letter of 1688. Edmund White wrote from London to Joseph Morton, two-time governor of the Carolina colony, offering the chance for investment in a slave ship which was sailing directly to the Guinea Coast, but acknowledging that Morton might rather venture his capital on Negroes already in the West Indies. If that were the case, White went on to recommend that Morton contact one Col. Johnson in Barbados, asking whether, "when any bargaine of negroes is to be had, he would buy them for you and keep them upon his plantation till he can send them." This, White assured Morton, "he can doe with much care & the negroes will be the better after they have been ashore for sometime and their work will be worth their keeping."[30] It is notable that White added, "let yʳ negroes be taught to be smiths shoemakers & carpenters & bricklayers: they are capable of learning anything & I find when they are kindly used & have their belly full of victualls and [possess suitable] clothes, they are the truest servants."[31]

The actual methods of obtaining black labor were quite varied at first, and many of the colony's earliest Negro slaves, like certain European and Indian workers, were secured by dubious means. Piracy was at its height in the Caribbean during the period of Carolina's settlement, and there is little doubt that colonists occasionally offered shelter and provision to buccaneers in exchange for portions of their spoils.[32] In 1684 the governor of Jamaica, protesting the increase of piracy to the Lords of Trade and Plantations, "represented to them the great damage that does arise in His Majesty's service by harbouring and encouraging of Pirates in Carolina."[33] A year later the Proprietors wrote their colony concerning some accused pirates, transported from Charlestown to London for trial, who reportedly "had negroes gould and other things which were seized in Carolina," all of which would fall to the Proprietors if the men were found guilty.[34] A large pirate fleet had plundered Vera Cruz in 1683, and according to the depositions made by several runaway English servants at St. Augustine in January 1686, South Carolina obtained roughly two hundred Negroes from this and other raids.[35] (The appearance of Spanish names among early slaves supports such testimony.) Raiding parties carried off Negroes from New Providence, the nearest English slave island in the Bahamas, twice during 1684, and again in 1703.[36]

A few Negroes no doubt came to Carolina through the practice of "salvaging" for resale slaves who had been abandoned to their own devices in the Caribbean as a result of natural disasters or shipboard rebellions.[37] Other blacks were imported to Carolina from as far away as England upon occasion.[38] As for imports directly from Africa, it is possible that interlopers in the slave trade who were turned away from Barbados by the Royal African Company might have traveled as far as Carolina, but this seems unlikely, for the colony's economy would not reach a scale capable of absorbing and paying for a large shipload of slaves on short notice until well after the turn of the century. One or two small vessels from Charlestown may have risked an Atlantic crossing to seek a cargo of African workers before 1700, but any such efforts were exceptional during the colony's first generation.

Throughout the first twenty-five years the documentary evidence suggests that most Negroes arriving in Carolina were brought in small numbers, by specific owners, from points in the western hemisphere. For example, in 1683 the ship Betty, "rideing att Anchor in the Roade of Barbadoes & bound for Ashley River in Carolina," took aboard six Negroes, along with two half-barrels of flour and two barrels of rum, for delivery "unto Bernard Schenckingh or to his Assignes." Upon their arrival, Schenckingh was to pay what must have been the standard shipping charge of fifty shillings per head for the group of slaves, which included four men (June, Meningo, Walle, Bache), one young woman (Cumboe), and a boy (Popler).[39] Because of the direction of Carolina's mercantile ties and the broader patterns of the English slave trade, Barbados served as the main source for this small-scale commerce in Negro labor. Due to the increased exertions of the Royal African Company and the growing number of separate traders, that island entrepot received more than seventy thousand slaves between 1670 and 1695.[40] Barbadian disdain for Irish labor ("commonly very idle") was expressed to the Lords of Trade and Plantations in 1676 by Sir Jonathan Atkins, who claimed that sugar planters had found by experience that black slaves worked better at one third the cost. In 1680 he observed that "since people have found out the convenience and cheapness of slave labour they no longer keep white men, who formerly did all the work on the Plantations."[41]

The preferences of the Caribbean landlords, although geared to a very different economy, must have been widely known to their Carolina cousins. Carolina's reliance upon Barbados for what slaves its white colonists could afford served to strengthen further the existing ties to the sugar island, and these bonds—in a circular fashion—helped predispose would-be planters in the mainland colony to black labor. Since little social hierarchy was possible at first in the southern wilderness, slave ownership quickly became a means for Englishmen to establish status distinctions in the mainland settlement. Their food, clothing, and shelter became more similar with migration; the destitute lived somewhat better, and the well-to-do somewhat worse, than they had before. At Bridgetown in Barbados, where more than 90 per cent of white householders owned Negroes—almost twice the percentage that possessed white labor[42]—the pattern counted for little, but in Charlestown, where white servants represented a smaller, safer, and more common investment than black, the possession of Negroes assumed additional social connotations.

Since an African retinue, however forlorn, served to distinguish and to reinforce authority patterns among whites, it is not surprising that at first local officials were among the largest individual importers of slaves. Among the early governors,

Sayle brought several slaves despite his brief tenure; Yeamans and Morton owned dozens between them. James Colleton employed black laborers on his extensive barony and probably left most of them there when he returned to Barbados; while Seth Sothell possessed at least ten slaves even before he replaced Colleton.[43] Sir Nathaniel Johnson, who would become governor in 1702, had imported over several decades more than one hundred "Servants & Negroes at Sundry times on his account in this parte of the province," and when the Rev. Samuel Thomas visited Johnson's Cooper River estate of "Silk Hope," he noted that "his family is very large many servants and slaves."[44]

Such status-seeking had certain implications for the slaves purchased to fill symbolic roles. Several hundred Negroes must have belonged to the handful of whites who each owned more than a dozen black workers before 1695. These slaves apparently lived upon large tracts in remote areas, where contacts with other Africans were limited but where the nucleus of a social unit larger than a family could already exist. Supervision was partial and activities varied, for new crops were being tried and new land cleared annually. (It is misleading to glorify—or damnify—any of these isolated seventeenth-century holdings as "plantations.") For slaves who had served on sugar plantations the uncertainties of the frontier must have posed a welcome contrast to the harsh routine of the islands, and for those who were dressed handsomely and employed superficially in ways calculated to enhance their master's stature, there were the small gratifications which the patronizing and the patronized always share. But labor was too scarce for any but the most highly placed to restrict Negroes to symbolic or genteel functions as yet. If certain masters purchased blacks to announce their social arrival, most employed them to better their economic well-being. In general, therefore, slaves simply shared the calling of the white household to which they were annexed, participating fully in the colony's growing number of specialized trades.[45]

IV

There were, however, numerous impediments to the use of African labor in Carolina, and widespread enslavement of Negroes was by no means a foregone conclusion from the start. An inexperienced Huguenot settler claimed that "any man who has a couple of negroes, a ready-made plantation, [and] a maid-servant . . . can live very happily . . . in this country at small outlay,"[46] but in fact the outlay required for black labor was by no means small. Indeed, it was their price, more than anything else, that limited the viability of slave laborers at first. If African labor was recognized in the Caribbean as potentially more profitable than European labor over the long run, it still entailed a larger initial investment, and many early settlers in Carolina who could not afford to bring slaves brought indentured servants instead. A Negro purchased outright for an unlimited period could be worked harder, maintained more cheaply, and retained longer than a white servant under a limited indenture, but only after several years of steady labor would these comparative advantages begin to carry weight. The additional cost and responsibility of such a purchase had limited appeal in a frontier colony where money was scarce, risks were high, and the future nature of the economy was still uncertain.

Whenever slave labor could be purchased cheaply, it usually represented an excessive gamble. The Canteys, an Irish family of small means who reached Carolina by way of Barbados in the 1670s, acquired along the way a slave named Marea and her infant son, Jacke. This "Sicke Dropsecall diseased Negro woman" was later appraised at two pounds and could hardly have been a valuable asset.[47] Moreover, even white Carolinians with sufficient capital to import healthy Negro labor could not always find sound investments at hand. Barbadian planters, who reckoned the mortality of their bondsmen at one in twenty annually, had prior call upon their island's expanding supply of imported slaves. As a result, other settlements, as close to Barbados as Nevis, complained about the price and quality of Negroes available through re-export. In the more distant and less wealthy mainland colony these problems were still greater.[48]

Foreign competition compounded these difficulties. Not only were the English colonies in the Caribbean, to which Jamaica had been added in 1655, exploiting Africans in growing numbers, but the mainland colonies of Spain were obtaining an increasing percentage of their slaves through British merchants. Although the Navigation Acts of 1661 excluded foreign ships from trading with English colonies, several thousand of the Royal African Company's slaves were annually diverted into "assientist" vessels, and in 1685 the Lords of Trade officially exempted from seizure "Spanish ships that are come to buy negroes"[49] at English ports in the Caribbean. Since the Spaniards could generally pay high prices in hard coin without requesting credit, they received priority over English planters and pushed the cost of Company Negroes upward. When the planters resorted to interlopers to supply their own demand, the expense of procuring slaves in Africa was also increased. Overall slave prices among the English appear to have risen more than 20 per cent during the 1680s.[50] Therefore, advantages related to employing Negroes in Carolina were largely offset by increasing demands for their services elsewhere.

And indeed, in Carolina itself the attraction of foreign demand was felt. Although the re-export of slaves from Charlestown for profit would not prove generally feasible for another three quarters of a century, the first generation of white settlers were never free from the thought of exchanging valuable Negro labor for Spanish bullion. Lord Shaftesbury, himself associated with the Royal African Company, had commerce with the Florida Catholic settlement in mind when he considered establishing his barony in Carolina. "You are to endeavour," he instructed Andrew Percivall in 1674, "to begin a Trade with the Spaniards for Negroes, Clothes or other Commodyties they want."[51] In the 1680s when eleven blacks (members of a larger contingent of "diverse negroe slaves" which had run away from South Carolina) appeared at St. Augustine, embraced Catholicism, and sought permanent asylum there, Maj. William Dunlop negotiated to sell them to the Spanish for sixteen hundred pieces of eight.[52] After the Spanish raid of 1686, in which thirteen of Landgrave Morton's slaves were carried off, his brother-in-law killed, and "great desolation . . . made in the South part of this Settlem,"[53] Gov. Colleton reopened trading relations so quickly that eyebrows were raised.[54] "The truth is," confirmed a later report, "there was a design on foot to carry on a Trade with the Spaniard."[55] Strategic considerations finally outweighed commercial interests, however, and no regular profits came to the English from selling slaves to their nearby Spanish rivals.

Next to the high initial cost, it was the frequency of disappearances which presented the greatest drawback to employing black labor, and these two factors were of course related. The unlimited term which raised the price of the slave also increased his motivation to escape; unlike the indentured servant's his situation contained no prospect of predictable improvement. Since settlement conditions were harsh and means of social control superficial, disappearances were frequent for all varieties of unfree labor in the new province, but the departure of a servant with several years left to serve was less costly to his white master than the absence of a lifetime slave.[56] Some newcomers were undoubtedly deterred from running away by ignorance of local geography, but many were knowledgeable and realistic about the prospects for escape, if only because of the regulations which forbade it. The likely refuge of St. Augustine was a constant subject of public discussion in early years, and the appearance of Carolina slaves and servants there gives evidence that its whereabouts was not overlooked.[57] Although more distant and less inviting, Virginia was also known, particularly to those laborers who had been brought from that direction. As early as 1671, when Yeamans sent Dr. Henry Woodward on a secret overland journey to the north, Gov. West had expressed concern to Lord Ashley that "if he arrives safe in Virginia, there is a way laid for or Serv^ta to range in, wee have lost two allready."[58]

Similar concerns are borne out in the colony's first legislation devoted entirely to slavery, an "Act for the Better Ordering of Slaves" passed by the Assembly in 1690 and quickly disallowed by the Proprietors for political reasons.[59] This statute represented little more than a reworking by the local West Indian faction of a strict law drawn up by whites in Barbados after a suspected Negro plot in 1688.[60] Significantly, the law initiated a system of tickets for slaves sent on errands, despite the absence of any effectual means of enforcement, and it sanctioned such brutal corporal punishments as branding, nose-slitting, and emasculation at a time when very few slaveowners in the wilderness colony were yet in a secure enough position to resort to punishments more severe than whipping.[61] [. . .] it is worth noting here that pirates occasionally conspired with Negroes to mutual advantage.[62] Having benefited in some instances from the slaves' arrival, the buccaneers were not above profiting from their escape, and more than one black was transported away to be sold again elsewhere or retained as a crewman. Nor was the line between pirate and non-pirate particularly clear in this turbulent era. The French pirate ship La Trompeuse, which included Negroes and Indians as well as Europeans among its crew, served briefly as an official man-of-war in 1684.[63] On the other hand, H.M.S. Drake, although assigned to protect the Carolina coast, engaged in this illegal traffic on the side. A letter of 1690 denounces her commander as a "Piraticall villain" who "seases carys abroad and receaves of Negros Runing from their Masters 2000 lib [pounds] worth to the ruining [of] many famalies."[64]

The attitudes of neighboring Indians, more than the activities of pirate groups, were crucial to the retention of black labor during this first generation. Local tribes could assist runaway Negroes or else capture and return them, depending upon a variety of factors. It quickly became apparent to white colonists that the nature of this response would in large measure determine the frequency and success of slave departures, and efforts were undertaken to have the surrounding native population assume, in effect, the confining function performed by the sea in the West Indies.[65] The Proprietors, through selfish concern for the growing fur trade, offered constant reminders that without good Indian relations "you can never get in yoʳ Negroes that run away."⁶⁶ By the 1690s, as Negro numbers expanded and the trade in furs opened up, the white colonists took concrete steps to set black and red at cross purposes. Gov. Thomas Smith reported to the commons at the start of its fall session 1693 that he had "by the Advice of the Councill Sumond all yᵉ neighbouring Indians to Receive Some Comands from yᵉ Councill relateing to Runaway slaves." Yet despite such dealings, Indian relations with the white slavemasters remained ambiguous, and the disappearance of black servants from the isolated colony continued. An inventory compiled the following spring for an extensive Charlestown estate includes, at a value of twenty-nine pounds, "one negro man named will now rund away."⁶⁷

Despite these various drawbacks, hundreds of Negroes were brought to Carolina to supplement labor from other sources. Frequently during the first generation black and white workers were imported on the same boat by the same planter, as was the case with "Tom: Samboe: Betty & Peter," who arrived at Charlestown in September 1682 alongside their master and his six European servants.⁶⁸ Already it was generally understood that indentured servants were white and their terms were short, while nonwhite laborers served for life; but anomalies remained common. A European could be bound to a life term;⁶⁹ an Indian could obtain an indenture.⁷⁰ And regardless of formal status, the actual conditions of life and labor did not yet vary greatly between servant and slave, free and unfree. The fact that few new residents were so well stationed as to be exempt from hardship, or so insignificant as to be expendable, is underscored by the letter of a young Huguenot girl who arrived in 1685. Judith Giton wrote to her brother in Europe, "*J'ai bien été dans ce pais six mois sans avoir goûté de pain, et que je travaillois à la terre comme une esclave.*"⁷¹

Where white migrants "worked like slaves," black arrivals labored in many respects like hired hands, and there were numerous households in which captured Indians, indentured Europeans, and enslaved Africans worked side by side during these first years. For example, the estate of John Smyth, who died in 1682, included nine Negroes, four Indians, and three whites.⁷² Even though such dependants were not all engaged in the same tasks or accorded equal status, they must have fulfilled complementary functions at close quarters. In the final balance, therefore, no one form of labor seemed sufficiently cheap or superior or plentiful to preclude the others.

V

Just as no single type of manpower predominated within the colony at first, no single economic activity preoccupied the varied work force of the early years. Given this context, the large-scale transitions to a slave labor force and to a rice-growing economy during the second generation take on particular interest. Both changes depended upon a great number of separate variables, and it is certainly conceivable that these parallel developments, so thoroughly intertwined in later years, had little causal relation at the outset. Every colony was in search of a staple, and South Carolina's commitment to rice developed only gradually; as late as 1720 there was probably more labor engaged in the production of meat exports and naval stores than in the growing of rice. Likewise every colony was in search of labor, and if each obtained from the nearest source workers who were accustomed to the prevailing climate, it was natural that the northern colonies would draw servants from Europe while the southern colonies were taking slaves from the West Indies and Africa. In South Carolina, there were logical reasons for the appearance of black laborers irrespective of the tasks intended for them. More than any mainland colony, its roots of settlement and early commercial ties stretched toward Barbados and the other islands of the English Caribbean. African labor was already in steady supply there, and English colonists from the West Indies who were economically unable to bring Negroes with them at least brought along the social aspiration of slave ownership. Laborers from the British Isles were in shorter supply during the period of South Carolina's early settlement than they had been during the initial years of the Virginia or Maryland colonies, and after the end of the government monopoly on the slave trade in 1699, the mainland colony closest to the Caribbean stood to benefit most from the participation of private English traders in the traffic in unfree labor.

Even reduced to briefest form, these points are logical enough, and in themselves they suggest little more than a temporal association between the development of rice and slavery. But one possible link has never been fully explored. Scholars have traditionally implied that African laborers were generally "unskilled" and that this characteristic was particularly appropriate to the tedious work of rice cultivation. It may well be that something closer to the reverse was true early in South Carolina's development. Needless to say, most of the work for all colonists was what one Scotsman characterized as simple "labor and toyl of the body,"[73] but if highly specialized workers were not required, at the same time there was hardly a premium on being unskilled. It seems safe to venture that if Africans had shown much less competence in, or aptitude for, such basic frontier skills as managing boats, clearing land, herding cattle, working wood, and cultivating fields, their importation would not have continued to grow. Competence in such areas will be considered elsewhere, but it is worthwhile to suggest here that with respect to rice cultivation, particular know-how, rather than lack of it, was one factor which made black labor attractive to the English colonists.

Though England consumed comparatively little rice before the eighteenth century, the cheap white grain had become a dietary staple in parts of southern Europe by 1670, and Carolina's Proprietors were anticipating a profit from this crop even before the settlement began.[74] The colonists sent out from London in 1669 did not possess rice among their experimental samples, although an enticing pamphlet for the Cape Fear settlement several years earlier had suggested that "The meadows are very proper for Rice."[75] Nevertheless, a single bushel or barrel of rice was shipped by the Proprietors along with other supplies aboard the *William & Ralph* early in 1672. This quantity may have been planted rather than eaten, for one of several servants who defected to St. Augustine two years later told the Spanish governor that the new colony produced "some rice" along with barrel staves and tobacco.[76] But by 1677 the colonists still had little to show for their experimental efforts, and their sponsors wrote impatiently from London: "wee are Layinge out in Severall places of ye world for plants & Seeds proper for yor Country and for persons that are Skill'd in plantinge & producing . . . Rice oyles & Wines." There is no direct evidence, however, that the Proprietors followed through on this promise, or that they responded helpfully to later requests for guidance.[77]

During the 1680s, perhaps after the arrival of a better strain of rice seed from Madagascar, the colonists renewed their rice-growing efforts.[78] The mysteries of cultivation were not unraveled quickly, however, as is shown by several letters from John Stewart in 1690.[79] Stewart had been managing Gov. James Colleton's "Wadboo Barony" and was taking an active part in rice experimentation.[80] He claimed to have cultivated the crop in twenty-two different places in one season to ascertain the best location and spacing of the plant. Stewart boasted, perhaps truthfully, that already "Our Ryce is esteem'd of in Jamaica," but even this arch promoter did not yet speak of the grain as a logical export staple. Instead he proposed that rice could be used for the distilling of beer and ale ("from what I observ'd in Russia"), and he went on to suggest that planters "throw by Indian corne to feed slaves with rice as cheaper."

The processing as well as the planting of rice involved obstacles for the Europeans, which may explain why they had discarded the crop initially. "The people being unacquainted with the manner of cultivating rice," recalled an Englishman during the eighteenth century, "many difficulties attended the first planting and preparing it, as a vendable commodity, so that little progress was made for the first nine or ten years, when the quantity produced was not sufficient for home consumption."[81] Similarly, Gov. Glen would later claim that even after experimenters had begun to achieve plausible yields from their renewed efforts around 1690, they still remained "ignorant for some Years how to clean it."[82]

By 1695 Carolina was not yet one of the sources from which England drew her moderate supply of rice, and the colonial legislature was still urging diversity of output as it cast about for a suitable economic base.[83] In 1698 the Assembly was seeking information on such possible activities as whale fishing and the raising of Smyrna currants. Although a request was also made that the Proprietors "Procure and Send . . . by y^e: first oppertunity a moddell of a Rice mill,"[84] it is doubtful that any such thing was ever found or sent. More than a decade later, Thomas Nairne mentioned the practice of cleaning rice in mills turned by oxen or horses, but no such labor-saving machines came into common use. It is notable that Nairne, like many others in South Carolina at the start of the eighteenth century, continued to view rice in large part as an adjunct to the livestock economy. "'Tis very much sow'd here," he wrote in 1710, "not only because it is a vendable Commodity, but thriving best in low moist Lands, it inclines People to improve that Sort of Ground, which being planted a few Years with Rice, and then laid by, turns to the best Pasturage."[85]

In contrast to Europeans, Negroes from the West Coast of Africa were widely familiar with rice planting. Ancient speakers of a proto-Bantu language in the sub-Sahara region are known to have cultivated the crop. An indigenous variety (*Oryza glaberrima*) was a staple in the western rain-forest regions long before Portuguese and French navigators introduced Asian and American varieties of *O. sativa* in the 1500s.[86] By the seventeenth and eighteenth centuries, West Africans were selling rice to slave traders to provision their ships. The northernmost English factory on the coast, James Fort in the Gambia River, was in a region where rice was grown in paddies along the riverbanks. In the Congo–Angola region, which was the southernmost area of call for English slavers, a white explorer once noted rice to be so plentiful that it brought almost no price.[87]

The most significant rice region, however, was the "Windward Coast," the area upwind or westward from the major Gold Coast trading station of Elmina in present-day Ghana. Through most of the slaving era a central part of this broad stretch was designated as the Grain Coast, and a portion of this in turn was sometimes labeled more explicitly as the Rice Coast. An Englishman who spent time on the Windward Coast (Sierra Leone) at the end of the eighteenth century claimed that rice "forms the chief part of the African's sustenance." He went on to observe, "The rice-fields or *luqars* are prepared during the dry season, and the seed sown in the tornado season, requiring about four or five months growth to bring it to perfection."[88] Throughout the era of slave importation into South Carolina references can be found concerning African familiarity with rice. Ads in the local papers occasionally made note of slaves from rice-growing areas,[89] and a notice from the *Evening Gazette*, July 11, 1785, announced the arrival aboard a Danish ship of "a choice cargo of windward and gold coast negroes, who have been accustomed to the planting of rice."[90]

Needless to say, by no means every slave entering South Carolina had been drawn from an African rice field, and many, perhaps even a great majority, had never seen a rice plant. But it is important to consider the fact that literally hundreds of black immigrants were more familiar with the planting, hoeing, processing, and cooking of rice than were the European settlers who purchased them. Those slaves who were accustomed to growing rice on one side of the Atlantic, and who eventually found themselves raising the same crop on the other side, did not markedly alter their annual routine. When New World slaves planted rice in the spring by pressing a hole with the heel and covering the seeds with the foot, the motion used was demonstrably similar to that employed in West Africa."[91] In summer, when Carolina blacks moved through the rice fields in a row, hoeing in unison to work songs, the pattern of cultivation was not one imposed by European owners but rather one retained from West African forebears.[92] And in October when the threshed grain was "fanned" in the wind, the wide, flat winnowing baskets were made by black hands after an African design.[93]

Those familiar with growing and harvesting rice must also have known how to process it, so it is interesting to speculate about the origins of the mortar-and-pestle technique which became the accepted method for removing rice grains from their husks. Efforts by Europeans to develop alternative "engines" proved of no avail, and this process remained the most efficient way to "clean" the rice crop throughout the colonial period. Since some form of the mortar and pestle is familiar to agricultural peoples throughout the world, a variety of possible (and impossible) sources has been suggested for this device.[94] But the most logical origin for this technique is the coast of Africa, for there was a strikingly close resemblance between the traditional West African means of pounding rice and the process used by slaves in South Carolina. Several Negroes, usually women, cleaned the grain a small amount at a time by putting it in a wooden mortar which was hollowed from the upright trunk of a pine or cypress. It was beaten with long wooden pestles which had a sharp edge at one end for removing the husks and a flat tip at the other for whitening the grains. Even the songs sung by the slaves who threshed and pounded the rice may have retained African elements.[95]

In the establishment of rice cultivation, as in numerous other areas, historians have ignored the possibility that Afro-Americans could have contributed anything more than menial labor to South Carolina's early development. Yet Negro slaves, faced with limited food supplies before 1700 and encouraged to raise their own subsistence, could readily have succeeded in nurturing rice where their masters had failed. It would not have taken many such incidents to demonstrate to the anxious English that rice was a potential staple and that Africans were its most logical culti- vators and processors. Some such chain of events appears entirely possible. If so, it could well have provided the background for Edward Randolph's comment of 1700, in his report to the Lords of Trade, that Englishmen in Carolina had "now found out the true way of raising and husking Rice."[96]

Notes

1 Glen, *Description*, p. 95. See Gray, *Agriculture*, II, 1021–23.
2 This claim, unnoticed by historians, is contained in a letter of Nov. 4, 1726, from Jean Watt in Neufchatel to M. le Col. de Valogne in London, BPRO Trans., XII, 156–57. For other claims, see BPRO Trans., XVII, 165; *Gentleman's Magazine*, XXXVI (1766), 287; Gray, *Agriculture*, I, 277.
3 Abbé Raynal, *Philosophical and Political History of the Possessions and Trade of Europeans in the Two Indies*, 6 vols. (2nd edn., London, 1798), VI, 59. (The first edition in 1772 offered only the shipwreck theory.)
4 Crane, *Southern Frontier*, p. 22.
5 Craven, *Colonies in Transition*, p. 292. Craven continued, "Although experiments with rice date from very early in the colony's history, success apparently came only in the last decade of the century, when new channels for the supply of Negro labor to the North American colonies also opened."
6 Sirmans, *Colonial S.C.*, p. 24; cf. Appendix A.
7 Anbrey C. Land, ed., *Bases of the Plantation Society* (paperback edn., New York, 1969), p. 206. Cf. Frank Robert Hawkins, "Legislation Governing the Institution of Slavery in Colonial South Carolina," unpublished master's thesis (University of Wisconsin, 1968), p. 1.
8 Gascoyne, *True Description*, p. 3. Louis Thibon's letter of Sept. 20, 1683, SCL, described the European settler's situation:

> If he wishes to hunt or to have an Indian hunt for him there is no lack of venison or game. An Indian will provide a family of 30 with enough game and venison, as much as they can eat, all the year round for 4 crowns . . . We have 15 or 16 nations of Indians round us who are very friendly and the English get on well with them; the largest number is not more than 500 strong. They bring them a great quantity of deer skins and furs.

9 Southeastern Indians had long accepted a pattern of forced servitude for criminals, debtors, and war prisoners, but it appeared to Europeans that "Their Slaves are not over-burden'd with Work." Lawson, *New Voyage*, p. 240; cf. p. 210. The standard work on Indian slavery is Almon W. Lauber, *Indian Slavery in Colonial Times within the Present Limits of the United States* (*Columbia University Studies in History, Economics and Public Law*, LIV, no. 3, New York, 1913). See also Crane, *Southern Frontier*: John T. Jurieck, "Indian Policy in Proprietary South Carolina: 1670–1693." unpublished M.A. thesis (University of Chicago, 1962); and the following unpublished Ph.D. dissertations: Lawrence Foster, "Negro-Indian Relationships in the Southeast" (University of Pennsylvania, 1935); William Robert Snell, "Indian Slavery in Colonial South Carolina, 1671–1795" (University of Alabama, 1972).
10 One disadvantage of unfettered livestock was the antagonism they aroused among the Indians. Wandering herds damaged Indian crops as they had done in the Caribbean during the previous century and in New England more recently. Local tribes occasionally stole

troublesome stock, and recriminations were constant. The Europeans, however, were not above turning these annoyances to advantage. The disappearance of several hogs could offer a helpful pretext for slaving raids like those made among the Coosas (Kussos) in 1671 and the Westoes in 1672. See BPRO *Trans.*, I, 174; Crane, *Southern Frontier*, p. 123; Waring, *First Voyage*, pp. 38, 46–47.

11 See Lauber, *Indian Slavery*, p. 288.

12 Edward McCrady, "Slavery in the Province of S.C.," p. 641, points out that this process was familiar elsewhere: "In 1650, Indians who failed to make satisfaction for injuries in Connecticut were ordered to be seized and delivered to the injured party, 'either to serve or to be shipped out and exchanged for negroes, as the case will justly bear.'"

13 RSP (1675–95), pp. 36–37. Maurice Mathews and James Moore, who undertook the venture, were both associated with Indian trading.

14 *Coll.*, V, 367; *Journal of the Grand Council, 1671–1680*, p. 80.

15 BPRO *Trans.*, I, 289; II, 59–60.

16 BPRO *Trans.*, II, 184; McCrady, *Proprietary Govt.*, p. 190. Cf. Louis R. Smith, "South Carolina Indian Trade Regulations, 1670–1756," unpublished M.A. thesis (University of North Carolina, 1968).

17 *Coll.*, V, 153. Southwell's credibility as an agent was enhanced "because they know I never had anything to due with the West India trade, but have ransomed many of them that have beene snatched up and privately conveyed on board the ship bound that way." Yet even this was not enough.

18 If previous abuses complicated the recruitment process in England, so did efforts to regulate the system of "voluntary servitude" there. In 1682 the king and council issued an order, renewed in 1686, calling for all English indentures to be recorded before a magistrate and to be cleared with a guardian wherever minors were involved. The fact that the Navigation Laws prohibited direct trade by the American colonies with Ireland and Scotland added further to the difficulty of procuring labor from those two sources.

19 *Warrants*, II, 81. Hugh Carteret received a warrant for 325 acres on March 20, 1683, which included "70 acres for his wife arriveing a ser^t: upon his acco^{tt}; in August 1671 [and] 70 acres allowed his wife at the expiracon of her servitude." Cf. *Warrants*, I, 61.

20 Harlow, *Barbades*, pp. 190 n, 301 n.

21 MH "A" (1682–90), p. 7.

22 *SCCHJ, 1695*, p. 7.

23 Cf. Thomas J. Wertenbaker, *The Old South* (New York, 1942), p. 308 n.

24 *Statutes*, II, 30–31. These "freedom dues," like terms of service, had to be competitive between colonies seeking indentured labor. North Carolina's promise of "Corne & Cloathes" is mentioned in CRNG, I, 579. For laws elsewhere, see Gray, *Agriculture*, 1, 365–66.

25 *Journal of the Grand Council, 1671–1680*, p. 52; cf. *Coll.*, V, 318, McCrady, "Slavery in the Province of S.C.," p. 633, cites the case of a woman named Elizabeth Linning who was taken up at the dockside in Glasgow. A captain transporting thirty-two political prisoners who had been banished to the colonies sold Linning into service in May 1684, but she was able to petition successfully for her liberty within the same year.

26 *Coll.*, V, 358. How many white servants had been convicted of similar crimes elsewhere and then deported to Carolina has always been a matter of debate, but there is little doubt that some who arrived on indentures had criminal records. A memorandum in the British Public Record Office (BPRO *Trans.*, III, 204) dated July 2, 1697, reads: "This day a Letter was writ to Mr Thornburgh about some Women Convicts now lying in Newgate [prison] for transportation proposed to be sent to Carolina."

27 *Journal of the Grand Council, 1671–1680*, pp. 33–34; cf. 14, 22–23, 25, 47, 54–55, 63–64; also see Sirmans, *Colonial S.C.*, pp. 21–22. Masters felt the adds for such ill behavior to be stronger among certain groups than among others. Joseph West, for example, having complained openly about the first servants drawn from England, held those from Barbados in even lower repute. He wrote the Proprietors in 1671:

> I hope yor Honn^{ra} are thinking of sending a supply of Servta from England, for some of these wilbe out of their time the next yeare, and wee find that one of

our Servtta we brought out of England is worth 2 of ye Barbadians, for they are
soe much addicted in Rum y^t they will doe little but whilst the bottle is at their
nose.

Coll., V. 299; cf. 387, 436–37. A "Drinker's Dictionary" which appeared in SCG, May 7, 1737, listed "Been at Barbados" as one local expression for being drunk or hung over.

28 Gascoyne, *True Description*, p. 2; Salley, *Narratives*, p. 290. A general consideration of this theme appears in David Bertelson, *The Lazy South* (New York, 1967), esp. Chapter III.

29 For example, a century earlier (June 4, 1580) the Council of the Indies in Madrid, in urging that thirty slaves be sent out from Havana to work on the fortifications at St. Augustine, remarked that, "With regard to their food, they will display diligence as they seek it in the country, without any cost to the royal treasury." Jeannette Thurber Conner, trans. and ed., *Colonial Records of Spanish Florida* (De Land, Fla., 1930), II, 315.

30 *SCHGM*, XXX (1929), 3. (The term "seasoning" was used in different ways to cover the process of adjustment—physical and psychological—faced by Europeans and Africans entering the plantation colonies of the New World.)

31 *Ibid.*, pp. 3–4. Of course few Europeans in the seventeenth century were likely to concede —or even suspect—that such Negro skills with metal, leather, wood, and masonry could well be the result of prior familiarity. Still, it was soon granted among whites that, by one means or another, blacks seemed to "understand most handycrafts." The Rev. John Urmston, July 7, 1711, *CRNC*, I, 764.

32 *Journal of the Grand Council, April–Sept., 1692*, pp. 54, 60. *SCHGM*, XVII (1916), 15, 16; IX (1908), 187.

33 *CRNC*, I, 347.

34 BPRO *Trans.*, II, 31.

35 Cited in Childs, *Colonization*, p. 207. The date is misprinted there as Jan. 11, 1696.

36 *Ibid.*, pp. 195–96, 207; Mass. Hist. Soc., *Collections*, 5th ser., VI, 88 n. Cf. Shirley Carter Hughson, "The Carolina Pirates and Colonial Commerce, 1670–1740," *Johns Hopkins University Studies in Historical and Political Science*, 12th ser. (Baltimore, 1894).

37 It was a common practice aboard slave vessels in distress to nail down the hatches over the "live cargo." See "Life of Equiano," pp. 99, 113. For a description of the salvage of slaves from a wrecked Dutch ship, see E. B. O'Callaghan, ed., *Voyages of the Slavers St. John and Arms of Amsterdam* (New York Colonial Tracts, no. 3, Albany, 1867). Some abandoned Negroes were able to protect their independence. The Black Caribs who inhabited the island of St. Vincent before any Europeans were the survivors from a slave ship which sank near Bequia in 1675. Ehenezer Duncan, *A Brief History of St. Vincent* (Kingstown, St. Vincent, W.I., 1941; 4th edn., 1967), p. 2.

38 RSP (1675–95), pp. 239–41, 260, 272. Conceivably, a few of the black slaves removed from Mediterranean galleys and transported to the French West Indies during this period could have ended up in the Ashley River colony. Paul W. Bamford, "Slaves for the Galleys of France, 1665 to 1700," in John Parker, ed., *Merchants and Scholars: Essays in the History of Exploration and Trade* (Minneapolis, 1965), pp. 180–84.

39 RSP (1675–95), p. 128. In the next decade the master of the ketch *Mary* out of Boston was instructed to travel between Carolina and New Providence "or elsewhere with pork and beef and mind that he purchase three or four good negroes." Records of the Court of Ordinary (1692–1700), p. 26, cited in *SCHGM*, VIII (1907), 171.

40 In the last quarter of the seventeenth century Barbados accounted for almost 40 per cent of the British slave trade, a trade which itself still represented less than 30 per cent of the entire Atlantic commerce in Africans during the period. Curtin, *Atlantic Slave Trade*, pp. 55, 119, 122, 124, 129.

41 Harlow, *Barbados*, pp. 309, 308 *n.*

42 Dunn, "The Barbados Census of 1680," 23.

43 On Colleton, see *SCHGM*, XII (1911), 43–52; *SCHGM*, XXXII (1931), 21–22. On Sothell, see BPRO *Trans.*, I, 208.

44 *Warrants*, II, 215; cf. 107, 116, 212, and *SCHGM*, XVIII (1917), 12–13; *SCHGM*, IV (1903), 226.

45 Some prosperous craftsmen owned whole black families, more than one member of which may well have been employed in the business. Stephen Fox, a tanner from Barbados, brought four men, four women, and four children with him aboard the Mary in May 1679; the extensive estate left by James Bearner, a "joyner," in 1694 included three men, three women, and six children; a carpenter named Thomas Gunstone owned two men, two women, and four children who were sold together in 1698. *Warrants*, II, 56; WIMR (1692–93), p. 208; RRP (1696–1703), pp. 100–101.

46 Letter of Louis Thibou, Sept. 20, 1683, SCL. Cf. note 8 above, where Thibou refers expansively to "a family of 30."

47 RSP (1675–95), pp. 61, 69.

48 Donnan, *Documents*, I, 205; Higham, *Leeward Islands*, p. 161.

49 Lords of Trade to colonial governors, April 10, 1685, *Calendar of State Papers, America and West Indies, 1685–1688*, p. 28. Jamaica, as the westernmost island of the English, became the logical center for this commerce, and by the first decade of the eighteenth century it had swept past Barbados as a slave entrepot and consumer of British goods. In the late 1600s, however, it remained common for Spanish sloops to roam as far east as Barbados to acquire Negroes and cloth. Curtis Nettels, "England and the Spanish-American Trade, 1680–1715," *Journal of Modern History*, III (1931), 3 n, 28; Harlow, *Barbados*, p. 311 n.

50 Nettels, "England and the Spanish-American Trade," pp. 5, 7, 11. At times interlopers were carrying as much as a third of the trade. Curtin, *Atlantic Slave Trade*, p. 125.

51 *Coll.*, V. 442.

52 *SCHGM*, XXXIV (1933), 24. There were two women and a three-year-old child, along with eight men, listed as Conano, Jesse, Jaque (Jack), Grun Dumlugo, Cambo, Mingo (suspected of killing an Englishman), Dique (Dick), and Robi.

53 Quoted in Rivers, *Sketch*, p. 425. Two of the slaves escaped and returned. Salley, *Narratives*, p. 205. The others included eight men named Peter, Scipio, Doctor, Cushi, Arro, Emo, Caesar, and Sambo, plus three women listed as ffrank, Bess, and Mammy, *SCHGM*, XXXIV (1933), 4. The eleven remained in St. Augustine and were rumored to be "actually imployed in buildinge a Fort." Rivers, *Sketch*, p. 425.

54 Assemblymen informed Seth Sothell when he arrived to replace Colleton in 1690: "wee are of oppinion wee ought not to be angry at a trade with the Spaniards, but as Englishmen . . . [we wonder] y^t soe exercrable a barbarity . . . should be buryed in silence for the hopes of a little filthy lucre." Rivers, *Sketch*, p. 425.

55 Edward Randolph to the Board of Trade, June 28, 1699, BPRO *Trans.*, IV, 90.

56 The difficulties posed to English Carolinians by black runaways had already been felt in older colonies. As far back as 1648 a traveler touching at Barbados had noted that there were "many hundreds of Rebell negro slaves in the woods." Force, *Tracts*, II, no. 7, p. 5. Yet the Caribbean experience was not entirely analogous. Island runaways were ultimately circumscribed in a way which may have made them more united, resourceful, and desperate at times but which limited their alternatives for escape. Mainland servants, on the other hand, had no absolute natural barrier, and both black and white took advantage of the coastal passages and overland trails that stretched beyond the edges of the colony. Regulations controlling shipboard departures, comparable to those passed in Barbados in 1670, could not have the same effect they had in the island settlement. *Journal of the Grand Council, 1671–1680*, pp. 20, 32–33; *Coll.*, V, 222.

57 By 1689 the red, white, and black populations of the Spanish settlement totaled almost fifteen thousand, and outside St. Augustine there already existed the makings of a distinct Negro community which would grow with time. Charles W. Arnade, *The Siege of St. Augustine in 1702* (Gainesville, Fla., 1959), pp. 9–11; "Dispatches of Spanish Officials Bearing on the Free Negro Settlement of Garcia Real de Santa Teresa de Mose, Florida," *JNII*, IX (1924), 144 ff.: translation of a letter in Spanish from Don La Reano de Torres, governor of St. Augustine, to John Archdale, Jan. 24, 1696, Archdale Papers, mfm, SCDAH, item 13.

58 *Coll.*, V, 338.

59 The first act to mention slaves in its title had been ratified Sept. 25, 1682, and was similar to subsequent acts passed in 1687, 1692, and 1696. All were aimed at "inhibiting the Trading with Servants and Slaves" and reflected the difficulty of imposing strict controls in a wilderness environment. *Statutes*, II, v–viii, acts 7, 34, 81, 135.

The tendency to associate "Servants" and "Slaves" together in these statutes may derive from the loose structure of the labor system in early Carolina, or it may stem from the fact that "all negroes and slaves" were accounted as freehold property rather than chattel property. This meant that, contradictory to the Fundamental Constitutions, a master owned the right to a slave's services but not to his person, and could not transfer or dispose of him at will. Such a legal nicety was by no means thoroughly recognized in daily practice, but it does reflect Carolina's affinity with the Caribbean, where the freehold definition of slavery was commonplace. Sirmans, "Legal Status of the Slave in S.C., 1670–1740," 465; *Statutes*, VII, 344.

60   Richard Hall, comp., *Acts Passed in the Island of Barbados, from 1643, to 1762, inclusive* (London, 1764), act no. 82; John Poyer, *The History of Barbados, from the First Discovery of the Island, in the Year 1605, till the Accession of Lord Seaforth, 1801* (London, 1808), pp. 128–44. Slave uprisings had already been undertaken on the island in 1649 and 1675 and rumored in 1683. When a larger conspiracy was uncovered there in 1692 (Poyer, pp. 155–57), assemblymen in Charlestown considered prohibiting importation "of such slaves as have been Conserned in any plott in Barbados." *SCCHJ*, 1693, p. 15.

61   Section V of the law required masters to search regularly for weapons in "all their slaves houses" at a time when it is likely that few Carolina Negroes yet lived in such separate and solid dwellings. Other portions of the act, however, pertained more closely to the local situation: masters were ordered to issue every slave a convenient set of clothes annually and to refrain from giving slaves Saturday afternoons free as had been the custom in Carolina until that time.

62   There is even an instance on record of a Negro and an Indian helping a captured pirate to escape. McCrady, *Proprietary Govt.*, p. 609.

63   Violet Barbour, "Privateers and Pirates of the West Indies," *AHR*, XVI (1911), 564.

64   John Stewart to Maj. William Dunlop, April 27, 1690, *SCHGM*, XXXII (1931), 25.

65   The fact "that the Indians will be of great Use to ye Inhabitants of our province for the fetching in againe of such Negro Slaves as shall Runn away from their masters" (BPRO *Trans.*, I, 174) was regarded by the Proprietors as grounds for improving relations with the Indians and curtailing their enslavement. A proprietary letter of 1683 hints that many would-be migrants "cannot see how in a large Contingent yo' negroes when Run away shall bee brought in againe, unless y' Indians be preserved." BPRO *Trans.*, I, 260. (The reference to "a large Contingent" of runaways is significant. Even if a clerical error altered what should have read, "a large Continent," as is possible, the passage would still be a notable commentary on the complications of mainland slavery.)

66   BPRO *Trans.*, 11, 293.

67   *SCCHJ*, 1693, p. 27; RSP (1692–1700), p. 164.

68   RSP (1675–95), p. 116. A sample of 45 Negroes imported during the 1670s shows that at least 40 belonged to persons who transported white labor as well.

69   *Ibid.*, p. 123. In 1682 one Mathew English, who had arrived as a servant from Barbados in 1671 and risen to be provost marshal, got a laborer named Robert Midling to agree in writing to work "in all or any manner of Service . . . dureing the whole terme and time of his Naturall life, for which . . . Mathew English doth covenant . . . to finde him . . . Sufficient meat drinke Washing lodgeing and apparrell."

70   *Ibid.*, p. 188. The 1683 will of William Jackson, a farmer who had come from London in 1673 and whose holdings after ten years were primarily in hogs and cattle, reads in part: "I give upto my two servts one breeding sow per piece & I doe moreover Acquitt them from any service they bringing the crop well into the house & my Indian Dan serveing time as per Indenture & my Indian boy serveing seaven years unto . . . Milleson Jackson & then to be ffree."

71   Charles W. Baird, *History of the Huguenot Emigration to America*, 2 vols. (New York, 1885), II, 297. A portion of Baird's translation of the Citon letter (II, 182–83) reads:

> After our arrival in Carolina we suffered all sorts of evils. Our eldest brother
> died of a fever, eighteen months after coming here, being unaccustomed to the
> hard work we were subjected to. We ourselves have been exposed, since leaving

France, to all kinds of afflictions, in the forms of sickness, pestilence, famine, poverty, and the roughest labor. I have been for six months at a time in this country without tasting bread, laboring meanwhile like a slave in tilling the ground. Indeed, I have spent three or four years without knowing what it was to eat bread whenever I wanted it.

72 RSP (1675–95), pp. 21–22. Smyth was a merchant-planter who had brought five Negroes and several servants with him from New York in 1671. He eventually became a member of the grand council and a Lord Proprietor's Deputy. (The inventory for his estate is reprinted in Appendix B.) Even after 1700 the employment of Negro men and Indian women was being commended to would-be planters as "profitable advice." See Crane, *Southern Frontier*, p. 113 n.

73 John Stewart to William Dunlop, April 27, 1690, *SCHGM*, XXXII (1931), 7.

74 Most of what little rice northern Europeans had seen came from the Mediterranean basin at this time, and Carolina, as her promoters enjoyed emphasizing, stood in roughly the same latitude as Jerusalem. The Duke of Albemarle must have spoken for all the Proprietors when he wrote to the governor of Barbados in 1663 that their new domain might be expected to produce "wine, oyle, reasons, currents, rice, silke &c; . . . as well as . . . beefe and poorke." *Coll.*, V, 15.

75 Salley, *Narratives*, p. 69 and note 2.

76 *Coll.*, V, 389–90; Childs, *Colonization*, p. 137.

77 BPRO *Trans.*, 1, 59; cf. note 84 below.

78 Evidence left by white Carolinians concerning the start of rice production can be found in A. S. Salley, *The Introduction of Rice Culture into South Carolina* (*Bulletins of the Historical Commission of South Carolina*, no. 6, Columbia, 1919); Gray, *Agriculture*, 5, 277 ff.; Clowse, *Ec. Beginnings*, pp. 123–32. The Madagascar tradition has been popularized in Duncan C. Heyward, *Seed from Madagascar* (Chapel Hill, N.C., 1937). On slaves from that region, see Virginia B. Platt, "The East India Company and the Madagascar Slave Trade," *WMQ*, 3rd ser., XXVI (1969), 548–77. St. Julien R. Childs, long familiar with these matters, suggests in a letter to the author (June 14, 1973) "that about 1693–1696, two and possibly more 'privateers' came into Charlestown from Madagascar, bringing booty captured from ships along the east coast of Africa. They probably also brought Madagascar rice and Negroes. It is even possible that some of the men who came on these vessels had engaged in growing rice in Madagascar."

79 For the two letters to William Dunlop quoted in this paragraph, see *SCHGM*, XXXII (1931). The extraordinary Stewart was a Scottish frontiersman possessed of boundless energy, supreme vanity, and an outrageously florid prose style, who sought credit for such things as the introduction of silk culture and the initiation of trade with the Upper Creek Indians. (See BPRO *Trans.*, II, 248; Crane, *Southern Frontier*, p. 46 n.) He professed expertise and optimism about every possible resource from buffalo to caviar, and he once listed all his "experiments projections and Rationale for Inriching the Inhabitants . . . wherein yow'l sie 51 projects, all holding test to reason and truth." *SCHGM*, XXXII (1931), 86.

80 For "Wadboo Barony" at the head of the western branch of Cooper River, see *SCHGM*, XII (1911), 43 ff. With respect to rice, Stewart's suggestions included draining swamps, manuring with swamp-mud, and planting the seeds more thickly than had been customary. "The Governor," he noted in his letter (p. 86), "both in Sevanoh and swamp sow'd his Rice thin after the Gooscreek philosophers' old measurs." Stewart asserted (p. 17) that both Colleton and Sir Nathaniel Johnson were converted to his design for using at least "3 bushels Ryce sowen on an nere . . . and all our neighborhood follow'd."

81 *Gentleman's Magazine*, XXXVI (1766), 278–79. Thomas Lamboll recalled how in 1704, as a ten-year-old boy walking to school near Charlestown, "he took notice of some planters, who were essaying to make rice grow."

82 *Description*, p. 94. In 1691 a Frenchman named Peter Jacob Guerard received a two-year patent on "a Pendulum Engine, which doth much better, and in lesse time and labour, huske rice; than any other [that] heretofore hath been used within this Province," but there is no indication that the device itself succeeded, or that it helped to spur further invention

as hoped. *Statutes*, II, 63. Guerard came to South Carolina in April 1680 aboard the *Richmond* with a group of French Huguenots. He was a goldsmith by trade and served as collector of the port in 1696. *SCHGM*, XLIII (1942), 9–11. His pendulum device may have been nothing more than a pestle attached to the limb of a tree so that it would swing back up after each stroke into the mortar below.

83 *SCCHJ*, Nov., 1695, pp. 12, 13, 15.

84 *SCCHJ*, 1698, p. 36.

85 Nairne, *Letter from S.C.*, p. 11.

86 Daniel F. McCall, *Africa in Time-Perspective* (Boston, 1964), p. 69. See the articles on the history of sub-Saharan food crops by J. Desmond Clark, H. G. Baker, and W. B. Morgan in the *Journal of African History*, III (1962), 211–39. (The *Journal* gives data on the detailed research on African rice by R. Portères on pp. 237–38.)

87 Grant, *Fortunate Slave*, pp. 24–25. Lydia Parrish, *Slave Songs of the Georgia Sea Islands* (New York, 1942), p. 227 n. Parrish is one of the few writers to have hinted that African people may have known what to do with rice seeds in Carolina.

88 Joseph Corry, *Observations upon the Windward Coast of Africa* (London, 1807; rpt. in London, 1968), p. 37. Cf. Christopher Fyfe, *Sierra Leone Inheritance* (London, 1964), pp. 20, 29, 77.

89 Donnan, *Documents*, I, 375, 377–80, 413, 428, 438, 442. An ad for the arrival in Charlestown of 250 Negroes "from the Windward & Rice Coast" is reprinted in Daniel P. Mannix and Malcolm Cowley, *Black Cargoes: A History of the Atlantic Slave Trade, 1518–1865* (New York, 1962), plates following p. 146. The caption observes that these slaves were "valued for their knowledge of rice culture."

90 The most dramatic evidence of experience with rice among enslaved Africans comes from the famous rebels aboard the *Amistad* in the nineteenth century. Thirty-six slaves from the Sierra Leone region were shipped illegally from Lomboko to Cuba, and in the wake of their successful shipboard uprising they eventually found themselves imprisoned in New Haven, Conn. There they were interrogated separately, and excerpts from the interviews drive home this familiarity with rice in personal terms. John W. Barber, *A History of the Amistad Captives* (New Haven, 1840; rpt. in New: York, 1969), pp. 9–15:

> He was a blacksmith in his native village, and made hoes, axes and knives; he also planted rice.

> There are high mountains in his country, rice is cultivated, people have guns; has seen elephants.

> He was caught in the bush by four men as he was going to plant rice; his left hand was tied to his neck; was ten days going to Lomboko.

> He was seized by four men when in a rice field, and was two weeks in traveling to Lomboko.

> He is a planter of rice.

> His parents are dead, and he lived with his brother, a planter of rice.

> He was seized by two men as he was going to plant rice.

> 5 ft. 1 in. high, body tattoed, teeth filed, was born at Fe-baw, in Sando, between Mendi and Konno. His mother's brother sold him for a coat. He was taken in the night, and sold to Garlobá, who had four wives. He staid with this man two years, and was employed in cultivating rice. His master's wives and children were employed in the same manner, and no distinction made in regard to labor.

91 Mclville J. Herskovits, *Life in a Haitian Valley* (New York, 1937), illustrations opposite p. 100; William R. Bascom, "Acculturation among the Gullah Negroes," *American Anthropologist*, XLIII (1941), 49.

92 Bascom, "Acculturation," p. 45; Henry Glassie, *Pattern in the Material Folk Culture of the Eastern United States* (University of Pennsylovania Monographs in Folklore and Folklife, no. 1, Philadelphia, 1968), p. 117.

93 Nathan I. Huggins, Martin Kilson, Daniel M. Fox, eds., *Key Issues in the Afro-American Experience*, 2 vols. (New York, 1971), I, illustrations opposite p. 128; Melville J. Herskovits. *The Myth of the Negro Past* (2nd edn.: Boston, 1958), p. 147. Much of this work had been done by women in Africa, though by no means all of it, as note 90 above makes clear. Female involvement with rice culture could help explain why men and women were more nearly equal in numbers and in money value in South Carolina than in the West Indies. It is also possible (as Paul Wrobel has pointed out to me) that certain African men, such as the Mende from Sierra Leone, may have found forced involvement in the cultivation of swamp rice to be particularly demeaning by their own values.

94 Glassie, *Pattern in the Material Folk Culture*, pp. 116–17, even suggests a Russian derivation, citing Dimitry Zelenin, *Russische* (*Ostslavische*) *Volkskunde* (Berlin and Leipzig, 1927), pp. 84–86.

95 Herskovits, *Myth*, p. 147; Parrish, *Slave Songs*, pp. 13, 225–33, and plates 7 and 8. In 1969 the linguist David Dalby observed (London Times, July 19): "The verb 'sock,' in the sense of 'to strike,' especially with something, has recently been popularized in the black American phrase 'sock it to me' (with an obscene connotation), and is reminiscent of a similar-sounding verb in Wolof meaning 'to beat with a pestle.'"

96 BPRO *Trans.*, IV, 189–90.

PART FOUR

Family, Gender and Community

I N T H E U S S O U T H, the separation and sale of slave family members was perhaps the most bitterly felt and long-remembered pain of slavery. Yet the slave family was, like slavery itself, made in the Americas. Africans arrived on the slave ships alone, not in family groups. Within the space of a few generations, however, not only had the slave family become an inescapable landmark in all slave societies, but it had established itself as a critical institution in slave culture. The concept of 'family' is, of course, more problematic than we might initially imagine, not least because there were (and are) so many different forms of family structure. In the era of slavery, Europeans (even those living close to slaves) often had trouble identifying the slave family because it frequently differed from the model idealised by Europeans. In their turn, historians, until relatively recently, failed to accept the slave family. Thanks to a major scholarly shift, and thanks especially to the rise of sophisticated demographic research, we can now locate forms of slave family with some precision.

The historiography of the slave family effectively began with Herbert Gutman's classic study of 1975. Michael Craton's essay (1997) is an important overview of how slave families emerged from the confusion of African arrivals, through to the mature, final stages of slavery in the Caribbean in the early nineteenth century. Cheryll Cody's essay (1987) on slave-naming customs among slaves is an innovative contribution to the study of the slave family.

Philip D. Morgan's essay (1999) on kin shifts our attention to the Old South. In a study of unrivalled sweep, Morgan imposes a clearer sense of what kinship means (to slaves and to us) from a confusion of research materials. He illustrates both the complexity of kinship ties and their importance in the shaping of everyday slave life and culture.

246 PART FOUR: FAMILY, GENDER AND COMMUNITY

INTRODUCTION TO PART FOUR

AFRICANS WERE BOUGHT AND SOLD into and from the slave ships as individuals, not as family groups. They were prized and valued individually, though slave owners in the Americas often bought them in batches. Even before they met the Europeans on the coast, Africans had been wrenched from their families and kinship groups long before they settled into the routines of labour in their new homes throughout the Americas. They landed and settled in the Americas alone, though they often developed important ties to other Africans who had made the Atlantic journey with them. Yet from these unpromising circumstances, slaves were to develop communal and, most importantly, family systems which became the bedrock of slave society across the enslaved Americas. Historians have, however, struggled with the history of the slave family, not least because the very terminology 'the family' presupposes a freedom in relationships, yet those relationships were rooted in slavery.[1] Until the past generation of scholarship, the historiographical trend was to minimise the importance of the slave family. More recently, major advances in slave demography and a fresh approach to the social history of slave relationships have shaped a different, more positive approach to the slave family and also to the slave community.[2] In well-established slave societies, it was deemed a great cruelty to separate enslaved husbands and wives. Indeed, some of the best-remembered abuses of slave owners' power concerned the separation, splitting up and selling of individual members of slave families. Initially, therefore, the slave family found it difficult to thrive in the harsh human and social environment of the early slave colonies.

The aim of the Atlantic slave trade was to supply robust labour for the backbreaking work of settlement and agriculture in the tropical and semi-tropical Americas. The Atlantic slave system developed with that in mind: to supply, as far as possible, healthy, strong Africans. Not surprisingly, then, the bulk of Africans shipped across the Atlantic fitted that pattern. Of all the African slaves transported, two-thirds were male and three-quarters were adults.[3] But these figures varied enormously across time and from place to place along the African coast. Slave owners and shippers generally wanted male slaves, but as we have seen, the supply of Africans was determined by factors within Africa. Far fewer African women than men were offered for sale on the African coast (largely because of demand for women within Africa). This, obviously, had major consequences for the development of slave family and community in the Americas. Increasingly however, and despite what they said to the contrary, planters took whatever slaves they could get. The passage of time saw ever more women and young Africans arriving in the Americas. This also meant that (again contrary to the language of slave owning) women were employed in all categories of slave work in the Americas. In the words of Herbert Klein, 'the American slave populations were the least sexually constrained laboring population in Western society up to the modern period.'[4]

Potential purchasers of Africans thus faced an unpredictable variety of Africans when the slave ships arrived. Slave owners had, quite simply, to make do with whichever Africans were available. But how did family and social life emerge from among the 10 million African survivors of the Atlantic crossing – the great majority of whom were young men – with only a small percentage, initially, of women for companions?

The patterns of African enforced migrations and settlement were basic to the development of the slave family and society. In a world where African men outnumbered African women, not surprisingly, slave reproduction was low. Understandably, too, those women took to the Americas the cultural habits of their homelands; in this case, most importantly, prolonged breast-feeding habits which inhibited conception. That, coupled with high infant mortality among African slave women, ensured a very low rate of slave reproduction. Where imported Africans dominated a local slave society, slave women simply did not give birth to the numbers of children necessary to maintain, still less to increase, the local slave population. Slave numbers could only be maintained by yet more importations of Africans. From one region to another (North America, Brazil, the West Indies) the early days of local slave societies were characterised by a dominance of males, the failure of local women to reproduce 'normally', and the continuing reliance on imported Africans. Slave owners everywhere recognised the problem. It seemed that slave labour could be maintained only via the Atlantic slave trade, hence the powerful plantocratic and metropolitan support for that trade and a dogged refusal to contemplate abolition.

The first generation of slaves in most regions of the Americas was characterised, then, by a failure to increase their numbers as might be expected. This in its turn explains why the Atlantic slave trade was so important to their owners. The tropical produce of the Americas simply could not be cultivated in the volumes required by the voracious appetite of the Western world without ever more Africans shipped across the Atlantic. As the volume of tropical produce increased, so too did the importation of African slaves.

Gradually, locally born (creole) communities began to emerge in the Americas. When they did, where creoles began to outnumber African slaves, the slave birth rate increased and the decline in slave population was halted. This took place most strikingly in North America where by about 1750 local slaves were increasing in numbers, and local slave owners could gradually cease to depend on imports of African slaves. This was also the case in certain regions of Brazil. The pattern was clear enough: where creole slaves came to dominate the local population the reliance on Africans declined. And where the local population grew naturally (as opposed to importing Africans), a balance emerged between men and women. Something like a normal population structure emerged, at the heart of which was the slave family.

In North America, the slave population increased naturally from the mid-eighteenth century onwards. There, slave women soon adopted the European habit of short periods of breast-feeding, with a consequent increase in the number of babies born to local slave women. This suggests that North American slaves were socially closer to – and more influenced by – their owners and by white society in general. In its turn, this may be explained by the fact that North American slaves (until the coming of cotton in the nineteenth century) were owned in smaller numbers and tended to live closer to white people. Slaves on West Indian and Brazilian plantations, by contrast, tended to be owned in large numbers and to live in slave villages at some remove from white residences. Moreover, North American slaves lived longer than slaves elsewhere. Social and health conditions in North America seem to have been better (for both blacks and whites) than in other regions of the settled Americas. Of course, once the slave trade had been abolished, and where Africans were no longer available to slave owners, the local slave populations changed in the course of a generation from being dominated by Africans to being predominantly local-born.

These changing patterns of slave population were basic to the development of the slave family and society. Inevitably, Africans brought with them memories and habits of their varied cultural backgrounds. In time, those habits hardened into distinctive local practice in the Americas. And this was as true of language, religion and social customs (cooking and dress, for example) as it was of family structure.

The settler slave societies were dominated by men. Not surprisingly, local slaves complained about the absence of women, and life was scarred by inevitable disputes about access to them. From the first it was obvious that slaves were happier in a stable domestic environment, but such stability was virtually impossible in the rough, wild days of frontier settlement. However, that changed: planters realised their interests were best served by promoting slaves' domestic happiness, but they took little direct interest in the slave family until quite late in the history of slavery. As more women became available, slaves expected their owners to allow them to live together in whatever unions they formed, or to allow them to visit each other when separated. In time, the initial communal living quarters (barracks, for example) gave way to individual slave cabins, and as women became less scarce, family units evolved among the slaves. They built their own dwellings, using whatever materials came to hand (often with material assistance from their owners) and the broad outlines of slave communities and villages began to sprout, close to the places of work. Where slaves were owned and worked in large gangs, as they did in the sugar colonies of the Caribbean and Brazil, planters liked their slaves to live at some distance from their homes, though whites were invariably surrounded by domestic slaves in and around the family home. The language of family – the use of the words 'husband' and 'wife' – came to dominate the vernacular of slavery, whatever differences might exist between types of slave family, and between European and slave patterns of family life.

The slave family thus slowly emerged from the most unpromising of material and human circumstances. Slaves named their children after fathers, mothers and grandparents. Lines of inheritance were established for the meagre material possessions of slave life and, more important, for the bequeathing of working skills from father to son, mother to daughter. The slave cabin was the centre of the slave community which spread out, like a spider's web, into distant corners of the region and even further afield. Because slaves were the property of others, they often had to travel to meet loved ones. The literature of slavery is filled with accounts of slaves running away to meet husbands, wives, children and lovers. Many walked huge distances to spend time with a partner. Some tried to divide their time between where they were employed and where a distant partner lived. Planters sometimes bought slaves in order to unite man and wife (or, conversely, separated them as punishment) and generally agreed to slave requests to cohabit. Of course, many slaves travelled as part of their work: transporting goods and produce, corralling beasts back and forth, visiting local towns and seaports to deliver goods and collect items for their owners, or moving between different properties. In the process, they naturally established links with other slaves. Major networks thus developed in all slave colonies of migratory and transient slaves moving, by land and water, from their main residence out into the wider local and regional area. Through all this, slaves' contact with other slaves was crucial. A slave on the move – a working man simply travelling to a distant workplace, a slave woman walking to see her husband, a young male seeking out a girlfriend – all knew that they could secure help and sustenance en route from other slaves. Relatives, friends, acquaintances, strangers even, became staging posts for migratory slaves between one point in a slave colony and another. This was especially noticeable at festivals and holidays, when slaves headed for loved ones and friends, gathering in large numbers to enjoy their rare days free from toil.

Yet all this could be threatened at a stroke, without warning, by their owners. Though slave owners quickly accepted the benefits, to them, of maintaining and encouraging slave family life, they might for economic, personal or capricious reasons disrupt or even destroy the basis of slave family life. A planter's death and subsequent rearrangement of his property (among which, of course, were the slaves), relocation, economic hardship and resulting property sales, all this, in addition to unpredictable acts of spite, could threaten slaves' domestic stability.

The pattern of family and community consolidation varied enormously from one slave society to another. The pioneering days of settlement were, everywhere, dominated by young men, black and white, free and slave (and indentured), working closely together, hacking some form of habitat and manageable cultivation from a hostile wilderness. The creation of export crops and the development of plantations to cultivate those crops saw local slave society transformed into a more settled and orderly community. But as long as it was dominated by Africans, as long as the population could only be sustained and expanded by imports of African labour, there remained an element of instability at the heart of the slave community. However, as the proportion of women increased, as the ratio of young men and women became more balanced, stable family units became the norm, with a consequent change in the patterns of reproduction among the slaves, and the lessening of the planters' dependence on newly imported African slaves.

To European eyes, slave families sometimes looked unusual. Slaves married, in the words of John Woolman 'after their own way'.[5] Slaves brought to their relationships, as they did to all aspects of their lives, the memories and practices of their African homelands, but all of it moderated and changed by life in the Americas, most notably through contact with white society. The closer they came to local whites, the closer the slaves came to approximating what whites regarded and expected as the norm for social behaviour. This was particularly the case among North American slaves who, from an early date, accommodated themselves more closely to the social conventions of local white life – for example, in language, religion and family.

Throughout the slave colonies, there was an inevitable tension between the simple economic imperatives of slavery and the clear desire of slaves to establish and maintain personal relationships within a family structure. Wherever it emerged, the slave family took the form of the two-parent household. Slave history passed through phases where men had few opportunities of access to female companionship, to a more settled phase in the mature years of slavery, when slave men and women found companionship with each other in a single household. That house-hold, in its turn, became the focal point for the rearing of children. There, in the slave family home, the young learned from older slaves the lessons for life which were vital for peaceful survival in the dangerous and hostile world of slavery: the 'dos' and 'don'ts', the conventions and limits, the social skills necessary for survival and for avoiding unnecessary trouble, all were learned from parents and grand-parents within the family home. Even apparently single-parent homes often masked the fact that the resident slave had a partner – a husband or wife – on another property.

In time, slave families became ever more extended, with that familiar entourage of relatives living close to hand. Grandparents were especially important in the evolution of extended kinship ties among the slaves. And those kinship ties inevitably spread out from the plantation into a much wider geographical setting, linking slaves from one plantation to another and between country and town.

The slave family was, inevitably, recognised both in law and social convention. Slave owners accepted that slaves wanted and needed their families and all the relationships which flowed from them. It was in the planters' own interests, as far as possible, to encourage the slave attachment to family. A happier slave was a better slave, more likely to remain rooted to the property, cautious about giving too much offence or injury to their owners and anxious not to prejudice the safety and well-being of immediate relatives and loved ones. Planters came to recognise the value of the slave family to the successful operation of the whole slave system. Of course, this did not mean that they always respected the slave family, or that their economic policies inevitably protected or nurtured the slave family. Often they did not. From first to last, the slave family was under threat. It was, in the words of Philip Morgan, 'held together by threads that a master might cut at any time'.[6] The most serious, ubiquitous threat came with the death of the slave owner. Most at risk were older children, and those slaves hired out to labour on other proper-ties. Yet most slaves tended to move, or be moved, only short distances. This changed, however, in the nineteenth-century United States, when the expansive cotton frontier absorbed huge numbers of slaves shipped westward from the states of the Old South. That apart, most slaves born in the Americas seem to have spent their lives in a small, restricted region. But in their social lives, they were much more mobile than we might expect.

Within the slave family, men and women chose their own partners, marrying in a variety of ceremonies which were, of course, limited by their material well-being. Thereafter, they lived in a family group dominated by the man, but where the woman exercised a strong role, often working as an equal in plantation labour as well as raising children (sometimes alone when the man was employed else-where). Slaves everywhere sought to enhance the material well-being of their families, to acquire property for and around the family home. We know that slaves valued their families, were fiercely protective of their children, going to great lengths to protect and sustain them, especially when faced with threats of separation or otherwise harmed. In their turn, slave children, as adults, took on the familiar role of caring for their ageing parents. Equally, slave siblings stuck together, both in childhood and adult life. The degree to which these important kinship ties reflected patterns of attachment derived from Africa is hard to tell. Yet here, as in all other forms of slave life, Africa was moderated by life in the Americas. But whatever their origins, the slaves' kinship ties provided networks which formed a social and human geography for slave life throughout the Americas.

Notes

1   Philip D. Morgan, *Slave Counterpoint,* Chapel Hill, 1998, p. 499.
2   The beginnings were Herbert Gutman, *The Black Family in Slavery and Freedom, 1750–1925,* New York, 1976. See also B.W. Higman, *Slave Populations of the British Caribbean, 1807–1834,* Baltimore, 1984.
3   Herbert S. Klein, *The Atlantic Slave Trade,* Cambridge, 1999, p. 161.
4   *Ibid.,* p. 162.
5   Philip D. Morgan, *Slave Counterpoint,* Chapel Hill, 1998, p. 498.
6   *Ibid.,* p. 512.

Chapter 13

Herbert Gutman

PERSISTENT MYTHS ABOUT THE AFRO-AMERICAN FAMILY

W E START WITH ALEXANDER HAMILTON. He was neither a historian nor a sociologist. Surely he would not be classified as an expert on the history of the Afro-American family. But a single sentence of his remains relevant to the theme of this paper. "The contempt we have been taught to entertain for the blacks," Hamilton observed nearly two centuries ago, "makes us fancy many things that are founded neither in reason nor in experience."[1]

Just now, such "things" and much else in the Afro-American past are being subjected to fresh examination by persons dissatisfied with inadequate but widely approved "explanations." Controversy and polemic range over many subjects. There is dispute about the "docility" of the slaves, the origins of segregation, the personality of Nat Turner, the content of Radical Reconstruction, the objectives of Booker T. Washington, and much else. One subject essential to an enriched and deepened understanding of historic Afro-American subculture has remained thus far immune from serious discussion and controversy. That is the history of the Afro-American family. This paper reopens that subject on two separate but also connected levels: first, by a reexamination of certain major themes in E. Franklin Frazier's classic study, *The Negro Family in the United States*, and second, by the presentation of a sample of much new evidence concerning Afro-American family and household composition at a given moment in several parts of the United States but especially in the South between 1860 and 1880 and in one northern city, Buffalo, New York, between 1855 and 1925.

Although the data have not yet been entirely analyzed, preliminary study casts serious doubt on several central theoretical conceptions that guided Frazier's approach to the Afro-American family's past. Much is at issue that cannot adequately be discussed in these few pages: the anthropological distinctions between "folk culture" and "urban culture" common in the 1920s and 1930s; the relationship between economic structure and social and cultural change; and, especially, the sociological "models" shaped by Park and other University of Chicago social scientists, which profoundly affected Frazier's work.[2] Here we shall focus on Frazier's central arguments that two streams of Afro-American family life developed out of the slave experience, that one of them—the "matriarchy"—was the more important in the nineteenth century, and that "class" affected family structure in a simple and direct way. This new evidence suggests, furthermore, the pressing need for a full reexamination of the Afro-American's family history, slave as well as free, and, perhaps even more importantly, a reconsideration of the social and class structure of varied nineteenth- and early twentieth-century black urban and rural communities.

Much has been written about the history of the Afro-American family, but little, in fact, is really known about its composition and household at given historical moments, and even less is known about how and why it changed over time. Without such knowledge, it is difficult to assess historic family roles or the changing relationship between family life and the larger culture that shaped it. Despite such deficiencies, most historians and sociologists consider these questions closed and settled. Moynihan and his critics, for example, quarreled bitterly over the contemporary structure of the "Negro family," but all shared a common view of its recent and distant history.[3] They did not dispute about Afro-American family life 100 or even 50 years ago but shed angry words over the relationship between past patterns of black family life and present conditions in the black ghetto. The past remained fixed in their bitter arguments. For instance, Hauser, a sociologist, summed up the conventional wisdom that informed this dispute and much else written about the history of the Negro family:

> Family disorganization and unstable family life among Negro Americans is a product of their history and caste status in the United States. During slavery and for at least the first half century after emancipation, the Negro never had the opportunity to acquire the patterns of sexual behavior and family living which characterize middle-class white society. African family patterns were, of course, destroyed during slavery, when it was virtually impossible to establish any durable form of family organization. This historical tendency toward a matrifocal family structure has been reinforced by the continued inability of the Negro male, because of lack of opportunity and discriminatory practices, to assume the role of provider and protector of his family in accordance with prevailing definitions of the role of husband and father. The Negro male has, in a sense, been the victim of social and economic emasculation which has perpetuated and reinforced the matriarchal Negro family structure created by slavery.[4]

Such views draw in a somewhat distorted fashion upon Frazier's major arguments. They are not serious historical and sociological analyses; instead, they serve as mere diachronic speculation about the relationship between slavery and twentieth-century Afro-American life. Despite my quarrel with Frazier's work as a *historian* of the black family, his reputation as a distinguished sociologist and pioneer student of Afro-American family life remains secure—for good reason. His scholarship and that of W. E. B. DuBois were the most significant in refuting widely approved racial "explanations" of Afro-American marital and family institutions. In a long and intimate connection with "this folk," Shaler, who rose to head Harvard's Lawrence Scientific School, said, "I have never heard a [Negro] refer to his grandfather, and any reference to their parents is rare. The Negro must be provided with these motives of the household; he must be made faithful to the marriage bond, and taught his sense of ancestry."[5] Such views were regularly repeated by "social scientists" and popular writers on the black family before Frazier tackled the subject.

A single illustration suffices to explain why much of this literature, quite properly, now is read by students of racial prejudice, not students of the black family. Odum's highly praised study of the *Social and Mental Traits of the Negro* insisted that "in his home life, the Negro is filthy, careless, and indecent, . . . as destitute of morals as many of the lower animals, . . . [and with] little knowledge of the sanctity of home or marital relations."[6] Frazier was the first to challenge seriously the work of Odum, Hoffman, Tillinghurst, Elwang, Weatherford, Thomas, and others of similar persuasion.[7]

Burgess did not exaggerate when he called Frazier's 1939 study "indispensable" because it "explodes completely, and it may be hoped once and for all, the popular misconception of the uniformity of behavior among Negroes. It shows dramatically the wide variation in conduct and in family life by social classes."[8] More than this, when we search for comparative material on the history of white lower-class families, we cannot find a single study that compares in scope or detail with Frazier's work on the black family. It remains the best single historical study of the American family, black or white, published to date.

To say this, however, is not to insist that Frazier's history was without serious fault. Quite the contrary. Frazier did not use careful methods in developing a historical explanation for the condition of the black family in the 1920s and the 1930s. Instead, he read that "condition" back into the past and linked it directly to the nineteenth-century slave experience. His most significant contributions included an analysis of the development of a "matriarchal" family structure as an adaptation to the conditions of slavery and those of post-emancipation rural and urban southern life together with a detailed examination of the interplay between that "way of life" and the urban experience of migrating blacks between 1910 and 1940. Frazier respected the historical record, so he also described the presence of a two-parent, male-centered household among certain nineteenth-century free blacks, North and South. But his evidence concerning these two strands was quite limited. He depended largely upon the testimony of white travelers and missionaries, the writings of ex-slaves, the oral recollections of blacks many decades after that time, and a printed historical record heavily colored by racial and class preconceptions and biases.

In essence, Frazier found two streams of historic Afro-American family life— one more important than the other. The more dominant stream was nurtured by slavery and the conditions of rural southern life; a "matriarchal family" was its most characteristic form. A subordinate "stream" was the two-parent, male-headed household that existed among a small minority of Afro-Americans who owned property, enjoyed middle-class occupations, or had independent artisan and craft skills. Thus, Frazier directly linked the two-parent, Afro-American household to property ownership, and skill to "class." Since so few Afro-Americans owned property or retained traditional skills, Frazier found the first stream to be the more important of the two trends and drew large conclusions from his two-stream theory. He rooted much of Afro-American difficulty in family life in the dominance of the one pattern:

> The widespread disorganization of family life among Negroes has affected practically every phase of their community life and adjustments to the larger white world. Because of the absence of stability in family life, there

is a lack of traditions. Life among a large portion of the urban Negro population is casual, precarious, and fragmentary.

"It lacks," Frazier concluded, "continuity, and its roots do not go deeper than the
contingencies of daily living."[9]

Since the appearance of Frazier's work, little else of value has been written
about the history of the Afro-American family. Impressed by it, Myrdal and his co-
workers gave little space to the black family in *An American Dilemma*; instead, they
advised readers to study Frazier's book.[10] Historians of slavery in recent decades
have added little to the traditional picture of the slave family because they have not
yet studied slave culture fully.[11] Superior studies of the antebellum southern and
northern free blacks such as those by Franklin and Litwack say little about family
relations. The same is true of such penetrating monographs about postbellum
southern blacks as the works of Taylor, Wharton, and Tindall. In their recent books
on South Carolina during Reconstruction, Rose and Williamson have broken the
silence about the Afro-American family and added significant new data, but these
are exceptions to the rule.[12] More common is the general view put forth in
the late Gilbert Osofsky's *Harlem*. What happened to the black migrant family is
summed up in a single sentence: "Slavery initially destroyed the entire concept of
family for American Negroes and the slave heritage, bulwarked by economic conditions, continued into the twentieth century to make family instability a common
factor in Negro life." A similar argument threads two recent general studies of the
Afro-American family by Billingsley and by Bernard. The former deals with the
Afro-American family between 1865 and the great migration in fewer than three
pages; Bernard's volume is a tangle of sociological jargon and misused historical
evidence. In truth, historians and sociologists have said little new about the history
of the Negro family since Frazier published his work thirty-five years ago. Glazer
was correct to write: "We have the great study of E. Franklin Frazier, *The Negro
Family in the United States*—aside from that precious little."[13]

If, as Frazier and others insisted, the slave household developed a "fatherless,"
matrifocal pattern sufficiently strong to become self-sustaining over time and to be
transmitted from generation to generation among large numbers of blacks, such a
condition necessarily must have been common among those Afro-American closest
in time and in experience to actual chattel slavery. Subnuclear and, generally, matrifocal family ties rather than conjugal and nuclear bonds should regularly appear in
the quantitative data that describe family and household composition among antebellum northern and southern free blacks and among rural and urban freedmen
during and just after Reconstruction. For this reason, my larger study focuses
intensely on the years between 1850 and 1880. It is there that the effects of chattel
slavery on personality and family structure should have been most severe. By
starting with these decades, my study tells nothing *directly* about either slave family
life or the family arrangements among post-Reconstruction blacks. But the findings
indirectly call into question many views on both of these subjects.

We turn first to the dominant historical view of the Afro-American family between
1850 and 1880 and especially the way in which most historians and sociologists
saw it in the aftermath of emancipation. Frazier's argument deserves attention at
the start. Afro-American family patterns following freedom offered a critical test

for his "two-stream" theory. Frazier insisted that "normal" family patterns had developed among small groups of antebellum free blacks, especially those of "mixed color" who had some economic opportunity in northern and southern cities or who lived in isolated "racial islands." Although Frazier admitted that emancipation increased their numbers, especially with those among ex-slaves who had been house servants or artisans and found in freedom the occasion to build stable, two-parent households, his major argument took exactly the opposite direction: The slave experience blocked "normal" family life for most freedmen. In the 1930s, readers of *The Negro Family in Chicago* learned from Frazier that "the Negro family, which was at best an accommodation to the slave order, went to pieces in the general break-up of the plantation."[14] Frazier later expanded this point:

> What authority was there to take the place of the master's in regulating sex relations and maintaining the permanency of marital ties? Where could the Negro father look for sanction of his authority in family relations which had scarcely existed in the past? . . . Emancipation was a crisis in the life of the Negro that tended to destroy all his traditional ways of thinking and acting. . . . The mobility of the Negro population after emancipation was bound to create disorder and produce widespread demoralization. . . . When the yoke of slavery was lifted, the drifting masses were left without any restraint upon their vagrant impulses and wild desires. The old intimacy between master and slave, upon which the moral order under the slave regime had rested was destroyed forever. . . . Promiscuous sexual relations and constant changing of spouses became the rule with the demoralized elements in the freed Negro population. . . . Marriage as formal and legal relation was not a part of the mores of the freedmen.[15]

Similar but briefer arguments appeared a decade later in *The Negro in the United States*. "The Civil War and Emancipation," Frazier concluded, "destroyed the discipline and the authority of the masters and uprooted the stable families from their customary mode of living."[16]

Frazier was neither the first nor the last to put forth such views. Contemporary enemies and even many friends of the freedman saw nothing but chaos and breakdown in his postbellum family life. Historians at the turn of the century joined to stamp final approval on this "truth." Unlike Frazier, however, their explanations turned on "race." "Negro he is, negro he always has been, and negro he always will be," said George Fitzhugh in 1866. Fitzhugh believed that racial inferiority and the withdrawal of paternal protection together doomed blacks.

> They [Negro orphans] lost nothing in losing their parents, but lost everything in losing their masters. Negroes possess much amiableness of feeling, but not the least steady, permanent affection. "Out of sight, out of mind" is true for them all. They never grieve twenty-four hours for the death of parents, wives, husbands, or children.[17]

Others echoed Fitzhugh. A rural Georgia newspaper (1865) mockingly approved a reader's suggestion that Negro marriages be legalized: "If *he can*, let him confer upon them the sanctity of the marriage relation; let him make them all

virtuous and chaste and continent; let him teach them to read the Bible and Shakespeare and then let him confer upon them liberty and white skin." Robert Toombs was no less direct, "Now," he asked *Atlanta Constitution* readers in 1871, "what does the negro know about the obligations of the marriage relation? No more, sir, than the parish bull or village heifer."[18] Toombs' animal analogy found a resonant friend in Bruce whose *Plantation Negro as Freeman* Frazier quoted as an authoritative source on Negro social life. Planters, Bruce insisted, could no longer "compel" black "parents to prevent their offspring from running wild like so many young animals," Whatever its deficiencies, moreover, slavery had offered more protection against "promiscuous intercourse" than freedom, "Marriage under the old regime," said Bruce, "was very like unlawful cohabitation under the new, only that the master, by the power he had, compelled the nominal husband and wife to live together permanently."[19] Fleming shared this belief and helped to legitimize it as historical "fact." The absence of a single shred of evidence did not prevent Fleming from insisting that in 1865 and 1886 "the fickle negroes, male and female, made various experiments with new partners" so that soon thousands "had forsaken the husband and wife of slavery times and 'taken up' with others." Again, without evidence of any sort, Fleming told that black "foeticide and child murder were common crimes." Not surprisingly, he concluded that "the marriage relations of the negroes were hardly satisfactory, judged by white standards."[20]

We cite these *opinions* not to say that Frazier shared them but to show instead that persons of quite different perspectives accepted as "fact" that chaos and disorder typified family life and marital relations among "freedmen" of both sexes. And this view continues to saturate historical and sociological writing and therefore smothers the past. Richardson wrote of Florida blacks during Reconstruction: "Through no fault of their own some of the freedmen had little conception of marital and family obligations. . . . The ex-slaves saw no particular reason for changing the practices by which they had always lived." Billingsley admits that "Emancipation had some advantages for the Negro family" but calls it "a catastrophic social crisis for the ex-slave" and finds "Reconstruction . . . a colossal failure," Mostly racist sources convinced Donald that freedmen and women had "no traditions or experience of marriage and family mores" and "had not yet developed that feeling of concern and sympathy which kinsmen ordinarily have for one another." Sociologists Broom and Green put it differently when they asserted that "many Negro males used their new freedom of movement to desert their wives and children, and some demoralized mothers abandoned their children." Bernard wants us to believe that "so far as *anomie* is concerned, there does seem to be one period in American history when this term could adequately serve: the tragic Reconstruction Era." Then, "the Negro male was put in a situation which forbade his becoming a mature human being, and then was both rewarded and punished for not becoming one. The result was a classic case of the self-fulfilling prophecy. . . . For over a generation after emancipation, the Negro obliged his detractors by acting out time prophecy." Lincoln says the same: "Freedom did not improve the image of the Negro male or give him a sense of security as the head of the family. He remained a semi-slave." What matters is not the truth of these observations but the fact that they reinforce and strengthen Frazier's conception of two streams of historic Afro-American family life.[21] New evidence lets us test in significant ways the conventional picture of the Afro-American family composition between 1850 and 1880. But, first, a few words

about the data. The discrete pieces of information gathered about individual blacks and their families from manuscript state, federal, and Freedmen's Bureau censuses number in the tens of thousands because nearly every Afro-American household has been reconstructed in twenty-one distinct urban and rural communities.[22] In each city and rural area, percentage distributions have been calculated for thirty types of Afro-American families, ranging from an augmented-extended family headed by a black father, to a subnuclear family headed by a black mother living in a white household. Five major types have been studied: nuclear, extended, augmented, households, and subfamilies living with either other black or white families. Each of these larger types has been broken down into subsets to tell just how many nuclear families, for example, were composed of a husband and wife, a husband, wife and their children, a father and his children, or a mother and her children. In addition, the age, sex, occupation, and, where available, real and personal property have been recorded for each individual black.

The scope of the study has widened over time. In a preliminary but unpublished study, Glasco and I reconstructed the household structure for the entire black population in Buffalo in 1855 and 1875, and sampled households in 1905 and 1925 (in all, 684 households).[23] A comparison of all items of significance between the 1855 black population and more than 15,000 natives and Irish and German immigrants followed. In addition, comparative materials were collected for portions of the 1860 New York City (128 households) and Brooklyn (191 households) black community, and for the entire 1860 free black community in Mobile, Alabama (212 households). Critics of this early study worried because the 1860 manuscript census failed to delineate exact family relationships. They also correctly argued that its selection was biased because free blacks, North and South, however close in time to slavery, nevertheless may have been distinct from the slaves and later freedmen in their aspirations. Thus, the study was expanded to confront the ex-slave and much else more directly. From his own unpublished work, Daniel Walkowitz supplied full demographic data on the Troy, New York, black community in 1860 and 1880 (253 households). Despite its limitations, full census data were gathered for the 1860 free black community in Richmond, Virginia (633 households), and Charleston, South Carolina (623 households). And, more important, the 1880 federal manuscript census permitted the reconstruction of thousands of rural and urban southern households inhabited by mostly ex-slaves: St. Helena's Island (904 households), St. Helena's Township (491 households), and the town of Beaufort, South Carolina (461 households); Natchez, Mississippi (769 households); all of rural Adams County, Mississippi (3,093 households); Mobile, Alabama (3,235 households); and finally, Richmond, Virginia (5,670 households).[24]

Additional material of unusual significance gathered from the Freedman's Bureau records in the National Archives added independent evidence. These data fell into two categories. First, exceedingly detailed manuscript censuses of the freedmen were gathered by Virginia Bureau officials in 1865 and 1866. Those for York (994 households), Montgomery (500 households), and Princess Anne (375 households) counties permitted careful examination of the household composition among Virginia blacks just after emancipation. In addition, marriage registers kept by Bureau officials revealed otherwise inaccessible information about prior family arrangements among more than 800 couples in Rockbridge and Nelson counties,

Virginia; a similar number in Washington, D.C.; and more than 2,000 black men and women in and near Vicksburg, Mississippi.

In all, but not including the marriage registers or the 1905 and 1925 Buffalo census data, information has been gathered about the composition of nearly 19,000 Afro-American households between 1855 and 1880. It is a more than adequate sample. Only the time factor is held constant. The range is far-reaching and covers distinct social and economic environments that affected Afro-American life differently. Virginia counties that sold off "surplus" slaves before the Civil War are included. So are northern industrial (Troy) and port (Buffalo) cities. Charleston was a decaying southern city in 1860. That year and twenty years later, Mobile was a booming Gulf port. Richmond in the same years allowed an examination of the family life of black factory workers. Beaufort and Natchez told about the small town: one a river port and the other, a predominantly black village. The South Carolina Sea Island townships were densely black in population and a repository of African "survivals." Only 59 whites, for example, lived among St. Helena Island's 4,267 Negroes. And rural Adams County was Deep South and had its own particular social structure. So diverse a setting allows us to ask and answer many questions. We can compare the household composition of antebellum free blacks in northern and southern cities and contrast particular southern cities. Rural and urban patterns among the freedmen and women can be distinguished. So can differences within a city: for example, the densely black wards in Richmond (Marshall and Jackson wards) and in Mobile (the seventh ward) show a more regular two-parent household than the "integrated" wards in these cities. Most important for this article are the answers to the questions posed earlier. Were there two streams of Afro-American family life? How widespread was the matriarchal household? What were the relationships between class and household composition?

The findings in this study dispute vigorously the general view of the black family and household composition between 1850 and 1880 because most antebellum free blacks, North and south, lived in double-headed households, and so did most poor rural and urban freedmen and women. Female-headed households were common but not typical. Some of the evidence for these conclusions may be summarized briefly.

The communities studied consisted overwhelmingly of urban and rural lower-class families; an occupational analysis of male and female income earners makes this fact clear. In rural Adams County, only 141 of 2,971 Mississippi black males had occupations other than farmer, farm laborer, farm worker, or laborer. Of these, only twenty-two were non-workers, including the coroner and the sheriff. The same was true for the Sea Island rural blacks. Only 26 of St. Helena's 850 adult males were neither farmers nor farm laborers. In the cities, except for the antebellum southern towns, black males worked mostly as unskilled laborers or domestic servants. The free black males of Charleston, Mobile, and Richmond counted many artisans and craftsmen among them: 32 percent in Richmond, 43 percent in Mobile, and 70 percent in Charleston. A quite tiny percentage held "middle-class" occupations (1 percent in Mobile and Richmond and 4 percent in Charleston).

Northern cities showed the opposite picture. There, the typical black male was an unskilled laborer or a service worker: The percentages in these occupational categories in Buffalo (1855 and 1875), Troy (1860 and 1880), and New York and Brooklyn (1860) ranged from 68 percent to 81 percent. Mostly unskilled male laborers also worked in the reconstructed southern cities. Only Beaufort had a substantial nonworking class, 12 percent of adult males. Half of one percent of Natchez's black males fell into this category; the percentage was a bit higher in Richmond and Mobile. Three of five Beaufort males worked as unskilled laborers or as domestics; in Natchez, four of five; in Mobile, nearly nine often. Richmond's factories made its black labor force more complex. One of every five adult males was a factory worker, and, including them, at least 80 percent of Richmond's male workers were dependent wage earners.

Such occupational information together with scattered but still useful data on income and property ownership casts serious doubts on the simple proposition that "class" factors *alone*—income, skill, property, and middle-class occupations—*determined* the presence of a two-parent household. To say this is not to minimize the importance of such factors but rather to assess their significance and to reject Frazier's crude economic determinism. To cite an example: The typical male head of an antebellum northern black family was an unskilled laborer or a domestic servant; his southern counterpart more probably was a skilled artisan. But a much higher percentage of Negro children younger than 18 in 1860 lived in male-present households in Buffalo, Troy, and Brooklyn than in Charleston and Richmond. Not just "economic" factors affected the shape of these households. For the entire period studied, a large proportion of the families and households analyzed had at their head poor, unskilled rural and urban laborers and domestic servants. Black males with artisan skills or real and personal property obviously had a better chance to build stable, two-parent households than others less fortunate. But it does not follow that unskilled black males, despite numerous obstacles, found it impossible to build and sustain such households. Actually, since most black households were headed by just such persons, it seems clear that the composition of the black household was affected by, but independent of, income, skill, and property. If most black families studied were male-present households, then it follows that that kind of household belonged to other nineteenth-century blacks than just a small black "elite"—those whom Frazier called the "favored few" who had "escaped from the isolation of the black folk."[25] As a result, the concept of two separate "streams" of Afro-American family life developing quite separately over time is, at best, misleading.

We therefore disregard the two-stream theory and instead ask a simple question: How *common* was the two-parent household among the thousands of Afro-American households examined between 1855 and 1880? Percentages vary for fourteen different northern and Southern black communities but reveal a consistent pattern everywhere. Depending upon the particular setting, no fewer than 70 percent and as many as 90 percent of the households contained a husband and wife or just a father (Table 13.1). In the Virginia counties surveyed by the Freedmen's Bureau in 1865 and 1866, male-present households ranged from 78 percent to 85 percent. Northern cities did not fall below 85 percent (and in Buffalo, significantly, the percentage remained that high in 1905 and 1925). The southern towns and cities revealed the lowest percentage of male-present households, but Beaufort, Natchez, Mobile, and Richmond all ranged between 70 percent and 74 percent. Southern rural two-parent households were more common, ranging from 81 percent to

Table 13.1   Percentage of male-present Negro households, 1855–1880

Place and date	Number of households	Male-present households (%)	Male-absent households (%)
Buffalo, N.Y., 1855	145	90	10
Buffalo, N.Y., 1875	159	85	15
Troy, N.Y., 1880	128	85	15
York County, Va., 1865	994	85	15
Montgomery County, Va., 1866	500	78	22
Princess Anne County, Va., 1865	375	84	16
Natchez, Miss., 1880	769	70	30
Beaufort, S.C., 1880	461	70	30
Richmond, Va., 1880	5,670	73	27
Mobile, Ala., 1880	3,235	74	26
Rural Adams County, Miss., 1880	3,093	81	19
St. Helena's Township, S.C., 1880	491	87	13
St. Helena's Island, S.C., 1880	904	86	14

87 percent in Mississippi and in South Carolina. Not surprisingly, most black children lived in two-parent households. In 1880, for example, 69 percent of black Natchez children younger than 6 lived with a father; the percentage was even higher, 77 percent each, in Richmond and Mobile.

To turn from the male-present household to the types of households that blacks lived in (whether or not an adult male was present), means again to unearth new findings that upset conventional views. Black households and family systems were exceedingly complex in the aftermath of emancipation. Arrangements within them varied greatly, but "chaos" and "disorder" are not useful concepts in understanding them. Only the 1880 manuscript census, however, is precise enough in defining family relationships to allow us to reconstruct some of this complexity. And even that source is deficient because it tells nothing about kinship ties between separate households. Yet, it reveals a great deal when sorted according to nuclear, extended, and augmented households as well as subfamilies living either with other black or white families (Table 13.2). The patterns are clear. Except for Richmond, very few black families lived in white households. One of every nine or ten urban black families lived with another black family. Together, extended and augmented families never accounted for more than 30 percent of the households in any area. Most black households were *nuclear* in composition: The range spreads from 50 percent in Natchez to 80 percent in St. Helena's Township; Richmond, Mobile, Beaufort, rural Adams County, and St. Helena's Island fall in between.

That so large a percentage of southern black households had two parents and were nuclear in composition tells more than that the double stream is a fiction. Most adults in these families were illiterate, and, unless we give unwarranted credit to northern evangels, their behavior had to be profoundly shaped by tradition and custom. So it becomes clear that the new data pose significant questions about the consciousness, the culture, and the family life of enslaved Afro-Americans. Unless we are prepared to believe that most slave owners taught their chattel the value

Table 13.2   Types of Afro-American households by percentages, 1880

Place	Nuclear	Extended	Augmented	Sub-black	Sub-white
Richmond, Va.	52	10	19	9	10
Mobile, Ala.	60	14	11	10	5
Natchez, Miss.	50	17	20	10	3
Beaufort, S.C.	63	17	10	9	1
Rural Adams County, Miss.	58	15	15	10	2
St. Helena's Island, S.C.	76	14	2	8	0
St. Helena's Township, S.C.	80	12	4	4	0

of a two-parent nuclear household and sustained it in practice, then we must reject Elkins' conception of American slavery as a "closed system" that let masters remake slaves in their image. Elkins' "significant other" may have been a husband or a father, not just a master. That so many rural South Carolina and Mississippi blacks lived in two-parent nuclear families is hard to reconcile with Stampp's conclusion that slave family life was "a kind of cultural chaos," was "highly unstable," and often revealed "the failure of any deep and enduring affection to develop between some husbands and wives." Similarly, there is difficulty in agreeing with Wade that urban slave marriage involved "a great deal of fiction" and that "family ties were weak at best." "Male and female slaves found their pleasure and love," Wade argues, "wherever they could. . . . Generally, relations were neither prolonged nor monogamous. . . . The very looseness of their mating . . . made a meaningful family unit even more difficult. . . . For the children of such a marriage, there could be no ordinary family life."[26] Such arguments do not square easily with the fact that fifteen years after slavery's end three of every four Richmond and Mobile black families, nearly all headed by adult ex-slaves, were two-parent households.

It is hazardous to read history backward, but such data indicate that the final word has yet to be written about slave family life and culture in the cities and on the farms and plantations. Important new evidence about the attitudes of freedmen and women toward marriage and family life as well as their marital condition as slaves is found in the Freedmen's Bureau manuscripts. Registers that listed the marriages of former slaves in Washington, D.C., and Rockbridge and Nelson counties, Virginia, between 1865 and 1867 show that models of stable marriages existed among the slaves themselves, not just among their masters, other whites, or free blacks. Some had lived together as husband and wife for more than forty years in slavery. In all, registers recorded the dates of 1,721 marriages: 46 percent in the Nelson county, 43 percent in Rockbridge county, and 36 percent in Washington, D.C, had resided together at least ten years. The Washington register tells even more. It listed 848 marriages, and of them only 34 were between men and women who had lived in the District before emancipation. The rest had moved there, probably as families, mostly from nearby rural counties in Maryland and Virginia. Asked by the registrar, who had married them, some did not know or could not remember. Others named a minister, a priest, or, more regularly, a master. Most important, 421, nearly half, responded, "no marriage ceremony," suggesting clearly that slaves could live together as husband and wife in a stable (though hardly secure and ideal) relationship without formal religious or secular rituals. The Vicksburg,

Mississippi, marriage registers for 1864 and 1865 give even more significant information. Freedmen and women whose slave marriages had been disrupted told how long they had lived together in an earlier marriage, the cause for its termination, and the number of children resulting from a prior marriage. Although these registers have not yet been fully analyzed, they have already yielded valuable information. Answers given by more than 2,100 ex-slaves who were taking new spouses show that 40 percent of the men and 35 percent of the women had been married for at least five years, and some for more than twenty years. "Death" (40 percent for the men and 57 percent for the women) and "force" (i.e., physical separation) (48.5 percent for the men and 31 percent for the women) explained the rupture of most of these marriages, but one of every twenty men and women gave as the reason "mutual consent."

Death and force broke up many slave marriages, but it does not follow that such severe disruption shattered slave *consciousness* of normal slave marriage relations and of the value of a two-parent household. The 1866 Freedmen's Bureau census in Princess Anne County, Virginia, sheds clear light on the consciousness. Bureau officials gathered detailed demographic data on 1,796 black men, women, and children. Only the occupational data were limited in use (all of the employed adult males were listed simply as "laborers"). Of these blacks, 1,073 were fifteen years and older, and of them 2 percent were of "mixed color," 6.3 percent had been free before 1863, and 3.5 percent could read. In other words, the adult population consisted almost entirely of black, illiterate ex-slaves. The census also recorded the names of former owners and where each person had lived before emancipation. Sixty-three percent, nearly two-thirds, of the entire population had not resided in Princess Anne County before emancipation. Most migrants had lived nearby in Virginia and North Carolina counties; a few came from Maryland and three from as far as Kentucky, Georgia, and Texas. Despite such extraordinary mobility, no more than one in ten lived apart from a larger black household. Ninety percent of the migrants and local residents lived in 375 families, 84 percent of which housed a husband and his wife. Part of the reason for so much physical movement was the reconstitution of former slave families. Not one of the female-headed households was composed of persons who had belonged to different owners. The two-parent households tell a different story. Of 291 households headed by a former male slave, 193, two-thirds in all, came from separate owners. Some came together from more than two owners, but in most instances the wife and children were from a single master and the husband from another master. Just how many of these families were reconstituted and how many were new marriages cannot be known without additional information, but even by itself these data help to explain the geographical mobility of so many freedmen in 1865 and 1866, movement widely misinterpreted by white contemporaries and, until quite recently, by historians. What many white contemporaries thought of such behavior often drew upon sources other than the behavior itself. So we are not surprised to read in the *New York Times* in 1865: "The Negro misunderstands the motives which made the most laborious, hard-working people on the face of the globe clamour for his emancipation. You are free, Sambo, but you must work. Be virtuous, too, oh, Dinah! 'Whew! Gor Almighty! bress my soul!'"[27] It may be in reexamining the consciousness, culture, and family life of slaves and freedmen, marriage registers and census tracts will prove more valuable than the *New York Times* and other traditional sources.

Let us turn finally to a portion of another world which figured so prominently in Frazier's sociohistorical model: the female-headed black household in the rural and urban South between 1855 and 1880. In this period and for still another generation, Frazier argued, the "Matriarchate" ("the House of the Mother") flourished. Property-owning Negro farmers became black Puritan fathers, and small numbers of Negro males headed households in the South's urban bourgeois enclaves, but these did not count as much as the "matriarchal" households that surrounded them. Five chapters argued that matriarchy became a *legitimized counter-norm.* "Motherhood outside of institutional control was accepted by a large group of Negro women with an attitude of resignation as if it were nature's decree." Such were "the simple folkways of . . . peasant folk." "In the rural areas of the South," Frazier said again, "we find the maternal family functioning in its most primitive form as a natural organization." The three-generation female household—grandmother–daughter–grandchildren—counted for much in this construct and Frazier insisted that the older Negro woman headed "the maternal family among a primitive peasant people."[28]

It is difficult to dispute when Frazier writes that "the maternal-family organization, a heritage from slavery, . . . continued on a fairly large scale" because this critical assertion rested on almost no historical evidence. Seventy pages of text on the post-slavery "matriarchy" include just six pieces of historical data on the critical decades between 1870 and 1900: a letter, from Elizabeth Botume; an extract from A. T. Morgan's *Yazoo* (Washington, D.C., 1884); and two quotations each from Philip Bruce and J. Bradford Laws, a Department of Labor investigator who studied two small Louisiana plantations at the turn of the century. (Frazier neglected Laws' comments that the plantation Negroes were "grossly animal in their sexual relations" and that "very few . . . appear capable of deep emotion; sorrow over the dead dies with the sun. . . .") Despite the lack of evidence, Frazier's arguments about matriarchy have gained widespread approval. Glazer for example, writes in 1966 that Frazier's main proposition "remains solid and structures all our thinking on the Negro family." Glazer even wants readers to believe that an "extension of the matriarchy" took place after emancipation.[29] Although these and similar propositions remain unproven, they nevertheless need to be seriously tested.

Three objective measures of matriarchy as a form of household and family organization are available: male presence, the presence of older female relatives in the household, and the earning power of women as contrasted with men. Males, as seen, most usually husbands, were found in at least 70 percent of the households examined. That so few were extended households suggests the infrequency of older female relatives as household members. Income is another matter. Unskilled black laborers earned two or three times more a week than female servants or washerwomen, but little is yet known of the regularity of male employment, so that this question remains open.

There are other ways to examine these female-headed households in order to see them in historical perspective. We do not regularly find large numbers of children in female-headed households (Table 13.3). In 1880, for example, female-headed households among women aged 30–49 usually had one or two children younger than 18. Furthermore, the overall age distribution of all female household heads studied in 1880 suggests that a good portion of them were heads because their husbands had died and for no other reason. Between 23 percent and 30 percent

Table 13.3   Size of female-headed black households, including all children younger than 18 for mothers aged 30–49, 1880

Place	Total	One or two children (%)	Three or more children (%)
Beaufort, S.C.	50	72	28
St. Helena Island and St. Helena Township, S.C.	85	65	35
Richmond, Va.	658	72	28
Natchez, Miss., Wards I–III	92	61	39

Table 13.4   Household status of all black women, aged 20–29 in 1880

Area	Number	Married with/without children (%)	Head of household with children (%)	Single, boarder, or daughter (%)
Beaufort, S.C.	243	54	18	28
Natchez, Miss.	227	31	14	55
Mobile, Ala.	1,570	52	13	35
Richmond, Va.	3,400	39	9	52
St. Helena's Island, S.C.	393	70	9	21
St. Helena's Township, S.C.	172	80	8	12
Kingston and Washington Township, Adams Co., Miss.	478	68	21	11

of the households studied in each rural and urban area had as its head a woman of at least age 50. An even more significant test of the matriarchal ethos and of the conceptions of family and marriage held by black men and women can be constructed by asking how many women aged 20–29 in 1880 headed households in relationship to all black women of that age. They are a good group to examine. Born between 1851 and 1860, they grew up as slave children and matured as young women in the "chaos" and "disorder" of the Reconstruction era. They fall into three categories: those married, with or without children; those with children and heading households; and single women boarding with white or black families or living with their parents (Table 13.4). Except in rural Adams County, single women far outnumbered those who headed households with children. More than this, four times as many Richmond and Mobile women were married, with or without children, than headed households with children. The proportions were higher in the rural Sea Islands and somewhat lower in Natchez, Beaufort, and rural Adams County. These relationships take on even greater significance when the extremely unfavorable female sex ratio is considered. For reasons as yet not entirely clear, black women between the ages of 15 and 40 far outnumbered males in the same age group. This imbalance was not nearly as marked in the southern rural areas as in the southern cities where it was astonishing. For every 100 Negro women aged 20–29 in Beaufort, Natchez, Mobile, and Richmond, there were only 57 black males! In any modern social system, such a ratio weakens the position of the woman and, by itself, spawns prostitution and illegitimacy. When we realize that this un-favorable sex ratio existed in the "Redeemed" and "Bourbon" southern cities, then the matriarchy ethos loses more of its "potency" and we ask ourselves, instead, why were there so *few* female-headed Negro households?

Similar computations about the household status of all black women older than 50 test Frazier's notion of the three-generation matriarchal household, the "classic" grandmother–daughter–grandchildren arrangement. If we ask in 1880 what percentage of black women aged 50 and older headed such households or cared alone for their grandchildren, we find a relatively significant number only in Beaufort where 16 percent (21 of 134 women) headed such households. The percentage dwindles in all other places: 9 percent each in St. Helena's Island and Natchez, 6 percent each in St. Helena's Township and rural Adams County, and 5 percent in Richmond. Everywhere, the number of black widows aged 50 and more living just with their children was greater, but an even larger proportion lived alone with a husband or still shared full family life with a husband and their children. The total picture in rural Adams County is revealing for other places, too. Of 843 women aged 50 and older who resided there, half lived with husbands, with or without children and other relatives; another 15 percent, widowed, lived with married children; 19 percent boarded with relatives and non-relatives or lived alone; 10 percent headed households that contained just their children or their children and distant kin; just 6 percent fit the "classic" model sketched by Frazier and so many others. None of this is surprising in light of the larger pattern uncovered.

Because so many black women worked, the relationship between their occu-pation and family position tells something important about the question of "matriarchy." We concentrate only on the cities and, in particular, on the Richmond washerwomen and domestic servants. The data are still raw, but certain tentative observations can be reported. Not all women worked; mostly married women with children did not work. But still, slightly more than 6,000 Richmond women labored. Fewer than expected worked in the tobacco factories; one of every five was a washerwoman; two of every three were domestic servants. Married women, with or without children, and female heads of households worked more as wash-erwomen; 37 percent of Richmond's washerwomen were married and most often mothers; 28 percent headed households. Only 12 percent of the nearly 4,000 servants were married women. Fifty-three percent of all servants lived as individ-uals with white families. When we study their ages, patterns emerge. Washer-women tended to be older as a group than servants. They may have preferred toil over the tub and the dignity of their own poor homes to daily demeaning servant relationships outside the home. The typical black servant was an unmarried young woman. Just as many girls younger than age 15 worked as house servants as women aged 60 and older. Only 13 percent of Richmond's servants were aged 50 and older; 57 percent were less than 30. As "single" women, most servants either supported themselves or contributed to family incomes. Few black female servants fit the classic "Mammy" stereotype. Either whites preferred younger black women, or older black women stayed away from such work.

So much for an obsolete sociohistorical model that has told much about the history of the Afro-American family but nevertheless confused or blinded scholars as well as citizens. To dispute this model, however, is not the same as to offer another. Before that is done, new questions have to be answered and much material examined in fresh, systematic ways. The slave family is just one example. *Historical* comparisons with white lower-class families, immigrant and native-born, as well as with black families in other cultures are needed. Glasco and I compared the 1855 Buffalo Negro family with that of Irish and German immigrants and native whites and found significant similarities and differences, and strengths as well as weaknesses. But this is just a start.[30] More importantly, the quality of culture and family life cannot be constructed by a desk calculator. Whole ranges of non-quantitative data must be examined. But there are difficulties. Few nineteenth-century white Americans reported findings consistent with the data in these pages. When they did, they expressed "surprise," even shock. Why so few whites saw the Afro-American family as, in fact, it existed is a significant and complex question. Part of the reason reflects a curious coincidence between anti-slavery and pro-slavery arguments. White abolitionists denied slaves a family life or *even* a family consciousness because for them marriage depended only on civil law, not on culture. Pro-slavery apologists said free blacks could not build wholesome marriages for racial reasons. Together, these arguments blurred white perception of black families. Race and slavery were involved, but so was class.

Plumb has reminded us that racial stereotypes of Negroes had their counterpart in eighteenth- and nineteenth-century England. "Even the Sambo mentality," Plumb notes, "can be found in the deliberately stupid country yokel or in the cockney clown of later centuries. So, too, the belief, as with Negroes, that they were abandoned sexually, given to both promiscuity and over-indulgence." Slaves and free workers "were the objects of exploitation. . . . Hence we should not be surprised to find similar attitudes."[31] Race and class, however, mixed together so meanly for many whites that what they believed had little connection to what they saw. A single example from many serves this point. During Reconstruction, a British traveler heard a Macon, Georgia, black condemn a former master whom others praised:

> I was dat man's slave; and he sold my wife, and he sold my two chill'un; yes, brudders, if dere's a God in heaven, he did. Kind! yes, he gib me corn enough, and he gib me pork enough, and he neber gib me one lick wid de whip, but whar's my wife?—whar's my chill'un? Take away de pork, I say; take away de corn, I can work and raise dese for myself, but gib me back de wife of my bosom, and gib me back my poor chill'un as was sold away.

The same writer who reported these words said most freedmen and women "have no conception of the sacredness of marriage" and lived "in habitual immorality." He and others like him further validate Gramsci's dictum that "for a social elite the features of subordinate groups always display something barbaric and pathological."[32] So we must use traditional historical sources with great care. In addition, we must not isolate the Afro-American family from both the black and the larger white social and class structure that profoundly affected it. Even though his application of it was faulted, Frazier's insistence upon such approaches must be retained. Take the question of occupational mobility. Glasco and I have completed an occupational analysis of the Buffalo black community in 1855, 1875, 1892, 1905, and 1925. The trend between 1855 and 1905 was not encouraging. Occupational opportunities narrowed relatively and absolutely for Buffalo blacks over time (Table 13.5). They could not penetrate the city's dynamic industrial and construction sectors. Although the number of black males older than 15 increased by more than 300 percent, the number of barbers fell from twenty-two to six, sailors from eleven to none, building-trades craftsmen from eight to seven, and so forth. In 1855, barbers were 16 percent of all employed black males; in 1905, 1.4 percent. Skilled building-trades workers fell from 6 percent to 1.6 percent in the same years. Factory labor was not available to black males: in 1855, 1875, and 1892, census takers did not record a single black factory worker; in 1905, only 2, of 425 males were listed as factory workers. Just as black males were closed off from the building trades and factory labor between 1855 and 1905, so, too, were they blocked from occupations with a higher status. Black professionals, usually ministers and doctors, fell from six percent) to four (0.9 percent) between 1855 and 1905, and the retail trades found no blacks at all in these years.

Such occupational depression and disadvantage were not isolated trends that happened only in Buffalo. In Troy, of 162, black males employed in 1880, 123 were menial workers or laborers; only two were iron workers. And this in a city that gave employment to several thousand immigrant and native white iron workers. Occupational exclusion of blacks actually began *before the Civil War*. In an unpublished study, Weinbaum has demonstrated conclusively such exclusion and decline for Rochester, New York, blacks between 1840 and 1860.[33] My own work shows a similar decline in Charleston, South Carolina, between 1850 and 1860. And these trends continued in the southern cities during Reconstruction: a crucial story that has yet to be told. The 1870 New Orleans city directory, Woodward pointed out, listed 3,460 black carpenters, cigarmakers, painters, shoemakers, coopers, tailors, bakers, blacksmiths, and foundry hands. By 1904, less than 10 percent of that number appeared even though the New Orleans population had increased by more than 50 percent.[34] The process of enclosing ex-slaves began during Reconstruction and is part of any larger study of the Afro-American family. Mobile, Alabama, for example, had among its 1880 residents 139 black carpenters. Only 29 percent were younger than 40 years of age. What matters is that 6 percent of Mobile's native white carpenters and 76 percent of its carpenters who were sons of European immigrants were younger than 40. Thirteen percent of Mobile's black carpenters were younger than 30; 58 percent of the same city's black male servants were younger than 30. Because similar patterns emerge in other crafts *and* in other 1880 southern cities, it is clear that Afro-American fathers were not able to pass accumulated skills to their sons at this early date. The Buffalo study also shows the absence of a local entreprenurial and professional class among the blacks. Although the occupational structure was more diverse in southern cities, few blacks were non-workers. More than 6,500 black males earned income in Richmond in 1880: among them, a single physician, a single lawyer, twelve teachers, thirteen clergymen, and sixteen store clerks. Artisans made up the "elite" among blacks in the northern and southern postbellum cities. But institutional racism shattered that "elite" in these years.

The implications of these findings are significant for the reconstruction of the history of the Afro-American family. Such occupational patterns may be a clue to

Table 13.5 Selected occupations of blacks in Buffalo, N.Y., 1855–1925

Occupation	1855. N: 133 % Negro		1875. N: 188 % Negro		1892. N: 346 % Negro		1905. N: 425 % Negro		1925. N: 211[c] % Negro	
	N	Males 1855	N	Males 1875	N	Males 1892	N	Males 1905	N	Males 1975
Barbers	21	16.0	16	8.5	9	2.6	6	1.4	3	1.4
Sailors	11	8.0	7	3.7	3	0.9	0	0.0	0	0.0
Musicians	1	0.8	3	1.5	10	3.0	18	4.2	0	0.0
Building trades	8	6.0	8	4.3	7	2.0	7	1.6	10	4.7
Masons	1	0.8	0	0.0	2	0.6	14	3.3	2	1.0
"Crafts"[a]	6	4.5	5	2.7	6	1.7	10	2.4	25[b]	11.8
Factory labor	0	0.0	0	0.0	0	0.0	2	0.5	47	22.0
Clerk, messenger	0	0.0	0	0.0	13	3.7	7	1.6	1	0.5
Storekeeper	0	0.0	0	0.0	0	0.0	0	0.0	1	0.5
Professional	6	4.5	3	1.5	5	1.4	4	0.9	3	1.4

Notes: [a] Some of those listed under particular crafts must have labored in factories or work-shops, but the census did not make such distinctions. [b] Does not include railroad firemen and brakemen. [c] The 1925 data area sample that drew all Negro males older than 15 residing in every twentieth Negro-headed household in wards 6, 7, and 8.

an American variant of what Smith found in his outstanding study of Negro family life in British Guiana:

> In rigidly stratified societies such as that of British Guiana, where social roles are largely allocated according to ascriptive criteria of ethnic characteristics, the lower-class male has nothing to buttress his authority as husband-father except the dependence upon his economic support. The uncertainty of his being able to carry out even this function adequately, because of general economic insecurity, undermines his position even further.[35]

But occupational segregation undermined more than the male's position in the household. The absence of a complex occupational hierarchy may have so weakened the Afro-American community as to prevent it from successfully organizing to compete with native whites and immigrant groups. At best, the Afro-American structure was "two-dimensional." Its width was a function of the numbers of blacks in the entire community; its depth a function of a complex family system. But it was denied the "height" derived from a complex class structure based on occupational diversity. As a result, the family system *may* have been more important in giving cohesion to the black than to the white lower-class community. Significantly, the occupational disability that victimized Buffalo blacks did *not* shatter their family system. In 1905, for example, 187 of Buffalo's 222 black households, 8 percent, were headed by males. Nevertheless, the decline of the black artisan and the absence of a significant middle class in all cities studied had significant implications that distinguish the black lower class from the white lower class, immigrant and native-born alike. Among the lower classes in the nineteenth and early twentieth centuries, the artisans were the dynamic and organizing element. Some became manufacturers, others became factory workers. Voluntary associations found leaders among them. Local politicians came from the artisans and skilled workers, so did leaders of trade unions and reform and radical movements. But the black skilled worker was blocked from playing these roles. Before that enclosure occurred, he had held a significant place in such movements. Unpublished studies demonstrate this fact in important ways. White has shown that black artisans led a protest movement against Buffalo's segregated school system between 1839 and 1968. Even more important Magdol has recently uncovered a pattern of artisan and craft leadership among the rural, town, and village blacks of the South between 1865 and 1870.[36] The destruction of artisan traditions wiped out such leadership and distorted the black community structure *above* the level of its family organization. Much that flows from this fact may help us in understanding black political and social behavior between 1870 and 1910.

We return to the beginning. Let us follow Alexander Hamilton's advice and set aside views about blacks "founded neither in reason nor in experience." Evidence from Buffalo, other Northern cities, and, more important, Southern rural regions, towns, and cities refutes the argument that makes of black family life little more than a crude speculation about the relationship between slavery and twentieth-century black experience. Such theorizing rests on faulty historical knowledge. Silberman, for example, said:

Slavery had emasculated the Negro males, had made them shiftless and irresponsible and promiscuous by preventing them from asserting responsibility, negating their role as husband and father, and making them totally dependent on the will of another. There was [after emancipation] no stable family structure to offer support to men or women or children in this strange new world. With no history of stable families, no knowledge of even what stability might mean, huge numbers of Negro men took to the roads as soon as freedom was proclaimed. . . . Thus there developed a pattern of drifting from place to place and woman to woman that has persisted (in lesser degrees, of course) to the present day.[37]

There is no reason to repeat such nonsense any longer. Ellison has answered the assumptions on which it rests in an eloquent and authoritative fashion: "Can a people . . . live and develop over 300 years by simply reacting?" he asks. "Are American Negroes simply the creation of white men, or have they at least helped create themselves out of what they found around them? Men have made a way of life in caves and upon cliffs, why can not Negroes have made a life upon the horn of the white man's dilemma?"[38]

Slavery and quasi-freedom imposed countless burdens upon American blacks, but the high proportion of two-parent households found among them between 1855 and 1880 tells how little is yet known about the slave family, its relationship to the dominant white family structure, and the ways in which freedmen and freedwomen adapted, transformed, retained, or rejected older forms of family life. Finally, if the family transmits culture from generation to generation, then black subculture itself needs to be reexamined. It is too simple to say with Frazier: "Because of the absence of stability in [Negro] family life, there is a lack of traditions."[39] The composition of the Afro-American family and household between 1855 and 1880 suggests compelling reasons to reexamine historic Afro-American community life and the very meaning of American black culture.

Notes

1   Quoted in W. E. B. DuBois, *Negro-American Family* (Atlanta, 1909), opposite title page.
2   See, for example, Robert E. Park, "The Conflict and Fusion of Cultures with Special Reference to the Negro," *Journal of Negro History*, IV (1919), 111–133.
3   The most convenient collection of materials on this report—a volume which includes the full text of Daniel Patrick Moynihan's *The Negro Family: The Case for National Action* (Washington, D.C., 1965), and the responses of diverse critics—is Lee Rainwater and William L. Yancey, *The Moynihan Report and the Politics of Controversy* (Cambridge, Mass., 1967).
4   Philip M. Hauser, "Demographic Factors in the Integration of the Negro," *Daedalus* XCIV (1965), 854.
5   Nathaniel Shaler, "The Nature of the Negro" and "The African Element in America," *Arena*, II, III (1890), 664–665, 23–35.
6   Howard Odum, *Social and Mental Traits of the Negro: Research into the Basic Condition of the Negro Race in Southern Towns* (New York, 1910), *passim*, but esp. 36–42, 150–176, 213–237.
7   See, for example, Frederick L. Hoffman, *Race Traits and Tendencies of the American Negro* (New York, 1896); Joseph A. Tillinghurst, *The Negro in Africa and America* (New York, 1902); William W. Elwang, *The Negroes of Columbia, Missouri: A Concrete Study of the Race*

Problem (Columbia, 1904); William H. Thomas, *The American Negro, What He Was, What He Is, and What He May Become* (New York, 1904); W. D. Weatherford, *The Negro from Africa to America* (New York, 1924).

8 Ernest Burgess, "Introduction," in E. Franklin Frazier, *The Negro Family in the United States* (Chicago, 1939).

9 Frazier, *The Negro in the United States* (New York, 1949), 636.

10 Gunnar Myrdal, *An American Dilemma: The Negro Problem and Modern Democracy* (New York, 1944), 930–935.

11 Since this article was written, the following works dealing with various aspects of the slave family have appeared: John W. Blassingame, *The Slave Community: Plantation Life in the Antebellum Community* (New York, 1972); Robert W. Fogel and Stanley L. Engerman, *Time on the Cross: The Economics of American Negro Slavery* (Boston, 1974), 2v.; Eugene D. Genovese, *Roll, Jordan, Roll: The World the Slaves Made* (New York, 1974). These works differ significantly in their treatment of the slave family, but all are "positive" in their emphasis. These works, however, contain inadequate explanatory "models" in describing slave familial life and behavior. All revise the "traditional picture of the slave family," but the evidence offered is largely descriptive and not analytic.

12 See, for examples, John Hope Franklin, *The Free Negro in North Carolina, 1790–1860* (Chapel Hill, 1943); Leon F. Litwack, *North of Slavery: The Negro in the Free States, 1790–1860* (Chicago, 1961); Alrutheus A. Taylor, *The Negro in South Carolina during the Reconstruction* (Washington, D.C., 1924), *The Negro in the Reconstruction of Virginia* (Washington, D.C., 1926), *The Negro in Tennessee, 1865–1880* (Washington, D.C., 1941); Vernon Lane Wharton, *The Negro in Mississippi, 1865–1890* (Chapel Hill, 1947); George Tindall, *South Carolina Negroes, 1877–1900* (Columbia, 1952); Willie Lee Rose, *Rehearsal for Reconstruction: The Port Royal Experiment* (Indianapolis, 1964); Joel Williamson, *After Slavery: The Negro in South Carolina during Reconstruction, 1861–1867* (Chapel Hill, 1965), The following important more recent studies have shed additional light on the Afro-American family in the aftermath of the general emancipation: Robert H. Abzug, "The Black Family during Reconstruction," in Daniel Fox, Nathan Huggins, and Martin Kilson (eds.), *Key Issues in the Afro-American Experience* (New York, 1971), II, 26–41; Peter Kolchin, *First Freedom: The Responses of Alabama's Blacks to Emancipation and Reconstruction* (Westport, Conn., 1972), 56–79; John Blassingame, *Black New Orleans, 1860–1880* (Chicago, 1973), 79–106.

13 Gilbert Osofsky, *Harlem: The Making of a Ghetto (Negro New York, 1890–1930)* (New York, 1963), 133–134. Andrew Billingsley, *Black Families in White America* (Englewood Cliffs, N.J., 1968), 69–71; Jessie Bernard, *Marriage and Family among Negroes* (Englewood Cliffs, N.J., 1966), *passim*; Nathan Glazer, "Introduction," in Stanley M. Elkins, *Slavery: A Problem in American Institutional and Intellectual Life* (New York, 1963), xv.

14 Frazier, *The Negro Family in Chicago* (Chicago, 1932), 33–34.

15 Frazier, *The Negro Family in the United States*, 89.

16 Frazier, *The Negro in the United States*, 627.

17 George Fitzhugh, "Camp Lee and the Freedmen's Bureau," *DeBow's Review*, II (1866), 346–355.

18 Quoted in Allan Conway, *Reconstruction of Georgia* (Minneapolis, 1966), 65–66.

19 Philip A. Bruce, *The Plantation Negro as Freeman* (New York, 1889), 4, *passim*.

20 Walter L. Fleming, *Civil War and Reconstruction in Alabama* (New York, 1905), 763–764.

21 Joe M. Richardson, *The Negro in the Reconstruction of Florida, 1865–1867* (Tallahassee, 1965). Billingsley, *Black Families in White America*, 69–71; Henderson H. Donald, *The Negro Freedman* (New York, 1952), 56–75; Leonard Broom and Norval Glenn, *The Transformation of the Negro American* (New York, 1967), 15–21; Jesse Bernard, *Marriage and Family Among Negroes*, 70–75; C. Eric Lincoln, "The Absent Father Haunts the Negro Family," *New York Times Magazine* (Nov. 28, 1965), 60, 172–176.

22 Data also have been gathered on all single blacks who lived alone or in white households.

23 Herbert G. Gutman and Laurence A. Glasco, "The Buffalo, New York, Negro, 1855–1875: A Study of the Family Structure of the Free Negroes and Some of Its Implications," unpub. paper prepared for the Wisconsin Conference on the History of American Political and Social Behavior (May, 1968); *idem*, "The Negro Family, Household, and Occupational

Structure, 1855–1925, with Special Emphasis on Buffalo, New York, but Including Comparative Data from New York City, Brooklyn, Mobile, and Adams County, Mississippi," unpub. paper prepared for the Yale Conference on Nineteenth-Century Cities (Nov., 1968).

24 In gathering data from the 1880 federal census, the author was greatly assisted by Elizabeth Ewen, Ursula Lingies, and Mark Sosower.

25 Frazier, *Negro Family in the United States*, 479.

26 Elkins, *Slavery* (Chicago, 1959), 81–88, 115–139; Kenneth M. Stampp, *The Peculiar Institution: Slavery in the Antebellum South* (New York, 1956), 340–349; Richard C. Wade, *Slavery in the Cities: The South, 1820–1860* (New York, 1964), 117–120.

27 *New York Times* (May 17, 1865), quoted in Myrta L. Avery, *Dixie after the War* (New York, 1906), 210.

28 Frazier, *Negro Family in the United States*, 106–107, 121, 127; see, esp. , chs. 5–8.

29 J. Bradford Laws, *The Negroes of Cinclaire Central Factory and Calumet Plantation, Louisiana* (Washington, D.C., 1903), 120–121, Nathan Glazer, "Foreword" to revised and abridged edition, Frazier, *The Negro Family in the United States* (Chicago, 1966), viii.

30 See note 23.

31 J. H. Plumb, "Slavery, Race, and the Poor," *New York Review of Books*, XII (March 13, 1969), 3–5.

32 William Macrae, *Americans at Work*, 316–320. Antonio Gramsci quoted in Charles Tilly, "Collective Violence in European Perspective," in Hugh Graham and Ted R. Gurr (eds.), *Violence in America* (New York, 1969), 12.

33 Unpublished paper, by Paul Weinbaum, "Rochester, New York, Blacks before the Civil War," 1968, in the author's possession.

34 C. Vann Woodward, *Origins of the New South, 1877–1913* (Baton Rouge, 1951), 361.

35 Raymond T. Smith, *Negro Family in British Guiana* (New York, 1956), 73.

36 Arthur White, "Antebellum School Reform in Boston: Integrationists and Separatists," *Phylon*, XXXIV (1973), 203–219; Edward Magdol, "Local Black Leaders in the South, 1867–75: An Essay toward the Reconstruction of Reconstruction History," *Societas*, IV (1974), 81–110.

37 Charles E. Silberman, *Crisis in Black and White* (New York, 1964), 94–95.

38 Ralph Ellison, *Shadow and Act* (New York, 1964), 315.

39 Frazier, *Negro in the United States*, 636.

Michael Craton

CHANGING PATTERNS OF SLAVE FAMILY IN THE BRITISH WEST INDIES

Introduction

THIS ESSAY, DATING FROM 1978, if not being quite the first to discover the existence of slave families in the British West Indies, shares with the work of Barry Higman, the credit of extending to the Caribbean the work on slave families in the USA initiated by Herbert Gutman. It [. . . singles] out the formation of slave families from other factors in the complex equation determining the nature and quality of slave life, taking into account demographic realities and the variations in work, climate and disease regimes at opposite ends of the Caribbean and over time. Although it is subject to the familiar problems of patchy documentation and of certainly distinguishing true families from mere households, the clinching argument for the importance of family is thought to rest on the essay's so far unique comparison of the experience of a single set of families transferred from one colony to another. At the very least it challenges received interpretations of the roles of Africans, white masters and the system of slavery in the formation of slave families. It might also lead future scholars to face the problem of explaining why, if slavery was not so inimical to formal close-knit families as previously suggested, the structure and cohesion of Caribbean families became progressively weaker rather than stronger after slavery ended.

> any Attempt to restrain this Licentious Intercourse between the Sexes amongst the Slaves in this Island in the present State of their Notions of Right and Wrong, by introducing the Marriage Ceremony amongst them, would be utterly impracticable, and perhaps of dangerous Consequence, as these People are universally known to claim a Right of Disposing themselves in this Respect, according to their own Will and Pleasure without any Controul from their Masters.[1]

Writers on the West Indies have echoed the negative statements of Alexis de Tocqueville and E. Franklin Frazier on slave and modern black families in the USA.[2] In this vein, Simey, Henriques and Goode exaggerated the matrifocality and instability of modern Caribbean families as 'deviant' results of an alleged absence of family life in slavery, while Smith and Patterson confidently backed up their

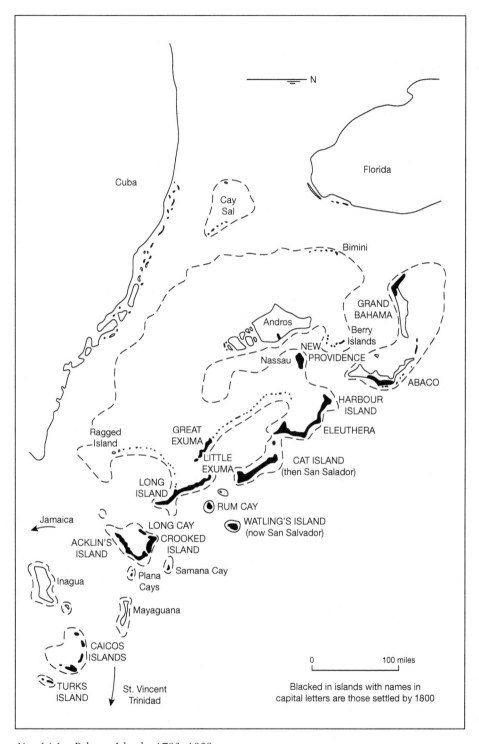

Map 14.1   Bahama Islands, 1783–1838

analyses of modern family with assertions that 'the women normally acted as the sole permanent element in the slave family, whether or not the male partner was polygynous', and that 'the nuclear family could hardly exist within the context of slavery'.[3]

In work published since 1973, Higman has proved these assertions to be wrong and thus has reopened the whole study of the West Indian family and its roots. Although concentrating on sugar plantation colonies and the period of slave amelioration and registration (1807–34), he has shown that family life – even in patterns recognisable to Europeans – was then the norm for British West Indian slaves. Although polygyny and other African practices persisted, the nuclear, two-headed household was extremely common among the African-born as well as creole slaves. More remarkably, single-headed maternal households were in a minority in every area studied by Higman, save for the towns. The frequency of matrifocal families and the general disruption of slave families had become exaggerated, he suggested, because of the practices of those slaves with whom whites were most familiar: domestics and urban slaves.[4]

The purpose of this present paper is fourfold. It adds to Higman's evidence by using material chiefly from the Bahamas, a non-sugar, largely non-plantation colony. It also summarises the evidence hitherto gathered, sketches the varieties of slave family from place to place and time to time, and, finally, discusses developmental models. Despite great variations according to location, employment and ownership (not to mention the difficulties presented by fragmentary and uneven evidence) a consistent pattern does emerge. This suggests both the place that the rediscovered West Indian slave family of the late slave period occupies in the continuum between West African roots and the modern West Indian black family, and some of the ways in which the dynamics of West Indian black family have differed from those of the USA and Latin America.

As Stephen noted as early as 1824, slave conditions in the Bahama Islands were at the benign end of a scale on which the sugar colonies further south – particularly the newly acquired colonies of Trinidad and Guyana – represented the opposite extreme. An influx of Loyalist planters after 1783 had changed the tone and pace of the archipelagic colony, doubling the white population and trebling the number of slaves; but the population density remained a twentieth of that of Jamaica and a fiftieth of that of Barbados, while the ratio of black slaves to white freemen and the average size of slave holdings remained among the lowest in the British West Indies.[5]

Most of the Loyalist emigrés settled their slaves on Bahamian 'Out Islands' until then unpopulated, attempting to replicate the plantation conditions they had left behind in the Carolinas, Georgia and Florida. They found the climate ideal for growing sea island cotton, but the exhaustion of the thin soil and the depredations of the chenille bug left them unable to compete with American cotton once Whitney's gin became effective after 1800. Although a local planter, Joseph Eve, invented a wind-powered variant of the gin, Bahamian cotton production had almost faded away by 1820. Plantations were turned over to stock or the growing of grains and other provisions, and many of the slaves had to fend for themselves.

Those planters who could, sold up and migrated once more. Many of them attempted to transfer their slaves to the old colony of Jamaica or the new sugar plantations in Trinidad and St Vincent, where fresh slaves were at a premium after the African supply had been cut off by the abolition of the Atlantic slave trade in

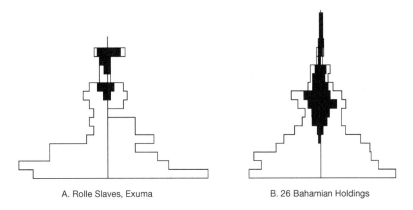

Figure 14.1   Population pyramids, Rolle slaves and 26 Bahamian holdings

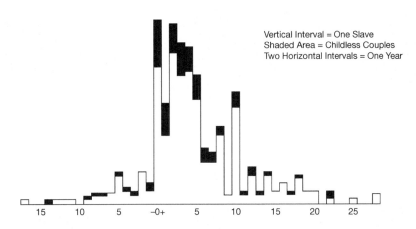

Figure 14.2   Bahamas, 26 holdings, 1822; Age differences between males and their mates

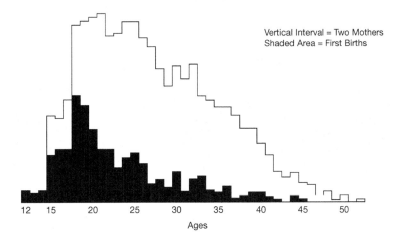

Figure 14.3   Bahamas, 26 Holdings, 1822; Ages of mothers at births of their children

1808. Although slaves were registered in the Crown Colony of Trinidad as early as 1813, this opportunistic trade was not revealed until the first returns under the Bahamian Slave Registration Act of 1821 reached London, after which it was effectively scotched by the abolitionists under Stephen Lushington in 1823. By then, perhaps 2,000 Bahamian slaves (a fifth) had already been transferred.[6]

The meticulous triennial returns of British West Indian slaves produced by the registration laws were of great value to the emancipationists, who were able to prove the persistence of 'natural decrease' as well as to end the intercolonial trade. Modern demographers, however, can put them to much wider use, reconstituting and comparing whole colony populations by age, sex, African or creole birth, mortality, fertility and life expectancy. In at least two colonies, Trinidad and the Bahamas, it is also possible to discover and compare patterns of slave family. Unlike the Trinidadian instructions, the Bahamian law did not require the listing of slaves' families or households-by-name. But approximately a quarter of Bahamian slaves were voluntarily listed by their owners in such a way as to indicate family relationships, though with limits on the range of family types identifiable. Comparison between the original lists of 1821 and 1822 and those of 1825, 1828, 1831 and 1834, moreover, allows both for corroboration of relationships and the testing of their permanence.[7]

In all, it has proved possible to analyse 26 slave holdings in the first Bahamian census of 1821–22 in which owners listed slaves in family groups, rather than by alphabetical order, age, sex or any other method. This sample comprised 3,011 out of a Bahamas grand total of about 12,000, an average of 116 slaves per holding, but with a range between 20 and 840, drawn from 11 different islands. The findings not only illustrate the contrasts between the Bahamian slave population and those in sugar plantation colonies farther south, but also point up the typicality of the only Bahamian slave group previously studied, that of the slaves owned by Lord John Rolle on the island of Exuma.[8]

Ten times the size of the Rolle holding, this widespread fourth of the Bahamian slave population exhibited almost as balanced, 'modern', and 'unslavelike' a demographic pattern, with a broad base of youngsters and a fair number of elderly slaves. The sexes in the fertile age ranges were almost as equally balanced as Rolle's slaves, and the only features reminiscent of slave populations farther south were a slight 'bulge' in the age range from 40–54, representing in this case survivors from the migration of Loyalists' slaves in the 1780s, and a substantial remnant of Africans, 18.8 per cent of the total. Unlike the Rolle holding, there also was evidence of considerable miscegenation, 6.9 per cent of the 3,011 slaves being listed as 'mulatto' or 'yellow'.[9]

These slight differences and the less optimal work and living conditions accounted for a rather lower average net population increase than with Lord Rolle's slaves, but the incidence of family in the sample of 26 holdings was very similar. As Table 14.1 shows, 85.0 per cent were found in some type of family, with no less than 54.1 per cent of the 3,011 slaves over 20 years old, 854, or 63.1 per cent, were listed in couples. The normal pattern was for males to be a few years older than their mates. On the average, males were some four-and-one-half years older, but this figure was skewed by some much older males and by the few older females. Of 397 couples who were the parents in nuclear families or were childless, in 303 cases the males were from zero to ten years older, with an average of three

Table 14.1 Household patterns, Rolle slaves, and 26 Bahamian holdings, 1822

Family type	Rolle slaves, Exuma				26 Bahamian holdings			
	Total slaves	Number of units	Mean size of units	Percent of total in type	Total slaves	Number of units	Mean size of units	Percent of total in type
1. Man, woman, children	110	26	4.23	46.6	1,629	308	5.29	54.1
2. Man, woman	14	7	2.00	5.9	178	89	2.00	5.9
3. Woman, children	40	12	3.33	16.9	377	95	3.97	12.5
4. Man, children	11	2	5.50	4.7	16	3	5.33	0.5
5. Three-generation groups	29	5	5.80	12.3	358	46	7.78	11.9
6. Men alone, or together	11	–	–	4.7	264	–	–	8.8
7. Women alone, or together	9	–	–	3.8	173	–	–	5.8
8. Children separately	12	–	–	5.1	16	–	–	0.5
Totals	236	–	–	100.0	3,011	–	–	100.0
A. Nuclear family (1, 2, 5)	153	38	4.03	64.8	2,165	443	4.89	71.9
B. Denuded family (3, 4)	51	14	3.64	21.6	393	98	4.01	13.0
C. No family (6, 7, 8)	32	–	–	13.6	453	–	–	15.1

years and ten-and-one-half months. Although the presence of elderly mothers whose first children had left the household or had died makes it difficult to count exactly, the average age of mothers at the birth of their first children appears to have been under 20 years. As Table 14.2 shows, the spacing between children was regular and healthy, with the overall average almost exactly three years. Of all women in the age range 15–49, a high proportion, 65.8 per cent, were indicated as mothers, having had on the average almost exactly three children.[10]

Besides these basic statistical findings, a study of the Bahamian returns allows for some general observations and analysis along lines followed by Gutman and other scholars of slavery in the USA. First, important implications concerning the incidence of endogamy and exogamy – or at least of in-group and out-group mating – arose from the tendency of slave families to appear most clearly in the records of the larger and more isolated holdings, which were mainly in islands distant from Nassau, the colonial capital.[11] In contrast, on New Providence (Nassau's island) and the nearer, long-established settlements of Harbour Island and Eleuthera, conjugal patterns seem to have been more disrupted. Many of the holdings were too small to include whole families and this clearly contributed to the custom of choosing mates from other holdings. But there were other factors. Among a heavily creolised population (with some slaves six generations removed from Africa), in small units, marital mobility was not only possible but probably seen as desirable to avoid too close a consanguinity. Miscegenation was also rather more common in New Providence and Eleuthera than farther afield, those slaves listed as mulatto or yellow constituting eight per cent of the few holdings analysed, and probably more than ten per cent overall.[12]

In general, it seems that these conditions led not to familial cohesion but the reverse, with many male mates absent or even temporary. Female-headed families were most common in the listings for New Providence (where almost a quarter of all Bahamian slaves lived), not only in the several holdings that consisted solely of slave mothers and their children, but also in such groups as the 37 slaves of Elizabeth Mary Anderson, where nine men aged from 22 to 60 were listed together but separately from five female-headed families averaging five children each. Only in the exceptional holding of William Wylly at the isolated western end of New Providence, were families distinct and clearly permanent.

In the distant, more recently established settlements, populations were on the average larger, more isolated and, perhaps of necessity, more cohesive. The choice of mates was limited, and thus relationships were likely to be not only well known but also more permanent. In relatively large populations, consisting in most cases primarily of first and second generation creoles, such enforced in-group mating would not yet come into conflict with any customary ban on cousin-mating that may have existed (whether derived from Africa or Europe). In all, it is possible that conditions in the Out Islands, which Nassauvians, both white and black, might consider primitive, were more conducive to stable family formation than those closer to the colonial centre. Certainly, in modern times, Otterbein has documented a greater awareness of the value of stable families in 'primitive' Andros Island than that to be inferred in the less affluent sections of modernised Nassau, which include large groups of displaced Out Islanders. Yet these conditions seem to have also obtained in slavery days, a conclusion that runs counter to Gutman's contention that the dislocating effects of urbanisation postdated emancipation, at least in the USA.[13]

Table 14.2   Bahamas, 26 slave holdings, 1822 – average ages of mothers at births and child spacing

Which child	Number of mothers	Percent total mothers in each group	Average ages at births	Average spacing (years)
1st	479	100.0	22.37	
2nd	356	74.3	26.53	3.36
3rd	244	50.9	30.00	2.93
4th	170	35.5	32.60	2.93
5th	105	21.9	33.38	2.42
6th	59	12.3	35.22	2.81
7th	31	6.5	40.10	2.95
8th	8	1.7	43.46	2.67
9th	2	0.4	38.75	1.87
10th	1	0.2	38.00	1.00
Averages			34.84	3.02

The listings of families headed by single females may disguise the existence of serially shifting, or even polygynous, relationships. But in the series of five censuses spread over 12 years (1822–34) there is very little positive evidence of serial monogamy, and only rare and equivocal evidence of polygyny.[14] Naming practices were little help in tracing family patterns. Bahamian slaves did not universally adopt surnames before emancipation, and then it is by no means certain that surnames were patronymics in the modern style.[15] The practice of taking the surname of the former owner tends to exaggerate consanguinity as well as to confuse relationships – the most extreme case being Lord Rolle's 372 slaves, all of whom took the surname Rolle in order to share common rights in their former master's land. The discernment of immediate relationships was aided, however, by the frequent practice of naming a male child after his father or grandfather, and the occasional custom of naming a female after her grandmother.[16]

Such three-generation links sometimes allowed for the identification of extended family units, but the positive evidence of wider kinship links was disappointingly meagre, and the direct evidence from the records of related families living close together in clusters of huts or 'yards' was non-existent, although such groupings are known to have been a feature of Out Island life in later times. However, the frequent listing of a young girl with her first child in the household of her parents, or mother, does permit some inferences about sexual customs. Few girls under 20 cohabited with their mates; few mothers over 20 lived with their parents, and most, as we have seen, lived with mates. Nearly all girls who bore their first children in their mothers' households began separate cohabitation at, or shortly before, the birth of their second children. It therefore seems likely that premarital sex was not uncommon, and even that virginity at marriage was not excessively prized; but that separate cohabitation in a nuclear household was the accepted norm for couples over the age of 20.[17]

The evidence proves the vigorous existence of families among Bahamian slaves during the registration period and, indeed, points to the existence of types of families classified as 'modern' by Europeans among the least modernised groups of slaves. It remains to be decided, though, whether this was a social pattern chosen by the slaves themselves – and thus likely to have existed before the recorded period – or one determined, or at least encouraged, by the Eurocentric, pro-natalist, or publicity-conscious masters.

Strong evidence for the latter conclusion is found in the case of the slaves of William Wylly, Attorney-General of the Bahamas. An ardent Methodist who arranged for a minister to preach regularly to his slaves, he came to be regarded as a crypto-emancipationist by his fellow planters because of a legal decision made in 1816, and was at the centre of a bitter wrangle between the plantocratic Assembly and three successive governors, lasting until 1820. Close examination of the evidence, however, shows that Wylly was a strict paternalist, and suggests that if he wished to turn his slaves loose it was because they were no longer profitable.[18]

By 1818, Wylly's three estates in western New Providence had ceased to grow cotton, Tusculum and Waterloo being turned over to stock raising and Clifton, the largest, being devoted to growing provisions for the slaves and the Nassau market. The Attorney-General's many enemies accused him both of allowing his slaves more time to work for themselves than laid down by Bahamian law, and of supplying them with less than the provisions specified. In response, Wylly produced convincing proof of the degree to which his slaves were self-supporting, and stated: 'My principal object has been, to accustom them to *habits of Industry and Oeconomy* – which I am convinced, never will be found to exist among any Slaves, in this part of the World, who are victualled by their Masters.'[19]

At the same time, Wylly forwarded a revealing set of regulations for his slaves which he had caused to be printed and published in Nassau in 1815. Apart from his concern for religious instruction and regular prayers, and details of clothing, feeding, work and punishment regulations, these clearly illustrated his views on slave marriage, sexual continence and motherhood. 'Every man, upon taking his first wife,' read Article VII of the regulations, 'is entitled to a well built stone house, consisting of two apartments, and is to receive a sow pig, and a pair of dunghill fowls, as a donation from the proprietor.'[20]

'In cases of Adultery,' read Article XI, 'the man forfeits his hogs, poultry, and other moveable effects; which are to be sold, and the proceeds paid over to the injured husband. Both offenders are moreover to be whipt; their heads to be shaved, and they are to wear *Sack cloth* (viz. gowns and caps made of Cotton bagging) for the next half year; during which time they are not to go beyond the limits of the plantation, under the penalty of being whipt.'

With far less Mosaic severity, Article XIX enjoined that, 'On working days, the children are to be carried, early every morning, by their mothers, to the Nursery, where proper care will be taken of them during the day; and their mothers are to call for them when they return from their work in the afternoon. Women who have children at the breast, are never to be sent to any distance from the homestead.'

Predictably, Wylly's slave lists in the registration returns disclose a neat pattern of families and a healthy natural increase. Since his regulations were published and his views on slave management became well known, it is possible that they became normative. The very decision to list slaves according to families and households may indicate owners who shared Wylly's concerns. Certainly, the other two

Bahamian owners known to have engaged in correspondence on the management of their slaves, Lord Rolle of Exuma and Burton Williams of Watling's Island, demonstrated an awareness of the value of stable families in producing healthy, fertile and contented slaves.[21]

It is likely, though, that such planters as Wylly, Rolle and Williams were self-deluding if not self-serving. The widespread incidence and consistent form of slave families suggest customary choice on the part of the slaves rather than the dictates of the masters. Few plantations were owner-managed, especially in the Out Islands, and it seems strange that orderly patterns of slave family should be more common the further from Nassau (where slaves were commonly under the daily scrutiny of their owners), unless this was the slaves' own choice. Nor can the growing influence of Christianity be given unequivocal credit. The established Anglican Church, which held a monopoly on formal weddings until 1827, did not proselytise the slaves, and the few sectarian missionaries concentrated on Nassau and the nearer islands. The underground 'Native Baptist', who were active among the Loyalists' slaves in Nassau as early as in Jamaica, may have had more widespread influence. But they were known to be tolerant about informal marital ties, being regarded by whites as hardly Christians at all. Indeed, the common impression held by the whites of the mass of the slaves was that those who were not heathen practisers of obeah were infidel 'followers of Mahomet'.[22]

This at least suggests strong African cultural retentions, particularly in the Out Islands. Numerically the Africans were few by the registration period but, as elderly survivors, seem to have been highly respected members of the slave community. Indeed, it became clear on further analysis of the 26 holdings that the African slaves had influence out of all proportion to their numbers, and even that they were dominant in shaping family life in the Bahamas. Although most of the African-born slaves were grouped together towards the end of the rolls, in more than a third of the slave holdings analysed an African couple was at the head of the list. Thus usually indicated that the owner had chosen the most prestigious married African as head driver.[23]

As in all slave communities the role of such leaders was ambivalent. They were chosen for what was termed 'confidentiality' – fidelity, reliability and respectability. But they were known to be effective because they commanded respect and 'reputation', among creoles as well as African blacks. For example, Wylly's African head driver and under-driver, Boatswain and Jack, practically ran his estates. Strong family men, they were expected to lead prayers at Sunday services and conduct funerals. Boatswain at least was literate, and was paid for each slave taught to read; both were rewarded with 12 guineas a year, the right to own and ride a horse, and the power to inflict punishment on their own initiative up to 12 stripes. But did their authority, ultimately, stem from their paternalistic master, or from their position as family heads and from African roots? And what did the family pattern at Clifton, Tusculum and Waterloo owe, respectively, to memories of Africa, the examples of Boatswain and Jack, and the encouragement of Wylly?

Strong clues emerged from the discovery that, when African-headed families – those in which both parents, either parent, or the only parent were African-born – were separated from purely creole families, it became obvious that Africans were considerably more inclined towards family formation than creole slaves. Of the Africans, 65.3 per cent lived in couples, compared with less than 60 per cent of the creoles over the age of 20. Of all African-headed families, 61.0 per cent were of the simple nuclear type, with an additional 9.4 per cent indicated as extended family households. This compared with 48.4 per cent in nuclear units and 14.4 per cent in extended households among creole families. Only 11.9 per cent of Africans lived alone, compared with 16.7 per cent of adult creoles.

By a Bahamian law of 1824, owners were forbidden to separate slave husbands from wives by sale, gift, or bequest, or to take their children away from them before they were 14 years old. Although the act did not expressly forbid the splitting of families by shifting slaves from island to island, or the separation of children from single parents, it would seem to have provided owners with a motive for discouraging rather than encouraging slave families. Yet the evidence strongly suggests that masters were not only forced to acknowledge slave marital arrangements and to sell or transfer slaves only in families, even before 1824, but also to consider carefully the social consequences before they shifted slaves from their customary houses, plots and kin at all.[24]

Wylly, although an alleged emancipationist, only manumitted three of his slaves after 1822 and did not scruple to scatter them by sale and transfer between 1821 and his death in 1828. Families, however, were carefully kept together. In another case, Rolle proposed an ingenious scheme in 1826 to shift all of his slaves to Trinidad, where they were to work to earn their freedom in the Spanish style. Fortunately for the slaves, the project was vetoed by the Colonial Office. But the word must have filtered down to Exuma, for in 1828 when Rolle's agent set about transferring some slaves to Grand Bahama, all of the slaves, fearing a move to Trinidad, became so mutinous that troops had to be sent down to keep order. Two years later, when they heard that the agent planned to ship them from Exuma to Cat Island, 44 slaves (five men, eight women, and their families) actually rebelled. Under the leadership of a slave called Pompey they first fled to the bush, then seized Rolle's salt boat and sailed to Nassau to put their case to Governor Smyth, who was widely thought to be a friend of the slaves. The fugitives were thrown into the workhouse and the leaders flogged (including the eight women). But Smyth was angry when he heard about it and none of the slaves in the end were sent to Cat Island; so it can be said that Pompey and his fellows won the principle that Bahamian slaves could not with impunity be shifted against their will.[25]

The largest single transfer of slaves had been the shipment in 1823 of most of the 840 slaves of James Moss from Acklin's Island and Crooked Island to Jamaica, where their fate remains obscure. Yet the most interesting of all Bahamian transfers was that to Trinidad between 1821 and 1823 of the majority of the slaves of Burton Williams of Watling's Island and his family, since it allows for comparisons between the fortunes of those transferred and other slaves in Trinidad, and between all those and the slaves left behind in the Bahamas.

Early in 1825, after he had been in Trinidad three-and-half years, Williams gave evidence to the Trinidad Council about his slaves. He claimed that in '30 odd' years of Bahamian residence he had seen the group of seven slaves inherited and 'about 100' bought augmented by 224 through natural increase. This remarkable growth (as rapid as that indicated for Rolle's slaves, and sustained over a longer period) was attributed by Williams to his own residence among the slaves, to firm management, and to the encouragement of marriage 'by giving a feast to the Gang when they come together and a sharp punishment when they part'.[26]

Table 14.3 Bahamas, 26 slave holdings, 1822 comparison between African-headed and creole families

Family type	A. African headed families[a]				B. Creole families			
	Total slaves	Number of units	Mean size of units	Percent of total in type	Total slaves	Number of units	Mean size of units	Percent of total in type
1. Man, woman, children	830[a]	154	5.39	61.0	799	154	5.19	48.4
2. Man, woman	138[a]	69	2.00	10.2	40	20	2.00	2.4
3. Woman, children	91	21	4.33	6.7	278	72	3.86	16.8
4. Man, children	11	2	5.50	0.8	5	1	5.00	0.3
5. Three-generation groups	128[a]	19	6.73	9.4	238	29	8.21	14.4
6. Men alone, or together	114	–	–	8.4	150	–	–	9.1
7. Women alone, or together	48	–	–	3.5	125	–	–	7.6
8. Children separately	–	–	–	–	16	2	8.00	1.0
Totals	1,360	–	–	100.0	1,651	–	–	100.0
A. Nuclear family (1,2,5)	1,096	242	4.53	80.6	1,077	203	5.31	65.2
B. Denuded family (3,4)	102	23	4.43	7.5	283	73	3.88	17.1
C. No family (6,7,8)	162	–	–	11.9	291	–	–	17.7

Notes: [a] African-Headed Families were taken to be those in which both parents, either parent, or the single parent were of African birth. Thus in categories 1, 2, and 5 in Section A mixed couples were included.

Certainly, the 450 Williams slaves found in the Bahamian in 1821 exhibited an even healthier demographic balance and a higher incidence of family formation than the Bahamian average, as is shown in Figure 14.4 and Table 14.4. The proportion of young children was higher, there were only two-thirds as many Africans, and yet a fair number were very elderly slaves. The proportion of slaves in nuclear families, 55.8 per cent, was some two per cent higher than the average for the 26 holdings analysed earlier, and the total in some kind of family more than five per cent higher, at 90.2 per cent. Yet by Williams' account, the situation in the Bahamas had become economically and demographically critical by 1821, so that he could neither clothe nor feed his slaves adequately, although he owned 13,000 acres of land. Taking advantage of the inducements offered by Trinidad, he therefore transferred 324 of his slaves in five cargoes between 1821 and 1823.[27]

Although one or two couples were split and an unknown number of extended family members separated, Williams clearly attempted to transfer his slaves predominantly in family units. Comparison of the slaves settled at Williamsville, his new estate in Naparima, in the Trinidadian returns of 1825 with those left behind listed in the Bahamas returns of the same year, indicates also that the majority of the elderly and Africans were left behind, and that rather more young females were carried than young males. The transferred population therefore exhibited many characteristics sharply different from those of the generality of Trinidad slaves. Only 5.3 per cent of the Williamsville slaves were African-born, compared with the Trinidadian average of over 40 per cent, and females outnumbered males by 7.8 per cent, more than reversing the general Trinidadian pattern. Whether using the categories used elsewhere in this paper or those employed by Higman, the contrast in family formation is even more noticeable. Because of the greater detail given in the Trinidadian registration returns, more types could be differentiated, but the total of Williamsville slaves in some type of family was as high as in the Bahamas sample, and almost twice as high as the Trinidadian average indicated by Higman. The percentage in simple nuclear households, 57.3 per cent, was slightly higher than in the Bahamas, and three times as high as the Trinidadian average. Mothers living alone with their children accounted for only six per cent of the Williamsville slaves, half of the Bahamas figure, and little more than a quarter of that for Trinidad as a whole.

As a consequence of the division of the Williams slaves, those left behind in the Bahamas were less well-balanced in composition than the Bahamian average and therefore increased in number rather less rapidly after 1823. Yet those transferred were less healthy than those left behind and increased even more slowly. However, they did increase, in contrast to Trinidadian slaves in general, who suffered an alarming depletion throughout the registration period. By the end of 1826, 33 of Williams' Trinidadian slaves had died, while 57 were born (49 having been sold and two manumitted), an annual rate of natural increase of roughly 16 per thousand. This was half the Bahamian rate, and compared with an annual net decrease at least as high for Trinidadian slaves on the average.[28]

Although his 1825 evidence was twisted to justify the transfer, Williams had to admit that the health and morale of his slaves had suffered in the first three years – the seasoning period. 'Fevers and Agues and bowel Complaints', as well as unfamiliar 'Sores', although not great killers, were common among the transferred slaves. These ills Williams attributed to his having arrived in the middle of the wet

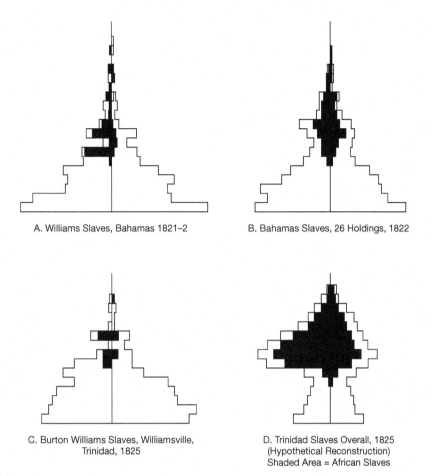

A. Williams Slaves, Bahamas 1821–2

B. Bahamas Slaves, 26 Holdings, 1822

C. Burton Williams Slaves, Williamsville,
Trinidad, 1825

D. Trinidad Slaves Overall, 1825
(Hypothetical Reconstruction)
Shaded Area = African Slaves

Figure 14.4   The Burton Williams slaves, 1822 and 1825, compared with Bahamas and Trinidad slaves, 1825; population pyramids

season, settling in a wooded and marshy area, and being forced to feed his slaves on plantains and saltfish rather than their customary guinea corn (millet or sorghum). He deplored the laxity of Trinidadian morals and the effects on family life of the disparity in the sex ratio. He also pleaded that the demoralising effects of Colonial Office regulations would encourage the idleness of slaves and limit the powers of correction of their masters. Against the evidence, he denied that the work required of slaves was harder than in the Bahamas, and claimed that slaves had more opportunity in Trinidad to dispose of the surplus food that they grew on their own allotments. However, he admitted that most of the slaves would have returned to the Bahamas if they had been given the choice.[29]

The research undertaken so far not only indicates a far wider existence of family in slave society than hitherto expected, but has also clarified the varieties of family within the range of West Indian slave communities in the late slave period. At one end of the scale were the virtual peasants of the Bahamas, Barbuda, and, perhaps, the Grenadines, with locational stability, a small proportion of African slaves, natural increase, and a relatively high incidence of nuclear and stable families. At the opposite pole were the overworked slaves of new plantations such as those of

Table 14.4 Bahamas, family formation, Williams slaves 1822 and 1825 compared with 26 holdings, 1822

Family type	A. Williams slaves, 1822				B. Williams slaves, bahamas, 1825				C. 26 Bahamian holdings, 1822			
	Total slaves	Number of units	Mean size of units	Percent of total in type	Total slaves	Number of units	Mean size of units	Percent of total in type	Total slaves	Number of units	Mean size of units	Percent of total in type
1. Man, woman, children	251	47	5.34	55.8	103	20	5.15	46.0	1,629	308	5.29	54.1
2. Man, woman	28	14	2.00	6.2	10	5	2.00	4.5	178	89	2.00	5.9
3. Woman, children	45	10	4.50	10.0	38	14	2.71	17.0	377	95	3.97	12.5
4. Man, children	2	1	2.00	0.5	0	0	—	—	16	3	5.33	0.5
5. Three-generation	80	9	8.88	17.8	25	4	6.25	11.2	358	46	7.78	11.9
6. Single men	15	—	—	3.3	22	—	—	9.8	264	—	—	8.8
7. Single women	14	—	—	3.1	8	—	—	3.5	173	—	—	5.8
8. Separate children	15	—	—	3.3	18	5	3.60	8.0	16	—	—	0.5
Totals	450	—	—	100.0	224	—	—	100.0	3,011	—	—	100.0
A. Nuclear family (1,2,5)	359	70	5.13	79.8	138	29	4.75	61.6	2,165	443	4.89	71.9
B. Denuded family (3,4)	47	11	4.27	10.4	38	14	2.71	17.0	393	98	4.01	13.0
C. No family (6,7,8)	44	—	—	9.8	48	—	—	21.4	453	—	—	15.1

Table 14.5 Family structure, Williams Trinidadian slaves, 1825 compared with Trinidadian total, 1813 (Higman, 1978)[a]

Family type	A. Williams slaves, 1825				B. Trinidadian slaves total, 1813			
	Total	Units	Mean size	Percent in type	Total	Units	Mean size	Percent in type
Man, woman, children	142	24	5.9	57.4	4,675	1,162	4.0	18.3
Man, woman	6	3	2.0	2.4	1,036	518	2.0	4.0
Woman, children	15	3	5.0	6.0	5,690	2,066	2.8	22.2
Man, children	0	0	–	–	357	138	2.6	1.4
Polygynists	0	0	–	–	31	7	4.4	0.1
Three-generation and extended[b]	47	8	5.9	18.9	445	97	4.6	1.7
Siblings	14	4	3.5	5.7	547	197	2.8	2.1
Siblings, children	9	2	4.5	3.6				
Man, woman, cousins	5	2	2.5	2.0	0	0	–	–
No family[c]	10	–	–	4.0	12,892	–	–	50.2
Totals	248	–	–	100.0	25,673	–	–	100.0

Notes: [a] Data from Public Record Office, London, T. 71/513 (1825); T. 71/501–503; Higman, "Family Patterns in Trinidad," 32. [b] In the Williams Population: Man, Woman, Children, their Children (8); Man, Woman, Children, Man's Sister, her Children (7); Man, Woman, Children, Woman's Brother, his Spouse (6); Man, Woman, Child, Man's Brother, his Spouse (5); Man, Woman, Man's Sister, her Child (4); Woman, Children, her Children (5). In the Higman Total: Woman, her Children, her Grandchildren (227); "Extended" (218). [c] In the Williams Population, Men and Women living alone, unrelated separated Children.

Trinidad, Guyana and St Vincent, with a high rate of natural decrease, a majority of slaves living alone or in 'barrack' conditions, and a high proportion of 'denuded', female-headed families. In between came the mass of West Indian slaves, all but ten per cent living on plantations of one sort or another, with a wide range of demographic patterns but a generally declining rate of natural decrease and a rapidly dwindling African population, and varying degrees of practical exogamy, miscegenation with whites, and family formation.[30]

Unfortunately, statistical information on West Indian slave families is practically limited to the registration period, 1813–34, after the slave trade with Africa had ended, when all plantations were starting to decline, amelioration measures were being applied, and missionaries were beginning to make their influence felt. It remains to be seen whether a morphology of slave family during the entire period of slavery can be inferred, or projected, from this material alone; what additional light is shed by the white-produced literary sources from an earlier period; and, finally, what other arguments can be adduced, including the incorporation of West African material.

Earlier speculation led the present writer and Higman to postulate, and then to refine to the point of dismissal, two successive models. First, if one took the

Table 14.6   West Indian family from slavery to the present: a comparison of Trinidad, Jamaica, and the Bahamas in slavery days with Barbuda immediately after slavery, and with modern rural Jamaica, 1813–1955.

	A. Trinidad, 1813				*B. Montpelier, Jamaica, 1825*			
Family[a] *type*	*Total slaves*	*Number of units*	*Mean size of units*	*Percent of total in type*	*Total slaves*	*Number of units*	*Mean size of units*	*Percent of total in type*
1	4,675	1,162	4.0	18.3	204	50	4.1	25.1
2	1,036	518	2.0	4.0	76	38	2.0	9.31
3	5,690	2,066	2.8	22.2	328	70	4.7	40.3
4	357	138	2.6	1.4	0	0	–	–
5	445	97	4.6	1.7	24	6	4.0	2.9
6 7 8	12,892	–	–	50.2	182	–	–	22.4
Others	578	204	2.8	2.2				
	25.673	–	–	100.0	814			100.0
A	6,156	1,777	3.5	24.0	304	94	3.2	37.3
B	6,625	2,408	2.8	25.8	328	70	4.7	40.3
C	12,892	–	–	50.2	182	–	–	22.6

Note: [a] 1 = Man, Woman, Children; 2 = Man, Woman; 3 = Woman, Children; 4 = Man, Children; 5 = Three-Generation Groups; 6 = Men Alone, or Together; 7 = Women Alone, or Together; 8 = Children Separately; A = Nuclear Family (1, 2, 5); B = Denuded Family (3,4); C = No Family (6, 7, 8). [b] Edith Clarke, *My Mother Who Fathered Me* (London, 1957), 191–194.

nuclear two-headed family as the quintessentially modern family form, it was beguilingly easy to propose its different incidence during the registration period as relating to the degree of maturation, creolisation, or modernisation of each slave unit, and thus to suggest a historical progression from some aboriginal African form of family. Such a progression initially seemed borne out by the closer parallels among the modern Jamaican rural communities analysed by Edith Clarke and the Exumian slaves of Rolle, as compared with Jamaican slave plantation examples, and by the highly developed family patterns traced by Colin Clarke and Lowenthal among the completely creolised peasants of Barbuda in 1851.[31]

However, the discovery by Higman, amply corroborated by the Bahamian material examined here, that Africans were at least as likely as creoles to form nuclear families, modified the original mode. This revision, coupled with the likelihood that the registration records largely concealed the existence of extended families, and the apparent paradox that creole men were more likely to be polygynous than Africans, led Higman to a second developmental model, based on the seemingly progressive differences between Trinidad, Jamaica and Barbados.[32] By this formulation, the establishment of 'elementary nuclear families' was the primary response of the displaced Africans in the first slave generation. This was the stage

Table 14.6   (continued)

C. Bahamas, 26 holdings, 1822				*D. Barbuda, 1851*				*E. Rural Jamaica, 1955[b]* 1. *"Sugartown"* 2. *"Mocca"*	
Total slaves	*Number of units*	*Mean size of units*	*Percent of total in type*	*Total slaves*	*Number of units*	*Mean size of units*	*Percent of total in type*	*Percent of total pop. in type*	*Percent of total pop. in type*
1,629	308	5.3	54.1	425	76	5.6	67.7	} 46	41
178	89	2.0	5.9	28	14	2.0	4.5		
377	95	4.0	12.5	50	12	4.2	8.0	16	17
16	3	5.3	0.5	6	1	6.0	0.7	3	3
358	46	7.8	11.9	90	18	5.0	14.3	18	30
246	–	–	8.8	7	7	1.0	1.1	} 17	} 9
173	–	–	5.8	10	10	1.0	1.6		
16	–	–	0.5	13	6	2.2	2.1		
3,011			100.0	629	144	4.7	100.0	100	100
2,165	443	4.9	71.9	543	108	5.0	86.3	65	71
393	98	4.0	13.0	56	13	4.3	8.6	19	20
453	–	–	15.1	30	23	1.3	3.1	17	9

of fictive kin such as the 'shipmate' relationship described by Edwards. Owing to high mortality, the further shifting of slaves and a high male ratio, families were able to practise polygyny. A second slave generation began to establish extended families based on the formation of virilocal 'yards' within single plantations; but, because mortality remained high and fresh Africans were continually arriving, the elementary family continued to be the dominant norm. At this stage polygyny may actually have increased, as an index of status and property. In subsequent generations, kinship networks expanded as slaves increasingly practised exogamy. This occurred earliest and most rapidly where holdings were small and contiguous and the proportion of creoles high. The process tended towards matrifocality rather than the nuclear family, especially where lack of slave-controlled provision grounds, money and property deprived slaves of the chance of 'marriage strategies'.[33]

It was clearly right to de-emphasise the normative role of the slave-owners and to stress that slaves largely determined their own family arrangements. Higman's schematic formulation also properly recognised that a wide variety of family types coexisted in all periods, since different islands and sectors developed at different rates and in different ways. A closer study of the Bahamian materials, however, suggested that it was the Bahamas rather than Barbados which represented the forward extreme of slave family development. Higman's most recent analysis of the 1813 registration returns also suggested that Trinidad was a more special case than previously thought: an area directly supervised and rapidly expanding on the eve of emancipation and changing technology, rather than a frontier area exactly analogous to Barbados in 1650 or Jamaica in 1720. In particular, his scrutiny pointed up three conclusions apparent or latent in the Bahamian material considered here: the critical importance of slave family development of plantation size; the effects of urbanisation; and the difficulty of tracing simple cultural transfers from Africa. Even more critically, Higman's earlier model underestimated the formative changes that occurred over the century and a half before the slave trade ended. These included great changes in the intensity of the plantation system and the gradual evolution of systems of slave management aimed at greater efficiency in general, and thus at increasing slave fertility as well. Perhaps most important of all was the filtering down into the West Indies of evolving concepts of the 'modern' family, which gradually gained hold in the practice of creolised slaves, as well as in the minds of white masters.

It is notable that the two most important early writers on British West Indian slavery gave sympathetic accounts of the slaves' society and customs. Ligon (1657) and Sloane (1707) described the early slaves as having a great sense of decorum. Unlike Europeans, they were not ashamed of nakedness and, although with a healthy sex drive, fastidiously avoided public displays of 'wantonness'. They married when they could, and had a rigorous distaste for adultery. Sloane wrote:

> They have every one his Wife and are very much concern'd if they prove adulterous, but in some measure satisfied if their Masters punish the Man who does them the supposed injury, in any of his Hogs, or other small wealth. The care of the Masters and Overseers about their Wives, is what keeps their Plantations chiefly in good order, whence they even buy Wives in proportion to their Men, lest the Men should wander to neighbouring Plantations and neglect to serve them.

The males appeared to be dominant and the practice of polygyny by no means uncommon, being enjoyed, 'by certain brave fellows . . . of extraordinary qualities', from the earliest days. In contrast to later reports there was a strong bond of affection between parents and children, particularly between mothers and infants, who, in African fashion, were carried to work in the fields and not weaned for two years or even longer. Great respect and care were shown for the aged, whether or not they were actual kin.[34]

Ligon and Sloane wrote with exceptional objectivity before the plantation system was intensified, and also in a period when extended families were more important than nuclear families in Europe itself, and modern ideas of childhood and parental affection were still relatively strange. Besides, during Ligon's period in Barbados and Sloane's in Jamaica, miscegenation had not yet become institutionalised because there was still a sizeable proportion of whites of both sexes in the labouring population, and the majority of blacks were unacculturated Africans.

Echoes of Ligon and Sloane could still be heard in later writings, but most gave a far less sympathetic account of the slaves. As Barbados, followed by the Leeward Islands and Jamaica, became dominated by sugar plantations, the planters became more callous and indifferent to slaves' social arrangements. Spurred by the plantations' demands, the slave trade also intensified, and now men imported outnumbered women by three to two. Meanwhile, bourgeois social values increasingly added insult to injury. As far as they were concerned at all, planters disparaged, as natural faults, characteristics in their slaves for which the whites themselves were chiefly to blame, and often similarly guilty. Thus, although marriage and family life were practically discouraged and forcible miscegenation was rife, planters condemned the slaves' 'promiscuity', 'polygamy' and apparent indifference to their children, or even to having children at all.

Behind the planters' ignorance and exaggeration, however, lay the undoubted truth that the quality of slave life had nearly everywhere deteriorated seriously. In this phase, West Indian families were probably at a low point of integration – before extended new kinships had been built up and laws passed forbidding the separation of husbands and wives, and mothers and children. Except for the polygynous favours enjoyed by privileged slaves like drivers – the slaves' 'worst domestic tyrants' – conjugal unions were rare and impermanent, and the majority of infants lived with single mothers or grandmothers – up to ten per cent of whom were, or had been, the casual mates of plantation whites.

In the last phase of slavery, as the profits of plantations dwindled, the price of slaves rose, and in 1808 the supply of fresh Africans was cut off and the West Indian slave-owners came under economic constraints at the same time as they were coming under pressure from metropolitan philanthropists. Writers on slave society attacked or defended plantation customs, or proposed methods of raising the dismal level of slave fertility. The encouragement of Christianity and family life were seen by some as methods for making slaves contented, peaceable and fertile. Some measure of local reform would, moreover, vitiate the arguments of the emancipationists and undermine the sectarian missionaries, who shared none of the establishment's reluctance to proselytise the slaves and promote respectable marriage. Accordingly, in the 1820s, plantocratic Assemblies passed acts ostensibly encouraging slave marriage and actually authorising fees to Anglican ministers for slave baptisms.

Few writers, though, acknowledged the slaves' own motives. Since all slaves yearned chiefly to be free, if adherence to the Church and its formulas were conditions of freedom, a growing number of slaves would aspire to baptism and formal marriage, with their official registrations, as potent indicators of improving social status. Most writers also ignored the degree to which slaves actually possessed property and virtual tenure of houses and plots, which they were able, in custom if not in law, to bequeath to whomever they wished. Long before emancipation, a fair proportion of West Indian slaves had ample reasons, on the grounds of respectability and conformability to the laws of inheritance, to adopt the familial norms of the master class.

But nearly every commentator, from Ligon and Sloane to 'Monk' Lewis and Mrs A. C. Carmichael, did share two absolute certainties: that as to marriage, whatever the masters did, the slaves always had and always would (in the words of the Jamaican, John Quier) 'claim a Right of disposing of themselves in this Respect, according to their Own Will and Pleasure without any Controul from their Masters'; and that within certain obvious constraints these voluntary arrangements were African rather than European. 'We restrain their Actions sufficiently, to our conveniences,' wrote Lindsay, Rector of St Catherine's, Jamaica, 'tho' we inslave not the Inclinations of the Heart, against their Natural Habits and Native Customs, which may well be injoy'd separately from their Obedience to us.'[35]

Few Africans carried their children with them in slavery, and fewer still accompanied marital partners from West Africa into West Indian plantations, let alone the members of the extended family and kinship groups which were of prime importance in West Indian society. The ethnic mixing which was standard plantation policy meant additionally that the legacies of Africa were transmitted in a haphazard or generalised way. Yet the impress of Africa was indelible, and African patterns were replicated where possible, and reconstituted as soon as possible where not, surviving slavery itself in modified forms.

On large plantations there were sometimes subcultural groups – such as 'Ibo' or 'Congo' – and some forceful cultural traditions, particularly the Akan (or 'Coromantee'), seem to have been normative. Yet the very variety of West African roots allowed for creative syncretism, or the choice of alternative customs – for example, concerning the role of women, and the acceptability of cousin-mating and premarital intercourse – as the slaves made the necessary adjustments to the new environment, the dictates of the plantation system and the shifting demographic conditions.[36]

Some features of the plantation system, such as the expectation that women would work in the fields, that men would monopolise the skilled and privileged roles, and that slave drivers and other élite slaves such as head craftsmen would be likely to practise polygyny, actually facilitated the continuation of West African customs. Other continuities were of necessity more covert, having to exist in the narrow scope of private life left to the slaves by the master class: rites of passage, courtship and premarital negotiations, marriage ceremonies and celebrations, and the role of elderly slaves as 'councils of elders' to determine custom and settle domestic disputes. While the slave trade lasted, direct links with Africa were never cut, native Africans being brought in groups to expand plantations or, more commonly, arriving in ones and twos to make up the shortfall in slave fertility.

As Edwards testified, these Africans were welcomed into family units, especially those of their own tribe and language.[37]

From the simple pairings which were all that the planters provided for, the slaves built up extended family relationships beyond the masters' ken or concern and, in the course of generations, whole new kinship networks based on the cohesive 'village' of a single plantation holding but gradually extending beyond the plantation's bounds into nearby groups. In Barbados, a small island covered with small contiguous plantations, the process of social diffusion had gone on longest; but even there, as in Africa, the primary allegiance remained the village, the birthplace, the home and burial-place of closest family, kin and ancestors.

In 1808 the direct connection with Mother Africa was cut, but by that time the area of social autonomy had significantly expanded for most slaves. Slaves owned their own property (in some colonies even in law), bequeathed and inherited houses and land, and in some islands virtually controlled the internal market system. On declining plantations they were encouraged to be as nearly self-sufficient as possible, and on decayed plantations were left almost entirely to their own devices. Yet, contrary to the masters' pessimism, the young and the aged were better cared for than under more rigorous slave regimes, and the unfavourable ratio between deaths and births began to reverse. In the phrase of Sidney Mintz, the most fortunate British West Indian slaves were proto-peasants long before slavery ended, and made an easy transition into 'full freedom' in 1838.[38]

Four influences militated against the continued development of peasant lifestyles and family systems: the breakup of the old slave quarters and the consequent 'marginalisation' of many ex-slaves; the persistence of plantations in a more impersonal form; an accelerated urbanisation; and the spread of the canons of respectability. The closing down of the slave cantonments after emancipation, as plantations decayed or turned to less intensive forms of agriculture (particularly, grazing 'pens'), or as ex-slaves who refused to work on the planters' terms were evicted from houses and plots, was as traumatic a change as the cutting of the African link or the ending of formal slavery itself. The more fortunate ex-slaves were able to form their own villages and develop a healthy peasant society; but many others without land of their own were forced into a marginal existence, depending on the increasingly mechanised plantations for wages, but competing with each other, and with newly imported indentured labourers, in a cruelly seasonal economy. Far fewer women worked as plantation labourers, and most of the men became transients, living in barracks or strange villages during crop-time and being unable to form permanent or stable attachments, while women provided the only permanence and stability for children. A similar continuation of the worst features of the slave period occurred among the poor of the towns, which burgeoned after emancipation. The new towns had a high proportion of migrants from the countryside, a disproportionately high ratio of women, and thus a majority of impermanent, fractured and matrifocal families.

As we have noticed, many slaves in the last phase of slavery were attracted by the apparent advantages of respectable, European-type families. After emancipation these became the norm among the small emergent middle class, many of the members of which were the coloured descendants of domestic slaves who had engaged in miscegenous relationships. Under the growing influence of the churches, a far wider spectrum of the ex-slaves continued to subscribe outwardly to the canons of respectability, especially in islands like Barbados where the Anglican Church was deeply entrenched and conditions were unfavourable for true peasant development. Yet, as Wilson has plausibly argued, the subscription to respectability is superficial among the majority of British West Indian blacks. Far more deeply engrained are the tenets of 'reputation': those elements of custom which place greater stress on community, kinship and extended family, and place greater value on social worth, than on introspective family forms, bourgeois manners and material wealth. In this analysis, reputation provides a continuous thread of tradition passing back through slavery to Africa itself.[39]

Therefore, in assessing the nature of slave family and its place in the continuum, we emphasise not the ways that slavery destroyed or distorted family, but the ways in which the slaves' own forms of family triumphed over adversity. In this light, we evaluate slavery not by the manner in which it controlled and shaped slaves' destinies, but by the degree to which it allowed slaves to make family lives of their own.

Notes

1 John Quier, 'Report of the Jamaican House of Assembly on the Slave Issues', in Lt Governor Clarke's No. 92, Nov. 20, 1788; Public Record Office, London, C.O. 137/88, Appendix C.

2 Herbert G. Gutman, *The Black Family in Slavery and Freedom, 1750–1925*, New York, 1976, xxi.

3 Thomas S. Simey, *Welfare and Planning in the West Indies*, Oxford, 1946, 50–51, 79; Fernando Henriques, *Family and Colour in Jamaica*, London, 1953, 103; William J. Goode, 'Illegitimacy in the Caribbean Social Structure', *American Sociological Review*, XXV, 1960, 21–30; M. G. Smith, *The Plural Society in the British West Indies*, Berkeley, 1965, 109; H. Orlando Patterson, *The Sociology of Slavery*, London, 1967, 167.

4 Barry W. Higman, 'Household Structure and Fertility on Jamaican Slave Plantations: A Nineteenth-Century Example', *Population Studies*, XXVII, 1973, 527–550; idem, 'The Slave Family and Household in the British West Indies, 1800–1834', *Journal of Interdisciplinary History*, VI, 1975, 261–287; idem, *Slave Population and Economy in Jamaica, 1807–1834*, Cambridge, 1976. Higman's 'Family Property: The Slave Family in the British Caribbean in the Early Nineteenth Century', unpublished paper (1976) is now largely superseded by his 'African and Creole Slave Family Patterns in Trinidad' paper delivered at the Tenth Conference of Caribbean Historians, 1978. See ibid, 12.

5 James Stephens, *The Slavery of the British West India Colonies Delineated*, London, 1824, I, Appendix III, 454–474. The Bahamas, with almost exactly the same total land area as Jamaica (4,400 square miles), had approximately 10,000 slaves against 300,000 in Jamaica, Barbados with only 166 square miles, had 65,000 slaves. In 1800, the ratio between blacks and whites in the Bahamas was about 4:1; in Barbados it was 8:1; in Jamaica 12:1.

6 David Eltis, 'The Traffic in Slaves between the British West Indian Colonies, 1807–1833', *Economic History Review*, XXV, 1972, 55–64. Perhaps through a misunderstanding, there was a partial census of Bahamian slaves in 1821. Most of these were relisted in 1822, but not all. The 1822 census book gives a grand total of 10,808 slaves, but this seems to omit the slaves listed in 1821 and not relisted in 1822. The intercolonial migration was at its peak between 1821 and 1822; its volume may never be known with complete accuracy.

7 Archives of the Bahamas, Nassau; Register of Returns of Slaves, Bahama Islands, 1821–1834. It was fortunate that the Bahamas Registration Act of 1821 required the listing of all slaves every three years, not just an initial census and subsequent triennial increases and decreases as in most other colonies. The act specified what information should be given but not the order of the lists. Despite this, there seems to have been a remarkable

uniformity in the method used by those owners who chose to list their slaves in family and household groups. An absolutely certain distinction between family and household was scarcely possible, but a comparison of the data on slaves transferred from the Bahamas to Trinidad (where the registration returns gave fuller details), and corroboration between the triennial Bahamas censuses, suggested that although extended families were understated, the listings concentrated on families rather than mere cohabitation, and the groups listed were almost invariably cohabiting families, rarely mere 'housefuls'.

8 Michael Craton, 'Hobbesian or Panglossian? The Two Extremes of Slaves Conditions in the British Caribbean, 1783–1834', *William and Mary Quarterly*, 25, 1978, 324–356; idem, *Searching for the Invisible Man: Slaves and Plantation Life in Jamaica*, Cambridge, MA 1978, 60–118.

9 The proportions of African and coloured slaves in the 26 holdings in 1822 were remarkably close to those in the overall slave population, 20.0 and 6.9 per cent.

10 The average age of mothers at the birth of their first children given in Table 14.2, 22.37 years, is clearly overstated since the 479 mothers included many whose earlier children were old enough to have left the parental household, and were thus not recorded. When the 251 mothers aged 35 or more at the time of the census were excluded, the average age of the remaining 228 mothers at the birth of their first surviving child was 19.27 years. Of the females in the age range 15–49, 65.6 per cent were indicated as mothers. In all, the 479 mothers listed had 1,456 listed children, an average of 3.02 children each.

11 Of the 26 holdings analysed, 20 were established in the farther islands, with a total of 2,643 slaves, an average of 132 per holding. Six were established in New Providence and Eleuthera, with a total of 367 slaves, an average of 61. In 1834 (the only year for which figures have been tabulated), 481 of the 730 Bahamian holdings of five or fewer slaves, and 692 of the 1,088 of 20 or fewer, were in New Providence and Eleuthera (including Harbour Island), but only 26 of the 107 Bahamian holdings of more than 20 slaves, Archives of the Bahamas, Nassau; Register of Returns of Slaves, Bahama Islands, 1834. The 1834 tabulation has been made by Gail Saunders.

12 The figure for 1834 was 9.6 per cent, but by that date a considerable number had been manumitted.

13 Keith F. Otterbein, *The Andros Islanders: A of Family Organization in the Bahamas*, Lawrence, KS, 1966. There is as yet no scholarly study of family in New Providence, or of the huge migration that has concentrated more than half the Bahamian population in the capital. Gutman, *Black Family*, 444–445, 489–491.

14 In the 1822 sample of 26 holdings, five possible cases of polygyny occurred. One such was Jack Stewart, a mulatto slave aged 66 belongings to James Moss at Acklin's Island, who appeared to live with Phoebe, an African aged 55, Kate, a creole aged 37, and 10 children aged between one and 15, all listed as mulattoes.

15 Permanent mates and their children generally shared a surname, but in female-headed families and transient unions a practice common later in the Bahamas may have been followed; children went by their mother's surname until they were 21 and then adopted their father's surname.

16 Craton, 'Hobbesian or Panglossian?', 19. Today there are thousands of Rolles in the Bahamas, including, it is said, two-thirds of the population of Exuma. Male children often had a prefix or suffix added, as with Young Bacchus, Jack Junior, Little Jim, or the African-sounding Jim Jim, son of Jim. Males were often named after their fathers, females more rarely after their mothers. Out of the 67 family units of the Williams group of slaves transferred to Trinidad there were 22 males named after their fathers and at least one after a grandfather; four females were named after their mothers, at least three after a grandmother, and one after a mother's sister.

17 In the population studied, 28 young mothers lived with their parents, their average ages being 18 years and 9 months. Only five were over 20-years-old, and the average age at the birth of their first children was 17 years and 8 months. Only one of the 28 had a second child.

18 Michael Craton, *A History of the Bahamas*, London, 1962, 173–174, 194–196.

19 William Wylly to President W. V. Munnings, Aug. 31, 1818, C.O. 23/67, 147.

20 *Regulations for the Government of the Slaves at Clifton and Tusculum in New Providence, Printed at the Office of the New Gazette*, 1815, enclosed in ibid.

21 Of Wylly's 67 slaves in 1821, as many as 53 lived in eight two-headed households (in two of which the family included a teenage single mother), with one female-headed family and a maximum of nine slaves living alone, averaging 49 years old and including six elderly Africans. Almost certainly, three of the household units at Clifton were the extended family of jack, the African under-driver, and his wife Sue. Twenty of the 67 slaves were under the age of ten in 1821.

22 D. W. Rose, reporting on the slaves of Exuma, 1802; Craton, *History of the Bahamas*, 183.

23 Besides ten African couples, there were three holdings in which an African male headed the list with his creole mate. In these 13 holdings (half of the total) there were 187 Africans out of a total of 805 slaves or 23.2 per cent, not significantly more than the overall average, 18.8 per cent.

24 Act of 4 Geo. IV, c. 6; *Acts of the Assembly of the Bahama Islands*, Nassau, 1827, V, 227–228.

25 Archives of the Bahamas, Manumissions Index; Register of Returns of Slaves, 1825, 1828, 1831, 1834; Public Record Office, London; Register of Returns of Slaves, St Vincent, 1822, 1825. Craton, 'Hobbesian or Panglossian?' 19–20; C.O. 295/67, 219; 295/71, 26–35; 295/78, 233–265; Governor James Carmicheal Smyth to Lord Stanley, Oct. 27, 1830, C.O. 23/82, 368–420.

26 Evidence given on Jan. 18, 1825, C.O. 295/66, 53–59. A population of 107 increasing at the Rolle rate for 1822–34, 34.5 per thousand per year, would have reached 331 in the 34th year.

27

		Men	Women	Boys	Girls	Infants	
July	1821	27	43	7	5	23	
February	1822	9	11	6	4	24	
July	1822	6	11	3	3	14	
March	1823	10	10	7	5	33	
June	1823	6	11	6	7	33	
Total		58	86	29	24	127	324

This compilation was made on Sept. 27, 1823. By that time, 19 children had been added to Williams' slaves by birth, and only seven of the total had been lost by death. This indicated a crude annual birth rate of 29 per thousand and a death rate around 11 per thousand. However, of 3,239 slaves imported into Trinidad from all sources between 1813 and 1822 (1,678 being males and 1,561 females), 232 males and 156 females had died, 388 in all, against only 236 births; C.O. 295/59, 252–255.

28 'Return showing the number of Negroes imported into this Island by Burton Williams Esq.', enclosed in Governor Sir Ralph Woodford to William Huskisson, March 7, 1828, C.O. 295/77, 33–49.

29 C.O. 295/66, 57.

30 Craton, 'Hobbesian or Panglossian?' 19–21; Cohn Clarke and David Lowenthal 'Barbuda; the Past of a Negro Myth', in Vera Rubin and Arthur Tuden (eds), *Comparative Perspectives on Slavery in New World Plantation Societies*, New York, 1977, 510–534.

31 The argument is proposed in Craton, 'Hobbesian or Panglossian?', which was first delivered at the conference on Comparative Perspectives in New World Plantation Societies, New York, 1976. Edith Clarke, *My Mother Who Fathered Me*, London, 1957. [See Table top page 299.]

32 What follows is the argument proposed by Higman, 'Family Property', now superseded by his Slave Family Patterns in Trinidad', 1977. The change was based on the analysis of the full 1813 slave population of 25,673 (a quarter of whom lived in Port-of-Spain), rather than the rural sample of 1,296 previously used.

33 Bryan Edwards, *The History, Civil and Commercial of the British Colonies in the British West Indies*, London, 180, II, 155.

Table [for note 31]   Barbuda household types, 1851

Household type	No. of units	No. of persons	Persons per unit	% total persons per unit type
1. Man, woman, children	76	425	5.59	67.57
2. Man and woman	14	28	2.00	4.45
3. Woman and children	12	50	4.17	7.95
4. Man and children	1	6	6.00	0.95
5. Three generations (in two women and children)	18	90	5.00	14.31 (95.23)
6. Men alone	7	7	1.00	1.11
7. Women alone	10	10	1.00	1.59
8. Women together	6	13	2.17	2.07 (4.77)
	144	629	4.73	100.00

Source: Colin Clarke and Lowenthal, private correspondence (Codrington records, Gloucester County Record Office, England).

34   Richard Ligon, *A True and Exact History of the Island of Barbadoes*, London, 1957, 47; Hans Sloane, *A Voyage to the Islands Madera, Barbados, Nieves, S. Christophers and Jamaica*, London, 1725, II, xlviii; Stanley L. Engerman, 'Some Economic and Demographic Comparisons of Slavery in the United States and the British West Indies', *Economic History Review*, XXIX, 1976, 258–275.

35   Quier, 'Report', 492; Lindsay, 'A Few Conjectural Considerations upon the Creation of the Human Race, Occasioned by the Present Quixotical Rage of setting the Slaves from Africa at Liberty', unpublished ms. dated Spanish Town, July 23, 1788, British Museum, Additional Mss. 12439.

36   Higman, 'Slave Family Patterns in Trinidad', 14–18, 33–35. This strongly stressed the melding effect of the African slave trade to Trinidad. Only among the Ibo was there a recognisable transfer of specific African family patterns, and this was attributed to their high numbers and comparatively even sex ratio. When the African slaves were broken down by seven general regions of origin there were no really significant variations in the proportions of family types recreated in Trinidad.

37   Edwards, *British West Indies*, II, 155.

38   Sidney W. Mintz, *Caribbean Transformations*, Chicago, 1974, 151–152.

39   Peter J. Wilson, *Crab Antics: The Social Anthropology of English-Speaking Negro Societies of the Caribbean*, New Haven, 1973.

Chapter 15

Cheryll Ann Cody

THERE WAS NO 'ABSALOM' ON THE BALL PLANTATIONS
Slave-naming practices in the South Carolina Low Country, 1720–1865

FOR HISTORIANS OF THE BLACK EXPERIENCE under slavery, the process by which Africans became Afro-Americans presents an intriguing set of questions. Many students of this transition have turned to some version of an "encounter model," to borrow the term anthropologists use, to identify and weigh the relative contributions of African and white American cultures to black societies of the New World.[1] Historians have long recognized that white "American" culture did not entirely subsume African culture, a fact made evident by the retention of African influences in black music, dance, language and speech patterns.[2] Afro-American slaves nevertheless came to share many values and beliefs with their owners, including Christianity.[3] An examination of the naming of slaves offers one way of viewing the cultural transformation in the early generations of black slavery and focuses on a stage of the process that scholars have often neglected.

This examination of the names and naming practices of slaves considers the subject from three perspectives. First, plantation records reveal the size, content, and continuity of the pool of names that slaves used. As parents selected names for their children, they may have reflected religious convictions, cultural antecedents, or contemporary heroes and events. Shifts in naming practices may indicate changes in the values and world view of the slaves. Second, the rules a society uses in the selection and transmission of family names indicate the value that the parent or the individual selecting the name attached to the preservation of ties to the namesake. As Daniel Scott Smith observed, "The desire to recognize familial continuity spans a range of intensities and a variety of naming practices in different societies."[4] Some cultures express continuity by linking the child to the grandparent or extended kin, others by linking the child to the parent. With slaves, the study of naming practices includes a third dimension that speaks directly to the issue of acculturation: the extent to which the names used by slaves represented an agenda of names and naming patterns determined by owners or, more broadly, by white American practices, as well as the extent to which the names reflected African naming systems retained or transformed by life under the institution of slavery.[5]

This study draws on the records of the slave populations on the Ball family rice plantations, located on the Cooper River in St. John's Berkeley Parish, South Carolina. Between 1698 and 1865, the Ball family owned at various times nine rice plantations in the Low Country that are partially or fully documented. Comingtee, the home plantation, was inherited in 1698 and remained in the Ball family until 1896. Stoke, a quarter of Comingtee, was a separate unit between 1805 and 1840. Kensington and Hyde Park were built in the 1740s and remained in the family until 1842. Limerick was purchased in 1764 and retained until 1891. Jericho (or Back River) was in the family from 1774 through 1842, Quinby from 1817 to 1842, and Cedar Hill and Halidon Hill were acquired in 1837 and 1842, respectively. The history of the plantations' settlement and the growth of their populations is detailed elsewhere, but several critical features need to be noted for the analysis that follows.[6] The birth and death registers of the Ball plantations span the years 1720 to 1865. Although extremely rich in some ways, these registers do not regularly record the name of a child's father. In some cases, this information can be gleaned from other sources, but a full genealogical reconstruction of the slave populations cannot be accomplished. The Ball records are nonetheless among the best documentation available of the earliest generations of American-born slaves.

The Ball family's slave population was subjected to few of the disruptions that came to other slaves through sales and the transmission of property from generation to generation. Before 1770, the Balls purchased slaves to increase the population. After 1770, additions other than by births came from a marriage gift in 1774, the purchase of a Tory cousin's slaves in 1784, and the inheritance of 140 slaves in 1812. In each instance, the source of the slaves was another member of the Ball family. A major disruption of the slave population came with the auction of 366 slaves from the estate of John Ball, Sr., in 1819. His sons purchased 126 of the slaves, as John Ball, Jr., noted, "because they were related by connection with those that were owned by me before the sale."[7] After 1840, the slaves at three plantations were no longer included in the surviving registers. As a result, a portion of the population disappears from this reconstruction. During the nineteenth century, the evidence becomes fuller with a column added to the register in which the date of death was recorded. Only for the last fifteen years, 1849 to 1865, and for one plantation, Comingtee, were the fathers of children regularly recorded. Beginning with these registers, 620 maternal histories were reconstituted. These histories were supplemented by distribution lists, estate inventories, division lists, and other documents that systematically enumerated populations in an attempt to locate evidence on the fathers of children. If a woman was linked in these documents with the same man over the period of her childbearing years without breaks in either her history of births or her linkage to the man, it was assumed that he fathered her children. Though somewhat unorthodox, this method takes advantage of the owner's practice in recording slave names by modifying the names of women with the names of their husbands. By this method, I identified the husbands of 194 women or about one-third of the families.

The analysis of slave names uses four sets of the Ball slave reconstitution. One set includes the names of 2,344 slaves born on the plantations who lived long enough to receive a name in the birth register. This set is used in the analysis of the content and continuity of the name pool itself. The second set uses only maternal histories with full death registration and includes only families begun after 1800 and completed in 1865. This subset of families is used in the analysis of patterns of necronymic naming. The third set uses only families in which the name of the father or fathers of all children are known and includes a total of 194 families. A final subset of this third set includes only families in which all four grandparents

Table 15.1   Leading names for Ball family children

Rank	Name	N	Percent	Cumulative percent
Sons (N = 76)				
1st	John	21	27.6	27.6
2d	Elias	10	13.2	40.8
3d	William	9	11.8	52.6
4th	Isaac	6	7.9	60.5
Daughters (N = 76)				
1st	Elizabeth-Eliza	11	14.5	14.5
2d	Anne	8	10.5	25.0
3d	Eleanor	7	9.2	34.2
3d	Lydia	7	9.2	43.2
5th	Martha	5	6.6	49.8
5th	Mary	5	6.6	56.4

are known. The last two data sets are used in the analysis of kin-naming patterns among slaves.

To assess the impact of owner names and naming systems on slaves, I turn first to the naming practices of the Ball family.[8] Members of the Ball family chose the names for their own sons and daughters from a small group of family names. More than 60 percent of the sons received one of four names: John, William, Elias, or Isaac. John and William were common English names and popular among white American populations in both the eighteenth and nineteenth centuries.[9] Both Elias and Isaac were first names that were somewhat unusual for white populations of the Low Country, but each name held significance in the family history of the Balls. Elias I was the first member of the Ball family to immigrate to South Carolina in the late 1690s. He was the most commonly shared ancestor and the source of the family's wealth, and thus his name was important in a society that emphasized both kinship and property. Isaac, whose death at age twenty-one made him both a tragic and romantic figure in the family history, was also a popular namesake for Ball children, tapping a budding strain of sentimentalism in the planter family.[10]

Although not as restricted as the pool of male names, the group of common names for daughters was small. Six names, Elizabeth, Anne, Eleanor, Lydia, Martha, and Mary, accounted for 56 percent of the names selected for Ball daughters. Elizabeth, Anne, and Mary were among the leading English names for women and also were dominant in eighteenth- and nineteenth-century American populations.[11] Lydia and Eleanor were perpetuated both as kin names and as namesakes because of the attributes of the first American-born ancestors to bear the names. Lydia Child Chicken's marriage to Elias II came after years of unrequited love, and she was thus a romantic figure in the family's history.[12] Eleanor Ball was the best-known individual in the family lineage, male or female. She was the recipient of a necronymic name, that is, she shared the name of her half-sister, who had died at age sixteen, seven years before Eleanor's birth. The only child of her father's second marriage to survive to adulthood, Eleanor married Colonel Henry Laurens.

Her marriage not only linked the family to power and wealth, it also produced four children of prominence: John Laurens, a hero of the Revolutionary War; Henry II, a wealthy planter and politician; Martha, the wife of Dr. David Ramsey, the first historian of the state; and Mary Eleanor, the wife of Governor Charles Pinckney. By choosing Eleanor as the namesake for their daughters, the Balls perpetuated a family name and at the same time linked the family to the powerful political past of the Laurens, Ramseys, and Pinckneys.

The Balls relied heavily on family names, especially those of the paternal lineage, in selecting both first and middle names. By the nineteenth century, middle names had come into common use, increasing the ability of parents to perpetuate family names. Since 1714, the Balls had used the middle name Coming for sons named John to make clear that the child shared the name of John Coming, from whom the Balls originally inherited their land in South Carolina, as well as to continue the surname of the first owner of Comingtee, albeit transposed as a middle name. The first of the Balls to use middle names consistently were John Ball and his second wife, Martha Carolina Swinton Ball. Whereas only one of the five children of John's first union, with his cousin, received a middle name, John and Martha gave ten of their eleven children middle names. The middle names selected fell into three categories: traditional first names, family surnames, and Latin names for numerals, such as Septimus. John and Martha gave five of their daughters middle names that were traditional first names, including the first set of twins, Carolina Olivia and Martha Angelina, each of whom shared one of their mother's names.[13]

One indication of the preference for paternal kin names is the frequency with which sons received the names of their fathers. Six of the eight families with one or two sons passed on the father's name to the next generation. All fourteen families with three or more sons named a son for his father. Members of the Ball family frequently used the paternal grandfather's name. In families with only one or two sons, three of eight named a child for his paternal grandfather. Among large families, the use of the paternal grandfather as a namesake was more prevalent, with 78.6 percent including a son who shared the name of his father's father. Maternal grandfathers rarely saw their name used for a child in families with one or two sons, but, again among larger families, more than half named a male child for his maternal grandfather. Considered together, nine out of ten families transmitted the name of the father to the next generation. About six of ten named a son for a paternal grandfather and four in ten for the maternal grandfather. Thus, in naming sons, the Balls relied on kin names with great frequency and preferred the immediate connection of father to son.

Because parents could not anticipate the number of children of each gender they would produce, the order in which they used kin names reveals not only the intensity of kin naming but also the priorities held. In selecting the names of first sons, members of the Ball family turned to the names of the fathers in more than two-thirds (68.2 percent) of the families. First-born sons who did not receive the names of their fathers (27.3 percent) often received the names of their paternal grandfathers but only rarely those of maternal grandparents (4.5 percent). Even though parental and grandparental names were chosen less frequently for second sons, families that had failed to name a first son for his father used the opportunity of the birth of a second boy to perpetuate the father's name. Again, the families seldom turned to the maternal grandfather as the source of a second son's name.

Table 15.2 Percentage of Ball Family Children Sharing a Kin Name by Gender, Family Size, and Kin Connection

Sons

	1–2		3 or more		All	
	N	Percent	N	Percent	N	Percent
Father	8	75.0	14	100.0	22	90.9
Paternal Grandfather (FAFA)	8	37.5	14	78.6	22	63.3
Maternal Grandmother (MOFA)	8	12.5	14	57.1	22	40.9

Daughters

	1–2		3 or more		All	
	N	Percent	N	Percent	N	Percent
Mother	13	53.8	12	91.7	25	72.0
Paternal Grandmother (FAMO)	13	23.1	12	66.7	25	44.0
Maternal Grandmother (MOMO)	13	30.8	12	75.0	25	52.0

Percent of first and second sons sharing name

	N	Father	FAFA	Both	MOFA	Neither Parent nor Grandparent
1st Son	22	68.2	27.3	{13.6}	4.5	13.6
2nd Son	19	36.8	26.3	{ 5.3}	5.3	36.9

Percent of first and second daughters sharing name

	N	Mother	MOMO	Both	FAMO	Neither Parent nor Grandparent
1st Daughter	25	44.0	32.0	{8.0}	28.0	0
2nd Daughter	22	22.7	18.2	{ 0}	13.6	45.5

Kin naming was not practiced as intensely for daughters as it was for sons. Slightly more than half (53.8 percent) of families with one or two daughters named a child for her mother. Among larger families, however, more than nine in ten used the mother's name. The maternal grandmother and the paternal grand mother served as namesakes with nearly equal frequency. Among families with only one or two daughters, 30.8 percent named one girl for her maternal grandmother, while 23.1 percent named a girl for her paternal grandmother. In families with three or more daughters, nine of twelve perpetuated the maternal grandmother's name and eight of twelve the name of the paternal grandmother.

A study of the naming priorities for first and second daughters reveals a Ball family preference for replication of the name of the mother over that of either grandmother, but the pattern of parental naming overall is weaker than that found for sons. All first-born daughters who shared the name of their mother or a grandmother did so in the following order of frequency: mother, maternal grandmother, and paternal grandmother. The small number of cases, the number of shared names, and the relatively slight differences detected suggest, however, that no clear-cut pattern of preference between parental or grandparental or between maternal and paternal lineage can be discerned. Furthermore, while all first-born daughters received a kin name, nearly half of the second-born daughters were given a name other than that of their mother or grandmother.

In selecting names for their children, the Balls valued perpetuation of the kin name above preservation of the individual identity of a child. One indication of this attitude is the frequency of necronymic sibling naming. David Scott Smith noted a trend away from the use of sibling necronyms by the nineteenth century among the Hingham population.[14] The Balls, however, continued to reuse the name of a dead child, taking advantage of six of twenty-six opportunities for replacement (23.1 percent) presented by the birth of a child of the same gender. The intensity of kin naming among the Ball family and the emphasis placed on perpetuating the paternal lineage can be seen in the names chosen for the children of William James Ball. In 1842, William James married Julia Cart, and, over the next eight years, the union produced five sons. The first four boys received the four family names used most frequently for male children and in order of kin relationship. The first son was named for his father, William James; the second for his paternal grandfather, Isaac; the third for his paternal great-grandfather, John; and the fourth for his paternal great-great-grandfather. In addition to directly replicating the paternal line, these four boys also shared the names of other paternal kin. Julia's father was John Cart; thus, the maternal grandfather also received a namesake among the Ball children. Because no daughter was born to William James and Julia, there was no opportunity to perpetuate Julia's name or the names of the grandmothers.

A second marriage allowed William James to broaden the scope of his use of kin names. Four years after Julia's death, he married his first cousin, Mary Huger Gibbs. This union produced one son and six daughters. The son shared the name of his maternal grandfather. The Balls were able to use the maternal grandfather's name for their first-born son because William James had completed his naming agenda for his male ancestry during his first marriage. The paternal line dominated the names selected for the six daughters. The first daughter shared the name of her paternal grandmother. The maternal line was not represented among William James's children until the seventh child (the second daughter, Maria Louisa, named

Table 15.3 Children of William James Ball

Rank	Gender	Gender-Rank	Name	Relationship	Status
wife Julia Cart (married 1842)					
1st	Son	1st	William James	Father	living
2d	Son	2d	Isaac	Paternal Grandfather (FAFA)	dead
				Paternal Uncle	dead
3d	Son	3d	John	Paternal Great-Grandfather (FAFAFA)	dead
				Paternal Uncle	living
4th	Son	4th	Elias	Paternal Great-Great-Grandfather (FAFAFAFA)	dead
				Paternal Great-Uncle	dead
5th	Son	5th	Francis Guerrin	Paternal Cousin	unknown
wife Mary Huger Gibbs (married 1862)					
6th	Daughter	1st	Eliza Catherine	Paternal Grandmother (FAMO)	living
				Paternal Aunt	dead
7th	Daughter	2d	Maria Louisa	Maternal Grandmother (MOMO)	unknown
8th	Daughter	3d	Jane	Paternal Great-Grandmother (FAFAMO)	dead
9th	Son	6th	Mathurin Guerrin	Maternal Grandfather	unknown
10th	Daughter	4th	Mary	Mother	living
11th	Daughter	5th	Lydia Child	Paternal (distant)	—
12th	Daughter	6th	Eleanor	Paternal (distant)	—

for her maternal grandmother). The third daughter, Jane, shared the name of her paternal great-grandmother, the fourth was named for her mother, and the fifth was Lydia Child, the infant's paternal great-great-grandmother. The sixth daughter received the name Eleanor, from a kin relationship even more distant.

The motivation of slaveowners in the selection of names for their own children seems fairly simple—the perpetuation of kin names, particularly, paternal kin— but the names chosen for slave children stem from afar more complex set of influences and values, some held by owners and others by slaves. For their part, owners needed to identify each slave by a single given name to simplify the allo- cation of tasks and provisions. If this need had totally governed the selection of names for slave children, it would have meant that no slave would have shared a first name with another slave on the same plantation, and no child would have shared the name of a parent, a living grandparent, or a cousin. On large planta- tions, this rule would require a broad pool of names, equal to the total population.

The desire to identify slaves uniquely accounted for the variety of names and the diversity of sources that the Balls used when they purchased slaves or named the first generation born in South Carolina.[15] It conflicted with any desire slaves may have had to use family names for their children. Even so, the first generation of South Carolina-born slaves on the Ball plantations seems to have asserted its influence by using kin names for its children.[16] Indeed, the slaves made use of family names not only between the generations but among extended kin of the same gener- ation as well, thus quickly undermining an effort to create a unique identity for each slave. When slaves on the same plantation shared the same first name, some form of modification was added to one or both names to distinguish between the two individuals. Name duplication was a common but easily resolved problem when a father and son, or grandfather and grandson, shared a name. They would be iden- tified, for instance, as "Big Pompey" and "Little Pompey." Other modifiers could be equally descriptive, including color, place of birth (either Africa or another plan- tation), or occupation. A comparison of the use of name modifiers can be made between a list from 1755 to 1758 of slaves receiving blankets at Comingtee and a blanket list from 1835 to 1837 at the same site. Although few slaves on the eigh- teenth-century list shared a name, Comingtee plantation recorded "Ebo Sylvia" and "Ebo Dy." Surnames were applied to three slaves, Jenny Buller, Tom White, and Hannah Shubrick. Age was used to differentiate six slaves. By the nineteenth century, modifiers were more frequently applied and, in more than half of the instances, were given to slaves who did not share the first name of another slave. Nearly two-thirds (63.7 percent) of the adult male slaves had some form of modi- fier applied to their names, with occupation and kinship accounting about equally for the type of modification. Seven out of ten female adults had their names modi- fied as well. Kinship was most often the form of modification, with the name of the woman's husband or her mother chosen with about equal frequency.

In a society in which one's history and position were transmitted orally, the selection of the name of a child may have held more significance than in a society with a written history. The selection of an African "day-name," for example, would give a child a name used solely by blacks in the community and would serve also as a reminder of an African past. Sharing a kin name was a useful device to connect children with their past and place them in the history of their families and communities. Because both slaveowner and slave used shared names as evidence of kinship, the Ball slaves appear to have avoided names uniquely associated with their male owners and the Ball lineage. This pattern of avoidance did not hold for female slaves, whose maternal parentage would be unquestioned, nor was it practiced when the male owner's name was common, since sharing such a name would not necessarily identify the owner as the father of the child.[17]

In addition to these patterns of choice and avoidance, the Ball slaves' conversion to Christianity added an additional dimension to naming practices. The lessons of the Bible presented not only a new or revitalized pool of names for slaves but also a model of family organization that stressed male roles and paternal ties. The selection of a biblical name and the emphasis on the paternal line in the choice of a kin name brought slaves closer in some ways to the familial values of owners.

The evolution of these influences on naming practices can be seen in the family history of Windsor and Angola Ame, slaves on the Comingtee plantation.[18] Windsor and Angola Ame had two sons and five daughters between 1743 and 1758. Each of the children received a name chosen, most likely, by the plantation owner or, at least, at his suggestion. The first son and daughter were given names that scholars label Anglicized day-names. Christmas, born on 25 December 1743, received a name appropriate for his date of birth. He was followed by a sister, Easter, born the Saturday before Easter Sunday. These names preserved the African form of day-naming or naming a child for an event, but the content of the name was that of a Christian religious holiday.[19] The selection of these names indicates either direct owner interference or the recognition of the Christian and work holidays of Christmas and Easter by Windsor and Angola Ame, who applied the content of the holiday to an African form.

Although slaves generally avoided the use of male names uniquely associated with their owners, female slaves occasionally received the name of an owner's sweetheart, wife, or daughter. Windsor and Angola Ame's second daughter was named Lydah (Lydia), sharing a form of the name of her owner's bride, Lydia Child Chicken Ball.[20] The appearance of Lydia as a slave name at Comingtee suggests that either Windsor and Angola Ame or Elias II used the opportunity of the birth of a female child to name a child for the owner's bride.

The sources for the names of the next four children are more literary than personal or religious and reflect the breadth of sources used by owners for slave names. Windsor and Angola Ame's second son, Surry, like his father, was given an English place name. Diana (Dye) is the Latin name for the moon goddess and also a common English name. Subrinagoddard (later shortened to Sabrina, Sabina, and possibly Binah) may have its origin in German or Scandinavian mythology. Cleopatra (later Patra), for the Queen of the Nile, was one of the few female figures from ancient history available as a namesake.

This initial group of nine names (Windsor, Angola Ame, Christmas, Easter, Lydah, Surry, Dye, Subrinagoddard, and Cleopatra) was repeated among the children of the next generation, demonstrating that slaves reused owner-influenced names as kin names and in this way made them their own. The names of Windsor and Angola Ame were used by their children in naming the couple's grandchildren, thus connecting the second generation of American-born slaves with their African-born grandparents. Each of the four daughters who survived to bear children named a son for the maternal grandfather, Windsor. Easter's third son, who shared the

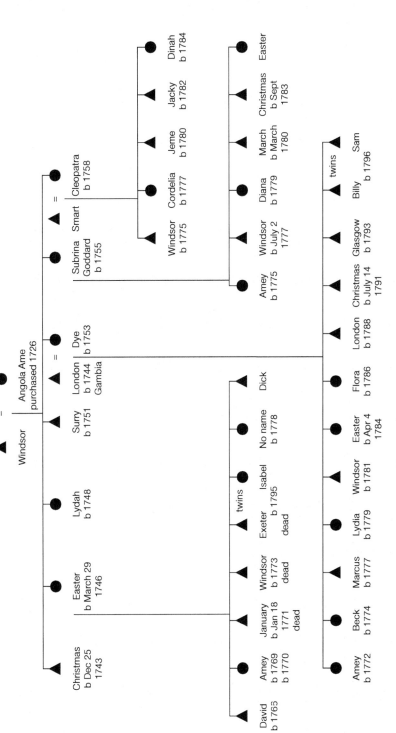

Figure 15.1 Three generations of the family of Windsor and Angola Ame

name Windsor, died shortly after birth in 1773; two years later, Cleopatra's first son, Windsor, also died as an infant. When Subrinagoddard's two sisters were unable to perpetuate their father's name, she changed the name of her oldest son from July (he was born on 2 July 1777) to Windsor. Dye and London's second son, born in 1781, also shared the name of his maternal grandfather. The efforts these four women made to perpetuate the name of their father, including changing the name of July, indicates that they placed a high priority on the preservation of family names. This desire may have been intensified by the elder Windsor's death prior to 1778. In reusing the name of their father for their sons, the four sisters attempted to ensure that his memory would be kept alive into the next generation.

The daughters of Windsor and Angola Ame also chose their mother as a namesake for their daughters. Easter, Dye, and Subrinagoddard all named their first-born daughters for Angola Ame. Significantly, none of them named a daughter for herself, Cleopatra did not reuse her mother's name, although she had two opportunities. Perhaps she felt that, since a living namesake existed, she could carry out another naming agenda.

Unlike the Balls, whose naming practices reflected depth but little breadth, the slaves emphasized kin ties that included both generational depth and breadth. Dye named daughters for her dead sister Lydah and for Easter, and a son for her brother, Christmas. She named a son London, after his father. Although Easter and Cleopatra seem to have been less involved in kin naming, Subrinagoddard gave five of her six children names for maternal kin. She named a daughter for each of her older sisters and a son for her only living brother.

Day-names and event names appeared seven times among the third generation of this family, illustrating the use of Anglicized day and event names and the perpetuation of this type of name as a kin name. July (later, Windsor) and March, the sons of Subrinagoddard, were born in the months for which they were named. Similarly, the name of Easter's son January was consistent with his month of birth. Although Windsor and Angola Ame's children Christmas and Easter received their names because of their dates of birth, the names were perpetuated as kin names. Sons of Subrinagoddard, and those of London and Dye born in July and September, were named Christmas. The name Easter was perpetuated as a kin name during April of 1784 and again in 1785.

The daughters of Windsor and Angola Ame were successful in transmitting kin names through the maternal line. Their brother Christmas probably shared a similar desire to name his offspring for his parents and siblings, but, unlike his sisters, Christmas had few opportunities to find a spouse on the plantation, and he may not have fathered a child in a recognized union at Comingtee. Between 1750 and 1780, Christmas lived on a plantation where the adult males outnumbered females, and it may have been difficult for him to form a stable union. A list of Ball slaves in 1784 places him at Comingtee, where the ratio was 210 males per 100 females, and men over the age of fifteen outnumbered women of the same age group twenty-three to seven. The list also placed him as head of a family that included the children of his deceased sister, Easter.[21]

The inability of some male slaves to form unions on their home plantations means that any family names they were able to pass on to their children would have been on another plantation and would not be reflected in the Ball family

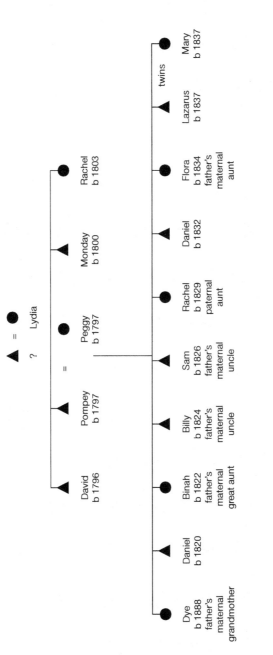

Figure 15.2 The family of Pompey and Peggy

Table 15.4   Persistence of names given at birth for male and female slaves born on the Ball plantations, 1720–1865 by gender and cohort

Birth cohort	Total no. named	Total no. of names used	New names	1740–59		1760–79		1780–99		1800–19		1820–39		1840–65	
				N	Per-cent	N	Per-cent	N	Per-cent	N	Per-cent	N	Per-cent	N	Per-cent
Male children (N = 1163)															
1720–39	32	31	31	25	80.6	24	77.4	24	77.4	23	75.0	21	66.7	21	66.7
1740–59	42	37	29			22	75.9	22	75.9	22	75.9	15	51.7	9	31.0
1760–79	73	59	44					35	79.5	33	75.0	28	63.6	20	45.5
1780–99	86	64	21							15	71.4	12	57.1	4	19.0
1800–19	285	163	88									44	50.0	31	35.2
1820–39	402	150	25											4	16.0
1840–65	243	108	16												
Female children (N = 1181)															
1720–39	26	21	21	20	95.2	20	95.2	20	95.2	20	95.2	20	95.2	18	85.7
1740–59	42	32	29			23	79.3	23	79.3	22	75.9	19	65.5	16	55.2
1760–79	90	66	42					36	85.7	36	85.7	35	83.3	31	73.8
1780–99	77	57	20							10	50.0	8	40.0	6	30.0
1800–19	273	143	70									38	54.3	26	37.1
1820–39	396	137	29											9	31.0
1840–65	277	115	12												
All children (N = 2344)															
1720–39	58	52	52	45	86.5	44	84.6	44	84.6	43	82.7	41	78.8	39	75.0
1740–59	84	69	58			45	77.6	45	77.6	44	75.9	34	58.6	25	43.1
1760–79	163	125	86					71	82.6	69	80.2	63	73.3	51	59.3
1780–99	163	121	41							25	61.0	20	48.8	10	24.4
1800–19	558	306	158									82	51.9	57	36.1
1820–39	798	287	54											13	24.1
1840–65	520	223	28												

records. Although this gap in the evidence produces an apparent bias in favor of the recognition of maternal kin, even for instances in which both spouses were born on Comingtee, no paternal preference in kin naming as seen among the Ball family can be found during this early period (see Tables 15.8 and 15.9).

Evidence suggests that, by the fourth and fifth generations, slaves began gradually to shift kin naming from a bilateral system to one that emphasized the paternal line. Lydia, the daughter of London and Dye, was the mother of four children: David, Pompey, Monday, and Rachel. The records do not reveal their father or fathers nor do the children bear names that were shared by maternal kin. In selecting the names of their children, Lydia's son Pompey and his wife Peggy reflected a transitional system that emphasized the maternal line while beginning a shift in favor of paternal kin names. They named five of their ten children for paternal kin and turned to Pompey's mother's family for four of their children's names. They named Dye for Pompey's maternal grandmother. Billy and Sam were named for Pompey's maternal uncles and Flora for his maternal aunt. Only one daughter, Rachel, shared the name of a relative in the immediate paternal line, specifically, Pompey's sister who had died. They gave Binah a common name for slave girls on the Ball plantations, but, again, they may have used Pompey's maternal great-aunt, Subrinagoddard, as a namesake. When selecting names from the extended kin group, Pompey chose the names of his mother's family. No child of Pompey and Peggy shared the name of a parent or grandparent. Kin names were used to link children born in the 1820s and 1830s with a more distant ancestry.

The size, continuity, and composition of the slave-naming pool developed out of these influences on the selection of slave names. While the Balls drew from a small pool of names, the slaves drew from a large one, a consequence of the desire of owners to provide each slave with a unique identity. As in the case of the children of Windsor and Angola Ame, the sources of these names were diverse. This need for a large pool of names may have enhanced the ability of slaves, at least among the first generation, to maintain African names as well as African practices of day-naming. For 1,163 male children born between 1720 and 1865, a total of 254 different names were used. The slightly larger number of 1,181 female children received their names from a smaller pool of 223 names. Prior to 1780, slaves born on the Ball plantations were given names that reflected the owner's desire for diversity. During these years, approximately three of four slaves (74.2 percent) received a name that had not been used before for an American-born child. Not all of these names were necessarily "new," in that some were used for slaves who had been purchased during that period, but they were new among slaves born on the Ball plantations. Between 1780 and 1800, the slaves began to name their own children, and they used a kin system. About two-thirds (66.1 percent) of the children were given names that had been used previously. The first two decades of the nineteenth century saw another shift in the structure of naming. But, after 1820, few names were given to slaves that had not been chosen continuously since they first entered the pool.

The chronological pattern is highly suggestive of the shift. Prior to 1780, slaves born on the Ball plantations received names that, in their diversity, failed to reflect generational ties. As was the case in the family of Windsor and Angola Ame, few children shared the name of a parent or, in fact, of any other living slave born on the Ball plantations. After 1780, the pattern was altered as a smaller percentage of "new" names was introduced and the use of kin names became more common. This was the second generation of American-born slaves to share the names of grandparents, aunts, and uncles. Between 1800 and 1820, more "new" names were introduced on the Ball plantations, but, after 1820, few names were brought into use, perhaps because the slight surge of names between 1800 and 1820 increased and diversified the pool of names to accommodate nearly everyone's naming agenda.

One measure of the continuity of names on the Ball plantations is the reuse of the group of names given to the first generation of American-born slaves for children born in the nineteenth century. Because this group of names was selected by owners in the interest of creating a distinct identity for each individual, the rate of persistence of these names indicates the long-term influence of owners on slaves' names. The repetition of names, family names in particular, depended on the size of slave families, the level of mortality, and the stability of the population under observation, and is difficult to measure; nonetheless, some comparisons are possible.

The method devised to capture the persistence of male and female names on the Ball plantations consists of recording the appearance of each name (results reported in Table 15.4). If a name was reused within forty years of its first appearance, it was counted as an "active" name. If a name was not reused within forty years, it was counted as removed from the "active" pool during the first twenty-year period it was not used for a child born on the plantations. For example, the name Caesar was used for one child born between 1720 and 1740. It was not reused during the next twenty-year period but appeared twice as the name of boys born between 1760 and 1780. Again, the next twenty years saw no child named Caesar, but two children born between 1800 and 1820, three between 1820 and 1840, and six between 1840 and 1865 shared the name. Caesar, then, was counted as a new name in the 1720 to 1740 period and as one of twenty-one of the original thirty-one names still active in 1865. Another classical name, Cato, was first used for a child born on the Ball plantations between 1760 and 1780. It was one of the forty-four male names that were "new" (had not been used previously for a child at birth) during that twenty-year period. "Cato" was reused during the next twenty years, but no slave born on the Ball plantations after 1800 was named Cato. Cato, then, was one of the two names first introduced between 1760 and 1780 and reused during the following period that was not used again after 1800.

Male and female names show a substantial difference in continual use on the Ball family plantations: male names were far more likely to disappear than were female names. In every period (see Table 15.4), more female names that were new to the pool of names were reused and remained in use up to the Civil War. Of greatest interest to the point under consideration is the persistence of the owner-influenced names that appeared before 1780. Of the thirty-one names given to male children between 1720 and 1739, two-thirds were active in 1865 and had been active for more than a hundred years. Female names once used for a slave on the Ball plantations continued to be reused with greater frequency, and 85.7 percent of those introduced between 1720 and 1739 remained active until 1865.

One explanation for the difference in the rates of persistence of male and female names can be found in the shifts in the frequency of some categories of names among slaves. I have classified names as biblical, classical, common English, Spanish, or French in origin; as place-names, day-names, or African names.[22] Biblical names that were in common English usage were classified as English names, thus defining the biblical category narrowly and including only names that were clearly biblical in origin. Both the African day-names and their Anglicized translations, such as Monday and Friday, have been categorized together, and the day-name category was expanded to include names that were used because they linked the child with an event that occurred at its birth. For this reason, months of the year, seasons and holiday names, such as Christmas and Easter, have been designated as day-names.

Most striking is the increased use of biblical names for male children of slaves. During the first hundred years, 1720 to 1819, biblical names were chosen for between 20 and 25 percent of male children. In the same period, biblical names accounted for less than 20 percent of all female names. After 1820, the number of biblical names for boys increased dramatically, accounting for four out of ten names. No comparable increase in the use of biblical names for females appears during the nineteenth century.[23]

The gender difference in the use of biblical names can be seen in the names chosen by John Ball, Jr., in 1805 and 1806 for two groups of newly purchased Africans. The six male slaves were all namesakes of figures from the Old Testament, including Nathan, Ishmael, and two sets of brothers, Moses and Aaron, Israel and Esau. The seven female slaves received names derived from a variety of sources— Roxena, Juno, Judy, Tenah, Pallas, Bobbet (presumably, Babette), and Molly.[24]

By the nineteenth century, place-names and day-names, two types of names that were used by slaves but did not appear among the white population, declined in use among the Ball slaves. Place-names such as Windsor, London, Glasgow, and Dublin were common among the first slaves born on the Ball plantations and accounted for about one in four names given to males between 1720 and 1740. Most often, place-names reflected the English and Irish roots of the slaveowners. When the names persisted in use—they constituted about 10 percent of all male names after 1740—they were usually transmitted as kin names. Place-names were almost exclusively male, with only Cuba (possibly the African name Cooba) appearing among females.

Day-names in all their forms also declined in popularity and did not account for more than 5 percent of all male names after 1800. They were rarely used for female slaves. Most day-names, as well as names for holidays, months, and seasons, entered the pool of names as actual day-names but were continued in usage as kin names. Eleven of the fourteen children (78.6 percent) who received Anglicized day-names during the eighteenth century were given names appropriate for their day of birth. By the nineteenth century, the percentage of day-names that accurately recorded the day, month, season, or holiday of a child's birth had declined to fourteen of thirty-five (40 percent). The decline suggests that, although day-naming persisted into the nineteenth century, among the Ball slaves, more often than not, the name was selected for another reason, frequently, as in the case of Christmas and Easter, as a kin name.

African day-names that survived in usage in the African form rarely retained the meaning associated with the day. Cuffee ("born on a Friday") was a popular name for male children on the Ball plantations, appearing eight times. However, it was used only once for a boy born on a Friday. Mimba, by African naming rules a name bestowed on girls born on a Saturday, was also a common name, but it

Table 15.5 Percentage of names given to slave children at birth on the Ball plantations, 1720–1865 by gender, classification, and cohort

Name type	1720–39	1740–59	1760–79	1780–99	1800–19	1820–39	1840–65	1720–1865
Males	N = 32	N = 42	N = 73	N = 86	N = 285	N = 402	N = 243	N = 1163
Biblical	18.6	23.8	26.0	20.1	26.3	43.3	39.5	34.2
Classical	15.6	23.8	15.1	22.1	10.5	9.5	10.0	11.8
English	12.5	9.5	13.7	15.1	17.9	24.6	21.0	19.9
Spanish	–	2.4	–	3.5	2.0	0.2	2.1	1.5
French	–	2.4	2.7	3.5	1.8	2.5	1.2	2.1
Place-name	25.0	4.8	8.2	9.3	6.0	3.5	7.0	6.2
Day-name	6.3	9.5	6.8	10.4	4.6	3.7	2.5	4.6
African	–	4.8	–	–	1.1	0.4	0.4	0.7
Unclassified	21.9	19.0	27.4	15.1	29.1	17.2	16.5	18.9
Females	N = 26	N = 42	N = 90	N = 77	N = 273	N = 396	N = 277	N = 1181
Biblical	19.2	11.9	16.7	16.9	15.8	21.0	15.2	17.4
Classical	7.7	14.3	5.6	5.2	10.6	5.6	10.8	8.3
English	38.5	40.5	44.4	40.3	39.6	41.7	44.8	41.9
Spanish	26.9	4.8	10.0	7.8	8.8	7.1	14.4	9.8
Floral	–	4.8	5.6	1.3	3.7	1.3	2.9	2.6
Day-name	–	2.4	1.1	2.6	2.2	1.8	–	1.4
African	2.7	4.8	6.7	9.1	7.3	6.8	5.8	6.7
Unclassified	2.7	16.7	10.0	16.9	12.1	14.9	6.1	11.8

was used only two of eight times for a girl born on Saturday, a weak pattern at best, since even a random use of the name would result in an appropriate day-name use in one out of seven instances.

Peter Wood's suggestion that some common slave names survived because they closely resembled the sound of more traditional African day-names is not supported by the evidence of the Ball plantations.[25] If these names did persist because of their sound, they rarely retained the African meaning Wood implied. Jack, a name that Wood argued may have persisted among slaves because it was derived from Quaco ("boy born on a Wednesday") was given to a child born on that day in only two of twelve instances. The name Phoebe, which Wood maintained was derived from Phiba, for a girl born on a Friday, was used eight times but never for a girl born on that day.

Classical names declined in use after 1800 as well. Like place-names and day-names, classical names were rarely found among the slaveowners. These names were associated almost exclusively with slaves. Prior to 1800, classical names accounted for about 20 percent of names given to male slaves born on the Ball plantations. During the nineteenth century, the share of classical names declined to about 10 percent. The gender difference in the frequency of classical names illustrates how these names came into use. As elsewhere in the colonial South, favorite names included Pompey, Cato, and Caesar, indicating that the Balls were well acquainted with *Plutarch's Lives* and turned to the classics and ancient history as a means of creating a diverse pool of slave names. Female characters are rare in these sources and provided few potential namesakes for slaves.[26]

Other slaves born in the eighteenth century received names that reflect the literary tastes of their owners. The plays of Shakespeare provided the names Cordelia, from *King Lear*, and possibly Celia, from *As You Like It*, as well as for one child, Romeo. Evidence suggests that the Balls also selected characters from popular contemporary fiction as namesakes for their slaves. The list of slaves in 1784 at Limerick plantation records an adult male slave named Gil Blas, whose name was continued into the next generation by his son. Since it is unlikely that the slaves had access to Alain Rene Le Sage's *History and Adventures of Gil Blas of Santillane*, the probable source for the name was the owner's library.[27]

The transition from slave names to names more widely used by other populations appears in a comparison of the leading names for the Ball slaves with those of their owners and the most common names in Hingham in Massachusetts and Middlesex County in Virginia.[28] The leading names for male and female children born on the Ball plantations for 1720 to 1799, 1800 to 1865, and the entire period are reported in Tables 15.6 and 15.7.[29] Male names on the Ball plantations between 1720 and 1799 bear only a partial resemblance to the most common names among blacks and whites in the Middlesex and Hingham populations of the eighteenth century, reflecting both the distinctive quality of black names and perhaps the local character of the slaves and slaveowners. Only six names, Tom, Dick, John (Jack), Jemme (James), Peter, and Charles, rank among the leading fifteen names for both Middlesex slaves and the Ball family slaves. These common English names were also among the leading names for whites in Middlesex. With one exception, the same six names were among the leading names in eighteenth-century Hingham (Smith's 1741 to 1780 parental marriage cohort). Names that were used exclusively among slaves did not overlap the two slave populations. Cupid, Alix, Prince, and Cuffee were popular names only among Ball slaves and were not shared to a large degree by slaves in Middlesex. The choice of "Maurey" and "Maurice" for Ball slaves may be attributed to the French Protestant influence present in the Low Country but not felt in either Middlesex or Hingham.[30] Regional variations in the Euro-American population evidently could affect the names of slaves.

The set of male names for slaves born between 1800 and 1865 on the Ball plantations shares many elements with the leading names in Hingham (Smith's 1781 to 1820 parental marriage cohort). Nine of the most popular fifteen names appear in both populations, which selected the same three leading names, William, John, and Thomas. The two populations also shared the common English names Charles, George, and James and the names of the biblical patriarchs, although "Abraham" is curiously absent from the Hingham list. Only one name that is obviously reserved exclusively for slaves appears among the leading names for Ball slaves—Prince.

Female slaves on the Ball plantations consistently shared a smaller group of names with both the Hingham population and earlier generations of whites and blacks in Middlesex. Prior to 1800, the Ball slaves shared only the names Mary, Betty, Jenny, Hannah, and Beck with slaves born and entering Middlesex. For roughly the same period (Smith's 1741 to 1780 parental marriage cohort), they also shared five names with Hingham women (Mary, Betty/Elizabeth, Hannah, Rebecca, and Rachel). The most popular names for female Ball slaves born in the nineteenth century overlapped to a greater extent with those found for Middlesex blacks of the eighteenth century than they did with the white populations of Hingham or Middlesex's residents. Six of the most frequent fourteen names were shared with Hingham, and five of those names with one addition were also in common use among Middlesex's whites. Six names were shared by Middlesex's native-born blacks, and eight of the leading fourteen names can be found among slaves entering eighteenth-century Middlesex County or the Ball slaves born in the nineteenth century. One explanation for this pattern may be that some of the names used by slaves were uniquely identified with slave women. "Binah" may have had West African origins in the names Binta or Beneba, or it may have been derived from the name Subrinagoddard.[31] Binah appears on none of the lists of leading names in Hingham or Middlesex. Hagar, the servant who bore the biblical Abraham's son Ishmael, would be an unlikely choice of name for a white woman.

Despite the shifts in choices of slave names, especially the names of male slaves, the long-term impact of the initially diverse pool of names can be detected well into the nineteenth century. One way to index the comparative size of the pool of names and the frequency with which the most common names were used is to determine the percentage of names concentrated at the top of each cohort. As previously noted, members of the Ball family relied so heavily on family names that more than half of the family's sons received one of four names and half of the daughters received one of six names. Because a high degree of name concentration within a lineage is only logical, a more useful comparison can be made with the Hingham population (Smith's 1781 to 1820 parental marriage cohort). In Hingham, 16.3 percent of the male children were given one of the three leading names, William, John, or Thomas. The same names, which were also the leading names for Ball slaves born after 1800, accounted for a total of 7.1 percent of all male names, or less than half the concentration at the top as seen in Hingham.

Table 15.6   Leading names for male slave children born on the Ball plantations, 1720–1865

1720–1799 (N = 233)

Rank	Name	N	Percent
1st	Cupid	6	2.6
2d	Alix	5	2.1
2d	Charles-Charley	5	2.1
2d	Cuffee	5	2.1
2d	Dick-Dicky	5	2.1
2d	John-Johnny	5	2.1
2d	Maurey	5	2.1
2d	Prince	5	2.1
2d	Tom	5	2.1
10th	David	4	1.7
10th	Devonshire	4	1.7
10th	Fortune	4	1.7
10th	Jacob	4	1.7
10th	Jimmy	4	1.7
10th	Peter	4	1.7
10th	Pino	4	1.7
10th	Windsor	4	1.7
Total		83	35.6

	Percent
3 Leading Names	6.9
5 Leading Names	11.2
10 Leading Names	21.9

1800–1865 (N = 930)

Rank	Name	N	Percent
1st	William-Billy	27	2.9
2d	John-Johnny	22	2.4
3d	Nathan-Nat	21	2.3
3d	Robert-Bob	21	2.3
3d	Thomas-Tom	21	2.3
6th	Abraham	19	2.0
7th	Isaac	17	1.8
8th	Benjamin-Ben	16	1.7
8th	Jacob	16	1.7
10th	Charles	15	1.6
10th	Richard-Dicky	15	1.6
10th	George	15	1.6
10th	Jacky	15	1.6
10th	James-Jimmy	15	1.6
10th	Prince	15	1.6
16th	Joseph	14	1.5
16th	Samuel-Sam	14	1.5
18th	Maurice-Maurey	13	1.4
18th	Peter	13	1.4
Total		324	34.8

	Percent
3 Leading Names	7.5
5 Leading Names	12.0
10 Leading Names	21.0

1720–1865 (N = 1163)

Rank	Name	N	Percent	Cohort*
1st	William-Billy	30	2.6	1800–19
2d	John-Johnny	27	2.3	1780–99
3d	Thomas-Tom	26	2.2	1800–19
4th	Nathan-Nat	24	2.1	1800–19
5th	Robot-Bob	23	2.0	1800–19
6th	Abraham	20	1.7	—
6th	Charles-Charley	20	1.7	1720–39
6th	Jacob	20	1.7	—
6th	Prince	20	1.7	—
10th	Benjamin-Ben	19	1.6	1800–19
11th	Isaac	18	1.5	—
11th	James-Jimmy-Jim	18	1.5	1760–79
11th	Maurice-Maurey	18	1.5	1740–59
14th	Richard-Dicky-Dick	17	1.5	1800–19
14th	George	17	1.5	—
14th	Jack-Jacky	17	1.5	—
14th	Peter	17	1.5	—
14th	Samuel-Sammy-Sam	17	1.5	1820–39
19th	Alexander-Alix	15	1.3	1840–65
19th	Joseph-Josey	15	1.3	1800–19
Total		398	34.2	

	Percent
3 Leading Names	7.1
5 Leading Names	11.2
10 Leading Names	19.6

* Cohort in which formal name first appeared.

Table 15.7 Leading names for female slave children born on the Ball plantations, 1720–1865

	1720–1799 (N = 235)				1800–1865 (N = 946)				1720–1865 (N = 1181)				Cohort[†]
Rank	Name	N	Percent	Rank	Name	N	Percent	Rank	Name	N	Percent		
1st	Mary-Maria	13	5.5	1st	Mary-Maria	38	4.0	1st	Mary-Maria	51	4.3		—
2d	Hannah	8	3.4	2d	Elizabeth-Betty	35	3.7	2d	Elizabeth-Betty	41	3.5		1820–39
3d	Jenny	7	3.0	3d	Binah	30	3.2	3d	Binah	32	2.7		—
4th	Betty-Betsy	6	2.6	4th	Susanna-Sue-Susey	24	2.5	4th	Susanna-Sue-Susey	29	2.5		1800–19
4th	Dolly	6	2.6	5th	Rebecca-Beck-Becky	23	2.4	5th	Rebecca-Beck-Becky	28	2.4		1800–19
6th	Beck-Becky	5	2.1	6th	Judy	21	2.2	6th	Diana-Dye	25	2.1		1760–79
6th	Diana-Dye	5	2.1	7th	Diana-Dye	20	2.1	7th	Judy	23	1.9		—
8th	Amey	4	1.7	8th	Sarah-Sarey	19	2.0	8th	Hannah	21	1.8		—
8th	Celia	4	1.7	9th	Hagar	16	1.7	8th	Sarah-Sarey	21	1.8		1740–59
8th	Clarinda	4	1.7	9th	Nancy	16	1.7	10th	Molly-Molsy	19	1.6		—
8th	Molly	4	1.7	11th	Lucy	15	1.6	10th	Nancy	19	1.6		—
8th	Peggy	4	1.7	11th	Molly-Molsy	15	1.6	10th	Rachel	19	1.6		—
8th	Rachel	4	1.7	11th	Rachel	15	1.6	13th	Hagar	18	1.5		—
8th	Sally	4	1.7	14th	Bella	14	1.5	14th	Jenny	17	1.4		—
8th	Sylvia	4	1.7	15th	Cate	13	1.4	10th	Lucy	17	1.4		1820–39
8th	Tenah	4	1.7	15th	Flora	13	1.4	16th	Catherine-Cate-Catey	16	1.4		—
8th	Tenang	4	1.7	15th	Hannah	13	1.4	16th	Flora	16	1.4		—
				15th	Harriet	13	1.4	16th	Harriet	17	1.4		—
				19th	*			19th	Bella	15	1.3		—
								20th	**				
Total		90	38.3			353	37.3			443	36.2		

	Percent		Percent		Percent
3 Leading Names	11.9		10.9		10.5
5 Leading Names	17.1		15.8		15.4
10 Leading Names	26.4		25.5		24.6

Notes: * "Lydia" appeared eleven times as a name for a girl born on the Ball plantations between 1800 and 1865. Four names were used ten times; Jenny, Amey, Tenah, and Sylvia. The name Jenny, which ranked third prior to 1800, declined to twentieth (tied with three others for the position). ** Between 1720 and 1865, the names Amey, Sylvia, Tenah, and Lydia were used fourteen times each. † Cohort in which formal name first appeared.

The twenty most frequent names at Hingham contributed more than half (53.1 percent) of all names given to the community's boys. On the Ball plantations, about one-third (34.8 percent) of the boys received one of the nineteen leading names. Female names on the Ball plantations and at Hingham were more heavily concentrated among leading names. Nearly one in four girls (24.6 percent) of Hingham received one of the three leading names—Mary, Lydia, or Hannah. On the Ball plantations, 10.5 percent of the girls received one of the three leading names— Mary, Elizabeth, or Binah. More than 70 percent of the girls in Hingham as compared to 36.2 percent of the Ball slave girls bore one of the twenty most common names.

Comparison with the leading names for slaves and whites in other populations indicates that male slaves on the Ball plantations, especially after 1800, were beginning to share a common set of names with white populations, especially that of Hingham, in which a strong biblical influence was felt. Female slaves maintained many names that were associated exclusively with their slave status and that set them apart from white populations. Although a weak trend toward biblical and common English names can be detected, the infrequent use of the most popular names suggests a stronger influence. Slaves continued to perpetuate as kin names those names that originated in the existing name system based on owner-selected names for the first and second generations.

By far the most intriguing shift in the pattern of slave naming is the increased use of biblical names. Although planters' records fail to reveal the precise timing and the process by which the Ball slaves were converted to Christianity, they do reveal that, by the 1830s, a black preacher with his own church was active at Comingtee plantation. Efforts to convert the slaves may have begun as early as the 1780s, when British abolitionists and anti-abolitionists published essays linking the successful reproduction of slave populations in the New World with the conversion of slaves to Christianity and the promotion of stable marriages among slaves. The Balls were well acquainted with these writings. An inventory in 1817 of more than 400 volumes in John Ball, Sr.'s library included both the works of British abolitionist James Ramsey and the pro-slavery writings of Bishop Beilby Porteus.[32] Ramsey's "Essay on the Treatment and Conversion of the African Slaves in the British Sugar Islands," published in 1784, recommended the conversion of the slave population as part of a humanitarian program to improve the quality of slave life.[33] Bishop Porteus saw the conversion of slaves as one means of reducing promiscuity and increasing fertility among Caribbean slaves.[34] Whatever the influence of these authors, the demographic records suggest that, by 1780, the Balls were developing a policy of maintaining and increasing their labor force through natural increase by adjusting plantation populations to a more balanced sex ratio.[35]

The timing of the rise in the use of biblical names for male slaves on the Ball plantations is consistent with the conversion of slaves during the first two decades of the nineteenth century. In fact, the biblical names that slaves chose indicate not a mere acquaintance with but a clear understanding of a set of Bible stories, primarily from the Old Testament. The evidence is strong enough to show that these stories were the core of the oral religious instruction given the slaves. The lessons provided new names, a set of character values, and a model of the structure of a patriarchal society.

To analyze most effectively the use of biblical names, I have grouped them by Bible stories. Families of the Old Testament patriarchs, Moses and the Israelites, King David, Adam and Eve, Samson and Delilah, Lazarus, Mary, and Martha provided names and examples of vice and virtue. Names associated with the patriarchs were most popular: Abraham, Isaac, Jacob, and Joseph. The story of Abraham mentions his wife, Sarah, their son, Isaac, Sarah's Egyptian servant, Hagar, and the son of Abraham and Hagar, Ishmael. Isaac's stories name his wife, Rebecca, and twin sons, Esau and Jacob (later, Israel). Jacob's stories detail his marriages to Laban's daughters, Leah and Rachel, and the births of his daughter, Dinah, and his twelve sons, including Joseph and Benjamin.

In selecting biblical names for their children, the slaves avoided some names, especially those of figures who exhibited deep flaws of character or appearance. From the story of Samson, slave parents chose the name of the hero for their sons but never the name Delilah for their daughters. From the stories of King David, slaves broke the continuity of the line of leadership—Hannah, Samuel, Saul, David, and Solomon—by omitting Saul. For those who heard his story recounted, Saul's jealousy, his erratic behavior, and suicide on the field of battle probably outweighed his positive qualities. Slaves avoided other namesakes from the King David stories. There was no Absalom on the Ball plantations. No slave parents used as a biblical namesake this disloyal son who rose in rebellion against his father. Nor did slave parents name a daughter for the adultress Bathsheba, though Uriah, the wronged husband, provided the name for one Comingtee slave.

Biblical stories supplied not only names for slaves but also a model of a system of kinship that emphasized the paternal line, as in the stories of the Old Testament. The link between conversion to Christianity and a paternal preference in naming is evident in the family of Preacher Brawley and his wife, Bina. Preacher Brawley worked as a hog minder at Comingtee. He built and preached in a "rough little clap-board church." According to his owners, he "professed and retained a certain amount of faithfulness to his master, but it was of a limited kind. As a preacher, he had considerable influence on the plantation; and, though tricky, was of great use, after the war, in inducing the hands to sign contracts."[36]

Preacher Brawley and Bina preferred biblical characters and paternal kin as namesakes for their children. Two sons, Trinity and Luke, were given names of biblical origin and new to the Ball slave population. Brawley, the first-born son, shared the name of both his father and paternal grandfather. After the death of the first young Brawley, Preacher Brawley and Bina reused the name for their fifth son, attempting to ensure the name replication of the paternal line into the next generation. They named their first daughter Hagar, for her paternal grandmother, reflecting a preference for paternal kin naming. No daughter shared the name of her mother or maternal grandmother, and, despite the birth of eight grandsons, Bina's father, Adonis, did not have a child named for him.

The preference for biblical names, especially those of the Old Testament patriarchs, brought a potential conflict with one of the rules that governed the selection of names. Ball family slaves avoided or were forbidden the use of their owner's name during his lifetime, as well as family names that were unique to the owner's lineage. This prohibition would be logical, given the emphasis the Balls placed on protecting and perpetuating family names. For example, no slave at any of the plantations received the name of the family patriarch and first immigrant,

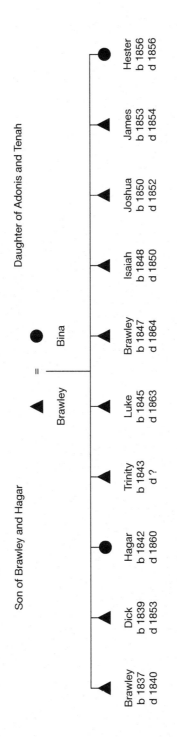

Figure 15.3   Children of Preacher Brawley and Bina

Elias. The use of the name Isaac is more instructive. The first appearance of Isaac as a slave name occurred in 1778, two years after Elias's son Isaac died. The Ball family reused "Isaac" in 1785 and again in 1818. During the period 1780 to 1825, Ball slaves avoided the name. After both Isaac Balls died in 1824 and 1825, respectively, the slaves began to use the name for their children, naming ten boys Isaac over the next decade. Two slave families used Isaac as a necronymic sibling name. Although, for more than forty-five years, the slaves avoided using the name Isaac, they increasingly used biblical names, especially the names of the Old Testament patriarchs and the women associated with them. Names from the stories of Isaac run through the records: Abraham (six children), Sarah (ten), and Hagar (ten); Rebecca, Isaac's wife (thirteen), although "Rebecca" was popular prior to the transition to biblical naming. The biblical Isaac's sons, Esau and Jacob, were also sources of names. Jacob was the name for fourteen children, while the less fortunate Esau, only one.

The stories of the Old Testament place great emphasis on paternal kin reckoning and may have influenced a shift toward a paternal preference in the selection of kin names among slaves. In selecting kin names for their children, the Ball family slaves made a transition after 1800 from a system that favored the grandfather as a namesake to one that emphasized ties to the father. In addition, they preferred paternal over maternal kin in selecting family names, more nearly replicating the naming practices of their owners.

A look at kin naming among the Ball slaves before and after 1800 suggests kin naming never achieved the intensity that it did among members of the Ball family. Before 1800, when they selected a kin name, the Ball slaves more often turned to a grandfather as the namesake than to the father and were equally likely to select the paternal and maternal grandfathers. In only 15.2 percent of the thirty-three families in which the first child was born prior to 1800 did the slaves name a son for his father. In the thirteen fully reconstructed families, only 15.4 percent transmitted the name of a father to his son. More than 60 percent of the slave families succeeded in reusing the paternal grandfather's name for a son. Similarly, 60 percent of the families transmitted the name of the maternal grandfather. This pattern, albeit based on a small number of cases, suggests that the first generations of American-born slaves selected as kin names for their children names that linked the child to a more distant and, in some cases, African past, without preference for patrilineality.

When the slave families named daughters, they preferred grandmothers as namesakes. Only three of the thirty-three families (9.1 percent) used the mother as a namesake. Among the seventeen fully reconstructed families, only 11.8 percent transmitted the name of the mother to her daughter. Furthermore, slaves rarely used the paternal grandmother's name, preferring by far the mother's mother (in 70.6 percent of the families).

Slaves revealed their naming priorities when they named their first and second children. Most significantly, about 60 percent of the first and second sons and more than 70 percent of the first and second daughters did not share either the name of parent or grandparent. Kin names, then, were perpetuated by subsequent children. One explanation for this pattern could be a necronymic naming system extended among a broadly defined kin.[37] The daughters of Windsor and Angola Ame appear to have practiced a system of kin replacement during the eighteenth century.

Table 15.8 Percentage of Ball slaves sharing a kin name by gender, family size, and kin connection, 1720–1799 and 1800–1865

Sons

	1–2		3 or more		All	
	N	Percent	N	Percent	N	Percent
1720–99						
Father	14	7.1	19	21.1	33	15.2
(fully reconstructed families*)						
Father	4	0	9	22.2	13	15.4
Paternal Grandfather (FAFA)	4	75.0	9	55.5	13	61.2
Maternal Grandfather (MOFA)	4	25.0	9	77.7	13	61.2
1800–65						
Father	57	7.0	76	42.1	133	27.1
(fully reconstructed families)						
Father	11	9.1	27	66.7	38	50.0
Paternal Grandfather (FAFA)	11	9.1	27	48.1	38	36.8
Maternal Grandfather (MOFA)	11	18.2	27	7.4	38	10.5

Daughters

	1–2		3 or more		All	
	N	Percent	N	Percent	N	Percent
1720–99						
Mother	12	0	21	14.3	33	9.1
(fully reconstructed families)						
Mother	6	0	11	18.2	17	11.8
Paternal Grandmother (FAMO)	6	0	11	9.1	17	5.9
Maternal Grandmother (MOMO)	6	0	11	81.8	17	70.6
1800–65						
Mother	49	4.1	82	22.0	131	15.3
(fully reconstructed families)						
Mother	12	0	28	17.9	40	12.5
Paternal Grandmother (FAMO)	12	33.0	28	39.3	40	37.5
Maternal Grandmother (MOMO)	12	16.7	28	21.4	40	20.0

Note: * Includes only families in which all four grandparents are known.

Table 15.9 Percentage of first- and second-born Ball slave children sharing a kin or biblical name by gender, family size, and kin connection, 1720–1799 and 1800–1865 (includes only fully reconstructed families)

Percentage of first and second sons sharing kin names

	N	Father	FAFA	Both	MOFA	Neither parent nor grandparent
1720–99						
1st Son	13	8.7	15.4	0	15.4	61.5
2d Son	12	0	8.3	0	33.3	58.3
1800–65						
1st Son	38	21.1	15.8	7.9	5.3	65.0
2d Son	35	17.1	11.4	2.9	0	74.4

Percentage of first and second sons receiving biblical names

	N	Biblical	Biblical non-kin*
1720–99			
1st Son	13	15.4	15.4
2d Son	12	25.0	16.7
1800–65			
1st Son	38	39.5	26.3
2d Son	35	24.3	22.9

Percentage of first and second daughters sharing kin names

	N	Mother	MOMO	Both	FAMO	Neither parent nor grandparent
1720–99						
1st Daughter	17	0	29.4	0	0	70.6
2d Daughter	14	0	21.4	0	0	78.6
1800–65						
1st Daughter	40	0	5.0	0	22.5	72.5
2d Daughter	35	5.7	8.6	0	8.6	77.1

Percentage of first and second daughters receiving biblical names

	N	Biblical	Biblical non-kin
1720–99			
1st Daughter	17	17.6	17.6
2d Daughter	14	14.3	14.3
1800–65			
1st Daughter	40	35.0	25.0
2d Daughter	35	25.7	17.1

Note: * Biblical names were categorized as non-kin it they were not shared by parent or grandparent.

The mortality evidence for slaves born on the Ball plantations during the eighteenth century is, unfortunately, too weak to test this hypothesis.

After 1800, the Ball slaves altered these naming patterns to emphasize paternal ties, adopting the naming preferences of the owners. Among the 133 slave families that began after 1800, 27.1 percent named a son for his father. Families with three or more sons transmitted the father's name to the next generation for 42.1 percent of the families. In the thirty-eight fully reconstituted families, the pattern is stronger, with half of all families and two-thirds of the families with three or more sons reusing the father's name in the next generation. The paternal grandfather was also a common namesake for slave sons; the maternal grandfather was, however, rarely chosen. For all families, 36.8 percent succeeded in naming a son for his paternal grandfather, while only 10.5 percent perpetuated the name of the mother's father. This pattern suggests that a transition was occurring from a naming system favoring grandfathers' names to one favoring fathers' names and, within the selection of a grandfather's name, a clear preference to replicate the paternal line.

In naming daughters, the Ball slaves persisted in a pattern favoring the name of the grandmother over the name of the mother. Only 15.3 percent of the 131 families in which both parents were known and 12.5 percent of the fully reconstructed families named a daughter for her mother. They perpetuated both the paternal and maternal grandmothers' names, with more than one in three (37.5 percent) of the families naming a daughter for her father's mother. One in five families used the name of the mother's mother. The preference for the paternal grandmother as a namesake is a reversal of the trend discerned for the eighteenth century favoring the maternal line and suggests that confirming ties to the paternal lineage grew in importance during the nineteenth century.

One indication of the strength of commitment to kin naming is the relatively low percentage of families with only one or two sons or daughters who used the name of a parent or grandparent for a child. Because no couple could predict the number of children of each gender they would produce, the selection of names for their first children reflect their priorities. In the nineteenth century as in the eighteenth, Ball slaves named only about three in ten first and second sons and daughters for kin. There is some indication that, in selecting kin names, the Ball slaves may have extended back beyond grandparents to confirm ties to more distant kin. The children of Pompey and Peggy are a case in point. Of the five children who received a kin name on the paternal side, four shared the name of kin extending back more than two generations. Systematic evidence of this depth of kin recognition cannot be obtained from the Ball records, but the example suggests both the depth and breadth of slave kin naming. As slaves began to prefer paternal kin, at least some began to subordinate kin naming to biblical naming. Such slave couples delayed the use of parental and grandparental names for their children. In families begun after 1800, slave parents named almost as many first and second sons and daughters for non-kin biblical namesakes as for a parent or grandparent.

Previous studies of slave-naming practices reveal one pattern common to the slaveowners that was avoided by slaves—the naming of another child in a nuclear family to replace a deceased sibling. Although the Ball family used necronyms, they took advantage of only about 20 percent of the opportunities presented. This proportion does not suggest an avoidance of the practice but indicates some reluctance to reuse the name of a deceased child. Slaves on the Ball plantations also engaged in necronymic sibling naming. Thirty-six families were involved in the practice and a total of thirty-eight children shared the name of a deceased sibling. As was the case with the Ball family, this represents about a 20 percent use of opportunities to name a child for a dead sibling. It should be noted, however, a family-by-family examination of slaves who practiced necronymic naming reveals that, in thirty of the families, at least one parent in each family was on the "blue list," that is, was a skilled slave who received a higher quality cloth when allocations were made. Skilled slaves such as drivers, carpenters, poultry keepers, and domestic servants were either more fully acculturated to the naming practices of their owners than were field hands or they experienced greater owner interference when selecting a name for a child.

Once Africans arrived in the New World, they began the process of transforming their African culture into an Afro-American one. Although they were unable to reproduce many of the artifacts of their African slave systems, they preserved the hidden structures by which a society functions. Their values as well as some of their African practices could be retained in the names they selected for their children. The naming practices of the Ball family slaves suggests that the system of slave naming evolved from one based on owner selection, with perhaps some slave participation, to one in which the slaves chose the names of their own children. In this process, the slaves turned first to the preservation of kin names. The first generation of American-born slaves used the names of their children to connect grandparent with grandchild, second generation American-born to African-born. By drawing kin connections to a wide network of family, slaves developed a kin-naming system that was distinctive from that of their owners.

This distinction was to be short-lived as slaves were exposed to other forces that influenced the names they selected and the naming practices they chose. Like other slave populations, the slaves on the Bali plantations were exposed to the teachings of the bible, which provided not only names but also a model of patrilineal society. As they turned to biblical names with greater frequency, slaves revealed a preference for some characters, a distaste for others, and structured a kin system that emphasized the connections between father and son and among broader relations of paternal kin. In transforming their naming system from one that was based on bilateral kin reckoning and that sought significant ties between the present and more distant past, slaves changed their naming practices to resemble more closely those of their owners.

Notes

Earlier versions of this article were presented to faculty colloquiums at the University of New Mexico and the University of California, Berkeley. I wish to thank Kermit Hall, Howard Rabinowitz, Darren Rutman, Daniel Scott Smith, Edward Tebbenhoff, George Terry, Eldon Turner, and Bertram Wyatt-Brown for their helpful comments. Figures were drawn by Mark Scialo of the Office of Instructional Resources, University of Florida.

1   Sidney W. Mintz and Richard Price, "An Anthropological Approach to the Afro-American Past: A Caribbean Perspective," Institution for the Study of Human issues, *Occasional Papers in Social Change*, 2 (Philadelphia, Pa., 1976), 4–11; Melville Herskovits, *The Myth of the Negro Past* (Boston, 1958); George M. Foster, "Peasant Society and the Image of Limited Good," *American Anthropologist*, 67 (1965): 293–315; Robert Redfield, *The Primitive World*

and Transformation (Ithaca, N.Y., 1953), 51–58. Mintz and Price suggested that a simple encounter model positing a cultural unity of West Africa whose elements could be transferred or modified in the New World must be rejected as a useful approach to the problem. They maintained that scholars may be better served by focusing more on values and attitudes that define social relations—the underlying principles that govern family, kinship, and communal activities—as the source of cultural unity in West Africa and cultural continuity with an African past

2 See John Blassingame, *The Slave Community: Plantation Life in the Antebellum South* (New York, 1972), 1–40; Peter Wood, *Black Majority: Negroes in Colonial South Carolina from 1670 through the Stono Rebellion* (New York, 1974), 167–91; Charles Joyner, *Down by the Riverside: A South Carolina Slave Community* (Urbana, Ill., 1984), 196–224; and Lynne Emery, *Black Dance in the United States from 1619 to 1970* (Palo Alto, Calif., 1972). Lawrence Levine, *Black Culture and Black Consciousness: Afro-American Folk Thought from Slavery to Freedom* (New York, 1977), 3–5, 60–61, addressed the issue of Afro-American cultural transformation directly by suggesting that, regardless of its origins, slave music was a "distinctive Cultural form" that contained not so much African survivals as transformations. Eugene Genovese, *Roll, Jordan, Roll: The World the Slaves Made* (New York, 1972, 1974), 309–13, 318–19, 322–24. Herbert Gutman, *The Black Family in Slavery and Freedom, 1750–1925* (New York, 1976), 194–201. Gutman most nearly followed Mintz and Price's agenda by searching for the hidden structures that governed slave family life.

3 See Robert Fogel and Stanley Engerman, *Time on the Cross: The Economics of American Negro Slavery*, 2 vols. (Boston, 1974), 1: 126–57. Fogel and Engerman found acceptance by Afro-Americans of both a Protestant work ethic and a system of kin organization that emphasized the nuclear family. See also Genovese, *Roll, Jordan, Roll*, 162–63, 283. Genovese argued that the religion of slaves manifested many African traits and exhibited a continuity with African ideas; it also produced a sense of self-worth in a belief system that was shared with the slaveowners.

4 Daniel Scott Smith, "Child-Naming Practices, Kinship Ties, and Change in Family Attitudes in Hingham, Massachusetts, 1641 to 1880," *Journal of Social History*, 18 (1985): 548. The Hingham population is white.

5 Studies of slave-naming practices include Newbell Niles Puckett, "Names of American Negro Slaves," *Studies in the Science of Society*, George Murdock, ed. (New Haven, Conn., 1937): 471–94; Stephen Gudeman, "Herbert Gutman's *The Black Family in Slavery and Freedom, 1750–1925*," *Social Science History*, 2 (1979): 56–65; Mary Beth Norton, *Liberty's Daughters: The Revolutionary Experience of American Women, 1750–1800* (Boston, 1980), 85–87; Darrett Rutman and Anita Rutman, *A Place in Time: Explicatus* (New York, 1985), 97–103; Allan Kulikoff. *Tobacco and Slaves: The Development of Southern Cultures in the Chesapeake, 1680–1800* (Chapel Hill, N.C., 1986), 325–26. Four studies of slave names have focused on the Carolinas: Wood, *Block Majority*, 181–86; Joyner, *Down by the Riverside*, 217–22; Orville Vernon Burton, *In My Father's House Are Many Mansions: Family and Community in Edgefield, South Carolina* (Chapel Hill, N.C., 1985), 165–66; and John C. Inscoe, "Carolina Slave Names: An Index to Acculturation," *Journal of Southern History*, 49 (1983): 527–54. Both Wood and Joyner are particularly interested in the use of African "day-names" in eighteenth and nineteenth-century South Carolina. Inscoe uses names to date a transition to biblical names among Carolina slaves in the early nineteenth century. Gutman's work and my own have focused on the use of family names by slaves. See Gutman, *The Black Family*, 185–201; and Cheryll Ann Cody, "Naming, Kinship and Estate Dispersal: Notes on Slave Family Life on a South Carolina Plantation, 1786 to 1833," *William and Mary Quarterly*, 3d ser., 39 (1982): 192–211.

6 See my unpublished dissertation, "Slave Demography and Family Formation: A Community Study of the Ball Family Plantations, 1720–1896" (Ph.D. dissertation, University of Minnesota, 1982), for details of the years of documentation for each site. On the impact of the 1819 sale of John Ball's slaves, see Cheryll Ann Cody, "'Painful Though It Might Be': Inheritance Practices and Slave Families on the Ball Plantations," Working Papers of the Social History Workshop, 86–3, Department of History, University of Minnesota; and Cody, "Slave Demography and Family Formation," 323–57.

7 More than 600 maternal slave histories were reconstituted from plantation records of the Balls housed in several archives, including Plantation Journal 1720–1782; and Blanket and

Cloth Book 1833 to 1844, both in Miscellaneous Papers, Private Collection of Mr. Elias Ball (now at the South Carolina Historical Society). John and Keating S. Ball Plantation Books, vols. 1–10; and William J. Ball Plantation Books, vols. 1–2, both in Southern Historical Collection, University of North Carolina, Chapel Hill. Blanket Book and Register of Isaac Ball for Midway, Limerick, Jericho, Quinby and Hyde Park (ca. 1804–1821); and Clothing and Blanket Book of John Ball's Slaves, 1830–1833, both in Ball Family Papers, South Carolina Historical Society, Columbia. Keating S. Ball, Comingtee Plantation Book, 1849–1896, Ball Family Papers, 1696–1800, South Caroliniana Library, University of South Carolina, Columbia. Keating S. Ball Plantation Book, 1860–1867, Ball Family Papers, 1792–1834, William Perkins Library, Duke University, Durham, N.C. Record series include: Wills; and Inventories, Charleston District; South Carolina Department of Archives and History, Columbia. The first register runs from 1720 to 1735 and lists the names of slaves born at Comingtee and slaves purchased by Elias Ball during each year. The second register spans 1735 to 1785 and for each child lists the date of birth, child's name, and mother's name, noting occasionally the death of the child. A third register, which overlaps the second, includes births from 1735 to 1817 with similar information.

8   See John and Keating S. Ball Plantation Books, vol. 5, Southern Historical Collection, University of North Carolina, Chapel Hill; Anne Simons Deas, *Recollections of the Ball Family of South Carolina and the Comingtee Plantation* (Charleston, S.C., 1978)

9   Smith, "Child-Naming Practices," 565; Rutman and Rutman, *A Place in Time: Explicatus*, 86.

10   Deas, *Recollections of Comingtee*, 72–77.

11   Smith, "Child-Naming Practices," 566; and Rutman and Rutman, *A Place in Time: Explicatus* 87, 99.

12   Deas, *Recollections of Comingtee*, 66–69.

13   The use of middle names also brought a new dimension to necronymic naming. Among the children of John Ball, Sr., and Martha Carolina Swinton, Angelina Matilda received the middle name of her recently deceased sister as her first name, and Edward William shared the two names of his deceased half-brothers. Other children were given surnames as their middle names, including Coming, Swinton, and Splatt. The use of Latin names also increased the opportunities for necronymic naming. One son, who shared the first name of his deceased half-brother, was called Elias Octavius.

14   Smith has altered his interpretation of the nineteenth-century decline in the practice of necronymic naming. He originally equated the practice with a parental failure to recognize the child as a unique being; Daniel Scott Smith, "Child Naming Patterns and Family Structure Change; Hingham, Massachusetts, 1640–1880," Newberry Papers in Family Community History, 76–5 (January 1977), 6. Smith later argued that, as death became romanticized, the intensity of grieving increased, and the connection between child and name more binding, families felt it was no longer appropriate to reuse a name. Smith, "Child-Naming Practices," 546–47.

15   The number of plantations, size of slave populations, and regular absenteeism of the owners all make it unlikely that the Balls continued to select the names of slave children after the first generation born in South Carolina. For example, the inventory of the estate of John Ball, Sr., in 1817 lists 669 slaves at nine plantations and in Charleston. In Burton's recent study of Edgefield County, South Carolina, he avoided taking a position on whether slaves or owners named slave children; Burton, *In My Father's House*, 166. Only one of twenty-four entries of births to slave mothers in Thomas Chaplin's diary of Tombee plantation notes that Chaplin named the slave infant. Theodore Rosengarten, *Tombee: A Portrait of a Cotton Planter; with the Journal of Thomas B. Chaplin (1820–1890)* (New York, 1986), 330, 358, 364, 496, 501, 504, 533, 536, 589, 612, 633, 635, 640, 669, 674, 695, 711–12.

16   There is some evidence to suggest that the selection of a child's name did not rest solely with slave parents. Joyner argues that some slaves were named by their grandparents, a continuation of an African practice; *Down by the Riverside*, 220–21. A notation made by Keating S. Ball in 1876 lends support to the view that the selection and ritual recording of a child's name may have included a broader kin, in this instance the child's maternal grandmother. He recorded, "Mother Judy Johnson formerly of this place now at Hagan St. Thomas; Nov 22; male; Ben entered at the request of Dorcus Pinckney the grandmother"; Keating S. Ball, Comingtee Plantation Book, 1849–1896.

17 Inscoe, "Carolina Slave Names," 539–40. Inscoe detected a pattern of avoidance of owners' names on the plantations he studied.

18 Angola Ame was brought to Comingtee in 1726 when she was probably less than ten years old. Windsor does not appear in either the birth or purchase records for 1720 through 1735, suggesting that his birth occurred before 1720 or that he was purchased sometime between 1735 and 1743. Either scenario would be consistent with the record of the births of his children.

19 Wood, *Black Majority*, 181–82.

20 Deas, *Recollections of Comingtee*, 66–71.

21 "A List of Negroes the Property of Elias Ball, Made the 12th Day of May 1784," Ball Family Papers, South Carolina Historical Society; Cody, "Slave Demography and Family Formation," 50–55.

22 George R. Stewart, *American Given. Names: Their Origin and History in the Context of the English Language* (New York, 1979), 29–31.

23 Inscoe, "Carolina Slave Names," 541–46.

24 John Ball Plantation Books, Southern Historical Collection, Chapel Hill.

25 Wood, *Black Majority*. 182–83; Joyner, *Down by the Riverside*, 218–19.

26 "Catalogue of Books at Marshland Farm Belonging to John Ball," Ball Family Papers, Perkins Library, Duke University, Durham, N.C.

27 *Ibid.*

28 Smith, "Child-Naming Practices"; and Rutman and Rutman, *A Place in Time: Explicatus*, 83–106.

29 Three features of these distributions should be noted. First, as a result of the large size of the pool of names and the relatively small number of cases, many of the rankings are shared by two or more names. Second, names used, with less frequency and ranked lower than the leading names have an even greater number of tied rankings. These two features render more powerful a statistical approach to the comparative ranking and ordering of the names of limited value. The Rutmans compute Spearman's rho and Pearsonian r as correlation coefficients between each period and the preceding period for which they have naming evidence. This method is problematic in distributions with a large number of tied rank-ings. The result of such computations is an apparently higher level of correlation. On the uses and misuses of Spearman's rho. see John Mueller, Karl Schuessler, and Herbert Coster, *Statistical Reasoning in Sociology* (Boston, 1977). 260–63. Third, formal names and diminu-tives that are counted together should be considered related names but not interchangeable in the written record of the slave population maintained by the Balls. Thus, Mary, Maria, Maryanne, and Marion were four individuals who shared a name that was common in root but not used interchangeably. Because slaveowners were interested in maintaining a broad pool of names, they carefully and consistently recorded all variations in the sound of a name as a distinctive name. This is not to say that nicknames were not in use; however, the written record does not indicate this type of variation for individuals.

30 On the Huguenot influence in South Carolina, see Jon Butler. *The Huguenots in America: A Refugee People in New World Society* (Cambridge. Mass., 1983).

31 Wood cites J. L. Dillard in suggesting that the popularity of Binah as a South Carolina slave name may have as its root the African day-name Cubena, for girls born on a Tuesday. See Wood, *Black Majority*, 183; and J. L. Dillard, *Black English* (New York, 1972), 129–30.

32 "Catalogue of Books at Marshland Farm."

33 James Ramsey, "An Essay on the Treatment and Conversion of the African Slaves in the British Sugar Islands" (London, 1784); see Folarin Shyllon, *James Ramsey: The Unknown Abolitionist* (Edinburgh, 1977).

34 Beilby Porteus, "A Letter to the Governors, Legislatures, and Proprietors of Plantations in the British West India Islands" (London, 1808).

35 In 1784, only Comingtee had a gross imbalance between the sexes. At Kensington, also owned by Elias Ball, the sex ratio among adults was 91 males per 100 females. Cody, "Slave Demography and Family Formation," 51–54.

36 Deas, *Recollections of Comingtee*, 166–167.

37 Cody, "Naming, Kinship and Estate Dispersal," 198–203. Slaves on the Gaillard plantation seem to have used the repetition of kin names to link a child with deceased kin or a family member who had been sold or removed from the plantations.

Chapter 16

Philip D. Morgan

THE SIGNIFICANCE OF KIN

IT IS ONE THING TO HAVE KINFOLK around, but it is another entirely to recognize and regulate relationships with them in such a way as to demonstrate their significance. When slaves can be shown to be aware of, and openly making use of, kin ties, it is possible to speak of a kinship system coming into being and of its being passed from one generation to the next. Visiting is important, then, because it provides one measure of the quality of kinship relationships among slaves. To explore further the meaning attached to kin, four relationships are worth investigating in more detail: husbands and wives, parents and children, siblings, and extended kin. By way of conclusion, the possible African influences on this emerging kinship system can then be assessed.[1]

Although slave unions were put under extraordinary pressure by slavery, marriage was a vital institution in the slave community. In general, slaves chose their own marital partners. When Henry Laurens sent one young woman to his Mepkin plantation, he told the overseer to allow her 'to be a Wife to whome she shall like the best amongst the single men.' Slaves acted not only independently but with dispatch. Two 'New Negroes,' bought in South Carolina and destined for an East Florida plantation, 'chose each other for man and wife' before they arrived. As she was being transferred from one John Carter's quarters to another, a Virginia girl fell ill and "before there was another opportunity of sending her" got one of the "Negro fellows for her husband." The rather perfunctory nature of slave courtship is also suggested in an incident on Robert Carter's estate. One Monday, Abraham of Dickerson Mill quarter visited Gemini quarter and "prevailed" with Milly "to go with him" back to his quarter "he calling Milly his wife." Carter consented to the transfer. In fact, masters rarely interfered. David Ross spoke for many when he declared that his "young people might connect themselves in marriage, to their own liking," although he added, "with consent of their parents who were the best judges." Most young slaves, then, acted voluntarily; rarely were they forced into marriage by a master; they required a master's consent but apparently parental consent, too.[2]

Particularly common in the Chesapeake was the slave who came to a master to ask permission to marry another owner's slave. In 1789, Frank did precisely this, asking "leave" of his master, Colonel Francis Taylor of Orange County, to "have Miss M. Conway's Pat for a Wife." Taylor employed Frank as his messenger and errand-runner, a valuable slave whose wishes ought to be respected if possible and who already traveled off the plantation. Thus Taylor "did not object," particularly when Frank told him that he "had the necessary consent" from Miss Conway. Frank must have anticipated his master's approval, because he had already arranged the wedding for the following evening.[3]

The ceremonial element of slave marriages was necessarily constrained. The origins of the nineteenth-century custom of "jumping the broomstick"—as a way of signifying a marriage—may well lie in the eighteenth century, but no trace of its existence has been found. One of the few firsthand observations is rather dismissive of any ritualistic quality to slave marriages. John Brickell, the historian of early North Carolina, explained that slave marriages were "generally performed amongst themselves, there being very little ceremony used upon that Head." However, he noted one common feature: "The Man makes the Woman a Present, such as a *Brass Ring* or some other Toy, which if she accepts of, becomes his Wife; but if ever they part from each other which frequently happens, upon any little Disgust, she returns his present." James Barclay, who acted as an overseer on a Lowcountry plantation in the early 1770s, also detected little ceremony, but much conviviality, in slave marriages. Marriages took place at night in his neighborhood, and a couple with many acquaintances might draw "several hundred" slaves from surrounding plantations. The owner often allowed a hog or two, the slaves served land tortoises and rum bought from their Sunday earnings, and the whole night was spent "eating and drinking, singing, dancing, and roaring."[4]

If slave courtships and weddings appeared perfunctory, the same cannot be said of the slaves' view of marriage. When the colony of Virginia demanded a female slave replacement for every man sent to aid South Carolina in the Yamassee War of 1715, Carolinians rejected the request on the grounds that slave husbands might rebel. In 1723, the governor of Virginia thought that transportation would be an effective punishment for the ringleaders of a slave conspiracy because "separation from their wives and children is almost as terrible to them as death itself." A Maryland slave, destined to be taken to Virginia to satisfy a debt, spoke in exactly these terms. He had such "a great Affection" for his family that he "declar'd Several times that he will Loose his life, or had rather Submit to Death then go to Virginia to leave his Wife and Children." When his removal appeared imminent, he asserted that he "had much rather be hang'd than come to Virginia." The loss of a chosen partner was the occasion for grief. When the wife of one of James Habersham's male slaves died, the husband was "inconsolable." Slaves clearly took marriage very seriously.[5]

Within and without marriage, slave women were strong figures. They often brought up their children alone; in that sense, many slave families were matrifocal. Women worked alongside men in the fields, even predominated in some field gangs, which might well have inclined them to think themselves the equals of men. The self-reliance and self-sufficiency of many slave women impressed white contemporaries. Henry Laurens attributed the transgressions of his slave March, who apparently had "a placid and obliging disposition," to his recent "Union" with Mary, a woman of "very great abilities" but who had long been "the bane" of Laurens's "Negro families." Not only had she "corrupted and ruined March," but she had schooled Cuffee, one of her sons, to follow in her footsteps. James Barclay marveled at the hardiness of slave women, many of whom turned out to work the day after childbirth, bearing their infants on their backs. Because slave men lacked much of the power that flows from the ownership and distribution of property, often failed to gain recognition as fathers, and were largely denied the role of provider, a picture of relative equality between the sexes under slavery may be plausible.[6]

If slavery bred strong women, however, it hardly emasculated black men. For one thing, as Jacqueline Jones has argued, the state of powerlessness that affected all slaves renders "virtually meaningless the concept of equality as it applies to marital relations." Furthermore, the male monopoly on most skilled and privileged positions cannot be ignored. Lorena Walsh, speaking of the late-eighteenth-century Chesapeake, wryly observes that black women indeed "shared the doubtful advantages of greater equality with black men—usually the equal privilege of working with hoes and axes in the tobacco, corn, and grain fields." In fact, as men gained opportunities for more varied work, more women spent time in monotonous drudgery. In large part because of their greater work opportunities, men traveled more than women. In divided-residence households, husbands, not wives, were the routine visitors. The growing importance of two-parent, male-centered households is indisputable. The naming practices of families, explored below, suggest the importance of the father and husband. Finally, in most rebellions and conspiracies that did materialize in early America, men rather than women dominated. Virtually no black woman, for example, was implicated in Gabriel's conspiracy in Virginia, and indeed one male conspirator required a recruit not to divulge their secrets to a woman.[7]

Slave husbands tended to be older than their wives. In the eighteenth-century Chesapeake, eight of ten husbands were older than their wives by an average of nine years. In the few cases in which wives were older than husbands, the age gap was much smaller—an average of four years. Similarly, in the eighteenth-century Lowcountry, seven of ten husbands were older than their wives by an average of eight years, two of ten wives were older than husbands by four years, and in one of ten marriages the spouses were the same age. Such large age differences owed much to the imbalance of the sexes in these two eighteenth-century societies, although African customs might also have played a role, for large age gaps between spouses were commonplace in many African societies. Whatever the origins, the major implication seems clear. In North America (and in Africa, too, it might be added), authority clearly followed age. For better or ill, then, slave husbands were in a more powerful position than their wives.[8]

Masters, in fact, often saw slave husbands as domineering. Perhaps these observations owed something to the patriarchal assumptions of the day, but their very pervasiveness suggests some basis in life. In Virginia, thirty-seven-year-old Charles "took" his nineteen-year-old wife with him when he ran away; Will "carried" away his wife and young child; fifty-year-old Tony and his forty-year-old wife, Phillis, were expected to make for Lancaster because that is where *he* wished to return. A master of an African couple, a twenty-year-old man and a sixteen-year-old woman, "imagine[d]" that the wife was "entirely governed" by the husband. Even when the wife was older, the husband apparently assumed the dominant role, for twenty-one-year-old Mack "carried with him" his thirty-three-year-old wife, Molly. Likewise, in South Carolina, husbands appear to have been the dominant partners: Cupid "inticed" his wife to run away; Toby came to Samuel Bonneau's plantation and removed his wife and young child; Binah's husband "persuaded her" to abscond with him.[9]

African beliefs concerning the respective roles of husbands and wives probably contributed to the upper hand held by men. In the Lowcountry, Charles Ball encountered a creole woman named Lydia, who had been "compelled" to marry an African. Her husband was atypical in that he "had been a priest in his own nation, and had never been taught to do any kind of labour." He also claimed to have "had ten wives in his own country, who all had to work for, and wait upon him." As a result, he "refused to give" Lydia "the least assistance in doing anything." Although this African man's view of marriage was probably unusual, it was not singular: Ball noted that Lydia was just "one of the women whose husbands procured little or nothing for the sustenance of their families." Her husband's stipulation that she "do all the little work that it was necessary to perform in the cabin; and also to bear all the labour of weeding and cultivating the family patch or garden" was one apparently shared by other of his countrymen.[10]

Some slave men adopted a cavalier attitude to matrimony itself. When Robert Carter sent three young men to the Baltimore Company ironworks in 1783, he described them to the manager as "all men of gallantry, Polygamists, and they may now want Physick proper in the venereal disease." Similarly, when twenty-one-year-old Jack of Dinwiddie County ran away to Prince George County in 1777, he was "supported and concealed . . . by several Negro Women whom he calls his Wives; his greatest Favourite amongst them belongs to Robert Bates." In South Carolina, the Reverend Francis Le Jau had trouble with a slave man who "had vowed to keep to his lawful Wife" (the reference to "lawful," a significant comment in itself) but "thro' love for another Man's wife . . . has been quite distracted and furious." Rather than trying to deal with the man, Le Jau significantly attempted to keep the "Adultress" away from him. Other slave men apparently used their privileged occupational status to their advantage. Cambridge was a boatman and had "a wife at almost every landing on Rappahannock, Mattapony, and Pamunkey Rivers"; Billy Barber was a much-traveled waiting man who lived in Urbanna but had a wife in Norfolk and in Hampton as well as in his hometown. Male promiscuity may conceivably reflect an assertion of masculinity in the face of feelings of inadequacy, but it hardly contradicts the domineering demeanor otherwise noted of slave men.[11]

Consider a young slave named Nero who formed liaisons with a number of women in the late-eighteenth-century Lowcountry. In March 1779, John M'Illraith advertised for two runaways from his plantation at Four Holes: Nero and a young woman named Marianne. At about the same time, Martin Pfeniger, also of Four Holes, declared his twenty-year-old woman Bynah missing. In early April, Pfeniger resorted to the advertisement columns yet again to announce the departure of his twenty-four-year-old woman, Cloe, who had been seen with Nero. Finally, a third owner from Four Holes, Thomas Caton, made sense of these seemingly separate scraps of information when he advertised for a twenty-four-year-old woman who had left him in May. According to Caton, the precocious mulatto Nero had "deluded or led away" all these women, "and it is supposed and partly proved by account, that the said fellow supports and provides for them all." For the past six months, Nero and his female companions had been seen at James Island, Sullivan's Island, Saint James Goose Creek, and Charleston. Quite who provided for whom is made less clear when Caton observed that these slaves found employment by washing and ironing for white folk. This was women's work, so perhaps Nero lived off the labors of his consorts.[12]

Finally, although slavery in general denied slave families the ability to function as self-subsisting units, men were occasionally able to look out for their families. Slave ironworkers in the Chesapeake purchased small luxuries and domestic items for their wives. During the 1730s, one skilled hand at the Baltimore Company iron-works in Maryland used his overwork pay to purchase a bed, two blankets, and a rug for his wife and children. In 1797, a slave named Phil, who worked at John Blair's foundry in Virginia, bought shoe leather and seven and a half yards of ribbon for his wife. Even ordinary field hands could provide for their womenfolk. Charles Ball's father came to see his family on a Saturday night, always bringing "some little present," such as "apples, melons, sweet potatoes, or, if he could procure nothing else, a little parched corn." North Carolina slaves "allowed to plant a sufficient quantity of *Tobacco* for their own use" and to gather snake-root used the proceeds to purchase "*Linnen, Bracelets, Ribbons*, and several other Toys for their Wives and Mistresses." Slave men were not totally bereft of the ability to provide small favors for their women.[13]

What is important to notice, however, no matter which sex provided these small domestic items, is their existence at all. The ability of even unskilled slave families to acquire a little property that they could call their own was important. Consider Caesar and Kate, both born in Virginia in the early 1730s. Neither possessed a skill, although both were "smooth tongued, and very sensible." Of what their domestic life consisted we cannot know, except for two small details. The first may suggest that they enjoyed smoking tobacco together after a long day of field labor, for both had "Teeth somewhat worn with Pipes." The second is more telling, for in 1772, when they decided to abscond together from their home in King William County, they were thought likely to go by water at least part of the way, for they took with them a "Variety of Clothes, and Articles for House keeping not very portable." Even families divided by ownership could own property in common. A slave couple who lived apart in piedmont Virginia still shared posses-sions, for the wife was convicted of receiving stolen goods from her husband and storing them in his chest, which was in her custody. Similarly, when Jemmy absented himself from the fields one day, wearing only his shirt and trousers, "which were of very good rolls, much wore," by rights his master ought to have been able to provide a good description. However, Jemmy then went to a neighboring plan-tation, and carried off "other clothes, together with his wife, and a boy of 12 to 14 years old, with all the luggage." Two South Carolina fugitives—Bess and Berwick —were seen passing through Ponpon on a Monday morning, each on horseback, with their clothes, blankets—and pets! Housekeeping items, substantial furniture, luggage, even pets: slaves would not be denied a semblance of domesticity.[14]

Much more important than taking along a few domestic items, fugitives took family members with them. Many runaways aimed to visit a spouse, but just as significant were those who ran away *with* a spouse. About one in ten of the fugi-tives advertised in South Carolina and Virginia newspapers ran away with family members. Half of these family groups consisted of a husband and wife, sometimes with children. Although groups were conspicuous and slow-moving, the desire to keep a family together overrode the dangers. Indeed, by the late eighteenth century, slaves even risked moving in larger groups. Thus, in 1784, Polidore and his wife, Betty, together with their three young children, another couple, Cyrus and his wife, Charity, and a woman named Hannah with her son, Job, fled Charleston, apparently hoping to make their way together to Camden. A year later, Robin and his wife, Charity, together with their two young sons and another couple, Jack and his wife, Hannah, all fled the same plantation in Charlotte County, Virginia, apparently with forged passes and in hopes of passing as free people.[15]

Slaves went to extreme lengths to maintain their marriages. Poignantly and expressively, slaves tell us what was dearest to their hearts. None spoke more eloquently than Chesapeake slaves, who faced even more forced separations than their Lowcountry counterparts. When James belonging to Fleet Coxe heard that his wife and two children were about to be removed to Frederick County, he visited her master and proposed that he be exchanged for another male slave so that he might accompany his family. After Christopher Collins bought a slave woman named Judy, he received repeated visits from her husband, Tobit, who made "several applications to me to endeavour to keep him and his wife together." Indeed, Collins observed in a letter written to Tobit's master, "He is now here pressing me." Sam, a carpenter on Robert Carter's Cancer plantation, deserted his post to be near his wife, who belonged to Charles Carter. Sam's complaint that it was "a hard case to be separated from his wife," together with the intercession of his overseer, carried the day, and Carter acceded to the transfer.[16]

When Charles Ball first learned that he would be sold from Maryland to Georgia, his first thoughts were of his wife and children. As he put it, "My heart died away within me." Shocked and numbed, "I felt incapable of weeping or speaking," he later recollected, "and in my despair I laughed loudly." Hands bound, Ball set out southward that same day, his request to see his family one last time rudely denied. On his journey he dreamed of his wife and children "beseeching and imploring my master on their knees not to carry away from them." Ball had only his memories to keep alive his sense of family affiliation. And, in time, those memories inevitably dimmed. Symbolic perhaps was the day he decided to lay aside his old straw hat, the one "my wife had made for me in Maryland," so as to "avoid the appearance of singularity" among his fellow cotton hands. The discarding of this concrete reminder of family feeling—an important way for slaves to affirm family ties—probably weighed on Ball more than even he knew and accounted for his recollection of the event many years later.[17]

Lowcountry slaves were equally distraught at the thought of family separation. When seven or eight slave families were on the verge of being "torn to pieces," Henry Laurens predicted "*great distraction* among the whole." Similarly, when Thomas Wright, on his deathbed, decided to bequeath a slave to his friend, he determined not to do it in the presence of the slaves, "observing that it might occasion *some uneasiness*" among them. The news of a prospective separation was like a stone thrown into a lake: the ripples of concern extended far and wide. And once a separation had occurred, Lowcountry slaves, like their Chesapeake cousins, strove to put right the damage. Two planters in the Cheraws district agreed to an exchange of slaves in order to reunite a wife and her husband. The impetus for the exchange apparently came from below, because one master agreed to it "for Peace sake." In 1764, William Simpson, a resident of Savannah, was "disobliged" by one of his male slaves, which induced him to sell the man along with his son. During the next three years, the bondman wrote "to his wife frequently, and appear[ed] by his letters to be in great distress for want of her." Believing sufficient punishment had been wrought, Simpson inquired of the new owner whether the two slaves had behaved well enough "to intitle them to any favour or indulgence." If so, Simpson offered to sell the man's wife and four other children in order to reunite the family. Ending on a moralistic note, unbefitting his earlier action, Simpson declared, "A separation of those unhappy people is adding distress to their unfortunate condition."[18]

The lengths to which slaves went to keep marriages together testifies to the strength of the bond between husband and wife. Slaves invariably chose their partners, underwent some form of ceremony to signify a marital union, and showed great distress when forced separations occurred. Women were not submissive: they often raised children alone, they did the same kind of work as men, and they were —often had to be—self-reliant. Men were not emasculated: they monopolized skilled posts, they were generally much older than their wives, they often domineered and sometimes exploited their womenfolk, but most often they headed families and tried as best they could to support them. For the most part, slave men and women took marriage very seriously.

They also took their responsibility as parents seriously, even though the realities of slavery always made caring for children difficult. Crèvecoeur, for instance, argued that slaves "have no time, like us, tenderly to rear their helpless offspring, to nurse them on their knees, to enjoy the delight of being parents. Their paternal fondness is embittered by considering, that if their children live, they must live to be slaves like themselves." Perhaps the distance that slave parents had often to place between themselves and their children accounts for one slave couple's willingness to part with their son Primas, "and he with them," when their master, then resident in London, requested the services of a boy as a personal servant. Perhaps also the opportunities involved in metropolitan service and proximity to an influential master outweighed the pains of separation. Some slave parents might have become so embittered at their offsprings' prospects that they took their children's lives. In 1760, Jenny of King George County was tried for murdering her daughter; thirteen years later, the Brunswick County court found Sall guilty of killing her child; and, in 1779, the Caroline County court tried Patt for the same offense, although she was eventually acquitted. To be sure, accusing slave mothers of crimes, in the context of the far larger crime of slavery, reflected the authorities' hypocrisy. An old slave woman's answer to a question about how many children she had was a most effective riposte. She replied that she had "five to her present Mistress and three to her last—the father was left out of the question."[19]

Although a measure of callousness and passivity was almost inherent in a parent–child relationship under slavery, most slave parents were loving and caring. They might well have been bitter, but not generally toward their children. Charles Ball encountered a slave mother who carried her young child all day on her back, while working with the hoe, because she could not bear hearing the child's cries if left at the end of the row. When a slave child died at Nomini Hall, the parents were so distraught, so overwhelmed with "overflowing Grief," that they did not appear at the funeral. The response of "an old, stooped, worn-out Negro" on a Georgia plantation to the Reverend Henry Muhlenberg's suggestion that the minister become the owner of the old man's "half-grown daughter" also revealed strong parental feelings. Although Muhlenberg promised to treat the girl as his "own child," the father "showed by his fearful countenance and gestures that he would rather lose his own life than be separated from his daughter." His conscience pricked, a chastened Muhlenberg confided to his journal that he had never intended to carry out the proposal.[20]

By their actions, many runaway slaves demonstrate that they, too, were not about to be separated from their children. Families that included quite old children sometimes ran away together. The record for the largest eighteenth-century fugitive family goes to forty-five-year-old Bacchus and his thirty-five-year-old wife, Betty, who, in 1789, fled in a six-oared canoe, apparently making their way to Georgia. They took with them six offspring: twenty-year-old Andrew, eighteen-year-old Sarah, fifteen-year-old Little Bacchus, twelve-year-old Bess, seven-year-old Kate, and two-year-old Grace. More common than two-parent families with children were single parents, usually mothers, and children. Occasionally, women like Jenny, "very big with child," summoned the resolve to elope: she left with a toddler in tow. These pregnant women perhaps wanted to be near their husbands when the baby was born. Mothers sometimes ran off with large numbers of children. Twenty-six-year-old Lucy gathered up her four children—two boys, aged eight and six, and two younger girls—for the long trek from Saint Thomas Parish in South Carolina to Savannah in Georgia, where she had sisters and other relations. Only one fugitive slave was reported to have left children behind when running away: she was a forty-year-old woman named Hannah, the mother of two young children and a resident of Charleston. However, she might not have abandoned her offspring, because she was "frequently" seen in the city as a runaway. Few single fathers ran away with children. Forty-year-old Bow, who fled Charleston with his twelve-year-old son Sandy, and forty-six-year-old Bristol, who took along his thirteen-year-old son, also named Bristol, for the trip from Horse Savannah to Johns Island, were the exceptions. Most male fugitives were unencumbered by children, in part because these men were too young to have married.[21]

As adults, slaves maintained ties to their parents. About nine of every ten slaves said to be visiting parents in both Virginia and South Carolina were adults, and most (like other fugitives) were in their twenties or early thirties. Jemmy was typical: age twenty-eight, a resident of Charleston, purchased as a boy from a Black River plantation where his parents still resided, and thought likely "to pay them a visit during his absence." Quite elderly slaves turned to their parents for support. Thirty-six-year-old Saucy, a Maryland slave, made his capture that much harder by changing his clothing, courtesy of his father, who lived on a quarter fourteen miles away. In South Carolina, forty-year-old Robin was thought to have gone to a plantation where his mother and other relations lived, while fifty-two-year-old Hesther, her master concluded, had long prepared her "jaunt" to mother and family. The parental bond was obviously vital for many adult slaves, even at advanced ages. Most runaways who were said to be visiting a parent ran to a mother, but slightly more than a third were thought to be running either to fathers or to both parents.[22]

The few slaves who penned autobiographies in the eighteenth century spoke fondly of their parents. Boston King, a South Carolina slave, especially respected his African father, who never swore in front of others and prayed with his family every night. "To the utmost of his power," King recalled, "he endeavored to make his family happy, and his death was a very great loss to us all." James Carter, a former Virginia slave, recalled conversations with his parents when searching for his fugitive brother, who had been killed by his overseer. His mother, for instance, had addressed him as follows: "Do my Son try and get home by sun set we may hear of your brother and you can help your father to get him home." In the early nineteenth century, Carter observed that his mother, then aged sixty-four, had just been freed, no longer being "of any service" to the Armistead family. He had attempted to purchase his father, then aged sixty-seven, in order that he might "go and Live with [his] Mother." Carter obviously retained strong ties of affection to his parents.[23]

Younger children, by word and deed, reveal similarly strong attachments to parents. In 1740, Robert Pringle, a Charleston merchant, decided to sell his girl Esther, who was a good house servant, because "she had a practice of goeing frequently to her Father and Mother, who Live at a Plantation I am concern'd in about Twenty Miles from [Charles] Town." Esther's frequent visits are eloquent reminders of the pain young children felt at being separated from parents, pain put into words by a Virginia slave boy named Bob. In the early 1800s, St. George Tucker replaced his waiting man, Johnny, with the boy Bob. Tucker traveled around Virginia as a lawyer, and Bob was separated from his mother, who lived in Williamsburg. The boy wrote to his mother; once he awakened Tucker by calling out in his sleep as he dreamed about his "mammy"; and on another occasion, he greeted a returning Tucker by saying, "I am mighty glad to see you, Sir, . . . I couldn't have been gladder to see anybody but my mammy and my sister." Bob's "affectionate temper" toward his mother touched the heart of his master.[24]

Masters were quick to recognize slave parents, mothers in particular, as protective and caring of their children. Landon Carter wondered whether slave mothers were not too indulgent toward their offspring. He believed that slave children were prone to sickness from being allowed to "press their appetites" and eat "loads of Gross food." Thus, when, in 1774, a slave mother came "bellowing" about her six-year-old girl "all swelled up to the eyes," Carter suspected that she had "been stuffing Potatoes [down her child] for some time." The master of Sabine Hall also engaged in a tussle of wills with his "Suckling wenches" about the frequency and duration of their absences from the field to attend to their infants. They wanted five feeding times, he only three. He was also aware that the death of a child was not easily passed off, for he observed that Winny was much "affected" by the loss of her daughter. Other members of the Carter clan came to understand the strong attachments that bound slave mothers to their children. In 1778, for example, Robert Carter of Nomini Hall sent a young woman and her two small children to the Baltimore Company ironworks because she would "not agree that her children stay with her relations." Twelve years later, the same master faced an angry mother who complained that her son and another boy who lived with her had been beaten unnecessarily by an overseer. Carter ordered the overseer to correct more moderately in the future and to "make a proper allowance for the Feelings of a Mother."[25]

Nor could masters ignore the important role of fathers. Landon Carter's plowman, a slave named Manuel, broke open the hut in which his daughter Sarah had been confined and freed her. On another occasion, the master of Sabine Hall lamented the roguery of his slave Johnny and "all his family bred under him," a comment that hardly suggests powerless slave fathers. On the Nomini Hall estate, carpenter George remarried but did not forget his child of a former marriage. When, in 1781, his former wife died, he asked his master to let his seven-year-old daughter Betty live with him and his new wife. Earlier on the same estate, Philip Fithian, the resident tutor, admitted Dennis, "the Lad who waits at Table," into school at his father's request. These fathers were important figures in their households.[26]

Some slave parents, and particularly fathers, could pass on to their children one important possession—their skill. They made the most of the opportunity. Woodworking was the most common trade in which a son might follow his father, but others gradually opened up even to mothers and their children. England and his two sons—twenty-one-year-old Prince and nineteen-year-old Prosper—were bricklayers. Two of George Washington's young ditchers were sons of Boatswain, the head ditcher. Bess, in her seventies, still practiced midwifery, along with daughter Flora, who was in her late forties, on the Pinckney plantations. By the late eighteenth century, slave families with a range of skills were beginning to emerge. Although some skilled slaves might have been passive recipients of masters' favors, others were active agents in passing on their trades to their children. Thus, when his son turned twelve and of working age, John Thomas, a slave blacksmith who resided on Robert Carter's Nomini Hall plantation, asked that his son be transferred from an outlying quarter to join him in the smith shop. Carter fell in with John's "scheme." A North Carolina cooper, put up for sale with his fifteen-year-old son, who had been "bred to the same work," continually called out, "Who buys me must buy my son too."[27]

Some parents were apparently so successful in passing on their skills to their children that a few families came to monopolize privileged positions on some plantations. When one Chesapeake planter transferred slaves from one quarter to another, he mentioned at least six skilled slaves who were part of just two families. There was "an old fellow called Charles and his son Anthony who have been employed always at the carpenters business," as well as Charles's wife, Betty, who was a house servant and assisted "in overlooking some spinning, her Girls knit, and do Needle Work," together with "Mulatto Milly who was the principal Spinner" and one of her children, who could "spin and work at her Needle." On the Carroll estate in Maryland, in 1773, more than half the tradesmen under age twenty-five learned their trades from kinsmen who were also skilled mechanics.[28]

Fathers passed not only their skills but also their names to their children. Many South Carolina slave families bear out the common practice of naming a son for a father. The first slave families on record in the Carolinas—dating to 1670 in South Carolina and to 1709 in North Carolina—both had sons named for fathers. Among Ball family slaves in the eighteenth century, one in six named a son for a father, whereas fewer than one in ten named a daughter for a mother. Similarly, three of the thirty-three families on the Ravenel plantations named sons for fathers, but only one named a daughter for a mother. On the Pinckney estate, five of a possible nine families (those in which names of fathers and sons are known) transmitted the name of a father to a son, whereas only one of a possible eleven families bequeathed a mother's name to a daughter. Over the course of the colonial period, slave families in South Carolina inventories were four times as likely to pass on a father's name to a son as a mother's name to a daughter, and five times as likely by the 1760s and 1770s.[29]

A similar pattern can be discerned among Virginia slaves, although it grew less pronounced over time. A listing of the Jones family slaves, taken in 1740, indicates that five families named a son for a father (of a possible twenty-one cases in which fathers and sons were named); no family named a daughter for a mother (of a possible twenty cases). In his diary, Landon Carter mentioned in passing that four of his male slaves shared a name with a son; he failed to observe a comparable pattern among his female slaves. Three of William Byrd's slave families, listed in 1772, named sons for fathers; again, no daughter assumed the name of her mother. Even a slave family divided by ownership—perhaps because it was divided by ownership—exhibited this pattern. Thus, when thirty-three-year-old Beck and her seven-year-old son Glasgow, formerly the property of a York County master but since sold to a Hanover County resident, ran away, it should have surprised no one that they were later seen in Hampton, where the head of the family, also named Glasgow, lived. Although the sample sizes are small, on some late-eighteenth-century estates the practice of naming children for parents seems to have become bilateral. At least as many daughters were named for mothers as sons for fathers.[30]

Two explanations may be offered for these patterns. First, naming sons for fathers rather than daughters for mothers may be partly an imitation of white practices. The available evidence suggests that whites did indeed name sons for fathers—on a much greater scale than among slaves—but they also named daughters just as frequently for mothers. If slave practices are considered imitative, then only late-eighteenth-century Virginia slaves approach correspondence to white patterns. Second, the sheer fact of slavery explains the differential naming of sons for fathers as opposed to daughters for mothers. Masters recognized the kinship relationship of a mother to her offspring, not that between a father and his children. Slaves named sons for fathers as their way of asserting that a child had relatives through both paternal and maternal lines. The practice also, of course, points to a more influential role for fathers than a matriarchal view of slave family life would permit.[31]

No doubt there were irresponsible and embittered slave parents, but most were protective and caring. Slave parents assiduously bequeathed the few things they had to their children—their knowledge, their skills, their names. They cared for their infants in the fields, made sure they got enough food, grieved over their death, and feared separation from them. And the children responded to their parents' efforts. They spoke kindly of their parents and ran away to visit them. Slavery severely tested the link between parent and child but never broke it.

The bond between siblings seems to have been particularly strong among slaves. Brothers and sisters played a significant role in some slaves' lives well into adulthood. Thus, Bristol, a young man, who ran away from his master in the Cape Fear region of North Carolina in December 1765, was still at large twenty months later and thought to be in the Northern Neck of Virginia, supported by his three brothers. Peter, in his midtwenties, absented himself from his master for more than a year, roaming widely throughout the South-side region of Virginia, and he ran away again only five days after being captured. He was thought to be with a brother in Surry County or with "several brothers and sisters in North Carolina." Twenty-two-year-old South Carolina slave Will, absent for six weeks before his master advertised for him as a runaway, was thought to have taken refuge with either of his two sisters or a brother in order "to get provisions." A network of brothers and sisters was obviously helpful to the slave runaway.[32]

Even slaves well advanced in years retained close ties to brothers and sisters. Thirty-five-year-old Maria was spotted at a plantation on the Santee River where she had a brother; Jenny, also in her middle to late thirties, was seen going in a wagon from Charleston to inland plantations where two of her brothers resided; forty-year-old Dickey left Saint Stephen Parish and was observed at Dr. Fausseaux's plantation in adjoining Saint John Parish, the residence of his brother. Most notable was fifty-year-old Peter, "somewhat grey, but particularly so in his side locks," a former driver and patroon, who absented himself on March 24, 1796, and remained at large seventeen months later. He had a wife at Goose Creek, where it was thought he spent most of his time, but he had also been seen in Savannah, where he had a sister.[33]

Some siblings made particularly strenuous efforts to renew acquaintances. In 1772, a twenty-two-year-old Virginia-born slave named Kit ran away from his master in Northampton County, North Carolina, and joined up with his brother Tom, who lived in Prince George County, Virginia. Together, they stayed out at least a year and, according to their owners, "committed many Outrages" on or near the Rappahannock River. Similarly, in August 1798, Peter ran away from Charleston, and his master had no doubt about his intentions, for, the previous fall, Peter had made his way to Santee, near Murray's Ferry, where his family resided, and from there to the Canal, where they were working. Peter had followed his old track, his master concluded, because "his brother, named Fortune, was seen with him in town, a noted run-away, belongs to Archibald Campbell, near Murray's Ferry."[34]

Masters recognized and often made use of slaves' strong sibling bonds. When Toby's state of health was pronounced "helpless," his master, Robert Carter, transferred him to Billingsgate quarter so that he could be "under the Care of his Sister Judith, who lives there." John Channing observed that his slave men preferred to have their wives *or* sisters make up their clothes. When masters separated adolescents from their families and transferred them to new quarters, they often kept siblings together. A number of households on the larger Chesapeake and Low-country plantations, in particular, consisted of siblings.[35]

Strong sibling bonds were important to extended family networks. As Herbert Gutman has suggested, they may represent an adaptation of "West African kinship beliefs where particular adult siblings ('mother's brother' and 'father's sister') retained important social functions in families headed by brothers and sisters." At any rate, the role of aunts and uncles in the lives of nieces and nephews appears to have been prominent; even cousins could occasionally be seen cooperating with one another.[36]

Extended kin not only grew more numerous over time, but slaves also increasingly recognized and made use of extended kin in their families. Far more pervasive than naming sons for fathers, for example, was the slave practice of naming children for extended kin. As slaves named for kin, inevitably their pool of names narrowed. This took time, for, in the early formation of any slave plantation, the pool tended to be large, since masters aimed to give each slave a distinctive name that would facilitate easy identification. In 1727, Robert "King" Carter told his overseers to "take care that the negros" recently purchased "always go by the names we gave them." So often were the new names repeated that he was convinced that "every one knew their names and would readly answer to them." Over time, however, as slaves assumed the right to name within families, the pool narrowed considerably. Before 1780, 423 slaves were named in the Ball family record, but 259 shared a name with another slave. In Chesapeake estates by the second half of the eighteenth century, the pool of names tended to be even smaller. Landon Carter mentioned the names of 165 of his slaves in his diary, of which 106, or 64 percent, shared a name (there were 8 Toms, 6 Sarahs, and 6 Bettys). As slaves named for kin, so masters began to use modifiers (place names, ethnic designations, skin color, former owners, and size) to differentiate slaves who shared names. Perhaps that is why they also began to note surnames among their slaves.[37]

The pattern of naming children for extended kin became much the most important way in which the pool of slave names narrowed. Thus, among Ball family slaves in South Carolina, more than 60 percent of families reused the name of a paternal and maternal grandfather for their sons, whereas 71 percent transmitted the name of a maternal grandmother to a daughter. Among Ravenel family slaves, naming for extended kin was widespread. Gibby and Nanny, for example, had twelve children. One child was given the same name as Nanny's brother, two were named for Gibby's sisters, and one shared the same name as Gibby's mother. Savey and Sarry had six children. Two sons were named after uncles (paternal and maternal), two daughters were named for aunts (again, in both lines), while a fifth child took the name of Sarry's mother. Three other Ravenel slave families passed on the names of grandparents to grandchildren. Among Gaillard family slaves, where two-generation kinship networks have been constructed, seven children were named for parents, as opposed to seventy for more extended kin. In 1808, Charles Cotesworth Pinckney listed his slaves, one of whom was Old Anthony. He was the son of Isaac and Molly. Old Anthony had two daughters, Rinah and Molly, the latter named for her grandmother. Rinah named one of her sons Anthony for her father, while Molly named her son after her great-grandfather Isaac, born almost a century earlier. The predominant pattern among eighteenth-century South Carolina slaves was the naming of children for more distant kin in both paternal and maternal lines. Presumably, they wished to link their children to a more distant and, in many cases, an African past.[38]

The greater kinship density present among Chesapeake, as against Lowcountry, slaves is reflected in an even more tightly knit pattern of kin naming. On the Carroll plantations of Anne Arundel County, Maryland, sixty-one slaves were named for blood relatives: nineteen bore the names of grandparents, sixteen of uncles and aunts, nine of great-grandparents and grand uncles or aunts, as opposed to only seventeen for parents, usually the father. Similarly, among Jefferson family slaves at the turn of the century, thirty carried the names of uncles and aunts, twenty-five the names of grandparents, two the names of granduncles, and four the names of great-grandparents, as opposed to twenty-three who assumed their parents' names. By naming their children predominantly for more distant kinfolk, Chesapeake slave parents linked new to past generations. As Gutman has observed, "Slavery had not obliterated familial and social memory."[39]

Extended kin played a particularly active role in a number of Chesapeake slave families. In a dispute between a slave girl and an overseer that came to the attention of Landon Carter, the girl's grandmother manufactured a story to discredit the white manager. The girl begged Carter not to let it be known that she had confessed to the influence of her "Granny," who "would whip her for it." Carter's refusal to remove the girl from under the overseer's charge prompted the grandmother to take revenge by turning loose all of Carter's cattle. She also had the "impudence" to tell Carter that the overseer "starved" her granddaughter. When a mother at Robert Carter's Cancer plantation wanted a nurse for her two-year-old child, Carter arranged for the baby's seventy-one-year-old grandfather to be transferred and "live at Suckey's house he to have the care of both his grand Children." Seventeen-year-old John fled Williamsburg, making for a plantation in Warwick where not just his father but also his grandmother resided.[40]

More remote kin—in-laws, cousins, uncles and aunts, nephews and nieces—cooperated in the Chesapeake, indicating that distant ties could be meaningful. Thus, Landon Carter's slave Tom was reluctant to work in his master's garden, because he did not wish to replace his father-in-law. A decision by two slaves to attend a Baptist meeting without their master's approval was probably made a little easier because the two could rely on each other; they were, after all, cousins. In 1781, when two slaves—Carter Jack, aged about thirty-five, and London, about fifteen—ran away, their master assumed not unnaturally that the adult instigated this flight; Jack also happened to be London's uncle. When one of Robert Carter's slaves gained his freedom, he petitioned his former master to have his wife and twelve-year-old niece come and live with him. He promised to "make an allowance" for both members of *his* family.[41]

Extended kin ties, if less pervasive in the Lowcountry than in the Chesapeake, became of increasing importance to that region's slaves as the century wore on. As early as 1753, a young woman named Doll who ran away from a plantation in Horse Savannah was thought to be harbored by her relations in Charleston, one of whom was an aunt belonging to Mr. Thomas Else. Three years later, twenty-one-year-old Ketch ran away to visit either his father on James Island or his grandmother in Saint George Dorchester. In the decade before the American Revolution, Sam sought support from an aunt and several cousins among Jonathan Scott's slaves, Toby headed for Willtown, where he had an uncle, Jack was "probably" among some of his in-laws, and an apprentice mulatto boy named Richard Collis was thought to have made for Ponpon, where his brother-in-law resided.[42]

By the second half of the century, extended family groups occasionally ran away together in South Carolina. Thus, in 1762, a twenty-three-year-old black male slave named Crack ran away with his free Indian wife, their two-year-old child, and his fifty-year-old mother. In 1783, forty-year-old Clarinda turned up at a plantation in Cheehaw to be with her husband, who had taken her as his wife in Virginia during the Revolutionary war. Clarinda had her twenty-one-year-old daughter Sarah and her sixteen-year-old son Charles in tow, together with her grandchild, Sarah's child in arms. Most remarkable was the four-generational family group that ran away from a Charleston master in 1785: an elderly woman named Jenny, her thirty-five-year-old daughter Dido, her granddaughter Tissey, and her great-granddaughter, Tissey's suckling child.[43]

The important role of extended kin in slaves' lives may derive in part from African beliefs. The slaves' propensity for thinking in kinship forms—the use of familial terms, particularly "aunt" and "uncle," in addressing nonkin or the important role of fictive kinfolk where kin were absent altogether—corresponds with what is known about basic assumptions concerning kinship in West African societies. Two sets of beliefs, as Sidney Mintz and Richard Price have emphasized, were particularly central: "the sheer importance of kinship in structuring interpersonal relations and in defining an individual's place in his society" and the vital "importance to each individual of the . . . lines of kinsmen, living or dead, stretching backward and forward through time." Conversely, the circumstances of eighteenth-century slavery kept some slaves rooted to the same spot and scattered others across the land, both of which either surrounded slaves with kin or gave them access to far-flung kin networks. How much traditional beliefs, as opposed to or in combination with the exigencies of slavery, produced the slaves' distinctive stress on the role of kinship, and particularly extended kin, is hard to assess.[44]

Similarly, the age gaps between husbands and wives and the close bonds between siblings and sibling families may owe something to African influences. Yet, slavery itself—whether the sexual imbalances of the slave trade that led inevitably to a pattern of older husbands and younger wives or the disruption of families that led siblings to bond together and masters to place older siblings together in households—may just as easily explain these traits. In these instances, perhaps the compatibility of homeland beliefs and the imperatives of slavery combined to produce these behavioral patterns.

One distinctive family form—polygyny—was transferred across the Atlantic, but only partially and incompletely. Though it was never widespread, polygyny was more common among Lowcountry slaves than among any others in British North America. Early in the eighteenth century, the Reverend Francis Le Jau warned South Carolina slaves that "the Christian Religion dos not allow plurality of Wives." Some bondpeople continued to ignore the minister's admonition throughout the century. In 1772, Mary Bull's estate listed a slave man Pompey with "his wife Alvira, and five children, Flora, July, Lisbon, Sue and Monmouth and another wife Ackey." Seven years later, James Parson's Bob headed a household that consisted of "his wife Nelly and their children Caesar and Sibbey, his other wife Elsey and child Bob." Such arrangements do not seem to have been a privilege conferred solely on skilled slaves. Whereas Jehu Elliot's driver had two wives, as did Isaac Godin's carpenter, two of the field hands on Hugh Thomson's plantation had two wives apiece, as did other field hands on a number of other estates. Henry Laurens mentioned his field hand Mathias's two wives only when one, in a fit of jealousy, poisoned the other.[45]

Instances of polygyny were much less common in the Chesapeake. The few cases that have materialized come, as might be expected, from the early eighteenth century, when Africans were more numerous. Thus, in the 1740s, a few men on the Eastern Shore of Maryland seem to have lived with more than one woman, and one of the 243 men—a foreman—belonging to Robert "King" Carter in 1733 had two wives. More indirectly, it has been suggested that slave women in turn-of-the-century Maryland might have nursed infants for three or four years, a common practice in polygynous societies. However, this is indirect evidence at best; what is more impressive is the speed with which Chesapeake slave women approximated Anglo-American nursing patterns, in the same way presumably as they rejected polygynous marriages.[46]

Another marriage pattern may also have had African antecedents. Slaves appear to have shared particular exogamous beliefs that dictated their selection of marital partners. Unlike whites, slaves seem to have had a taboo against marriage between cousins. Admittedly, no precise West African origins have been identified for this pattern, but it is difficult to see the behavior as originating in the exigencies of slavery or under Anglo-American influence, particularly when marriages between cousins were increasingly common among both gentry and plainfolk throughout the eighteenth century.[47]

In general, then, it cannot be claimed that African influence was fundamental to African American familial development. What is more interesting is that slaves created a distinctive form of family life, irrespective of the derivation of particular influences. There is no better example of this than the naming patterns of slaves. As we have seen, some African names were retained, but they were never more than a fraction of the names employed by eighteenth-century slaves. Yet, at the same time as slaves were employing standard Anglo-American names, they were naming in ways that were distinctive, whether it was the naming of sons for fathers far more than of daughters for mothers or the naming for extended kin in particularly tight-knit ways.

Also distinctive was the relative absence of the white pattern of necronymic naming among slaves. Among South Carolina slaves, this practice has been discovered only among the more assimilated house slaves and artisans in the nineteenth century. In the Chesapeake, three newborn Jefferson slaves bore the names of recently deceased siblings, and a blood cousin carried the name of a dead kinsman. Landon Carter's personal body servant, Nassau, used the name Nat twice for his sons: the first died in 1757, and the second seems to have begun working alongside his father in the early 1770s, suggesting that Nassau reused the name at the first opportunity. That the practice can be found in the Chesapeake at all is evidence of the greater assimilation of that region's slaves to white practices, but it should be emphasized that it was never more than a minor occurrence.[48]

Another distinctive pattern, forced on slaves as much as anything else, was the absence of surnames. Last names were least common in the Lowcountry. Only a few of the more acculturated South Carolina runaways had surnames. Two brick-layers, a mustee and a mulatto, belonging to Christopher Holson, were known as William Saunders and Jack Flowers, respectively; a Charlestonian master advertised for his runaway "Jack, sirnamed Ryan"; and a mulatto fugitive named Jemmy took the name James Freeman, an indication of the status to which he aspired. A new name obviously meant much to a slave: in 1756, Frank ran away and assumed the name John Williams; six years later he ran away again, also as John Williams. Overall, however, only 1 percent of advertised runaways in South Carolina newspapers were said to have surnames. Last names were just as scarce among slaves in plantation listings and inventories. Jack and Tom Stuard were the only bond-people with surnames among John Peacom's 65 slaves; Dick Williams, a field hand, was similarly conspicuous among John McKenzie's 210 slaves, as were Jack Outerbridge and Jack Green among Thomas Godfrey's 112 slaves. Only three of the few hundred bondpeople mentioned by Henry Laurens had a surname: Andrew Dross and Jemmy Holmes were mariners, and Scipio became Robert Scipio Laurens when he was taken to England as a waiting man.[49]

Slaves with surnames were somewhat more widespread in Virginia. There, one in ten runaways was known either to have a surname or to be using one in passing as free. Thus, Charles Bruce matter-of-factly advertised for his fifty-year-old "Negro fellow called Harry Spencer," and Anthony Martin referred to his slave Will, who, when absent, added a surname and a little more dignity to his forename by passing as William Cousins. Slaves clearly took the initiative in assuming surnames. Robert Rawlings advertised for his runaway "negro fellow by the name of GEORGE, but calls himself GEORGE LEWIS," Alexander Baugh for his slave Ben, who "calls himself Ben Sharp," Edward Carter for his "likely Negro man, who calls himself John Cellars," Thomas Walker for his man Frank "but frequently calls himself Frank Waddy." Surnames, though never wide-spread, dotted the pages of inventories and plantation listings in the Chesapeake. Three slaves with the surname Parrott (together with Will Coley, Jack Tooth, Sue Miller, and Jack Sambo) belonged to James Burwell's estate in York County; three mulattoes with the surname Bond were the only slaves on John Gildy's estate in Essex County; four slaves, all with separate surnames, lived on John Spotswood's estate in Spotsylvania County; and four Stewarts (as well as Barton Cocheno) belonged to Colonel Richard Jones's estate in Amelia County. On large estates in Virginia by the turn of the century, many slaves possessed surnames. There were Carys, Johnsons, Newmans, Smiths, and at least seven Joneses among Robert Carter's slaves, while Samuel Harrison and his wife, Judith Harrison, so liked their surname that they named one of their sons Harrison. On William Fitzhugh's plantations in 1810, forty-two of ninety-four adults shared surnames: Carters, Tripletts, Douglasses, and Bossees were present on most of his quarters.[50]

Most interestingly, however, few slaves shared a surname with their current owner. Highly exceptional were Jenny Carter, belonging to Landon Carter, and Robert Laurens, belonging to Henry Laurens. Significantly, both these slaves were personal servants, closely identified with their masters. Slaves generally followed a more independent and inventive path: George took the surname America; John thought in monetary terms and became John Twopence; Sharper in fragrant terms, becoming Henry Perfume; a mariner in religious terms, becoming John Baptist; Jack Dismal might have named himself after the swamp; Tim became James Traveller, highly appropriate for a fugitive. In other cases, slaves assumed the last name of a former, often their first, owner. Thus, a mulatto sailmaker formerly named Cubbina, who was sold by Joshua Lawson of the island of Saint Christopher to Thomas Mace and then to Josiah Smith of South Carolina, adopted the name John Lawson when he decided to pass as a free man. A Jamaican-born slave named Gloucester who served as hostler and cook to the Fox family in Gloucester County, Virginia, and whose services were then rented out in the city of Richmond, took the name John Baker when he ran away. Apparently, his first Virginia master was Dr. John Baker, with whom "he lived some years in Williamsburg." Taking the name of an earlier owner was, as Genovese and Gutman have emphasized, a way for slaves to recapture their history, to establish a link to a family of origin, and to forge a social identity separate from that of successive owners. A South Carolina slave, born in 1852 and able to trace his ancestry to an African great-grandfather, spoke eloquently of these concerns when he said: "I do not know the name my great grandfather bore in Africa, but when he arrived in this country he was given the name Clement, and when he found he needed a surname—something he was not accustomed to in his native land—he borrowed that of the man who brought him. It was a very good name, and as we have held the same for more than one hundred and fifty years, without change or alteration, I think, therefore, we are legally entitled to it."[51]

That it was a South Carolina and not a Virginia slave who recalled an African great-grandfather is indicative of the difference in familial experiences of the two areas' bondpeople. More solitaries, the existence of polygyny, fewer surnames, and the absence of necronymic naming all point to a more widespread African presence in South Carolina than in Virginia. There were other differences, too. Coresident two-parent households were more widespread in the Lowcountry, divided-residence and one-parent families more widespread in the Chesapeake. Chesapeake slaves enjoyed greater kinship density than their Lowcountry cousins, but they also faced more family disruptions through sale, bequest, estate division, and forced migration. Slave family life was far from uniform throughout the plantation South.

Nevertheless, slaves everywhere experienced similar pressures and responded in similar ways. Although enslavement denied slaves essential familial choices and essential knowledge about their pasts, they never accepted that denial. As Edmund Morgan shrewdly observed, "Human nature has an unpredictable resiliency, and slaves did manage to live a life of their own within the limits prescribed for them." If the limits were constricting, they were never "so close as to preclude entirely the possibility of a private life." Many slaves were prevented from enjoying much of a family life, particularly early in the eighteenth century, and many others had their family lives disrupted by masters. But by the late eighteenth century, more than half of the slaves in both Lowcountry and Chesapeake had formed families. That so many lived as faithful husband and wife, as devoted parent and child, and as supportive extended kin, even under the most trying circumstances, is remarkable. The immediate family and the enlarged kin group were, in Gutman's words, "central binding institutions within slave communities." They helped shape and support a separate culture.[52]

Abbreviations cited in Notes

AHR	*American Historical Review*
BL	British Library, London
CC	College of Charleston
City Gaz	*Cit Gazette* (Charleston)
City Gaz and DA	*City Gazette, and [or] Daily Advertiser* (Charleston)
CLS	Charleston Library Society
CW	Research Library, Colonial Williamsburg Foundation, Williamsburg, Va.
Duke	Duke University, Durham, N.C.
Ga Gaz	*Georgia Gazette* (Savannah)
Gaz of State of SC	*Gazette of the State of South-Carolina* (Charleston)
GHQ	*Georgia Historical Quarterly*
GHS	Georgia Historical Society, Savannah
HSP	Historical Society of Pennsylvania, Philadelphia
JAH	*Journal of American History*

Laurens Papers	Philip M. Hamer et al., eds., *The Papers of Henry Laurens* (Columbia, S.C., 1968–)
LC	Library of Congress, Washington, D.C.
Md Gaz	*Maryland Gazette* (Annapolis)
MHM	*Maryland Historical Magazine*
MHR	Maryland Hall of Records, Annapolis
MHS	Maryland Historical Society, Baltimore
NCDAH	North Carolina Division of Archives and History, Raleigh
NYHS	New-York Historical Society, New York
NYPL	New York Public Library
PRO	Public Record Office, London
Royal Gaz	*Royal Gazette* (Charleston)
SC and AGG	*South-Carolina and American General Gazette* (Charleston)
SCDAH	South Carolina Department of Archives and History, Columbia
SCG	*South-Carolina Gazette* (Charleston)
SCG and CJ	*South-Carolina Gazette: And Country Journal* (Charleston)
SCG and DA	*South Carolina Gazette and Daily Advertiser* (Charleston)
SCG and GA	*South-Carolina Gazette and General Advertiser* (Charleston)
SCG and T and MDA	*South-Carolina State-Gazette and Timothy and Mason's Daily Advertiser* (Charleston)
SCG and TDA	*South-Carolina State-Gazette, and Timothy's Daily Advertiser* (Charleston)
SCHM	*South Carolina Historical Magazine*
SCHS	South Carolina Historical Society, Charleston
SC Weekly Gaz	*South-Carolina Weekly Gazette* (Charleston)
SC State Gaz	*South-Carolina State-Gazette* (Charleston)
SPG	Society for the Propagation of the Gospel, London
State Gaz of SC	*State Gazette of South-Carolina* (Charleston)
UNC	University of North Carolina, Chapel Hill
USC	University of South Carolina, Columbia
UVa	University of Virginia, Charlottesville
VaG (C and D)	Clarkson and Davis's *Virginia Gazette* (Williamsburg)
VaG (D and H)	Dixon and Hunter's *Virginia Gazette* (Williamsburg)
VaG (D and N)	Dixon and Nicolson's *Virginia Gazette* (Williamsburg)
VaG (Hunter)	Hunter's *Virginia Gazette* (Williamsburg)
VaG (P and D)	Purdie and Dixon's *Virginia Gazette* (Williamsburg)
VaG (Parks)	Parks's *Virginia Gazette* (Williamsburg)
VaG (Pinkney)	Pinkney's *Virginia Gazette* (Williamsburg)
VaG (Purdie)	Purdie's *Virginia Gazette* (Williamsburg)
VaG (Rind)	Rind's *Virginia Gazette* (Williamsburg)
VaG (Royle)	Royle's *Virginia Gazette* (Williamsburg)
VaG and GA	*Virginia Gazette, and General Advertiser* (Richmond)
VaG and WA	*Virginia Gazette, and [or] Weekly Advertiser* (Richmond)
Va Ind Chron	*Virginia Independent Chronicle* (Richmond)
Va Ind Chron and GA	*Virginia Independent Chronicle and General Advertiser* (Richmond)
VBHS	Virginia Baptist Historical Society, University of Richmond

VHS   Virginia Historical Society, Richmond
VMHB   *Virginia Magazine of History and Biography*
VSL   Virginia State Library, Richmond
W and M   College of William and Mary, Williamsburg, Va.
WMQ   *William and Mary Quarterly*
WPA   Works Progress/Work Projects Administration

Notes

1   Peter Laslett, *Family Life and Illicit Love in Earlier Generations* (Cambridge, 1977), 260.

2   *Laurens Papers*, IV, 148; John Bartram to William Bartram, Apr. 5, 1766, Bartram Family Papers, HSP; John Carter to George Carter, July 6, 1737, Carter-Plummer Letter-book, UVa; Robert Carter Journal, 1784–1789, Jan. 13, 1785, 30, LC (six years later, the couple was still together, parents to four children, one aged four, twins aged three, and the last a six-month-old infant named after his father); Ross to Robert Richardson, Apr. 30, 1812, David Ross Letterbook, 1812–1813, VHS, as cited in Charles B. Dew, "David Ross and the Oxford Iron Works: A Study of Industrial Slavery in the Early Nineteenth-Century South," *WMQ*, 3d Ser., XXXI (1974), 211.

3   Diary of Colonel Francis Taylor, Jan. 30, 1789, VSL.

4   John Brickell, The Natural History of North Carolina (Dublin, 1737), 274; James Barclay, *The Voyages and Travels of James Barclay, Containing Many Surprising Adventures, and Interesting Narratives* (Dublin, 1777), 27; Gutman, *Black Family*, 270–284.

5   Records in the British Public Record Office Relating to South Carolina, 1663–1782, VI, 262–263, SCDAH, as quoted in Wood, *Black Majority*, 128–129; Hugh Drysdale to Commissioners for Trade and Plantations, June 29, 1723, CO5/1319, fol. 115, PRO; Adams to Washington, Mar. 15, 1775, Papers of George Washington, 4th Ser., microfilm, reel 33, Manuscript Division, LC, and Lund Washington to George Washington, Jan. 17, 1776, in possession of the Mount Vernon Ladies' Association, as cited in Lee. "The Problem of Slave Community," *WMQ*, 3d Ser., XLIII (1986), 357; *The Letters of Hon. James Habersham, 1756–1775*, GHS, Collections, VI (Savannah, Ga., 1904), 23. See also Betts, ed., *Jefferson's Farm Book*, part 2, 19; Edwin Morris Betts and James Adam Bear, Jr., eds., *The Family Letters of Thomas Jefferson* (Columbia, Mo., 1966), 131; Henry Lee to Col. Robert Goode, May 17, 1792, Executive Letterbook, 1792–1794, 4–5, VSL; and John Sutton to Robert Carter, Apr. 3, 1782, Carter Family Papers.

6   *Laurens Papers*, VIII, 89, 101, 290, XI, 487, 492, 561–562, 565, XIII, 539–540, XIV, 134, 181; Barclay, Voyages and Travels, 25.

7   Jacqueline Jones, *Labor of Love, Labor of Sorrow: Black Women, Work, and the Family from Slavery to the Present* (New York, 1985), 42; Lorena S. Walsh, "The Experiences and Status of Women in the Chesapeake, 1750–1775," in Walter J. Fraser, Jr., R. Frank Saunders, Jr., and Jon L. Wakelyn, eds., *The Web of Southern Social Relations: Women, Family, and Education* (Athens, Ga., 1985), 13. For other critiques of slave women as dominant, see Christie Farnham, "Sapphire? The Issue of Dominance in the Slave Family, 1830–1865," in Carol Groneman and Mary Beth Norton, eds., *"To Toil the Livelong Day": America's Women at Work, 1780–1980* (Ithaca, N.Y., 1987), 68–83; and Elizabeth Fox-Genovese, *Within the Plantation Household: Black and White Women of the Old South* (Chapel Hill, N.C., 1988), esp. 48–50. On the masculine world of Gabriel's conspiracy, I have benefited from reading James Sidbury, *Ploughshares into Swords: Race, Rebellion, and Identity in Gabriel's Virginia, 1730–1810* (New York, 1997).

8   The age difference between husbands and wives comes from two sources: plantation listings and runaway slave advertisements. In Virginia, the ages of husbands and wives were reported for 74 couples in the records of the Jones family (1730s). Paul Carrington, Edmund Randolph (1784), Robert Carter (1788), and William Fitzhugh (1810), and for 13 runaway couples in newspaper advertisements between 1736 and 1739. Of these 87, 73 husbands were older than wives by 8.6 years, 12 wives were older than husbands by

4.4 years, and 2 couples were the same age. Similarly, Kulikoff found that on three late-18th-century Maryland plantations, 47 husbands were on average 6.8 years older than their wives (*Tobacco and Slaves*, 374n). In the Lowcountry, the ages of husbands and wives were reported for 151 couples in the plantation listings of Alexander Vanderdussen, George Austin, Samuel Waddingham, Pierce Butler, Hannah Bull, and Colonel Stapleton and for 21 runaway couples in the newspaper advertisements between 1732 and 1799. Of these 172, 126 husbands were older than wives by 8.1 years, 32 wives were older than husbands by 4.4 years, and 14 couples were the same age. The evidence from South Carolina indicates some narrowing of the age difference over time. For remarking on the African evidence, and noting correctly that age differences were much smaller in the 19th century, see Stanley L. Engerman, "Studying the Black Family," *Jour. Fam. Hist.*, III (1978), 96, although also see Wayne K. Durrill, "Slavery, Kinship, and Dominance: The Black Community at Somerset Place Plantation, 1786–1860," *Slavery and Abolition*, XIII (1992), 9; and Malone, *Sweet Chariot*, 169–170, 230.

9 Joseph Jones, *VaG* (P and D), May 14, 1767 (Charles); Francis Jerdone, *VaG and WA*, Apr. 17, 1784 (Will); Cuthburt Bullitt, *VaG* (Rind), Nov. 8, 1770 (Tony); William Watt, ibid. (P and D), Sept. 10, 1772 (two Africans); Josiah Garey and Lucy Clark, *VaG and WA*, Oct. 30, 1784 (Mack); William Lloyd, SCG, Dec. 11, 1756, supplement (Cupid); Samuel Bonneau, *SC and AGG*, July 30, 1778 (Toby); E. McClellan, *City Gaz*, July 13, 1797 (Binah).

10 Charles Ball, *Fifty Years in Chains* (New York, 1970), 157, 263–264. This African husband, "a morose, sullen man," "often beat and otherwise maltreated his wife." The overseer "refused to protect her, on the ground, that he never interfered in the family quarrels of the black people." Perhaps, for the same reason, there were few recorded 18th-century rapes by black men on black women. An exception was 19-year-old Christopher, who was found guilty of raping Sarah and sentenced to hang but was later pardoned. Westmoreland County Orders, 1776–1786, 57, VSL; and Robert Carter to Governor Patrick Henry, June 3, 1778, and to Clement Brooke, July 27, 1778, Carter Letterbook, III (3), 35, 45. Duke. For another case, also in Westmoreland, see Thomas D. Morris, *Southern Slavery and the Law, 1619–1860* (Chapel Hill, N.C., 1996), 306.

11 Robert Carter to Clement Brooke, Jan. 7, 1783, Carter Letterbook, V, 91–93, Duke; James French, *VaG* (D and H), Oct. 31, 1777 (Jack); Rev. Francis Le Jau to the SPG, July 10, 1711, A6/103, 318–319; John Holladay, *VaG* (P and D), Apr. 21, 1768 (Cambridge); Bennett Browne, ibid. (D and H), July 15, 1775 (Billy Barber).

12 John M'Illraith, *Gaz of State of SC*, Mar. 17, 1779; Martin Pfeniger, *SC and AGG*, Mar. 18, May 29, 1779; Thomas Caton, ibid., Sept. 10, 1779. For other examples of creole slaves with more than one wife, see James Kennedy, *State Gaz of SC*, Feb. 18, 1790; and Allard Belin, *City Gaz*, May 10, 1797.

13 Inventory of Ben Tasker at Baltimore Co., 1737, Carroll-Maccubbin Papers, MHS, and Ledger of John Blair, 1795–1797, W and M, as cited in Ronald L. Lewis, "Slave Families at Early Chesapeake Ironworks," *VMHB*, LXXXVI (1978), 172; Ball, *Fifty Years in Chains*, 18; Brickell, *Natural History of North Carolina*, 275.

14 Robert Ruffin, *VaG* (P and D), Sept. 24, 1772; trials of Deborah, Nov. 23, 1743, Feb. 20, 1744, Orange County Court Order Book, 1743–1746, 22–23, 47–48; Augustine Moore, *VaG* (Purdie), June 23, 1775; Roger Pinckney, *SC and AGG*, Mar. 9, 1772. For other slaves with pets, see John Harrison, ibid., May 22, 1776; and Charles Harris, *SCG*, July 14, 1777. For a slave's conveying many of his clothes to his wife's home on another plantation, see John Hales, *VaG* (D and H), Apr. 1, 1775.

15 George Bedon, *Gaz of State of SC*, Apr. 15, 1784; John Olives, *VaG or AA*, Sept. 24, 1785. Between 1732 and 1779, I count 403 South Carolina runaways as members of family groups—12% of all advertised fugitives. Of these, 48% consisted of spouses alone or with children (24% alone, 24% with children), 43% mothers and children, 4% father and children, 4% siblings, and 2% extended family groups. In Virginia between 1736 and 1779, I count 78 members of family groups—7% of all advertised fugitives. Of these, 51% consisted of spouses alone or with children (36% alone, 15% with children), 20% mothers and children, 20% siblings, and 8% extended family groups.

16 Robert Carter to Fleet Cox, Jan. 2, 1788, Carter Letterbook, VIII, 61, Duke; Christopher Collins to Robert Carter, Jan. 11, 1788, Carter Family Papers: Robert Carter to John Pound, Mar. 16, 1779, Letterbook, III (3), 110. See also Erasmus Gill to Duncan Rose, Jan. 24, 1801, Haxall Family Papers, VHS.

17 Ball, *Fifty Years in Chains*, 36, 39, 147.

18 *Laurens Papers*, IV, 595; Thomas Wright's deed of gift, Oct. 28, 1775, Miscellaneous Record Book, RR, 349; depositions of William Davis and William Allston, Oct. 24, 1777, Miscellaneous Records, RR, 452–453; William Simpson to Governor James Grant, June 15, 1767, Papers of General James Grant of Ballindalloch, 0771/243. See also David Yeats to James Grant, Apr. 6, 1774, ibid., 0771/370.

19 J. Hector St. John Crèvecoeur, *Letters from an American Farmer*, ed. W. P. Trent and Ludwig Lewisohn (New York, 1925 [orig. publ. 1782], 228; Robert Raper to Thomas Boone, Mar. 15, 1770, Robert Raper Letterbook, West Sussex Record Office, microfilm, SCHS; Governor Fauquier's appointment of the Justices in King George County, Oct. 11, 1760, photostat, CW; Court of Oyer and Terminer, Brunswick County, Jan. 11, 1773, Colonial Papers, VSL; Caroline County Court Order Book, 1777–1780, Jan. 14, 1779, 147, VSL; Dick Journal, Dec. 18, 1808, UVa. I have found only one South Carolina slave trial that refers to a mother's alleged murder of her child (in this case, her bastard) (trial of Mellum, Sept. 18, 1754, Miscellaneous Record Book, KK, 90–91).

20 Ball, *Fifty Years in Chains*, 151; Hunter Dickinson Farish, ed., *Journal and Letters of Philip Vickers Fithian, 1773–1774: A Plantation Tutor of the Old Dominion* (Williamsburg, Va., 1957), 239, 241; Henry Melchior Muhlenberg, *The Journals of Henry Melchior Muhlenberg*, trans. Theodore G. Tappert and John W. Doberstein, 2 vols. (Philadelphia, 1942–1958), II, 675.

21 Alex Cameron, *City Gaz*, July 8, 1789 (this family had escaped in a canoe in 1781 [Mrs. Holmes, *Royal Gaz*, Aug. 15, 1781]); Allen Freedman, *VaG* (Purdie), Apr. 11, 1777 (Jenny); James Akin, *SC and AGG*, Aug. 16, 1780 (Lucy); Christopher McDonald, *SCG and TDA*, Dec. 15, 1798 (Hannah); John Edwards, *SCG*, Apr. 17, 1762 (Bow); John Haly, ibid., Aug. 4, 1766 (Bristol). Of the 1,004 women listed as both fugitives and captives in South Carolina newspapers between 1732 and 1782, 113, or 11%, were accompanied by their children (78 with 1 child, 24 with 2, 9 with 3, and 2 with 4). In Virginia newspapers between 1736 and 1779, only 7 of 112 women, or 6%, were said to have been accompanied by children. I have found 8 cases of a father's running away with 1 or more sons—all are from colonial South Carolina newspapers. For the pattern in Georgia, which was much like South Carolina's, see Betty Wood, "Some Aspects of Female Resistance to Chattel Slavery in Low Country Georgia, 1763–1815," *Historical Journal*, XXX (1987), 610.

22 John Strobel, *City Gaz*, July 11, 1799 (Jemmy); Samuel Wortington, *Maryland Journal and Baltimore Advertiser*, Aug. 7, 1781 (Saucy); William Ekells, *Gaz of State of SC*, Sept. 3, 1778 (Robin); Peter Spence, ibid., Aug. 26, 1778 (Hesther). In colonial South Carolina, there were 80 cases (counting any group as one case) of slaves who were thought to be visiting a parent or parents. Of these 80, 89% were adults above 16 years of age; 65% were said to be visiting a mother, 20% a father, and 15% both parents. In Virginia from 1736 to 1779, there were 24 such cases: 92% were adults; 63% were said to be visiting a mother, 29% a father, and 8% both parents.

23 "Memoirs of the Life of Boston King, a Black Preacher," *Methodist Magazine*, XXI (1798), 105–106; Linda Stanley, ed., "James Carter's Account of His Sufferings in Slavery," *Pennsylvania Magazine of History and Biography*, CV (1981), 336–338.

24 Walter B. Edgar, ed., *The Letterbook of Robert Pringle*, I (Columbia, S.C., 1972), 247; Mary Haldane Coleman, ed., *Virginia Silhouettes: Contemporary Letters concerning Negro Slavery in the State of Virginia . . .* (Richmond, Va., 1934), 9–10.

25 Greene, ed., *Carter Diary*, 194, 218, 496, 865; Robert Carter to Clement Brooke, July 27, 1778, Carter Letterbook, III (3), 46, Duke; Robert Carter to Newyear Branson, Feb. 13, 1790, ibid., X, 93.

26 Greene, ed., Carter Diary, 385, 777; Robert Carter to Samuel Carter, Mar. 10, 1781, Carter Letterbook, IV, 48, Duke; Farish, ed., *Journal and Letters of Philip Vickers Fithian*,

184, 240. See also Mechal Sobel, *The World They Made Together: Black and White Values in Eighteenth-Century Virginia* (Princeton, N.J., 1987), 163.

27   Joseph Wragg, SCG, Oct. 13, 1739; Donald Jackson and Dorothy Twohig, eds., *The Diaries of George Washington*, IV (Charlottesville, Va., 1978), 277–283 (see also John C. Fitzpatrick, ed., *The Writings of George Washington from the Original Manuscript Sources, 1745–1799*, 39 vols. [Washington, D.C., 1931–1944], XXXVII, 256–268); C. C. Pinckney Plantation Book, LC; Robert Carter to Newyear Branson, Aug. 22, 1788, Carter Letterbook, VIII, 170, Duke; Johann David Schoepf, *Travels in the Confederation [1783–1784]*, trans. and ed. Alfred J. Morrison, 2 vols. (Philadelphia, 1911), I, 148. For father and son woodworkers, see will of Lewis Burwell, York County Deeds, Orders, and Wills, no. 14, 60–64; inventory of Robert Carter, November 1733, Carter Papers, VHS; Greene, ed., *Carter Diary*, 367; *Laurens Papers*, IV, 579; and diaries of Charles Drayton, Mar. 14, 1792, Drayton Family Papers, Historic Charleston Foundation.

28   John Norton to B. Muse, Dec. 23, 1781, Battaille Muse Papers, Duke; Kulikoff, *Tobacco and Slaves*, 373; Dew, "David Ross and the Oxford Iron Works," *WMQ*, XXXI (1974), 212–213; Lewis, "Slave Families," *VMHB*, LXXXVI (1978), 177; Norton, Gutman, and Berlin, "Afro-American Family," in Berlin and Hoffman, eds., *Slavery and Freedom*, 181–182.

29   John C. Inscoe, "Carolina Slave Names: An Index to Acculturation," *Journal of Southern History*, XLIX (1983), 529–530; Ball Account Book, Ball Family Papers, SCHS; John and Keating Simons Ball Books, Southern Historical Collection, UNC; Ravenel Account Book, B1–1, Ravenel Papers; C. C. Pinckney Plantation Book. There were 304 cases of naming children for parents in colonial South Carolina inventories. In the 1730s and 1740s, the ratio of sons named after fathers as compared to daughters after mothers was less than 3:1 (29:11). In the 1760s and 1770s, the ratio had increased to more than 5:1 (164:33). See also Gutman, *Black Family*, 345–346; Cheryll Ann Cody, Chapter 15, this volume; "Generation and Gender as Reflected in Carolina Slave Naming Practices: A Challenge to the Gutman Thesis," *SCHM*, XCIV (1993), 252–263, who emphasizes that the majority of slave families did not name sons for fathers, though he recognizes that names of slave mothers were very infrequently passed on to daughters. For other marked differentials between naming sons for fathers more frequently than daughters for mothers, see Kay and Cary, *Slavery in North Carolina*, 163; and Jerome S. Handler and JoAnn Jacoby, "Slave Names and Naming in Barbados, 1650–1830," *WMQ*, 3d Ser., LIII (1996), 685–728.

30   Jones Family Papers, microfilm, CW; among Landon Carter's slaves, foreman George, Joe, and carpenters Ralph and Toney all passed their names on to one of their sons (Greene, ed., *Carter Diary*, 159, 219, 749–750, 1072); deed of trust between William Byrd and Peyton Randolph and Benjamin Harrison, Dec. 9, 1772, Charles City County Records, 1766–1774, 471–472, VSL; Jennings Pulliam, *VaG and WA*, Sept. 25, 1784. Two late-18th-century Chesapeake slave lists in which the incidence of sons named for fathers roughly equaled daughters named for mothers are those of Edmund Randolph, 1784, and Robert Carter, 1787–1788.

31   Cody, "There Was No 'Absalom,'" *AHR*, XCII (1987), 563–596; Gutman, *Black Family*, 93–95, 180–181, 189–191; Gudeman, "Gutman's *Black Family*," *Soc. Sci. Hist.*, III (1979), 61.

32   George Moore, *VaG* (P and D), July 9, 1767; Samuel Sherwin, ibid. (Rind), May 9, 1771; Thomas Legare, Jr., *City Gaz*, Feb. 12, 1799; Theodore Gaillard, Sr., ibid., Aug. 23, 1799. For siblings running away together, see John Nelson, *VaG and WA*, Aug. 6, 1785; and Thomas Barksdale, *SCG*, Sept. 22, 1798.

33   Robert Johnston, SCG, July 9, 1763; William Sams, SC and AGG, Dec. 24, 1778; John Sinkler, State Gaz of SC, May 11, 1786; Anthony Bourdeaux, City Gaz, Aug. 24, 1797. See also Benjamin Singellton, SCG and CJ, June 23, 1772; John Austin Finnie, VaG (P and D), July 4, 1771; and John Lewis, ibid. (Purdie), July 10, 1778.

34   Samuel Meredith, Sr., *VaG* (P and D), Apr. 21, 1772; Robert Giles, *City Gaz*, Sept. 19, 1798.

35   Robert Carter to Richard Dozier, Dec. 7, 1778, Carter Letterbook, III (3), 78, Duke; John Channing to William Gibbons, June 26, 1770, William Gibbons, Jr., Papers, Duke; and see Tables 30 and 31.

36 Gutman, *Black Family*, 200–201.

37 Robert Carter to Robert Jones, Oct. 10, 1727, Carter Letterbook, 1727–1728, VHS; I have made my own calculations from the Ball family papers located in the SCHS and UNC, but see also Cody, "There Was No 'Absalom,'" *AHR*, XCII (1987), 563–596; and Greene, ed., *Carter Diary*. In all, Henry Laurens named 147 slaves in his correspondence; only 35, or 24%, shared a name with another slave (*Laurens Papers*, III, 203, IV, 319, and account book of Henry Laurens. 1766–1773, April 1771, 377, CC).

38 Ball, Ravenel, and Pinckney sources are listed in note 29, above; the Gaillard data come from Cheryll Ann Cody, "Naming, Kinship, and Estate Dispersal: Notes on Slave Family Life on a South Carolina Plantation, 1786–1833," *WMQ*, 3d Ser., XXXIX (1982), 192–211. For a precise African analog for naming children after grandparents, see John Thornton, "Central African Names and African-American Naming Patterns," *WMQ*, 3d Ser., L (1993), 727–742. esp. 740–742. For a likely matrilineal emphasis in naming-children for kin, see Handler and Jacoby, "Slave Names and Naming in Barbados," *WMQ*, 3d Ser., LIII (1996), 685–728.

39 Norton, Gutman, and Berlin, "The Afro-American Family," in Berlin and Hoffman, eds., *Slavery and Freedom*, 180, 183; Gutman, *Black Family*, 93.

40 Greene, ed., *Carter Diary*, 760, 762; Robert Carter to Charles Haynie, Apr. 21, 1784, Carter Letterbook, V, 201, Duke; Robey Coke, *VaG* (Purdie), July 25, 1777; Kulikoff, *Tobacco and Slaves*, 377.

41 Greene, ed., *Carter Diary*, 547, 575, 842, 854 (see 731 for the mention of a young boy's grandfather and uncle); Robert Carter Daybook, Apr. 22, 1778, XV, 15–16, Duke; Robert Pleasants to General Arnold, Jan. 30, 1781, Robert Pleasants Lettercopy Book, W and M; Robert Carter Daybook, 1790–1792, Aug. 27, 1792, LC; Gutman, *Black Family*, 200–202.

42 Andrew Letch, *SCG*, June 12, 1753 (Doll); Jonathan Copp, ibid., Jan. 22, 1756 (Ketch); Francis Roche, *SCG and CJ*, Oct. 20, 1767 (Sam); John Chapman, ibid., July 26, 1774 (Toby); William Hort, ibid., July 25, 1775 (Jack); Richard Lamput, *SCG*, Oct. 24, 1775 (Richard Collis).

43 Joseph Allston, *SCG*, Feb. 20, 1762 (Crack et al.); Charles Skirving, *SC Weekly Gaz*, Mar. 8, 1783 (Clarinda et al.); Charles H. Simmons, *State Gaz of SC*, Aug. 8, 1785 (Jenny et al.).

44 Gutman, *Black Family*, 91, 154, 194, 217–220; Sidney W. Mintz and Richard Price, *An Anthropological Approach to the Afro-American Past: A Caribbean Perspective*, Institute for the Study of Human Issues, Occasional Papers in Social Change, no. 21 Philadelphia, 1976), 34.

45 Rev. Francis Le Jau to SPG, Oct. 20, 1709, A5/49, SPG; inventory of Mary Bull, Jan. 16, 1772, Inventory Book, Z, 177–187, SCDAH; inventory of James Parson, Nov. 9, 1779, ibid., BB, 190–201: inventory of Jehu Elliott, Mar. 27, 1762, ibid., V, 180–184; inventory of Isaac Godin, Jan. 22, 1778, ibid., CC, 320–326; inventory of Hugh Thomson, Dec. 21, 1774, ibid., &, 480–483. It is difficult, in other cases, to know whether African tradition or forced separation accounted for a male slave's having more than one wife.

46 "Eighteenth Century Maryland as Portrayed in the 'Itinerant Observations' of Edward Kimber," *MHM*, LI (1956), 327; Robert Carter inventory, 1733, Carter Papers, VHS; Menard, "Maryland Slave Population," *WMQ*, 3d Ser., XXXII (1975), 41; Herbert S. Klein and Stanley L. Engerman, "Fertility Differentials between Slaves in the United States and the British West Indies: A Note on Lactation Practices and Their Possible Implications," *WMQ*, 3d Ser., XXXV (1978), 369–371.

47 Gutman, *Black Family*, 88–91; Kulikoff, *Tobacco and Slaves*, 252–255, 374. But for a skeptical assessment of the African origins of the slaves' supposed taboo against cousin marriage, see Engerman, "Studying the Black Family," *Jour. Fam. Hist.*, III (1978), 89–91.

48 Cody, "There Was No 'Absalom,'" *AHR*, XCII (1987), 595; Norton, Gutman, and Berlin, "The Afro-American Family," in Berlin and Hoffman, eds., *Slavery and Freedom*, 183; Greene, ed., Carter Diary, esp. 159, 345, 348–349, 373. The relative absence of necronymic naming among 18th-century slaves argues against its African origin, a point of view supported strongly by Inscoe, "Generation and Gender," *SCHM*, XCIV (1993), 260; and Gutman, *Black Family*, 193–194.

49   Christopher Holson, SCG, July 21, 1757; Joseph Tobias, ibid., Aug. 4, 1758; Thomas Whitesides, ibid., Nov. 7, 1761; Thomas Smith, ibid., May 29, 1756, Nov. 13, 1762 (there were 64 runaway slaves with surnames in colonial South Carolina newspapers); inventory of John Peacom, Dec. 8, 1752, Inventory Book, WPA, CXXXIV, 491–494; inventories of John Mackenzie, June 19-Aug. 10, 1771, ibid., CLXXXIV, 102–114; inventory of Thomas Godfrey, Aug. 20, 1776, ibid., CXCII, 110–115; *Laurens Papers*, VII, 231, VIII, 1, 34, 37, 60, 348, 370, 412, 612. I am skeptical about the argument that West African traditions were reflected in the adoption of surnames: Handler and Jacoby, "Slave Names and Naming in Barbados," *WMQ*, 3d Ser., LIII (1996), 685–728.
50   Charles Bruce, *VaG* (P and D), May 21, 1767 (Harry Spencer); Anthony Martin, ibid., June 21, 1770 (William Cousins); Robert Rawlings, *VaG and WA*, Sept. 4, 1788 (George Lewis); Alexander Baugh, *Va Ind Chron and GA*, July 7, 1790; Edward Carter, *VaG* (Rind), Oct. 31, 1771 (John Cellars); Thomas Walker, Jr., *VaG or AA*, July 12, 1783 (Frank Waddy) (there were 107 slaves with surnames among Virginia fugitives); inventory of James Burwell, Mar. 10, 1718, York County Deeds, Orders, and Wills, no. 15, 421 (42 slaves); inventory of John Gildy, Feb. 21, 1726, Essex County Wills and Inventories, no. 4, 202; inventory of John Spotswood, Dec. 5, 1758, Spotsvylania County Will Book, D, 88; inventory of Col. Richard Jones, November 1780, Amelia County Will Book, no. 3, 5 (48 slaves). The best data on slave names in the Robert Carter material come from his manumission document of 1791, Duke; and for the Harrison family, see "Valuation of Nomony Hall," in Robert Carter's Memo Book, 1788–1789, LC; see also John Randolph Barden, "'Flushed with Notions of Freedom': The Growth and Emancipation of a Virginia Slave Community, 1732–1812" (Ph.D. diss., Duke University, 1993), 352–353, where the author notes 56 family names emerging from the Nomini Hall community as they were manumitted; for Fitzhugh, see Donald Mitchell Sweig, "Northern Virginia Slavery: A Statistical and Demographic Study" (Ph.D. diss., College of William and Mary, 1982), 116–121. See also Sobel, *The World They Made Together*, 159.
51   Greene, ed., *Carter Diary*, 810 (Jenny Carter); Thomas Watkins, *VaG* (Purdie), Apr. 11, 1766 George America); Robert Beverley, ibid. (D and H), Apr. 11, 1777 (John Twopence); John Edloe, ibid. (Purdie), Mar. 10, 1775 (Henry Perfume); Paris Boillat, *SCG*, June 27, 1774 (John Baptist); Robert Burwell, *VaG* (P and D), Feb. 18, 1773 (Jack Dismal); Catesby Jones, *VaG and WA*, Oct. 25, 1783 (James Traveller); Thomas Mace, *SCG and CJ*, May 13, 1766 (John Lawson: John Fox, *Va Ind Chron and GA*, July 28, 1790 (John Baker); Eugene D. Genovese, *Roll, Jordan, Roll: The World the Slaves Made* (New York, 1974), 445–447; Gutman, *Black Family*, 250–256, esp. 252.
52   Edmund S. Morgan, *Virginians at Home: Family Life in the Eighteenth Century* (Charlottesville, Va., 1952), 66; Gutman, *Black Family*, 260.

PART FIVE

Slave Culture

DEFINITIONS OF CULTURE ARE notoriously elusive and confusing. Slave culture is even more challenging. First, because there were many forms of slavery in the Americas, inevitably there were different varieties of slave culture. Second, the cultures which emerged among slaves in the Americas were located in an African past, yet moderated and changed by life in the Americas, more especially by contact with the dominant local European cultural forms. Yet even those European cultures were themselves utterly changed by life in the Americas.

Africans, like their white owners, carried their own, highly personal cultural baggage with them into the Americas, in the form of their languages, their memories of an African past, their beliefs. The work of Edward Kamau Brathwaite was critical in establishing the importance of slave culture in the Americas, and is represented here in his pioneering piece of 1971.

The importance of African beliefs among slaves in the Americas is explored in the essay by Sylvia Frey and Betty Wood (1998). For their part, Europeans generally refused to regard Africans' beliefs as religions in any meaningful sense. Though whites in a number of slave colonies resisted converting slaves to Christianity (the British West Indian planters were especially reluctant), Christianity eventually made a massive impact in the slave quarters. However, it came relatively late to Jamaican slaves, largely because of plantocratic resistance.

Religion, however important, was only one form of cultural expression. Other scholars have seen in slave customs and practices a firmer, clearer African influence which cut across specific African divisions and helped to give slaves a sense of cultural unity. A recent analysis of slave music by Shane White and Graham White (1999) significantly advances the study of slave culture, for it classifies music as an integral theme in a more broadly based slave aesthetic, located in Africa, but finding its distinctive voice in the Americas.

Through all of this, there was the intellectually challenging issue of social change. How did Africans and their offspring born in the Americas change? How did they become different people? In his masterly essay of 1996, Ira Berlin suggests the broad cultural transformations which saw Africans become African-Americans.

INTRODUCTION TO PART FIVE

S LAVE CULTURE THROUGHOUT the Americas emerged from a combination of African cultures blended with, and transformed by, elements of various
European cultures (imported by the slaves' local owners). But whites in their
turn found their cultures transformed in the Americas. The English who had settled
in late eighteenth-century Virginia, the Portuguese in Brazil or Spaniards in Cuba
at the same time, were different from their contemporaries in their homelands. It
is hardly surprising that large numbers of people who relocated (by choice or against
their will) thousands of miles away from their homes, and often in a hostile, alien
environment, found themselves utterly changed. It was, inevitably, a complex
process which saw the survival of critical areas of *all* migrants' cultural life in the
Americas (religion and language, for example) but which, equally, encouraged the
disappearance of other cultural traits. In the process, the migrant English, Irish,
Scots and others became American, just as the Portuguese became Brazilian. But
what did African slaves become?

The question is rendered even more complex by historians' confusion about the
slaves' origins. Africans were drawn from a host of different cultures. From the
earliest days of the Atlantic system, planters and slave traders developed strong
preferences for certain kinds of slaves. They did not, for example, want Africans
from what they regarded as 'warlike peoples'. Yet many slaves were captured,
initially, through military engagements. One difficulty is that slave owners' preferences were often described in generic terms which were inaccurate reflections of
the actual ethnic groupings within Africa itself. Precisely how Africans are to be
grouped and classified has posed huge problems for historians (not least because
historians of American slavery are rarely experts in African history).[1] Moreover,
it is abundantly clear that the slave experience differed greatly for different peoples.
In the words of Michael Gomez, 'Africans did not all experience American slavery
in the same way.'[2]

The simple term 'African' is often misleading. The concept of being African was
not something most slaves would recognise. Indeed, the term did not become commonplace among slaves and ex-slaves in the Americas until the late eighteenth
century. Even then it was clearly adopted from the European habit of using that
generic term. For their part, Africans viewed themselves as something altogether
more specific: Igbo or Kongo, for example. 'Africa' and 'Africans' were concepts
used by outsiders. By the late eighteenth century, however, the terms had gained
usage among numbers of slaves and ex-slaves in North America and Europe. Equiano
and his friends in London described themselves as African. Earlier, when the enslaved
Equiano was employed in Montserrat to greet newly arrived Africans on the slave
boats, he talked about meeting 'my own country men'; that is, fellow Igbo.[3]

The slave cultures of the Americas depended then on the specifics of African
origins, blended together with elements from European cultures, and the whole
transmuted by life in the particular locale in the Americas (and often moderated
by dealings with local Indian peoples). There has, furthermore, been a reluctance
to analyse slave social life as culture because of the heavily loaded tendency to
think of high culture; to imagine that what existed in Africa, and what emerged
in the Americas, was too simple, too crude, to warrant the term 'culture'. This is

in large degree merely one aspect of a Eurocentric outlook which has traditionally dismissed African civilisations, and which has, in its turn, prompted such fierce reaction in recent years. Today, however, no serious historian could deny the existence of a vital and important African aesthetic.[4]

Slaves brought to the Americas not merely their specific African backgrounds, but their personal experiences and memories of African life, of enslavement and of the Atlantic crossing, all of which were woven into the collective folk memory and culture of slave society. Africans arrived as individuals (not, in general, in family groups) though many were grouped together with other Africans of similar backgrounds through the process of enslavement and sale on the coast. For example, in the years of British domination of the slave trade in the eighteenth century, perhaps 80 per cent of Africans shipped into British possessions were Igbo peoples from the Bight of Biafra.[5] If true, this would have had enormous ramifications for the emergence of slave culture in those colonies, not least because most of those Africans would share similar languages.

The development of slave culture has to be placed in the context of African arrivals in the Americas. Everywhere, the slaves arrived alone, mainly sick and almost certainly traumatised by the protracted experiences of the past months (from the point of enslavement through to landfall). They were virtually naked with no or few material possessions. From such miserable circumstances there were to emerge, among the survivors, the rich and varied cultures of slave society.

Like working people everywhere, a prime element in local slave culture was the nature of work. Slave labours were, as we have seen, varied, though the great bulk of African slaves was destined, initially, to work in sugar production. The precise nature of slave work clearly determined the broad contours of slave culture. The onerous toil of the first gang in the sugar fields, or the unpleasantness of task work in the rice fields, was utterly different from enslaved life as a domestic, a nurse or a navigator. Work varied enormously, depending on crop (and therefore geography), location (town or country), age, gender and health. The culture of sugar slaves, toiling in large gangs which were dominated for much of the slave period by Africans, was quite distinct from that of smaller groups (handfuls really) of local-born slaves working side-by-side with white people (free and indentured) on smallholdings such as small tobacco plantations. Everywhere, the nature, pace and rhythms of work determined distinctions in local slave culture. Since work dominated slave life, it inevitably played a key role in shaping slave culture.

Cultural life came, in time, to pivot on the slave family. This was not imported from Africa but created in the Americas (but from African elements). The creation of family life, however, posed more difficulties than we might imagine. There was, first and foremost, the problem of sexual ratios and age groups. In the days of pioneering settlement and in frontier life, young African males heavily outnumbered women, and the recurring slave complaint was the need for more women. Even when local demography was more favourable, the development and maintenance of family life (nuclear or otherwise) were no easy matters. Securing partners, setting up and controlling the physical arrangements of domestic life, maintaining relationships with partners and children posed difficult problems in societies where each slave was at the beck and call of owners. In time, slave owners came to accept that contented slaves (those able to maintain relationships with chosen partners and with their own family groups) made for easier management. But there was, throughout, a tension between the need to allow slaves autonomy in their private lives (a concept which slave owners would have found hard to envisage) and the economic imperatives of slavery, which meant owners viewing their human capital as items they needed to shuffle and reorder according to changing economic circumstances.

Despite these and other difficulties, the slave family came to dominate the slave quarters. And the slave community, close by the place of work (notably the plantation), formed the crucible from which emerged the broad strands of local social and cultural existence. Slave owners often belittled the slave family, because those families seemed so different from anything Europeans recognised as familiar. Yet it was from the slave family, and the slave community of which it was an integral part, that there emerged a slave culture: beliefs, organisations and social values, enabling slaves to deal with the peculiar problems of their lives. Indeed, the importance of the slave family can be gauged by the bitterness and anguish which greeted the break-up of slave families by slave owners. This became a particular problem in the first half of the nineteenth century in the United States. To supply the cotton frontier with yet more slaves for the expansive cotton industry, slave owners in the Upper South – the old slave colonies – sold their 'surplus' slaves to traders who moved them westward. Abolitionists throughout the English-speaking world made great play of this, the break-up of slave families, as one of the most resented of all affronts to decency.

The other core feature of slave culture was religion; though, again, the term can be misleading. First, Europeans resolutely resisted the idea that, with the exception of Islam, Africans had religions at all. They were, by and large, regarded as pagans, adhering to superstitions which were not worthy of the name of religion. Indeed, this apparent lack of religion provided a simple rationale for enslavement: Christians were justified in enslaving pagans who were beyond the pale of civilised life. Yet many slave owners were equally insistent on not allowing Africans and their local-born offspring into their Christian churches. (There were, however, marked differences between Catholic and Protestant societies: the former, by and large, encouraged slave baptism while the latter resisted it.) British slave owners, for example, especially in the Caribbean, worried that baptism would lead to black freedom. In the event, the sugar planters had very good reasons to distrust the rise of enslaved Christianity. A church provided an alternative meeting-place for slaves, off the plantation. The Bible, and preachers, provided ideals which might (and, in the event, did) prove corrosive of plantocratic control. This resistance was less striking in British North America, though there the black:white ratio was quite different. Whites in colonial North America were rarely outnumbered by local slaves as they were throughout the Caribbean, and slaves therefore lived closer to white social life and became acculturated to it more quickly and more widely. In the sugar islands, the slaves remained separate, distinct – quite different – clinging to cultural habits (belief systems, for example) which owed more to Africa than to Europe. All that was to change with the ending of the slave trade in 1807, the rise of a local-born population and the inevitable numerical decline of the Africans. As they died out, the cultural links to African became ever more attenuated but were never fully severed.

Africans brought their own beliefs and practices into the slave colonies, mystifying (and alarming) slave owners with their private and communal practice of beliefs which seemed pagan and threatening. This was especially true of *vodun* in the French islands and *obeah* (a form of African-based sorcery) in the British, but existed in different forms in slave societies throughout the Americas. African slaves placed great importance on magical beliefs – notably those which harmed people – again alarming slave owners throughout the Americas. These beliefs survived the intrusion of Christianity among the slaves.[6] As long as the slave trade continued, such beliefs would also continue, refreshed and maintained by newly arrived Africans eager to seek out and cling to ideas, habits and customs which they recognised and valued from their African past.

Yet it would be wrong to think of slave religion as a stark set of alternatives: African religions on the one hand, European (Christian) on the other. More usual was the blending of the two. Even then, it was an unusually complex process, as yet not fully explained (not least because the nature of African beliefs in the Americas is still poorly understood). Even when slaves were wooed to Christianity (for example, to nonconformity in the British West Indies in the early nineteenth century), local whites worried that the tone and style of black Christianity seemed more African than they liked or found acceptable. Slaves invested their new Christianity with an enthusiasm, with ecstatic responses and calls, which sat uneasily with more traditional Christian ceremonials. Moreover, the Bible provided slaves with a language and imagery which transformed black life. So many biblical stories and images spoke to the enslaved condition and they became, in popularised and musical form, the vernacular not merely of slave devotion but of slave social aspiration. Similarly, the Sabbath became important: a day of rest from life's grinding toil when slaves gathered away from the place of work (and slavery) to meet with other slaves, to organise socially as they wished, to listen to preachers, increasing numbers of whom were black, and all untrammelled by slave owners. Around the Christian calendar – notably Christmas and Easter – slaves evolved a cycle of local social life with a focus on the church, the Bible and communal worship, with prayers and hymns which addressed the slaves' condition. It was in brief a marked shift towards independence from the slave owners' direct control (the very reason why slave owners resisted black Christianity in the first place). In the British West Indies, many slave rebels in the early nineteenth century proved to be Christians. Where slave owners had once feared Africans, now they worried at the disruption and corrosion caused by the rise of black Christianity. Also alarming was that the slaves seemed to have incorporated elements of their traditional African beliefs into their new-found Christianity. It was an illustration, as Philip Morgan has shown for key regions of British North America, of how slaves managed 'to preserve some deep-level principles drawn from their African heritage'.[7] This was obviously not a Christianity familiar in Europe.

The adoption of Christianity, then, did not cause any great reduction in the practice of African spiritual and folk practices, including the use of naturalistic medicine, local healers and the casting of spells – a range of 'superstitions' which had survived the migrations into the Americas. Other cultural features were transplanted, understandably enough, because they were integral to the slaves themselves: language and folk memory, facial markings, foodstuffs and cooking, domestic and labouring skills, all entered the Americas with the Africans. Of course, they changed in contact with local whites and with other Africans. Some were driven out. In time, for example, native languages gave way to the varied European-based tongues of the Americas, to local patois, even though certain words and phrases lived on to show their direct African lineage.[8]

Sometimes, Africans' personal possessions, material artefacts from Africa, may have survived enslavement and the Atlantic crossing, but most Africans arrived in the Americas with nothing. Yet within a very short time those same people began to fill their new homes with familiar items: clothing, cooking implements, decorative pieces and musical instruments. In the main they were able to do this through their own efforts, in their gardens and plots, using their skills and labours, to produce artefacts, foodstuffs and animals which they traded with other slaves and whites. To put the matter simply, slave culture reflected a culture of ownership and individual possessiveness which, even if only at a humble and mundane level, provides evidence of the remarkable changes in slaves' lives since first stepping from the slave ships.

The focus of slave culture became the slave family. For a long time, and until fairly recently, some historians doubted whether the slave nuclear family had even been possible in the hostile conditions of the plantations.[9] It is clear enough that the emergence of the slave family was shaped from remembered African habits and the dictates of American circumstances. Moreover, the terminology of family life (derived from assumptions about free choice) might not apply under slavery.[10] Nevertheless, in time, slaves moved towards family systems, with more extended kinship links which reached out into the local and wider slave community, and which formed the bedrock of slave life throughout the mature slave societies of the Americas.

Patterns of naming, marriage, funeral rites and family celebrations, like lessons for the young, and the ties of affection for kinsfolk, formed a cultural system which derived directly from the slave family. A slave culture developed with clear moral and practical precepts, although slave owners were often unable to see it (not least, of course, because so much slave culture was fashioned as a shield against slavery's greatest dangers). Whites were generally puzzled by slave behaviour which seemed so often contrary to all the whites held dear: slave deception, footdragging, formed a stark contrast to the social values slave owners expected and wanted from their slaves. Here was, in effect, a code of behaviour for slaves which, however much disliked and challenged by whites, was well suited to slave life. Moreover, it was, throughout the Americas, reflected in an oral culture, of tales, songs and rhymes which have survived to this day. Children's stories that tell of the weak deceiving and defeating the strong, and of the wily outfoxing the predator, were important elements of slave culture, forming, in effect, the very principles for slave life.

Though the focus of slave culture was the family, that family was part of a slave community which was, in effect, a world within a world. The community was a small social unity which tried as best it could to keep slavery at arm's length and offered a reprieve from its difficulties. It was here, too, that slave social life evolved in its more public forms: those more elaborate and memorable occasions of collective enjoyment, at important times in the local agricultural (sometimes urban) calendar, the cycle of the Christian year, and at high points of personal, family and communal life. It was on such occasions that we see glimpses of slave culture in its most eye-catching form: the music-making, merriment, lavish drinking and eating, elaborate dressing-up at moments which amazed contemporaries for their zest and expense. How could slaves (people who seemed to have little more than the mere basics of everyday life) afford such pleasures? We now know, of course, that one critical aspect of slave culture was independent work which provided slaves with the where-withal to improve their material lot. One feature of slavery throughout the Americas was the development of a striking material culture.

Notes

1   See Douglas Chambers, '"My Own Nation": Igbo Exiles in the Diaspora', *Slavery & Abolition*, *18* (1997); David Northrup, 'Igbo and Myth Igbo: Culture and Ethnicity in the Atlantic World, 1600–1850', *Slavery & Abolition, 21* (2000).
2   Michael A. Gomez, *Exchanging our Country Marks*, Chapel Hill, 1998, p. 29.
3   James Walvin, *An African's Life: The Life and Times of Olaudah Equiano, 1745–1797*, London, 1998, p. 112.
4   For a discussion of African aesthetic see John Thornton, *Africa and Africans in the Making of the Atlantic World, 1400–1680*, Cambridge, 1992, pp. 221–234.
5   Douglas B. Chambers, '"My Own Nation": Igbo Exiles in the Diaspora', in David Eltis and David Richardson, eds, *Routes to Slavery*, London, 1997.
6   Philip D. Morgan, *Slave Counterpoint*, Chapel Hill, 1998, p. 657.
7   *Ibid.*, p. 657.
8   For an introduction to the study of African-based languages in the Americas see, for example, R.B. Le Page and Andree Tabouret-Keller, *Acts of Identity: Creole-based Approaches to Language and Ethnicity*, Cambridge, 1985; Maureen Warner-Lewis, *Guinea's Other Suns,* Dover, Mass., 1991.
9   Orlando Patterson, *The Sociology of Slavery*, London, 1967, p. 167.
10 Philip D. Morgan, *Slave Counterpoint,* chapter 9.

Chapter 17

Edward Kamau Brathwaite

THE 'FOLK' CULTURE OF THE SLAVES

THE VAST MAJORITY OF JAMAICA'S slaves came from West Africa. No attempt will be made in this study, to enter the argument about African 'survivals', 'retentions', 'adaptations' and so on, within creole society. But the habits, customs, and ways of life of the slaves in Jamaica, derived from West Africa, will be seen in this context as a 'folk' culture—the culture of the mass of ex-Africans who found themselves in a new environment and who were successfully adapting to it.

Some understanding of the nature of this folk culture is important, not only in terms of the creole society to which it was to contribute within the time-limits of this study, but also because the changes in Jamaican society after 1865 involved the beginning of an assertion of this folk culture which was to have a profound effect upon the very constitution of Jamaican society. This assertion has become increasingly articulate since the gaining of political independence in 1962 and is now the subject of some study by scholars and intellectuals. This 'folk culture' is also being made use of by many Jamaican and West Indian artists and writers, though the nature of the creolization of this culture has made the effective validation of it more difficult than might be supposed. This is because, in M. G. Smith's phrase, 'the Creole culture which West Indians share is the basis of their division'. White (European) and 'mulatto' (creole) values are still preferred to black folk values—even by black West Indians themselves.

The African orientation of Jamaican folk culture

Folk culture, though usually autochthonous, may be said to be dependent upon a 'great tradition', in the sense defined by Redfield, for its sanctions, its memories, its myths. In the case of Jamaica's slaves, the 'great tradition' was clearly in Africa, in the same way that white Jamaicans' was in Europe—both, in other words, external to the society.

> Have you ever heard African Negroes speak of their own country?
> —I have heard them speak very much in favour of their own country, and express much grief at leaving it. I never knew one but wished to go back again.

Did you know any instances of African Negroes expressing themselves with affection of their native country, and desiring to return to it?

—I did, as I brought a Guinea woman to England who wished much to be sent back to her own country; and it is very common for Negroes when they are sick to say, they are going back to their own country.

Did they say it with apparent satisfaction?

—They certainly do, as they express always a great deal of pleasure when they think they are going to die, and say, that they are going to leave this Buccra country.

Slave customs connected with the life cycle

(i) Birth

When a child was born, the placenta and navel string were carefully disposed of. 'The mother must guard it carefully and, after three days to a year from the time of birth, must bury it in the ground and plant a young tree over the spot, which henceforth becomes the property of the child and is called his "navel-string tree"'. The newborn was regarded as not being of this world until nine days had passed. 'Monk' Lewis was told by a slave midwife: 'Oh, massa, till nine days over, we no hope of them'. Dr. Dancer in his *Medical Assistant*, said: 'The negro usage, of tying up the cut Navel-string with burnt rag, and never examining it for nine days, is attended sometimes with bad consequences.' After this period, the child was exposed 'to the inclemency of the weather, with a view to render [him] hardy'. But was it as simple and crude as this? Dr. Patterson, in discussing the nine-day period of neglect, says it was due to the fear of tetanus in Jamaica. On the other hand M. J. Field, describing the birth customs of the Ga people, has this account which corresponds, not insignificantly, with the Jamaican experience:

> After the child is born it is 'kept like an egg' indoors for seven days. It is then held to have survived seven dangers, and is worthy to be called a person.
>
> On the eighth day very early in the morning, about four o'clock, two women of the father's family are sent to bring the child from the mother's home, where it was born and where it will be suckled, to its father's house. The friends and relatives assemble in the yard outside the house for the *kpodziem*, or 'going-out' ceremony . . .
>
> . . . the child is laid naked on the ground under the eaves. . . . Then the 'godfather' takes water in a calabash and flings it three times on the roof, so that it trickles down on the child like rain. This is to introduce the child to the rain and to the earth. Then the child as it lies on the ground is blessed. . . . The child is now a member of the family and has assumed its own name. If it dies before the eighth day it is considered as having never been born and has no name, but it can die on the ninth day and its father and mother for the rest of their lives be called by its name—'*Dede* mother', '*Tete* father.'

Martha Beckwith's *Black Roadways*, in fact, describes a Jamaican 'outdooring' observed in the 1920s:

> The momentous time in an infant's life arrives on the ninth day after birth, when for the first time he is taken out of doors. During the first nine days the mother eats only soft food, like arrowroot, bread, and milk. On the ninth day, a bath is prepared for the child, a little rum thrown into it, and each member of the family must throw in a bit of silver 'for the eyesight'.
> . . . To ward off evil spirits, indigo blue is added to the bath, and the forehead marked with a blue cross . . . the midwife offers a prayer before bringing the baby out into the air.

(ii) Sexual/Domestic unions

> It is a truth well known, that the practice of polygamy, which universally prevails in Africa, is also very generally adopted among the Negroes in the West Indies; and he who conceives that a remedy may be found for this, by introducing among them the laws of marriage as established in Europe, is utterly ignorant of their manners, propensities, and superstitions. It is reckoned in Jamaica, on a moderate computation, that not less than ten thousand of such as are called Head Negroes (artificers and others) possess from two to four wives.

But

> one only is the object of particular steady attachment; the rest, although called wives, are only a sort of occasional concubines, or drudges, whose assistance the husband claims in the culture of his land, sale of his produce, and so on; rendering to them reciprocal acts of friendship, when they are in want. They laugh at the idea of marriage, which ties two persons together indissolubly.

(iii) Children

> They exercise a kind of sovereignty over their children, which never ceases during life; chastizing them sometimes with much severity; and seeming to hold filial obedience in much higher estimation than conjugal fidelity.

> I can affirm, that the affections between the mothers and even spurious offspring are very powerful as well as permanent . . . and with respect to black children, nothing is so sure to irritate and enrage them as cursing their mothers. . . .

> negroes absolutely respect primogeniture; and the eldest son takes an indisputed possession of his father's property immediately after his decease . . .

they are in general [so] attached to their families, that the young will work with cheerfulness to maintain the sickly and the weak, and . . . they are much disposed to pay to age respect and veneration.

(iv) Death, funerals and burial

Before burial, a dead person was, if possible, laid out in state:

> an assemblage of slaves from the neighbourhood appears: the body is orna-mented with linen and other apparel, which has been previously purchased, as is often the custom, for this solemn occasion; and all the trinkets of the defunct are exposed in the coffin. . . .

A wake usually took place at this time, accompanied by what white observers called 'every kind of tumult and festivity'—dirges, drumming, horn-blowing in the West African style, praise-songs for the deceased, sacrifices of poultry and libations. Interment took place in Negro burial grounds, if these were provided by the author-ities, or 'promiscuously in the fields, and [near] their near and dear relations at the back of their huts, and sometimes under their beds'. According to Lewis, they were

> always buried in their own gardens, and many strange and fantastical cere-monies are observed on the occasion. If the corpse be that of a grown person, they consult it as to which way it pleases to be carried; and they make attempts upon various roads without success, before they can hit upon the right one.

Dr. Field's description of a Ga funeral procession is almost exactly similar:

> When the time comes for burial the body is put into a coffin—it used to be a basket—and is carried round the town. If any one is responsible for the death either by witchcraft, poison, or bad medicine, the coffin will lurch and plunge towards the house of the offender and refuse to pass it. Even when it has no accusation of this kind to make a coffin is always an unruly burden.

At the graveside, libations were offered:

> The manner of the Sacrifice is this: The nearest Relation kills [a hog], the Intrails are buried, the four Quarters are divided, and a kind of Soup made, which is brought in a Calabash or Gourd, and, after waving it Three times, it is set down; then the Body is put in the Ground; all the while they are covering it with Earth, the Attendants scream out in a terrible manner, which is not the Effect of Grief, but of Joy; they beat on their wooden Drums and the Women with their Rattles make a hideous Noise . . .

The dead body's spirit, however, would not yet be at rest. A period of forty days had to elapse before this would be accomplished. As in parts of West Africa, therefore, the first burial was considered temporary, and food was left by the grave-side for the succour of the 'traveller':

> After the Grave is filled up they place the Soup which they had prepared at the Head, and a Bottle of rum at the Feet. . . .

There then followed the period of mourning—again West African in character (though Long thought that he recognized in it the Scottish highland 'late-wake').

> When the deceased is a married woman, the husband lets his beard remain unshaved, and appears rather negligent in his attire, for the space of a month; at the expiration of which, a fowl is dressed at his house, with some messes of good broth, and he proceeds, accompanied by his friends, to the grave.

Here now, about a month (or forty days) after the first interment, the 'second', final (often symbolic only), burial took place.

> Then begins a song, purporting, that the deceased is now in the enjoy-ment of compleat felicity; and that they are assembled to rejoice at her state of bliss, and perform the last offices of duty and friendship. They then lay a considerable heap of earth over the grave, which is called *covering it*; and the meeting concludes with eating . . . drinking, dancing and vociferation.

Because of this 'two-burial' custom, some white Jamaican observers, lacking understanding, received the impression that the slaves did not care for their dead, but merely covered them lightly with a little earth. The 'happy' songs and up-tempo rhythms used when returning from the graveside also contributed to this impression.

Religious ideas

'The African negroes of the West Indies,' Stewart wrote,

> whatever superstitious notions they may bring with them from their native country, agree in believing the existence of an omnipotent Being, who will reward or punish us in a future life for our good or evil actions in this. . . .

Another writer confirmed this, but went on to assume that this Being was not worshipped:

> The Africans all acknowledge a Supreme Being; but they suppose him endowed with too much benevolence to do harm to mankind, and there-fore think it unnecessary to offer him any homage. . . .

The slaves also believed that

> after death, they shall first return to their native country, and enjoy again
> the society of kindred and friends, from whom they have been torn away
> in an evil hour. . . .

This led, as in Africa, to the recognition of the ancestors as active spirits or forces
and to the connected belief (or superstition) in duppies and other forms of visible
ghosts; 'Monk' Lewis in 1818 having to wonder if his slaves' general resistance
to Christian doctrine did not betoken some religious beliefs of their own. Such a
possibility, however, was not easy for white creoles to accept, though De la Beche
found that

> Some negroes entertain ideas of the transmigration of the soul; an old
> woman on my estate . . . stated her belief that people when they died
> turned into dust like brickdust; that those who behaved ill during their
> lives became mules, horses, flies, etc.; but that those who had led a
> good life were born again, and occupied similar situations to those they
> had previously filled; that blacks would be blacks again, and whites
> whites.

Religious practice

As Lewis said, it was difficult to know if the slaves had any real religious beliefs
or practice, since the only external sign of a 'priest', was the obeah-man. Lewis
was perhaps nearer than he knew to the truth about his slaves' religious beliefs
and practices, but he did not understand the function of the obeah-man, since he
was associated in the Jamaican/European mind with superstition, witchcraft, and
poison.

But in African and Caribbean folk practice, where religion had not been
externalized and institutionalized as in Europe, the obeah-man was doctor, philoso-
pher, and priest. Healing was, in a sense, an act of faith, as it was in the early
Christian church, and the fetish (*suman*) had come to mediate (in many instances
to replace and obscure the connection) between man and god. More generally,
however, the fetish was regarded as an attribute or token of the god. Each man
was also, in a way not understood by Europeans, a priest, and through possession
(induced by communal dancing to drums) could not only communicate with the
gods, but become and assume the god. In Jamaica, Black Baptist worshippers
were often possessed, as were 'pagan' cultists, and not always under the prompting
of drums:

> During the sermon, a heathen woman began to twist her body about, and
> make all manner of Grimaces. I bore it all for sometime till she disturbed
> the congregation, when I desired one of the assistants to lead her out,
> thinking she was in pain. When the service was over, I inquired what ailed
> her, and was told, that it was a usual thing with the negroes on M. estate,
> and called by them Conviction.

Music and dance

Music and dance, though recreational, was functional as well. Slaves, as in Africa, danced and sang at work, at play, at worship, from fear, from sorrow, from joy. Here was the characteristic form of their social and artistic expression. It was secular and religious. There was no real distinction between these worlds in the way that a post-Renaissance European was likely to understand. And because this music and dance was so misunderstood, and since the music was based on tonal scales and the dancing on choreographic traditions entirely outside the white observers' experience—not forgetting the necessary assumption that slaves, since they were brutes could produce no philosophy that 'reach[ed] above the navel'—their music was dismissed as 'noise', their dancing as a way of (or to) sexual misconduct and debauchery. On the other hand, the 'political' function of the slaves' music was quickly recognized by their masters—hence the banning of drumming or gatherings where drumming took place—often on the excuse that it disturbed the (white) neighbours, or was bad for the bondsmen's own health, or both.

On the whole, therefore, the available descriptions of the slaves' music and dancing are picturesque only, though now and then a hint comes through of grace of form and discipline:

> nothing could be more light, and playful, and graceful, than the extempore movements of the dancing girl. Indeed, through the whole day, I had been struck with the precision of their march [Lewis is here describing a Christmas carnival], the ease and grace of their action, the elasticity of their step, and the lofty air with which they carried their heads. . . .

> The dances performed tonight seldom admitted more than three persons at a time: to me they appeared to be movements entirely dictated by the caprice of the moment; but I am told that there is a regular figure, and that the least mistake, or a single false step, is immediately noticed by the rest.

Dancing usually took place, as in Africa, in the centre of a ring of spectator-participants, performers entering the ring singly or in twos and threes. Sometimes male dancers expressed themselves acrobatically, but more often, especially at private entertainments, the shuffle step was employed, the dancers stylistically confining themselves to a very restricted area indeed. 'Sometimes there are two men dance with one woman; they follow, fan her with their handkerchiefs, court her and leave her alternately, and make you understand, as perfectly as any ballet-dancer in Europe, what they mean.' As is still the custom in parts of West Africa, where coins are placed on the forehead of excellent performers, 'presents of ryals [were] thrust into [the] mouths or bosoms' of dancers who gave particular satisfaction to the audience, 'some officious negro going round the circle to keep back intruders'.

Improvisation was also a feature of many of the slaves' songs. 'Guinea Corn' is an excellent example of this genre:

Guinea Corn, I long to see you
Guinea Corn, I long to plant you

Guinea Corn, I long to mould you
Guinea Corn, I long to weed you
Guinea Corn, I long to hoe you
Guinea Corn, I long to top you
Guinea Corn, I long to cut you
Guinea Corn, I long to dry you
Guinea Corn, I long to beat you
Guinea Corn, I long to trash you
Guinea Corn, I long to parch you
Guinea Corn, I long to grind you
Guinea Corn, I long to turn you
Guinea Corn, I long to eat you

The climax of the song came with the word *eat*, when 'as though satiated with the food, or tired with the process for procuring it', the singers bestowed 'an hearty curse on the grain, asking where it came from'.

Many of these 'impromptus' were, like 'Guinea Corn' (above) or like

Hipsaw! my deaa! you no do like a-me!
You no jig like a-me! you no twist like a-me!
Hipsaw! my deaa! you no shake like a-me!
You no wind like a-me! Go, yondaa!

and

Ying de ying de ying,
Ying de ying de ying,
Take care you go talk oh,
Min' you tattler tongue,
Ying de ying,
Min' you tattler tongue,
Ying de ying,
Min' you tattler tongue,
Ying de ying . . .

songs of entertainment, used in ring games or while dancing. Some songs, on the other hand, had rebellious overtones or intentions, while many of them carried on the West African tradition of ridicule. Some of these were merely concerned at laughing at Europeans, like the song Renny reported hearing off Port Royal:

As soon as the vessel in which the author was passenger arrived near to Port Royal in Jamaica, a canoe, containing three or four black females, came to the side of the ship, for the purpose of selling oranges, and other fruits. When about to depart, they gazed at the passengers, whose number seemed to surprise them; and as soon as the canoe pushed off, one of them sung the following words, while the other joined in the chorus, clapping their hands regularly, while it lasted:

> New-come buckra,
> He get sick,
> He tak fever,
> He be die
> He be die
>   New-come buckra, etc.

The song, as far as we could hear contained nothing else and they continued singing it, in the manner just mentioned, as long as they were within hearing.

But very often the ridicule was turned as much against the masters as the singers themselves:

> If me want for go in a Ebo,
> Me can't go there!
> Since dem tief me from a Guinea,
> Me can't go there!

> If me want for go in a Congo,
> Me can't go there!
> Since dem tief me from my tatta,
> Me can't go there!

> If me want for go in a Kingston,
> Me can't go there!
> Since massa go in a England,
> Me can't go there!

Or

> Sarragree kill de captain,
> O dear, he must die;
> New rum kill de sailor,
> O dear, he must die;
> Hard work kill de neger,
> O dear, he must die.

> La, la, la, la
> La, la, la, la . . .

and

> Bun-go Moo-lat-ta,
> Bun-go Moo-lat-ta,
> Who dé go married you?
> You hand full a ring
> An' you can't do a t'ing.

A closer approximation to the African character of slave songs, however, may be observed in this phonetic transcription of a *cumina* invocation recorded by a field researcher in the Morant Bay area of St. Thomas (in-the-East) in the early 1950s.

Cumina is a memorial ceremony for calling down ancestral spirits and African gods and is similar to, say, *vodun*, in Haiti.

> Tangε langε Jeni di gal εva
> Wang lang mama o
> Di le kuwidi pangε le
>   So-so langε widi gal
> So-so langε mama o
> Owɔt kuqelaa zɔmbi di gal ɔlɔk
> O widi pangε le
> Galɔmɔt widi pangε le
> Di le konakunda pangε langε e
> Di lɔ wɔtɔ widingga le
> Mɔnukɔ di lɔ kuwidi pangε le.

> Dance tall Jenny gal
> Walk tall mama o
> The dead come to greet you
> Water long like the dead, gal
> Water long, mama o
> Look how the spirits look on the gal there
> O the dead greet her
> The gal who greets the dead
> They all come tall to greet her
> The black ancestors from the water
> Manuka of the spirits greets her.

As in Africa, these songs were usually built on a statement and response pattern and except for work and digging songs, were customarily the province of women:

> The style of singing among the negroes, is uniform: and this is confined to the women; for the men very seldom, excepting upon extraordinary occasions, are ever heard to join in chorus. One person begins first, and continues to sing alone; but at particular periods the others join: there is not, indeed, much variety in their songs; but their intonation is not less perfect than their time.

Musical instruments

These were almost entirely African. There were flutes: from the long bassoon-like 'Caramantee flute', to the small 'Maroon' nose-flute; the *abenghorn*; a mouth violin or 'bender' (Twi: *bentá*); the banjo (banja or bangil); a box (tambourine) filled with pebbles, 'which they shake with their wrists'; the *rookaw* and scraper (similar instruments), corrugated sticks across which were (and are) rubbed a plain stick; *jenkoving* (from the Ga *kofen*) 'which is a way of clapping their Hands on the Mouth of two Jars'; and the 'jawbone': the lower jaw of a horse, 'on the teeth of which, a piece of wood [was] passed quickly up and down, occassioning [*sic*] a rattling noise'. Above all, there were the various drums: the *cotter* or *cotta*, the Eboe (Ibo) drum, the *bon* or *panya* (played with sticks), the gomba (goombah, gumbie or goombay played with the hands. One commentator claims that the gomba, goombah and goombay were different drums. But this seems unlikely, though it is possible that the word 'gomba' (conga? congo?) might have been applied generically to a certain kind of dance drum. In any case, there are conflicting descriptions of the gomba. In *Marly* it appears played with 'a single stick'. The confusion seems to have started with Long, (usually reliable in description). His is the first extant description of the gomba. But what he appears to have described is the gomba ('tabor') and a kind of *etwie* drum 'which is played by rubbing the drum head with a stick':

> The goombah . . . is a hollow block of wood, covered with sheep-skin stripped of its hair. The musician holds a little stick, of about six inches in length, sharpened at one end like the blade of a knife, in each hand. With one hand he rakes it over a notched piece of wood, fixed across the instrument, . . . whilst a second performer beats with all his might on the sheep-skin, or tabor.

Belisario's description (in view of the modern equivalent) is probably more accurate:

Creolization

> [A] small square wooden frame, over which a goat's skin is tightly strained . . ., and being briskly struck several times in quick succession with one hand, and once only with the other, produces a . . . sound with but little vibration:—it is supported by a Bass-drum: *very unlike* that in the band at the 'Horse-Guards' in London. . . .

There were also various rattles ('Shaky-shekies and Kitty-katties'), made of gourds or cylindrical tin boxes, 'pierced with small holes, and filled with beads, shots or gravel' used, as in African music, as a kind of metronome.

It was in this area of most intense 'culture focus', however, that, paradoxically, the greatest amount of creolization took place. As Stewart observed in 1823:

> In a few years it is probable that the rude music here described will be altogether exploded among the creole negroes, who shew a decided preference for European music. Its instruments, its tunes, its dances, are now pretty generally adopted by the young creoles, who indeed sedulously copy their masters and mistresses in every thing. A sort of subscription balls are set on foot, and parties of both sexes assemble and dance country dances to the music of a violin, tambarine, etc.

But a distinction must be made here between public slave entertainment, like Christmas 'John Canoe' processions and the balls described by Stewart, and the more intransigent 'cult' observances of the slaves that were necessarily secret, or at any rate, private, and which centred around the drum. It was this drumming, which the authorities and the missionaries tried unsuccessfully to eradicate by legislation and persuasion, respectively, which retained and transmitted important and distinctive elements of African/folk culture into the period after Emancipation.

Private entertainments

Dec 24, 1812
Being Christmas-eve, our evening-service was attended by most of our people from Elim, Two-mile-wood, Lancaster, and this place [Bogue]. The glad tidings of great joy . . . [were] heard with great attention. . . . [But] Scarcely was our worship closed, before the heathen negroes on the estate began to beat their drums, to dance, and to sing, in a most outrageous manner. The noise lasted all night, and prevented us from falling asleep.

Dec 25, 1812
After breakfast, I went down and begged the negroes to desist, but their answer was: 'What, Massa, are we not to dance and make merry at Christmas. We always did so.' I represented to them that this was not the way to celebrate the birth of our Saviour, and expressed my surprise, that having heard the word of God for so many years, they still continued their heathenish customs. But all I could say was in vain. . . .

Dec 26, 1813
These Christmas rejoicings among the negroes have certainly a very bad influence, even among Christian negroes, several of whom will find excuses for joining in what they call an innocent dance. . . .

'Crop-over' and the 'Habit of rambling to what are called Negro Plays, or nocturnal Assemblies', the annual yam festival, and wrestling, were also among the entertainments of African origin in this category, as were games of chance like *warri* (Twi: *ware*; Fante: *aware*) which, like the musical instruments described above, survived the Middle Passage.

Public entertainments

These took place during the legal seasonal holidays: Christmas, Easter, and Whitsun. They took the form, usually of street processions with music, dancing and costumes as in the Trinidad and similar carnivals in the Catholic Caribbean today. As in Carnival, these entertainments were a brilliant fusion of African and European elements, deriving their energy and motifs, not from Catholicism in Protestant Jamaica, but from Africa, where many of their prototypes can still be observed, especially in the festivals of the coastal towns and villages.

In Jamaica, these Carnivals (Belisario uses the word) rapidly became the cultural expression, *par excellence*, of the creole slaves and the free blacks and coloureds, rather than of the African or 'new' Negroes. The 'new' Negroes influenced by their African Great Tradition, tended to regard festivals as essentially religious in nature, and so kept them secret (or as secret as possible); thus forming the basis of the various 'cults' that were to emerge after Emancipation. Many creole slaves and the bulk of the free people, on the other hand, tended to be grateful for the seasonal licence and encouragement given them publicly by the white Establishment, and so responded enthusiastically to the occasion:

> The Negroes enjoy the time from Christmas to new-Year's-day as holidays and the streets were now crowded with splendid processions, or choked up with crowds of dancers. . . . Their processions are really elegant, but as far as I could learn, they consisted principally of free Negroes. [The author is here writing of the North Coast, a dense plantation area.] They were well attired in muslins and silks, accompanied with bands of music. They walked arm in arm, males and females. Sometimes a female with a good voice sung a song, and the whole procession joined in the chorus. They carried, at certain intervals, large artificial trees, stuck full of burning tapers. They usually made a halt at the doors of the wealthier inhabitants, and after chanting some stanzas in praise of the occupant, received . . . gratuity in money.

Perhaps because of these factors (participation by the free groups, Establishment encouragement), public entertainments in the island became increasingly orientated (externally, at least) towards European forms (silks, muslins, bands of music); at the same time reflecting the unquestionably *creole* colour/class divisions of the society. In the various costumed bands, for instance,

> the *colours* were never blended in the same set—no blackie ever interloped with the browns, nor did the browns in any case mix with the sables— always keeping in mind—black *woman*—brown *lady*.

This process of creolization from African motif to something local but (externally) European-influenced may be studied in the development of the masked (masque) bands like John Canoe. Edward Long, writing just before the beginning of our period, described this manifestation as follows:

> In the towns, during Christmas holidays, they have several tall robust fellows dressed up in grotesque habits, and a pair of ox-horns on their head, sprouting from the top of a horrid sort of vizor, or mask, which about the mouth is rendered very terrific with large boar-tusks. The masquerader, carrying a wooden sword in his hand, is followed with a numerous croud of drunken women [*sic*], who refresh him frequently with a sup of aniseed-water, whilst he dances at every door, bellowing out *John Connu*! with great vehemence. . . . This dance is probably an honourable memorial of John Conny, a celebrated cabocero at *Tres Puntas*, in Axim, on the Guiney coast; who flourished about the year 1720.

In 1769 'several new masks appeared; the Ebos, the Pawpaws, etc., having their respective Connús, male and female. . . .' By 1815, however, when 'Monk' Lewis was writing his Jamaica *Journal*, this 'primitive' Connú had been creolized into a Merry-Andrew dressed in a striped doublet, and bearing upon his head a kind of pasteboard house-boat, filled with puppets, representing, some sailors, others soldiers, others again slaves at work on a plantation . . . ,

while De la Beche (1825) records an even further stage in the process:

I was much amused on Easter Monday by a party which came to my house from a neighbouring property, consisting of musicians, and a couple of personages fantastically dressed to represent kings and warriors; one of them wore a white mask on his face, and a part of the representation had evidently some reference to the play of Richard the Third; for the man in the white mask exclaimed, 'A horse, a horse, my kingdom for a horse!'

In true Carnival spirit, however,

The piece . . . terminated by Richard killing his antagonist, and then figuring in a sword dance with him.

The most beautiful moment in these seasonal festivities came, perhaps, with the procession of the Red and Blue 'Set Girls', originating, according to Lewis, in the Red and Blue divisions of the Royal Navy, and coming later to represent the English (Red) and Scots (Blue) in Kingston and elsewhere. There were also French Sets, Golden Sets, Velvet Sets, Garnet Ladies, etc.; and each set represented some variation of the society's complexity of colour:

They danced along the streets, in bands of from fifteen to thirty. There were brown sets, and black sets, and sets of all the intermediate gradations of colour. [The girls in each] set [were] dressed pin for pin alike, and carried umbrellas or parasols of the same colour and size, held over their nice showy, well-put-on *toques*, or Madras handkerchiefs, all of the same pattern, tied round their heads, fresh out of the fold.—They sang, as they swam along the streets, in the most luxurious attitudes . . . beautiful creatures . . . elegant carriages, splendid figures,—full, plump, and magnificent.

Here, too, it was the brown girls who predominated, with their 'clear olive complexions, and fine faces'. These, at least, were the ones most noticed, representing as they did, the Euro-tendency of this part of creole society.

First marched Britannia; then came a band of music; then the flag; then the Blue King and Queen—the Queen splendidly dressed in white and silver . . . his Majesty wore a full British Admiral's uniform, with a white satin sash, and a huge cocked hat with a gilt paper crown upon the top of it. . . .

Jack-in-the-Green and the May-pole dance (using a 'spike of the yellow flowers of the American aloe' as pole), were also popular forms of public amusement by the end of our period. These were post-1807 developments, reflecting the cutting off of demographic and cultural renewal from Africa, and the increasing influence of those browns and privileged blacks who could afford to spend time and money on costumed processions, and who wished, or tended, to imitate European models in these matters.

But the African influence remained, even if increasingly submerged, as an important element in the process of creolization. European adaptations or imitations could never be whole-hearted or complete. There might be apparent European forms, but the content would be different. There was developing a European-orientated creole form (Euro-creole) and an African-influenced creole form (Afro-creole); and they existed together within, often, the same framework. It was a Negro fiddler who usually led the costumed bands; and it was the music of 'negroe drums, the sound of the pipe and tabor, negroe flutes, gombas and jawbones', that moved them along. There were also large areas of public entertainment that remained intransigently African or Afro-creole. Those bands, for instance, who continued to dramatize or satirize aspects of the slave society—their and their masters' condition. Outside the sets and masquerades, large groups of slaves 'from different districts in Guinea' wandered about, 'diverting themselves with their own peculiar singing, instruments and dances'.

Dress

> The general Clothing in Jamaica is what is called Osnaburgh Linen. On every well-regulated Estate, the annual Allowance is from Ten to Twenty yards to every Man; from Seven to Fifteen Yards to every Woman; and in proportion to the younger People. To every Negro, a Worsted Cap, Bonnet, or Hat, besides a Woollen Jacket, or Welch Blanket, to the Men; and a Petticoat and Blanket to the Women. The Petticoat is on many Estates of Perpetuana; a Quantity of common Check Linen is given on some Estates to the principal Negroes, such as Boilers, Drivers, Waggoners and Tradesmen; and several of our Planters furnish Handkerchiefs, Knives, Scissors, Thread, Needles, and short Tobacco Pipes. The Jamaica law enjoins sufficient Clothing to be given, and inflicts a Penalty on such Owners as disobey that Injunction. In general, the Negroes in Jamaica are well clothed; and there are very few Sugar Estates where the Negroes do not from their own private Earnings provide themselves with extra Clothes for Sunday and Holidays.

In some houses, male domestics wore 'a coarse linen frock which buttons at the neck & hands, long trowsers of the same, a checked shirt, & no stockings'. Servant maids appeared usually in 'cotton or striped Holland gown[s]'; though of course there was often considerable variation between house and house, estate and estate, and town and country.

Slave women, as in Africa, were 'fond of covering [their head] at all times, twisting one or two handkerchiefs round it, in the turban form . . .', and at festivals, according to Lewis, they tended to dress in white—an Akan colour of celebration; though Christian missionary influence cannot be ruled out here. They also appeared during their holidays, according to Lewis, 'decked out with a profusion of beads and corals, and gold ornaments of all descriptions'. Where the gold came from is not indicated or suggested. Is it possible that it could have been smuggled over on slave ships and accumulated over the years in the island? Writing of St. Vincent, Mrs. Carmichael noted that

> The real value of their jewellery is considerable; it consists of many gold ear-rings, and rings upon their fingers. Coral necklaces, and handsome gold chains, lockets, and other ornaments of this description.

Besides the usual ear-rings and necklaces, the slave belles produced African-influenced creole decorations of their own:

> the women have at different times used as beads, the seeds of *Jobstears*, *liquorice*, and *lilac*; the vertebrae of the shark; and lately red sealing wax, which in appearance nearly resembles coral. Sometimes they sportively affix to the lip of the ear, a *pindal* or ground nut, open at one end; at other times they thrust through the hole bored for the ear-ring, the round yellow flower of the opopinax . . .,

while many slaves proudly displayed their tribal marks

> with a mixture of ostentation and pleasure, either considering them as highly ornamental, or appealing to them as testimonies of distinction [from] Africa; where, in some cases, they are said to indicate free birth and honourable parentage.

Under slavery, needless to say, these marks were supplemented with planters' initials on the shoulder or breast, stamped into the flesh 'by means of a small silver brand heated in the flame of spirits. . . .'

Hair style was presumably 'Afro' or plaits, many females taking 'great pleasure in having their woolly curled Hair, cut into Lanes or Walks as the *Parterre* of a Garden . . .'; as is still done in West Africa.

Slave children, as children in West Africa still do, wore 'party-coloured beads tied round their loins'. Sandals, 'cut from an ox-hide, which they bind on with thongs', were also worn on occasion by adults. In general, however, slaves went barefoot and many of them, especially 'new' Africans and field slaves when working, were described as being naked or almost naked. As in Africa, babies were often carried 'ty'd to their [mothers'] Backs, in a Cloth [used for that] purpose, one Leg on one side, and the other on the other of their Mother'.

Houses and furniture

> The cottages of the Negroes usually compose a small village, the situation of which, for the sake of convenience and water, is commonly near the buildings in which the manufacture of sugar is conducted. They are seldom placed with much regard to order, but, being always intermingled with fruit-trees, particularly the banana, the avocado-pear, and the orange (the Negroes' own planting and property) they sometimes exhibit a pleasing and picturesque appearance.

In general, a cottage for one Negro and his wife, is from fifteen to twenty feet in length, and divided into two apartments. It is composed of hard posts driven into the ground, and interlaced with wattles and plaister. The height from the ground to the plate being barely sufficient to admit the owner to walk in upright. The floor is of natural earth, which is commonly dry enough, and the roof thatched with palm . . ., or the leaves of the cocoa-nut-tree; an admirable covering, forming a lasting and impenetrable shelter both against the sun and the rain.

By the end of our period, some of these huts were boarded, instead of wattle and daubed; and shingles ('wood split and dressed into the shape of slates, and used as a substitute for them) were in evidence on the roofs.

Of furniture they have no great matters to boast, nor, considering their habits of life, is much required. The bedstead is a platform of boards, and the bed a mat, covered with a blanket.

Many slaves, in fact, slept on the floor or ground, causing a wit to remark that they don't go to *bed*, they simply go to sleep. Other items inside the house included

a small table; two or three low stools; an earthen jar for holding water; a few smaller ones; a pail; an iron pot; *calabashes* of different sizes (serving very tolerably for plates, dishes, and bowls). . . .

According to the slave laws, certainly for the towns, slave huts, for control and security reasons, were not supposed to have more than one window and door. This, plus the very limited height of the structure, meant that little more than sleeping could be enjoyed inside the houses. 'Cookery', relaxing, story-telling, singing, etc., were all 'conducted in the open air'.

This account of their accommodation, however, is confined to the lowest among the field-negroes: tradesmen and domesticks are in general vastly better lodged and provided. Many of these have larger houses with boarded floors, and are accommodated (*at their own expence it is true*) with very decent furniture:—a few have even good beds, linen sheets, and musquito nets, and display [such was the progress of their creolization] a shelf or two of plates and dishes of queen's or Staffordshire ware.

The making of these houses was, as in a great deal of public Negro activity, communal. Ingenuity and improvisation, as is so often the case in 'pre-industrial' situations, went into their construction—skills which were also applied to the building of plantation houses. The wood used in building, for instance, was often first burnt to prevent it from rotting. When nails could not be easily obtained, a notch was cut in the top of each post to receive the wall-plates, 'bestowing very little labour on any of their timber, except squaring one or two sides'. The beams which crossed the wall-plates were held in their proper position by notches at the end where they overlapped. A ridge pole was placed in the forks of the uprights, at the ends and middle of the structure. The rafters, often of sweet-wood were 'flatten'd at the upper ends and connected in pairs by wooden pins'. The laths were bound to the rafters by strong withes, easily obtained from the surrounding woods.

> The structure being thus far completed, the next concern is furnishing the sides with wattles. . . . Between every two posts in the wall, a small stick is placed perpendicularly & another nailed on each side of every post. The wattles are placed alternately; both ends of one bending inward, the next in a contrary direction. The interstices among the wattles are filled with clay and earth, into which some fibres of dried plantain leaves are rubbed to render the same more cohesive; and both the surfaces of the wall plaistered smoothly with the same composition: the whole is white washed when the mountain affords lime stone and the owner will be at trouble to burn it; otherwise the surface is left of its natural colour, a pale reddish yellow, red, or gray, as the loam employed in plaistering happens.

Where hinges were unobtainable, un-dressed leather straps or wooden pivots were used. Locks, keys and bolts could also be made of wood. In the kitchen, which, as pointed out earlier, was out of doors, the trivet for supporting cooking-pots was replaced (as it still is in many rural areas) by three large stones. Ovens were made 'by scooping hollows in perpendicular sides of a bank; and covered with a shade of sticks & leaves to keep off rain. By frequent heating the cavity acquired sufficient hardness to answer its intention'. Where the in-door householder used shelves, the 'kitchen-garden cook' had to improvise with forked sticks placed in the ground. An earthenware water jar hung from the 'stem of a small tree with three prongs, fixed in one corner of [the] house'. The water-cup (and one can still remember using these as a small boy) was a calabash, or small coconut shell, with a stick thrust through the sides. There were also calabashes, gourds, wooden plates, and bowls, *yabbas* (Twi: *ayawa*; earthenware vessels, crudely glazed, coming in all sizes), and the wooden mortar for pounding Indian corn, plantain, etc., into *fufu* and *tumtum*.

Language

It was in language that the slave was perhaps most successfully imprisoned by his master, and it was in his (mis-)use of it that he perhaps most effectively rebelled. Within the folk tradition, language was (and is) a creative act in itself; the word was held to contain a secret power, as 'Monk' Lewis discovered one day on his estate:

> The other day, . . . a woman, who had a child sick in the hospital, begged me to change its name for any other which might please me best: she cared not what; but she was sure that it would never do well so long as it should be called Lucia.

'Perhaps', Lewis speculated,

> this prejudice respecting the power of names produces in some measure their unwillingness to be christened.

Lewis, like most Europeans in Jamaican slave society, was really unable to conceive of the possibility that the slaves did not wish to be christened because they had their own *alternative* to Christianity. The Bantu concept of *nommo* was unknown to him, though he did recognize that *some* principle of belief was at work.

> They find no change produced in them [by Christianity], except the alteration of their name, and hence they conclude that this name contains in it some secret power; while, on the other hand, they conceive that the ghosts of their ancestors cannot fail to be offended at their abandoning an appellation, either hereditary in the family, or given by themselves.

It is interesting to observe, though, how *nommo* was quickly creolized by Anancy into a secular device to avoid responsibility. This may be illustrated with the instance of the slave who, after having been baptized by a missionary, declared (the story is no doubt apocryphal, but it serves its turn):

> Me is new man now; befo me name Quashie, now me Thomas, derefo Thomas no pay Quashie debt.

The Rev. G. W. Bridges recognized and analysed another aspect of *nommo* in discussing the power of Negro preachers over their congregations:

> so susceptible are the Africans of the influence of that art which variously affects the mind by the mysterious power of sound, . . . they will scarcely give any attention to a religious instructor who possesses a harsh or discordant voice. Every good speaker, independently of the softness of his tones, raises and lowers them in strict musical intervals; so that, in fact, his discourse is as capable of being noted in musical characters as any melody whatever, becoming disagreeable only when those intervals ear uniformly the same, or when the same intonations are used to express sentiments of the most opposite import.

'Of this qualification', the Negro congregations, with their African background of tonal speech (though Bridges did not know and certainly did not admit this) were 'naturally most extraordinary judges'.

In their everyday lives, also, the slaves observed carefully the courtesies of language. Their greetings—'Good morning; how is family', followed by the asking after each member in turn, their polite modes of address—'compliments of respect and friendship, when speaking of or to each other' (Uncle, Aunty, Granny, Tatta)— all had their roots in West African forms of etiquette.

Then there was flattery (*Congo-saw*), as when an old slave woman, wanting to impress on 'Monk' Lewis her gratitude to him for a small favour, addressed him as '*my husband*' instead of Massa. There were also proverbs and sayings such as 'Massa's eye makes the horse grow fat'; the response of the old man who, wakened from sleep by another with the question, '*You no hear Massa call you?*', replied, '*Sleep hab no Massa*' and returned to his dreams; and the accurate description by the woman who, asked by a Baptist minister if she still felt sin, now that her heart was changed, admitted: 'It trouble me too much—it tick to me Massa, as close as de clothes to me back'.

This language attained its freest expression in the folk tales, many, but not all, featuring the Akan spider-hero, Ananse, and known in the island as Anancy stories. Stories involving magic and rivers, and featuring spirit persons like the River Maid or Water Mama, were (and are) also very common, since these elements ('magic' and rivers in flood) play such an important part in the life of the folk.

an, a so dem do. Dem kal de gyal, an she come. An im seh, Yu nyaam me peas today? Him seh, nuo ma, me no eat non. Him se, a'right, come, we go down a gully ya. We wi' find out. Him tek de gal an im go down a de gully. An when goin down to de gully, im go upan im laim tree, an im pick trii laim. Im guo in a im fowl nest, im tek trii eggs. Him guo in a geese nest, im tek trii. Das nine egg. An im tek trii dok eggs, mek wan dozen egg! An im staat, an haal im sword, an im go doun a de gully. An im go doun in a di gully. Him pu' down de gyal in a di lebl drai gully, an seh, See yal tan op dey. Me de go tell you now, ef you eat me peas, you de go drownded, bot ef you nuo eat e, notn wuon do you. So swie, you bitch! swear! Seh you no eat e, while you know you eat e. An she lit [lick] doun wan a de laim a doti [dirty; earth. ground] so, *wham*! An de drai gully pomp op wata, cova de gyal instep. De gyal seh, Mai! puo me wan! A weh me de go to die? Him se, Swie! Swie! you bitch! An im lik doun wan nida laim so, *wham*! An de wata mount di gyal to im knee. De gyal seh,

   laad ooi! Me Wilyam ooi!

(e im sweetheart im de kall)

   me Wilyam ooi!
   puo me wan ooi! Peas ooi!
   oo, me dearis Wilyam oo!
   ring doun peas oi ai A ring doun!
   oo, ring doun.

Chapter 18

Sylvia R. Frey and Betty Wood

THE AMERICAS
The survival of African religions

J ON BUTLER HAS RECENTLY ARGUED that the transatlantic slave trade shattered African systems of religion, describing it as "a holocaust that destroyed collective religious practice in colonial America." It would not have been altogether surprising had those who experienced the trauma of separation and sale in West and West Central Africa, who were herded like cattle on to the slave ships, completely lost their faith in gods who seemed to have abandoned them and in deities who appeared unwilling or unable to protect them. Some, believing perhaps that their gods had indeed forsaken them or that the superior "magic" of their European oppressors had prevailed, might have lost their faith, either permanently or temporarily; the majority did not.

Enslaved Africans turned to their gods and deployed their religious convictions in ways that gave structure and meaning to the present and challenged the total authority over their persons being claimed by Europeans. By remembering and recreating the past, they produced hope for the future, whatever that future might hold. That those taken on board the slave ships had been torn from the institutional frameworks of their traditional religious cultures is patently obvious. However, those who survived the Middle Passage showed enormous courage, resilience, and ingenuity in devising new religious structures to cope with the demands that enslavement in the British plantation colonies made on them.

Millions of Africans were forcibly removed from cultural, social, economic, and political contexts that were not precisely identical and fed into the international slave trade. Indeed, the trade thrived on often violent antagonisms among different ethnic groups and African nations, which sometimes resurfaced in the New World. But there were also some highly significant similarities in the religious cultures and languages of many of those shipped to British America. Profits dictated that slave ships be filled and dispatched as quickly as possible, and this usually involved loading at a single port rather than "coasting." That did not necessarily mean that all those taken on board a particular vessel came from the immediate vicinity of the port, but they had probably been obtained "from a restricted and culturally quite homogeneous zone." The "comparative cohesiveness" of the religious and linguistic traditions that crossed the Atlantic would be critically important in the reformulation of traditional West and West Central African religious cultures in the New World. Those cultures would retain some "explicitly West African . . . forms."

Most Africans transported from their homeland before the closing of the slave trade in the early nineteenth century subscribed to traditional religious cultures, and they would encounter Christianity for the first time in the Americas. However, the slave ships also included a smattering of people who adhered to their own versions of Islam and Christianity. These religious convictions would also survive the Middle Passage and take their place alongside traditional beliefs and practices in the very different contexts of the New World.

Capture and sale of slaves in Africa usually destroyed the ties of family and kinship that were of such significance to African peoples, and the personal and communal cost of that destruction to those who remained as well as to those who were taken should be neither forgotten nor underestimated. But the physical, psychological, and emotional brutality of the Middle Passage did not destroy memory, beliefs, experience, and expertise. Although stripped of much of their material culture, every African who survived the Middle Passage retained cultural attributes that could be put to creative use in the Americas.

The captains and crews of British slave ships felt no burning sense of mission to proselytize, but they were neither ignorant of nor indifferent to the often religiously inspired behavior of their human cargoes. Most were acutely conscious of the fact that those on board their vessels were not totally demoralized but at any moment might seek what was their common objective: their return to Africa. The arrangements on the slave ships made organized resistance difficult but not totally impossible once the vessels had left African waters. There is no record of the number of uprisings that occurred on the Middle Passage, but during the eighteenth century they averaged two a year on British slavers. Many involved women as well as men, and some depended upon traditional religious beliefs and practices for their inspiration and execution.

Throughout the duration of the slave trade most ships carried more men than women: somewhere between two-thirds and three-quarters of all the Africans transported to the Americas were men. The consequences of this imbalance for shaping the contours and dynamics of slave culture in the New World were to be manifold. On slave ships, however, it is highly relevant that captains and crews mistakenly assumed that the women on board their vessels posed little danger to them. In fact, African women from a wide spectrum of ethnic backgrounds were deeply involved in many of the insurrections that occurred on the Middle Passage. As Lucille Mathurin Mair has commented, whatever else it might have entailed, the Middle Passage involved "a crude levelling of sexual distinctions" that served to ensure that from the outset African women would "share every inch of the man's physical and spiritual odyssey."

Whether or not they involved women, some shipboard rebellions were spontaneous; others were planned over hours, days, or even weeks. Some relied very heavily indeed upon the potency of various African beliefs, symbols, and rituals for the secrecy and solidarity deemed essential for their success. In 1751, for example, the crew of the *Duke of Argyll*, a slaver bound for Antigua, was "alarmed with a report that some of the men slaves had found means to poison the water in the scuttle casks upon deck." They were both relieved and amused when they discovered that the men concerned "had only conveyed some of their country fetishes . . . or talismans into one of them, which they had the credulity to suppose must inevitably kill all who drank it." These African men, who might have included some experienced practitioners of witchcraft, were probably not trying to physically poison the white crew but had laid a form of curse or spell upon them.

In 1789 James Arnold, who was employed as a surgeon on the *Ruby*, gave a graphic account of an uprising that also included a profoundly important West African component. What is remarkable but not necessarily unique about this episode is that it involved the taking of a blood oath. West and West Central African oaths varied somewhat in their character and purpose, but all were taken immensely seriously. Ritual oaths, such as the blood oath taken by the men on the *Ruby*, were highly significant instruments for the creation of moral solidarity. In this case, the oath served as a major "weapon" in the men's struggle to secure their freedom.

The men on the *Ruby* failed in their bid for freedom, however. One of their leaders was shot and killed when he confronted the crew "with a Knife in each of his hands." Another, who held out for eight hours despite being "severely scalded with a Mixture of boiling Water and Fat, which was repeatedly thrown down upon him," was chained to the foremast, denied food or medical care, and after three days thrown overboard, possibly while still alive. These men were killed for one purpose and one purpose only: to convince their compatriots of the futility of such defiance. These two men may not have wished to die, but they had sworn to each other in the most solemn African terms their eternal brotherhood and their willingness to die together as brothers. No doubt they were greatly fortified by the belief that even if they could not secure their bodily freedom, at least their death would ensure the return home of their souls to Africa.

Several men and women on board the slave ships made quite calculated decisions to die by their own hand. Some may have killed themselves, or tried to kill themselves, because of indescribable fear or deep clinical depression; many must have been comforted, if not prompted, by their unshakeable convictions concerning the hereafter. West and West Central African peoples did not necessarily regard suicide as a negative act that placed the immortal soul in jeopardy. Among the Yoruba and Ashanti peoples, for example, suicide could be "acclaimed as praiseworthy." The Yoruba gave "great credit and honour" to those who killed themselves because they found "life burdensome, disgraceful and perilous."

There is no record of the number who committed suicide en route to the Americas. However, much can be gleaned about their motives and methods from the observations of white crew members as well as from the few extant African accounts of the Middle Passage. The three most common ways women and men tried to kill themselves were by starvation, refusing "medicines when sick," and by throwing themselves overboard. For reasons that had everything to do with profits and nothing whatsoever with Christian beliefs, crew members used the most ruthless means to prevent suicides. Those who would not eat were likely to be whipped, force-fed, or both. On one ship two women who tried to starve themselves were flogged until they "fainted away with the pain," but still they would not take food. These women found the death they sought in another way: They "fold[ed] themselves in each others arms [and] plunged over the poop of the vessel into the sea, and were drowned." Other women who observed this scene "cried out in the most affecting manner [and] many of them were [prepared] to follow their compatriots."

Thomas Phillips, captain of the *Hannibal*, which sailed from Whydah to Barbados in 1693/1694, remarked that on this particular voyage "about 12 Negroes did wilfully drown themselves, and others starved to death." Phillips failed to mention whether those who threw themselves off the *Hannibal* did so at different times or, as was the case with "about an hundred Men Slaves" on another slave ship, *The Prince of Orange*, had committed mass suicide. Europeans who witnessed these scenes may have been unfamiliar with African understandings of suicide, but they readily acknowledged that there were those on board their vessels who were totally unafraid of death, who "wished to die" and who, as they were dying, said "with pleasure" that they were "going home."

The captains of slave ships sometimes tried to prevent suicides by employing a form of spiritual coercion. For example, it was not uncommon for Africans to be forced to watch the decapitation or dismembering of one of their number who had either mutinied or committed suicide. The rationale informing this threat to the living by mutilating the dead was perfectly simple. As Captain William Snelgrave explained, "Many blacks believe that if they are put to death and not dismembred [*sic*], they shall return again to their own Country." By the mid-seventeenth century a similar form of coercion was being employed in the British plantation colonies.

There are relatively few clues as to the hopes and fears that passed through the minds of those on board the slave ships as the New World coastline came into view. Many must have believed that their death, and the return of their soul to Africa, was imminent, for, as Job Ben-Solomon commented, Africans "entertained a Notion, that all who were sold for Slaves were either eaten, or murdered, [by Europeans] since none ever came back." Probably the first reliable evidence that they would not be "eaten by these ugly [white] men" came some time after their arrival in the Americas.

For captive Africans, in one sense the arrival of a slave ship in the New World marked the end of one stage in their journey and the beginning of another. On another level, however, surviving the Middle Passage proved to be but one point, albeit a critically significant one, in a continuum of religious beliefs and practices. Once they were in the New World, the convictions that had so fortified these men and women while they were en route to the Americas were neither casually forgotten nor discarded as unnecessary or irrelevant. The ritualistic expressions of these convictions would be broadly similar to West and West Central African ones, but the local circumstances in which enslaved Africans found themselves dictated that they could never be identical. Nowhere in the Americas would Africans be able to duplicate their traditional religious systems. What they were able to do, and often very successfully, was to piece together new systems from the remnants of the old.

There were significant variations in the plantation economies that evolved in British America through the middle years of the eighteenth century. Thousands upon thousands of Africans entered against their wills public worlds that increasingly they helped to shape and define and private worlds that they struggled to create for themselves. The precise ethnic mix on particular estates and in particular neighborhoods was of obvious importance, as was the size and proximity of those estates. Sex ratios and age structures played a critical role in the formation of sexual partnerships, in the definition of family and kinship networks, and in the reconstitution of spiritual community. Mortality rates, together with the attitude of slave owners toward the disposal of their human property, profoundly influenced the duration of partnerships, the integrity of family and kinship networks, and the precise composition of spiritual communities. All of these factors interacted in an infinitely complex, ever-changing fashion with traditional African beliefs and practices to shape the domestic and communal lives of bondpeople. The private worlds that evolved in the slave quarters of the British Caribbean and Southern mainland between the mid-seventeenth and mid-eighteenth centuries differed not so much in kind as in the degree to which it proved possible for enslaved people to draw upon their African pasts to deal with present realities and future possibilities.

Before the closing of the transatlantic slave trade, at least 500,000 Africans were shipped to British North America. Between 1627 and 1775 approximately 1,500,000 Africans were landed in the British Caribbean, of whom around 50 percent remained there. The others were reexported to various destinations in the New World, including the mainland American colonies. The volume of imports into the different plantation colonies varied over time, but everywhere they were comparatively high during the initial stages of plantation formation.

The conditions experienced by Africans imported into Barbados during the seventeenth century were so horrendous that their life expectancy was a mere seventeen years. Avaricious sugar planters could easily afford to work their slaves to death and to purchase replacements as and when they needed them. Between 1670 and 1695 around 70,000 Africans were shipped to Barbados. During the next three-quarters of a century annual imports ranged from a low of 1,027, between 1708 and 1710, to a high of 5,101, between 1766 and 1770. Slave imports into Jamaica, whose plantation economy included the so-called 'minor staples' as well as sugar, increased from around 2,000 per annum in 1700 to approximately 8,000 per annum in 1790. A surge in imports between 1792 and 1807, to 10,700 per year, was indicative of continuing high mortality rates as well as the impending closure of the British slave trade.

Before the late seventeenth century Africans were demographically and economically insignificant in the Chesapeake. In 1650, for example, they accounted for only around 3 percent of the region's population, a proportion that increased to 15 percent in 1690 as the transition from indentured to involuntary servitude began to get under way. By 1710 the estimated 23,118 Africans in Virginia accounted for under 42 percent of the colony's population. Between 1700 and 1740 around 49,000 Africans were shipped to Virginia and Maryland, and by the latter date they accounted for approximately 28 percent of the total population of these two colonies. Both in absolute and in relative terms this growth rate was of a very different order to that which characterized the British Caribbean.

As early as 1660 the black population of Barbados numbered around 20,000 and accounted for just over 47 percent of the island's inhabitants. Jamaica, taken from Spain five years earlier, had a total population of 3,500 and was around 17 percent black. The 2,000 Africans in the Leeward Islands of Antigua, St. Kitts, Nevis, and Montserrat accounted for one-fifth of the population. Within a few years each of these British islands had a black majority: by 1670 in Barbados, by 1680 in Jamaica, and by 1690 in the Leeward Islands. By 1713 Barbados was almost 74 percent black, Jamaica was roughly 89 percent black, and the Leeward Islands were around 77 percent black. In the Southern mainland, only the Low Country of South Carolina and Georgia would come close to approximating these proportions.

Principally because of the Barbadian connection, chattel slavery was sanctioned from the outset in South Carolina. Small numbers of Africans were brought to the

Map 18.1   The Caribbean

Low Country, mainly from the British Caribbean, during the first three decades of settlement, but it was only with the development of rice culture that South Carolina planters began to rely heavily on the transatlantic slave trade. By 1708 South Carolina's population of 8,000 was half black. This trend intensified after 1720 as rice emerged as the Low Country's premier staple crop. Between the mid-1720s and 1740 around 29,000 Africans were imported into South Carolina, with annual imports ranging from a low of 439 (in 1725) to a high of 3,097 (in 1736). By 1740 South Carolina's black population was estimated at 39,155 and the colony was roughly two-thirds black.

In the 1750s and 1760s South Carolina's slavery-based rice economy expanded into Low Country Georgia. In 1750 the Georgia trustees were forced to abandon their prohibition on slavery, and thereafter South Carolina planters and their slaves poured across the Savannah River. By the eve of the American Revolution Georgia's predominantly African-born enslaved population totaled around 16,000.

Just as significant in the definition of slave culture as the total number of Africans imported and the ebb and flow of imports over time were the ethnic origins of those taken to the plantation colonies. Africans, wrote Richard Ligon in the mid-seventeenth century, were "fetched [to Barbados] from . . . Guinny and Binny, some from Cutchew, some from Angola, and some from the River of Gambia." They spoke "several languages, and by that means, one of them under-stands not another." Toward the end of the century an anonymous British author explained that "the safety of the Plantations depends upon having Negroes from all parts of Guiny, who not understanding each others languages and Customs, do not, and cannot agree to Rebel, as they would do . . . when there are too many Negroes from one Country." These two commentators were right about the diverse back-grounds of the Africans being shipped to Barbados, but they failed to record the often highly significant similarities between their "languages and Customs." These similarities reflected a combination of factors operating in West and West Central Africa together with evolving planter preferences for Africans from particular regions and ethnic groups.

The ethnic origins of the Africans shipped to the British plantation colonies varied regionally and over time. However, the ultimately reconcilable ethnic identities of many newly enslaved Africans are readily apparent. Before the mid-eighteenth century three regions of Africa, the Windward Coast, the Gold Coast, and the Bight of Benin, supplied roughly two-thirds of the Africans transported to the Americas by British slavers. By 1807, however, "approximately two-thirds of the African-born populations" of the British Caribbean had been drawn from the Bight of Biafra and central Africa. However, there were important variations in the African origins of the enslaved peoples of the British sugar islands. Thus, "the Bight of Biafra was the most important source of slaves [for] the southern Caribbean, but in the Leeward Islands Central Africa and Senegambia dominated." Just under half of all the Africans landed in Jamaica before 1807 were Ibos from the Bight of Biafra or BaKongo people from Central Africa.

In the Southern mainland, around 60 percent of the Africans imported into Virginia between 1718 and 1726 were from the Bight of Benin; during the 1730s roughly 85 percent came from the Bight of Biafra or Angola. Under 70 percent of the 8,045 Africans shipped to Charleston during the late 1730s had been brought from Angola, and another 6 percent are known to have originated in the Gambia region. Around 40 percent of the 2,500 Africans landed in Savannah between 1766 and 1771 came from Gambia, 16 percent came from Sierra Leone, and 10 percent came from Angola. Another 6 percent were said to be from "Gambia and Sierra Leone," while 3 percent had been brought from Senegal. Of the remainder, 14 percent were identified as having come from the "Rice Coast," 5 percent from the "Grain Coast," and the others simply from "Africa."

The African regions that predominated in the slave trade to the British plantation colonies were not ethnically monolithic, but "a single ethnic group often accounted for a large proportion of the slaves from a particular region." The extent to which particular groups were able to preserve their "cultural habits" once in the New World depended upon many factors, one of the most important of which was their concentration on any given estate or in any given neighborhood.

The precise local mix of ethnic origins in particular colonies varied, as did the size and the proximity of the estates upon which enslaved Africans found themselves. Slaveholdings in the Southern mainland were much smaller and far more dispersed than they were in the British Caribbean. Local ratios of Europeans to Africans also varied, but everywhere in the Southern mainland they were much higher than in any of the sugar islands. In the early eighteenth century, for example, the South Carolina parish of Goose Creek contained around 500 enslaved Africans but about twice that number of Europeans; in Barbados and Jamaica, on the other hand, a single sugar plantation was likely to be worked by two or three hundred slaves under the direction of one white overseer. Colonial Georgia's largest slaveholder, Governor James Wright, held 523 bondpeople, thereby putting himself on a par with premier sugar planters. His slaves, however, were employed not on one but on eleven different plantations, indicative of the belief that the optimum number of workers per unit of rice production was between thirty and forty. Eminent rice and sugar planters may have held similar numbers of slaves, but they organized their operations very differently and in ways that were to be highly significant in the definition of the private lives constructed by their workforces.

Sex ratios and age structures were important in shaping many aspects of life in the slave quarters. As we have seen, most slave ships carried at least two men for every woman, and this imbalance persisted for varying lengths of time in the New World. For instance, during the 1730s, a decade of particularly heavy slave imports in Prince George's County, Virginia, the sex ratio was in the order of 187 men to every 100 women. On estates with more than ten slaves it soared to 249 to 100. Between 1755 and 1775 the ratio of men to women on Georgia estates was around 146 to 100, but on plantations with more than forty slaves it rose to 152 to 100. Depending upon the slaves' ethnic mix, the preservation of "cultural habits" might have been more viable on larger plantations, but it is also possible that their imbalanced sex ratios may have generated intense rivalries among men who were in search of sexual partners.

Richard Ligon and the anonymous pamphleteer of 1694 believed that varied African "languages and customs" could be used by Europeans as a highly effective means of securing racial control. Their arrogant assumption was that Africans were intellectually incapable of transcending the linguistic and cultural differences that existed among them. In fact, these linguistic differences were not always as severe, or as insurmountable, as these contemporary commentators imagined them to be. Some Africans could find themselves in the unenviable position of Olaudah Equiano, who upon his arrival in Virginia discovered that he "had no person to speak to that I could understand," but many more, and perhaps the majority of those arriving in the plantation colonies through the middle years of the eighteenth century, did not.

The practice of loading slave ships at a single West African port meant that planters were often making their choices from among Africans who, if not "culturally homogeneous," were in all probability culturally compatible. These choices, especially in the case of eminent planters, usually involved the purchase of more than one person from any given shipment. Such purchases often resulted in the separation of couples, families, and friends, but they could also mean that "on large estates . . . slaves would typically have no trouble finding members of their own nation with whom to communicate." Subsequent purchases from slave ships that had set sail from a different African port could introduce to the plantation representatives from other ethnic groups. The resulting linguistic and cultural variations may have reflected a deliberate policy of ethnic mixing, but they could also have reflected nothing more than pragmatic decisions to satisfy labor requirements as and when the opportunities to do so arose.

The manner in which the transatlantic slave trade was organized and the purchasing habits of planters meant that enslaved Africans could be both united and divided by language. The reconciliation of linguistic differences was achieved in each of Britain's plantation colonies with a speed and a facility that often astounded Europeans. The spread of Islam in West and West Central Africa was a particularly important part of this process, providing as it did the fragments of a common vocabulary, if not of a common language. Within a comparatively short time, each of the plantation colonies had developed its own lingua franca.

The resolution of linguistic differences went hand in hand with the recognition and interaction of often compatible African pasts. However, some European writers remarked on the persistence of clashes directly attributable to those pasts. In 1689, for example, Edward Littleton implied that in Barbados, encounters between different ethnic groups often resulted in physical violence. Two later writers, Griffith Hughes and James Barclay, also remarked on the continuing significance of ethnic origins in the slave quarters. But neither of these commentators repeated Littleton's claim that ethnic antagonisms could be so bitter as to totally preclude any possibility of constructive cultural interaction.

Writing in 1750, Hughes, the Anglican rector of the Barbadian parish of St. Lucy, noted that the "Mirth and Diversions" of the island's enslaved population "differ according to the Customs of so many Nations intermixed." He added that "the Negroes in general are very tenaciously addicted to the Rites, Ceremonies and Superstitions of their *own Countries*," but he did not suggest that these strongly held religious convictions were a source of overt physical conflict. Nor did he conclude, as have some recent scholars, that the communal performance of "Rites" and "Ceremonies," which he did not describe in detail, "may well have been occasions to recall national religions." Instead, Hughes chose to emphasize a different aspect of these religious celebrations that surely must have been as obvious to those in the ethnically commingled slave quarters of Barbados as it was to him: the essential compatibility of many of these "Rites, Ceremonies and Superstitions."

It was, Hughes remarked, the "universal Custom" in Barbados for slaves, regardless of their ethnic origin, to adorn themselves with talismans and fetishes that usually took the form of "Strings of Beads of various Colours . . . in great Numbers twined around their Arms, Necks and Legs." In the case of "the richer sort of House Negroes" these "Beads" might be "interspersed . . . with Pieces of Money." Moreover, there was something else upon which the captive peoples of "so many Nations . . . all agree." According to Hughes, without exception they stood "in much Awe of such as pass for *Obeah* Negroes, they being a sort of Physicians and Conjurers, Who can, as they believe not only fascinate them, but cure them when they are bewitched by others."

Twenty-five years later James Barclay, an Englishman who worked as an overseer on a rice plantation near Dorchester, South Carolina, remarked that he found it "diverting to hear" bondpeople "in their quarrels, reproaching one another with their respective countries." Like Littleton, Barclay attributed these "quarrels" to the "violent antipathy" that he thought existed between the peoples of different African "provinces." He believed that when "the people . . . are brought over here, the same antipathy subsists," and he claimed that this was particularly the case with "those of Gulli or Gully, and Iba." The latter, he reported, would goad the former with the taunt that "'You be Gully Niga, what be the use of you, you be good for nothing'" and receive the reply that "'You be Iba Niga; Iba Niga great rascal.'"

These comments suggest that at a time when both Barbados and the Lower South still depended heavily upon the transatlantic slave trade, African-born people identified strongly with their ethnic origins and grouped themselves accordingly. Common African roots provided the most logical reference point for the understanding and organization of present realities and future possibilities. The broad similarity of many of the religious beliefs and the ritualistic expression of those beliefs that Hughes and Barclay alluded to ultimately made it possible for people from different African backgrounds to devise mutually acceptable ceremonies for marrying each other, naming their children, and burying their dead.

In the early 1680s Morgan Godwyn, a churchman who was instrumental in persuading the Anglican hierarchy in London of the necessity and the desirability of proselytizing enslaved Africans, had claimed that bond-people in Barbados and Virginia clung tenaciously to their "*Heathen Rites*," to their "barbarous . . . behaviour and practice in *Worship* and *Ceremonies* of *Religion* . . . their *Polygamy* . . . their *Idolatrous Dances*, and *Revels*." They had "brought out of Africa," Godwyn continued, various "*Recreations* and *Customs*" that demonstrated beyond any shadow of a doubt their "*Impiety*" and their "*Barbarity*." Among the three "*Recreations* and *Customs*" specifically mentioned by Godwyn, probably because they were the best known to him, were the "*Idolatrous Dances*, and *Revels*; in which they usually spend their *Sunday* after the necessity of labour for their Provisions . . . has been complied with."

Godwyn acknowledged that "the *Gentiles* anciently did esteem and practice *Dancing*, as a part of *Divine Worship*; and no less also did the *Jews*," but he claimed that the dances performed by Africans in Barbados and Virginia were but one of the more obvious manifestations of their "Idolatry." He based his "Conjecture" on the fact "that they use their Dances as a *means to procure Rain*," presumably for their provision grounds rather than for their owners' cane and tobacco fields. Godwyn did not describe these ritual dances, but Ligon did. He emphasized that, in Barbados at any rate, there was "no mixt dancing" but that men and women performed their dances separately and "may dance a whole day [to] their Musick." As for "Their motions," Ligon recorded that "their hands [have] more of motion than their feet, and their heads more than their hands."

Writing a quarter of a century after Godwyn, Sir Hans Sloane made no mention of men and women dancing separately, but he did comment that their ritual dances entailed "great activity and strength of Body, and keeping time if it can be." The dancers had "Rattles ty'd to their Legs and Wrists, and in their Hands, with which they make a noise, keeping in time with one who makes a sound answering it on the mouth of an empty Gourd or Jar with his hands." In addition, it was "very often" the case that "they . . . tie Cow Tails to their Rumps, and add such other things to their Bodies in several places, as to give them a very extraordinary appearance." European commentators would continue to be both fascinated and repelled by what they regarded as the eroticism of the ritual dances performed by enslaved Africans. Unfortunately, their descriptions of these dances were usually so generalized as to preclude any possibility of linking them to specific African antecedents.

Just as distasteful to Morgan Godwyn as ritual dancing was the "confidence" placed by enslaved Africans "in certain Figures and ugly Representations, of none knows what besides themselves." In the absence of "more *Magnificent Temples*," these "Deities" were "usually enshrined[ed] in some *Earthern Potsherds*." Such was the power attributed to these "Deities," continued Godwyn, that "Fugitives and Runaways" were utterly convinced that they were "able to protect them in their Flight, and from Discovery." Godwyn failed to mention who had made and supplied these "Representations," but almost certainly they had been sanctified, if not made, by sacred specialists in the slave quarters.

The third of the "Customs" that Godwyn correctly surmised had been "brought out of Africa" was what he mistakenly referred to as "*Polygamy*." The main point at issue here was not the absence of sexual morality but the absence of a particular sexual morality: that predicated upon Anglican beliefs and assumptions concerning sexuality and marriage. In Barbados, Godwyn maintained, neither planters nor Anglican churchmen took much interest in the sexual partnerships formed by slaves. Bond-people entered into such partnerships "by mutual agreement amongst themselves" and with a "frequent *repudiating* and changing of . . . Wives, usual amongst most *Heathens*." Godwyn concluded that it was principally because of the "*Connivance* and Toleration" of their owners that enslaved Africans continued to practice "Polygamie." Most planters, he charged, "esteeming them but as Cattle, and desirous of their *Encrease*, are apter to encourage, than to restrain them from it."

Godwyn erroneously believed that in Tidewater Virginia enslaved Africans had already chosen to abandon their traditional marriage patterns. There, he claimed, the "*Negro's* . . . tho imported from the same places [as those shipped to Barbados] are not (so far as I could learn) addicted to *Polygamies*; but rather of themselves choosing to follow the Custom of the *English*." That this was not nearly true is suggested by an episode in 1712 or 1713 when a slave named Roger "hanged himself . . . not any reason he being hindred from keeping other negroes men wifes beside his owne."

Reports from early-eighteenth-century South Carolina confirm the persistence, and universal occurrence, of polygyny in the British plantation colonies. Like Godwyn, Reverend Francis Le Jau talked in generalities and confused polygamy and polygyny. But he asserted that in his parish of Goose Creek "and elsewhere" in the Low Country there was "a constant and promiscuous cohabiting of slaves of different Sexes and Nations together: When a Man or Woman's fancy dos [*sic*] alter about this party they throw up one another and take others which they also change when they please." This, he added, was "a General Sin, for the exceptions are so few they are hardly worth mentioning." A year later he wrote that "One of the most Scandalous and common Crimes of our Slaves is their perpetual Changing of Wives and husbands." This "Crime" was no more unique to South Carolina than it was to Barbados and Virginia. Enslaved Africans everywhere in British America continued to engage in polygynous relationships through the eighteenth century.

Most European commentators, including the clergy, had little to say about the formation of family and kinship ties by slaves, including the patterns of courtship that preceded the taking of a marriage partner, whether the widespread African convention of dowries persisted, or the circumstances that might result in the voluntary dissolution of a marriage. However, from the few clues left by contemporary Europeans, it is clear that traditional African assumptions and practices were adapted to meet the requirements of the slave quarters. As John Woolman commented of the Chesapeake colonies in the 1740s, "Negroes marry after their own way."

One of the earliest descriptions of a marriage ceremony devised by slaves in the Southern mainland dates from 1731. The ritual took place in North Carolina and, in its fundamentals, would have been instantly recognizable in many parts of West and West Central Africa. According to John Brickell's account, "Their *Marriages* are generally performed amongst themselves, there being very little ceremony used upon that Head; for the Man makes the Woman a Present, such as a *Brass Ring* or some other Toy, which if she accepts of becomes his Wife; but if ever they part from each other, which frequently happens, upon any little Disgust, she returns his Present: These kind of Contracts no longer binding them, than the woman keeps the pledge give her."

Writing of Low Country marriage practices on the eve of the American Revolution, James Barclay endorsed Brickell's observation that there appeared "to be no particular ceremony . . . but the married pair acknowledging themselves man and wife." A private ritual not dissimilar to that described by Brickell persisted in the Low Country into the early nineteenth century. There, "the man would go to the cabin of the woman he desired, would roast peanuts in the ashes, place them on a stool between her and himself, and while eating propose marriage." If the woman accepted his proposal, "the couple repaired to his cabin immediately, and they were regarded as man and wife."

These fragmentary reports suggest that everywhere in the Southern mainland the exchange of tokens, the taking of the marriage vow, was an essentially private matter. However, marriage was also a cause for public celebration, which affirmed and reaffirmed, at the same time it created, ties of family, kinship, and friendship that often extended beyond the boundaries of the plantation or plantations upon which the couple resided. In the 1740s, for example, Thomas Bacon wrote of the "small congregations . . . brought together" by slave marriages on Maryland's Eastern Shore. Almost forty years later, James Barclay remarked of the custom in the Carolina Low Country that if the couple to be married were "well acquainted in the place, multitudes of men, women and children, to the amount of several hundreds," would "flock together from the neighbouring plantations" to participate in the festivities. He added that marriages were usually "kept in the night," not for any specifically religious reason but "because in the day-time [slaves] must work for their masters."

The slaves who lived on the estate on which the marriage took place provided most of the hospitality and often spent several weeks beforehand making their preparations. They "commonly" fattened "a number of land tortoises" for the wedding feast and spent "what money they have got for their labour on Sundays on rum." Sometimes their owner would "allow them a hog or two to entertain the company." The assembled guests would spend "the whole night . . . in eating and drinking, singing, dancing and roaring, 'till all the victuals and drink are done, when each departs to his own home." Owners did not "interfere on these occasions, except they become riotous, and then the ringleaders are sure to pay for it."

The rituals surrounding death attracted more, and more unfavorable, comments from Europeans than those involving marriage. Like their contemporaries who described burials in West and West Central Africa, Anglican clergy particularly were shocked at what they depicted as the depravity with which slaves buried their dead. They were especially scandalized by the feasting, drinking, music making and dancing that took place on these occasions. Unfortunately, even the commentators such as Thomas Bacon who claimed to "have attended several" slave burials provided few details about the funeral rites devised by Africans in the Southern mainland.

Compared with the often lengthy descriptions of slave burials in the British Caribbean, only a few fragments of literary evidence survive from the colonial South. However, this limited documentation indicates that, as in the sugar islands, the rituals surrounding death, the joyous assertion and reassertion of the essential continuity between past, present, and future generations, drew heavily from what in their fundamentals was a common African heritage. Little is known about the ceremonials that might have occurred in the time between death and burial, but it may be safely inferred that the work demanded of the living by their owners precluded what Europeans depicted as the lengthy mourning that preceded burials everywhere in West and West Central Africa. Similarly, there is little detailed record from the colonial South of the way in which the corpse was prepared for burial, conveyed to the burial site, and subsequently interred.

As in Barbados, archaeological excavations of African burial sites in both the Chesapeake and the Lower South have revealed talismans, beads, and similar objects that probably had a profound religious significance. Evidence from Jamaica and Barbados also documents the practice of providing food and drink to sustain the dead on their journey. In 1707, for example, Sir Hans Sloane remarked that in the British Caribbean "Rum and Victuals" might be buried "in gourds" with the corpse or "at other times" spilt "on the grave." In Jamaica, these "Victuals" included "casader bread . . . sugar, rum, tobacco, & pipes with fier [sic] to light his pipe." Sometimes, "After the Grave is filled up . . . a kind of Soup" was placed "at the Head, and a Bottle of Rum at the Feet."

The ex-slave Charles Ball's graphic description of the burial of an infant that took place on a South Carolina plantation around the turn of the eighteenth century indicates that the practice was also observed in the Southern mainland. The child's father, who was African-born and claimed to have "been a priest in his own nation," conducted the burial ceremony. His wife, a country-born woman named Lydia, and Ball assisted him in preparing the body for interment. Ball did not say what this process entailed, but once the body had been made ready the father "buried" with his son

> a small bow and several arrows; a little bowl of parched meal; a minia-ture canoe, about a foot long, and a little paddle, (with which he said it would cross the ocean to his own country) a small stick with an iron nail, sharpened and fastened into one end of it; and a piece of white muslin, with several figures painted on it in blue and red, by which, he said, his relations and countrymen would know the infant to be his son, and would receive it accordingly on its arrival amongst them.

The "funeral service" ended with the father placing "a lock of hair from his head . . . upon the dead infant, and clos[ing] the grave with his own hands." The burial of this child with various grave goods to ensure his safe return to Africa, was typical; the apparent privacy of his burial was not.

There is plentiful evidence from the British Caribbean and the American South that demonstrates that the three elements commonly associated with the interment of a slave—the procession with the body to the grave, the burial, and the subse-quent festivities—usually involved everyone on the plantation and often attracted large numbers of bondpeople from the immediate neighborhood. In mid-eighteenth-century Antigua, for example, it was the usual practice for the corpse to be "carried to the grave attended by a numerous concourse." Some of those who processed to the burial site played "an instrument . . . resembling a Drum, called a 'Gumba'; others . . . what they call a 'Shake, Shake' . . . and all singing some heathenish account of the Life & Death of the deceased." In 1740 Charles Leslie spoke of the "vast Multitude" of slaves who processed to burials in Jamaica. Singing "all the way," they carried the corpse, which if not in a coffin would be wrapped in cloth, "on their Shoulders" to the grave. After the interment "the songs grow more animated, dancing and apparent merriment commence."

Just as in European accounts of burials in Africa, reports of interments in the plantation colonies often emphasized the prominent part women played in the proceedings. For example, according to Leslie, throughout the burial "the Attendants scream out in a terrible Manner, which is not the Effect of grief but of Joy; they beat on their Wooden Drums, and the Women with their rattles make a hideous Noise." Sometimes one of the women would sing "a melancholy dirge, the chorus of which is performed by the whole of the other females, with admirable precision, and full-toned and not unmelodious voices." This "dirge" did not take "the strain of a hymn, or solemn requiem" but was "a loud and lively African air."

The evidence that has survived from the colonial South strongly suggests the continuing significance of grave goods and points to four other similarities to the much more richly documented burial rites of West and West Central Africa and the Caribbean: the holding of a second burial ceremony, often some months after the interment of the corpse; the large numbers of slaves who attended both burials; the importance of instrumental and vocal music at graveside ceremonials; and the almost universal practice of holding both the first and the second burial after dark.

Unfortunately, European reporters provided very few details about what actually happened at slave burials in the early South. However, what evidence is available indicates that graveside rituals were highly reminiscent of those known to have taken place in the British Caribbean. In 1766, for example, Georgia's Grand Jurors complained about the "rioting" that occurred at slave "funerals," by which no doubt they meant singing and dancing as well as feasting. A decade later Janet Schaw, a Scottish traveler, attended the funeral of Jane Corbin, a white woman, at Point Pleasant Plantation in North Carolina. According to Schaw's account, "the Negroes assembled to perform their part of the funeral rites" for their mistress, "which they did by running, jumping, crying and [doing] various exercises." Presumably, these "rites" were broadly similar, if not identical, to those they would have performed for one of their compatriots.

One of the earliest extant accounts of a second burial in the American South was penned by Henry Knight, who visited Virginia in 1816. Knight implied that when a planter's slave died it was usual for him to give "the rest a day, of their own choosing, to celebrate the funeral." This, he continued, was "perhaps a month after the corpse is interred." It was "a jovial day," on which those present "sing and dance and drink the dead to his new home, which some believe to be in old Guinea."

Later reports suggest that, as in West and West Central Africa and the British Caribbean, there was no hard and fast rule in the American South as to the time allowed to elapse between first and second burials. An undated report from Gloucester, Virginia, intimated that the second burial might be "three days after death, or six months." A similar variation was also mentioned by ex-slaves from Georgia. Caroline Gilman was probably close to the truth of the matter when she commented that the precise timing of second burials, "where religious ceremonies are performed, and refreshments provided," depended upon the distance that family members and friends who were able to attend had to travel.

In some instances deceased ancestors were commemorated annually. In mid-eighteenth-century Antigua, for example, they were venerated "on Christmas mornings." The choice of Christmas day had no specifically Christian connotations. It was selected for the performance of this ritual simply because it was the custom in Antigua, as it was in all the plantation colonies, for slaves to be given Christmas day off. According to one report, "The Grave yards & burying places, both in Town & Country, would be crowded . . . with the friends and relatives of deceased persons strewing quarters of boiled, and roasted, meat; of fowls & yams & pouring bottles of Rum, upon the graves of their departed friends." Very similar rituals, described by one contemporary as "the principal feasts . . . [the slaves] ever give," took place elsewhere in the British Caribbean.

By the mid-eighteenth century another calendrical celebration associated with time off work at Christmas that some scholars believe was an adaptation of West and West Central African yam festivals was taking place: what became known variously in the New World plantation colonies as *John Canoe*, *John Cornu*, or *Jonkonnu*. First described by Edward Long in the mid-1770s as taking place in Jamaica, the *Jonkonnu* festival was held "in the towns during the Christmas holidays." According to Long's description, *Jonkonnu* involved a parade consisting of "several tall robust fellows dressed up in grotesque habits, and a pair of ox-horns on their head, sprouting from the top of a horrid sort of vizor, or mask, which about the mouth is rendered very terrific with large boar-tusks." These men would go about the town, each of them "followed with a numerous crowd of drunken women, who refresh him frequently with a sup of aniseed water, whilst he dances at every door, bellowing out *John Connu*! with great vehemence." Perhaps because of what Long had gleaned from the participants, he concluded that the parade was "probably an honourable memorial of John Conny, a celebrated cabocero at *Tres Puntas*, in *Axim*, on the Guiny Coast."

By the end of the eighteenth century *Jonkonnu* was well established in Jamaica and was celebrated elsewhere in the Caribbean in various forms. As Elizabeth Fenn has recently pointed out, *Jonkonnu* fulfilled similar functions to certain seasonal rituals performed by European underclasses. It entailed "sharp criticism of the privileged classes," and when the participants wore "white masks" or powdered their faces a "racial inversion" occurred that "turned plantation society into a world in which nothing was as it seemed—a world of uncertainty, confusion, and unlimited potential."

For reasons that are not clear, *Jonkonnu*, in its elaborate Caribbean form, did not emerge as a major calendrical ritual in the Southern mainland. Music making and dancing were a part of the Christmastime festivities of slaves in the American South, but the costumes and parading associated with *Jonkonnu* seem to have been comparatively rare occurrences, and references to them date from the nineteenth century rather than the eighteenth. With one notable exception, the versions of *Jonkonnu* that were reported took place in North Carolina and Virginia rather than in the Lower South. In 1843 Henry Benjamin Whipple, a visitor to St. Mary's, a town on the Georgia/Florida border, commented that December 27 was the "last day" of the slaves' Christmas holiday and that they referred to it as the " 'great day.' " His description of what took place on that day closely resembles accounts of Caribbean *Jonkonnu* festivals. The slaves, Whipple wrote, "have paraded, with a corps of staff officers with red sashes, mock epaulettes & goose quill feathers, and a band of music composed of 3 fiddles, 1 tenor & 1 bass drum, 2 triangles & 2 tambourines and they are marching up & down the street in great style. They are followed by others, some dancing, some walking & some hopping, others singing, all as lively as can be." If any one refused to "join them they seize him & have a mock trial & sentence him to a flogging which is well laid on. Already they have had several such court martials." Any whites they encountered were expected to give them cash "& thus [they] find themselves in pocket money." Whether this version of *Jonkonnu* was brought to this part of the Low Country directly from Africa or by slaves imported from the Caribbean and how long it had been performed there is not recorded. Nor is there any firm evidence that it was replicated elsewhere in the Low Country.

From the mid-seventeenth century in Barbados and by the late seventeenth century in the Chesapeake and South Carolina, the gathering together of "large numbers" of slaves for the celebration of religious rituals, especially after dark, was a matter for widespread white consternation. In 1687 nighttime burials were banned in Westmoreland County, Virginia, because the local authorities were convinced that they provided ideal cover for the planning and execution of rebellions. Virginia planters may have known about the uprisings in Barbados in 1675, but had they not, Bacon's Rebellion, in which Africans participated, provided an alarming image of black militancy much closer to home.

Whether for spiritual or secular reasons, or a mixture of both, slaves could and did evade legislation that sought to prevent them from associating with those on neighboring estates. They continued to congregate in significant numbers during the hours of darkness to celebrate the marriage of the living and the burial of their dead. If they so chose, planters and slave patrols could make life difficult for those who wished to attend such celebrations. However, in practice there was comparatively little they could do to prevent slaves from leaving their plantations after dark. As Charles Ball explained, all that had to be done was to wait until the owner or overseer was asleep and then slip off the plantation.

Yet, as James Barclay's comments suggest, not all slaves had to resort to this kind of subterfuge in order to attend religious gatherings. Owners usually knew of the arrangements being made in the slave quarters for the celebration of a marriage; in fact, sometimes they contributed to the festivities. And they must have known, or suspected, that these festivities would not be confined to their own slaves. Similarly, they almost certainly knew of the arrangements that would be made for the interment of dead slaves. Their main concern was not to prevent these celebrations but to try to ensure that they did not get out of hand.

Exactly the same was true of slave owners' dealings with those in the slave quarters whose influence rivaled, and arguably surpassed, their own: the sacred specialists who, by design or chance, had been placed on board the slave ships destined for the New World. The reputation of priests, prophets, herbalists, rainmakers, witch doctors, and witches and the reverence and fear in which they were held by African peoples survived the Middle Passage largely intact. In the Americas it was to these people, with their specialized and intimate knowledge of the spiritual "pasts" of Africa, that enslaved Africans turned, as they had always turned, for physical and spiritual curatives, for guidance and support, for protection, and for the mediation of their differences. The authority and prestige of sacred specialists varied both regionally and over time. However, for varying lengths of time in each of the plantation colonies they wielded a power that planters and the Anglican clergy alike could only envy.

By the mid-eighteenth century sacred specialists figured prominently in virtually every European account of Africans in the British Caribbean. Europeans

frequently confused the activities and precise significance of different sacred special-
ists, more often than not employing the generic term Obeah, or Obi, abbreviated
forms of the Ashanti word *Obaye*. However, they were accurate on several points:
It was generally held that "the Professors of *Obi* are, and always were, Natives of
Africa, and none other" and that they had "brought the Science with them." This
"Science," claimed Europeans, was "universally practiced" in the British Caribbean.

In describing Obeah, Europeans wrongly applied the term to witchcraft or
sorcery and often confused witches with Myalmen and women. In fact, Obeah was
the result of a fusion of religious offices, several of which originally had overlapping powers and functions, and shared common beliefs and practices of different
African peoples. The fusion of functions is apparent in the powers that were ascribed
to them by European observers. They included diagnosing and treating diseases—
in Africa usually the work of a medicine man or a herbalist and sometimes a diviner;
obtaining revenge for injuries or insults, or curing the bewitched—in Africa the
responsibility of the witch doctor; the discovery and punishment of theft or adultery
—in Africa the work of the diviner; and the prediction of future events—in Africa
the work of highly trained mediums or diviners.

The cultural traditions of the various religious specialists were preserved
directly through the slave trade, the vehicle by which they were transported to the
New World. Under the disintegrating effects of bondage, most of the regalia of
the sacred specialists and the paraphernalia of their practices was lost. However,
many, if not most, of the ancient remedies, magical potions and ornaments, rattling
gourds, and feathers and animal parts used in the conduct of religious offices,
survived. The sacred offices themselves also survived, but they too began to change.
By the eighteenth century they reappeared in a different form known in all the
plantation colonies as Obeah.

Most plantations in the British Caribbean were said to have at least one prac-
titioner of Obeah, and Europeans generally agreed that those who inspired "the
greatest Devotion and Confidence were the oldest and the most crafty." It was also
reported that there were a significant number of women among them. The
"Devotion and Confidence" inspired by female sacred specialists was deeply rooted
in African religious pasts and was unbroken by the Middle Passage. In their capacity
as sacred specialists, as females, and as mothers, African women were to play a
pivotal, and eventually a dual, role in the definition of the religious lives bondpeople carved out for themselves in the plantation colonies. They were "essential
bearers of tradition" and among the "primary agents" in preserving and promoting
"traditional (African-derived) culture [and] conventionally accepted modes of behaviour." During the second half of the eighteenth century they would also become
highly visible as agents of change and cultural redefinition.

Great secrecy surrounded the usually private practice of Obeah, but it seems
clear that the conventional conceptions of male and female religious roles was reaffirmed in the New World. The majority of spiritual practitioners were probably
men, but women continued to be prominent in the conduct of religious affairs. A
"considerable part" of the African women sold into slavery in the Americas was
reported to have been convicted of witchcraft. Many of them were found "distributing drugs; in particular such as occasion abortion." Edward Long, a member of
the Jamaican planter class and an early and powerful advocate of slavery, attributed the low birthrate among Jamaican slaves to various causes, among them a high

ratio of men to women, the "unskillfulness and absurd management of the Negro midwifes," and the fact that many West African women—most of whom he thought were "common prostitutes"—"take specifics to cause abortions."

Male and female sacred specialists used their knowledge of drugs and magic to attempt to heal the physical ailments suffered by their compatriots. In Jamaica, for example, it was said to be the usual practice on many plantations for slaves who suffered from "certain disorders—as yaws, ulcers, bone-ache, etc" to be cared for by "an elderly negro woman who professes a knowledge of this branch of physic." That same knowledge of drugs and magic could also be used to manipulate and control relationships with owners or to intimidate fellow bondpeople. Quite exceptionally, given the secrecy surrounding Obeah, in Jamaica in 1775 an enslaved woman informed on "her Step-Mother (a woman of the *Popo* Country)" who "had put *Obi upon her*." Convinced of her impending death, the younger woman "thought herself bound in Duty" to reveal to her owner "the true Cause of her Disorder." She also claimed that her "Step-Mother" had "put *Obi* . . . upon those who had lately died; and that the old Woman had practiced *Obi* for as many years past as she could remember."

Some women continued to function as mediums, or oracles trained in possession by spirits of the gods or ancestors. The enslaved population of Surinam reportedly had "*locomen*, or pretended prophets," who were generally male, as well as "a kind of *Sibyls*." A European account of "these sage matrons dancing and whirling round in the middle of an assembly, with amazing rapidity, until they foam at the mouth, and drop down as convulsed" is an apparent description of mediumistic possession. In Africa the medium's power was benign, used to carry messages from the spirit world or to offer guidance to those who sought help. In the slave societies of the British Caribbean it was often used against the oppressors. According to one European account, "Whatever the prophetess orders to be done during this paroxysm, is most sacredly performed by the surrounding multitude; which renders these meetings extremely dangerous, as she frequently enjoins them to murder their masters, or desert to the woods."

After witchcraft became pervasive during the rebellion of 1760, Myalism was introduced into Jamaica. The Myal society, a cult whose purpose was to identify and negate the influence of evil spirits that threatened danger or harm to the community as a whole and that sought to break the power of the witches, had its roots in the traditional West African religion, wherein the ceremony of public burial and resurrection culminated the long and complex training of witch doctors. In Edward Long's decidedly unsympathetic description of Myalism, "The lure hung out was, that every Negro, initiated into the Myal society, would be invulnerable by [sic] the white men; and, although they might in appearance be slain, the Obeah-man could, at his pleasure, restore the body to life." Long's account of the initiation rite of the Myal society sounds remarkably like the principal rite in the initiation of Azande witch doctors: "The method, by which this trick was carried on, was by a cold infusion of the herb *branched colalue*, which, after the agitation of dancing, threw the party into a profound sleep," or apparent death, which sometimes lasted for several hours.

A possession-inducing "Myal dance" formed part of the ceremony. One of the earliest descriptions of the dance as performed in Jamaica was written by Matthew Gregory Lewis, an absentee sugar planter who visited his estate in 1815/1816 and again in 1817. According to Lewis, the ministrations of the "chief Myal-man" were accompanied by "a great variety of grotesque actions, and chanting all the while something between a song and a howl, while the assistants, hand-in-hand, dance slowly round them in a circle, stamping the ground loudly with their feet to keep time with his chant." In time the initiate was restored to consciousness by the application of more medicine ("as yet unknown to whites"), and the Myal dance concluded. Armed with the secrets of magical potions and ointments, the newly initiated witch doctor was then prepared to fight against the malign activities of witches and heal those people who had been bewitched. Myalism, and the frenzied possession-inducing Myal dance associated with it, later became the "Cumina" cult.

Information on pre-Christian life in the Southern mainland is fragmentary. As with the communal rituals associated with marriage and death, what little survives suggests close similarities to that of the African peoples of the British Caribbean. Divination and healing were practiced; a rudimentary version of Obeah still functioned; and traditional male and female ritual leadership roles survived, particularly in the Low Country, which continued to receive African peoples until 1808. "Root doctors" played a prominent, if somewhat ambiguous, role in black and white life throughout the American South. Colonial governments sought both to repress and to exploit their skills; whites both feared and sought the herb-based skills of enslaved African "Doctors." The superiority of certain African cures over those prescribed by European doctors was tacitly conceded by the granting of cash payments, freedom from bondage, and sometimes both to slaves who revealed their knowledge of a remedy deemed to be in the public interest. In 1733, for example, an unnamed slave in Virginia was freed and granted a lifetime pension of £30 for discovering an "effectual Cure for all Distempers arising from an inveterate Scurvy, such as the Yawes, Lame Distemper, Pox, Dropsy etc." In the same year in South Carolina Caesar was freed by the General Assembly and awarded an annual allowance of £100 for life for his discovery of a "cure" for poison and "the bite of a rattlesnake." Both men were probably African diviners or medicine men, perhaps former members of a religious cult whose purpose was to treat and cure specific diseases. Almost certainly their wide knowledge of the curative properties of herbs, plants, and roots had been handed down to them from other African medicine men, and they, in their turn, would pass on their knowledge to chosen members of the next generation. Like other sacred specialists, however, they were obliged to adapt their herbal expertise to the different ecosystems of British America.

Traditional African healers, female as well as male, normally employed their extensive knowledge of medicinal herbs and poisonous substances for therapeutic relief, or as a defense against witchcraft and sorcery. But under conditions of New World bondage they also used their expertise to harm others. The skill, or art, of poisoning was one of the most powerful weapons available to enslaved Africans, and it was one that they were by no means reluctant to employ.

Although there are many authenticated cases from both the British Caribbean and the American South of whites being poisoned by slaves, the actual number can never be known, if only because a growing white obsession with such a possibility meant that many unexpected deaths were mistakenly attributed to this cause. Court records offer a few clues but do not tell the whole story. In Virginia between 1740 and 1785, for example, a total of ninety slaves were accused of poisoning whites; thirty-five were convicted and sentenced to death. They comprised a microscopic proportion of Virginia's enslaved population. Yet white fears of being poisoned by slaves were not entirely irrational. "Poisoning Offences" happened infrequently, but they happened often enough to intensify white anxieties.

Slaves did not restrict the use of poison to their white "status enemies." As in Africa, for those who had the knowledge, means, and opportunity poison was a convenient way of disposing of, or threatening, an adversary in the slave quarters. It is as difficult to determine how often slaves used poison against one another as it is to determine how often they used it against whites. Between 1745 and 1785 in Virginia, for example, forty-four, or under a quarter, of those tried for "Poisoning Offences" were charged with poisoning, or attempting to poison, another slave. How many other undetected cases there might have been is a moot point. Similarly, there are few clues as to the precise nature of the jealousies and enmities that prompted the use, or the threatened use, of poison. Some of those who survived to tell the tale did so perhaps because they hoped to secure protection from their owners or to gain revenge on their assailants. In 1712, for example, a slave named George, who lived in King William County, Virginia, claimed that "his country men had poysened him for his wife."

Although the details remain obscure, it is evident that the ability to administer poison and the herbal expertise that this often presupposed was a potent source of power within the slave quarters. As Matthew Gregory Lewis recorded, one of his slaves, a man named Adam, was "strongly suspected of having poisoned twelve negroes, men and women." Sometimes Adam administered the poison himself; sometimes he prevailed on others in the slave quarters to do it by threatening to take their lives. According to Lewis, "The terror thus produced was universal throughout the estate" and "several" bondpeople believed that "their lives were not safe while breathing the same air with Adam." Eventually Adam was put on trial, "but all the poisoning charges either went no further than strong suspicion, or . . . were not liable by the laws of Jamaica to be punished, except by flogging or temporary imprisonment." The situation was resolved, however, when a gun, some ammunition, and "a considerable quantity of materials for the practice of Obeah," were found in Adam's cabin. For these offenses Adam was sentenced to be transported from Jamaica and, according to Lewis, few, if any, of the enslaved people on the plantation were sorry to see him go.

Herbal expertise employed for malevolent purposes was a source of power that directly threatened the lives and property interests of owners, and, for these most pragmatic of reasons, it was something that they and the colonial governments they dominated sought to destroy. No clear distinction was made, and by definition could not be made, by colonial legislators between benign and malevolent herbal practitioners; all were potentially suspect. The resultant legislation enacted by various colonial governments during the course of the eighteenth century differed only in detail. In addition to sanctioning the death penalty for slaves found guilty of "procuring, conveying or administering poison," colonial governments tried to prevent the spread of herbal expertise within and between generations by making it a capital offense for "any slave [to] teach or instruct another slave in the know-ledge of any poisonous root, plant, herb, or other poison whatsoever." In an attempt to deny slaves easy access to deadly substances, whites were often forbidden to employ slaves "in the shops or places where they keep their medicines or drugs." Despite these organized efforts to repress them, traditional African healers continued to ply their skills. Indeed, in the Southern mainland they succeeded in establishing a legacy for the black physicians trained through apprenticeships who began to appear during the Revolutionary War years and for the black medical profession that emerged in the mid- to late nineteenth century.

It might have been expected that the Anglican clergy, who would have been incredulous at the proposition that Africans had been stripped bare of their religious cultures as a result of the Middle Passage, would sing the praises of planters and colonial governments for their attacks on the sacred specialists whose activities so appalled them. But, in fact, beginning with Morgan Godwyn, the clergy reserved some of their most vituperative language for the slave-owning members of their flocks. Anglican churchmen wanted something more than the suppression of sacred specialists and the total eradication of traditional African beliefs and practices. They insisted that these beliefs and practices be replaced in their entirety by Anglican beliefs and rituals. According to Godwyn, owners had to bear much of the responsibility for the fact that their slaves were not "being made *Christians*." He would not be the last churchman to underestimate the strength of enslaved Africans' commitment to their traditional religious culture and sacred specialists or their antipathy to the Anglicanism deemed fit for their consumption.

Beginning in the last two decades of the seventeenth century saving the souls of enslaved Africans became an increasingly important imperative of the Church of England. The diametrically opposed agendas of the planters who the clergy sought to convince and of the slaves who they strove equally hard to convert combined to ensure that before the mid-eighteenth century Protestant Christianity would feature scarcely at all in the private lives of the enslaved populations of the British plantation colonies.

Chapter 19

Shane White and Graham White

'US LIKES A MIXTERY'
Listening to African-American slave music

O N 18 OCTOBER 1821, before a crowd of some 700 whites and 1500 blacks, the sheriff of Princess Ann, in Somerset County, Maryland, executed Jenny, a 70-year-old African-American woman. Seconds before Jenny was hung 'several hundreds of the colored people' turned their backs to the gallows, squatted on the ground, 'covered their faces with their hands, and uttered a simultaneous groan, which while it expressed their feelings, added not a little to the horror of the scene'.[1] In June 1820 an English traveller, W. Faux, sojourning among the plantations along the South Carolina coast, reported in his diary that close to sunset there 'suddenly burst upon my ear an earth-rending shout. It proceeded from negroes shouting three times three, on finishing their task.'[2] In the course of his journey through South Carolina in the years before the Civil War, Frederick Law Olmsted encountered a group of African-American slaves, members of a railroad work gang gathered around a fire. Suddenly, one of the men 'raised such a sound as I never heard before, a long, loud, musical shout, rising, and falling, and breaking into falsetto, his voice ringing through the woods in the clear, frosty night air, like a bugle call'. The cry sounded, Olmsted would later write, like 'Negro jodling'.[3] In these three almost random cases (an examination of the records of the plantation South will turn up many such examples), the sounds created by slaves induced in while observers feelings of cultural dissonance. In this article we aim to begin the necessarily speculative process of recovering the role of sound in African-American slave culture, to chart some significant ways in which slaves experienced their environment differently from their Euro-American owners.

As the WPA interviews of the 1930s readily show, the sounds of the plantation and its surrounds were an important part of the remembered fabric of slavery, giving both shape and texture to former slaves' recollections of their early lives. Some of those sounds originated in the natural environment. A very young Uncle Stepney, eluding the dreaded patrollers by hiding out in the woods near his Alabama plantation, told how he had listened anxiously to 'de panthers a screamin' a way off in de fores' an' de wildcats a howlin'. More ominous, however, had been the cry of a screech owl, a sure sign of impending death. Quickly, the boy had turned the pockets of his overalls inside out and the cry had ceased.[4] Other memories related to the ordinary business of plantation life. Charley Williams could recall 'de anvil start dangling in de blacksmith shop; "Tank! Deling-ding! Tank! Deling-ding!"' 'Course you can't hear de shoemaker awling and pegging, and de card spinners, and de old mammy sewing by hand,' he added, 'but maybe you can hear de old loom going "frump, frump",' and if you did you knew that 'you gwine to git new britches purty soon!'[5] Mingo White explained that 'ever' body knowed when wash day was 'case dey could hear de paddle for 'bout three or four miles. "Pow-pow-pow," dat's how it sound.'[6] But the workaday soundscape of the plantation was punctuated by much starker aural reminders of the slaveholder's presence and power: the cries of children who were being sold away from their families; the sounds of cruel beatings ('Folks a mile away could hear dem awful whippings.');[7] the baying of hounds on the trail of slave runaways; and, most insistently, the sounds that marked the day's toil: 'Bells and horns! Bells for dis and horns for dat!' Charley Williams expostulated 'All we knowed was go and come by de bells and horns!'[8] Decades later, the Rev. W. B. Allen recalled the sound of the first of the day's bells, waking the slaves at 3 o'clock in the summer, and that of the second bell an hour later, signalling that it was time to trudge to the fields. But for Allen, still too young to work, the bells marked an hour's grace in which he would lie in bed and listen to his mother singing as she bent over the open fire making breakfast:

> Our troubles will soon be over,
> I'm going to live with Jesus – after while;
> Praying time will soon be over.
> I'm going home to live with Jesus – after while.[9]

Allen's reference to music is suggestive; few subjects appear as frequently in the recollections of former slaves. Our intention here is to begin an examination of this aspect of slavery's soundscape, to look at the deeper cultural significance of various forms of slave music, and then to trace some of the ways in which the sounds created by slaves related to other dimensions of African-American culture.

In his famous autobiography, ex-slave Frederick Douglass observed that 'apparently incoherent' slave songs actually held 'deep meanings'. In saying this, Douglass was not alluding primarily to the verbal content of these songs; the meanings to which he referred were to be found, rather, in the 'wild notes' of the singers, the 'tones, loud, long and deep,' every one of which constituted 'a testimony against slavery, and a prayer to God for deliverance from chains'. Those who wished 'to be impressed with a sense of the soul-killing power of slavery', Douglass suggested, should 'go to Col. Lloyd's [Douglass's Maryland owner's] plantation, and, on allowance day,' as the slaves, singing all the while, passed by on their journey to collect their rations, 'place [themselves] in the deep, pine woods, and there . . . in silence, thoughtfully analyze the sounds that shall pass through the chambers of [their] soul[s]'.

Douglass assumed here that the 'deep meanings' of slave songs were transmissible as between blacks and whites. He believed, in other words, that the sounds of slaves' songs could serve as a point of entry into their cruel and oppressive world; that the wild and plaintive tones of the singers 'told a tale of grief and sorrow' that would reveal, to those who cared to listen, much about the peculiar institution's devastating psychological impact.[10] But to African-American slaves, the musical sounds their compatriots created had meanings that were much more culturally specific, and vastly more powerful.

We can make an initial attempt to 'hear' those cultural messages, however imperfectly, if we 'listen', as best we can, to a type of slave vocal music that frequently assumed the character of 'pure sound', by which we mean no more than that the music contained no words at all. Many of the calls, cries, and hollers that echoed throughout the rural and urban South wherever African Americans were held captive were of this broad type.

Not surprisingly, the West African practice of using a variety of calls to announce important events, greet friends, summon meetings, and so on, was carried over to the New World.[11] As deployed by North American slaves, these elemental kinds of musical expression took various forms, ranging from the relatively simple to the complex, and served a range of purposes not all of them readily appreciated by outsiders. Particularly when African influences were strong – in the early years of slavery, for example, or wherever groups of newly arrived slaves were kept together – calls functioned as an alternative communication system, conveying information through the medium of sounds that whites could neither confidently understand nor easily jam. Calls constructed from the languages of the slaves' homeland were, of course, unintelligible to whites. Moreover, just as West African drums could 'talk' by imitating the rhythmic and tonal characteristics of speech, so too, in all probability, could the wordless calls of North American slaves. As Harold Courlander, who interviewed a number of elderly African Americans in the rural South earlier this century, has pointed out, this process could become extremely complex.

> It is now well understood that African signal drumming is based largely on simulation, through rising and falling inflection, of speech tones. Voice signaling in Africa is sometimes based on this same principle, and signal horns are used in the same manner. In some instances, voice signals are not modeled directly on speech tones, but on the sound of instruments imitating speech. Many of the early day slave calls and cries in the United States may have utilized these communicative devices. In such disguise, seemingly wordless messages could have been quite unintelligible to outsiders.[12]

As slaves became acculturated, their calls incorporated English-language words, a development that would have made them intelligible to whites, at least in some degree. Such calls were often simple expressions of loneliness, pain, or despair. Harold Courlander was told that a slave 'working under the hot sun might give voice to such a cry on impulse, directing it to the world, or to the fields around him, or perhaps to himself'. The call 'might be a phrase like "I'm hot and hungry,"' or could, as in the case of the following Alabama cry, contain a more detailed message:

Ay-oh-hoh!
I'm goin' up the river!
Oh, couldn't stay here!
For I'm goin' home![13]

Other calls had a more obvious practical purpose. Yach Stringfellow, formerly a field slave in Texas, told his WPA interviewer how, 'ef de oberseer wuz comin', a slave named Ole man Jim, the possessor of 'a big boom voice', would 'wail out loud like an say: "Look-a long black man, look-a long; dere's trouble comin shore."'[14] Calls were also commonly used to aid work routines. Soon after the 'strange cry' of the black railroad worker whom Olmsted encountered had died away, Olmsted heard another member of the work gang 'urging the rest to come to work again, and soon he stepped towards the cotton bales, saying, "Come, bredern, come; let's go at it: come now, coho! roll away! eeoho-eeoho-weeioho i!" and all the rest taking it up as before, in a few moments they all had their shoulders to a bale of cotton and were rolling it up the embankment'.[15]

But even after slaves had become relatively well acculturated, they continued to employ calls that contained either no or very few English words; if a few such words were included, they tended to function as do syllables in scat singing, as pure sound, rather than as vehicles for the conveying of information. The former slave Julia Frances Daniels revealed that her brother, a skilled hunter, used a celebratory but wordless call to broadcast his success. 'We would know when we hear him callin', "OooooOOOooo-da-dah-dah-ske-e-e-e-t-t-t-ttt,' that he had sumpin''. That was just a make-up of his own, but we knowed they was rabbits for the pot.'[16] The boastful Hector Godbold incorporated some English words into the call he reproduced for his WPA interviewer, but those words were obviously valued for sound rather than sense. 'I was one of de grandest hollerers you ever hear tell bout. . . . Here how one go: O – OU – OU – O – OU, DO – MI – NICI – O, BLACK – GA – LE – LO, O – OU – OU – O – OU, WHO – O – OU – OU. Great King, dat ain' nothin.'[17]

It is important to realize here that contemporary white observers of the peculiar institution, as well as those who managed later to interview former slaves, were able to give only a very imperfect representation of the calls they heard. On many occasions, interviewers appear to have recorded only or mainly the words of a particular cry. African-American voices could, however, transform such words into richly detailed patterns of sound. As visually represented by Yach Stringfellow's interviewer, Ole man Jim's warning call: 'Look-a long black man, look-a long; dere's trouble comin shore' seems simple in form and straightforward in meaning, but rich tonal and melismatic embellishment, which the interviewer may have lacked the time or ability to represent, could easily have translated this call into a complex, vocal utterance.[18] Again, the wordless 'plantation holler' that ex-Texas slave Jeff Calhoun performed for his interviewer, was merely written down as 'Uh, . . . Uh . . . Uh . . . Uh . . . Uh . . . Uh.'[19] However, as Harold Courlander points out, apparently simple wordless calls of this type – he instances a call consisting merely of a long 'Hoo-Hoo' – could be 'filled with exuberance or melancholy', and 'stretched out and embellished with intricate ornamentation of a kind virtually impossible to notate'.[20]

In fact, wordless or near-wordless slave calls were often elaborate vocal creations which drew heavily, as Ashenafi Kebede points out, on 'many African vocal devices, such as yodels, echolike falsetto, tonal glides, embellished melismas, and microtonal inflections that are often impossible to indicate in European staff notation'.[21] In Willis Lawrence James's estimation, these more complex or 'coloratura' calls rank 'among the most amazing and remarkable vocal feats in folk music'.[22] It was a coloratura call that had attracted Olmsted's attention as he came upon the group of African-American railroad workers; the yodelling sounds that so intrigued him originated with the rainforest Pygmies of Central Africa, whose musical styles influenced, in turn, the Kongo peoples of West Africa, and, ultimately, broad segments of the North American slave population.[23] As we have seen, Olmsted had been puzzled by the lone railroad worker's richly filigreed cry; the more interesting issue, however, is what meanings that cry had communicated to those African Americans who heard it.

At the deepest cultural level, coloratura slave calls were emblematic African (and African-American) sounds, and deeply evocative on that account. Robert Farris Thompson's comment that 'the textlessness of [Pygmy] yodeling, unshackling sound from words, unlock[ed] extraordinary freedom of voice' is applicable to many of the more complex New World calls as well.[24] These, too, were free musical forms, allowing virtually limitless scope for improvisation, for the admixture of the vocal leaps, glides, moans, yells, and elisions that gave to African-American musical expression its characteristic rhythmic and tonal complexity, its perennial inventiveness and love of surprise. Slave calls exemplified, that is to say, what Olly Wilson has termed 'the heterogeneous sound ideal', defined by Wilson as an 'approach to music making' that deploys 'a kaleidoscopic range of dramatically contrasting qualities of sound [which is to say, timbres]', qualities that characterized the West African tonal languages from which that music was derived.[25]

In West African societies, dramatic variations in timbre or tone 'colour' had been in evidence, of course, not merely in calls, but whenever music was made, and most saliently in the African dancing ring, the symbol, as Samuel A. Floyd, Jr. points out, of 'community, solidarity, affirmation, and catharsis'.[26] In the New World, the African circle or ring was initially shattered, as members of cultural groups were deliberately dispersed or indiscriminately distributed among competing buyers. The ring would take periodic physical shape again in the ring shout and, most publicly and dramatically, in the dancing formations of slaves at New Orleans's Place Congo, but to those who remained outside the ring – who lived relatively isolated lives or belonged to owners determined to suppress 'primitive' ritual – the calls, cries and hollers that drifted across an often hostile Southern soundscape constituted an idiom with which African-Americans must have felt a high degree of aesthetic affinity. In emotional terms, slave calls fleetingly reconstituted the West African ring, the centre of communal life and locus of culture-affirming movement and sound. They evoked, that is to say, not merely a time-honoured African and African-American means of communication but deep-seated cultural memory.[27]

There is little reason to expect that former African-American slaves, interviewed by employees of the federal government, would have attempted to put such feelings into words, but an anecdote from the writings of Willis Laurence James conveys in some imperfect degree the evocative power of wordless but culturally compelling sound. The incident that James relates occurred during a conference on African-American folk music.

> One morning at a lecture of mine on Negro cries . . . I sang a florid Negro cry. Mr. [Eubie] Blake leaped halfway from his seat and yelled, 'Oh, professor, professor, you hit me, you hit me.' He placed both hands over his heart and continued with great emotion: 'You make me think of my dear mother. She always sang like that. I can hear her now. That's the stuff I was raised on.'[28]

For African-American slaves the more complex sonic textures of communal, inter-active singing held still deeper meanings.

In May 1865 an official party, dispatched by President Andrew Johnson to investigate conditions in the South in the aftermath of the Civil War, reached the island of St Helena, off the South Carolina coast. The group's immediate purpose was to assess the condition of the island's African-American inhabitants, who, under the guidance of Major General Rufus Saxton, the Union General in command of Port Royal area, had worked the land since the hurried flight of their former owners some years before. Included in the party were General Saxton, Secretary of the Treasury Salmon P. Chase, the Reverend Doctor Richard Fuller, former owner of some hundreds of the island's slaves, and the northern journalist Whitelaw Reid. It is on Reid's sound-rich account of the day's events that the following discussion largely relies.

Arriving, without notice, on a Sunday, the official party found the roads thronged with African Americans, 'gay with holiday attire', heading for the island's main church. When Reid and the others reached the church they found large numbers of African Americans massed in front of it, the building being too small to contain them. Presently, a 'white-wooled deacon' arrived and informed General Saxton that 'De people is gathered, sah, and was ready for de suvvices to begin'. Saxton then led the official group to a small platform under some live-oaks, and after its members had taken their seats, 'a quaint old African' moved to the front of it as if to welcome them.

Instead of delivering an address, the old man began to sing. 'Leaning, like a patriarch, on his cane', Reid recorded, 'and gently swaying his body to and fro over it, as if to keep time, he struck up, in a shrill, cracked voice, a curiously monotonous melody, in which, in a moment, the whole congregation were ener-getically joining.' Reid quickly found himself agreeing with those who held 'that the language of these sea islanders (and I am told that, to some extent, the same is true of the majority of plantation hands in South Carolina), is an almost unin-telligible patois'; the journalist found it 'impossible, for a time, to make out [the song leader's] meaning'. Not only this, but 'the vocal contortions to which the simplest words seemed to subject' the aged singer were 'a study that would have amazed a phonetic lecturer'.[29]

The first person whose presence the former slaves acknowledged in their song was the Rev. Dr Fuller, who had earlier won their affection by giving up his law practice in order to preach to them. The singing followed the usual call-and-response pattern, which Reid, in his later account, represented as best he could.

    Ma-a-a-assa Fullah a sittin' on de tree ob life,
    Ma-a-a-assa Fullah a sittin' on de tree ob life,
       Roll, Jordan, roll.
    Ma-a-a-assa Fullah a sittin' on de tree ob life,
       Roll, Jordan, roll.
    Ma-a-a-assa Fullah a sittin' on de tree ob life,
       Ro-o-oll, Jordan, roll,
       Ro-o-oll, Jordan, roll,
       Ro-o-oll, Jordan, roll.

Eventually, after 'repetitions that promised to be endless' the lyrics changed, and the name of General Saxton, who had assisted the former slaves as they struggled to adjust to a dramatically changed post-slavery world, was substituted for that of Master Fuller.

> Gen-e-ul Sa-a-axby a sittin' on de tree ob life;
>> Roll, Jordan, Roll,
> Gen-e-ul Sa-a-axby a sittin' on de tree ob life;
>> Ro-o-oll, Jordan, roll,
>> Ro-o-oll, Jordan, roll,
>> Ro-o-oll, Jordan, ro-o-oll!

When it came the turn of the Treasury Secretary to be honoured, the song leader 'struck out in harsher tones, and more indescribably bewildering difficulties of pronunciation than ever', and the answering chorus was sung, Reid wrote, 'with a vehemence that pierced the ears'.

> Me-is-ta-ah Che-a-ase a sittin' on de tree ob life,
> Me-is-ta-ah Che-a-ase a sittin' on de tree ob life,
>> Roll, Jordan, roll;
> Me-is-ta-ah Che-a-ase a sittin' on de tree ob life,
>> Roll, Jordan, roll,
> Me-is-ta-ah Che-a-ase a sittin' on de tree ob life,
>> Roll, Jordan, roll,
>> Roll, Jordan, roll,
>> Ro-o-oll, Jordan, ro-o-oll.[30]

Following this impromptu musical performance, a decided shift in musical styles occurred. A white teacher from one of the island's schools led the slave congregation in the singing of some of 'the ordinary hymns of the church', and soon, Reid observed, 'great volumes of sound rang like organ peals through the arches of the oaks'. If Reid now found the tones of the singers 'harsh', or their diction difficult to follow, or the repetitions in the songs tedious, he did not say so.

After some questions as to their well-being had been asked of the audience, Dr Fuller pronounced the blessing to end the day's formal proceedings. No sooner had he done so than he was surrounded by about one hundred of his former slaves, who 'pushed up against him, kissed his hands, passed their fingers over his hair, crowded about, eager to get a word of recognition'. Whitelaw Reid attempted to capture the ex-slaves' speech in dialecticized English. 'Sure, you 'member me, Massa Rich'd; I'm Tom.' 'Laws, Massa Rich'd, I mind ye when ye's a little 'un.' 'Don't ye mind, Massa Rich'd, when I used to gwine out gunnin' wid ye?' 'How's ye been dis long time?' ''Pears like we's never gwine to see 'ou any more; but, bress de Lord, you'm cum.' 'Oh, we's gittin' on cumf'able like; but ain't 'ou gwine to cum back and preach to us sometimes?'[31]

Whitelaw Reid's narrative of these events returns us, in some senses, to what Ronald Radano has termed the 'sound-filled, preliterate past' of a people not long out of slavery.[32] It does so, of course, in only a partial and unsatisfactory way. As Winthrop Jordan has pointed out, we cannot really recover the sounds of 'the long past'. The music of slaves (or, as in this case, of people not long out of slavery) could be described by whites but not recorded, except through conventional transcriptions, which, in the despairing words of William Francis Allen, a compiler of the volume entitled *Slave Songs of the United States* (1867), were 'but a faint shadow of the original'. The slaves' voices, Allen declared, 'have a peculiar quality that nothing can imitate; and the intonations and delicate variations of even one singer cannot be reproduced on paper'.[33] Slave speech has, to a degree, been preserved in written, and often, as in Reid's narrative, in dialecticized form, but, as Winthrop Jordan has warned, such visual records tell us nothing of its nuances and cadences, of 'the nearly infinite variety of human inflections and accents as they resonated in different places, situations, and time'. Even if 'something of [the] timbre and rhythm' of slave speech can be approximated 'by listening to twentieth-century audio electromagnetic recordings', Jordan cautions, 'there is always danger in listening backward in time by a process of extrapolation from the sounds of later years'.[34]

Though we are attempting, in some measure, to 'listen' once more to the sounds of the past, our main objective is to reach an understanding of what those sounds meant to enslaved African Americans. Limitations in the historical record often require historians to 'look' at slavery through the eyes of whites; the same limitations mean that we shall often have to 'hear' it through their ears, in the present instance, fortunately, through the ears of a shrewdly observant and more than usually perceptive journalist, one who knew, however, very little about a people large numbers of whom he was encountering for the first time.

In the main, Reid reacted negatively to the manner in which St Helena's former slaves sang and spoke. In that respect, of course, he was hardly unique. If Reid disliked the harsh tones and vehement delivery of the African-American singers, so also had the Scottish traveller Laurence Oliphant, who, after touring the South in 1856, objected that slaves' religious songs were performed 'with great vehemence and unction', and that, where they were mentioned, sacred names 'were generally screamed rather than sung, with an almost ecstatic fervour'.[35] Such comments become a testy refrain in white contemporaries' accounts of slave life. Occasionally a more sympathetic observer detected deeper messages in these apparently dissonant tones; like Frederick Douglass before her, Lucy McKim, who, with her abolitionist father, Rev. James Miller McKim, visited the Carolina Sea Islands in 1862, concluded that 'the wild, sad strains' of slave song 'tell, as the sufferers themselves never could, of crushed hopes, keen sorrow, and a dull daily misery which covered them as hopelessly as the fog from the rice swamps'.[36] Even in such cases, however, the more fundamental importance of tone and tonal variation in African-American music was not understood.

Underlying whites' objections to the 'harsh' and 'aberrant' tones of slave vocal music lay a different conception of the role of sound in musical performance. In the slaves' African homelands, Francis Bebey has argued, musicians sought 'not . . . to combine sounds in a manner pleasing to the ear', but 'simply to express life in all its aspects through the medium of sound', to 'translate everyday experiences into living sound',[37] 'to render emotions and desires as naturally as possible'.[38] Reflecting the tonal nature of African languages, on which much African music is based, the tones employed by an African singer, Bebey writes, 'may be soft or harsh as circumstances demand'. Thus, a 'mellow tone' may be used 'to welcome a new bride; a husky voice to recount an indiscrete adventure'.[39] In the same way, impassioned falsetto might effectively express grief, a grainy rasp anguish, a sonorous wail despair. If, as we might anticipate, southern slaves too made freer use than did whites of different tones (strictly timbres, or tone 'colours') to express the pain and emotional trauma that must have been part and parcel of their lives, it is not surprising to find whites describing such sounds as 'wild and barbarous',[40] 'uncouth',[41] a 'dismal howl'[42] or 'hideous noise'.[43] The African and African-American practice of weaving a variety of wordless intensifiers – shouts, cries, yells, groans – into a melody, translating, thereby, their strongly felt emotions into sound, can only have increased whites' sense of alienation.

African-American vocal music sounded dissonant to many whites not only because of its use of harsh, impassioned, or gravely tonalities, but also because slave singers inflected the pitches of notes 'in ways quite foreign to regular melodic practice in Western art music'. Observing that the use of inflected pitches and pitch play is common among people of African origin in North America, but not among those in South America or the West Indies, Paul Oliver has argued that these musical tendencies were brought to North America by Muslim slaves from the savannah areas in Africa, rather than by slaves from the rain forest areas of the Guinea coast, whose music did not display these characteristics and who, though they arrived in far greater numbers, came later. Pitch play and inflected pitches were characteristic also of English and Irish American folk music, to which Muslim slaves were also exposed. In the event, William Tallmadge argues, later slave arrivals from West Africa 'were unable to dominate and suppress the combined tonal practice of the white-English and Scotch-Irish folk singers and savannah Negro slaves'.[44]

William Francis Allen, one of the compilers of *Slave Songs of the United States*, remarked that 'like birds', slaves often seemed 'to strike sounds that cannot be precisely represented by the gamut, and abound in "slides from one note to another, and turns and cadences not in articulated notes"'.[45] It was a view echoed by many others. After accompanying a slave funeral procession through the woods on her Virginia plantation in 1861, Mrs Roger Pryor reached a similar conclusion, declaring the mourners' song to be 'a strange, weird tune no white person's voice could ever follow'.[46] This tendency of black singers (and instrumentalists) to 'play' with pitch, to worry, for example, the third degree of the scale by 'slurring or wavering between flat and natural', was disconcerting to those whites who first encountered it in the musical performances of slaves.[47] To Mrs C. J. B., who transcribed the spiritual 'The Day of Judgment' for the publication *Slave Songs of the United States*, for instance, a 'tone' that would later have been described as a worried third merely sounded like 'a sort of prolonged wail'.[48]

Similarly disconcerting to whites were what Lucy McKim termed the 'odd turns made in the throat' of black singers, another of the characteristics which, like the presence of 'worried' notes, made it 'difficult to express the entire character of . . . negro ballads by mere musical notes and signs'.[49] Lucy McKim may have been referring, here, to various forms of vocal embellishment practised by slaves, the use of yodels, bends, or slides, for instance, or most probably to melisma, the practice of carrying one syllable of a word over several different tones (or fractions of tones). When Whitelaw Reid called attention to the 'vocal contortions to which the simplest words seemed to subject' the former slave who led the St Helena blacks in song, he may have been describing certain difficulties of pronunciation, or alluding to the leader's Gullah or Gullah-inflected speech.[50] But it is more likely that Reid too was referring to the African-American practice of extending the number of syllables in a sung word in order to give greater scope for melismatic play. By representing the song leader's enunciation of the word 'Massa' as 'Ma-a-a-assa', Reid reveals that the man had turned a two-syllable word into a five-syllable one. And when, instead of singing 'Mr. Chase', the caller sang 'Me-is-ta-ah Che-a-ase', he had effectively transformed three syllables into seven. The carrying of African-American voices over the additional tones these extra syllables allowed for may have produced the 'odd turns in the throat', those puzzling, and to whites 'unnatural' sounds to which McKim had alluded.

Like Reid, many whites regarded the words of slaves' songs as almost meaningless, a melange of mispronunciation, trivial content, and pointless repetition. In 1842 Rev. Charles Colcock Jones, anxious to replace the slaves' religious songs with 'approved hymns', described the former as 'extravagant and nonsensical chants'.[51] In similar vein, Colonel Thomas Wentworth Higginson, commander of the first African-American regiment to fight in the Civil War, a man whose general attitude towards black Americans was notably sympathetic, characterized the nightly singing of his troops as 'incomprehensible negro methodist, meaningless, monotonous, endless chants, with obscure syllables recurring constantly'.[52] So generally 'absurd and unmeaning' were the lyrics of the 'so-called hymns' in the recently published volume *Slave Songs of the United States*, a reviewer complained in March 1868 'that it would be as well for the teachers in the schools and meeting-houses where they are sung to commence, as speedily as possible, the destruction of the entire lot'.[53] Even slaves, it sometimes seemed, did not comprehend the meaning of the words they sang. Puzzled by the term 'cater nappen', included in the song line 'Wid a white a cater nappen tied "roun" he [Jesus's] wais', school teacher Elizabeth Kilham and her companions inquired of several of the slave singers as to its meaning, but 'received no further explanation than, "Why, dat's jes' in de hymn"'. Kilham was similarly bemused by the way in which slaves appended a hymn chorus – 'Shall we know each other there?' – of which they were particularly fond to 'almost everything, sometimes in rather startling association'. She cited the following examples:

> Hark from the tombs a doleful sound, –
> Chorus – Shall we know each other there?

And

> Hell is a dark an' a drefful affair,
> An' ef I war a sinner I wouldn't go dar, –
> Chorus – Shall we know each other there?[54]

Such seemingly odd alignments of song lines would not have seemed incongruous to blacks. On being asked by a white woman what an African American had preached about at a camp meeting, 'Jenny', a recently freed slave, had replied that, while she could not 'tell de particulars' (though 'I's got dem all in my heart'), she could 'sing some of de hymns I larned dar'. Encouraged to do so, Jenny began:

I hears a rumblin' in de skies,
Jews, screws, de fi dum!
I hears a rumblin' in de skies,
Jews, screws, de fi dum!

When asked the meaning of the second and fourth lines (which were the same in each of several additional verses), Jenny replied, with some impatience: 'La, dear soul, don't you know what dem is? Dem is de chorus!' Further efforts to secure a satisfactory reply provoked the following rejoinder: 'Mean?' cried Jenny, with a deprecating glance at the inquisitive mistress, 'dey don't mean nothin', as I knows on, dey's de chorus, I tell you!' Later, the white woman learned that the 'correct' words of the chorus were 'Jews crucified him'.

In all probability, the song Jenny described had originally been a white hymn that had been recast by an African-American gathering into the familiar call-and-response format. In this context, the main function of the chorus (response) was not to 'make sense', when placed after every call line that preceded it, but to provide a stable foundation against which the lyrical, melodic and rhythmic improvisations of the caller would be set. The chorus that Jenny used could adequately perform this task even if the 'words' of which it was composed had been scrambled in translation.[55]

But something deeper was involved here. To Elizabeth Kilham, the surprising juxtaposition of different elements within African-American songs seemed almost deliberate; the slaves made nearly 'all their hymns into this kind of patchwork', she wrote, 'without apparently, the slightest perception of any incongruity in the sentiments thus joined together'. She speculated that the future publication of a collection of African-American religious songs would prompt the question as to whether they were 'composed as a whole, with deliberate arrangement and definite meaning, or [were] fragments, caught here and there, and pieced into mosaic, haphazard as they come?'[56] To Texas schoolteacher William P. Stanton, too, his black students' hymns 'seem[ed] to be a sort of miscellaneous patchwork, made up from the most striking parts of popular Methodist hymns'.[57] And, endeavouring to describe the singing of companies of black soldiers as they marched along, Colonel Thomas Higginson wrote that 'for all the songs, but especially for their own wild hymns, they constantly improvised simple verses, with the same odd mingling, – the little facts of to-day's march being interwoven with the depths of theological gloom, and the same jubilant chorus annexed to all'.[58]

Once again, the bemused or hostile reactions to slaves' religious songs measure the cultural gap between black and white. The kind of spontaneous 'sampling' in which the creators of spirituals engaged reflected the imperatives of a culture that prized improvisation and was not bound by the processes of linear thought. In the manner of slave quilt-makers, slave musicians pieced their compositions from different, often provocatively juxtaposed elements.[59]

Whitelaw Reid was scarcely alone in finding the St Helena blacks' singing 'curiously monotonous', in expressing puzzlement over 'repetitions that promised to be endless'.[60] In similar vein, for instance, Thomas Wentworth Higginson referred to the nightly singing of his troops as 'monotonous, endless chants'.[61] Again, such judgments reflect impatience at the apparent sameness of slave music, its lack of lyrical progression, and prolonged reiteration of single melodic sequences. Yet, as we have seen, repetition, through the time-honoured practice of call-and-response, facilitates improvisation, rather than hindering it. As John Miller Chernoff points out, in African music 'a repeated rhythmic response provides a stable basis to clarify the rhythms which change'.[62] That is to say, it is against the regularly recurring rhythmic chorus or response that the varying rhythms of the caller are set, creating a more complex rhythmic pattern. For instance, overlapping antiphony, a feature of slave choral music which occurs, for example, where the lead singer's call over-laps the response, or begins before the chorus's response has ended, introduces in the music an element of polyrhythmic, as well as polyphonic (that is, many voiced) complexity. To the extent to which the St Helena blacks' lead singer's call ('Ma-a-a-assa Fullah a sittin' on de tree ob life') overlapped the crowd's response ('Roll, Jordan, Roll'), a more complex rhythmic structure would have been created. It was this kind of rhythmic complexity that African-Americans prized, but that whites 'heard' merely as discord and confusion. Criticisms of the repetitive nature of slave singing miss, also, the elements of tonal variety and imaginative forms of vocal embellishment — melisma, yodels, glides, falsetto swoops, and other vocal tech-niques — that invariably characterized the lead singer's performance.

Repetition enabled the creation of a fluid, non-linear musical form; singing was cyclical, continuing not, as in Western practice, until the song was finished, but until the singers had accomplished their purpose. In the case of the St Helena blacks, the reiteration in song of the names of each of the white men who either helped them in the past or now intended to do so was exuberantly prolonged until the former slaves' celebration of those individuals was complete. This was not some-thing to hurry over.

It was, among other things, the complex rhythmic structure of slave music that made it so difficult to notate in conventional European form. Such music was 'almost as impossible to place on score, as the singing of birds, or the tones of an Aeolian Harp', Lucy McKim declared, in large part because of the additive rhythmic effect created by 'voices chiming in at different irregular intervals'.[63] William Francis Allen did attempt to score slave music. As Ronald Radano has revealed, in Allen's own copy of *Slave Songs of the United States*, a number of loose-leaf tran-scriptions were discovered, representing his attempts to capture the melodies of slave shouts probably performed around the area of Beaufort, South Carolina. In one of these transcriptions, 'Bell Da Ring', Allen has reproduced, under the stan-dard, five-line bars of music, the words the slaves sang. These words are set in two or sometimes three rows of horizontal lines, arranged one under the other, and distributed laterally in such a manner that the words in the three lines frequently overlap. In *Slave Songs of the United States*, the first section of the lyrics of 'Bell Da Ring' reads as follows (the bracketed words have been added; 'yedde' is a Gullah word meaning 'hear'):

(introduction) I know, member, know, Lord, I know I yedde de bell
   da ring
(call) Want to go to meeting,   Bell da ring, (response)
(call) Want to go to meeting,   Bell da ring, (response)
(call) Road so stormy,   Bell da ring, (response)
(call) Road so stormy,   Bell da ring, (response)

In Allen's private formulation, on the other hand, the lyrics are shown thus:

    I know member, know Lord   I want to go to meeting
      I know I yedde de bell da ring   Bell da ring

What Allen illustrates here is overlapping call and response, a common, if not ubiquitous, slave practice. (In his introduction to Slave Songs of the United States, Allen
remarked that slaves 'overlap in singing . . . in such degree that at no time is there
any complete pause'.) Overlapping of this kind created thicker sonic textures and
a more complex interweaving of rhythms, characteristics that, as Lucy McKim and
others quickly discovered, rendered slave singing virtually impossible to score.[64]

Listening, in bemused fashion, to the performance of the St Helena ex-slaves.
Whitelaw Reid almost certainly missed not only the complex rhythmic colloquy
between lead singer and chorus, and the polyphonic effect of other voices chiming
in at irregular intervals, but also the purpose of the former slaves' performance.
The message of their song – celebratory, profound – was that those who had helped
them and whose names they now honoured had, like the members of that great
African-American church congregation, won the right to the tree of life. It was a
message worthy of repetition.

There is a striking uniformity in whites' reactions to African and African-
American vocal music not only in United States across time, but also in the diaspora.
Whitelaw Reid's complaints had been anticipated, decades earlier, by George
Pinckard, who, in 1796, described the singing of a group of Africans on the deck
of a slave ship at anchor in Carlisle Bay, Jamaica, on its way to Georgia. 'Their
song', Pinckard declared, 'was a wild yell, devoid of all softness and harmony, and
loudly chanted in harsh monotony.'[65] Here again are the objections to harsh tones,
to timbres that clash rather than blend, to dissonance, and to repetition. There is
more than a rough similarity, too, between the recollections of Jeanette Robinson
Murphy and those of George Pinckard, Whitelaw Reid, and numerous other white
observers. As a child during the early post-bellum years, Murphy had listened to
the singing of aged former slaves who had either come directly from Africa or
whose parents had been born there. A more sympathetic observer, Murphy had
been enchanted by the sounds of the former slaves' voices, by 'all the intonations
and tortuous quavers of [their] beautiful music' (use of contrasting timbres and
tremolo). To her, 'some of the strange, weird, untamable, barbaric melodies'
possessed 'a rude beauty and . . . charm'. It would, however, be futile for whites
to attempt to reproduce these sounds, since, to be effective, a singer's voice needed
to be made 'exceedingly nasal and undulating' (harsh tones and yodelling) and
'around every prominent note' there needed to be placed 'a variety of small notes'
(use of melisma). It would also be necessary for such a white singer to 'sing tones
not found in our scale' (pitch inflection) to 'drop from a high note to a very low
one' (possibly yodelling, but more likely octave leaping or swooping to inject an
element of surprise) to 'intersperse his singing with peculiar humming sounds' (use
of wordless intensifiers) and to 'carry over his breath from line to line and from
verse to verse, even at the risk of bursting a blood-vessel' (possibly overlapping
call-and-response, but more probably the overlapping, by some of the singers, of
the end of one line with the beginning of the next, producing polyphony and cross
rhythmic complexity).[66]

What whites who criticized slave music failed to realize was that blacks were listening to different things. Where whites wanted intelligible lyrics, accurate pitch, and purity of tone, blacks needed to hear the complex rhythmic patterns, inflected pitches, and timbral diversity that delighted them, the sorts of characteristics that could create what Olly Wilson has termed 'a kaleidoscopic range of dramatically contrasting qualities of sound'.[67] Whites' attempts to discover a clear melody were defeated not only by vagaries of pitch and odd tonal shadings, but by melismatic embellishment and a seemingly inexhaustible repertory of vocal interjections – moans, shouts, grunts, hollers, and screams – used to intensify musical expression. Listening for harmony, whites heard instead a strange form of heterophony, as many voices sang in unison (often an octave apart), but others wove melodic and tonal improvisations into the fabric of sound. Harmony in slave singing meant not a structured system, as in western music, but moments of blend forever being transformed by vocal improvisation, the intermittent and ever-changing harmonies of singers who refused to be bound. 'I despair of conveying any notion of a number singing together', William Francis Allen had written, since 'no two appear to be singing the same thing', and the basers 'seem to follow their own whims, beginning when they please and leaving off when they please . . . or hitting some other note that chords, so as to produce the effect of a marvellous complication and variety'.[68] To the whites who heard him, the St Helena song leader's shrill, cracked notes may have been disconcerting, but in those sounds the African-American congregation would have 'heard', in those apparently harsh and discordant sounds, sincerity, intensity, and emotional fervour, meaning expressed, as in West Africa, through timbre and tone.

After listening to St Helena's former slaves, led by a white teacher, sing a conventional hymn. Whitelaw Reid had made no complaint. In all probability, the words of this song, one of the 'ordinary hymns of the church', would have been familiar to Reid and, because of the influence of the island's white churchmen on St Helena's African-Americans, easily comprehended by him. (After the hymn had been sung, the white clergyman had the African-American children sing 'My country, 'tis of thee.') The hymn would have been composed by a white, and although the black singers may well have introduced variations here and there to make the song more to their liking, the extent of any changes was probably not great. Reid's only comment on the blacks' rendition of the hymn was an approving one: 'great volumes of sound', he noted with some enthusiasm, 'rang like organ peals [presumably 'harmonious' ones, from whites' perspective] through the arches of the oaks'.[69] How different was all this from the earlier, impromptu musical performance of St Helena's former slaves, with its harsh tones, clashing rhythms, chant-like repetitions and antiphonal style, and from Whitelaw Reid's reaction to it. In all likelihood, many blacks lived this double musical life, conforming to white expectations when it was prudent to do so, but reverting to their own musical performance styles where and when they could.

It was at the slave dances at Place Congo in New Orleans that the sounds of slave music – not just vocal music, as in the singing that Whitelaw Reid and his party heard at St Helena, but instrumental music as well – were broadcast in the most public and uninhibited way. While out walking in the city on a Sunday afternoon in 1819, the architect and engineer Benjamin Latrobe was affronted by a 'most extraordinary noise, which I supposed to proceed from some horse Mill, the horses trampling on a wooden floor'. Following this sound to its source, Latrobe came upon an area of open ground adjacent to the city, on which some five or six hundred blacks were 'formed into circular groupes in the midst of four of which was a ring'. Within these rings slave instrumentalists were playing while other African-Americans danced.

In one of the dancing rings, 'an old man sat astride of a Cylindrical drum about a foot in diameter, and beat it with incredible quickness with the edge of his hand and fingers', and a second man beat an 'open staved' drum in a similar manner, while holding it between his knees. The resulting noise, Latrobe declared, was 'incredible'. Other unfamiliar sounds issued from a 'curious' stringed instrument, which Latrobe felt must have come from Africa, and which was being played by an old man. 'On top of the finger board [of the instrument] was the rude [carved] figure of a Man in a sitting posture, and two pegs behind him to which the strings were fastened. The body [of the instrument] was a Calabash.' To add to the din, some 'women squalled out a burthen [refrain] to the playing, at intervals, consisting of two notes, as the Negroes working in our cities respond to the Song of their leader'.

Two of the other rings contained ensembles of this general type, but at the last and the largest, Latrobe discovered instruments of markedly different design. One resembled 'a block cut into something of the form of a cricket bat with a long and deep mortice down the Center'. Another was 'a square drum looking like a stool'. The noise of the first, which was being 'beaten lustily on the side by a short stick', was 'considerable'; that of the second 'abominably loud'. The ensemble was completed by 'a Calabash with a round hole in it, the hole studded with brass nails', on which a woman beat with two sticks. Meanwhile, as a raucous complement to the sound these instruments made, a man 'sung an uncouth song to the dancing which I suppose was in some African language, for it was not french', and some women 'screamed a detestable burthen on one single note'.[70]

Latrobe's account clearly indicates the strongly percussive and rhythmic character of slave music, but what also distinguishes the instrumental ensembles in evidence at Place Congo, and, indeed, those that former slaves have described, is their ability to create a mix of strikingly different sound qualities (a necessity if the individual rhythms were to be 'heard'). Since they were constructed differently and from different materials, the cylindrical and open-staved drums in the first of Latrobe's dancing rings would in any case have yielded sharply varying tones. But by using a variety of hand and finger movements, for instance, or beating the drum membrane in a different place, the drummer of each would have been able to alter, even more dramatically, his instrument's sonic range. As J. H. Kwabena Nketia explains, on many drums a broad range of tone quality and pitch may be obtained through a drummer's use of 'the cupped hand, the palm, palm and fingers, or the base of the palm in different positions on the drum'.[71] The player of the open-staved drum, the sides of which appear, from a sketch that Latrobe made, to have been composed of strips of wood, could have achieved additional tonal differentiation by applying pressure with his knees, between which the drum was held, squeezing the sides of the drum to increase tension on the membrane and relaxing such pressure when lower tones were desired. Just such a method is used by players of the Yoruba two-headed hour-glass drum, which is held under one arm and beaten with a curved stick. 'Variations in tension of the skins are obtained', Bebey writes, 'by exerting pressure with the forearm on the longitudinal thongs that connect the skins', a procedure so effective that it 'gives different sonorities which can produce all the tones of speech'.[72] The open staves that formed the sides of the drum that Latrobe described would seem to correspond very closely to the 'longitudinal thongs' mentioned by Bebey, and were almost certainly worked on in the same way.

The 'cricket bat' drum (actually a struck idiophone) in the largest of the Place Congo dancing rings bears at least some resemblance to the African slit drum, which, Nketia tells us, is 'made out of a hollowed log of wood, a section of which is slit open to provide it with a pair of "lips" that can be struck with beaters'. Lips of different thickness produce different tones when struck.[73] But whatever sounds this Place Congo drum was capable of producing, they were certain to have differed considerably from those made by the drum which 'resembled a stool', and even more so from those of the 'calabash with a round hole in it, the hole studded with brass nails which was beaten by a woman with two short sticks'. The singing that Latrobe heard as he inspected the slave dancing rings would have created even more complex sonic textures, 'kaleidoscopic' in their 'range of dramatically contrasting qualities of sound'.[74]

Yet something more subtle may also have been going on. According to Robert Farris Thompson, West African dance and musical performance possess 'a dynamic sensibility', both of these artistic forms 'seem[ing] to fuse energy and decorum in a manner that confounds the either/or categories of Western thinking'. Developing this insight, John Miller Chernoff has pointed out that, whereas 'a Westerner might find rhythmic conflict an overwhelmingly intense experience[,] in an African musical context, rhythmic conflict brings coolness to communication'. Coolness 'calls for mediated involvement rather than concentrated attention, collectedness of mind rather than self-abandonment . . . In African music, the emphasis shifts from rhythm to rhythm or part to part. Without balance and coolness, the African musician loses aesthetic command, and the music abdicates its social authority, becoming hot, intense, limited, pretentious, overly personal, boring, irrelevant, and ultimately alienating.' Individual performers may drum, or sing, or dance 'apart' – may improvise – but they must do so without losing touch with the whole. In this context, Thompson writes, call-and-response becomes 'a means of putting innovation and tradition, invention and imitation, into amicable relationships with one another', and 'in that sense, it, too, is cool'. Musical 'conversations' of the type we have been considering at Place Congo – voice with voice, voice with instrument, instrument with instrument, instrument with body, and so on – are 'additive', rather than disruptive, and, as Thompson expresses it, 'cool in [their] expressions of community'.[75]

None of these things could Benjamin Latrobe have appreciated. Exposed to the unfamiliar sights and sounds of Place Congo, he experienced only an overwhelming sense of cultural alienation. The sound of the drums was 'abominably loud'; the singing 'uncouth', 'detestable'; the notes screamed rather than sung. 'I have never', the traveller concluded, 'seen any thing more brutally savage, and at the same time dull and stupid than this whole exhibition.'[76] The hundreds of African-Americans who came each Sunday to Place Congo, however, heard not a frenzied cacophony of ear-splitting noise, but an exciting, but at the same time cool, mix of culturally evocative sound.

In explaining to Jeanette Robinson Murphy how spirituals were created, one of the former slave women, to whose singing Murphy had listened appreciatively, pointed to a significant difference between the religious music of African Americans and that of whites. 'Notes is good enough for you people', the woman declared, 'but us likes a mixtery.'[77] It may have been that, in using the word 'mixtery', the woman was referring to the process by which the lyrics of spirituals were composed, a process that often seemed to whites to entail an almost haphazard piecing together of texts drawn from the whole bible – 'fragments, caught here and there, and pieced into mosaic', as Elizabeth Kilham had expressed it.[78] It seems likely, however, that, in juxtaposing the words 'notes' and 'mixtery', the woman had more than lyrical content in mind, that the 'notes' she deemed 'good enough' for whites referred to the sounds of a simple tune sung in a straightforward manner (a style typical of much white hymn singing), whereas the 'mixtery' preferred by blacks was the more complex sonic texture of the slave spiritual, with its overlapping rhythms, sharp timbral contrasts, and liberal tonal embellishment. Whether this was so or not, there are clear indications that North American slaves did like a 'mixtery', and that in so doing they were reflecting West African cultural preferences.

West African musicians also mixed sounds of great range and diversity. In their efforts to replicate the world of sound, Nketia points out, African singers exploit 'the prosodic features of speech', using 'explosive sounds or special interjections, vocal grunts, and even the whisper'.[79] Players of African musical instruments, Francis Bebey observes, 'experiment with unusual sonorities', seeking 'to produce all manner of weird and complex sounds that often strike Western ears as being impure. Metal jingles may be attached to instruments or dried seeds placed in the sound-box to add their dancing rhythms to the music; drums sometimes have snares. All manner of contrivances are used to produce a variety of sounds – muted, nasal, or strident – that are intended to bring the music as close as possible to the actual sound of nature.'[80]

But the principle of mixing has a wider application, extending to cultural spheres as diverse as textile design, speech, and dance. In textile production, West Africans mix colours and designs in ways that whites often find disconcerting. As Robert Farris Thompson has pointed out, 'African cloth has for centuries, as it is today, been distinguishable by deliberate clashing of "high affect colors," . . . in willful, percussively contrastive, bold arrangements.' In the widely influential Mande culture, Thompson asserts, 'visual aliveness' and vibrancy in textile production are achieved not only by the aggressive mixing of colours, but by the apparently haphazard placement of the variously designed narrow strips of which the material is made. In the so-called 'rhythmized' cloth of West Africa, rhythms are irregular, mixing elements of colour and design in ways that disturb white sensibilities.[81]

In the early nineteenth century, when North American slaves became involved in the manufacture of cloth and clothing, they also mixed colours and patterns in ways that whites found strange. Former South Carolinian slave Charlie Meadow explained to his WPA interviewer that, whereas the slaves' winter clothing had been 'drab and plain', 'for our summer clothes we plaited de hanks to make a mixtry of colors'.[82] Lizzie Norfleet, interviewed in Mississippi, remembered that the dresses slave women made for themselves were 'beautiful', with 'one dark stripe and one bright stripe'. 'Folks them days', she averred, 'knowed how to mix pretty colors.'[83] Whites, however, were less impressed. Fanny Kemble, resident on her husband's Georgia plantation in the late 1830s, called the 'sabbath toilet' of the slaves

the most ludicrous combination of incongruities that you can conceive
. . . every color of the rainbow, and the deepest possible shades blended
in fierce companionship . . .; head handkerchiefs, that put one's very eyes
out from a mile off; chintzes with sprawling patterns, that might be seen
if the clouds were printed with them; beads, . . . flaring sashes, and, above
all, little fanciful aprons, which finish these incongruous toilets with a sort
of airy grace, which I assure you is perfectly indescribable.[84]

Kemble alluded here not just to the propensity of slaves to create seemingly bizarre
mixtures of colour and design, but also to combine various items of clothing within
the one ensemble in ways that whites often considered wildly inappropriate.

The slaves' creation of such mixed and odd-seeming clothing ensembles
reflected not simply privation, a sort of catch-as-catch-can mentality, but a tendency, also observable in West Africa and particularly among the elite, to add to
their garb any garment that caught the wearer's fancy or that she or he happened
to acquire, without any Westernized sense that such an item should co-ordinate in
style, colour, or anything else with whatever else they were wearing. Writing
shortly after the end of the Civil War, an anonymous correspondent of *Harper's
New Monthly Magazine*, who had spent several years in Guinea, mocked this very
practice. 'What a union of civilized and barbarous costume was here!' he declared,
referring to the garb of one 'Hamitic Dandy', who had offset more usual African
forms of dress with a European-style hat and cane and a prominently displayed
collection of keys. In this writer, the juxtaposition of items of European clothing
or accessories, or items of European manufacture, with more recognizably African
garments excited feelings of bemusement and disdain.[85]

As we have seen, slave singers also mixed musical sounds in ways that defeated
whites' attempt to score their songs. So also did African-American instrumentalists. Slaves on former slave Wash Wilson's Texas plantation, for example, used a
variety of substances (animal bone of various types, a piece of iron, a kettle, a
gourd, a section of a tree trunk and a barrel, both with animal skins stretched over
one end, and a buffalo horn), beaten or otherwise played in a variety of ways (with
fingers, hands, feet, sticks, or mouth), to create a combination of sounds of sharply
different pitch and timbre.[86]

The kind of apparently haphazard mixing to which whites took bemused objection also characterized some forms of black speech, notably slave sermons. In rural
South Carolina in 1863, Charles Raymond, a white clergyman, was invited to attend
a 'funeral preaching' for a slave woman who had died two years earlier, the oration
to be delivered by a famed slave preacher known as 'Uncle Phil'. Having listened
to Phil's address, Raymond readily conceded that, although the sound of the man's
voice had deeply affected the large black congregation ('to see Phil and hear him
preach', Raymond wrote, 'was to rouse and stir all the tenderest depths of your
nature'), intellectually the oration had been 'mere trash', a 'jumble of thoughts',
analytically 'ridiculous'. For this reason, any attempt systematically to reproduce
one of Phil's sermons, or indeed those of any 'genuine Southern negro', would,
prove, Raymond declared, quite futile.[87] (The clergyman's comments recall claims
by whites that slave religious songs were 'a kind of patchwork', and that slave music
was impossible to score.)

If Raymond felt alienated by the apparently jumbled content of the funeral sermon and the lack of temporal connection between the death and the preaching, Phil found the expectations of the dominant culture equally strange. Some time earlier, Raymond had given him a book of sermon skeletons, hoping to encourage in him a more structured presentation of ideas, but Phil had merely been non-plussed, reacting with incredulity to the notion that sermons could be planned and delivered in this way. As the slave well knew, he would be judged by different standards. His audience would be listening to the metrics of delivery. They would understand that the repetitive rhythms of the chanted sermon were needed to evoke the necessary audience response, that without the requisite rhythms the Spirit would not come. Phil's audience would be concerned, too, with the aesthetics of his performance, with the way he wove formulaic expressions, whether spontaneously created or drawn from Scripture or the spirituals, into his own metrical style.[88] A representative of a predominantly oral culture, he had stored in his memory a vast repertoire of phrases and ideas which awaited artful use. The success of his performance would be measured not simply for the poetic fit of the expressions he sampled (and mixed together), but for their connotative referencing, the associations those words had conjured, their effectiveness in bringing meanings from other contexts to a particular moment in his address, to the story he was unfolding. Controlled, linear organization was far less important than congregational involvement, imaginative sampling, and cumulative rhythmic and associational effect. As with slave music, so also with slave preaching: the African Americans and whites who heard it were listening to different things.

This discussion illustrates how an aesthetic first identified by Robert Farris Thompson in his studies of African cultures was exemplified in all aspects of slave music, not only in the 'off-beat phrasing of melodic accents', to which Thompson specifically refers, but in the overlapping of rhythmic patterns, the apparently haphazard construction of the lyrics of slave songs, and, in the case of both slave singers and instrumentalists, in the incessant mixing of dramatically contrasting timbres and tones. Our discussion also suggests that this same idiom is observable in other forms of black cultural expression: in the way slaves combined colours and patterns in the quilts and clothing they created, in the odd-seeming way they combined items of clothing within the one ensemble; in the non-linear manner in which slave preachers 'joined the words' as they preached the Christian gospel to their own people. To be sure, we have centred our discussion on best-case scenarios; the main sites of our study – the Sea Islands, Place Congo, and rural South Carolina – were areas of dense slave concentration, where it has long been acknowledged that African influences were strongest. As well, we have written here only of the nineteenth century. For a variety of reasons, sources for this period are comparatively rich. An increased number of travellers criss-crossed the South during these years, whose heightened concern over the nature of the 'peculiar institution', and generally more sympathetic attitude towards the slaves themselves, led them to observe and record closely the details of African-American life. From the early years of the Civil War, various Northerners went to conquered areas of the South to teach or otherwise assist newly freed slaves, and out of their experiences came several lengthy descriptions of the music of the slaves. In addition, for the nineteenth century we have available to us the words of former slaves themselves, as recorded in ex-slave autobiographies and Works Progress Administration interviews conducted in the 1930s.

The temptation may be great simply to assume that African elements in North American slave culture were even more important in the seventeenth and eighteenth centuries, than in the nineteenth, but recent work on slavery has demonstrated that slave culture did not travel in such conveniently straight temporal lines.[89] A fuller examination of the cultural significance of slavery's sounds must await further work not only among other nineteenth-century sources, but also among the much more sparse and problematical sources for the colonial period. At this stage we would suggest, however, that much the same underlying principles that have emerged from this study animated slave culture elsewhere in the South, although that may often have been far less obvious.

From our perspective, what is most striking in all this is the links that exist between different cultural spheres, links that are starkly demonstrated by the similarity of whites' reactions to diverse aspects of slave life. Whites' contemptuous dismissal of slaves' colour and clothing preferences, and their criticisms of the apparently analytically chaotic nature of slave sermons, are analogues, in the sartorial and verbal realms, of their disdainful reaction to slave music – to its lack of harmony, seemingly ill-assorted lyrics, bewildering rhythmic complexity, and sharp timbral dissonance. But these reactions are merely a sign, pointing us to something much more significant: the continuing importance of a distinctive cultural aesthetic in the lives of North American slaves. For African-Americans who danced to makeshift musical ensembles in the slave quarters or at Place Congo, or joined in the antiphonal singing, or clapped or patted to intensify the basic pulse, the mixed sounds and rhythms of the music they made fit easily into a cultural aesthetic that gave a reassuring sense of unity to their lives and offered a brief respite from the rigours of a hard and often capricious existence.

Notes

1   *National Advocate*, 8 Nov. 1821.
2   W. Faux, *Memorable Days in America: Being a Journal of a Tour to the United States* (London: W. Simpkin & R. Marshall, 1823), p. 84.
3   Harvey Wish (ed.), Frederick Law Olmsted, *The Slave States* (New York: Capricorn Books, 1959 [orig. pub. 1856]), pp. 114–15.
4   George P. Rawick (ed.), *The American Slave: A Composite Autobiography*, VI: Alabama and Indiana Narratives (41 vols. and index; Westport. CT, and London: Greenwood, 1972–1981). Alabama Narratives. 395.
5   Rawick (ed.), *The American Slave*. VII: Oklahoma and Mississippi Narratives, Oklahoma Narratives. p. 335.
6   Rawick (ed.), *The American Slave*, VI: Alabama and Indiana Narratives, Alabama Narratives, pp. 416–17.
7   Ibid., p. 129.
8   Rawick (ed.), *The American Slave*, VII: Oklahoma and Mississippi Narratives, Oklahoma Narratives, p. 335.
9   Rawick (ed.), *The American Slave*, Supplement Series 1, III: Georgia Narratives, Pt.1, pp. 9–10.
10 Frederick Douglass, *My Bondage and My Freedom* (New York: Dover Publications, 1969 [orig. pub. 1855]), pp. 97–9.
11 Samuel A. Floyd. Jr., *The Power of Black Music: Interpreting Its History from Africa to the United States* (New York: Oxford University Press, 1995), p. 46.
12 Harold Courlander, *Negro Folk Music, U.S.A.* (New York and London: Columbia University Press, 1963), p. 85.

13 Ibid., p. 82.
14 Rawick (ed.), *The American Slave*, Supplement Series 2, IX. Texas Narratives, Pt.8, p. 3752.
15 Olmsted, *The Slave States*, Wish (ed.), p. 115.
16 Rawick (ed.), *The American Slave*, Supplement Series 2, IV: Texas Narratives, Pt.3, p. 1022.
17 Rawick (ed.), *The American Slave*, II, South Carolina Narratives, Pt.2, p. 146.
18 Rawick (ed.), *The American Slave*, Supplement Series 2, IX, Texas Narratives, Pt.8, p. 3752.
19 Rawick (ed.), *The American Slave*, Supplement Series 2, III, Texas Narratives, Pt.2, p. 610.
20 Courlander, *Negro Folk Music*, p. 81.
21 Ashenafi Kebede, *Roots of Black Music: The Vocal, Instrumental, and Dance Heritage of Africa and Black America* (Englewood Cliffs, NJ: Prentice Hall, 1982), p. 47.
22 Willis Lawrence James, 'The Romance of the Negro Folk Cry in America', in Alan Dundes (ed.), *Mother Wit from the Laughing Barrel: Readings and Interpretation of Afro-American Folklore* (Englewood Cliffs, NJ: Prentice Hall, 1973), p. 438.
23 Robert Farris Thompson, 'The Song That Named the Land: The Visionary Presence of African-American Art', in *Black Art Ancestral Legacy: The African Impulse in African-American Art* (Dallas, Texas: Dallas Museum of Art, 1989), p. 97.
24 Ibid.
25 Olly Wilson, 'The Heterogeneous Sound Ideal in African-American Music', in Josephine Wright (ed.), *New Perspectives on Music: Essays in Honor of Eileen Southern* (Warren, MI: Harmonie Park Press, 1992), p. 329.
26 Floyd, *Power of Black Music*, p. 21.
27 Ibid., pp. 8–9.
28 James, 'Romance of the Negro Folk Cry', p. 443.
29 C. Vann Woodward (ed.), Whitelaw Reid, *After the War: A Tour of the Southern States, 1865–1866* (New York: Harper and Row, 1965), pp. 100–3.
30 Ibid., pp. 104–5.
31 Ibid., pp. 108–11.
32 Ronald Radano, 'Denoting Difference: The Writing of the Slave Spirituals', *Critical Inquiry*, 22, 3 (Spring 1996), p. 507.
33 William Francis Allen, Charles Pickard Ware and Lucy McKim Garrison (comp.), *Slave Songs of the United States* (New York: Oak Publications, 1965 [orig. pub. 1867]), pp. 9–10.
34 Winthrop D. Jordan, *Tunnels and Silence at Second Creek: An Inquiry into a Civil War Slave Conspiracy* (Baton Rouge and London: Louisiana University Press, 1993), p. 20.
35 Quoted in Dena J. Epstein, *Sinful Tunes and Spirituals: Black Folk Music to the Civil War* (Urbana and Chicago: University of Illinois Press, 1981 [orig. pub. 1977]), pp. 227–8.
36 Lucy McKim, 'Songs of the Port Royal Contrabands', in Bruce Jackson (ed.), *The Negro and His Folklore in Nineteenth-Century Periodicals* (Austin and London: University of Texas Press, 1967), p. 62.
37 Francis Bebey, *African Music: A People's Art* (London: Harrap, 1975 [orig. pub. 1969]). pp. 2, 115.
38 Quoted in Bebey, *African Music*, p. 5.
39 Bebey, *African Music*, p. 115.
40 Arthur M. Schlesinger (ed.), *Frederick Law Olmsted, The Cotton Kingdom: A Traveller's Observations on Cotton and Slavery in the American South* (New York: Alfred A. Knopf, 1953), p. 36.
41 Quoted in Epstein, *Sinful Tunes*, p. 72.
42 Reid, *After the War*, p. 523.
43 Quoted in Epstein, *Sinful Tunes*, p. 84.
44 William Tallmadge, 'Blue Notes and Blue Tonality', *The Black Perspective in Music*, 12, 2 (Fall 1984), pp. 155, 159–62.
45 Allen, *Slave Songs of the United States*, p. 10.
46 Quoted in Epstein, *Sinful Tunes*, p. 236.
47 Quoted in Tallmadge, 'Blue Notes and Blue Tonality', p. 155.
48 Radano, 'Denoting Difference', p. 536.
49 Quoted in Epstein, *Sinful Tunes*, p. 261.
50 Reid, *After the War*, 103.

51 Quoted in Epstein, *Sinful Tunes*, p. 201.
52 Quoted in Epstein, *Sinful Tunes*, p. 281.
53 Unsigned review of *Slave Songs of the United States* in *Lippincott's Magazine*, 1 (Philadelphia, March 1868), pp. 341–3 reprinted in Jackson (ed.), *The Negro and His Folklore*, p. 107.
54 Elizabeth Kilham, 'Sketches in Color', *Putnam's Magazine*, 5 (March 1870), p. 309.
55 *Christian Watchman and Reflector*, 18 July 1867, p. 4.
56 Kilham, 'Sketches in Color', p. 308.
57 Quoted in Epstein, *Sinful Tunes*, p. 276.
58 Quoted in Eileen Southern, *The Music of Black Americans* (New York and London: Norton & Co., 1983), p. 210.
59 Shane White and Graham White, *Stylin': African American Expressive Culture From Its Beginnings to the Zoot Suit* (Ithaca and London: Cornell University Press, 1998), pp. 5–36, 63–84.
60 Reid, *After the War*, pp. 103, 104.
61 Quoted in Epstein, *Sinful Tunes*, p. 281.
62 John Miller Chernoff, *African Rhythm and African Sensibility: Aesthetics and Social Action in African Musical Idioms* (Chicago and London: University of Chicago Press, 1979), p. 111.
63 McKim, 'Songs of the Port Royal Contrabands', p. 62.
64 Radano, 'Denoting Difference', 538; Allen, *Slave Songs*, pp. 75, 14.
65 Quoted in Epstein, *Sinful Tunes*, p. 10.
66 Jeanette Robinson Murphy, 'The Survival of African Folk Music in America', in Jackson (ed.), *The Negro and His Folklore*, pp. 328, 331–2.
67 Wilson, 'Heterogeneous Sound Ideal', p. 329.
68 Allen, *Slave Songs*, p. 10.
69 Reid, *After the War*, p. 108.
70 Edward C. Carter II, John C. Van Horne, and Lee W. Formwalt (eds.), Benjamin Henry Latrobe, *The Journals of Benjamin Henry Latrobe, 1799–1820: From Philadelphia to New Orleans*, Vol. 3 (New Haven and London: Yale University Press, 1980), pp. 203–4.
71 J. H. Kwabena Nketia, *The Music of Africa* (London: Gollancz, 1975), p. 89.
72 Bebey, *African Music*, p. 94.
73 Nketia, *The Music of Africa*, p. 73.
74 Wilson, 'Heterogeneous Sound Ideal', p. 329.
75 Robert Farris Thompson, 'An Aesthetic of the Cool: West African Dance', *African Forum*, 2, 2 (Fall, 1966), pp. 87, 98: Chernoff, *African Rhythm*, p. 140.
76 Latrobe, *Journals*, p. 204.
77 Murphy, 'Survival of African Folk Music', p. 329.
78 Kilham, 'Sketches in Color', p. 308.
79 Nketia, *The Music of Africa*, p. 178.
80 Bebey, *African Music*, pp. 40–1.
81 Robert Farris Thompson, *Flash of the Spirit: African Art and Afro-American Art and Philosophy* (New York: Vintage Books, 1984), pp. 208–10.
82 Rawick (ed.), *The American Slave*, Vol. 3 South Carolina Narratives, Pts 3 & 4, Pt 3, 180 (our italics).
83 Rawick (ed.), *The American Slave*, Supplement Series 1, Vol. IX, Mississippi Narratives, 1641–42.
84 John A. Scott (ed.), Frances Ann Kemble, *Journal of a Residence on a Georgian Plantation in 1838–1839* (New York: New American Library, 1975), pp. 93–4.
85 'The Fashions in Guinea', *Harper's New Monthly Magazine*, 37, 218 (July 1868), pp. 166–7.
86 Rawick (ed.), *The American Slave*, Vol. V. Texas Narratives, Pt.4, p. 198.
87 Charles A. Raymond, 'The Religious Life of the Negro Slave', *Harper's New Monthly Magazine*, 27, 161 (October 1863), pp. 677–79.
88 Bruce A. Rosenberg, *Can These Bones Live? The Art of the American Folk Preacher* (Urbana and Chicago: University of Illinois Press, 1988 [1970]). pp. 142–4.
89 Ira Berlin's recent work has been particularly disruptive of such linear interpretations of African-American culture. See this volume, Chapter 20, and *Many Thousands Gone: The First Two Centuries of Slavery in North America* (Cambridge, MA: Harvard University Press, 1998). See also White and White, *Stylin'*, pp. 5–36.

Ira Berlin

FROM CREOLE TO AFRICAN
Atlantic creoles and the origins of African-American society in mainland North America

I N 1727, ROBERT "KING" CARTER, the richest planter in Virginia, purchased a handful of African slaves from a trader who had been cruising the Chesapeake. The transaction was a familiar one to the great planter, for Carter owned hundreds of slaves and had inspected many such human cargoes, choosing the most promising from among the weary, frightened men and women who had survived the transatlantic crossing. Writing to his overseer from his plantation on the Rappahannock River, Carter explained the process by which he initiated Africans into their American captivity. "I name'd them here & by their names we can always know what sizes they are of & I am sure we repeated them so often to them that every one knew their name & would readily answer to them." Carter then forwarded his slaves to a satellite plantation or quarter, where his overseer repeated the process, taking "care that the negros both men & women I sent . . . always go by the names we gave them." In the months that followed, the drill continued, with Carter again joining in the process of stripping newly arrived Africans of the signature of their identity.[1]

Renaming marked Carter's initial endeavor to master his new slaves by separating them from their African inheritance. For the most part, he designated them by common English diminutives—Tom, Jamey, Moll, Nan—as if to consign them to a permanent childhood. But he tagged some with names more akin to barnyard animals—Jumper, for example—as if to represent their distance from humanity, and he gave a few the names of some ancient deity or great personage like Hercules or Cato as a kind of cosmic jest: the most insignificant with the greatest of names. None of his slaves received surnames, marks of lineage that Carter sought to obliterate and of adulthood that he would not admit.[2]

The loss of their names was only the first of the numerous indignities Africans suffered at the hands of planters in the Chesapeake. Since many of the skills Africans carried across the Atlantic had no value to their new owners, planters disparaged them, and since the Africans' "harsh jargons" rattled discordantly in the planters' ears, they ridiculed them. Condemning new arrivals for the "gross bestiality and rudeness of their manners, the variety and strangeness of their languages, and the weakness and shallowness of their minds," planters put them to work at the most repetitive and backbreaking tasks, often on the most primitive, frontier plantations. They made but scant attempt to see that slaves had adequate food, clothing, or shelter, because the open slave trade made slaves cheap and the new disease environment inflated their mortality rate, no matter how well they were tended. Residing in sex-segregated barracks, African slaves lived a lonely existence, Without families or ties of kin, isolated from the mainstream of Chesapeake life.[3]

So began the slow, painful process whereby Africans became African-Americans. In time, people of African descent recovered their balance, mastered the circumstances of their captivity, and confronted their owners on more favorable terms. Indeed, resistance to the new regime began at its inception, as slaves clandestinely maintained their African names even as they answered their owner's call.[4] The transition of Africans to African-Americans or creoles[5]—which is partially glimpsed in the records of Carter's estate—would be repeated thousands of times, as African slavers did the rough business of transporting Africa to America. While the transition was different on the banks of the Hudson, Cooper, St. Johns, and Mississippi rivers than on the Rappahannock, the scenario by which "outlandish" Africans progressed from "New Negroes" to assimilated African-Americans has come to frame the history of black people in colonial North America.[6]

Important as that story is to the development of black people in the plantation era, it embraces only a portion of the history of black life in colonial North America, and that imperfectly. The assimilationist scenario assumes that "African" and "creole" were way stations of generational change rather than cultural strategies that were manufactured and remanufactured and that the vectors of change moved in only one direction—often along a single track with Africans inexorably becoming creoles. Its emphasis on the emergence of the creole—a self-sustaining, indigenous population—omits entirely an essential element of the story: the charter generations, whose experience, knowledge, and attitude were more akin to that of confident, sophisticated natives than of vulnerable newcomers.[7] Such men and women, who may be termed "Atlantic Creoles"[8] from their broad experience in the Atlantic world, flourished prior to the triumph of plantation production on the mainland—the tobacco revolution in the Chesapeake in the last third of the seventeenth century, the rice revolution in the Carolina lowcountry in the first decades of the eighteenth century, the incorporation of the northern colonies into the Atlantic system during the eighteenth century, and finally the sugar revolution in the lower Mississippi Valley in the first decade of the nineteenth century. Never having to face the cultural imposition of the likes of Robert "King" Carter, black America's charter generations took a different path—despite the presence of slavery and the vilification of slave masters and their apologists. The Atlantic creole's unique experience reveals some of the processes by which race was constructed and reconstructed in early America.

Black life in mainland North America originated not in Africa or America but in the netherworld between the continents. Along the periphery of the Atlantic—first in Africa, then in Europe, and finally in the Americas—African-American society was a product of the momentous meeting of Africans and Europeans and of their equally fateful encounter with the peoples of the Americas. Although the countenances of these new people of the Atlantic—Atlantic Creoles—might bear the features of Africa, Europe, or the Americas in whole or in part, their beginnings, strictly speaking, were in none of those places. Instead, by their experiences and sometimes by their persons, they had become part of the three worlds that came together along the Atlantic littoral. Familiar with the commerce of the Atlantic, fluent in its new languages, and intimate with its trade and cultures, they were cosmopolitan in the fullest sense.

Atlantic creoles originated in the historic meeting of Europeans and Africans on the west coast of Africa. Many served as intermediaries, employing their linguistic skills and their familiarity with the Atlantic's diverse commercial practices, cultural conventions, and diplomatic etiquette to mediate between African merchants and European sea captains. In so doing, some Atlantic creoles identified with their ancestral homeland (or a portion of it)—be it African, European, or American—and served as its representatives in negotiations with others. Other Atlantic creoles had been won over by the power and largesse of one party or another, so that Africans entered the employ of European trading companies and Europeans traded with African potentates. Yet others played fast and loose with their diverse heritage, employing whichever identity paid best. Whatever strategy they adopted, Atlantic creoles began the process of integrating the icons and ideologies of the Atlantic world into a new way of life.[9]

The emergence of Atlantic creoles was but a tiny outcropping in the massive social upheaval that accompanied the joining of the peoples of the two hemispheres. But it represented the small beginnings that initiated this monumental transformation, as the new people of the Atlantic made their presence felt. Some traveled widely as blue-water sailors, supercargoes, shipboard servants, and interpreters—the last particularly important because Europeans showed little interest in mastering the languages of Africa. Others were carried—sometimes as hostages—to foreign places as exotic trophies to be displayed before curious publics, eager for firsthand knowledge of the lands beyond the sea. Traveling in more dignified style, Atlantic creoles were also sent to distant lands with commissions to master the ways of newly discovered "others" and to learn the secrets of their wealth and knowledge. A few entered as honored guests, took their places in royal courts as esteemed councilors, and married into the best families.[10]

Atlantic creoles first appeared at the trading *feitorias* or factories that European expansionists established along the coast of Africa in the fifteenth century. Finding trade more lucrative than pillage, the Portuguese crown began sending agents to oversee its interests in Africa. These official representatives were succeeded by private entrepreneurs or *lançados*, who established themselves with the aid of African potentates, sometimes in competition with the crown's emissaries. European nations soon joined in the action, and coastal factories became sites of commercial rendezvous for all manner of transatlantic traders. What was true of the Portuguese enclaves (Axim and Elmina) held for those later established or seized by the Dutch (Fort Nassau and Elmina), Danes (Fredriksborg and Christiansborg), Swedes (Karlsborg and Cape Apolina), Brandenburgers (Pokoso), French (St. Louis and Gorée), and English (Fort Kormantse and Cape Coast).[11]

The transformation of the fishing villages along the Gold Coast during the sixteenth and seventeenth centuries suggests something of the change wrought by the European traders. Between 1550 and 1618, Mouri (where the Dutch constructed Fort Nassau in 1612) grew from a village of 200 people to 1,500 and to an estimated 5,000–6,000 at the end of the eighteenth century. In 1555, Cape Coast counted only twenty houses; by 1680, it had 500 or more. Axim, with 500 inhabitants in 1631, expanded to between 2,000 and 3,000 by 1690.[12] Small but growing numbers of Europeans augmented the African fishermen, craftsmen, village-based peasants, and laborers who made up the population of these villages. Although mortality and transiency rates in these enclaves were extraordinarily high, even by the standards of early modern ports, permanent European settlements developed from a mobile body of the corporate employees (from governors to surgeons to clerks), merchants and factors, stateless sailors, skilled craftsmen, occasional missionaries, and sundry transcontinental drifters.[13]

Established in 1482 by the Portuguese and captured by the Dutch in 1637, Elmina was one of the earliest factories and an exemplar for those that followed. A meeting place for African and European commercial ambitions, Elmina—the Castle São Jorge da Mina and the town that surrounded it—became headquarters for Portuguese and later Dutch mercantile activities on the Gold Coast and, with a population of 15,000 to 20,000 in 1682, the largest of some two dozen European outposts in the region.[14]

The peoples of the enclaves—both long-term residents and wayfarers—soon joined together genetically as well as geographically. European men took African women as wives and mistresses, and, before long, the offspring of these unions helped people the enclave. Elmina sprouted a substantial cadre of Euro-Africans (most of them Luso-Africans)—men and women of African birth but shared African and European parentage, whose combination of swarthy skin, European dress and deportment, knowledge of local customs, and multilingualism gave them inside understanding of both African and European ways while denying them full acceptance in either culture. By the eighteenth century, they numbered several hundred in Elmina. Farther south along the coast of Central Africa, they may have been even more numerous.[15]

People of mixed ancestry and tawny complexion composed but a small fraction of the population of the coastal factories, yet few observers failed to note their existence—which suggests something of the disproportionate significance of their presence. Africans and Europeans alike sneered at the Creoles' mixed lineage (or lack of lineage) and condemned them as knaves, charlatans, and shameless self-promoters. When they adopted African ways, wore African dress and amulets, and underwent ritual circumcision and scarification, Europeans declared them outcasts (*tangomãos*, renegades, to the Portuguese). When they adopted European ways, wore European clothing and crucifixes, employed European names or titles, and comported themselves in the manner of "white men," Africans denied them the right to hold land, marry, and inherit property. Yet, although *tangomãos* faced reproach and proscription, all parties conceded that they were shrewd traders, attested to their mastery of the fine points of intercultural negotiations, and found advantage in dealing with them. Despite their defamers, some rose to positions of wealth and power, compensating for their lack of lineage with knowledge, skill, and entrepreneurial derring-do.[16]

Not all *tangomãos* were of mixed ancestry, and not all people of mixed ancestry were *tangomãos*. Color was only one marker of this culture-in-the-making, and generally the least significant.[17] From common experience, conventions of personal behavior, and cultural sensibilities compounded by shared ostracism and mercantile aspirations, Atlantic creoles acquired interests of their own, apart from their European and African antecedents. Of necessity, Atlantic creoles spoke a variety of African and European languages, weighted strongly toward Portuguese. From the seeming babble emerged a pidgin that enabled Atlantic Creoles to communicate widely. In time, their pidgin evolved into Creole, borrowing its vocabulary from all parties and creating a grammar unique unto itself. Derisively called "*fala de Guine*" or "*fala de negros*"—"Guinea speech" or "Negro Speech"—by the Portuguese and "black Portuguese" by others, this creole language became the lingua franca of the Atlantic.[18]

Although jaded observers condemned the culture of the enclaves as nothing more than "whoring, drinking, gambling, swearing, fighting, and shouting," Atlantic Creoles attended church (usually Catholic), married according to the sacraments, raised children conversant with European norms, and drew a livelihood from their knowledge of the Atlantic commercial economy. In short, they created societies of their own, *of* but not always *in*, the societies of the Africans who dominated the interior trade and the Europeans who controlled the Atlantic trade.

Operating under European protection, always at African sufferance, the enclaves developed governments with a politics as diverse and complicated as the peoples who populated them and a credit system that drew on the commercial centers of both Europe and Africa. Although the trading castles remained under the control of European metropoles, the towns around them often developed independent political lives—separate from both African and European domination. Meanwhile, their presence created political havoc, enabling new men and women of commerce to gain prominence and threatening older, often hereditary elites. Intermarriage with established peoples allowed creoles to construct lineages that gained them full membership in local elites, something that creoles eagerly embraced. The resultant political turmoil promoted state formation along with new class relations and ideologies.[19]

New religious forms emerged and then disappeared in much the same manner, as Europeans and Africans brought to the enclaves not only their commercial and political aspirations but all the trappings of their cultures as well. Priests and ministers sent to tend European souls made African converts, some of whom saw Christianity as both a way to ingratiate themselves with their trading partners and a new truth. Missionaries sped the process of christianization and occasionally scored striking successes. At the beginning of the sixteenth century, the royal house of Kongo converted to Christianity. Catholicism, in various syncretic forms, infiltrated the posts along the Angolan coast and spread northward. Islam filtered in from the north. Whatever the sources of the new religions, most converts saw little cause to surrender their own deities. They incorporated Christianity and Islam to serve their own needs and gave Jesus and Mohammed a place in their spiritual pantheon. New religious practices, polities, and theologies emerged from the mixing of Christianity, Islam, polytheism, and animism. Similar syncretic formations influenced the agricultural practices, architectural forms, and sartorial styles as well as the cuisine, music, art, and technology of the enclaves.[20] Like the stone fortifications, these cultural innovations announced the presence of something new to those arriving on the coast, whether they came by caravan from the African interior or sailed by caravel from the Atlantic.

Outside the European fortifications, settlements—the town of Elmina as opposed to Castle São Jorge da Mina, for example—expanded to provision and refresh the European-controlled castles and the caravels and carracks that frequented the coast. In time, they developed economics of their own, with multifarious systems of social stratification and occupational differentiation. Residents included canoemen who ferried goods between ships and shore; longshoremen and warehousemen who unloaded and stored merchandise; porters, messengers, guides, interpreters, factors, and brokers or *makelaers* (to the Dutch) who facilitated trade; inn keepers who housed country traders; skilled workers of all sorts; and a host of peddlers, hawkers, and petty traders. Others chopped wood, drew water, prepared food, or supplied sex to the lonely men who visited these isolated places. African notables occasionally established residence, bringing with them the trappings of wealth and power: wives, clients, pawns, slaves, and other dependents. In some places, small manufactories grew up, like the salt pans, boatyards, and foundries on the outskirts of Elmina, to supply the town and service the Atlantic trade. In addition, many people lived outside the law; the rough nature and transient population of these crossroads of trade encouraged roguery and brigandage.[21]

Village populations swelled into the thousands. In 1669, about the time the English were ousting the Dutch from the village of New Amsterdam, population 1,500, a visitor to Elmina noted that it contained some 8,000 residents. During most of the eighteenth century, Elmina's population was between 12,000 and 16,000, larger than Charleston, South Carolina—mainland North America's greatest slave port at the time of the American Revolution.[22]

The business of the creole communities was trade, brokering the movement of goods through the Atlantic world. Although island settlements such as Cape Verde, Principé, and São Tomé developed indigenous agricultural and sometimes plantation economics, the comings and goings of African and European merchants dominated life even in the largest of the creole communities, which served as both field headquarters for great European mercantile companies and collection points for trade between the African interior and the Atlantic littoral. Depending on the location, the exchange involved European textiles, metalware, guns, liquor, and beads for African gold, ivory, hides, pepper, beeswax, and dyewoods. The coastal trade or cabotage added fish, produce, livestock, and other perishables to this list, especially as regional specialization developed. Everywhere, slaves were bought and sold, and over time the importance of commerce-in-persons grew.[23]

As slaving societies, the coastal enclaves were also societies with slaves. African slavery in its various forms—from pawnage to chattel bondage—was practiced in these towns. Both Europeans and Africans held slaves, employed them, used them as collateral, traded them, and sold them to outsiders. At Elmina, the Dutch West India Company owned some 300 slaves in the late seventeenth century, and individual Europeans and Africans held others. Along with slaves appeared the inevitable trappings of slave societies—overseers to supervise slave labor, slave catchers to retrieve runaways, soldiers to keep order and guard against insurrections, and officials to adjudicate and punish transgressions beyond a master's reach. Freedmen and freedwomen, who had somehow escaped bondage, also enjoyed a considerable presence. Many former slaves mixed Africa and Europe culturally and sometimes physically.[24]

Knowledge and experience far more than color set the Atlantic creoles apart from the Africans who brought slaves from the interior and the Europeans who carried them across the Atlantic, on one hand, and the hapless men and women on whose commodification the slave trade rested, on the other. Maintaining a secure place in such a volatile social order was not easy. The creoles' genius for intercultural negotiation was not simply a set of skills, a tactic for survival, or an attribute that emerged as an "Africanism" in the New World. Rather, it was central to a way of life that transcended particular venues.

The names European traders called Atlantic creoles provide a glimpse of the creole's cosmopolitan ability to transcend the confines of particular nations and cultures. Abee Coffu Jantic Seniees, a leading African merchant and politico of Cape Coast on the Gold Coast in the late seventeenth century, appears in various European accounts and account books as "Jan Snees," "Jacque Senece," "Johan Sinesen," and "Jantee Snees." In some measure, the renderings of his name—to view him only from the perspective of European traders—reflect phonic imperialism or, more simply, the variability of transnational spelling. Senices probably did not know or care how his trading partners registered his name, which he may have employed for commercial reasons in any case. But the diverse renderings reveal something of Abee Coffu Jantie Seniees's ability to trade with the Danes at Fredriksborg, the Dutch at Elmina, and the English at Cape Coast, as well as with Africans deep in the forested interior.[25]

The special needs of European traders placed Atlantic creoles in a powerful bargaining position, which they learned to employ to their own advantage. The most successful became principals and traded independently. They played one merchant against another, one captain against another, and one mercantile bureaucrat against another, often abandoning them for yet a better deal with some interloper, all in the hope of securing a rich prosperity for themselves and their families. Success evoked a sense of confidence that observers described as impertinence, insolence, and arrogance, and it was not limited to the fabulously wealthy like Jantie Seniees or the near sovereign John Claessen (the near-ruler of Fetu), who rejected a kingship to remain at trade, or the merchant princes John Kabes (trader, entrepreneur, and dominant politico in Komenda) and John Konny (commanding ruler in Pokoso).[26] Canoemen, for example, became infamous among European governors and sea captains for their independence. They refused to work in heavy surf, demanded higher wages and additional rations, quit upon insult or abuse, and abandoned work altogether when enslavement threatened. Attempts to control them through regulations issued from Europe or from local corporate headquarters failed utterly. "These canoemen, despicable thieves," sputtered one Englishman in 1711, "think that they are more than just labour."[27]

Like other people in the middle, Atlantic creoles profited from their strategic position. Competition between and among the Africans and European traders bolstered their stock, increased their political leverage, and enabled them to elevate their social standing while fostering solidarity. Creoles' ability to find a place for themselves in the interstices of African and European trade grew rapidly during periods of intense competition among the Portuguese, Dutch, Danes, Swedes, French, and English and an equally diverse set of African nationals.

At the same time and by the same token, the Atlantic creoles' liminality, particularly their lack of identity with any one group, posed numerous dangers. While their middling position trade them valuable to African and European traders, it also made them vulnerable: they could be ostracized, scapegoated, and on occasion enslaved. Maintaining their independence amid the shifting alliances between and among Europeans and Africans was always difficult. Inevitably, some failed.

Debt, crime, immortality, or official disfavor could mean enslavement—if not for great men like Jantie Seniees, Claessen, Kabes, or Konny—at least for those on the fringes of the creole community.[28] Placed in captivity, Atlantic creoles might be exiled anywhere around the Atlantic—to the interior of Africa, the islands along the coast, the European metropoles, or the plantations of the New World. In the seventeenth century and the early part of the eighteenth, most slaves exported from Africa went to the sugar plantations of Brazil and the Antilles. Enslaved Atlantic creoles might be shipped to Pernambuco, Barbados, or Martinique. Transporting them to the expanding centers of New World staple production posed dangers, however, which American planters well understood. The characteristics that distinguished Atlantic creoles—their linguistic dexterity, cultural plasticity, and social agility—were precisely those qualities that the great planters of the New World disdained and feared. For their labor force they desired youth and strength, not experience and sagacity. Indeed, too much knowledge might be subversive to the good order of the plantation. Simply put, men and women who understood the operations of the Atlantic system were too dangerous to be trusted in the human tinderboxes created by the sugar revolution. Thus rejected by the most prosperous New World regimes, Atlantic creoles were frequently exiled to marginal slave societies where would-be slaveowners, unable to compete with the great plantation magnates, snapped up those whom the grandees had disparaged as "refuse" for reasons of age, illness, criminality, or recalcitrance. In the seventeenth century, few New World slave societies were more marginal than those of mainland North America.[29] Liminal peoples were drawn or propelled to marginal societies.

During the seventeenth century and into the eighteenth, the Dutch served as the most important conduit for transporting Atlantic creoles to mainland North America. Through their control of the sea, they dominated the commerce of the Atlantic periphery. Stretching mercantile theory to fit their commercial ambitions, the Dutch traded with all comers, commissioned privateers to raid rival shipping, and dealt openly with pirates. The Dutch West India Company, whose 1621 charter authorized it to trade in both the Americas and west Africa, cast its eye on the lucrative African trade in gold, ivory, copper, and slaves even as it began to barter for furs and pelts in the North Atlantic and for gold and sugar in the South Atlantic. In 1630, the Dutch captured Portuguese *capitanias* in northeastern Brazil, including Pernambuco, the site of the New World's first sugar boom. About the same time, the West India Company established bases in Curaçao and St. Eustatius. To supply their new empire, the Dutch turned to Africa, supplementing their outposts at Mouri on the Gold Coast and Gorée in Senegambia by seizing the Portuguese enclaves of Elmina and Axim in 1637, Luanda and Príncipe in 1641, and São Tomé in 1647. They then swept the Angolan coast, establishing trading factories at Cabinda, Loango, and Mpinda.[30]

Although ousted from the Gold Coast, the Portuguese never abandoned their foothold in central Africa, and they and their Brazilian successors regrouped and counterattacked. In 1648, the Portuguese recaptured Luanda and forced the Dutch to evacuate Angola. They expelled the Dutch from Pernambuco in 1645 and completed the reconquest of Brazil in 1654.

Still, the short period of Dutch dominance—roughly, 1620 to 1670—had a powerful impact on the Atlantic world. During those years, the Dutch took control of Portuguese enclaves in Africa, introduced their commercial agents, and pressed their case for Dutch culture and Calvinist religion on the ruling Kongolese Catholics and other remnants of Portuguese imperialism. Although unsuccessful for the most part, the Dutch established ties with the Atlantic creoles and preserved these link-ages even after the Portuguese reconquest, keeping alive their connections along the African coast and maintaining their position as the most active agents in slavery's transatlantic expansion during the seventeenth century.[31]

The Dutch transported thousands of slaves from Africa to the New World, trading with all parties, sometimes directly, sometimes indirectly through their base in Curaçao. Most of these slaves came from the interior of Angola, but among them were Atlantic creoles whose connections to the Portuguese offended the Dutch. Following the Portuguese restoration, those with ties to the Dutch may have found themselves in similar difficulties. During the Dutch invasions, the subsequent wars, and then civil wars in which the Portuguese and the Dutch fought each other directly and through surrogates, many creoles were clapped into slavery. Others were seized in the Caribbean by Dutch men-of-war, privateers sailing under Dutch letters of marque, and freebooting pirates.[32] While such slaves might be sent anywhere in the Dutch empire between New Netherland and Pernambuco, West India Company officers in New Amsterdam, who at first complained about "refuse" slaves, in time made known their preference for such creoles—deeming "Negroes who had been 12 or 13 years in the West Indies" to be "a better sort of Negroes."[33] A perusal of the names scattered through archival remains of New Netherland reveals something of the nature of this transatlantic transfer: Paulo d'Angola and Anthony Portuguese, Pedro Negretto and Francisco Negro, Simon Congo and Jan Guinea, Van St. Thomas and Francisco Cartagena, Clues de Neger and Assento Angola, and—perhaps most telling—Carla Criole, Jan Creoli, and Christoffel Crioell.[34]

These names trace the tumultuous experience that propelled their owner: across the Atlantic and into slavery in the New World. They suggest that what-ever tragedy befell them, Atlantic creoles did not arrive in the New World as deracinated chattel stripped of their past and without resources to meet the future. Unlike those who followed them into slavery in succeeding generations, trans-planted creoles were not designated by diminutives, tagged with names more akin to barnyard animals, or given the name of an ancient notable or a classical deity. Instead, their names provided concrete evidence that they carried a good deal more than their dignity to the Americas.

To such men and women, New Amsterdam was not radically different from Elmina or Luanda, save for its smaller size and colder climate. A fortified port con-trolled by the Dutch West India Company, its population was a farrago of petty traders, artisans, merchants, soldiers, and corporate functionaries, all scrambling for status in a frontier milieu that demanded intercultural exchange. On the tip of Manhattan Island, Atlantic creoles rubbed elbows with sailors of various nationali-ties, Native Americans with diverse tribal allegiances, and pirates and privateers who professed neither nationality nor allegiance. In the absence of a staple crop, their work—building fortifications, hunting and trapping, tending fields and domestic animals, and transporting merchandise of all sorts—did not set them apart from workers of European descent, who often labored alongside them. Such encounters made a working knowledge of the creole tongue as valuable on the North American coast as in Africa. Whereas a later generation of transplanted Africans would be linguistically isolated and de-skilled by the process of enslavement, Atlantic creoles found themselves very much at home in the new environment. Rather than losing their skills, they discovered that the value of their gift for intercultural negotiation appreciated. The transatlantic journey did not break creole communities; it only transported them to other sites.[35]

Along the edges of the North American continent, creoles found slaves' cultural and social marginality an asset. Slaveholders learned that slaves' ability to negotiate with the diverse populace of seventeenth-century North America was as valuable as their labor, perhaps more so. While their owners employed creoles' skills on their own behalf, creoles did the same for themselves, trading their knowledge for a place in the still undefined social order. In 1665, when Jan Angola, accused of stealing wood in New Amsterdam, could not address the court in Dutch, he was ordered to return the following day with "Domingo the Negro as interpreter," an act familiar to Atlantic creoles in Elmina, Lisbon, San Salvador, or Cap Françis.[36]

To be sure, slavery bore heavily on Atlantic creoles in the New World. As in Africa and Europe, it was a system of exploitation, subservience, and debasement that rested on force. Yet Atlantic creoles were familiar with servitude in forms ranging from unbridled exploitation to corporate familialism. They had known free people to be enslaved, and they had known slaves to be liberated; the boundary between slavery and freedom on the African coast was permeable. Servitude generally did not prevent men and women from marrying, acquiring property (slaves included), enjoying a modest prosperity, and eventually being incorporated into the host society; creoles transported across the Atlantic had no reason to suspect they could not do the same in the New World.[37] If the stigma of servitude, physical labor, uncertain lineage, and alien religion stamped there as outsiders, there were many others—men and women of unblemished European pedigree prominent among them—who shared those taints. That black people could and occasionally did hold slaves and servants and employ white people suggested that race—like lineage and religion—was just one of many markers in the social order.

If slavery meant abuse and degradation, the experience of Atlantic creeks provided strategies for limiting such maltreatment—contrary to notions that they were libidinous heathens without family, economy, or society—and even for winning to freedom. Freedom meant not only greater independence but also identification with the larger group. Although the routes to social betterment were many, they generally involved reattachment to a community through the agency of an influential patron or, better yet, an established institution that could broker a slave's incorporation into the larger society.[38] Along the coast of Africa, Atlantic Creoles often identified with the appendages of European or African power—be they international mercantile corporations or local chieftains—in hopes of relieving the stigma of otherness—be it enslavement, bastard birth, paganism, or race. They employed this strategy repeatedly in mainland North America, as they tried to hurdle the boundaries of social and cultural difference and establish a place for themselves. By linking themselves to the most important edifices of the nascent European-American societies, Atlantic creoles struggled to become part of a social order where exclusion or otherness—not subordination—posed the greatest dangers. To be inferior within the sharply stratified world of the seventeenth-century Atlantic was understandable by its very ubiquity; to be excluded posed unparalleled dangers.

The black men and women who entered New Netherland between 1626 and the English conquest in 1664 exemplified the ability of people of African descent to integrate themselves into mainland society during the first century of settlement, despite their status as slaves and the contempt of the colony's rulers. Far more than any other mainland colony during the first half of the seventeenth century, New Netherland rested on slave labor. The prosperity of the Dutch metropole and the opportunities presented to ambitious men and women in the far-flung Dutch empire denied New Netherland its share of free Dutch immigrants and limited its access to indentured servants. To populate the colony, the West India Company scoured the Atlantic basin for settlers, recruiting German Lutherans, French Huguenots, and Sephardic Jews. These newcomers did little to meet the colony's need for men and women to work the land, because, as a company officer reported, "agricultural laborers who are conveyed thither at great expense . . . sooner or later apply themselves to trade, and neglect agriculture altogether." Dutch officials concluded that slave labor was an absolute necessity for New Netherland. Although competition for slaves with Dutch outposts in Brazil (whose sugar economy was already drawing slaves from the African interior) placed New Netherland at a disadvantage, authorities in the North American colony imported all the slaves they could, so that in 1640 about too blacks lived in New Amsterdam, composing roughly 30 percent of the port's population and a larger portion of the labor force. Their proportion diminished over the course of the seventeenth century but remained substantial. At the time of the English conquest, some 300 slaves composed a fifth of the population of New Amsterdam, giving New Netherland the largest urban slave population on mainland North America.[39]

The diverse needs of the Dutch mercantile economy strengthened the hand of Atlantic creoles in New Netherland during the initial period of settlement. Caring only for short-term profits, the company, the largest slaveholder in the colony, allowed its slaves to live independently and work on their own in return for a stipulated amount of labor and an annual tribute. Company slaves thus enjoyed a large measure of independence, which they used to master the Dutch language, trade freely, accumulate property, identify with Dutch Reformed Christianity, and—most important—establish families. During the first generation, some twenty-five couples took their vows in the Dutch Reformed Church in New Amsterdam. When children arrived, their parents baptized them as well. Participation in the religious life of New Netherland provides but one indicator of how quickly Atlantic creates mastered the intricacies of life in mainland North America. In 1635, less than ten years after the arrival of the first black people, black New Netherlanders understood enough about the organization of the colony and the operation of the company to travel to the company's headquarters in Holland and petition for wages.[40]

Many slaves gained their freedom. This was not easy in New Netherland, although there was no legal proscription on manumission. Indeed, gaining freedom was nearly impossible for slaves owned privately and difficult even for those owned by the company. The company valued its slaves and was willing to liberate only the elderly, whom it viewed as a liability. Even when manumitting such slaves, the company exacted an annual tribute from adults and retained ownership of their children. The latter practice elicited protests from both blacks and whites in New Amsterdam. The enslavement of black children made "half-freedom," as New Netherland authorities denominated the West India Company's former slaves who were unable to pass their new status to their children, appear no freedom at all.[41]

Manumission in New Netherland was calculated to benefit slave owners, not slaves. Its purposes were to spur slaves to greater exertion and to relieve owners of the cost of supporting elderly slaves. Yet, however compromised the attainment of freedom, slaves did what was necessary to secure it. They accepted the company's terms and agreed to pay its corporate tribute. But they bridled at the fact that their children's status would not follow their own. Half-free blacks pressed the West India Company to make their status hereditary. Hearing rumors that baptism would assure freedom to their children, they pressed their claims to church membership. A Dutch prelate complained of the "worldly and perverse aims" of black people who "wanted nothing else than to deliver their children from bodily slavery, without striving for piety and Christian virtues."[42] Although conversion never guaranteed freedom in New Netherland, many half-free blacks secured their goal. By 1664, at the time of the English conquest, about one black person in five had achieved freedom in New Amsterdam, a proportion never equalled throughout the history of slavery in the American South.[43]

Some free people of African descent prospered. Building on small gifts of land that the West India Company provided as freedom dues, a few entered the landholding class in New Netherland. A small group of former slaves established a community on the outskirts of the Dutch settlement on Manhattan, farmed independently, and sold their produce in the public market. Others purchased farmsteads or were granted land as part of the Dutch effort to populate the city's hinterland. In 1659, the town of Southampton granted "Peeter the Neigro" three acres. Somewhat later John Neiger, who had "set himself up a house in the street" of Easthampton, was given "for his own use a little quantity of land above his house for him to make a yard or garden." On occasion, free blacks employed whites.[44]

By the middle of the seventeenth century, black people participated in almost every aspect of life in New Netherland. They sued and were sued in Dutch courts, married and baptized their children in the Dutch Reformed Church, and fought alongside Dutch militiamen against the colony's enemies. Black men and women— slave as well as free—traded on their own and accumulated property. Black people also began to develop a variety of institutions that reflected their unique experience and served their special needs. Black men and women stood as godparents to each other's children, suggesting close family ties, and rarely called on white people —owners or not—to serve in this capacity. At times, established black families legally adopted orphaned black children, further knitting the black community together in a web of fictive kinship.[45] The patterns of residence, marriage, church membership and godparentage speak not only to the material success of Atlantic creoles but also to their ability to create a community among themselves.

To be sure, the former slaves' prosperity was precarious at best. As the (Dutch transformed their settlement from a string of trading posts to a colony committed to agricultural production, the quality of freedpeople's freedom deteriorated. The Dutch began to import slaves directly from Africa (especially after the Portuguese retook Brazil), and the new arrivals—sold mostly to individual planters rather than to the company—had little chance of securing the advantages earlier enjoyed by the company's slaves.[46]

The freedpeople's social standing eroded more rapidly following the English conquest in 1664, demonstrating the fragility of their freedom in a social order undergirded by racial hostility. Nonetheless, black people continued to enjoy the benefits of the earlier age. They maintained a secure family life, acquired property, and participated as communicants in the Dutch Reformed Church, where they baptized their children in the presence of godparents of their own choosing. When threatened, they took their complaints to court, exhibiting a fine understanding of their legal rights and a steely determination to defend them. Although the proportion of the black population enjoying freedom shrank steadily under English rule, the small free black settlement held its own. Traveling through an area of modest farms on the outskirts of New York City in 1679, a Dutch visitor observed that "upon both sides of this way were many habitations of negroes, mulattoes and whites. These negroes were formerly the property of the (West India) company, but, in consequence of the frequent changes and conquests of the country, they have obtained their freedom and settled themselves down where they thought proper, and thus on this road, where they have ground enough to live on with their families."[47]

Dutch vessels were not the only ones to transport Atlantic creoles from Africa to North America. The French, who began trading on the Windward Coast of Africa soon after the arrival of the Portuguese, did much the same. Just as a creole population grew up around the Portuguese and later Dutch factories at Elmina, Luanda, and São Tomé, so one developed around the French posts on the Senegal River. The Compagnie du Sénégal, the Compagnie des Indes Occidentales, and their successor, the Compagnie des Indes—whose charter, like that of the Dutch West India Company, authorized it to trade in both Africa and the Americas—maintained headquarters at St. Louis with subsidiary outposts at Galam and Fort d'Arguin.[48]

As at Elmina and Luanda, shifting alliances between Africans and Europeans in St. Louis, Galam, and Fort d'Arguin also ensnared Atlantic creoles, who found themselves suddenly enslaved and thrust across the Atlantic. One such man was Samba, a Bambara,[49] who during the 1770s worked for the French as an interpreter —maître de langue—at Galam, up the Senegal River from St. Louis. "Samba Barbara" —as he appears in the records—traveled freely along the river between St. Louis, Galam, and Fort d'Arguin. By 1722, he received permission from the Compagnie des Indes for his family to reside in St. Louis. When his wife dishonored him, Samba Bambara called on his corporate employer to exile her from St. Louis and thereby bring order to his domestic life. But despite his reliance on the company, Samba Bambara allegedly joined with African captives in a revolt at Fort d'Arguin, and, when the revolt was quelled, he was enslaved and deported. Significantly, he was not sold to the emerging plantation colony of Saint Domingue, where the sugar revolution stoked a nearly insatiable appetite for slaves. Instead, French officials at St. Louis exiled Samba Bambara to Louisiana, a marginal military outpost far outside the major transatlantic sea lanes and with no staple agricultural economy.[50]

New Orleans on the Mississippi River shared much with St. Louis on the Senegal in the 1720s. As the headquarters of the Compagnie des Indes in main land North America, the town housed the familiar collection of corporate functionaries, traders, and craftsmen, along with growing numbers of French engagés and African slaves. New Orleans was frequented by Indians, whose canoes supplied it much as African canoemen supplied St. Louis. Its taverns and back alley retreats were meeting places for sailors of various nationalities, Canadian *coureurs de bois*, and soldiers—the latter no more pleased to be stationed on the North American frontier than their counterparts welcomed assignment to an African factory.[51] Indeed, soldiers' status in this rough frontier community differed little from that on the coast of Africa.

In 1720, a French soldier stationed in New Orleans was convicted of theft and sentenced to the lash. A black man wielded the whip. His work was apparently satisfactory, because five years later, Louis Congo, a recently arrived slave then in the service of the Compagnie des Indes, was offered the job. A powerful man, Congo bargained hard before accepting such grisly employment; he demanded freedom for himself and his wife, regular rations, and a plot of land he could cultivate independently. Louisiana's Superior Council balked at these terms, but the colony's attorney general urged acceptance, having seen Congo's *"chef d'oeuvre."* Louis Congo gained his freedom and was allowed to live with his wife (although she was not free) on land of his own choosing. His life as Louisiana's executioner was not easy. He was assaulted several times, and he complained that assassins lurked everywhere. But he enjoyed a modest prosperity, and he learned to write, an accomplishment that distinguished him from most inhabitants of eighteenth-century Louisiana.[52]

Suggesting something of the symmetry of the Atlantic world, New Orleans, save for the flora and fauna, was no alien terrain to Samba Bambara or Louis Congo. Despite the long transatlantic journey, once in the New World, they recovered much of what they had lost in the Old, although Samba Bambara never escaped slavery. Like the Atlantic creoles who alighted in New Netherland, Samba Bambara employed on the coast of North America skills he had learned on the coast of Africa; Louis Congo's previous occupation is unknown. Utilizing his knowledge of French, various African languages, and the ubiquitous creole tongue, the rebel regained his position with his old patron, the Compagnie des Indes, this time as air interpreter swearing on the Christian Bible to translate faithfully before Louisiana's Superior Council. Later, he became an overseer on the largest "concession" in the colony, the company's massive plantation across the river from New Orleans.[53] Like his counterparts in New Amsterdam, Samba Bambara succeeded in a rugged frontier slave society by following the familiar lines of patronage to the doorstep of his corporate employer. Although the constraints of slavery eventually turned him against the company on the Mississippi, just as lie had turned against it on the Senegal River, his ability to transfer his knowledge and skills from the Old World to the New, despite the weight of enslavement, suggests that the history of Atlantic creoles in New Amsterdam—their ability to escape slavery, form families, secure property, and claim a degree of independence—was no anomaly.

Atlantic creoles such as Paulo d'Angola in New Netherland and Samba Bambara in New Orleans were not the only products of the meeting of Africans and Europeans on the coast of Africa. By the time Europeans began to colonize mainland North America, communities of creoles of African descent similar to those found on the West African *feitorias* had established themselves all along the rim of the Atlantic. In Europe—particularly Portugal and Spain—the number of Atlantic creoles swelled, as trade with Africa increased. By the mid-sixteenth century, some 10,000 black people lived in Lisbon, where they composed about 10 percent of the population. Seville had a slave population of 6,000 (including a minority of Moors and Moriscos).[54] As the centers of the Iberian slave trade, these cities distributed African slaves throughout Europe.[55]

With the settlement of the New World, Atlantic creoles sprouted in such places as Cap Françis, Cartagena, Havana, Mexico City, and San Salvador. Intimate with the culture of the Atlantic, they could be found speaking pidgin and creole and engaging in a familiar sort of cultural brokerage. Men drawn from these creole communities accompanied Columbus to the New World; others marched with Balboa, Cortés, De Soto, and Pizarro.[56] Some Atlantic creoles crisscrossed the ocean several times, as had Jerónimo, a Wolof slave, who was sold from Lisbon to Cartagena and from Cartagena to Murica, where he was purchased by a churchman who sent him to Valencia. A "*mulâtress*" wife and her three slaves followed her French husband, a gunsmith in the employ of the Compagnie des Indes, from Gorée to Louisiana, when he was deported for criminal activities.[57] Other Atlantic creoles traveled on their own, as sailors and interpreters in both the transatlantic and African trades. Some gained their freedom and mixed with Europeans and Native Americans. Wherever they went, Atlantic creoles extended the use of the distinctive language of the Atlantic, planted the special institutions of the creole community, and propagated their unique outlook. Within the Portuguese and Spanish empires, Atlantic creoles created an intercontinental web of *cofradias* (*confradias* to the Spanish), so that, by the seventeenth century, the network of black religious brotherhoods stretched from Lisbon to São Tomé, Angola, and Brazil.[58] Although no comparable institutional linkages existed in the Anglo- and Franco-American worlds, there were numerous informal connections between black people in New England and Virginia, Louisiana and Saint Domingue. Like their African counterparts, Atlantic creoles of European, South American, and Caribbean origins also found their way to mainland North America, where they became part of black America's charter generations.

The Dutch were the main conduit for carrying such men and women to the North American mainland in the seventeenth century. Juan (Jan, in some accounts) Rodrigues, a sailor of mixed racial ancestry who had shipped from Hispaniola in 1612 on the *Jonge Tobias*, offers another case in point. The ship, one of the several Dutch merchant vessels vying for the North American fur trade before the founding of the Dutch West India Company, anchored in the Hudson River sometime in 1612 and left Rodrigues either as an independent trader or, more likely, as ship's agent. When a rival Dutch ship arrived the following year, Rodrigues promptly shifted his allegiance, informing its captain that, despite his color, "he was a free man." He served his new employer as translator and agent collecting furs from the native population. When the captain of the *Jonge Tobias* returned to the Hudson River, Rodrigues changed his allegiance yet again, only to be denounced as a turncoat and "that black rascal." Barely escaping with his life, he took up residence with some friendly Indians.[59]

Atlantic creoles were among the first black people to enter the Chesapeake region in the early years of the seventeenth century, and they numbered large among the "twenty Negars" the Dutch sold to the English at Jamestown in 1619 as well as those who followed during the next half century.[60] Anthony Johnson, who was probably among the prizes captured by a Dutch ship in the Caribbean, appears to have landed in Jamestown as "Antonio a Negro" soon after the initial purchase. During the next thirty years, Antonio exited servitude, anglicized his name, married, began to farm on his own, and in 1651 received a 250-acre headright. When his Eastern Shore plantation burned to the ground two years later, he petitioned the county court for relief and was granted a substantial reduction of his taxes. His son John did even better than his father, receiving a patent for 550 acres, and another son, Richard, owned a 100-acre estate. Like other men of substance, the Johnsons farmed independently, held slaves, and left their heirs sizable estates. As established members of their communities, they enjoyed rights in common with other free men and frequently employed the law to protect themselves and advance their interests. When a black man claiming his freedom fled Anthony Johnson's plantation and found refuge with a nearby white planter, Johnson took his neighbor to court and won the return of his slave along with damages from the white man.[61]

Landed independence not only afforded free people of African descent legal near-equality in Virginia but also allowed them a wide range of expressions that others termed "arrogance"—the traditional charge against Atlantic creoles. Anthony Johnson exhibited an exalted sense of self when a local notable challenged his industry. Johnson countered with a ringing defense of his independence: "I know myne owne ground and I will worke when I please and play when I please." Johnson also understood that he and other free black men and women were different, and he and his kin openly celebrated those differences. Whereas Antonio a Negro had anglicized the family name, John Johnson—his grandson and a third-generation Virginian—called his own estate "Angola."[62]

The Johnsons were not unique in Virginia. A small community of free people of African descent developed on the Eastern Shore. Their names, like Antonio a Negro's, suggest creole descent: John Francisco, Bashaw Ferdinando (or Farnando), Emanuel Driggus (sometimes Drighouse; probably Rodriggus), Anthony Longo (perhaps Loango), and "Francisco a Negroe" (soon to become Francis, then Frank, Payne and finally Paine).[63] They, like Antonio, were drawn from the Atlantic littoral and may have spent time in England or New England before reaching the Chesapeake. At least one, "John Phillip, A negro Christened in *England* 12 yeeres since," was a sailor on an English ship that brought a captured Spanish vessel into Jamestown; another, Sebastian Cain or Cane, gained his freedom in Boston, where he had served the merchant Robert Keayne (hence probably his name). Cain also took to the sea as a sailor, but, unlike Phillip, lie settled in Virginia as a neighbor, friend, and sometimes kinsman of the Johnsons, Drigguses, and Paynes.[64]

In Virginia, Atlantic creoles ascended the social order and exhibited a sure-handed understanding of Chesapeake social hierarchy and the complex dynamics of patron–client relations. Although still in bondage, they began to acquire the property, skills, and social connections that became their mark throughout the Atlantic world. They worked provision grounds, kept livestock, and traded independently. More important, they found advocates among the propertied classes—often their owners—and identified themselves with the colony's most important institutions, registering their marriages, baptisms, and children's godparents in the Anglican church and their property in the county courthouse. They sued and were sued in local courts and petitioned the colonial legislature and governor. While relations to their well-placed patrons—former masters and mistresses, landlords, and employers—

among the colony's elite were important, as in Louisiana, the creoles also established ties among themselves, weaving together a community from among the interconnections of marriage, trade, and friendship. Free blacks testified on each other's behalf, stood as godparents for each other's children, loaned each other small sums, and joined together for after-hours conviviality, creating a community that often expanded to the larger web of interactions among all poor people, regardless of color. According to one historian of black life in seventeenth-century Virginia, "cooperative projects . . . were more likely in relations between colored freedmen and poor whites than were the debtor–creditor, tenant–landlord, or employee–employer relations that linked individuals of both races to members of the planter class."[65] The horizontal ties of class developed alongside the vertical ones of patronage.

Maintaining their standing as property-holding free persons was difficult, and some Atlantic creoles in the Chesapeake, like those in New Netherland, slipped down the social ladder, trapped by legal snares—apprenticeships, tax forfeitures, and bastardy laws—as planters turned from a labor system based on indentured Europeans and Atlantic creoles to raw Africans condemned to perpetual slavery. Anthony Johnson, harassed by white planters, fled his plantation in Virginia to establish the more modest "Tonies Vineyard" in Maryland. But even as they were pushed out, many of the Chesapeake's charter generations continued to elude slavery. Some did well, lubricating the lifts to economic success with their own hard work, their skills in a society that had "an unrelenting demand for artisanal labor," and the assistance of powerful patrons. A few of the landholding free black families on Virginia's Eastern Shore maintained their propertied standing well into the eighteenth century. In 1738, the estate of Emanuel Driggus's grandson—including its slaves—was worth more than those of two-thirds of his white neighbors.[66]

Atlantic creoles also entered the lowcountry of South Carolina and Florida, carried there by the English and Spanish, respectively. Like the great West Indian planters who settled in that "colony of a colony," Atlantic creoles were drawn from Barbados and other Caribbean islands, where a full generation of European and African cohabitation had allowed them to gain a knowledge of European ways. Prior to the sugar revolution, they worked alongside white indentured servants in a variety of enterprises, none of which required the discipline of plantation labor. Like white servants, some exited slavery, as the line between slavery and freedom was open. An Anglican minister who toured the English islands during the 1670s noted that black people spoke English "no worse than the natural born subjects of that Kingdom."[67] Although Atlantic creole culture took a different shape in the Antilles than it did on the periphery of Africa or Europe, it also displayed many of the same characteristics.

On the southern mainland, creoles used their knowledge of the New World and their ability to negotiate between the various Native American nations and South Carolina's European polyglot—English, French Huguenots, Sephardic Jews —to become invaluable as messengers, trappers, and cattle minders. The striking image of slave and master working on opposite sides of a sawbuck suggests the place of blacks during the early years of South Carolina's settlement.[68]

Knowledge of their English captors also provided knowledge of their captors' enemy, some two hundred miles to the south. At every opportunity, Carolina slaves fled to Spanish Florida, where they requested Catholic baptism. Officials at

St. Augustine—whose black population was drawn from Spain, Cuba, Hispaniola, and New Spain—celebrated the fugitives' choice of religion and offered sanctuary. They also valued the creoles' knowledge of the countryside, their ability to converse with English, Spanish, and Indians, and their willingness to strike back at their enslavers. Under the Spanish flag, former Carolina slaves raided English settlements at Port Royal and Edisto and liberated even more of their number. As part of the black militia, they, along with other fugitives from Carolina, fought against the English in the Tuscarora and Yamasee wars.[69]

Florida's small black population mushroomed in the late seventeenth and early eighteenth centuries, as the small but steady stream of fugitives grew with the expansion of lowcountry slavery. Slaves from central Africa—generally deemed "Angolans"—numbered large among the new arrivals, as the transatlantic trade carried thousands of Africans directly to the lowlands. Although many were drawn from deep in the interior of Africa, others were Atlantic creoles with experience in the coastal towns of Cabinda, Loango, and Mpinda. Some spoke Portuguese, which, as one Carolinian noted, was "as near Spanish as Scotch is to English," and subscribed to an African Catholicism with roots in the fifteenth-century conversion of Kongo's royal house. They knew their catechism, celebrated feasts of Easter and All Saint's Day or Hallowe'en, and recognized Christian saints.

These men and women were particularly attracted to the possibilities of freedom in the Spanish settlements around St. Augustine. They fled from South Carolina in increasing numbers during the 1720s and 1730s, and, in 1739, a group of African slaves—some doubtless drawn from the newcomers—initiated a mass flight. Pursued by South Carolina militiamen, they confronted their owners' soldiers in several pitched battles that became known as the Stono Rebellion.[70] Although most of the Stono rebels were killed or captured, some escaped to Florida, from where it became difficult to retrieve them by formal negotiation or by force. The newcomers were quickly integrated into black life in St. Augustine, since they had already been baptized, although they prayed—as one Miguel Domingo informed a Spanish priest—in Kikongo.[71]

Much to the delight of St. Augustine's Spanish rulers, the former Carolina slaves did more than pray. They fought alongside the Spanish against incursions by English raiders. An edict of the Spanish crown promising "Liberty and Protection" to all slaves who reached St. Augustine boosted the number of fugitives—most from Carolina—especially after reports circulated that the Spanish received runaways "with great Honors" and gave their leaders military commissions and "A Coat Faced with Velvet." In time, Spanish authorities granted freedom to some, but not all, of the black soldiers and their families.[72]

Among the unrewarded was Francisco Menéndez, a veteran of the Yamasee War and leader of the black militia. Frustrated by the ingratitude of his immediate superiors, Menéndez petitioned the governor of Florida and the bishop of Cuba for his liberty, which he eventually received. In 1738, when a new governor established Gracia Real de Santa Teresa de Mose, a fortified settlement north of St. Augustine, to protect the Spanish capital from the English incursions, he placed Menéndez in charge. Under Captain Menéndez, Mose became the center of black life in colonial Florida and a base from which former slaves—sometimes joined by Indians—raided South Carolina. The success of the black militia in repelling an English attack on Mose in 1740 won Menéndez a special commendation from the governor, who declared that the black captain had "distinguished himself in the establishment, and cultivation of Mose." Not one to lose an opportunity, the newly literate Menéndez promptly requested that the king remunerate him for the "loyalty, zeal and love I have always demonstrated in the royal service" and petitioned for a stipend worthy of a militia captain.[73]

To secure his reward, Menéndez took a commission as a privateer, with hopes of eventually reaching Spain and collecting his royal reward. Instead, a British ship captured the famous "Signior Capitano Francisco." Although stretched out on a cannon and threatened with emasculation for alleged atrocities during the siege of Mose, Menéndez had become too valuable to mutilate. His captors gave him 200 lashes, soaked his wounds in brine, and commended him to a doctor "to take Care of his Sore A-se." Menéndez was then carried before a British admiralty court on New Providence Island, where "this Francisco that Cursed Seed of Cain" was ordered sold into slavery. Even this misadventure hardly slowed the irrepressible Menéndez. By 1752, perhaps ransomed out of bondage, he was back in his old position in Mose.[74]

Meanwhile, members of the fugitive community around St. Augustine entered more fully into the life of the colony as artisans and tradesmen as well as laborers and domestics. They married among themselves, into the Native American population, and with slaves as well, joining as husband and wife before their God and community in the Catholic church. They baptized their children in the same church, choosing godparents from among both the white and black congregants. Like the Atlantic creoles in New Amsterdam about a century earlier, they became skilled in identifying the lever of patronage, in this case royal authority. Declaring themselves "vassals of the king and deserving of royal protection," they continually placed themselves in the forefront of service to the crown with the expectations that their king would protect, if not reward, them. For the most part, they were not disappointed. When Spain turned East Florida over to the British in 1763, black colonists retreated to Cuba with His Majesty's other subjects, where the crown granted them land, tools, a small subsidy, and a slave for each of their leaders.[75]

In the long history of North American slavery, no other cohort of black people survived as well and rose as fast and as high in mainland society as the Atlantic creoles. The experience of the charter generations contrasts markedly with what followed: when the trauma of enslavement, the violence of captivity, the harsh conditions of plantation life left black people unable to reproduce themselves; when the strange language of their enslavers muted the tongues of newly arrived Africans; and when the slaves' skills and knowledge were submerged in the stupefying labor of plantation production. Rather than having to face the likes of Robert Carter and the imposition of planter domination, Paulo d'Angola, Samba Bambara, Juan Rodrigues, Antonio a Negro, and Francisco Menéndez entered a society not markedly different from those they had left.[76] There, in New Netherland, the Chesapeake, Louisiana, and Florida, they made a place for themselves, demonstrating confidence in their abilities to master a world they knew well. Many secured freedom and a modest prosperity, despite the presumption of racial slavery and the contempt of their captors.

The charter generations' experience derived not only from who they were but also from the special circumstances of their arrival. By their very primacy, as members of the first generation of settlers, their experience was unique. While they came as foreigners, they were no more strange to the new land than were those who enslaved them. Indeed, the near simultaneous arrival of migrants from Europe and Africa gave them a shared perspective on the New World. At first, all saw themselves as outsiders. That would change, as European settlers gained dominance, ousted native peoples, and created societies they claimed as their own. As Europeans became European-Americans and then simply Americans, their identification with—and sense of ownership over—mainland society distinguished them from the forced migrants from Africa who continued to arrive as strangers and were defined as permanent outsiders.

The charter generations owed their unique history to more than just the timing of their arrival. Before their historic confrontation with their new owner, the men and women Robert Carter purchased may have spent weeks, even months, packed between the stinking planks of slave ships. Atlantic Creoles experienced few of the horrors of the Middle Passage. Rather than arriving in shiploads totaling into the hundreds, Atlantic creoles trickled into the mainland singly, in twos and threes, or by the score. Most were sent in small consignments or were the booty of privateers and pirates. Some found employment as interpreters, sailors, and grumeter on the very ships that transported them to the New World.[77] Although transatlantic travel in the seventeenth and eighteenth centuries could be a harrowing experience under the best of circumstances, the profound disruption that left the men and women Carter purchased physically spent and psychologically traumatized was rarely part of the experience of Atlantic creoles.

Most important, Atlantic Creoles entered societies-with-slaves, not, as mainland North America would become, slave societies—that is, societies in which the order of the plantation shaped every relationship.[78] In North America—as in Africa—Atlantic creoles were still but one subordinate group in societies in which subordination was the rule. Few who arrived before the plantation system faced the dehumanizing and brutalizing effects of gang labor in societies where slaves had become commodities and nothing more. Indeed, Atlantic creoles often worked alongside their owners, supped at their tables, wore their hand-me-down clothes, and lived in the back rooms and lofts of their houses. Many resided in towns, as did Paulo d'Angola, Samba Bambara, and Francisco Menéndez. The proportion of the mainland's black population living in places such as New Amsterdam, Philadelphia, Charleston, St. Augustine, and New Orleans was probably higher during the first generations of settlement than it would ever be again. Urban slaves, for better or worse, lived and worked in close proximity to their owners. The regimen imposed the heavy burdens of continual surveillance, but the same constant contact prevented vented their owners from imagining people of African descent to be a special species of beings, an idea that only emerged with the radical separation of master and slave and the creation of the worlds of the Big House and the Quarters. Until then, the open interaction of slave and slaveowner encouraged Atlantic creoles, and others as well, to judge their enslavement by its older meaning, not by its emerging new one.

The possibility of freedom had much the same effect. So long as some black people, no matter how closely identified with slavery, could still wriggle free of bondage and gain an independent place, slavery may have carried the connotation of otherness, debasement, perhaps even transgression, iniquity, and vice, but it was not social death. The success of Atlantic creoles in rising from the bottom of main-land society contradicted the logic of hereditary bondage and suggested that what had been done might be undone.

The rise of plantation slavery left little room for the men and women of the charter generations. Their efforts to secure a place in society were put at risk by the new order, for the triumph of the plantation régime threatened not inequality—which had always been assumed, at least by European—but debasement and permanent ostracism of the sort Robert "King" Carter delivered on that Virginia wharf. With the creation of a world in which peoples of African descent were presumed slaves and those of European descent free, people of color no longer had a place. It became easy to depict black men and women as uncivilized heathens outside the bounds of society or even humanity.[79]

Few Atlantic creoles entered the mainland after the tobacco revolution in the Chesapeake, the rice revolution in lowcountry Carolina, and the sugar revolution in Louisiana. Rather than being drawn from the African littoral, slaves increasingly derived from the African interior. Such men and women possessed little under-standing of the larger Atlantic world: no apprenticeship in negotiating with Europeans, no knowledge of Christianity or other touchstone of European culture, no acquaintance with western law, and no open fraternization with sailors and merchants in the Atlantic trade—indeed, no experience with the diseases of the Atlantic to provide a measure of immunity to the deadly microbes that lurked everywhere in the New World. Instead of speaking a pidgin or creole that gave them access to the Atlantic, the later arrivals were separated from their enslavers and often from each other by a dense wall of language. Rather than see their skills and knowledge appreciate in value, they generally discovered that previous experi-ence counted for little on the plantations of the New World. Indeed, the remnants of their African past were immediately expropriated by their new masters.

In the stereotypes that demeaned slaves, European and European-American slaveholders inadvertently recognized the difference between the Atlantic creoles and the men and women who followed them into bondage, revealing how the meaning of race was being transformed with the advent of the plantation. Slaveholders condemned creoles as roguish in the manner of Juan Rodrigues the "black rascal," or arrogant in the manner of Antonio a Negro, who knew his "owne ground," or swaggering in the manner of "Signior Capitano Francisco," who stood his ground against those who threatened his manhood. They rarely used such epithets against the postcreole generations that labored on the great plantations. Instead, slaveholders and their apologists scorned such slaves as crude primitives, devoid of the simple amenities of refined society. The failings of plantation slaves were not those of calculation or arrogance, but of stark ignorance and dense stupidity. Plantation slaves were denounced, not for a desire to convert to Christianity for "worldly and perverse aims" as were the half-free blacks in New Netherland or because they claimed the "True Faith" as did the Carolinians who fled to St. Augustine, but because they knew nothing of the religion, language, law, and social etiquette that Europeans equated with civilization. The unfamiliarity of the post-Atlantic creole cohort with the dynamics of Atlantic life made them easy targets for the slaveholders' ridicule. Like the Virginia planters who slammed Africans for the "gross bestiality and rudeness of their manners," an eighteenth-century chronicler of South Carolina's history declared lowcountry slaves to be "as great strangers to Christianity, and as much under the influence of Pagan darkness, idolatry and superstition, as they were at their first arrival from Africa." Such a charge, whatever its meaning on the great lowcountry rice plantations, could have no relevance to the runaways who sought the True Faith in St. Augustine.[80]

In time, stereotypes made were again remade. During the late eighteenth century, planters and their apologists rethought the meaning of race as more than a century and a half of captivity remolded people of African descent. As a new generation of black people emerged—familiar with the American countryside, fluent in its languages, and conversant in its religions—the stereotype of the artful, smooth-talking slave also appeared. Manipulative to the point of insolence, this new generation of African-Americans peopled the slave quarter, confronted the master on their own terms, and, in the midst of the Revolution, secured freedom. African-Americans reversed the process of enslavement—among other things, taking back the naming process (although not the names) that "King" Carter had usurped.[81]

Their story—whereby Africans became creoles—was a great one and one that Americans would repeat many times in the personages of men as different as David Levinsky, the Godfather, or Kunta Kinte—as greenhorns became natives. Historians, like novelists and film makers, have enjoyed retelling the tale, but in so doing, they lost the story of another founding generation and its transit from immigrant to native. While the fathers (and sometimes the mothers) of European America, whether Puritan divines or Chesapeake adventurers, would be celebrated by their posterity, members of black America's charter generations disappeared into the footnotes of American history. Generations of Americans lived in the shadow of John Winthrop and William Byrd, even Peter Stuyvesant and Jean Baptiste Bienville, but few learned of Paulo d'Angola, Samba Bambara, Juan Rodrigues, Antonio a Negro, and Francisco Menéndez. If Atlantic creoles made any appearance in the textbook histories, it would be as curiosities and exceptions to the normal pattern of American race relations, examples of false starts, mere tokens.

The story of how creoles became Africans was lost in a chronicle that presumed American history always moved in a single direction. The assimiliationist ideal could not imagine how the diverse people of the Atlantic could become the sons and daughters of Africa. The possibility that a society-with-slaves was a separate and distinct social formation, not a stage in the development of slave society, was similarly inconceivable in a nation in which wealth and power rested upon plantation slavery.

The causes of creole anonymity ran deep. While Carter initiated newly arrived Africans to the world of the plantation, the descendants of the charter generations struggled to maintain the status they had earlier achieved. To that end, many separated themselves from the mass of Africans on whom the heavy weight of plantation bondage fell. Some fled as a group, as did the creole community in St. Augustine that retreated with the Spanish from Florida to Cuba following the British takeover in 1764.[82]

Others merged with Native American tribes and European-American settlers to create unique biracial and triracial combinations and established separate identities. In the 1660s, the Johnson clan fled Virginia for Maryland, Delaware, and New Jersey. John Johnson and John Johnson, Jr., the son and grandson of Anthony Johnson, took refuge among the Nanticoke Indians and so-called Moors, among whom the Johnson name has loomed large into the twentieth century. Near one

Nanticoke settlement in Delaware stands the small village of "Angola," the name of John Johnson's Virginia plantation and perhaps Anthony Johnson's ancestral home. Similar "Indian" tribes could be found scattered throughout the eastern half of the United States, categorized by twentieth-century ethnographers as "tri-racial isolates."[83]

Others moved west to a different kind of autonomy. Scattered throughout the frontier areas of the eighteenth century were handfuls of black people eager to escape the racially divided society of plantation America. White frontiersmen, with little sympathy for the nabobs of the tidewater, sometimes sheltered such black men and women, employing them with no questions asked. People of African descent also found refuge among the frontier banditti, whose interracial character —a "numerous Collection of outcast Mulattoes, Mustees, free Negroes, all Horse-Thieves," by one account—was the subject of constant denunciation by the frontier's aspiring planters.[84]

While some members of the charter generations retreated before the expanding planter class, a few moved toward it. At least one male member of every prominent seventeenth-century free black family on the Eastern Shore of Virginia married a white woman, so the Atlantic creoles' descendants would, perforce, be lighter in color. Whether or not this was a conscious strategy, there remains considerable, if necessarily incomplete, evidence that these light-skinned people employed a portion of their European inheritance—a pale complexion—to pass into white society.[85]

Retreat—geographic, social, and physical—was not the only strategy members of the charter generations adopted in the face of the emergent plantation régime. Some stood their ground, confronting white authorities and perhaps setting an example for those less fortunate than themselves. In 1667, claiming "hee was a Christian and had been severall years in England," a black man named Fernando sued for his freedom in a Virginia court. The case, initiated just as tidewater planters were consolidating their place atop Virginia society, sent Virginia lawmakers into a paroxysm that culminated in the passage of a new law clarifying the status of black people: they would be slaves for life and their status would be hereditary. In succeeding years, such Atlantic creoles—men and women of African descent with long experience in the larger Atlantic world—would continue as Fernando continued to bedevil planters and other white Americans in and out of the court room, harboring runaway slaves, providing them with free papers, and joining together matters slaveholders viewed as subversive. In 1671, New York authorities singled out Domingo and Manuel Angola, warning the public "that the free negroes were from time to time entertaining sundry of the servants and negroes belonging to the Burghers . . . to the great damage of their owners." It appears that the warning did little to limit black people from meeting, for several years later New York's Common Council again complained about "the frequent randivozing of Negro Slaves att the houses of free negroes without the gates hath bin occasion of great disorder." As slaveholders feared, the line between annoyance and subversion was a thin one. Atlantic creoles were among the black servants and slaves who stood with Nathaniel Bacon against royal authority in 1676.[86]

The relentless engine of plantation agriculture and the transformation of the mainland colonies from societies-with-slaves to slave societies submerged the charter generations in a régime in which African descent was equated with Slavery.

For the most part, the descendants of African creoles took their place as slaves alongside newly arrived Africans. Those who maintained their freedom became part of an impoverished free black minority, and those who lost their liberty were swallowed up in an oppressed slave majority.[87] In one way or another, Atlantic creoles were overwhelmed by the power of the plantation order.

Even so, the charter generations' presence was not without substance. During the American Revolution, when divisions within the planter class gave black people fresh opportunities to strike for liberty and equality, long-suppressed memories of the origins of African life on the mainland bubbled to the surface, often in lawsuits in which slaves claimed freedom as a result of descent from a free ancestor, sometimes white, sometimes Indian, sometimes free black, more commonly from some mixture of these elements.[88] The testimony summoned by such legal contests reveals how the hidden history of the charter generations survived the plantation revolution and suggests the mechanisms by which it would be maintained in the centuries that followed. It also reveals how race had been constructed and reconstructed in mainland North America over the course of two centuries of African and European settlement and how it would be remade.

Notes

1   Carter to Robert Jones, Oct. 10, 1727 [misdated 1717], Oct. 24, 1729, quoted in Lorena S. Walsh, "A 'Place in Time' Regained: A Fuller History of Colonial Chesapeake Slavery through Group Biography," in Larry E. Hudson, Jr., ed., *Working toward Freedom: Slave Society and the Domestic Economy in the American South* (Rochester, N. Y., 1994), 14.

2   For the names of Carter's slaves see the Carter Papers, Alderman Library, University of Virginia, Charlottesville. The naming of Chesapeake slaves is discussed in Allan Kulikoff, *Tobacco and Slaves: The Development of Southern Cultures in the Chesapeake, 1680–1800* (Chapel Hill, 1986), 325–26, and John Thornton, "Central African Names and African-American Naming Patterns," *William and Mary Quarterly*, 3d Ser., 50 (1993), 727–42. For surnames see Walsh, "A 'Place in Time' Regained," 26–27 n. 18. The pioneering work on this subject is Peter H. Wood, *Black Majority: Negroes in Colonial South Carolina from 1670 through the, Stono Rebellion* (New York, 1974), 181–86. Henry Laurens, the great South Carolina slave trader and planter, followed a similar routine in, naming his slaves; Philip Morgan, "Three Planters and Their Slaves: Perspective on Slavery in Virginia, South Carolina, and Jamaica, 1750–1790," in Winthrop D. Jordan and Sheila L. Skemp, eds., *Race and Family in the Colonial South* (Jackson, Miss., 1987), 65.

3   Gerald W. Mullin, *Flight and Rebellion: Slave Resistance in Eighteenth-Century Virginia* (New York, 1972), chaps. 1–3; Kulikoff, *Tobacco and Slaves*, esp. 319–34; Russell R. Menard, "The Maryland Slave Population, 1658 to 1730: A Demographic Profile of Blacks in Four Counties," *WMQ*, 3d Ser., 32 (1975), 29–54; Lois Green Carr and Walsh, "Economic Diversification and Labor Organization in the Chesapeake, 1650–1820," in Stephen Innes, ed., *Work and Labor in Early America* (Chapel Hill, 1988), 144–88. Quotation in Hugh Jones, *The Present State of Virginia, from Whence Is Inferred a Short View of Maryland and North Carolina*, ed. Richard L. Morton (Chapel Hill, 1956), 36–38, and Philip Alexander Bruce, *Institutional History of Virginia in the Seventeenth Century* . . . 2 vols. (New York, 1910), 1:9. See a slightly different version in "The Journal of the General Assembly of Virginia," June 2, 1699, in W. N. Sainsbury et al., eds., *Calendar of State Papers, Colonial Series, America and West Indies*, 40 vols. (London, 1860–1969), 17:261.

4   In the summer of 1767, when two slaves escaped from a Georgia plantation, their owner noted that one "calls himself GOLAGA," although "the name given him [was] ABEL," and the other "calls himself ABBROM, the name given him here BENNET." For evidence that the practice had not ended by 1774 see Lathan A. Windley, comp., *Runaway Slave*

Advertisements: A Documentary History from the 1730s to 1790, 4 vols. (Westport, Conn., 1983), 4:22 ([*Savannah*] *Georgia Gazette*, June 3, 1767). 62 (ibid., Apr. 19, 1775).

5   "Creole" derives from the Portuguese *crioulo*, meaning a person of African descent born in the New World. It has been extended to native-born free people of many national origins, including both Europeans and Africans, and of diverse social standing. It has also been applied to people of partly European but mixed racial and national origins in various European colonies and to Africans who entered Europe. In the United States, creole has also been specifically applied to people of mixed but usually non-African origins in Louisiana. Staying within the bounds of the broadest definition of creole and the literal definition of African American, I use both terms to refer to black people of native American birth: John A. Holes, *Pidgins and Creoles: Theory and Structure*, 2 vols. (Cambridge, 1988–1989), 1:9. On the complex and often contradictory usage in a single place see Gwendolyn Midlo Hall, *Africans in Colonial Louisiana: The Development of Afro-Creole Culture in the Eighteenth Century* (Baton Rouge, 1992), 157–59, and Joseph G. Tregle, Jr., "On that Word 'Creole' Again: A Note," *Louisiana History*, 23 (1982), 193–98.

6   See, for example, Mullin, *Flight and Rebellion*, and Mullin, *Africa in America: Slave Acculturation and Resistance in the American South and the British Caribbean, 1736–1831* (Urbana, Ill., 1992), 208, which examines the typology of "African" and "creole" from the perspective of resistance. See also the 3 stages of black community development proposed by Kulikoff, "The Origins of Afro-American Society in Tidewater Maryland and Virginia, 1700–1790," *WMQ*, 3d Ser., 35 (1978), 226–59, esp. 229, and expanded in his *Tobacco and Slaves*, chaps. 8–10. Although the work of Sidney Mintz and Richard Price, which has provided the theoretical backbone for the study of African acculturation in the New World, begins by breaking with models of cultural change associated with "assimilation" and, indeed, all notions of social and cultural change that have a specific end point, it too frames the process as a progression from African to creole; *Anthropological Approach to the Afro-American Past: A Caribbean Perspective*, Institute for the Study of Human Issues Occasional Papers in Social Change (Philadelphia, 1976). Others have followed, including those sensitive to the process of re-Africanization. See, for example, Wood, *Black Majority*; Kulikoff, *Tobacco and Slaves*; Ira Berlin and Ronald Hoffman, eds., *Slavery and Freedom in the Age of Revolution* (Charlottesville, 1983); and Berlin, "Time, Space, and the Evolution of Afro-American Society on British Mainland North America," *American Historical Review*, 85 (1980), 44–78. Thornton's work represents an important theoretical departure. He distinguishes between the African and the Atlantic experiences, maintaining the "Atlantic environment was . . . different from the African one." He extends the Atlantic environment to the African littoral as well as the Americas, in *Africa and Africans in the Making of the Atlantic World, 1440–1680* (Cambridge, 1992), quotation on 211.

7   The use of charter groups draws on T. H. Breen, "Creative Adoptions: Peoples and Cultures," in Jack P. Greene and J. R. Pole, eds., *Colonial British America: Essays in the New History of the Early Modern Era* (Baltimore, 1984), 203–08. Breen, in turn, borrowed the idea from anthropologist John Porter.

8   "Atlantic creole," employed herein, designates those who by experience or choice, as well as by birth, became part of a new culture that emerged along the Atlantic littoral—in Africa, Europe, or the Americas—beginning in the 16th century. It departs from the notion of "creole" that makes birth definitive (see n. 5 above). Circumstances and volition blurred differences between "African" and "creole" as defined only by nativity, if only because Africans and creoles were connected by ties of kinship and friendship. They worked together, played together, inter-married, and on occasion stood together against assaults on their freedom. Even more important, men and women could define themselves in ways that transcended nativity. "African" and "creole" were as much a matter of choice as of birth. The term "Atlantic creole" is designed to capture the cultural transformation that sometimes preceded generational change and sometimes was unaffected by it. Insightful commentary on the process of creolization is provided by Mintz, "The Socio-Historical Background to Pidginization and Creolization," in Dell Hymes, ed. *Pidginization and Creolization of Languages: Proceedings of a Conference Held at the University of the West Indies. Mono, Jamaica, April 1968* (Cambridge, 1971), 481–96.

9   For ground-breaking works that argue for the unity of working peoples in the Atlantic world see Peter Linebaugh, "All the Atlantic Mountains Shook," *Labour/Le Travailleur*, 10 (1982), 82–121, and Linebaugh and Marcus Rediker, "The Many-Headed Hydra: Sailors, Slaves, and the Atlantic Working Class in the Eighteenth Century," *Journal of Historical Sociology*, 3 (1990), 225–52. Thornton, *Africa and Africans in the Making of the Atlantic World*, adopts a similar perspective in viewing the making of African-American culture. A larger Atlantic perspective for the formation of black culture is posed in Paul Gilroy, *The Black Atlantic: Modernity and Double Consciousness* (Cambridge, Mass., 1993).

10 A. C. de C. M. Saunders, *A Social History of Black Slaves and Freedmen in Portugal, 1441–1555* (Cambridge, 1982), 11–12, 145, 197 n. 52, 215 n. 73 (for black sailors and interpreters in the African trade); P. E. H. Hair, "The Use of African Languages in Afro-European Contacts in Guinea, 1440–1560," *Sierra Leone Language Review*, 5 (1966), 7–17 (for black interpreters and Europeans' striking lack of interest in mastering African languages); George E. Brooks, *Landlords and Strangers: Ecology, Society, and Trade in West Africa, 1000–1630* (Boulder, Colo., 1993), chap. 7 (particularly for the role of *grumetes*), 124, 136–37; Wyatt MacGaffey, "Dialogues of the Deaf: Europeans on the Atlantic Coast of Africa," in Stuart B. Schwartz, ed., *Implicit Understandings: Observing, Reporting, and Reflecting on the Encounters between Europeans and Other Peoples in the Early Modern Era* (Cambridge, 1994), 252 (for hostages); Kwame Yeboa Daaku, *Trade and Politics on the Gold Coast, 1600–1720: A Study of the African Reaction to European Trade* (Oxford, 1970), chap. 5, esp. 96–97 (for ambassadors to the United Provinces in 1611); Anne Hilton, *The Kingdom of Kongo* (Oxford, 1985), 64; Paul Edwards and James Walvin, "Africans in Britain, 1500–1800," in Martin L. Kilson and Robert 1. Rotberg, eds., *The African Diaspora: Interpretive Essays* (Cambridge, Mass., 1976), 173–205 (for African royalty sending their sons to be educated in Europe). See also Shelby T. McCloy, "Negroes and Mulattoes in Eighteenth-Century France," *Journal of Negro History*, 30 (1945), 276–92. For the near-seamless, reciprocal relationship between the Portuguese and the Kongolese courts in the 16th century see Thornton, "Early Kongo-Portuguese Relations, 1483–1575: A New Interpretation," *History in Africa*, 8 (1981), 183–204.

11 For an overview see Thornton, *Africa and Africans in the Making of the Atlantic World*, chap. 2, esp. 59–62. See also Daaku, *Trade and Politics on the Gold Coast*, chap. 2; Brooks, *Landlords and Strangers*, chaps. 7–8 (see the Portuguese crown's penalties against *lançados* for illegal trading, 152–54); Philip D. Curtin, *Economic Change in Precolonial Africa: Senegambia in the Era of the Slave Trade* (Madison, Wis., 1975), chap. 3; Ray A. Kea, *Settlements, Trade, and Polities in the Seventeenth-Century Gold Coast* (Baltimore, 1982); John Vogt, *Portuguese Rule on the Gold Coast, 1469–1682* (Athens, Ga., 1979); C. R. Boxer, *Four Centuries of Portuguese Expansion, 1415–1825: A Succinct Survey* (Johannesburg, 1961); and Boxer, *The Dutch Seaborne Empire, 1600–1800* (New York, 1965). *Lançados* comes from a contraction of *lançados em terra* (to put on shore); Curtin, *Economic Change in Precolonial Africa*, 95. As the influence of the Atlantic economy spread to the interior, Atlantic creoles appeared in the hinterland, generally in the centers of trade along rivers.

12 Kea, *Settlements, Trade, and Polities*, chap. 1, esp. 38.

13 Ibid.; Vogt, *Portuguese Role on the Gold Coast*; Harvey M. Feinburg, *Africans and Europeans in West Africa: Elminans and Dutchmen on the Gold Coast during the Eighteenth Century*. American Philosophical Society, *Transactions*, 79. No. 7 (Philadelphia, 1989). For mortality see Curtin, "Epidemiology and the Slave Trade," *Political Science Quarterly*, 83 (1968), 190–216, and K. G. Davies, "The Living and the Dead: White Mortality in West Africa, 1684–1732," in Stanley L. Engerman and Eugene D. Genovese, eds., *Rare and Slavery in the Western Hemisphere: Quantitative Studies* (Princeton, 1975), 83–98.

14 Kea, *Settlements, Trade, and Polities*, chap. 1, esp. 38–50, 133–34; Vogt, *Portuguese Rule on the Gold Coast*; Feinberg, *Africans and Europeans in West Africa*. Eveline C. Martin, *The British West African Settlements, 1750–1821: A Study in Local Administration* (New York, 1927), and Margaret Priestley, *West African Trade and Coast Society: A Family Study* (London, 1969), describe the English enclaves in the, 18th and 19th centuries, casting light on their earlier development.

15 Brooks, *Landlords and Strangers*, chap. 7–9, esp. 188–96, and Brooks, "Luso-African Commerce and Settlement in the Gambia and Guinea-Bissau Region," *Boston University*

African Studies Center Working Papers (1980), for the connection of the Luso-Africans with the Cape Verde Islands; Daaku, *Trade and Politics on the Gold Coast*, chaps. 5–6; Vogt, *Portuguese Rule on the Gold Coast*, 154; Feinberg, *Africans and Europeans in West Africa*, 32, 88–90; Curtin, *Economic Change in Precolonial Africa*, 95–100, 113–21 (for Afro-French). For the development of a similar population in Angola see Joseph C. Miller, *Way of Death: Merchant Capitalism and the Angolan Slave Trade, 1730–1830* (Madison, Wis., 1988), esp. chaps. 8–9, and Miller, "A Marginal Institution on the Margin of the Atlantic System: The Portuguese Southern Atlantic Slave Trade in the Eighteenth Century," in Barbara L. Solow, ed., *Slavery and the Rise of the Atlantic System* (Cambridge. Mass., 1991), 125, 128–29. By the mid-17th century, the hierarchy of Kongolese Catholics was largely mixed African and European ancestry or *pombeiros*; Hilton, *Kingdom of Kongo*, 140–41, 154. See also Allen F. Isaacman, *Mozambique: The Africanization of a European Institution: The Zambezi Prazos, 1750–1902* (Madison, Wis., 1972). The number of such individuals in west Africa is difficult to estimate. Brooks, in his study of the Grain Coast and its interior, estimates "hundreds of Portuguese and Cabo Verdean traders were admitted to western African communities by the close of the fifteenth century." Probably the same could be said for other portions of the African coast at that time. By the middle of the 16th century, Atlantic creoles were more numerous. In 1567, when the English adventurer John Hawkins launched a raid on an African settlement on the Cacheu River, he was repulsed by a force that included "about a hundred" *lançados*; Brooks, *Landlord and Strangers*, 137, 230–31. By the 19th century, the Afro-Europeans had become to a "remarkable extent soundly and politically integrated" and "occupied their own 'quarter' of the town" of Elmina; Larry W. Yarak, "West African Coastal Slavery in the Nineteenth Century: The Case of Afro-European Slaveowners of Elmina," *Ethnohistory*, 36 (1989), 44–60, quotation on 47; J. T. Lever, "Mulatto Influence on the Gold Coast in the Early Nineteenth Century: Jim Nieset of Elmina," *African Historical Studies*, 3 (1970), 253–61.

16 Daaku, *Trade and Politics on the Gold Coast*, chaps. 4–5; Brooks, *Landlords and Strangers*, chaps. 7–9, esp. 188–96; Curtin, *Economic Change in Precolonial Africa, 95–100*. See also Miller's compelling description of Angola's Luso-Africans in the 18th and 19th centuries that suggests something of their earlier history, in *Way of Death*, 246–50. Brooks notes the term *taugomãos* passed from use at the end of the 17th century, in "Luso-African Commerce and Settlement in the Gambia and Guinea-Bissau," 3.

17 Speaking of the Afro-French in Senegambia in the 18th century, Curtin emphasizes the cultural transformation in making this new people, noting that "the important characteristic of this community was cultural mixture, not racial mixture, and the most effective of the traders from France were those who could cross the cultural line between Europe and Africa in their commercial relations," in *Economic Change in Precolonial Africa*, 117.

18 Holm, *Pidgins and Creoles*; Thornton, *Africa and Africans in the Making of the Atlantic World*, 213–18; Saunders, *Black Slaves and Freedman in Portugal*, 98–102 (see special word—*ladinhos* —for blacks who could speak "good" Portuguese, 101); Brooks, *Landlords and Strangers*, 136–37. See also Robert A. Hall, Jr., *Pidgin and Creole Languages* (Ithaca, 1966); David Dalby, "The Place of Africa and Afro-America in the History of the English Language," *African Language Review*, 9 (1971), 280–98; Hair, "Use of African Languages in Afro-European Contacts in Guinea," 5–26; Keith Whinnom, "Contacts De Langues et Emprunts Lexicaux: The Origin of the European-Based Pidgins and Creoles," *Orbis*, 14 (1965), 509–27, Whinnom, "Linguistic Hybridization and the 'Special Case' of Pidgins and Creoles," in Hymes, ed., *Pidginization and Creolization of Languages*, 91–115, and Whinnom, "The Context and Origins of Lingua Franca," in Jürgen M. Meisel, ed., *Langues en Contact— Pidgins—Creoles* (Tübingen, 1975); and J. L. Dillard, "Creole English and Creole Portuguese: The Early Records," in Ian F. Hancock, ed., *Readings in Creole Studies* (Ghent, 1979), 261–68. For another theory on the origins of the west African pidgin see Anthony J. Naro, "The Origins of West African Pidgin," in Claudia Corum, T. Cedric Smith-Stark, and Ann Weiser, eds., *Papers from the Ninth Regional Meeting*, Chicago Linguistic Society (1973), 442–49.

19 Daaku, *Trade and Politics on the Gold Coast*, chaps. 3–4; Feinberg, *Africans and Europeans in West Africa*, chap. 6, quotation on 86; Kea, *Settlements, Trade, and Politics*, esp. pt. 2; Curtin, *Economic Change in Precolonial Africa*, 92–93.

20   Vogt, *Portuguese Rule on the Gold Coast*, 54–58; Daaku, *Trade and Politics on the Gold Coast*, 99–101; Thornton, "The Development of an African Catholic Church in the Kingdom of Kongo, 1491–1750," *Journal of African History*, 25 (1984), 147–67; Hilton, *Kingdom of Kongo*, 32–49, 154–61, 179, 198; MacGaffey, *Religion and Society in Central Africa: The BaKongo of Lower Zaire* (Chicago, 1986), 191–216, and MacGaffey, "Dialogues of the Deaf," 249–67. Pacing the cultural intermixture of African and Europe was the simultaneous introduction of European and American plants and animals, which compounded and legitimated many of the cultural changes; Alfred W. Crosby, *Ecological Imperialism: The Biological Expansion of Europe*, 900–1990 (Cambridge, 1986).

21   The history of one element of this population, the canoemen, is discussed in Peter C. W. Gutkind, "The Boatmen of Ghana: The Possibilities of a Pre-Colonial African Labor History," in Michael Hanagan and Charles Stephenson, eds., *Confrontation, Class Consciousness, and the Labor Process: Studies in Early Procolonial Class Formation* (Westport, Conn., 1986), 123–66, and Gutkind, "Trade and Labor in Early Precolonial African History: The Canoemen of Southern Ghana," in Catherine Coquery-Vidrovitch and Paul E. Lovejoy, eds., *The Workers of African Trade* (Beverly Hills, Calif., 1985), 25–49; Robert Smith, "The Canoe in West African History," *J. African Hist.*, 11 (1970), 515–33; and Robin Law, "Trade and Politics behind the Slave Trade: The Lagoon Traffic and the Rise of Lagos," ibid., 24 (1983), 321–48. See also Daaku, *Trade and Politics on the Gold Coast*, 103–04, 121–22. For an overview of the coastal towns see Kea, *Settlements, Trade, and Polities*, esp. chap. 2; Daaku, *Trade and Polities on the Gold Coast*, chap. 4; and Curtin, *Economic Change in Precolonial Africa*, 119–20, for the relation between European trading communities acid African towns. Since Africans would not rent outsiders more land than needed for a house or a store, food production and other services remained in African hands; Brooks, *Landlords and Strangers*, 189–90. For bandits see Kea, "'I Am Here to Plunder on the General Road': Bandits and Banditry in the Pre-Nineteenth Century Gold Coast," in Donald Crummey, ed., *Banditry, Rebellion, and Social Protest in Africa* (London, 1986), 109–32.

22   Feinberg, *Africans and Europeans in West Africa*, 84–85 (for Elmina): Joyce D. Goodfriend, *Before the Melting Pot: Society and Culture in Colonial New York City, 1664–1730* (Princeton, 1992), 13 (for New Amsterdam); Peter A. Coclanis, *The Shadow of a Dream: Economic Life and Death in the South Carolina Low Country, 1670–1920* (New York, 1989), 115 (for Charleston).

23   Kea, *Settlements, Trade, and Polities*, esp. chap. 6.

24   Feinberg, *Africans and Europeans in West Africa*, 65, 82–83; Kea, *Settlements, Trade, and Politics*, 197–202, 289–90. On the Cape Verde Islands, free blacks obtained the right to hold public office in 1546. Racial distinctions did not appear until the emergence of a plantation society in the mid-16th century, when the preoccupation with skin color and hair texture emerged along with racially exclusionary policies; Brooks, *Landlords and Strangers*, 158–59, 186–87; Dierdre Meintel, *Race, Culture, and Portuguese Colonialism in Cabo Verde* (Syracuse, N. Y., 1984), 96–103.

25   Kea, *Settlements, Trade, and Polities*, 233–35, 315–16, 319–20. Daaku notes that "difficulties arise in establishing the exact nationalities" of Gold Coast traders, as European "writers tended to 'Europeanize' the names of some of the Africans with whom they traded and those in their service, while some of the Africans fancifully assumed European names," in *Trade and Politics on the Gold Coast*, 96.

26   Daaku, *Trade and Politics an the Gold Coast*, chaps. 5–6; David Henige, "John Kabes of Komenda: An Early African Entrepreneur and State Builder," *J. African Hist.*, 18 (1977), 1–19.

27   Gutkind, "Boatmen of Ghana," 131–39, quotation on 137, and Gutkind, "Trade and Labor in Early Precolonial African History," 40–41 (for canoemen who pawned themselves and later became successful traders).

28   For enslavement of canoemen for violation of Portuguese regulations see Gutkind, "Trade and Labor in Early Precolonial African History," 27–28, 36. Okoyaw, a canoeman who pawned himself to the Royal African Company in 1704 to redeem a debt, agreed in return "to attend Dayly the Company's Work"; cited in Kea, *Settlements, Trade, and Polities*, 243. Because there was no established system of commercial law, creditors might seize the slaves

or even the fellow townsmen of their debtors to satisfy an obligation: Curtin, *Economic Change in Precolonial Africa*, 302–08.

29 The northern North American colonies often received "refuse" slaves. For complaints and appreciations see Goodfriend, "Burghers and Blacks: The Evolution of a Slave Society at New Amsterdam," *New York History*, 59 (1978), 139; Sainsbury et al., eds., *Calendar of State Papers, Colonial Series, 1708–1709*, 24:110; Lorenzo J. Greene, *The Negro in Colonial New England, 1620–1776* (New York, 1942), 35: Jeremias van Rensselaer to Jan Baptist van Rensselaer, ca. 1659, in A. J. F. Van Laer, ed., *Correspondence of Jeremias Van Rensselaer, 1651–1674* (Albany, 1932), 167–68, 175; William D. Pierson, *Black Yankees: The Development of an Afro-American Subculture in Eighteenth-Century New England* (Amherst, Mass., 1988), 4–5; Edgar J. McManus, *Black Bondage in the North* (Syracuse, N. Y., 1973), 18–25, and McManus, *A History of Slavery in New York* (Syracuse, N. Y., 1966), 23–39; James G. Lydon, "New York and the Slave Trade, 1700 to 1774," *WMQ*, 3d Ser., 35 (1978), 275–79, 281–90; Darold D. Wax, "Negro Imports into Pennsylvania, 1720–1766," *Pennsylvania History*, 32 (1965), 254–87, and Wax, "Preferences for Slaves in Colonial America," *J. Negro Hist.*, 58 (1973), 374–76, 379–87; and Sharon V. Salinger, *"To Serve Well and Faithfully": Labour and Indentured Servitude in Pennsylvania, 1682–1800* (Cambridge, 1987), 75–78.

30 Boxer, *The Dutch in Brazil, 1624–1654* (Oxford, 1957); Johannes Menne Postma, *The Dutch in the Atlantic Slave Trade* (Cambridge, 1990), chaps. 2–3, 8; Cornelis C. Goslinga, *The Dutch in the Caribbean and on the Wild Coast, 1580–1680* (Gainesville, Fla., 1971).

31 Boxer, *Four Centuries of Portuguese Expansion*, 48–51, and Boxer, *Dutch in Brazil*: P. C. Emmer, "The Dutch and the Making of the Second Atlantic System," in Solow, ed., *Slavery and the Rise of the Atlantic System*. 75–96, esp. 83–84; Thornton, *Africa and Africans in the Making of the Atlantic World*, 64–65, 69–77. Albert van Danzig, ed. and trans., *The Dutch and the Guinea Coast, 1674–1742: A Collection of Documents from the General, State Archives at the Hague* (Accra, 1978), provides insight into the operation of the Dutch West India Company and the role of the Dutch on the Gold and Slave coasts.

32 Thornton, *The Kingdom of Kongo: Civil War and Transition. 1641–1718* (Madison, Wis., 1983), esp. 72–74, chaps. 6–7 passim; Hilton, *Kingdom of Kongo*, chaps. 6–7: Ernst Van Den Boogaart and Pieter C. Emmer, "The Dutch Participation in the Atlantic Slave Trade. 1596–1650," in Henry A. Gemery and Jan S. Hogendorn, eds., *The Uncommon Market: Essays in the Economic History of the Atlantic Slave Trade* (New York, 1979), 353–71. The best survey of the Dutch trade is Postma, *Dutch in the Atlantic Slave Trade*.

33 Goslinga, *Dutch in the Caribbean and on the Wild Coast*; Van Laer, ed., *Correspondence of Jeremias Van Rensselaer*, 167–68, 175, quotation on 167; Elizabeth Donnan, ed., *Documents Illustrative of the History of the Slave Trade to America*, 4 vols. (Washington, D. C., 1930–1935), 3:421; Goodfriend, "Burghers and Blacks," 139.

34 Names are drawn from E. B. O'Callaghan, comp., *The Documentary History of the State of New-York*, 4 vols. (Albany, 1849–1851); O'Callaghan, ed., *Documents Relative to the Colonial History of the State of New-York*, 15 vols. (Albany, 1853–1887) (hereafter *N. Y. Col. Docs.*); O'Callaghan, comp., *Laws and Ordinances of New Netherland. 1638–1674* (Albany, 1868); O'Callaghan, ed., *Calendar of Historical Manuscripts in the Office of the Secretary of State, 1630–1664* (Albany, 1865); Berthold Fernow, ed., *The Records of New Amsterdam from 1653 to 1674*, 7 vols. (New York, 1897); Fernow, ed., *Minutes of the Orphanmasters Court of New Amsterdam, 1655–1663*, 2 vols. (New York, 1907); Kenneth Scott and Kenn Stryker-Rodda, comps., *New York Historical Manuscripts; Dutch*, vols. 1–4 (Baltimore, 1974–); Charles T. Gehring, ed., *New York Historical Manuscripts: Dutch Land Papers* (Baltimore, 1980): New York Genealogical and Biographical Society, Collections, *Marriages from 1639 to 1801 in the Reformed Dutch Church of New York* (New York, 1890); I. N. Phelps Stokes, *Iconography of Manhattan Island, 1488–1909*, 6 vols. (New York, 1914–1928). A few names suggest the subtle transformation as the Atlantic creoles crossed the ocean and assumed a new identity that was unfamiliar to its hosts. For example, Anthony Jansen of Salee or Van Vaes, a man of tawny complexion—"mulatto," per below—who claimed Moroccan birth, became "Anthony the Turk," perhaps because Turks were considered fierce—as Anthony's litigious history indicates he surely was—but, more important, because he was alien in status and brown in pigment; Leo Hershkowitz, "The Troublesome Turk: An Illustration

of Judicial Process in New Amsterdam," *N. Y. Hist.*, 46 (1965), 299–310. But if names of
new arrivals in New Netherland reflect their lived experience rather than an owner's designation, they also have nothing of the ring of Africa: no Quaws, Phibbis, or any of the day
names that Africans later carried. Such names would become familiar to northern slaveholders when the slave trade reached into the interior of Africa. In Portugal, the names
slaves bore do not seem different from those of native Portuguese; Saunders, *Black Slaves
and Freedmen in Portugal*, 89–90. The practice of attaching a national modifier to a given
name was employed for others besides Africans. See Edmund S. Morgan, *American Slavery,
American Freedom: The Ordeal of Colonial Virginia* (New York, 1975), 153–54

35 Nothing evidenced the circles' easy integration into the mainland society better than the
number who survived into old age. There are no systematic demographic studies of people
of African descent during the first years of settlement, and perhaps because the numbers
are so small, there can be none. Nevertheless, "old" or "aged" slaves are encountered again
and again, sometimes in descriptions of fugitives, sometimes in the deeds that manumit—
i.e., discard—superannuated slaves. Before the end of the 17th century, numbers of black
people lived long enough to see their grandchildren.

36 Fernow, ed., *Records of New Amsterdam*, 5:337, cited in Goodfriend, *Before the Melting Pot*,
252 n. 25.

37 Suzanne Miers and Igor Kopytoff, eds., *Slavery in Africa: Historical and Anthropological
Perspectives* (Madison, Wis., 1977); Paul E. Lovejoy, *Transformations in Slavery: A History of
Slavery in Africa* (Cambridge. 1983); Patrick Manning, *Slavery and African Life: Occidental,
Oriental, and African Slave Trader* (Cambridge, 1990); Thornton, *Africa and Africans in the
Making of the Atlantic World*, chap 3; Claude Meillassoux, *The Anthropology of Slavery: The
Womb of Iron and Gold* (Chicago, 1991); Martin A. Klein, "Introduction: Modern European
Expansion and Traditional Servitude in Africa and Asia," in Klein, ed., *Breaking the Chains:
Slavery, Bondage, and Emancipation in Modern Africa and Asia* (Madison, Wis., 1993), 3–26;
Toyin Falola and Lovejoy, "Pawnship in Historical Perspective," in Falola and Lovejoy,
eds., *Pawnship in Africa: Debt Bondage in Historical Perspective* (Boulder, Colo., 1994), 1–26.
A dated but still useful critical review of the subject is Frederick Cooper, "The Problem
of Slavery in African Studies," *J. African Hist.*, 20 (1979), 103–25.

38 Miers and Kopytoff, eds. *Slavery in Africa*, chap. 1, esp. 17.

39 Goodfriend, *Before the Melting Pot*, 10, chap. 6; Van Den Boogaart, "The Servant Migration
to New Netherland, 1624–1664," in Emmer, ed., *Colonialism and Migration: Indentured
Labour before and after Slavery* (Dordrecht, 1986), 58; O'Callaghan, ed., *N. Y. Col. Docs.*,
1:154.

40 Goodfriend, *Before the Melting Pot*, chap. 6: Goodfriend. "Burghers and Blacks," 125–44;
Goodfriend, "Black Families in New Netherland," *Journal of the Afro-American Historical and
Genealogical, Society*, 5 (1984), 94–107; Morton Wagman, "Corporate Slavery in New
Netherland," *J. Negro Hist.*, 65 (1980), 34–42; McManus, *Slavery in New York*, 2–22;
Michael Kammen, *Colonial New York: A History* (New York, 1975), 58–60; Van Den
Boogaart, "Servant Migration to New Netherland," 56–59, 65–71; Vivienne L. Kruger,
"Born to Run: The Slave Family in Early New York, 1626 to 1827" (Ph. D. diss., Columbia
University, 1985), chap. 2. esp. 46–48. chap. 6, esp. 270–77: Oliver A. Rink, *Holland
on the Hudson: An Economic and Social History of Dutch New York* (Ithaca, 1986), 161 n. 33.
Between 1639 and 1652, marriages recorded in the New Amsterdam Church represented
28% of the marriages recorded in that period—also note one interracial marriage. For
baptisms see "Reformed Dutch Church, New York, Baptisms, 1639–1800," New York
Genealogical and Biographical Society, *Collections*, 2 vols. (New York, 1901), 1:10–27,
2:10–38; for the 1635 petition see Stokes, *Iconography of Manhattan Island*, 4:82, and No.
14, Notulen W1635, 1626 (19–11–1635). inv. 1.05.01. 01. (Oude), Algemeen
Rijksarchief, The Hague. A petition by "five blacks from New Netherland who had come
here [Amsterdam]" was referred back to officials in New Netherland. Marcel van der Linden
of the International Institute of Social History in Amsterdam kindly located and translated
this notation in the records of the Dutch West India Company.

41 Petition for freedom, in O'Callaghan, ed., *Calendar of Historical Manuscripts*, 269. White
residents of New Amsterdam protested the enslavement of the children of half-free slaves,

holding that no one born of a free person should be a slave. The Dutch West India Company rejected the claim; O'Callaghan, ed., *N. Y Col. Docs.*, 1:302, 343; O'Callaghan, ed., *Laws and Ordinances of New Netherland*, 4:36–37. For the Dutch West India Company's "setting them free and at liberty, on the same footing as other free people here in New Netherland," although children remained property of the company, see Van Den Boogaart, "Servant Migration to New Netherland," 69–70.

42   For black men paying tribute to purchase their families see O'Callaghan, ed., *Calendar of Historical Manuscripts*, 45, 87, 105; O'Callaghan, ed., *N. Y. Col. Docs.* 1:343; Goodfriend, "Burghers and Blacks," 125–44, and "Black Families in New Netherlands," 94–107; McManus, *Slavery in New York*, 2–22; Wagman, "Corporate Slavery in New Netherland," 38–39; quotation in Gerald Francis DeJong, "The Dutch Reformed Church and Negro Slavery in Colonial America," *Church History*, 40 (1971), 430; Kruger, "Born to Run," chap. 1, esp. 90–92; Henry B. Hoff, "Frans Abramse Van Salee and His Descendants: A Colonial Black family in New York and New Jersey," *New York Genealogical and Biographical Register*, 121 (1990), 65–71, 157–61.

43   Goodfriend estimates that 75 of New Amsterdam's 375 blacks were free in 1664, in *Before the Melting Pot*, 61.

44   Kruger, "Born to Run," 50–55, 591–606, tells of the creation of a small class of black landowners as a result of gifts from the Dutch West India Company and direct purchase by the blacks themselves (quotation on 592); Goodfriend, *Before the Melting Pot*, 115–16, 253 n. 36; Peter R. Christoph, "The Freedmen of New Amsterdam," *J. Afro-Amer. Hist. Gen. Soc.*, 5 (1984), 116–17. See also Stokes, *Iconography of Manhattan Island*, 2:302, 4:70–78, 100, 104–06, 120–48, 265–66; Gehring, ed., *New York Historical Manuscripts*; and Van Den Boogaart, "Servant Migration to New Netherland," 56–59, 65–71. For the employment of a white housekeeper by a free black artisan see ibid., 69; Fernow, ed., *Minutes of the Orphanmasters Court*, 2: 46; and Roi Ottley and William J. Weatherby, eds., *The Negro in New York: An Informal Social History* (New York, 1967), 12.

45   O'Callaghan, ed., *Calendar of Historical Manuscripts*, 87, 105. 269 (for manumission, dubbed "half slaves"), 222 (adoption), 269 (land grants). See also Goodfriend, *Before the Melting Pot*, chap. 6, and Fernow, ed., *Records of New Amsterdam from 1653 to 1674*, 3:42, 5, 172, 337–40, 7, 11 (for actions in court); Goodfriend, "Burghers and Blacks," 125–44, and "Black Families in New Netherlands," 94–107; Van Den Boogaart, "Servant Migration to New Netherland," 56–59, 65–71; McManus, *Slavery in New York*, 2–22; DeJong, "Dutch Reformed Church and Negro Slavery in Colonial America," 430; Kruger, "Born to Run," 46–48; 270–78; Hoff, "Frans Abramse Van Salee and His Descendants"; Kammen, *New York*, 58–60. For blacks using Dutch courts early on see Rink, *Holland on the Hudson*, 160–61—e. g., in 1638, Anthony Portuguese sued Anthony Jansen for damages done his hog; soon after, one Pedro Negretto claimed back wages. For adoption of a black child by a free black family see Scott and Stryker-Rodda, eds., *The Register of Salmon Lachaire, Notary Public of New Amsterdam, 1661–1662* (Baltimore, 1978), 22–23; O'Callaghan, ed., *Calendar of Historical Manuscripts*, 222, 256; and Kruger, "Born to Run," 44–51.

46   Until New Netherland developed an agricultural base, slavery did not seem to take hold, and settlers admitted in 1649 that slaves imported at great cost "just dripped through the fingers" and "were sold for pork and peas"; O'Callaghan, ed., *N. Y Col Docs.*, 1:302. For the change that took place during the 1650s and the beginning of direct African importation in 1655 see O'Callaghan, ed., *Calendar of Historical Manuscripts*, 268, 289, 293, 307, 331. New York sharply limited manumission in 1712. Few slaves were freed before then. One careful enumeration counted 8 manumissions between 1669 and 1712; Kruger, "Born to Run," 593.

47   James B. Bartlett and J. Franklin Jameson, eds., *Journal of Jasper Danckaerts, 1679–1680* (New York, 1913), 65. See also Goodfriend, *Before the Melting Pot*, 115–16 (land). After the English conquest, black people continued to present their children for baptism, although they changed to the Anglican church; ibid., 131.

48   Curtin, *Economic Change in Precolonial Africa*, 104–05, 121–27; Jean Mettas *Répertoire des Expéditions Négrières Françaises au XVIIIe Siècle*, 2 vols. (Paris, 1984); Marcel Giraud, *A History of French Louisiana: The Reign of Louis XIV, 1698–1715*, trans. Joseph C. Lambert (Baton

Rouge, 1974); Hall, *Africans in Colonial Louisiana*, chaps. 2–4. For the French slave trade see Robert Louis Stein, *The French Slave Trade in the Eighteenth Century: An Old Regime Business* (Madison, Wis., 1979).

49   The Bambaras had complex relations with tire French. Although many Bambaras—usually captives of the tribe whom the French also deemed Bambaras (although they often were not)—became entrapped in the international slave trade and were sold to the New World, others worked for the French as domestics, boatmen, clerks, and interpreters in the coastal forts and slave factories. Their proud military tradition—honed in a long history of warfare against Mandingas and other Islamic peoples—made them ideal soldiers as well as slave catchers. Along the coast of Africa, "Barbara" became a generic word for soldier; Hall, *Africans in Colonial Louisiana*, 42, and Curtin, *Economic Change in Precolonial Africa*, 115, 143, 149, 178–81, 191–92: see the review of Hall in *Africa*, 64 (1994) 168–71.

50   The evidence of Samba's participation in the Fort D'Arguin insurrection is insubstantial and contradictory, but he got himself into enough trouble to be enslaved and deported; Hall, *Africans in Colonial Louisiana*, 109–10; Le Page du Pratz, *Histoure de la Louisiane*, 3 vols. (Paris, 1758). 3:305–17; Daniel H. Usner, Jr., "From African Captivity to American Slavery: The Introduction of Black Laborers to Colonial Louisiana," *La. Hist.*, 20 (1979), 37. On the Afro-French community in St. Louis and other enclaves on the Senegal see Curtin, *Economic Change in Precolonial Africa*, 113–21.

51   The first census of the French settlement of the lower Mississippi Valley comes front Biloxi in 1699. It lists 5 naval officers, 5 petty officers, 4 sailors, 19 Canadians, 10 laborers, 6 cabin boys, and 20 soldiers; Hall, *Africans in Colonial Louisiana*, 3, and esp. chap. 5. Usner makes the point in comparing the use of black sailors on the Mississippi and the Senegal, in "From African Captivity to American Slavery," 25–47, esp. 36, and more generally in *Indians, Settlers, and Slaves in a Frontier Exchange Economy: The Lower Mississippi Valley before 1783* (Chapel Hill, 1992). See also James T. McGowan, "Planters without Slaves: Origins of a New World Labor System," *Southern Studies*, 16 (1977), 5–20; John G. Clark, *New Orleans, 1718–1812: An Economic History* (Baton Rouge, 1970), chap. 2; and Thomas N. Ingersoll, "Old New Orleans: Race, Class, Sex, and Order in the Early Deep South. 1718–1819" (Ph. D. diss., University of California at Los Angeles, 1990), chaps. 2–3.

52   Hall, *Africans in Colonial Louisiana*, 131–32.

53   Ibid., 106–12; du Pratz, *Histoire de la Louisiane*, 3:305–17; Usner, "From African Captivity to American Slavery." 37, 42.

54   Charles Verlinden, *The Beginnings of Modern Colonization: Eleven Essays with an Introduction* (Ithaca, 1970), 39–40; Saunders, *Black Slaves and Freedmen in Portugal*, chap. 1, esp. 55; Ruth Pike, "Sevillian Society in the Sixteenth Century: Slaves and Freedmen," *Hispanic American Historical Review*, 47 (1967), 344–59, and Pike, *Aristocrats and Traders: Sevillian Society in the Sixteenth Century* (Ithaca, 1972), 29, 170–92; P. E. H. Hair, "Black African Slaves at Valencia, 1482–1516," *History in Africa*, 7 (1980), 119–31; Thornton, *Africa and Africans in the Making of the Atlantic World*, 96–97; A. J. R. Russell-Wood, "Iberian Expansion and the Issue of Black Slavery: Changing Portuguese Attitudes, 1440–1770," *AHR*, 83 (1978), 20. During the first two decades of the 16th century, about 2,000 African slaves annually entered Lisbon and were sold there. By the 1530s, most slaves brought to Lisbon were sent to the New World via Seville.

55   In the mid-16th century, black people entered the periphery of Europe; Verlinden, *Beginnings of Modern Colonization*, chap 2. England developed a small black population that grew with English involvement in the African trade; see James B. Walvin, *Black and White: The Negro and English Society*, 1555–1945 (London, 1973), chap. 1, and F. O. Shyllon, *Black Slaves in Britain* (London, 1974), and *Black People in Britain 1555–1833* (London, 1977). For France see William B. Cohen, *The French Encounter with Africans: White Response to Blacks, 1530–1880* (Bloomington, 1980), and Sue Peabody, "'There Are No Slaves in France': Law, Culture, and Society in Early Modern France, 1685–1789" (Ph. D. diss., University of Iowa, 1993).

56   J. Fred Rippy, "'The Negro and the Spanish Pioneer in the New World," *J. Negro Hist.*, 6 (1921), 183–89; Leo Wiener, *Africa and the Discovery of America*, 3 vols. (Philadelphia, 1920–1922).

57   Saunders, *Black Slaves arid Freedmen in Portugal*, 29; for sailors see 11, 71–72, 145 and Hall, *Africans in Colonial Louisiana*. 128. A sale of 6 slaves in Mexico in 1554 included one born in the Azores, another born in Portugal, another born in Africa, and the latter's daughter born in Mexico; Colin A. Palmer, *Slaves of the White God: Blacks in Mexico, 1570–1650* (Cambridge, Mass., 1976), 31–32; "Abstracts of French and Spanish Documents Concerning the Early History of Louisiana," *Louisiana Historical Quarterly*, 1 (1917), 111.

58   Saunders, *Black Slaves and Freedmen in Portugal*, 152–55; Russell-Wood, "Black and Mulatto Brotherhoods in Colonial Brazil," *Hisp. Amer. Hist. Rev.*, 54 (1974). 567–602, and Russell-Wood, *The Black Man in Slavery and Freedom in Colonial Brazil* (New York, 1982), chap. 8, esp. 134, 153–54 159–60. See also Pike, *Aristocrats and Traders*, 177–79. In the 16th century, some 7% (2,580) of Portugal's black population was free; Saunders, *Black Slaves and Freedmen in Portugal*, 59.

59   Simon Hart, *The Prehistory of the New Netherland Company Amsterdam Notarial Records of the First Dutch Voyages to the Hudson* (Amsterdam, 1959), 23–26, 74–75, quotations on 80–82; Thomas J. Condon, *New York Beginnings: The Commercial Origins of New Netherland* (New York, 1968), chap. 1, esp. 30; Rink, *Holland on the Hudson*, 34, 42; Van Cleaf Bachman, *Peltrier or Plantations: The Economic Policies of the Dutch West India Company in New Netherland, 1623–1639* (Baltimore, 1969), 6–7.

60   Wesley Frank Craven's investigation determined that the first black people to arrive at Jamestown were prizes taken by a Dutch man-of-war in consort with an English ship somewhere in the eastern Caribbean. Craven maintains they were born in the West Indies and stolen from there. J. Douglas Deal suggests they may have been taken from a Portuguese or Spanish slaver. Craven, *White Red, and Black: The Seventeenth-Century Virginian* (Charlottesville, 1971), 77–81; Deal, *Race and Class in Colonial Virginia: Indians, Englishmen, and Africans on the Eastern Shore during the Seventeenth Century* (New York, 1993), 163–64. In 1708, a Virginia planter remembered "that before the year 1680 what negros were brought to Virginia were imported generally from Barbados for it was very rare to have a Negro ship come to this Country directly from Africa"; Donnan, ed., *Documents Illustrative of the Slave Trade*, 4:89.

61   Anthony Johnson's primacy and "unmatched achievement" have made him and his family the most studied members of the charter generation. The best account of Johnson and his family is found in Deal, *Race and Class in Colonial Virginia*, 217–50. Also useful are T. H. Breen and Stephen Innes, *"Myne Owne Ground": Race and Freedom on Virginia's Eastern, Shore, 1640–1676* (New York, 1980), chap. 1; Ross M. Kimmel, "Free Blacks in Seventeenth-Century Maryland," *Maryland Magazine of History*, 71 (1976), 22–25; Alden Vaughan, "Blacks in Virginia: A Note on the First Decade," *WMQ*, 3d Ser., 29 (1972), 475–76; James H. Brewer, "Negro Property Owners in Seventeenth-Century Virginia," ibid., 12 (1955), 576–78; Susie M. Ames, *Studies of the Virginia Eastern, Shore in the Seventeenth Century* (Richmond, 1940), 102–05: John H. Russell, *The Free Negro in Virginia, 1619–1865* (Baltimore, 1913); and Russell, "Colored Freemen as Slave Owners in Virginia," *J. Negro Hist.*, 1 (1916), 233–42. Indirect evidence of the baptism of Johnson's children comes from the 1660s when John Johnson replied to challenges to his right to testify in court by producing evidence of baptism. He may have been baptized as an adult.

62   Quotation in Breen and Innes, *"Myne Owne Ground,"* 6. The statement is generally attributed to Johnson but may have been uttered by Francis Payne. See Deal, *Race anal Class in Colonial Virginia*, 266–67. For John Johnson's Angola see Kimmel, "Free Blacks in Maryland," 23.

63   Deal, *Race, and Class in Colonial Virginia*, 205–406, 265–67 (for Payne), 305 n. 2 (for the Driggus name), and Deal, "A Constricted World: Free Blacks on Virginia's Eastern Shore, 1680–1750," in Lois Green Carr, Philip D. Morgan, and Jean B. Russo, eds., *Colonial Chesapeake Society* (Chapel Hill, 1989), 275–305: Breen and Innes, *"Myne Owne Ground,"* esp. chap. 4, 69 (names).

64   The nature of the slave trade in the Chesapeake was summarized by Maryland's governor in 1708: "before the year 1698, this province has been supplyd by some small Quantitys of Negro's from Barbados and other her Ma'tys Islands and Plantations, as Jamaica and New England Seaven, eight, nine or ten in a Sloope, and sometymes larger Quantitys, and

sometymes, tho very seldom, whole ship Loads of Slaves have been brought here directly from Africa by Interlopers, or such as have had Lycenses, or otherwise traded there." Most of the latter had arrived in the previous decade; Donnan, ed., *Documents Illustrative of the Slave Trade*, 4:21–23. 88–90; Menard, "From Servants to Slaves: The Transformation of the Chesapeake Labor System," *Southern Studies*, 16 (1977), 363–67; Deal, *Race and Class in Colonial Virginia*, 164–65; Breen and Innes, "*Myne Owne Ground*," 70–71. On Phillip see Robert McColley, "Slavery in Virginia, 1619–1660: A Reexamination," in Robert H. Abzug and Stephen E. Mazlish, eds., *New Perspectives on Race and Slavery in America* (Lexington, Ky., 1986), 15–16, and Vaughan, "Blacks in Virginia," 470; on Cain see Deal, *Race and Class in Colonial Virginia*, 254–55, 317–19, and Robert C. Twombly and Robert H. Moore. "Black Puritan: The Negro in Seventeenth-Century Massachusetts," *WMQ*, 3d Ser., 14 (1967), 236.

65   Deal, *Race and Class in Colonial Virginia*, 205–405, quotation on 209, and Deal, "A Constricted World," 275–305; Michael L. Nicholls, "Passing Through This Troublesome World: Free Blacks in the Early Southside," *Virginia Magazine of History and Biography*, 92 (1984), 50–70.

66   Deal, *Race, and Class in Colonial Virginia*, 225–35, quotation on 208, and Deal, "A Constricted World," 290; Breen and Innes, "*Myne Owne Ground*," 79–82, 86, 90.

67   Morgan Godwyn, *The Negro's and Indian's Advocate* (London, 1680), 101, quoted in Breen and Innes, "*Myne Owne Ground*," 70, 130 n. 8.

68   Wood, *Black Majority*, chaps. 1, 4, esp. 97, for a reference to a slave master who "worked many days with a Negro man at the Whip saw." See also Clarence L. Ver Steeg, *Origins of a Southern Mosaic: Studies of Early Carolina and Georgia* (Athens, Ga., 1975), 105–07.

69   Jane Landers, "Spanish Sanctuary: Fugitives in Florida. 1687–1790, *Florida Historical Quarterly*, 62 (1984), 296–302, and Landers, "Gracia Real de Santa Teresa de Mose: A Free Black Town in Spanish Colonial Florida," *AHR*, 95 (1990), 9–30; John J. TePaske, "The Fugitive Slave: Intercolonial Rivalry and Spanish Slave Policy, 1687–1764," in Samuel Proctor, ed., *Eighteenth-Century Florida and Its Borderlands* (Gainesville, 1975) 2–12; I. A. Wright, comp., "Dispatches of Spanish Officials Bearing on the free Negro Settlement of Gracia Real de Santa Teresa de Mose, Florida," *J. Negro Hist.*, 9 (1924), 144–93, quotation on 150; Zora Neale Hurston, "Letters of Zora Neale Hurston on the Mose Settlement, and Negro Colony in Florida," ibid., 12 (1927), 664–67; J. D. Duncan, "Slavery and Servitude in Colonial South Carolina, 1670–1776" (Ph. D. diss., Emory University, 1964), chap. 17, quotation on 664; and J. G. Dunlop, "William Dunlop's Mission to St. Augustine in 1688," *South, Carolina Historical and Genealogical Magazine*, 34 (1933), 1–30. Several of the slaves who rejected freedom and Catholicism in St. Augustine and returned to South Carolina were rewarded with freedom, creating a competition between English and Spanish colonies that redounded to the fugitives' advantage. See Duncan, "Slavery and Servitude in Colonial South Carolina," 381–83.

70   Wood, *Black Majority*, chaps. 11–12; Thornton, "African Dimensions of the Stono Rebellion," *AHR*, 96 (1991), 1101–11, quotation on 1102. Thornton makes a powerful case for the Kongolese origins of the Stono rebels in their military organization and the nature of their resistance. For the pretransfer conversion of slaves from central Africa to Christianity see Thornton, "Development of an African Catholic Church in the Kingdom of Kongo," 147–50, and *Kingdom of Kongo*, 63–68; MacGaffey, *Religion and Society in Central Africa*, 198–211; and Hilton, *Kingdom of Kongo*, 179–98.

71   Thornton, "African Dimensions of the Status Rebellion," 1107; Landers, "Gracia Real de Santa Teresa de Mose," 27; Michael Mullin, ed., *American Negro Slavery: A Documentary History* (New York, 1976), 84.

72   Landers, "Spanish Sanctuary," 296–302; Landers, "Gracia Real de Santa Teresa de Mose" 9–30; Duncan, "Servitude and Slavery in Colonial South Carolina," chap. 17, quotations on 659, 663.

73   Landers, "Gracia Real de Santa Teresa de Mose," 15–21, quotation on 20; Larry W. Kruger and Robert Hall, "Fort Mose: A Black Fort in Spanish Florida," *The Griot*, 6 (1987), 39–40.

74   Landers, "Gracia Real de Santa Teresa de Mose," 21–22, quotations on 22.

75   Ibid., quotations on 21, 23–30; Theodore G. Corbett, "Population Structure in Hispanic St. Augustine," *Florida Historical Quarterly*, 54 (1976), 265, and "Migration to a Spanish

Imperial Frontier in the Seventeenth and Eighteenth Centuries: St. Augustine," *Hisp. Amer. Hist. Rev.*, 54 (1974). 420–21.

76 I have been unable to locate female analogues of Paulo d'Angula, Sandra Baunbara, Juan Rodrigues, Antonio a Negro, and Francisco Menéndez. Their absence does not, however, reflect the experience of Atlantic creoles, as small shards of evidence indicate that women played central roles in the production of creole culture, the transmission of language, the facilitation of trade, and the accumulation of capital. The best study derives from the 18th century. See George E. Brooks, Jr., "The *Signares* of Saint-Louis and Gorée: Women Entrepreneurs in Eighteenth-Century Senegal," in Nancy J. Hafkin and Edna G. Bay, eds., *Women in Africa: Studies in Social and Economic Change* (Stanford, Calif., 1976), 19–44. For an interpretation of 17th-century Chesapeake society that stresses the critical role of women in the shaping of race relations and the emergence of slavery see Kathleen Mary Brown, "Gender and the Genesis of a Race and Class System in Virginia, 1670–1750" (Ph.D. diss., University of Wisconsin, 1990).

77 Writing about the forced transfer of Africans to the New World, W. Jeffrey Bolster observes that "many of the slaves who left Africa with no maritime skills acquired rudimentary ones on the Middle Passage, along with some knowledge of European work-routines and social organization," in *Black Jacks: African-American Seamen in the Atlantic World, 1740–1865* (forthcoming).

78 For a useful distinction between societies with slaves and slave societies see Keith Hopkins, *Conquerors and Slaves: Sociological Studies in Roman History*, 2 vols. (Cambridge, 1978), 1:99, and Moses I. Finley, "Slavery," *International Encyclopedia of the Social Sciences* (New York, 1968), and *Ancient Slavery and Modern Ideology* (New York, 1980), 79–80.

79 Jordan, *White over Black: American Attitudes toward the Negro* (Chapel Hill, 1968), chaps. 1–6, traces the initial appearance of such notions among the transplanted English and their later triumph.

80 Quotations in Bruce. *Institutional History of Virginia in the Seventeenth Century*, 1:9, and Alexander Hewatt, *An Historical Account of the Rise and Progress of the Colonies of South Carolina and Georgia*, 2 vols. (London, 1779), 2:100.

81 Their story is told by Mullin, *Flight and Rebellion, and Africa in America*. On renaming see Berlin, *Slaves without Masters: The Free Negro in the Antebellum South* (New York, 1974), 51–52; Gary Nash, Forging Freedom: The Formation of Philadelphia's *Black Community, 1720–1840* (Cambridge, Mass., 1988), 79–88, and "Forging Freedom: The Emancipation Experience in the Northern Seaport Cities, 1775–1820," in Berlin and Hoffman, eds., *Slavery and Freedom in the Age of Revolution*, 20–27; and Cheryll Ann Cody, "Kin and Community among the Good Hope People after Emancipation," *Ethnohistory*, 41 (1994), 28–33.

82 Corbett, "Migration to a Spanish Imperial Frontier in the Seventeenth and Eighteenth Centuries," 420; Wilbur H. Siebett, "The Departure of the Spaniards and Other Groups from East Florida, 1763–1764," *Florida Historical Quarterly*, 19 (1940), 146; Robert L. Gold, "The Settlement of the East Florida Spaniards in Cuba, 1763–1766," ibid., 42 (1964), 216–17; Landers, "Gracia Real de Santa Teresa de Mose," 29. For the northward migration of free people of color from the Chesapeake region see Deal, *Race and Class in Colonial Virginia*, 188.

83 The accepted anthropological designation for the these communities is "tri-racial isolates." Scholars have traced their origins to Virginia and North Carolina in the 17th century and then their expansion into South Carolina, Kentucky, and Tennessee with various branches moving north and south. A recent survey by Virginia Easley DeMarce provides an excellent overview; "'Verry Slitly Mixt': Tri-Racial Isolate Families of the Upper South— A Genealogical Study," *National Genealogical Society Quarterly*, 80 (1992), 5–35.

84 Rachel N. Klein, *Unification of a Slave State: The Rise of the Planter Class in the South Carolina Backcountry, 1760–1808* (Chapel Hill, 1990), 18–21, 62–72.

85 For Johnson's whitening see Deal, *Race and Class in Colonial Virginia*, 258–69, esp. 277. See, for example, the case of Gideon Gibson, a mulatto slaveholder who during the mid-18th century was in the process of transforming himself from "black" to "white," in Jordan, *White over Black*, 171–74; Klein, *Unification of a Slave State*, 69–71; Robert L. Meriwether,

The Expansion of South Carolina, 1729–1765 (Kingsport, Tenn., 1940), 90, 96. As a group, free people of color were getting lighter in the Chesapeake during the late 17th century and into the 18th, perhaps as part of a conscious strategy of successful free men who married white women. See, for example, Deal, *Race and Class in Colonial Virginia*, 187, 276, n. 20, and Berlin, *Slaves without Masters*, 3–4.

86   Quotation from William W. Hening, comp., *The Statutes at Large Being a Collection of All the Laws of Virginia*, 13 vols. (Richmond, 1800–1823) 2:260; Warren M. Billings, "The Cases of Fernando and Elizabeth Key: A Note on the Status of Blacks in Seventeenth-Century Virginia," *WMQ*, 3d Ser., 30 (1973), 467–74; Billings, ed., *The Old Dominion in the Seventeenth Century: A Documentary History of Virginia, 1606–1689* (Chapel Hill, 1975), 165–69; David W. Galenson, "Economic Aspects of the Growth of Slavery in the Seventeenth-Century Chesapeake," in Solow, ed., *Slavery and the Rise of the Atlantic System*, 21; Fernow, ed., *Records of New Amsterdam*, 6:146, 286; Herbert L. Osgood, ed., *Minutes of the Common Council of the City of New York*, 8 vols. (New York, 1905), 1:134, 276–77; J. B. Lyon, ed., *Colonial Laws of New York from 1664 to the Revolution*, 5 vols. (Albany, 1894–1896), 1:356–57; Goodfriend, *Before the Melting Pot*, 120–21. After warning Domingo and Manuel Angola not to repeat their behavior, the court ordered them to communicate its admonition to "the other remaining free negroes"; ibid.

87   Goodfriend, *Before the Melting Pot*, 116–17; Nicholls, "Passing Through This Troublesome World," 50–53; Deal, "A Constricted World," 275–305; Breen and Innes, "*Myne Owne Ground*," chaps. 4–5.

88   Berlin, *Slaves without Masters*, 33–34; Shane White, *Somewhat More Independent The End of Slavery in New York City, 1770–1830* (Athens, Ga., 1991), 117–18; Nash and Jean R. Soderlund, *Freedom by Degrees: Emancipation in Pennsylvania and Its Aftermath* (New York, 1991), 115–36. Also see the papers of the Pennsylvania Society for Promoting the Abolition of Slavery (Historical Society of Pennsylvania), and the New York Manumission Society (New York Historical Society), for the upsurge of suits for freedom. For naming patterns within free black families that reached from the Revolutionary era back to the mid-17th century see Deal, *Race and Class in Colonial Virginia*, 342.

PART SIX

Slave Economy and Material Culture

THE ECONOMIES OF THE SLAVE COLONIES were determined in large
part by slave owners and their metropolitan backers. But beneath this rather
obvious generalisation lay an economic complexity which historians are in the
process of exploring. The most striking feature of the historiography of economic
life in the slave societies is not so much the debate about planters', slave traders'
or metropolitan profits, but the remarkable diversity and significance of the slave
economy.

Slaves everywhere engaged in independent economic activity which was, at
once, an important feature of broader social life and a crucial addition to their
own (often marginal) material well-being. Slaves improved their material lives by
work in their spare time, in gardens and plots, in cultivating foodstuffs and tending
livestock, and in capitalising on whatever skills or energies they were able to offer.
Slaves fed themselves, as Woodville Marshall explains in his essay (1991) on the
Windward Islands, from the fruits of their own labours. In the process, of course,
they helped to relieve planters of the burden. Such independent labour had enormous consequences for the development of independent economic and social life
among slaves, and later among freed slaves.

Hilary Beckles's essay (1991) concentrates on Barbados and argues that slave
hucksters became a cornerstone of local economic life while also helping to shape
an independent life for themselves. The habits of independent labour in the British
islands bred a culture of independence and self-sufficiency. More than that, as
Roderick McDonald illustrates in his piece (1991) on Louisiana, the culture of
independent labour, with rewards for the labourer and his family, rather than for
the owner, greatly enhanced the social as well as the economic lives of the slaves
involved.

The routes which slave produce and goods travelled to the consumer – the
simple movement of people from slave garden and plot to the point of purchase or
exchange – laid the foundation for local marketing systems. In the case of Jamaica,
illustrated in Sidney Mintz's classic essay (1974 edition), the world of independent
slave cultivation, and the marketing system which evolved to service that cultivation, established the foundations for the post-slave marketing system of the
nineteenth and twentieth centuries.

INTRODUCTION TO PART SIX

S LAVES INHABITED A WORLD partly shaped by their owners, but which
was improved and enhanced by the slaves' own efforts. It is no surprise to learn
that slaves' material lives were spartan. Their homes, their clothing, their immediate social environment and community, all were characterised by mean conditions:
by the feel and smell of poverty. And this was true whichever region of the Americas
we study. However, in time the slaves' material conditions improved and by the
time slave systems were ended, life for many slaves had improved markedly (if not
universally). Such improvements were derived, first, from slave-owners' efforts at
amelioration (from knowing that it made economic sense to care for their slaves)
but also from the slaves' own labours. There were, of course, enormous variations.
Some slaves seemed relatively well cared-for and materially comfortable while
others lived in material misery. Moreover, material comforts were shared unevenly
among slaves. More privileged slaves – skilled workers, favourites, domestics –
usually enjoyed better circumstances than their contemporaries toiling in the fields.
In time, however, as the sheer volume of goods disgorged by the material revolution of the seventeenth–nineteenth centuries increased, it was inevitable that items
once regarded as luxuries would pass into slave hands: clothing, household fixtures,
furnishings and a range of hand-me-downs, passing from white to black.

This world of slave material consumption is captured in any number of contemporary illustrations: drawings and sketches of slave life revealing slaves dressed in,
or enjoying, 'luxury' items on festivals and holidays, and of glimpses into their
homes. It is an image confirmed by the continuing work of archaeologists working
on slave sites and able to retrieve the range of goods which circulated in and around
the slave quarters.[1]

It is, however, worth repeating a point made elsewhere: that the millions of
Africans who stepped ashore in the Americas did so with virtually no material
possessions. Thus, the slaves' material culture was shaped entirely in the Americas,
though, obviously, it drew inspiration from African backgrounds and utilised goods
and artefacts acquired locally and from all corners of the globe. The story of slave
housing is a case in point. Early slave dwellings tended to be simple, communal
barracks (an obvious way to organise housing in frontier, pioneering conditions).
But the emergence of more settled communities, especially plantations, led to a
change in slaves' domestic arrangements. Slaves everywhere demanded more
private, more family-based living units. This was itself a clear indication of the
emergence of slave families and the associated need for domestic privacy. Slave
cabins and huts, generally built by the slaves and therefore incorporating a number
of African features, emerged in groups. These small clutches of buildings formed

the core of the wider slave community. Slaves' social lives developed around these homes; they generally cooked and gathered outdoors in the evenings after work. Such communal space, close to the home, became central to the social life of slaves across the Americas. The more stable the local economy, the more permanent were the slave homes. In regions where slaves were owned in small numbers, on tobacco properties or in towns, for example, slaves lived in outbuildings close to their owners/masters, at the back of the white home.

Slaves' domestic conditions varied enormously, according to their owners' well-being (or poverty), and the slaves' own status and skills. Slave owners quickly grasped the importance of allowing slaves a degree of privacy within their homes, and of allowing the heads of the family an element of authority inside that house-hold. The fact that slave homes often had locks on the doors clearly suggests the slaves' determination to safeguard their own possessions. Of course, such personal or family items were often little more than life's basic essentials: cooking and eating utensils, minimal clothing and bedding (often, though, not even a bed). Slave owners distributed eating and cooking utensils to slaves, normally by family grouping. Knives and cooking pots, like slave clothing, were imported, but other tools (sieves, graters, strainers, colanders) seem to have been home-made from pieces of metal and wire used in other parts of the property.[2]

Slaves with greater skills and status clearly enjoyed superior levels of material comfort and possessions. By the mid- to late eighteenth century, a range of European pottery had found its way into the slave quarters, in both North America and the Caribbean.[3] Eighteenth-century ceramics, imported from Britain, have been excavated from Montpelier plantation in Jamaica.[4] Gradually, slave homes began to contain more than life's basic essentials. We know, for example, that some slaves stole from other slaves, and that the stolen goods were not always basic essentials. One slave in Jamaica in the 1780s stole a clock from another slave.[5]

Pictures and contemporary descriptions of slaves at work tell us a great deal about slave dress. Slaves worked in the roughest and simplest of work clothes, the clothing generally provided by the slave owners. Plantation papers record the volumes of textiles (and hats) imported by plantations, some of it transshipped through Europe from Asia for distribution to the slaves. Imported textiles were often made up by slave seamstresses, or by women in the family groups (only women tended to be issued with sewing equipment), into basic clothing.[6] West Indian slaves were rarely given shoes, unlike their contemporaries in North America, where the colder winters required both warmer clothes and protection for the feet. Even this simple distribution of life's essentials revealed differences among the slaves. Skilled and high-status slaves received more and superior rations of clothing and food-stuffs than slaves lower down the slave hierarchy.[7] But work clothes inevitably remained basic and simple. Yet the basic, dull functionalism of slave clothing was sometimes brightened by individual changes in a slave's clothing. Slaves occasion-ally adorned their clothing with personal items – buttons, beads, patches and dyes.

This basic impression of slave dress – the clothing worn by slaves throughout the working day – is in sharp contrast to the image of slaves when they enjoyed themselves. Contemporary pictures show slaves elaborately dressed for their various festivals and moments of enjoyment at family celebrations, weekends, crop-over or Christian festivals. The simplicity of working life was set aside for an altogether more elaborate personal and communal lifestyle. When slaves enjoyed their holidays and breaks, alcohol, music and dance and gambling (in North America, horse-racing) all played major roles. All involved cost, and slaves spent money on more than life's essentials, on 'luxuries'. Clearly, not all slaves had the ability to enjoy such luxuries. But others, somehow, acquired the material wherewithal to enjoy themselves. This was reflected particularly in the elaborate clothing some of them wore on high days and holidays. Women dressed in eye-catching clothes and headware, highlighted by personal touches of strings of beads, buckles, bracelets, bangles, anklets, buttons and other colourful decorations. Slaves sought to create a more pleasing appearance, an aesthetic, in all forms of material culture from their domestic furnishings through to their personal appearance on special occasions. Slaves decorated their tableware and their homes with pictures and carvings. But the most notable slave efforts to create a pleasing aesthetic were undoubtedly in their dress and body adornment.[8]

This slave dressing-up reached remarkable heights at Christmas and New Year, with groups of West Indian slaves opting for particular coloured materials as they organised themselves into 'sets'. On such occasions, elaborate materials, colours, hats, coats, shoes and a variety of accoutrements characterised the slaves' public enjoyments. Many of these items were obviously acquired from slave owners and other whites. But, like much of the material culture of American slaves, a great deal was acquired by the slaves' own efforts. It was slave work, in their spare time, which enabled them to acquire their material possessions. But how were slaves able to do this?

Slaves everywhere made the most of whatever opportunities were afforded by the land, and by the skills and qualities they possessed. Slaves hunted and fished for food and pelts, for barter and trade. Food acquired in this way augmented foodstuffs supplied by masters. So too did the food grown on slave plots and in their gardens. In time a wide range of vegetables, fruits and crops was established across the slave societies, enhancing the local diet and mollifying slave feelings. From what we know of slave cooking utensils, these foodstuffs often ended in stews, part of a one-pot dish to serve the family group. Through all this, it seems clear enough that the slave diet was worse than that of their white contemporaries, but it is also true that it would have been worse still had slaves not become horticulturalists in their spare time on their own plots.[9] This also enabled slaves to become an important part of the domestic economy.

Slaves acquired money. We know that cash became common among slaves, though it obviously did not amount to substantial savings. Slaves bought and sold the animals they reared and the crops they grew. They were also sometimes paid for services rendered. Thomas Thistlewood often paid slave women for their services after his myriad sexual encounters. Exceptionally, certain slaves made large sums from major transactions, placing the cash in boxes left with trusted friends or associates for safety. Slaves who worked in towns were often paid in cash. On Worthy Park Plantation, the local planter sought to encourage slave reproduction by giving a dollar to each slave woman who gave birth in 1794.[10] Equiano – admittedly an exceptional slave – regularly saved cash when working at sea, keeping the money in his sea chest. Phibbah, another remarkable slave who lived in western Jamaica in the 1760s, sold a horse (to another slave) for £5.10 down, the outstanding amount to be paid in three months' time. More remarkably still, she gave her English lover a gold ring as a keepsake.[11] Thomas Thistlewood acted as executor for a slave's will which specified how the man's animals were to be distributed to other slaves.[12] Though slave owners frequently denounced their slaves as lazy, slaves displayed numerous signs of industry, application and even acquisitiveness, in their own time, and when working for themselves.

This slave energy could be seen in the columns of slaves heading for local markets or to the nearest town, with produce, animals and other items for sale. Thistlewood, again, told how, in September 1763, the road running past his property was filled 'with an abundance of Negroes', heading for the 'large Negro market by Tony's gate'.[13] Slaves — women especially — hawked their goods from door to door in towns. Some became specialist hawkers, selling only particular items, walking the streets of the major towns or ports, selling garden produce or food they had baked, or choosing their favourite spot on the street to sell their wares. They were sometimes encouraged by their owners, who wanted the consequent income earned by the slaves. Some slaves acted as the hawkers of their owners' produce.

Most contemporaries were agreed that slaves were best (i.e., most usefully) employed by working at staple production: by cultivating the sugar, tobacco or rice which formed the core of slave work throughout colonial America. Yet as local slave society matured, as the economies diversified, as money spread, and as local industries prospered and expanded, there were inevitable social and economic opportunities which slaves exploited, even at the humblest of levels, say of music-making or cooking.

There were obvious benefits which slaves acquired from these various economic activities, but this independent slave economy, which was clearly linked to the broader economy, brought much more than material benefits. Curiously, though, in many respects slave owners needed this slave autonomy, especially in the cultivation of foodstuffs. By feeding themselves or supplementing their food allowances, slaves saved their owners a great deal of money. More than that, slaves developed critical forms of independent social life which others, notably their owners, did not control. Here was an area of slave life which was beyond the reach of the slave owner. It also encouraged a degree of acquisitiveness among slaves, a feature which became more noticeable as ever more material artefacts began to move around the broader Atlantic economy. The slave colonies were, after all, an integral part of the Atlantic economy, producing goods primarily for Europe, in return for a vast range of imported European (and even Asian) goods. Many of those goods were imported for slave use, from tools and equipment through to clothing and tableware. Slaves clearly developed a taste for many of those items and even aspired to other items, notably the luxuries, which were imported (or sometimes produced locally) for their owners' homes and persons. Slaves were, like working people elsewhere, the recipients of hand-me-downs from their employers: clothes, shoes, decorations, household items. Slave owners who paraded their own possessions, and who sought to impress the outside world with their material successes, clearly impressed some of their slaves to the extent that they too wanted to join in.

This slave involvement in the consumer revolution of the eighteenth century may seem a marginal issue. Yet contemporaries were struck by the degree to which the habits of acquisitiveness had permeated the slave communities. Slaves wanted to improve themselves by the possession of personal items – clothing and household fittings, luxury decorations and finery to be displayed on holidays – by the accumulation of cash, of animals and produce. In an Atlantic world which, by the mid-eighteenth century, was changing markedly because of the rise of new forms of consumption, in both the domestic and civic spheres, it was inevitable that slaves would be drawn into such consumption. Slaves were naturally attracted to that range of material artefacts which proved so alluring to people on both sides of the Atlantic[14] Some thought that this urge to acquisitiveness among slaves would act as a 'civilising' force.[15]

The slave economy, the slaves' economic activities in their own time and in their own interests, was the foundation on which a much broader independent slave culture was built. Yet even here, in an apparent sphere of independent activity, slaves could not sever their links to the slave system that ensnared them. Though slave owners came to respect the conventions of slave independence (allowing slaves free time on certain days or at particular periods), such conventions were granted on the strict understanding that slaves returned to their chores and routines, at their owners' behest, when their free time ended. It was a pattern of obligation and freedom which paralleled the social conventions of pre-modern *chiavari*: of governing and propertied orders allowing their inferiors to turn the world upside-down, briefly, for particular festivals, on the understanding that mundane reality was instantly restored. Thus, the slaves who paraded in their most colourful finery for those prolonged bouts of communal pleasure, of music and drink, or for the more sober displays of Christian devotion in the Christianised slave societies, slipped back to work the day after in their drab and ragged working apparel. Frederick Douglass, for one, did not like what he saw. 'So, when the holidays ended, we staggered up from the filth of our wallowing, took a long breath, and marched to the field, feeling, upon the whole, rather glad to go.'[16]

Yet slaves also made their lives more acceptable, sometimes more comfortable and certainly more pleasurable in the time and freedom they secured away from their owners' demands. Slaves everywhere were filled with a deep-seated antipathy to the world of slavery they inhabited. The world of slave independent culture and economy may have provided, for brief moments, an antidote to the woes of slavery, but the fundamental grievances always remained.

Notes

1   Anne Elizabeth Yentsch, *A Chesapeake Family and Their Slaves: A Study in Historical Archaeology*, Cambridge, 1994; B.W. Higman, *Montpelier, Jamaica: A Plantation in Slavery and Freedom, 1739–1912*, Kingston, 1998.
2   B.W. Higman, *Montpelier*, pp. 216–221.
3   Philip D. Morgan, *Slave Counterpoint*, Chapel Hill, 1998, p. 115; Bryan Edwards, *The History, Civil and Commercial, of the British Colonies in the West Indies*, 3 vols, 3rd edn, London, 1801, II, p. 165.
4   B.W. Higman, *Montpelier*, p. 224.
5   National Library of Jamaica, *Slave Trials*, St Ann, Jamaica, 29 August 1788.
6   See Higman, *Montpellier*, pp. 229–233.
7   See the distribution of provisions, listed in *Worthy Park Plantation Book, 1787–1792*, Jamaica Archives, Spanishtown, Jamaica.

8   B.W. Higman, *Montpelier*, pp. 244–257.

9   Philip D. Morgan, *Slave Counterpoint*, pp. 139–145.

10 Michael Craton and James Walvin, *A Jamaican Plantation: Worthy Park, 1670–1970*, London, 1970, pp. 140–141.

11 D.G. Hall, ed., *In Miserable Slavery: Thomas Thistlewood in Jamaica, 1750–1786*, London, 1989, pp. 94, 79, 80.

12 Ibid., p. 83.

13 Ibid., p. 60.

14 See essays in John Brewer and Roy Porter, eds, *Consumption and the World of Goods*, London, 1993.

15 Bryan Edwards, *The History, Civil and Commercial*, III, p. 283.

16 *Narrative of the Life of Frederick Douglass, an American Slave*, Boston, 1845 edn, p. 76.

Chapter 21

Woodville K. Marshall

PROVISION GROUND AND PLANTATION LABOUR IN FOUR WINDWARD ISLANDS
Competition for resources during slavery

THE ROLE OF THE PROVISION ground and internal marketing system in the context of plantation slavery has been a subject of increased interest during the last generation. Recent findings have greatly enriched comprehension of slave subsistence patterns, internal markets, the slaves' 'proto-peasant' activities, and even the quality of the slaves' diet.[1] However, no scholar has yet provided a full description of the provision-ground system, and only Sidney Mintz has attempted to link slaves' proto-peasant activities with post-slavery developments.[2]

A description and analysis of the provision-ground system in the four Windward Islands of Grenada, St Lucia, St Vincent and Tobago during the last 50 years of slavery offer insight into these large subjects. Three tentative conclusions are reached: first, echoing Mintz, that the provision-ground and internal marketing system provided an extensive stage, as in Jamaica, for slaves' participation in independent activities; second, that the slaves' attempts to exploit the potential of these activities inevitably created intense competition between themselves and plantation owners and managers for labour services and land resources;[3] third, that slaves' success in creating and defending corners of independent existence fostered the growth of attitudes to plantation labour and to independent activities which affected labour relations in the post-slavery period.[4]

The four Windward Islands were, like Jamaica, 'home fed' colonies.[5] Most of the slaves subsisted not on rations of imported or locally grown food but on the produce of own-account cultivation of provision grounds, supplemented by weekly allowances of salt provisions – mackerel, cod, shad, or herring – provided by their owners. In emergencies caused by flood and drought or depletion of soil of the provision grounds, masters were usually expected (and often compelled by law) to supply weekly food rations of imported foodstuffs (grains, cornmeal or plantains), the amounts of which were not specified until the amelioration of slavery in the 1820s.[6] This pattern of slave feeding was firmly in place in Grenada, St Vincent, and Tobago by 1790; witnesses before the parliamentary committee said it was 'universally the custom'.[7]

However, the four Windwards adopted provision-ground system at different times, reflecting the differential rates of conversion to full slave-plantation economies. In general, it would appear that the first stage of plantation establishment (as well as the seasoning of all slaves) involved the feeding of slaves from rations of either imported food or a combination of imported food and ground provisions produced by gang labour. When land for the staples was cleared and planted, the provision-ground system took root, and continued to co-exist with other methods of slave feeding. In Grenada, where the plantation economy was well established by the 1750s, the provision-ground system was being subjected to legal regulation by 1766, suggesting that law was catching up with practice.[8] From St Vincent, where the plantation was established after 1763, the governor, James Seton, indicated that by 1789 the provision-ground system was the dominant method of slave feeding among others.[9] In both Tobago and St Lucia, where full plantation exploitation was constrained by frequent exchanges of ownership between England and France, the remnants of the original method of slave feeding could be found in slave laws as late as 1794 for Tobago and 1825 for St Lucia. In both cases the law directed planters to produce a quantity of provisions by gang labour in a fixed proportion to their slave population.[10]

Several factors influenced the adoption of the system. First, as Mintz points out, slaveowners had an obvious interest in maximizing 'their returns from the slave labour' in a situation where the demand for slave labour was not constant all year round and where the cost of imported provisions represented a significant and regular outlay of capital.[11] Planter witnesses before the parliamentary committees of 1789–91 often linked the existence of provision grounds to reduced importation of foodstuffs, indicating that they were aware of the savings they had achieved.[12] Second, such savings became most important during the crisis of slave subsistence between 1776 and 1783, and again between 1794 and 1815. Wars and the effects of wars on established trading arrangements triggered a steep rise in the price of imported food, caused malnutrition and starvation, increased slave mortality, and forced planters to allocate more estate land to the production of food supplies.[13] Provision grounds therefore saved money and reduced the planters' risks.[14]

Third, slaves' preference for provision grounds also merged with masters' self-interest. For slaves, the advantages of a more secure and plentiful food supply, cash from the sale of surpluses and periods of unsupervised activity were apparent. Indeed, slaves may have taken the initiative in modifying the patterns of feeding on some estates. In 1789 Ashton Warner Byam, a leading judicial official in Grenada and a proprietor in St Vincent, told the parliamentary committee that when his slaves had made complete provision grounds for themselves '*they of their own accord offered to me that if I would give them the Saturday afternoon, out of crop time, they would require nothing but salt provisions from me*'.[15] Such an expressed preference enabled masters to perceive quickly the value of provision grounds as a mechanism for control. One year later Alexander Campbell, one of the leading proprietors in Grenada, observed that it was 'the custom' in Grenada to grant slaves as much land as they could work because it had been 'universally considered the greatest benefit to a planter that his Negroes should have a sufficient quantity of provisions, and the more money the Negroes got for themselves, the more attached they were to the property'.[16]

The topography of the Windwards was perhaps the most important factor in the planters' adoption and the slaves' consolidation of the provision-ground system. Grenada, St Vincent, and St Lucia were mountainous and Tobago at least hilly; all possessed wooded, mountainous interiors which restricted settlement to the coasts and coral lowlands, to the volcanic foothills, and to well-watered valleys leading to the sea.[17] The plantations, usually located in shore-facing valleys, often possessed land which ran into the foothills and 'new ground' or 'mountain runs' that were marginal or unsuited to sugar or other staple cultivation.[18] Lowland plantations, which were not so well endowed, often possessed 'little vacant spots' on which, as David Collins, a St Vincent physician, said, slaves were permitted to cultivate on their own account.[19] In those few cases where these vacant spots proved inadequate planters purchased mountain land 'for the purpose of negro ground'.[20] Allocation of this type of land for provision cultivation was sometimes justified by the disingenuous argument that 'these broken and steep places' did 'answer very well for provisions'.[21] But this inversion of the laws of husbandry could neither fully deflect criticism of the adequacy of slave feeding methods nor obscure the fact that planters recognized that such an allocation advanced their vital interests in low production costs and social control.

Provision grounds could consist of three different types of land allowance – yam grounds, gardens and mountain land or mountain ground. Yam grounds, apparently distributed only in St Vincent as customary allowances, may have been a remnant of earlier slave feeding methods, which featured provision production by gang labour. These grounds were small portions, not exceeding 40 square feet, of cane land being prepared for planting. Allotments were distributed to slaves on a declining scale according to age, and on these allotments slaves were expected to raise a yam crop before the new cane crop was planted. The allowance therefore served a dual purpose. It increased the slave's subsistence by assuring him of 'a fair crop' out of the cultivation of good land and it reduced the planter's labour costs by providing him with a 'clean and ameliorated surface to plant first crop canes'.[22]

Gardens, which can be confused with provision grounds because contemporaries sometimes used the terms interchangeably, were in the main not a land allowance at all.[23] In general, slaves created gardens from the land surrounding their houses, but sometimes garden allotments were provided by planters as partial substitutes for provision grounds. In Grenada, a 1788 law directed planters, who were prevented by the nature of soil or the 'particular situation' of estates from providing provision grounds, to allot each adult slave at least one-fortieth of an acre 'contiguous to the Negro Houses for the purpose of cultivating gardens for their sole use and benefit'.[24]

Sketchy and contradictory contemporary comment makes difficult any assessment of the size, exploitation and value of these gardens. Mrs Carmichael, the wife of a West Indian planter, and John Bowen Colthurst, a special magistrate on St Vincent, both of whom seemed intent on proving that slaves and apprentices were 'plentifully maintained' by their own-account activities, described the St Vincent gardens as of 'a very comfortable size'. For them, the gardens offered space for raising poultry and small stock and for cultivating tree crops, vines and vegetables, which could meet the short-term food needs of the cultivators.[25] Another observer, John Anderson, noted that these gardens were generally neglected and unappreciated.[26] The point turns, no doubt, on the size and quality of this land. Since broken ground of the estate would most likely be the site planters preferred for slave villages, as abolitionist James Stephen argued, the garden's main utility would be to provide yards and passages between houses.[27] Gardens, therefore, had value to the extent that they contained conveniently located space for raising small stock and poultry.

Mountain ground was the characteristic provision ground, and its location created problems for optimal cultivation. Distance between the grounds and slaves' residences was one problem. No direct information exists on the distance slaves had to walk to their grounds, but the inference may be drawn from various estate papers, slave codes and local abolition acts that it was often 'considerable', probably as much as ten miles.[28] Such distances posed problems for the most efficient use of labour time and for the security of growing crops. Time consumed in a long trek to and from provision grounds meant loss of labour and under-exploitation of the grounds; distant residence from growing crops also reduced the possibility of effective policing and increased the risk of theft.

More important, difficulties with mountain grounds arose from the natural constraints on cultivation which such a location imposed. As the name suggests, such land was mainly forest and mountain: difficult of access because of steep slopes, difficult to clear because of virgin forests, difficult to cultivate because of boulders and stones, and impossible to protect against threats of land slippage and erosion. No doubt, as John Bowen Colthurst suggested, some provision grounds were established in 'deep rocky glens' containing some of the richest deposits of soil in St Vincent, but the search for these locations could consume valuable time.[29] Moreover, success in the search might compound the problem of inconvenient distance from residence.

Planters apparently cared little about the selection of the actual location of provision grounds. Only two contemporary commentators suggest that any criteria were applied in its selection. James Baillie, proprietor of estates in Grenada and St Vincent, allotted 50 acres of 'the most valuable seasonable part' of his Grenada estate for provision grounds; Sir William Young 'set apart' 46 acres of 'the richest ground' on his St Vincent estate for 'the negro gardens'.[30] Those planters who possessed mountain runs, which automatically recommended themselves as provision grounds; seem to have left the exact locations to drivers and field slaves. The viability of the soil for provision grounds did not have to be pre-tested because of the presumed fitness of the land for the purpose. It was the slaves' responsibility to check its possibilities, identify its deficiencies, and indicate when new ground was required.[31] On lowland and smaller estates inattention could not be the rule. Choices had to be made: how much land could be spared, whether gardens should substitute for provision grounds, and whether a specific quantity and quality of mountain land should be leased. No doubt planters in general paid more attention to the distribution of individual lots, but that attention was probably misplaced because the location of the ground could determine the adequacy of the provisions to be derived from the individual lot.

The law did not define the size of the individual allotments until the last years of slavery. Late eighteenth-century legislation in Grenada directed that adult slaves (over 14 years) should receive 'his or her proper ground', but the assessment of its size and adequacy for maintenance was left to a loose inspection procedure controlled by planters themselves.[32] In the 1820s, under abolitionist pressure for greater precision, 'a sufficient portion of land adapted to the growth of provisions' was stipulated and the size of allotment was fixed at one-quarter acre for adult slaves in Grenada and Tobago.[33] The greatest precision and most liberal provisions were achieved in St Lucia: land *properly* adapted for provision cultivation and a half acre in size became the legal requirement.[34] This was a consequence of the island's constitutional position; direct British rule made possible by Crown Colony status prevented planters from obstructing the will of the British government to an extent that was impossible in the other islands. The local abolition legislation generally echoed these provisions, though the Tobago legislature found it 'desirable' to follow St Lucia's example and increase the size of the allotment to a half acre for adult slaves.[35] Only in St Vincent did vagueness about the allowance persist until the end of slavery. On St Vincent the local abolition act defined the size of the acreage and its quality in negative terms: the 'sufficient portion' of provision ground would be 'deemed adequate and proper for maintenance and support of every praedial apprentice *unless good and sufficient cause be shown to the contrary*'.[36]

Customary practices undoubtedly influenced the legal definition of the allowance. Some planters, eager to exonerate themselves from charges of underfeeding their slaves, loosely suggested that the islands' topographical variety ensured that slaves had access to 'great quantity' of ground and to 'considerable tracts' which they cultivated 'for their own benefit'.[37] It is probable that planters recognized that a restrictive policy could be self-defeating; they could hardly spare the resources of personnel and time to enforce it. In any event, they could resume possession or restrict the size of the allotment whenever the imperatives of plantation expansion or slave discipline warranted. Moreover, the brute fact remained that the size of the allotment was effectively limited by its location, the quality of its soil, the available labour time and the labour requirements of the particular cultigens.[38] Therefore, the amount of land that individual slaves managed to cultivate was probably no more than a quarter acre. In 1790 Alexander Campbell told the parliamentary committee that the provision-ground allowance in Grenada was never less than one acre for a family of six; two years later Sir William Young reported that each household on his St Vincent estate had access to about half an acre; and John Bowen Colthurst suggested that a slave family in St Vincent may have had access to a maximum of two acres during the 1830s.[39]

Throughout the slave period, the time allowed for slaves to cultivate provision grounds was both minimal and seasonal. Before the 1820s it amounted to between 14 and 19 working days which could be utilized only 'out of crop' when the sugar canes had been reaped. After April or May the designated time, usually Saturday, was then doled out on the basis of a half day weekly or a full day fortnightly. Planters expected, as various witnesses explained to the parliamentary committees in 1790, that slaves would supplement the allowance by their 'spare hours' – the afternoon rest period, after sunset out of crop, on Sundays and in the three-day holiday at Christmas.[40] This allocation and schedule reflected planters' prejudices and priorities. According to Alexander Campbell, 'very little labour' was required for planting and weeding the provision ground; therefore 'the Negroes need not work half of the time allowed them in their gardens'. Further, because provisions could not be planted before the rains in May and June slaves had 'no occasion to work in their gardens, but out of crop-time'.[41] In brief, planters did not intend for their production schedule to be affected by any inconvenient dispersal of the labour force. Mrs Carmichael declared that 'no sugar could be made on Friday, Saturday or Monday', if labour time was granted during the grinding season: 'the sugar made on Friday must be potted on the following morning, and canes cut on Friday would be sour by Monday morning'.[42]

Abolitionist pressure forced a roughly 50 per cent increase in the allowance during the 1820s – from 14 and 19 days to between 26 and 35 days. But, while 'full working days' were substituted for the optional weekly half-day, the seasonal stipulation was retained.[43] Little alteration occurred during the apprenticeship period, the final phase of slavery. The seasonal stipulation was dropped in Grenada, St Vincent, and St Lucia, but in Tobago the allowance was reduced from 35 to 14 full working days and the seasonal restriction on the use of the allowance was extended to six months – July to December.[44]

Slaveowners did not supervise or assist slaves in the cultivation of provision grounds. Planters, as individuals or as official 'guardians', had responsibility for providing land enough for the slaves' maintenance.[45] But that responsibility was discharged in perfunctory fashion. Planters did lay out ground and distribute lots to individuals and families, but they paid little or no attention to the precise location of lots and seldom bothered to demarcate their boundaries clearly.[46] Although some planters probably sent their gangs to assist in the heavy work of clearing forests for the establishment of provision grounds, the main business of clearing and preparation of the ground was left to the slaves themselves.[47] Planters needed to be satisfied that provision grounds were productive if only to ensure that their gangs would be fit for labour and that plantation stores and fields would not be raided for food. Their interest in the slaves' practices of husbandry was excited only to the extent that slaves broke the prohibition against cultivation of staple crops or created fire hazards for central plantation property by 'slash and burn' methods of cultivation.[48] As a result, planters seldom inspected the grounds to check on the state of cultivation or the fertility of the soil and slaves were left to indicate when soil was depleted and new ground required.[49] Plantation supervisory staff probably mustered slaves for provision-ground duty on Saturday afternoons and on Sundays, but that action was probably more a police exercise against the threats of desertion and malingering than a deliberate effort to ensure the adequacy of slave maintenance. Planters, in spite of Dr Collins' advice to the contrary, apparently offered little or no assistance to slaves in regard to supplies of plants and seeds, information about crop selection, rotation and preservation, or protection of crops against theft.[50] Therefore, slaves were generally forced to rely on their own scanty resources. How they coped with institutionalized neglect was illustrated by John Jeremie, president of the Royal Court in St Lucia in 1825. Jeremie found that the slaves on St Lucia were 'extremely careful of their provision grounds', cultivating them 'with assiduity' and guarding them 'night and day', that they 'never forgive a theft on them', and that 'nothing is more likely to keep them at home than the cultivating of their gardens'.[51]

Slaves' choice of crops reflected the pressure and circumstances which created and sustained the provision-ground system. The main staples of the slave diet were dominated by root crops and starches (yams, eddoes, cassava, sweet potatoes), tree crops (plantain, banana and breadfruit), and grains and legumes (Indian and Guinea corn, many varieties of peas and beans).[52] In addition, slaves produced some vegetables and fruit. Dietary preference was one element in the slaves' choice, as the yam and plantain, traditional staples of the West African diet, were 'a favorite and good food', or 'what the potato is to the lower classes in Britain'.[53] Quality of soil was another determinant. Cassava, arrowroot, peas and vines could subsist in poor soil, therefore occupied land that was perceived as unfit for staple crop cultivation.

Restricted labour time both determined the amount of land that could be culti-vated and constrained the choice of crop. Slaves preferred crops that did not require close and constant attention, such as high-yield crops like plantains and bananas that quickly propagated themselves. Not surprisingly, the yam and sweet potato, whose growth inhibited weeds, were featured in the slaves' crop regime. Moreover, most slaves raised a variety of small stock in their gardens and backyards and exploited the fishing resources of the islands' rivers.[54]

The produce of the provision ground and yard or garden formed the basis for an expanding local market. In the Windward islands eighteenth-century slave laws show that those markets, as in Jamaica, made their appearance early in the life of the plantations. Legislation, which had as its rationale the discouragement of theft, also sought to outlaw door-to-door peddling by slaves, to reduce marketing by slaves through enforcement of the pass laws and to prohibit the trading of cattle, plantation staples, precious metals and jewellery by slaves entirely. But these prohibitions themselves confirm the existence of unsupervised marketing by slaves. Moreover, the marketing of 'logs of wood, firewood, fresh fish and dunghill fowls, goats, hogs, and vegetables of any sort' by slaves was not interdicted.[55] This division in the productive function provided unintended incentives for slaves to produce and trade surpluses. By 1790 planters pointed to the slaves' virtual monopoly of the internal markets for locally produced food, firewood and charcoal, and fodder. Urban dwellers purchased much of their food from slaves and the planters them-selves depended on slaves for the greater part of their supply of poultry and fresh meat.[56] 'A few poultry and crops', Alexander Campbell observed, 'were raised by the proprietors, about their homes, but their chief consumption is bought of the slaves'.[57] By the end of slavery this 'breach' in the slave system was virtually complete: while the restriction on the trade in plantation produce was retained, slave participation in the internal markets was officially recognized by the formal concession of the slaves' right to attend market on a designated day, and slaves were openly protesting the choice of market day and the organization of markets. Customary arrangements had overturned legal restrictions, and what had grown outside the law had become recognized in law.[58]

Scattered evidence suggests that produce grown by plantation slaves animated elaborate urban markets in the Windward Islands.[59] Slave supply and urban demand stimulated commodity exchange and increased slaves' purchasing power. This in turn sustained an expanding distributive network linking slave producers to free and slave consumers, plantation to town, and slave to market. Plantation slaves, mainly women, marketed produce, either utilizing hucksters as intermediaries or selling in the markets on their own account. Itinerant traders, usually coloured slaves and freed persons, based in town or on the plantations, hawked dry goods around the countryside, tapping the savings of slaves or bartering their 'finery' for the slaves' produce. Urban slave hucksters, operating either as slave hirelings or as agents for their owners, sometimes functioned as retailers of the plantation slaves' produce and were a steady source of the small items needed by plantation slaves. Merchants and shopkeepers furnished imported goods which increasing purchasing power brought within the reach of plantation slaves. Towns were central to this network – as sites of the main markets, as the main source of demand for slaves' produce and as mercantile and financial centres. Slaves thus heightened the scale of urban activity in commodity exchange and increased employment and accumulation in internal markets.

Competition for market shares between small and large urban operators and between urban retailers and rural producers was a natural consequence of this expanding market. Barry Higman demonstrates that *free* merchants and shopkeepers sought to confine *slave* hucksters to the sale of locally produced goods. For example, in 1815 hucksters selling bread about the streets of St George's, the capital of Grenada, had to be licensed.[60] For similar reasons, urban traders strongly supported the closure of Sunday markets, since they too perceived that their abolition would increase their own market share. Slave producers often did their retailing in the Sunday market, selling in the central market or in the street, effectively eliminating the urban middlemen. After 1823, when the British government, in response to abolitionist pressure, ended or curtailed Sunday markets as a means of ameliorating the slaves' moral and material condition, it received strong support from urban traders. These traders reasoned that the abolition of Sunday markets would reduce competition offered by rural retailers on that day. Moreover, the substitution of a weekday as the new market day would strengthen their position in the exchange of slave produce, because the change of market day would disrupt the slaves' traditional commercial routine and deprive them of access to the large volume of business that was transacted on a weekend. Events on Grenada illustrate how this advantage was exploited. After 1828 hucksters in St George's engrossed the produce brought into town by the rural slaves on Thursday, the new official market day, and then retailed it at inflated prices.[61]

The slaves' reaction to the formal abolition of the Sunday markets reveals the extent to which they competed with free traders and perceived the effect on their own interests of a disturbance of traditional arrangements. By 1825 market day had been switched in Grenada and Tobago to Thursday and to Saturday in St Lucia, while in St Vincent the main market in the capital, Kingstown, was closed from ten on Sunday mornings. But four years later the governor of St Vincent ruefully reported that he was issuing 'the most peremptory orders' to the Clerk of Market and to the Chief Constable 'to carry the law into complete effect'.[62] In St Lucia, in 1831, marketing on Sunday was still outlawed, but the governor was being directed by the Colonial Office to 'appoint' a market day, even though the Legislative Council had recently switched the market from Saturday to Monday.[63] Slave resistance in the form of complaint and open defiance to such changes explains the gap between legislative enactment and implementation. In Grenada slaves greeted the change in the market day with 'much dissatisfaction'.[64] In St Vincent the governor admitted that 'nothing but absolute force' would shift slaves 'from a long customary enjoyment (as it is estimated by them) of marketing on Sunday'. Slaves had indicated that they thought 'the abolition of this privilege' constituted 'one of the greatest hardships imposed on them'. The governor was fully alive to the economic implications of the switch in the market day, in that prices of provisions also were increased 'to the great injury of domestics and other slaves in Kingstown, who rely upon the market for subsistence'. Therefore he concluded that the moral issue was likely to lose out to the economic: 'until the Negroes shall have acquired a sufficient degree of religion to induce them to observe the Sabbath from a principle of morality, they will not give up their habits of trafficking on Sundays'.[65]

The imprecision of available evidence makes it difficult to assess the slaves' material gains from provision grounds. Most contemporary observers, planter and official alike, suggested that the annual returns were substantial enough to provide 'comparative wealth', 'an approach to real comfort' and that accumulation did take place.[66] Witnesses before the parliamentary committees of 1789–91 estimated the slaves' annual earnings at £6 to £20, with 'industrious' slaves on fertile soil earning as much as £30 to £40.[67] James Baillie, a Grenada planter, claimed that some slaves on his estate possessed property 'worth forty, fifty, one hundred and even, as far as two hundred pounds sterling' and that such property was 'regularly conveyed from one generation to another, without any interference whatever'.[68] Alexander Campbell, impressed with the slaves' 'fine clothes' and lavish 'entertainments', concluded that *'one half of the current specie'* in the ceded islands (Dominica, Grenada, St Vincent, and Tobago) *'is the property of the Negroes'*.[69] Later commentators, like Mrs Carmichael and John Bowen Colthurst, echoed these sentiments. For Mrs Carmichael, any St Vincent slave could earn £30 annually, 'and very many may save much more'.[70] For Colthurst, the returns were less ample – £2.10 for any family and £7.10 for the 'industrious' family.[71] For both of them, however, each element of the slaves' domestic economy brought material benefit and possibilities for accumulation. Provision-ground and garden produce fed slaves and stock; surplus produce was exchanged for dietary supplements, for 'finery' and for the 'little articles' like candles, soap and tobacco; small stock and poultry were marketed for cash which was saved or employed in the purchase of small luxuries. Therefore, according to Mrs Carmichael and Colthurst, some slaves saved 'large sums', as much as £100 or £150.[72]

The accuracy of these estimates and the conclusions they underpin must be queried for at least three reasons. First, these observers were partisans of one stripe or another. Witnesses before the parliamentary committees of 1789–91 were, like Sir William Young and Mrs Carmichael, apologists for slavery. Colthurst, a self-proclaimed abolitionist, was perhaps eager to inflate the significance of evidence that slaves had adopted capitalistic values and had therefore vindicated all that their supporters hoped of them.[73] Second, the claims took little account of the disparities in quality and size of provision grounds and of the capacity (or industry) of the slaves to exploit them. Most observers did qualify their more liberal estimates by linking them to the performance of 'industrious' slaves. But, as Dr Collins and James Stephen suggested, the terms 'industrious slave' and 'bad' and 'lazy' slave carried special connotations.[74] The apparently ample returns of the industrious slave might relate as much to the quality of the land and to the availability of labour for its cultivation as to the drive and determination of the slave. Similarly, the poor returns achieved by lazy slaves who, by the estimate of the Chief Justice of St Vincent, constituted the bulk of the slave population, might have been a consequence of depleted soils, debility induced by malnutrition, hunger and overwork, or a simple lack of interest. Third, the planter's evidence was internally inconsistent, if not contradictory. On the one hand they pointed to an 'abundance' of provisions, to well-stocked internal markets, 'dimity jackets' and 'muslins', furniture and substantial savings; on the other hand they asserted that slaves 'in general are subject to thieving' and accepted that there was a correlation between the incidence of theft and the adequacy of slaves' nutrition.[75] 'All the estates', Alexander Campbell claimed, 'are obliged to keep guards on the Negro provision gardens and to guard the cattle pens, storehouses, and rum cellars'.[76] Finally, these sanguine conclusions overlooked the extreme vulnerability of the provision-ground sector of the economy. Provision grounds had no defence against drought or flood: crops burned in drought and floods washed away the mountain ground. In Grenada, after the 1831 hurricane, hunger drove slaves on the Lataste estate to eat unripe provisions, which made them ill, forcing them to rely on their masters for rations of expensive imported grain. Eventually the slaves had to re-establish provision grounds on new land.[77] Provision grounds thus may have provided slaves with a more secure source of nutrition and some, but not all, slaves were hardy enough to cope with the competing labour demands of plantations and provision ground and could therefore create opportunities for the improvement of their standard of living.[78]

The participation of slaves in provision-ground cultivation and marketing exposed, as Mintz has often pointed out, the contradiction and inconsistencies of the slave regime.[79] Slaves cultivated land and disposed of its produce without supervision from their owners. Slaves worked their provision grounds in family groups. Slaves selected crops and determined the methods of cultivation, the extent of provision saving and cash accumulation. They did so, moreover, with an energy and enthusiasm that sharply contrasted with their work habits and low productivity in gang labour plantation export staples.

Slave families in 'the constant occupation' of provision ground forced their owners to recognize rights of occupancy to portions of plantation ground.[80] Slaves would not move from their ground without notice or without replacement grounds being provided, and they could bequeath rights of occupancy as well as property.[81] The increasing ability of slaves to produce marketable food surpluses and to consume imported goods created and sustained markets, and their involvement in those markets eventually secured a legal right of participation.

These achievements were particularly remarkable because they were secured mainly by the slaves themselves. Their owners contributed land and grudgingly donated small portions of the slaves' labour time, but they did not intend or expect more from the provision-ground system than a reduction in the cost of slave maintenance. In extending proto-peasant activity, slaves often had to cope with planter hostility; the best that they could hope for was the unintended complicity of indifference. Therefore, while it may be possible to accept Bryan Edwards' 'coalition of interests' in the elaboration of the plantation complex, it is difficult to see how it was a 'happy' arrangement. Rather, its existence involved a barely disguised persistent and unequal competition for resources.

The competition was predicated upon, on the one hand, the slaves' perception that provision-ground cultivation and marketing offered a partial escape from the hard and long routine of supervised plantation labour, and, on the other hand, their recognition of the ever-present limitations on their ability to exploit this means of escape fully. The demand for regular plantation labour naturally deprived them of the time and energy to optimize the material and psychological returns from provision cultivation and marketing. The prime limiting factor was, of course, slavery itself. But, if most slaves were seldom disposed towards suicidal confrontation with their owners and overseers, then resistance took the form of continuous efforts to explore and exploit what little the social system offered – to cope with slavery, not by direct confrontation, but by attempts to make lives of their own.[82]

Resistance therefore may have been subsumed under a competition and scramble for land and labour resources.

Competition for land did not usually involve claims to larger portions of plantation ground. Rather competition revolved around the quality of land allotted to slaves, the distance of that land from slaves' residences, and rights of occupancy to that land. In 1831 a confrontation between slaves and the manager-attorney on the Lataste estate in Grenada – which may be regarded as a form of industrial action – provides an excellent view of that competition. On that estate the slaves' provision ground was mountain land, but its occupancy had been rendered insecure by the dismissed attorney, William Houston, 'who made no scruple at saying he would turn them away from those grounds at ten days' warning'. In June 1831 the provision grounds were badly damaged by floods spawned by a hurricane. By September the slaves faced starvation, and they indicated that they were 'quite dissatisfied' with the quality and location of their provision grounds, that they were 'anxious to get a new piece of land' and were cultivating the damaged grounds with 'reluctance'. In response, the manager-attorney admitted the validity of the complaints – 'the land is poor and is now run out' – and, though he chided the slaves for murmuring at 'the will of the Almighty', he quickly sought replacement ground. By late September he had succeeded in leasing 'a piece of excellent new land for the Negroes', which was two miles nearer the estate than the old ground and with which the slaves seemed 'well pleased'.[83] Slaves had invoked their customary rights, and the manager-attorney had recognized the policy of satisfying them.

Essentially, slaves wanted what they did not control but what was within their masters' power to concede: adequate maintenance to be provided by provision grounds with good soil in a convenient location, and full rights to crops through secure occupancy of grounds. Laws designed to guarantee them minimal levels of maintenance – the periodic inspection of provision grounds – were a dead letter. Slaves thus took it upon themselves to remind their masters that inadequate maintenance would be met with theft, desertion and even insurrection. Their tactics included persistent complaint, 'reluctance' (the go-slow), and desertion, perhaps in that order. The most commonly used tactic, however, was self-help. Some slaves took advantage of the negligible restrictions on the appropriation of land for provision ground by scouring the mountains and high valleys for suitable provision ground. Therefore, what John Bowen Colthurst saw as the indulging of a 'wandering propensity' was often the exercise of initiative, the far-ranging search for the adequate maintenance that masters failed to provide.[84]

Available evidence does not indicate the effectiveness of any of these tactics. However, inferences may be drawn from two developments. First, slaves consolidated the provision grounds and marketing complex, and this required rising production and, perhaps, productivity of provision grounds. Therefore the slaves' success may have forced planters to respond to their statements of grievance. Second, legislation near the end of slavery (usually in the local abolition acts) promised improvement in levels of maintenance. This was mainly the achievement of the abolitionists, and of James Stephen in particular. In 1824 his monumental work, *The Slavery of the British West India Colonies Delineated*, dissected as never before the practices of the slave system. But the story Stephen told was the story of the plight and struggle of West Indian slaves; so, to the extent that Stephen's work stimulated reform, the slaves' actions must be held partly responsible for the amelioration of their own condition.

Scramble for labour services was probably more intense than the competition for land, because labour was the slaves' scarcest resource. Supervised plantation labour normally occupied 55 hours in a six-day week. It left little for slaves themselves; the portion they controlled was small and intermittent and might be reduced without notice by demands from their masters for extra duty or other chores on a Sunday.[85] Yet slaves were faced with competing claims on their time – recuperation from the plantation routine, provision-ground cultivation, marketing, and leisure time activities. If slaves gave priority to one claim, the effect on maintenance or health could be disastrous. Sickness or distance from provision grounds or markets could aggravate the situation. Therefore the slaves' existence must have been hectic and full of frustrations; it required some ingenuity to juggle competing claims and conserve energy for the tasks that awaited the small amount of time they controlled. Their problem, as rural producers, was how to maximize the use of available labour time in own-account activities and how, in the face of supervised plantation labour, to gain extra time for those activities.

Slaves tried to solve this double problem in at least three ways. The first tactic involved co-operation with masters and other slaves. Slaves in supervisory positions were permitted by masters either to *hire* or freely avail themselves of the labour services of other slaves.[86] Non-elite creole slaves sought their masters' patronage and may have competed with each other for the temporary labour services of newly arrived slaves during their seasoning period. Masters apprenticed new slaves to creole slaves and, according to Sir William Young, the creoles' scramble for an allocation 'was violent, and troublesome in the extreme'.[87] The second tactic stressed co-operation among slaves. Observers remarked on the higher average earnings which 'Negroes and slaves having children' achieved compared to those of 'single slaves'.[88] Obviously the pooling of land and labour resources in family groups created possibilities for a more efficient deployment of labour and for more intensive exploitation of provision ground and internal market. Children may have been mainly employed around the yards and gardens, tending the stock; women were the main market-people preparing, transporting and selling produce; and men presumably bore the major responsibility for clearing and preparing the grounds.

The third tactic was 'theft' of masters' labour time. Slaves stole constantly because independent economic activities expanded even though the allowance of labour time did not increase before the 1820s. This theft could not often be obvious – absence from gang or late return from meal breaks – though these actions may have played a part. Supervision and the certainty of punishment for malingering and temporary desertion most likely checked the incidence of overt malingering. Theft had to be subtle – theft through energy conservation and the deliberate reduction of performance levels. If one takes account of the length and intensity of the plantation work schedule, slaves' success in energy conservation must be a main explanation for the contrast between their 'sodden, stupid and dull' demeanour in the plantation fields and their 'lively, intelligent and even happy' behaviour in their provision grounds and in the markets.[89] No doubt, as Mintz argues, unsupervised provision-ground cultivation did give slaves opportunities to express fully their humanity, but both that expression and provision-ground cultivation required reasonably high energy levels to sustain them.[90]

Proto-peasant activity, the competition this generated, and the limited gains which slaves made in that competition nurtured and confirmed their attitudes about those activities and their relationship to plantation labour. These own-account activities and coerced labour, in an uneven mix, dominated the slaves' experience; and slaves employed proto-peasant activity continuously during slavery to reduce the extent and impact of coerced labour. Therefore, from the slaves' perspective, their own-account activities were probably as important as coerced labour in defining their status, their humanity and their notions of freedom. Perhaps it is not too fanciful to suggest that humanity and freedom may have been equated by them with their independent activities. Further, slaves doubtless perceived that their forced involvement in plantation labour was the factor which constrained their exploitation of the potential in proto-peasant activity and was the critical limiting factor on their acquisition of freedom and full expression of humanity. Therefore, they may have concluded that when they had a choice in the matter they should rearrange the allocation of labour time to give priority to the transforming element of own-account activities.

Post-slavery labour relations reveal the influence of such attitudes. Both apprentices and ex-slaves utilized the greater control of the labour time which slavery abolition conferred to de-emphasize regular plantation labour and to emphasize own-account activities.[91] However, they tried to do all this *within the confines of the plantation* which was still dependent on regular gang labour. This suggests that the scope of that competition was to some extent culturally determined.

Notes

1   See Sidney W. Mintz and Douglas G. Hall, *The Origins of the Jamaican Internal Marketing System*, Yale University Publications in Anthropology, No. 57 (New Haven, 1960), 3–26; Mintz, *Caribbean Transformations* (Chicago, 1974); 'Caribbean Marketplaces and Caribbean History', *Nova Americana*, 1 (1978), 333–44; 'Was the Plantation Slave a Proletarian?' *Review*, 2 (1978), 81–98; Robert Dirks, *The Black Saturnalia: Conflict and Its Ritual Expression on British West Indian Slave Plantations* (Gainesville, 1987); 'Regional Fluctuations and Competitive Transformations in West Indian Societies' in C.D. Laughlin and I.A. Brady (eds.), *Extinction and Survival in Human Populations* (New York, 1978); B.W. Higman, *Slave Populations of the British Caribbean, 1807–1834* (Baltimore, 1984); Kenneth F. Kiple, *The Caribbean Slave: A Biological History* (New York, 1984); Richard B. Sheridan, *Doctors and Slaves: A Medical and Demographic History of Slavery in the British West Indies, 1680–1834* (New York, 1985).

2   See, in particular, Sidney W. Mintz. 'Slavery and the Rise of Peasantries', *Historical Reflections*, 6 (1979), 213–42.

3   What is meant by 'competition' is not much different from what Dirks outlines in *Black Saturnalia*, 98–102. But I am not sure how the ecological formulation clarifies the political issues that were present.

4   The primary sources for a description and analysis of the provision ground system in the Windward Islands are limited. The earliest description can be found in absentee proprietor, Sir William Young, 'A Tour through the several Islands of Barbados, St. Vincent, Antigua, Tobago and Grenada in the years 1791 and 1792' in Bryan Edwards, *History, Civil and Commercial of the British Colonies in the West Indies* (London, 1801), 3: 249–84. A second was produced by David Collins, a successful doctor-planter, resident in St Vincent for over 20 years, who published *Practical Rules for the Management and Medical Treatment of Negro Slaves in the Sugar Colonies* (Freeport, NY, 1971 [1803]). The fullest account is provided by Mrs A.C. Carmichael in her *Domestic Manners and Social Condition of the White, Colored,*

and Negro Population of the West Indies, 2 vols. (London, 1833). She lived in St Vincent for over two years between 1820 and 1823, and was a keen observer and assiduous collector of information, although favouring the planters' side of the abolition question. The final description can be found in the journal of a Special Magistrate in St Vincent, John Bowen Colthurst, who served during the last seven months of the Apprenticeship: W.K. Marshall (ed.), *The Colthurst Journal* (Millwood, NY, 1977).

Two supplementary sources can amplify this information: the slave laws, particularly those enacted under abolitionist pressure for slavery amelioration, and the testimony provided by witnesses before the parliamentary committees of (1789–91) on the slave trade and slavery. See Sheila Lambert (ed.), *House of Commons Sessional Papers of the 18th Century* [*HCSP*], Vols. 69, 70, 71, 77, 82. Nine witnesses gave evidence on conditions in Grenada, St Vincent, and Tobago, and these included leading proprietors and officials, nearly all of whom qualified for expert status because of their professional experience and long residence in the islands.

5 James Stephen, *The Slavery of the British West India Colonies Delineated*, 2 vols. (London, 1824), 2: 261.

6 Higman, *Slave Populations*, 204.

7 *HCSP*, Vol. 71, 114, 147, evidence of Alexander Campbell. See also evidence of Gilbert Francklyn (Tobago), 85, and of James Seton, Governor of St Vincent (Vol. 69, 427).

8 See Grenada Act No. 2 of 1766, quoted in B.A. Marshall, 'Society and Economy in the British Windward Islands, 1763–1823', Ph.D. Diss. (University of the West Indies, 1972), 302.

9 *HCSP*, Vol. 69, 427, evidence of Governor Seton.

10 *British Parliamentary Papers* [*BPP*] (Dublin, 1969, 1971), Vol. 71, 155, Vol. 77, 435; B. Marshall, 'Society and Economy', 303. In Tobago, the stipulation was one acre 'well planted with provisions' for every five slaves. In St Lucia, it was 500 plants of manioc or other vegetable for each slave.

11 Mintz, 'Caribbean Marketplaces', 335.

12 See evidence of Gilbert Franklyn and Ashton Warner Byam (*HCSP* Vol. 71, 85, 105).

13 Richard B. Sheridan, 'The Crisis of Slave Subsistence in the British West Indies during and after the American Revolution', *William and Mary Quarterly*, 3rd series, 33 (1976), 615–41.

14 Mintz and Hall, *Origins*, 3.

15 *HCSP*, Vol. 71, 105. Emphasis added.

16 Ibid., Vol. 71, 144. See Edward Kamau Brathwaite, 'Controlling Slaves in Jamaica', unpublished paper, Conference of Caribbean Historians, Georgetown, 1971.

17 J.D. Momsen, 'The Geography of Land Use and Population in the Caribbean with special reference to Barbados and the Windward Islands', Ph. Diss. (University of London, 1969), 132–3; D.L. Niddrie, *Land Use and Population in Tobago* (Bude, Cornwall, 1961), 17, 43; W.M. Davis, *The Lesser Antilles* (New York, 1926), 8.

18 See evidence of Alexander Campbell and James Bailie (*HCSP*, Vol. 71, 144, 199).

19 Collins, *Practical Rules*, 76.

20 *Parliamentary Papers* (*PP*), 1842, Vol. 13. Evidence of Henry Barkly before the Select Committee on West India Colonies (Q. 2661).

21 *HCSP*, Vol. 69, 428, evidence of Governor Seton. See *PP*, Vol. 13, evidence of H.M. Grant before the Select Committee on West India Colonies (Questions 31–72).

22 *Colthurst Journal*, 171. See John Anderson, 'Journal and Recollections', 26, Aberdeen University Library, Scotland.

23 For example, Sir William Young in Edwards, *History*, 3: 248; John Jeremie, First President of the Royal Court in St Lucia, in *BPP*, Vol. 71, 223; and W.C. Mitchell, Attorney of Lataste estate in Grenada in Mitchell to Baumer, 3 Sept. 1831, *Lataste Estate Papers*, Moccas Court Collection, National Library of Wales.

24 *HCSP*, Vol. 70, 132, Grenada Act of 3 Nov. 1788; B. Marshall, 'Society and Economy', 319.

25 *Colthurst Journal*, 170; Carmichael, *Domestic Manners*, 1: 135–7.

26 Anderson, 'Journal', 26.

27 Stephen, *Slavery*, 2: 262.

28 The Grenada Abolition Act referred to provision grounds located 'a considerable distance from their place of abode'. See Higman, *Slave Populations*, 204.
29 *Colthurst Journal*, 171.
30 *HCSP*, Vol. 71, 199; Edwards, *History*, 3: 271.
31 *HCSP*, Vol. 71, 132, evidence of Gilbert Francklyn; *Lataste Estate Papers*, Moccas Court Collection, Mitchell to Baumer, 3 and 25 Sept. 1831.
32 *HCSP*, Vol. 70, 131, Grenada Acts of 10 Dec. 1766 and 3 Nov. 1788. Inspectors, later called Guardians, were given the responsibility of inspecting provision grounds, of determining their adequacy for maintenance, and of fining planters for infractions of the law.
33 *BPP*, Vol. 77, 140, Tobago Slave Act, 1829.
34 Ibid., Vol. 77, 369, St Lucia Second Supplementary Ordinance, 1830; ibid., Vol. 79, 126, Order in Council, 1831. The local ordinance in 1830 had stipulated 'at least one *carré* [3⅓ acres] for every two full grown slaves', but the Order in Council of 1831 reduced the size to half an acre for each slave 15 years and over.
35 Section 10 of Tobago Slavery Abolition Act.
36 Section 10 of St Vincent Slavery Abolition Act. Emphasis added.
37 *HCSP*, Vol. 71, 85, 199, evidence of James Baillie and Gilbert Francklyn; Edwards, *History*, 3: 274.
38 Dirks, *Black Saturnalia*, 75.
39 *HCSP*, Vol. 71, 172, 182; Edwards, *History*, 3: 271; *Colthurst Journal*, 170.
40 *HCSP*, Vol. 71, 105–6, 145, 148, 199–200, evidence of James Baillie, Alexander Campbell and Ashton Warner Byam; ibid., Vol. 69, 428, evidence of Governor Seton; ibid., Vol. 82, 164, evidence of Drewery Ottley.
41 Ibid., Vol. 71, 146, evidence of Alexander Campbell; also evidence of Ashton Warner Byam (104–7); Carmichael, *Domestic Manners*, 1: 174–5.
42 Carmichael, *Domestic Manners*, 1: 174.
43 *BPP*, Vol. 71, 57, 95, Grenada Consolidated Slave Law, 1825; ibid., Vol. 77, 140, 369, Tobago Slave Act, 1829 and St Lucia 2nd Supplementary Ordinance, 1830.
44 Section 11 of Tobago Abolition Act.
45 B. Marshall, 'Society and Economy', 301–3, 318–22.
46 *HCSP*, Vol. 71, 146, 199–200, evidence of James Baillie and Alexander Campbell; Collins, *Practical Rules*, 87–99.
47 *HCSP*, Vol. 71, 132, 199–20, evidence of Gilbert Francklyn and James Baillie.
48 *BPP*, Vol. 71, 106, 228, St Vincent Consolidated Slave Act, 1825 and St. Lucia Ordinance, 1825.
49 *HCSP*, Vol. 71, 132, evidence of Gilbert Francklyn; *Lataste Estate Papers*, Mitchell to Baumer, 3 and 25 Sept. 1831.
50 *HCSP*, Vol. 71, 145, 200, evidence of Alexander Campbell and James Baillie; Collins, *Practical Rules*, 91–9.
51 *BPP*, Vol. 71, 223, enclosed in Acting Governor to Bathurst, 30 Aug. 1825.
52 *HCSP*, Vol. 71, 146, evidence of Alexander Campbell; Carmichael, *Domestic Manners*, 1: 162–78.
53 *HCSP*, Vol. 71, 146, evidence of Alexander Campbell; Carmichael, *Domestic Manners*, 1: 152.
54 Carmichael, *Domestic Manners*, 1: 51–3, 179.
55 *HCSP*, Vol. 70, 149, St Vincent Act for the Better Government of Slaves, 11 July 1767, Section X; B. Marshall, 'Society and Economy', 292–6.
56 *HCSP*, Vol. 71, 86, 107–8, 191, evidence of Gilbert Francklyn, Ashton Warner Byam, James Baillie.
57 Ibid., Vol. 71, 173, evidence of Alexander Campbell.
58 Mintz, 'Caribbean Marketplaces', 336; Mintz and Hall, *Origins*, 12–13.
59 This paragraph is based mainly on the analysis of Higman.
60 *St George's Chronicle*, 13 May 1815, quoted in Higman, *Slave Populations*, 238.
61 *Grenada Free Press*, 19 Aug. 1829, quoted in Higman, *Slave Populations*, 241.
62 *BPP*, Vol. 77, 136, Brisbane to Murray, 22 May 1829. Emphasis added.
63 Ibid., 366, 1st Subsidiary Ordinance, 1830 to HM's Order in Council; Vol. 79, 101–3, Order in Council, 1831.

64 Ibid., Vol. 71, 78, Patterson to Bathurst, 23 Nov. 1825.
65 Ibid., Vol. 77, 136, Brisbane to Murray, 22 May 1829. For comparable response in Antigua, see D.B. Gaspar, 'Slavery, Amelioration, and Sunday Markets in Antigua, 1823–1831', *Slavery and Abolition*, 9 (1988), 11–21.
66 Edwards, *History*, 3: 271; Carmichael, *Domestic Manners*, 1:5.
67 *HCSP*, Vol. 71, 107–8, evidence of Alexander Campbell, Ashton Warner Byam; Vol. 82, 163–4, evidence of Drewery Ottley.
68 Ibid., Vol. 71.
69 Ibid., Vol. 71. Emphasis added.
70 Carmichael, *Domestic Manners*, 1: 176–9.
71 *Colthurst Journal*, 163, 171.
72 Ibid., 171; Carmichael, *Domestic Manners*, 1: 194–7.
73 For example, Drewery Ottley, (*HCSP*, Vol. 82, 163–4), suggested that, on a 200-slave estate, only about 12 to 18 slaves would earn annually the £6 to £8 which was within the reach of 'an industrious but ordinary Field Slave'.
74 Collins, *Practical Rules*, 77–9; Stephen, *Slavery*, 2: 264–71.
75 *HCSP*, Vol. 71, 145, 148, evidence of Alexander Campbell. See also evidence of John Giles (ibid., Vol. 82, 75).
76 Ibid., Vol. 71, 151. See also evidence of Gilbert Francklyn (Vol. 71, 87) and of Drewery Ottley and John Giles (ibid., Vol. 82, 75, 176).
77 *Lataste Estate Papers*, Mitchell to Baumer, 3 and 25 Sept. 1831.
78 Stephen, *Slavery*, 2: 270–71; Higman, *Slave Populations*, 212–18.
79 See Mintz, 'Was the Plantation Slave a Proletarian?' and 'Caribbean History'.
80 *Colthurst Journal*, 10.
81 *Lataste Estate Papers*, Mitchell to Baumer, 3 and 25 Sept. 1831; Carmichael, *Domestic Manners*, 1: 197; *HCSP*, Vol. 71, 95, 191, evidence of James Baillie and Gilbert Francklyn.
82 Mintz, *Caribbean Transformations*, 212.
83 *Lataste Estate Papers*, Mitchell to Baumer, 3 and 25 Sept. 1831.
84 *Colthurst Journal*, 171.
85 *HCSP*, Vol. 82, 75, 109, evidence of John Giles and John Terry. Both observed that the plantation chore of 'picking of grass' on Sundays and in the afternoon break was 'a great hardship on slaves'. Giles also complained that slaves received no compensation in time for the loss of their Sundays to guard duty.
86 Ibid., Vol. 71, 107, evidence of Ashton Warner Byam; Higman, *Slave Populations*, 212.
87 Edwards, *History*, 3: 272; *HCSP*, Vol. 71, 147–8, evidence of Alexander Campbell.
88 *HCSP*, Vol. 71, 148. See also Gilbert Francklyn's evidence (87, 95–6), and *Colthurst Journal*, 171.
89 Mintz, 'Was the Plantation Slave a Proletarian?', 94.
90 Mintz, 'Caribbean Marketplaces', 340; *Caribbean Transformations*, 151–2.
91 See W.K. Marshall, 'Commentary One' on 'Slavery and the Rise of Peasantries' in *Historical Reflections*, 6 (1979), 243–8; and 'Apprenticeship and Labor Relations in Four Windward Islands' in David Richardson (ed.), *Abolition and Its Aftermath* (London, 1985), 202–24.

Chapter 22

Roderick A. McDonald

INDEPENDENT ECONOMIC PRODUCTION BY SLAVES ON ANTEBELLUM LOUISIANA SUGAR PLANTATIONS

DURING THE LATE ANTEBELLUM PERIOD slaves on Louisiana sugar plantations organized extensive and integrated economic systems, accumulating and disposing of capital and property within internal economies they themselves administered. Such economic systems probably functioned on every sugar estate in Louisiana, and their importance far outweighed the often limited pecuniary benefits slaves derived. The internal economy not only reflected the ways in which slaves organized their efforts to earn and spend money, but also influenced the character and development of slave family and community life. The slaves' economy thus shaped patterns of slave life, providing the material basis for African-American culture in the sugar-producing region.

Louisiana was the foremost sugar-producing state in the antebellum South. Between 1824 and 1861 cane sugar — which was climatically unsuited to cultivation in most of the North American continent — became the principal crop in southern Louisiana. Sugar production quintupled to more than 500,000 hogsheads annually, and the number of sugar estates increased almost seven-fold, from 193 to 1,308. The slave population of the sugar region rose dramatically from just over 20,000 to around 125,000.[1]

Sugar production was confined to the southern part of Louisiana, the location of some of the largest and richest plantations in the South. Although only 24 of the state's 64 parishes grew sugar, and less than 50 per cent of their improved lands were ever in cane cultivation, the sugar region had a disproportionate number both of slaves and large estates. Louisiana's slave population numbered about 69,000 in 1820 and rose to 109,600 in 1830, 168,500 in 1840, and 244,800 in 1850. On the eve of the Civil War, it stood at 331,700. Slaves who worked on sugar estates numbered 21,000 in 1827 and by 1830 had reached 36,100 (about one-third of the state's total slave population). Thereafter the number of sugar plantation slaves increased to approximately 50,700 in 1841, 65,300 in 1844, and by 1852 and 1853 stood at some 125,000, or one-half of all slaves in Louisiana.[2]

Land consolidation and the growth of large estates paralleled the sugar boom. Small holdings were common in the 1820s, even in prime sugar land that fronted the rivers and bayous. After 1830, however, small farms gave way to large estates and by 1860 the average sugar plantation contained 480 improved acres compared to 128 improved acres for non-cane farms. With this consolidation, the number of slaves on each plantation increased steadily. By the Civil War plantations with slave populations numbering in the hundreds were commonplace. Sugar production soared and the great estates, where most southern Louisiana slaves lived and worked, dominated the sugar economy.[3]

The cultivation of sugar was a race against time. Sugar cane cannot withstand the frosts which occur annually in Louisiana. Consequently, the sugar cane harvest came but nine or ten months after the date of planting (compared to the fourteen to eighteen months necessary for full maturation). Yet the longer the crop stayed in the ground, the higher its sugar content. Louisiana planters thus sought to plant the sugar crop as early as possible in the year and to harvest it at the last conceivable moment. Crucial to the determination of when to start the harvest were the planter's estimate both of the speed with which the crop could be cut and processed, and the date of the first killing frost.

The work routine of Louisiana sugar plantation slaves reflected the intensity of the sugar crop's cycle. Immediately following their annual Christmas and New Year holidays slaves ploughed the fields in preparation for planting the canes, opening furrows some six to eight feet apart into which they placed seed cane set aside from the previous year's crop. Usually Louisiana planters allowed a given cane plot to ratoon for no more than two years before replanting.[4] Ratoons yielded less sugar than cane grown from seed, but ratooning also demanded less labour than planting, and thus permitted cultivation of many more acres. After two years low sugar yields required that the ratoons be dug up and the cane replanted from seed. Slaves thus planted about one-third of the estate's acreage of cane every year.

Slaves usually completed planting by the end of February and, after the plant cane and ratoons sprouted, tended the crop through the first months of its growth. Tending the canes involved hoeing and ploughing between the rows to keep the cane piece free of grass and weeds. By late June or early July the cane had grown tall enough to withstand weeds. Slaves then ploughed and hoed – 'threw up' – the rows of cane in ridges to permit better drainage from the plant's roots. The cane was then 'laid by' and left to grow untended until harvest time.

Tending the crop required less work than either planting or harvesting, which monopolized the time of the estate's labour force. During spring and early summer planters diverted some labour to such tasks as growing provisions and secondary cash crops, preparing for the sugar harvest and maintaining and improving the estate. Through spring and summer slaveholders had the slaves plant one or two crops of corn, as well as perhaps potatoes, pumpkins, sweet potatoes and other vegetables. Slaves harvested these crops and cut hay for fodder before the sugar harvest began. Slaves also mended roads and fences, built and repaired levees, made bricks for the construction and refurbishment of plantation buildings, dug and cleaned ditches, and gathered wood both for fuel and for use by the estate's coopers.

After the sugar crop was laid by slaves also began preparing for the sugar harvest. Before its commencement planters sought to have everything ready to see them through the harvest: sufficient wood to fuel the sugar mill, enough barrels and hogsheads to hold the crop and adequate roads to transport the cane from field to works. Out of crop (the non-harvest stage of production), slaves worked from sunup to sundown, with half-an-hour off for breakfast and a dinner break at noon, for five-and-a-half to six-and-a-half days per week, with time off on Saturdays and Sundays.

The sugar harvest usually began by mid-October. Once underway, the work of cutting canes and processing the crop continued without stop until completion. Slaves first cut and mat-layed (seed cane was literally laid out in mats and covered with a layer of earth to protect it from frost) the cane that was to be set aside for the next year's seed. Thereafter the harvest began in earnest. Slaves worked 16 or more hours a day, seven days a week, although factors such as bad weather, impassable roads and breakdowns at the mill could disrupt this schedule. In addition to their tasks in the fields slaves performed all the labour involved in processing the crop, from feeding and stoking the mill to loading hogsheads of sugar and barrels of molasses onto the river steamers at the plantation wharf.

Because of the threat of frost, harvest proceeded at a furious pace with slaves working in shifts through the night every day from late October through December. Freezing temperatures were most likely in the first couple of months of the new year, so planters tried to finish the crop by Christmas, at which time the slaves had their annual holidays. Often, however, harvest continued until January. Thomas Hamilton, a British military officer who visited Louisiana in 1833, noted that 'the crop in Louisiana is never considered safe till it is in the mill, and the consequence is that when cutting once begins, the slaves are taxed beyond their strength, and are goaded to labour until nature absolutely sinks under the effort'.[5]

The gang system prevailed on Louisiana sugar plantations. Planters organized gangs according to the capacity of the slave labour force, incorporating their notions of the appropriate sexual division of labour. All adults worked in the fields, but the two most burdensome tasks on the estate, ditching and wood-gathering, were men's work. Slave children also worked in gangs. Supervised by female slave drivers, they performed such light tasks as cleaning-up around the sugar works and picking fodder. The work schedule of women with unweaned children accommodated their babies' feeding routine. Such women either had additional time off from labour in the gangs, or worked in a 'suckler's gang'.

The combination of agriculture and industry required in sugar cultivation and processing placed tremendous demands on slave workers. Louisiana sugar plantations earned a dreadful reputation throughout the South. 'The cultivation of sugar in Louisiana', commented Hamilton, 'is carried on at an enormous expense of human life. Planters must buy to keep up their stock, and this supply principally comes from Maryland, Virginia, and North Carolina'. Frances Trollope, a committed abolitionist, claimed that 'to be sent south and sold [was] the dread of all the slaves north of Louisiana'. E. S. Abdy, an Englishman who travelled through the South in the early 1830s, related how planters in the seaboard South disciplined slaves by threatening to sell them 'down the river to Louisiana', while slaves incorporated the Louisiana sugar region's unenviable reputation in the chorus of a song:

> Old debble, Lousy Anna,
> Dat scarecrow for poor nigger,
> Where de sugar-cane grow to pine-tree,
> And de pine-tree turn to sugar.[6]

Sugar slaves suffered overwork often compounded by undernourishment, harsh punishment, inadequate housing and clothing, high infant mortality, ill-health and a life-span shortened by the grim plantation regime.

Slaves struggled to transcend the brutality of plantation labour, the planters and their agents. Slave community life throughout sugar's reign in Louisiana exhibited extraordinary creativity; the thousands of men and women who lived and died in bondage displayed resourcefulness, endeavour, dignity and courage – the full array of humanity's most prized attributes. The independence slaves displayed in their art and music, family and community development and religion was also manifest in their economic activities. As their houses, gardens and grounds provided the focus for slave family and community life, so too were they the base for their own economy.

While their independent economic activities had no basis in law, slaves secured the tacit assent and approval of the planters. In much the same way as slaves used what control they had over the processes of production – by withholding their labour or labouring inefficiently – to get the planters to accede, for example, to better working conditions and standards of food, clothing and shelter, planters also conceded to slaves the opportunity, during their time off from plantation labour, to work for themselves, to market the produce of their labour and to keep the proceeds. Although subject to constant negotiation, the internal economy developed by sugar slaves expanded steadily until the Civil War.

Agricultural endeavours were a central component of the slaves' independent economic production. On most Louisiana sugar estates slaves controlled some land, where they raised livestock and grew crops for their personal consumption and sale. Slaves almost always had a small patch surrounding their house where they tended gardens and kept some poultry and livestock. Travellers often commented on these gardens. 'In the rear of each cottage, surrounded by a rude fence', observed journalist T. B. Thorpe in 1853, 'you find a garden in more or less order, according to the industrious habits of the proprietor. In all you notice that the chicken-house seems to be in excellent condition.' Describing the slave village on a Louisiana sugar estate, London *Times* correspondent William Howard Russell noted 'the ground round the huts . . . amidst which pigs and poultry were recreating'. A former slave, Elizabeth Ross Hite, confirmed Thorpe's and Russell's accounts, recalling that she and her fellow slaves 'had a garden right in front of our quarter. We planted ev'rything in it. Had watermelon, mushmelon, and a flower garden'. Similarly, ex-slave Catherine Cornelius remembered the 'garden patch, wid mustard greens, cabbage, chickens too'.[7]

Louisiana slaves put their kitchen gardens to diverse uses, raising fruits, vegetables, small livestock and poultry. The close proximity of these gardens to the cane fields meant that slaves could work them at odd times through the week, during the midday break and in the evenings. Moreover, elderly slaves, who had few responsibilities for plantation work, could spend considerable time in the kitchen gardens. One former slave recalled that her grandmother did not go to work in the fields but 'would tend to the lil patch of corn, raise chickens, and do all the work around the house'.[8]

Besides their kitchen gardens, slaves had more extensive allotments of land elsewhere on the plantation which were often known as 'Negro grounds'. There they generally cultivated cash crops, most commonly corn, although they also raised some minor crops such as pumpkins, potatoes and hay. While slaves consumed some of the kitchen-garden crops, they sold most of their provision-ground crops.

The 'Negro grounds' were less accessible than the kitchen gardens, and slaves normally could not spend time in them during the regular work week Often they were located on the periphery of the plantation, beyond the land in sugar, sometimes a great distance from the sugar works, cane fields and slave villages. Only on weekends (primarily on Sundays, but also sometimes on part of Saturdays) could slaves tend them. Russell observed that slaves had 'from noon on Saturday till dawn on Monday morning to do as they please'. On some estates, however, slaves did regular plantation work for six days and light work for part of Sunday. Ex-slave Elizabeth Ross Hite recalled that 'de Sunday wurk was light. Dey would only pull shucks of corn'. Sunday work usually entailed the performance of a specific task such as shelling corn, gathering fodder, branding livestock, or making hay, after which slaves had the rest of the day to themselves. Ex-slave Catherine Cornelius recalled that on the West Baton Rouge Parish estate where she lived the task work system applied to Saturdays, but slaves invariably had Sunday off except during the harvest: 'dat [Saturdays] was de day fo' ourselves', Cornelius explained. 'We all had certain tasks to do. If we finished dem ahead of time, de rest of de day was ours'.[9]

Slaves used their time off to cultivate their crops. Sometimes, generally just before the sugar harvest, slaves secured additional time off from the regular plantation schedule either to harvest or market their crop. For example, slaves on Duncan Kenner's Ashland Plantation 'gathered their corn, made a large crop' one Sunday in early October 1852. Two days later 'all but a few hands went to Donaldsonville', a nearby town, either to market their crop or spend their earnings. The next day the sugar harvest began. From mid-October until at least the end of December slaves harvested cane every day, including Sundays and Christmas.[10] The seven-day labour schedule, of course, precluded slaves from working in their grounds for the duration of the sugar harvest. Slaves, however, sometimes received compensation, getting days off at the end of the harvest equal to the number of Sundays worked.[11]

Slaves valued time off prior to the sugar harvest, since it allowed them to secure their own crops before labouring full-time cutting and grinding cane. Slaves on Isaac Erwin's Shady Grove Plantation in Iberville Parish spent the two days' holiday before the 1849 sugar harvest 'dig[g]ing their Potatoes & Pinders', while on Valcour Aime's St James Parish plantation on the day preceding the commencement of the 1851 sugar harvest the slaves had a 'free day to dig their potatoes'. When such free time was not available slaves did the best they could on their regularly scheduled days off. Slaves also worked for themselves during other annual holidays, which usually fell at Christmas and New Year, as well as at the end of the cane planting and when the sugar crop was laid by in midsummer.[12]

The plantation was not only the source of the slaves' independent production but also the principal market for the goods they produced. The growing and retailing of corn was the most lucrative dimension of the internal economy on Louisiana sugar plantations and the one that involved the largest proportion of the slave population. Slaves marketed most of their produce on their home estate, as both they and the planters benefited from retailing the corn crop there. Planters wanted the crop since corn meal comprised a large proportion of the standard slave ration and by purchasing it on the plantation they were freed from the various fees attendant to buying through an agent, while slaves were saved the expense of shipping and marketing. Less frequently, slaves marketed their crop off the plantation. In 1849 Elu Landry recorded that he 'gave [the slaves] permission & pass to sell their corn in the neighborhood – lent them teams for that purpose', while slaves on a Bayou Goula plantation sold their 1859 crop of 1,011 barrels of corn to the neighboring Nottoway Estate of J. H. Randolph for $758.[13] Although in these years the price slaves got for their corn – from 37½ cents to 75 cents a barrel – was somewhat below the commodity's market price in New Orleans, it was probably the equivalent of a local market price.[14]

Slave-grown corn was essential to the operation of many plantations. Because of its importance slaves sometimes managed to obtain protection for their crops in case of loss or damage. In 1859, Lewis Stirling's Wakefield Estate accounts recorded that 12 slaves 'lost all their corn' (a total of 47 barrels). They were, however, recompensed by the planter at the full price of 50 cents a barrel. When, in a similar instance two years previously, plantation hogs had destroyed their corn crop, six slaves received payment of $22 from the planter as compensation. Such arrangements document the importance to the plantation of the slaves' private agricultural endeavours and the extent of planters' commitment to the slaves' continued involvement.[15]

Slaves grew and marketed a number of other cash crops. Some slave-controlled land was put into pumpkins. Although they sold for only pennies apiece, pumpkins could bring in a tidy sum. On Benjamin Tureaud's estate a slave named Big Mathilda received $10 for the 700 pumpkins she sold to the plantation in 1858, while the accounts of slaves for the Gay plantation in Iberville Parish reveal that in 1844 seven of the 74 slaves derived part of their earnings from the sale of pumpkins. In the previous year the plantation's accounts record 'Pumpkins 4000 bought of our Negroes . . . $80'.[16] Slaves also raised potatoes and their hay crops found a ready market on the plantation. In 1844 about the same proportion of the Gay plantation slaves as raised pumpkins sold hay to the estate at $3 a load, while a year previous the total crop was 10 loads or 3,000 pounds.[17]

Poultry and hogs, the animals most commonly raised by slaves in Louisiana, also found their principal market on the plantation. Raising poultry was ideally suited to the economy of the slave community, since it demanded little investment of time or effort, required minimal capital outlay, and provided a steady income through marketing both eggs and the birds themselves. Few travellers failed to comment on the slaves' proclivity to keep poultry. and their descriptions of slave villages on Louisiana sugar plantations invariably mention the chickens, ducks, turkeys and geese ranging through the quarters. The prices paid by planters for fowl varied little during the antebellum years. Chickens sold at anywhere from 10 cents to 25 cents each and the price of eggs was from 12½ cents to 15 cents a dozen, On W. W. Pugh's Woodlawn Plantation in Assumption Parish, muscovy ducks fetched 37½ cents each in the early 1850s.[18]

Judging from the scene which William Howard Russell witnessed, slaves showed a trading acumen consistent with their position as independent retailers, 'An avenue of trees runs down the negro street' on John Burnside's Houmas Plantation in Ascension Parish, Russell observed, 'and behind each hut are rude poultry hutches, which, with the geese and turkeys and a few pigs, form the perquisites of the slaves, and the sole source from which they derive their acquaintance with currency'.

In the slaves' business transactions 'their terms are strictly cash. . . . An old negro brought up some ducks to Mr. Burnside', Russell related,

> and offered the lot of six for three dollars. 'Very well, Louis; if you come tomorrow, I'll pay you'. 'No massa, me want de money now'. 'But won't you give me credit. Louis? Don't you think I'll pay the three dollars?' 'Oh, pay some day, massa, sure enough. Massa good to pay de tree dollar; but this nigger want money now to buy food and things for him leetle family. They will trust massa at Donaldsonville, but they won't trust this nigger'.

'I was told', Russell continued, 'that a thrifty negro will sometimes make ten or twelve pounds a year from his corn and poultry'.[19]

This exchange reveals the slave as a shrewd retailer with a knowledge both of the value of his commodity and the terms of the transaction. Indeed, Louis did not hesitate to contradict the planter in the course of the negotiations. The money Louis accrued from the sale was earmarked for purchases for himself and his family and, although he found a market for his goods on the plantation. Louis apparently planned to spend his cash off the estate in the nearby town of Donaldsonville, where, by virtue of his understanding of the terms demanded by the merchants there, he had traded before.

The sale of crops, poultry and livestock to the planter was not the only source of revenue for the slaves' independent economic activities on the plantation. Within the confines of the estate slaves had the opportunity to engage in various other money-making activities. Technological developments in the sugar industry that mechanized the grinding and milling of sugar gave slaves the opportunity to earn money, since the machines consumed huge quantities of fuel – almost without exception locally felled timber. The vast amounts of wood required by the Louisiana sugar mills can be estimated, since it took from two to four cords of wood to make one hogshead of sugar, and twice in the decade preceding the outbreak of the Civil War the sugar crop topped 400,000 hogsheads. The amount of wood that could be collected during regular plantation hours rarely met the estates' needs, and contracting for wood off the plantation was expensive. Buying wood that slaves chopped on their own proved the most efficient means for planters to supplement their fuel supply. It also gave slaves the opportunity to earn substantial amounts of money. Payments to slaves for cutting wood on the Uncle Sam Plantation in St James Parish, for example, totalled over $1,000 in 1859. In July 1860 53 slaves received some $600 for wood-cutting and four months later $436 was paid to 58 slaves, while in the following year 61 slaves cut nearly 1,600 cords and were paid about $800 (the going rate in these years being 50 cents per cord). The most wood any one slave cut in 1861 was 80 cords and the least 3 cords, with the majority of slaves cutting between 15 and 40 cords.[20]

Slaves found advantages and disadvantages in lumbering. Although their compensation (from 50 to 75 cents per cord) was below the market price, slaves used the plantation's axes and saws, and also had access to the estate's flat-boats, work animals and the tackle necessary to carry the wood out of the swamp and back to the mill. Moreover, they felled trees on land owned by the planters. Thus, since planters covered most of the slaves' capital costs, the price paid for wood may have been more equitable than it appears.[21] Woodcutting, however, was onerous, unpleasant work, since the wood had to be carried from swamps and bayous abutting the river-front plantations. Slaves either worked from a flat-boat or stood in the water, and they had to float or boat the wood out. Invariably, only men did this work.

Woodcutting was just one of many services for which planters would pay slaves. Planters also paid slaves to dig ditches, since sugar estates needed well-maintained irrigation systems and the amount of ditching done as part of the regular plantation labour schedule usually proved insufficient. Planters were thus obliged either to contract ditchers or pay slaves on the plantation for any ditching done on their time off.[22] On W.W. Pugh's estate slaves made shingles, staves, pickets and boards, and Pugh bought slave-made shuck collars, barrels and hogsheads. Slaves were also paid to haul wood, as well as to do regular work for the plantation on Sundays or holidays.[23] Slaves on the Gay family's sugar estate in Iberville Parish similarly were paid for work done on their time off from plantation labour. The proliferation of jobs included sugar-potting, coopering, fixing and firing kettles, collecting fodder, forging iron hoops, mending shoes, counting hoop-poles and serving as watchmen. Skilled slaves, moreover, made money during sugar harvest. In the mid-1840s the plantation sugar-maker received $30 for his services at harvest, while his deputy received $15; the chief engineer and the kettle-setter each got $10. The firemen, kettle-tenders and the second engineer all received $5 for their harvest season work.[24] On his estate, Benjamin Tureaud paid slaves for making bricks, hogsheads, shuck-collars and baskets, while on the Wilton Plantation in St James Parish, estate accounts note cash payments to slaves for ditching, 'levying', and making rails and handbarrows.[25]

Skilled slaves had an especially wide range of opportunities to work for themselves. Slave carpenters, coopers and blacksmiths could use their training for their own profit, undertaking large-scale lucrative projects. For example, on the Gay family's plantation a slave named Thornton received $20 for making a cart.[26] On some estates slave tradesmen did piece-work, producing a specific quantity of items. On John Randolph's Nottoway Plantation coopers received cash payments for producing more than an agreed upon number of barrels. In December 1857 Cooper Henry received payment of $19.50 for making 26 barrels and 13 hogsheads above his quota, while his fellow tradesmen, Cooper William and Cooper Jack, earned $16 and $8 respectively for their extra production.[27]

Many paying jobs required physical stamina if not trained skills. Except for some tasks such as counting hoop-poles and collecting fodder, slaves lacking strength or skills had few opportunities other than making themselves available for day labour. Such work would take into consideration the abilities of the individual slaves since it was voluntary. Many slaves chose not to work for the plantation, however, preferring to tend to their farming, gardening, poultry and livestock-raising, and domestic crafts, while others combined working for themselves and for the plantation.

Cash could enter the internal economy from various other sources. Many sugar-plantation slaves found profit in nearby swamps and streams. Hunting and fishing supplemented the pork and corn ration supplied by planters, and also offered slaves an opportunity to supplement their income since they could sell or barter some of their catch to fellow slaves, traders or planters.[28]

At Christmas some slaves received cash payments as a holiday bonus. Such was the case for the 150 slaves on the Nottoway Estate where, through the early 1850s, John Randolph made regular payments to the slaves. Indeed, extant plantation manuscripts contain numerous references to cash paid to slaves. An 1854 memorandum from the Stirling family's sugar plantation lists 95 slaves, 50 women and 45 men, receiving cash payments totalling $314. Most payments compensated slaves for goods and services; some of the larger amounts went to two partners for wood-cutting. A similar list, probably dating from the following year, shows 78 slaves receiving a total of $258. Similarly, in the early 1840s there were a number of cash payments to slaves on the Gay family plantation. For example, between December 1841 and January 1842 34 men received a total of some $200, with individual payments ranging from $1 to $20. The money was probably paid either for slave crops or for harvest work, but may have included holiday or Christmas bonuses and gifts.[29] Within the confines of the plantation slaves thus had a wide range of opportunities to earn money which planter gifts supplemented.

Slaves also bypassed the plantation and sold their commodities elsewhere. Some were involved in marketing at major ports on the Mississippi River, as well as at local town markets and in the neighbourhood of the plantation. They also transacted business with the traders who plied the waterways and highways of southern Louisiana.

Throughout the sugar region slaves worked for themselves collecting and drying Spanish moss, a plant that grew in profusion. Picking moss from the trees was relatively easy, since with the assistance of a long staff the plant could readily be detached from a tree's trunk and limbs. After it had been dried in the sun slaves bound the moss into bales weighing 250 to 350 pounds ready for shipment. Hunton Love, who for the first 20 years of his life had been a slave on John Viguerie's sugar plantation on the Bayou Lafourche, testified to the importance of the collection and sale of moss. 'Once I heard some men talkin', he recalled in the 1930s, 'an' one sed, "You think money grows on trees", an' the other one say, "Hit do, git down that moss an' convert it into money", an' I got to thinkin' an' sho' 'nuff, it do grow on trees.'[30] The records of various plantations show slaves exploiting this market for moss. On Robert Ruffin Barrow's Bayou Lafourche estates slaves spent Sundays working their moss crop, while the accounts of Magnolia Plantation also recorded payments to slaves for moss.[31] Slaves consigned their dried moss to major entrepôts on the Mississippi, chiefly St Louis, New Orleans and Natchez, where they transacted business with the cities' retail agents.

The records of the Gay family's sugar estate contain rich documentation of moss-gathering, including the collection and marketing patterns, and payment schedules. In the mid-1840s Colonel Andrew Hynes and Joseph B. Craighead ran the plantation, while Edward Gay lived in St Louis and acted as agent for the estate's produce. In 1844 Gay wrote to Hynes and Craighead suggesting that the slaves pick moss and forward it to St Louis where he guaranteed it would sell for a good price. Thereafter, moss became an integral part of his slaves' internal economy. Within a few months the first shipment of dried moss sold in St Louis at 2 cents a pound with 22 slaves, two of whom were women, sending in all 9,705 pounds of moss and receiving a total of $162 ($196 less $34 freight and commission).[32] From 1844 to 1861 slaves on the Gay estate continued to send their moss to St Louis for sale, where the price per pound ranged from 2 cents to 1¼ cents. Mississippi steamers took an average of four or five shipments per year. Slaves paid for the cartage aboard ship and the agent's sales commission, which totalled from 75 cents to $1.25 a bale. When the receipts arrived at the plantation slaves received the total net proceeds, usually around $4 to $5 a bale.[33]

A record book documenting moss-gathering and sale on the Gay plantation between the years of 1849 and 1861 shows the extent of the slave community's involvement. During that period 160 slaves – 41 of whom were women – sold 1,101 bales of moss, with individual slaves selling between 1 and 48 bales. More than these 160 slaves were involved, however. Some of the shipments were sent jointly by husbands and wives, whose children and kin also assisted them in the project. Since the total slave population on the estate stood at 224 in 1850 and 240 in 1860, the great majority of adult slaves on the plantation were participating in this venture, from which, during the period, at least $4,000 entered the internal economy, an average of some $300 a year.[34]

Another commodity sold by slaves was molasses. On Duncan Kenner's Ashland Plantation the overseer recorded that in January 1852 he 'sold the negroes molasses' and bought flour for them with the proceeds. Slaves on the Gay plantation also regularly shipped molasses for sale in St Louis where it fetched $8 to $12 a barrel. One such shipment consigned 19½ barrels which netted the 15 slaves involved a total of $148.[35]

Slaves on Louisiana sugar estates had other options for marketing their crops and goods. Some transacted business in the general locale of their home plantation. Slaves on the Ventress estate, for example, contracted with a neighbouring planter for the sale of their sizable corn crop of 1,011 barrels, while slaves on Elu Landry's plantation borrowed the estate's draft animals and wagons to peddle their crops throughout the neighbourhood.[36] Others who lived near towns could trade at the village markets that were held on Sunday, the slaves' traditional day off. In 1860 the Reverend P. M. Goodwyn, a resident on Edward Gay's plantation, was amazed and horrified at the prevalence of Sunday trading. He saw slaves 'going to and from the place of trade – wagons & carts, loaded and empty – servants walking and riding, carrying baskets – bundles – packages etc.', and asked,

> why all this? – Can it be possible that there is a necessity for it? – If so, then it is excusable – and, vice versa, – Has the Master gone, or is he going to the house of God today? – How will he – how *ought* he to feel – as the thought comes up while he is attempting to worship – My Servant, or Servants, have a *permit* from me, – and now, while I am here, they are trading and trafficking in the stores of the town.[37]

Despite the misgivings of Goodwyn and other men of the cloth, Sunday remained the principal trading day for slaves able to journey to nearby towns. These markets were important to slaves as places both to sell their wares and to spend their earnings. The slave Louis, who had sold his ducks to John Burnside, was obviously well acquainted with the retail outlets in the nearby town of Donaldsonville. He insisted on a cash payment for the poultry, since he intended spending the money in the town's stores where 'they will-trust massa [with credit] . . . but they won't trust [him]'.[38]

The market-day activities of Louisiana sugar slaves were not confined to retailing and purchasing goods. Some slaves used the day to shake the routine and restrictions of the plantation and at market spent some of their earnings on liquor, gaming and other pleasures. The Mayor of Plaquemine added his voice to that of other local officials when he complained that 'Several Negroes were lately caught in this town drunk and gambling on Sunday in the day time in the house of a Free Negro woman'. These illicit 'shebeens' were, no doubt, a feature of market towns throughout the Louisiana sugar region.[39]

Even when their Sabbatarian scruples proscribed Sunday trading, slaves still retailed their goods in town. In 1853 planter William Weeks reported that a slave named

> Amos has heard of the flat boats [trading vessels] being in New Town & has asked my permission to spend a portion of his crop on them – In consideration of his faithful services on all occasions, and his really conscientious scruples about trading on Sunday, I have concluded to let him go tomorrow.

On Monday, a working day on the plantation, Amos went to town to trade on his own behalf.[40]

The vastness of Louisiana's sugar region and its paucity of towns meant that most slaves did not have recourse to urban markets for buying and selling goods. Nevertheless, by transacting business with itinerant peddlers slaves established trade networks over which planters had no control. Ex-slave Martha Stuart remembered the salesmen who 'come thru the country', while another former slave, Catherine Cornelius, recalled how the slaves on the plantation where she lived would 'git down to de ped'lers on de riber at nite tuh buy stuff'. In fact, river traders had more extensive contact with plantation slaves than highway traders. Inadequate roads made travel by land difficult, while the large sugar plantations had direct access to navigable waterways. Moreover, river traders could move quietly and quickly and thus trade clandestinely in illicit goods. On the eve of the Civil War a Canadian traveller, William Kingsford, left an excellent description of river traders. From the deck of a Mississippi steamer he observed

> the small vessels which, owned by pedlars, pass from plantation to plantation, trading with the negroes principally, taking in exchange the articles which they raise, or, when the latter are sold to the boats, offering to their owners the only temptations on which their money can be spent.

Kingsford related how 'now and then you come upon one of them, moving sluggishly down stream, or moored inshore, where the owner is dispensing his luxuries, in the shape of ribbons, tobacco, gaudy calicoes, and questionable whiskey'.[41]

Slaves found the independence the external trading network conferred extremely useful. It allowed slaves to divest themselves of the constraints of the plantation and engage in an independent economic system which they themselves controlled. Planters had influence over neither the form of the trade nor the goods being traded. Indeed, often the river trade was carried on in violation of both plantation regulations and state law. Clandestine trading provided slaves the opportunity to sell goods planters would not buy and to buy goods planters would neither sell nor order. For example, while slaveholders rarely sold slaves liquor, river traders did, despite laws banning its sale. In turn, traders purchased a variety of commodities, including stolen goods, not traded between slaves and planters.[42]

Sugar planter Maunsell White revealed the disparity of interests between planters and river traders on the one hand and the identity of interests between slaves and river traders on the other when some of his slaves 'were caught stealing molasses to sell to a Boat or "Capota". White kept them under surveillance until 'they were found on board the Boat, where they had hid themselves & were secreted by the owner; a man who called himself "Block", a German & another who called himself Bill"'. (Block's German nationality was not unusual, since many of these traders were immigrants.) When White and his companions searched 'the Boat, an other negro was also found, who said he belonged to the Boat as did also the Men who owned it; but we soon found on arresting the whole of them, that the Boy confessed or said he belonged to [a fellow planter, George Lanaux]'. White interrogated Lanaux's slave the following morning, and he found that the man had been a runaway 'for 4 months; the whole of which time he said he spent in the City [New Orleans?] at work. Thirty five dollars and 50/100 was found on his Person, & a Silver Watch . . . he afterwards said it was only 2½ months'. River peddlers therefore not only gave slaves a means of enriching their lives in slavery, but also provided them with an opportunity to escape slavery entirely.[43]

Theft played an integral role in the internal economy. Many slaves had no compunction about taking the planters' property, since they believed that in appropriating plantation property they were taking what was rightly theirs. Transactions in stolen goods between slaves and peddlers were, according to Frederick Law Olmsted, common throughout the South. Olmsted noted, however, that there was a higher incidence of such trading in the Louisiana sugar region, because the sugar estates had navigable waterways and peddlers could more easily transport and conceal themselves. He observed that 'the traders . . . moor at night on the shore, adjoining the negro-quarters and float away whenever they have obtained any booty, with very small chance of detection'.[44] River peddlers had few inhibitions regarding what they were willing to purchase. The character of the trade militated against bulky consignments, the loading of which would require time and therefore increase the likelihood of detection. If they could avoid such logistical problems, however, peddlers were willing to purchase whatever slaves had to sell. Few of the planter's possessions were safe from the depredations of those involved in the trade. According to Olmsted, one planter had 'a large brass cock and some pipe . . . stolen from his sugar-works'. The planter 'had ascertained that one of his negroes had taken it and sold it on board one of these boats for seventy-five cents, and had immediately spent the money, chiefly for whisky, on the same boat'. It cost the planter $30 to replace the machinery. Another sugar planter informed Olmsted

> that he had lately caught one of his own negroes going towards one of the 'chicken thieves,' (so the traders' boats are called) with a piece of machinery that he had unscrewed from his sugar works, which was worth eighty dollars, and which very likely might have been sold for a drink.[45]

Plantation records reveal the prevalence of slave theft and profile its most popular targets. Most thefts involved the plantations' produce and livestock. Slaves on Maunsell White's plantation stole molasses to sell to river traders, and William

Weeks grumbled about 'Simon that prince of runaways & troublesome negroes . . . [whose] last offence was to go into the sugar house & steal a portion of the little sugar I had kept for home use'.[46] Livestock and poultry ranged free providing particularly easy prey for slaves. Joseph Mather, superintendent of Judge Morgan's Aurora Plantation, recorded the 'theft of chickens' and Ellen McCollam noted that she had 'had 8 hens stowlen out of the yard'. The threat of having his livestock stolen prompted Maunsell White to urge his overseer to make a picket pen 'in order to save our hogs, pigs & sheep from all sorts of "*Varmints*" two-legged as well as four'. Similarly, planter J. E. Craighead complained that 'the negroes steal our sheep as we have no safe place to keep them'. One can judge the extent to which stealing poultry was viewed as characteristic of slaves by a claim incorporated in the lines of a Louisiana song:

> Negue pas capab marche san mais dans poche,
> Ce pou vole poule –
> Negro cannot walk without corn in his pocket,
> It is to steal chickens –[47]

Slaves stole the slaveholders' personal property as well. Planter Andrew McCollam and his wife Ellen, for example, lost items from their laundry. Once they had '8 shirts stolen out of the wash', and later 'had a pair of sheets table cloth stolen out of the garden', whereas a visitor to Colonel Andrew Hynes' plantation had a trunk full of clothing stolen while his luggage was being loaded onto the steamer.[48]

Some stolen property supplemented the slaves' diet. Planter F.D. Richardson alluded to this in writing about slaves 'committing depredations in the way of robberies', and claiming that 'the whole matter is no doubt attributable to the high price of pork – for many planters will not buy at the present rates & depend upon a little beef and other things as a substitute'. Martha Stuart, formerly a slave on a Louisiana sugar plantation, recalled that 'ma Marster had a brother, they called him Charles Haynes and he was mean and he didn't feed his people . . . he didn't give 'em nuthin; 'twas the funniest thing tho; his niggers was all fat and fine cause dey'd go out and kill hogs – dey'd steal dem from de boss'.[49] In addition to improving slaves' diet, clothing and lodgings directly, goods stolen by slaves were traded for other commodities or for cash. Theft made an important contribution both to the slaves' economy and to their well-being.

Like the plantation economy, the slaves' independent economic production varied with the seasons. Fall and winter saw the injection of large sums of money into the internal economy, since slaves gained most of their income when they sold their cash crops and when they delivered wood prior to the beginning of the sugar harvest. Valcour Aime, a St James Parish planter, paid $1,300 to slaves on his plantation for their 1848 corn crop, and in October 1859 slaves on the Uncle Sam estate received over $1,000 for cutting wood and making barrels and bricks. The following year slaves on Uncle Sam earned about $500 for wood, bricks and barrels, and the year after, the total paid was $843. Similar payment schedules, involving sums from a few dollars to hundreds, occur regularly in plantation records.[50]

Stealing from the sugar house also was seasonal, since it had to be carried out between the time the crop was processed and was shipped off the estate.

Furthermore, gifts from planters were usually distributed at the end of harvest or at Christmas. Christmas, according to T. B. Thorpe, was

> the season when the planter makes presents of calico of flaming colors to the women and children, and a coat of extra fineness to patriarchal 'boys' of sixty-five and seventy. It is the time when negroes square their accounts with each other, and get 'master' and 'mistress' to pay up for innumerable eggs and chickens which they have frome time to time, since the last settling day, furnished the 'big house', In short, it is a kind of jubilee, when the 'poor African' as he is termed in poetry, has a pocket full of silver, [and] a body covered with gay toggery.[51]

Not all of the entry of cash occurred in late fall and early winter. Poultry provided year-round earnings, as did theft, day labour, moss-collecting and other commercial ventures. The sugar harvest, however, was another matter. The uninterrupted labour schedule left slaves little, if any, free time to devote to their own economic interests. At this time, slaves had to be preoccupied with the basic necessities of survival – food and rest. Apart from those paid for their services during harvest (such as kettle-men, firemen, sugar-makers and engineers), and those able to 'appropriate' some of the sugar and molasses for themselves, slaves had little opportunity to advance their economic position. Additionally, they had little time to spend their money during harvest.

The internal economy, therefore, had a distinct seasonal profile. Earnings fluctuated considerably since the labour demands of sugar slavery, especially during harvest, overlaid the seasonal nature of income derived from growing and marketing crops. Earnings potential also varied from year to year, since the slaves' cash crops were subject to the vagaries of the weather. Poor growing years diminished profitability for the slaves as well as the planters.

Not all slaves participated in the internal economy equally and some may not have participated at all, although it was an integral part of community life on every sugar plantation in Louisiana. Considerable disparities existed in the earnings of slaves even within the same plantation. The money accumulated by individual slaves on Benjamin Tureaud's estate for 1858–1859 ranged from $170 to $1 (during this period, 104 slaves on the estate earned a total of $3,423, with most adult slaves earning between $15 and $50). Some slaves, including 22 of the 30 women and two of the 98 men, earned no money, although, since many received credit, there was the expectation of future earnings. Similarly, cash earned by slaves on the Gay family plantation in 1844 ranged from $82 to $1 with some slaves also getting credit: 66 slaves earned a total of $864 and ten slaves received $32 in credit in that year. The 23 slaves paid for cutting wood on the Stirling estate in 1849 received sums of from $10 to $1 as their share of the total of $103 paid, while an 1854 list records payments of from $15 to 10 cents in the total of $314 paid the 50 women and 45 men.[52]

Plantation records, however, provide only a partial reckoning of the slaves' earnings, containing payments for certain commodities or work performed. They do not record income earned off the plantation. Other earnings would also have been unevenly distributed, although they did not necessarily benefit the same slaves. Those slaves who derived the greatest profit from dealings with river traders or through theft, for example, may not have been the same slaves who made the most money in transactions with the planter.

The internal economy permitted slaves to enjoy substantial material benefits. Slaves used their earnings for self-improvement – to eat and dress better and to live in more comfortable homes, caring in these and other ways for themselves and for members of their families. Although earnings were often small and purchases modest – sugar plantation slaves could not, for example, expect to earn enough to purchase freedom for themselves or their families – they reflect the independent actions of slaves as consumers and offer insight into the way slaves dealt with their lives in bondage.

The purchases made by Louisiana slaves fell principally into six categories: food and drink, pipes and tobacco, clothing and other personal items, housewares, tools and implements, and livestock. Within these six categories, however, slaves chose from a wide range of goods. They bought such foodstuffs as flour, molasses, meat, fish, coffee, beans, rice, potatoes, fruit and bottles of cordial. They also purchased a variety of clothing and cloth from which they made their 'best clothing'. Among more elaborate purchases were 'Elegant Bonnets', 'fine Summer Coats', 'Fine Russian Hats', 'Chambray', white and coloured shirts, jackets and waistcoats, silk dresses, gloves, oiled-cloth and 'log cabin' pantaloons, and oiled-cloth winter coats. More usually, however, slaves purchased plainer goods: lengths of calico, checked, plain, and striped cotton, linen, cottonade, 'domestic', blue drilling and thread, as well as simpler ready-made clothing like dresses, hose, shirts, pants, hats, shoes and boots, kerchiefs, suspenders and shawls. Besides clothes, slaves bought such personal items as pocket knives, combs, fiddles and umbrellas. Patrick, a slave 'Engineer and Overseer' on the Gay family's plantation, even paid $15 for a watch. Slaves bought an equally diverse range of housewares. Their purchases included furniture, bedspreads, blankets, baskets, tin cups and buckets, copper kettles, chairs, bowls and pots, cutlery, locks, mosquito bars, soap and tallow, and spermaceti candles. Furthermore, Louisiana slaves made extensive use of chewing and pipe tobacco, which they bought along with pipes. Some of the purchases slaves made represented an investment in their economic activities, including various implements and tools, such as shovels, saddles, bridles and bits, wire, twine, fishing hooks and line, 'mud boots' and mitts. They also invested in pigs, shoats and poultry.[53]

Obviously not every slave bought such a wide range of goods. The foregoing derives from the records of purchases made by hundreds of slaves on some 20 Louisiana sugar plantations in the years between 1834 and the Civil War. This extensive listing, however, does indicate overall trends in slave purchases.

Slaves' buying practices underwent little change over time. Throughout the period they placed high priority on a limited number of commodities – specifically flour, cloth and tobacco – with other goods given primacy, including shoes and various items of ready-made clothing. This general pattern held not only over time but also from plantation to plantation. When slaves had only limited purchasing power they tended to buy these few staple commodities, whereas slaves with larger earnings purchased other goods in addition to the staples.

Rations distributed by planters could, in specific cases, alter slaves' buying habits; slaves obviously did not have to buy goods if they were given them by the planter. On the Gay plantation, for example, slaves received a regular ration of tobacco and hence an extensive itemization of purchases on that estate reveals them buying none.[54] The slaves' buying habits reveal that they wanted to enrich their diet, dress better, smoke tobacco and drink liquor. Slaves considered the purchase of the more elaborate personal goods, housewares and other items, of secondary import. They bought such goods only if they had money left over after buying the 'staples'.

Various plantation accounts provide evidence of this pattern. On one of Benjamin Tureaud's sugar plantations, for example, of the 93 men who bought goods through the plantation, 76 (82 per cent) spent part of their earnings on tobacco, 77 (83 per cent) bought shoes, and 70 (75 per cent) bought either meat or flour. In addition, the majority of the slaves (51 out of the 93 – 55 per cent) bought some cloth or clothing other than shoes. Conversely, a minority of slaves bought such items as mosquito bars, locks, buckets and sheet-tin. The records of the Weeks family's Grande Cote Island sugar estate substantiate this pattern. The principal commodities slaves bought there were striped cotton, handkerchiefs, tobacco, flour and coffee. Records of other Louisiana sugar plantations reveal similar purchasing patterns.[55]

Slaves managed their own earnings, purchasing needed goods and saving the rest. Planters co-operated with slaves in establishing plantation accounts which credited slaves for work or goods and which slaves could use as depositories for earnings made off the plantation. Planters also acted as intermediaries in many of the expenditures made by slaves; that is, slaves made their purchases through the planter, the cost being debited from the slaves' personal accounts. Similarly, any money accrued from intracommunity transactions, such as T. B. Thorpe alluded to ('the time when negroes square their accounts with each other'), could be deposited with the planter. Given the extent to which slaves withdrew and deposited cash, the plantation slave communities were familiar with the medium of hard currency, albeit in small denominations, and were acquainted with both a barter system and a cash economy.[56]

Slaves were also conversant with the operation of a credit economy. On the Gay plantation, for example, nine slaves received a total of $32 in credit in 1844. Six of the slaves used their credit to obtain flour and coffee, two withdrew theirs in cash, while one slave, Elias, spent part of his $4 of credit on a 'Fine Russian Hat bt. in N. Orleans' that cost him $3. The other dollar went to pay a previous balance he owed on clothes. Similarly, on the Tureaud estate two slaves, Nash and David Big, received flour, meat, handkerchiefs, check cloth, shoes and tobacco on credit, while another slave, Charles Yellow, who had earned only $2 cutting wood, bought tobacco, flour, shoes, hose, meat, handkerchiefs, cotton cloth and a hat. Since the bill for these goods came to $15.50, the planter extended credit to Charles Yellow for the balance of $13.50.[57]

Debiting systems and purchasing patterns indicate that the slave accounts were family accounts designated under the name of the head of household, almost always a man. Few slave women had accounts listed in their own names. On the Tureaud estate, for example, 98 men all transacted business in their own names in 1858 and 1859, whereas of the 30 women listed in the ledger only eight accumulated any earnings; the other 22 had neither debits nor credits. Similarly, the Gay plantation records show only a handful of women with accounts in their own names, either in comparison to the number of men (six women and 70 men), or in comparison to the total number of 70 adult women living on the estate.

That few women held accounts, of course, neither reflects their lack of involvement in the system nor suggests that they accrued fewer benefits from it.[58]

Wives had recourse to accounts listed under their husbands' names and made purchases through them. On John Randolph's Nottoway Plantation, for example, three slave women had their purchases of shoes deducted from the accounts of slave men. Two of these women, Mahala and Susan, each received a pair of shoes at the cost of $1, which was debited from the accounts of George and Gus respectively, while in another case, the journal records, 'Long William got one pr. Shoes (for Leana) – $1'. An 1864 'List of Negroes' shows that George and Mahala were husband and wife, and one may assume that Gus and Susan and Long William and Leana were also married or closely related, although it is also possible that they had some sort of non-kin working or contractual relationship. The accounts of slaves on the Gay plantation provide further evidence. In 1841 William Sanders had his account debited to pay for a 'White Cambrice dress for wife'. In 1839 Little Moses' account paid for shoes for his wife, Charity; five years later Ned Davis was charged for 'Coffee by your wife'. A slave named Willis bought children's shoes from his account on the Tureaud estate, while Kenawa Moses, a slave on the Gay estate, paid for 'meat for [his] children' from the money he earned. Other slaves on the Gay estate who were charged for goods for family members included Harry Cooper, who bought shoes for his wife and his daughter Tulip, and Alfred Cooper, who purchased calico for his daughter Louisiana and two 'Elegant Bonnets' costing $2 each, presumably for his wife Dedo and his daughter.[59]

The debiting systems and the purchasing patterns thus indicate that the slave accounts were family accounts to which the family of the account-holder had access. Purchases went to improve the lives and comfort not only of the slaves who were debited for the goods, but also of members of their families. Staple foodstuffs – meat and flour for example – fed the entire family, while the lengths of cloth bought through the accounts would have been sewn by the women of the family to provide garments for all. Similarly, furniture, cutlery and other tableware, cooking utensils, blankets, locks, mosquito bars, soap and candles would have been used by the household. Even where the records make no mention of kin-relationship, as in the debit of $12.50 from the account of Woodson, a slave on W. W. Pugh's estate, for a 'Silk Dress for Rachel', and in the 'cash [paid] to Aunt Julia' from Patrick's account on the Gay plantation, it seems likely that the men and women were kin.[60]

Records of the Gay estate reveal the familial basis of the slaves' accounts. A comparison of the 1844 slave accounts on the plantation with other slave lists compiled around the same time shows the family relationships of the account-holders. Seventy-six people earned money and held accounts, 70 of whom were men. Of these 70 male, account-holders, 37 were heads of households, six were sons in male-headed households, three were sons in female-headed households and 18 were single males without family affiliation. (The status of the remaining six men is unclear.) Of the six women holding accounts, two were heads of households, one was a daughter in a female-headed household, and one a single woman. The two other women held joint accounts; Clarissa with her husband Toney (Toney also held an account with another slave, Ned Teagle, who was a son in a female-headed household) and Anna with William, neither of whom can be traced elsewhere in the plantation records. Some of the slaves recorded as single and without family affiliation nevertheless had families who drew on their accounts. The slave named Kenawa Moses, for example, who was listed as single, paid from his account for 'meat for [his] children'. The accounts held by sons in either male- or female-headed households suggests a 'coming of age' pattern. Young adults may have been listed individually, for example, when they assumed sole responsibility for a specific money-making endeavour.[61]

Slaves did not rely on the planters for all their purchases. Although they may or may not have kept accounts on the plantation, slaves frequently found reasons to buy elsewhere. Ex-slave Catherine Cornelius recalled that on the plantation where she lived the owner 'wouldn't gib us combs en brushes, but we got some from pedlin'.[62] Slaves also bought and traded for alcohol. Markets outside the plantation were usually the only source from which slaves could obtain liquor, since planters did not usually supply it (although they occasionally distributed it on holidays, like Christmas) and rarely allowed slaves to buy it through the plantation accounts.[63] Doubtless some of the cash slaves withdrew from their accounts went to purchase alcohol from river traders, illicit 'shebeens' and grog shops, or 'moonshiners, either on or off the plantation. Slaves also spent money gambling, as evidenced by reports of slaves 'drunk and gambling' on Sunday in Plaquemine township. Cultural and religious items and locally crafted artifacts made by slave artisans were also purchased through agencies other than the planter.[64]

Participation in the internal economy offered slaves a number of less tangible benefits. Slaves who worked for themselves and accumulated money and goods not only supplemented their often meagre rations and compensated for deficiencies in food and other necessities, but also derived satisfaction from controlling a portion of their own lives. In assuming responsibility for structuring their independent economic activities, slaves chose the manner and extent of their involvement, decided which crops they would grow and how to distribute time between small-holding agricultural pursuits and work for which planters paid them, when to sell and what to buy: decisions not normally allowed them. Although the internal economy operated within the constraints imposed by chattel bondage, the opportunity for independent economic activity gave slaves a degree of control and independence at variance with the basic tenets of servitude. Slaves *qua* slaves operated within a structure of social and labour relations that deprived them of personal rights, autonomous actions, decision-making and self-motivated work regimes. As independent economic agents, however, they structured their own efforts, controlled 'their' land and the manner of its cultivation, and decided how to market produce and dispose of the accumulated profits.

The independent activities of slaves on Mavis Grove Estate in Plaquemines Parish provide a telling example of the disparity between the slaves' lives as slaves and their lives as independent producers. On Sunday 13 September 1857 the plantation journal recorded 'Boys not cutting wood today, resting from the fatigues of last night's frolic'. Although slaves on Mavis Grove normally spent Sunday chopping wood for sale to the planter, they themselves agreed to take that Sunday off. This balancing of work with social concerns demonstrates that slaves working within the confines of the internal economy determined how to order their time and labour and shows their priorities. Indeed, the structure of the slaves' internal economy, where they assumed the responsibility of deciding how to organize their work, resembled the economy of a landed peasantry.[65]

The processes by which slaves controlled their independent economies doubt-less proved cathartic. Although involvement had potentially deleterious effects, such as overwork and physical stress, slaves found independent production rewarding. They derived great satisfaction from working for themselves, pacing their work and organizing their own efforts, as well as controlling the disposal of, and profiting directly from, the fruits of their labour. The independent economic activities, more-over, established the material foundations for slave family and community life. Patterns of production and marketing permitted not only economic independence and distance from the planters' control but also helped establish unique patterns of life within slave communities, providing an independent material basis for their society and culture. The diversity and ubiquity of the economic activities of slaves in Louisiana testifies to their creative initiative. Although planters no doubt found benefits in the slaves' internal economy, this system of independent production prompted enterprise not subservience. Whereas the plantation economy followed the planters' will, the slaves' economy contradicted the very premises of chattel bondage and helped to shape patterns of African-American life, culture and economy that endured from slavery to freedom.

Notes

1   J. Carlyle Sitterson, *Sugar Country: The Cane Sugar Industry in the South* (Lexington, 1953), 28–30, 60.
2   Ibid., 48; *Hunt's Merchant's Magazine and Commercial Review*, 7:2 (Aug. 1842). 133–47; 7:3 (Sept. 1842), 242; 30:4 (April 1854), 499; 31:6 (Dec. 1854), 675–91; 35:2 (Aug. 1856), 248–9; *De Bow's Review*, 1 (1846), 54–5; Joseph C.C. Kennedy, Population of the United States in 1860; compiled from the Original Returns of the *Eighth Census* (Washington, DC, 1864), 188–93. Here and subsequently numbers have been rounded off.
3   Sitterson, *Sugar Country*, 30, 48–50; *De Bow's*, 1 (1846), 54–5; 19 (1855), 354; *Hunt's*, 30:4 (April 1854), 499; 35:2 (Aug. 1856), 248–9; 42:2 (Feb. 1860), 163.
4   Sugar cane did not have to be replanted following each harvest since the stubble left after cutting sprouted new shoots or ratoons.
5   Captain Thomas Hamilton, *Men and Manners in America* (Edinburgh and London, 1833), 2: 229–30.
6   Ibid., 2: 229; Frances Milton Trollope, *Domestic Manners of the Americans*, ed. by Donald Smalley (New York, 1949), 246; E.S. Abdy, *Journal of a Residence and Tour in the United States of North America, from April 1833 to October 1834* (London, 1835), 3: 103–4.
7   T.B. Thorpe, 'Sugar and the Sugar Region of Louisiana', *Harper's New Monthly Magazine*, 7 (1853), 753; William Howard Russell, *My Diary North and South* (London, 1863), 371; Interview conducted under the auspices of the Slave Narrative Collection Project, Federal Writers' Project, Works Progress Administration. Interviewee – Elizabeth Ross Hite: Interviewer – Robert McKinney: Date – c. 1940, Louisiana Writers' Project File, Louisiana State Library, Baton Rouge, Louisiana (LWPF, LSL); Interview conducted under the auspices of a Slave Narrative Collection Project organized by Dillard University (DUSNCP) using only black interviewers. This project developed alongside the Federal Writers Project program. Interviewee – Catherine Cornelius: Interviewer – Octave Lilly Jr: Date – c. 1939, Archives and Manuscripts Department, Earl K. Long Library, University of New Orleans, New Orleans, Louisiana.
8   Interviewee – Melinda (last name unknown): Interviewer – Arguedas: Date – c. 1940: F.W.P. Interviews, Federal Writers' Project Files, Melrose Collection, Archives Division, Northwestern State University of Louisiana, Natchitoches, Louisiana (LWPF, NSU).
9   Russell, My *Diary*, 399; Interview with Elizabeth Ross Hite, LWPF, LSL; Plantation Diary, Vol. 1, 1838–40, Samuel McCutcheon Papers, Department of Archives and Manuscripts, Louisiana State University, Baton Rouge; Interview with Catherine Cornelius, DUSNCP.

10 Ashland Plantation Record Book, Archives, LSU.

11 Isaac Erwin Diary, Archives, LSU; Plantation Diary of Valcour Aime, Louisiana Historical Center, Louisiana State Museum, New Orleans.

12 Plantation Diary and Ledger, Elu Landry Estate, Archives, LSU.

13 Plantation Diary and Ledger, Landry Papers; Journal 6, Plantation Book 1853–63, John H. Randolph Papers. Archives, LSU.

14 *De Bow's Review*, 4 (1847), 393; 6 (1848), 436; 7 (1849), 420; 9 (1850), 456; 11 (1851), 496; 13(1852), 512; 15 (1853), 528; 17 (1854), 530; 19 (1855), 458; 21 (1856), 368; 23 (1857), 365; 25 (1858), 469; 27 (1859), 477; 29 (1860), 521; Sam Bowers Hilliard, *Hog Meat and Hoecake* (Carbondale. Ill., 1972). 155.

15 'Negroes Corn for 1857', Box 9, Folder 54; 'Negroes Corn 1859', Box 9, Folder 57, Lewis Stirling and Family Papers, Archives, LSU.

16 Ledger 1858–72, Benjamin Tureaud Papers, Archives, LSU; Daybook 1843–47 (Vol. 5), Edward J. Gay and Family Papers, Archives, LSU.

17 Plantation Diary of Valcour Aime; Daybook 1843–47 (Vol. 5), Gay Papers.

18 Thorpe, 'Sugar and the Sugar Region', 753; Russell, *My Diary*, 373; Thomas Haley to Mrs Mary Weeks, 11 April 1841, Box 9, Folder 29, David Weeks and Family Papers, Archives, LSU; Notebook 1853–57 (Vol. 9), The Weeks Hall Memorial Collection, David Weeks and Family Collection, Archives, LSU; Daybook 1843–47 (Vol. 5), Gay Papers; Ledger 1851–56 (Vol. 18), George Lanaux and Family Papers, Archives, LSU; Cashbook for Negroes 1848–55 (Vol. 6), W.W. Pugh Papers, Archives, LSU.

19 Russell, *My Diary*, 396.

20 'Statements of the Sugar and Rice Crops Made in Louisiana', by L. Bouchereau (New Orleans, 1871) in Box 1, Folder 1, UU-211, No. 555, Pharr Family Papers, Archives, LSU; Box 7, Folder 39, Stirling Papers; Boxes 1 and 2. Uncle Sam Plantation Papers, Archives, LSU; Joseph K. Men, *The Large Slaveholders of Louisiana – 1860* (New Orleans. 1964), 353–4; Plantation Record Book 1849–60 (Vol. 36), Gay Papers; Journal 1851–60 (Vol. 14), Lanaux Papers.

21 Plantation Diary 1842–59, 1867, William T. Palfrey & George D. Palfrey Account Books, Archives, LSU.

22 Diary 1847 (Vol. 1), Kenner Family Papers, Archives, LSU; Plantation Record Book 1849–60 (Vol. 36), Gay Papers; Cashbook for Negroes 1848–55 (Vol. 6), W.W. Pugh Papers.

23 Cashbook for Negroes 1848–55 (Vol. 6), W.W. Pugh Papers; Plantation Record Book 1849–60 (Vol. 36), Gay Papers.

24 Daybook 1843–47 (Vol. 5); Plantation Record Book 1849–60 (Vol. 36); 'Memorandum relative to payments to negroes Dec. 1844', Box 11, Folder 81, Gay Papers.

25 Ledger 1858–72, Tureaud Papers; S-124 (9) No. 2668, Bruce, Seddon and Wilkins Plantation Records, Archives, LSU.

26 Plantation Record Book, 1849–60 (Vol. 36), Gay Papers.

27 Journal 6, Plantation Book 1853–63, Randolph Papers.

28 Interviewee – Martha Stuart: Interviewer – Octave Lilly Jr: Date – c. 1938: DUSNCP; Interview with Elizabeth Ross Hite, LWPF, LSU.

29 Journal – Plantation Book 1847–52 (Vol. 5); Journal 6, Plantation Book 1853–63, Randolph Papers; Box 8, Folder 49; Box 8. Folder 51, Stirling Papers; Estate Record Book 1832–45 (Vol. 8); Cashbook/Daybook 1837–43 (Vol. 18), Gay Papers.

30 Interviewee – Hunton Love: Interviewer – unknown: Date – c. 1940; LWPF, LSL.

31 J.L. Rogers to Robert Ruffin Barrow, 29 Oct. 1853, Box 2, Folder 1850 s–20; Residence Journal of R.R. Barrow, 1 Jan, 1857–13 June 1858, (copied from original manuscript in Southern Historical Collection, University of North Carolina, Chapel Hill, North Carolina), Department of Archives, Tulane University, New Orleans: Book of Accounts of the Magnolia Plantation 1829–53, Louisiana State Museum.

32 Edward Gay to Hynes and Craighead, 6 April 1844: 'Account 1844, Memorandum, Sale of moss for the negroes', Box 11, Folder 81, Gay Papers.

33 Moss Record Book 1849–61 (Vol. 35); Boxes 11–13, Folders 81–96, Gay Papers; Residence Journal of R.R. Barrow, 1857–58, Barrow Papers.

34 Moss Record Book 1849–61 (Vol. 35); Estate Record Book 1848–55 (Vol. 34), Gay Papers: Menn, *Large Slaveholders*, 244–5.
35 Ashland Plantation Record Book; Daybook 1843–47 (Vol. 5); Box 12, Folder 86; 'Sales of Moss & Molasses belonging to the Negroes, Box 13, Folder 100; Box 12, Folder 93; Box 13, Folder 96, Gay Papers.
36 Journal 6, Plantation Book 1853–63, Randolph Papers; Plantation Diary and Ledger. Landry Papers.
37 Rev. P.M. Goodwyn, to Edward Gay. 27 Aug. 1860, Box 29, Folder 255, Gay Papers.
38 Russell, My *Diary*, 396.
39 Ibid., 373; P.E. Jennings to Edward Gay, 25 Aug. 1858, Box 25, Folder 221, Gay Papers.
40 W.F. Weeks to Mary C. Moore, 31 Jan. 1853, Box 31, Folder 82, Weeks Papers.
41 Interviewee – Frances Doby: Interviewers – Arguedas–McKinney Date – 1938: LWPF, NSU; Interview with Catherine Cornelius, DUSNCP; (William Kingsford), *Impressions of the West and South during a Six Weeks' Holiday* (Toronto, 1858), 47–8.
42 U.B. Phillips (comp.), *The Revised Statutes of Louisiana* (New Orleans, 1856), 48–65.
43 Maunsell White to G. Lanneau, 15 April 1859, Box 3. Folder 1, Lanaux Papers.
44 Frederick Law Olmsted. *A Journey in the Seaboard Slave States* (New York, 1856), 674.
45 Ibid., 675.
46 William F. Weeks to Mary C. Moore, 20 June 1860, Box 36, Folder 180, Weeks Papers.
47 Joseph Mather Diary 1852–59, Archives, LSU; Diary and Plantation Record of Elicit E. McCollam, Andrew and Ellen E. McCollam Papers, Archives, LSU; Maunsell White to James P. Bracewell, 10 Aug. 1859, Maunsell White Letterbook, Archives, LSU; J.E. Craighead to John B. Craighead. 11 Sept. 1847, Box 14, Folder 102, Gay Papers; Lyle Saxon (comp.), *Gumbo Ya-Ya* (Boston, 1945), 430.
48 Diary and Plantation Record of Ellen McCollam, McCollam Papers; Plantation Diary and Ledger, Landry Papers; Nicholas Phipps to Colonel Andrew Hynes, Feb. 1847, Box 13, Folder 97, Gay Papers.
49 F.D. Richardson to Moses Liddell, 18 July 1852, Safe 12, Folder 3, Moses and St John R. Liddell and Family Papers, Archives, LSU; Interview with Martha Stuart, DUSNCP.
50 Plantation Diary of Valcour Aime 1847–52; Boxes 1 and 2, Uncle Sam Papers.
51 T.B. 'Thorpe, 'Christmas in the South', *Frank Leslie's Illustrated Newspaper*, 5 (26 Dec. 1857), 62.
52 Ledger 1858–72, Tureaud Papers; Daybook 1843–47 (Vol. 5); Moss Record Book 1849–61 (Vol. 35), Gay Papers; 'List of Wood Cut by Slaves and Payment Made', Box 7, Folder 39; Box 8, Folder 39, Stirling Papers.
53 Ledger 1858–72, Tureaud Papers; Daybook 1843–47, Gay Papers; Journal – Plantation Book 1848–52, Randolph Papers; Plantation Record Book 1849–60, Gay Papers; Wilton Plantation Daily Journal 1853, Bruce, Seddon and Wilkins Records; Journal 1851–60, Journal 1851–56, Lanaux Papers; Cashbook for Negroes 1848–55, W.W. Pugh Papers.
54 P.O. Daigre to Edward J. Gay, 15 Aug. 1858, Box 25, Folder 221, Gay Papers.
55 Ledger 1858–72, Tureaud Papers; Notebook 1853–57 (Vol. 9), Weeks Collection.
56 Ledger 1858–72, Tureaud Papers; Daybook 1843–47, Gay Papers; T.B. Thorpe, 'Christmas', 62.
57 Ledger 1858–72, Tureaud Papers; Daybook 1843–47, Gay Papers.
58 Ledger 1858–72, Tureaud Papers; Daybook 1843–47, Gay Papers.
59 Ledger 1862–65 (Vol. 8), Randolph Papers; Memorandum Book 1840–41 (Vol. 28); Estate Record Book 1831–45 (Vol. 8), Gay Papers.
60 Cashbook for Negroes 1848–55, W.W. Pugh Papers; Daybook 1843–47, Gay Papers.
61 Estate Record Book 1831–45 (Vol. 8); Cashbook/Daybook 1837–43 (Vol. 18), Gay Papers.
62 Interview with Catherine Cornelius, DUSNCP.
63 Kingsford, *Impressions*, 47–8; V. Alton Moody, *Slavery on Louisiana Sugar Plantations* (New Orleans, 1924), 68. Slaves on the Gay family's estate, for example, were occasionally given whiskey. On 28 Dec. 1846 'whiskey for Negroes dinner' cost $1.50, and on 25 Dec. 1850 'Whiskey for Negroes' cost $2.50. The planter paid for these items. Estate Record Book 1842–47 (Vol. 12); Estate Record Book 1848–55 (Vol. 34), Gay Papers.
64 P.E. Jennings to Edward J. Gay, 25 Aug. 1858, Box 25, Folder 221, Gay Papers.
65 Journal of Mavis Grove Plantation 1856, Louisiana State Museum.

Chapter 23

Hilary McD. Beckles

AN ECONOMIC LIFE OF THEIR OWN
Slaves as commodity producers and distributors in Barbados

S TUDIES OF PATTERNS of property ownership and resource use in the Caribbean slave societies have generally focused on the nature of economic conditions within the free, mostly white, communities. Particular attention has been given, for example, to the manner in which economic relations developed between the dominant mercantile and planting communities. Scholars who have examined the economic experiences of free people of colour have reinforced opinions held about the tendencies of the white elite to monopolize the market. The slaves' independent economic behaviour, especially for the English colonies, has received less attention. The neglect of this subject is surprising, since slave hucksters had great influence over the informal commercial sector of most island economies. Comprehending the economic role of slave marketing practices will provide both a more realistic understanding of slave life and a firmer basis for interpreting the nature of master–slave relations in the economic sphere of plantation culture.

Much evidence exists to illustrate that slaves, like free persons, sought to increase their share of colonial wealth by participating in the market economy as commodity producers and distributors, with and without their owners' permission. Although they were undoubtedly the primary victims of colonial economies, in which they were defined and used as property, generations of slaves managed, none the less, to identify and pursue their own material interests.[1] By combining their work as fieldhands, artisans, domestics, or whatever with their own productive and commercial activities, slaves made economic decisions as 'free' persons. At least such was the case on the island of Barbados.

For slave owners, the largely independent activities of slaves at times complicated the generally understood terms and conditions of chattel slavery. In nearly all instances, property owning whites, who dominated colonial governments in the Caribbean, objected to market competition from slaves and enacted legislation that gradually proscribed their economic activities.[2] Since slave owners considered the slaves' subordination critical to the island's system of control, they sought to assert their dominance in all economic relations, no matter how petty. On Barbados, slaves tenaciously resisted such legislative assaults upon this aspect of their independent economic activities and made from the outset a determined effort to maintain their market participation. At times, Barbadian slave owners adopted concessionary policies, prompted generally by their desire to secure the wider goals of social stability and high levels of labor productivity. Slaves, in turn, converted the most limited concessions into customary rights and defended them adamantly.

Huckstering, the distributive dimension of small-scale productive domestic activity, was familiar to Africans. It was certainly as much part of their culture as other more well-known aspects of Afro-American life, such as religion and the arts. Its attractiveness to slaves, however, had much to do with the social and material conditions of their enslavement. Huckstering afforded slaves the opportunity to improve the quantity and quality of their nutrition in environments where malnutrition was the norm.[3] It allowed them to possess and later own property, which in itself represented an important symbolic offensive against the established order. It enabled them to make profitable use of their leisure time. And it afforded them the chance to travel and normalize their social lives as much as possible under highly restrictive circumstances.

The relations between slaves' independent production and huckstering provides the context in which the development of the internal marketing systems can be understood. In what accounts to a typology of food production, Sidney Mintz and Douglas Hall[4] have shown how the autonomous economic life of slaves in Barbados, and other smaller sugar monoculture plantation colonies, differed from that of their Jamaican counterparts. Within this analysis, they divided plantation systems into two basic categories: first, those in which slaves were fed by their masters, such as Barbados; and, second, those in which slaves were largely responsible for producing their own subsistence, such as Jamaica.

In Barbados especially, planters allotted 'land to food cultivation only by impinging on areas which, generally, could be more profitably planted in cane'. The planters' policy was to 'restrict the land at the disposal of the slaves to small house plots', import food for the slaves, and include 'some food production in the general estate program'.[5] In Jamaica, owners allotted their slaves large tracts of land unsuited to cane production in the foothill of the mountain ranges and there encouraged slaves to produce their own food. These provision grounds or polinks represented the primary form of food cultivation, and slaves were given managerial authority in this activity. In addition to these provision grounds, which were generally located miles from their homes, Jamaican slaves also cultivated little 'house spots'.

The provision grounds on which Jamaican slaves became experienced proto-peasants constituted the basis of their entry into, and subsequent domination of, the internal marketing system. White society came to depend heavily upon the slaves' produce. There was, as a result, no persistent legislative attempt to arrest and eradicate the slaves' commercial activities and, by the mid-eighteenth century, the slaves' domination of the provisions market was institutionalized.[6]

The experience of slaves in Barbados was somewhat different in scale and character than that of those in Jamaica. Barbadian slaves had no provision grounds. They were fed from the masters' stocks, which were both imported and locally produced. Imported salted meat and plantation grown grain were allocated to slaves by their overseers, sometimes on Friday night, but mostly on Sunday morning. Slaves possessed only little house spots, generally no more than 25 yards square, on which to root their independent production and marketing activity. They could not therefore be defined as anything more than 'petty proto-peasants', and yet the vibrancy of their huckstering activities was no less developed than that in Jamaica where slaves cultivated acres of land.

Several visitors to Barbados paid attention to the relationship between slaves' receipt of food allowances and their huckstering. Dr George Pinckard, who toured the island during the mid-1790s, was especially perceptive. He noted that slaves received their subsistence on a weekly basis, 'mostly guinea corn, with a small bit of salt meat or salt fish', which served for 'breakfast, dinner and supper'. This diet, he added, was 'for the most part the same throughout the year', though 'rice, maize, yams, eddoes, and sweet potatoes form an occasional change'. But the slaves, 'in order to obtain some variety of food', were often seen 'offering guinea corn for sale' and using the proceeds obtained to 'buy salt meat or vegetables'. When slaves were asked why they preferred to sell or barter their food allocations, Pinckard declared, they would commonly

> express themselves: 'me no like for have guinea corn always! Massa gib me guinea corn too much – guinea corn today – guinea corn tomorrow – guinea corn eb'ry day – Me no like him guinea corn – him guinea corn no good for guhyaam'.[7]

In his 1808 *History of Barbados*, John Poyer, a white creole social commentator, agreed with Pinckard that slaves would generally 'barter the crude, unsavory, substantial allowance of the plantations for more palatable and nutritious food'.[8]

Pinckard, however, recognized that slaves did not rely fully on food rations in creating supplies of marketable goods. Rather, he observed, 'those who are industrious have little additions of their own, either from vegetables grown on the spot of ground allotted to them, or purchased with money obtained for the pig, the goat, or other stock raised about their huts in the negro yard'.[9] He regarded it as 'common for the slaves to plant fruit and vegetables, and to raise stocks'. At one hut on the Spendlove estate Pinckard 'saw a pig, a goat, a young kid, some pigeons, and some chickens, all the property of an individual slave'. He observed the advantages of these activities for both slave and master, for he thought garden plots and livestock afforded slaves 'occupation and amusement for their leisure moments', and created 'a degree of interest in the spot'.[10]

Thirty years later F.W. Bayley's account of the slaves' domestic economy, like that of Pinckard's, emphasized the raising of poultry and animals, as well as the cultivation of roots, vegetables and fruits. He described as 'pretty well cultivated' the 'small gardens' attached to slave huts. For him, 'slaves have always time' to cultivate their 'yams, tannias, plantains, bananas, sweet potatoes, okras, pineapples, and Indian corn'. To shade their homes from the 'burning rays and scorching heat of the tropic sun', noted Bayley, slaves planted a 'luxuriant foliage' of trees that bear 'sweet and pleasant fruits', such as the 'mango, the Java plum, the breadfruit, the soursop, the sabadilla and the pomegranate'. In 'every garden' could be found 'a hen coop' for some 'half dozen of fowls' and, in many, 'a pigsty', and 'goats tied under the shade of some tree'. Bayley also observed that while the animals were 'grazing or taking a nap' a watchful 'old negro woman was stationed near' to ensure that 'they were not kidnapped'.[11]

Retailing was the slaves' principal means of raising the cash necessary for their purchases, and many produced commodities specifically for sale. Sunday was their main market day (until 1826, when it became Saturday), although it was customary for 'respectable overseers and managers' to grant slaves time off during the week when 'work was not pressing' in order to market 'valuable articles of property'.[12] The established Anglican Church was never happy with Sunday marketing. In 1725 the catechist at Codrington Plantation informed the Bishop of London, under whose See Barbados fell: 'In this Island the Negroes work all week for their masters, and on the Lord's Day they work and merchandize for themselves; in the latter of which they are assisted, not only by the Jews, but many of those who call themselves Christians'.[13] Efforts made by the estate's managers to prevent Sunday trading were unsuccessful, and many insubordinate slaves went to their beds 'with very sore backsides unmercifully laid on'. The catechist suggested that the 'force of custom' among slaves in this regard would inevitably break through 'managerial resolve'.[14]

Descriptions of slave huckstering illustrate the extent to which these fettered entrepreneurs made inroads into the colony's internal economy. William Dickson reported in the late eighteenth century that slaves were seen all over the island on Sundays walking 'several miles to market with a few roots, or fruits, or canes, sometimes a fowl or a kid, or a pig from their little spots of ground which have been dignified with the illusive name of gardens'.[15] J.A. Thome and J.H. Kimball, who witnessed the disintegration of Barbados slavery in the nineteenth century, had much to say about the role of black people – slave and free – in the internal marketing system. Thome and Kimball were impressed by the spectacle of these 'busy marketeers', both 'men and women', 'pouring into the highways' at the 'crosspaths leading through the estates'. These plantation hucksters were seen 'strung' all along the road 'moving peaceably forward'. Thome and Kimball described as 'amusing' the 'almost infinite diversity of products' being transported, such as 'sweet potatoes, yams, eddoes, Guinea and Indian corn, various fruits and berries, vegetables, nuts, cakes, bundles of fire wood and bundles of sugar canes'. The women, as elsewhere, were in the majority. They mentioned one woman with 'a small black pig doubled up under her arm'; two girls, one with 'a brood of chickens, with a nest coop and all, on her head', and another with 'an immense turkey' also elevated on her head. Thome and Kimball were not only impressed with the 'spectacle' of this march to the Bridgetown market, but also with the hucksters' commercial organization, especially the manner in which their information network conveyed 'news concerning the state of the market'.[16]

Huckster slaves dominated the sale of food provisions in the Bridgetown market. Numerous urban slaves, however, retailed for their owners, mainly in the supply of non-agricultural foodstuffs, such as cakes, drinks, and a range of imported goods. According to Bayley, many Bridgetown inhabitants gained a livelihood by sending slaves about the town and suburbs with articles of various kinds for sale. These hucksters, mostly women, carried 'on their heads in wooden trays' all sorts of 'eatables, wearables, jewelry and dry goods'. Bayley also commented on the social origins of free persons who directed huckster slaves. Most, he stated, were less fortunate whites, but it was common for members of 'the higher classes of society' to 'endeavour to turn a penny by sending their slaves on such money-making excursions'.[17] Such slaves retailed exotic items such as 'pickles and pre-serves, oil, noyau, anisette, eau-de-cologne, toys, ribbons, handkerchiefs, and other little nick-knacks', most of which were imported from the neighbouring French island of Martinique.

Town slaves, who sold on their own account, marketed items such as 'sweets and sugar cakes'. Bayley described these items as 'about the most unwholesome eatables that the West Indies produce'. Hucksters could be found 'at the corner of almost every street' in Bridgetown, 'sitting on little stools' with their goods neatly displayed on trays. Plantation hucksters, then, posed no competition for their urban counterparts. There was a mutually beneficial relationship in which each provided a market for the other's goods.[18]

From the early eighteenth century, government policies respecting slave hucksters were informed by the planters' beliefs that a significant proportion of the goods sold at the Sunday markets were stolen from their estates. The assumptions that the tiny garden plots cultivated by slaves could not support the quantity of produce marketed and that hucksters were not sufficiently diligent and organized to sustain an honest trade throughout the year underpinned the debates in the Assemblies and Legislative Councils. It was more in the slaves' nature, planters argued, to seek the easier option of appropriating plantation stocks. The charge of theft, therefore, featured prominently in the planter's opinions and policies towards slave hucksters.

The acquisition of plantation stocks by slaves was one likely way to obtain items for the Sunday markets, though such acts of appropriation were difficult to separate from scavenging by malnourished slaves looking to improve their diet. There was little planters could do to eradicate the leakage of stocks into slave villages. In spite of the employment of numerous watchmen and guards to protect their property, they complained constantly about the cunning and deviousness of slaves in this regard.

Contrary to the planters, Pinckard found evidence of a sort of moral economy in which slaves asserted a legitimate right over a satisfactory share of the produce of their labour. Many slaves, he stated, were firm in the opinion that it was not immoral to appropriate plantation stock, but rather it was the master's inhumanity that denied them what was rightfully theirs, an adequate proportion of estate production. Slaves, he said, 'have no remorse in stealing whensoever and wheresoever' and do not accept the notion of 'robbing their masters'. They would commonly respond to the charge of theft, Pinckard added, with the expression: 'me no tief him; me take him from massa'.[19] The slaves' perception of the planter as the guilty party may have fuelled the highly organized system through which they sought redress by the clandestine redistribution of resources. The lavish overconsumption by the planter elite also enhanced the moral imperative implicit in the slaves' responses.

A case illustrative of the slaves' determination to increase their share of estate produce can be extracted from events on the Newton plantation between 1795 and 1797. During this time the manager, Mr Wood, made several references to the confiscation of stocks by slaves and considered it a major problem. Wood's account of the slaves' organized appropriation under the management of his predecessor, Mr Yard, provides a detailed view of extensive contact between plantation thief and huckstering. Dolly, the daughter of Old Doll, the estate's retired housekeeper, was brought into the house by Yard and kept as his mistress. On account of their intimate relations, Dolly obtained access to all stores, and it was believed that she 'pilfered' for the enrichment of her family. Sir John Alleyne, the estate's attorney, discovered the sexual relation between Yard and Dolly on a surprise visit to the property, and Yard's services were terminated. Dolly was removed from the household, but the flow of goods continued. When Wood conducted his investigation he realized that Billy Thomas, Dolly's cousin, who worked for Yard and was held 'in great confidence' and 'trusted with everything', was the culprit. Billy, noted Wood, 'had an opportunity of stealing the key of the box which held the key of the building'. This gave him and his family access to 'the rum, sugar, corn, and everything else which lay at their mercy'. Billy's aunt, Betsy, also a plantation slave, was married to a free black huckster who, 'through these connections', was 'supplied plentifully with everything'. Old Doll also did some huckstering and her home was described by Wood as a 'perfect out-shop for dry goods, rum, sugar, and other commodities'.[20]

A greater problem was posed for planters, however, when their slaves plundered the property of other persons, which was also another way of obtaining articles – especially fresh meat – for sale. Such cases involved more than estate discipline, and at times required criminal litigation. The records of Codrington Estate, for example, show that neighbouring planters commonly sought compensation outside of court when Codrington slaves were presumed guilty of theft. In some instances, however, courts settled such matters. In 1746, for example, Richard Coombs was paid £1 by the estate 'for a hog of his kill'd by the plantation negroes'. The following year James Toppin was paid 3s 9d 'for a turkey stolen from him by the negro John', and in 1779 the manager paid William Gall £8 when he agreed not to sue at law 'for a bull stolen' from him by a group of field slaves.[21] It was suspected that these stocks found their way onto the market through white intermediaries who worked in league with slaves.

Most contemporaries believed that the typical huckster's income, outside of what was earned from the occasional sale of high priced fresh meats, was meagre.[22] Bayley offered an account of their annual earnings by estimating the values of produce sold. In normal times, he noted, 'a tray of vegetables, fruits, calabashes, etc.' brought in gross annual receipts of six or seven shillings. The sale of poultry and animals, in addition to 'cane, cloth, and sugar', would increase receipts to about 'ten shillings'.[23] Such an income level, Bayley suggested, could not sustain a slave's life without plantation allowances. Free blacks or poor whites with such an income would have had to resort to the parish for relief.

Bayley, however, considered such modest incomes the result of the slave huckster's lack of the accumulationist spirit. Slavery, he believed, was responsible for the suppression of their acquisitive impulse. He made reference to slaves who had 'the power of earning' but 'frequently neglected it'. He attributed this to 'the cursed spirit of slavery' which 'leaves too many contented with what they deem sufficient for nature, without spurring them to exert themselves to gain an overplus'. Such persons, he added, would 'only cultivate sufficient ground to yield them as much fruit, as many vegetables as they require for their own consumption'. As a result, according to Bayley 'they have none to sell'.[24]

Bayley believed a minority of 'more enterprising' hucksters, who 'strive to make as much as they can', generally do very well. Some even accumulated enough cash to purchase their freedom. Most financially successful slaves in Bayley's opinion, however, lacked the appetite for freedom. 'I have known several negroes', he averred, who had accumulated large sums of money, more than enough to purchase their emancipation, but that as they saw no necessity for changing their condition, and were very well contented with a state of slavery, they preferred remaining in that state and allowing their money to increase.[25]

Bayley's belief was tempered by his recognition that many slaves realized that the free black's material and social life was frequently not an improvement over their own. Consequently, for some slaves it made more sense to seek the amelioration of their condition by the purchase of a 'host of comforts'. The use of cash to facilitate the education of their children was as important as the purchase of a 'few luxuries for their huts', Bayley concluded.[26] Plantation hucksters, who were mostly field slaves, did not live as well as the mechanics, artisans, domestics and drivers or other members of the slave elite. One was more likely to find a driver in a position to offer a visitor 'a glass of wine and a bit of plumcake' than a huckster.[27]

The poor white, living on the margins of plantation society, developed the most noticeable contacts with slave hucksters. From the seventeenth century, many white women labourers, mostly former indentured servants and their descendants, made a living by selling home-grown vegetables and poultry in the urban market. Largely Irish Catholics, they were discriminated against in the predominantly English Protestant community. They formed their own communities in back country areas of the St Lucy, St John, St Andrew, St Joseph, and St Philip parishes, where they cultivated crops as subsistence peasants on a variety of rocky, wet and sandy, non-sugar lands. Descriptions of their huckstering activity differ little from those of the slaves.

William Dickson, who studied the poor whites closely, offered a detailed account of their huckstering culture. Labouring Europeans, both men and women, he stated, 'till the ground without any assistance from negroes', and the 'women often walk many miles loaded with the produce of their little spots, which they exchange in the towns for such European goods as they can afford to purchase'.[28] Their gardens were generally larger than those utilized by slaves, as was the volume of commodities they traded. But in spite of their disadvantage, slaves offered their white counterparts stiff competition especially at the Sunday markets.

The relationship between slave and white hucksters was complex. Both Dickson and Pinckard commented that the marketing patterns and customs of the two showed similarities. White women hucksters were typically seen carrying baskets on their heads and children strapped to the hip in a typical African manner, which suggests some degree of cultural transfer. Dickson stated that some white hucksters owned small stores in the towns and most of these depended upon the exchange of goods with slaves. These hucksters, he said, 'make a practice of buying stolen goods from the negroes, whom they encourage to plunder their owners of everything that is portable'.[29]

Dickson made a strong moral plea for the protection of slave hucksters in their unequal relationship with their white counterparts. Until 1826 slaves had no legal right to own property, and they suffered frequent injustices in their transactions with whites. Many white hucksters, Dickson stated, 'depend for a subsistence on robbing the slaves' by taking their goods 'at their own price' or simply 'by seizing and illegally converting to their own use, articles of greater value', which the 'poor things may be carrying to market'. 'For such usage', he added, 'the injured party has no redress' and so 'a poor field negro, after having travelled eight or ten miles, on Sunday, is frequently robbed, by some town plunderer, within a short distance of his or her market, and returns home fatigued by the journey, and chagrined from having lost a precious day's labor'.[30] Slave owners were not prepared to offer huckster slaves – even those who sold on their account – protection from these white 'plunderers'. Many saw the matter as nothing more than thieves stealing from thieves, from which honest folk should distance themselves.

The detailed descriptions and accounts of slave huckstering offered by visitors to Barbados present a static image which underestimates the social and political tension and conflict that surrounded it. Concealed in these reports was an important social crisis. However common, huckstering was never fully accepted, and slaves struggled to maintain their marketing rights against hostile legislation. From the mid-seventeenth century Barbadian lawmakers designed legislation to prevent slave huckstering by linking it directly to a range of illicit activities. In addition, author-ities formulated policies to mobilize the entire white community against the slaves' involvement in marketing by stereotyping slaves as thieves and receivers of stolen goods. Against this background of persistent efforts to criminalize huckstering, slaves attempted to maintain an economic life of their own.

Initially, legislators considered it possible to prevent slaves going from 'house to house' with their 'goods and wares'. But a difficulty was recognized in that so many whites declared a willingness to accept slave hucksters. Legislators, there-fore, had to differentiate this 'deviant' element within the white community and target it for legal consideration. The 1688 Slave Code provided, for instance, that justices of the peace were required to identify such whites and warn them against transacting business with slave hucksters.[31] The law also empowered justices to take legal action against persistent offenders.

In 1694 an assemblyman who considered the 1688 provisions insufficient intro-duced two bills designed to remove slaves from the internal market economy. The first bill prohibited 'the sale of goods to negroes' and the second barred 'the employment of negroes in selling'.[32] The debate over this legislation focused on the need to prevent the employment of slaves in activities other than those related to plantations. Some planters, however, expressed concern that a curtailment of slaves' 'leisure' would impair already fragile labour relations on the estates. Slaves had grown accustomed to considerable freedom of movement during non-labouring hours and marketing was a direct consequence of this independent use of leisure time. The implementation of the proposed restrictions would entail closer surveil-lance of slaves – undoubtedly a major administrative task for local officials and slave owners alike.

The legislation never became law, but persistent complaints from small-scale white cash-crop producers, urban shopkeepers, and other of the slaves' competitors kept the subject at the forefront of discussion concerning the 'governing' of slaves. In 1708 the first of many eighteenth-century laws was finally passed attempting to undermine the huckstering culture of slaves. This 1708 law tackled every aspect of slave huckstering, both as a planter-controlled enterprise and as an independent slave activity. The preamble to the act linked huckstering to slave insubordination and criminality, stating that 'sundry persons do daily send their negroes and other slaves to the several towns in this island to sell and dispose of all sorts of Quick stock, corn, fruit, and pulse, and other things', with the result that slaves 'traffick among themselves, and buy, receive and dispose of all sorts of stolen goods'. The 1708 law, therefore, flatly disallowed any white person from sending or employing a slave to sell, barter, or dispose 'of any goods, wares, merchandize, stocks, poultry, corn, fruit, roots, or other effects, or things whatsoever'.[33]

While provisions were made for the punishment of whites – who either transacted with or employed slave hucksters, as well as for the hucksters themselves, the law of 1708 also implicitly recognized the hucksters' existence by stating conditions and terms under which they could legally function. Offending white persons found guilty could be fined £5, while slaves convicted for selling or bartering could receive 'one and 20 stripes on his or her bare back upon proof thereof made by any white person'. Exempted hucksters were allowed to sell 'stocks' to their masters, overseers and managers, and 'milk, horse meat or firewood' to any person. But this concession was also granted on terms that dehumanized the huckster and symbolized criminality, for the huckster had to wear 'a metaled collar' locked about his or her neck or legs. The collar had to display the master's and maker's name and place of residence.[34]

Legislators were concerned specifically with plantation slaves huckstering in Bridgetown, as they had suspected collusion between these slaves, white hucksters and shopkeepers. The 1708 law thus required 'the clerk of the market' to hire annually two able men to apprehend slaves that 'come into the said town to sell' without 'a metal collar' or accompanied by a white person. Magistrates were also empowered to remove all slaves from 'tippling houses, huckstering shops, markets, and all other suspected place' where they might trade with whites.[35]

During the eighteenth century elements in the white community and their elected representatives remained dissatisfied with the ineffectual nature of the 1708 law. Bridgetown continued to attract large numbers of hucksters from the countryside, who, like the residents in the town, appeared determined to ignore the law. During the 20 years after 1708 reports reaching the government confirmed the continued expansion of huckstering in Bridgetown. In 1733 the island's assembly passed a new law to strengthen and expand the provisions of the 1708 act. This time the law enumerated the foodstuffs and other items that hucksters were allowed to sell. It also enlarged the range of commodities which slaves could not trade, either on their own or their masters' account.[36]

The 1733 law was undoubtedly a response to the growing number of slave hucksters in the years after 1708. It suggests that the planter-controlled government saw hucksters as a threat to efficient slave control and its own economic dominance. The list of commodities that constables and market clerks were empowered to confiscate from slave hucksters now included sugar cane, 'whole or in pieces, syrup, molasses, cotton, ginger, copper, pewter, brass, tin, corn and grain'. Particular concern was expressed for the welfare of petit white and small planters, whose profits were adversely affected by intense slave competition. In order to protect these persons, the act made it unlawful for slaves to plant crops for the use of anyone but their masters. Cotton and ginger were singled out, and any slave found selling these two crops could be charged for selling 'stolen goods'.[37] In addition, white persons who purchased such items from slave hucksters could be prosecuted for receiving stolen goods. The 1733 Act was amended in 1749, making it illegal for slaves to assemble 'together at Huckster shops' for any reason.[38] Still slaves refused to comply, rendering these provisions ineffective. For example, in 1741 the manager of Codrington plantation, reporting on his slaves' attitudes towards these laws, stated that nothing short of 'locking them up' could keep slaves away from the markets, and such an action would probably result in a riot.[39]

In spite of these laws, then, slaves continued to participate actively in the internal marketing system. In 1773 the legislature came under pressure from Bridgetown merchants who claimed that slave and white hucksters posed unfair competition for their businesses and a public nuisance on account of the noise and litter the slaves' created. The legislative Assembly responded by appointing a committee to 'settle and bring in a bill for putting a stop to the Traffick of Huckster Negroes'.[40] The committee's bill became law in 1774, proscribing 'free mulattos and negroes', who hitherto were not singled out for legal discrimination, from the marketplace.[41]

The 1774 act sought to diffuse three decades of accumulated grievances among the island's merchants. This time, however, the legislature's emphasis was not to attempt the impossible – that is, eradicate huckstering – but to seek its containment. Provisions were made for the punishment of slaves and free people of colour who sold meat to butchers and who operated on 'Sunday, on Christmas Day and Good Friday'. The 1774 law also outlawed slave huckstering 'in or about any of the streets, alleys, passages, or wharfs of any of the towns' and on 'any of the highways, broad-paths and bays'.[42] Slaves found guilty of these offences were to be imprisoned and have their goods confiscated.

The small measure of legitimacy given 'country' hucksters by the 1733 act was retained in 1774. Such slave hucksters could 'sell firewood and horse meat', items which posed no competition to small white merchants and planters. No mention was made of milk, the sale of which had been allowed under the 1708 act. To those enterprising hucksters, however, who were accused of creating commodity shortages and inflating prices, legislators were particularly hostile. They singled out slave hucksters 'who go on board vessels' and who 'go a considerable way out of the respective towns to meet' country hucksters, in order to 'buy up and engross' produce with the result that 'the price of stock and provisions are greatly advanced'. Such attempts by slaves to manipulate, even corner, the market were outlawed. Offending slave hucksters were liable to receive 21 lashes. Since some offenders were likely to be women, law makers, sensitive to the ameliorative spirit of the time, included a provision that 'the punishment of slaves with child may, in all cases, be respited'.[43]

Established Bridgetown merchants remained dissatisfied with these legal provisions and they lobbied for still tougher measures. In 1779 the 1774 act, like its predecessors, was amended.[44] The new law aimed to end the 'traffick carried on by slaves' and limit the number of free hucksters – white, coloured, and black. For the first time white hucksters were subject to official regulation, and categorized with free coloureds and free blacks. All free hucksters were now required to obtain a trade licence from the treasurer at an annual cost of £10, in addition to a processing fee of 25 shillings. This levy, which also served as a revenue measure, sought to eliminate marginal hucksters. In 1784 an amendment to the 1779 act provided for a penalty of up to three months imprisonment for white persons convicted of buying 'cotton or ginger' from slaves.[45] In November 1784, shortly after the 1779 act was amended, the *Barbados Mercury* reported that the number of hucksters on the streets of Bridgetown continued to increase.[46] The Court of

Quarter Session subsequently urged the government to adopt a policy towards huckstering which emphasized formal organization and legitimization rather than opposition. The government agreed, and hucksters in Bridgetown were instructed to confine themselves to the 'public market place called the Shambles adjoining the Old Church Yard'.[47]

John Poyer, a local historian, opposed the reasoning behind the legislative provisions of 1774, 1779 and 1784, and welcomed the institutionalization of the huckster market. Attempts to eradicate slave hucksters and penalize free hucksters, he argued, reflected the monopolistic thinking and tendencies of the commercial elite, which ultimately burdened the majority of the island's inhabitants. Both free and slave hucksters, he insisted, displayed survival skills and energy under adverse circumstances which should be encouraged. White hucksters, he stated, were in great part 'aged and infirm' and women whose capital 'in very few instances' was equal to the 'sum required for a licence'.[48] These persons, he added, could not afford to pay such a levy, and would be forced out of business, resulting in their families becoming 'burdensome to their parish'.[49] As for the slaves, the huckster trade allowed them an income with which they could vary their nutrition. 'Let not the hapless slave', he argued, 'be denied these needful comforts by absurd and unnatural policies.'[50] Poyer led the lobby which in 1794 succeeded in repealing the 1774 and 1779 laws. As a result, huckster markets, such as the Shambles, became accepted in law, and a victory against discriminatory legislation partly won.

During the June 1811 sittings of the Assembly, members were informed that 'Roebuck (a central Bridgetown street) was as much crowded as ever by country negroes selling their goods'.[51] Reportedly, hucksters refused to be confined to the Shambles, which they considered out of the way of pedestrians. From their perspective, Roebuck Street was ideally situated, and it attracted hucksters in spite of stiff penalties attached to street vending. The Assembly also learned that slave hucksters 'do not like to go there [Shambles] because the persons about the market set whatever price upon their commodities and the poor negroes are compelled to take that price'. Hucksters associated the old market with consumer domination, something they were determined to destroy. Freedom of movement, they believed, was the most effective way of gaining some measure of control over prices.

The Shambles became a place of open hostility between hucksters and constables. Disagreements among hucksters and between hucksters and customers sometimes resulted in affrays. In these instances the clerk of the market would instruct constables to arrest offending hucksters and confine them to the stocks. Stocks were eventually fixed adjoining the market where 'disorderly' hucksters were imprisoned and flogged. In 1811 the Grand Session was notified that the Shambles had become a public flogging place to the great disgust and annoyance of all who go there and buy and sell.

By the beginning of the nineteenth century the huckster market had become an entrenched institution within the colony, commonly described by visitors as colourful, exciting and attractive. Alongside this formal arrangement, street vending proliferated, and each was an important part of the internal marketing system. In 1826 the 'Sunday and Marriage Act', designed to accelerate the pace of slave Christianization, finally outlawed Sunday markets and Saturday became the major market day until the present time. After emancipation hucksters continued to dominate in the marketing of food provisions, although plantations sometimes sold food directly to the public. As in other Caribbean colonies, former slaves took to other types of work, but huckstering remained an attractive occupation.[52] It was an economic niche which they had identified and protected during slavery, and which, in freedom, became a cornerstone in the survival strategies for many households.

During slavery the Barbadian internal marketing system revealed the slaves' struggle to achieve an economic life of their own. Unlike their Jamaican counterparts, Barbadian slaves pursued this objective within the context of persistently hostile legislative interventions from their owners. Evidence confirms the aspect of the Mintz and Hall account which shows that in the sugar monoculture colonies of the English Caribbean slave owners did not or could not make provisions that would enable slaves to produce their own subsistence. A close look at slave huckstering in Barbados, however, requires an important revision of the Mintz and Hall analysis by demonstrating that, in spite of the land handicap suffered by 'small island' slaves, they too were able to establish their own vibrant economic culture based upon the exchange of food allocations, the raising of poultry and stocks, and the intensive cultivation of lands that surrounded their huts.

Notes

1   Hilary Beckles, *Natural Rebels: A Social History of Enslaved Black Women in Barbados* (New Brunswick, NJ, 1989), 72–7; Robert Dirks, *The Black Saturnalia: Conflict and Its Ritual Expression on British West Indian Slave Plantations* (Gainesville, 1987), 69–80; Jerome S. Handler, *The Unappropriated People: Freedom in the Slave Society of Barbados* (Baltimore, 1974), 125–33; Hilary Beckles and Karl Watson, 'Social Protest and Labor Bargaining: The Changing Nature of Slaves' Responses to Plantation Life in 18th Century Barbados', *Slavery and Abolition*, 8 (1987), 272–93; Edward Brathwaite, *Contradictory Omens: Cultural Diversity and Integration in the Caribbean* (Kingston, 1974), 41–3; Sidney W. Mintz and Douglas Hall, *The Origins of the Jamaican Internal Marketing System*, Yale University Publications in Anthropology No. 57 (New Haven, 1960); Sidney W. Mintz, 'Caribbean Market Places and Caribbean History', *Nova Americana*, 1, (1980–81), 333–44; John H. Parry, 'Plantation and Provision Ground: An Historical Sketch of the Introduction of Food Crops in Jamaica', *Revista de Historia de America*, 39 (1955), 15–18.

2   In 1711, the Jamaican Assembly prohibited slaves from owning livestock, or from selling meat, fish, sugar cane, or any manufactured items without their masters' permission. In 1734 and 1735, the St Lucian Assembly prevented slaves from selling coffee or cotton. Between 1744 and 1765, the French Antillean slave owners passed laws prohibiting slaves from huckstering in towns or trading in coffee. In 1767, the St Vincent Assembly forbade slaves to plant or sell any commodities that whites export from the colony. See Franklin Knight, *The Caribbean: the Genesis of a Fragmented Nationalism* (New York, 1978), 92; Hilary Beckles, *Black Rebellion in Barbados: The Struggle Against Slavery, 1727–1838* (Bridgetown, 1984), 71–2; Edward Long, *The History of Jamaica . . .* 3 vols. (London, 1974 [1774]), 2: 486–7; Woodville Marshall's essay in this volume.

3   For an account of slave nutrition, see Kenneth F. Kiple, *The Caribbean Slave: A Biological History* (Cambridge, 1984). On the impact of malnutrition upon mortality levels, see Richard B. Sheridan, *Doctors and Slaves: A Medical and Demographic History of Slavery in the British West Indies, 1680–1834* (Cambridge, 1985); 'The Crisis of Slave Subsistence in the British West Indies during and after the American Revolution', *William and Mary Quarterly*, 3rd series, 23 (1976), 615–43.

4   Mintz and Hall, *Origins*, 23.

5   Ibid., 10.

6   Mintz and Hall note that the laws in force during the seventeenth century 'make plain that a number of markets were established, formalized, and maintained under government

provision . . .', and that 'formal legal acknowledgement of the slaves' right to market had been in negative form at least, as early as 1711'. Restrictions were applied to the slaves' sale of beef, veal and mutton, but they were allowed to market provisions, fruits, fish, milk, poultry and small stocks. Ibid., 15.

7   George Pinckard, *Notes on the West Indies . . .*, 3 vols. (London, 1806), 2: 116.

8   John Poyer, *The History of Barbados . . .* (London, 1971 [1808]), 400.

9   Pinckard, *Notes*, 2: 116–17.

10   Ibid., 1: 368.

11   F.W. Bayley, *Four Years Residence in the West Indies* (London, 1830), 92.

12   *Report of a Debate in Council on a Dispatch from Lord Bathurst* (Bridgetown, 1822), 8.

13   J. Harry Bennett Jr. *Bondsmen and Bishops: Slavery and Apprenticeship on the Codrington Plantations of Barbados, 1710–1838*, University of California Publications in History, 62 (Berkeley, 1958), 26.

14   Ibid., 24–5.

15   William Dickson, *Letters on Slavery* (London, 1814), 11.

16   J.A. Thome and J.H. Kimball, *Emancipation in the West Indies: A Six Month's Tour in Antigua, Barbados, and Jamaica in the Year 1837* (New York, 1838), 66.

17   Bayley, *Four Years Residence*, 60–1.

18   Ibid.

19   Pinckard, *Notes*, 2: 118.

20   Sampson Wood to Thomas Lane, 1796, M523/288, Newton Papers, Senate House Library, University of London.

21   Bennett, *Bondsmen and Bishops*, 25.

22   In 1822, Mr Hamden, a member of the Legislative Council, reported, 'The goods which they have to take to market are comparatively insignificant; nor are the supplies which they procure from thence less so. The poultry which they raise with the superfluity of their allowance, or the surplus of allowance in kind, which can never be considerable, are the only objects of honest traffic which they have', *Report of a Debate in Council*, 8.

23   Bayley, *Four Years Residence*, 422.

24   Ibid., 423.

25   Ibid., 424.

26   Ibid., 425. See also Hilary Beckles, 'The Literate Few: An Historical Sketch of the Slavery Origins of Black Elites in the English West Indies', *Caribbean Journal of Education*, 11 (1984), 19–35; Claude Levy, *Emancipation, Sugar, and Federalism: Barbados and the West Indies, 1838–1876* (Gainesville, 1980), 19.

27   Bayley, *Four Years Residence*, 425.

28   Dickson, *Letters*, 41.

29   Ibid., 41–2. In 1741, Abel Alleyne, manager of Codrington Plantation informed the estate owner that the white hucksters are 'often worse than the negroes, by receiving all stolen goods'. Alleyne to the Society for the Propagation of the Gospel in Foreign Parts. 9 Dec. 1741, Letter Book, Vol. B8, 51, SPGFP Archives, London. Whites were protected by law from slaves' evidence; also, white hucksters could not be prosecuted if their slave suppliers informed legal authorities. In 1788, Joshua Steele informed Governor Parry that 'under the disqualification of Negro evidence the crime of *receiver of stolen goods* cannot be proven against' white hucksters, and that this acts as an encouragement to them. Reply of Joshua Steele to Governor Parry, 1788, *Parliamentary Papers*, 1789, Vol. 26, 33 (italics in original).

30   Dickson, *Letters*, 41–2.

31   An Act for the Governing of Negroes, 1688, in Richard Hall, *Acts Passed in the Island of Barbados from 1643–1762 inclusive* (London, 1764), 70–1.

32   Journal of the Assembly of Barbados, 17 Oct. 1694, Colonial Entry Book, Vol. 12, 484–6, Public Record Office, London. Also, *Calendar of State Papers, Colonial Series*, 1693–6, 381.

33   An Act to Prohibit the Inhabitants of this Island from employing their Negroes and other slaves in selling and Bartering; passed 6 Jan. 1708. Sec Hall, *Laws*, 185–7.

34   Ibid., 185–6.

35   Ibid., 187.

36 An Act for the Better Governing of Negroes, and the more Effectual Preventing the Inhabitants of this Island from Employing their Negroes or Other Slaves in Selling and Bartering, Passed 22 May 1733, Hall, *Laws*, 295–9.
37 Ibid., 298.
38 An Act for Governing Negroes, 1749, in Hall, *Laws*, 355–6.
39 Bennett, *Bondsmen and Bishops*, 24–5.
40 Minutes of the House of Assembly, 6 July 1773, HA 3/15, 1772–4, Barbados Archives.
41 'An Act for the better to Prohibit Goods, Wares, and Merchandize, and other things from being carried from House to House, or about the roads or streets in this Island, to be sold, bartered, or dispose of . . . and to remedy the mischief and inconveniences arising to the Inhabitants of this Island from the Traffic of Huckster Slaves, Free Mulattos, and Negroes', passed 15 March 1774, in Samuel Moore, *The Public Acts in Force, Passed by the Legislature of Barbados, from May 11th, 1762 to April 8th, 1800, inclusive* (London, 1801), 154–71.
42 Ibid., 164.
43 Ibid., 167.
44 Ibid., 212–17.
45 Ibid., 251–5.
46 *Barbados Mercury*, 20 Nov. 1784.
47 Ibid.
48 Poyer, *History of Barbados*, 398–419.
49 Ibid., 400, 401.
50 Ibid., 400.
51 Minutes of the House of Assembly, 14 June 1811, CO 31/45, PRO.
52 See Handler, *The Unappropriated People*, 125.

Chapter 24

Sidney W. Mintz

THE ORIGINS OF THE JAMAICAN MARKET SYSTEM

THIS CHAPTER DEALS WITH the origins and growth of the Jamaican internal market system and the local small-scale agriculture which is served by that system. The Jamaican census of 1943 indicated that out of an agricultural labor force of 221,376, there were 49,200 peasants who operated holdings of ten acres or less, while 16,972 peasants had larger holdings. In addition, a significant proportion of the agricultural labor force listed as wage earners was simultaneously engaged in cultivating owned land in plots of less than one acre or in cultivating rented land.

The Jamaican peasantry of today originated two centuries ago within the physical boundaries of the slave-worked sugar estates and within the normal pattern of slave-estate administration. Since the slave plantation elsewhere in much of the Caribbean region—in Puerto Rico for example—served to destroy rather than to create the peasantry, the forces at work in the Jamaican case are of particular interest. Jamaican internal marketing is closely intermeshed with the rise of that country's peasant class.

Under slavery, the owners and managers of estates in the British Caribbean faced the problem of feeding their slaves. The alternative extremes were either to have the slaves produce as much as possible of the food they ate or to import all of their food. Of these two courses the first, though not always practicable, was the more desirable. If the slaves could feed themselves, the estates would save the cost of imported foods and avoid the risks contingent upon importation. When warfare disturbed merchant shipping, a frequent occurrence in the eighteenth century, and shortages of imported food resulted, food prices rose. Moreover, when import shortages existed, the slaves could not be adequately fed even if the planter could afford high food prices. Prolonged interference with the importation of food introduced a vicious circle of high prices, malnutrition, and reduced production and profits.

Yet there were often difficulties in the way of local food production, and it is no accident that today in the British Caribbean, the peasantry and food production sites are found chiefly in mountain areas or in areas otherwise unsuitable, by reason of location, or of soil or weather conditions, for sugar production. Until the 1830s land and slave labor were the essential factors of sugar production. Capital equipment and technical know-how became important only after the Emancipation and the opening of the British sugar market to foreign competition in the second half of the nineteenth century.

The sugar planters wanted to plant sugar wherever it could be planted profitably but at the same time had either to provide land on which food could be raised for the labor force or risk the uncertainties of importing food. Generally speaking, where land was flat and fertile, the cane was planted; where it was not, food was grown for the slaves and dependence on food imports was considerably reduced. Thus, throughout the archipelago, the flat or gently sloping islands (e.g., Barbados, Antigua, St. Kitts) were almost entirely planted to sugar, whereas on the mountainous islands (e.g., Grenada, St. Vincent, Jamaica), where sugar cultivation was limited by topography planters had at their disposal relatively extensive areas on which food crops might be grown.

Jamaica, the largest of the British islands, contains distinctive coastal plains and interior valleys as well as mountain areas. On this island, therefore, both patterns developed. On the few estates which lay quite apart from steep mountain slopes the use of food imports tended to prevail; but on those estates (the majority by far) which included rough hills or slopes or other poor-quality sugar land within their boundaries, the tendency was to produce food. Clearly, whatever the individual planter's preference as between importing and producing food for his slaves, his actual practice was much influenced by sugar prices, the lay of his land, and the condition of the soil.

Where food production was undertaken, the planter had to decide whether to include the work in the regular supervised agricultural program of the estate or to offer the slaves inducements to undertake it voluntarily. As will be demonstrated, a thoroughgoing dependence on the regulated production of food was never achieved; in large measure, food crops were raised by the slaves in the absence of compulsion, and under conditions which implicitly acknowledged their responsiveness to the same incentives as those which operated for the free Jamaican.

In short, there was no generally accepted policy for supplying the slaves with food. Where an estate had land not wanted for cane, the slaves were usually allowed to cultivate food crops on it in their spare time. When war threatened or when for other reasons food imports were insufficient to meet the demand for them, laws were usually passed requiring estate owners to undertake the cultivation of a stipulated quantity of land in foodstuffs as an estate operation. Since in years of warfare the prices offered for sugar tended to rise, thus encouraging the expansion of cane fields, in Jamaica the laws requiring local food production were customarily honored only in the breach. In all the islands, and especially in those in which the food-import system prevailed, the provident planter attempted to time his purchases of imported foods judiciously in order to keep his costs down and his stocks ready in case of shortage. At the same time, the unsupervised cultivation of food stocks by the slaves themselves grew steadily more important whenever the estate contained land to support this activity.

The slaves used such land to produce a variety of foods, such as tree crops, vegetables, and edible herbs and roots, as well as craft materials. These foods and materials were raised primarily for their own use. But eventually—and the details of the process are regrettably dim—surpluses came to be taken to local markets and exchanged for other commodities or sold for cash. The proceeds of these transactions accrued entirely to the slaves, apparently from the very first. Market day, customarily held on Sunday so as not to interfere with estate cultivation, became an important social and economic institution.

Consideration of the system of agricultural production and marketing by slaves briefly noted above raises questions which are a prime concern of this chapter. It is not at first apparent, for instance, why food production should have been left to the slaves' initiative and not have been more commonly regulated as a part of the estate's program of cultivation. It is even less apparent why the slaves were permitted to go to market, sell or exchange surplus produce, and retain the goods or money received. Further, there is the question of the origins of the markets themselves. Also, we may ask precisely what crops the slaves chose to cultivate, why these were chosen, and with what skill and proficiency the enterprises of production and marketing were executed.

Exact and wholly satisfying answers to these questions are not yet possible. For most of them, however, we have been able to formulate reasonable answers based on the available data, and it is convenient to begin with the subjects of crops and agricultural skills.

There had been a background for cultivation and its associated processes before the English conquest of Jamaica and the rise of plantation agriculture, and even before the Spanish discovery and conquest of the island. To some extent at least, later patterns of subsistence were derived from these older adjustments.

Jamaica was occupied by Arawak Indian cultivators at the time of its discovery and early colonization by Spain. Parry writes that the native Arawak cultivated cassava (manioc) and perhaps a soft variety of maize, and gathered shellfish, roots, and berries. Further information suggests that the Jamaican aboriginal crop repertory included "tannier" (*Xanthosoma* sp.), sweet potatoes, beans, capsicum, and a variety of uncultivated fruits. The diet was apparently sufficient and well-balanced.

The Spanish settlement of Jamaica substantially eliminated the Arawak, but not their crops. Las Casas and others note the continued cultivation of the foods mentioned above, and the only important innovations mentioned are the raising of livestock and the curing of pork and bacon. Nonetheless, some of the earliest references to cultivated plants after the English occupation in 1655 make it clear that new crops had been added during the Spanish period or introduced soon after the English landed. The Spaniards certainly were responsible for the introduction of the banana, nearly all the then known varieties of citrus, the sugarcane, and probably arrowroot. The English may, perhaps, be accredited with the introduction of the potato, as well as bread-fruit, dasheen (*Colocasia esculenta*), and the mango.

Some of the root crops so important in later peasant agriculture and diet spanned the three periods. Cassava and sweet potatoes, as we have noted, were cultivated aboriginally. The "yampee," or "cush cush," a true New World cultivated yam (*Dioscorea trifida*), is popular to this day in Jamaica. Sloane did not mention it in his exhaustive botanical work (1707), and Parry thinks it fair to assume that it was introduced from the American mainland after that time. Sloane did mention *Dioscorea cayenensis*, the "yellow Guinea yam," which Parry believes came to Jamaica from Oceania, probably via West Africa, in the eighteenth century. By the start of the nineteenth century, there were at least six cultivated yam varieties in Jamaica, as well as the taros—the so-called "eddoes, dasheens, and cocoes or cocoyams" – which are of Oceanian origin and probably became established in Jamaican peasant cultivation and cuisine in the eighteenth century. Finally, there are several important plants whose dates of entry can be precisely fixed. Parry refers to the akee (from West Africa, 1778), the mango (from Oceania, 1782), and the bread-fruit (from Oceania, 1793, carried by Bligh on his second voyage).

The slaves as a proto-peasantry

From these enumerations, it will be seen that the crop possibilities open to Jamaican cultivators were considerable indeed. But very little, unfortunately, is ever afforded in the early reports concerning the agricultural methods themselves. Beckford, writing in 1790, probably provides the fullest description, and that all too sketchy and vague:

> When a tract of negro-provisions is regularly planted, is well cultivated, and kept clean, it makes a very husbandlike and a beautiful appearance; and it is astonishing of the common necessaries of life it will produce. A quarter of an acre of this description will be fully sufficient for the supply of a moderate family, and may enable the proprietor [read "cultivator"] to carry some to market besides; but then the land must be of a productive quality, be in a situation that cannot fail of seasons, be sheltered from the wind, and protected from the trespass of cattle, and the theft of negroes.
>
> If a small portion of land of this description will give such returns, a very considerable number of acres, if not attended to, will on the contrary, yield but little; and those negroes will hardly ever have good grounds, and of consequence plenty of provisions, who are not allowed to make for themselves a choice of situation, and who are not well assured that it will be well guarded and protected.

At a later point, Beckford states:

> All kinds of ground provisions and corn are, as well as the plantain, success-fully cultivated in the mountains; but as this is done by the negroes in their own grounds [i.e., provided individually by the owner or overseer] and on those days which are given to them for this particular purpose, it does not enter into the mass of plantation-labor.

And further:

> The manner in which the negroes occupy themselves in their grounds is rather an employment than a toil, particularly if the wood be felled, and the land be cleared; but if they have heavy timber to cut down, the labour will be much, and the danger will be great; for they often get maimed or killed in this precarious operation, in which are required not only strength but likewise foresight.
>
> They generally make choice of such sorts of land for their ground as are encompassed by lofty mountains; and I think that they commonly prefer the sides of hills, which are covered with loose stones, to the bottoms upon which they are not so abundant. Some will have a mixture of both,

and will cultivate the plantain-tree upon the flat, and their provisions upon the rising ground; and some will pursue a contrary method; for in the choice as well as change of situation, they seem to be directed more by novelty and caprice, than by convenience or expediency.

They prepare their land, and put in their crops on the Saturdays that are given to them, and they bring home their provisions at night: and if their grounds be at a considerable distance from the plantation, as they often are to the amount of five or seven miles, or more the journey backwards and forwards makes this rather a day of labour and fatigue, than of enjoyment and rest; but if, on the contrary, they be within any tolerable reach, it may be said to partake of both.

The negroes, when working in their grounds, exhibit a picture of which it will be difficult to give a minute description. They scatter themselves over the face, and form themselves into distinct parties at the bottom of the mountains; and being consequently much divided their general exertions can only be observed from a distance.

If the land be hilly, it is generally broken by rocks, or encumbered by stones; the first they cannot displace, but the last they gently remove as they proceed in their work, and thus make a bed for the deposit of the plantain-sucker and the coco, or of the corn and yarn.

Upon these occasions they move, with all their family, into the place of cultivation; the children of different ages are loaded with baskets, which are burdened in proportion to their strength and age; and it is pleasing to observe under what considerable weights they will bear themselves up, without either murmur or fatigue. The infants are flung at the backs of the mothers, and very little incommode them in their walks or labour.

The provision-grounds in the mountains, or polinks as they are called in the Island, admit of not much picturesque variety. Upon these are cultivated, and particularly upon those in Liguanea (a fertile tract of ground in the neighborhood of Kingston), all kinds of fruit and garden stuff, or coffee, coco, ginger and other minor productions of the country.

It is known that the slave cultivators burned off the land they were preparing to plant. This technique, contemptuously referred to as "fire-stick cultivation" in Jamaica, is of doubtful origin. It may have been continuous with aboriginal practice, but this cannot be easily proved.

The provision grounds, which normally lay at some distance from the huts of the slaves grouped near the center of the estate, were set apart agriculturally from the tiny house plots, or "yards." On the patches of land around their huts, the slaves cultivated fruit trees, garden herbs, and crops which were very easily stolen or very delicate. The distinction between house plot and provision ground persists to the present and is characteristic of Jamaican peasant agriculture. Stewart, writing in the first quarter of the nineteenth century, makes clear reference to the distinction between house plot and "polink":

Adjoining to the house is usually a small spot of ground, laid out into a sort of garden, and shaded by various fruit-trees. Here the family deposit their dead, to whose memory they invariably, if they can afford it, erect a rude tomb. Each slave has, besides this spot, a piece of ground (about half an acre) allotted to him as a provision ground. This is the principal means of his support; and so productive is the soil, where it is good and the seasons regular, that this spot will not only furnish him with sufficient food for his own consumption, but an overplus to carry to market. By means of this ground, and of the hogs and poultry which he may raise (most of which he sells), an industrious negro may not only support himself comfortably, but save something. If he has a family, an additional proportion of ground is allowed him, and all his children from five years upward assist him in his labours in some way or other.

This use of the term *polink*, which H. P. Jacobs believes to be related to the Spanish *palenque* (a palisade or palisaded village; later, a fortified runaway slave village, as in Cuba or Colombia), is interesting in itself, symbolizing the link between independent cultivation and the status of the slaves. In any case, the major local sources of food appear to have been the provision grounds, or polinks. That these normally lay upon the slopes where cane was not grown suggests that the particular techniques of cultivation were adjusted to the terrain, a pattern which persisted long after Emancipation and still largely characterizes peasant agriculture in Jamaica. This is of more than passing importance. Peasant agriculture in Jamaica has been repeatedly criticized for its erosive effects. It is true that failure to make long-range investments of labor and materials on such land is destructive. But it ought to be borne in mind that it is not necessarily the cultivation methods as such, or even the crops, which are destructive.

The "choice" of hilly land for such cultivation followed from the monopolization of coastal plains and interior valleys by the plantations. It has never been conclusively proved, in fact, that the small-scale production of the Jamaican peasantry is in itself inherently less productive or more destructive than other systems of production *on the same land*. (This does not contradict the justifiable claim that productivity would be increased and erosion slowed by proper terracing, crop rotation, manuring, the building of retainer structures, and so on.)

Sauer has written very explicitly of the *conuco*, or garden plot of the Antilles:

When Indians gave way to Negro slaves, the latter took over for themselves, rather than for their masters, the cultivation of the Indian crops, and added thereto such African things as the greater yam, the pigeon pea or *guandul* [sic], okra, and the keeping of fowls.

The food potential of the traditional *conuco* planting, or provision ground, is hardly appreciated by ourselves, be we agricultural scientists, economists, or planners, because its tradition as well as content are so different from what we know and practice. Yields are much higher than from grains, production is continuous the year round, storage is hardly needed, individual kinds are not grown separately in fields but are assembled together in one planted ground, to which our habits of order would apply neither the name of field or garden. And so we are likely to miss the merits of the system.

The proper *conuco* is, in fact an imitation by man of tropical nature, a many-storied cultural vegetation, producing at all levels, from tubers underground through the understory of pigeon peas and coffee, a second story of cacao and bananas, to a canopy of fruit trees and palms. Such an assemblage makes full use of light, moisture, and soil—its messy appearance to our eyes meaning really that all of the niches are filled. A proper planting of this sort is about as protective of the soil as is the wild vegetation. The *conuco* system can make intensive use of steep slopes and thereby may encounter erosion hazards that should not be blamed on the system itself, as commonly they have been.

Sauer's contentions, while unproved, certainly demand reflection. In fact, the adjustment of Caribbean peasantries to the aftermath of slavery, to the circumstances of a ruined economy, and to freedom deserves more study than it has yet received. Such study can profitably examine the view that the patterns of human and horticultural occupancy, the system of cultivation, the paths of distribution of products, and the economic relationships of the peasantry to other classes form one interwoven system. We contend that this system had begun to evolve long before the Emancipation.

Information on the agricultural implements used by the slaves is discouragingly scanty. The most important were the bush knife, or cutlass, and the short-handled hoe. We have been unable to ascribe an origin to these tools; a case might be made for either England or Africa. It is likely that at first they were provided by the plantation, and this might argue against an African origin.

With regard to the crops generally preferred for cultivation and cuisine, our information is again less than satisfactory. Several early authors suggest that the slaves preferred to cultivate plantains (and bananas?), corn, and vegetables rather than root crops, attributing this preference to either imprudence or laziness. The planters themselves preferred to see root crops planted since these would better survive hurricanes. Renny believed it was the slaves' preference for plantains and corn that led them to neglect the root crops. And yet yams, sweet potatoes, dasheen, tanniers, cassava, and the like could hardly have become established as preferred peasant foods only after the start of the nineteenth century. It seems fair to suppose, therefore, that any favoritism the slave cultivators may have shown for plantain, corn, and vegetables over root crops could have arisen as much from the market situation as from anything else, and it is possible that these items were supplied in significant quantities to naval and merchant vessels. That the planters never actively interfered with the slave cultivators' crop choices is in any case of great interest, and seems to underline the mutual respect for customary arrangements which held between the estate owners or managers and the slaves. It also explains the vagueness of the accounts of the provision grounds given by Beckford and others. The only points which these commentators make with clarity are the distinction between house plots and polinks, the "high" productivity of the latter if conscientiously cultivated, and the fact that the slaves were allowed to take surpluses to market, dispose of them, and keep the proceeds.

The first of these points is of interest because it indicates that even where estates were limited in size and did not contain slave provision grounds, the slaves were not absolutely dependent on imports. Even in Barbados and St. Kitts, for example, there were house plots. But it was upon the polinks that the foundations of the free peasantry were established, and here we turn to the local trading of the slaves and the origins and early growth of the marketplaces.

Extracts from the writings of two West Indian proprietors of the late eighteenth century will serve to give the planter's view of the relative advantages of food production as against food importation and to suggest one very powerful motive for the reluctance of masters to supervise production on the polinks.

> *Friday Feb. 10th, 1792.* My voyage to Antigua has put me in full possession of the question concerning the best mode of feeding the negroes. I am speaking of the difference in this situation in regard to plenty and comfort, when fed by allowance by the master, as in Antigua; or when by provision grounds of their own, as in St. Vincent. In the first case, oppression may, and certainly in some instances and in different degrees doth actually exist, either as to quantity or quality of food; besides the circumstances of food for himself, the negro too suffers in his poultry and little stock, which are his wealth. The maintenance of his pigs, turkeys, or chickens must often subtract from his own dinner, and that perhaps a scanty one, or he cannot keep stock at all; and a negro without stock, and means to purchase tobacco, and other little conveniences, and some finery too for his wife, is miserable.
>
> In the second case, of the negro feeding himself with his own provisions, assisted only with salt provisions from his master (three pounds of salt-fish, or an adequate quantity of herrings, per week as in St. Vincent's) the situation of the negro is in proportion to his industry; but generally speaking, it affords him with a plenty that amounts to comparative wealth, viewing any peasantry in Europe.

Bryan Edwards, a contemporary observer whose main experience was of Jamaica, wrote on the same subject:

> The practice which prevails in Jamaica of giving the Negroes lands to cultivate, from the produce of which they are expected to maintain themselves (except in times of scarcity, arising from hurricanes and droughts, when assistance is never denied them) is universally allowed to be judicious and beneficial; producing a happy coalition of interests between the master and the slave. The negro who has acquired by his own labour a property in his master's land, has much to lose, and is therefore less inclined to desert his work. He earns a little money, by which he is enabled to indulge himself in fine clothes on holidays, and gratify his palate with salted meats and other provisions that otherwise he could not obtain; and the proprietor is eased, in a great measure, of the expense of feeding him.

Both these observers mention the advantage of having the slaves produce their own food, but it is interesting that Edwards, the Jamaican planter, is more explicit about the consequent savings enjoyed by the master. In the small, relatively flat, arable islands, such as Barbados or Antigua, the planter could allot land to food cultivation only by impinging on areas which, generally, could be more profitably planted in cane. He tended therefore to restrict the land at the disposal of the slaves to small house plots, to depend heavily on imports of food, and, when the food trade was disturbed, to include, however reluctantly, some food production in the general estate program.

In St. Vincent and the other mountainous islands of the Windwards, the planter's decision was affected by the relative unsuitability of his land for sugar production. The "sacrifice" of allotting land to food cultivation was not so strong a deterrent, and the advantages of having a comparatively well-fed slave force and of reduced dependence on food imports were clear.

In Jamaica, the largest of the British islands, with the largest estates and the greatest variety of soil, topography, and climate, the planter usually had land on his estate which, except in periods of unusually high sugar prices, he would never consider using for cane. There is much evidence that in Jamaica the area in sugar cultivation expanded and contracted under the influence of rising and falling sugar prices. As prices fell, marginal sugar areas became submarginal and were, at least temporarily, thrown out of cane cultivation. But even when the process worked the other way, and cane fields were extended in responses to the promise of higher prices, there was generally a significant area which, because of its high unsuitability, would remain beyond the sugar line.

It is worth noting that in Barbados and the Leewards (except mountainous Montserrat) there is still a heavy reliance on food imports; that in the Windward Islands and Montserrat the sugar industry declined under the competitive conditions of nineteenth-century free trade in sugar and that these islands now export foodstuffs to Barbados and the Leewards; and that only in Jamaica have both food production and sugar production managed to survive.

But from the two extracts quoted above, it appears that deciding whether or not to allow the slaves to cultivate foodstuffs was affected by more than "classical" economic considerations of diminishing returns to land. We have shown that even where polinks were not usually allowed, house plots were, and many of the contemporary explanations account for the system by a sort of medievalism modified by the realities of colonial slave-plantation life in the eighteenth century. There is the implied concept of the estate community, of the advantages to be gained from "a happy coalition of interests between the master and the slave"; and indeed, the eighteenth-century sugar estate, with its great house and surrounding fields, its "village" of workshops and slave quarters, its unfree agricultural population, and its complement of skilled craftsmen, was, superficially, not unlike the medieval manor. Even further, although sugar cultivation was the basic occupation, the workers had access to estate "waste" land (the polinks), where they labored on their own behalf, not only growing food but also grazing small livestock and collecting the raw materials for their handicraft products.

But superficialities apart, there was a very important reason why masters should be concerned with securing this happy coalition of interest. It was simply that, since there was neither an ethical nor an economic basis for any such coalition (and here we diverge from the ostensible medieval pattern), they must try to introduce and stimulate it. At any rate, the wiser masters would because, as our two writers argued, the slave with a better diet, a small source of income, and a feeling of proprietorship in land was less discontented, less likely to run away, and less dangerous as a potential rebel. It would be of interest to test this opinion by comparing data on slave desertions, riots, and other indices of disaffection in, for example, Antigua and St. Vincent. But such a comparison would have to take into account the disincentives to desertion and other forms of slave resistance in flat, fully occupied, and small islands, and the greater chances for successful resistance in the larger, mountainous, and less fully occupied islands.

The slave was not supervised in his food cultivation, and this activity was never included, except in brief periods of shortage or threatening shortage of food, in "the mass of plantation-labor." Supervised field labor was repugnant to the slaves, and in the social hierarchy of the slave population the field slaves occupied the lowest rung. Supervised cultivation of food would have necessitated either a reduction of the time spent in cane cultivation, which the masters would not have willingly conceded, or an increase in the daily hours of compulsory estate labor, which would have encouraged disaffection and rebellious sentiments among the slaves.

But the accounts quoted above were written more than a century after the practice of allowing slaves to cultivate estate backlands, or polinks, had been established. The writers, therefore, might simply have been trying to explain, in the light of their own experience, the reasons for a custom whose beginning and original intention were unknown to them. They tell us not how the practice began but only why it was still favored in the late eighteenth century.

Blome, writing in 1672 from the notes of Governor Sir Thomas Lynch, in Jamaica, gives detailed instructions for the setting up of a "Cocao [sic] Walk" or plantation, and his advice includes careful explanations of the need for provision grounds for servants and slaves. Sloane's introductory notes to his great work on the flora of Jamaica, published 1707–25, say of the slaves:

> They have *Saturdays* in the Afternoon, and *Sundays*, with *Christmas* Holidays, *Easter* call'd little or Piganniny Christmas, and some other great Feasts allow'd them for the Culture of their own Plantations to feed themselves from Potatoes, Yams and Plantains, etc., which they plant in Ground allow'd them by their Masters, beside a small Plantain-Walk they have by themselves.

Leslie, writing in 1739, states:

> Their owners set aside for each a small Ground, and allow them the Sundays to manure it: In it they generally plant Maiz, Guiney Corn. Plantanes, Yams, Cocoes, Potatoes, Etc. This is the food which supports them.

Though we have not been able to establish a precise date for the beginning of this practice, Blome's statements, coming but 17 years after the English occupation, make it clear that it was generally adopted even on the earliest estates.

We do not know, however, whether it became the practice to provide slaves with provision grounds immediately upon the establishment of a new plantation. Conceivably; the managers of a new estate might have attempted to institute food production as a matter of course at the time the estate was set up. But this is not likely to have been the case. When a new estate was being established, when slaves were being bought, land cleared, buildings erected, and factory machinery installed, managerial attention would probably have been directed almost exclusively toward the main objective of getting the first sugar off to market. Imported foods probably bulked large in an estate's first years. If food production by the estate slaves was undertaken in those years, it was presumably in the slaves' free time. Much of this is surmise, but thus far we have found no contrary evidence. Estate-supervised production of provisions never seems to have been undertaken without pressure from the island legislature and, as we have stressed, unsupervised cultivation by the slaves goes back to the early years of the occupation and may have been conjoined with the start of the estates. By the late eighteenth century what might have begun as a conveniently casual system of industrial feeding had become a tradition with which it would have been profitless and dangerous to interfere.

The slaves as marketers

In these circumstances the emergence of local marketing arrangements is not surprising. The unsupervised production of food crops by slaves provided the very basis of an open market system. Each slave cultivated as, and what, he wanted to cultivate. His primary concern, originally, might well have been his own household needs. But because his neighbors also had free choice of whether to plant, what to plant, and how much to plant, the range of small transactions which might take place even among the slaves of a single estate must have been considerable. For instance, the volume of exchange would have been increased by the fact that some slaves would prefer to produce minor handicrafts, some to raise small livestock, some to grow food, and some to act as intermediaries among these diverse producers. The Jamaican higgler, or middleman, also finds his prototype in the slave society. Under a system of estate-organized food production this specialization could never have emerged. It would have been choked off by the routine and the compulsory conformity of estate agriculture.

Exactly how the first slave producers came to market their surplus stock is not known; nor can we pin down with assurance the founding date of the first market in Jamaica. The first legally established marketplace, however, was created in Spanish Town (Santiago de la Vega) in the year 1662, seven years after the English occupation, at the request of English settlers.

> Whereas the settlement of our Island of Jamaica is much hindered or obstructed for want of a Faire or Markett for the sale and buying of Horses, Mares, Mules, Assinegoes, Cowes, Bulls and other Cattle and many other necessaries for the use of our subjects there and whereas our Towne of Snt. Jago de la Vega in our said Island is commodiously situated for the keeping of such a Faire or Markett therein . . . [we] by this our present Charter doe grant and confirm that . . . [the] inhabitants of our said Town of Snt. Jago de la Vega for ever have a Faire or Markett in our said Towne . . . four times in every year . . . for the sail of horses, mares, mules, assinegoes, cows, bulls, and all or any other cattle and all or any other goods and commodities whatsoever of the groweth or produce of our said Island and all or any goods, wares and merchandizes whatsoever with all liberties . . . according to the usage and customs of our kingdome of England.

The emphasis in this statement is on the establishment of a market for livestock. Furthermore, this is a quarterly market only, and one may judge that its original intent was to serve the free population of Jamaica. Yet we learn that the need for a marketplace had been recognized and acted upon less than a decade after the occupation; it is also worth noting that the market here described was set up quite matter-of-factly according to English law. Though the slaves came to play a central role in Jamaican internal marketing, it is clear that this first legal market was English, not African, in conception and form.

Edward Long, describing events in the 1660s, tells of large numbers of small cultivators who produced food for the markets of Spanish Town (the capital) and of Port Royal, then a headquarters of the buccaneers where

> the great consumption of provisions of all sorts in that town, and for the outfit of so many privateers, created a very large demand for cattle, sheep, hogs, poultry, corn, and every other similar supply furnished by planters and settlers. And it is owing to this cause that we find such a prodigious number of these little settlements grouped together in all the environs of St. Jago de la Vega [Spanish Town], and in the maritime parts not far from Port Royal harbour, which were then full of people, all subsisting well by their traffic with that town.

But, he continues, the suppression of the buccaneers and the founding of the sugar industry led to "the declension of Port Royal, and the dissipation of the petty settlers, who from that period began to spread themselves more into the island parts," while the establishment of large estates led to the buying out of many of these small settlers "by the more opulent planters or merchants".

But as settlement and the sugar industry and trade increased, activity in the capital town and in the ports of the island would also have grown. New demands for food supplies would have been met, not by those early European small-scale farmers whom Long described, and in whose interest this first market had been officially established, but by their successors in the business of food production. The great majority of these successors, we believe, were slaves who sold in officially designated and other marketplaces the produce they raised in their spare time on estate lands.

Since it was the individual slaves or slave households who produced provisions on the estate backlands, then clearly they would be the sellers of surplus produce. Either individual slaves would go marketing, or else they would make voluntary agreements among themselves for marketing one another's produce. Certainly no sane estate manager would ever have conceived the idea of collecting and selling produce from separate slave provision grounds. The effort would have been pointless. If the estate kept all or even a share of the proceeds, voluntary food production by the slaves would have fallen off. In any case, the prevention of transactions between slaves of the same estate, or even of adjacent estates, would have been physically impossible for the limited and generally inefficient subordinate managerial staff.

Undoubtedly, the earliest transactions between slave producers were not conducted in markets. What seems probable is that the establishment of markets on the English model afforded a setting in which the slave producer could most readily buy and sell what he wished. The slave's part in market activity probably grew swiftly in importance, but the details are nearly all obscure. Hickeringill and Blome, two of the earliest observers, do not refer directly to markets, though Blome did state that provisions were "very dear" in Kingston, and the reference seems to have been to locally produced foodstuffs. Cundall makes a revealing reference to a market for the year 1685, less than a quarter of a century after the first legally recognized market was established; asserting "In May, the negroes at a usual Saturday market at Passage Fort having made some little disturbance, the market was suppressed by the Council". Note that this market was "usual" and that Negroes participated in it.

Leslie provides an abstract of laws in force under the second government of Sir Thomas Lynch (1671–74), and these laws make plain that a number of markets were established, formalized, and maintained under government provision even in this early period. Laws regarding the weighing of meats, occasions of sale, market days, and so on were put into effect in the seventeenth century.

Formal legal acknowledgment of the slaves' rights to market had been given, in negative form at least, as early as 1711: "Hawking about and selling goods (except provisions, fruits, and other enumerated articles) to be punished, on conviction before a magistrate, by whipping, not exceeding *thirty-one lashes*". The exception is more important than the law, since it read: "This restraint is construed to extend only to beef, veal, mutton and saltfish; and to manufactures, except baskets, ropes of bark, earthen pots and such like". In 1735, the law is stated in positive terms: "Slaves may carry about, and sell, all manner of provisions, fruits, fresh milk, poultry, and other small stock of all kinds, having a ticket from their owner or employer."

It is interesting to compare the lists of goods in which slaves were allowed to trade. The purpose of restriction was, of course, to prevent them from dealing in stolen goods. A slave with a carcass of beef was, prima facie, guilty of having slaughtered his owner's cattle. A slave offering metalware or saltfish, neither of which was produced on the island, was clearly suspect of having raided the estate stores. But clearly, between 1711 and 1735 there was some change. In the former year, slaves are forbidden to sell "beef, veal, mutton and saltfish"; in 1735, they are permitted to trade "fresh fish, milk, poultry, and other small stock of all kinds." This suggests either a belated legal acknowledgment of the range of slave production or—more likely, since the laws were generally permissive and not restrictive in this matter—a fairly rapid extension of productive activities by the slaves in response to a growing market for their produce. Accounts of the late eighteenth century and after almost invariably list pigs, goats, fish, poultry, eggs, and milk as products sold by the slaves. This last item may have been goats' milk or perhaps cows' milk bought by the slaves from the estate owners for retail trading. Yet the cattle may have been owned by the slaves themselves. In his journal entry for March 2, 1816, Lewis (1861: 102–3) writes that he purchased from his slaves, at fifteen pounds per head, cattle which they owned and grazed on the estate's pasture. As will be discussed further, later laws restricting the free movement of slaves always excepted their marketing operations.

The importance of slaves to the Jamaican domestic economy in the third quarter of the eighteenth century, is revealed at length in the intelligent and thorough discussions provided by Long, one of the most careful and thoughtful writers of the eighteenth century. In 1774, by Long's estimate, of the 50,000 pounds in currency circulating in the island at least 10,000 pounds, or 20 percent, was in the hands of the slaves, most of it in the form of small coins. Money was scarce, and this scarcity adversely affected daily commerce and interfered with transactions. The island had serious need of small silver to "enable the housekeepers and Negroes to carry on their marketing for butchers meat, poultry, hogs, fish, corn, eggs, plantain and the like."

> A small copper coin might be found extremely convenient here, as enabling the lower class of inhabitants not only to exchange their silver without a drawback, but likewise to keep down the prices of the small necessaries of life: which is a matter that has been thought of great importance to every trading community; and is especially of moment to this island, where the Negroes, who supply the market with small stock, and other necessaries, as well as the white families supplied from those markets, must be very much distressed, if they should ever be wholly deprived of a minor currency accommodated to their dealings with each other.

Long describes a number of markets, but his description of Kingston market is particularly revealing:

> At the bottom of the town, near the water side, is the market place, which is plentifully supplied with butchers meat, poultry, fish, fruits, and vegetables of all sorts. Here are found not only a great variety of American, but also of European, vegetables: such as pease, beans, cabbage, lettuce, cucumbers, French beans, artichokes, potatoes, carrots, turnips, radishes, celery, onions, etc. These are brought from the Liguanca mountains, and are all excellent in their kind. Here are likewise strawberries, not inferior to the productions of our English gardens; grapes and melons in the utmost perfection; mulberries, figs, and apples exceedingly good, but in general gathered before they are thoroughly ripe. In short, the most luxurious epicure cannot fail of meeting here with sufficient in quantity, variety, and excellence, for the gratification of his appetite the whole year round. The prices are but little different from those of Spanish Town: but where they disagree, they are more reasonable at Kingston, the supplies being more regular, and the market superintended by the magistracy. The beef is chiefly from the pastures of Pedro's, in St. Ann's: the mutton, from the salt-pan lands, in St. Catherine's: what they draw from the penns in St. Andrew's parish being very indifferent meat.

Long did not criticize the virtual monopoly which the slaves had come to exercise in internal marketing: rather, he repeatedly suggested means to broaden and extend it. He objected to the pay system in country barracks of the Army, where the officers disbursed the pay. It would have been better, he argued, had the common soldiers received their pay directly:

> With the money in their hands, the men might purchase much better in quality, and more in quantity, of fresh meat and wholesome victuals . . .

every country-barrack would attract a market for the sale of hogs, poultry, fresh fish, fruits, and roots, which are articles produced and vended by almost all the Negroes.

Indeed, by the time Long was writing, the slaves were not only central to the economy, as the producers of the cash export commodities, principally sugar, but had also become the most important suppliers of foodstuffs and utilitarian craft items to all Jamaicans.

The customs of slave-based subsistence farming and marketing clearly provided the slaves with their best opportunities to accumulate liquid capital, as Hall and others have demonstrated. Long, too, writes:

> Even among these slaves, as they are called, the black grandfather, or father, directs in what manner his money, his hogs, poultry, furniture, cloaths, and other effects and acquisition, shall descend, or be disposed of, after his decease. He nominates a sort of trustees, or executors, from the nearest of kin, who distribute them among the legatees, according to the will of the testator, without any molestation or interruption, most often without the enquiry, of their master; though some of these Negroes have been known to possess from £50 to £200 at their death; and few among them, that are at all industrious and frugal, lay up less than £20 or £30. For in this island they have the greatest part of the small silver circulating among them, which they gain by sale of their hogs, poultry, fish, corn, fruits, and other commodities, at the markets in town and country.

Thus, one century after the first legal Jamaican market was created, the slaves had made a place for themselves in the free economic activity of the country which would never thereafter be challenged.

Our continuing emphasis on the slaves' role in supplying and maintaining the internal markets, however, should not obscure another aspect of the economy as it was constituted under slavery. At the end of the eighteenth century, Jamaica's major exports, measured either in bulk or in value, were typically plantation products: cotton, coffee, ginger, and pimento to a lesser extent and, most important, sugar and rum. But other items also reached foreign markets, and quantities of these were derived from slave holdings; that is, they were produced on estate backlands by the slaves. Here may be mentioned gums, arrowroot, castor oil, turmeric, hides, supplejacks, oil nuts, cows' horns, goatskins, and wood products. These items were exported through a growing class of small merchants who lived in towns and did their business in conjunction with local markets. There is scarcely any descriptive information on these traders and their commercial relationships with slave producers; yet such relationships, well reported in the years after Emancipation, must have taken on their characteristic form under slavery. Large quantities of imported goods consumed by the slaves passed through the hands of local importers, the largest traffic being in clothes, household wares, and other items of comfort and convenience not provided by the estate owners.

By the start of the nineteenth century, reports by observers on slave production of provisions and slave buying power had become quite matter-of-fact in character. Dallas, writing in 1803, reports:

> Every proprietor is compelled by law, to cultivate in ground provisions (of course indestructible by hurricanes) one acre for every ten negroes; besides the allotment of negro territory. To cultivate this allotment, one day in every fortnight, belongs to the slaves, exclusive of Sundays and holidays. Thus they raise vegetables, poultry, pigs, or goats, which they consume, bestow, or sell. While some raise provisions, others fabricate coarse chairs, baskets, or common tables. These are bartered for salted meat, or pickled fish, utensils, or gaudy dresses; of which they are very fond. Their right of property in what they thus acquire, is never questioned; but seems completely established by custom.

It will be seen that certain customary arrangements had been secured, and these appear to have been observed by master and slave alike. The marketing arrangements, the increasing dependence of townspeople and free people on slave production, the customary system of slave inheritance, and the slave's attitudes concerning his property rights in the fruits of his labors, all must have grown up gradually and to some extent at least outside the law. They were maintained and accepted by the small group which wielded overwhelming power in the society because they were economically and socially convenient, even necessary, once they had begun to take shape.

By the time the nineteenth-century observers had begun to write of the markets and the slaves' role in them, the pattern had well over a century of traditional practice behind it. No really important new crops entered into the slaves' cultivation, diet, or marketing after 1800; and the slave code which guaranteed rights to market had long been in force. After Emancipation, many new markets would appear, and the scope of economic activity open to the freedmen would be much increased. But Emancipation, insofar as marketing and cultivation practices were concerned, only widened opportunities and increased alternatives; apparently it did not change their nature substantially.

Mathew Gregory ("Monk") Lewis, an estate owner, reported on his 1815–17 visit to his Jamaica estates:

> In my evening's drive I met the negroes returning from the mountains, with baskets of provisions sufficient to last them for the week. By law they are only allowed every other Saturday for the purpose of cultivating their own grounds, which, indeed, is sufficient; but by giving them every alternate Saturday into the bargain, it enables them to perform their task with so much ease as almost converts it into an amusement; and the frequent visiting their grounds makes them grow habitually as much attached to them as they are to their houses and gardens. It is also advisable for them to bring home only a week's provisions at a time, rather than a fortnight's; for they are so thoughtless and improvident that, when they find themselves in possession of a larger supply than is requisite for their immediate occasions, they will sell half to the wandering higglers, or at Savannah la Mar, in exchange for spirits; and then, at the end of the week, they find themselves entirely unprovided with food, and come to beg a supply from the master's storehouse.

Lewis's comments indicate that the slaves were inclined to make much of their provision grounds. Certainly they must have found it a relief to escape from the regimen of labor in the cane fields and to work on "their own" cultivations. Lewis's observations on their attachment to these far-off fields are even shrewder than he realized. The assumption some observers had made that the slave, once free, would be unable to give up his residence at the center of the estate because of his emotional attachment to his house and garden there, proved to be very mistaken. The slaves must also have responded well to the feeling of autonomy which work on their provision grounds afforded. As Emancipation approached, other observers, particularly missionaries intent on establishing the slaves' capacity for freedom, tried to confirm this:

> If the vices of the slave belong then to his condition, that condition should be changed before the nature of the negro is deemed incapable of elevation, or susceptible of improvement. That his defects are redeemed by no good qualities would be a bold assertion; that they are mingled with so many good ones as they are, is to me a matter of the greatest wonder.
>
> To say that he is not industrious without reference to the object for which his exertions are employed would be an absurd remark; to say he is indolent, where his labour is exacted without reward, is to prove nothing.
>
> But where the negro labours on his own ground, for his own advantage,—where his wife and children have the price of his own commodities to fetch him from the market-town, no matter how many miles they have to trudge, or how heavy the load they have to bear,—where the wages he received for his services are at his own disposal,—where his own time is duly paid for, not in shads and herrings, but in money a little more than equivalent to the advantages he deprives his own ground of, by transferring his extra time to the estate he is employed on—the negro is not the indolent slothful being he is everywhere considered, both at home and in the colonies.

In fact, the marketing system in which the slave had been long involved not only prepared him for freedom but demonstrated his capacity to live as a freedman.

At the same time that the missionaries were working courageously for Emancipation, they deplored the Sunday markets. Their mournful pronouncements provide some useful information on the markets themselves. Bickell describes a market in Kingston on the day of his arrival in August 1819:

> It was on a Sunday, and I had to pass by the Negro Market, where several thousands of human beings, of various nations and colours, but principally Negroes, instead of worshipping their Maker on His Holy Days, were busily employed in all kinds of traffick in the open streets. Here were Jews with shops and standings as at a fair, selling old and new clothes, trinkets and small wares at cent. per cent. to adorn the Negro person; there were some low Frenchmen and Spaniards, and people of colour, in petty shops and with stalls; some selling their bad rum, gin, tobacco, etc.; others, salt provisions, and small articles of dress; and many of them bartering with

the Slave or purchasing his surplus provisions to retail again; poor free people and servants also, from all parts of the city to purchase vegetables, etc., for the following week.

Concern that the slave did his marketing on Sunday was not restricted to the missionaries, however. The shopkeepers who kept the Sabbath were effectively cut off from sharing in the consumer market the slave represented. Long, in 1774, had sought to demonstrate that there was more to the profaning of the Sabbath than met the eye. He noted the comment of a contemporary:

> It is certain that the sabbath-day, as at present it is passed, is by no means a respite from labour: on the contrary, the Negroes, either employing it on their grounds, or in travelling a great distance to some market, fatigue themselves much more on that day, than on any other in the week. The forenoon of that day, at least, might be given to religious duties; but I think it rather desirable than otherwise, that the after-part of it should be spent on their grounds, instead of being uselessly dissipated in idleness and lounging, or (what is worse) in riot, drunkenness, and wickedness. If such an alteration should take place, Thursday might be assigned for the market day, instead of the sabbath, and prove of great advantage to all Christian shop-keepers and retailers; the Jews now grossing the whole business of trafficking with the Negroes every Sunday, at which time there is a prodigious resort of them to the towns, and a vast sum expended for drams, necessaries, and manufactures. This alteration would therefore place the Christian dealers upon an equal footing, which they do not at present enjoy.

"No Sunday markets" was probably the only issue in Jamaican history on which missionaries and proslavery writers were able to agree, though their reasons were wholly different.

The significance of this concern is the proof it offers that the marketing activities of the slaves were in fact very important to the Jamaican economy. The economy itself rested on the plantation system and slave labor; but the circumstances were such that the slaves could make a second valuable capital-building contribution through their individual efforts. And the same observers who debated whether the slaves were capable of learning even the fundamentals of Christian teaching were surely aware of their very human capacity for creating and employing wealth by cultivation and commerce. Had it not been for the slaves' skills as producers and distributors and their needs as consumers, there could scarcely have appeared in the Jamaican economy a numerous class of middlemen, import and export dealers, and retailers. The importance of slave marketing was legally recognized in the laws which regulated the behavior of the slave population. Renny cites a law revelatory of this:

> And whereas it is absolutely necessary, that the slaves in this island should be kept in due obedience to their owners, and in due subordination to the white people in general, and, as much as in the power of the legislature, all means and opportunities of slaves committing rebellious conspiracies,

and other crimes, to the ruin and destruction of the white people, and others in this island, prevented, and that proper punishments should be appointed for all crimes to be by them committed; be it further enacted by the authority aforesaid, that no slave, *such only excepted as are going with firewood, grass, fruit, provisions, or small stock and other goods, which they may lawfully sell, to market, and returning therefrom* [italics added], shall here after be suffered or permitted to go out of his or her master or owner's plantation or settlement, or to travel from one town or place to another, unless such slave shall have a ticket from his master, owner, employer, or overseer.

Thus even the sharpest vigilance was relaxed to facilitate the marketing practices of the slaves, and the exceptions cry for explanation. It would be hard to explain them completely and with certainty. But it may be fair to contend that the growth of town populations and the increased demand for the products of the slaves' spare time labor encouraged the participation of slaves as sellers and suppliers; that the growth of the market and the emergence of new demands enlarged the quantity and variety of items which reached the markets; that the activity of the markets increased the slaves' buying power, and that this led in turn to increases in the number of local merchants, retailers, moneylenders, etc., who became dependent on the slaves' surpluses and buying needs for their income; that the free people in the towns gradually came to depend on the slaves' marketing activities for the satisfaction of their daily needs; and that long before Emancipation, the markets and all of the related institutions which maintained them had become core features of Jamaican society and economy. Such seems to have been the situation in Jamaica in 1834, when slavery ended and the Apprenticeship system began.

Freedom and constraint

In most of the British West Indian colonies, an attempt was made to bridge the gap between slavery and freedom by an intervening number of years of Apprenticeship during which masters and slaves were to condition themselves for the new order of a free society. But the Apprenticeship system asked too much of mere mortals. It allowed the masters the labor of their slaves for a stated number of hours per week. Beyond this limit, the slaves (or "apprentices") had the right either to refuse to work for their masters or to demand wages for the work they did. The Apprenticeship system failed to serve its purpose, however, and was curtailed. It was too much to ask that a man should be a slave on weekdays and a wage earner over the weekend. The Apprenticeship system ended at midnight, July 31, 1838, exactly four years after it was inaugurated. At its conclusion, the expected disagreements between ex-masters and ex-slaves began.

The great variety of those disagreements need not detain us. They have been fully described elsewhere, and our present concern is with only one of the sources of discontent. Estate slaves had been housed in huts or tenements provided by their owners, and they had been allowed to cultivate estate backlands. Now, as free wage workers, they were asked to pay rents for huts and land, and ex-masters and ex-slaves faced each other as landlord employers and tenant employees.

A vast potential for misunderstanding and conflict was created by the new situation. Under slavery, the Jamaican planters had made much of the freedom which they allowed the slaves in the cultivation of the backlands.

> I do not believe that an instance can be produced of a master's interference with his Negroes in their peculium thus acquired. They are permitted also to dispose at their deaths of what little property they possess; and even to bequeath their grounds or gardens to such of their fellow-slaves as they think proper. These principles are so well established, that whenever it is found convenient for the owner to exchange the negro-grounds for other lands, the Negroes must be satisfied, in money or otherwise, before the exchange takes place. It is universally the practice.

There, precisely stated, are three points of immediate and important relevance to the post-Emancipation squabbles over rents and wages. The first is that slaves were allowed to acquire and bequeath property of various kinds; the second, that they were even allowed to bequeath their provision grounds, or gardens; and the third, that planters so fully recognized the slaves' rights to these grounds that they offered compensation whenever it became necessary to convert an area of slave cultivation to estate purposes.

There is no need to discuss further the reasons why the slaves were allowed to keep the money and goods they received in their marketing transactions, but since they were allowed to keep them it was only logical to allow bequests. The alternative would have been an unworkable estate tax system of one hundred percent death duties on the "property" of deceased slaves. And without the full cooperation of the slaves themselves, it would have been impossible to assess the property of any individual slave, given the crowded living conditions of the slave quarters and the circumstances of a lifetime of unaccounted small purchases and transactions.

The fact that planters usually compensated slaves who were made to give up provision grounds to estate uses is reasonable enough. If the slaves were required to provide most of their own food, they clearly had to have the necessary resources at their disposal. If they were deprived of certain plots of provision grounds, they would have to be given other grounds yielding crops, or a supply of food, or money with which to fulfill their needs until other land was allowed them and they could collect their first harvest. From the planter's point of view—unless he were disposed to see his slaves starve—the need would be obvious.

It is the fact that slaves were allowed to bequeath provision grounds which is most difficult to explain. At first glance, this would seem to imply that for each estate a time would come when, all of the backlands having been appropriated, there would be no marginal areas left free for cultivation by newly arrived slaves. Yet this could never happen, in part because of the high rate of slave mortality, and more so because of the way in which newly imported slaves were absorbed into the estate organization. "The practice is that of distributing the newly-imported Africans among the old Negroes, as pensioners (with some little assistance occasionally given) on their little *peculium*, and provision-grounds." Thus, new arrivals were simply taken into the existing pattern of provision ground production, and slave importation did not necessitate the setting aside of more land for spare-time cultivation.

The system appears to have been favored by all concerned. From our point of view, it is of interest because it was the course of action least likely to encourage continued introduction of West African methods into Jamaican slave estate agriculture. Admittedly, the newly arrived slaves would, by their language and behavior, revive memories of Africa among a few of the longer enslaved, but in their new households they were the newcomers, the trainees, and the minority voice. Edwards claims that the new slaves were in fact pleased with the arrangement,

> and ever afterwards considered themselves as the adopted children of those by whom they were thus protected, calling them parents, and venerating them as such; and I never knew an instance of the violation of a trust thus solicited and bestowed. In the course of eight or ten months, provided they are mildly used and kept free of disease, new people, under these circumstances, become reconciled to the country; begin to get well established in their families, their houses and provision-grounds; and prove in all respects as valuable as the native or Creole negroes.

The new slaves thus became operators on the household's provision grounds, and later, perhaps, as heads of the households in a succeeding generation, inherited the right of use of the land. And this is where the emphasis must be placed, for as Edwards himself showed, no slaves held provision grounds by legal right of property in land. The land belonged to the estate owner. The use of it was allowed to the slaves. What slaves were permitted to bequeath was certainly not a plot of land, but rather the right to continue to cultivate a certain piece of land for as long as the owner or estate manager permitted that land to be cultivated in provisions. The slaves, never disillusioned in the matter, may well have considered a certain piece of land as their "property"; the master, under no illusions, recognized the arrangement for what it was, namely, a free letting of land in return for which he hoped to have a well-fed and contented slave-labor force. After Emancipation, of course, employers were no longer directly concerned with the condition of their workers' minds and stomachs, the *peculium* was quickly forgotten, and money rents were imposed.

The Emancipation was the most important event in Jamaican history after the English conquest of the island. The Jamaican freedman of 1838 had to work out his style of life anew. The material needs of daily living would be met by personal effort and because of personal motivation; the hated compulsion of the planter was no longer a spur to effort, and the freedman easily learned to live without it.

The freedman's most important means for establishing his independence was by repudiating his previous status as an estate laborer and becoming a peasant, that is, an agriculturist who produced, wholly or mainly on his own land, the bulk of his own food needs and a surplus for sale. The inspiring transformation of the Jamaican people into a free and independent peasantry has been described at length many times; but our concern here is with the freedman's preparation for this transformation. Aside from funds for the acquisition of land and housing, the freedman had to have skills and knowledge which would enable him to live independently. In this he had been prepared for independence by certain conditions of slavery, notably the initial insistence or concession that he provide his own food. At the same time, it must be made clear that newly enslaved Africans carried to Jamaica and absorbed into the estate system and the slave household did not have to learn everything anew. Some of native America's most important foods, such as maize and cassava, were carried to West Africa as early as the sixteenth century and were adopted there with incredible rapidity and success. Later, food-bearing plants had been brought from West Africa to the West Indies. In certain major crops, therefore, and perhaps in the technology and equipment of cultivation, there was much that was already familiar to newly arrived slaves.

Nevertheless, we have largely avoided dealing with the important question of Africanisms, either in agriculture or in marketing. In the case of Jamaican agriculture, the available historical data have not yet been totally and thoroughly analyzed, while sufficient data simply are not available to assess the degree to which Jamaican marketing might have been derived directly from West African practices. Such common West African features as separate royal and commoner markets, royal monopolies in certain products, and price fixing by the court were of course absent and could not have been expected to occur. The first formally established marketplace, with its schedules and regulations, appears to have been a wholly English innovation.

This is neither to argue that prior marketing activities by slaves (or, for that matter, English colonists) did not occur, or that African traditions played no part in the conduct of marketing activity. Especially interesting, perhaps, is the fact that women carry on most marketing activity today in Jamaica, as they did, and do, in much of West Africa. But specification of the role of the African past in shaping the Afro-Caribbean present will require much careful historical research, to free the argument from simple comparisons of trait similarities, and to deal with complex functional relationships between modes of behavior and the attached values and attitudes of those who carry out such behavior. There is no evidence that women outnumbered men among the slaves trafficking in Jamaican marketplaces in the eighteenth century; during the first part of the nineteenth century, most of the descriptions cite male marketers or whole families in the marketplaces, as they cite whole slave families at work on the provision grounds. Women may have become predominant as the freedmen acquired land of their own and became independent peasant cultivators. Hence, the resulting division of labor might parallel African patterns in some cases, without necessarily being derived from them in any simple, invariant fashion.

Enslavement, and slavery itself, meant removal from familiar landscapes, the breakdown of institutions dependent on specific groups of personnel (a priesthood, a court and king, a legal profession), and the forced separation of the members of kin groups of all kinds. It meant sudden and forcible introduction into an estate system and a social order with economic objectives entirely foreign to the newly arrived slaves. And because among each shipload of new arrivals the men usually far outnumbered the women, slavery demanded a total reconsideration of the place and roles of men and women in society, beginning with fundamental questions about new patterns of mating and domestic organization, which the slaves themselves had to resolve under what were often viciously repressive conditions.

Within the plantation, life was supposed to be lived as the master ordered; and to a large extent, this was the case. But we have amassed evidence to demonstrate that the patterns of cultivation and marketing developed largely outside the formal demands of the plantation regimen, either with the overt and explicit cooperation of the planter class or, in some cases, without it. Most interesting, perhaps, the remarkable economic performance of Jamaican slaves made their society dependent on the slave group in ways that no early planter could have predicted—or might have been willing to concede. We see here, then, a clear instance in which the internal contradictions of the plantation system made possible the development of adaptive patterns by the slaves themselves, patterns which might be said to have contributed both to the effective operation of the system on the one hand and to its progressive weakening on the other.

In all this, we still remain uncertain as to the role of the African heritage. Neither slaves nor masters—and it is too often forgotten that the difference in this respect was one of degree—could retain their entire past under the new conditions of plantation life. For the slaves, of course, the difficulties were multiplied by the oppressiveness of slavery itself, as well as by the diversity of their ethnic and cultural origins. Yet slavery made the slaves alike—it inevitably lent a commonality to their suffering; and we have sought to show how the resourcefulness and creativity of the slaves were employed to make their situation somewhat less intolerable. In spite of important recent work (e.g. Brathwaite, this volume), the unraveling of the ways in which the Caribbean's diverse cultural origins were reworked into new patterns remains largely unfinished. Instead of a simple search for like elements in isolation, or the assertion of rather vague generalizations of a philosophical order, what is needed is more thorough historical research on both sides of the Atlantic, to discover what was, and thereupon to determine how the present came to be.

We shall attempt to carry the description of Jamaican markets and marketing further forward in time in the next chapter. Here we have sought to outline some of the fundamental features of the market system in the early period of Jamaica's history as a British possession. We think that both the peasant economy and its marketing pattern originated within the slave plantation. We feel that a tendency to overattribute features of Jamaican peasant culture to the African culture stream may have slighted the role of European culture and culture history. This is not at all to diminish or undervalue what must have been a very substantial African contribution, nor is it to argue that the African past was irrelevant to life on the plantation —within which these patterns probably took on their new forms. But the real question is not one of fractions or proportions; it is, rather, one of documenting precisely the ways in which new cultural patterns are actually created out of older substances, as an aspect of the development of a general theory of culture.

Adequate study of the Jamaican peasantry, both in its historical roots and its ethnographic present, has only begun. As the grand lay historian of Jamaica, the late Ansell Hart, has written:

Plantation economy, absentee proprietorship and the overlordship of the British combined to produce Jamaican traits of delegation, dependence, and 'tek a chance,' above which however, tower the Jamaican's humor, sentiment, physique, capacity for hard work and generosity. There are of course many strands to the story of the undesirable traits which emerges from the plantation economy: neglect, economic insufficiency, malnutrition, disease, etc. Subsistence economy on the other hand developed into the main source of supply of staple food; and besides giving the slave a 'bellyful,' produced directly by himself for himself, also gave him access to the Sunday market, a money economy, important social contacts in field and market and some degree of self-reliance and independence. The cultural and economic effect of what began as subsistence production was immense.

PART SEVEN

Slave Resistance

THE HISTORY OF SLAVE RESISTANCE is the story of slavery itself. In only one case did slaves utterly overthrow and destroy slavery in the Americas: in St Domingue (Haiti) in 1791. Yet the entire history of slavery and the Atlantic slave trade was characterised by slave resistance of one form or another. Whereas historians once looked for slave resistance in the more obvious, overt acts of violence, rebellion and destruction, recently they have sought a more nuanced approach to (and definition of) slave resistance. This reassessment has been greatly influenced by other areas of social investigation and by the spreading awareness among scholars in other disciplines (notably sociology and anthropology) that the rituals of resistance might even be built into the deceptively peaceful fabric of everyday life. It is now commonly accepted that resistance took many forms, some not immediately apparent. We need, as Stuart Schwartz shows in his essay of 1977, to consider slave accommodation alongside slave resistance.

Atlantic slavery was a rapacious system which used (and needed) violence at every turn. Africans were enslaved violently and they were transported across the Atlantic under the daily threat of violence. They were sold and then finally kept at their tasks by rituals of managerial violence. In effect, violence was the lubricant of the slave system. It was hardly surprising that the system prompted violent responses among the slaves.

Too often historians have concentrated on male slave resistance, largely because they conceived of resistance in traditional violent, masculine terms. In her study of lowcountry Georgia (1987), Betty Wood reminds us of the strategies of resistance which were part of the female history of local slavery. Recent research conveys a *different* impression of the patterns of female accommodation/resistance, and prompts us to rethink the social experience of female slaves more broadly.

The essay by Edward A. Pearson (1996) on the 1739 Stono Rebellion in South Carolina forms an important call for historians to look to the African origins of slave resistance in the Americas. The African backgrounds of slaves, and especially the common experience of warfare among many of them, may be a more important explanation for slave rebellions than historians have generally allowed.

More common than the slave rebel, however, was the slave runaway. Whereas historians once thought of runaways as an indication of escape from brutality or misery, recent studies have developed a more subtle analysis. Many were running *to* someone, often a distant loved one. Gad Heuman (1986) in his study of Barbados explains the complexity of the phenomenon. Most troublesome of all to authorities were runaway communities, the so-called maroon societies (discussed here in a ground-breaking essay of 1973 by Richard Price), which emerged in a number of slave colonies.

————•◆•————

INTRODUCTION TO PART SEVEN

THE STUDY OF SLAVE RESISTANCE has yielded important discoveries in recent years, not merely about the way slaves resisted their bondage, but about the very nature of slavery itself and about the relationships between slaves and their owners. Of course, we need to know more exactly what we mean by 'resistance', for it has often been used by historians to embrace a huge range of slave reactions, from outright and bloody rebellion to the most unknowable or secretive of private thoughts and hidden gestures. One way of beginning is to turn the formula round, and to ask how slave owners, masters and mistresses, and slave traders (indeed most free people who came into contact with slaves) viewed the reality or the threats and possibilities of slave resistance? It is a simplification – but a core reality – that slave owners tended to view their slaves either with fear or deep-seated suspicion. Moreover, this seems to have been true throughout the history of black slavery in the Americas, and across the historical geography of slavery, from the moment of African enslavement through to daily life on the remotest of American frontier settlements.

In a sense, any social history of slave life is itself a study in resistance, for, to use the words of Philip Morgan, 'In work and in play, in public and in private, violently and quietly, slaves struggled against masters'. In extracting from their masters an admission of their own humanity, slaves were resisting 'the dehumanization inherent in their status'.[1] Resistance has been viewed, then, by a number of key historians, as a defining characteristic of slavery, not so much a consequence of slavery but integral to slavery itself.

Slavery in the Americas was a violent institution. It was conceived in violence, in the African interior, far from the view of Europeans on the coast. It was continued in violence in the enforced migration, by land and then especially by water, and it heaped further violence on the slaves at landfall, at resale in the Americas and, finally, at the point of settlement. This does not mean that all slaves received cuffs and blows at each step of the way (though many did) but rather that here, manifestly, was an institution, from initial enslavement to resettlement in the Americas, whose lubricant was institutional and personal violence. Atlantic slavery could not have functioned without that violence. Most Africans were seized through acts of violence. Their transportation was managed by the realities and threat of violence. And, certainly on the plantations, no planter could have hoped to work his slaves without the ultimate penalty of physical punishment. Similarly, legal and penal systems from one slave colony to another made critical use of violence (corporal and capital) for the maintenance of their system. It is hard to tabulate the incidence of slave uprisings, the severity of whippings, the number of executions.

Moreover, the slaves themselves knew that they lived in a violent culture. Throughout slave societies in the Americas, slave folklore and parents' lessons for their enslaved offspring were aimed at warning the young of the risks and dangers of slave life, and how to avoid them. For millions of slaves, Africans and local-born, life itself was dangerous. The slaves responded accordingly.

Yet it would be wrong to think of slave resistance solely in physical terms. Though physical resistance (rebellion, destructiveness) is the most obvious, it is only one element in a complex spectrum of slave resistance. It seems remarkable, therefore, given the levels of violence endemic to American slavery, that slaves rarely overthrew the system. For their part, slave owners assumed the worst of their slaves, fearing resistance, planning for it and devising local and society-wide regulations to prevent, curb or punish it. African slaves were generally enslaved through violent acts (warfare, seizure, kidnapping). The movement to the slave coast, the shipboard encounters and Atlantic crossing, the auctions in the Americas – all involved physical violation to some degree. So, too, did learning to work on the plantations. To the slaves, violence and physical aggression must have seemed basic to their dealings with white people from first to last. Slave reactions had to be tempered, however, by the knowledge of what happened to slaves who overstepped the mark. Young slaves and new arrivals were taught, by parents and friends, the ever-present dangers of too hasty or intemperate reaction to life's injustices. Those who ignored those lessons (or who could take no more) and who flared up were likely to encounter more trouble. This was a particular problem for young men.

Life's daily miseries were doled out by whites or others in authority on the ground, at the place of work or in the community. The cuffs, blows and other indignities generally came from people the slaves knew. But their dealings with outsiders (at market, in towns, on their travels) also contained a fair share of dangers for slaves.[2] More than that, however, slave societies were organised around the principle that slaves were likely to resist and that the law needed to be in place to deal with it. Stated crudely, slave owners everywhere viewed their slaves as dangerous and unpredictable. Those who thought otherwise were often disabused of their ideas.

Africans posed the greatest dangers. Some had been seized in warfare and clearly had had military experience in Africa. The loading and corralling of Africans on and in the slave ships sought to blend economic utility (the pressing need to keep the slaves fit and well for sale in the Americas) with physical safety for the crew. We know of 313 voyages on which slaves rebelled, and of other rebellious slave incidents on the coast itself.[3] This was quite apart from unsuccessful acts of resistance and individual defiance by Africans on board ship. More than this, the time spent on board the ships was a seminal experience for slaves; it was, in effect, the first contact between African slaves and white men. Thereafter, daily working life on plantations (especially sugar plantations) was overshadowed by the threat of physical punishment. Men in authority armed with whips and sticks patrolling their slave gangs were ubiquitous.

This is the context in which we need to consider slaves' physical resistance. They did so most spectacularly in the Haitian revolution of 1791. Yet that revolt was exceptional, in scale and success. More common were unsuccessful slave uprisings (notably in Jamaica – helped, like Haiti, by local geography). In rugged terrain, in mountainous islands or in South American settlements where the vast interior beckoned, rebellious slaves might secure an untraceable escape. In such places, maroon communities of runaway slaves evolved into independent black communities which were fiercely resistant to white attack and proud of their independence. In some slave colonies, such escape routes were impossible. Where, for example, could runaways escape to on the small island of Barbados? Nevertheless, slave revolts flared up throughout the Americas. Even in North America – where slave violence was noticeably less frequent and widespread – slave revolts periodically erupted: South Carolina (1739), French Louisiana (1763), Virginia (1800), Charleston (1822) and Nat Turner's rebellion in Virginia in 1831.

The Caribbean islands were homes to slave violence of an altogether different kind. It was no coincidence that in the islands (and Brazil) Africans dominated the slave quarters until the late years of slavery. Time and again, slave violence had to be put down by that characteristic mix of plantocratic repression and help from the resident military. The European naval presence enabled white society to move men and arms relatively quickly from one trouble spot to another. Indeed, the dependence of local whites on outside military assistance against the slaves weighed heavily, in 1776, when some voices were raised in support of the rebellious North American colonists. West Indian whites, unlike their North American counterparts, simply could not manage without metropolitan help when facing the slaves.

British West Indian slave owners faced a confusing problem: slave violence would not go away. It was commonplace when the slaves were primarily African, but it also flared up when the slave population had begun to change in the early nineteenth century (after the abolition of the slave trade in 1807), and when an increasing proportion of slaves were local-born and Christian. Major slave rebellions (Barbados (1816) with 400 slaves dead; Demerara (1823) with 250 slaves dead; and, most destructive of all, Jamaica (1831–32) when 500 were killed – each death toll vastly exceeding local white deaths) shook plantocratic control and alarmed metropolitan opinion. Each act of slave rebellion was followed by a predictable white reaction: repression and violence on an ever more sickening scale, with slaves killed out of hand or executed in their droves by crude and quickly summoned legal proceedings. Though slave violence and subsequent white repression (in the British case) did not overthrow the slave system, it helped to persuade increasing numbers of people in Britain that slavery was not worth preserving. Throughout the eighteenth century, few had doubted that, whatever the difficulties, slavery was worth the effort and trouble. By the 1820s that no longer seemed to be the case. And in that definitive shift towards questioning and doubting the value, utility or morality of slavery, slave rebellion and resistance had played an important role.

More common perhaps than actual revolts was the fear of slave rebellion. Rumours of plots, fears of rebellion, imaginary slave threats, all and more flit in and out of the history of slavery. Such evidence speaks to the planters' mentality: of deep-seated fear and distrust of their slaves, especially of Africans, whom they scarcely knew and yet whom they needed for their well-being and daily care. Sudden death, and in the tropics death often came swiftly and unexpectedly, was often imputed to slave malevolence rather than nature. Slaves who spent their lives in close proximity to whites, notably domestic servants, bore the brunt of such worries in addition to the irritations of white people living cheek by jowl with others they rarely understood, and distrusted at every turn. Such living arrangements (common everywhere in the Americas) were a recipe for misunderstanding and friction.

Slaves ran away in all slave societies, but these acts of escape were more frequent, widespread and complex than historians once imagined. They went away by foot, by boat, cart or horse when available.[4] Some newly arrived Africans escaped in groups, but most escaped alone. Curiously, some runaways took off at particular times of the year, and their owners (free of the burdens of feeding them in hard times) often delayed searching for them. In many slave societies there was clearly a degree of latitude shown towards runaways. Many, of course, were not so much running away from someone (owners or the plantation) as towards someone: a sibling, a loved one, a parent, relative or friend. Slave societies everywhere had their regular quota of runaways. Local newspapers were peppered with advertisements seeking the return of runaways or issuing threats against people who harboured them.[5] The number of fugitive slave advertisements is remarkably high. Moreover, it is clear that not all runaways were recorded in this fashion.

Plantation papers, like contemporary newspapers, regularly list slaves as 'runaways': slaves who absconded, but who came back time and again (normally to face inevitable punishment). Of course, slaves tried to escape long before they reached their final home (say, a plantation): they ran away from their captors in Africa, they tried to flee from the slave ships or en route from the slave auctions. Sometimes slaves were branded 'R' for runaway. And yet despite the practical difficulties and dangers, some slaves managed to stay away for considerable periods. Some even escaped from one island to another. Runaways seeking to return might negotiate with their owner, through an intermediary, conditions for their return. Here, and elsewhere in slave society, we see dispossessed slaves exercising levels of choice and autonomy in ways we had not imagined possible until recently.

Runaway slaves had to fend for themselves as best they could. More likely, however, they could rely on the remarkable slave networks which operated throughout slave societies, linking one slave community to another, sometimes operating across great distances. Friends, relatives, shipmates, workmates, slaves in transport trades, all and more formed a web of slave contacts which enabled information to travel quickly among the slaves. It also allowed slaves to move more easily from place to place. There were enormous risks involved for the fugitives and for those slaves who harboured or aided them, but slave networks were vital, offering advice, shelter, food and clothing to the runaway slave. It seems clear enough that runaways often would not have got very far, or survived for long, if left to their own devices. Thus, though running away seemed a solitary decision and affair, it was often sustained by the wider slave community.

Slaves had to learn how best to steer a path through the dangers of slave life. Insults, blows, threats, small and daily irritations (quite apart from major dangers and problems) had to be borne, accepted and dealt with. Slaves developed their own ways of dealing with such problems: insults were tolerated with a sullen silence, threats heeded by turning away. Slaves everywhere evolved a culture of resistance which cushioned them against slavery's most painful blows. Incomprehension, foot-dragging and feigned incompetence played their parts in allowing slaves to pace themselves and distance themselves from their owners' demands and expectations. Slaves effectively devised conventions of slave life – accepted also by their owners – as part of the complex negotiations with the slave system. Cutting corners, not working too hard, wilfully misunderstanding, half-truths, all formed strands in the slaves' resistance to the hostile world around them.

Rarely did slave owners and their hired managers/overseers have full and free control over the slaves. Rarely could they do precisely what they wanted, and rarely did they exact from their slaves the levels of work, obedience and deference they would have liked. This is not to claim that the slaves were any less oppressed or brutalised by the slave system. But it was a system through which slaves negotiated a modus vivendi. This, the harshest of human conditions, could paradoxically function effectively only by tolerating degrees of slave resistance. There was a point, though, for each slave and for each enslaved community, beyond which they could not trespass. Anything beyond that point (too insolent, rough, lazy, deceitful) and they could expect the inevitable white reaction. Again, we return to the point made at the beginning: slave resistance was not so much a distinct, separate aspect of slave experience, but an integral element of slave society itself.

Notes

1   Philip D. Morgan, *Slave Counterpoint: Black Culture in the Eighteenth-Century Chesapeake and Lowcountry*, Chapel Hill, 1998, p. xxii.
2   A sense of this can be gauged from incidents of maltreatment in Equiano's everyday life. See James Walvin, *An African's Life: Olaudah Equiano, 1745–1797*, London, 1998.
3   Herbert S. Klein, *The Atlantic Slave Trade*, Cambridge, 1999, p. 159.
4   Philip D. Morgan, *Slave Counterpoint*, pp. 56–57.
5   Gad Heuman, ed., *Out of the House of Bondage: Runaways, Resistance and Marronage in Africa and the New World*, London, 1986.

Chapter 25

Betty Wood

SOME ASPECTS OF FEMALE RESISTANCE TO CHATTEL SLAVERY IN LOW COUNTRY GEORGIA, 1763–1815

ALTHOUGH OFTEN DIFFERING DRAMATICALLY in their methodologies and conclusions, most studies of the slave societies of the American South either draw to a close by the middle years of the eighteenth century or begin their story only in the 1820s and 1830s. Moreover, whilst some scholars have differentiated between particular patterns of black behaviour, as for example between African- and country-born slaves, field hands and domestic slaves, until quite recently comparatively little interest has been shown in delineating the ways in which black women perceived and responded to their status and condition.[1]

Barbara Bush has commented of West Indian slave women that 'Popular stereotypes . . . have portrayed them as passive and downtrodden work-horses who did little to advance the struggle for freedom. The "peculiar burdens" of their sex allegedly precluded any positive contribution to slave resistance.'[2] Such 'stereotypes' are as untrue of the Georgia Low Country between 1763 and 1815 as they are of the sugar islands between 1790 and 1838.

The story of the Low Country's slave society before 1815 may be broken down into three, not altogether distinct, phases. The years down to the mid-1770s saw the creation of a slave-based plantation economy; the War for Independence severely disrupted that economy and the black workforce upon which it depended; and, finally, the post-war years witnessed the rebuilding of that economy and workforce.

Two things did not change dramatically during these years; the modes of resistance which theoretically, if not always in practice, were open to black men and women and, secondly, certain white assumptions about the institution of slavery. Few whites doubted that the Low Country's prosperity stemmed from the employment of slaves or that the ownership of land and slaves comprised the main route to economic, social, and political preeminence. These assumptions emerged virtually unscathed from the challenge posed by the ideas and events of the American revolution. Insofar as the white Georgians of the Revolutionary and early National periods were 'worried' about slavery then it was only in the albeit critically important sense of determining how they might ensure that the economic benefits of that institution were secured at a minimal cost to the white community.

Despite the bitter debate that had preceded the introduction of slavery into Georgia in 1751 there were, by the 1760s and 1770s, few dissenters.[3] Black dissidents, male or female, young or old, could expect little sympathy, let alone positive assistance, from any white Georgian.

I

Between 1751, when the restrictions imposed by the Trustees on land, labour and credit were finally lifted, and the mid-1770s the Georgia Low Country experienced sustained demographic and economic growth. The white population grew from less than 3,000 to roughly 18,000 whilst the black element soared from under 350 to approximately 16,000.[4] The Georgia settlers, as one of the Trustees' supporters had put it back in 1746, were 'stark Mad after Negroes'.[5]

As the Low Country became embroiled in the War for Independence this growth came to a fairly dramatic halt. Loyalist departures and wartime casualties took their toll of the white population, and possibly as many as 90 per cent of the region's slaves were removed by their Loyalist owners or the British, stolen, or managed to escape.[6] However, the vast majority of black men and women ended the war as they had begun it; as chattel slaves.

As during the colonial period so after 1783 Low Country rice planters clamoured for slaves, now to replenish wartime losses. By 1790 Georgia's black population totalled 29,264 but, as Sylvia Frey has pointed out, 'whereas in 1775 two-thirds of Georgia's slaves lived within twenty miles of the coast, by 1790 over half of all Georgia's slaves lived in the backcountry'.[7] This infilling was to have important consequences for black resistance.

Both before and immediately after the war rice planters depended upon the African and domestic slave trades, rather than on natural increase, for the bulk of their black workers and, demographically, there were to be important similarities in the composition and structure of the pre- and post-war black populations of the Low Country.

Between 1752 and 1765 upwards of 3,000 blacks, most of whom appear to have been African-born, were brought by their owners, or shipped, to a labour-hungry Georgia from elsewhere in British America. In 1766 blacks began to be imported directly from West Africa.[8] After 1783 what Sylvia Frey has termed the 'pent-up demand' for slaves was also largely satisfied by recourse to the African slave trade.[9]

The Low Country's black population throughout this period was predominantly African-born, male, young, and unskilled. The main requirement was for workers who could undertake the arduous physical labour involved in rice and indigo cultivation and, by the 1760s, planters had a clear idea as to precisely which Africans fitted that bill. As in South Carolina, certain modes of black behaviour were associated with particular tribes and regions of West Africa.[10] But as, if not more, important was the African's age and state of health upon arrival in America. The constant plea of planters and merchants involved in the slave trade to Georgia was for 'prime Men & Women, with a few Boys & Girls, the Men and Women not exceeding twenty five years of age'.[11]

Unfortunately there is no detailed record of the sex ratios and age structure of the slave cargoes landed in Georgia during these years. However, such evidence as there is confirms four crucial points. First, the great majority of black men and women had a knowledge, and often a recent knowledge, of freedom in Africa. In this context, the sheer novelty of Georgia's slave system as of the mid–late eighteenth century cannot be overemphasized.[12] Second, and vitally important in shaping various aspects of black life, the slave population conformed closely to the age structure specified by planters and merchants. Only 2 per cent of the 3,042 adult slaves listed on 235 colonial inventories of estates (records which, it must be said, seldom indicated the exact or even approximate ages of slaves) were said to be 'old'. The same was true of just under 5 per cent of the 1,563 men and women listed on ninety-eight inventories from Chatham County covering the years between 1776 and 1796.[13]

The last two points concern the size and sex ratios of slave-holdings in the Low Country. In neither respect was there a dramatic change between the 1760s and the end of the eighteenth century. Within a decade or so of the introduction of slavery into Georgia the Low Country already contained 'a pyramid shaped distribution of landholders with a handful of large slave-owning rice planters at the apex and small family farms with one or no slaves at the bottom', a social structure which endured down to the Civil War.[14]

At the top of this 'pyramid' 5 per cent of masters owned more than fifty slaves whilst at the other end of the spectrum 11 per cent before, and 6 per cent after, the war held just one slave. The average size of holdings increased from fifteen between 1755 and 1777 to around twenty by the turn of the century. But throughout this period as many as 70 per cent of Low Country slaves lived on estates containing more than twenty (but seldom more than fifty) slaves.[15]

In the black population as a whole, men outnumbered women. Before the war the sex ratio on the 235 estates surveyed was in the order of 148 men to every 100 women; on those drawn from Chatham County during the 1780s and 1790s it was 145 to 100. But there were significant variations. Men outnumbered women in the countryside, but the reverse appears to have been true in Savannah, as indeed it was in Charleston also.[16] In the countryside, the larger the slave-holding the larger the imbalance between the sexes.[17]

Twelve per cent of pre-war, and 5 per cent of post-war Chatham County estates contained only male slaves; those consisting only of women fell from 9 per cent before the war to around 5 per cent during the 1780s and 1790s. Men outnumbered women on 48 per cent of colonial, and 54 per cent of post-war, estates. The reverse was true of 10 and 17 per cent of holdings, respectively.

Both before and after the war numbers were equal on 17 per cent of estates. On the remaining holdings the slaves' sex was not mentioned by those compiling the inventory. Obviously these local, as well as Low Country-wide, sex ratios were to be of enormous significance in shaping patterns of black family life and, moreover, resistance.

Although the distinction between rural and urban slavery was not always clearcut, the vast majority of Low Country slaves lived and worked in the countryside on a permanent basis. Sometimes, especially on smaller estates, they might perform more than one type of work but no more than about 10–15 per cent of rural slaves were allowed, or required, to acquire skills. However, there was a crucial distinction between male and female slaves; insofar as it is possible to talk of an occupational elite, then that elite was predominantly male.

On large plantations as many as one-quarter of adult male slaves worked as artisans or as domestic servants of one sort or another. Certain skills and functions were effectively limited to men; plantation records do not reveal any women who worked as drivers, coopers, carpenters, brickmakers, and so on. Some, but by no means all, household jobs were reserved for women. On large estates upwards of 10 per cent of women were employed as cooks, maids, washerwomen, nurses, midwives, and seamstresses.[18] But even so, there was a very real sense in which black women were tied to the rice and indigo fields. Most had no specialized occupational skills such as might help them to secure an albeit precarious independence should they decide to take flight or, for that matter, take them legitimately off the plantation.

Although both the pre- and post-war demand for black women under the age of twenty five could be interpreted as an explicit interest in securing women of child-bearing age, there is no evidence that this was the case. Women were regarded primarily as workers rather than as potential mothers. Planters were certainly aware of the economic value of slave children but did not allude, at least not in print, to the reproductive capacity of black women, to their value as 'breeders'.[19]

Not least because of the continuing availability of 'surplus' slaves from the Upper South, Low Country planters, who were agitating for labour, very occasionally complaining about the low rate of natural increase of their slaves and, after the 1760s, coming under heavy external pressure to close the African slave trade, do not appear to have seriously contemplated the possibility that their labour needs might be largely, and more cheaply, satisfied were they to emulate Jamaican sugar planters and positively encourage black women to have more children.[20] Neither did they suggest that deliberate abortion or infanticide might be partially responsible for the low rate of natural increase of their slaves.

But although not making a substantial contribution to the overall growth rate of the black population natural increase, or more specifically the black partnerships and parenthood it signified, played a key role in shaping both the character and the incidence of black resistance. An essential, continuing, and often successful aspect of the struggle waged by black men and women was that of trying to ensure the integrity of their family life.

Whilst not self-consciously encouraging their slave women to 'breed', Low Country planters did take an interest in the sexual and family lives of their slaves. Many, and probably the majority, refused to grant, or impose upon, their slaves a Christian wedding ceremony but were by no means averse to the formation of monogomous relationships. They appreciated that 'such relationships [and] especially the sexual order and stability they conferred on the slave quarters, were very much to [their] advantage'.[21] They recognized, moreover, the extent to which the enforced separation of black couples, and parents from their children, comprised a powerful motive for running away. But death, indebtedness, or the prospect of profit could and did result in partnerships being broken and families torn asunder. The only small crumb of comfort offered to black mothers was that in all probability they would not be separated from their children before the latter reached the age of seven or eight.[22]

How much choice black men and women had in their selection of a marriage partner is debatable. Masters were not keen on their slaves leaving the plantation for any reason, including visits to a spouse, and it is probable that, sex ratios and age structure permitting, wedlock usually involved slaves who lived on the same estate.[23] Inventories give no indication of how, when, and why particular partnerships were formed, but they do offer some revealing insights into the incidence of slave marriage, black parenthood, and the separation of couples.

Of the 738 women listed on those colonial inventories which recorded marital and familial relationships, 196 were married and living with their husbands – 18 per cent of the men on those estates. 112, or 57 per cent, of these couples had at least one child who lived with them. The remainder either had no children or had been separated from them: it is impossible to tell which. Women known to have given birth to at least one child totalled 272, but 59 per cent of these mothers appear not to have had a husband, or the father of their children, living with them at the time the inventory was taken. There is no way of knowing whether the men in question were dead, living on a neighbouring estate, or had been sold away. Only 7 men (less than 1 per cent of those on the estates surveyed) lived 'alone' with their child or children.

A similar pattern characterized Chatham County in the 1780s and 1790s. Almost exactly one-third of the women on those estates where marital and familial relationships were recorded were married; their husbands accounted for 24 per cent of the men on these holdings. Two-thirds of the 188 couples listed had at least one child living with them. Fractionally under 42 per cent of women are known to have given birth at least once, and 47 per cent of these mothers (a drop of 12 per cent on the pre-war figure) lived 'alone' with their offspring. The same was true of 2 per cent of men.

The salient points to be drawn from this data would seem to be these; somewhere between one-quarter and one-third of Low Country slaves had no reason to take flight in search of their spouse. But roughly half the women known to have been mothers appear to have been living apart from their husbands. For both partners separation, however close or distant, provided a compelling reason to run away. But for mothers, especially of young children, even if they knew where their husband was living, and how to reach him, running away could prove problematical. Some mothers elected to take their children with them; virtually none were prepared to abandon them in the hope of thereby facilitating their own escape.[24]

Slave mothers did not lack the will to run away in search of their husbands, or permanent freedom, but were often obliged, or felt themselves obliged, to express their discontent by malingering and feigning illness rather than by absconding. The torment of separation was no less severe for slave husbands and fathers, but the circumstances of that separation often meant that when contemplating whether or not to take flight in search of their loved ones they were not confronted by the same logistical problems faced by the mothers of their children.

Many factors shaped the character and frequency of slave resistance in the Georgia Low Country between the early 1760s and 1815 but, in the final analysis, the decision as to whether, when, and how to resist rested with the individual slave. Unfortunately, a dearth of first-hand black evidence means that to some degree motives and the process of decision-making must remain matters for speculation. However, the one thing which made absolutely no difference whatsoever in determining the will to resist was the slave's sex. Women, just as much as men, could hope to run away, fire a gun, and destroy property. But did they so decide in the same numbers as men? If not, why not?

II

Between 1755 and 1770 the Georgia Assembly enacted a series of increasingly repressive laws designed to regulate the institution of slavery.[25] These laws, like those of the other Southern colonies, were predicated not on the belief that Africans were docile, submissive creatures but, on the contrary, that each and every one of them was a potential rebel. There was no suggestion in the slave codes that black women might behave differently from, or present a lesser threat than, black men. Neither was any provision made for the lighter punishment of female offenders.

Georgia's slave laws enumerated the kinds of black misconduct serious enough to warrant public attention. Capital crimes included insurrection and attempted insurrection, murder, assault, the destruction of certain types of property and, after 1770, the rape, or attempted rape, of a white woman. Capital courts were instructed to select 'such manner of Death' as would be 'most Effectual to deter others', and most opted for death by hanging or burning. Non-capital crimes, for which convicted slaves could expect to be whipped, included such offences as petty theft, being absent without a ticket, and working without a badge.[26]

The punishment of those misdeeds which comprised 'day to day resistance' was left to the discretion of individual owners. But the slave codes offered some guidelines. The castration, cutting out the tongue, putting out an eye, scalding, or burning a slave was deemed to be excessive 'Cruelty'; acceptable punishments included 'whipping or beating with a Horse Whip Cow Skin Switch or Small Stick', 'Putting Irons on', and imprisonment.[27] Beginning in 1763 those owners who, for whatever the reason, did not wish to whip their slaves themselves could obtain this service for a modest fee at the Savannah Work-house.[28]

The mode of resistance which white Georgians feared above all others, organized rebellion on a scale which threatened to topple their society, was that which by the 1760s and 1770s was least likely to occur.[29] The most serious outbreak of slave violence in the Low Country between 1763 and 1815 occurred in St Andrew Parish in 1774 when eleven 'New Negroes' and a country-born slave killed four whites. The group was soon taken up, and the two men deemed to be the ringleaders burned alive.[30] This 'revolt' had a significance out of all proportion to the numbers involved; it reminded white Georgians of the need for constant vigilance and black slaves of the gruesome fate which awaited unsuccessful rebels. But in the present context it is also significant that two of the participants were women. We know nothing about them, not even their names. Yet their involvement suggests that far from being placid 'workhorses' some black women were prepared to kill, and run the risk of being killed in the most brutal fashion, in order to secure their freedom.

The failure of Georgia's black men and women to mount a rebellion during this period, and especially during the War for Independence when, on the face of it, the Low Country's white society was peculiarly vulnerable, should not be taken to mean that they were so psychologically devastated by their experience of slavery that they had given up all hope of regaining the freedom which so many of them had known in Africa. But by the 1760s and 1770s there were already virtually insurmountable obstacles to the launching of such uprisings, obstacles that were not significantly diminished by the onset of war and which were added to by the rapid infilling of the Backcountry during the post-war years.[31]

During the War blacks saw the British, who elsewhere in the mainland had shown their willingness to arm male slaves belonging to Patriots, as offering them the best prospect of freedom. But, as Sylvia Frey has argued, the wholesale emancipation of Georgia's slaves was never regarded by the British as a viable, or even as a wholly desirable, possibility.[32] On the Patriot side, the Laurens Plan, which envisaged freeing a maximum of 4,000 male slaves in South Carolina and Georgia, was a virtual non-starter in both states.[33]

An unknown number of black men and women took advantage of wartime dislocations not to rebel but to run away – if not to the British then to the Backcountry or into the coastal and river swamps. For most, that freedom was to prove both tenuous and temporary. Yet at least one of the runaway communities established in the river swamps not too distant from Savannah managed to survive until the mid-1780s, supporting itself partly by growing its own foodstuffs and partly by raiding outlying plantations. As white Georgians appreciated, such a community, if allowed to persist, would attract other slaves and possibly come to comprise the nucleus of the large scale rebellion which they so feared.

This community, which contained 'a number of women', was organized along strict military lines under the leadership of Lewis and Sharper, the latter referring to himself as 'Captain Cudjoe'. In this community the women 'planted rice' and 'stayed in Camp'. When the settlement was attacked by whites in 1787 'all' the women, by their own account, were 'ordered . . . in the Canes' by their menfolk and took no part in the fighting which resulted in the death of 'Captain Cudjoe' and the capture of Lewis. How many managed to remain at large is uncertain. Two of those who were taken up testified at Lewis's trial, whether voluntarily or under duress is debatable.[34]

In effect, the war years witnessed and facilitated not organized rebellion but the amplification of what was undoubtedly the most common expression of black rage and black despair; running away. Although by no means indicative of the total number of runaways, newspaper advertisements provide the best source of information about this mode of black behaviour.

During the thirteen years before the War for Independence advertisements for 453 runaways were placed in Georgia's only newspaper, *The Georgia Gazette*. Between 1783 and 1795 the same newspaper contained advertisements for 528 adult fugitives. The imbalance between the numbers of male and female runaways is immediately apparent. In the pre-war period only 61, or 13 per cent, were women; a proportion which increased to fractionally over 24 per cent between 1783 and 1795. These proportions did not reflect a similar sex ratio in the black population as a whole. Peter Wood has suggested that women were 'more likely than men to visit . . . and return of their own accord in a pattern less likely to prompt public advertising',[35] and it is probable that, not least because of the constraints imposed by motherhood and occupation, this was indeed the case.

Less readily explained is the virtual doubling of advertisements for female runaways between 1783 and 1795. The available evidence offers no neat explanation. However, two possibilities lend themselves to consideration. First, it is conceivable that, mainly because of wartime dislocations and separations, more women were actually running away. Second, owners might have been more willing to advertise for the return of their female slaves, especially during the immediate post-war years when they were particularly hard-pressed for workers.

Table 25.1   The destinations of slave runaways, 1763–75

Destination	Men	Women	Country-born	African-born	New Negro	Un-known	Total
In, near, or heading for Savannah	31	5	13	3	3	17	36
To family, friends, former residence	11	1	5	–	1	6	12
Harboured/hiding out in countryside	3	2	–	–	–	5	5
Master uncertain, assumes in Georgia	24	2	3	10	5	8	26
Will try to pass as free	10	–	3	1	–	6	10
Will try to escape by sea; heading for coast (other than ports)	16	4	1	2	10	7	20
To Backcountry; Indian Nation; going 'upriver'	15	1	2	–	–	14	16
To coast *or* Backcountry	3	3	–	–	6	–	6
To join other runaways	5	2	–	–	6	1	7
Other							
'Southerly'	1	–	–	–	–	1	1
Savannah *or* Carolina	1	–	–	–	–	1	1
Killed slave	1	–	–	–	–	1	1
Killed overseer	1	–	–	–	–	1	1
'Northward'	3	1	–	–	–	4	4
South Carolina	1	–	1	–	–	–	1
Harboured/stolen by white person	–	1	–	–	–	1	1
Total	126	22	28	16	31	73	148

Broadly speaking, slaves ran away in order to be reunited with their family and friends; to join up with bands of fugitive slaves; to escape to the Back-country, possibly in the hope of being harboured by Indians; or headed for, or remained in, Savannah, either with a view to blending into the black 'urban crowd' or making their escape by sea (see Tables 25.1 and 25.2). Men might have predominated among the advertised runaways but, with one or two exceptions, the proportions of men and women making for each of these destinations did not differ dramatically.

The destinations and motives of 305 (or 67 per cent) of colonial runaways were not mentioned by those placing the advertisement. Of the remainder (126 men and 22 women), fractionally under 25 per cent of men, and just over 22 per cent of women, were said to be in, near, or heading for Savannah (see Table 25.1). Another 41 slaves were said to be 'well known' in that town and its environs.

Table 25.2 The destinations of slave runaways, 1783–95

Destination	Men	Women	Country-born	African-born	New Negro	Un-known	Total
In, near, or heading for Savannah	35	20	13	1	—	41	55
To family, friends, former residence	33	8	8	2	—	31	41
Harboured/hiding out in countryside	53	19	9	6	3	54	72
Will try to pass as free	14	—	8	—	—	6	14
Will try to escape by sea; heading for coast (other than ports)	7	—	—	2	1	4	7
To Backcountry; Indian Nation; going 'upriver'	15	5	1	5	—	14	20
To join other runaways	7	—	2	1	2	2	7
Florida	7	1	1	2	—	5	8
Indian Nation *or* Florida	5	—	—	1	—	4	5
South Carolina	9	1	3	1	—	6	10
Other							
Skidaway	2	—	—	—	—	2	2
Ebenezer	1	—	—	—	—	1	1
Waynesborough	1	—	—	—	—	1	1
Tybee	1	—	—	—	1	—	1
'Southward'	1	—	—	—	—	1	1
South Carolina *or* Backcountry	1	—	—	—	—	1	1
Countryside *or* Florida	—	1	—	—	—	1	1
Carolina *or* Savannah	—	1	—	—	—	1	1
Total	192	56	45	21	7	175	248

Eight per cent of male runaways, and just 1 woman, were believed to be making their way to a member of their family (usually their spouse), a friend or friends, or back to a previous owner. The same proportion of men, but no women, were thought to be trying to pass as free blacks. This might involve eking out a precarious living in Savannah or attempting to escape by sea from the port of Savannah. Four women (18 per cent of those whose destination was mentioned) and 13 per cent of men were said quite specifically by their owners or overseers to be trying to do the latter. Another 12 per cent of men, and one woman, were thought to be making for the Backcountry, presumably also with a view to securing their permanent freedom from bondage.[36]

The destinations of runaways did not change dramatically after the War for Independence (see Table 25.2). In 53 per cent of cases owners and overseers did not mention the likely destination of their slaves. In the remaining cases (192 men and 56 women) 18 per cent of men, and 35 per cent of women, were thought to be in, or making for, Savannah. According to their owners, another 41 male, and 18 female, runaways were 'well known' in the town. One-third of the female fugitives whose destination was mentioned, and just over 27 per cent of men, were thought to be 'harboured', or hiding out, in the countryside. Roughly the same proportion of men (17 per cent) and women (14 per cent) were believed to be trying to reach a relation, friend, or former owner. The Backcountry still attracted some runaways; 7 per cent of men, and 8 per cent of women, were said to be making for the 'Upcountry' or the 'Indian Nation'. Fourteen, or 7 per cent, of male fugitives, but no women, were thought to be trying to pass as free blacks. As during the colonial period, other destinations, usually in Georgia and South Carolina, continued to attract smaller numbers of runaways.

A slave's sex, marital status, occupational experience, and place of residence all helped to define the options that were open to would-be runaways. But as important throughout this period was the slave's birthplace and, if African-born, the length of time spent in America.

During these years the Low Country's slave population remained predominantly African-born but, just as significant, contained a high proportion of 'New Negroes'. All the available evidence suggests that the behaviour of this population both before and immediately after the War for Independence conformed closely to that predicated by Mullin for eighteenth-century Virginia.[37]

'New Negroes', male and female, whether 'out of a sense of shock and bewilderment . . . or a more aggressive intent to escape' tried to 'put as many miles as they could between themselves and their owners and . . . to avoid contact with whites'.[38] Newly imported Africans, who often absconded in groups which shared a common African origin, spoke little or no English and at best had only a hazy knowledge of the Georgia landscape. Although at least one party, including a woman, set off in the hope of finding their way back to Africa,[39] most must have taken flight with little idea of their ultimate destination or even of what awaited outside the immediate confines of their owner's estate.

Their linguistic ability, and greater knowledge of the white world, opened up possibilities for country-born and acculturated blacks which were effectively closed to 'New Negroes'. For example, an awareness of the existence of Savannah or Charleston offered the prospect of some degree of personal autonomy as well as the possibility of escape by sea. The ability to speak English, and the realization that there was an albeit minute free black community in Georgia,[40] meant that there was some chance of passing as free and, if apprehended, of talking one's way out of trouble.

But even for those country-born and acculturated women who were not, or who did not feel themselves to be, constrained by maternal responsibilities there could be additional constraints imposed by their sex and occupational experience. For example, even if a woman, unhindered by small children, made her way to Savannah, without some help from family or friends it could prove immensely difficult for her to survive. Despite the regulations governing the hire of slaves, unskilled men could hope to find casual employment as porters and carters without too many questions being asked of them.[41] Similarly, some whites would employ skilled male slaves even if they knew, or suspected, that they were fugitives. At best, all that unskilled women could hope for was occasional work as washerwomen and domestics. But even then, it was most unlikely that an 'unknown' slave would be taken into a white household, at least on a permanent basis, without some recommendation from a previous employer.

Black women, be they from the town or countryside, might have had sufficient English to try and pass as free but, unlike men, they could not easily use Savannah as a springboard for escape by sea. Male slaves, who could often quite legitimately claim 'a knowledge of the sea', might be taken on as crew by ships' captains who were not too fussy about those they employed as sailors. This did not mean was that escape by sea was totally impossible for women. But what it did mean was that women like Flora, said by her owner to be 'harboured under the Bluff by Sailors', had to devise different stratagems if they were to make good their escape.[42]

The published advertisements for runaways give some indication of the courage, resourcefulness, and determination displayed by black men and women alike. Fugitives adopted different names and, whenever possible, changed their clothing in the hope of thereby avoiding detection. If challenged, they might try to pass as a free black. Even when identified as a runaway, some women refused to give up without a struggle. They may not have had the physical strength to overpower their captors but, if the opportunity presented itself, they seized the chance to escape. Sometimes this meant taking flight again in leg irons or handcuffs.[43] On at least one occasion some female runaways joined with male slaves in breaking out of Savannah Gaol.[44]

If organized rebellion was the most feared, and running away the most common, mode of resistance what about the other offences itemized in the slave codes? What was the incidence of such capital crimes as murder, assault, and arson and ostensibly less serious, but for whites often extremely worrying, offences such as theft, drunkenness, and being absent without a ticket?

The scanty evidence that has survived from the colonial period suggests that no more than about a dozen white Georgians met their deaths at the hands of slaves and that between 1766 and 1774 a minimum of seventeen slaves were executed for crimes which included murder, attempted murder, arson, robbery, and attempted insurrection. The lists of payments made to owners of executed slaves do not always indicate the slave's sex. However, it appears that at least one black woman, 'a household Negress', was burned alive after having been convicted of attempting to poison her owner, Pastor Rabenhorst, and his wife.[45] There is no evidence that the pastor interceded on her behalf by, for example, petitioning the Royal Governor to commute her death sentence to deportation.

The colonial evidence concerning non-capital crimes is even thinner. No court records have survived (assuming that written records were kept) and contemporary accounts and complaints about such offences as theft seldom referred to the perpetrators' sex. Arguably the most complete evidence concerning the incidence of both capital and non-capital crimes in the post-war period comes in the form of the Savannah Gaol Book, a volume which lists the name, owner, place of residence, and alleged offence of every slave lodged in the gaol between April 1809 and May 1815. It also indicates the length of time each slave spent in prison, the number who escaped, and those who died.[46]

Obviously it would be foolish to extrapolate from the Gaol Book, which lists just under 3,800 offences, a pattern of black behaviour which characterized the years between 1763 (or even 1783) and 1815 or, for that matter, the Low Country as a whole. The black inmates of Savannah Gaol during these six years came from many different parts of Georgia and South Carolina, but around 84 per cent of male offences, and 92 per cent of female offences, were committed by slaves who were, or had owners who were, resident in Savannah. But even so, the Gaol Book offers unique insights into the range of offences committed by black men and women as well as into the role assigned to prisons in the attempt to maintain racial discipline.

Three features of the material contained in the Gaol Book are particularly note-worthy; the total number of slaves who were taken, or sent, to prison; the imbalance between the number of male and female inmates; and, finally, what appears to have been a relatively low incidence of capital crimes. (Low, that is, in the context of the anxieties expressed by white Georgians.)

As far as can be ascertained, at least 3,048 different slaves (2,366 men and 682 women) were taken to Savannah Gaol at least once during this six-year period.[47] For men and women alike, the two most common reasons for imprisonment were running away and 'safe-keeping'; together they accounted for around 86 per cent of all the offences recorded in the Gaol Book.

'Safe-keeping' was cited as the reason for the imprisonment of 59 per cent of men and 60 per cent of women. Slaves could be committed to gaol by their owners (which was the case with 47 per cent of the men and 51 per cent of the women imprisoned for 'safe-keeping') for three main reasons; for corporal punishment, prior to sale, or because adequate supervision could not be provided for them. Unfortunately the Gaol Book does not distinguish clearly between them.

Obviously, imprisonment, for whatever reason, meant the loss of often valuable workers, and most owners were reluctant to keep their slaves in gaol for longer than was absolutely necessary. Thus 17 per cent of the men, and 20 per cent of the women, sent to prison for 'safe-keeping' by their owners were released on the same day; 43 per cent of men, and 40 per cent of women, spent less than one week in gaol. Only 11 per cent of men, and 4 per cent of women, were kept in prison for more than a month by their owners.

A quarter of all the offences (male and female) listed in the Gaol Book related to slaves who had been picked up by the Savannah Watch or one of the rural slave patrols and taken to prison for 'safe-keeping'. In the majority of cases (60 per cent of men and 59 per cent of women) the slave was released on the same day, apparently without having been either charged or punished.

The rest of the slaves who were sent, or taken, to prison for 'safe-keeping' were committed either by individuals other than their owners or as the result of various legal orders. Although, in each category of 'safe-keeping', men outnumbered women, there was little difference in the length of time that they spent in gaol. Much the same was true of the other offences mentioned in the Gaol Book (see Table 25.3).

Ever since 1763 Savannah's Workhouse and Gaol had played a central role in the processing of black runaways. Fugitives who could not be identified, or who refused to identify themselves, were interned, advertised and, if not reclaimed, sold at public auction to recoup the cost of their imprisonment.[48]

Table 25.3   The length of time spent by black slaves in Savannah Gaol, April 1809 to May 1815 (all offences)

Time in gaol	Men		Women		All slaves	
	n	*%*	*n*	*%*	*n*	*%*
Released on same day	861	29.35	245	29.55	1,106	29.39
One night	364	11.79	108	13.02	472	12.54
2–6 nights	693	23.62	190	22.91	883	23.47
7–13 nights	282	9.61	91	10.97	373	9.91
14–20 nights	169	5.76	44	5.30	213	5.66
21–27 nights	114	3.88	25	3.01	139	3.69
28 or more nights	325	11.08	93	11.21	418	11.11
Not mentioned/unknown	125	4.26	33	3.98	158	4.19
Total	2,933	–	829	–	3,762	–

Between 1809 and 1815 runaways accounted for around one-quarter of all the offences (male and female) listed in the Gaol Book. It is of note, however, that apprehended runaways were distributed fairly evenly over this six-year period. Although, as Clarence Mohr has argued, Low Country blacks made their way to the British forces during the War of 1812 in the hope of securing their freedom, this was not reflected in a dramatic upsurge in the number of fugitives taken to Savannah Gaol during the months when the British were operating off the Georgia coast.[49]

Clearly, the length of time that runaways spent in prison depended upon how long it took their owners to reclaim them. But the gaol served a second function in respect of runaways; slaves who had taken flight and been recaptured might be sent there by their owners in the hope that a harsh prison regime might persuade them of the error of their ways. At least 56 slaves (47 men and 9 women) were gaoled by their owners. Most spent less than a week in prison (which suggests corporal punishment) and only four men spent more than a month there.

The extent to which imprisonment, and the corporal punishment which it might have entailed, deterred slaves from running away again, or committing other offences, is difficult to determine. All that can be said with certainty is that at least 450 slaves (361 men and 89 women) who between them had committed, or who were believed to have committed, 1,164 offences (928 by men and 236 by women) were sent, or taken, to Savannah Gaol at least twice between 1809 and 1815.

It seems that no slave was taken to prison more often than Nancy, a woman who belonged to a Mr Gotong. She found herself in gaol on no less than eleven occasions during this six-year period; for running away (eight times) and for 'safe-keeping' (imprisoned once by her owner and twice by the Savannah Watch). Altogether she spent six weeks in gaol. Another woman, Nanny, who ran away eight times was in prison for a total of two months.[50] Sally, who was owned by a Mr Driscoll, was committed to gaol seven times between July, 1809 and December, 1814; for running away (twice), for 'safe-keeping' (four times) and for working without a badge (once). As far as can be ascertained, only one man, Adam, who was owned by a Mr Hulet, was taken to gaol eight times and none appear to have surpassed Nancy's record.

Table 25.4   The length of time spent by black slaves in Savannah Gaol for running away and the indebtedness of their owners

Time in gaol	Men		Women		All slaves		All offences (%)
	n	%	n	%	n	%	
(A) Running away (excluding those runaways committed to gaol by their owners)							
Released on same day	109	14.78	31	14.76	140	14.78	29.39
1 night	78	10.58	29	13.80	107	11.29	12.54
2–6 nights	199	27.00	57	27.14	256	27.03	23.47
7–13 nights	98	13.29	36	17.14	134	14.14	9.91
14–20 nights	74	10.04	18	8.57	92	9.71	5.66
21–27 nights	35	4.74	7	3.33	42	4.43	3.69
28 or more nights	110	14.92	19	9.04	129	13.62	11.11
Not mentioned/ unknown	34	4.61	13	6.19	47	4.96	4.19
Total	737	–	210	–	947	–	–
(B) Indebtedness							
Released on same day	3	3.12	1	2.43	4	2.91	29.39
1 night	4	4.16	5	12.19	9	6.56	12.54
2–6 nights	15	15.62	2	4.87	17	12.40	23.47
7–13 nights	5	5.20	3	7.31	8	5.83	9.91
14–21 nights	3	3.12	–	–	3	2.18	5.66
21–27 nights	16	16.66	3	7.31	19	13.86	3.69
28 or more nights	43	44.79	24	58.53	67	48.90	11.11
Not mentioned/ unknown	7	7.29	3	7.31	10	7.29	4.19
Total	96	–	41	–	137	–	–

As mentioned above, roughly 86 per cent of the offences cited in the Gaol Book had to do either with running away or with 'safe-keeping'. Of the remainder, 3.6 per cent reflected on offence (usually indebtedness) on the part of the owner rather than the slave. At least 137 slaves (96 men and 41 women) were imprisoned through no fault of their own. These slaves, together with those runaways whose owners could not be readily identified, were liable to spend the longest time in gaol (see Tables 25.3 and 25.4).

With one or two exceptions, the remaining non-capital offences involved fewer than ten slaves each. They ranged from 'drunkenness' (one man), 'impertinance' and 'abuse' (three women), and 'fighting' (two men) to harbouring runaways (two men and two women) and working without a badge (eighteen men and eighteen women). Virtually none of these offences could be described as exclusively, or typically, 'male' or 'female' in character.

Less than 1 per cent of the offences mentioned in the Gaol Book were capital crimes. There were 5 men awaiting trial or execution for murder, 2 for attempted murder, and 3 for arson; 9 were suspected, or had been found guilty of, assault and 125 of theft, offences which, under certain circumstances, might have been capital crimes. In most instances, however, release dates were given indicating non-capital, as opposed to capital, offences. No women were in prison on charges of murder or attempted murder; one was accused of assault and another of arson. Twenty-two were thought to have committed theft.

What on the face of it appears to have been a relatively low incidence of violent crimes, especially by women, should not be construed as evidence of black, or female, docility. All slaves, men and women, knew full well the penalty for such offences; to commit them, and to be caught, was 'tantamount to committing suicide and, understandably, this was a path which few chose to follow'.[51] But, as Eugene Genovese has argued, it was the fact, rather than the actual number, of violent crimes against white persons and their property which was so significant.[52] The murder or attempted murder of just one white person, the burning down of just one house 'served to reinforce white fears and to remind [whites] of the arbitrary and often unpredictable violence that might be indulged in by any of their slaves'.[53]

Largely through an often difficult process of trial and error, black men and women in the Georgia Low Country learned how they might assert themselves and their individuality in ways which did not invite barbaric retribution. To some degree, the options open to women, who did not lack the will and determination to resist, were restricted if not by their sex *per se* then by motherhood and occupational experience. But overt resistance was not the sole preserve of black men. Black women, albeit in smaller numbers, also rebelled, rioted, and ran away. There were those like Nancy, Nanny and Sally who, regardless of the floggings, irons, and imprisonment which was their lot, refused to submit, refused to be broken, but continued to offer resistance of the most stubborn and uncompromising kind.

Notes

1 Although attention has been paid to various aspects of the life and labour of black women in the American South there has been a dearth of detailed studies which address the slavery experience from their perspective. For two studies which go a long way towards remedying this deficiency see Deborah Gray White, *Ar'n't I a woman? Female slaves in the plantation South* (New York, 1985) and Jacqueline Jones, *Labor of love, labor of sorrow. Black women, work, and the family from slavery to the present* (New York, 1985). Unfortunately, neither of these authors has much to say about black women in the eighteenth-century South.

2 Barbara Bush, 'Towards emancipation: slave women and resistance to coercive labour regimes in the British West Indian colonies, 1790–1838', in David Richardson, ed., *Abolition and its aftermath: The historical context, 1790–1916* London, 1985), pp. 27–54.

3 For a recent discussion of the debate which preceded the introduction of slavery into Georgia, see Betty Wood, *Slavery in colonial Georgia, 1730–1775* (Athens, 1984), pp. 1–87.

4 The demographic and economic growth of Georgia during the years of Royal government is dealt with by Wood, *Slavery in colonial Georgia*, pp. 89–98, 104–9 and Julia Floyd Smith *Slavery and rice culture in Low country Georgia, 1750–1860* (Knoxville, 1985), pp. 15–29, 93–100.

5 John Dobell to the Trustees, Savannah, 11 June 1746, in Allen D. Candler and Lucian L. Knight, eds., *The Colonial records of the state of Georgia*, ?6 vols. (Atlanta, 1904–16), XXIV, 72 (hereafter *Col. Recs.*).

6 Sylvia Frey, '"Bitter fruit from the sweet stem of liberty": Georgia slavery and the American revolution' (paper presented to the Annual Meeting of the American Historical Association held in New York City, Dec., 1985), p. 13.

7   Ibid., p. 15.
8   As Robert S. Glenn Jr. has observed, Georgia 'approximated the pattern of the other southern colonies in that it did not develop a direct slave trade with Africa until its economy was advanced enough to absorb cargoes of 150 to 200 slaves at a time', Glenn, 'Slavery in Georgia, 1733–1793 (Senior thesis, Princeton University, 1972), pp. 63–4. Between 1766 and 1771, the only pre-war years for which there is detailed evidence, 2487 Africans were landed in Georgia and an unknown number of 'New Negroes' purchased by Georgia planters and merchants in the South Carolina slave markets. For discussions of the slave trade to Georgia in the eighteenth century see Wood, *Slavery in colonial Georgia*, pp. 98–104; Smith, *Slavery and rice culture*, pp. 93–8; and Darold D. Wax, '"New negroes are always in demand": the slave trade in eighteenth-century Georgia', *Georgia Historical Quarterly*, LXVIII (1984).
9   Frey, '"Bitter fruit"', p. 14.
10 Wood, *Slavery in colonial Georgia*, pp. 103–4; Elizabeth Donnan, 'The slave trade into South Carolina before the Revolution', *American Historical Review*, XXXIII (1928), 816–17; Daniel C. Littlefield, *Rice and slaves: ethnicity and the slave trade in colonial south Carolina* (Baton Rouge, 1981).
11 Telfair, Cowper and Telfair to Robert Macmillan, Savannah, 2 Sept. 1773; to Thomas Wallace, Savannah, 2 Sept. 1773. Telfair papers, Item 43, Cover 2, Letterbook, 11 Aug. 1773 to 11 May 1776. Georgia Historical Society, Savannah.
12 Clarence L. Mohr, 'Slavery and Georgia's second War of Independence' (paper presented to the Annual Meeting of the American Historical Association held in New York City, Dec., 1985), p. 5.
13 The colonial inventories are taken from Inventory Book F (1754–1771) and FF (1771–1778), Georgia Department of Archives and History, Atlanta and from the Telamon Cuyler Collection, Box 7 (special heading Georgia. Colonial. Estate Papers) and Boxes 38A and 38B (special heading Georgia. Governor. Wright, James, 1760–1776) held in the Manuscript Room, University of Georgia Library. The Chatham County inventories were consulted at the Chatham County Courthouse, Savannah.
14 Ralph Gray and Betty Wood, 'The transition from indentured to involuntary servitude in colonial Georgia', *Explorations in Economic History*, XIII (1976), 363.
15 Based on an analysis of the inventories cited in note 13 (above).
16 In Savannah women outnumbered men by around 115 to 100. For a rare contemporary account of the sex ratio of Savannah's slave population see the census of 'all the people of color above the age of Fifteen in the City of Savannah' (dated 28 May 1798) in the Negro History Files, File 2: 1773–1800 folder, Georgia Department of Archives and History, Atlanta. For the sex ratio of Charleston's slaves see Philip D. Morgan, 'Black life in eighteenth-century Charleston', *Perspectives in American History*, new series, 1, (1984), 188–9.
17 On estates with more than twenty adult slaves the ratio of men to women was in the order of 161 to 100; on those with fewer than ten slaves it dropped to roughly 127 to 100. Based on an analysis of the inventories cited in note 13 (above). Thomas R. Statom Jr. has estimated that between 1755 and 1764 the sex ratio on all estates was 160:100 and between 1764 and 1776 134:100. His analysis is based on Inventory Books F and FF. Statom, 'Negro slavery in eighteenth-century Georgia' (unpublished Ph.D. dissertation, University of Alabama, 1982), pp. 180–1.
18 For the occupational structure of one of colonial Georgia's largest holdings see *The Georgia Gazette*, 13 Feb. 1781, which lists the possessions of John Graham, Lieutenant-Governor of the colony. 18.5 per cent of his male slaves filled skilled or semi-skilled positions and another 7 per cent were 'Usually employed and kept around the House'. Of the women owned by Graham 23.5 per cent worked as seamstresses, washerwomen, cooks, midwives, and 'house wenches'. For the occupational structure of one of Chatham County's larger post-war holdings see the inventory of James Mackay's estate, drawn up on 1 January 1787. Seventeen, or 51.5 per cent, of Mackay's male slaves were skilled or semi-skilled. Only three, or 9 per cent, of his slave women worked as cooks (one), nurses (one), and maids (one).

19   None of the advertisements placed in *The Georgia Gazette* between 1763 and 1795 for the sale or hire of a slave woman, or the return of a runaway, mentioned the woman's value as a 'breeder'.

20   For a rare contemporary comment about the rate of increase of Low Country slaves see James Habersham to William Knox, Savannah, 24 July 1772. *Collections of the Georgia Historical Society*, VI, 193–4. For late eighteenth-century Jamaican attempts to boost the rate of natural increase of the island's slave population, and the inducements offered to black women to produce more children, see Betty Wood and Roy Clayton, 'Slave birth, death and disease on Golden Grove Plantation, Jamaica, 1765–1810', *Slavery and Abolition*, VI (1985), 99–121.

21   Wood, *Slavery in colonial Georgia*, p. 155.

22   Klaus G. Loewald, Beverly Starika, and Paul S. Taylor, trans. and eds., 'Johann Martin Bolzius answers a questionnaire on Carolina and Georgia', *William and Mary Quarterly*, 3rd ser., xiv (1958), 236, 256. An analysis of newspaper advertisements, wills, and miscellaneous bonds (which recorded the transfer of slaves by deed of gift and sale) strongly suggests that this practice continued throughout the period under consideration here.

23   Wood, *Slavery in colonial Georgia*, p. 156.

24   Between 1763 and 1775 six of the female runaways advertised in *The Georgia Gazette* took at least one of their children with them. The same was true of eight women who ran away between 1783 and 1795. Another six women, who absconded with men who might or might not have been their husbands, also took children with them. The only advertised runaway between 1763 and 1795 said to have abandoned one of her children was Hannah, who ran away in 1786. Hannah's owner, Martha M. Melven, commented that although she had taken her daughter Lydia, 'about five years old', she had 'inhumanly' left 'a child at her breast'. Hannah had 'extensive acquaintances . . . in and around Savannah', and her mistress believed that she was being 'harboured by some ill-intentioned person'. *The Georgia Gazette*, 20 Apr. 1786.

25   For a discussion of the framing and content of Georgia's slave laws see Wood, *Slavery in colonial Georgia*, pp. 110–30.

26   Ibid., 120–2, 124–7, 129.

27   AN ACT For the better Ordering and Governing Negroes and other Slaves in this Province. March, 1755. *Col. Recs.*, XVIII, 131–5.

28   AN ACT For Regulating a Work House, for the Custody and Punishment of Negroes. April, 1763, ibid. 558–66. The Act permitted owners to send their 'stubborn, obstinate or incorrigible Negroes' to the workhouse, where they would be 'kept to hard Labour or otherwise . . . corrected'. Owners would be charged 6*d.* per diem for their upkeep and an additional 'one Shilling and fourpence for each Chastisement'.

29   For white fears of organized slave rebellions, and the difficulties confronting would-be black rebels, see Wood, *Slavery in colonial Georgia*, pp. 125–8, 188–98.

30   The only contemporary account of the St Andrew Parish 'revolt' is in *The Georgia Gazette*, 7 Dec. 1774.

31   Frey, '"Bitter Fruit"', pp. 14–15.

32   Ibid., *passim*.

33   For a discussion of the Laurens Plan and its reception in South Carolina and Georgia see Donald Robinson, *Slavery in the structure of American politics, 1763–1820* (New York, 1979), pp. 118–20.

34   There had been runaway communities in the colonial period which greatly alarmed white Georgians. For the 'depradations' committed by the members of these communities, and white attempts to root them out, see *Col. Recs.*, XIV, 292–3. For a description of the post-war community headed by Lewis and 'Captain Cudjoe' see 'Trial of Negroe Man Slave Named Lewis the Property of Oliver Bowen for the Murder of John Casper Hersman, Robbing Philip Ulsmer, John Lowerman of Ga. & Col. Borquin of South Carolina, 1787', in Slave File, Telamon Guyler Collection, Manuscript Room, University of Georgia Library. Lewis was sentenced to death.

35   Peter H. Wood, *Black majority: negroes in colonial south Carolina from 1670 through the Stono rebellion* New York, 1974, p. 241.

36   For a detailed discussion of black runaways in colonial Georgia see Wood, *Slavery in colonial Georgia*, pp. 169–87.

37   Gerald W. Mullin, *Flight and rebellion: slave resistance in eighteenth-century Virginia* (New York, 1972), *passim*.

38   Wood, *Slavery in colonial Georgia*, p. 180.

39   The fate of this group is unknown, but their overseer thought it 'probable' that those concerned would 'keep along shore and be taken up either to the southward or northward of Savannah'. *The Georgia Gazette*, 25 Jan. 1775.

40   In 1790 there were 398 free blacks in the 'District of Georgia', of whom 180 lived in Wilkes County and 112 in Chatham County. 'Census of the District of Georgia', *The Augusta Chronicle*, 5 Nov., 1791.

41   For legislation regulating the hiring out and casual employment of slaves see Wood, *Slavery in colonial Georgia*, pp. 131–2, 142–5.

42   *The Georgia Gazette*, 13 July 1774, 24 May 1775.

43   See for example ibid., 4 Apr. 1764.

44   The break-out in question occurred on 7 Oct. 1789 and involved five men and two women. Both women, Satira, who belonged to Levi Sheftall, and Eve, who was owned by Dr Beecroft, were said to be 'well known in and about Savannah', and no further description was given. One of the men, Tom, who belonged to Matthew McCallister, had 'a large iron on one leg' and another, a boy named Charles, was said to have 'lost one leg'. It is not clear from the published account precisely how they managed to engineer their escape or how long they remained at large. *The Georgia Gazette*, 8 Oct. 1789.

45   Theodore G. Tappert and John W. Doberstein, trans. and eds., *The journals of Henry Melchior Muhlenberg*, 2 vols. (Philadelphia, 1942, 1958), II, 575, 576.

46   The Gaol Book (which is unpaginated) is in the possession of the Georgia Historical Society, Savannah.

47   There is no sure way of knowing how many of these slaves might have changed hands between 1809 and 1815. Also, on some larger holdings it was not unusual to find more than one slave with the same name.

48   See note 28 (above). Virtually every issue of *The Georgia Gazette* between 1763 and 1795 carried an advertisement for runaways whose owners could not be identified.

49   Mohr, 'Slavery and Georgia's Second War of Independence', pp. 5–6.

50   Nanny was owned by Mary Barnet.

51   Wood, *Slavery in colonial Georgia*, p. 198.

52   Eugene D. Genovese, *Roll, Jordan Roll: The world the slaves made* (London, 1975), pp. 616–17.

53   Wood, *Slavery in colonial Georgia*, p. 197.

Chapter 26

Edward A. Pearson

'A COUNTRYSIDE FULL OF FLAMES'

A reconsideration of the Stono Rebellion and slave rebelliousness in the early eighteenth-century South Carolina lowcountry

T HE REBELLION BEGAN SOMETIME before the dawn broke across the South Carolina lowcountry on Sunday, 9 September 1739. In those hours, a group of about twenty enslaved men, some of whom had been members of a gang working on a road, gathered by the bridge that spanned the Stono River in the coastal parish of St. Paul's, a rural plantation district that lay some twelve miles south of Charles Town. Nearby stood Hutchenson's store, a modest structure occupied that night by Mr Gibbs and Robert Bathurst and containing 'many small Arms and Powder'.[1] Led by an Angolan named Jemmy, the slave men attacked the building, took weapons and other supplies before decapitating its occupants and depositing their severed heads on the steps.[2] This assault heralded a rebellion that struck 'terror and consternation' into local planters and their families.[3] Heading toward St. Augustine in Spanish Florida and the promise of freedom offered by its governor, the rebels gathered about a hundred slaves to their cause, burning plantations and houses, killing their inhabitants and leaving 'the countryside full of Flames'.[4] Only the militia's mobilization by Lieutenant-Governor William Bull, who had eluded capture by the rebels as he travelled from his country estate to Charles Town that morning, prevented the revolt from spreading across the lowcountry.[5]

The end came late on Sunday afternoon when planters and militia men caught the rebels in a field where they had 'set to Dancing, singing and beating Drums' as they celebrated the early success of their enterprise.[6] In the skirmish that followed, the militia gunned down a large number of the insurgents; those who escaped were relentlessly pursued and summarily executed. The authorities had restored some semblance of order to the parish, leaving some forty-four slaves and twenty-one whites dead as night fell. In the days that followed, Bull hired Chickasaw and Catawba Indians to track down rebels who had sought sanctuary in the forests and swamps of coastal Carolina and Georgia. Despite these measures, however, the minister of the small settlement of Ebenezer in Georgia, noted several weeks later that a number of rebels were still 'roaming around in gangs in the Carolina forests' while others had reached the 'border of this country'.[7]

Although it lasted less than twenty-four hours, the Stono rebellion stands as a significant act of collective resistance by enslaved Africans in British North America.[8] While 'every breast' was allegedly 'filled with concern' by the uprising and it 'awaken'd the attention of the most unthinking' about the realities of slave rebelliousness, the collective action at Stono did not prompt Anglo-Carolinians to pick up their pens and record their thoughts on paper.[9] Unlike other rebellions, this one did not produce a flurry of newspaper editorials or pamphlets in which civic leaders reflected upon the events of that bloody Sunday. Nor were there any trials of captured rebels. What we know of this insurrection comes from a small archive: a brief report that Lieutenant-Governor Bull filed for his imperial masters in London, an anonymous account enclosed in a letter from General James Oglethorpe, a letter that appeared in *The Gentleman's Magazine*, and a post-mortem discussion held in the colonial assembly.

Despite the dearth of sources, the Stono insurrection has attracted the attention of a number of historians.[10] Alexander Hewatt, author of the colony's first history, suggested that, had the rebels not been defeated, the entire lowcountry would 'have fallen sacrifice to their great power and indiscriminate fury'.[11] In his now-classic account of lowcountry slave culture, Peter Wood devotes much attention to the uprising, concluding that the significant rise of slaves directly from Africa combined with formal and informal restrictions against this growing slave population provided a context for rebellion.[12] For Wood, Stono acts as a watershed in the lowcountry's history, demarcating a period of racial fluidity associated with frontier life from the severity and discipline of plantation agriculture. Some scholars, however, do not regard the rebellion as the pivotal moment in the history of slavery in the lowcountry. Both Michael Mullin and M. Eugene Sirmans disagree with the importance that Wood accords the rising, arguing it was 'less an insurrection than an attempt by slaves to fight their way to St. Augustine'.[13] Others have used it to explore additional facets of slave society. John Thornton has compared how Kongolese military skills shaped the organization and tactics of the Stono rebels, concluding that ethnic martial traditions had a profound influence on their conduct and the final outcome of the rising.[14]

Building on these contributions, this essay offers a reappraisal of the rebellion by considering the role that the gendered division of labour may have played in the creation of low country slave culture and the uprising itself. Gender, as Joan Scott has observed, offers a useful analytical tool that allows historians to explore how appropriate roles for women and men are socially constructed and the ways in which different societies ascribe value to certain activities according to the organization of labour along lines of sex.[15] I wish to suggest here that the transformation of the lowcountry's agricultural economy from a frontier to a plantation society may have had a dramatic impact on gender relations and that this rebellion can be understood in gendered terms as a moment in which enslaved African men articulated their masculinity. It should be noted, however, that as neither travellers, colonial officials nor planters directly addressed the gendered organization of labour on rice estates, the following discussion offers speculative rather than definitive conclusions.

Before the rice revolution of the early eighteenth century transformed the lowcountry's economy, a large number of male slaves experienced some degree of autonomy as cattle herders or foresters in their daily lives.[16] The rise of large-scale rice cultivation demanded that the organization of agricultural work be reconfigured. In addition to imposing a routinized work regime in the rice fields, planters used male slaves to grow and harvest this crop. By so doing, they violated the sexual division of labour that had customarily structured agricultural labour in the societies of western and west-central Africa from which a significant number of slaves who worked on lowcountry plantations originated. By transgressing the definitions of appropriate gender roles that prevailed in Atlantic Africa in the work place, lowcountry plantation owners may have galvanized male slaves to rebel against the social and cultural consequences of the rice revolution that swept across coastal Carolina in the early 1700s. I want to suggest, moreover, that the consequences of the rice revolution and the sexual organization of plantation work may be discerned in events surrounding the Stono uprising.

Second, this essay also offers a close reading of the few contemporary accounts on the rebellion to expose aspects of slave consciousness that have hitherto remained hidden. Adopting this approach to such moments of dramatic confrontation between the enslaved and their enslavers, historians can effect 'a persuasive reconstruction of the experiences of past actors'.[17] Problems clearly abound when using materials written by dominant groups to explain the world view of the dominated. The authorities do not view events from the perspective of the rebels; they impose their own narrative structure on events and infuse the text with their own ideological inclinations, 'authorizing' it for their own ends. In accounts written by officialdom, as Ranajit Guha has observed for episodes of collective resistance in India, the insurgent was 'denied recognition as a subject of his history in his own right even for a project that was all his own'.[18] By forcing the authorities to become involved in their protests, rebels not only demanded attention, but they also forcefully turned themselves into subjects whose values and beliefs we may glimpse by reading the records against the grain.

Every subordinate group, argues James Scott, generates a 'hidden transcript' that critiques and undermines the power of the dominant by engaging in subversive practices that range from petty insubordination to open rebellion.[19] Fashioned by slaves in their quarters from their various ethnic traditions and from the material circumstances of plantation life, this backstage discourse spoke against the authority of slaveholders. Not only did slaves attempt to subvert that authority through everyday acts of resistance (feigning sickness, insolence or vandalism), but they also engaged in more overt forms of protest that ranged from arson to poisoning to flight. The most vital expression of opposition – open rebellion – brought this discourse of dissent from the realm of the shadows and into the glare of centre stage. Reacting to their subordination as slaves as well as to the transgression of the gender division of labour that prevailed in Atlantic Africa, the Stono rebels demonstrated the incomplete nature of their masters' domination. The moment of insurrection that exploded in St. Paul's Parish in autumn 1739 stands as a 'rare moment of political electricity when, often for the first time in memory, the hidden transcript is spoken directly and publicly in the teeth of power'.[20]

For several decades after its establishment by English, and Afro-Barbadian pioneers in 1670, South Carolina remained, as Russell Menard has recently noted, 'a struggling, unimpressive, outpost colony'.[21] In addition to an indigenous population of some 7,500, the lowcountry was peopled by about 3,260 whites and 2,444 slaves by 1700 who depended primarily on subsistence farming, pastoral agriculture and the provisions trade (naval supplies, deer skins and dried goods) for their livelihoods.[22] As the backbone of the labour force, African and Afro-Caribbean slaves worked as cattle herders, foresters as well as field hands as their owners sought to discover a staple that would yield profits as large as those reaped by Caribbean sugar planters. Although experiments with various crops, such as citrus fruit, vines and cotton, had mixed results, many settlers established themselves as cattle ranchers. Hogs and cattle had become 'extremely plentiful [with] many Gentlemen owning from five Hundred to fifteen Hundred Head' by the 1680s.[23] Needing little capital to start a herd and few workers, cattle became an important export commodity with several thousand barrels of salted meat being shipped from Charles Town by the turn of the century.[24] The extensive grasslands and woods of the coastal plain, moreover, proved to be 'an exceeding good ground for stocks of cattle' throughout the year.[25]

The grass and woodlands that provided cattle with such an hospitable environment served another economic purpose. Naval surveyor Thomas Ashe saw these forests as raw materials for 'goodly Boxes, Chests, Tables, Scrittories and Cabinets'.[26] His fellow officers, however, believed that this raw timber could be converted into the masts, tar and pitch used in the building of ships of the line. Subsidised by a Parliamentary bounty passed in 1705 that sought to reduce the Royal Navy's dependence on European sources of these essential materials, settlers began to exploit the lowcountry's pine lands.[27] These commodities, noted traveller John Lawson in 1700, 'never fail of a Market'.[28] In addition to its strategic importance. Governor Robert Johnson observed that commerce in naval stores 'not only occasioned the greater consumption of British manufactories, but encouraged merchants abroad to import into the province great numbers of Negro slaves from Africa and brought a great concourse of ships into this port'.[29] Both the cattle and timber trades functioned as vehicles by which settlers were able to accumulate capital and served to integrate the region into the Atlantic trading system.

For the slaves who worked along the cattle frontier, gender played a primary role in the configuration of labour. Research by John Otto and Peter Wood has indicated that cattle ranchers used slave men as ranch hands. John Smyth, for example, owned fifty-three cattle that were tended by three white male servants and three slave men, James Joyner's three male slaves supervised a herd of some two hundred animals and Bernard Schenkingh's holdings on James Island included '134 Head of Cattle [and] One Negro man'.[30] After completing his indenture in 1672. Dennis Mahone became a small independent farmer who, after speculating in land and cattle with some success, sold 'fower calves & three steers, five sows and one boare & a negro man named Cato' to a new settler in 1681.[31] A sizeable number of slave men appear to have spent their working lives in the lowcountry's forests and on its savannas, herding cattle and hogs. Moreover, as many early settlers appear not to have held title to the land on which they grazed their animals, their cattle doubtless roamed freely across the 'thriving Range' of the coastal plain.[32] These slaves likely experienced a moderate degree of geographic mobility and modest levels of independence as they supervised the herds and built the wooden pens in which to house the animals against the appetites of 'the Tygar, Wolf and Wild Catt' that also roamed the region.[33] Unlike the discipline that would characterize plantation work, the semi-nomadic character of ranching resulted in greater autonomy for enslaved men. Lacking the acreage necessary for grazing cattle, most ranchers let their animals graze and forage 'wild in the woods'.[34] To prevent cattle from falling prey to predators and becoming feral, slave herdsmen would round up the herds at nightfall, blowing horns and luring them into the corral 'with a little Indian corn . . . Turnips and other roots'.[35] This daily routine would be punctuated by other tasks associated with pastoral agriculture. After the spring calving, herdsmen would 'ride out in search for them in the woods', returning the new animals to the cattle pens for branding.[36] In addition, slaves would maintain the pens, repairing gates and fences, as well as drive the animals to market.

The flexible routines of pastoral agriculture allowed these slaves to pursue a number of activities independent of their primary job. Apart from supervising calving early in the year and driving cattle to market in the fall, pastoralism did not place severe demands on their time.[37] At the centre of their lives stood the cattle pen itself. Often situated some distance from the 'Neighbourhood of Planters', these small settlements usually consisted of provision grounds, several buildings to house both animals and people and the pens themselves.[38] In his diary, Johann Martin Boltzius, a Lutheran minister at Ebenezer, wrote about the 'construction of a shelter in the woods for the cattle' while Captain John North's cattle pen on the Saltcatcher River was advertised as having the 'necessary buildings thereon' as well as 'some provisions and many necessary Cowpen and plantation utensils'.[39] Other evidence suggests that slave women formed part of this tiny community, working on the provision grounds or being 'employ'd either for the Dairy or to attend the Hogs'.[40] In addition to their duties as herdsmen, male slaves likely hunted, taking advantage of the lowcountry's abundance of wild animals and fish. These activities may have made the pens virtually self-sufficient, perhaps reinforcing the sensation of autonomy that slaves may have experienced as frontier herders.[41] These pens also functioned as focal points for loosely knit social and commercial networks that developed as slaves grazed their herds or drove them market. That a traveller, riding from Charles Town to Georgia, should spend some time at a cattle pen, described as a 'little sort of settlement', suggests that these places offered some rudimentary amenities. The other functions of these pens remain unknown, but it appears that milk and cheese were produced there. In addition to branding cattle, slaves may have butchered and salted carcasses for sale. It is more probable that the bulk of animal processing took place in Charles Town from where the 'fat Beeves' as well as tallow, cowhides and some tanned leather were shipped.[42] In the pens' ramshackle huts, slaves perhaps fashioned a congenial setting in which to exchange news, tell tales, and consume meals from the commodities that surrounded them. The long process of shaping some sense of community among lowcountry slaves may have started in the cattle pens dotted about the coastal lowlands.

In contrast, the small population of slave women (estimated at around 1,100 in the late seventeenth century) worked at a range of agricultural and domestic tasks that kept them within the farm or cattle pen. One promotional tract suggested that they cultivated the small kitchen gardens that surrounded the pens. In addition, female slaves performed tasks associated with animal husbandry, including milking, churning butter and making cheese.[43] This labour arrangement conformed to the broad pattern of female work in western Africa where women did domestic work, gathering water and fuel, preparing and processing food and raising, children. Not only did enslaved women supervise the slave household as plantation agriculture came to the low country, but their domestic role expanded to include the marketing of goods grown on their own provision grounds in Charles Town's markets.

Pastoral agriculture, moreover, demanded the acquisition and application of a number of skills associated with livestock management. If they had not mastered the skill already, slaves likely learned how to ride and maintain horses. Several probate inventories suggest that these animals played a part in cattle farming. The owner of seventy-two cattle, Thomas Greatback also used two horses and four slaves on his farm while Francis Turgis, with one hundred animals, used eight horses and fourteen slaves on his property.[44] Like cattle and hogs, horses were so common in the lowcountry that, as Peter Purry noted, 'you seldom see any body travel on foot, except *Negroes*, and they often on horseback'.[45] By this 'continual ranging [in] the Woods', slave herdsmen became 'better acquainted with the land than any other set of men' as their cattle moved between watering holes, grazing areas and market place.[46] The local knowledge that they gained may have been put to use later as some slaves established temporary maroon camps or planned escapes from South Carolina to Spanish Florida. As a vital and early form of agricultural labour that depended on enslaved Africans, the practice of pastoralism perhaps established the foundation upon which rural slaves in the lowcountry fashioned their culture.

The forests in which cattle and hogs roamed echoed to more than the sounds of grazing animals. The noise of axes was also present as slaves felled stands of pine that grew throughout the lowcountry.[47] As the 'most useful Tree in the Woods', pine could be made into pitch, tar, turpentine as well as 'Planks, Masts, Yards and a great many other Necessaries'.[48] The manufacture of tar and pitch often took place throughout the lowcountry as slaves set up kettles and kilns to process pine rosin into pitch and tar. Demanding both skill and perseverance, this work also gave male slaves some degree of autonomy as they went about a complicated task that took several days of close supervision lest the fire 'burn too quick which wastes the tar' or to prevent it 'from blazing out which also wastes the tar'.[49] Having completed this process, slaves ladled the finished product into barrels before taking it to Charles Town.[50] These forests also provided materials for a number of other trades, such as boat building, coopering and construction that were economically important.

The vast majority of the bound labourers who worked on the lowcountry frontier had already experienced slavery in the New World. Prior to their arrival in the colony in the 1670s and 1680s, a majority of these people had been slaves on the sugar plantations on Barbados. Although they arrived in the lowcountry from the West Indies, most had not been born in the Caribbean, but in the societies that bordered the Gulf of Guinea on the coast of West Africa. Shipped primarily from Kormantin or Whydah on the Gold Coast, these slaves found themselves firmly embedded in the order and discipline that the cultivation and production of sugar demanded.[51] As the English established a foothold in the lowcountry in the 1670s and 1680s, they depended heavily on the labour of slaves that arrived with the first waves of settlers, primarily from Barbados. For these slaves, the sugar plantation thus proved to be only a temporary sojourn in their long journey from west Africa to South Carolina. After the back-breaking toil of growing sugar, the work regime on the lowcountry frontier likely came as a relief to these first slave pioneers.

The working environment in which these pioneer slaves found themselves bore a number of similarities to that which prevailed in west Africa. The division of labour by sex was fundamental to economic and social life in both locales.[52] Men and women worked to meet the obligations of running their households, but the way they allocated their labour differed from that of their European counterparts. In observing how villagers on the Guinea coast ran their households, English traders and travellers, who wrote from the perspective of a society in which the association of female work with domestic tasks rendered it far less visible than men's labour, noted the significant amount of agricultural and domestic work African women performed. Travelling through Dahomey in the mid-eighteenth century, slave trader Robert Norris observed Yoruba women 'tilling the ground . . . they were also occupied in spinning cotton, weaving clothes, and brewing pitto [beer], in dressing victuals for sale, and carrying merchandises to market'.[53] This organization of work prevailed elsewhere in Atlantic Africa.[54] To the south, Girolama Merolla, a missionary in the Kongo, observed how men constructed houses, cared for trees that yielded cloth, utensils, medicines and palm wine while women provided food for both use at home and sale in local markets.[55] Women generally spent their days 'in a continual state of employment' as they worked in the field and house while men were engaged in other tasks to complement these activities.[56]

For a significant number of men along the Guinea coast, pastoral agriculture was central to the village economy. A task that often removed them from the vicinity of the village, herding demanded that men travel long distances in search of grazing and water along the Senegal and Gambia river valleys.[57] Men did perform work associated with certain aspects of arable farming, but the accounts of a number of travellers suggest that just as many African males were involved in other agricultural pursuits that did not conform to the organization of labour on English farms. This attitude perhaps prompted at least one English trader to observe how 'men for their parts do lead an idle kind of life'.[58] For these pastoralists, however, life was anything but idle as they cared for the animals that constituted an important part of their wealth.[59]

The social organization of labour for men in the societies of western and west-central Africa bore similarities to the ways in which ranchers arranged work on the lowcountry frontier. Among the ethnic groups who lived along the Upper Guinea coast, cattle played a vital role in the domestic and commercial economies of peoples like the Balantas, Djolas and Wolof. Around Cape Verde, French trader Jean Barbot observed how the traffic in cattle between the Wolof and people from the interior, possibly the nomadic Fulani who grazed their herds across the vastness of the western Sudan, stimulated a flourishing trade in hides.[60] Using techniques that would become familiar in the lowcountry, these herders would pasture the animals during the day and enclose them at night 'in pens formed in clearings . . . closed round with a fence of thorns and briars'.[61] These pens of Upper Guinea may have been the antecedents for those constructed by lowcountry slaves.

Men were also responsible for exploiting the rich resources of the forest. William Towerson, a Guinea trader, observed how men fashioned 'cordes, girdles, fishing lines, and all such like things' from the immense stands of trees around the Casamance River.[62] The forests also yielded other products important to the commerce of everyday life. A beverage 'more bounteous far than all the frantic juice that Bacchus pours', palm wine was integral to all forms of socializing.[63] Kola nuts, prized for their medicinal power and exchange value, also played a key cultural and commercial role in daily life.[64] Along the coasts and river estuaries of Upper Guinea, craftsmen fabricated ocean-going canoes in which to transport either the fruits of the forest or warriors from giant silk-cotton trees. For many slaves who came to the lowcountry from the Guinea coast, neither forest nor pastoral work would have been a novel experience.

The similarities between the male work culture of herding and forestry in Atlantic Africa and these pursuits in South Carolina had implications for slave life in the eighteenth-century lowcountry. The Afro-Caribbean slaves who initially peopled the frontier may have experienced enough independence for them to replicate certain aspects of the work culture of their native societies. Perhaps working at tasks with which they were familiar helped to vitiate the dishonour and degradation that played a central part in the psychology of domination and enslavement.[65] For slaves from the Caribbean, the fluid work arrangements of the frontier stood in stark contrast to the rigidities of the sugar plantation regime. Moreover, as many of these Caribbean imports originated from these same regions of west Africa, a return to the more familiar world of pastoral and arboreal agriculture may have fostered some sense of self-worth and restored some measure of dignity to lowcountry slaves.[66] This frontier world, however, was about to undergo profound changes as rice emerged as the colony's premier cash crop.[67]

The shift in the economy from ranching and lumbering to rice brought about a dramatic change in the ethnic composition of the slave population in the lowcountry. Slaves from the Caribbean no longer dominated the Charles Town market as rice planters began strengthening their ties to the Atlantic traders by purchasing labourers with some familiarity with rice cultivation in the early eighteenth century.[68] Some 257 slaves (44 per cent) out of the 582 slaves brought into the colony in 1717 came from Guinea while 217 (37 per cent) came from the Caribbean. By the next year, the difference in the origins of imports from these two regions had grown significantly with 74 per cent of slaves arriving in Charles Town originating from the Guinea coast.[69] This shift began the long process of the Africanization of the lowcountry's enslaved labour force as imports from Atlantic Africa first supplemented then supplanted Afro-Caribbean slaves.[70]

The provenance of African slave imports gradually shifted at the start of the eighteenth century. Ships carrying slaves from the rice-growing regions of the Senegambia and the Gulf of Guinea continued to arrive throughout the 1720s. As Daniel Littlefield has shown, these slaves were highly sought after by lowcountry planters.[71] By the 1730s, however, these planters also began buying slaves from British merchants who were active along the Loango coast of west-central Africa and were purchasing slaves from the kingdom of Kongo and Angola.[72] Of the 10,661 slaves imported between 1735 and 1739, traders designated 6,310 slaves (59 per cent) as Angolan; the remainder were listed as African (3,585 or 34 per cent), Gambian (615 or 6 per cent) or Caribbean (133 or 1 per cent). In 1738, the year before the rebellion, some 1,462 slaves landed in South Carolina, of which 906 slaves (62 per cent) were listed as from west-central Africa with the remainder being from Africa (28.5 per cent), the Gambia (8.5 per cent) or the Caribbean (1 per cent).[73] Although traders sold enslaved women and children, the correspondence of merchants like Henry Laurens and John Guerard as well as auction notices indicate that planters preferred young adult slave men over slave women. For the South Carolina trade, notes David Richardson, 'these age and sex preferences were not unusual: on the contrary, they were fairly typical of planter preferences throughout British America before the Revolution'.[74] Such patterns are entirely consistent with the Atlantic trade in which 179 male slaves were exported for every 100 enslaved women.[75]

Between 1670 and the late 1730s, the colony experienced three overlapping waves of slave importation. African and Afro-Caribbean slaves preceded slaves from the Senegambia and Gulf of Guinea who were, in turn, followed by captives from west-central Africa. As the first coerced labourers in the colony, Afro-Caribbean slaves constituted a 'charter group', able to create their own folkways from a combination of their own traditions and the circumstances of frontier life as well as to establish boundaries for the incorporation of newcomers.[76] The new imports from Guinea and the Senegambia encountered a society in which the basic contours for cultural innovation among slaves had already been broadly defined. As Sidney Mintz and Richard Price have noted on this aspect of slave culture, the arrival of 'massive new importations from Africa apparently had little more effect than to lead to secondary elaborations'.[77]

This is not to say that newcomers to lowcountry plantations had no impact on the process of cultural formation in the slave quarters. The final wave of slaves from Kongo and Angola appear to have enjoyed several advantages over those taken from western Africa. Unlike slaves from the Senegambia and the Gulf of Guinea, where the heterogeneous cultures of the region's numerous ethnic groups did not facilitate the making of broad cultural commonalities, these new arrivals from west-central Africa came from remarkably homogeneous societies. Drawn together by the common lexical base of Bantu languages, these people had also experienced some contact with Portuguese traders, Jesuit and Capuchin missionaries.[78]

Of the slaves taken from this region of Africa, it is likely that some were familiar with Roman Catholicism, even though Kongo Christianity was highly syncretic in nature, and some may have had some ability in either Italian, the language of the Capuchins, or Portuguese. Moreover, some slaves may have also had an acquaintance with English after the Royal African Company established trading posts along the Loango coast at Malimba and Kabinda, competing with its European rivals for trade at the turn of the eighteenth century.[79] This region subsequently became a major source of slaves for English possessions in the New World, with over 20 per cent of its imports coming from the lands between the Zaire River and Gabon Estuary. Many of these captives were young adult males as it was here, according to Paul Lovejoy, that 'the goal of purchasing twice as many males as females appears to have been realized for the first time'.[80] Like so many other prisoners of war in Atlantic Africa, a significant number of these men would have been soldiers who, on becoming captives of their enemies, were sold into slavery.[81] Both language and military skills, as we shall later see, would play major parts in the rebellion of 1739.

These men not only contributed to the reconfiguration of the lowcountry's ethnic landscape, but they also played a central role in the rice revolution that forever changed the social fluidity that had characterized the frontier. As planters began purchasing more land, consolidating holdings, clearing swamps and embarking on commercial rice farming, they depended on Afro-Carolinian and African-born slaves to provide the labour power. Male slaves felled cedar and cypress trees, cut irrigation ditches and dug rice fields from the lowcountry's 'black, greasy Mould' to create an environment that bore only a passing resemblance to Caribbean plantations or the landscapes of Atlantic Africa.[82]

Throughout the 1730s, planters continued to expand the commercial production of rice on estates laboriously carved from swamps and creeks by slaves.[83] Rice exports underwent explosive growth, rising from six hundred to ten thousand tons between 1709 and 1731, an average increase of 20 per cent per annum.[84] The lowcountry also underwent a demographic revolution as the number of slaves rose from 5,768 to around 20,000 over the same period.[85] Already a society dependent on slave labour prior to its commercial cultivation, rice transformed South Carolina into a plantation society.

That a large number of lowcountry slaves came from regions in which rice was grown and that these captives were preferred by planters has been well documented by Daniel Littlefield, Peter Wood and others.[86] The role played by women in its production has not received as much attention, however. A major staple throughout the Senegambia and, to a lesser degree, along the Grain, Ivory, Gold and Slave Coasts of the Gulf of Guinea, the crop was almost universally cultivated by women.[87] Trading with the Mende along the Sherbro coast of the Senegambia in the 1730s and 1740s, Irish trader Nicholas Owens saw women 'making plantations and beating out the rice'.[88] In his account of its cultivation among the Baga, Captain Samuel Gamble, who also traded in this region, observed how 'Women & Girls transplant the rice and are so dextrous as to plant fifty roots in a minute' and the manner by which they cultivated and harvested the crop.[89] Other traders and naval officers concurred with these observations: Thomas Winterbottom, a navy surgeon, noted that they 'not only cook, and wash and beat the rice, clean it from the husk, but they also cut down the underwood, assist in hoeing the ground, and they carry the produce to market'.[90] This grain, however, was not widely cultivated in either the Kongo or Angola. According to one traveller, rice was 'little thought of' and mainly used to provision slave ships.[91] Whatever crop was being grown, women rather than men played the central role in its cultivation in Atlantic Africa.

To meet the demands of rice cultivation, planters dissolved the gender division of labour that had characterized slave work along the ranching and lumbering frontier. The new configuration of work combined the imposition of the disciplined work routine of plantation cultivation with the violation of western African constructions of appropriate gender roles for agricultural work. Thomas Nairne, a planter from St. Helena Parish, demanded that 'slaves of both Sexes' labour in his fields while pastor Johann Martin Bolzius noted that slaves, regardless of their sex, were required to cultivate a certain acreage of land per day.[92] As rice fields and irrigation channels transformed the lowland countryside, both male and female slaves found themselves working side by side. This arrangement violated the cornerstone of the economic and social organization of village culture in western Africa. Already dishonoured by their status as captives, these new arrivals perhaps suffered another insult to their honour by having to perform tasks traditionally done by women.

The slaves who worked on the lowcountry frontier were able to create a climate in which they experienced certain amount of autonomy and could, to a limited extent, adapt African customs to the new circumstances. Even though the work they performed required much muscle power, these slaves retained some control over their lives. Comprising the first wave of settlers, these pioneers played a strategic role in defining the contours of Afro-Carolinian culture.[93] Familiar with English and expert in several trades, Afro-Caribbean and Afro-Carolinian slaves would have become slave drivers or assumed responsibility for skilled jobs on the plantation while new imports would have laboured in the rice fields.

The changes that rice cultivation brought to the lowcountry furnished the context in which the revolt occurred. Many slaves may have been only partly aware of the region's changing ethnic and demographic patterns, but they would have been very conscious of how rice cultivation was reshaping their working lives. The back-breaking nature of this work combined with the transgression of gender roles that had prevailed in Atlantic Africa gave male slaves a specific set of grievances against which to struggle.[94]

The 1730s was a decade of slave unrest throughout the New World plantation complex. Conspiracies were uncovered in the Bahamas in 1734 and in Antigua a year later while war between colonists and maroons broke out on Jamaica in 1730, and rebellions occurred on Saint John in 1733 and on Guadelope in 1737.[95] Part of the Atlantic system, South Carolina likewise experienced unrest and discontent among its slave population as well as military threats from the Spanish. A group of enslaved men near Charles Town 'conspired to Rise' in August 1730. Only apparent divisions between conspirators who wanted to 'destroy their own Masters' and those who believed that a 'Rising in a Body' would be more effective led to the rebellion's collapse and the arrest of its ringleaders.[96] Two years later, rumours about a rebellion prompted Governor Robert Johnson to order the militia 'to ride about to keep the Negroes in due order'.[97] Other plots against slaveholders were uncovered as the enslaved continued to challenge their owners' authority in the course of the decade.

The colony's authorities also had to face renewed threats from the Spanish in Florida. As the English gained a foothold in coastal Georgia, the borderlands between these new settlements and St. Augustine became, as David Weber has noted, 'a turbulent arena of contention between warring Europeans' as they competed for the upper hand in the Indian trade.[98] War clouds between these two nations began to gather over the lowcountry in the late 1730s. After capturing a spy in early 1737, the English learned that extensive preparations for an invasion of the mainland by Spanish soldiers from Havana were well in hand.[99] The crisis between the English and the Spanish came to a climax when, just hours before Jemmy and his followers struck Hutchenson's store, the War of Jenkins' Ear broke out.[100]

Lowcountry planters, however, found the policy pursued by the Spanish in St. Augustine to be as troubling as the threat of war as Port Royal trader Caleb Davis found out in 1738. Determined to recover his slaves who had run to Florida, he travelled to St. Augustine to reclaim his property. Governor Manuel de Montiano informed him that slaves who had escaped to the Spanish might expect their liberty in accordance with royal edicts.[101] Those who successfully completed the long and dangerous journey from South Carolina to the Spanish could become smallholders in the nearby settlement of Gracia Real de Santa Teresa de Mose.[102] At least one group who reached it found themselves 'received there with great honors, one of them had a Commission given to him, and a coat faced with Velvet'.[103] Reports about the 'Protection and Freedom to all Negroe Slaves who would report thither' clearly circulated in the lowcountry and influenced at least some slaves who, bent on reaching their destination in August 1739, stopped some Indians to ask directions to the Spanish settlement.[104]

These slaves were just a few of the hundreds who elected to free themselves from slavery. By the late 1730s, this form of liberation had become fairly commonplace. Among the repertoire of resistance, it was among the most significant acts of 'self-assertion'.[105] Planter Charles Pinckney believed that flight constituted 'a matter of very Ill Consequence to the Estates and Properties of the People'.[106] Frustrated by an inability to stem what they perceived to be an exodus, legislators hastily assigned a boat to guard 'Water Passages to the South' and offered rewards to those apprehending fugitives.[107]

Between 1732 and 1739, the *South Carolina Gazette* reported that 253 slaves had escaped slavery. Even though they constitute the tip of 'an otherwise indeterminate iceberg', these notices offer a rough profile of individuals who successfully 'stole themselves'.[108] As in every slave regime, male slaves comprised the majority of lowcountry fugitives, making up 77 per cent (or 194 slaves).[109] Over three-quarters of these men lived in the countryside and departed at the most arduous times of rice cultivation in January and February, when they had to clean ditches and prepare fields, and in September and October, when they worked long hours reaping, transporting and threshing the harvest. Perhaps it is no accident that rebellion occurred as plantation work reached its most intense and when slave men, reaping a bumper rice harvest in 1739, may have been provoked to contemplate flight.

The African origins of the advertised runaways provides further information on the relationship between resistance and ethnicity.[110] Although the provenance of some Stono rebels suggests that recently arrived African men were more likely to oppose slavery, we cannot definitively conclude that African-born slaves were more prone to escape than their American-born counterparts because information on ethnicity is often absent from the notices. Between 1732 and 1739, however, the available evidence indicates that enslaved Africans, who constituted the bulk of lowcountry slaves by the 1730s, also made up the majority of fugitives. Out of 192 men who ran, the paper reported 62 slaves (32 per cent) as being African (with 26 or 13 per cent of these being Angolan) and 17 (or 8 per cent) as being either native-born or from the Caribbean. Among the remaining 87 slaves (45 per cent), it is very probable that some were non-native born slaves.[111] In these eight years, therefore, 46 per cent of all male escapees came from some part of Atlantic Africa. What we know about the ethnicity of the rebels and their leader indicates that they came from Angola, but this does not preclude either slaves from other parts of Atlantic Africa or even the 'country born' from being among their ranks.[112]

In addition to growing problems in Anglo-Spanish relations and the presence of an increasingly restive slave population, the combination of bad weather and disease further added to the problems faced by the colonists. Torrential rains in the summer of 1737 contributed to poor harvests of rice and other staples, leading to a 'Great Scarcity of Corn, Pease, Small Rice, Flower and Bisket' and contributing to the death of some slaves from 'want'.[113] Although there was a poor harvest next year, it did not lead to any deaths. It was a smallpox epidemic that proved to be the killer in 1738, spreading throughout Charles Town and some rural areas during the summer and autumn months and leaving several hundred people, slave and free, dead. As the colony recovered from this outbreak, yellow fever erupted the following summer, leaving the colony in 'a deplorable state' in the closing months of the year.[114] Trade came to a virtual standstill, the Assembly removed itself from Charles Town for its sessions, the *South Carolina Gazette* closed temporarily and, as the first week of September ended, reports about the outbreak of hostilities between Spain and England arrived.[115] The continual traffic between the town and its hinterlands ensured that the trials besetting the colony would spread throughout the lowcountry.

The presence of epidemic disease and food shortages and the threat of attacks by the Spanish had an impact on enslaved as well as free people. For slaves, the possibility of war meant a further imposition on their freedom of movement as Governor Thomas Broughton, having informed imperial officials that 'our Negroes are . . . and more dreadfull to our safety than any Spanish invaders', doubled the number and strength of patrols and used Cherokee Indians to shore up the colony's internal security.[116] In addition to these patrols, scout boats stationed along the coast further impeded slave self-activity. Some lowcountry slaves may have interpreted the militia's presence along with the other misfortunes as portents of some undefined event of great magnitude. Others may have recognized that preparations for war signalled the start of a major challenge by the Spanish to English mastery in the region. Whether these slaves saw the soldiers at St. Augustine as an army of liberation is unknown, but these menacing events may have been perceived as heralding a moment of impending yet unknown change.[117]

The tocsin of rebellion rang in the early hours of Sunday morning on 9 September as rebellious slaves assembled outside Hutchenson's store under Jemmy's leadership. Described only as 'their Captain' and an Angolan, we know nothing else about this man. That no other rebel was individually identified perhaps indicates that he held a position of prominence on a plantation or among local slaves. Whatever his place in the community, he may have visited nearby estates to recruit slaves. Although Bull alluded to it thirty years after the insurrection, the rule that 'work on the public road', a task in which a number of rebels were apparently involved over the course of several days, played in the insurrection is worth considering.[118] Drawn from several local plantations and farms, the members of the road gang likely exchanged the laborious work of the rice harvest for the equally arduous labour of road work. Moreover, as these workers would have been male, Jemmy perhaps took advantage of the overseer's 'slack inspection' to convince his fellow workers to rebel.[119]

But did Jemmy intend to launch a full-scale rebellion or did he plan to escape with a number of other slaves? Jemmy may have aimed to lead some slaves across coastal Carolina and Georgia to St. Augustine. They may have intended to take supplies from Hutchenson's store and then effect their escape as the colonists prepared themselves for attack by Spanish forces.[120] By starting their action on Sunday, when many white people would have been at worship and when planters allowed slaves 'to work for themselves' on their provision grounds, the rebels would have been able to take advantage of a day when their masters may have been less vigilant and other enslaved people were engaged in their own unsupervised affairs. After the killings at the store, the slaves perhaps decided to fight their way to freedom. The rebels alternatively may have intended to inflict as much damage as possible on their owners and their property before striking south and the promise of liberation.

Whatever their original intention, the slaves transformed themselves from field hands into rebels in that moment of drama and violence at Hutchenson's store. Perhaps it was a moment in which they recovered a sense of martial identity that may have informed many of their lives in Africa. These killings and the display of the severed heads of Bathurst and Gibbs on the steps served as a public declaration.

From a practical standpoint, the raid furnished the rebels with the arms and ammunition necessary to conduct a successful rising. Their actions at the store spoke not just to pragmatic concerns, however. They also illuminated the consciousness of the insurgents. The murder and subsequent decapitation of the two men in the store indicate the presence of violent rage, but these acts likely also possessed some symbolic content for the rebels.

Through the ritual brutalization of these men, the rebels were able to invert the power relations in which they found themselves embedded. The very act of rebellion itself clearly threatened to turn the world upside down, but decapitation may have had a specific meaning for the rebels.[121] Often an integral part to the punishment that colonial authorities inflicted on slaves found guilty of serious offences, beheading was performed as a public spectacle. Both free and slave inhabitants of Charles Town saw the execution of a man named Quash for burglary in 1734. After the hanging, his 'Head was sever'd from his Body, and fixed upon the Gallows'.[122] A few months before the rising, the bodies of two executed slaves were 'hung in Chains by Hang Man's Point . . . in sight of all negroes passing and repassing by water'.[123] Away from the court room, slaveholders also occasionally administered this brand of justice. After killing an escaped slave in early 1732. Charles Jones was ordered by a judge to remove the head, 'fix it on a pole and set it near the crossroads'.[124] Reports of these executions no doubt reached slaves on lowcountry plantations. Appropriating this form of punishment for themselves, the rebels inverted patterns of discipline used by the authorities for their own purposes.

This incident may have held yet another symbolic meaning for the rebels. Decapitation not only played a part in the exercise of colonial justice; it was also integral to the martial culture of several western African societies. Robin Law has noted how warriors in Dahomey and neighbouring areas beheaded their enemies, displaying the severed heads as trophies of military prowess and preserving them for ritual display.[125] An English slave trader at Whydah on the Bight of Benin watched soldiers 'return from ravaging' carrying 'bags full of men, women, and childrens heads' into the royal compound which they proceeded to 'kick and sling about' with great energy.[126] By beheading the men and displaying their heads, the rebels may have been participating in a time-honoured tradition firmly grounded in their own martial culture.

After declaring their intent at the Stono Bridge, the rebels headed down the Pon Pon road and into the heart of St. Paul's Parish. As they marched through the countryside, they continued on their course of violence. After plundering the house of the Godfrey family and killing its inhabitants, they reached Wallace's Tavern and the Lemy house by daybreak. Instead of destroying both buildings and their residents, the insurgents elected to save the tavern keeper, who was 'a Good Man and kind to his Slaves' and kill Lemy, his wife and child.[127] The nature of Wallace's benevolence toward his slaves remains a mystery, but as a tavern keeper he may have broken the law, served alcohol to slaves and tacitly encouraged them to patronize his establishment in exchange for goods. Their decision to kill Lemy's family and spare Wallace's suggests the ways in which the rebels calculated the value of the people who had once presided over their lives.

The pattern established at the tavern continued throughout the day. That killing, burning and plundering constituted the modality of the rebellion is unsurprising. The widespread destruction of farm buildings and plantation houses in addition to the theft of alcohol, firearms and other goods all indicate the rebels' desire to destroy or acquire the insignias of their masters' power. By burning over-seers' houses, storehouses and other buildings, the rebels used arson, a time-honoured form of resistance to incinerate signs of their own oppression.

The incidents that transpired at the house inhabited by Thomas Rose reveal the ambiguous character of solidarity and community among lowcountry slaves. Rather than join the rebels. Rose's slave hid his master before stepping outside to pacify the rebels.[128] This slave was not alone in selecting this course of action. Several slaves owned by Thomas Elliott followed this example, demonstrating 'Integrity and Fidelity' to their owner rather than to their potential liberators.[129] For July, another of Elliott's slaves, this display of loyalty involved killing one of the rebels who had threatened his master. Citing his bravery, the Assembly rewarded July with 'his Freedom and a Present of a Suit of Clothes'.[130] Other slaves who had 'behaved themselves well' received not liberty but clothes made with 'blue Stroud, faced up with Red, and trimmed with brass Buttons'.[131] In all, the Assembly rewarded over thirty slaves for their 'great service in opposing the rebellious Negroes' in addition to a number of Indians who hunted and captured those rebels who escaped the final skirmish.[132]

These decisions by slaves raise questions about the degree to which lowcountry slaves had developed a sense of solidarity in the face of their collective oppression. The collusion between slave and slave holder suggests that expressions of solidarity and community among slaves across the lowcountry was fairly fragile. That several slaves came to the aid of their embattled owners suggests that they identified with the interests of their master and household rather than with their potential libera-tors. Slaves like July may have been acting in a purely pragmatic way. Those who could have joined the rebellion may have weighed the chances of its possible success against the retribution that failure would bring. A large number of prospective rebels perhaps elected to cling to the few rights and privileges that they had extracted from their masters rather than join an endeavour that may have seemed foolhardy.

As the ranks of the rebels 'increased every minute by New Negroes coming to them', some slaves clearly decided to take their chances with Jemmy.[133] Ambiguous about how many took this course of action, reports indicated that 'they were above Sixty, some a hundred' as the afternoon drew on.[134] The slaves of St. Paul's would have learned of the uprising in several ways. The rebels obtained some drums and flags – perhaps from Hutchenson's store – by which they announced their presence to the farms and plantations of St. Paul's Parish, enabling them to get a number of slaves to rally to their 'Colours displayed'. Moreover, as they marched in this formation, their consciousness revealed itself as they were reported 'calling out Liberty'. This idea, so powerfully symbolized by St. Augustine, suggests that Jemmy and his followers may have understood the political character of their actions. Alternatively, it is possible that this incident of the rebellion was fabricated by an official who, wishing to vindicate the militia's violent response, imbued the insurgents' actions with an ideological design. By placing an emphasis on the revolt's political content, the Assembly would believe itself to be fully justified by their aggressive suppression of the rebellions, the rough justice administered to the rebels and the draconian laws that they passed some months later.[135]

In addition to serving a practical purpose, the use of drums and banners were integral to methods of fighting in west-central Africa. It is worth repeating, moreover, that many African men who found themselves caught in the Atlantic trade were veterans of conflicts. Thus, it is entirely possible that some of the Stono rebels had prior military service and, as John Thornton has demonstrated, rebels tactics bore some hallmarks of the style of fighting practised by the armies of Kongo-Angola.[136] Just as Jemmy's followers beat drums to recruit other slaves to their cause, Kongo soldiers launched their attacks by striking 'large kettle drums . . . with small clubs of ivory'.[137] As ranks formed on the battlefield, other soldiers began 'dancing and beating drums' to inspire the army as fighting commenced. By employing similar tactics, the rebels reproduced aspects of the martial culture of their former lives through the use of banners and drums. As they adopted this posture, these men became, as Vincent Harding has observed, 'warriors again', perhaps resurrecting the masculine cast of military life that they had experienced in Africa.[138]

This moment was short-lived, however. Having 'discerned the approaching Danger with time enough to avoid it', Bull alerted the militia who, after posting pickets at strategic crossroads and ferry crossings, set out to find the rebels.[139] Hastily assembling themselves into a patrol, local farmers and planters joined the militia and together they stumbled on the rebels near the Jacksonborough ferry on the Edisto River's eastern shore at about 4 p.m.[140] Believing that they were 'victorious over the Whole Province' and intending 'to draw more Negroes to them', the slaves had begun to dance, sing and consume their plunder. Again, such behaviour not only has its ethnic antecedents in Kongo military tradition where victorious troops celebrated in similar ways, but it also gave the rebels further opportunity to undermine and invert the symbols of authority by engaging in actions deemed illegal by their masters.

This festive mood changed dramatically as well-armed militia men and planters stormed the field, bringing down about fourteen revellers with their first volley. It was a struggle in which, concluded a legislative committee, 'one fought for Liberty and Life, the other for their Country and every thing that was dear to them'.[141] In one episode during the fight, the character of relations between masters and slaves revealed themselves. Armed with a pistol, one rebel confronted his master who asked the slave whether 'he wanted to kill him'.[142] The enslaved man answered that he intended to do so and then 'snapped the Pistoll at him, but it mist fire'. Without any hesitation, the slave holder took his own gun and shot his adversary through the head.[143] For a very brief moment, the enslaved had held ultimate power over his master and by his words and actions had expressed the deadly rage that he harboured against his enslaver. Although the authorities noted that they 'behaved boldly', some slaves did not stand their ground, but fled into the woods, hoping to reach their home plantations before their absence was noticed. The militia moved through the countryside, seized those rebels who had managed to escape and sought to 'put a stop to further mischief'.[144] Several months elapsed before daily life in the district began to have the semblance of normality. The insurrection had prompted several to 'desert their habitations' while it had forced others 'to assemble together in numbers . . . for their better security and defence against those Negroes who are not yet taken'.[145] Perhaps seeking revenge for the decapitations at Hutchenson's store or simply wishing to reassert their power, some planters who captured escaped rebels 'cut off their Heads and set them on every Mile Post they came to'.[146] The events of the Stono rebellion had come full circle.

The transformation of the South Carolina lowcountry from a thinly populated frontier to a thickly inhabited plantation zone led to the degradation of slave work from a regime characterized by self-direction, semi-autonomy and skill into one notable for its routine and discipline. The partial reconstruction of the agricultural practices of Atlantic Africa along the lowcountry's ranching and lumbering frontier possibly ameliorated enslavement for the first generation of slaves. The gradual but steady rise in work regimentation as rice cultivation began to dominate the economy and slave life perhaps fostered feelings of frustration as plantation agriculture supplanted pastoral farming.

For subsequent arrivals of enslaved people (from the Guinea coast and then from Kongo and Angola), the transition to slavery in the New World was considerably more disorienting. In addition to the degradations of captivity and the middle passage, newly arrived slave men were then forced to work in a plantation regime in which the gender roles that prevailed in their homelands had been dissolved by their new owners. This infraction may have forced slave men to confront further dishonour as they performed work traditionally done by women. The fundamental negation of their masculinity and the transgression of their understanding of customary gender roles may have provided the circumstances that drove Jemmy and his followers onto a path of insurrection. As they crossed St. Paul's Parish, the rebels were able to reassert themselves as African men and to articulate a consciousness that was firmly rooted in their opposition to the social and cultural legacy of the rice revolution.

Notes

1   'An Account of the Negroe Insurrection in South Carolina', in Allan D. Candler (ed.), *The Colonial Records of the State of Georgia, Part Two* (Atlanta, 1913), 22, p. 234 [hereafter *CRG*]: for a description of this district, see 'James Sutherland to My Lord, 14 April 1729' *South Carolina Historical Magazine* 68 (April 1967), p. 82 [hereafter *SCHM*]. In a report filed in the aftermath of the rebellion, Lieutenant-Governor William Bull made no mention of the road gang, but he did mention it some thirty years later in a summary of the colony's trade, agriculture and settlement. See 'Governor William Bull's Representation of the Colony, 1770' in H. Roy Merrens (ed.). *The Colonial South Carolina Scene: Contemporary Views, 1697–1774* (Columbia, 1977), p. 260.

2   See 'A Ranger's Report of Travels with General Oglethorpe,' in Newton Mereness (ed.), *Travels in the American Colonies* (New York, 1916), pp. 222–3.

3   Alexander Hewatt, *An Historical Account of the Rise and Progress of the Colonies of South Carolina and Georgia*, in B.R. Carroll (ed.), *Historical Collections of South Carolina*, 2 vols., (New York, 1936), 1, p. 333.

4   Entry for 13 September 1739 in William Stephens. 'The Journal of Colonel William Stephens, 1737–1740', in Candler (ed.), *CRG*, 4, p. 412.

5   Reporting his narrow escape to London, Bull recounted how he and four travelling companions 'met these rebels at 11 o'clock in the forenoon, and fortunately discerned the approaching danger in time enough to avoid it'. Lieutenant-Governor William Bull to the Board of Trade, 5 October 1739, in Original Correspondence, Board of Trade. CO5/367/f114, British Public Record Office, London [hereafter PRO]. See also, Kinloch Bull, Jr., *The Oligarchs in Colonial and Revolutionary Charleston: Lieutenant Governor William Bull II and His Family* (Columbia, 1991), pp. 15–16.

6   Candler (ed.), 'Negroe Insurrection', p. 234.

7   Daily Register, 28 September 1739, in George Fenwick Jones and Renate Wilson, trans. and ed., *Detailed Reports on the Salzburger Emigrants Who Settled in America* (Athens, 1981), 6, p. 226.

8   On slave resistance in this period, see Peter Wood, *Black Majority: Negroes in Colonial South Carolina from 1670 through the Stono Rebellion* (New York, 1974), esp. pp. 239–70, 285–330; Michael Mullin, *Africa in America: Slave Acculturation and Resistance in the American South and the British Caribbean, 1736–1831* (Urbana, 1992); Gerald Mullin, *Flight and Rebellion: Slave Resistance in Eighteenth-Century Virginia* (New York, 1972).

9   'Report of the Committee to Inquire into the Causes and Disappointment of Success of the Late Expedition to St. Augustine', 1 July 1741 in J.H. Easterby (ed.), *The Journal of the Commons House of Assembly, 1741–1742* (Columbia, 1953), pp. 83–4 [hereafter JCHA].

10   For additional discussions, see Margaret Washington Creel. *'A Peculiar People': Slave Religion and Community-Culture Among the Gullahs* (New York, 1988), pp. 33–4, 114–16; Robert M. Weir, *Colonial South Carolina: A History* (Millwood, NY, 1983), pp. 193–4; Mullin, *Africa in America*, pp. 43–5.

11   Hewatt, *Historical Account* in Caroll (ed.), *Historical Collections of South Carolina*. 1, p. 333.

12   Wood, *Black Majority*, pp. 308–26. For Darold Wax, Stono was 'the most serious slave uprising in colonial America'. See Darold D. Wax, "The Great Risque We Run": The Aftermath of Slave Rebellion at Stono, 1739–1745', *Journal of Negro History* 67 (Summer 1982), pp. 136–47.

13   M. Eugene Sirmans, *Colonial South Carolina: A Political History, 1663–1763* (Chapel Hill, 1966), p. 208. Agreeing with Sirmans' assessment, Mullin writes that 'Stone was not a climax'. See Michael Mullin, *Africa in America: Slave Acculturation and Resistance in the American South and the British Caribbean, 1736–1831* (Urbana, 1992), pp. 317–18, n. 33.

14   John Thornton, 'African Dimensions of the Stono Rebellion', *American Historical Review* 96 (October 1991), p. 1113.

15   Joan Scott, 'Gender: A Useful Category of Historical Analysis', in Joan Scott, *Gender and the Politics of History* (New York, 1988), pp. 28–50.

16   The term 'rice revolution' is taken from Ira Berlin, 'The Slave Trade and the Development of Afro-American Society in English Mainland North America, 1619–1775', *Southern Studies* 20 (Summer 1981), p. 129.

17   On this aspect of historical inquiry, see 'Discourse on Method' in Rhys Isaac, *The Transformation of Virginia, 1740–1790* (Chapel Hill, 1988), p. 357.

18   Ranajit Guha, *Elementary Aspects of Peasant Insurgency in Colonial India* (Delhi, 1983), 3–4; idem., 'The Prose of Counter-Insurgency', in Nicholas B. Dirks, Geoff Eley, and Sherry Ortner (eds.), *Culture/Power/History: A Reader in Contemporary Social Theory* (Princeton, 1994), pp. 336–71; see also Douglas Haynes and Gyan Prakesh, 'Introduction: The Entanglement of Power and Resistance', in Douglas Haynes and Gyan Prakesh (eds.), *Contesting Power: Resistance and Everyday Social Relations in South Asia* (Berkeley, 1991), pp. 1–23.

19   James C. Scott, *Domination and the Arts of Resistance: Hidden Transcripts* (New Haven, 1990).

20   Ibid., xiii; see also idem., *Weapons of the Weak: Everyday Forms of Peasant Resistance* (New Haven, 1985).

21   Russell R. Menard. 'Financing the Lowcountry Export Boom: Capital and Growth in Early South Carolina', *William and Mary Quarterly*, 3rd ser., 41 (October 1994), p. 659 [hereafter *WMQ*]; see also Peter A. Coclanis, *The Shadow of a Dream: Economic Life and Death in the South Carolina Law Country, 1670–1920* (New York, 1989), p. 64.

22   On population, see Peter H. Wood, 'The Changing Population of the Colonial South: An Overview of Race and Region, 1685–1790', in Peter H. Wood, Gregory A. Waselkov, and M. Thomas Hatley (eds.), *Pawhatan's Mantle: Indians in the Colonial Southeast* (Lincoln, Neb., 1989), p. 38: see also Coclanis, *Shadow of A Dream*, p. 64.

23   George Milligen-Johnston, *A Short Description of the Province of South Carolina* (London, 1770), p. 28: see also Terry G. Jordan, *Trails to Texas: Southern Roots of Western Cattle Ranching* (Lincoln, Neb., 1981), pp. 25–31. On the development of cattle herding in the lowcountry, see John S. Otto, 'The Origins of Cattle Ranching in Colonial South Carolina. 1670–1715', *SCHM* 87 (April 1986), pp. 117–24: idem., 'Livestock Raising in Early South Carolina, 1670–1700: Prelude to the Rice Plantation Economy', *Agricultural History* 61 (Fall 1987), pp. 13–24 [hereafter *AH*]: John S. Otto and Nain E. Anderson, 'The Origins of Southern Cattle Grazing: A Problem in West Indian History', *Journal of Caribbean History*

21 (1987), pp. 138–53; Mart A. Stewart, '"Whether Wast, Deodand, or Stray": Cattle, Culture and the Environment in Early Georgia', *AH* 65 (Summer 1991), pp. 1–28.

24 See Converse D. Clowse, *Economic Beginnings in Colonial South Carolina, 1670–1710* (Columbia, 1971): [John Norris], 'An Interview with James Freeman', in Merrens (ed.), *Colonial South Carolina Scene*, p. 43.

25 'A Voyage to Georgia by A Young Gentleman Giving an Account of his Travels to South Carolina and Parts of North Carolina', in *Collections of the Georgia Historical Society*, 15 vols., (Savannah, 1840–to date), 3, p. 50; on the frontier, see also Verner Crane, *The Southern Frontier, 1670–1732* (Durham, 1928); W. Stitt Robinson. *The Southern Colonial Frontier, 1607–1763* (Albuquerque, 1979).

26 Thomas Ashe, *Carolina: Or A Description of the Present State of that Country* (London, 1682) in Carroll (ed.), *Historical Collections*, 2, p. 63.

27 Pine trees yielded a number of useful commodities. Apart from lumber, the tree's resin (turpentine) had a number of medicinal purposes as either a liniment or diuretic. Tar and pitch were its most valuable by-products, with the former being used as a lubricant and to coat ropes to prevent fraying; the latter was used to seal ships. These products go under the generic title of 'naval stores'. See John J. McCusker and Russell R. Menard, *The Economy of British America, 1607–1789* (Chapel Hill, 1985), pp. 179–80; see also Timothy Silver, *A New Face on the Countryside: Indians, Colonists, and Slaves in South Atlantic Forests, 1500–1800* (New York, 1990), pp. 121–2; G. Melvin Herndon, 'Naval Stores in Colonial Georgia', *Georgia Historical Quarterly* 52 (December 1968), pp. 426–33; idem., 'Timber Products of Colonial Georgia', ibid., 57 (Spring 1973), pp. 56–63; Wood, *Black Majority*, pp. 110–14.

28 John Lawson, *A New Voyage to Carolina*, edited by Hugh Talmadge Lefler (Chapel Hill, 1967), p. 167.

29 Governor Robert Johnson to Lords Proprietors, 17 December 1717, in W. Noel Sainsbury (ed.), *Records in the British Public Record Office Relating to South Carolina, 1719–1720*, p. 5.

30 Otto, 'Livestock Raising in Early South Carolina', p. 19; Wood, *Black Majority*, p. 31.

31 *Records of the Register and Secretary, 1675–1696*, cited in Aaron M. Shatzman, *Servants into Planters: The Origin of an American Image: Land Acquisition and Status Mobility in Seventeenth-Century South Carolina* (New York, 1989), p. 46. Wood also refers to this incident, although he calls the farmer Denys Omahone. See Wood, *Black Majority*, p. 31.

32 Shatzman, *Servants into Planters*, p. 113; Lawson, *New Voyage*, p. 34.

33 Ashe, *Carolina: or A Description* in Carroll (ed.), *Historical Collections*, 2, p. 73. As no tigers have ever lived in the Carolina lowcountry, Ashe presumably was referring to cougars.

34 James Glen, 'Estimate of the Value of South Carolina', in H. Roy Merrens (ed.), *Colonial South Carolina Scene*, p. 186.

35 Wilson, *An Account of the Province of Carolina* in Carroll (ed.), *Historical Collections*, 2, p. 30; Ashe, *Carolina* in ibid., 2, pp. 72–3. See also Mabel L. Webber (ed.), 'Letters from John Steward to William Dunlop', *SCHM* 32 (January 1931), p. 22; on cattle pen development, see Gary S. Dunbar, 'Colonial Carolina Cowpens', *AH* 3 (July 1961), pp. 125–31.

36 [John Norris], 'Interview with James Freeman', in Merrens (ed.), *Colonial South Carolina Scene*, p. 49.

37 For another perspective on pastoral agriculture, see Emmanuel Le Roy Ladurie's fascinating discussion on the life of the shepherd in the Pyrenees in *Montaillou: Cathars and Catholics in a French Village, 1294–1324* (London, 1980), pp. 103–35.

38 William DeBrahm, *Report of the General Survey in the Southern District of North America* (ed.), Louis DeVorsey, Jr., (Columbia, 1971), p. 95; *South Carolina and American General Gazette*, 18 February 1779. See also 'A Gentleman's Account of his Travels, 1733–1734', in Merrens (ed.), *The Colonial South Carolina Scene*, p. 119. This particular travellers noted how planters 'frequently settle their cow pens' on savannas, further observing that at least one pen stood six miles from the main plantation house.

39 Jones and Wilson (eds.), *Reports on the Salzburger Emigrants*, 6, p. 159; *South Carolina Gazette*, 18 July 1768: see also Dunbar, 'Colonial Carolina Cowpens'.

40 John Norris, *Profitable Advice for Rich and Poor* (London, 1712), p. 132: see also Thomas Naime, *A Letter From South Carolina* (London, 1711), p. 63.

41 These traditions of independent food production during slaves' free time may have played a critical role in the development of provision grounds and the task system that configured labour on rice plantations. See Philip D. Morgan, 'Work and Culture: The Task System and the World of Lowcountry Blacks, 1700 to 1880', *WMQ* 3rd ser., 39 (October 1982), pp. 563–99; idem., 'Task and Gang Systems: The Organization of Labor on New World Plantations', in Stephen Innes (ed.), *Work and Labor in Early America* (Chapel Hill, 1988), pp. 189–220.

42 Lawson, *New Voyage to Carolina*, p. 88.

43 [John Norris], *Profitable Advice for Rich and Poor, in a Dialogue between James Freeman, a Carolina Planter, and Slmon Question, a West Country Farmer* (London, 1712), p. 89.

44 Otto, 'Livestock Raising in Early South Carolina', p. 17.

45 Peter Purry, 'Proposals of Mr. Peter Purry [1731]', in Carroll (ed.), *Historical Descriptions*, 2, p. 133.

46 Cited in Robert L. Meriwether, *The Expansion of South Carolina, 1729–1765* (Kingsport, Ta., 1940), p. 12.

47 Silver, *New Face on the Countryside*, pp. 120–30.

48 Lawson, *New Voyage to Carolina*, p. 104; on the various types of pine in lowcountry forests, see Silver, *New Face on the Countryside*, pp. 123–9.

49 Mark Catesby, 'The Manner of Making Tar and Pitch', in Merrens (ed.), *The Colonial South Carolina Scene*, p. 107; see also Silver, *New Face on the Countryside*, pp. 121–3.

50 William Bartram, *Travels Through North and South Carolina, Georgia, East and West Florida* (London, 1791; reprinted, New York, 1988), p. 335.

51 Creel, *'A Peculiar People'*, pp. 30–1; Mullin, *Africa in America*, pp. 13–14; on slavery in the English Caribbean, see Richard Dunn, *Sugar and Slaves: The Rise of the Planter Class in the English West Indies, 1624–1713* (Chapel Hill, 1972); David Barry Gaspar, *Bondmen and Rebels: A Study of Master–Slave Relations in Antigua* (Baltimore, 1985).

52 John K. Thornton, *The Kingdom of Kongo: Civil War and Transition, 1641–1718* (Madison, 1983), p. 29.

53 Robert Norris, *Memoirs of the Reign of Bossa Ahadee, King of Dahomey* (London, 1798), 143. Norris later became an ardent anti-abolitionist. See Robin Law, *The Slave Coast of West Africa, 1550–1750: The Impact of the Atlantic Slave Trade on an African Society* (Oxford, 1991), pp. 1–2. For other observations about the role of women in the coastal regions of Atlantic Africa, see Henry Meredith. *An Account of the Gold Coast* (London, 1812), p. 76; Thomas Winterbottom, *An Account of the Native Africans in the Neighbourhood of Sierra Leone* 2 vols. (London, 1803), p. 145; Richard Jobson, *The Golden Trade, or a Discovery of the River gambra and the Golden Trade of the Aethiopians* (London, 1623), p. 49. For modern discussions of this topic, see Claude Meillassoux, 'Female Slavery', in Claire C. Robertson and Martin A. Klein (eds.), *Women and Slavery in Africa* (Madison, 1983), pp. 49–66; James F. Searing, *West African Slavery and Atlantic Commerce: The Senegal River Valley, 1700–1860* (New York, 1993), pp. 120–3.

54 Jan Vansina, *Paths in the Rainforest: Toward a History of Political Tradition in Equatorial Africa* (Madison, 1990), pp. 83–5.

55 Thornton, *Kingdom of Kongo*, p. 29. See also Walter Rodney, *A History of the Upper Guinea Coast, 1545 to 1800* (New York, 1970), pp. 18–19; Fililipo Pigafetta, *A Report of the Kingdom of Kongo and of the Surrounding Countries Drawn Out From the Writings and Discourses of the Portuguese, Duarte Lopez*, trans. and ed. by Margarite Hutchinson (London, 1970), p. 19; Joseph C. Miller, *Way of Death: Merchant Capitalism and the Angolan Slave Trade, 1730–1830* (Madison, 1988).

56 Meredith, *Account of the Gold Coast*, p. 76.

57 See Y. Person, 'The Coastal Peoples: From Casamance to the Ivory Coast Lagoons', in D.T. Niane (ed.), *The General History of Africa: Africa from the Twelfth to the Sixteenth Century* (Berkeley, 1984), pp. 310–23; Graham Connah, *African Civilizations: Precolonial Cities and States in Tropical Africa: An Archaeological Perspective* (New York, 1987), pp. 97–120.

58 Jobson, *Golden Trade*, p. 49.

59 Andrew B. Smith, *Pastoralism in Africa: Origins and Development Ecology* (London, 1992), pp. 72–98; John G. Galenty and Pierre Bonte, 'Introduction', in John G. Galenty and Pierre Bonte (eds.), *Herders, Warriors, and Traders: Pastoralism in Africa* (Boulder, 1991), pp. 3–30.

60 Jean Barbot, *Barbot on Guinea: The Writings of Jean Barbot on West Africa, 1678–1712* (eds.), P.E.H. Hair, Adam Jones, and Robin Law, 2 vols. (London, 1992), I, p. 103.

61 Barbot, *Barbot on Guinea*, p. 101: see also B. Barry, 'Senegambia from the Sixteenth to the Eighteenth Century: Evolution of the Wolof, Sereer and 'Tukuloor', in B.A. Ogot (ed.), *The General History of Africa: Africa from the Sixteenth to the Eighteenth Century* (Berkeley, 1992), pp. 262–99.

62 William Towerson, *The First Voyage to Guinea* in John William Blake (ed.), *Europeans in West Africa, 1450–1560: Documents to Illustrate the Nature and Scope of the Portuguese Enterprise in West Africa* (London, 1942), p. 379.

63 Winterbottom, *Account of Sierra Leone*, I, p. 61.

64 George E. Brooks, *Landlords and Strangers: Ecology, Society, and Trade in Western Africa, 1000–1630* (Boulder, 1993), pp. 52–3; Rodney, *Upper Guinea Coast*, p. 25.

65 See Orlando Patterson, *Slavery and Social Death: A Comparative Study* (Cambridge, Mass., 1982), p. 79.

66 The literature on Atlantic African ways in the lowcountry is fairly extensive, see, for example, Leland Ferguson, *Uncommon Ground: Archaeology and Early African America, 1650–1800* (Washington, DC, 1992); Creel, 'A Peculiar People'; Joseph Holloway, 'The Origins of African-American Culture', in Joseph Holloway (ed.), *Africanisms in American Culture* (Bloomington, 1990), pp. 1–18; Wood, *Black Majority*; Littlefield, *Rice and Slaves*. For more general discussions, see Robert Farris Thompson, *Flash of the Spirit: African and Afro-American Art and Philosophy* (New York, 1984), pp. 101–60; Roger Bastide, *African Civilizations in the New World* (New York, 1971); Sidney Mintz and Richard Price, *The Birth of African-American Culture: An Anthropological Perspective* (Philadelphia, 1976; reprint ed., Boston, 1992).

67 On work and dignity, see Patrick Joyce, 'The Historical Meaning of Work: An Introduction', in Patrick Joyce (ed.), *The Historical Meaning of Work* (Cambridge, 1987), pp. 1–30.

68 The literature on the slave trade to South Carolina is substantial, see Daniel C. Littlefield. *Rice and Slaves: Ethnicity and the Slave Trade in Colonial South Carolina* (Baton Rouge, 1981); idem., '"Abundance of Negroes of That Nation": The Significance of African Ethnicity in Colonial South Carolina', in David R. Chesnutt and Clyde N. Wilson (eds.), *The Meaning of South Carolina History: Essays in Honor of George C. Rogers, Jr.* (Columbia, 1991), pp. 19–38; idem., 'The Slave Trade to Colonial South Carolina: A Profile', *SCHM* 91 (April 1990), pp. 68–99; W. Robert Higgins, 'Charleston: Terminus and Entrepot of the Colonial Slave Trade', in Martin L. Kilson and Robert I. Rotberg (eds.), *The African Diaspora: Interpretive Essays* (Cambridge, Ma., 1976); idem., 'The Geographical-Origins of Negro Slaves in Colonial South Carolina', *South Atlantic Quarterly* 70 (Winter 1971), pp. 34–47; David Richardson, 'The British Slave Trade to Colonial South Carolina', *Slavery and Abolition* 12 (December 1991), pp. 125–72.

69 The information on slave imports into South Carolina is both incomplete and somewhat contradictory. Material on 1717 and 1718 slave imports drawn from Shipping Returns. CO5/508, PRO, and 'The Record of Annual Slave Imports, 1706–1739', *Gentleman's Magazine*, 25 (1755), 344, cited in Wood, *Black Majority*, p. 151. For further discussions on this topic, see previous note.

70 Russell R. Menard, 'The Africanization of the Lowcountry Labor Force', in Winthrop D. Jordan and Sheila L. Skemp (eds.), *Race and Family in the Colonial South* (Jackson, Ms., 1987), pp. 81–108.

71 Littlefield, *Rice and Slaves*; see also Peter H. Wood, '"It Was a Negro Taught Them": A New Look at African Labor in South Carolina', *Journal of Asian and African Studies* 9 (1974), pp. 160–9: Judith A. Carney, 'From Hands to Tutors: African Expertise in the South Carolina Rice Economy', *AH* 67 (Summer 1993), pp. 1–30.

72 On the Loango trade, see David Richardson, 'Slave Exports from West Africa and West-Central Africa, 1700–1810: New Estimates of Volume and Distribution', *Journal of African History* 30 (1989), pp. 19–20 [hereafter *JAH*]; Phyllis M. Martin, *The External Trade of the Loango Coast, 1576–1870: The Effects of the Changing Commercial Relations on the Vili Kingdom of Loango* (Oxford, 1972), pp. 73–92: Miller, *Way of Death*, pp. 549–51.

73 Entries of Negroes, 29 September 1738 to 29 September 1739, Records of the Public Treasurer, South Carolina Department of Archives and History [hereafter SCDAH]; see also Shipping Returns, CO5/511, PRO. John Thornton, however, has raised questions about the provenance of slaves labelled 'Angolan', arguing that the Portuguese in Angola traded primarily with Brazilian rather than English merchants. These slaves came instead from the kingdom of Kongo whose merchants traded with the English-based Royal African Company at Kabinda, near the mouth of the Zaire River. See Thornton, 'African Dimensions', 1104; K.G. Davies, *The Royal African Company* (New York, 1970), p. 231.

74 Richardson, 'British Slave Trade to Colonial South Carolina', p. 133.

75 See David Geggus, 'Sex Ratio, Age and Ethnicity in the Atlantic Slave Trade: Data From French Shipping and Plantation Records', *JAH* 30 (1989), p. 25. Although he looks primarily at the French trade, Geggus does draw some broad conclusions for the entire Atlantic commerce. With some qualification, these findings are generally supported by Paul Lovejoy who notes, throughout the course of the Atlantic trade, 'that 64.4% of the slaves were male and 35.6% were female'. See Paul Lovejoy. 'The Impact of the Atlantic Slave Trade on Africa: A Review of the Literature', ibid., p. 381.

76 On charter groups, see T.H. Breen, 'Creative Adaptations: Peoples and Cultures', in Jack P. Greene and J.R. Pole (eds.), *Colonial British America: Essays in the New History of the Early Modern Era* (Baltimore, 1984), pp. 195–232.

77 Mintz and Price, *Birth of African-American Culture*, p. 50.

78 Jan Vansina, *Kingdoms of the Savanna* (Madison, 1968), pp. 60–1, 151–2; Anne Hilton. 'European Sources for the Study of Religious Change in Sixteenth and Seventeenth Century Kongo', *Paideuma: Mineilungen zur Kulturkunde*, 33 (1987), pp. 289–312; John Thornton, 'The Development of an African Catholic Church in the Kingdom of the Kongo, 1491–1750', *JAH* 25 (1984), pp. 147–67.

79 Martin, *External Trade of the Loango Coast*, pp. 73–92; Davies, *Royal African Company*, pp. 231–2.

80 Lovejoy, 'Impact of the Atlantic Slave Trade on Africa', p. 382; see also Geggus, 'Sex Ratio, Age and Ethnicity', pp. 36–43.

81 See Paul Lovejoy, *Transformations in Slavery: A History of Slavery in Africa* (New York, 1983), pp. 68–96; John Thornton. 'African Soldiers in the Haitian Revolution', *Journal of Caribbean History* 25 (1993), pp. 58–80; idem., 'The Art of War in Angola, 1575–1680', *Comparative Studies in Society and History* 30 (April 1988), pp. 360–78.

82 James Glen, *A Description of South Carolina* in Carroll (ed.), *Historical Collections*, 2, p. 201.

83 See Joyee E. Chaplin, *An Anxious Pursuit: Agricultural Innovation and Modernity in the Lower South, 1730–1815* (Chapel Hill, 1993), pp. 37–8, 227–76; Coclanis, *Shadow of A Dream*, pp. 48–110; McCusker and Menard, *Economy of British America*, pp. 169–88.

84 *American Husbandry* (ed.), Harry Carmen (London, 1775; reprint, New York, 1939), p. 275. See also Series Z, pp. 481–5, 486–92, and 493–9 in U.S. Bureau of the Census, *Historical Statistics of the United States: Colonial Times to 1970*, 2 vols. (Washington, DC, 1975), 2, pp. 1192–3; James M. Clifton, 'The Rice Trade in Colonial America', *AH* 55 (July 1981), pp. 266–83; Henry C. Dethloff, 'The Colonial Rice Trade', ibid., 56 (January 1982), pp. 231–43; David O. Whitten, 'American Rice Cultivation, 1680–1980: A Tercentary Critique', *Southern Studies* 21 (Spring 1982), pp. 5–26.

85 Coclanis, *Shadow Of A Dream*, p. 64.

86 Wood, *Black Majority*, pp. 35–62; Littlefield, *Rice and Slaves*; Carney, 'From Hands to Tutors'; for an anthropological study of rice cultivation in southwestern Senegal, see Marc R. Schloss, *The Hatchet's Blood: Separation, Power and Gender in Ehing Social Life* (Tucson, 1988).

87 On rice production in Atlantic Africa, see Littlefield, *Rice and Slaves*, pp. 74–114; see also Wood, '"It was a Negro Taught Them": A New Look at Labor in Early South Carolina'.

88 Nicholas Owens, *Journal of A Slave Dealer* (ed.), Eveline Martin (London, 1930), p. 52; see also Brooks, *Landlords and Strangers*, pp. 282–319; Carol MacCormack. 'Wono: Institutionalized Dependence in Sherbro Descent Groups', in Suzanne Miers and Igor Kopytoff (eds.), *Slavery in Africa: Historical and Anthropological Perspectives* (Madison, 1977), pp. 181–204.

89   Captain Samuel Gamble, *A Journal of a Voyage from London to Africa in the Sandown* [1793–1794], Log M121. National Maritime Museum, Greenwich, London; see also Littlefield, *Rice and Slaves*, pp. 93–5; Carney, 'From Hands to Tutors', pp. 14–15.

90   Winterbottom, *Account of the Native Africans in the Neighbourhood of Sierra Leone* I: 145; see also John Matthews, *Voyage to the River Sierra Leone* (London, 1788), p. 56. In a 1620 account, there is some discussion of men working in the fields for a very limited time, helping with village and harvest, see Jobson, *The Golden Trade*, p. 49. Most travellers' accounts, however, describe women as the primary field workers.

91   Pigafetta, *Report on the Kingdom of Congo*, p. 67; Miller, *Way of Death*, p. 417.

92   Nairne, *Letter from South Carolina*, p. 59; Klaus G. Loewold, *et al.* (eds.), 'Johann Martin Bolzius Answers A Questionnaire on Carolina and Georgia', *WMQ* 3rd. ser., 14 (April 1957), p. 258. On the role of slave women and men in rice production, see Thomas Porcher Plantation Diary, Stoney Porcher Papers, Southern Historical Collection. University of North Carolina. Chapel Hill: 'Observations on the Culture of Rice', William Rutler Papers, Southern Historical Collection; List of Negroes. Charles Cotesworth Pinckney Papers, Duke University.

93   See Mintz and Price, *Birth of African-American Culture*.

94   See Scott, *Weapons of the Weak*, p. 43; Frances Fox Piven and Richard A. Cloward, *Poor People's Movements: Why They Succeed, How They Fail* (New York, 1977), p. 20.

95   Jan Rogozinski, *A Brief History of the Caribbean: From the Arawak and the Carib to the Present* (New York, 1992), p. 158.

96   'Extract of a Letter from South Carolina, August 20, 1730', in the *Pennsylvania Gazette*, 5 November 1730; Creel, '*A Peculiar People*', p. 114.

97   Cited in Walter J. Fraser, Jr., *Charleston! Charleston!: The History of A Southern City* (Columbia, 1989), p. 53.

98   David J. Weber, *The Spanish Frontier in North America* (New Haven, 1992), p. 179; see also Crane, *Southern Frontier*; Jane Landers, 'Gracia Real de Santa Teresa de Mose: A Free Black Town in Spanish Colonial Florida', *American Historical Review* 95 (February 1990), pp. 9–30.

99   Captain Digby Dent to Secretary of State, 30 March 1737, Original Correspondence. Secretary of State, CO5/384, PRO: see also John Jay TePaske, *The Governorship of Spanish Florida, 1700–1763* (Durham, 1964), pp. 139–40.

100 On the war itself, see Larry E. Ivers, *British Drums Along the Southern Frontier: The Military Colonization of Georgia* (Chapel Hill, 1974), pp. 90–150.

101 See Landers, 'Gracia Real de Santa Teresa de Mose', p. 14. A cedual (order-in-council) issued by the Spanish crown proclaimed that all runaways, male and female, who made it to Florida could obtain their freedom once they pledged alliegence to the Catholic church, see John J. Te Paske, 'The Fugitive Slave: Intercolonial Rivalry and Spanish Slave Policy, 1687–1764', in Samuel Procter (ed.), *Eighteenth-Century Florida and Its Borderlands* (Gainesville, Fla., 1975), pp. 1–12; on the Davis case, see 19 January 1738, *JCHA, 1736–1739*, p. 596.

102 See Landers, 'Gracia Real de Santa Teresa de Mose', pp. 23–9; see also Kathleen Deagan, *Spanish St. Augustine: The Archaeology of a Colonial Creole Community* (New York, 1983).

103 Candler, 'Account of the Negroe Insurrection', pp. 232–3.

104 Landers, 'Gracia Real de Santa Teresa de Mose', p. 19. That slaves knew of the Spanish emancipation proclamation is strongly suggested in 'An Account of the Negroe Insurrection in South Carolina', in Candler (ed.), *CRG*, 22: pp. 104, 232.

105 Wood, *Black Majority*, p. 239.

106 17 January 1739, *JCHA, 1736–1739*, p. 591.

107 2 April 1739, *JCHA, 1736–1739*, p. 70; 9 February 1739 in Candler (ed.), 'Journal of William Stephens', p. 277.

108 See Wood, *Black Majority*, pp. 239 70; Philip D. Morgan, 'Colonial South Carolina Runaways: Their Significance for Slave Culture', *Slavery and Abolition* 6 (December 1985), p. 57; see also Daniel Meaders, 'South Carolina Fugitives as Viewed Through Local Colonial Newspapers, 1732–1801', *Journal of Negro History* (April 1975), pp. 288–319. The data presented below was drawn from the *South Carolina Gazette* from February 1732

until September 1739. Using D-Base 3, I entered 253 cases, categorizing them by name, sex, date, age, place of birth, residence, owner, skin colour, method of escape, number in escape, goods stolen, destination, skill, mode of transportation and language abilities. See Edward A. Pearson. 'From Stono to Vesey: Slavery, Resistance and Ideology in South Carolina' (Ph.D. dissertation, University of Wisconsin, 1992), pp. 110–14.

109   Michael Johnson has noted that 'the typical runaway was a young man who absconded alone', see Johnson, 'Runaway Slaves and the Slave Communities in South Carolina, 1799 to 1830', *WMQ* 3rd. ser., 38 (July 1981), p. 418; Daniel E. Meaders supports this conclusion, noting that 'the average runaway was male, single, between the ages of eighteen and thirty', see Meaders, 'South Carolina Fugitives as Viewed Through Local Colonial Newspapers with an Emphasis on Runaway Notices, 1732–1801', *Journal of Negro History* 60 (Fall 1975), p. 292.

110   On this topic, see Mullin, *Flight and Rebellion.*

111   In his study of slave resistance in eighteenth-century Virginia, Gerald Mullin argues that 'accumulation – the changes by which African customs fell away as he acquired English and occupational specialization – ultimately created slaves who were able to challenge the security of the society itself.' See ibid., p. 161.

112   John Thornton has suggested that the rebels may have come from the Kongo, a kingdom that conducted its slave trade largely with the English-run Royal African Company, and not from Angola, whose traders sold slaves primarily to Portuguese merchants who shipped them directly to Brazil. The contemporary report, titled 'An Account of the Negroe Insurrection in South Carolina', that indicates the rebels to be 'some Angola Negroes' identifies them, Thornton argues, incorrectly. See Thornton, 'African Dimensions of the Stono Rebellion', 1103. On the relationship between the Angolan slave trade and Brazil, see Herbert S. Klein, *African Slavery in Latin American and the Caribbean* (New York, 1986), pp. 67–88; Katia M. de Queiros Mattoso. *To Be A Slave in Brazil, 1550–1888* (New Brunswick, 1986), pp. 7–32; Miller, *Way of Death.*

113   19–26 August 1737, Virginia *Gazette*; 4 October 1737, *JCHA, 1736–1739*, p. 330.

114   *South Carolina Gazette*, 5 October 1738; 24 August 1738 and 25 September 1738 in Candler (ed.), 'Journal of William Stephens', pp. 190, 423; see also John Duffy, 'Eighteenth-Century Health Conditions', *Journal of Southern History* 18 (August 1952), pp. 289–302.

115   Fraser, *Charleston! Charleston!*, pp. 64–5; Wood, *Black Majority*, p. 315.

116   Thomas Broughton to Lords Commissioners of Plantations, 6 February 1737, CO5/388, Original Correspondence, Secretary of State, CO5/388, PRO; see also *Pennsylvania Gazette*, 10 March 1737.

117   See Vincent Crapanzano, *Waiting: The Whites of South Africa* (New York, 1985), pp. 44–5; Guha, *Elementary Aspects of Peasant Insurgency*, p. 245.

118   'Governor Bull's Representation', in ibid., p. 260.

119   'Governor William Bull's Representation of the Colony, 1770', in Merrens (ed.), *Colonial South Carolina Scene*, p. 260.

120   A number of slaves who made this journey took various items with them, including blankets, tools and clothes.

121   See Scott, *Domination and the Arts of Resistance*, pp. 166–82; for further discussions of practices of inversion in a European setting, see Natalie Zemon Davis, *Society and Culture in Early Modern France* (Stanford, 1975), pp. 92–123; Emmanuel Le Roy Ladurie, *Carnival in Romans: A People's Uprising at Romans, 1579–1580* (New York, 1979).

122   *South Carolina Gazette*, 6 April 1734. On this practice, see Wood, *Black Majority*, pp. 283–4.

123   *South Carolina Gazette*, 5 April 1739.

124   Ibid., 22 January 1732.

125   Robin Law, '"My Head Belongs to the King": On the Political and Ritual Significance of Decapitation in Pre-Colonial Dahomey', *JAH* 30 (1989), pp. 399–415.

126   Law, *The Slave Coast of West Africa*, pp. 97–8; Thomas Phillips, *A Journal of the Voyage made in the Hannibal of London, Ann. 1693, 1694*, in Awnsham Churchill and John Churchill (eds.), *Collection of Voyages and Travels* (London, 1732), 6, p. 220, cited in Law, *Slave Coast*, p. 97.

127 Candler (ed.), 'Negroe Insurrection', p. 232.
128 Ibid., p. 235.
129 29 November 1739, *JCHA, 1739–1741*, pp. 50–1, 64–5.
130 28 November 1739, in ibid., p. 63.
131 29 November 1739, in ibid., p. 65.
132 29 November 1739, in ibid., pp. 64–5.
133 Candler (ed.), 'Negroe Insurrection', p. 234.
134 Ibid.
135 On the aftermath of the rebellion, see Wax. '"The Great Risque We Run"'; Wood, *Black Majority*, pp. 320–6.
136 Thornton, 'African Dimensions of the Stono Rebellion', pp. 1101–13; idem., 'The Art of War in Angola, 1575–1680', *Comparative Studies in Society and History* 30 (April 1988), pp. 360–78.
137 Pigafetta, *A Report on the Kingdom of Congo*, p. 35.
138 Vincent Harding, *There is A River: The Black Struggle for Freedom in America* (New York, 1981), p. 35.
139 Lt.-Gov. William Bull to Board of Trade, 5 October 1739, CO5/367, PRO.
140 Hewatt, *Historical Progress* in Carroll (ed.), *Historical Collections*, 1, p. 332.
141 Report of the Committee to Enquire into the Causes and Disappointment of the Late Expedition to St. Augustine [July 1741], in *Assembly Journal*, 1741–1742, p. 83.
142 'A Ranger's Report of Travels with General Oglethorpe', in Newton Mereness (ed.), *Travels in the American Colonies* (New York, 1916), p. 222.
143 Ibid., p. 223.
144 1 July 1741, *JCHA, 1739–1741*, pp. 83–4; Mereness (ed.), *Travels in the American Colonies*, 'A Ranger's Report', p. 223.
145 21 November 1739, *JCHA, 1739–1741*, p. 37.
146 Report of the Committee to Enquire into the Causes and Disappointment of the Late Expedition to St. Augustine', *JCHA, 1741–1742*, pp. 83–4.

Chapter 27

Gad Heuman

RUNAWAY SLAVES IN NINETEENTH-CENTURY BARBADOS

I

RUNAWAY SLAVES IN nineteenth-century Barbados were a significant aspect of the slave society. Little research has thus far been done on runaways in Barbados, in part because it is surprising that slaves managed to run away at all. Barbadian slaves did not have the possibilities of *grand marronage* which Richard Price, Silvia de Groot, and others have documented for Jamaica and Surinam.[1] By the nineteenth century, there was no scope for the establishment of communities of runaways. Barbados was a relatively small and settled colony; the forests and caves which may have helped earlier generations of slaves to escape no longer existed. In addition, the proportionately high ratio of whites to blacks which characterised Barbados must have made running away a distinctly difficult enterprise.

Yet the slave advertisements in the Barbadian press indicate that running away was hardly uncommon. It is impossible to quantify precisely the numbers of such slaves; but scarcely an issue of a Barbadian newspaper in the first two decades of the nineteenth century is without an advertisement for a runaway slave or a report of a slave being discovered or lodged in gaol.

Whatever their numbers, Barbadian runaways did not generally pose a threat to the slave system. Yet running away was a form of resistance to their enslavement. At the very least, it was a denial of labour to a particular master. At the other extreme, running away was an attempt to escape the system altogether. We therefore need to know about runaways – who they were, where they went, and who harboured them. But the evidence on running away is not just important in describing individuals; it is also suggestive about the nature of slavery in Barbados during this period. This paper will seek to address both points: the runaways themselves and some of the wider issues which they raise.

II

The statistical evidence on runaways was collected from advertisements in the Barbadian press at roughly five-year intervals from 1805 to 1830. As certain runs of newspapers were unavailable in the Barbados Archives, the years included in the

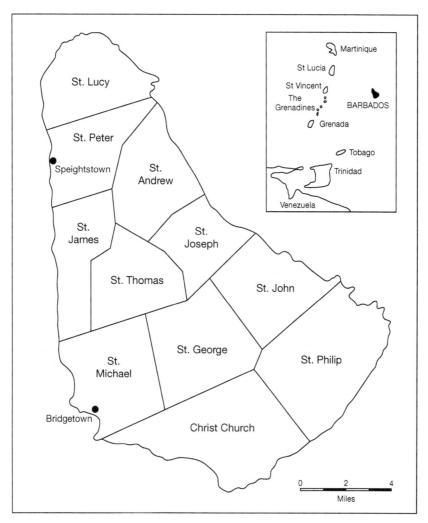

Map 27.1   Barbados parish boundaries
Source: Jerome S. Handler

survey were 1805, 1810, 1815, 1819, 1824 and 1830. Two newspapers, *The Barbados Mercury and Bridgetown Gazette* and *The Barbadian*, were the sources of the advertisements. Where it was possible, the press was also examined for other years during this period for general information on the runaways. The statistical material was coded and run through a computer, using the programme, SPSS.[2]

There are obvious hazards in using data of this kind. The information is often sketchy. It is usually possible to ascertain the name, the sex, and the date first advertised of any slave. Colour, country of birth, occupation, and age are to varying degrees less available. For the years after 1817, it was possible to examine the Slave Registers for additional data, especially for the slaves' occupation, colour, and age.[3] But this only added significant material for 1819. The most revealing information in the advertisements was often the description of the slaves rather than their age or sex; in many cases, however, there were no such data at all.

Other problems also arose with the material. In some cases, the country of birth was cited, especially when the slave was African. When this information was not cited, it was assumed that the slave was Barbadian. The evidence of origin in the Slave Registers reinforced this supposition. A more insoluble problem concerns the length of absence of any slave. All that is generally known is the elapsed time of the advertisements, although in some cases, the owner indicated the period the slave had already been away before the advertisement appeared in the press. The time that advertised slaves were away is therefore seriously understated, although the data do provide an indication of this important variable. As in the case of the Jamaican material, slaves who were caught had rarely been sought in advertisements, thus making it impossible to make use of this information to ascertain length of absence.[4] It is also likely that owners would have been more eager to get back their most valuable slaves; as a result, the sample includes more skilled and elite slaves than in the general population of runaways.

It could be argued that the descriptive material in the advertisements is itself not very reliable. In many cases, owners were guessing where their runaway slaves might be. Information must also have come from other slaves, some of whom may have sought to mislead their masters. Yet, as Michael Mullin has suggested, this data was unbiased; it was not intended for use by propagandists, let alone historians. With all its faults, the evidence from slave advertisements may therefore be 'more appropriate for the study of a people who could not or were not inclined to write things down'.[5]

The sample consisted of 368 slaves, a large proportion of whom were male (see Table 27.1).[6] Since the sex ratio of the Barbadian slave population had become balanced by the early nineteenth century, it is clear that males were disproportionately represented among the cohort of runaways. Similarly, creoles (who were slaves born on the island) made up the overwhelming majority of runaways. For those slaves for whom there are data on origins, over 90 per cent were creole while about 9 per cent were African. These figures are not very different from the proportions of creoles and Africans in the slave population generally in 1817; if anything, the proportion of African runaways is slightly larger than in the general population (see Table 27.1).

Most of the runaways were relatively young, if young is defined to include those under 30 years of age. Nearly three-fourths of all runaways were in this age-range. When the age ranges were broken down by sex, it was found that, male and female runaways were represented roughly in proportion to their respective percentages in the overall sample of runaways.

Not surprisingly, the percentage of coloured runaways was high:[7] 53 per cent of slaves for whom there is such evidence were of mixed colour while 47 per cent were black (see Table 27.1). Since the percentage of brown slaves in the Barbadian slave population was about 15, the large proportion of coloured runaways is immediately evident.[8]

The data for Jamaica provide an interesting contrast with some of these figures. While the male/female ratios in the Jamaican case are roughly similar to those of Barbados, the origins of the runaway slaves in the two colonies differ widely. Pat Bishop calculated that nearly 70 per cent of runaways in Jamaica had been born in Africa. Allowing for the longer time span of her study and the greater proportion

Table 27.1   Runaways in the slave population

	Runaways (%)	Total slave population (%)
Sex		
Males	63.5	45.6
Females	36.5	54.4
Nation		
African	9.2	7.1
Creole	90.8	92.9
Colour		
Black	46.8	85.1
Coloured	53.2	14.9
Population	360	77,493

Sources: B. W. Higman, *Slave Populations of the British Caribbean, 1807–1834* (Baltimore, 1984), pp. 413, 116; Sample Survey.

of Africans in the Jamaican slave population, the evidence nonetheless suggests very different origins for runaways in Jamaica and Barbados.[9]

Owners were often very clear about the type of slaves who escaped. They were generally creoles or behaved like creoles. For instance, Chloe was an African woman who had gone out to sell some glassware one day but had not been heard of since. Her owner, E. S. Bascom, could think of no reason for her disappearance; moreover, he noted that 'by her appearance and speech, she may be taken for a Barbadian'. Many slaves sought to pass as free people; this meant that they could usually act the part. Words like 'plausible' and 'artful' appear quite frequently in the advertisements to describe such slaves. Thomas 'is a very artful fellow, and may undertake to pass himself as a free man'.[10] The owner of the slave, Hamlet, put it another way: Hamlet 'has a [good] deal to say for himself, [and] may easily pass for a free man'. These were generally highly assimilated and often skilled slaves who could merge into the black and brown free community.

Skilled slaves were far more likely to escape. An analysis of 92 occupations listed in the advertisements reveals that the overwhelming number were skilled or semi-skilled. Just over 20 per cent were carpenters, 12 per cent sold goods of one kind or another, and nearly 9 per cent were tailors or domestic slaves. Other occupations represented in significant proportions included shoemakers, masons, and sailors; there were also smaller proportions of a wide range of other skilled workers. On the other hand, field slaves formed less than 5 per cent of this occupational cohort. The slave elite – and particularly the artisan elite – were therefore heavily represented in the occupations of the runaways, far more than their proportion of the total slave population.

A breakdown of the sex of the runaways for whom there are data on occupations is quite revealing. The only categories cited for female occupations were hucksters, house servants, and field slaves. Approximately three-fourths of those runaways who sold goods were women while just over 60 per cent of house servants were females. Only one-quarter of the runaway field slaves were females. In every other occupational category – most of which were skilled – no women were listed at all. The dominance of male runaways in the skilled occupations and in the slave elite reinforces what is known about the respective position of men and women in Caribbean slave society.

The colour of these slaves is also interesting. All of the field slaves were black as were three-fourths of the domestics. Women whose occupations are known were more likely to be black than brown. By virtue of their colour and their occupations, women generally would have had a more difficult time merging into the free community. The exception to this was runaway hucksters, nearly 70 per cent of whom were coloured.

As expected, most skilled runaways were coloureds: there were usually two skilled coloured to each one skilled black. This was the case for carpenters, cooks, masons, and tailors. Porters and fishermen violated this rule, as both categories included only blacks. Nearly all the runaway slaves for whom occupations were known were creoles: almost 95 per cent were in this category.

But where did the runaways go? In many cases, the owners did not know, but in a large number of instances, they were able to be quite specific about their slaves' possible destinations. One of the obvious places was a town, especially Bridgetown or Speightstown. For skilled slaves, towns probably offered greater possibilities of employment. The relatively large free black and brown communities there must have made it easier for a runaway to pass as a free person. Of those runaways whose destinations are known, more than a quarter of them were said to be in a town.

What is perhaps surprising is that a similar proportion – over 25 per cent of the runaways – found refuge in the country, presumably on other plantations. Roughly 6 per cent of runaways were either abroad or on a ship and a similar percentage were attempting to pass as free, most probably in a town. Owners knew nothing about the destination of another quarter of their slaves, and the remaining 8 per cent were thought to be employed either in a town or in the country. These categories clearly overlap, and many slaves were in more than one grouping. The figures suggest that running away to the country was a more significant destination than might have been expected.

It is also interesting to examine the destinations of slaves by sex. Table 27.2 demonstrates that more female runaways went to the country than to the town, while males favoured the towns. This correlates with earlier data about the occupations and colour of female and male runaways. Since the women were more likely to be in less skilled occupations than the men, female runaways seem to have escaped more frequently to the country where they may have had kin to harbour them. On the other hand, skilled males more often attempted to blend into the free urban community, looking for employment and trying to pass as free. Male runaways also sought to get abroad: 90 per cent of this cohort were male.

There are tantalising suggestions about slaves who fled abroad and who may have formed an earlier generation of 'boat-people'. In 1805, a slave was picked up in a boat by a Mr Todd near St Vincent. Since the runaway claimed to have a Barbadian master, Todd, who was from St Vincent, was prepared to have the slave returned on proof of ownership. Fourteen years later, a seaman slave named James Cuttery absconded from a mail boat. He stole a smaller boat, a bucket, and a sail and probably also headed for St Vincent. Cuttery had a good reason for getting to

Table 27.2   Destination of runaways by sex

	Town	Country	Pass as free	Abroad
No. M	68	55	17	10
%	71.6	60.4	77.3	90.9
No. F	27	36	5	1
%	28.4	39.6	22.7	9.1

Source: Sample Survey

St Vincent: he had formerly lived there. As the island was to the windward of Barbados, it is quite plausible that other slaves sought to escape in the same way.[11]

St Vincent was not the only foreign destination of Barbadian runaways. Nancy Efey was the mother of two mulatto children and perhaps therefore had a better chance of obtaining 'spurious papers'. Her owner reported that Nancy intended to go to Demerara, where she had a sister. Another owner thought that her slave, Jane Frances, would leave Barbados, but did not make any specific suggestions about where she might go. Jane 'endeavours to pass as a free woman, and, in all probability, will wish to quit the Island. All masters and owners of vessels are hereby cautioned not to take her off the Country, and other persons from harbouring or employing her'.[12]

This was a frequent warning, but it is unclear what effect it had. Jacob was a well known slave who worked on board English ships, and whose professional name was Samson. 'He went down the river on the 15th inst. on board the ship FAIRY, Capt. Francis, and has not since been heard of'.[13] Another slave, identified in the Slave Registers as John Maycock, was a 15-year-old butler. He seems to have 'imposed himself on the master of either the ship Constantine or Tiger, as a free man . . . [and] quitted the island'.[14] Ships' captains may have found it in their interest to have runaways on board. Runaways were potential extra hands, they could be sold at another port, or they could possibly pay for their passage. The constant warnings about the complicity of captains not only suggest that this was one of the possible escape routes for runaways but also that it was of considerable concern to Barbadian slaveholders.

Whether they fled abroad or remained in Barbados, runaway slaves seem to have been quite consistent in the month or the season they chose to escape (see Figure 27.1). Based on the month the owners first advertised for their runaways, the data reveal that slaves most frequently left in July and August. The least popular month for running away was February. One possible explanation for these various months, at least for plantation slaves, is related to the plantation cycle. Slaves may have escaped after the crop had been harvested in the early summer, partly because supervision was more lax or because the dead season meant fewer extra perks for slaves. Barry Higman's research adds weight to this view: he found that food supplies from the plantations as well as from the slaves' provision grounds were most stretched in this season. Since Barbadian slaves knew this time of year as the 'hungry-time' or 'hard-time', seasonal nutritional stress could have been an additional factor in increasing the number of runaways in July and August.[15] It is also important to note that owners may have been less concerned by slaves running away in the slow season. This view is supported by the unpopularity of February

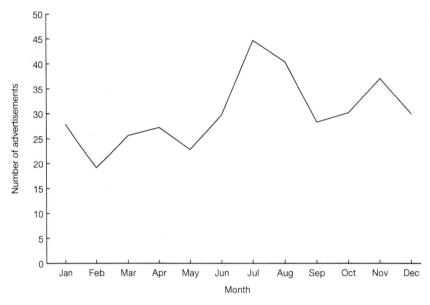

Figure 27.1   Runaways by month first advertised

as a time to escape; at that point, sugar was being harvested and the planters would have needed all their labour.

There are other data to support this interpretation. It is possible to examine the date each slave was first advertised and how long the advertisements continued. In this way, it can be shown in which months slaves were absent for the longest and the shortest periods of time. The analysis reveals that slaves were away for the greatest average time in December, January, and February and for the least number of days in August. July is in the middle range of this cohort. This evidence would suggest that planters may have been quite desperate to get back their labour for crop-time and therefore advertised heavily for their slaves during these winter months. Similarly, it adds weight to the belief that owners generally were less concerned about slaves' running away after the crop was over. Another possibility for the relative popularity of staying away during the winter months was the Christmas festivities and the importance of slave families and friends being together then. It may also be that slaves may have sought to avoid returning to the most difficult work of all: harvesting the crop.

Data on the slaves' length of absence are revealing in other areas as well, especially if the time elapsed is broken down into the following categories: short (under two weeks), medium (two weeks to three months), and long (over three months). In this case, a slightly higher proportion of female runaways is among the short stayers than their proportion in the overall runaway sample. Male runaways were more heavily represented in the medium and long categories. These figures reinforce the possibility that women may have escaped more often for relatively short periods to visit family or friends. On the other hand, males were more likely to have escaped for longer periods – seeking more frequently, as we have seen, to merge into the free community or to escape abroad. The data may also reflect the differential importance owners placed on male and female runaways. Males were usually more valuable economically, and this may have been reflected in the number of advertisements placed for them.

Other categories for the elapsed time slaves were gone are perhaps more predictable. The average figure for creoles' length of absence was twice as high as for Africans and that for coloured three times the figure for blacks. Slaves aged between 18 and 29 years of age were away considerably longer than those in the younger and older age ranges. According to the data, slaves over 40 were gone the least amount of time. For those slaves whose occupations are known, field slaves were away for among the shortest periods of time, while domestics and shoemakers were gone for twice the average of this occupational cohort. Carpenters, fishermen, hucksters, and tailors were all near the average length of absence. Again, it is clear that runaways who were creole, coloured, and skilled had a far greater chance of escaping for a longer duration than those who were African, black, and unskilled.

The evidence also suggests that the overwhelming majority of slaves were gone for a relatively short time. Nearly 65 per cent of runaways were in this category. It would be fair to assume that many of these slaves had left their owners temporarily and intended to return. But what of the 35 per cent of slave runaways who were gone for a longer period, and within that grouping, the 8 per cent who had escaped for at least three months?

It may be instructive to examine some cases of slaves who stayed away for a very long time, even within the confines of Barbados. One of the most striking examples involved a slave named Johnny Beckles, who was caught in 1805 on the Pool Plantation in St John. Beckles was about 45 years old, and the man who discovered him reported that 'from the best information I can collect, [Beckles] has been living in the Pool Negro-yard for many years before the storm of 1780'. This would mean that Beckles had run away at least 25 years previously. Another long-term runaway was a shoemaker named Sam, who was about 20 years old. Sam had been harboured by his father 'for nearly 16 years when by accident he was discovered to be a slave; and it was fairly proved that he was stolen by his parents when the mother was leased on Haymond's Plantation, and he a child'. For all those years, Sam had successfully passed as free, but was now possibly harboured with his mother.[16]

An even more curious case involved an African man named Buffy, who was discovered at Lancaster Plantation in St James in 1806. According to Buffy, his owner was a Frenchman in Jamaica who had died about six years previously. At that point and somewhat mysteriously, Buffy 'came over as a cook on board a vessel, and . . . has remained on the island ever since'. The advertiser pointed out that Buffy spoke broken English 'but plain enough to be understood by any person' and 'has his country marks on both cheeks'.[17] Buffy was hardly an assimilated slave, although he did have a profession. Yet he had been able to live for six years in Barbados before being discovered as a slave.

Even an unacculturated African slave was able to escape for nearly two months. Betsy 'can speak little or no English, having been purchased from a Guinea ship about 10 months ago'. The first advertisement for her appeared on 5 October 1805 and she was not caught until 23 November of that year. This is one of the few cases where an advertised slave was caught and for whom there was an additional advertisement. Betsy's experience suggests that slaves appearing in the advertisements were probably away a minimum of two months and perhaps longer.[18]

Table 27.3   Number of runaways advertised and their mean number of days gone by year

	1805	1810	1815	1819	1824	1830
No. runaways advertised	101	91	105	48	6	12
Mean length of stay in days	32.3	10	52	41	18	?

Source: Sample Survey

One of the interesting questions to ask is whether the pattern of running away altered in any way during the period 1805 to 1830. It is immediately clear that the highest number of advertisements, 105, appeared in 1815, with 101 advertisements in 1805 and 91 in 1810 (see Table 27.3). There were far fewer advertisements in the years after 1815. Although it is not possible to account for the significant drop in the number of advertisements after 1815, one of the consequences of the 1816 slave rebellion may have been an alteration in the system of dealing with runaways. The law may have changed, or the apprehension of slaves may have become more rigorous. It seems unlikely that the actual number of runaways would have dropped significantly in the period after the rebellion.

The year 1815 did not just experience the largest number of advertisements; it also witnessed the highest average length of stay for runaways, apart from 1830 which was distorted statistically (see Table 27.3). When absence is examined as previously by short, medium, and long stays, 1815 is the year with the largest number of slaves who were absent for the longest period of time. The destination of runaways in 1815 is also suggestive: far more than the statistical average went to the country than to the towns. Nearly 43 per cent of all the slaves escaping to the country in the sample went there in 1815, contrasted with only 31 per cent of slaves going to the towns. The 1816 Rebellion was not an urban phenomenon: it broke out in St Philip. The evidence about the number of runaways in 1815, their length of stay, and their destinations points to the conclusion that runaways were not simply merging into the free community or temporarily visiting kin. Although runaways did not normally pose a threat to the system, they apparently could do so. It would be unwise to correlate runaways with rebellion; however, the increase in the number of runaways in 1815 may have been symptomatic of the heightened tension in Barbados which ultimately resulted in the 1816 Rebellion.[19]

Owners were very aware of the dangers posed by runaways. The year after Bussa's Rebellion in 1816, the master of a female slave named Massey sought to warn planters about runaways generally and his escaped slave in particular. Massey probably had a forged pass and was working as a laundress. Her owner believed that 'gentleman proprietors and managers are not aware of the evil in suffering absent slaves about their property, as they certainly will imbibe pernicious maxims, and afterwards afford a ready asylum to such of their slaves as may abscond'.[20] One problem, then, was the potential example of successful runaways. But there were also more serious cases to worry about.

Appea was a tall, 50-year-old man with a

> surly countenance, has several scars about his head occasioned by fighting, and a piece off one of his ears, bit out by the same cause; he has been absent upwards of 12 months, and has eluded every vigilant attempt to take him. He is perhaps one of the most notorious villains the Country ever possessed; and a dangerous person to be at large amongst Plantation Negroes.

Yet this dangerous runaway – whose advertisement appeared in the middle of 1815 – was able to survive by 'drawing the figure of negroes on paper, by which means he gets a subsistence, going from one Estate to another; although he seldom stays long on any'.[21]

A final example reveals the potential danger of trying to arrest runaways as well as an important aspect of the system of apprehending escaped slaves. In October, 1815, the driver of Mount Wilton Plantation, Primus, was sent to search for a runaway and given a pass for ten days. 'Primus not returning home since, though invited to do so through his connections, it became necessary to seek him; he has a Wife at Mr. Searles' in St. Joseph'. The owner of Primus, Reynold Ellcock, hired Frank, the ranger of Pickering Plantation, and two other men in January 1816 to find the runaways.

> As they were returning at midnight, on Saturday the 20th instant, without finding the Runaways, they were suddenly attacked in the public road, not far from the buildings at Mount Wilton, and Frank, who seemed to be the sole object of their vengeance, was barbarously murdered by 5 or 6 men who had concealed themselves in a corn-field near the road. The subscriber offers a reward of £25 to any person or persons who will give evidence to convict the perpetrators of this horrid murder, it being natural to suppose Prince [the first runaway] and Primus had gotten notice of this search, and had waylaid the men sent after them.[22]

This murder followed a particularly difficult year in Barbados. Michael Craton has documented the economic problems as well as the political ferment in the island in 1815 over the act for slave registration.[23] These developments may have given Primus as well as Appea more determination to flee in the first instance and subsequently to resist arrest.

One other interesting point is worth noting about this case. Primus had been sent out to catch a runaway and then Frank had been sent to get him. Indeed, the system depended on drivers and other elite slaves helping to apprehend escaped slaves. But slaves often used this system to their own advantage: when running away themselves and when challenged, they claimed to be searching for escaped slaves.

Like many slaves, Primus had run away to kin; in his case, it was to his wife. More than twice as many slaves in the sample were supposedly harboured by family as by non-family members. While a significant proportion of runaways were harboured either by a wife or by a husband, it is interesting that a greater percentage of this cohort were thought to be with their parents. Siblings played a slightly lesser role than husbands and wives, but they too were not insignificant.

If these data are examined by length of absence, parents emerge as the kin who harboured runaways for the longest average time. Parents are above the mean time for the cohort of all families as harbourers (28 days) as are husbands, while wives are just below this figure. Siblings, grandparents and children are well below the mean figure for families generally.

Families were an obvious destination for runaways. But the evidence goes further than this: it points to the strength of family ties and to that of the extended family. Betty Beck was a mulatto slave who was 'supposed to be harboured in the Plantation of Richard Cobham, Esq called Stepney, where she was born, and many of her family belong'. Jack Charles was also well connected: he had numerous family in St Philip, St George and St Michael. His owner knew that Jack had already spent time with his wife in St Philip, but there was a mother and an uncle to worry about as well. Families not only hid their escaped kin; they sometimes put them to work. Bob was a carpenter who had 'been seen at work with his father, by the name of Johnny Gittens, living in Milk Market'. Bob's sister also lived in the same district.[24]

The data are also suggestive in other ways about the family relationships of escaped slaves. Nearly a third of all the slaves who were harboured by wives had more than one of them; in several cases, owners mentioned three wives for their runaways. It is also interesting that the harbouring family members were not necessarily all slaves; many slaves had free kin. Clarissa, who was about 20 years old, had a free black mother 'living under the green trees in the Roebuck; and her father a black man belonging to James Holligan, Esq. called Mingo – by either of whom it is supposed she may be harboured'. It was obviously a considerable help to have free kin: Sanco 'passes as a free man, having family of that description in town'. Mimbah was doing even better. She had been a retailer of dry goods and had a house where she lived with her free black husband.[25] These harbourers suggest a complex pattern of relationships. They provide evidence of the existence of the slave family and should redirect efforts to examine the intricate and connected world of slave and free people.

Many slaves were not harboured by kin, but by friends, by employers, or by the soldiers of the West India Regiment. Judged by the length of their absence, those runaways harboured by non-family may have been able to stay away longer than those hidden by families. In part, this was because of the relative success of the runaways harboured by whites.

Although there were not many slaves in this cohort, planters were concerned about the implications of whites harbouring runaways. Sarah Jane was thought to be harboured by her mother 'or by some evil-disposed white person or other in behalf of her mother'. April 'had been harboured at [Codrington] College and at a white man's house' in St John, although on a previous escape, he had been hidden by slaves. More important was the type of advertisement for Jacob: 'a further £10 to any person who will give information of any free subject who has employed him'.[26] The implication here is that whites may have often hired runaways; alternatively, that escaped slaves may have sought particular whites as employers. These slaves were not threatening the slave system generally but were making choices about their owners. White collusion with runaway slaves was not uncommon elsewhere as well; discussing runaways in the United States, Mullin concluded that a large number of runaway slaves were successful 'because for a variety of reasons, many whites who "harboured" them were willing to challenge the slave code at its weakest point'.[27]

It was not only whites who employed runaways; slaves did so as well. Ceafor was a mason who was 'supposed to be harboured by black masons employed upon the King's Works'. Another escaped slave named James was a fisherman who had lost his right leg and used crutches; nonetheless, he was thought 'to be employed and harboured by some of the fishermen about Fontabelle, particularly by a man belonging to Isaac Green'.[28] Slaves working for other slaves are indicative of a more elaborate structure of employment and harbouring than has previously been recognised.

Slaves were also harboured in and around the Castle, the home of the West India Regiment. Runaways could more easily pass as free among the black soldiers and among the free community which served them. There were some amusing cases in this group. For instance, Marissa 'had been repeatedly seen at St. Ann's [the Castle], and was once taken from there, and rescued by some soldiers, before she could be delivered up to her owner'. This was despite her being 'remarkably stout'. Fortune had escaped once before as well and 'by virtue of a certificate given by some evil-disposed person of his freedom, he enlisted in the black corps under the name of Thomas Panton, a native of Jamaica'. The Castle also offered a refuge for two Africans who had several countrymen there but who spoke little English.[29] For a variety of reasons, then, white West Indians may have been right to worry about the effects of free black soldiers on a slave society.[30]

III

It is clear from the evidence that the majority of advertised runaways were male, creole, coloured, and skilled slaves. Runaways escaped to the country as well as to the towns, with males apparently preferring the towns where they were more likely to pass as free men, gain employment, or try to get abroad. Women, on the other hand, opted more often for the country where they sought refuge among kin. Runaways more frequently chose to leave in the dead season, after the crop had been harvested. The majority seem to have stayed away a relatively short time, although a significant percentage of runaways were gone for over three months. There were also some prominent examples of slaves who managed to hide for several years, even within Barbados. More slaves in the sample left in 1815 than any other year and those slaves stayed away the longest period of time. This suggests a possible link to the 1816 slave rebellion and to the political ferment in Barbados in 1815. Slaves were harboured by both family and non-family; interestingly enough, whites as well as slaves were among the harbourers who hid and sometimes employed runaways. These are some of the conclusions of the study, but there are a number of other points worth emphasising.

On the one hand, it was sometimes in the masters' interest to allow slaves to run away. As we have seen, planters may well have regarded the July/August period as a more convenient time for slaves to be absent. Owners undoubtedly wanted to get rid of some of their runaways, and some runaways who were caught were apparently never claimed. Joe and William were two such runaways; they were arrested, put in gaol, and first advertised in January 1830. Almost a year later, they were still unclaimed and unsold.[31]

Other masters had specific reasons to get rid of their slaves. The owner of Nelly reported that she had escaped along with £104 worth of dry goods. He was prepared to 'dispose of her for £100, and her child, and give the goods into the bargain to the purchaser'. Another case involved Betty Phyllis: she 'was well known . . . to be the object who set on fire the bed and curtains of her former owner, Mrs. Griffith'. The owner of Ben reported he would probably try to pass as a free man and get employed, but she had clearly had enough and would 'be glad to dispose of the said Man'.[32]

On the other hand, there were many masters who were quite determined to get their slaves back. The owner of two runaways who were brothers offered the extraordinary reward of £50 for them. He also made it clear that 'if they will both or either of them return to their business of their own accord, I will freely pardon them, and inflict no kind of punishment upon them whatsoever, nor ask any questions where they may have been harboured'. John H. P. King was another anxious owner. His slave, Richard, had run away and was probably harboured by his father or mother. Richard's father had 'lately expressed a great wish that [Richard] be also sold to his present owners, the Messrs Cumberbatch'. However, King was not about to sell, 'it being the subscribers unalterable determination not to dispose of him'. King placed 16 advertisements in the press for Richard without apparent success.[33]

Richard's case suggests that some slaves ran away to put pressure on their owners to sell them. In some instances, masters promised that their runaways would be able to choose new owners on their return. Phill had run away, and was now offered for sale, but 'should he voluntarily return, the privilege of choosing an owner will be granted to him'. Similarly for Hamlet, 'if he will return of his own accord in 8 days from this date, he shall have a paper to look for another owner'. Or in the case of Charlotte, should she 'return home accompanied by a ready money purchaser, she will be pardoned, and sold reasonably'.[34]

Running away, then, could serve a variety of purposes. Some slaves managed to escape altogether; others used it to change their owners while most probably sought to make life more bearable for a while. In the process, runaways revealed the strength of family and personal ties in Barbadian slave society as well as the collusion of free people in their escape. While runaway slaves were clearly resisting aspects of the slave society, they were also testimony to 'the role of the powerless in affecting, and even controlling important parts of the lives of the masters'.[35]

Notes

1   Richard Price, ed., *Maroon Societies* (Garden City, N.Y., 1973) and Silvia W. de Groot, *From Isolation Towards Integration: The Surinam Maroons and their Descendants, 1845–1863* (The Hague, 1963). See also Alvin O. Thompson, 'Some Problems of Slave Desertion in Guayana, c. 1750–1814', Occasional Paper No. 4, *ISER* (1976) and David Barry Gaspar, 'Runaways in Seventeenth-Century Antigua, West Indies', *Boletin de Estudios Latinoamcricanos y del Caribe* 26 (June 1979): 3–13.
2   For a useful introduction, see Marija J. Norusis, *SPSS, An Introductory Guide* (New York, 1982).
3   T71/520–33; T71/540–46.
4   P.A. Bishop, 'Runaway Slaves in Jamaica, 1740–1807' (unpublished M.A. thesis, University of the West Indies, 1970), p. 151.

5   Gerald W. Mullin, *Flight and Rebellion: Slave Resistance in Eighteenth-Century Virginia* (London, 1972), p. x.

6   The statistical material in the paper is derived from the sample survey and from an SPSS analysis of this data.

7   *Coloured* is used here to mean slaves of mixed colour. Synonyms include browns and mulattoes.

8   B. W. Higman, *Slave Populations of the British Caribbean* (Baltimore, 1984), p. 116.

9   Bishop, 'Runaway Slaves', p. 22.

10 *The Barbados Mercury and Bridgetown Gazette* (hereafter BM): 4 March, 24 June 1817; 19 Aug. 1815.

11 BM: 8 June 1805; 6 Nov. 1819; see also Michael Craton, *Testing the Chains: Resistance to Slavery in the British West Indies* (Ithaca, 1982), p. 147.

12 BM: 6 April 1819; 14 Oct. 1817.

13 BM: 20 Aug. 1805.

14 T71/520, f. 456; T71/524, f. 271; BM, 24 April 1819.

15 Higman, *Slave Populations*, p. 215.

16 BM: 11 June 1805; 24 Oct. 1818.

17 BM: 19 July 1806.

18 BM: 5 Oct., 23 Nov. 1805.

19 For a further discussion of this argument, see Hilary Beckles, 'Emancipation by War or Law? Wilberforce and the 1816 Barbados Slave Rebellion' in David Richardson, ed., *Abolition and its Aftermath: The Historical Context 1790–1916* (London, 1985), pp. 80–104.

20 BM: 4 Oct. 1817.

21 BM: 15 July 1815.

22 BM: 27 Jan. 1816.

23 Craton, *Testing the Chains*, pp. 259–60.

24 BM: 30 Dec., 8 Aug. 1815; 19 Oct. 1805.

25 BM: 23 Feb. 1819; 3 June 1815; 17 Dec. 1805.

26 BM: 10 Nov. 1810; 21 Jan. 1815; 10 Nov. 1810.

27 Mullin, *Flight and Rebellion*, p. 106.

28 BM: 18 June 1805; 24 July 1816.

29 BM: 27 April, 16 Nov., 9 Nov. 1805.

30 For further information on these regiments, see Roger Norman Buckley, *Slaves in Red Coats: The British West India Regiments, 1795–1815* (New Haven, 1979).

31 *The Barbadian*: 19 Jan., 18 Dec. 1830.

32 BM: 9 Oct. 1810; 28 Nov. 1815; 24 Nov. 1810.

33 BM: 22 Dec. 1810; 6 Aug. 1805.

34 BM: 29 Nov. 1817; 1 Sept. 1810; 11 Feb. 1809.

35 Sidney W. Mintz and Richard Price, 'An Anthropological Approach to the Afro-American Past: A Caribbean Perspective', *ISHI Occasional Papers in Social Change* (1976), p. 16.

Chapter 28

Richard Price

MAROONS AND THEIR COMMUNITIES

WITH THE FLEET OF GOVERNOR OVANDO, bound for Hispaniola in 1502 to reinvigorate the faltering colony that Columbus had left behind the previous year, sailed "a few Negroes . . . brought out by their masters". Among them was the first Afro-American maroon, an anonymous slave who "escaped to the Indians" in the mountainous interior soon after setting foot in the New World. Today, some 470 years later, there still lives in Cuba a man named Esteban Montejo, who escaped from slavery in his youth and lived for years in the forests, and who must be the last surviving exemplar of this desperate yet surprisingly frequent reaction to slavery in the Americas—flight or *marronage*.

For more than four centuries, the communities formed by such runaways dotted the fringes of plantation America, from Brazil to the southeastern United States, from Peru to the American Southwest. Known variously as *palenques*, *quilombos*, *mocambos*, *cumbes*, *ladeiras*, or *mambises*, these new societies ranged from tiny bands that survived less than a year to powerful states encompassing thousands of members and surviving for generations or even centuries. Today their descendants still form semi-independent enclaves in several parts of the hemisphere, remaining fiercely proud of their maroon origins and, in some cases at least, faithful to unique cultural traditions that were forged during the earliest days of Afro-American history.[1]

During the past several decades, historical scholarship has done much to dispel the myth of the "docile slave." The extent of violent resistance to enslavement has been documented rather fully—from the revolts in the slave factories of West Africa and mutinies during the Middle Passage to the organized rebellions that began to sweep most colonies within a decade after the arrival of the first slave ships. And we are finally beginning to appreciate the remarkable pervasiveness of various forms of "day to day" resistance—from simple malingering to subtle but systematic acts of sabotage. Flight or *marronage*, however, has received much less attention, at least from North American scholars—in part no doubt because so much of the relevant data are in languages other than English but also because publications on maroons and their communities have so often been couched in what Curtin has called the "parochial tradition of ethnocentric national history."

Yet maroons and their communities can be seen to hold a special significance for the study of slave societies. For while they were, from one perspective, the antithesis of all that slavery stood for, they were at the same time everywhere an embarrassingly visible part of these systems. Just as the very nature of plantation slavery implied violence and resistance, the wilderness setting of early New World plantations made *marronage* and the existence of organized maroon communities a ubiquitous reality. Throughout Afro-America, such communities stood out as an heroic challenge to white authority, and as the living proof of the existence of a slave consciousness that refused to be limited by the whites' conception or manipulation of it.

From a European perspective, *marronage* appeared to be "the chronic plague" of New World plantation societies. Within the first decade of most colonies' existence, the most brutal punishments had already been reserved for recaptured runaways, and in many cases these were quickly written into law. An early eighteenth-century visitor to Surinam reported that

> if a slave runs away into the forest in order to avoid work for a few weeks, upon his being captured his Achilles tendon is removed for the first offence, while for a second offence . . . his right leg is amputated in order to stop his running away; I myself was a witness to slaves being punished this way.

And similar punishments for *marronage*—from castration to being slowly roasted to death—are reported from many different regions.

Yet *marronage* did not have the same meaning in all colonies at all times. As long as the numbers of slaves who took to the hills remained small, only the least skilled slaves were involved, and they did not interfere directly with plantation life, the maroons' existence might be tolerated or largely ignored, as Debien suggests for some of the French islands. Moreover, throughout the Americas, planters seem to have accepted as part of the system the common practice of *petit marronage*—repetitive or periodic truancy with temporary goals such as visiting a relative or lover on a neighboring plantation. For example, temporary flight of this type was clearly an everyday part of plantation life in the southern United States; the pattern is vividly brought to life in several of Faulkner's stories (for example, "Was," "Red Leaves"), and is more dryly attested to by Mullin's statistics on the "motives" of Virginia runaways.

It was marronage on the grand scale, with individual fugitives banding together to create independent communities of their own, that struck directly at the foundations of the plantation system, presenting military and economic threats that often taxed the colonists to their very limits. In a remarkable number of cases throughout the Americas, the whites were forced to bring themselves to sue their former slaves for peace. In their typical form, such treaties—which we know of from Brazil, Colombia, Cuba, Ecuador, Hispaniola, Jamaica, Mexico, and Surinam—offered maroon communities their freedom, recognized their territorial integrity, and made some provision for meeting their economic needs, demanding in return an agreement to end all hostilities toward the plantations, to return all future runaways and, often, to aid the whites in hunting them down. Of course, many maroon communities never reached this stage, being crushed by massive force of arms; and even when treaties were proposed they were sometimes refused or quickly violated. Nevertheless, new maroon communities seemed to appear almost as quickly as the old ones were exterminated, and they remained the "chronic plague," "the gangrene," of many plantation societies right up to final Emancipation.

It is important to keep in mind that maroon societies arose in reaction to *colonial* slavery, an institution significantly different from that of the ante bellum South, which until recently served so many North American scholars as *the* implicit model of plantation slavery. Colonial slave systems in the various parts of the Americas were much more similar to one another at the outset than they were to become later on, after locally born slaves came to predominate, and as whole plantation systems became more differentiated economically, legally, and politically. Early colonial systems shared, for example, a particularly high proportion of native Africans (with all that this implies culturally), a sex ratio heavily skewed in favor of males, and considerable craft specialization among the slaves. As Mullin concluded in a recent study, such factors made colonial slave populations "more alike than not and therefore highly comparable". And it is this comparability that is the ultimate justification for a hemispheric approach to maroon societies.

[. . . M]aroon societies form a class or type that can yield unique insights about the Afro-American experience. [. . .] I [. . .] suggest that those rebels who attempted to create communities of their own faced largely similar problems and arrived at broadly comparable solutions. I must admit at the outset that both personal and professional biases lead me to slight somewhat the European or colonial perspective, in favor of attempting to come to grips with maroon societies as much as possible on their own terms. Two years of field research with the largest surviving maroon group, the Saramaka "Bush Negroes" of Surinam, failed to prepare me for the frustrations of trying to achieve a "maroon perspective" on other communities, seen only through the screen of Eurocentric histories. Yet in spite of the difficulties, the effort seems well worth making. Since I have been unable to find any generalizing work on maroons and their communities from this perspective, I will try in the remainder of this [chapter] to survey some of the major themes and common problems and to point to topics for future investigation.

To be viable, maroon communities had to be almost inaccessible, and villages were typically located in inhospitable, out-of-the-way areas. In the southern United States, isolated swamps were a favorite setting; in Jamaica, the most famous maroon groups lived in the unbelievably accidented "cockpit country," where deep canyons and limestone sinkholes abound but where water and good soil are scarce; in the Guianas, seemingly impenetrable jungles provided a home for the maroons; and numerous other such "extreme" environments are mentioned as settings for communities [. . .].

It is worth suggesting that such locales were often inhospitable not only to pursuing troops (about which so much has already been written) but also to the original run-aways themselves. Reading Edwards on Jamaica or Stedman on Surinam one gets a romantic picture of sons and daughters of Africa perfectly adapted to an environment that generously provides water, crops, and game. But the maroon viewpoint, as we know it from a few precious accounts, suggests instead that the harsh natural environments of early communities at first presented terrifying obstacles, and that it was only with a great deal of suffering, and by bringing to bear the full range of their collective cultural experience and creativity that the remarkable adaptations that inspired Edwards and Stedman were finally achieved. In discussing their early history with Saramaka maroons in Surinam, I was often struck by the way that they emphasized their initial difficulties in fighting the environment (with few of the key tools—axes, hoes, guns—that they had known on the plantations) almost as much as they did their problems with pursuing troops. Something of the utter "alienness" of their new jungle home as it must have appeared to eighteenth-century Saramakas may be seen in a story still told today; the band of runaways who, after months of wandering, reached the Gaánlío (a river far in the interior along which they live today) were unable to drink the water because it was filled with tiny worms. It was only after performing major rituals, under the protection of what was to become the central oracle-deity of the region, that they were able finally to purify the river and to settle by its banks.

Successful maroon communities learned quickly to turn the harshness of their immediate surroundings to their own advantage for purposes of concealment and defense. Paths leading to the villages were carefully disguised, and much use was made of false trails replete with dangerous booby traps. In the Guianas, villages set in swamps were approachable only by an underwater path, with other, false paths carefully mined with pointed spikes or leading only to fatal quagmires or quicksand. In many regions man traps, and even dog traps, were used extensively in village defenses. And the villages themselves were often surrounded by a strong palisade (whence the generic name for hispanic maroon communities: *palenques*). The extensive use of natural features for defense is well illustrated by this account of the Leeward Maroons of Jamaica:

> [The Maroon] men were placed on the ledges of rocks that rose almost perpendicularly to a great height, on a ground which, compared to those precipices, might be called a plain, the extremity being narrowed into a passage, upon which the fire of the whole body might bear. This passage contracted itself into a defile of nearly half a mile long, and so narrow that only one man could pass along it at a time. Had it been entered by a line of men, it would not have been difficult for the Maroons from the heights to have blocked them up in the front and in the rear, by rolling down large rocks at both ends, and afterwards to have crushed them to death by the same means. . . . The entrance was impregnable, the continuation of the line of smaller cockpits rendered the rear inaccessible, and Nature had secured the flanks of her own fortification. In this dell were secured the Maroon women and children, and all their valuable things deposited. On the open ground before the defile the men had erected their huts, which were called Maroon town, or Cudjoe's town, whence, in case of an alarm, the people could fly in a minute to the ledges of the rocks at the mouth of the cockpit.

It is interesting that Saramakas, in Surinam, used a similar stratagem in building a palisaded village atop a hill and digging a single, sunken path as the only means of approach to its entrance. As the colonial troops advanced up this path, the maroons rolled large logs down it, crushing them (according to the account of an old Saramaka, recorded in 1968). In some places, maroons depended even more heavily on man-made defenses, of which the most formidable were probably those erected in the final years of Palmares in Brazil, at the end of the seventeenth century. An eyewitness wrote:

The line of defense was very strong, of 2,470 fathoms, with parapets of two fires at each fathom, complete with flanks, redoubts, redans, faces, sentry-boxes, . . . and the exterior terrain so full of caltrops [pointed stakes] and of pits full of them, at all levels—some at the feet, others at the groin, others at the throat—that it was absolutely impossible for anyone to come close to the said line of defense at all from any angle. . . . Nor was it possible for them [the soldiers] to make approaches, such was the density and the thickness of the underbrush in the woods; and indeed this factor had made it impossible for them to dig trenches.

Maroon men throughout the hemisphere developed extraordinary skills in guerrilla warfare. To the bewilderment of their European enemies, whose rigid and conventional tactics were learned on the open battlefields of Europe, these highly adaptable and mobile warriors took maximum advantage of local environments, striking and withdrawing with great rapidity, making extensive use of ambushes to catch their adversaries in crossfire, fighting only when and where they chose, depending on reliable intelligence networks among nonmaroons (both slaves and white settlers), and often communicating by horns. The two most detailed reports of actual battle tactics, from Jamaica and Surinam, describe strikingly similar evasive maneuvers of great ingenuity. Since it was imperative to maximize the effect of what little firepower they possessed, early maroon survival depended heavily on such general tactics. Many bands had only a few usable firearms, and the shortage of ammunition sometimes led to the use of buttons, coins, and pebbles instead of shot. In many areas, maroons used bows and arrows extensively as weapons, as well as home-made spears and Amerindian warclubs, and even, in some cases, "crooked stick[s] shaped something like a musket" to frighten the whites by their apparent force of arms.

The contrast between maroon and European styles of fighting can be seen in two accounts from Jamaica. A nineteenth-century writer, with the advantage of hindsight, noted that:

The [British] troops marched in their proper regimentals, as if they were going to fight a regular and civilized enemy, and sometimes had even the absurdity to traverse the mountainous roads with drums beating. . . . The customary accoutrements were too clumsy and burdensome for traversing the woods and clambering over the rocks, and the red coats were too conspicuous an object to the Maroon marksmen, who seldom missed their aim. . . . The regular soldiers . . . disdained for a time to have recourse to rocks and trees as a shield against their enemies' fire, accounting it base and unmanly in a soldier thus to shrink from danger.

Meanwhile, the Maroons, using classic guerrilla tactics,

disposed of themselves on the ledges of the rocks on both sides [of a canyon] . . . through which men can pass only in a single file . . . [They] lay covered by the underwood, and behind rocks and the roots of trees, waiting in silent ambush for their pursuers, of whose approach they had always information from their out-scouts. [The troops] . . . after a long march,

oppressed by fatigue and thirst, advance toward the mouth of the defile.
. . . A favorable opportunity is taken [by the Maroons] when the enemy
is within a few paces to fire upon them from one side. If the party surprised
return the fire on the spot where they see the smoke of the discharge
. . . they receive a volley in another direction. Stopped by this, and un-
decided which party to pursue, they are staggered by the discharge of a
third volley from the entrance of the defile. In the meantime, the concealed
Maroons, fresh, and thoroughly acquainted with their ground, vanish
almost unseen before their enemies have reloaded. The troops, after losing
more men, are under the necessity of retreating; and return to their posts,
frequently without shoes to their feet, lame, and for some time unfit for
service.

Maroons not only faced superior firepower, but were almost always heavily
outnumbered. Local European militias were often supplemented with imported
mercenaries. Indians were hired by colonists to track down and to fight maroons
in many areas—for example, Brazil, Dominica, Guatemala, the Guianas, Mexico,
and the United States. In Jamaica, the government went so far as to import several
shiploads of Miskito Indians from the Central American mainland for this purpose,
and Indians were relocated by colonists attempting to deal with maroons in Brazil,
and elsewhere as well. In addition, black troops—known variously as "rangers,"
"*chasseurs*," "black shot," etc.—were used widely by the Dutch, English, French,
and Spanish. Composed of slaves and freedmen, or sometimes of slaves who were
promised freedom in return for military service, these troops were considered far
and away the most effective of all the antimaroon forces. And finally, the maroons
in some areas (for example, Cuba and Jamaica) had to contend with trained dogs.

Reports by outsiders give only glimpses of what must have been the paramount
importance of religious beliefs and practices to the fighting maroons themselves.
We are told that in Cuba, attacking soldiers came upon "magical paraphernalia";
that in Jamaica, Nanny was able to attract and catch bullets between her buttocks,
where they were rendered harmless and that Tacky "caught all the bullets fired at
him in his hand, and hurled them back with destruction upon his foes"; and finally
that in Surinam, as in Haiti, Jamaica, and elsewhere, warriors underwent complex
rites and wore amulets intended to make them bulletproof. Saramakas, recounting
to me their ancestors' battles with colonial troops, made quite clear that as far as
they were concerned, it was their gods and obeahs that spelled the ultimate difference between victory and defeat.

The economic adaptations of maroons to their new environments were just as
impressive as their military achievements. Living with the ever-present fear of
sudden attack, they nevertheless succeeded in developing a wide range of innovative techniques that allowed them to carry on the business of daily life. Swidden
horticulture was the mainstay of most maroon economies, with a similar list of
cultigens appearing in reports from almost all areas—manioc, yams, sweet potatoes, and other root crops, bananas and plantains, dry rice, maize, groundnuts,
squash, beans, chile, sugar cane, assorted other vegetables, and tobacco and cotton.
These seem to have been planted in a similar pattern of intercropping—for
example, vegetables scattered in a field of rice—from one end of the hemisphere
to the other. Making gardens was one of the first tasks for each newly formed

maroon group; only nine months after having established a new village, Yanga's people in Mexico "had already planted many seedlings and other trees, cotton, sweet potatoes, chile, tobacco, corn, beans, sugar cane, and other vegetables." And pursuing troops, fully understanding the maroons' dependence on their gardens, often made their destruction the first order of business when attacking settlements. It should be noted, however, that in a few areas, communities seem to have been unable to achieve this degree of economic independence or were uninterested in seeking it, and instead lived directly off plantation society—for example, the economically "parasitic" *mocambos* around Bahia.

Maroons learned to exploit their environment in many other ways as well—from hunting and fishing to the development of a varied pharmacopoeia. Captain Stedman, who was positively awed by the environmental knowledge of his maroon adversaries in Surinam, provides several illustrations.

> Inconceivable are the many expedients which these people employ in the woods. . . . Game and fish they catch in great abundance, by artificial traps and springs, and preserve them by barbacuing; while their fields are even overstocked with rice, cassava, yams, plantains, &c. They make salt from the palm-tree ashes. . . . We have found concealed near the trunk of an old tree a case-bottle filled with excellent butter, which . . . they made by melting and clarifying the fat of the palm-tree worms; this fully answers all the purposes of European butter, and I found it in fact even more delicious to my taste. The pistachio or *pinda* nuts [peanuts] they also convert into butter, by their oily substance, and frequently use them in their broths. The palm-tree wine they have always in plenty; they procure it by making deep incisions of a foot square in the fallen trunk, where the juice being collected, it soon ferments by the heat of the sun; it is not only a cool and agreeable beverage, but sufficiently strong to intoxicate. The manicole or pine-tree [a palm] affords them materials for building; they fabricate pots from clay found near their dwellings; the gourd or callebasse tree procures them cups; the silk-grass plant and maurecee-tree supplies materials for their hammocks, and even a kind of cap grows naturally upon the palm-trees, as well as brooms; the various kinds of nebee supply the want of ropes; fuel they have for cutting; and a wood called *bee-bee* serves for tinder, by rubbing two pieces on each other; it is also elastic, and makes excellent corks; candles they can make, having plenty of fat and oil; and the wild bees afford them wax, as well as excellent honey.

A great many of these techniques for dealing with the environment clearly were learned, directly or indirectly, from American Indians. It is not yet possible to say how many had some sort of antecedents in the African homeland as well. I would suggest, however, that a good deal of maroon technology must have been developed on the plantations during slavery. Throughout Afro-America, Indians interacted with slaves, whether as fellow sufferers, as trading partners, or in other capacities. Indian technologies—from pottery making and hammock weaving to fish drugging and manioc processing—were taken over and, often, further developed by the slaves, who were so often responsible for supplying the bulk of their own daily needs. Life as maroons meant numerous new challenges to daily survival, but it was on a base of technical knowledge developed in the interaction between Indians and blacks on plantations that most of the remarkable maroon adaptations were built.

Yet in spite of their remarkable achievements in wresting a living from an alien environment, maroons remained unable to manufacture certain items that were essential to their continued existence. As long as the wars went on, the need for such things as guns, tools, pots, and cloth (as well as for new recruits, particularly women) kept maroon communities unavoidably dependent on the very plantation societies from which they were trying so desperately to isolate themselves. This inability to disengage themselves fully from their enemy was the Achilles heel of maroon societies throughout the Americas.[2] Whether located at a marching distance of several weeks from colonial centers (as were the early Saramakas or the Palmaristas) or within a few miles of major cities (as were the Bahian *mocambos* or André's village in French Guiana, successful communities worked out fairly extensive economic relations with colonial societies. Such relations ranged all the way from the guerrilla raids on outlying plantations (which were especially frequent in Surinam) or the extortion tactics common around Bahia, to the quasi-institutionalized clandestine exchange of goods and services that took place in many other parts of the Americas. Two points deserve special emphasis: the extent of maroon dependence on colonial society for certain essential items, and the surprising amount of collusion by members of almost all social classes with the rebels, whenever it served their individual self-interest.

While colonial governments, which were charged with protecting the plantation system, were generally in a position of outright enmity toward maroon communities, a large number of individual members of these societies found the maroons useful suppliers of goods and services and had few scruples about supplying them, in return, with the items they needed. Selected plantation slaves, who often included relatives and friends, were important allies of maroons in most areas. In Guadeloupe, slaves smuggled arms to maroons; in Cuba, slaves (as well as freedmen) served as their middlemen, selling their beeswax, honey, and leather in urban markets and supplying them, in return, with tools and firearms; and in Jamaica, slaves not only helped the maroons economically, but provided crucial intelligence information as well. Trade with white settlers was also common in most areas. Many Cuban communities traded directly with neighboring whites; Spanish middlemen sold game and fish in the towns of Saint-Domingue for the maroons of le Maniel, obtaining for them guns, powder, and tools; the settlers around Palmares carried on an extensive and complex illegal trade with the *quilombos*, exchanging guns for silver and gold taken by the Palmaristas on their raids closer to the coast; and in the southern United States the maroons of the Dismal Swamp carried on an active trade with the surrounding white populace.

In general, the social environments in which nascent maroon communities found themselves were as new and challenging as their natural surroundings, and success at survival depended in large part on how they responded to them. The colonial New World was a volatile social arena with many types of competing interest groups, and successful maroon communities were often able to play one off against another. In turn, of course, maroons often found themselves being used as pawns in struggles among the great European powers as well as among more special European or colonial interest groups. In eighteenth-century Amsterdam, for example, certain business interests periodically spread "false rumors about the imminent threat of violence from maroons . . . [causing] artificial drops in the prices of shares in Surinam on the stock market, for purposes of speculation."

One of the strangest of the "alliances of convenience" that arose in this setting was that between maroons in the Spanish territories and the pirates who represented Spain's enemies. This often close relationship was intermittent and based on opportunism by both sides; pirates were often slave traders or owners, and something of their general opinion of maroons might be inferred from the etymology of the verb "to maroon," which "came to mean the form of punishment meted out [by the pirates] to backsliders from their own numbers." Yet for three centuries, beginning in the early 1500s, there were maroons who fought alongside pirates in their naval battles, guided them in their raids on major cities, and participated with them in widespread, illicit international trade. We know that some maroons rose high in the pirate ranks; for example, the Cuban runaway Diego Grillo became Capitán Dieguillo, serving as an officer under the notorious Dutchman Cornelis Jol ("Kapitein Houtbeen"—"Captain Pegleg"), until the former maroon was convicted of illicit slaving along the coasts of Central America. The most famous collaboration between maroons and pirates, shrouded in legend like so much else about the man, involved Sir Francis Drake. On one major Panama adventure we are told that local maroons served him as hunters, carpenters, masons, nurses, scouts, and archers, providing him with thirty of his forty-eight fighting men. And, in return for helping him capture nearly thirty tons of Spanish silver and as much gold as each man could carry, Drake gave the maroon chief a "fair gilt scimitar" that had once belonged to the late French king, Henri II.

In many areas, maroons lined up even more directly with the European rivals of their former masters. In Jamaica, the Spanish maroons joined the British and played a decisive role in driving the Spaniards from the island; on Hispaniola, the maroons of le Maniel played off the French against the Spanish for decades; in Florida, the Spaniards welcomed maroons from the British and American colonies, and used them against their former masters; many other such examples could be cited.

Maroons in most parts of the Americas also found themselves dealing with native Americans—the Indians who were so often their reluctant neighbors. But while relations with Indians were a fact of life for most communities, such relations were diverse, varying from successful cooperation to all-out war. In a number of cases, groups of Indians and maroons "fused," both culturally and genetically, but their relative positions varied. The Miskito Indians of Honduras and Nicaragua, for example, kept a large group of maroons as domestic slaves in the seventeenth century, intermarrying with them and gradually absorbing them into their general population. In contrast, the Island Carib, who had also kept maroons as slaves initially, soon found themselves dominated by the blacks in terms of power, and later genetically as well; in the twentieth century, one ethnographer went so far as to describe the culture of these Black Carib, rather misleadingly, as "an African cake with Amerindian ingredients." Seminoles and maroons, during their long history of close collaboration and intermarriage, maintained their separate identities more clearly; they fought side by side but in separate companies against the whites, and maroons (even while being "domestic slaves") served as trusted advisers and counselors of Seminole chiefs. Cases of close military cooperation between maroons and Indians occurred in many other areas as well—for example, Mexico, Colombia, and Surinam. And throughout Brazil, groups of maroons and Indians merged in a wide variety of political and cultural arrangements.

Though relationships as close as those of maroons with Miskitos, Island Caribs, or Seminoles were not the rule, maroons and Indians did carry on commercial relations in many parts of the hemisphere, and maroon men, suffering from a shortage of women, often took Indian wives (see below). In at least one case, maroon-Indian trade has continued unabated for over two centuries; the Trio Indians of Surinam

> received all types of manufactured goods [acquired by the "Bush Negroes" from the whites], but in particular axes, knives, machetes, and bends, and the Bush Negroes collected in exchange dogs, cassava squeezers, pets, and basketwork. [Hunting] dogs were and still are the most valuable trade item; . . . in 1964, I saw a hunting dog sold for two axes, two machetes, a big knife, a metal canister with padlock, a litre bottle of salt, two mirrors, a pair of scissors, and a metal basin.

However, in other areas (and in many of these same areas at different periods) hostile relations were common, often encouraged by local whites. In British Guiana and parts of Brazil and Virginia, it was probably the mere presence of hostile Indians in large numbers that prevented the establishment of viable maroon communities, and, as mentioned earlier, Indians were commonly employed by the whites both to hunt down individual runaways and to serve as troops in major battles against maroon communities.

The internal organization of maroon societies has received relatively little scholarly attention. Yet enough is known to allow some generalization and to point to problems that deserve special attention in the future.

Early maroon societies, whether organized as centralized states (like Palmares), loose and shifting federations (like the Windward Maroons of Jamaica), or isolated bands (like that of André in French Guiana), were communities at war, fighting for their very existence. The state of continuous warfare strongly influenced many aspects of their political and social organization.

To assure the absolute loyalty of its members, each community had to take strong measures to guard against desertion and the presence of spies. New members, particularly those slaves liberated during raids, posed a special threat to security. We know that precautions were often taken to make it impossible for such people to return to their plantations and betray the group. In French Guiana, for example, new recruits "are brought to the village . . . by way of numerous detours without going on any real paths, so that once they are there, they cannot find their way back." And in maroon communities throughout the Americas, new recruits served probationary periods, often in some kind of domestic slavery. For example, in Cuba, new maroons underwent a two-year trial period during which they were not allowed out of the village; in Palmares, men freed on raids became slaves of the maroons until they succeeded in finding a substitute on another raid; among Chief Boni's men in Surinam, none "were trusted with arms until they had first served him some years as slaves, and given him unquestionable proofs of fidelity and resolution"; the Leeward Maroons of Jamaica kept new recruits in a type of isolation during which "They would not Confide in them, until They had served a

time prefixed for their Probation," which was sufficiently trying to make some of
them wish to return to their masters; and the Windward Maroons obliged new
recruits "to be true to them by an oath which is held very sacred among the negroes,
and those who refuse to take that oath, whether they go to them of their own
accord or are made prisoners, are instantly put to death." Throughout the hemisphere, desertion was commonly punished by death. In Palmares, "when some
Negroes attempt to flee, he [the king] sends *crioulos* after them and once retaken
their death is swift and of the kind to instill fear." In Cuba, the rebels "had the
custom of killing those who deserted the maroon bands, and those who did not
defend themselves against their pursuers," and the same penalty obtained among
the Windward maroons of Jamaica, in French Guiana, le Maniel, and elsewhere.
Moreover, I can report that even today, the theme of fear and distrust of new
runaways crops up repeatedly in Saramaka oral accounts of their own early history.

Internal dissension of any sort could also pose a fatal threat to a small
community at war. In the absence of developed institutions to maintain social
control, early maroon communities allowed a great deal of power and authority to
accrue to their leaders, and they learned to live with very harsh sanctions on internal
dissension. In Palmares, the "king rules . . . with iron justice" and "robbery,
adultery, and murder were punished uniformly with death." At the other extreme
in terms of size, André's small group in French Guiana also exhibited considerable
centralization of authority and strong internal discipline. In Jamaica, Cudjoe's
concern with maintaining absolute authority is stressed by all observers; he went
so far as to execute some of his own men who had murdered some whites contrary
to his orders, and at one point refused to allow a fleeing group of Eastern Maroons
to join his own group because "He had an absolute command of His People . . .
[while the eastern group] were Independent of Him, and Subject only to their own
chiefs, who would not Submit to Him." In Surinam, the great maroon leader Boni
"maintained the strictest discipline amongst his troops: he was . . . absolutely
despotic, and had [recently] executed two of his men . . . only upon suspicion of
having hinted some few words in favour of the Europeans." Finally, according to
the missionaries among the eighteenth-century Saramaka, the "choicest tortures,"
including dismemberment and burning at the stake, were used for those convicted
of serious crimes.

Perhaps the most serious threat to the internal peace of early maroon societies
involved rights over women. During the early colonial period throughout the
Americas, there was a severe imbalance of male to female slaves, and this proportion was further increased among the original bands of runaways because a
disproportionately large number of men successfully escaped from plantation life.
Moreover, polygyny was the prerogative of important maroon men in many areas
(for example, in Jamaica, French Guiana, Surinam, and Palmares), further reducing
the number of wives available for the rest of the community. Many groups tried
to solve this problem by capturing Indian women (as in Mexico, Panama, Colombia,
Brazil, and Peru). But until they were able to raise their own children to maturity,
almost all groups had to live with a severe shortage of women. Maroon men were
well aware that fights over women could have the most serious consequences. We
know, in fact, of one community in French Guiana that split up in the wake of just
such a dispute. And where we have information on the penalty for adultery in early
maroon communities, such as in Palmares or among the Windward Maroons of

Jamaica, it is invariably death. One additional and most unusual report about the regulation of rights in women deserves mention. It claims that among the Leeward Maroons of Jamaica, there were carefully codified rules regulating the sharing of one woman by more than one man, allotting each a specific number of nights with her, controlling rights in the offspring, and so forth. Though from a cultural viewpoint such practices might seem anomalous in the context of Afro-America, they give some indication of the severity of the shortage of women and of the recognition of the need for preventing it from rending communities apart.

A great deal can be learned by comparing maroon societies in a time perspective. For example, the date of a community's original formation as well as the length of its survival seem everywhere to be major influences on the form of its political organization. Communities formed in the sixteenth or seventeenth century seem to have differed from those formed later, both in the types of men they chose as leaders and in the models used to legitimize their authority. Before 1700, the great majority of maroon leaders on whom we have data were African-born. Moreover, four of the six major leaders (Ganga Zumba, Domingo Bioho, Yanga, and Bayano) claimed to have been kings in their African homelands. During this period, models of monarchy were frequently appealed to; in addition to the well-known case of Palmares, where King Ganga Zumba and his relatives formed a dynasty, the Venezuelan maroon leader, "el Rey Miguel," "formed a royal court with his cabinet and royal family . . . his mistress Guiomar was made Queen, and their son became the Heir Apparent"; Domingo Bioho in Colombia was styled "Rey del Arcabuco" [King of the Craggy Spot] or "Rey Benkos"; and in Panama King Bayano "was regarded with the reverance and obedience due a lord and natural king."

In contrast, after the beginning of the eighteenth century, maroon leaders only very rarely claimed princely descent from Africa, tending instead to style themselves captains, governors, or colonels rather than kings. Moreover, a striking number of leaders during this period were Creoles, quite out of proportion to the number of American-born men in the general slave population.

I would like to suggest, particularly for this period, that the nature of maroon (and colonial) society made the person who was skilled at understanding whites, as well as his fellow maroons, especially valuable as a leader. Although many Creole slaves—taught special skills and treated relatively well—may have disdained the company of African-born field hands, there were at least some who managed to achieve high status in the eyes of both planters and common slaves (for example, Toussaint l'Ouverture in Haiti or many of the rebel leaders in British Guiana). It was that trusted servant who was wise in the ways of the whites, but who also maintained close ties with the mass of slaves and could understand and use "African" modes of thought and action, who was particularly suited for maroon leadership. In fact, looking back over the historical records in Surinam, I find that almost all successful tribal chiefs possessed just this unusual combination of skill at handling whites and knowledge of "African" traditions. Even today in Saramaka, neither a man who is too Westernized in experience and attitudes nor one who is too exclusively committed to traditional, "African"-type values is considered appropriate for this office; within the system, the former receive little respect, while the latter typically take on important but specialized advisory or priestly roles.

Few maroon societies outlived their turbulent wartime years. However, those that did manage to survive for long periods represent case histories of special sociological significance, since their complete evolution from initial formation to full development can often be reconstructed. This developmental aspect of maroon societies has barely begun to be explored and presents one of the most challenging problems for future research.

It seems clear, for example, that wherever maroon communities survived for long periods, important aspects of their early social and political organization were altered as new institutions developed. In some cases, such as Yanga's group in Mexico or San Basilio in Colombia, documentation of these developments is scanty. In others, such as the "Bush Negroes" of Surinam or the Jamaican Maroons, the outlines are already beginning to emerge. For example, in Saramaka—the society I know best—the power and authority of early wartime leaders was gradually diffused into a number of developing institutions. Reading the reports of missionaries living with the Saramaka in the late eighteenth century, I get the distinct impression that kinship networks, which had existed in only attenuated forms during the earliest years of the society, were playing a major organizational role and determining to a large extent the distribution of authority; legal institutions, including "councils," ordeals, and other standardized judicial mechanisms, were operating smoothly; a complex but integrated system of ritual and belief held an important place in social and political control; and the harsh sanctions that typified early maroon societies were at least beginning to give way to more subtle pressures against deviance—the moral force of the community as a group and the threat of supernatural sanctions. And there was a still more general tendency during this period for the focus of religion (especially for men) to shift away from cults that stressed individual power and protection to ones having a stronger ethical component—a trend vastly accelerated by increasing contact with coastal society during the late nineteenth century.

Understanding the nature of long-range changes in the political ideology of maroons is a task for the future, but such studies are almost certain to throw light on current debates about the nature of "slave personality." The same immense difficulties that face the student trying to reconstruct slaves' thoughts and motives confront the student who is trying to interpret apparent shifts through time in the way maroons defined themselves vis-à-vis outsiders. Patterson touches on this problem in reviewing the famous confrontation between Cudjoe, the fierce war leader of the Western Maroons of Jamaica, and Colonel Guthrie, the white commander sent to make peace. And he suggests that Cudjoe's "contradictory" behavior—humbling himself at the white's feet—must be understood in the light of the essentially contradictory nature of slave personality more generally; he adds, however, that there may be a strong element of role-playing involved.[3] The complexities of interpretation become intensified when a time perspective is added. Following the treaties, these same Jamaican Maroons bought, sold, and owned substantial numbers of slaves, hunted new runaways for a price, managed to gain the hatred of much of the slave population, and in many respects may have deserved their common post-treaty nickname, "the King's Negroes" (post-treaty Maroons cooperated in hunting down new runaways in Hispaniola, parts of Surinam, and elsewhere as well). But we know almost nothing about the reality or the extent of changes in accompanying underlying attitudes or self-image. From reports of encounters between Saramakas and outsiders after the treaties, it is my own impression that there was less ambivalence or contradiction and more conscious role-playing than in Jamaica; until the late nineteenth century at least, most Saramakas seem to have retained a fairly firm belief in their own moral superiority over whites as well as coastal blacks and tended to view all relations with outsiders instrumentally. One is tempted to suggest that Saramakas were privileged by their greater isolation to live with less ambivalence toward Western society and with greater self-esteem than the Jamaican Maroons, who were subject to strong pressures for creolization as early as the mid-eighteenth century. But we cannot be certain. Considerably more field work among surviving maroons, as well as more sophisticated analysis of documentary sources, will be necessary before speculations of this sort can be converted into intellectually interesting and testable propositions. The importance of the broader issues, however, suggests that the effort is well worth making.

Maroon societies possess an unusually "synthetic" character because of the special, largely shared historical circumstances in which they were forged. In this final section, I want to turn from the consideration of external contingencies on their form—such as alien environments or pursuing troops—to a discussion of the cultural ideas and models that maroons brought with them to the forests and that were the ultimate determinants of the unique shape that their societies took on.

It is essential at the outset to underscore the diversity of values and points of view that must have been represented in most of the original maroon groups. Not only were African tribal affiliations quite diverse, but a wide range of slave adaptations was represented as well. Marronage was not a unitary phenomenon from the point of view of the slaves, and it cannot be given a single locus along a continuum of "forms of resistance." The meaning of marronage differed for slaves in different social positions, varying with their total perception of themselves and their situation, and this in turn was influenced by such diverse factors as their country of birth, the period of time they had been in the New World, their task assignments as slaves, and the particular treatment they were currently receiving from overseers or masters, as well as more general considerations such as the proportion of blacks to whites in the region, the proportion of freedmen in the population, the opportunities for manumission, and so forth.

Because of such considerations, the frequency of marronage differed significantly among different types of slaves. Although the relevant statistical data have only just begun to be explored, certain generalizations are already emerging that seem to hold throughout the Americas. First, the least acculturated slaves were among those most prone to marronage, often escaping within their very first hours or days on American soil, and often doing so in groups, sometimes in a vain attempt to find their way back to Africa. Second, native-born Africans who had spent some time in the New World were not particularly prone to flight, and when they did run off it was most often temporarily, in *petit marronage*. Finally, an unusually high proportion of Creoles and highly acculturated African-born slaves ran off, though it was less often to maroon communities than to urban areas, where their independent skills and relative ease in speaking the colonial language often allowed them to masquerade as freemen.

The typical early maroon community was, then, composed of Africans who were often literally just off the ships, unskilled plantation slaves born in Africa but who had lived for years in the Americas (and who, because of their numerical preponderance in colonial slave populations made up the bulk of most maroon communities), and some Creoles or highly acculturated Africans. We know, moreover, that this first group probably included an unusually high proportion of middle-aged men, which must have enhanced its influence on the shaping of maroon cultures and societies; that the second group included a large number of especially embittered slaves, since those slaves who had made some kind of long-range adjustment to the system tended to take definitive flight only when they had been victims of brutality considered excessive even by the ordinary standards of the plantation, or after being torn from their normal social context, for example by sudden sale to a new master; and that the third group probably included many people with particularly strong ideological commitments against the slave system itself, since most of these skilled slaves who joined maroon groups could have chosen the easier course of melting unobserved into urban populations.

Yet such generalizations tell us tantalizingly little about the actual processes of culture-building that must have gone on in these new societies. Such slave "types" as the newly arrived African or the Creole are abstractions which, though useful on one level, must be viewed with genuine caution. The alternatives open to slaves of any such category were much greater than has usually been supposed, and the individual adjustments achieved were often extremely complex. I doubt, therefore, that our understanding of "slave personality" can be furthered by attempts to force real individuals onto a unilinear gradient from "accommodation" to "resistance" to slavery. As Mintz reminds us, "the house slave who poisoned her master's family by putting ground glass in the food had first to become the family cook. . . . And the slaves who plotted armed revolts in the marketplaces had first to produce for market, and to gain permission to carry their produce there." In this context, it seems significant that some of the most "creolized" of maroon societies—those with the heaviest overlay of Catholicism, European language, Western dress, and so forth—seem to have been composed of a particularly high proportion of native-born Africans (for example, many of the sixteenth-century communities in the Spanish territories). We are dealing, then, with phenomena of great complexity, whose comprehension demands both considerably more acts than we currently have at our disposal and analytical thought of greater subtlety than has yet been brought to bear.

To my knowledge, Roger Bastide is the only scholar who has tried to come to grips with these broad issues, speculating on the dynamics of the formation of maroon cultures and societies and attempting to characterize their uniqueness. Bastide views maroon societies as somehow anomalous, perceiving in them a fundamental "split between the infra- and superstructures."

> Whereas in Africa there exists a functional connection between the various levels of what G. Gurvitch has termed "sociology in depth", and all strata—from the ecological to those embodying social values or group conscience—form part of the same continuum, in these maroon communities a quite different state of affairs prevails. Here, environmental determinism and the claims of collective memory come into direct conflict.

Moreover, he argues that, in examining maroon societies, "we find ourselves everywhere confronted with 'mosaic' cultures," with "one [African] culture predominant . . . [though] this still allows the coexistence of whole enclaves based on other civilisations."

It seems to me that, in these passages, Bastide oversimplifies the processes that contributed to the formation of maroon cultures and societies, misconstruing the nature of the principles that served to integrate them, and considerably under-estimating the maroons' creative resources. The notion of a "collective memory," apparently viewed as some sort of repository of African culture, does not cope adequately with the reality represented by the total cultural equipment brought by maroons to the forests. As we have seen, this equipment was in fact quite diverse, including contributions by Africans just off the ships who represented a variety of languages and cultures, as well as by long-term (African-born) slaves and Creoles with a wide range of individual adjustments to slavery, orientations to reality, and ways of handling problems. What the majority of these people did share was a recently forged Afro-American culture and a strong ideological (or at least rhetor-ical) commitment to things "African." Though the environments in which maroons found themselves were alien and hostile in many respects, these people were far from being completely unequipped to deal with them; as suggested above, much of the basic cultural knowledge necessary for the maroons' physical adaptation had already been developed throughout the New World on local plantations. The image of an unrelenting tension in maroon societies between the claims of "collective memory" and the necessity for new environmental adaptations is misleading, then, on several counts: its failure to recognize adequately the cultural diversity of the Africans involved; its confusion of ideological commitment to things African with the putative possession of some sort of generalized African culture; and its complete omission of nascent but already powerful plantation-forged Afro-American cultures.

Bastide's belief that these are "cultures in mosaic" or "mosaic cultures" is also misleading, and contains more than a hint of old-fashioned, mechanistic thinking about the nature of Culture itself (as Herskovits himself, late in life, recognized). Nor does Bastide's corollary image of "cultural enclaves" within a "dominant [African] culture" stand up to close scrutiny. I would suggest that by focusing on the diverse African origins of various "culture-traits" considered in isolation, Bastide has failed to see the principles that integrate these societies and gave them their characteristic shape. In studying maroon societies, I have always been struck by the earliness and completeness of their "functional integration," by very much the kind of fit between levels that Gurvitch writes of. And this remarkably rapid formation by maroon groups of whole cultures and societies was made possible, as I have suggested, by the previous existence throughout the hemisphere of rather mature local slave cultures combined with a widely shared ideological commitment to things African.

The development of rich, local slave cultures (which shared a great many features in the different colonies) is just beginning to receive the attention it deserves, but it is already clear that Africans in the New World, who at first often shared little more than a common continental origin and the experience of enslave-ment, developed distinctively Afro-American ways of dealing with life from the very beginning. We know, for example, that the national language of Surinam (Sranan, an English-based Creole) was already "firmly established" within the first sixteen years of the settlement of the colony. Further, I can cite as evidence for the early and rich development of Afro-American cults on plantations the fact that today, particular groups of Saramakas commonly visit, worship, and exchange ritual information with certain non-Bush Negroes—in each case, precisely those who are the descendants of the slaves who lived on the same plantation from which the ancestors of that particular group of Saramakas fled over two and a half centuries ago. Moreover, some characteristic modern forms of Afro-American social relations are conterminous with the Middle Passage itself; Saramaccan *máti* and *síbi*— forms of "ritual kinship" implying strong solidarity—referred originally to the experience of having shared passage on the same slave ship (cf. Bastide on the similar *malungo* relationship in Palmares). Far from being limited to the environmental realm, then, the contribution of plantation culture to maroon societies touched almost all areas of life.

Yet slave culture was restricted in certain key respects, providing maroons with few models, for example, for higher-level social or political organization. (There were important attempts at trial-based political organization among slaves in British Guinna, Jamaica, and elsewhere, sometimes culminating in major revolts, but for the hemisphere as a whole, these were the exception rather than the rule.) And slave culture provided maroons with only attenuated models for the arts, religion, and certain other aspects of culture of which full expression was impossible in the setting of the plantation. The uniqueness of maroon societies in the context of Afro-American culture stems in large part from the ways in which they overcame these particular limitations, and it is here that Bastide's "mosaic" metaphor seems weakest.

Maroons indeed drew on their diverse African heritages in building their cultures. But unlike other Afro-Americans, who were unable to pass on integrated patterns of traditional culture, maroons could and did look to Africa for deep-level organizational principles, relating to cultural realms as diverse as naming their children on the one hand, or systems of justice on the other. We still know almost nothing about the actual culture-building processes that took place. It seems likely, however, that such factors as the geographical range in Africa of particular cultural principles (or at least their mutual compatibility), and their potential adaptiveness for the special conditions of early maroon life influenced the outcomes. And the generally shared commitment to a "homeland" ideology must have been the cement that allowed practices and beliefs from different areas to be incorporated more or less harmoniously into these developing systems. (Bastide himself has written elsewhere that marronage involved more of a "nostalgia for Africa" than an attempt at exact reconstitution of it.)

Those scholars who have examined maroon life most closely seem to agree that such societies are often uncannily "African" in feeling, even if devoid of any directly transplanted systems. However "African" in character, no maroon social, political, religious, or aesthetic *system* can be reliably traced to a specific tribal provenience; they reveal, rather, their syncretistic composition, forged in the early meeting of peoples bearing diverse African, European, and Amerindian cultures in the dynamic setting of the New World. The political system of Palmares, for example, which Kent has characterized as an "African" state, "did not derive from a particular central African model, but from several." In the development of the kinship system of the Djuka of Surinam, "undoubtedly their West-African heritage played a part . . . the influence of the matrilineal Akan tribes is unmistakable, but so is that of patrilineal tribes . . . [and there are] significant differences between the Akan and Djuka matrilineal systems." And painstaking historical research has recently revealed that the woodcarving of the "Bush Negroes" of Surinam, long considered "an African art in the Americas" on the basis of many formal resemblances, is a fundamentally new, Afro-American art "for which it would be point-less to seek the origin through direct transmission of any particular African style."

Of course, maroon cultures do possess a remarkable number of direct and sometimes spectacular continuities from particular African tribes, ranging from military techniques for defense to recipes for warding off sorcery. These are, however, of the same type as can be found, if with lesser frequency, in Afro-American communities throughout the hemisphere. In stressing these isolated African "retentions" (which, taken together, are probably what make maroon cultures look like "mosaics" to Bastide) there is, I believe, a danger of ignoring cultural continuities of a far more significant kind. Bastide himself has divided Afro-American religions into those *en conserve* ("preserved" or "canned")—like Brazilian *Candomblé* or Cuban Santería—and those that are *vivantes* ("living")—like Haitian *Vaudou*. The former, he claims, represent a kind of "defense mechanism" or "cultural fossilization," a fear that any small change may bring on the end; while the latter are more secure of their future and freer to adapt to the changing needs of their adherents. I think it can be shown more generally that tenacious fidelity to "African" forms is, in many cases, an indication of a culture finally having lost meaningful touch with the vital African past. Certainly, one of the most striking features of West African cultural systems is their internal dynamism, their ability to grow and change. The cultural uniqueness of the more developed maroon societies rests firmly, I would argue, on their fidelity to "African" principles on these deeper levels, to underlying cultural principles—whether aesthetic, political, or domestic—rather than on the frequency of their isolated "retentions." With a rare freedom to extrapolate African ideas and adapt them to changing circumstance, maroon groups include what are in many respects both the most meaningfully African and the most truly "alive" of all Afro-American cultures. [. . .]

Notes

1   The English word "maroon," like the French *marron*, derives from Spanish *cimarrón*. As used in the New World, *cimarrón* originally referred to domestic cattle that had taken to the hills in Hispaniola and soon after to Indian slaves who had escaped from the Spaniards as well. By the end of the 1530s, it was already beginning to refer primarily to Afro-American runaways, and had strong connotations of "fierceness," of being "wild" and "unbroken."

2   In some cases, at least, maroon groups may have been less the victims of economic necessity than these statements imply. There is evidence that in some settings they could have survived physically with considerably less contact with colonial society than was the rule. For example, the Spanish maroons in Jamaica lived in virtual isolation for years without guns and most other Western manufactures. But even though some maroon groups could make their own cloth, pots, and so forth, they seem to have *preferred* Western manufactures and to have been willing to risk a good deal to obtain them. To some extent at least, then, the "economic dependence" of maroons on colonial society was a matter of choice, and it bespeaks a kind of "Westernization" which, though limited in scope, is more profound than simply the knowledge of new skills picked up on the plantation.

3   It is worth noting that Cudjoe's kissing of Guthrie's feet may be less revealing of his personality than of the standard symbolic behavior of the era. Foot-kissing was a common symbol of the relationship between vassal and lord, and appears matter-of factly in a later incident involving the then-pacified Jamaica Maroons during a performance of martial skills for Governor Lyttelton in 1764. After going through their maneuvers, the Maroons approached the governor with their muskets "and piled them in heaps at his feet, which some of them desired to kiss, and were permitted."

Chapter 29

Stuart B. Schwartz

RESISTANCE AND ACCOMMODATION IN EIGHTEENTH-CENTURY BRAZIL
The slaves' view of slavery

T O A GREAT EXTENT, despite an extensive and ever-increasing bibliography, the history of slavery in Brazil remains to be written. As an institution that persisted in Brazil for almost four centuries, the nature and conditions of slavery underwent a series of modifications related to changes in the economy, the social structure, and the dominant cultural norms. Moreover, we should not forget the continuous influence of the Africans themselves on the shape of the institution which molded their destiny as Brazilians. Within these four centuries of change there are certain constant themes and among them is the continuous struggle of African or Brazilian born slaves against the institution of slavery. The great *quilombo* of Palmares, the revolt of the Males in Bahia, and other such dramatic events are now relatively well known by historians of Brazil and students of slavery in general. However there were many others.[1] In this short article I wish to present some information concerning a long-forgotten slave revolt that occurred in Ilhéus (now a part of the state of Bahia) at the end of the eighteenth century. While the revolt itself was a relatively minor affair, it is especially significant because it produced the only contemporaneous document now known in which the slaves themselves commented on the nature of Brazilian plantation slavery. This document is appended here as Document II.

For a variety of reasons slave resistance in Bahia intensified in the period 1790 to 1840. Certainly, external events such as the French Revolution of 1789, the great slave rising in Saint Domingue in 1791, and other events in the Atlantic world influenced the aspirations of both slaveowners and slaves in Bahia.[2] Also, the rapidly expanding sugar economy, responding to the new market conditions caused by the elimination of Saint Domingue as a major producer, probably prompted increased demands on the servile population that adversely affected their lives. These conditions and the changing political situation at the beginning of the nineteenth century that eventually resulted in the demise of the colonial regime between 1821 and 1824 exposed the slave population to new motives and greater opportunities for overt resistance. The importation of significant numbers of slaves from the Mina coast including Hausa-speaking Muslims who, coming together and in quantity, were able to maintain much of their culture intact has also been offered as an explanation of much slave unrest in the late eighteenth and early nineteenth centuries.[3] Whatever the reasons, it is clear that in this period the slave regime of Bahia and the surrounding areas was being severely challenged.

As part of the unknown history of slave resistance in Bahia, I wish to present here information from two unpublished documents from the Arquivo Público da Bahia (Secção Histórica, Cartas ao Governo 207). The first of these is a letter from Desembargador Ouvidor Geral do Crime (royal magistrate) Claudio José Pereira da Costa to the Conde da Ponte, governor of Bahia. This letter relates the history of a group of slaves from Engenho Santana in Ilhéus who killed their overseer and fled to the forests establishing a *mocambo* (escaped slave community) from which they resisted all attempts to recapture them. The slaves knew how to disrupt the operations of their master's plantation, and they had carefully taken with them all the hardware (*ferramenta*) of the engenho so that the mill remained inactive (*fogo-morto*) for two years.

The existence of a group of fugitives on the perimeters of the plantations challenged the continued captivity of other slaves. The slave system could simply not permit fugitive communities that would serve as a beacon of freedom to those who remained enslaved. Thus, colonial authorities and individual planters sought to eliminate these *mocambos* by force and this is the course that was followed against the escaped slaves of Engenho Santana. In this case, the actions of the slaves and the response of the colonial authorities while interesting are not in any way extraordinary since they follow the general pattern of such incidents in Brazilian colonial history. What is extraordinary and singular, however, is the contents of the second document: a treaty of peace proposed by the escaped slaves to their former master, Manoel da Silva Ferreira, in which they sought to define the conditions under which they would return to captivity.

To place this treaty in proper perspective it is necessary to present here the background of the incident. The Engenho Santana of Ilhéus was one of the oldest sugar plantations in the central captaincies and probably the largest in Ilhéus. Established in the sixteenth century by Governor Mem de Sá, it had become the property of the absentee Count of Linhares and with the death of his wife and heir, Dona Felipa de Sá, passed into the control of the Jesuit College of Santo Antão of Lisbon. For most of its history it was administered by the Jesuits and was linked with their other great sugar mill, Engenho Sergipe do Conde in the Bahian Recôncavo.[4] After the expulsion of the Jesuits from Brazil in 1759 the *engenho* was sold to Manoel da Silva Ferreira who in 1789 still owed some 8,000 *mil-réis* to the royal treasury for the purchase. It was in this year that the crown magistrate of Ilhéus (Ouvidor Geral da Comarca de Ilhéus) reported that fifty of the three hundred slaves of Engenho Santana had fled to the forest and established a *mocambo* near the *engenho*.[5] The crown magistrate, fearing the effect of the *mocambo* on other slaves and on "public order (*sossego público*)" at first tried to persuade the fugitives to return. Failing this, he then organized a punitive expedition composed of slave hunters (*capitães do mato*) and Indians from the villages of Barcelos and Olivença. The use of Indians as shock troops against escaped slaves was a common tactic in Brazil throughout the colonial period. The expedition was placed under the command of Sargento-Môr da Comarca, Ignácio de Azevedo Pericoto.

Between the date of the letter of the Ouvidor Geral da Comarca de Ilhéus (June 12, 1789) and that of the Ouvidor Geral do Crime (January 22, 1806) published here as Document I, we have no further information. Still, Document I makes it clear that the punitive expedition must have failed and it narrates in some detail the manner in which the fugitives were finally moved to offer a treaty of peace to their former master stating the conditions under which they would return to slavery. It goes on to tell how Manoel da Silva Ferreira by deceit and dissimulation recaptured the slaves and sent their leader, a *cabra* named Gregório Luís, and fifteen or sixteen others to José da Silva Maia, a merchant in Salvador, so that he could sell them in Maranhão.[6] These events occurred at the end of 1789 or early in 1790. We do not know the ultimate fate of the fugitives with the exception of Gregório Luís who was imprisoned in Salvador. There he remained for some sixteen years and it was probably this long confinement without trial that led him to appeal to the Ouvidor Geral do Crime who in response drew up the two documents appended here.

The treaty of peace

A treaty of peace between escaped slaves and a colonial regime is not unknown in the history of slavery in the Americas. In Mexico and in Ecuador escaped slaves established their freedom and eventually forced colonial authorities to recognize it, usually with the condition that no other fugitives would be welcomed. Perhaps the most famous example of this phenomenon is provided by Maroon War of Jamaica in the eighteenth century, during which a large number of slaves under the leadership of the African Cudjoe won their freedom after a long guerrilla campaign.[7] The treaty presented here is quite different from these others in that it attempts to set out the conditions under which the slaves will return to captivity. It seems at first glance to be a simple attempt to ameliorate the conditions of slave labor in recognition of defeat. On closer examination, however, its content is far more revolutionary.

There are two aspects of the treaty that deserve special commentary. First, in that the treaty establishes a series of *desiderata* it offers us a vision of the conditions of life and labor on Brazilian sugar plantations at the end of the eighteenth century from the point of view of the slaves. Many of the articles of the treaty refer to specific conditions of labor and to the minimum needs of physical comfort—the clothing of the boatmen, the number of workers needed in the mill, the elimination of unpleasant tasks. In a number of paragraphs it is made clear that the slaves were accustomed to providing their own sustenance.[8] The demands for two days free from responsibility to the *engenho* with the right to fish, plant rice, and cut firewood indicate a certain degree of economic independence and self-sufficiency. The fact that these slaves were able to produce a marketable surplus is underlined by their demand that the plantation owner provide them with a large boat to carry their produce to the market in Salvador and free them of the usual transport costs. We have here evidence that even agricultural slaves participated directly in the market economy and were able to accumulate capital. This provides one explanation of how slaves acquired the funds necessary to purchase their freedom. Moreover, this evidence should raise some serious questions about the often repeated generalization that because slaves were unable to accumulate capital there existed no internal market in colonial Brazil, and that as a result there was no real opportunity for industrial development. Until we understand more about the relationship between slaves and the cash economy, this generalization is hypothetical at best.[9]

The greatest part of the treaty refers to the slaves' labor obligations. The paragraph that refers to the quantity of a *tarefa* of sugarcane is an example of the nature of these requests. The slaves demanded that the *tarefa de canas*, that is the amount of sugarcane to be cut in one day, should be "of five hands (*mãos*) and not of six, and ten canes in bundle (*feixe*)." Cane cutters measured their work in "hands" of cane. Each hand was equivalent to five "fingers," each of which was made up of ten bundles, with a dozen canes per bundle. Thus a hand of cane was equal to 600 canes. The slaves of Engenho Santana therefore were seeking a reduction in both the number of hands required for the daily quota and the number of canes required in each bundle. Instead of a daily quota of 3,600 canes ($6 \times 5 \times 10 \times 12$) they wanted a requirement of only 2,500 canes ($5 \times 5 \times 10 \times 10$), a reduction of thirty percent. In either case, both figures are substantially below the quota of seven hands of cane, or 4,200 canes, reported by Antonil as the *tarefa* expected of cane cutters in Bahia at the end of the seventeenth century. These very practical matters were of most concern in the proposed treaty.[10]

The articles of the treaty relating to work also illustrate two interesting aspects of slave life. First, the role of slave women as milling and agricultural laborers and not simply as house slaves is quite apparent from this document. Quotas for women in the planting of manioc and the role of women in the cutting of firewood are both mentioned. Also, it was common practice in Bahia for women to accompany the cane cutters and to bind the cane into bundles in the field. Second, it is also curious to note the continuous animosity between the various "nations" of slaves. The concept of "divide and conquer" was an old and efficient means of slave control. The runaways from Engenho Santana, led by a Brazilian-born *cabra*, apparently had little sympathy for their fellows from the Mina coast in Africa. Certain disagreeable tasks such as searching for crabs and shellfish in the tidal pools and saltwater swamps were particularly disliked by the slaves. The attitude of the fugitives expressed here was "leave these tasks to the Mina slaves."

Despite the practical and everyday nature of most of the treaty's articles, there are three paragraphs that warrant special attention. In one, the slaves declared clearly that they would not accept the present overseers. Perhaps this was a way to speak out against physical punishment, an aspect of slave life not mentioned directly in the proposals. The rebels also declared that the new overseers had to be chosen with the approval of the slaves. The threat that such a condition would impose on the slave regime is obvious. Even more revolutionary was the demand that the equipment (*ferramenta*) of the *engenho* also remain in their control. This would place control of the plantation entirely in their hands and would reduce the concept of slavery to a farce. To accept such conditions would be tantamount to the end of slavery. What the slaves of Engenho Santana sought was basically to establish acceptable conditions of life and labor including such modern concepts as a four-day work week. The control they hoped to obtain over their own servitude was far too revolutionary for any slave regime to accept. As Document I explains, they were finally tricked, captured and re-enslaved.

Finally, it is worth noting that within the context of a series of demands concerning the nature of work, the slaves of Engenho Santana also affirmed their humanity. The final article of the treaty seeks to protect their culture, or in their own words, "we will be able to play, relax, and sing any time we wish without your hinderance nor will permission be needed." This reference to the larger dimension of man, to his spirit and not only to the body, represents that which was perhaps the greatest contribution of the slaves to Brazilian culture, that is the desire to maintain these human dimensions intact under the most difficult conditions of life. Given the tragic end of the fugitives from Engenho Santana, this last article of the treaty becomes even more poignant.

Document I

Arquivo Público do Estado
    da Bahia: Secção histórica
    Cartas ao Governo, 207

Illustrious and most Excellent Sir

The Supplicant Gregorio Luís, a *cabra* finds himself a prisoner in the jail of this High Court where he was sent by his master, Captain Manoel da Silva Ferreira, resident on his Engenho called Santana in the district of the Town of Ilhéus; there coming at the same time with him, as I remember, some fifteen or sixteen other slaves. These were sent to the merchant José da Silva Maia, his commercial agent, so that he could sell them in Maranhão while the Supplicant came with the recommendation that he be held in prison while the Court of that district prepared the charges so that he could be given exemplary punishment. Taking a preliminary investigation of the Supplicant, I have determined the following facts. The above mentioned Manoel da Silva Ferreira being master and owner of the aforesaid *engenho* with three hundred slaves, including some of the Mina nation discovered the majority of them in rebellion refusing to recognize their subordination to their master. And, the principal leader of this disorder was the Supplicant who began to incite among them the partisan spirit against their master and against the Sugar Master. The Supplicant was able with a few of his followers to kill the latter and until now none know where they buried him. Taking control of part of the *engenho*'s equipment, they fled to the forest refusing not only to give their service or to obey their master, but even placing him in fear that they would cruelly take his life. For this reason the *engenho* has remained inactive for two years with such notable damage that its decadence is dated from that time forward, and, moreover, these damages added to the danger that the rest of the slaves might follow the terrible example of those in rebellion. Thus the majority of the slaves persisted divided into errant and vagabond bands throughout the territory of the *engenho*, so absolute and fearless that the consternation and fright of their master increased in consideration that he might one day fall victim to some disaster. Matters being in this situation, the rebels sent emissaries to their Master with a proposal of capitulation contained in the enclosed copy [see Document II] to which he showed them that he acceded: some came and others remained. The Supplicant as the most astute was able to extort from him a letter of Manumission which was granted at the time without the intention that it have any validity, at the same time he [the Supplicant] sought the District Judge who entering the *engenho* with eighty-five armed men sought out the house of his Master: The latter who could not now confide in the principal leaders of that uprising took advantage of a stratagem of sending the Supplicant Gregorio and fifteen others with a false letter to the Captain major of the militia, João da Silva Santos, who was in the Vila of Belmonte, telling them that they would receive from him some cattle and manioc flour for the *engenho*. Arriving at the said Vila all were taken prisoner with handcuffs despite the great resistance that they made almost to the point of much bloodshed. They were finally conducted to the jail of this High Court as I have said, that is, the Supplicant as the prime mover to be held until his charges were seen and the others with orders to the aforementioned merchant to be sold to Maranhão as they were.

Twice there has been required from this court an order to be sent the investigation or any other charges against the Supplicant and until now they have not arrived.

I must also tell Your Excellency that the Master of the said Engenho has on repeated occasions recommended with the greatest insistence that the Supplicant not be released from prison except by a sentence that exiles him far away because if he is freed he will unfailingly return to the *engenho* to incite new disorders, that may be irreparable.

That which is reported here seems to me enough to give Your Excellency a sufficient idea concerning the Supplicant and the reasons for his imprisonment. God Protect Your Excellency. Bahia 22 of January of 1806.

The Desembargador Ouvidor geral do Crime
Claudio Jose Pereira da Costa

Document II

Treaty Proposed to Manoel da Silva Ferreira
By His Slaves during the Time that They
Remained in Revolt

My Lord, we want peace and we do not want war; if My Lord also wants our peace it must be in this manner, if he wishes to agree to that which we want.

In each week you must give us the days of Friday and Saturday to work for ourselves not subtracting any of these because they are Saint's days.

To enable us to live you must give us casting nets and canoes.[11]

You are not to oblige us to fish in the tidal pools nor to gather shellfish, and when you wish to gather shellfish send your Mina blacks.

For your sustenance have a fishing launch and decked canoes, and when you wish to eat shellfish send your Mina blacks.

Make a large boat so that when it goes to Bahia we can place our cargoes aboard and not pay freightage.

In the planting of manioc we wish the men to have a daily quota of two and one half hands and the women, two hands.[12]

The daily quota of manioc flour must be of five level *alqueires*, placing enough harvesters so that these can serve to hang up the coverings.[13]

The daily quota of sugarcane must be of five hands rather than six and of ten canes in each bundle.[14]

On the boat you must put four poles, and one for the rudder, and the one at the rudder works hard for us.

The wood that is sawed with a hand saw must have three men below and one above.[15]

The measure of firewood must be as was practiced here, for each measure a woodcutter and a woman as the wood carrier.[16]

The present overseers we do not want, choose others with our approval.

At the milling rollers there must be four women to feed in the cane, two pulleys, and a *carcanha*.[17]

At each cauldron there must be one who tends the fire and in each series of kettles the same, and on Saturday there must be without fail work stoppage in the mill.

The sailors who go in the launch beside the baize shirt that they are given must also have a jacket of baize and all the necessary clothing.

We will go to work the canefield of Jabirú this time and then it must remain as pasture for we cannot cut cane in a swamp.

We shall be able to plant our rice wherever we wish, and in any marsh, without asking permission for this, and each person can cut jacaranda or any other wood without having to account for this.

Accepting all the above articles and allowing us to remain always in possession of the hardware, we are ready to serve you as before because we do not wish to continue the bad customs of the other *engenhos*.

We shall be able to play, relax and sing any time we wish without your hinderance nor will permission be needed.

Notes

1 The literature on slave revolts and escaped slave communities is growing rapidly. See, for example, José Alipio Goulart, *Da fuga ao suicídio: Aspectos da rebeldia dos escravos no Brasil* (Rio de Janeiro, 1972). The number of regional studies based on local sources is now increasing as can be seen in works such as Pedro Tomas Pedreira, "Os quilombos baianos," in *Revista Brasileira de Geografia*, N. 24 (1962), 79–93; José Antônio Soares de Sousa, "Quilombo de Bacaxá," *Revista do Instituto Histórico e Geográfico Brasileiro*, 253 (Oct.–Dec., 1961), 3–11; Armando Salles, *O Negro no Pará* (Rio de Janeiro, 1971). I have cited most of the standard sources in Stuart B. Schwartz, "The *Mocambo*: Slave Resistance in Colonial Bahia," *Journal of Social History*, 3 (1970), 313–333.

2 Documentary evidence of the Haitian revolution on blacks and mulattos in Brasil is provided by Luis Mott, "A escravatura: O propósitio de uma representação a El-Rei sobre a escravatura no Brasil," *Revista do Instituto de Estudos Brasileiros* v. 14 (1973), 127–136. The general intellectual situation is presented in Kenneth Maxwell, "The Generation of the 1790s and the Idea of Luso-Brazilian Empire," in Dauril Alden, ed., *Colonial Roots of Modern Brazil* (Berkeley, 1973), 107–146. See also Katia M. de Queiros Mattoso, *Presença francesa no*

movimento democrático baiano de 1798 (Bahia, 1969); Carlos Guilherme Mota, *Atitudes de inovaçao no Brasil—1798–1801* (Lisbon, no date [1969]).

3   This thesis is suggested most recently by Pierre Verger in his *Flux et reflux de la Traite des Negres entre le golfe de Bénin et Bahia de todos os santos* (Paris, 1968), pp. 325–350.

4   The best summary of the history of Engenho Santana and Engenho Sergipe do Conde are provided by Wanderley Pinho in "Testamento de Mem de Sá, Inventário de seus bens no Brasil," *Terceiro Congresso de História Nacional*, III (1938), 5–161. This article includes an inventory of Engenho Santana made in 1810. See also Serafim Leite, *História da Companhia de Jesus no Brasil*, 10 vols. (Lisbon, 1938–1950), V, 243–251.

5   Here we encounter a discrepancy between the reports of the Ouvidor Geral da Comarca de Ilhéus (1789) and that of the Desembargador Ouvidor Geral do Crime (1806) in reference to the actual number of "revolted" slaves. The former speaks of fifty slaves who participated in the resistance while the latter claims that the majority (*o maior número*) joined the rebels. It should be noted, however, that both agree that there were three hundred slaves at Engenho Santana. This is a number far above the average size of eighty to one hundred slaves characteristic of the Bahian *engenhos* of the period.

6   The booming cotton agriculture of the Amazonian region created the market in Maranhão for even troublesome slaves.
     José da Silva Maia was an important merchant in Salvador in the last decade of the eighteenth century. A man of wealth and position, he owned a number of ships in the coastal trade and had three vessels engaged in trans-Atlantic commerce. He was a lay brother of the Third Order of São Domingos and he became a brother of the Santa Casa da Misericôrdia in 1802. His will, drawn up in 1802, indicates that among his possessions were twenty-five slaves. See Arquivo Público do Estado da Bahia, Secção judiciária, maço 676, n. 5. The author wishes to thank Ms. Catherine Lugar for some of the information concerning José da Silva Maia.

7   For a comparison see David Davidson, "Negro Slave Control and Resistance in Colonial Mexico," *HAHR*, 46 (1966), 233–253. This and other essays have been collected in Richard Price, ed., *Maroon Societies* (New York, 1973). The treaty ending the first Maroon War in Jamaica signed in 1738 was reprinted in Bryan Edwards, *The History . . . of the West Indies* (London, 1807) and is included in the *Maroon Societies* volume, pp. 237–239.

8   The slaves in Bahia were often poorly fed. In 1606 and 1701 royal orders were issued that required slaveowners to feed their slaves properly, but observers in 1711, 1756, and 1807 all agreed that slaves were generally not given proper nourishment. Cf. Arquivo Público do Estado da Bahia, Ordens régias 6, n. 103; C. R. Boxer, *Race Relations in the Portuguese Colonial Empire, 1485–1825* (Oxford, 1963), p. 111.

9   This argument is perhaps best known from the works of Celso Furtado, especially his *Economic Growth of Brazil* (Berkeley, 1963), pp. 50–58.

10   Antonil's book was published in 1711 but the critical edition of Mlle. Andrée Mansuy indicates that most of the sections dealing with sugar date from the year 1689. See *Cultura e opulência do Brasil por suas drogas e minas* (Paris, 1968). Conditions of labor in the cane fields are described in Stuart B. Schwartz, "Free Labor in a Slave Economy: The Lavradores de Cana of Colonial Bahia," in Dauril Alden, ed., *Colonial Roots of Modern Brazil* (Berkeley, 1973), pp. 147–197.

11   The *tarrafa* or casting net is still widely used along the coast of Northeast Brazil. It is presently about 170 inches in length with a 480-inch circular bottom that is weighted. See Shepard Forman, *The Raft Fishermen* (Bloomington, 1970), pp. 58–59.

12   As with sugar cane, the daily quotas (*tarefas*) were measured in "hands," as a mnemonic device. While it is possible to establish the quantity of a *tarefa* of sugar cane, it has been impossible to do so for manioc.

13   The *alqueire* is a dry measure equal to 36.27 litres or approximately one English bushel. The reference to coverings (*tapetes*) is obscure, apparently referring to the processing of manioc flour.

14   See the text, p. 629.

15   The reference here is apparently to the ripsaw that was widely used in colonial Brazil. There is a good pictorial representation of its use by slaves in Jean Baptiste Debret, *Viagem*

Pitoresca e histórica ao Brasil, 2d ed., 3 vols. in 2 (São Paulo, 1949). The occupation of sawyer (*serrador*) was commonly listed for sugar plantation slaves since building and repairing the mill called for much carpentry.

16   Some idea of the quota of firewood required of slaves is provided by Antonil. He reported that the daily requirement was a pile of firewood seven *palmos* (*palmo* = nine inches) high by eight *palmos* deep of 63″ × 72″. This was the equivalent of one cartload. See Antonil, *Cultura e opulência*, p. 200.

17   *Moedeiras* were the women whose job it was to feed the cane through the milling rollers. At the time of Antonil only two women were employed at the rollers. The juice squeezed from the cane was collected in a large vat (*parol*) and was then taken out by buckets on a hoist (*guinda*) and poured into the cauldrons for boiling. The women employed in this task were called *guinda-deiras*. For a pictorial representation based on Antonil's account, see Hamilton Fernandes, *Açúar e Álcool ontem e hoje* (Rio de Janeiro, 1971), pp. 56–57. I have been unable to identify a *carcanha*.

PART EIGHT

Race and Social Structure

FEW TOPICS HAVE TROUBLED students of slavery more than the issue of 'race'. The concept of race itself has become unusually problematic. In the words of Ira Berlin, 'Of late, it has become fashionable to declare that race is a social construction.' Yet, as Berlin suggests, few people believe that statement – or act on it.[1] Whatever scholars may say or write about 'race', the popular vernacular remains undiminished and unabated. Common usage, political debate and media discussion continue to use the language of race unaffected by academic or historical doubts about its usefulness.

At first glance, the history of Atlantic slavery suggests that race – or colour – is a clear enough topic. By about 1700, black people in the Americas were assumed to be slaves; to be black was to be a slave. And to be a slave meant being black. At the height of the slave colonies, local laws and conventions allotted particular roles to black and white, defining human categories along the designated fault-lines of local colour. Here was a social structure which seemed simple and obvious: rank and status were defined by colour. But was that *race*? What did contemporaries mean by race? And how did they cope with those increasingly perplexing human borderlands between the stark alternatives of black and white ('people of colour')? Concepts of race differed enormously across time, from place to place and across the social structures of societies.

The most fundamental historical issue has been the role of race in the origins and development of Atlantic slavery. Were Africans relegated to an enslaved status because they were black? Or did colour become a retrospective justification for slavery after the establishment of African slavery? Conversely, did slavery create the racial divides of the Americas (and indeed of the wider Atlantic world)? In brief, did slavery racialise the Western world?

These complex issues are discussed here in a number of essays. Winthrop D. Jordan, arguably the most influential pioneer in this topic, illustrates in his essay of 1962 the variations in definitions and treatment of people of mixed race in the British colonies. Gad Heuman's piece from 1981 provides a case study of Jamaica's 'free coloureds' in the last years of colonial slavery. A related issue, but studied across the whole of Caribbean slave society, is addressed by Arnold Sio in his essay (1987).

While the question might appear more clear cut when dealing with imported Africans, David Northrup's essay (2000) suggests the elasticity of meaning and definition when contemporaries and historians have discussed African 'tribal' groupings.

The language of race and colour has a potency which has transcended the era which saw its evolution and immediate usefulness. Long after slavery had gone, the language of race, and the cultural values of colour, thrived in the Western world.

Note

1   Ira Berlin, *Many Thousands Gone: The First Two Centuries of Slavery in North America*, Cambridge, Mass., 1998, p. 1.

———•◆•———

INTRODUCTION TO PART EIGHT

S LAVERY IN THE AMERICAS is exclusively identified with people of African descent. From one slave society to another, and in the European heartlands which established those societies, it came to be assumed that black slaves, Africans and their New World descendants, alone were suited for slavery. Indeed, down to the present day there remains a popular association of slavery and blackness; when people think of slaves, they think of black slaves. Yet this association between race and slavery is, in the long span of history, unusual.[1] In many other slave societies (in the ancient world, Meso-America and Asia) there was no necessary link between colour and slavery. It was not always possible to distinguish a slave by his or her colour. However, slavery in the Americas did precisely that: it established a link between blackness and slavery. To be black was to be a slave; to be a slave was to be black. Behind this simple formula there lay, of course, a complex ideology of slavery. It was, in effect, a complicated process of justification which had its own dynamic, changing through time and place, but which was critical in establishing the simple proposition, namely that only black people could be slaves. But why should this be so when, as we have suggested, slaves elsewhere (and indeed even in the early days of settlement in the Americas) might not be identifiable by colour? What, in brief, was so distinctive about American slavery that it came to hinge on the question of race?

Stated simply, it could be argued that the Atlantic economy created and then fostered a dependence on African labour. There seemed no way of providing labour, in the required numbers and at affordable prices, for the settlements and economic developments in the Americas from other obvious sources of labour: European settlers (free or unfree) or the indigenous peoples of the Americas. But if Europeans wanted to cultivate tropical goods with African labour, why not settle and cultivate those crops in Africa itself, rather than transport millions of Africans across the Atlantic for the purpose? Europeans could not settle in sub-Saharan Africa because of the ferocious disease environment. Not until the development of modern tropical medicines in the late nineteenth century were Europeans able to settle on the West African coast and migrate into the interior. Before then, Africa was a dangerous place for Europeans, a fact amply confirmed by the mortality rates among white crew on those slave ships which lingered too long on the African coast. The association, then, between slavery and colour/race emerged as a cover, a justification, for the growing European reliance on African labour in the tropical colonies of the Americas. It was an ideology which changed with the waxing and waning of slavery itself. It became more racially assertive when slavery found itself under attack, from the late eighteenth century onwards.

There is ample evidence about white attitudes towards black humanity long before the European settlement of the Americas. Dislike, disapproval and outright hostility can be seen in a variety of pre-modern European sources. But it was life in the Americas which took older perceptions of black humanity and moulded them into something qualitatively different. The development of the slave settlements saw the emergence of views about mankind which sought to separate black from white, gradually consigning black humanity to the very edge of humanity itself.

Yet initial demand for labour in the pioneering settlements was colourblind. Indentured European labourers, transported European criminals, white landowners, groups of (reluctant) Indians, all worked alongside small bands of African slaves, sharing the same tasks, the same meagre returns of food and shelter, and the common hardships of pioneering life. In the British case, tens of thousands of indentured labourers, mainly young men bound for five to seven years to their masters in the Caribbean and the Chesapeake, were poured into the colonies. The British, like other Europeans, had no legal or moral qualms about using unfree labour to settle and develop their colonies. However, indentured labourers were not slaves, and local convention and law granted them distinct rights. Moreover, if indentured labourers survived, they became free at the end of their indenture. But the supply of such labour was not enough to satisfy local planters, especially following the sugar and tobacco revolutions, the expansion of plantations, and the growth of lucrative export trades in staples to Europe. Africans seemed to fit the planters' requirements perfectly, not least because their value had already been proved in the Atlantic islands. As a result, ever more Africans were imported into Brazil, the Caribbean and the Chesapeake. By the late seventeenth century, the economies in those regions had become characterised by the use of enslaved African labour. Local planters, and the local polities they dominated, therefore began to offer justifications for their growing reliance on African slave labour. Colour, and all it represented, offered an obvious visual means of justification and reached back to longstanding prejudices and antipathies.

The English had inherited powerful cultural assumptions about blackness. The language itself – English – associated blackness with evil, dirt and sin. It stood in sharp contrast to the imagery of purity, virtue and beauty denoted by whiteness.[2] There was, moreover, a growing awareness about black Africa prompted by that expanding genre of travel accounts from the mid-sixteenth century onwards. This flow of travelogues and (often fictional) stories about Africa published in English, with their mix of fantasy and bizarre reality, helped to confirm in people's minds the image of Africa as home to uncivilised and barbarous peoples. Here were pagans, devoid of any form of civilisation recognised by Europeans, possessing no 'proper' religion (save for Islam) and ideally suited, so it seemed, for toil in the tropical settlements of the Americas. There was a growing divide, cultivated by travellers' tales, between Europeans and Africans. And all seemed to be explained by the issue of colour. From this complexity of cultural forces there developed those distinctive relations between black and white in the course of the sixteenth and seventeenth centuries. More than that, European sailors and traders, including the English, had been actively buying and selling Africans as slaves – as objects – in Europe and the Atlantic islands even before the development of the American colonies. It involved no great change, no quantum leap, for Europeans to buy and sell Africans for labour in the Americas.

There was, then, a powerful disposition in England to regard Africans as occupying a distinctive role in cultural demonology. English sailors and merchants trading to Africa looked at Africans through eyes tinted by these cultural forces. It seemed easy and natural to point to the African's colour to explain the complex cultural differences between black and white. In time it came to be a *post-hoc* rationalisation for using Africans as slaves, though the basic reason was, of course, economic. There were voices which spoke out against African slavery, and who denied the association between colour and slavery, but they were few, and they were generally ignored as the planters cried out for ever more Africans to tap the lucrative developments in the colonies.

As slavery developed in the Americas, as local laws and social convention began to demarcate ever more clearly the contours of slavery and the boundaries between black and white, plantocratic ideologies emerged which needed to justify the local treatment of slaves. The slave systems of the Americas were, despite the differences between them, based on the chattel status of the slaves. They were bought and sold, inherited and bequeathed, gifted and received, like most other material possessions. The slaves were securely located beyond the pale of humanity. From the moment they were sold to European slave traders on the coast, in their oceanic transit stowed below decks as numbers, in their purchase and regulation by planters as objects with a financial value, the slaves were consigned to the level of property and chattel. Despite the obvious philosophical and moral contradictions inherent in this process, the Africans entered the Atlantic system (and their offspring were born into it) as commodities. The slave lobby, in Europe and the colonies, needed to justify the system they had brought into being, and on which they thrived. For that they needed to exclude slaves from the fraternity of humanity, to devise the pretence that Africans and their descendants were less than human. Anything which might contradict that philosophy (access as equals to the Church, for example) was to be resisted. And this complex process was most easily achieved by concentrating on colour: pointing to blackness as evidence and proof that the slave was outside the pale. In this way, black people slipped from being objects of cultural curiosity to being non-persons.

The transformation of the African from a person to a thing, from *Homo sapiens* to chattel, is the story of plantation slavery itself. It was a process which differed from one colony to another, but the overall pattern was similar. As local plantations developed, with their apparently insatiable appetite for more African slaves, local economic usage and legal practice confirmed the property status of the Africans and their local descendants. Moreover, each new act of slave resistance saw a progressive tightening of the plantocratic grip over their human property. New laws, sharper distinctions and differences between black and white became the bases of colonial life. Nor was this merely a matter of colonial practice, for the whole system was monitored, approved of or qualified by the metropolitan powers in Europe. London, for example, played an instrumental role in shaping the property status of black humanity. The laws passed by Parliament to govern the slave trade itself specifically defined the African as an object. Similarly, English colonies had their laws scrutinised, approved and altered by London. All this was in addition to the legal confusions which followed the haphazard transplanting of slaves into England itself: the arrival of small bands of slaves from Africa and the Americas in the company of their owners, and the consequent legal arguments about whether slavery was legal in England (or Scotland).[3]

By the early eighteenth century, it was clear enough that the law, broadly defined, had set the seal of property on the African. How could it be otherwise with so huge an Atlantic business, involving so many British ports, so many British vessels and men, so many slave plantations in the British Americas – all requiring Africans to work as slaves? The slave was now an object, and was most easily demarcated by his or her colour. Thus did blackness emerge as the defining characteristic of slavery in the Americas.

It is understandable that the plantocratic lobby should seek justifications for their distinctive system. For their part, planters, and the scribes they hired, garnished their arguments with details gleaned from the slave quarters of the Americas. They paraded before the reading public, especially in London, details about slaves' shortcomings, to persuade readers that the slave was capable of being no more than a slave; that blacks were born slavish and could only be kept at their tasks by the impositions of the slave regimes. It was, of course, self-interest masquerading as something else. And although it was a circular argument, it clearly worked, not least because a number of prominent eighteenth-century writers repeated the racial prejudices of the planters in a variety of publications. The assertion that the black was an inferior being, destined to work in perpetuity for whites, was repeated time and again throughout the eighteenth century and, despite occasional objections, was not fully confronted until the rise of abolitionist sentiment towards the end of that century. Until then, the racist ideology of the slave lobby remained effectively unchallenged.

Yet even in England, there was an abundance of evidence to refute the planters' racist ideology. There was, for example, a growing number of blacks, Africans and others, who began to make their presence felt in England. And many did not fit the caricature of slavishness so basic to the planters' ideology. It was clear enough, for those with eyes to see, that blacks were not destined by nature to be slaves to white people. London especially was littered with blacks who had made their ways in the world, who had become independent free people with a variety of attainments. A similar, indeed more striking, picture could be seen throughout the slave colonies. There, large numbers of slaves had, as we have seen, secured for themselves levels of economic well-being which would have surprised outsiders. The flourishing of independent slave economic life yielded the wherewithal for a better, more rounded life. When slaves were allowed to flourish as independent people, they often did so with great success. But such images, which could be seen in all corners of the plantation colonies, contradicted and subverted the planters' racist ideology.

What brought the question of race and slavery to a head were the early abolitionist attacks on slavery from the mid 1780s onwards. Those attacks, in London and Philadelphia, were helped forward, and given a specific edge, by the problems of black life in both those cities. Equally, the American Revolution was critical, with its arguments about political and social rights. As slavery came under fiercer attack from a small band of opponents led by the Quakers, its proponents were obliged to justify themselves and their use of slavery as never before. It was at this point that concepts of race surfaced and received their widest currency as a major justification for slavery. The debate, more complex than can be outlined here, was polarised between issues of social and human rights, on the one hand, and race and colour, on the other. And the whole complex argument was lifted onto a qualitative new plane by the impact of the French Revolution. The concepts of the rights of man – of liberty, equality and fraternity – had a seismic impact on the slave empires. If all men (and women) were equal, it must surely follow that blacks were equal to whites. The most dramatic impact of those ideals was to be seen in St Domingue (Haiti) in the 1790s, where the slave revolt led to the emergence of the first post-colonial black republic outside of Africa. And all was built on the ruins of what, up to 1789, had been the most buoyant of slave societies.

Demands for black freedom prompted some of the most abusive of plantocratic racist claims. Indeed, the debate about slavery and abolition became progressively more embroiled in questions of race. It seemed easy to dismiss the claims to black equality by a denigration of black life and potential. Such dismissive assertions were used, from the mid-nineteenth century onwards, in more overtly racist arguments which incorporated evidence from the new disciplines of natural and social science. As those sciences sought to perfect the categorisation of mankind (and the animal kingdom), older concepts, derived from the arguments about slavery, were absorbed into newer 'scientific' analyses. This development of scientific racism, though different from anything that had gone before, inherited ideas and assumptions from the heyday of the slave empires. In its turn, scientific racism bequeathed to the twentieth century a thriving debate about the nature of race. That debate was to become a central theme in political and social disputes throughout much of that century.

Clearly, the racism which so scarred the mid–late twentieth century was qualitatively different from the racist arguments which emerged from debates about slavery. Yet the two were linked, directly and unbroken, in ways which have often been overlooked. The racially determined world of Atlantic slavery was to leave its mark down to the present day.

Notes

1   The concept of 'race' is of course highly troublesome and problematic. For a recent interdisciplinary approach, see Les Black and John Solomos, eds, *Theories of Race and Racism: A Reader*, London, 2000.
2   See Winthrop Jordan, *White over Black*, New York, 1968.
3   James Walvin, *Britain's Slave Empire*, Stroud, 2000, ch. 5.

Chapter 30

Winthrop D. Jordan

AMERICAN CHIAROSCURO
The status and definition of mulattoes in the British colonies

THE WORD *MULATTO* IS NOT frequently used in the United States. Americans generally reserve it for biological contexts, because for social purposes a mulatto is termed a *Negro*. Americans lump together both socially and legally all persons with perceptible admixture of Negro ancestry, thus making social definition without reference to genetic logic; white blood becomes socially advantageous only in overwhelming proportion. The dynamic underlying the peculiar bifurcation of American society into only two color groups can perhaps be better understood if some attempt is made to describe its origin, for the content of social definitions may remain long after the impulses to their formation have gone.

After only one generation of European experience in America, colonists faced the problem of dealing with racially mixed offspring, a problem handled rather differently by the several nations involved. It is well known that the Latin countries, especially Portugal and Spain, rapidly developed a social hierarchy structured according to degrees of intermixture of Negro and European blood, complete with a complicated system of terminology to facilitate definition.[1] The English in Maryland, Virginia, and the Carolinas, on the other hand, seem to have created no such system of ranking. To explain this difference merely by comparing the different cultural backgrounds involved is to risk extending generalizations far beyond possible factural support. Study is still needed of the specific factors affecting each nation's colonies, for there is evidence with some nations that the same cultural heritage was spent in different ways by the colonial heirs, depending on varying conditions encountered in the New World. The English, for example, encountered the problem of race mixture in very different contexts in their several colonies; they answered it in one fashion in their West Indian islands and in quite another in their colonies on the continent.

As far as the continental colonies were concerned, the presence of mulattoes received legislative recognition by the latter part of the seventeenth century. The word itself, borrowed from the Spanish, was in English usage from the beginning of the century and was probably first employed in Virginia in 1666. From about that time, laws dealing with Negro slaves began to add "and mulattoes." In all English continental colonies mulattoes were lumped with Negroes in the slave codes and in statutes governing the conduct of free Negroes:[2] the law was clear that mulattoes and Negroes were not to be distinguished for different treatment—a phenomenon occasionally noted by foreign travelers.[3]

If mulattoes were to be considered Negroes, logic required some definition of mulattoes, some demarcation between them and white men. Law is sometimes less than logical, however, and throughout the colonial period only Virginia and North Carolina grappled with the question raised by continuing intermixture. In 1705 the Virginia legislature defined a mulatto as "the child, grand child, or great grand child of a negro," or, revealingly, merely "the child of an Indian." North Carolina wavered on the matter, but generally pushed the taint of Negro ancestry from one-eighth to one-sixteenth.[4] There is no reason to suppose that these two colonies were atypical, and in all probability something like these rules operated in the other continental colonies. What the matter came down to, of course, was visibility. Anyone whose appearance discernibly connected him with the Negro was held to be such. The line was thus drawn with regard to practicalities rather than logic. Daily practice supplied logic enough.

Another indication of the refusal of the English continental colonies to separate the "mixed breed" from the African was the absence of terminology which could be used to define a hierarchy of status. The colonists did, it is true, seize upon a separate word to describe those of mixed blood. They were forced to do so if they were to deal with the problem at all, even if they merely wished, as they did, to lump "mulattoes" with Negroes. If, however, an infusion of white blood had been regarded as elevating status, then presumably the more white blood the higher the social rank. Had such ranking existed, descriptive terminology would have been required with which to handle shades of distinction. Yet no such vocabulary developed in the American colonies. Only one word besides *mulatto* was used to describe those of mixed ancestry. The term *mustee* (*mestee, mustize, mestizo, mustizoe*) was used to describe a mixture which was in part Indian, usually Indian-Negro but occasionally Indian-white. The term was in common use only in the Carolinas, Georgia, and to some extent New York, that is, in those colonies where such crosses occurred with some frequency. Its use revealed the colonists' refusal to identify Indians and Negroes as the same sort of people, a refusal underlined by their belief that the two groups possessed a natural antipathy for each other.[5] Yet while the colonists thus distinguished persons of some Indian ancestry by a separate word, they lumped these *mustees* with mulattoes and Negroes in their slave codes.

Although legislative enactments provide a valuable index of community sentiment, they do not always accurately reflect social practice. An extensive search in the appropriate sources—diaries, letters, travel accounts, newspapers, and so on—fails to reveal any pronounced tendency to distinguish mulattoes from Negroes, any feeling that their status was higher and demanded different treatment. The sources give no indication, for instance, that mulattoes were preferred as house servants or concubines. There may well have been a relatively high proportion of mulattoes among manumitted slaves, but this was probably due to the not unnatural desire of some masters to liberate their own offspring. Yet all this is largely negative evidence, and the proposition that mulattoes were not accorded higher status than Negroes is as susceptible of proof as any negative. Perhaps the usual procedure of awaiting disproof through positive evidence may be allowed.

A single exception to these generalizations stands out sharply from the mass of colonial legislation. In 1765 the colony of Georgia not only undertook to

encourage immigration of free colored persons (itself a unique step) but actually
provided that free mulatto and mustee immigrants might be naturalized as white
men by the legislature, complete with "all the Rights, Priviledges, Powers, and
Immunities whatsoever which any person born of British parents" could have,
except the right to vote and sit in the Commons House of Assembly.[6] Thus a
begrudging kind of citizenship was extended to free mulattoes. That Georgia should
so distinguish herself from her northern neighbors was a measure of the colony's
weak and exposed condition. A small population with an increasingly high proportion of slaves and perpetual danger from powerful Indian tribes made Georgians
eager for men who might be counted as white and thus strengthen the colony. The
legislature went to great lengths in its search—perhaps too far, for it never actually
naturalized anyone under the aegis of the 1765 law.

Only rarely in the colonial period did the subject of mulattoes receive any
attention from American writers. Mulattoes were so fixed in station that their position apparently did not merit attention. The subject did come up once in the
South-Carolina Gazette, yet even then it was casually raised in connection with an
entirely different topic. An anonymous contributor in 1735 offered the public some
strictures on Carolina's *nouveau riche*, the "half Gentry," and attacked especially
their imitative and snobbish behavior. For illustration he turned to the character
of the mulatto.

> It is observed concerning the Generation of *Molattoes*, that they are seldom
> well beloved either by the Whites or the Blacks. Their Approach towards
> Whiteness, makes them look back with some kind of Scorn upon the
> Colour they seem to have left, while the Negroes, who do not think them
> better than themselves, return their Contempt with Interest: And the
> Whites, who respect them no Whit the more for the nearer Affinity in
> Colour, are apt to regard their Behaviour as too bold and assuming, and
> bordering upon Impudence. As they are next to Negroes, and but just
> above them, they are terribly afraid of being thought Negroes, and there-
> fore avoid as much as possible their Company or Commerce: and
> Whitefolks are as little fond of the Company of *Molattoes*.[7]

The writer's point, of course, was not that mulattoes were in fact superior to
Negroes, but that they alone thought they were. Apparently mulattoes thought
white blood to be a source of elevation, a proposition which whites (and Negroes
as well) were quick to deny. White blood secured one's status only if undiluted.

A somewhat different aspect of this problem came up in 1784 when it was
forced on the attention of a Savannah merchant, Joseph Clay. As executor of a will
Clay became responsible for the welfare of two young mulattoes, very possibly the
children of his deceased friend. Because the young people were both free, Clay's
letter to a gentleman in Ireland offers valuable evidence of what a combination of
personal freedom and some white ancestry afforded in the way of social position
in Georgia. "These young Folks are very unfortunately situated in this Country,"
Clay wrote, "their descent places them in the most disadvantageous situation, as
Free persons the Laws protects them—but they gain no rank in Life, White Persons
do not commonly associate with them on a footing of equality—so many of their
own Colour (say the mixt breed) being Slaves, they too naturally fall in with them,

and even the Negro Slaves claim a right to their acquaintance and Society." For Clay the situation was one of unrelieved gloom, even of horror: "thus a little reflection will present to you what their future Prospects here must be—neglected by the most respectable Class of Society, [they] are forced to intermix with the lowest, and in what that must end—we woud wish to draw a Veil—all the Care that can be taken of them cant prevent it, it arrises from our peculiar situation in regard to these people." Clay went on to recommend as "the most eligible plan" that the children be sent to Europe if his correspondent would accept them as wards. "The Boy might be Bound to some business . . . and the Girl might make a very good Wife to some honest Tradesman." It was essential that they cross the Atlantic: "this alone can save them . . . I think they might both be made usefull Members of Society, no such distinctions interfere with their happiness on your side the Water."[8] Clay added finally that several of his friends endorsed his proposal. Apparently America offered little opportunity for blacks to become whites through intermixture. American society, wedded as it was to Negro slavery, drew a rigid line which did not exist in Europe: this was indeed "our peculiar situation in regard to these people."

The existence of a rigid barrier between whites and those of Negro blood necessarily required a means by which the barrier could on occasion be passed. Some accommodation had to be made for those persons with so little Negro blood that they appeared to be white, for one simply could not go around calling apparently white persons Negroes. Once the stain was washed out visibly it was useless as a means of identification. Thus there developed the silent mechanism of "passing." Such a device would have been unnecessary if those of mixed ancestry and appearance had been regarded as midway between white and black. It was the existence of a broad chasm which necessitated the sudden leap which passing represented.

Fortunately it is possible to catch a glimpse of this process as it operated in the colonial period by following the extraordinary career of a family named Gibson in South Carolina. In 1731 a member of the Commons House of Assembly announced in the chamber that several free colored men with their white wives had immigrated from Virginia with the intention of settling on the Santee River. Free Negroes were undesirable enough, but white wives made the case exceptionally disturbing. "The house apprehending [this prospect] to be of ill Consequence to this Province," appointed a committee to inquire into the matter. Governor Robert Johnson had already sent for what seemed to be the several families involved, and the committee asked him to report his findings to the house.

"The people lately come into the Settlements having been sent for," Johnson duly reported, "I have had them before me in Council and upon Examination find that they are not Negroes nor Slaves but Free people, That the Father of them here is named Gideon Gibson and his Father was also free, I have been informed by a person who has lived in Virginia that this Gibson has lived there Several Years in good Repute and by his papers that he has produced before me that his transactions there have been very regular, That he has for several years paid Taxes for two tracts of Land and had seven Negroes of his own, That he is a Carpenter by Trade and is come hither for the support of his Family." This evident respectability so impressed the governor that he allowed the Gibson family to remain in the colony. "The account he has given of himself," Johnson declared, "is so Satisfactory that he is no Vagabond that I have in Consideration of his Wifes being a white woman and several White women Capable of working and being Serviceable in the Country permitted him to Settle in this Country upon entering into Recognizance for his good behaviour which I have taken accordingly."[9]

The meaning of Johnson's statement that "they are not Negroes nor Slaves but Free people" is not entirely clear. Certainly Gideon Gibson himself was colored; it seems likely that he was mulatto rather than Negro, but it is impossible to tell surely. At any rate Gideon Gibson prospered very nicely: by 1736 either he or a son of the same name owned 450 acres of Carolina land. He continued to own Negroes, and in 1757 he was described as owning property in two widely separated counties. By 1765 the status of Gideon Gibson (by this time definitely the son of the original carpenter) was such that he was appointed administrator of an estate.[10] His sister married a wealthy planter, and there is no evidence to indicate that Gibson himself was regarded by his neighbors as anything but white.[11] In 1768 he was leading a band of South Carolina Regulators on the field of battle. The commander dispatched to arrest Gibson was a planter and colonel in the militia, George Gabriel Powell, who ignominiously resigned his commission when his men sided with the Regulators. This latter worthy, apparently a kind master to his own Negroes, sought vindication by attacking Gibson's ancestry.[12] The exact nature of the attack is unclear, but the matter came up on the floor of the Commons, of which Powell was a member. The prominent merchant-patriot of Charles Town, Henry Laurens, recorded the conflict in a letter written some years later. Laurens was writing from England of his own conviction that slavery ought to be brought to an end, a conviction that inevitably raised the question of color.

> Reasoning from the colour carries no conviction. By perseverance the black may be blanched and the "stamp of Providence" effectually effaced. Gideon Gibson escaped the penalties of the negro law by producing upon comparison more red and white in his face than could be discovered in the faces of half the descendants of the French refugees in our House of Assembly, including your old acquaintance the Speaker. I challenged them all to the trial. The children of this same Gideon, having passed through another stage of whitewash were of fairer complexion than their prosecutor George Gabriel [Powell].—But to confine them to their original clothing will be best. They may and ought to continue a separate people, may be subjected by special laws, kept harmless, made useful and freed from the tyranny and arbitrary power of individuals; but as I have already said, this difficulty cannot be removed by arguments on this side of the water.[13]

Laurens showed both sides of the coin. He defended an individual's white status on the basis of appearance and at the same time expressed the conviction that colored persons "may and ought to continue a separate people." Once an Ethiopian always an Ethiopian, unless he could indeed change his skin.

Gideon Gibson's successful hurdling of the barrier was no doubt an unusual case; it is of course impossible to tell how unusual. Passing was difficult but not impossible, and it stood as a veiled, unrecognized monument to the American ideal of a society open to all comers. One Virginia planter advertised in the newspaper for his runaway mulatto slave who he stated might try to pass for free or as a "white man." An English traveler reported calling upon a Virginia lawyer who was "said to be" and who looked like a mulatto.[14] But the problem of evidence is insurmountable. The success of the passing mechanism depended upon its operating in silence. Passing was a conspiracy of silence not only for the individual but for a biracial society which had drawn a rigid color line based on visibility. Unless a white man was a white man, the gates were open to endless slander and confusion.

That the existence of such a line in the continental colonies was not predominantly the effect of the English cultural heritage is suggested by even a glance at the English colonies in the Caribbean. The social accommodation of racial intermixture in the islands followed a different pattern from that on the continent. It was regarded as improper, for example, to work mulattoes in the fields—a fundamental distinction. Apparently they were preferred as tradesmen, house servants, and especially as concubines.[15] John Luffman wrote that mulatto slaves "fetch a lower price than blacks, unless they are tradesmen, because the purchasers cannot employ them in the drudgeries to which negroes are put too; the colored men, are therefore mostly brought up to trades or employed as house slaves, and the women of this description are generally prostitutes."[16] Though the English in the Caribbean thought of their society in terms of white, colored, and black, they employed a complicated battery of names to distinguish persons of various racial mixtures. This terminology was borrowed from the neighboring Spanish, but words are not acquired unless they fulfill a need. While the English settlers on the continent borrowed one Spanish word to describe all mixtures of black and white, the islanders borrowed at least four—*mulatto, sambo, quadroon*, and *mestize*—to describe differing degrees.[17] And some West Indians were prepared to act upon the logic which these terms implied. The respected Jamaican historian, Bryan Edwards, actually proposed extension of civil privileges to mulattoes in proportion to their admixture of white blood.[18] Such a proposition was unheard of on the continent.

The difference between the two regions on this matter may well have been connected with another pronounced divergence in social practice. The attitude toward interracial sex was far more genial in the islands than in the continental colonies. In the latter, miscegenation very rarely met with anything but disapproval in principle, no matter how avid the practice. Sexual intimacy between any white person and any Negro (that "unnatural and inordinate copulation") was utterly condemned. Protests against the practice were frequent.[19] A traveler in New York reported that the citizens of Albany possessed a particular "moral delicacy" on one point: "they were from infancy in habits of familiarity with these humble friends [the Negroes], yet being early taught that nature had placed between them a barrier, which it was in a high degree criminal and disgraceful to pass, they considered a mixture of such distinct races with abhorrence, as a violation of her laws."[20] About 1700 the Chester County Court in Pennsylvania ordered a Negro "never more to meddle with any white woman more upon paine of his life." Public feeling on this matter was strong enough to force its way over the hurdles of the legislative process into the statute books of many colonies. Maryland and Virginia forbade cohabitation of whites and Negroes well before the end of the seventeenth century. Similar prohibitions were adopted by Massachusetts, North and South Carolina, and Pennsylvania during the next quarter-century and by Georgia when Negroes were admitted to that colony in 1750. Thus two Northern and all Southern colonies legally prohibited miscegenation.[21] Feeling against intercourse with Negroes was strengthened by the fact that such activity was generally illicit; Americans had brought from England certain standards of marital fidelity which miscegenation flagrantly violated.

The contrast offered by the West Indies is striking. Protests against interracial sex relations were infrequent. Colored mistresses were kept openly. "The Planters are in general rich," a young traveler wrote, "but a set of dissipating, abandoned, and cruel people. Few even of the married ones, but keep a Mulatto or Black Girl in the house or at lodgings for certain purposes."[22] Edward Long of Jamaica put the matter this way: "He who should presume to shew any displeasure against such a thing as simple fornication, would for his pains be accounted a simple blockhead; since not one in twenty can be persuaded, that there is either sin; or shame in cohabiting with his slave."[23] Perhaps most significant of all, no island legislature prohibited extramarital miscegenation and only one declared against intermarriage.[24] The reason, of course, was that white men so commonly slept with Negro women that to legislate against the practice would have been merely ludicrous. Concubinage was such an integral part of island life that one might just as well attempt to abolish the sugar cane.

Mulattoes in the West Indies, then, were products of accepted practice, something they assuredly were not in the continental colonies. In the one area they were the fruits of a desire which society tolerated and almost institutionalized; in the other they represented an illicit passion which public morality unhesitatingly condemned. On the continent, unlike the West Indies, mulattoes represented a practice about which men could only feel guilty. To reject and despise the productions of one's own guilt was only natural.

If such difference in feeling about miscegenation has any connection with the American attitude toward mulattoes, it only raises the question of what caused that difference. Since the English settlers in both the West Indies and the continental colonies brought with them the same cultural baggage, something in their colonial experiences must have caused the divergence in their attitudes toward miscegenation. Except perhaps for climatic disimilarity, a factor of very doubtful importance, the most fundamental difference lay in the relative numbers of whites and Negroes in the two areas. On the continent the percentage of Negroes in the total population reached its peak in the period 1730–65 and has been declining since. It ranged from about 3 per cent in New England, 8 to 15 per cent in the middle colonies, 30 to 40 in Maryland and Virginia, 25 in North Carolina, 40 in Georgia, to a high of some 60 per cent in South Carolina. The proportion of Negroes in the islands was far higher: 75 per cent in Barbados, 80 in the Leeward Islands, and over 90 in Jamaica.[25]

These figures strongly suggest a close connection between a high proportion of Negroes and open acceptance of miscegenation. South Carolina, for example, where Negroes formed a majority of the population, was alone among the continental colonies in tolerating even slightly conspicuous interracial liaisons.[26] Thoroughly disparate proportions of Negroes, moreover, made it inevitable that the West Indies and the continental colonies would develop dissimilar societies. The West Indian planters were lost not so much in the Caribbean as in a sea of blacks. They found it impossible to re-create English culture as they had known it. They were corrupted by living in a police state, though not themselves the objects of its discipline. The business of the islands was business, the production of agricultural staples; the islands were not where one really lived, but where one made one's money. By contrast, the American colonists maintained their hold on the English background, modifying it not so much to accommodate slavery as to winning the new land. They were numerous enough to create a new culture with a validity of its own, complete with the adjustments necessary to absorb non-English Europeans. Unlike the West Indians, they felt no need to be constantly running back to England to reassure themselves that they belonged to civilization. Because they were conscious of the solid worth of their own society, forged with their own hands, they vehemently rejected any trespass upon it by a people so alien as the Negroes. The islanders could hardly resent trespass on something which they did not have. By sheer weight of numbers their society was black and slave.

This fundamental difference was perhaps reinforced by another demographic factor. In the seventeenth century the ratio of men to women had been high in America and higher still in the West Indies, where the ratio was about three to two, or, as the sex ratio is usually expressed, 150 (males per 100 females). In the following century it dropped drastically. New England's sex ratio went below 100 as a result of emigration which was as usual predominantly male. Elsewhere on the continent the bounding birth rate nearly erased the differential: in 1750, except on the edge of the frontier, it was probably no more than 110 and in most places less. Perhaps not so well known is the fact that the same process occurred in most of the English islands. Emigration sapped their male strength until Barbados had a sex ratio in the 80s and the various Leeward Islands were balanced in the neighborhood of 100. A significant exception was Jamaica, where in mid-eighteenth century a plentiful supply of land maintained a sex ratio of nearly two to one.[27]

Male numerical predomination was surely not without effect on interracial sexual relations. Particularly where the white population was outnumbered by the black, white women formed a small group. Their scarcity rendered them valuable. The natural reaction on the part of white men was to place them protectively upon a pedestal and then run off to gratify passions elsewhere. For their part white women, though they might propagate children, inevitably held themselves aloof from the world of lust and passion, a world associated with infidelity and Negro slaves. Under no circumstances would they have attempted, nor would they have been allowed, to clamber down from their pedestal to seek pleasures of their own across the racial line. In fact the sexual union of white women with Negro men was uncommon in all colonies. When it did occur (and it did more often than is generally supposed) it was in just those areas to which the demographic factors point—America north of South Carolina, especially in New England, where white women even married Negroes. Such a combination, legitimized or not, was apparently unknown in the West Indies.[28]

If a high sex ratio contributed to the acceptability of miscegenation, it may well have enhanced the acceptablity of mulatto offspring. For example, there is the striking fact that Jamaica, the only colony where the sex ratio continued high, was the only colony to give legislative countenance to the rise of mulattoes. In 1733 the legislature provided that "no Person who is not above Three Degrees removed in a lineal Descent from the Negro Ancestor exclusive, shall be allowed to vote or poll in Elections; and no one shall be deemed a Mulatto after the Third Generation, as aforesaid, but that they shall have all the Privileges and Immunities of His Majesty's white Subjects of this Island, provided they are brought up in the Christian Religion."[29] In this same period Barbados was barring any person "whose original

Extract shall be proved to have been from a Negro" from voting and from testifying against whites.[30] Beginning in the 1730s the Jamaican legislature passed numerous private acts giving the colored offspring (and sometimes the colored mistress) of such and such a planter the rights and privileges of white persons, especially the right to inherit the planter's estate. There was objection to this blanching of mulattoes, however, for in 1761 the Assembly restricted the amount of property a planter might leave to his mulatto children, saying that "such bequests tend greatly to destroy the distinction requisite, and absolutely necessary to be kept up in this island, between white persons and negroes, their issue and offspring. . . ." The law failed to destroy the acceptability of the practice, however, for the private acts continued.[31] It was in Jamaica, too, that Bryan Edwards called for extension of civil privileges to mulattoes. And Edward Long, in his history of the island, wrote that those beyond the third generation were "called English, and consider themselves as free from all taint of the Negroe race."[32] Thus Jamaica, with the highest proportion of Negroes and highest sex ratio of all the English colonies, was unique in its practice of publicly transforming Negroes into white men.

The American continental colonist refused to make this extension of privilege. He remained firm in his rejection of the mulatto, in his categorization of mixed-bloods as belonging to the lower caste. It was an unconscious decision dictated perhaps in large part by the weight of Negroes on his society, heavy enough to be a burden, yet not so heavy as to make him abandon all hope of maintaining his own identity, physically and culturally. Interracial propagation was a constant reproach that he was failing to be true to himself. Sexual intimacy strikingly symbolized a union he wished to avoid. If he could not restrain his sexual nature, he could at least reject its fruits and thus solace himself that he had done no harm. Perhaps he sensed as well that continued racial intermixture would eventually undermine the logic of the racial slavery upon which his society was based. For the separation of slaves from free men depended on a clear demarcation of the races, and the presence of mulattoes blurred this essential distinction. Accordingly he made every effort to nullify the effects of racial intermixture: by classifying the mulatto as a Negro he was in effect denying that intermixture had occurred at all.

Notes

1   See, for example, Irene Diggs, "Color in Colonial Spanish America," *Journal of Negro History*, XXXVIII (1953), 403–427.

2   These statements are based on an examination of what I believe to be nearly all the colonial and state statutes concerning Negroes and slaves through 1807. For the use of *mulatto* see the *Oxford English Dictionary* and the private petition to the Virginia Assembly in "The Randolph Manuscript," *Virginia Magazine of History and Biography*, XVII (1909), 232. The word was first used in a statute in 1678: William Hand Browne and others, eds., *Archives of Maryland* (Baltimore, 1883–), VII, 76. Maryland actually created a legally separate class of persons known as "Mulattoes born of white women," and in doing so developed a severe case of legislative stuttering. The difficulty originated in 1664 when the Assembly declared that children were to follow the condition of the father (rather than the mother as in other colonies). It took 35 years to straighten out this matter, but meanwhile some provision had to be made for mulatto children of white mothers, for no one really wanted them to be slaves. The Assembly provided that they should serve until age 31. This group was sometimes treated legally as white and sometimes as Negro, a procedure which seems to have been followed only about through the 1730s. (Virginia in 1691 enacted similar

provisions for this class, but apparently abandoned them five years later.) The underlying intention was that mulatto children of white mothers should be free in status, though punished for their illegitimate origin. This was not discrimination between mulattoes and Negroes but between mulattoes of two different kinds of mothers, white and black. The legal confusion and inconsistencies on this matter may be followed in Browne and others, eds., *Archives of Md.*, I, 526–527, 533–534; VII, 176, 177, 203–205; XIII, 290, 292, 304, 306–307, 308, 323, 380, 394, 529, 546–549; XIX, 428; XXII, 551–552; XXVI, 254–261; XXX, 289–290; XXXIII, 111–112; XXXVI, 275–276; XXXVIII, 39; William Kilty, ed., *The Laws of Maryland* (Annapolis, 1799–1800), II, chap. 67, sec. 14. None of the standard secondary sources on the Negro in Maryland offer a satisfactory account of this matter. For Virginia, see William Waller Hening, ed., *The Statutes at Large: Being a Collection of All the Laws of Virginia* . . . (New York, Philadelphia, Richmond, 1819–23), II, 170; III, 87, 137–140, 252. A Virginia militia act of 1777 declared that free mulattoes might serve as "drummers, fifers, or pioneers" (Hening, ed., *Statutes of Va.*, V, 268), but this failure to refer to "negroes and mulattoes" was so unusual that one must suspect inadvertent omission. See also a clear case of such omission in Massachusetts: George H. Moore, *Notes on the History of Slavery in Massachusetts* (New York, 1866), 228–237.

3 Duc de La Rochefoucault Liancourt, *Travels through the United States of North America* . . . (London, 1799), I, 568; Kenneth and Anna M. Roberts, trans., *Moreau de St. Méry's American Journey, 1793–1798* (Garden City, N.Y., 1947), 301–302.

4 Hening, ed., *Statutes of Va.*, III, 252; Walter L. Clark, ed., *The State Records of North Carolina* (Goldsboro, N. C., 1886–1910), XXIII, 106, 160, 262, 345, 526, 559, 700, 882; XXIV, 61; XXV, 283, 445; William L. Saunders, ed., *The Colonial Records of North Carolina* (Raleigh, 1886–90), VII, 605, 608, 645. In 1785–87 Virginia altered the definition to one-quarter Negro, but there was no general trend in this direction during the 19th century; see Hening, ed., *Statutes of Va.*, XII, 184; Samuel Shepard, ed., *The Statutes at Large of Virginia, from October Session 1792, to December Session 1806, Inclusive*, New Ser., being a continuation of Hening (Richmond, 1835–36), I, 123.

5 See, for example, Hugh Jones, *The Present State of Virginia from Whence Is Inferred a Short View of Maryland and North Carolina*, ed. Richard L. Morton (Chapel Hill, N.C., 1956), p. 50; John Brickell, *The Natural History of North-Carolina* . . . (Dublin, 1737), pp. 263, 273; Anne Grant, *Memoirs of an American Lady; With Sketches of Manners and Scenes in America as They Existed Previous to the Revolution*, ed. James G. Wilson (New York, 1901), I, 134; [George Milligen-Johnston], *A Short Description of the Province of South-Carolina* (London, 1770), in Chapman J. Milling, ed., *Colonial South Carolina; Two Contemporary Descriptions by Governor James Glen and Doctor George Milligen-Johnston*, South Caroliniana, Sesquicentennial Series, No. 1 (Columbia, 1951), p. 136; Parish Transcripts, Box III, bundle: Minutes of Council in Assembly (1755), p. 3, New-York Historical Society, New York City. See also Kenneth W. Porter, "Relations between Negroes and Indians within the Present Limits of the United States," *Jour. of Negro Hist.*, XVII (1932), 298–306, 322–327.

6 Allen D. Candler, comp., *The Colonial Records of the State of Georgia* (Atlanta, 1904–16), XVIII, 659. The wording of the act is ambiguous, and though free Negroes might have fallen under its provisions, the legislature was apparently thinking only of mulattoes and mustees.

7 *South-Carolina Gazette* (Charleston), Mar. 22, 1735.

8 Joseph Clay to John Wright, Savannah, Feb. 17, 1784, in *Letters of Joseph Clay, Merchant of Savannah, 1776–1793* . . . (Georgia Historical Society, *Collections*, VIII [1913]), 203–204. Further testimony that mulattoes considered themselves superior to Negroes may be found in William Logan to Lord Granville, London, Aug. 13, 1761, Logan Papers, XI, 60, Historical Society of Pennsylvania, Philadelphia.

9 Parish Transcripts, Box II, bundle: S. C., Minutes of House of Burgesses (1730–35), 9.

10 *South-Carolina Gazette*, Aug. 29, 1743, supplement; Nov. 26, Dec. 10, 1750; Mar. 3, 1757, supplement; "Abstracts of Records of the Proceedings in the Court of Ordinary, 1764–1771," *South Carolina Historical and Genealogical Magazine*, XXII (1921), 97, 127; see also XXIII (1972), 35; [Prince Frederick Parish], *The Register Book for the Parish Prince Frederick, Winyaw* (Baltimore, 1916), 15, 20, 32, 34.

11 For this point I am indebted to Dr. Richard M. Brown, of Rutgers University, who is currently publishing a study of the South Carolina Regulators. He also provided information and references on the younger Gideon Gibson's regulating activities and kindly pointed out to me a useful local history: Alexander Gregg, *History of the Old Cheraws* [2d Ed.] (Columbia, 1905). See this source, 72n, for the marriage of Gibson's sister.

12 For the Regulators' battle, see Gregg, *Old Cheraws*, 73–74, 139–156; Charles Woodmason, *The Carolina Backcountry on the Eve of the Revolution; The Journal and Other Writings of Charles Woodmason, Anglican Itinerant*, ed. Richard J. Hooker (Chapel Hill, N.C., 1953), 176–177. For biographical information on Powell and his kindness to his slaves, A. S. Salley, ed., "Diary of William Dillwyn during a Visit to Charles Town in 1772," *S. C. Hist. and Genea. Mag.*, XXXVI (1935), 35, and n.

13 Henry Laurens to William Drayton, Feb. 15, 1783, in David Duncan Wallace, *The Life of Henry Laurens; With a Sketch of the Life of Lieutenant-Colonel John Laurens* (New York and London, 1915), 454. The speaker was Peter Manigault.

14 Rind, *Virginia Gazette* (Williamsburg), Apr. 23, 1772; J[ohn] F. D. Smyth, *A Tour in the United States of America: Containing an Account of the Present Situation of that Country . . .* (London, 1784), I, 123.

15 [Thomas Tryon], *Friendly Advice to the Gentlemen-Planters of the East and West Indies* ([London], 1684), pp. 140–141; John Singleton, *A General Description of the West-Indian Islands, as far as Relates to the British, Dutch, and Danish Governments . . .* (Barbados, 1767), pp. 152–153; [Janet Schaw], *Journal of a Lady of Quality; Being the Narrative of a Journey to the West Indies, North Carolina, and Portugal, in the Years 1774 to 1776*, ed. Evangeline Walker Andrews, in collaboration with Charles M. Andrews, 3d Ed. (New Haven, 1939), p. 112; [Edward Long], *The History of Jamaica . . .* (London, 1774), II, 328–330, 332–335; William Beckford, *A Descriptive Account of the Island of Jamaica* (London, 1790), II, 322; Bryan Edwards, *The History, Civil and Commercial, of the British Colonies in the West Indies*, 3d Ed. (London, 1801), II, 18–31. The only place in the United States ever to develop an established institution of mulatto concubinage was New Orleans, where the influence of the Spanish and of French refugees from the West Indies was strong.

16 John Luffman, *A Brief Account of the Island of Antigua, together with the Customs and Manners of its Inhabitants, as Well White as Black* (London, 1789), p. 115.

17 *Mulatto* meant one-half white; *sambo*, one-fourth white; *quadroon*, three-fourths white; and *mestize* (which did not imply Indian mixture as it did on the continent), seven-eighths white. Long, *Jamaica*, II, 260–261; Edwards, *History*, II, 18; J[ohn] G. Stedman, *Narrative of a Five Years' Expedition, against the Revolted Negroes of Surinam, in Guiana* (London, 1796), II, plate opposite p. 98; *Jamaica, a Poem, in Three Parts* (London, 1777), pp. 22–23.

18 Edwards, *History*, II, 24n.

19 For a few examples: James Fontaine, *Memoirs of a Huguenot Family*, trans. and ed. Ann Maury (New York, 1872), p. 350; Eugene P. Chase, trans. and ed., *Our Revolutionary Forefathers; The Letters of François, Marquis de Barbé-Marbois during His Residence in the United States as Secretary of the French Legation, 1779–1785* (New York, 1929), p. 74; *South-Carolina Gazette*, Mar. 18, 1732; Mar. 28, 1743; May 22, 1749; Elhanan Winchester, *The Reigning Abominations, Especially the Slave Trade, Considered as Causes of Lamentation* (London, 1788), p. 22n; Klaus G. Loewald, Beverly Starika, and Paul S. Taylor, trans. and eds., "Johann Martin Bolzius Answers a Questionnaire on Carolina and Georgia," *William and Mary Quarterly*, 3d Ser., XIV (1957), 235.

20 Grant, *Memoirs*, I, 85.

21 Hening, ed., *Statutes of Va.*, II, 170; III, 86–87, 452–454; Browne and others, eds., *Archives of Md.*, I, 533–534; VII, 204–205; XIII, 546–549; XXII, 552; XXVI, 259–260; XXX, 289–290; XXXIII, 112; XXXVI, 275–276; Edward R. Turner, *The Negro in Pennsylvania, Slavery—Servitude—Freedom, 1639–1861* (Washington, 1911), p. 30n; *The Acts and Resolves, Public and Private, of the Province of the Massachusetts Bay* (Boston, 1869–1922), I, 578–579; *Acts and Laws of the Commonwealth of Massachusetts* (Boston, 1890–98), IV, 10; Clark, ed., *State Recs. of N. C.*, XXIII, 65, 106, 160, 195; Thomas Cooper and David J. McCord, eds., *Statutes at Large of South Carolina* (Columbia, 1836–41), III, 20; James T. Mitchell and others, eds., *Statutes at Large of Pennsylvania from 1682 to 1809* (Harrisburg, 1896–1915),

IV, 62–63; also X, 67–73, and the *Pennsylvania Packet* (Philadelphia), Mar. 4, 1779; Candler, comp. , *Col. Recs. of Ga.*, I, 59–60. Delaware, not considered a Southern colony or state by contemporaries, passed no outright prohibition until 1807 (repealed the next year) but provided for heavier fines in interracial bastardy cases than in such cases where only whites were involved; *Laws of the State of Delaware* (New Castle and Wilmington, 1797–1816), I, 105–109; IV, 112–113, 221.

22   Samuel Thornely, ed., *The Journal of Nicholas Cresswell, 1774–1777* (New York, 1924), p. 39.

23   Long, *Jamaica*, II, 328.

24   The exception was Montserrat; the law was probably disallowed: Colonial Office Papers, Ser. 391, LXIX, 51 (Feb. 16, 1762), Public Record Office, London, for which reference I am indebted to Frank W. Pitman, *The Development of the British West Indies, 1700–1763* (New Haven, 1917), p. 27, where the citation is given as C.O. 391/70, p. 51 (Feb. 16, 1762). This statement on the absence of antimiscegenation laws is based on a reading of the statutes of the various islands which, from the nature of the sources, is probably less complete than for the continental colonies. For obvious reasons only those islands settled primarily by Englishmen have been included: those captured from the French had a different cultural heritage. An act applying to all the Leeward Islands declared that no "Free Person" should be married to "any Slave," but this provision was in a section regulating the conduct of free Negroes and almost certainly applied only to them; *Acts of Assembly, Passed in the Charibbee Leeward Islands. From 1690, to 1730* (London, 1734), pp. 138–139. Bermuda in 1663 acted against miscegenation, but this fact merely gives additional confirmation to the pattern outlined above, since the island at the time had fairly close contact with Virginia and never became like the Caribbean islands in economic structure, proportion of Negroes, or social atmosphere. See J. H. Lefroy, comp. , *Memorials of the Discovery and Early Settlement of the Bermudas or Somers Islands, 1515–1685* (London, 1877–79), II, 190.

25   Population statistics for the colonial period are at best merely rough estimates in most cases. I have compiled tables showing the proportion of Negroes in the total population for the principal colonies settles by Englishmen, with figures drawn largely from the following sources: U. S. Bureau of the Census, *A Century of Population Growth, from the First Census of the United States to the Twelfth, 1790–1900* (Washington, 1909); Evarts B. Greene and Virginia D. Harrington, *American Population before the Federal Census of 1790* (New York, 1932); *Calendar of State Papers, Colonial Series, America and West Indies*, 37 vols. (London, 1860–); Alan Burns, *History of the British West Indies* (London, 1954), pp. 401, 454, 461, 465, 499, 500, 510, 511, 514, 515; Vincent T. Harlow, *A History of Barbados, 1625–1685* (Oxford, 1926), p. 338; C. S. S. Higham, *The Development of the Leeward Islands under the Restoration, 1660–1688; A Study of the Foundations of the Old Colonial System* (Cambridge, Eng., 1921), pp. 145, 148; Pitman, *West Indies*, pp. 48, 370, 374, 378; Edwards, *History*, II, 2. My figures are in substantial agreement with those which may be calculated from a table recently compiled by Stella H. Sutherland in U. S. Bureau of the Census, *Historical Statistics of the United States, Colonial Times to 1957* (Washington, 1960), p. 756, except in the case of North Carolina where her figures yield a proportion nearly 10 per cent higher than mine.

26   For a New Englander's comment on miscegenation in South Carolina see Mark Anthony DeWolfe Howe, ed., "Journal of Josiah Quincy, Junior, 1773," Massachusetts Historical Society, *Proceedings*, XLIX (Boston, 1916), 463.

27   Tables of the sex ratios in the various colonies have been calculated from the sources given in the previous note and, in addition, Pitman, *West Indies*, pp. 371–382; Long, *Jamaica*, I, 376.

28   I have found no cases of white women sleeping with colored men in the West Indies. For this combination on the continent, see extracts from the Court of General Sessions of the Peace [Suffolk County, Mass.], Apr. 4, 1704, Oct. 2, 1705, Apr. 6, 1708, July 4, 1710, Apr. 6, 1714, in Parish Transcripts, Box XVI; James Bowdoin to George Scott, Boston, Oct. 14, 1763, in Bowdoin-Temple Papers, XXVIII, 56, Mass. Hist. Soc., Boston in which Bowdoin wrote that "My Man Caesar has been engaged in an amour with some of the white ladies of the Town. . . ." so he was sending him to Grenada in exchange for produce or another Negro boy; W. H. Morse, "Lemuel Haynes," *Jour. of Negro Hist.*, IV (1919),

22; [Daniel Horsmanden], *A Journal of the Proceedings in the Detection of the Conspiracy Formed by Some White People, in Conjunction with Negro and other Slaves, for Burning the City of New-York in America, and Murdering the Inhabitants* (New York, 1744), pp. 2, 4; *Boston News-Letter*, June 25, 1741; Arthur W. Calhoun, *A Social History of the American Family from Colonial Times to the Present* (Cleveland, 1917–19), I, 211; Helen T. Catterall, ed., *Judicial Cases Concerning American Slavery and the Negro* (Washington, 1926), I, 89–91; II, 12; IV, 28, 32; *Maryland Gazette* (Annapolis), Aug. 19, 1746; James H. Johnston, Race Relations in Virginia and Miscegenation in the South, 1776–1860 (unpubl. Ph.D. diss., University of Chicago, 1937), pp. 199–202; John H. Franklin, *The Free Negro in North Carolina, 1790–1860* (Chapel Hill, N. C., 1943), pp. 37, 39; Saunders, *Col. Recs. of N. C.*, II, 704; "Johann Martin Bolzius,", p. 235. For this combination in actual marriage, see Lorenzo J. Greene, *The Negro in Colonial New England, 1620–1776* (New York, 1942), pp. 201–202; Morse, "Lemuel Haynes," p. 26; Grant, *Memoirs*, I, 86; Calhoun, *Family*, I, 211; Catterall, ed., *Judicial Cases*, II, 11; La Rochefoucault Liancourt, *Travels*, I, 602; *Maryland Gazette*, July 31, 1794; and the case of Gideon Gibson discussed above. A causal connection between the sex ratio and miscegenation has been suggested by Herbert Moller, "Sex Composition and Correlated Culture Patterns of Colonial America," *William and Mary Quarterly*, 3d Ser., II (1945), 131–137, but some of his conclusions must be treated with caution.

29 *Acts of Assembly, Passed in the Island of Jamaica; from 1681, to 1737, inclusive* (London, 1738), pp. 260–261; see also Long, *Jamaica*, II, 261, 321. This same definition of a mulatto was retained in 1780; *Acts of Assembly, Passed in the Island of Jamaica; from 1770 to 1783, inclusive* (Kingston, 1786), p. 174.

30 *Acts of Assembly, Passed in the Island of Barbados, from 1648, to 1718* (London, 1721), pp. 112, 153, 171, 213, 226, 267; Richard Hall, comp., *Acts, Passed in the Island of Barbados. From 1643, to 1762, inclusive* (London, 1764), p. 256.

31 *Acts of Assembly, Passed in the Island of Jamaica; from the Year 1681, to the Year 1769, inclusive.* 2 vols. in 1, with an *Appendix: Containing Laws Respecting Slaves* (Kingston, 1787), I, Table of Acts, 18, 20–25, 30–31; II, Table of Acts, 3, 7–11, 14–15; II, 36–39; *Acts of Assembly, Passed in the Island of Jamaica; from 1770, to 1783, inclusive*, Table of Acts, 8, 11, 13, 16, 18, 20, 22, 24, 26, 28, 30–31; *Acts of Assembly, Passed in the Island of Jamaica; from the Year 1784, to the Year 1788, inclusive* (Kingston, 1789), Table of Acts, vi–viii, xi, xv–xvi; *The Laws of Jamaica: Comprehending all the Acts in Force, Passed between the Thirty-Second Year of the Reign of King Charles the Second, and the Thirty-Third Year of the Reign of King George the Third* (St. Jago de la Vega, 1792), I, Table of Acts, no pagination; *The Laws of Jamaica, Passed in the Thirty-Third Year of the Reign of King George the Third* (St. Jago de la Vega, 1793), Table of Acts, no pagination; *The Laws of Jamaica, Passed in the Thirty-Fourth Year of the Reign of King George the Third* (St. Jago de la Vega, 1794), Table of Acts, no pagination. See also Long, *Jamaica*, II, 320–323; Edwards, *History*, II, 22–23.

32 Long, *Jamaica*, II, 332. This general picture of Jamaica is borne out by a work on a somewhat later period; Philip D. Curtin, *Two Jamaicas: The Role of Ideas in a Tropical Colony, 1830–1865* (Cambridge, Mass., 1955), chaps. 1–3.

Chapter 31

Gad Heuman

THE FREE COLOREDS IN JAMAICAN SLAVE SOCIETY

JAMAICAN SLAVE SOCIETY was dominated numerically by blacks and economically by whites. Africans had little choice about their importation to Jamaica; whites, on the other hand, often came to the island with little intention of settling there permanently. Many whites worked on the sugar plantations, with the hope of returning home as wealthy absentee owners. However, the majority of them never attained their goal. A contemporary observer has estimated that no less than four-fifths of the white settlers died before they had "realized a sufficiency while only a favoured few (perhaps no more than five or six in a hundred) ever returned to their native country with a fortune, or competency."[1]

In the eighteenth century, it seemed worth taking the risk. Jamaica's plantation economy was booming, and the dramatic increase in the number of slaves and in cane production was evidence of this rapid growth. In 1673, there were only 9,504 slaves on the island; this figure jumped to 86,546 by 1734, and within the next thirty years, the slave population almost doubled. Sugar output kept pace. While the island yielded an insignificant amount of cane in 1675, by 1739 there were 429 estates producing 33,000 hogsheads of sugar per annum. During the following two decades, the number of plantations rose to 640.[2]

Since sugar was the mainstay of the economy, planters played an important role in the life of the colony. Those who retired to England often sought to safeguard Jamaican and West Indian interests through the activities of the West India Committee.[3] Because many of them could afford to buy seats in Parliament, they formed a group that was able to influence colonial policymaking. Planters who remained in Jamaica dominated politics there as delegates to the local House of Assembly.[4] But not all whites on the Jamaican plantations were wealthy estate owners. Whites also served as bookkeepers, supervising the slaves in the field and in the boiling house; as overseers, superintending the planting and giving the daily orders; and as skilled artisans. In the absence of a resident proprietor, an attorney acted as the agent of the absentee. Since attorneys frequently had more than one plantation under their supervision, they were among the most important men on the island.[5]

Whites did other work as well. Edward Brathwaite has estimated that between 18,000 and 24,000 whites lived in Jamaica around the turn of the nineteenth century, not including an "upper class" of about 6,000 wealthy planters, merchants, and their families. Those in the towns accounted for a large proportion of this total: some of them were in the professions, while others were involved in a wide range of commercial and skilled activities. Brathwaite's conclusions suggest that the white population was larger and more diverse than previous research has indicated.[6] Nonetheless, many whites expressed a strong urge to return home; adhering to this ideal, the white offspring of planters were often sent to Europe for their education. Few probably ever came back to resettle on the island.[7]

The effect of this absentee mentality was apparent in the social life of the colony.[8] There was a shortage of white women in Jamaica, at least partly because of an unwritten rule that young planters arriving in the island remain single. With an overwhelming slave population and a scarcity of white females, intercourse between white males and black slave women became common.[9] The resulting brown population added another dimension to Jamaican society which was to prove a recurrent problem in the eighteenth and nineteenth centuries.

The offspring of whites and slaves at first merged into the slave population. Since the children of these unions inherited the status of their mothers, they were born slaves. However, colored slaves usually received preferential treatment, in part because whites believed that people of mixed color could not work in the fields as effectively as blacks. Brown slaves had a greater opportunity to learn skills, and many worked as house slaves. White attitudes toward the people of color also meant that they were more likely to gain their freedom than blacks. According to one contemporary estimate, 80 percent of freedmen were colored and 20 percent black.[10] The liberality of many white fathers added to the population of freedmen. Whites often manumitted their black or brown mistresses and their illegitimate children, sometimes at birth. But whatever their parentage, freedmen did not become the legal equals of whites; for them manumission meant only a release from ownership and was not a grant of full civil rights.[11]

In time, freedmen formed a separate group in Jamaican society with their own social hierarchies and a specific nomenclature to account for their varied racial origins.[12] While the law did not recognize these color distinctions, it divided the freedmen on the basis of birth. Blacks and browns born of free mothers were entitled to trial by jury, but those born as slaves and later freed were still subject to slave courts. In addition, manumitted freedmen could not give evidence in court against free-born coloreds and blacks. Despite these differences, the two groups of freedmen shared in common the other disabilities directed against the free nonwhite community.[13]

The restrictions limited the freedmen's political, economic, and social life. Like slaves, free blacks and coloreds could not participate in politics, which meant that they were not eligible to sit in the legislature and, after a law enacted in 1733, that they lost the right to vote. Freedmen were not allowed in court to give evidence against whites and were barred from serving on juries. Moreover, their participation in the economic life of the colony was severely restricted. An act passed in 1711 made it an offense to employ a free black or brown person in a public office. A year later, the Assembly approved a bill prohibiting them from acting as navigators or driving carriages for hire, probably to ensure that they would not encroach on jobs held by whites. More importantly, the deficiency legislation of 1715 served to exclude freedmen from supervisory positions on the plantations. The measure imposed fines on planters who did not retain a certain number of whites on each estate in proportion to the plantation's slave population. Even free colored estate owners had to employ whites in proportion to the slaves they owned, as the coloreds and their families did not qualify to avoid the deficiency fines. In the last half of the eighteenth century, planters increasingly chose to pay the fines rather than maintain the prescribed ratio of whites on their estates. Nonetheless, the general habit of barring freedmen from posts on the plantations continued.[14]

The Assembly also enacted legislation to differentiate free blacks and browns from the rest of society. One act stated that any freedman who did not own land and at least ten slaves had to wear a blue cross on his right shoulder.[15] Freedmen also had to register in a parish and to appear before a magistrate for proper certification of their freedom. Not surprisingly, freedmen regarded these requirements as degrading. They complained that the statutes created "an ignominious distinction, which can answer no purpose but to render them[selves] odious."[16]

The delegates to the House were not averse to making some minor improvements in the status of the freedmen. In 1748, the representatives therefore granted manumitted blacks and browns the same rights in court as those who had been born free.[17] This measure reflected the increasing wealth of at least part of the free black and brown population. Although there were restrictions on the freedmen's economic opportunities, planters on occasion left estates to their colored children or to their mistresses. As this trend increased, whites became alarmed at the amount of land the free coloreds and blacks were inheriting. An inquiry by the House of Assembly in 1761 substantiated these fears when the representatives found that property already bequeathed to freedmen was valued between £200,000 and £300,000. As a result, the assemblymen moved to counteract this development. They approved legislation that prohibited whites from leaving real or personal property worth more than £1,200 (sterling) to any colored or black. Combined with the earlier disabilities against the freedmen, this statute crippled their potential economic growth.[18] The whites had decided that it was more important to keep the land in European hands than to follow parental instincts.

But restrictive legislation against the freedmen did not apply to all of them. Some coloreds and blacks successfully appealed to the Assembly for a remission of the various enactments. The earliest example of this kind occurred in the 1707–1708 session and allowed two manumitted free blacks the right of trial by jury. Another bill which granted a free black similar concessions specified the reasons for the award: it noted that the recipient had discovered a French plot to invade the island and was a Christian as well. The next privilege bill passed in 1733 was more generous, as it accorded a brown man and his family all the rights of Englishmen born of white ancestors. While this was a considerable concession, the acts that followed it usually required the privileged freedmen to marry whites if their children were to inherit the same immunities. According to a later report, some freedwomen complied with this stipulation by marrying white husbands. Certainly most of those who applied for privileges after 1733 were mulatto or quadroon women and their children.[19]

The privileged freedmen presented a serious problem for the whites. Often better educated than the planters, the privileged blacks and coloreds generally adopted European values and rejected any association with slaves or any link with Africa.[20] Many of them were wealthy and owned slaves themselves. Yet, the position of the privileged freedmen upset the racial stereotype that was at the heart of the slave society. For the system to be successful, slaves had to associate the owner-ship of land and people with whites; slaveholding freedmen were dangerous because their existence suggested that browns and blacks were no different from whites. The situation was complicated because psychological considerations of parentage were involved. Without attempting to analyze these implications, it seems clear that the privileged coloreds and blacks raised the question of the freedman's place in Jamaica to its logical conclusion. In 1761, the delegates to the Assembly were no longer willing to face the issue. When they realized how much wealth was passing into colored and black hands, they not only put a limit on the size of wills but also ceased granting full civil rights to those who applied for them. After 1761, privileges were fewer and less generous. Many petitioners were not allowed to hold public office of any kind, and some privilege acts were limited to the right of testifying against whites in court.[21]

The legislation in 1761 significantly affected the legal status of the privileged blacks and coloreds as well as the economic development of the group as a whole. However, it did little to halt the freedmen's numerical growth. As Table 31.1 shows, the free brown population increased rapidly during the remainder of the eighteenth and early part of the nineteenth centuries. The growth was particularly evident in the period preceding emancipation. Even though the figures are un-reliable, it seems likely that the free colored population more than tripled during

Table 31.1   Estimates of the population in Jamaica, 1768–1844

Year	White	Free colored		Free black	Slaves	Total
1768	17,000	3,700	3,700	3,700	167,000	187,700
1789	18,000	10,000	10,000	10,000	250,000	278,000
1807	30,000	—		—	300,000	—
1825	—	28,800		10,000	—	—
1834	16,600	31,000		11,000	310,000	368,600

Census	Whites	Colored	Black	Total
1844	15,776	68,529	293,128	377,433

Sources: John Stewart, A *View of the Past and Present State of the Island of Jamaica* (Edinburgh, 1823), p. 23; Edward Long, *The History of Jamaica*, 3 vols. (London, 1774), 2:337; CO 318/76, Campbell to Hill, December 1825, Schedule B; CO 137/175, Lushington to Courtenay, September 17, 1826; Douglas Hall, "Jamaica," in David W. Cohen and Jack P. Greene (eds.), *Neither Slave Nor Free* (Baltimore, 1972), p. 194; Edward Brathwaite, *The Development of Creole Society in Jamaica, 1770–1820* (Oxford, 1971), p. 152; B. W. Higman, *Slave Population and Economy in Jamaica, 1807–1834* (Cambridge, 1976), pp. 142, 144; G. W. Roberts, *The Population of Jamaica* (Cambridge, 1957), p. 39; Sheila Duncker, "The Free Coloured and Their Fight for Civil Rights in Jamaica, 1800–1830" (unpublished M.A. thesis, University of London, 1960), p. 10. The eighteenth- and early nineteenth-century figures are based on contemporary accounts of the period, and the 1825 figures for free colored and free black on John Campbell's "Memorandum" of that year. The 1834 figure for whites is based on B. W. Higman's calculation for 1832; the figures for free colored and free black in 1834 tally roughly with the census of 1844, assuming, as Higman does, that 10 percent of the slaves were colored in 1834 and adopting G. W. Roberts' calculation of a 1 percent per annum growth rate for coloreds between 1834 and 1844 (although Roberts' figure was worked out for a slightly later period). The figures for free colored and free black in 1834 are higher than Hall's total of 35,000 freedmen and closer to Duncker's calculation of 44,435 freedmen in that year.

Table 31.2   The free population in four Jamaican parishes, 1812

Parish	Number			Percentage of free population		
	White	Free colored*	Free black	White	Free colored	Free black
St. George	379	343	32	50.3	45.5	4.2
Westmoreland	688	790	119	43.1	49.5	7.4
Portland	415	180		70.0	30.0	
St. Thomas in the East	434	463		48.4	51.6	

Note: * The figures for free colored for Portland and St. Thomas in the East include free black as well.

Source: CO 137/136, Morrison to Bathurst, January 28, 1813, no. 21, enclosures in CO 137/137.

the three decades after 1790 and that it surpassed the white population during the 1820s. There was also a considerable expansion of the free black population in this period.

Scattered figures for individual parishes reveal the extent of the free brown population in 1812 (Table 31.2). By then, they made up nearly half the total free population in St. George and Westmoreland. When the number of free blacks is taken into account, it is apparent that whites were already becoming a minority of the free population in Westmoreland as well as in St. Thomas in the East. More ominous for the whites was the number of free black and colored children. As Table 31.3 suggests, in two of the four parishes cited, the population of free black and brown children was three times that of the equivalent white group. In one parish, St. Thomas in the East, the number of free black and colored children was more than seven times that of white children. Since most of these children were free browns, the statistics must have caused concern among the whites about the future size of the free colored population.

The available figures are also suggestive about the sexual composition of the free brown population. According to John Campbell, a prominent free man of color from St. James, there were twice as many adult females as males among the free coloreds in 1825. Out of a total of 28,800 free people of color, Campbell estimated that there were 4,800 adult males and 9,600 adult females. G. W. Roberts has made use of more reliable statistics on the number and sex of slave

Table 31.3   Free children in four Jamaican parishes, 1812

Parish	Number		Percentage of free population	
	White	Free colored and free black	White	Free colored and free black
St. George	67	183	8.9	24.3
Westmoreland	127	373	8.0	23.4
Portland	102	49	17.1	8.2
St. Thomas in the East	16	114	1.8	12.7

Source: CO 137/136, Morrison to Bathurst, January 28, 1813, no. 21, enclosures in CO 137/137.

manumissions to make a similar point. Lumping together free browns and blacks, Roberts found that 2,566 females were manumitted between 1817 and 1829 compared with 1,445 males during the same period. These statistics provide further evidence of the sexual imbalance in the freedmen population.[22]

The nature of the legislation against the freedmen as well as the statistics on their distribution make it clear that free blacks and people of color lived primarily in towns. The deficiency legislation meant that it was difficult for them to become landowners, and the law of 1761 limited this possibility even further. Moreover, the towns offered them the best chance of employment. Kingston had the largest number of free coloreds and blacks; an estimate in 1788 put their numbers at 3,280, or 12 percent of the city's population. Since more than 2,700 of the freedmen were brown, there was a high proportion of free coloreds among the urban freedmen.[23] St. Catherine also had a significant freedmen population. In 1796, there were 1,902 free coloreds and blacks in the parish, most of them from Spanish Town.[24] Thus, nearly half of Jamaica's freedmen lived in Spanish Town or Kingston at the end of the eighteenth century. Freedmen also made their homes in the other towns around the island and constituted an important segment of the population in the parish of St. Elizabeth.[25] The early nineteenth century witnessed their continued expansion in the urban areas of Jamaica. In Kingston, for example, the free blacks and coloreds were the fastest growing part of the city's population during this period, with one report suggesting a total of nearly 10,000 freedmen in 1825.[26]

In the towns, many of the freedmen performed the same work as slaves. They found jobs in shops, they acted as servants and porters, and they were employed as boatmen and sailors. As elsewhere in the British Caribbean, the more fortunate freedmen occupied a middle ground between the upper ranks of the slaves and the poorer whites.[27] Women in this category became shopkeepers and sold provisions, millinery, confectionery, and preserves. They usually had two or three slaves who traveled into the interior of the island to sell commodities on the estates. In addition, freedwomen owned and managed lodging houses throughout the island.[28]

Many free colored and black men also had a small number of slaves working for them; these freedmen were often mechanics, artisans, or tradesmen. Sheila Duncker has reported on the predominance of tradesmen among this group. In the St. Catherine Register of Free Persons, she found a list of freedmen and their occupations, which included "two taylors, three masons, a farrier, two planters, four carpenters, a wheelwright, a tavern keeper and a 'Butcher near the Race Course.'"[29] Other free coloreds were finding different kinds of work. During the first few decades of the nineteenth century, more free browns were becoming clerks and there was an increasing number of brown schoolmasters. A significant proportion of the local merchants involved in the American-West Indian trade were colored. Several became creditors of the estate owners and then planters themselves when difficult economic conditions after the Napoleonic Wars forced many plantations into near bankruptcy. Free coloreds and blacks also were acquiring property in towns, some of which provided income in the form of rents.[30] Most of the freedmen who remained in the country, on the other hand, grew provisions for the weekday markets, although the wealthier free blacks and coloreds tended to cultivate pimento and ginger or raise cattle. Despite the bias against them, there were some brown overseers as well as a few colored estate owners who had inherited their properties before the limitation on legacies.[31]

The influx of free coloreds and blacks from St. Domingue at the end of the eighteenth century increased the range of occupations among the freedmen in Jamaica. Many of the refugees from the Haitian Revolution were skilled craftsmen; these included goldsmiths, cabinet makers, shoemakers, dyers, tanners, and bakers. While the women often kept shops that sold provisions and liquor, agriculturalists among the immigrant freedmen had a more lasting effect on Jamaican produce. They significantly improved techniques for growing coffee and for irrigating land.[32]

The free coloreds thus worked in a variety of occupations. As a group, they were better off economically than free blacks, but it is important to note that most of the free browns were at the lower end of the economic scale. One measure of this relative poverty was their contribution to the island treasury. The duke of Manchester (William Montagu), who was governor of Jamaica from 1808 to 1827, pointed out in 1823 that their share of the taxes was less than 3 percent of the total amount paid by whites.[33] John Campbell also provided evidence that the overwhelming majority of the people of color were in a difficult economic position. In 1825, he estimated that 22,900 free browns were "absolutely poor," while only 400 were "rich" and 5,500 in "fair circumstances."[34] Although there were clearcut economic differences among the coloreds, they shared a common goal. As Duncker has noted, "fundamental to all free colored was a desire to be measured by the same yardsticks as those used for people in similar positions who were white."[35] The nature of Jamaican slave society meant that it would be difficult to attain their goal.

But what was the position of the free coloreds in Jamaican slave society? While the evidence is slight on the "absolutely poor" people of color, more information is available on the rest of the free colored population. Relations between browns and whites are also better documented than those between browns and blacks. In general, the free people of color were excluded from the high society that existed on the island as well as from the society of the lower-class whites. It would not have occurred to the governor's wife, Lady Nugent, in 1803 to invite coloreds to her parties and dinners in Spanish Town, but she would receive brown women privately when visiting estates in the country. Even this behavior was not typical of that of less transient whites. The European Club, which admitted colonists of at least twenty-five years' residence in the island, pointedly invited "*Europeans only*" to an anniversary meeting in 1794.[36] Attitudes had not changed much three decades later. A Jamaican planter noted in 1827 that whites not only disliked "the contact and strong smell of a negro" but also had "been used from infancy to keep mulatto men at a distance."[37] The planters generally refused to mix with even wealthy or well-educated people of color, although this rule was relaxed in the case of a few privileged people of color.

Whites seem to have regarded the coloreds with a mixture of superstition and contempt. They maintained, for example, that the people of color were incapable of producing children. Although an absentee owner found that this was not the case, he concluded after a visit to Jamaica that coloreds were weak and effeminate. Governor Manchester also had doubts about the qualities of the people of color despite his numerous brown children. When the Colonial Office asked him to recommend free coloreds for overseas service in Africa, Manchester commented on their timidity and lack of resolution.[38]

Despite their belief that the people of color were inferior, the whites were uncertain whether the coloreds would prove a threat to their continued supremacy or a potential support for it. A well-traveled stipendiary magistrate, R. R. Madden, noted that the whites distrusted brown men because they were potential rebels in disguise.[39] Planters feared that the Jamaican people of color might follow the example of the Haitian coloreds and help to destroy the system of slavery. Some whites, however, argued that coloreds could serve as a protection against the slaves. The most important contemporary historians of eighteenth-century Jamaica and the British Caribbean agreed that the brown slaves should be freed and apprenticed in a trade or business. This would create a group between the whites and the blacks who "would naturally attach themselves to the white race as the most honourable relations, and so become a barrier against the designs of the Blacks."[40]

In spite of such ideas, the free people of color had little access to white society. Some groups of free coloreds, such as those who were educated abroad, were particularly bitter about their situation. Often accepted as whites in Britain, these coloreds were dismayed by their reception in Jamaica when they returned home. One of the most articulate of them who had spent time in England, Richard Hill, noted that the educated coloreds regarded themselves in Jamaica as "blasted trees— 'barkless, branchless, and blighted trunks upon a cursed root.'" The reaction of another man of color traveling home from Europe was less literary but nonetheless indicative of what was likely to happen. On landing in Barbados, he went ashore to a tavern with his fellow travelers, only to be singled out by the waiter who informed him that he could not sit down with gentlemen. Astonished, the colored man followed the waiter to another room and "burst into tears."[41]

Usually barred from the society of whites and often rejecting the company of blacks, the people of color staged their own entertainments. Like the whites, they organized balls and dinners that were as expensive and often more lively than those they could not attend. The planter and writer Monk Lewis described a ball that was limited to brown people; more often, colored women sponsored dances specifically for white men.[42] While these social events upset any generalizations about racial segregation, they did not alter the prevailing views about the inferiority of the people of color.

Free browns were constantly reminded of their lower status. Coloreds entered the theater by a different door than whites and sat apart from them; sometimes there were separate performances for whites and free coloreds. The people of color faced similar restrictions in the Anglican church. Although they worshipped together with whites, coloreds occupied special galleries or pews. This was a cause of much complaint not only because of the supposed brotherhood of all men but also because whites were often allotted more space than they could use. The separation of browns and whites continued after death. Each group had its own burial ground, and church bells rang longer for whites than for people of color.[43]

The Methodists proved to be more popular among the free coloreds, in part because of the Dissenters' lack of exclusiveness in seating arrangements and in the church hierarchy. In Kingston, free coloreds comprised half of the membership and two-thirds of the attendance at the Wesleyan missions. They often donated land for new chapels and subsidized the building of churches. Free people of color also held prominent positions as society officials, sometimes advising the missionaries and holding the societies together when illness or death among the missionaries interrupted their work. Yet, despite this help, the free browns were not treated as the social equals of the European missionaries. No missionary married a free colored woman, and the missionaries were accused in the 1830s of being prejudiced against the people of color.[44]

In contrast to this situation, the opportunities for the education of colored children seemed to provide a measure of equality between whites and people of color. Free coloreds were occasionally admitted to formerly white schools. In the case of Wolmer's Free School in Kingston, colored pupils formed the majority of the student body by 1822, only seven years after the first brown student was admitted. But Wolmer's was an exception, and even there white students seemed to leave in preference for segregated schools once the color bar had been breached. Elsewhere in the island, the educational facilities for the people of color were limited. A missionary noted that the means of education in the western district were inadequate even for white children "and still more for free browns, who could not mix with the others, and had long been treated as if they had no right to be free."[45] In St. James, the free coloreds sought to establish a school for poor colored students largely from their own funds but were unable to get any help from the parish vestry. The situation improved by the 1830s as more schools were open to brown children, especially in Kingston. Nonetheless, several years after emancipation there still remained a small handful of private schools that were limited to whites.[46]

Like the students at Wolmer's, the colored "housekeepers" also appeared to be on an equal footing with whites. This pattern of black or brown females cohabiting informally with white men was so widely accepted that one observer noted that it involved nine-tenths of the colored women on the island. The practice enabled some brown women to become economically secure. Monk Lewis described the colored landlady of an inn who was the mistress of an English merchant in Kingston and who owned a house of her own. Brown mistresses could have certain customary rights: whites would in some cases contract to pay large sums of money to them in case they married or left the island. Such economic rewards were greater than brown men could usually offer, and there was the prospect for colored women of children who were lighter in color. As in the contemporary Caribbean, these considerations were often more important than the question of legitimacy.[47]

Despite these advantages, the housekeeping system was not an equal partnership. On the contrary, it was a further example of the subordinate position of the free coloreds. Brown women were never accepted in white society. Apart from rare exceptions, they could not marry the men they lived with. In addition, the system served to debase men of color who were forced to cohabit with free blacks or slaves. As in the case of the Portuguese colonists in West Africa, the Jamaican planters' informal relations with colored women did not overturn the prevailing pattern of white superiority. Instead, the system of concubinage reflected the social inferiority of the people of color and their general exclusion from white society.[48]

Yet, there were free coloreds—like the privileged brown man James Swaby— who were not subject to these restrictions. Swaby was a rich planter who owned at least two estates and several hundred slaves; he was educated at Charterhouse and served in the British army. In supporting his application for special rights, the attorney general of Jamaica reported that Swaby "is highly esteemed by the different white inhabitants of Manchester and is admitted to their society and treated in every respect as a white person."[49] Thomas Drummond was in a similar positon. He was

also a wealthy colored planter who had inherited a large estate and was the proprietor in 1823 of a 1,200-acre estate and 115 slaves. Since he had "acquired the
respect of the Community in which he has resided." Drummond believed he was
"entitled to greater privileges than the general class of people of free condition."[50]

These examples suggest that it was possible for a few privileged browns to gain
entry into white society in spite of their color. Unlike the colonists in the United
States, white Jamaicans had begun to take account of class as well as color considerations in determining status. But the acceptance of a small number of brown
people into white society did not improve relations between whites and browns as
a whole.[51] The experience of a young man of color, Martin Halhead, was evidence
that problems between free coloreds and whites would continue as long as most
brown people were denied their rights.

In late May 1813, the Kingston Common Council declared that certain parts
of the Anglican church in Kingston would be set apart for whites. It is unclear
whether this was a new ruling or an alteration of an existing arrangement. A few
weeks later, Halhead refused to leave a pew reserved for whites during a regular
Sunday service. When he was eventually taken out, he warned white officials that
"your power is over or at an end; take care how you act." Once in court, Halhead
insulted the magistrates and was placed under custody. Another person of color
who was willing to serve as Halhead's bail was also arrested.[52]

Although Halhead was soon released, he continued to be a problem for the
authorities. Two years later, he was in jail again, this time because of a riot in front
of the Kingston Theater. A group of coloreds led by Halhead had picketed the
theater and collected signatures from people of color against possible new color
bar restrictions. The riot that accompanied the demonstration required the military
to quell the disturbance, and only the governor's clemency saved Halhead and a
fellow agitator from the pillory.[53] Yet, while Halhead's response to the segregation of the coloreds attracted considerable attention, his actions were not directed
toward a fundamental reform of the society. He was not attempting to abolish
slavery or even to ameliorate the condition of the slaves. Instead, Halhead joined
the overwhelming majority of coloreds who accepted the divisions between slave
and free and who wanted to have the same rights as whites.

Coloreds thus emphasized their affinity with the whites in a variety of ways.
For example, they sought to imitate European fashions, often in an exaggerated
form. Brown women frequently dressed in the latest and loudest English clothes
to outdo their white competitors. In addition, the people of color formed the largest
church-going group in Jamaica in proportion to their numbers and were more interested in European literary and cultural developments than were the white creoles.
They established various educational societies, including the Society for the
Diffusion of Useful Knowledge and the St. James Institute for Promoting General
and Useful Knowledge.[54] Even though whites probably did not participate in these
organizations, the societies were another way for brown men to differentiate themselves from blacks and to assimilate aspects of European civilization.

Free coloreds not only adopted white values but also tended to compensate
for their lower status by abusing slaves. Many travelers reported that brown
men were harsher masters than whites and were more likely to mistreat their slaves.
A common Jamaican saying reflected the feeling that slaves preferred white owners:
"If me for have massa or misses, give me Buckra one—no give me mulatto, dem

no use neega well."[55] Even so, brown slaveowners were concerned about being identified with the slaves and refused to do any work on the estates that could link them with slavery. Free coloreds would not "cut cane, load carts, drive mules, carry trash" or perform any other tasks which in their mind belonged to slaves.[56] A white planter claimed that "they would rather starve than engage in agricultural labour—of course I mean manual labour."[57]

Coloreds also frequently sought to maintain the same distinctions toward slaves which characterized relations between browns and whites. Two abolitionists who visited Jamaica in the 1830s reported that free brown settlers in St. Elizabeth refused to send their children to a school where brown and black pupils were treated equally. Similarly, the Baptist missionary William Knibb encountered problems with free colored parents who were opposed to sending their children to schools that mixed freedmen with slaves.[58] There were exceptions. Recent evidence suggests that the free colored men in Kingston and Spanish Town often mated with black slaves. As there were more whites in the towns, the coloreds had difficulty competing with them for free colored women and turned to blacks.[59] But the racial attitudes of the coloreds who sought to keep black and brown students apart were probably more typical. This type of prejudice was not confined to browns and blacks. Since browns themselves differed in shade and in status, those who were most like the whites emphasized their distance from the rest of the free colored population.

Governor Manchester was aware of the tensions between the lighter and darker brown people. In a dispatch to the Colonial Office, he noted that the dark coloreds and blacks were "indignant at the superiority which those of fairer complexion claim over them."[60] More than a decade later, the lighter complexioned coloreds were still maintaining the same posture. A letter writer to *The Herald and Literary Journal* directed his anger at the offending browns: "You boast of personal attractions, but even after you have added to your loveliness by the application of patent washes for the improvement of your skins, I can discover nothing in you but your ignorance and conceit."[61] As in the case of brown attitudes toward blacks, light-colored freedmen assumed a superiority on the basis of their superficial closeness to whites.

Thus, considerations of color were crucial to the people of color. The light-complexioned browns, the free coloreds who abused their slaves, and the privileged people of color all sought to identify with the whites and generally to distance themselves from the blacks. The result was not a closer union of whites and browns, but rather the advancement of a small group of coloreds who were legally differentiated from the people of color as a whole. Although the whites allowed a tiny fraction of the people of color to enjoy a special status in Jamaica, this did not alter the plight of the overwhelming majority of coloreds. The petitions and campaigns of the free coloreds for an improvement in their legal condition highlighted this situation even further.

Notes

1   John Stewart, *A View of the Past and Present State of the Island of Jamaica* (Edinburgh, 1823). p. 179.
2   Ibid.; W. J. Gardner, *A History of Jamaica* (London, 1873), p. 155.
3   Although there were separate groups of West Indian merchants and planters who met on occasion during the eighteenth century, the West India Committee was first established in

1775. For more information on it, see Douglas Hall, *A Brief History of the West India Committee* (Barbados, 1971) and Lillian Penson, *The Colonial Agents of the British West Indies* (London, 1924), Chapter 10.

4   The House of Assembly was an all-white body elected on a £10 franchise. Each parish in Jamaica was allowed two representatives; exceptions were Kingston, Port Royal, and St. Catherine which had three.

5   Stewart, *A View of Jamaica*, Chapter 12; Gardner, *History*, p. 120.

6   Edward Brathwaite, *The Development of Creole Society in Jamaica, 1770–1820* (Oxford, 1971), Chapter 10; Lowell J. Ragatz, *The Fall of the Planter Class in the British Caribbean, 1763–1833* (New York, 1928), p. 9.

7   Lowell J. Ragatz, "Absentee Landlordism in the British Caribbean, 1750–1833," *Agricultural History* 5 (January 1931): 7–9. For a critique of Ragatz's view on the effects of absentee landlordism, see Douglas Hall, "Absentee-Proprietorship in the British West Indies," *Jamaican Historical Review* 4 (1964): 15–35.

8   For a discussion of the effects of absenteeism, see Orlando Patterson, *The Sociology of Slavery* (London, 1967), pp. 38–44. Edward Brathwaite has critically examined Patterson's work in "Jamaican Slave Society, A Review," *Race* 11 (1968): 331–42.

9   Winthrop D. Jordan, "American Chiaroscuro: The Status and Definition of Mulattoes in the British Colonies," *The William and Mary Quarterly* 19 (April 1962): 195–98.

10 Arnold A. Sio, "Race, Colour and Miscegenation: The Free Coloured of Jamaica and Barbados," *Caribbean Studies* 16 (April 1976): 7. For a discussion of brown slaves and their greater chance of becoming free in the Leeward Islands, see Elsa V. Goveia, *Slave Society in the British Leeward Islands at the End of the Eighteenth Century* (New Haven, Conn., 1965), pp. 231–32.

11 Douglas Hall, "Jamaica," in David W. Cohen and Jack P. Greene (eds.), *Neither Slave Nor Free* (Baltimore, 1972), p. 195; Gardner, *History*, p. 171.

12 A mulatto was the result of a union between black and white, sambo between mulatto and black, quadroon between mulatto and white, mustee between quadroon and white. The union of a mustee and a white produced a musteefino who was legally white and enjoyed full civil rights. Samboes, mulattoes, quadroons, and mustees were legally classified as mulattoes and were subject to the same disabilities.

13 CO 137/91, Williamson to Dundas, June 4, 1793, no. 10, secret. enclosure: Memorandum by Bryan Edwards, May 16, 1793.

14 6 George II, c. 2 of 25 April 1733; 10 Anne, c. 4 of 19 May 1711: 11 Anne, c. 3 of 14 November 1712; [Richard Barrett], *A Reply to the Speech of Dr. Lushington* . . . (London, 1828), p. 36; Hall, "Jamaica," p. 202. I have adopted Barrett's date of 1715 for the deficiency legislation, although the act does not appear in the *Acts of the Assembly* for that year.

15 Edward Long, *The History of Jamaica*, 3 vols. (London, 1774), 2: 321. Bryan Edwards noted that by 1790 the law was no longer enforced. It was also questionable how rigorously it had been applied earlier. See Edwards' memorandum in CO 137/91, Williamson to Dundas, June 4. 1793, no. 10. secret, enclosure.

16 CO 137/91, Williamson to Dundas, June 4, 1793, no. 10, secret, enclosure: Memorandum by Bryan Edwards, May 16, 1793.

17 21 George II, c. 7 of 13 August 1748; CO 318/76, Sympson to Hill, n.d. [1825], p. 7; [Barrett], *A Reply*, p. 22.

18 2 George III, c. 8 of 19 December 1761; Gardner, *History*, p. 172.

19 CO 318/76, Sympson to Hill, n.d. [1825], Appendix: "A Table shewing the private privilege bills passed by the House of Assembly from time to time on the free blacks and coloured inhabitants of Jamaica"; *JAJ*, February 4 and 7, 1708, p. 438.

20 For a critical view of the privileged coloreds on this point, see the letter from a nineteenth-century brown man, Cato, in *The Watchman and Jamaica Free Press*, December 17, 1831.

21 Sheila Duncker, "The Free Coloured and Their Fight for Civil Rights in Jamaica, 1800–1830" (unpublished M.A. thesis, University of London, 1960), p. 37; CO 318/76, Sympson to Hill, n.d. [1825], Appendix.

22   CO 318/76, Campbell et al. to Hill, December 1825, Schedule D; G. W. Roberts, *The Population of Jamaica* (Cambridge, 1957), p. 71.

23   Wilma R. Bailey, "Power Relations in Pre-Emancipation Kingston," Paper presented to the Eighth Conference of Caribbean Historians (1976), p. 17.

24   Gerad Tikasingh, "A Method for Estimating the Free Coloured Population of Jamaica" (unpublished paper, University of the West Indies. Department of History [1968]), pp. 14, 16.

25   Brathwaite, *Creole Society*, p. 169.

26   Bailey, "Pre-Emancipation Kingston," p. 17; CO 318/76, Sympson to Hill, n.d. [1825], Appendix: Remark.

27   Goveia, *Slave Society*, p. 227. Goveia's discussion of the Leeward Islands parallels the situation of the freedmen in Jamaica on this point. See also the useful discussions in Jerome S. Handler, *The Unappropriated People* (Baltimore, 1974), Chapter 6 and Edward L. Cox, "The Shadow of Freedom: Freedmen in the Slave Societies of Grenada and St. Kitts, 1763–1833" (unpublished Ph.D. thesis, Johns Hopkins University, 1977), Chapter 4.

28   CO 318/76, Sympson to Hill, n.d. [1825], p. 12.

29   Duncker, "The Free Coloured," p. 79.

30   Ibid., p. 78; Hall, "Jamaica," pp. 202–203; Gardner, *History*, p. 371; CO 318/76, Sympson to Hill. n.d. [1825], pp. 12–13.

31   Brathwaite, *Creole Society*, p. 172; CO 318/76, Sympson to Hill, n.d. [1825], p. 12.

32   CO 318/76. Sympson to Hill. n.d. [1825], p. 13: Duncker, "The Free Coloured," pp. 85–86.

33   CO 137/154, Manchester to Bathurst, December 23, 1823, private.

34   CO 318/76, Campbell et al. to Hill, December 1825, Supplement to Schedule D. "Rich" meant those owning property worth more than £5,000, while those "in fair circumstances" had property valued between £1,000 and £2,500. Many of the "absolutely poor" free people of color possessed property worth £500.

35   Duncker, "The Free Coloured," p. 244.

36   Maria Nugent, *Lady Nugent's Journal*, edited by Philip Wright (Kingston, 1966), p. xxix: *Postscript to The Royal Gazette*, March 15, 1794.

37   [Barrett], *A Reply*, p. 48.

38   M. G. Lewis, *Journal of a West India Proprietor, 1815–17*, edited by Mona Wilson (London. 1929). pp. 94–95: CO 137/165. Manchester to Bathurst, April 1827, private; CO 137/163, Manchester to Bathurst, August 28, 1826.

39   R. R. Madden, Twelve Months' *Residence in the West Indies During the Transition from Slavery to Apprenticeship*, 2 vols. (London, 1835), 1: 113. Stipendiary magistrates were appointed to help adjudicate disputes between masters and their apprentices during the apprenticeship period which followed the abolition of slavery in 1834. Slaves were freed but served as apprentices to their former masters until 1838. For further background, see Chapter 8, pp. 97–98.

40   Bryan Edwards, *The History, Civil and Commercial, of the British Colonies in the West Indies*, 2 vols. (London, 1793), 2: 310; Long, *History*, 2: 333–35.

41   Richard Hill, *Lights and Shadows of Jamaica History* (Kingston, 1859), p. 104; Robert Renny, *An History of Jamaica* (London, 1807), p. 190n. Edward Long elaborated on the belief in England that colored schoolboys were really whites who had been tanned by the sun in *History*, 2: 274.

42   Lewis, *Journal*, p. 143; [J. Stewart], *An Account of Jamaica and Its Inhabitants* (London, 1808), pp. 302–303.

43   CO 137/175, Lushington to Courtenay, September 17, 1826; Brathwaite, *Creole Society*, p. 187; *The Watchman and Jamaica Free Press*, May 15, 1830; Duncker, "The Free Coloured," p. 119; David Lowenthal, *West Indian Societies* (New York, 1972), p. 49.

44   Mary Reckord, "Missions and Slavery, A Study of Protestant Missions in Jamaica, 1815–34" (unpublished manuscript), p. 38. Later controversies among the Methodists reinforced this view of the treatment of free coloreds. See, for example, the correspondence of the M.M.S., Edmondson to Beecham, July 20, 1837.

45 Reverend Hope Masterton Waddell, *Twenty-Nine Years in the West Indies and Central Africa* . . . (London, 1863), p. 34; *Appendix to the JAJ* (1841), p. 54; Brathwaite, *Creole Society*, pp. 173–74.

46 CO 318/76, Campbell, et al. to Hill, December 1825; James A. Thorne and Horace J. Kimball, *Emancipation in the West Indies* (New York, 1838), p. 88.

47 Stewart, *A View of Jamaica*, pp. 326–27; Lewis, *Journal*, p. 142; Mavis Campbell, *The Dynamics of Change in a Slave Society* (Rutherford, N.J., 1976), p. 54. For the modern West Indies, see Edith Clarke, *My Mother Who Fathered Me: A Study of the Family in Three Selected Communities in Jamaica* (London, 1957), and Fernando Henriques, *Family and Colour in Jamaica* (London, 1953).

48 Duncker, "The Free Coloured," pp. 58–59; James Kelly, *Voyage to Jamaica and Seventeen Years' Residence in That Island* (Belfast, 1838), p. 31; C. R. Boxer, *Race Relations in the Portuguese Colonial Empire, 1415–1825* (Oxford, 1965), p. 40; Goveia, *Slave Society*, p. 217. In his study of *Creole Society*, pp. 188–89, Brathwaite documents some exceptions to the rule against mixed marriages. See also *VAJ*, November 12, 1796, p. 43, for an example of a petition by a colored man who was married to a white woman.

49 Duncker, "The Free Coloured," pp. 42–43. Duncker claims that Swaby was a sambo, but this was unlikely. See [Barrett], *A Reply*, pp. 8–9.

50 *Postscript to The Royal Gazette*, November 8–15, 1823, Debates: November 12, November 13.

51 Duncker, "The Free Coloured," pp. 245–46.

52 *Postscript to The Royal Gazette*: May 29–June 5, 1813; June 12–19, 1813; August 21–28, 1813.

53 Brathwaite, *Creole Society*, p. 196.

54 William Beckford, *A Descriptive Account of the Island of Jamaica*, 2 vols. (London, 1790), 1: 389; M. G. Smith, "Some Aspects of Social Structure in the British Caribbean About 1820," *Social and Economic Studies* 1 (August 1953): 63; *The Watchman*, February 12, 1834.

55 Stewart, *A View of Jamaica*, pp. 331–32; CO 137/112, Nugent to Cooke, August 30, 1804, private; Edwards, *History*, 2: 25; H. T. de la Beche, *Notes on the Present Condition of the Negroes in Jamaica* (London, 1825), pp. 34–35.

56 R. C. Dallas, *The History of the Maroons*, 2 vols. (London, 1803), 2: 402–3.

57 [Barrett], *A Reply*, p. 29.

58 Joseph Sturge and Thomas Harvey, *The West Indies in 1837* (London, 1838), p. 247; Reckord, "Missions and Slavery," p. 115.

59 B. W. Higman, *Slave Population and Economy in Jamaica, 1807–1834* (Cambridge, 1976), pp. 146–47.

60 CO 137/154, Manchester to Bathurst, December 23, 1823, private.

61 CO 137/225, *The Herald and Literary Journal*, May 9, 1836.

Chapter 32

Arnold A. Sio

MARGINALITY AND FREE COLOURED IDENTITY IN CARIBBEAN SLAVE SOCIETY

THE STRUCTURE OF CARIBBEAN slave society consisted of a small minority of Europeans who dominated the majority of the population of enslaved Africans. Despite the profound differences in power, culture, and race between the masters and the slaves, the ideal of the masters that the two were to remain totally separate was never realized. The bipolar structure of the society was gradually altered through the genetic intermixture of the masters and the slaves and the emergence of an intermediate racial group. Over time a significant portion of this racial mixed population became legally free. This created an overlap between the free Europeans and the enslaved Africans and promoted questions regarding the boundaries of the respective groups, criteria of identification, and status allocation. In a society in which slavery was associated with race, a free coloured person was 'a third party in a system built for two'. The interpenetration of the masters and the slaves and the appearance of an intermediate group of freedmen or free coloured has been defined 'as one of the most critical problem-areas in the historical study of Afro-Caribbean societies'.[1]

Unlike the United States where the literature on the free Negro dates back to the turn of the century, research on this group in the Caribbean is relatively recent and less substantial. The Caribbean freedmen figure in two kinds of studies. The most extensive are those pertaining to race and colour in the Caribbean that often involve comparisons with the rest of the Americas, particularly the United States. Second, are those more recent studies that, although they may take up the matter of race and colour, are for the most part descriptive accounts of the freedmen that include their demographic characteristics, political–legal status, economic activity, religious life, education, and to some extent stratification, relations with whites and with slaves, and culture and social organization.

There are two general features of the research on the free coloured that have given rise to the issues discussed in this paper. The first is that the studies conform for the most part to the observation that much of what has been written is about the 'established free coloured, if not the elite',[2] and to the related observation that the 'plight of the free coloured majority . . . is seldom recorded'.[3] Many of the existing generalizations are based on a 'fraction of the whole'[4] that probably varied from five to seven per cent of the group and in some places might have consisted of a small number of families. The tendency to take the most visible, active and articulate 'as typical of the whole group'[5] has not gone unrecognized in the literature.[6] While it may be the case that in a particular study reference is made to the narrowness of its base, the implications are not always taken into account when generalizations are actually stated.

The second general feature pertains to the way in which the freedmen have been depicted in the literature. The people of colour were marginal to Caribbean slave society: neither black nor white, neither African nor European, and neither slave nor free. The consequences of this marginality for their identity constitute the content of the depictions of the group in the literature. Although it is recognized that their marginality did not produce a uniform response among the freedmen, including the leadership and the established segment of the group, the free coloured are generally portrayed, sometimes explicitly, more often implicitly, as having identified themselves with the dominant whites.[7] The defining features of this assimilationist depiction are to be found in the following: 'they were loyal to the establishment',[8] 'strongly identified with the master class',[9] 'tended to identify culturally with the whites',[10] and 'were very conscious of their European heritage and extremely proud of it'.[11] Although opposed to the white policy of exclusion based on racial ancestry, they favoured the existing society, including slavery, and 'tended to aspire to white plantocratic or managerial status'.[12]

The concern of this essay is with three problematic or neglected issues that relate to the question of the identity of the free people of colour: culture and social organization, unity and group consciousness, and the style and goals of their political activity. The existing research provides the basis for observations that are often of an exploratory and provisional nature. The tentative parts of this discussion reflect not only the need for more historical information that is comparative and generalizable, but also for more research that is guided by a view of the free coloured as of critical importance to an understanding of Caribbean slave society and Afro-American history.[13]

I

What we know about the culture of people of colour pertains to members of the upper stratum of the population who are said to have emulated the whites. Although this view of the free coloured culture is often extended by assumption and implication to the entire group, little is known about the culture of the majority of freedmen during slavery. It is apparent that this issue is considerably more complex than is conveyed by statements based on a segment of the group. Not only is it the least studied of the three issues, it is also the most difficult to approach. For that reason many of the observations in this section of the paper are likely to be the most exploratory and provisional.

In approaching the origin and nature of the culture of the free coloured we begin with the relationship between the free coloured and the slaves. Since the freedmen emerged in conjunction with slavery, their culture and social organization originally involved a transfer or carry-over from the slave community. The components of this Afro-creole complex were modified as the free coloured became differentiated into separate strata. However, since it appears that during slavery and after a substantial number of the people of colour remained generally removed from sustained interaction with the whites and the Euro-creole complex of that group, this cleavage served to maintain and reinforce the Afro-creole cultural complex among themselves and the slaves.

It is likely that in the early years of the group a number of the free coloured, many of them the miscegenated offspring of wealthy whites who had arranged for their freedom, conformed to the Euro-creole pattern of the dominant group. Even at a later date, however, the number who could adopt and sustain this way of life, as we shall note, must have been quite limited. Our conception of the culture of the freedmen is based largely on the minority who were in a position to take on the cultural complex of the ruling whites.

Within the boundaries created and maintained by the white structure of dominance, the life of the free people of colour was to a large extent removed from that of the whites. Indeed, members of the dominant group were peripheral to most of the relationships in which the freedmen were involved. The ratio of free coloured to whites, the concentration of the free coloured and of the coloured slaves in the towns, the location of most of the freedmen in the lower stratum of the free coloured social order, the racism of the dominant group and its control of the major sources of power – these were among the factors that singly and in combination determined the interaction of the free coloured people and the whites. With the exception of the interaction between free coloured women and white males and a small number of those of the upper stratum and whites, interaction with those of the dominant group was not an important element in the free coloured social structure.

It was the local community of the freedmen that constituted their primary environment, while the work experience, which was most likely to bring them into contact with the whites, was their secondary environment and less important for their life-ways. Considerable social interaction occurred between the freedmen and the slaves of the towns. Just as the distinction between the master and the slave tended to break down in the towns, so the line between the freedmen and the slaves became blurred. Not only did the town slaves have more mobility than those on the plantations, many also worked, lived and carried on a social life away from their masters. Interaction with the slaves on many levels and in a variety of ways rather than with the whites must then have been a feature of everyday life for most of the free people of colour. Given the concentration of the free coloured and the coloured slaves in the towns, it is likely that relations were mainly between the coloured members of each group.[14]

Many freedmen existed on the margins of an economy that was dominated by the plantation system.[15] They often found themselves and the slaves similarly situated in the towns, especially with regard to work and living conditions. They lived close to each other, they interacted more frequently with each other than either did with the whites and they shared the same familiar life-space. They often participated in the same religious, economic, educational, and social activites. Family and kinship relations based on common origin were another measure of the extensive network in which the freedmen and the slaves were involved. Then, too, there were the numerous informal contacts that must have marked the daily round of freedmen and slaves as they moved about the towns.[16] In spite of the growing difference in legal status and group membership, a substantial number of the free coloured and the slaves, who were concentrated in a similar economic, social, and ecological position, shared the Afro-creole pattern which was in turn reinforced by their participation in a wide range of institutions and activities.[17]

Thus, the conditions that functioned to largely confine the interaction of the majority of the freedmen to themselves and with the slaves, also served to perpetuate the Afro-creole complex of the free coloured group. Moreover, the structure of dominance maintained by the whites, especially their control of the economy and polity, was such that the life chances of the free people of colour were exceedingly limited. Their position was characterized by its static nature. This, too, furthered the stability and continuity of the group's life-ways.

Additions to the group from the slave population through manumission and self-purchase tended to have the same result. The change in status from slave to freedman was a shift from one subordinate group to another, both based on racial ancestry. It is likely that many of those who were freed became incorporated into the lower stratum of the free coloured community. Although an important change occurred in legal status and group affiliation, the freed slave could expect to find significant continuities of colour, cultural patterns and, if an ex-town slave, little change in environment. Given the network that existed between the slaves and the freedmen, the freed slave was likely to have been very familiar with the free coloured social and cultural life even as it changed, especially when, as must often have been the case, there were parents, children, other relatives, and friends among the freedmen. It is unlikely, then, that the change in status from slave to freedman involved a set of unfamiliar institutions and cultural understandings. The freed slave was a source of stability and continuity, for the movement of freed slaves into the free coloured group meant an infusion of Afro-creole life-ways. The transition for the freed slave was relatively simple, causing little personal or group disruption with integration into the group of freedmen being largely a matter of course.

Accretion to the freedmen population also occurred through the birth of children. Throughout the slavery period, the free coloured group appears to have been the only one capable of increasing through natural means. This was an important source of growth. When restrictions were placed on manumission, it became the primary source of population growth. The life-ways that were passed on through the socialization of the children contributed to the cultural continuity of the freedmen and promoted group identification.

The changes that gradually occurred among the free coloured during the slavery period included some degree of social, economic and cultural differentiation. As mentioned earlier, a small upper stratum emerged who participated in the Euro-creole culture of the dominant group. However, those who could adopt this cultural complex remained a small number throughout the period. Most of those who desired to do so were unable to acquire the education or wealth to maintain the life-ways of the ruling whites. The middle stratum that emerged in the process of differentiation developed a 'Synthetic-creole' culture that was a combination of elements derived from the Afro-creole and Euro-creole patterns.[18]

The process of differentiation did not involve a large number of the freedmen. No significant increase in interaction with the white population appears to have occurred. The social and kinship networks among the free coloured and between them and the town slaves remained relatively unchanged. A substantial proportion of the freedmen, varying in size from colony to colony, remained – and was to remain for a long time – Afro-creole in its life-ways.

II

The issue regarding the unity and consciousness of the freedmen is, like that relating to their culture, part of the larger question of their identity as a group. It has been said that they lacked a 'social organization' and that they were slow in developing a 'group consciousness'.[19] It is clear, however, that a sense of identity was a continuous process and developed with the freedmen's consciousness as a group. The growth of a group consciousness began quite early. Just as they were set apart from the beginning by the dominant group, so they set themselves apart. Their consciousness largely coincided with their position in the society. They were a people of colour, neither black nor white, but coloured and consciously so. Like their counterparts in the United States, they were 'new people'.[20] Since the boundaries between themselves and the slaves were vague and fluid, the continuation of relations with slaves was not a barrier to a free coloured identity. By the late eighteenth century, the larger society was aware that the free coloured had begun to develop a separate identity and were becoming a solidary people.

The development of a group consciousness among the freedmen occurred in conjunction with an increase in population size and density and with the growth of social organization. Over time the increasing size and concentration of the free coloured in the towns meant more than an aggregation of large numbers of people of one's own kind. For there gradually emerged a sense of a sizeable group and a perception of being part of a discernible whole with a distinct history, common origin, and shared concerns.[21] This perception was also fostered by the creation of organizations and associations that contributed to the development of a group identification. The racism of the whites that was institutionalized in the structure of dominance and exclusion reinforced patterns of association and identification among the free people of colour. The limited occupational differentiation among them made for common social and economic interests and for a similarity of life-ways. Thus, the limitations on the economic development of the freedmen that kept them marginal to the main economy of the society contributed to their consciousness as a group and to their solidarity.

As they became conscious of themselves as a group an identity developed that embodied a distinct sense of difference. The sense of identity manifested itself in the definitions of acceptable behaviour among themselves, the terms they used to define themselves, and in their view of themselves in relation to whites, to a particular island, and to the Caribbean region as a whole.

In the course of time, norms and values developed that were seen as contributing to group identity and pride and that were intended to govern the actions of the freedmen. Those who deviated from these norms and values aroused the displeasure of others. The freedmen of Jamaica who applied for and were granted special privileges by the Assembly, removing various disabilities normally attached to the status of the free coloured, incurred the displeasure of the rest of the group. The practice was scorned by the free coloured newspaper where those 'who chose to avail themselves of *such means* to be blanched' were referred to as having participated in an 'infamous delusion'. While those who were granted the special privileges viewed themselves as having been rewarded for achieving a mode of living that conformed to that of the dominant group and won its approval, the press viewed them as dupes and as a threat to the solidarity of the group. They had been subjected to the '*acme* of political juggling' by the ruling whites.[22]

The terms with which they distinguished themselves as a group reveal that their sense of identity very much involved attachment to a homeland or territory and a region. Most of all they perceived themselves as genuinely indigenous to the area, indeed, as native sons. They were 'natives of the soil', a particular island was 'our native country' or 'native land'. 'This is our native country – we have nowhere else to go.' They were creoles of colour expressing a new ethnicity.

On the other hand, the whites were perceived as 'alien', as 'transient', and as 'foreigners'. The freedmen of Grenada expressed it as having more of a vested interest than the 'transient white foreigners'. Moreover, 'they', the whites, were aliens and interlopers not only to particular islands but to the Caribbean region as a whole. Throughout, the free coloured make it clear that central to their identity was that 'we', the free coloured, are native sons and our homeland is an island and region, while 'they', the whites, are alien to both.

The regional dimension of the free coloured sense of identity was grounded in an extensive network of similar groups in the Spanish, French, Dutch and Danish colonies as well as the British. Information was communicated through this network regarding the general situation, political activities, and goals of the several groups in the region. The value of this network was enhanced by the immigration and travel of freedmen to the different colonies where much exchange of information took place and their presence tended to heighten the group consciousness and identity of the free coloured.[23]

The evolution of a separate identity included the way the free coloured conceived of their place in the structure of the society. The whites, of course, intended that they be located between themselves and the slaves, with the free people of colour having their primary identification with the whites. However, although the free coloured accepted their intermediateness in terms of 'colour' and, indeed, made it a central feature of their distinctive identity, they had no intention of occupying an intermediate position in the society. Such a position would have been inherently unstable, with severe limitations on their civil rights and aspirations. Their aggressive pursuit of the rights of citizenship made it apparent to the dominant group that the freedmen rejected being relegated to an intermediate place in the society.

Thus, while they identified themselves as native sons, they also considered themselves as British citizens. Was this a matter of confused identity? That the freedmen may have subscribed to the political values of the dominant group and claimed equal rights as British citizens is hardly to be taken as evidence that they did not perceive of themselves as having a separate and distinctive identity. It did not mean that the free coloured identified with the whites and that the acquisition of citizenship was to be the initial step toward acceptance in the existing society. Rather it was that the rights and privileges of citizens were seen as instrumental not only to inclusion in the polity and as crucial to their efforts in the economy, but potentially as providing access to the power resources with which to have an independent impact on the society and on their future as a group with its own identity. Recent research indicates that the freedmen did not entirely share the white view of Caribbean society and its future, despite the subscription of some of them to the Euro-creole pattern.[24]

We have referred to those of the freedmen who in the course of time were able to assimilate the cultural patterns of the ruling whites. Even by the 1830s, however, when the free coloured had gained their civil rights, the ability to adopt those life-ways was limited to a minority of the group. With the Afro-creole and Synthetic-creole patterns predominating, the differences in culture among the freedmen may not have been very great. It is conceivable that the freedmen shared a view of themselves as native sons and as British citizens who valued and sought equal rights as a means to the realization of their aspirations as individuals and as a group. There is no evidence of a confused identity resulting from their identification of themselves as a distinct people and as British citizens.

III

Their political activity was aimed at gaining the rights and privileges of British citizens, which would resolve the political and legal contradictions confounding their position in the society. Only a small number of the group were involved in articulating the goals of the freedmen and in providing the political leadership. Much of the research has been centred on the activities of these freedmen.

The politicization of the freedmen occurred in connection with certain changes in their situation. These included the growth in the size of the group, the appearance of a significant number of free-born people of colour, the increasing concentration of freedmen in the towns, the social and economic differentiation that meant some economic success and growth in the wealth of the group, and their involvement in the activities of the mission churches.[25] These changes raised their expectations regarding their life chances which, however, came up against the continued exclusionary policies and practices of the dominant white group. The effects of these changes were reinforced and intensified by the restiveness of the freedmen in the other colonies, the revolutionary disturbances in the French colonies, and the changes in the British colonial policy in response to the movement for amelioration and emancipation.

The goals of the freedmen and the means they employed have been depicted as conservative.[26] However, in seeking to gain civil and political rights for themselves – and acting on the premise that they had a legitimate claim to such rights – the freedmen were in fundamental opposition to the existing structure of the society as it was being maintained by the power and racial ideology of the ruling whites. Moreover, the goals and political activity of the free coloured could very well be taken as an indirect attack on slavery, for the same power and ideology informed and maintained the system of slavery. To pursue these goals, then, was to challenge the power and ideology that were integral to the identity, cohesion, and dominance of the whites. To attempt to bring the free coloured into the power structure of Caribbean slave society under these circumstances was hardly a conservative or moderate goal and the whites were quick to perceive it as the radical goal that it, indeed, was at the time. The presence of a politically aggressive group of freedmen pursuing issues that challenged the stability and continuation of the existing political, economic, and social organization of the society convinced the whites that they had been correct from the beginning in their view of the free coloured as potentially as great a threat to the established order as the slaves.[27]

The freedmen engaged in individual, uncoordinated acts of protest and organized political action to gain their civil rights. There was persistent opposition by individuals and small, groups of the free coloured to segregation in churches and places of public recreation and to the generally discriminatory behaviour of the whites. The organized political action carried on by the freedmen was legal and aimed primarily at constitutional change: petitions, appeals, expressions of grievances, lobbying in England, and testifying before imperial commissions. Action directed at constitutional change was the primary means used by the freedmen.

The freedmen were fundamentally opposed to living in a society in which 'the structure was rooted in the biogenetic conception of group superiority–inferiority – in short, racism'.[28] From the vantage point of the whites, of course, this represented a rejection of the principle that was fundamental to the hierarchical organization of the society. The status of the free coloured was ascribed on the basis of their non-white ancestry. The whites intended that their status and racial ancestry would correspond in that not only would freedmen be relegated to a subordinate group, but the group would also remain undifferentiated. However, the free coloured did become internally differentiated to the point where, in terms of certain social and economic criteria, there were freedmen who were at the same level or a level above the whites. Yet, since racial ancestry was intended to determine the structure of the society, they were excluded from certain rights that would have been theirs had they been white. It was not that the freedmen were opposed to living in a stratified society. Rather, through their political activity they hoped to create a situation in which their individual efforts and achievements – given full rein as a result of having the rights of citizens – would largely determine their position in the society and not their racial ancestry.

Slavery and the relations with slaves were very much involved in the strategy pursued by the freedmen in their campaign for civil rights. This is especially evident in the way in which they portrayed themselves to the whites and in the methods used to bring about change. It is clear from the previous discussion of the relations between the slaves and the free coloured that the complex issue of the place and meaning of slavery in the life of the freedmen is far from settled. Some of what follows, then, is of necessity tentative and provisional.

With regard to the direct involvement in slavery through the ownership of slaves, the most recent research indicates that the free coloured owned relatively few slaves, were no more than 20 per cent of the owners in 1832, and owned a much smaller proportion of the slave population than did the whites. A relatively large proportion of the coloured slaves belonged to the freedmen which, as we noted earlier, reflected the concentration in the towns of the two groups. More free coloured females than males owned slaves. They were most likely to have owned slaves in units of rarely more than 10, many of whom would have been domestics. Their owner may well have been someone to whom they were related and who was not wealthy. While there were those among the free people of colour who saw the ownership of slaves as the way to wealth and prestige in a slave society, there were few planters among them.[29]

Challenging the slavery system directly was not one of the goals in the otherwise aggressive, persistent, and lengthy campaign carried on by the freedmen for their civil rights. Freedmen were not to become involved in political alliances with the slaves. Unless they were willing to challenge the slavery system head on, the freedmen were aware that improvement in their life chances depended on setting themselves apart from the slaves. It seems doubtful, however, that they could have expected to attain equality in the sense that their racial ancestry would no longer be a factor in their life chances. For that would be a long time in coming and called for the unity of all those with African ancestry and the abolition of slavery. Nevertheless, it was perceived that substantial gains were to be made within the existing society by separating themselves from the slaves.

Separating themselves from the slaves meant more than not entering into alliances with the slaves or not attacking slavery. Distinguishing themselves from the slaves socially, culturally, and ideologically was crucial for the image they projected of themselves in their approach to the ruling whites. Thus we find that while, on the one hand, the free coloured expressions of group identity emphasized their separateness – a third group in the society – and tended to be cast in ethnic terms and in language often critical of the whites and of colonialism, in their numerous and various appeals for equal rights, on the other hand, they stressed their identity with the whites.

In validating their claim to the rights of British citizens they portrayed themselves as having achieved ownership of land, property and slaves, and as sharing many of the values, sentiments, and attitudes of the whites. Throughout they stressed that they had remained an orderly and loyal people. It was an approach to the dominant group that involved refraining from an attack on slavery, distinguishing themselves from the slaves, expressing their identity with the whites, and exploiting the desire of the whites to have the free coloured serve as a buffer group between themselves and the slaves.

The free coloured portrayals of themselves in their approach to the colonial authorities tell us much about their conduct of the campaign for civil rights. They are much less reliable as sources of information about their life-ways, attitudes toward whites, and particularly their views on slavery. After all, the campaign was designed and conducted to bring the ruling group around to the point of granting the freedmen their rights as citizens.[30] Therefore, with the possible exception of those directly involved in the various petitions and addresses, we do not know the extent to which there was acceptance within the free coloured community, particularly among the lower stratum, of a set of goals that prohibited political alliances with slaves and expressions of opposition to slavery.

Although political alliances with the slaves are likely to have been infrequent, we do have some evidence of freedmen becoming allied with slaves, and expressing their opposition to slavery in other ways. Unfortunately, very little research has been done on free coloured involvement in slave rebellions, conspiracies, runaways, and marronage. We have information on alliances of slaves and freedmen in revolts in Grenada,[31] Barbados,[32] and Jamaica,[33] and in aborted plots in Antigua[34] and Tobago,[35] and on the harbouring of runaways.[36] These alliances extended from 1736 in Antigua to 1832 in Jamaica and into the period when the free people of colour were granted their civil rights. What appears to have happened is that, as the freedmen gained their civil rights in the late 1820s and early 1830s, especially the franchise and access to the Assembly, and as their sense of a separate identity continued to develop, there was an increase in their opposition to slavery.

Contrary to what the whites had come to expect after they had granted the freedmen their civil rights, in the end the freedmen did not join with them in a united front against the abolition of slavery. Nor were the expectations of the free coloured fully realized. Caribbean society continued to be one in which the life chances of its people would be determined to a large extent by their racial ancestry. There were gains for the freedmen. While these gains varied from colony to colony, there was a general reduction in the scope of white regulation of the polity and the economy, though they continued to control both areas. Sharing political and legal rights with members of the dominant group did not, of course, mean full acceptance. The exclusion of people of colour from the primary and institutional life of the whites remained almost complete. For 'they continued to suffer the stigma of slave and partial black ancestry'.[37]

IV

At the centre of the research on the free coloured is the marginality of their position in Caribbean slave society. They have been depicted as responding to their marginality by identifying with the whites. Although it is recognized that their response was not entirely uniform, it is the free coloured as assimilationist that is the most prominent, explicitly and implicitly, in the scholarly research and in the popular view of the group. A discussion of this interpretation of their identity has been the objective of this essay. It has involved observations grounded in the documentary materials as well as assertions that are tentative and speculative.

The question of the identity of the free coloured must be examined in relation to the evolving and changing character of the group. The history of the freedmen during slavery is the evolution and assimilation to a new identity.[38] From the beginning they were defined as a marginal people. Accepting this definition of themselves was also the beginning of their consciousness as a new people. As their marginality dissolved during the slavery period, they gradually developed an identity as a people who were creole in colour and culture and in their views of Caribbean society, its people, and its future. Some final observations on these dimensions of their identity are in order.

In making their phenotype a vital part of their identity the free coloured, it has been said, failed to develop a consciousness of their own worth. For they had made as their own the racist ideology and practices of the dominant white group. The 'white bias' of the freedmen, then, is evidence of their identification with the whites.[39]

While there may have been a similarity in form, the so-called white bias of the freedmen did not have the same meaning and purpose as among the whites. To begin with, given the focus of the present research, we know only that during slavery this bias existed among some of the established freedmen. Second, the slaves as well as the free blacks and free coloured – whether free by manumission, self-purchase or birth – were all subjected to the racism of the whites. The legal disabilities and discriminatory practices of the whites applied to all free non-whites. Likewise, no distinctions were made by the whites between free coloured and free blacks in the extension of civil rights over the years. Third, slaves, free blacks and free coloured were often joined by an extensive network of ties, including kinship, and similar life situations. Fourth, the freedmen carried on a vigorous campaign for their civil rights and against their exclusion from full participation in the society on the basis of their racial ancestry. Most important, the phenotypic bias of the free persons of colour was not justified and supported by a racist ideology as were the racial values and practices of the whites. It was apparent even before they gained their civil rights and before Emancipation, that the freedmen did not intend to institutionalize their bias in a structure of dominance devoted to the maintenance of an hierarchial order based on gradations of colour and the permanent exclusion of those who did not have the proper phenotype. The phenotype, it may be suggested, had the same meaning and purpose, though perhaps not the same weight during slavery, as the socioeconomic criteria usually associated with 'class': occupation, income, wealth, education, lifestyle. That is, among the freedmen the value of the phenotype did not derive from an ideology of biogenetic superiority, but rather from its importance as a determinant of a person's life chances in a society where race was used to justify slavery.

The freedmen were creoles of culture as well as colour. The focus of the existing research gives the impression that they identified culturally exclusively with the dominant white sector in adopting the Euro-creole culture.

Largely missing from the discussion of the culture of the free coloured group are the lower and middle strata. Given the limited differentiation of the free coloured sector and the restricted interaction with the whites for most of the slavery period, interaction occurred mainly among the freedmen themselves and between those of the lower stratum and the slaves who shared the Afro-creole culture. A substantial number of the freedmen, varying from colony to colony, were involved in this relationship, which continued in the towns after Emancipation and into the twentieth century.

The segmented nature of free coloured culture became pronounced as the group became differentiated and gradually gained its civil rights. The result was the Afro-creole, Synthetic-creole and the Euro-creole cultural segments. Most important in this process was the emergence of a middle stratum and the development of the Synthetic-creole pattern. Much later a century or more after the free coloured had gained their civil rights and the slaves their freedom – when the middle stratum finally gained political control, as in Jamaica, the Synthetic-creole culture was articulated as a national culture and as the basis for solidarity and the integration of all parts of the society.[40]

The development of an identity of their own among the freedmen required that they be free and in order to be free they had to belong – to have their rights as British citizens. It is important, however, that the conflict between themselves and the whites not be seen as limited to the acquisition of civil rights for the freedmen, as part of a drive toward the 'maximization of their status' and eventual incorporation into the existing society, but as a conflict having to do with the way the society was ordered and its future. Their support of the abolition of slavery, the pivotal institution in the society, and their opposition to racism, the ideology that justified both slavery and the severe restrictions on their freedom, involved a conception of society very different in important respects than the existing one, and was a manifestation of their strong identification with the colony as their homeland.

The insular dimension of their identity became most evident in the post-Emancipation years when they opposed the ruling whites, whose identity remained predominantly metropolitan, concerning the issues facing the society, especially those pertaining to the newly freed slaves, and the future direction of the society. Rather than identify their interests with those of the whites, they 'engaged in a politics of opposition, of alternative proposals and policies, and enacting rather than reacting'.[41] Moreover, they had a different view of themselves than the whites who were bent on keeping them and the former slaves in a position of subordinancy, while they looked forward to 'ascendancy' in the society for themselves and the freemen. At the same time, however, their commitment to pluralism is evident in their stress on the importance of the whites and certain of their values to the well-being and development of the post-Emancipation society.

Notes

1 Sidney W. Mintz and Richard Price, *An Anthropological Approach to the Afro-American Past: A Caribbean Perspective*, Philadelphia, 1976, p. 3. The terms free coloured, free people of colour, and freedmen refer to persons of mixed racial ancestry who gradually came to be defined as a separate socioracial group.

2 *Neither Slave Nor Free: The Freedman of African Descent in the Slave Societies of the New World*, ed. David W. Cohen and Jack P. Greene (Baltimore, 1972), p. 15.

3 David Lowenthal, 'Free Coloured West Indians: A Racial Dilemma', *Studies in Eighteenth-Century Culture* (Cleveland, 1973), p. 347.

4 Edward Brathwaite, *The Development of Creole Society in Jamaica, 1770–1820* (Oxford, 1971), p. 174.

5 Cohen and Green, *Slave Nor Free*, p. 15.

6 Jerome S. Handler, *The Unappropriated People: Freedmen in the Slave Society of Barbados* (Baltimore, 1974), pp. 212–13; Gad J. Heuman, *Between Black and White: Race, Politics and the Free Coloreds in Jamaica, 1792–1865* (Westport, Conn.) 1981, p. xvi.

7 The most systematic assimilationist interpretation is Mavis Christine Campbell, *The Dynamics of Change in a Slave Society: Sociopolitical History of the Free Coloreds in Jamaica, 1792–1865* (Rutherford, NJ, 1976), pp. 10, 144–5, 176, and esp. 368. A contrasting interpretation of the free coloured response to their marginality is Heuman, *Between Black and White*, esp. Appendix A, and 'Slavery and Emancipation in the British Caribbean', *Journal of Imperial and Commonwealth History*, 6 (1978), 170–1. See Arnold A. Sio, 'West Indian Politicians of Color', *Plantation Society*, 2 (1983), 91–7.

8 Brathwaite, *Development of Creole Society*, p. 193.

9 Orlando Patterson, *Slavery and Social Death* (Cambridge, 1982), p. 257.

10 B.W. Higman, *Slave Populations of the British Caribbean* (Baltimore, 1984), p. 112.

11 Philip D. Curtin, *Two Jamaicas* (Cambridge, 1955), p. 45.

12 Cohen and Greene, *Slave Nor Free*, p. 12.

13 The interpretation presented in the section that follows owes much to Handler, *Unappropriated People*, an especially creative and insightful study of the freedmen during the slavery period, and to the dialogue created by the studies of Campbell, *Dynamics of Change* and Heuman, *Between Black and White*.

14 Very little has been written on either the cultural or social relations between slaves and freedmen. However, see Handler, *Unappropriated People*, pp. 79–80, 98–9, 153, 201–8, and the observations in the more recent study by Edward Cox, *Free Coloreds in the Slave Societies of St. Kitts, and Grenada, 1763–1833* (Knoxville, 1984), pp. 25, 45, 71, 75. The emerging research on urban slavery in the Caribbean undoubtedly will involve relations between slaves and freedmen. Heuman has observed that 'an examination of manumission data as well as of free coloured wills might also reveal the close bonds between many free people and slaves. Such research would help to offset the portrayal of the free coloured and slave communities as totally divided and at odds with each other.' See his 'Robert Osborn of Jamaica', Paper presented at the Fifteenth Conference of Caribbean Historians, University of the West Indies (Jamaica), 1984, p. 3. The terms Euro-creole, and

Afro-creole are from Brathwaite, *Development of Creole Society*, pp. 297–305, 309. Also Handler, *Unappropriated People*, p. 216. Similar terms and distinctions are to be found in Curtin, *Two Jamaicas*, pp. 25, 42, and Orlando Patterson, 'Context and Choice in Ethnic Allegiance', *Ethnicity*, ed. Nathan Glazier and Daniel P. Moynihan (Cambridge, 1975), pp. 316–19.

15   Arnold A. Sio, 'Race and Colour in the Status of the Free Coloured in the West Indies: Jamaica and Barbados', *Journal of Belizean Affairs*, 4 (1976), pp. 35–7; Celia Karch, 'London Bourne of Barbados', Paper presented at the Fifteenth Conference of Caribbean Historians, University of the West Indies (Jamaica) April, 1984, 12. It is not clear from the study of Grenada and St. Kitts to what extent the freedmen were economically marginalized as in Jamaica and Barbados. Indeed, according to Cox, it was not the exclusion of the freedmen from the economy that brought them into contact with the slaves, but rather their central position in the economy. Thus, 'meaningful ties with the slaves' were not only to be found among the lower stratum of the free coloured community (*Free Coloreds in the Slave Societies*, p. 75).

16   Minutes of evidence, Select Committee of the House of Lords, the Laws and Usages of the Several West Indies Colonies in Relation to the Slave Population, Part 11, 14 July–9 August, 1832, p. 710.

17   Initially, the free coloured were simply no longer the property of another Beyond that they had no rights and often were treated legally as slaves. Only gradually did the legal status of the free coloured begin to diverge from that of the slaves.

18   The term 'Synthetic-creole' is from Patterson, 'Context and Choice', pp. 317–19. I have retained his definition. However, I view this pattern as emerging before the free coloured gained their civil rights and Emancipation. At the same time, I agree with Patterson that the process of creolization was not as advanced during slavery as some have assumed. Moreover, as he and others have pointed out, it was a segmented process that produced Afro-creole, Synthetic-creole, and Euro-creole patterns. It was with the gradual differentiation of the free coloured group that a middle stratum emerged whose limited resources would not allow for the adoption of the Euro-creole life-ways. The result was the synthetic pattern. What I am suggesting is that a significant percentage of people of colour were to be found in the lower stratum adhering to the Afro-creole pattern during slavery and well into the twentieth century.

19   Cohen and Greene, *Slave Nor Free*, p. 12.

20   'You must take us for ourselves – we are new people.' Charles Waddell Chesnutt, *The House Behind Cedars* (Ridgewood, NJ, 1900), 1968, p. 83.

21   Leonard P. Curry, *The Free Black in Urban America 1800–1850* (Chicago, 1981), pp. 239–43 describes a similar development among free Negroes in the United States.

22   *Watchman and Jamaica Free Press*, 17 Dec. 1831. Italicized in the original. Also Heuman, 'White Over Brown Over Black: The Free Coloureds in Jamaican Society During Slavery and After Emancipation', *Journal of Caribbean History*, 1981, pp. 14, 57.

23   Cox, *Free Coloreds in the Slave Societies*, pp. 100, 142.

24   This is the main argument presented by Heuman, *Between Black and White* and Karch, 'London Bourne'. It was made much earlier by Curtin, *Two Jamaicas*, p. 44.

25   The importance of the Protestant missions in the politicization of the freedmen – their consciousness and organizational skills – warrants a separate study. In this connection see the excellent study by Mary Turner, *Slaves and Missionaries* (Urbana, Ill.), 1982, pp. 15, 27, 57, 85, 91, 163, 179, 198; Handler, *Unappropriated People*, pp. 154–61; Cox, *Free Coloreds in the Slave Societies*, pp. 111–22 for the role of the Catholic Church as well as the missions; Brathwaite, *Development of Creole Society*, pp. 208–11.

26   This a widely held view. Handler, *Unappropriated People*, pp. 216–17, is representative.

27   Cohen and Greene, *Slave Nor Free*, pp. 16–17.

28   *The Origins of American Slavery and Racism*, ed. Donald L. Noel (Columbus, Ohio, 1972), pp. 9, 27.

29   Higman, *Slave Populations*, pp. 101, 107, 112, 153.

30   The major shortcoming of the source materials on the free coloured is that much of it consists of whites who were writing for whites, whether in public documents or travel

accounts, and of petitions and addresses prepared by the free coloured leadership for white consumption. These petitions and addresses are important in that they were produced by the freedmen themselves and, therefore, are of value, especially with regard to their political goals and activities and for the manner in which they portrayed themselves to the ruling whites.

31 Cox, *Free Coloreds in the Slave Societies*, Ch.5.

32 Hilary Beckles, 'On the Backs of Blacks: The Barbados Free Coloured Pursuit of Civil Rights and the 1816 Slave Rebellion', *Immigrants and Minorities*, 3 (1984), 167–85; Handler, *Unappropriated People*, pp. 85–6; Michael Craton, *Testing the Chains* (Ithaca, 1982), p. 260.

33 Craton, *Testing*, p. 316.

34 David Barry Gaspar, *Bondmen and Rebels* (Baltimore, 1985), pp. 12, 28, 43–61.

35 Craton, *Testing*, p. 157.

36 Gad Heuman, 'Runaway Slaves in Nineteenth-Century Barbados', in *Out of the House of Bondage*, ed. Gad Heuman and *Slavery and Abolition*, 6, 3, (Dec. 1985), p. 107.

37 Patterson, *Slavery and Social Death*, p. 257. Indeed, white racism may have intensified after the freedmen gained their civil rights and after Emancipation. See David Lowenthal, *West Indian Societies* (New York, 1972), p. 67. Also David Barry Gaspar, '"The Best Years of My Life:" James Johnston of St. Lucia and Antigua, 1819–1832', pp. 2, 4, 5–6, Paper presented at the Fifteenth Conference of Caribbean Historians, University of the West Indies (Jamaica) April 15, 1983.

38 Campbell, on the other hand, concluded that a combination of factors led to an increase in the identification with whites from the 1820s onward. *Dynamics of Change*, p. 368.

39 Fernando Henriques, *Family and Colour in Jamaica* (London, 1953), p. 49.

40 Patterson, 'Context and Choice', p. 319.

41 Sio, 'West Indian Politicians', p. 97. Also Swithin Wilmot, 'Race, Electoral Violence and Constitutional Reform in Jamaica, 1830–1854', *Journal of Caribbean History*, 1982, 17, 1–13.

Chapter 33

David Northrup

IGBO AND MYTH IGBO
Culture and ethnicity in the Atlantic world, 1600–1850

T HE CONSTRUCTION OF GROUP IDENTITY in pre-colonial Africa and colonial African America is a hot topic. Considering the limitations and complexity of the evidence, it is not surprising that recent studies have led to divergent conclusions. While many scholars of African identity are arguing that sub-national or 'tribal' identities are a creation of the twentieth century, historians of African America have been positing the development of similar cultural identities in seventeenth- and eighteenth-century America. This essay seeks to resolve some misunderstandings and confusions that have arisen in discussions of cultural identity by taking a critical look at the terms that Africans and Europeans used to identify communities in the West African region north of the Bight of Biafra between 1600 and 1850. Its main thesis is that the ethnographic labels commonly used by Europeans greatly enlarged and simplified African identity groups in the era of the Atlantic slave trade. It argues that historians need to examine the development of African-Americans' ethnic identity with greater sensitivity to the identities that people from this important trading coast would have brought with them.

Recent studies of the evolution of ethnolinguistic identities within sub-Saharan Africa have argued that the 'tribal' identities generally considered typical of Africa are in fact quite recent creations. One influential body of work argues modern African ethnicities were products of the colonial era, fostered by the spread of missionary education in standardized African languages, by colonial policies seeking to create simpler units of administration, by widespread African labour migration that expanded identity horizons, and by anti-colonial agitation by African intellectuals.[1] While initially devised to describe conditions in southern Africa, this model has validity for much of West Africa, where very similar processes were at work. In southern Nigeria, for example, twentieth-century colonial forces and post-colonial politics fostered solidarity among the millions of Yoruba- and Igbo-speaking peoples that had no pre-colonial counterpart. The process has taken place more imperfectly among the Anang, Ibibio, and Efik peoples of south-eastern Nigeria, who speak dialects of a common language, but accept no common name for themselves. In this essay these three and related peoples will be called Efik-speaking, because that was the first dialect to be recorded.

Underlying larger simplified identities 'created' during the twentieth century, historians recognize forces for integration and differentiation that have been shaping

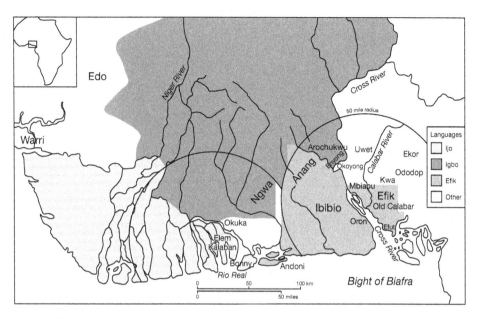

Map 33.1   Hinterland of the Bight of Biafra

and reshaping West African ethnic identities for many centuries. The languages that are basic to modern West African 'tribal' identities have existed for thousands of years. In places in West Africa, pre-colonial state formation was as important and as instrumental in shaping group identities as in early modern Europe. The growth of Asante, Dahomey, and the new Yoruba kingdoms of the nineteenth century instilled a degree of national identity in those who were incorporated into them. However, the people north of the Bight of Biafra experienced no such political centralization in pre-colonial times, although considerable economic and cultural exchange took place in pre-colonial times. Anthropologist Igor Koyptoff argues that 'certain pan-African cultural principles' were the product of long historical processes during which 'the effects of common origins, diffusion, similarities through convergence, and a functional relationship among cultural features [have] been equally powerful in the historical shaping of African societies'.[2] The region's rapid expansion of overseas and internal trade after 1500 and especially after 1750 further increased cultural interaction and exchange. The bottom line is that people from the region who were forcibly transported to the Americas brought with them many similar cultural practices, some common languages, a tradition of group identity that was fluid not static, but did not possess the ethnolinguistic 'tribal' identities of today.

Scholarship about the formation of African-American identities during slavery has been moving in quite different directions. Rejecting an older interpretation of enslavement in the Americas as having stripped Africans of their cultural heritage, recent scholars have sought to demonstrate the persistence of historical African identities. Some have moved beyond pinpointing particular cultural 'survivals' to positing the transportation to the Americas of identifiable African cultures.

Recent studies of the transfer of African identities from the Bight of Biafra to the Americas have taken three quite different lines of analysis. Some have followed the approach put forward by Sidney Mintz and Richard Price a quarter-century ago, which has much in common with the creation-of-tribalism approach among Africanists. Rejecting the idea that Africans were able to transfer intact cultures from their homelands or bring widely shared regional cultural 'complexes' (as once argued by M. J. Herskovits). Mintz and Price argue that essentially new African-American identities emerged in the Americas out of disparate African elements and European-based creole cultures. Acknowledging that enslaved Africans brought individual beliefs and practices and unconscious 'basic assumptions about social relations' from their homelands, they suggest that plantation cultures were much more the product of Africans' common experiences on the Middle Passage and early incorporation to plantation life, their interaction with European and/or creole ruling classes, and their interaction with creolized African-Americans. Despite the brevity of Mintz and Price's essay and the limited historical evidence it marshals (heavily drawn from the somewhat exceptional experiences of Surinam), its clear and carefully reasoning has dominated studies even of parts of the Americas quite distant and different from the Caribbean societies Mintz and Price studied.[3]

Given these limitations of Mintz and Price's model and the diversity of slave systems in the Americas, it is hardly surprising that some scholars have put forward different models of identity formation among enslaved Africans in the Americas. Coming out of studies emphasizing African-American roots and cultural survivals in North America, one challenge has revived the 'tribal' approach that Mintz and Price (and their modern Africanist counterparts) reject. Essentially these studies argue that something closely resembling the ethnolinguistic 'tribes' of twentieth-century nationalist politics emerged in the Americas and made important contributions to the development of African-American cultures.

A recent article by Douglas Chambers exemplifies the 'tribal' approach with regard to slaves from the Bight of Biafra. Chambers argues that the Igbo of the eighteenth century were 'a distinct ethno-historical group who shared a distinctive set of ancestral traditions' and 'a people whom modern scholars can study as a separate "nation" in the transatlantic diaspora'. While fully aware of the political fragmentation of Igbo communities in pre-colonial Africa, he argues that, once they were abroad, the Igbo 'embraced a collective identity'. Chambers seeks to build a case for the importance of an Igbo identity group in the Americas by three questionable manipulations of the evidence.

The first is to inflate the number of Igbo transported, by arbitrarily assuming that 80 per cent of all slaves from the Bight of Biafra in the eighteenth and nineteenth centuries were Igbo. For this to be true every single slave from the two main ports of Bonny and Old Calabar would have to have been an Igbo, which, as is shown below, is demonstrably untrue. His second methodological misstep is to see the triumph of Igbo culture in the meagre survivals of a handful of stray words that might arguably be assigned to their language, whereas a more realistic assessment might see in this same evidence proof of how little of the ancestral language survived. Finally Chambers cites foods and religious practices that are common throughout West Africa as evidence of Igbo influence. In one case, he even sees a demonstrably non-Igbo usage as Igbo influenced: acknowledging that *buckra*, a common term for 'white man', derives from the Efik word *mbakara* (the equivalent Igbo word is *beke*), he still asserts without evidence. 'It was Igbo people who brought the term into English', even suggesting that they used the borrowed term with a full understanding of its root meaning in Efik. The most curious part of his thesis is the argument that previously isolated Igbo-speaking groups not only coalesced into a cultural nation in the Americas, but they also 'Igboized' Africans of other origins.[4]

A similar argument has been put forward by Michael Gomez. Though likewise displaying an impressive awareness of the cultural and linguistic diversity of the region north of the Bight of Biafra from which American slaves came, Gomez attributes to the Igbo a 'profound impact on African American society' in the eighteenth century that appears to be out of proportion to their numbers and in disregard of Igbo cultural diversity. Gomez refers to the enslaved Africans from Bight of Biafra who were imported into the Chesapeake Bay colonies as 'Igbo/Biafrans', acknowledging that the Igbo were only a portion of those taken from this area, but he is disinclined to explore any other ethnolinguistic groups. Like Chambers, Gomez insists on the exceptional 'homogeneity of the Biafran region', without specifying what biological or cultural traits he means. Although citing percentages only half those claimed by Chambers, Gomez also misconstrues evidence to inflate the percentage of Igbo immigrants, arguing that Virginia's 'importation of the Igbo between 1710 and 1760 constituted some 38 per cent of its total importation of African captives' – or even 40 per cent, whereas both percentages refer to the total slaves exported from Bight of Biafran ports, not just to the Igbo.[5]

Gomez apparently believes that enough of those shipped from the Bight of Biafra were Igbo that one need not always make the distinction clear. He attaches no importance to the contemporary use of 'Calabar,' considering it a synonym for Igbo.[6] He also is quite ready to accept the cultural/temperamental stereotypes voiced by contemporary Europeans and North Americans, without questioning whether these have any factual base. Finally, he assumes that those individuals called 'Eboe' by European colonists in the Chesapeake already possessed the pan-Igbo identity of modern times, as though neither time nor circumstance made any difference.[7]

A third position, taken by John Thornton in his aggressively revisionist *Africa and Africans in the Making of the Atlantic World*, tries to avoid the pitfalls of the 'tribal' approach while still taking issue with the Mintz and Price thesis. Dealing with Atlantic trade before 1680, Thornton disputes the older idea that the Middle Passage 'randomized' the Africans of various origin and broke their connections to Africa. He accepts that slaves taken by a single ship from a single coast represented more than one 'tribe', but explicitly revives Herskovits's thesis about large culture complexes in arguing that such enslaved persons would have been drawn very largely from a single culture zone.

As he reconstructs the situation before 1680, the Atlantic coast of Africa consisted 'at most' of three culture zones (Upper Guinea, Lower Guinea, and Angola) and seven 'often quite homogeneous' subgroups. Thornton proposes the existence of broad cultural homogeneity, but his evidence is almost exclusively linguistic. Thus he notes that the peoples of Lower Guinea, from the Gold Coast to Cameroon, spoke languages belonging to the Kwa sub-family of Niger–Congo, which he believes can be subdivided into an Akan zone and an Aja zone – the latter including the Fon, Yoruba, Edo, [Ijo] and Igbo speaking peoples. Thornton builds his case on some rather tenuous assertions that people within these subzones could understand each other's languages, while ignoring contrary evidence and testimony from later times that brings his West African zones into question.[8] Problems of evidence aside, Thornton's argument is circular:

> Using *language*, we can divide the parts of Atlantic Africa that participated in the slave trade into three culturally distinct zones, which can be further divided into seven subzones. From this analysis one can then say that although Africans may have been *linguistically* diverse, there were only three different cultures that contributed to the New World, and among them only seven distinct subcultures.[9]

Although Thornton's approach avoids the problem of assuming the existence of modern 'tribal' identities in an earlier period, for West Africa generally and for the Bight of Biafra in particular, his analysis is quite untrustworthy.[10]

To a considerable extent Thornton's problems result from over-simplifying the testimony of his principal source, the Jesuit missionary Alonso de Sandoval, who collected information from Africans in early seventeenth-century Peru. As Paul Hair demonstrated some time ago, place names, ethnicities, and languages of coastal West Africa mentioned by Sandoval and other early writers correspond to a remarkable extent to places and peoples recorded in twentieth-century ethnographic research.[11] This considerable degree of ethnolinguistic continuity also means that languages along the Gulf of Guinea could have been no more permeable in the sixteenth and seventeenth centuries than in more recent times.

While Thornton's construction of an Akan linguistic cluster of Western Kwa languages can be supported by the generally accepted linguistic classifications of Joseph Greenberg (who places Ewe, Akan and other languages in a single subgroup of Kwa). Thornton's Eastern Kwa lumps together Yoruba, Edo, Igbo, and Ijo, which Greenberg classifies as four different subgroups.[12] Anthropologist Ray Bradbury agrees that the several dialects of Edo are closely related, but, in direct contradiction of Thornton's thesis about the Eastern Kwa languages, he denies that there exists anything approaching 'mutual intelligibility between Edo and the neighbouring Kwa languages. Yoruba, Igbira, Igala, Ibo, and Ijaw, though frontier populations are frequently bilingual'.[13] The synoptic comparison in Table 33.1, based on the earliest systematic collection of the region's languages, reveals the wide divergence of Eastern Kwa vocabulary. A list of the same words from the major Romance and Germanic languages of Europe would provide far more obvious similarities, yet would anyone seriously propose that French and German were mutually intelligible in the seventeenth century or are so today?

The problems with Thornton's interpretation are most pronounced east of the Niger. Not only does his thesis greatly understate the linguistic and cultural diversity in the region bordering the Bight of Biafra, it also misconstrues the early evidence concerning the peoples east of the Niger who were involved in the early Atlantic slave trade. Before one can consider what cultural baggage Africans from this region may have transported to the Americas, one needs a more accurate and detailed understanding of identities in their home area. A review of the major ethnolinguistic terms, *Calabar*, *Moko*, and *Igbo*, used by contemporary sources, reveals much about the underlying realities of the region.

Table 33.1   Comparative vocabulary of the eastern Kwa languages

III.C.1.d English	V.A.1 'Yoruba'	V.B.3 'Isoama' (Igbo)	V.C.1 'Beni' (Edo)	'Okuloma' (Ijo)
one	eni	ote	ovo	nge
two	edshi	abo	eva	me
three	eta	afo	eha	tere
four	eri	ano	ene	ini
five	aro	isa	ise	sona
ten	ewa	ili	igbe	ate
twenty	ogu	ogo	uge	shi
man	akore/okori	nguoke	okpea	oubo
woman	obere	ndiom	ogwoko	erebo
head	oli/ori	ishi	obunu	dsibe
mouth	eno/enu	ono	unu	bebe
leg	ese	oko	owe	buo
bone	egu	obobo	uve	ngbe
market	odsha	ahia	eki	ogumebili
pot	igogo	ite	ngwagwa	bele
God	oloru	dshuku	oisa	ogono
water	omi	mmele	ame	mingi

Source: S.W. Koelle, *Polyglotta Africana, or a Comparative Vocabulary of Nearly 300 Words and Phrases in More Than 100 Distinct African Languages* (London: Church Missionary House, 1854), pp. 1–79. Koelle's spelling conventions are simplified by writing ng for a dotted 'n' and sh for s over a dot, and by not including his stress accents and vowel quality marks.

Calabar – I

Sandoval reports that in the early seventeenth century Africans in the eastern Niger Delta were known as *Caravalies*, but came in two distinct types. The first were the 'native or pure Caravalies' with whom Europeans traded, whose location and name make them readily identifiable with the Elem Kalabari, an Ijo-speaking community known to be active in the Atlantic trade from an early date. The second type were a heterogeneous assemblage of 'forty or fifty villages of various and different groups and nations [*castas y naciones*] . . . who are called *caravalies particulares*, even though they really are not [*caravalies*]; because they appear and come to trade with the [pure] *caravalies*, we take them for such'. Sandoval records the names of eighteen *caravalies particulares*, who, he says, 'are innumerable and don't understand each other nor do they commonly understand the *caravalies puros*'.[14] As Paul Hair pointed out 30 years ago, most of the names on this list can be identified with other Ijo-speaking communities in the eastern Niger Delta. A few are more distant peoples: the *ibo*, presumably an Igbo-speaking group bordering the delta: the *done*, likely the Andoni, a coastal fishing people who speak a dialect of Efik: and the *moco*, a name that would later be widely used on both sides of the Atlantic. (It is argued below that *moco* most likely refers to speakers of another Efik dialect at this time.)[15]

Although Sandoval overstates the problems Ijo speakers among the *caravalies particulares* would have had in understanding each other, he is certainly correct with regard to the mutual unintelligibility of the Igbo, Ijo, and Efik. Indeed, Efik and its dialects do not belong to the Kwa branch of Niger Congo at all but are a distant cousin of the Bantu languages of equatorial and southern Africa. Very curiously, Thornton ignores all this modern scholarship as well as all of Sandoval's interesting information concerning the Bight of Biafra. While declaring 'I have not tried to locate individual places' associated with Sandoval's list of *caravalies particulares*, Thornton treats them all as 'Igbos', apparently because he believes that 'some of [the names] are recognizably of the Igbo linguistic group'. Other than '*ibo*' it is hard to imagine which ones he has in mind. Thornton also ignores Sandoval's statement that because of the tremendous linguistic variety in this area, most communication is conducted in a corrupted form of Portuguese that all the coastal Africans speak and understand.[16]

This review of the evidence of the early seventeenth century leads to a number of conclusions. First, the inhabitants of the coastal region east of the lower Niger spoke several distinct and mutually unintelligible languages. Second, despite their transformative experience of the Middle Passage and slavery, the enslaved persons from this region whom Sandoval interviewed in South America still identified themselves in terms of small communities, not large language groups. Third, such divisions were no impediment to intercourse: the residents of the coastal region were avid traders and quickly adopted a Portuguese pidgin to facilitate communication. Fourth, contemporary Europeans masked this complexity by using one name, Caravali or Calabar, for everyone from the region. Fifth, Sandoval's lists of the *caravalies particulares* confirms what would be expected about the origins of the slaves drawn from the Bight of Biafra: they came from areas within 50 miles of Elem Kalabari. If the different communities mentioned are roughly indicative of numbers, most of those sold away were from Ijo-speaking communities in the Niger Delta with a few Igbo and Efik-speakers obtained from areas that abut the delta. As Table 33.2 suggests, this is roughly proportional to the distribution of languages in the catchment area.

Calabar – II

The Efik-speaking port of Old Calabar, a cluster of settlements just off the Cross River estuary, strikingly illustrates the mobility of broad ethnolinguistic labels. It is not clear from the historical record precisely when or why Europeans began to designate the older port of Elem Kalabari as *New* Calabar, while giving the name *Old* Calabar to the Efik towns that began selling slaves to the English around the 1660s. Nor is there evidence of any historical or linguistic connection between Old Calabar and Elem Kalabari. Nevertheless, by the eighteenth century all slaves from Old Calabar were being designated as 'Calabars', although some Europeans continued to apply that to people from Elem Kalabari.[17]

As the volume of trade along the Bight of Biafra grew substantially from the middle of the seventeenth century, Bonny and Old Calabar rivalled and then displaced Elem Kalabari as the coast's premier trading ports. There is no direct evidence of the origins of the slaves shipped from Old Calabar before the late eighteenth century, but the Efik towns would naturally have traded with surrounding communities: the densely populated Ibibio and Igbo peoples west of the Cross River and the more thinly populated and ethnolinguistically diverse peoples east of the

Table 33.2 Estimated percentages of slave exports from the Bight of Biafra by language group, 1600–1800

| Language | 50-mile catchment radius | | | | 100-mile catchment radius | | | |
| | Elem Kalabari | | Old Calabar | | Bonny | | Old Calabar | |
	By area	Adjusted	By area	Adjusted	By area	Adjusted	By area	Adjusted
Ijo	60	30			25	5		
Igbo	25	45	10	15	43	60	40	60
Efik	10	15	40	60	25	30	10	15
Other	5	10	50	25	7	5	50	25

Note: The surface area occupied by different languages is adjusted to reflect population density. All adjustments are rough approximations intended for illustrative purposes only.

river. From the late eighteenth century some details are known. The diary entries made by the Old Calabar trader Antera Duke that survive for the years 1785–87 name several sources of slaves, which appear to be the markets where they were obtained rather than their individual places of origin. The places most often mentioned were 'Orroup' (the Ododop, a people 30 miles east of Old Calabar, who traded slaves from as far as the Cameroon Grasslands). 'Curcock' (Ekrikok, i.e., the Mbiabo Efik to the northwest of Old Calabar), 'Boostam' (Umon, 30 miles north of Old Calabar), and 'Enyong' (an Efik-speaking people about 30 miles up the Cross River, who had connections to trading networks west of the river).[18] The heterogeneity of the resulting slave-cargoes can be judged from a report that among the first 150 captives taken aboard an English ship at Old Calabar in 1790 'fourteen different tribes or nations' were represented, all of whom became 'Calabars' when exported.[19]

Information about the diversity of the slaves exported from Old Calabar becomes more abundant in the last decades of the Atlantic slave trade. The agent of the African Association there in 1805 named the groups who made up 'most of the slaves Calabar people get[:] Eericock [Ekrikok, i.e., Mbiabo Efik]. Tobac [Oron Ibibio]. Eericock Boatswain [Umon], and Ebeo [Igbo]; sometimes some Brassy [Ijo] slaves, and Cameroon [Efut] slaves'.[20] The registration lists of persons liberated from three ships seized by British patrols in 1821–22 provide further information about the ethnic origins of slaves from Old Calabar. Given how much other sources emphasize the diversity of peoples Old Calabar traded, it is striking that the Slave Trade Commissioners registered 56 per cent of the liberated Africans as Igbo-speaking and 42 per cent as 'Calabar', assigning other identities to only two per cent. However, these identifications were most likely based on individuals' ability to understand these languages. Since Efik and Igbo were widely used as trading languages by other peoples along the Cross River, such a system of assigning identities would have jumped other liberated Africans in with native Igbo and Efik speakers.[21]

Further information about slaves from Old Calabar comes from the Church Missionary Society missionary Sigismund W. Koelle, who devoted himself to the collection and classification of the languages spoken by liberated Africans the British patrols resettled in Sierra Leone in the first part of the nineteenth century. Among the more than 100 languages he recorded, Koelle recognized the connections among the Kwa group, which, much like Greenberg, he subdivided into Liberian. Dahomean, and Aku[Yoruba]-Igala clusters. Koelle grouped the Edo, Igbo, and Ijo languages in a separate Niger Delta division. In line with modern classification, he put in a class by itself the language known as 'Calaba' in Sierra Leone (i.e., Efik), which he believed should properly be called 'Anang'.[22] The missionary's decision to call the language Anang perhaps indicates how numerous people from this dialect of Efik were among recaptives in Sierra Leone. Located at the western end of Efik-speaking lands, the Anang would have been more likely to furnish slaves through Bonny than through Old Calabar.

The transfer of *Calabar* from Elem Kalabari to the distant and linguistically quite different port of Old Calabar is a vivid reminder of the imprecision of such terminology. Just as Sandoval's 'Caravalies' designated two different categories of persons, this new sense of *Calabar* was applied variously to Efik-speakers and to the entire cluster of peoples drawn from Old Calabar's catchment area.

Moko

The odyssey of the name *Calabar* through the centuries is paralleled by the changing identities designated by *Moko* (or Moco), first recorded by Sandoval as one of the *caravalies particulares* trading at Elem Kalabari. The name continued to be used on both sides of the Atlantic during the following centuries. In an appendix on 'The Problem of the Provenance of African Slaves Brought to British America'. Michael Mullin concludes that the 'Moco' of British America came from the hinterland of the Bight of Biafra in the eighteenth century, but he is unable to decide from the evidence if they were Igbo, lbibio, or from the cluster of upper Cross River peoples. He finds confusing the testimony from Jamaica in the last quarter of the eighteenth century about a person identified as Igbo who 'speaks Moco [and] may pass as Moco' and another person who is 'Moco, but speaks Ebo [Igbo]'.[23] It is possible to improve on Mullin's research and resolve many of the problems he encounters.

One of the puzzling facts Mullin encountered was Koelle's statement that the people known as Moko in Sierra Leone in the early nineteenth century were all speakers of sixteen languages belonging to two small linguistic sub-families found on the upper Cross River. However, not long after, the Scottish missionary Hugh Goldie assigned much broader definition to Moko: 'a name given in Sierra Leone to all people coming from the region of the Calabar and Cameroons rivers'.[24] Other pre-nineteenth-century sources located the Moko further west, nearer to the eastern Niger Delta. The great compiler of information about coastal Africa in the seventeenth century, Olfert Dapper, placed 'the Province of Moco' inland of the Okrika, who lived on the eastern edge of the delta. Seventeenth- and eighteenth-century maps and accounts also support a location close to the Niger Delta.[25]

As it happens, evidence crucial for identifying the Moko comes from the same period and provenance as Mullin's Jamaican evidence. C.G.A. Oldendorp, a missionary in the Danish West Indies in 1767–68, collected information about the customs and languages of the enslaved Africans he met. The 'Mokko', he learned from his informants, lived near the Ijo of New Calabar and were distinct from both the Igbo and the 'Bibi' (presumably the Ibibio). Oldendorp's list of words

Table 33.3   Linguistic evidence for the identity of the eighteenth-century Moko

English	Oldendorp's 'Mokko'	Koelle's 'Mokko'	Goldie's Efik
one	kia	ket	kiet
two	iba	iba	iba
three	ita	ita	ita
four	inan	ina	inang
five	uttin	itien	itiun
six	ituekee	itieket	itioket
seven	ittiaba	itiaba	itiaba
eight	itteiata	itieita	itiaeta
nine	huschuki-et	anangket	osukiet/usukiet
ten	bub	duob	duup
God	Abassi	Abasi	Abasi

gathered from 'Mokko' speakers sharply narrows the possibilities for their identity (see Table 33.3). Although many Cross River peoples use the word he recorded for God (*Abassi*), the numbers from one to ten are uniquely those of Efik speakers.[26]

The conclusion that in the second half of the eighteenth century *Moko* referred to some or all Efik-speaking people is also supported by the testimony of the Captain John Adams, an Englishman who made ten voyages from western Africa to the West Indies between 1786 and 1800. In describing what he knew of the geography and ethnography of the coastal plain between the Niger and the Cross River, Adams placed the 'country inhabited by a nation called Ibbibby, or Qwaw (the Mocoes of the West Indies) [bordering the Igbo] territory on the east'.[27] Thus, Adams confirms that the Moko were Efik-speakers, even though he counts the Ibibio as Moko, while Oldendorp suggests that the Moko were distinct from the Ibibio. It is clear from the discussion of *Calabar* that such names can have both general and particular meanings. A narrow sense of Moko, tied to the Anang, would be consistent with the testimony that puzzled Mullin. In the eighteenth century, the Anang lived along an unstable frontier with the Ngwa Igbo, whose traditions are quite explicit about their penetration and incorporation of Anang peoples. The Anang and Ngwa lay along important trade routes from Arochukwu to Bonny. Thus, an Ngwa Igbo might well speak Moko and look like a Moko. Similarly there would be nothing odd about an Anang (Moko) who could speak Igbo as a second language.[28]

Could Sandoval's 'Moco' two hundred years earlier also have been Efik-speaking? Since 'Moco' designated people trading with (or sold to) Elem Kalabari in the early seventeenth century, they must have lived within the 50-mile radius of the port that included his other *caravalies particulares*. Thus, they could not possibly have been from the distant upper Cross River nor could they have come from Old Calabar at that date. His 'Moco' (and 'Ibo') might have been generic terms, encompassing all the many related communities, but it seems more likely that the terms referred to particular communities near Elem Kalabari. Like Oldendorp who distinguished the Moko from the Bibi (Ibibio), Sandoval distinguished the 'Moco' from the 'Doni', the coastal Andoni who were the closest

Efik-speakers to Elem Kalabari. Only slightly farther away were Ibibio and Anang communities, whose members were enslaved in large numbers in later times.

Since Moko was not a name any people in the region used for themselves but one they acquired when they travelled abroad, where did the name come from? Such nicknames can have various origins. Some designate the port or coast that people came from: Calabar, Popo, Cormantee. In other cases strangers conferred a nickname because of something people said. Thus Yoruba-speakers in Sierra Leone were called 'Aku', a name derived from their greeting. The name Moko might well derive from the Efik words *kom* (to thank) or *kop* (to hear), as in the common conversational phrases *mokom* (I thank you) or *mokop* (I hear/understand).[29] Whatever its origins, it would appear that in the Americas Moko referred to Efik-speakers, and perhaps particularly to the Anang, although it is important to bear in mind that it was in the nature of such terms to be used in imprecise and changeable ways.

Igbo

The term *Igbo* differs from *Calabar* (after 1750) and *Moko* in that it has indigenous validity since some (but not all) Igbo-speakers used it for themselves and their language in the pre-colonial era. As Koelle noted, some of the people called 'Ibo' in Sierra Leone had never heard of that name in their own country, knowing 'only the names of their respective districts or countries'. He listed five 'Ibo countries' plus 15 others that 'are called Ibo, whereas this name is not used by any one of these tribes'. All but one of these 15 can be identified with Igbo-speaking communities. The exception, 'Bom', was the Ozuzu Igbo name for New Calabar (Elem Kalabari), which by the nineteenth century had absorbed a great many Igbo-speakers.[30]

Despite its lack of currency in much of their homeland, *Igbo* was a name that Igbo-speaking people seem to have readily accepted abroad. The famous Olaudah Equiano did so and the explorer William Baikie reported, 'In Igbo each person hails, as a sailor would say, from the particular district where he was born, but when away from home all are Igbos',[31] a statement as true in the Americas as in Sierra Leone. The experience of becoming conscious of a pan-Igbo identity is also a recurrent theme in the colonial period for those who moved to Nigerian cities or went abroad. The experience was perhaps not unlike that of an Englishman or an American today, who, after a bit of hesitation, might accept the basis of a Frenchman's portrayal of them both as 'Anglo-Saxons'. But it is not likely that people who were not native speakers of Igbo would have adopted that identity.

Even though Igbo-speakers were taken from the hinterland of the Bight of Biafra in large numbers during the course of the Atlantic slave-trade, as should already be clear, it is unwarranted to neglect the importance of other ethnolinguistic communities in the region. There is little direct evidence of the origins of slaves, but it is possible to calculate the relative percentage of speakers of the major languages in the catchment basins of the region's major slaving ports and to adjust these purely topographical calculations with information about population densities and slaving operations.

Table 33.2 suggests that by the late eighteenth century, Old Calabar's slave exports may have been well over half Igbo. From the 1730s the eastern Delta port of Bonny became the most important slaving port in the Bight of Biafra and the principal source of Igbo slaves. During the century after 1730, Bonny supplied nearly half of the slaves from this region, with Igbo-speakers accounting for perhaps 60 per cent of that port's total.[32] Slaves reached Bonny via land and water routes from markets and fairs in Igbo and Efik lands as well as in more distant regions.[33] Of the slaves on four ships from Bonny captured by the British patrol in 1821, fully 74 per cent were registered in Sierra Leone as 'Ebo' or 'Heboo' (Igbo) and 20 per cent as 'Calabar' (Efik-speaking). As in the case of the captured ships from Old Calabar, the method by which the registrars established who was an Igbo would have inflated the percentage somewhat by including individuals of smaller groups who also understood Igbo.

This evidence suggests that the proportion of Igbo speakers among slaves entering the Chesapeake would have been more like 25 per cent than Gomez's 38 to 40 per cent or Chambers's 80 per cent. Besides underestimating the language diversity of the Bight of Biafra, these authors may have been misled by the tendency of their American sources to simplify African ethnolinguistic complexities. As Michael Mullin points out, whites in British Caribbean and mainland colonies used 'Ebo' or 'Ibo' to include the 'Ibo, Ibibio, and Efik and Cross River peoples' and rarely used and little understood the meaning behind names such as 'Calabar' or 'Moko'.[34] However, first-generation slaves would have preserved a much richer idea of who they were in terms both of their particular origins and of any broader identities they may have adopted during their journey to the Americas.

Identities at home and abroad

This survey demonstrates that *Calabar*, *Moko*, and *Igbo* had imprecise, shifting, and overlapping meanings during the era of the Atlantic slave-trade. Popular with outsiders wanting to categorize the diverse peoples of the northern hinterland of the Bight of Biafra before 1850, the terms would meant little or nothing to most inhabitants of the region, who, as careful interviewers from Sandoval to Koelle reported, identified themselves in terms of small, kinship-based units. Thus these same blanket terms, used even more loosely in the Americas, cannot be taken to represent ready-made identities brought from Africa. Instead of hypothesizing rigid, boxed cultures, historians of African America would be better advised to pay attention to the dynamic process of culture adaptation that was well established in this part of Africa. It is beyond the scope of this essay to explore the particular processes by which identities evolved during the Middle Passage and enslavement in different parts of the Americas, but it does seem useful to address some conceptual issues that have muddled exploration of those processes. Foremost among these is the assumption that languages defined African 'nations' that had discrete cultures.

It has long been apparent that a common language would have been very important for communication among Africans during the Middle Passage as well as after their arrival in the Americas, and thus would likely have fostered some sort of common bond. Although Thornton's notion that large numbers of West African languages were mutually intelligible is demonstrably untrue, native speakers would have been able to manage communication across the many dialects of languages such as Igbo or of Efik. Many non-native speakers would have been able to join in because Igbo and Efik came to be used as trading languages by many adjoining peoples. Trading contacts had spread the knowledge of even remote inland languages such as Hausa and Igala along the lower Niger by the eighteenth century or earlier.

However, indigenous languages were not the only means of communication among people from the Bight of Biafra. Many captives would have known a European-derived trading language or would have learned one during the course of their captivity. In the early decades of the trade, Sandoval notes, when slave cargoes were gradually assembled on the island of São Thomé, captives learned to speak a 'corrupt and mixed Portuguese' while awaiting shipment across the Atlantic. This 'São Thomé tongue' was also widely used along the coast. By the eighteenth century, an English-based pidgin was common enough along this coast that the Efik trader Antera Duke kept his diary in it,[35] and many Africans could have learned pidgin English before their capture or while awaiting shipment. Given the limited roles that African languages appear to have played in North America and other parts of the New World, it is worth paying more attention to Thornton's suggestion that pidgins brought from Africa may have played a significant role in the development of colonial creoles.[36]

Misleading ideas about broad and enduring bonds based on ancestral languages can be compounded by the use of the term *nation*. This usage begins innocently enough with Sandoval and Equiano and has been taken up by modern scholars such as Chambers and Thornton.[37] It is an attractive word, far preferable to *tribe* when speaking of large ethnolinguistic units, but it can also introduce concepts that are both elusive and inappropriate for much of pre-colonial Africa. Indeed, even in modern European historiography the origins of *nations* are a matter of some controversy.[38]

The concept becomes particularly elusive when applied to populations like those in the hinterland of the Bight of Biafra that neither possessed centralized political institutions nor were in the process of creating them.[39] Although some nineteenth-century Europeans speculated that large Igbo and Efik kingdoms must have disintegrated under the impact of the slave trade leaving only autonomous communities,[40] modern historical research finds no basis for such interpretations. As events in twentieth-century Africa show, language groups are capable of developing nationalist (and 'tribalist') identities, but calling language groups *nations* risks assuming what needs to be proved.[41]

The key question is whether African language groups or 'nations' were (or were capable of becoming) coherent cultural units. In most cases, language is a poor surrogate for culture, because languages change so much more slowly than other cultural institutions. It is reasonable to expect that the evolution of numerous dialects of Igbo and Efik over many centuries would have been accompanied by far greater changes in other cultural institutions, especially since this region lacked 'national' courts, festivals, or other institutions that could have reinforced cultural unity. Thus, the expectation of some historians, African nationalists, or pre-colonial European traders that language, culture, and identity coincide is very problematic.

The historical study of pre-colonial culture in the region is in its infancy, and it is surely a very complex story.[42] Too little direct evidence exists for there to be conclusive proof, but there seems little reason to believe that people who spoke Igbo or Efik in pre-colonial times would have regarded language as an important basis for mutual solidarity. For one thing, local traditions suggest that warfare between communities speaking the same language may have been about as common as across linguistic frontiers. Moreover, alliances often transcended linguistic frontiers. For example, the traditions of the Aro people of Arochukwu, describe their community as a mergers of Efik-speaking Enyong. Igbo-speaking Abam, and other Cross River peoples. While Arochukwu itself came to be primarily Igbo-speaking, the Aro trading-diaspora operated freely across language lines. Among other frontier communities, similar amalgamations (and much cultural borrowing) took place across language lines during centuries of contact: between the Efik of Old Calabar and their neighbours, between the Anang and their Ngwa Igbo neighbours, between the southern Igbo and their Ijo neighbours, and between the western Igbo and their Edo neighbours.[43]

In addition, economic exchanges had been building ties across linguistic boundaries in the hinterland of the Bight of Biafra for some centuries before 1850. Exchanges across ecological frontiers probably began the process: salt and fish from the coast for cultivated crops and forest products such as palm oil. The products of specialized crafts also circulated widely, notably metalwork, but also pottery and canoes. Centuries before the arrival of the first Europeans, the area was criss-crossed by trading networks and markets that had links far outside the region. Atlantic trade greatly increased interaction among communities. Fishing villages became important maritime ports, their populations swollen by slaves from the hinterland. Markets grew larger, some becoming fairs, as trading peoples like the Old Calabar Efik and the Aro built up widespread connections across the region. The Aro in particular excelled at established extensive trading colonies throughout the region and by establishing pacts with prominent families and 'big men' through oaths (including blood-brotherhoods), economic ties, and marriage connections, as well as by intimidation and occasionally warfare. In the vicinity of Old Calabar, a quasi-corporate structure was established: the graded secret society of Ekpe, whose lodges included a variety of Africans, free and slave, and some Europeans.[44]

The borrowing of cultural practices was another product of expanding trade. The Aro, for example, actively promoted the cult of the Oracle at their hometown Arochukwu. There is clear evidence from the early colonial period that other religious practices, including masquerade styles, the names of deities, and cults were regularly borrowed across 'tribal' lines.[45] In short, while there were similarities in the cultural practices of many Igbo- or Efik-speaking communities, this should not be taken to mean that there was any clearly defined or long-lasting cultural frontier between one linguistic group and another. Looked at another way, it is possible to find as much cultural diversity among Igbo or Efik communities as it is to find commonality.

Given these complex issues, how can one talk about culture, cultural identity, and the transfer of culture overseas? There will always be good reasons for scholars to disagree, but much current disagreement seems tied to the inconsistent use of language. For example, while Gomez correctly notes that the Bight of Biafra was 'an area of some cultural and economic diversity' and that the larger groups such as Igbo, Ibibio, and Ijo 'can be further subdivided into many cultural communities', a page later he argues for the existence of pan-Igbo 'cultural unity' on the basis of Equiano's having found his native language spoken almost all the way to the coastal port he was sold from.[46] As seen earlier, Thornton goes much further, positing the existence of even broader culture zones based on families of related languages. This use of *culture* to refer to small-scale communities, to large-scale language groups, and to zones and subzones based on language-families, is no different than the very loose way the word is used in talking of other parts of the world (e.g., New York Jewish culture, American culture, Western culture), but such imprecision impedes a meaningful examination of the cultural dynamics created by the Atlantic slave trade.

The distinction suggested by Mintz and Price, between a 'culture' consisting of institutionalized beliefs and practices observed and transmitted by a community and a cultural 'heritage' of uninstitutionalized shared beliefs or practices, seems particularly appropriate for describing this African region and useful for understanding how identities evolved in the Americas.[47] The analytical distinction may be arbitrary, but it performs the useful function of focusing attention on the process of cultural dynamics and away from assumptions about pre-packaged static cultures.

Given the paucity of relevant evidence on both sides of the Atlantic, the important question of how cultural identities developed among Africans in the Americas may never receive a fully satisfactory answer. However, by clarifying the terminology used to discuss these issues and by drawing out more fully the implications of the cultural baggage Africans brought with them, it may be possible to shed light on some issues. Despite the attraction of using *language* as a surrogate for *culture* and *nation*, there is no credible evidence that Africans from the Bight of Biafra came pre-packaged in large identity units. The names with which Europeans on both sides of the Atlantic conveniently labelled Africans misrepresent African cultural diversity and reinforce stereotypes of African cultures as static. Africans from the hinterland of the Bight of Biafra brought to the Americas ancestral languages and tradition of language-learning, specific cultural identities and a tradition of cultural borrowing, particular communal identities and the ability to reconceptualize themselves in new social contexts. A dynamic model of linguistic, cultural, and social change seems more useful for studying the development of African-American cultures in the Americas. It is moreover a model that avoids the false opposition of cultural continuity and cultural change. In the real world, both continuity and change are the hallmarks of living societies.

Notes

1   Leroy Vail, 'Introduction', in Leroy Vail (ed.), *The Creation of Tribalism in Southern Africa* (Berkeley, California: University of California Press, 1989), pp. 7–16. The late Professor Vail's plan to assemble a new volume on African identity provided the initial inspiration for this essay, which in its small way is a tribute to his continuing influence.

2   Igor Kopytoff, 'The Internal African Frontier: The Making of African Political Culture', in Igor Kopytoff (ed.), *The African Frontier: The Reproduction of Traditional African Societies* (Bloomington, Indiana: Indiana University Press, 1987), p. 15.

3   Sidney M. Mintz and Richard Price, *An Anthropological Approach to the Afro-American Past: A Caribbean Perspective* (Philadelphia: Institute for the Study of Human Issues 1976), pp. 1–11. The primacy of this paradigm is noted, for example, by Philip D. Morgan, 'The Cultural Implications of the Atlantic Slave Trade: African Regional Origins, American Destinations and New World Developments', *Slavery and Abolition*, 18 (1997), pp. 141–2, citing more recent writings by Mintz and Price.

4   Douglas B. Chambers, '"My Own Nation": Igbo Exiles in the Diaspora', *Slavery and Abolition*, 18 (1997), pp. 73–7.

5   Michael A. Gomez, *Exchanging Our Country Marks* (Chapel Hill, North Carolina and London: University of North Carolina Press, 1998), p. 115. One of the works Gomez cites, James A. Rawley, *The Trans-Atlantic Slave Trade* (New York: W.W. Norton, 1981), p. 335, actually states that 'Virginians from 1710 to 1760 received . . . about 38 per cent [of their slaves] from the Bight of Biafra': Rawley is generally uninterested in the African end of the slave trade and does not even include a reference to the Igbo in his index. Gomez's other source, Michael Mullin, *Africa in America: Slave Acculturation in the American South and the British Caribbean 1736–1831* (Chicago: University of Illinois Press, 1992), p. 24, actually writes, 'Iboes came from the Bight of Biafra, a region that supplied 40 percent of all new Negroes imported to the Chesapeake'.

6   His index entry is revealing: 'Calabar. See Bight of Biafra; Igbo, the': Gomez, *Exchanging*, p. 361.

7   A third work exploring the Bight of Biafra–Chesapeake connection calculates that 'approximately 60 percent of Africans entering the York River between 1718 and 1726' were from the Bight of Biafra. While generally judicious in its treatment and indicating such slaves were 'Ibo, Ibibio, Efik, or Moko' in origin, this work also confines its examination of their cultural heritage to the Igbo: Lorena S. Walsh, *From Calabar to Carter's Grove: The History of a Virginia Slave Community* (Charlottesville, Virginia and London: University Press of Virginia, 1997), pp. 67–8, 71–5.

8   John Thornton, *Africa and Africans in the Making of the Atlantic World, 1400–1800*, 2nd ed. (Cambridge: Cambridge University Press, 1998), pp. 183–91. The second edition adds a chapter on the Americas that goes to 1800, but no other aspects of his thesis are updated, not even his consistent misspelling of Herskovits's name (pp. 183, 187, 209, 210, 337).

9   Thornton, *Africa and Africans*, pp. 186–7, emphasis added. Here and on Map 5 (p. xiv). Thornton specifies only six subzones.

10 See the review of the first edition of Thornton's book by Richard Rathbone, *Journal of African History*, 34 (1993), pp. 495–6.

11 P.E.H. Hair, 'Ethnolinguistic Continuity on the Guinea Coast', *Journal of African History*, 8 (1967), pp. 247–68.

12 Joseph H. Greenberg, *The Languages of Africa*, 2nd ed. (Bloomington, Indiana: Indiana University Press, 1966), p. 8.

13 R.E. Bradbury, *The Benin Kingdom and the Edo-speaking Peoples of South-western Nigeria*, Ethnographic Survey of Africa. Western Africa. Part XIII (London: Oxford University Press, 1957), p. 14.

14 S.J. Alonso de Sandoval, *De Instauranda Aethiepum Salute* (Bogota: Empressa Nacional de Publicaciones, 1956), pp. 17, 94; this is a reissue of Sandoval's 1627 work.

15 Hair, 'Ethnolinguistic Continuity', p. 263.

16 Thornton, *Africa and Africans*, p. xxiv; Sandoval, *De Instauranda*, p. 94.

17 A.J.H. Latham, *Old Calabar, 1600–1891* (Oxford: Clarendon Press, 1973), pp. 1–18. At least 650 slaves from Old Calabar arrived in Jamaica between 1685 and 1691; David Buisseret. 'Slaves Arriving in Jamaica, 1684–1692', *Revue Française d'Histoire d'Outre-mer*, 54 (1977), pp. 85–8.

18 'The Diary of Antera Duke', in D. Forde (ed.) *Efik Traders of Old Calabar* (London: Oxford University Press, 1956), pp. 30–41 and *passim*.

19 William Butterworth [pseudonym for Henry Schroeder], *Three Years Adventures of a Minor in England, Africa, the West Indies, South-Carolina and Georgia* (Leeds: Thomas Inchhold, 1831), p. 85.

20 Henry Nicholls to African Association, 15 February 1805, in Robin Hallett (ed.), *Records of the African Association 1788–1831* (London: Thomas Nelson, 1964), p. 204. Hugh Goldic, *Dictionary of the Efik Language* (Edinburgh: United Presbyterian College, 1862), p. xlii, similarly emphasizes the existence of 'eight . . . distinct languages, besides the Efik and its various dialects' within a hundred-mile radius of Old Calabar, viz., 'Usahadet (Bakasey), Efut (Kameroons), Aqua (Kwa), Akayong, Uwet, Umon (Boson), Ekoi and Unene (Ibo)'.

21 David Northrup, *Trade Without Rulers: Pre-Colonial Economic Development in South-Eastern Nigeria* (Oxford: Clarendon Press, 1978), pp. 60–62, 231. According to a missionary to Old Calabar in 1850. 'The number of languages in this country is extraordinary. From Tom Shotts point at the mouth of the [Cross] river up to Uwet and Umon, a distance of about 120 or 130 miles, there are eight different tongues', not counting Igbo, but all the smaller groups speak 'Calabar'; Hope Masterton Waddell, 'Journal of the Old Calabar Mission', Vol. 8. United Presbyterian Church papers, National Library of Scotland, MS7741. This refers only to variation along a north/south axis: variation was about as great along the coastals west and southeast of Old Calabar.

22 Greenberg, *Languages*, p. 8, classifies Efik and Ibibio as a branch of the Cross River division of Benue-Congo, which also includes all of the Bantu languages of central and southern Africa.

23 Mullin, *Africa in America*, pp. 30, 31, 287.

24 Goldie, *Dictionary*, p. 260.

25 For more detailed references see David Northrup, 'New Light from Old Sources: Pre-Colonial References to the Anang Ibibio', *Ikenga*, 2 (1973), pp. 1–5.

26 Christian Georg Andreas Oldendorp, *History of the Mission of the Evangelical Brethren on the Caribbean Islands of St. Thomas, St. Croix, and St. John* (Ann Arbor, Mich.: Karoma Publishers, 1987), pp. 166–70, 203–6. See the comparative vocabulary lists of Cross River languages (including Efik) in P. Amaury Talbot, *In the Shadow of the Bush* (London, 1912), Appendix F.

27 John Adams, *Remarks on the Country Extending from Cape Palmas to the River Congo* (London: G. & W.B. Whittaker, 1823), p. 132. The 'Qwaw' are the Kwa, a name used for Efik-speakers by the people of Bonny: Daryll Forde and G.I. Jones, *The Ibo and Ibibio-speaking Peoples of South-Eastern Nigeria*. Ethnographic Survey of Africa, Western Africa. Part III (London: Oxford University Press, 1950), p. 68. This Kwa should not be confused with the unrelated Kwa people east of the Cross River nor with the Kwa subfamily of Niger–Congo.

28 Northrup, *Trade Without Rulers*, pp. 33–4.

29 The source of the use of Moko for upper Cross River people is a game by that name played by Cameroonians with counters on a board, according to Christopher Fyfe, *A Short History of Sierra Leone* (London: Oxford University Press 1962), p. 170, citing the *Sierra Leone Weekly News* of 9 Oct. 1915.

30 Koelle, *Polyglotta*, pp. 7–8: this identification of 'Bom' was recorded by the explorer William Balfour Baikie, *Narrative of an Exploring Voyage up the Rivers Kwóra and Bínue in 1854* (London: John Murray, 1856), p. 309.

31 Baikie, *Narrative*, p. 307.

32 David Eltis and David Richardson, 'West Africa and the Transatlantic Slave Trade: New Evidence of Long-Run Trends', *Slavery and Abolition*, 18 (1997). Tables 1 and 2. The rest of the slaves from the Bight of Biafra were drawn from ports southeast of Old Calabar (11 per cent) and from smaller Niger Delta ports (1 per cent).

33 Northrup, *Trade Without Rulers*, pp. 85–176.

34 Mullin, *Africa in America*, p. 286, and personal communication. For the use of 'Calabar' see Philip D. Morgan. *Slave Counterpoint: Black Cultures in the Eighteenth-Century Chesapeake and Lowcountry* (London: University of North Carolina Press, 1998), pp. 62–5, 447. Mullin's observation (p. 281) that 'ordinary people [in the Americas] identified Africans as members of particular societies more carefully than scholars have given them credit for doing' may be relevant here.

35 For the use of English in Old Calabar see Paul Lovejoy and David Richardson, 'Trust, Pawnship, and Atlantic History: The Institutional Foundations of the Old Calabar Slave Trade', *American Historical Review*, 104 (1999), pp. 341–5.

36 Thornton, *Africa and Africans*, pp. 328–9.

37 Chambers, '"My Own Nation"', p. 73.

38 Benediet Anderson, *Imagined Communities* (London: Verso, 1983); E.J. Hobshawm, *Nations and Nationalism since 1780: Programme, Myth, Reality*, 2nd ed. (Cambridge: Cambridge University Press, 1992); Adrian Hastings, *The Construction of Nationhood: Ethnicity, Religion and Nationalism* (Cambridge: Cambridge University Press, 1997).

39   Some form of nationalism in eighteenth-century West Africa was associated with the growth of Asante on the Gold Coast and Dahomey on the Slave Coast.

40   Goldie, *Dictionary*, p. xlii.

41   After an imaginative description of how African 'nations' recreated themselves on the basis of language. Thornton, *Africa and Africans*, pp. 320–9, acknowledges that in North America and some other places, African languages were not transmitted to the generation born in the Americas.

42   See A.E. Afigbo. 'Prolegomena to the Study of the Cultural History of the Igbo', in B.K. Swartz Jr. and Raymond E. Dumett (eds.), *West African Culture Dynamics: Archaeological and Historical Perspectives* (The Hague: Mouton, 1978, 1980).

43   Forde and Jones, *Ibo and Ibibio, passim*; Northrup, *Trade Without Rulers*, pp. 30–49.

44   Northrup, *Trade Without Rulers*, pp. 16–29, 85–113; Latham, *Old Calabar*, pp. 39–41, 80–1.

45   Herbert M. Cole and Chike C. Aniakor, *Igbo Arts: Community and Cosmos* (Museum of Cultural History, University of California, Los Angeles, 1984).

46   Gomez, *Country Marks*, pp. 124–5.

47   Mintz and Price, *Anthropological Approach*, pp. 7–9.

PART NINE

Africans in the Atlantic World

FOR TOO LONG THE STUDY of Atlantic slavery has, like most areas of academic history, been neatly divided into its various constituent areas. In part, this
is because the subject is so vast – spread over three continents for the best part
of four centuries – that few historians have felt able to study the whole. This professional reluctance has been compounded by the intellectual difficulty of locating
any overarching, integrating theme. In recent years, however, a way forward has been
offered by historians of Africa. That continent, and the historical experience of its
people, provides a new way of looking at the development of the wider Atlantic world.
Indeed, the concept of an Atlantic world begins to take shape, and make intellectual
sense, if we begin with Africa. It was, after all, the people of Africa who dominated
the migratory patterns across the Atlantic until the early nineteenth century. It was
Africans who pioneered and then made profitable enormous sweeps of the tropical
and semi-tropical Americas. And it was the people of Africa who found themselves
(against their will) scattered to all corners of the Atlantic rim. The historical, human
and cultural world of the Atlantic was borne of African experience.

It is impossible to recognise that fact without a fuller appreciation of African
history itself. The growing appreciation of the African past is analysed in Joseph
Miller's essay (1999). Miller explains how the Western discovery of that past had
consequences for historical understanding far beyond the study of Africa itself.
More than that, the rise of modern African historiography forced Western historical
scholarship to confront its own assumptions and shortcomings.

Europe's involvement with Africa throughout the era of slavery inevitably
skewed the Western appreciation of the African past. Slavery and the supply of
Africans as slaves seemed the dominant themes of African life. It is not to deny
the partiality of that impression to concentrate, here, on the history of Atlantic
slavery. Moreover, so enormous was the European appetite for Africans, so vast
and deep its impact on Africa, that economic and social systems waxed and waned
on the back of it. Slavery within Africa was, of course, utterly transformed by the
European coastal demand for slaves destined for the Americas.

To facilitate the movement and sale of Africans to the European settlements,
new social and economic groups emerged on both sides of the Atlantic. In their
essay (1999), Robin Law and Kristin Mann look at the new commercial/social

groupings that served the Atlantic trade in West Africa. More remarkably, perhaps, Daniel Schafer (1999) describes how family and commercial ties spanned the South Atlantic.

John Thornton's essay (1998) reminds us that Africa continued to exert an influence over the history of American life despite the physical distance travelled, and the traumas suffered, by the imported Africans.

———— •◆• ————

INTRODUCTION TO PART NINE

THE ENFORCED MOVEMENT of African peoples into the Americas was, as we have seen throughout this volume, a critical experience for the peoples of three continents. In recent years, historians have tried to move beyond simply tabulating the data of that epic transformation. Recently, the raw statistics have been the subject of pioneering and revisionary research, and it is important to acknowledge the importance of that evidence. We now know in some precise detail the movement of African peoples across the Atlantic over a period of four centuries.

It is tempting to think of Atlantic slavery as merely a scattering of millions of Africans around the Atlantic rim, in the process creating new communities in a random fashion wherever Europeans settled and found themselves short of labour for their agricultural endeavours. Recently, considered historical reflection has sought to integrate this historical process more closely: to see the apparently unconnected pieces of this historical experience as part of a closely integrated social and economic phenomenon. The European incursions into the tropical and semi-tropical Americas helped to create a cohesive economic system which drew together European finance and deep-water maritime abilities and the commercial potential of lands in the Americas. But all this came to profitable fruition and was given economic rationale by the labour of millions of imported Africans.

The economic analysis of Atlantic slavery has long been concerned with integrating all sides of Atlantic society. Indeed, the core of Eric Williams's pioneering thesis, expounded as long ago as 1944, was to try to assess the economic consequences of African labour in the Americas for the transformation of a major European economy (Britain). It is now apparent that the integration of the separate parts of Atlantic society operated at a more varied and often more subtle level than the mere economic. It is also clear that the unifying element in the whole system was the population of Africa.

The most critical element in scholarly rethinking of the Atlantic has been the transformation in the historiography of Africa. Since the mid-1960s, the development of African historiography has been astonishing. The scholarly interest in the African past has resulted in some of the most innovative and revisionary of historical writing. Initially, the historical interest in Africa had to overcome deep-seated cultural prejudices about Africa itself. For scholars whose researches inevitably concentrated on the written word, or on the artefacts of material culture, Africa seemed to offer little prospect of satisfactory historical findings. The historical cultures of Africa presented a host of different challenges to researchers: challenges which many viewed as insurmountable obstacles. Those who took a different tack and embarked on historical research on Africa (and *in* Africa) prompted the rise of a new African historiography.

In the English-speaking world, no one was more influential than Philip Curtin and his students. Even if we calibrate their work in quantitative terms – simply describing how much more we know about Africa's past – theirs has been a remarkable achievement. But our new appreciation of the African past is, obviously, not merely an accumulation of previously unknown data. The work of Africanists over the past forty years has relocated the people of Africa to the centre of historical considerations. A vast continent which had previously been seen almost as an accidental bystander in a historical drama unfolding in the Atlantic world has now been given its rightful place in the reconstruction of the past. In the early twenty-first century, this may seem obvious, even indisputable. In the mid-twentieth century, however, it was much less apparent, and much less accepted.

If we discuss the development of the Atlantic world, we must then begin with Africa. But what do we mean by Africa? Too often scholars and commentators prefer to use the generic terms – Africa and Africans – to describe phenomena which need more specific classification. This is especially important because, throughout the era of the slave trade, the Africans imported into the Americas would not have recognised, or described, themselves as Africans. Their identity was shaped by much more specific ethnic, tribal or cultural characteristics. Outsiders – Europeans and Americans – tended to lump Africans together for convenience, but also because they knew so little about the specifics of African identities. Recent scholarship has emphasised the importance of being precise in the historical reconstruction of Atlantic slavery; and, thanks to that scholarship, we now know much more about the exact cultural dimensions of the people fed into the maws of Atlantic slavery. We know where people came from, where exactly they embarked and departed the African coast, where they were landed and resettled (if they survived). We know in great detail about their maritime transit into the Americas. And we know the degree to which their specific African cultural roots helped to shape their identities as slaves in the Americas. Much of this information has flowed from the work of Africanists. It is one of the striking features of recent slave scholarship that the most important revelations about slaves in the Americas have derived from work on Africa and the slave trade.

To repeat, this was not the obvious way to proceed in the 1960s (the period when slave scholarship began to take off in a major way). Part of this same process (the development of a new and innovative history of Africa) also revealed the varied economic history of the continent, and especially of the European interest in Africa's resources. It may seem a curious point to make in a book devoted to slavery, but we need to recall that Europeans turned to Africa for much more than its enslaved humanity. Clearly, the sheer scale of Atlantic slavery, and its impact on the Americas, remained pre-eminent, but African raw materials, from gold to palm oil, were important attractions for the expansive European economies. Long before the development of the Atlantic slave trade, Europeans had sought a number of African commodities.

Historians of Africa, then, have been the seminal force in recasting the history of Atlantic slavery. This has involved not simply uncovering long-ignored data, nor the research field-work pioneered by Africanists, but derives from the cumulative impact of their work. Africanists have, in effect, brought about a major transformation in the study of Atlantic slavery. We can, for example, now speak with precision about the history of slavery within Africa (before, during and after the Atlantic slave trade), where previously such debate had been largely based on informed guess work. Put simply, we now understand much more about the history of Africa. In its turn, this historical transformation has enabled other historians to re-evaluate their specialised corners of slave studies. For example, historians of slavery on plantations in the Americas – peopled for much of their history by Africans – have been forced to rethink their work in the light of emergent research on Africa itself. Again, it seems logical and obvious now, but it was not always so.

Europeans looking for African slaves on the vast stretches of the West African coast offered in exchange a host of goods, some of which had been transshipped through Europe from the most distant point of European trade in Asia. Cowrie shells from the Maldives and textiles from India were favourite items of trade and barter on the African coast. Goods from Asia thus found their way into African communities. Similarly, they were to be found scattered throughout the societies of the Americas: cool calicoes worn by white women in the American tropics, Indian textiles provided for slaves on the plantations, and a range of baubles and eye-catching jewellery exchanged with North American Indian peoples in return for furs and pelts. All this, of course, was in addition to the remarkable number of Asian commodities, most notably tea and tableware from China, which helped to transform social life in Europe itself. Clearly, the Atlantic economy, which hinged on African labour, did not thrive in isolation but was part of an interdependent global trading system.

Above all else, the colonial Americas needed Europe. Pioneering settlers needed the maritime links to their metropolis, first for vital supplies and military defence (primarily against other marauding colonial powers). Even when those American communities matured into complex societies, the ties to Europe remained vital. Dominated by plantation production, the societies addicted to slavery needed an endless list of manufactured goods to maintain the fabric of daily life: clothing, instruments and tools, seeds, medicines, books and even foodstuffs. Similarly, European markets were vital for their export produce: sugar and rum, tobacco and rice, coffee, indigo and wood. For much of the colonial period, the slave colonies were, in effect, westerly dependencies – counties almost – of Europe, integrated into the domestic European economies.

In time, however, the apparent simplicity of this arrangement became increasingly complex. Flows of trade and people, movements of money and credit, the shipment of crops and commodities began to criss-cross the Atlantic economy in varied and sometimes confusing ways. What had once seemed a relatively straightforward triangular system was replaced by a confusion of trading and migratory routes. Ships moved goods and people back and forth in direct lines between Brazil and Africa. Vessels from North America sailed directly to Africa and back. Goods bound for the Caribbean were shipped south from New England; produce from the Caribbean flowed northwards into North America. And at each point of this increasingly complex system there emerged local mercantile and commercial communities, in all the major entrepôts of the Americas: groups of men well versed and experienced in the skills and conventions of long-distance maritime trade and finance.

At the heart of this ever more complex Atlantic trading system were, of course, the major European centres of trade and finance, most notably (in turn) Amsterdam, Lisbon, Seville, London and Paris – but each with a number of key local ports which sustained and received Atlantic trade. From all of those ports, the produce of the enslaved Americas, and of Africa, passed into the most distant recesses of local life. And so too did the people of Africa. The Africans were initially cast ashore in Europe more like the flotsam and jetsam of European overseas expansion: hapless people caught up in epic events they could not control. In time, however, there developed black communities in all points of the Atlantic economy. Though they generally took on the trappings of local life (British or French colonial, for example), they were, at heart, Africans in exile. Here was the early formation of an African diaspora which saw African communities proliferate at all points of the Atlantic economy. Nor were those communities simply isolated scatterings of people. We now know that Africans kept in touch with each other across the vast distances of the Atlantic. In part this was because numbers of Africans were employed as sailors (free and enslaved), while others moved around the Atlantic – between Africa and the Americas, between the North American and West Indian colonies – as servants and personal slaves, with the military or colonial officials. There was, in short, a remarkable migration of Africans back and forth. And wherever they settled, worked, lived or visited, they inevitably developed ties with other Africans. They took news from one part of the Atlantic to another, keeping each other in touch with people and events thousands of miles away. There was, in effect, a flow of information along the extended lines of the African diaspora which, in time, was to have major political consequences. This was especially important when concepts of equality and freedom began to move across the Atlantic, first from North America in 1776 and then from France after 1789. In a world dominated by slavery, ideas of freedom were to prove contagious and simply could not be restricted, not least because the diaspora had become so vast and so vital a movement of peoples.

The African diaspora was not simply the involuntary removal of large numbers of Africans around the Atlantic. It was, for all its violence and inhumanity, an energetic social system which fed the peoples and cultures of one part of the world into other regions. But the process of violent, long-distance migration and resettlement inevitably changed the people involved. The black communities of the Americas were not only different one from another (between, say, Brazil and Barbados, or between Jamaica and Virginia), but were each different from their African origins. However many cultural features of their African homelands survived among the slaves of the Americas, they were, in time, fundamentally transformed by the altered circumstances of life in the Americas.

The number of Africans forcibly transshipped across the Atlantic hugely outnumbered Europeans travelling in the same direction. But only in unusual circumstances did slave populations reproduce themselves faster than local whites. The explanations for this lie, of course, in the peculiarities of slave demography, work and treatment. Yet whatever the growth of slave populations, whether by transatlantic importation of still more Africans or by natural increase, it was the Africans and their descendants who dominated the human landscape of all the slave colonies of the Americas. In Europe, Africans formed only a small minority, but even there their importance transcended their numbers. They were, in effect, a local reminder that it was the people of Africa who made possible the slave-grown produce of the Americas, itself so integral to social life on both sides of the Atlantic in the course of the seventeenth and eighteenth centuries. Again, we are led back to the integrated nature of the Atlantic world itself.

The tendency among an older generation of historians was to tease apart, and to treat separately, the constituent themes in the history of the Atlantic world in these years. More recently, historians have struggled to reintegrate those strands and to see the Atlantic world as a whole. It was a dynamic historical process which brought together the peoples of three continents into a mutual economic and social dependency. The aim was the material advancement of the Western world: the flowering of European expansion and colonial settlement for the material betterment of Western Europe. It all took place at the expense of the peoples of Africa and the Americas, though few contemporary Europeans viewed it that way. How that system worked can only be fully appreciated by trying to see the era of Atlantic slavery in the round; by viewing it as a historical phenomenon which tied utterly different Atlantic societies together in an integrated social and economic entity.

Chapter 34

Joseph C. Miller

HISTORY AND AFRICA/AFRICA AND HISTORY

ISTORICAL CONSCIOUSNESS IN AFRICA is—of course—quite literally as old as time, but in Europe and the Americas awareness of Africa's past has dawned only more recently. In the United States, African Americans during the nineteenth century first attended to Africans' pasts in the face of the racialized skepticism of the era. Writing more than a hundred years later as an Africanist historian here in the journal of the American Historical Association for colleagues in all fields, I want to suggest some of the intellectual pathways along which they and their successors have brought Africa within the practice of professional history at the end of the twentieth century and thus what learning to do history in a place as remote—affectively, culturally, geographically, and intellectually—as Africa was for the founders of the historical discipline may reveal about history itself as process and as epistemology. It will become clear that I write of history in a humanistic vein that has become meaningful to me as I have matured—or perhaps merely aged—in our profession, speaking personally with what seems to be an executive privilege that the American Historical Association accords to presidents on this occasion.[1] I do so without intent, thereby, to excommunicate colleagues who may balance in other ways the complex combinations of personal insight, techniques of inquiry, research data, engagement with popular memory, and practical application through which historians discern and disseminate meanings in evidence from the past.

The story that follows begins against the familiar background of the birth of the modern discipline of history at the end of the nineteenth century, torn as it was then between theological-philosophical speculation and faith in empirical data as evidence that would satisfy lingering cravings for certainties about the past, confirmed scientifically; both tendencies specifically excluded most of Africa from the human progress that they celebrated. Those whose own lives confirmed that Africans belonged within universal history had to circumvent the exclusionary particularity of the discipline by adapting aspects of other more comprehensive—though also abstract, static, less humanistic—generalizing epistemologies to bring Africa within the realm of academic respectability. From such academically alien beginnings, they only slowly and haltingly restored the humanism, the sense for change, and the sensitivity to contexts of time and place that distinguish history's way of knowing. But in relying, *faute de mieux*, on mythological oral traditions, reified languages, mute archaeological artifacts, and presentist ethnographic descriptions, they tested multiple limits of how they thought as historians. Looking back, their struggles highlight complex balances among several epistemological aspects of historians' craft: between particularity and generality, theory and data, sequence and chronology, internal subjectivities and unavoidable (whether or not "real") externalities, and empathetic similarity and curiosity-stimulating (or fear-provoking) differentiation in the relationship between historians and their subjects. I hope to suggest here how bringing Africans within the orbit of historical discipline may remind historians in any field of what is most historical about how we all have come to think.

Africans and African Americans adapted the progressive historiographies current at the end of the nineteenth century to write about Africa, while historians in Europe and the United States were laying out standards of the modern discipline.[2] The problem they faced was that, following Hegel, the meta-narrative of the emerging discipline excluded Africa's past as morally unedifying and methodologically unverifiable, leaving Africans outside its exultation in European superiority as "people without history."[3] The search for an African past sculpted in these progressive terms meant highly selective emphasis on monumental achievements comparable in antiquity, size, and military power to what Europeans then celebrated with acknowledged inspiration from Hegel. about their own past.[4] They drew, first, on their contemporaries' appreciation for ancient Egypt and the mysterious lands to the south, some of them biblical—Punt, Nubia, Kash, and Ethiopia or Abyssinia —and sought monumental ruins comparable to what they knew of the "glory that was Rome" and the Egyptian antiquities publicized in the wake of Napoleon's 1798 invasion of the lower Nile.[5] They limited research to written texts, which in Europe's experience conveyed direct impressions from remote times in relatively unchanged, or reconstructible, forms that met the demanding standards of verifiability emergent in scientific history. But writing also testified to the intelligence of its authors, otherwise suspect as illiterate "natives" living out mindless lives of changeless, endless barbarity. They accepted durable archaeological evidence as also providing similarly irrefutable credibility against the currents of racist skepticism then flowing. In retrospect, the prestige that progressive historians accorded continuities from ancient origins seems a singularly contradictory way to validate the recent advances on which they prided themselves, while in Africa the same perpetuation of ancient custom explained only contemporary primitiveness. The implicit accent on continuity undermined the progressives' insistence that devotion to change as a centrally revelatory element in human experience distinguished their discipline from theology and other competing epistemologies of their era. The roots of the paradox lay, of course, in the premises of biological racism on which its logic rested: priority in achievement demonstrated inherent racial superiority, and subsequent continuity in culture reassuringly paralleled transmission of the knack for civilization by genetic means.

The only possible source of evidence from the other side, turn-of-the-century anthropology, redoubled the challenge to those who would discover a meaningful past in Africa by validating its moral distance from the modern West. The first phases of anthropological investigation in Africa grew out of German idealism and received no small romantic impetus from European self-exiles disillusioned by the failing promise of industrialized capitalist society at the *fin de siècle*.[6] Broadly inspired by Hegel's "universal history" of the development of the human spirit, one historically oriented group of German ethnologists derived "advanced" cultural traits from primal centers of civilization in the ancient Middle East and explained apparently "civilized" achievements reported from other parts of the world as products of a quasi-historical dynamic of "diffusion" of their unique inspiration. Diffusionist theories linked what people had done indissolubly to who they were, and so they accounted for historical change only in terms of "migrating" groups, mysterious conquerors who had spread "civilized" culture into remote corners of the world, or by imitative natives "borrowing" from them.[7] To construct a "history" for Africa meaningful by these high and ancient standards, but independent of presumed origins in southwestern Asia, meant positing an independent font of inspiration south of the Sahara, primary either because it was older than Egypt or because it possessed virtues more estimable than modern Europe's mechanized military power.

The German ethnologist Leo Frobenius became an erratic champion of Africa in these errantly historical terms.[8] Frobenius shared his contemporaries' disdain for the "degenerate" colonial Africans of his own time, but he nonetheless found them fascinating "because he thought them to be living documents of an otherwise unrecoverable universal human past."[9] In the course of repeated research trips to Europe's new African colonies around the turn of the century, he sensed traces of a creative, simple, and unspoiled local form of civilization higher than his embittered assessment of modern Europe. To account for the anomaly, he hypothesized an ancient, since-vanished civilization in West Africa known to its Mediterranean contemporaries, the Etruscans, hence anterior to Rome, and remembered later in the European myth of a lost Atlantis.[10]

Frobenius's "African Atlantis" reversed the diffusionist "Hamitic hypothesis" dominant in progressive history's vision of Africa. This pseudo-historical Hamitic theory reconciled older faith in the Christian Bible with newer, scientifically styled studies of language, physical type, and political economy to account for what Europeans could recognize in Africa as vestiges of "civilization" understood in modern terms. From the moment that self-styled European "explorers" and colonial armies had set foot in Africa, they encountered formidable opponents, leaving the would-be "civilizers" with considerable and perplexed respect for African military power, political leadership, and even monumental architecture, the litmus tests of progress. All of these contradicted the low rankings that the racial classification schemes of the time accorded dark-skinned people. Only a "white" residue in Africans' cultures could explain so unanticipated a suggestion of competence among "Negroes." By the convenient logic of diffusionist inference such "Caucasian" influence could have reached sub-Saharan Africa through historical contact with emigrant "whites" of Mediterranean origin, long enough ago to match the presumed antiquity of authentic originators and to leave time for their salutary influence to have degenerated to the faint traces still evident in the otherwise universal genetic and cultural gloom.[11] In the United States, where God-fearing Southerners justified the violent racism of the "Jim Crow" era on their faith "that God had shaped the Negro's physical and emotional makeup at the beginning of existence and rendered him forever inferior to whites,"[12] these biblical, evolutionary, environmental, and racial determinisms hung heavily in the immediate background to nineteenth-century thinking about the past in Africa.

The scholarly W. E. B. Du Bois led several African-American colleagues at the beginning of this century in creating a professional history for Africa against the backdrop of American racism. As an undergraduate at Fisk University, where the "natural inferiority [of people of African descent was] strenuously denied," it had been Bismarck who struck Du Bois as a model of the "strength and determination under trained leadership" that would "foreshadow . . . the kind of thing that American Negroes must do" for themselves. But as Du Bois entered Harvard's graduate history program in 1888, he found "Africa . . . left without culture and without history."[13] With no alternative, Du Bois concentrated his studies on American history and politics but oriented his thesis research toward Africa by taking up the "suppression of the African slave-trade to the United States of America, 1638–1870." He read his first academic paper on the subject to the annual meeting of this Association in 1891, in Washington, D.C.[14] Realizing "what in my education had been suppressed concerning Asiatic and African culture," Du Bois followed the German pilgrimage of the time among historians in America for two years' study at the University of Berlin (1892–94).[15] There, he must have heard metropolitan echoes of Germany's wars of colonial conquest, seen the published reports of nineteenth-century German scientific expeditions in Africa, and drawn on contact with German ethnology to frame the first continental-scale history of Africa in his sweeping, racially unified history, The Negro.[16]

In The Negro, Du Bois described ancient African kingdoms comparable to Europe in civilization. But the glories of such earlier accomplishment cast an unavoidable dark shadow over a contemporary Africa recently subjugated to European colonial rule. Du Bois found an explanation for this painful realization in historical reasoning: he attributed contemporary Africans' apparent degradation to damage done by subsequent European and Muslim slaving, a theme prominent in the writings of eighteenth-century opponents of the slave trade that he must have encountered in researching his doctoral dissertation. Du Bois' horror at the loss of "100,000,000 souls,[17] . . . the rape of a continent to an extent never paralleled in ancient or modern times," led to his tragic concession, by the standards of progressive historiography, "of the stagnation of culture in that land since 1600!"[18] Without personal experience on the continent, not even Du Bois could escape the European and American judgment of contemporary Africans' backwardness by contemporary standards. But asserting a retrogressive narrative of damage and decline by historical agents, albeit external ones, at least allowed him to avoid the eternal burden of inferiority by reason of race.

"Progressive" history early in this century thus confined even this brilliant—defended of the "Negro" to a salvage operation, a search for racial respect by interpreting specifics from ancient Africa to support modern, European valuation of the national state, military power, and monument buildings The result corresponded to historical thinking at the end of the twentieth century only in its contemplation of times past. It lacked African contexts of time and place independent of presentist projections, or inversions, of European racial presumption. Du Bois could attribute recent initiative only to outsiders, European (and Muslim) slavers, and thus left Africans in roles perilously close to passive victims, without agency of their own. Du Bois', and Frobenius's, concessions of the recent stagnation of Africa's cultures—or of a singularized "African culture," as the rubric of racism usually homogenized them—all but excluded current ethnographic description of Africans since their fall into backwardness as a source of insight into the earlier but vanished glories. Without human, African context to stimulate motive and action, even Du Bois' prodigious reading in published writings left his story of triumphal political leadership in Ghana, Mali, and Songhai—the empires of Africa's medieval Sudan, cut down at the threshold of modernity—a fable not of tragedy but rather of failure.

African teachers and scholars, and the Europeans and Americans who worked in Africa with them after World War II, gradually distinguished modern African history from the liberalizing intellectual currents that swept Europe and the United States during the waning years of colonial rule They did so by adding empirical evidence focused on issues arising from circumstances particular to Africa.[19] This postwar generation of academics, intent on preparing colonies in Africa for political independence and African youth for future civic responsibility, lived amid intense preoccupation with politics. African politicians, several of them trained in the United States in Du Bois' vision of African history under Leo Hansberry, who had introduced the first academic courses in African history at Howard University in the early 1920s, capitalized on its nationalist spirit to justify Africans' political accountability.[20] These pioneering historians of Africa overwhelmed the regional historical traditions of the colonial era and adapted basic progressive assumptions to African purposes, demonstrating political centralization and expansion in political scale in Africa of European proportions.[21]

The academic institutions in the colonial metropoles in Europe, which held authority to validate these teachers' efforts as professional "history," expressed fewer reservations than previously about Africans' inherent eligibility for history, but they showed strong hesitation about the lack of evidence from Africa that seemed to meet the historical discipline's positivist standards.[22] As in all history, only disciplined recourse to voices independent of the present, to primary evidence understood in terms of its originators in the past, could convey Africans' agency and the contexts to which they reacted. Research strategies that might historicize Africa's past had to start in Africa, draw on African sources, and array the new information around historical hypotheses focused on concerns of Africans. Objections on such technical grounds presented challenges that the first Africa-based generation of professional historians welcomed with enthusiastic inventiveness.

They regarded the prized documentary sources of the progressives as highly suspect for these purposes in Africa. Europeans had written about Africans since they had arrived in the fifteenth century, but documents became sufficiently comprehensive to bear the weight of historical interpretation alone only much later, since about the 1880s, with the advent of government records accompanying the establishment of colonial authority. However, these writings of modern Europeans were alien and self-interested, as well as tainted by the use made of them in colonial and imperial history to lionize Europe's civilizing political mission around the globe. Nationalist historiography rejected them as very nearly polar opposites of the Africans' history that they sought.

What little research drew on colonial government files, even though it reached monumental proportions in isolated instances, was administrative and sociological, not historical.[23] Narratives of the colonial governments' economic "development" programs, or, alternatively, the success of nationalist politicians at mobilizing popular opposition to them, since the nineteenth century, were "case studies" in a social-science mode, with primarily comparative and theoretical implications. They tended to extract "variables" relevant to the "models" and theories they tested from their full historical contexts. The enabling generation of post-World War II historians had little choice but to appropriate these other disciplines for their own historical purposes, even—as was repeatedly the case—when their sociological accents tempted them to phrase arguments in terms of aggregated behavior and abstractions.

Social-science "models" tempted historians also because they offered the alluring logical coherence of theory to paper over the initial lack of enough empirical evidence from the African past to make sense on its own terms, and to distract from the dubious standing, by conventional historical standards, of what there was. Still more seductive of historical epistemology were the equilibrium assumptions of much mid-twentieth-century sociology, with its stable institutions and equilibrium models. In terms of change, these amounted to social-scientific analogs of the timeless "primitive" African cultures that they sought to replace. Structural logic thus diverted historians' attention from their own discipline's reliance on change as a primary mode of explaining, observing transience as a fundamental aspect of human existence.

Yet, out of this initial reliance on methods, conceptualization, and narratives distinctly ahistorical in logic and alien to Africa, historians gradually added context, change, and African agency, the three epistemological elements that together distinguish history from other disciplines, to create a more historicized African past.[24] Driven back in time by the unacceptability of colonial-era documents and by progressive history's respect for ancient origins, aspirant historians of Africa had to confront the technical challenges of making responsible use of unwritten sources. As historians, they sought to identify properties in these novel forms of evidence familiar from documentary records. Their need to justify themselves by disciplinary standards alien to Africa distracted them from these sources' distinctively African characteristics, and thus from their historicity.

Narrative oral traditions—recountings of events attributed to a past beyond the experience of living witnesses and presumed to have passed down to the present through multiple tellers and hearers[25]—seemed particularly authentic voices from Africans' pasts. Their narrative form made them seem subject to critical methodologies developed for reconstructing primary versions of the similarly discursive written sources familiar to historians elsewhere.[26] However, application of this documentary analogy to "traditional" narratives revealed that Africans told their tales so creatively, at least in the politically charged circumstances of talking to the powerful European outsiders who recorded them, that the scenes they portrayed amounted to outright fabrications.[27] They structured their accounts by aesthetic, rhetorical, and interpretive strategies more than by chronological sequence, and they tended to account for change by radical, magical-appearing transformations rather than by detailing the incremental sequences plausible as change to historians.

Once historians recognized that they could not read oral narratives as histories or reconstitute them as wholes, they reexamined their elements to see how they might offer valid pointers to circumstances—if not the actors or events narrated —in the past. But historians prepared to extract evidence from traditions by dissecting them faced a cross-disciplinary challenge from anthropologists eager to claim the same oral representations for theoretical purposes of their own as social, conceptual, and performative entities.[28] British structural-functional anthropologists, authors of much of the ethnography on which the first generation of historians drew in their search for African historical context, emphasized the presentist aspects of narratives constructed to legitimate privilege and power, often by deploying metaphors of antiquity to assert the inalterability of current inequalities.[29] Structuralist anthropologists influenced by French symbolic anthropology joined the cause against traditions' historicity by interpreting the logic and language of the same materials as cosmological speculation, even as expressing fundamental structures of mind untouched by any specific experience or conscious reflection, present or past.[30] Historians responded that narratives need not directly describe times gone by to contain elements bearing marks of origins in times past, even without the performers' awareness of the antiquity on which they drew. Anthropologists exaggerated the presentist aspects of oral performances only by selectively emphasizing the tales' narrative meanings and aesthetic strategies, or the political and intellectual reasons why performers might displace into former times narratives fabricated in—or even deliberately constructed as metaphors for—the present.

In the oblique and mutually stimulating way in which divergent disciplines interact, historians historicized their use of oral traditions by converting the anthropologists' emphasis on compositional strategies to understand how Africans selected, preserved, and shared collectively important knowledge through time in mnemonic environments.[31] Mnemonic techniques of preserving knowledge, for example, distributed vital information among several individuals, all responsible together for mutual verification of essential points, however made.[32] Individual performers engaged existentially with their auditors around the immediate occasion, against backgrounds of current power, rank, and privilege, but arguments for the exclusively presentist idiosyncrasy of oral performances could be sustained only by isolating them from their distinctive communal context, by restricting analysis to a single performer along lines that presumed individual artistry comparable to performance in literate cultures.[33] By analyzing the compositional strategies of oral performers as group processes, historians replaced abstracted oral traditions with intellectual history contextualized in African environments.[34]

The centrality of precise chronology to progressive methods of inferring (possible) cause and consequence from contemporaneity and sequence led the first generation of professional historians at work in Africa down obscure paths in search of proxies for calendrical dates that would bring African evidence up to accepted standards. Lists of kings common in the royal traditions of African political systems seemed convertible to calendrical years on the supposition that succession in royal lineages exhibited demographic regularities. Historians might then count the rulers named and multiply assumed average lengths of reigns back from recent monarchs of known date to estimate dates of earlier rulers.[35] That African dynasties might have exhibited greater order, and hence more regular sequences, than unpredictable struggles over power elsewhere in the world proved a vain hope, nurtured in part by the illusion conveyed by colonial-era social anthropology of mechanistic, functionally integrated political institutions in Africa.[36] But in following Africans' ways of speaking about the past, historians gradually abandoned such artificial and abstracted chronologies in favor of contextualizing pastness as people in mnemonic cultures experienced it: as absence, as broad contrasts between what is proximate and what is remote, mixing space with time accordingly.[37]

Historians looked also to Africans' 1,500 different languages for the aspects of linguistic change that might yield calendrical dates.[38] The resulting chronologies were, of course, similarly mechanistic artifices and proved imprecise as historians' needs grew more refined. They also riveted historians' attention on classifications of abstracted *Languages of Africa* rather than on the people who created them.[39] But other historical aspects of Africans' linguistic behavior—"language communities always in contact and constantly evolving"—spoke more directly about their experiences in the past.[40] The marked contrasts among Africa's five major language families gave sharp definition and multiple dimensions to the discrete, specific linguistic innovations that produced Africa's diverse linguistic heritage. Phonetic shifts in the way that people pronounced old words, or mispronounced words they appropriated from neighbors, are key markers of historical experience, and changes for many areas of collective life can be reliably sequenced by reconstructing them. Sets of novel words that clustered in conceptual fields within this phonetic framework pointed to specific technology, political institutions, fashions in apparel, or moments of enduring human inventiveness in the past, including the kinds of people who might have changed the ways they talked and the reasons why their descendants preserved their linguistic habits down to the languages of the present.[41] This historicizing transition from statistical analysis of abstracted vocabularies to historical inferences from reconstructed past linguistic behavior paralleled historians' abandonment of the formal properties of oral narratives in favor of sensing how narrators drew on inherited memories to compose them.

The preoccupations and enthusiasms, circumstantial worries and collective accomplishments of ancient parents literally echo in the present through the speech habits they taught their children. Moreover, their accents express historical experience without conscious intent and hence, unlike the ideological distortions characteristic of oral narratives, are unfalsifiable. Historical inference from linguistic reconstruction is attaining degrees of detail, depths in time, and regional comprehensiveness that outline a coherent narrative—though with increasing selectivity as the focus lengthens to more remote eras—of who in Africa experienced what in times past as long as 20,000 years ago.[42] Historical inferences from linguistic evidence thus approach the threshold of intentionality as a significant determinant of human experience, the dawn of dependence on communication for collective welfare, and reliance on self-conscious creativity through cultural consensus, all marking the beginnings of history understood as deliberate, effective agency. In another ironic interplay of disciplines, historians' failure to extract chronologies from languages useful for history in the progressive style left them with powerful linguistic techniques for hearing about the past as Africans experienced it.

Chronology-dependent historians also embraced archaeology in significant part because it produced datable stratigraphy and artifacts. In Africa's predominantly rural areas, that hope rested on the physical dating of radioactive isotopes of carbonized organic materials, such as wood charcoal, and then inferring likely relationships of these material remains to human issues of interest to historians.[43] Beyond the imprecision of the dates calculable from these radiocarbon techniques, the uncertain associations of materials thus dated to specific human activities left their conclusions far from historical in style.[44] The search for hard evidence to civilize Africans by European standards also turned historians of Africa to archaeology for traces of early metallurgy, a technology of undeniable accomplishment by modern industrial standards. This line of investigation gained momentum when iron smelting turned up in Africa earlier than anticipated, five centuries or more before the Common Era in several regions. Africans had thus smelted iron—as was nearly always emphasized in the lingering competitive spirit of the quest—before much of western Europe replaced bronze with ferrous metals. African smelting techniques also arguably derived from local inspiration, and iron workers there primarily fabricated agricultural implements. This last purposive nuance rescued Africa—it was hinted—from the retardation implied by the still more ancient dating of iron in Anatolia, but there for less reputable use as weapons. Subsequently, study of the African contexts of iron production, with emphasis on culture and environment, has replaced "early enthusiasms" about iron artifacts in Africa with historicized comprehension of African metal workers and their metal-working strategies.[45]

The progressive impulse to unearth African evidence of antique monuments respectable in European terms showed little promise south of the Nile corridor and Ethiopia, with the exception of massive thirteenth- and fourteenth-century stone walling in southern Africa centered at "Great Zimbabwe,"[46] in towns that dotted Africa's Indian Ocean coastline since at least the eighth century, and such famed thirteenth- to sixteenth-century West African cities as Timbuktu, along the southern fringes of the Sahara Desert. These town centers had attracted attention as sub-Saharan prototypes of modern, Western-style urbanity since Du Bois' initial attempt at African historiography. However, the classic archaeological research at these sites focused on the imported wares found in their ruins, on Muslim building in Arab and Persian styles, and on other evidence of datable foreign contacts. Because archaeologists then contemplated their findings in terms of abstract typological contrasts rather than as historical products of human creativity, few remarked on the faint aroma of the discredited "Hamitic hypothesis" that emanated from attempting to give Africans credit only for taking up the good ideas of immigrants from southwest Asia.[47]

Archaeologists, like linguists, have learned to interpret their findings according to the mental maps of the Africans who built these towns.[48] The West African cities, once treated as isolated outposts of North African Muslim traders in search of sub-Saharan gold valuable in Mediterranean markets, have been revealed as late elaborations on African patterns of urbanization that arose from desiccation and local exchanges across the region's increasingly sharp environmental gradients two millennia before they attracted foreign merchants.[49] All these centers expressed distinctively African communal strategies of production, distribution, and provisioning necessary to support dense settlement.[50]

In the beginning, historians had turned to ethnography for data distinguishable as "African" among the prevailing written Europeans' impressions of Africa. They accepted the theorized social structures, mental worlds, and cultures in which anthropologists phrased these descriptions as enduring determinants of African behavior rather than as modern, Western constructs about them. Moreover, the urgency of their search for evidence from the past predisposed them to overlook the contemporaneity of the mid-twentieth-century circumstances that ethnography in fact described. Ethnographers' assertions that they abstracted aspects of Africans' lives as they had existed before European modernity intruded gave an illusion of pastness—however static—that dulled the sense of change critical to history.

In particular, the hoary colonial fallacy that Africans could usefully be understood as belonging to enduring, homogeneous ethnic aggregates—the "tribes" still current in popular discourse—further distracted historians from positioning ethnographic evidence firmly in its historical present. Although historians rejected the connotations of backwardness conveyed by the colonial idea of "tribes," the functional integrity of African "societies" rendered every element of the contexts in which people "must have" lived so essential to all others that reference in a conventional dated source to one of them seemed to allow historians to assume the connected presence of most, or surely some, of the rest in the otherwise undocumented past.[51] Functional "tribal" integration of this sort allowed historians, further, simply to bundle the conclusions of all the other disciplines they had engaged, assuming that conclusions from one could verify inferences from others without considering the specific contexts that might have generated each.

This rationalization, however well-intended and cautiously applied, placed even the scattered direct evidence then available for earlier times squarely within the timeless vision of Africa's past that historians meant to refute. The few options for accommodating change that such "tribes" offered were familiar from progressive history: like "civilizations" and "races," they had "origins" locatable in time and space, subsequently acted primarily as groups by "migrating" to wherever their members currently lived, "conquered" anyone they encountered along the way, and reliably passed "traditional" behavior through the generations. African sources offered few ways out of this time trap of "tribal" logic, since traditions everywhere expressed the inviolable integrity of current groups as enduring ethnic antiquity. To historians working in the pressure cooker of trying to confirm scattered information by the rules of a doubting discipline, the documented presence of a few elements of a current ethnographic "society" or "culture" appealed seductively as the visible tip of a likely ethnic iceberg of associated (even if unremarked) behavior and institutions in the past.

Even now, in an era that emphasizes the contingent and constructed character of groups of any sort, anywhere in the world, a lingering reliance on "tribes," though long rejected among Africanists,[52] still sometimes substitutes for historicized context among nonspecialists drawn to consider Africa's past. As appreciation of Africa's relevance to history beyond its own shores has grown, historians of other world regions have necessarily approached so unfamiliar a subject through simplifying assumptions that they reject in areas they know better. "Tribes" now usually lie concealed behind polite euphemisms—"cultures," "ethnic groups," and neo-logistical "ethnicities," even "communities"—but politesse does not eliminate the time-defying, history-denying static logic of the notion: stereotyped Africans confined within abiding structures, individuals submerged in depersonalized, abstracted aggregates, who act mostly by realizing social (or cultural) norms, that is, by preserving unchanged what colonial-era language reified as "tradition."[53]

Definitive historicization of ethnography came not only from situating ethnographic descriptions in time and context[54] but also from seeing the African strategies colonial ethnography had reified as institutions as Africans' ways of achieving specific historical objectives.[55] Africans compose "traditions," for example, by adapting popular memories about the past to apply the ideological force of claimed antiquity and stability for discernible purposes of the moment.[56] Historicization has transmogrified such ethnographic staples as African "kinship," and its common expression as "lineages," from functional frameworks within which Africans thought into collective entities that they created and adapted to secure valued resources in land, in political standing, or in people themselves. Anthropologists and historians together have sensed that "witchcraft" in Africa was a historical reaction against the danger that individuals grown wealthy, powerful, and independent posed not only to their relatives and neighbors but also to the ethos of collective responsibility itself; commercialized exchanges with the Atlantic economy since 1600 or so and the colonial-era introduction of a monetary economy raised public alarm about abuses of private accumulation to haunting intensity.[57]

African politicians and intellectuals created ethnicity itself by manipulating supple collective identities to meet historical circumstances.[58] A capsule history of ethnicity in Africa would trace the oldest of the collective identities that colonial ethnographers froze in time as "tribes" to ancient adaptations of basic agricultural and other productive technologies to local environments, wherever these were so successful that whoever later lived in those areas carried on in terms of the community arrangements that the first settlers worked out. Others derive from a wave of political consolidation that swept through Africa from the thirteenth to the fifteenth centuries, wherever people continued to rely on political solutions derived from the early states that had attracted Du Bois' admiration. Still others date from seventeenth- and eighteenth-century conflicts and population movements, as people fled slave-raiding and reorganized their collective lives around the straitened circumstances it created. Others again formed as communities gathered around commercial, agricultural, and extractive enterprises of the nineteenth century. Colonial conquest once more challenged men and women in Africa to transform the group identities dominant at the opening of the twentieth century, to resurrect some that had drifted into latency, and to invent others out of momentary conjunctures to exploit cash economies and European political power. Where nominal continuity is evident,[59] new personnel frequently (one suspects always!) adapted "tradition" to dramatically shifting circumstances, if only to preserve viable aspects of shared heritages and wrap themselves in the legitimacy of the ages. Even the stereotypically unchanged hunters in the Kalahari (so-called "Bushmen") have survived by adapting,[60] and Africa's nomadic forest people turn out to have maintained their strategic flexibility only by innovating against heavy odds.[61]

In no small irony, the methodological distractions of using the blueprints of other disciplines,[62] not yet historicized, to construct a past for Africa left historians vulnerable to haste in handling evidence in familiar written forms. The founding generation's intense commitment to an autonomous African history—led by inexperienced research students, sometimes by faculty of necessity trained in other fields,[63] nearly always institutionally isolated from their historical colleagues in area-studies programs—insulated them from the discipline in the rest of the world, and from the methodological caution that prevailed in departments of history.[64] This liberal generation of aspirant historians acquired too easy a sense of having met their professional responsibility for source criticism by exposing the racist biases of European writings about Africa. Although fighting racism was an unavoidable component of constructing a history of Africa, even the passing racist ambiance of the time still distracted historians of Africa from the critical methods of their discipline.

The limits of well-intended innocence as historical method appeared as soon as the initially high yields of plowing virgin documents for superficially accessible content about Africans' interactions with their European authors began to decline. The second generation of Africanist historians—or, often, in fact, the first gener- ation, wiser with experience—took up positions in departments of history where they encountered the questions of historical methodology that underlay their search for answers in Africa. With tenure and with the outline of an African past becoming clearer in their minds, more of them found time to follow through on doubts raised, but not resolved, by their uses of documentary sources in their early research.[65] By the 1970s, their students had to reinterpret the same limited corpus of written sources more closely for their implications for new, more subtle questions that an increasingly complex history of Africa was raising. The increased awareness of African contexts at the same time enabled them to read the written sources—and not only "European" documents—against the grain of their authors' ignorance for the shadows that Africans' activities cast over what they reported.[66] Unsurprisingly to historians of the ancient Mediterranean and medieval Europe,[67] even the author- ship and chronology of seemingly familiar publications of known dates have proved very uncertain without thorough *explication do texte*.[68]

As historians of Africa re-engaged their discipline's text-based methodologies, they also incorporated the content of early modern and modern European (and American) history as context for Africa's past.[69] At the birth of modern history in Africa, when ignorance of what had happened there left historians little alternative, they cited the relative isolation of one continent from the other, intercommuni- cating regions of an Old World "ecumene" to explain Africa's apparent failure to share in the advances under way elsewhere.[70] Stimulating contact with, ideas different from one's own, as this liberal meta-history of diversity ran, accounted for progress throughout Eurasia. Africa's presumed historical isolation saved its inhabitants from the racist condemnation of "Hamitic" contact but only at the cost of once again conceding backwardness and exclusion from the world of progress. Further, by limiting stimulating interactions to Europe and its Asian partners, this history imposed a pan-African homogeneity, at least congruent with the racial stereotype it tried to avoid, that ignored intense, animating communication across many cultural borders within Africa.[71] The assumption of isolation also underesti- mated Africans' intercontinental contacts and missed the creativity with which they had appropriated from outsiders what made sense in the contexts in which they lived, not least their adaptations of Islam since the eighth century and of Judaism and Christianity in the millennium before then.[72]

History nonetheless emerged, even from research that had strained so hard against the distractions of alien disciplines during the 1960s to meet the standards of historical method that inspired it. Historians gradually discerned sufficiently prob- able patterns of past African actions that their successors could place imported artifacts, world religions, and international capital in historical contexts indepen- dent of modern values. A breakthrough of sorts came in the 1970s, when French neo-Marxist anthropology highlighted dysfunctional tensions within structural func- tionalists' harmonious ethnographic families, distinguished the diverse actors formerly homogenized within "tribes"—communities with and without lands of their own,[73] elders and youth,[74] slaves,[75] richer and poorer,[76] even ambitious and successful individuals[77]—and positioned them in dynamic, historicized tensions[78] Systematic neo-Marxist emphasis on material differentiation within Africa broke through the racialist homogenization lingering from earlier formulation of the subject as "the Negro" and moved beyond conflicts stereotyped as "tribal." Differentiation by gender, after first missing its full potential by celebrating African women who excelled in normatively male power roles, focused on sex-specific inequalities of colonial rule and gradually explored the distinctive experiences of the larger half of the African population to add a pervasive, vivifying dialectical tension to the context of Africa's recent past.[79] With these frustrations and other motivations in view, Africans emerged as active historical agents, in ways recognizable to historians practiced in the politics and processes of European and American history, where struggles over sharply differentiated ambitions are axiomatic.

But Africans also acted on intellectual premises and constructed historical contexts with salient aspects very different from those of progressive Europeans and maximizing materialists: prominently among many such contrasts, behind and against all of the practical tensions, was an ethos of collective responsibility rather than modern individualistic autonomy.[80] The community values of Africans' histories constitute a kind of moral historiography[81] that exhibits precisely the "ideological" qualities social anthropologists cited as evidence of ahistoricity in oral narratives. The sense in which historical "agency" may be attributed to Africans is prominently—though never exclusively—a collective one, especially during centuries before the nineteenth. Archaeological data are nearly always anonymous and interpreted generically, and words are by definition standardized products of recurrent collective practice.[82] Africans recollect their experiences communally, and performers of oral traditions publicly address shared concerns. Although oral performers characteristically build their narratives around figures of dramatically distinctive character—culture heroes, monarchs, and others, these apparent personages are in fact stock figures who reflect subsequent consensus about them more than particular persons in the past, even the individuals who may in fact have inspired such commemoration. Beginning in the sixteenth century, documents mention individually some of the Africans who met Europeans or at least characterize the specific roles they assumed in approaching literate outsiders, and from the seventeenth century onward they allow increasingly nuanced interpretations of personality in African contexts.[83] But the collective aspect of the people otherwise detectable in the more remote epochs of Africa's past means that individual agency must often be understood in terms of its effects rather than its motivations, and that the effects remembered are public rather than private.

The anonymity of individuals in much of the evidence available thus becomes less a deficiency of the sources than a window opening onto Africans' collective ways of thinking. Even though individuals pursued personal ambition in Africa no less than elsewhere, they did so by subtly evoking responses from those around them rather than by asserting their autonomy too obviously. Autonomous success invited suspicion of "witchcraft" rather than admiration. This African emphasis on collective responsibility also had its own history, with individualism becoming more effective and more acknowledged since about the eighth century, when a few Africans took advantage of outsiders—mostly Muslim and then later Christian merchants from commercial, literate backgrounds—who were prepared to deal with them on a personal basis. More than coincidentally, these foreign visitors also left the documentary records from which historians may now derive evidence of African agency as individual.

From recognizing Africans' distinctive mental worlds, historians could also appreciate their experiences of change itself as more abrupt and discontinuous than their own notions of processual incrementalism. The smaller the alterations modern historians can note, the more individuated and specific the changes, and—as a logical complement—the greater the multiplicity of their aspects, the more plausible and historical they find the process thus defined. Perception of change in such nuanced form relies on dense and continuous runs of documentary records and, beyond them on habits of writing that preserve momentary impressions of every step along the way.[84] Mnemonic notions of change in Africa more resembled what nominally literate historians in Europe before the seventeenth century accepted as "miracles"; both elided progressive history's processual stages of modification into sudden transitions between preceding and succeeding (but other than that timeless) states, sequenced but not otherwise connected.[85] Both depersonalized the human-scale agency of processual change by displacing causation into extra-human realms, usually taken seriously in Europe as "religious" but in Africa for many years dismissed, with connotations of superstitious irrationality, as "magical." Subsequent liberal revision of this pejorative characterization rationalized causation of this African sort as "cosmological" or as respectably "spiritual" but did not interpret its implications for historical thought.

Within these frameworks of causation and historical agency, Africans' strategies of action focused on ends rather than means, which they left mysterious though not beyond human access. Africans acted on the premise that humans did not themselves possess transformative power, but they might nonetheless convert existing states into desired ones by gaining personal access to a limitless pool of potentiality inherent in the world around them, a force personalized to varying degrees as "spirits."[86] Europeans, who restricted the idea of historical efficacy to human initiative, misconstrued individual action conducted in these terms as "sorcery." But African action was in fact efficacious socially as intended, that is, to the often-considerable extent that people feared the ability of individuals to tap the imagined pool of natural potency and acted on their apprehensions. Once historians accepted Africans' strategies of acting, they recognized that the ways in which they applied reasoned inquiry, calculated experimentation, and close observation of effect to transform their situations paralleled—though within the limits of detection imposed by their reliance on only the human senses—the microscopic, chemical, and eventually nuclear and electronic techniques of observation that seventeenth-century Europeans elaborated as "science."[87]

It would be misleading to overdraw these subtle distinctions in emphasis between European and African historical ways of thinking. Modern general theories of human behavior and abstracted processual models of causation are hardly less naturalizing and impersonal than Africans' metaphors of change. They internalize the power Africans see inherent in nature as inalienable human "rights" and as "sociological" or "psychological" constants; they understand agency to include manipulating "human nature" by influencing consciousness and belief. Nor do Africans' attributions of agency to collective culture heroes and founding kings in oral narratives differ in their implicit dynamics of causation from charismatic "great man" theories in Western philosophies of history. The collective solidarities that Africans represent as "ancestors," or the kings they view as embodying entire polities, produced historical effects, just as people everywhere change their worlds by acting together in groups of similar proportions. Strict rationalist observers dismissed African behavior as timeless "ritual" or "religion," hence unreflective, inexplicable, and pointless "traditional" failed attempts at agency. But contexualizing efficacy, change, and causation in these non-modern—and also postmodern, and only incidentally African—terms makes it plausible by historicizing it. The postmodern embrace of cultural history, social constructivism, memory, and collective consciousness throughout the historical profession has now brought these universal aspects of human existence clearly into view in other parts of the world.

The implications of Africa's past for history as a discipline do not, of course, arise only from the earlier eras on which nearly all of the present discussion has concentrated. The bulk of historical research in Africa has in fact shifted during the last twenty years to modern times, roughly since the mid-nineteenth century, but early Africa exemplifies the process of historicizing its study more dramatically than does the colonial era.[88] Its historiography reaches back more than a century, long enough to reveal the dynamics of the process, while modern Africa has been subject to historical study for barely more than two decades. Further, the formidable technical challenges of eliciting evidence from Africa's more remote eras reveal more sharply the challenges of maintaining disciplinary integrity while drawing on other academic epistemologies than do the interviews, colonial documents, and other relatively familiar sources employed for the twentieth century. In addition, distinctively African historical processes visible only over spans of time reaching back to ancient eras frame all interpretations of recent periods.[89] These processes decidedly do not constitute a static, "pre-colonial" past, defined only negatively by contrast to European political authority, but rather the centuries when Africans developed solutions to problems of their own times, some of which their descendants have struggled to adapt to contemporary challenges.[90] Without early history to give African context to recent experience, Africans' appropriation of current opportunities falls by default into projections of Europe's dreams of "modernization," or lapses into pessimistic resurrections of meta-histories of terminal decline—as predictions for the future![91]—to explain their failure. Whatever the ethical and political overtones of distorting modern Africa to fit into these alien terms, they fail as history because they perpetuate the teleological and ahistorical premises of the racist progressivism and liberal structuralism from which they grew.

Frictions in Africa, however effective they may have been in generating historical dynamics in Africa's past, exacted a considerable price by separating African from African-American history, making two fields from the one that Du Bois had presented generically and genetically as the history of the "Negro." African history now appeals to other professionals in terms of the, discipline and methodology that characterize the academy, more than it reflects the memories of its popular audience in the African-American community. Ambiguities arising from tensions in Africa, formerly concealed behind the American racial mask of "the Negro," seem to expose disharmonies inappropriate for public discussion in Western societies still redolent of the intolerance that Du Bois wrote to refute, to compromise commitment, to reduce the vigilant solidarity necessary for community survival in an unwelcoming world. But since Africa looms integrally in the background of African-American history as a unified ancestry reflecting the racial sense of community forced by American prejudice on African Americans,[92] for many professionalization of the subject leaves a distinct sense of loss.

History reinvented from African circumstances resonates throughout the profession, perhaps even revealingly because of the distinctive intensity with which Africa challenged the exclusionary premises of the classic, progressive form of the discipline at the end of World War II. The ahistoricity, even anti-historicity, of the social-science disciplines with which aspirant Africanist historians had to begin forced them to look deep into their own professional souls as well. Their experience of inventing a history for Africa, not by rejecting established standards but by embracing and extending them to integrate the unconventional forms in which the world's "people without history" had remembered their pasts, exposed inner logics of historical reasoning.[93] Inclusive liberalism brought "others" formerly segregated in the separate spheres of "ethnohistory" within a single, comprehensive, and seamless history of humanity. It also replaced the artificial barrier between 'history" and "pre-history" set by limiting evidence to its documentary form with a processual threshold for history defined in terms germane to how historical inquiry proceeds, that is, in terms of human agency: historical method gradually becomes productive of understanding ancient women and men as calculation supplemented biological evolution, animal instinct, and random accident as a coherent, significant source of intended—and unintended—change in the affairs of those thereby rendered human.

Historical inquiry—and historians are, above all, questioners—requires to challenge of the unknown to spark the curious imagination. History derives its essential energy from explaining difference, from the tension of the distance that separates historian and subject. All knowledge gains clarity and coherence from the elementary binary mental function of discriminating like from unlike, of course, and history is distinctive primarily in focusing on distance across time, between then and now, between the historian's and subjects' eras. The centrality of difference to the wellspring of history's epistemology underlies the reflexive appreciation, recently prominent in all historical fields, of the complexity of relations between historian-observer and observed subject, between selves and others. Progressive Europe's and America's praise of their own ways of doing things prevented historical inquiry from drawing fully on this core potential, by coding cultural behavior as biological absolutes, by limiting its subjects to the relatively familiar, by celebrating selves rather than exploring others.

Such exclusion distracts attention from the equally important, countervailing premise of historical inquiry: the shared humanity that links otherwise distanced, but not alienated, historians and their subjects. History is fundamentally humanistic in the sense that its way of knowing depends on an intuitive sense of commonality, of sheer comprehensibility, beyond the differentiation by which it defines in order to explain. This connective aspect of history's method binds historians to their subjects in multiple ways. Affectively, it appears in the emotionally engaged fascination that attracts scholars—or the horror and dismay that repel them no less engagingly—to the parts of the past that they choose to investigate. Cognitively, it sustains their inquiring interest to the point of inspiring them to impose order on chaotic evidence. Historians convey this sense of understanding by presenting their subjects as people like themselves and their audience, by touching readers and hearers intuitively, evoking contradictions, paradoxes, and ironies of life that they understand because they share them. All history is thus ethnic, part of the creation of group identities by authors who claim affinity with the subjects about whom, and for whom, they write.[94] The prominence of the past in the rhetorics of nationalism, racism, "culture wars," and chauvinisms of every sort amply confirms the extent to which history is inherently about "us."

But never exclusively so. Historical curiosity and understanding start together, from the tension of holding the opposing sensations of difference and similarity, distance and intimacy in the precarious, productive balance that makes inquiry conducted in this spirit productive. The delicate equilibrium of historical thinking makes its practice dependent on the training, poise, and control of professionals. But clarifying contrasts is so basic to human thought that carrying the same mental process to extremes allows nonprofessionals to imitate history by emphasizing either of the two tendencies of its dialectic, claiming its appeal while violating its dynamic epistemological equilibrium. Since both parts are always present and hence available to employ one-sidedly, imitators' claims may be difficult to distinguish from those of historians balanced on the tightrope of professionalism. History's humanism is so intuitive, and its legitimating intimacy so powerful, that it gives enormous popular appeal to versions of the past that draw only on commonalities, distorting the evidence in response to what the community, or the historian, wants to believe, ideologically proclaiming their obviousness as truth or more openly acknowledging them as entertaining fiction. When historians differentiate excessively by projecting onto "others" their own envy, fears, or hopes, they betray the integrity of the discipline no less than when they proclaim similarities beyond those that in fact exist. They then merely generate obscurantism, stereotyping "others" to stress difference, as Africans—who have lived with alienating histories—and African Americans —who have been excluded by racist association—know all too well.

Recent critical examination of this reflexivity—enriched by literary, hermeneutic, or psychoanalytic theories (but not by theory from the empirical social sciences)—offers productive ways to examine these inevitable, and essential, subjectivities. Taken alone, however, even informed self-awareness loses touch with the discipline's equally essential focus on others, on people in the past understood as unlike themselves. The epistemological function of empirical data for historians is to draw them outside their own imaginations. No objective reality may lurk out there, awaiting "discovery," but externalities inevitably intrude on consciousness sufficiently to differentiate and provoke curiosity. The subtle distinction that places history among the humanities rather than the sciences turns on its use of induction to test insight rather than its deploying intuition to interpret data.[95] The empirical aspect of this subtle interplay may be similarly intensified to extremes, and in the positivist phase of the discipline documents attained a sanctity that had nightmarish consequences for Africa. Novelty and sheer abundance on the empirical side of historical scrutiny have repeatedly tempted the leaders of advances into new ranges of evidence, from the written documents of the founding "scientific" generation to the unwritten sources that beguiled historians of Africa. The social historians of the 1960s struggled to comprehend data in quantities incomprehensible to unaided human cognitive faculties, and some limited themselves to conclusions in the forms in which electronic technologies and statistical techniques—necessary to detect patterns hidden within these sources—delivered them. Quantitative methods framed critical aspects of historical context by describing aggregate tendencies in human behavior, but by themselves they seldom generated historical insight into the human experience.

History turns data into evidence not by pursuing the technical attributes of data but by substituting a distinctively intuitive, humanistic, holistic strategy for the experimental method of science. It assesses meaning by qualitatively contextualizing evidence in the complex, multivariant circumstances of the past in which people created it. History ultimately fails as "science," since historians can assemble only random evidence from the debris of the past that reaches them through processes far beyond their control. They cannot replicate the closely regulated conditions of laboratories, in which their scientific counterparts precisely measure varying outcomes of exact, determining circumstances. Rather, they can compare only approximately, among the few aspects of past conditions known to them, of only general similarity, and seldom in instances numerous enough to establish levels of statistical probability beyond the plausibility inferable from intuition alone. Auras of ambiguity hover over all bits of evidence considered out of context, removed from the human creativity from which they come. Even the apparent precision of timing establishes only correlations based on chronologies, not cause or effect. History's holistic methodology thus makes sense of the data at hand by setting all information available, considered simultaneously together, in the context of the human moment from which it originated. The more information at hand, the richer the context it creates and the greater its potential thus to explain. The more intuitive the historian, the more contradictions and paradoxes in the assemblage she or he is able to reconcile.

Contemplating history without calendrical chronologies in Africa generalizes the discipline's sense of time beyond sequence according to numbered dates. History's fundamental sense of change emphasizes not dates but rather the ephemerality of the human experience and the processual aspects of historical contexts, the becomingness, the remembered absences. No human being can escape the imposing imponderability of change itself: everyone orients himself or herself to the inaccessibly fleeting present in which they live by trying to apply perceptions of past experience, to prepare for an impending future foreseeable only as projections from the here and now, which events will render irrelevant before the limited "lessons of the past" can be applied. Sequential narrative modes of exposition render these settings coherent in the flow of time, but only by invoking irony, actions with consequences unintended, tragic fates for those who cling to efforts after they have failed, uncertainty and fear, and causes arising from circumstances far beyond human control replace ineluctable progress and all the comforting regularities of theory: all very unlike the uncomplicated sense of progress that gave birth to the modern discipline.

History is thus neither empirical nor imaginative but rather a continual dialectical confrontation of insight with evidence, of intuition and empirical induction, of past and present, of mutually challenging awarenesses of the self and of the world. The meanings that historians seek are similarly multiple and distinct, simultaneously those of their subjects, those of their audience, and private ones, unconscious as well as conscious. Professional history must constantly, exhaustively, test its intuitive aspect against evidence and awareness external to both historians and their publics, in order to keep the actions of the others that it is held to reveal at safe, respected distances from their interpreters. Once historians acknowledged Africans' human accessibility and plunged into the uncertain contexts of alien disciplines and of data in half-understood forms from unfamiliar cultures, they encountered contrasts, less absolute than race, that energized their inquiries. The cultural originality that challenged anthropologists to understand Africans as exotic "others" whom time—understood only as progress toward modernity—seemed to have forgotten became a source of revealing contrasts when historians recognized it as products of the creativity of people like themselves. Scholars with personal backgrounds in the cultures of Africa gained a parallel sense of understanding from their mastery of Western historical method and often led colleagues from Western backgrounds in understanding Africans' histories that were their own.[96]

Historians achieved a similarly subtle, biased balance between history and its sister disciplines as they generated historical ways of contemplating Africa's past out of anthropology, political science, archaeology, linguistics, and other ways of knowing characterized by the primacy of theory. In sharp contrast to history, theory achieves coherence largely by abstracting selected elements from their historical contexts, to expose the logical relationships among them. Because history's core subject is the human experience, that of the historian as well as those of the historian's subjects, because all human situations exhibit multiple facets, and because historical actors shift their attention selectively among them and act momentarily in relation to many different ones, historians therefore must appropriate theories and models in eclectic multiples, not to test any one of them on its own terms but rather to apply the relevant insights of all, pragmatically, to the compound ambiguity of past experience—in combinations that are historical because each is unique to its moment. Because the external rationality of any single theory may explain behavioral tendencies of large aggregates of people over long periods of time, the theorized disciplines—philosophical as well as social and psychological sciences—reveal the *longue durée* tendencies, cultural assumptions, and general human inclinations that are vital aspects of historical context.

The disciplinary distractions of historians' early efforts in Africa thus derived not from inherent limits of the social-science theory and structure they employed but rather from their having to substitute conclusions from them for evidence from the past. Historians simply lacked sufficient data independent of their own imaginations to hold generalizing disciplines in heuristically secondary positions, supportive of their primary project of particularizing moments. In pursuit of the illusion of "tribes," they also attempted to blur distinctions among the distinct epistemologies by treating them as if they focused on the same elements of past historical contexts. For example, historians hoped that momentous subjects consciously remembered in oral tradition might directly confirm evidence of the thoroughly unremarkable aspects of life retrieved through archaeological methods; or, historians and anthropologists—in efforts recurrent as both disciplinary camps confronted their need for the other—thought it possible to synthesize a "historical anthropology" or an "anthropological history." But they learned that the dialectic of thinking inter-disciplinarily does not resolve on the plane of method. Rather, Africanists of all academic persuasions maintained their academic composures separate from others and applied the insights of all simultaneously or, as they became relevant, to complex historical contexts. There, each contextualized and thereby rendered plausible conclusions reached independently through others. Engaged historically through intuitive application to human contexts, scrupulous respect for inherent differences among academic disciplines preserved the integrity of each and enriched the productivity of all. The balance among them paralleled history's differentiated affect of scholar and subject and its mutual testing of intuition and induction.

Once historians learned enough about African local and regional dynamics to juxtapose them against Europe's experience, they engaged perhaps the most dynamic differential contrast of all. Africans seen as living in coherent "worlds of their own," fully integral but not isolated, stood in fertile tension with broader currents of world history. Africans had in fact lived in broader historical contexts long before colonial rule in the twentieth century, and before their contact with the Atlantic economy over the preceding three hundred years. They had interacted with the Islamic world in transformative degrees for nearly a millennium before that, and they had drawn significantly on contacts with the Indian Ocean and the Mediterranean in the classical eras of both neighboring regions. Saharans fleeing a growing desert had entered the Nile Valley during the millennia preceding the consolidation of classical Egyptian civilization there. The interpretation of these historical interactions as Africans borrowing "traits" abstracted from their historical contexts had generated no fruitful dynamic, nor had the effort to endow Africans with agency by isolating them within separated spheres of autonomy. Equally, single-sided "domination" by European colonialism, "modernization" by industrial civilization, or feminized "penetration" by world capitalism had left Africans passive, reactive subordinates. But balanced tension between regional and global rhythms of change in African contexts summoned up the proximate differences, distanced intimacies, of active historical inquiry.[97]

The differences exploited by contemplating Europeans' experiences in Africa together with Africans' experience of global historical processes[98] suggest that change in the large, persisting "civilizations" favored by progressive history in fact originates on their fringes, not in their relatively stable centers. Just as the Kuhnian process in science operates at the margins of awareness and intelligibility and as the unknown stimulates historical curiosity, it is at the edges of what is familiar that people in history encounter others different enough from themselves to appear baffling, where strangers pose challenges they are not prepared to meet, and to which they may respond with innovation.[99] The alternative reaction—hatred, denial, incomprehension—leads only to the loss of perspective from which unduly ethnic history—African as well as European—suffers. But history's humanistic premise of commonality, of intelligibility, turns dread of the unknown into a quest for explanation. In the case of Africa, differences had exceptional power to challenge the historical discipline, since they assumed extreme forms, wrapped in the emotional garb of race that lurked at the core of progressive history, appeared to transgress its apotheosis of evidence in documentary form, confronted modernists with present practices like witchcraft presumed left behind by the advance of civilization in Europe, and—far beyond what Africans in fact were doing—represented fanciful projections of private subjectivities that progressive historians' insistence on rational objectivity most obscured from themselves. Explanation of anomalies as multiple and sensitive as these that Africa seemed to present could not but deepen professional historical sensibilities and broaden historians' skills.[100]

Finally, historians turn to the past to implement their tragic sensibility to transitoriness only in part because ephemerality and contingency appear there in demonstrable ways. The past matters equally to the epistemology of history because evidence rooted firmly and inalterably in times gone by remains inaccessibly impervious to the inquirer's imagination in the present. Strict respect for the pastness of evidence renders it inaccessible and thus immunizes historians against the constant temptation to manipulate it in the service of concerns of their own, created by history's contravening metaphors of continuity and contiguity. It thus preserves the distance that makes historians of those who engage the lives of others, back then. Time, or—as Africans see it—absence within communities of empathy, makes the difference from which the vitality of historical inquiry flows.

Africans thus historicized as people with pasts of their own, with autonomous contributions distinguishable from the passivity assigned them by slavery, and with identities no longer rendered invisible by its racial sequels, are poised to enter the world's longer-established historical regions. More Africans than Europeans reached the Americas until sometime early in the nineteenth century, as we have known for long enough to think more carefully than most have done about the implications of the fact, and recent evidence confirms that 80 percent of the women and 90 percent of the children coming before 1800 to the New World from the Old traveled in the holds of slaving vessels.[101] Historical insights are now passing in both directions between Africa and Europe and the Americas, no less than Europeans and Africans have long interacted across the Mediterranean and all around the Atlantic.[102] The regional fields that once confined action within contexts distortingly narrow are becoming "globalized." Once historians recognize Africans as people with stories of their own, they expand their vision of lame parts of mainland North American colonies to take account of the Africans who helped, however involuntarily, to make those places what they became. The significant presence of their African-American descendants, whatever their nominal exclusion by reason of race, then follows ineluctably. With Africans brought in from the cold beyond the periphery, Atlantic history stands solidly on three legs,[103] and Africans join others around the world as intelligible participants in themes central to European history,[104] beyond their former bit parts as foils for European follies overseas. By the maxim of history's enrichment by diverse and comprehensive context—"research locally, but think globally"—all need all the others, and to equal degrees.

I am not the first president of the American Historical Association to acknowledge—at least implicitly through my confidence that lessons learned from doing history in Africa matter to historians specialized in fields once considered remote—the opportunity that the American Historical Association presents, distinctively among our many other, more specialized professional societies, to deepen understanding by providing a forum for cultivating awareness of the full historical context in which all whom we study in fact lived.[105] The AHA has taken fruitful steps in recent years to "globalize regional histories," in the phrase of one recent initiative, in the pages of the *American Historical Review*, and in supporting development of sophisticated historical thinking on a world scale.[106] The "Atlantic context" of North American history and the global aspects of modern European history, not to mention the position of Christian Europe for a millennium before on the periphery of the Islamic world, and the Indo-centric and Afro-Eur-Asian dynamics around the Mediterranean long before the age of Philip V of Spain, all thrive on the stimulus of balancing, without abandoning, perspectives inherent in each against pulses of change in the others. The subjectivity essential to history comes alive in this interplay; we realize ourselves most fully when we engage with others unlike ourselves. Historians have achieved productive diversity as the discipline has matured, but —as progressive history showed—stark differentiation without compensating engagement is sterile. As the inclusive arena in which historians can avoid disintegrating into isolated, inert fragments, the American Historical Association keeps newer styles of history from taking older ones for granted and exposes older ones to resonances of the new that animate what they have already accomplished. Africa offers historians a rich challenge as part of this process, a place not fundamentally opposed to "ourselves," as progressive history once constructed it, but one stimulatingly distinct in modulated ways from which all historians gain by including, just as Africanists thrive on being included.

Notes

1   I limit references in these notes to recent works illustrative of the steps along the way to writing history in Africa; those will orient the reader in turn to the many other authors, not all historians by any means, who historicized Africa's past. I regret my inability to acknowledge by name the legions of important contributions to the substantive historiography of Africa. For an introduction to the literature, see the still reasonably current "Africa" section (Margaret Jean Hay and Joseph C. Miller, eds.) in Mary Beth Norton, ed., *American Historical Association Guide to Historical Literature*, 2 vols. (New York, 1995), sect. 19, 1: 560–616. It is also necessary here to omit references to relevant works in other regional fields, familiarity with which I trust to the expertise of my intended readers.

2   I employ the term "progressive," not capitalized, in a sense broader than Peter Novick, *That Noble Dream: The "Objectivity Question" and the American Historical Profession* (New York, 1988), who capitalizes the phrase as "Progressive Historians" to explore the senses it acquired among historians in the United States after World War I. I include the nineteenth-century German rigorous critics of documentary sources whom Novick characterizes as "scientific historians." "Progressive" here connotes, above all, a teleological orientation of the story of the world's past to culminate in modern Europe and, in its American extension, the United States. This style of history was confident in the value of progress and modernity, optimistic, positivistic in its certainty that critical rigor might establish scientifically verifiable "truths" about the past, but also romantic, nationalistically centered on political identities, idealist. An Africanist can only be all too aware of the caricatured effect of compressing the many distinctions and controversies among those in Europe who claimed the mantle of such history into a single phrase. The way I use the label, largely for contrastive purposes, in particular blurs the "idealist"-empiricist/positivist distinction that animated many of these debates; the conclusion to this essay will, I hope, make clear why that blurring is deliberate.

3   Eric Wolf's now-classic phrase, in *Europe and the People without History* (Berkeley, Calif., 1982), with acknowledged inspiration from Hegel.

4   Europeans did not take seriously the efforts by mission-trained Africans in the 1890s to frame local histories in European historical models; see Paul Jenkins, ed., *The Recovery of the West African Past: African Pastors and African History in the Nineteenth Century; C. C. Reindorf and Samuel Johnson* (Basel 1998); also Toyin Falola, ed., *Yoruba Historiography* (Madison, Wis., 1991).

5   Edward W. Said, *Orientalism* (New York, 1979); "Orientalism Reconsidered," in Francis
    Barker, Peter Hulme, Margaret Iversen, and Diana Loxley, eds., *Europe and Its Others*,
    2 vols. (Colchester, 1985), 1: 14–27.

6   French sociology, primarily Emile Durkheim, influenced the African anthropology read in
    the U.S. mainly through its British adaptations. Early French interest in Africa had drawn
    a pejorative distinction in *mentalités* between rational Europeans and "pre-logical" savages,
    like Africans; see Lucien Lévy-Bruhl, *Les fonctions mentales dans les sociétés inférieures* (Paris,
    1910). Although later French anthropologists emphasized sophisticated cosmological
    thought in Africa, this crude distinction continued to confine historians' understanding of
    African thought within typologically contrasted "mental structures" much later.

7   Such trait tracing, of course, still resonates in American history in studies of African
    "survivals" in the New World.

8   Suzanne Marchand, "Leo Frobenius and the Revolt against the West," *Journal of Contemporary
    History* 32 (1997): 153–70.

9   Marchand, "Frobenius and the Revolt against the West," 161.

10 Based on prodigious, if also random and even unscrupulous collecting of artifacts and verbal
    arts; for example, Leo Frubenius, *Und Afrika Sprach*, 2 vols. (Berlin, 1912–13), culmi-
    nating in the huge *Atlantis: Volksmärchen und Volksdichtungen Afrikas*, 12 vols. (Jena,
    1921–28). Marchand characterizes these works as "mix[ing] highly insightful ethnological
    analyses with wildly conjectural global histories"; "Frobenius and the Revolt against the
    West," 159. For a rehabilitation of Frobenius as ethnographer, see J. M. Ira, "Frobenius
    in West African History," *Journal of African History* 13 (1972): 673–88.

11 Wyatt MacGaffey. "Concepts of Race in the Historiography of North Africa," *Journal of
    African History* 7 (1966): 1–17; Edith B. Sanders, "The Hamitic Hypothesis: Its Origin and
    Functions in Time Perspective," *Journal of African History* 10 (1969) 521–32.

12 Daniel Joseph Singal, "Ulrich Bunnell Phillips: The Old South as the New," in John David
    Smith and John C. Inscoe, eds., *Ulrich Bonnell Phillips: A Southern Historian and His Critics*
    (Westport, Conn., 1990), 223.

13 W. E. B. Du Bois, *Dusk of Dawn: An Essay toward an Autobiography of a Race Concept* (New
    York, 1940), 32, 41 49, 55, 97–98. On this as with all succeeding comments on Du Bois,
    see the lively, insightful and suitably appreciative life story by David Levering Lewis,
    W. E. B. Du Bois: Biography of a Race, 1868–1919 (New York, 1993).

14 Du Bois, *Dusk of Dawn*, 44; Lewis, *W. E. B. Du Bois*, 155–61. The dissertation of course,
    became *The Suppression of the African Slave-Trade to the United States of America, 1638–1870*
    (New York, 1896).

15 Du Bois, *Dusk of Dawn*, 99.

16 W. E. Burghardt Du Bois, *The Negro* (New York, 1915), 244, citing Frobenius's eulo-
    gies of an African "Atlantis" with approbation. Also see Werner J. Lange, "W. E. B. Du
    Bois and Leo Frobenius on Africa: Scholarship for What?" *Abhandlungen und Berichte des
    Staatlichen Museums für Völkerkunde* (Dresden) 41 (1984): 262–77. The work of the West
    African historians (note 4), which was appearing by the later 1890s, seems not to have
    attracted Du Bois' attention. Had it done so, it is not clear how these historians' uncrit-
    ical presentation of local oral materials would have struck the scientifically trained Du Bois.
    For African-American public writing and lecturing transitional from oral performance of
    community memory during the second half of the nineteenth century, see Dennis Hickey
    and Kenneth C. Wylie, *An Enchanting Darkness: The American Vision of Africa in the Twentieth
    Century* (East Lansing, Mich., 1993), chap. 7. George Shepperson's introduction to the
    1970 edition of *The Negro* (London) frames the intellectual context in which Du Bois wrote
    in terms of existing studies of Africa citing as his source Dorothy B. Porter, "A
    Bibliographical Checklist of American Negro Writers about Africa," in John A. Davis, ed.,
    Africa from the Point of View of American Scholars (Paris, 1959), 379–99.

17 Heated references to this figure in ongoing debates about the numerical dimensions of the
    Atlantic slave trade may merit a digressive comment on what Du Bois employed so large
    a number to denote. He offered 100,000,000 as an inclusive estimate of all losses "[t]hat
    the slave trade cost Negro Africa," including exports to Muslim lands estimated at two-
    thirds the size of the European trade (that is, 40/60), multiplied by six to reflect his

assumption that "every slave imported represented on the average five corpses in Africa or on the high seas"; Du Bois, *The Negro*, 155. Du Bois acknowledged that the "total number of slaves imported" to the Americas through the Atlantic portion of the several trades in slaves from Africa "is not known." He went on to summarize others' estimates to speculate that "perhaps 15,000,000 in all" might have arrived, and that "at least 10,000,000 Negroes were expatriated" across the Atlantic from Africa. In *The Atlantic Slave Trade: A Census* (Mad on, Wis., 1969), Philip D. Curtin made sophisticated inferences from reports of arrivals in the Americas and from reports of New World slave populations to estimate imports at 9.566 million people, with a confidence interval of +/−20 percent, essentially confirming Du Bois' minimal estimate; Curtin then used evidence on shipboard mortality to estimate the numbers of people taken on board in Africa at 11.2 million. Thirty years of subsequent archival research have yielded details on more than 27,000 Atlantic slaving voyages, perhaps two-thirds to three-quarters of all the ships leaving Europe or ports in the Americas with the intent of taking on slaves in Africa. On the basis of this massively expanded primary documentation of the trade—in significant part, data on European origins and on departures from Africa independent of Curtin's import-based research strategy, the compilers of these data at Harvard's W. E. B. Du Bois Institute estimate that 9.683 million people reached the Americas alive, the survivors of 11.349 million exported, once again confirming the minimum range that Du Bois suggested in 1915. See David Eltis, David Richardson, Stephen D. Behrendt, and Herbert S. Klein, eds., *The Atlantic Slave Trade: A Database on CD-ROM Set and Guidebook* (New York, 1999, forthcoming); for the most current estimate, see David Eltis, Stephen D. Behrendt, and David Richardson, "The Volume of the Transatlantic Slave Trade: A Reassessment with Particular Reference to the Portuguese Contribution" (unpublished paper, conference on "Rethinking the African Diaspora: The Making of a Black Atlantic World in the Bight of Benin and Brazil," Emory University, Atlanta, April 17–18, 1998).

18   Du Bois, *The Negro*, 156. The exclamation point is Du Bois'.

19   Particularly in the relatively prosperous British colonies of Nigeria, the Gold Coast, and Uganda. These were also sites of considerable African production of written works that employed oral traditions about the past as precedent to defend the prerogatives of various political interests in the "native authorities" created under Indirect Rule. A recently studied example is Jacob U. Egharevba, *A Short History of Benin* (Benin, 1934, originally in Edo); see Uyilawa Usuanlele and Toyin Falola, "The Scholarship of Jacob Egharevba of Benin," *History in Africa* 21 (1994): 308–18.

Graduates of Britain's colonial schools in Africa found less opportunity to study African history in the United Kingdom. The principal academic degree relevant to Africa there was in anthropology, and its most prominent holder Jomo Kenyatta; see *Facing Mount Kenya: The Tribal Life of the Gikuyu* (London, 1938). No similar Africa-oriented history took shape in the educational systems in the colonies of France, where training was in geography and other "human sciences"; rev. edn. (London, 1956); M. Delafosse, *Haut-Sénégal-Niger* (Paris, 1912); R. Mauny, *Tableau géographique de l'ouest africain au moyen âge* (Dakar, 1961). Belgium and Portugal, which viewed their colonies as continuing under European control for many years into the future, focused resolutely on the Europeans' "civilizing mission."

20   Hansberry's African history derived directly from Du Bois' inspiration and inspired a number of young African students, including Kwame Nkrumah (future president of Ghana) and Nnamdi Azikiwe (nationalist leader in Nigeria); William Leo Hansberry, "W. E. B. DuBois' Influence on African History," *Freedomways* 5 (1965): 73–87; Joseph Harris, ed., *Pillars in Ethiopian History* (Washington, D.C., 1974), 18–22.

21   African historians now look back on this formative phase of historicized study of Africa's past as its "nationalist" era, since its neo-progressive themes not only demonstrated Africans' sophistication in governing themselves but also gave Africa's nascent "nations," often led by former students of history turned politicians, the deep, popular historical roots that the theory of nationalism prescribed.

22   A. H. M. Kirk-Greene, ed., *The Emergence of African History at British Universities* (Oxford, 1995); Roland Oliver, *In the Realms of Gold: Pioneering in African History* (Madison, Wis.,

1998); and for a revealing incident in 1947, John D. Hargreaves, "African History: The First University Examination," *History in Africa* 23 (1996): 467–65, with support from Aberdeen and Oxford examiners, in 1947. The founding generation of Africans earning British doctorates in history—Kenneth O. Dike, Saburi Biobaku, B. A. Ogot, Jacob Ajayi, Ado Boahen, and many others shortly thereafter—have not published memoirs that would reveal their experiences of those years or of their subsequent academic leadership in Africa. For the principal African-directed synthesis, see UNESCO *General History of Africa* (Los Angeles, 1981–93), 8 vols. Bogumil Jewsiewicki and David Newbury, eds., *African Historiographies: What History for Which Africa?* (Beverly Hills, Calif., 1986), took up the distinctions between Africans' histories and the developing international historiography of Africa.

23 For example, William Malcolm (Lord) Halley, *An African Survey of Problems Arising in Africa South of the Sahara* (London, 1938).

24 The substantive themes by which historians have interpreted Africans and the intellectual resources on which they drew are familiar enough to specialists, and the theoretical perspectives of African historiography would present few surprises to historians familiar with the conceptual trajectories of the field in other parts of the world. Arnold Temu and Bonaventure Swai, *Historians and Africanists: A Critique* (London, 1981), and Caroline Neale, *Writing "Independent" History: African Historiography, 1960–1980* (Westport, Conn., 1985), present contrasting general outlines. Several contributors, many of them African, test that structure against national and other "African" perspectives in Jewsiewicki and Newbury, *African Historiographies*. The dominant figure in the intellectual history of African studies is V. Y. Mudimbe; see *The Invention of Africa: Gnosis, Philosophy, and the Order of Knowledge* (Bloomington Ind., 1988), edited with Bogumil Jewsiewicki; *History Making in Africa* (Middletown, Conn., 1993); and *The Idea of Africa* (Bloomington, 1994).

25 And thus distinct from the "oral history;" or interviews drawing on living memory with which historians sometimes supplement inaccessible written evidence for recent periods.

26 Jan Vansina, *De la tradition orale: Essai de méthode historique* (Tervuren, 1961), trans, as *Oral Tradition: A Study in Historical Methodology* (Chicago, 1965).

27 For an early critique of practices attained, see David P. Henige, "The Problem of Feedback in Oral Tradition: Four Examples from the Fame Coastlands," *Journal of African History* 14 (1973): 223–35.

28 Sally Falk Moore, *Anthropology and Africa: Changing Perspectives on a Changing Scene* (Charlottesville, Va., 1994).

29 A prominent example from Bantu-speaking regions of Africa was T. O. Beidelman "Myth, Legend, and Oral History: A Kaguru Traditional Text," *Anthropos* 65 (1965): 74–97.

30 Luc de Heusch, *Le roi ivre: ou, L'origine de l'Etat; Mythes et rites bantous* (Paris, 1972), trans. by Roy Willis as *The Drunken King* (Bloomington, Ind., 1982). The historian's critique is found in Jan Vansina, "Is Elegance Proof? Structuralism and African History," *History in Africa* 10 (1983): 307–48.

31 "Mnemonic" rather than "oral," because the relevant focus is on how people preserved knowledge, by devising ways of remembering it, rather than the contrast in the form of transmission—"oral"—against written sources, thus retained as the implicit standard.

32 Jan Vansina, *Oral Tradition as History* (Madison, Wis., 1985). This work integrated Vansina's revisions of his own *Tradition orale* over two decades in an essentially new synthesis covering many aspects or oral tradition beyond the point accented here.

33 For an example of a strong statement of this neo-presentist case, see Elizabeth Tonkin, *Narrating Our Pasts: The Social Construction of Oral History* (New York, 1992).

34 For exemplary insight along these lines see Steven Feierman, *Peasant intellectuals: Anthropology and History in Tanzania* (Madison, Wis., 1990); compare Feierman's earlier presentation of related materials in *The Shambaa Kingdom: A History* (Madison, 1974), to sense the shift in emphasis away from structure toward historians and their intellectual strategies. Also Isabel Hofmeyr, *"We Spend Our Years as a Tale That Is Told": Oral Historical Narrative in a South African Chiefdom* [a Ndebele state in the Northern Transvaal] (Portsmouth, N.H., 1994). E. J. Alagoa, "An African Philosophy of History in the Oral Tradition," in Robert W. Harms, Joseph C. Miller, David S. Newbury, and Michele D.

Wagner, eds., *Paths toward the Past: African Historical Essays in Honor of Jan Vansina* (Atlanta, Ga., 1994), 15–25; Ralph A. Austen, ed., *In Search of Sunjata: The Mande Oral Epic as History, Literature, and Performance* (Bloomington, Ind., 1998).

35   The first volume of the *Journal of African History* anticipated most of these lines of subsequent inquiry: G. S. P. Freeman-Grenville, "East African Coin Finds and Their Historical Significance," 1 (1960): 31–43; Margaret Priestley and Ivor Wilks, "The Ashanti Kings in the Eighteenth Century: A Revised Chronology," 1 (1960): 83–96; Roger Summers, "The Southern Rhodesian Iron Age," 1 (1960): 1–13, concluding with an "Appendix on Chronology"; and the first of a long series of "Radiocarbon Dates for Sub-Saharan Africa—I," 2 (1960): 137–39.

36   None convertible to precise chronology, though sometimes reliable with regard to sequence; *The Chronology of Oral Tradition* was, as David P. Henige wondered rhetorically, a *Quest for a Chimera?* (New York, 1974). For a sequence broadly confirmed by dated documents back to the early seventeenth century, see Joseph C. Miller, "Kings, Lists, and History in Kasanje;" *History in Africa* 6 (1979): 51–96. For the classic effort to correlate the king lists of several neighboring, interacting—and hence presumably mutually verifying—dynasties, see the summary by David W. Cohen, "A Survey of Interlacustrine Chronology," *Journal of African History* 11 (1970): 177–201; response by David P. Henige, "Reflections on Early Interlacustrine Chronology: An Essay in Source Criticism," *Journal of African History* 15 (1974): 27–46. Recent extensions of discussion in this style include David Newbury, "Trick Cyclists? Recontextualizing Rwandan Dynastic Chronology," *History in Africa* 21 (1994): 191–217.

37   For example, Tamara Giles-Vernick, *Vines of the Past: Environmental Histories of the Sangho River Basin in Equatorial Africa* (forthcoming).

38   Derek Nurse "The Contributions of Linguistics to the Study of History in Africa," *Journal of African History* 38 (1997): 359–91, figure given on p. 362. Allowing fur the subtleties of distinguishing languages from dialects, a figure in the range of 1,500 represents a surprising degree of consensus; compare Paul Newman, "Language Families: Overview," in *Encyclopedia of Africa South of the Sahara*, John Middleton, ed., 4 vols. (New York, 1997), 2: 501; Christopher Ehret, "African Languages: A Historical Survey," in *Encyclopedia of Precolonial Africa*, Joseph O. Vogel, ed. (Walnut Creek, Calif., 1997), 159.

39   The classic is Joseph H. Greenberg, *The Languages of Africa* (The Hague, 1963).

40   For a recent, comprehensive introduction to historical linguistics in Africa, written for historians, see Nurse "Contributions of Linguistics," 360.

41   Jan Vansine, "New Linguistic Evidence and 'The Bantu Expansion,'" *Journal of African History* 36 (1995): 173–95.

42   Jan Vansina, *Paths in the Rainforests: Toward a History of Political Tradition in Equatorial Africa* (Madison, Wis., 1990), is a tour-de-force application of this technique to 4,000 years of the past in a vast region all but inaccessible through any other source. Christopher Ehret and several former students at UCLA are now consolidating two decades of working from similarly humanistic and historical premises in other parts of Africa; see David Lee Schoenbrun, *A Green Place, a Good Place: Agrarian Change, Gender, and Social Identity in the Great Lakes Region to the 15th Century* (Portsmouth, N.H., 1998). Most generally and suggestively, Christopher Ehret, *An African Classical Age: Eastern and Southern Africa in World History, 100 B.C. to A.D. 400* (Charlottesville, Va., 1998); *The Civilizations of Tropical Africa: A History* (forthcoming).

43   So-called "radiocarbon or ^{14}C, dating," with the laboratory "dates" it produced, was recorded faithfully in the *Journal of African History* for more than three decades. Other chemical and nuclear traces were put to similar use, though mostly at time-depths before human intentionality, and therefore historical methods, become central to explaining change.

44   See the critique of older styles of archaeology in Jan Vansina, "Historians, Are Archeologists Your Siblings?" *History in Africa* 22 (1995): 369–408.

45   Duncan E. Miller and Nikolaas J. van der Merwe, "Early Metal Working in Sub-Saharan Africa: A Review of Recent Research," *Journal of African History* 35 (1994): 1–36. The most adventurous integration of archaeology with ethnography, linguistics, and other disciplines

toward a humanistic history is that of Peter R. Schmidt, most recently *Iron Technology in East Africa: Symbolism, Science, and Archaeology* (Bloomington, Ind., 1997); also, but less historically, Eugenic W. Herbert, *Iron, Gender and Power: Rituals of Transformation in African Societies* (Bloomington, 1993). And for iron workers rather than iron working (the title notwithstanding), see Colleen E. Kriger, *Pride of Men: Ironworking in 19th-Century West Central Africa* (Portsmouth, N.H., 1998).

46   In the modern country taking its name from its leading national monument. See Peter Garlake, *The Kingdoms of Africa*, rev. edn. (New York, 1990); and Thomas N. Huffman, *Snakes and Crocodiles: Power and Symbolism in Ancient Zimbabwe* (Johannesburg, 1996). A recent overview of the debates that swirled early in this century over whether Africans might have built these striking stone constructions is Henrika Kuklick, "Contested Monuments: The Politics of Archaeology in Southern Africa" in George W. Stocking, Jr., *Colonial Situations: Essays on the Contextualization of Ethnographic Knowledge* (Madison, Wis., 1991), 135–69. Graham Connah, *African Civilization: Precolonial Cities and States in Tropical Africa: An Archaeological Perspective* (New York 1987), extends this classical analysis of "civilizations" throughout sub-Saharan Africa in thoughtful, enlightened tones.

47   Until Derek Nurse and Thomas T. Spear, *The Swahili: Reconstructing the History and Language of an African Society, 800–1500* (Philadelphia, 1985).

48   Recent examples along the Indian Ocean coast are Mark Horton, *Shanga: The Archaeology of a Muslim Trading Community on the Coast of East Africa* (Nairobi, 1996); and John Sutton, "The African Lords of the Intercontinental Gold Trade before the Black Death: Al-Hasan bin Schuman of Kilwa and Mansa Musa of Mali," *Antiquaries Journal* 77 (1997): 221–42. The title of the latter conveys Sutton's humanizing end historicizing strategy, in this case moving beyond the ruins to the contexts in which the original structures were built, and to the men who built them. A conference on "The Growth of Farming Communities in Africa from the Equator Southwards," Cambridge University, 1994, marked the shift in archaeologists' attention to priorities of rural Africans; see (partial) proceedings published in *Azania* 29–30 (1994–95).

49   For an early, accessible statement of this approach, see Susan Keech and Roderick J. McIntosh, Finding West Africa's Oldest City," *National Geographic* 162 (September 1982): 396–418; for an accessible short survey, see "Cities of the Plain," in Oliver, *African Experience*, 90–101. The leading interpreters are Susan K. McIntosh and Roderick J. McIntosh, "The Early City in West Africa: Towards an Understanding;" *African Archaeological Review* 2 (1984): 73–98; and "Cities without Citadels: Understanding Urban Origins along the Middle Niger," in Thurstan Shaw, Paul Sinclair, B. Andah, and A. Okpoko, eds., *The Archaeology of Africa: Food, Metals and Towns* (London, 1993), 622–41.

50   A single example is abandonment of the modern, European assumption that dense settlements, particularly political capitals, need be permanent; David Conrad, "A Town Called Dakajalan: The Sunjata Tradition and the Question of Ancient Mali's Capital," *Journal of African History* 35 (1994): 355–77.

51   Historians' use of linguistic evidence in terms of holistic languages, classified in single-dimensioned arrays of standardized, and hence inherently ahistorical, vocabulary, further selected for its assumed stability, created no cognitive dissonance against this background.

52   Led by anthropologists; Aidan Southall, "The Illusion of Tribe," *Journal of African and Asian Studies* 5 (1970): 28–50.

53   For the limited kinds of change conceivable within this paradigm—homeostatic cyclical deviations followed by self-regulating restoration of equilibrium conditions, see Max Gluckman, "Some Processes of Social Change, illustrated with Zululand Data," *African Studies* 1 (1942): 243–60. African ethnicity begs specific comment on uses of the concept in American and African-American history, which is only beginning to historicize the concept; beyond Michael A. Gomez, *Exchanging Our Country Marks: The Transformation of African Identities in the Colonial and Antebellum South* (Chapel Hill, N.C., 1998), which does so more thoroughly for the Americas than for Africa, see Robin Law, "Ethnicity and the Slave Trade: 'Lucumi' and 'Nago' as Ethnonyms in West Africa," *History in Africa*, 24 (1997): 205–19. Forthcoming work in this and other regions will further demonstrate the complex and dynamic sources of collective identities attributed to, and sometimes claimed by, Africans in the slaving era.

54 Jan Vansina, *The Tio Kingdom of the Middle Congo, 1880–1892* (London, 1973), applied ethnographic method to historical sources from a single decade, the 1880s, to one African region in a "historical ethnography" that emphasized the historicity of the moment thus describable. Also see Vansina's *Children of Woot: A History of the Kuba Peoples* (Madison, Wis., 1978). More recently, Sharon E. Hutchinson, *Nuer Dilemmas: Coping with Money, War, and the State* (Berkeley, Calif., 1996), won the 1997 Amaury Talbot prize of the Royal Anthropological Institute of Great Britain and Ireland for setting E. E. Evans-Pritchard's classic Nuer ethnography in the context of the Sudan in the 1930s.

55 That ethnography and anthropology in Africa have also become more historical since the 1950s forms a major theme of Moore, *Anthropology and Africa*.

56 E. J. Hobsbawm and T. O. Ranger, eds., *The Invention of Tradition* (New York, 1983). Subsequently, Martin Chanock, *Law, Custom, and Social Order: The Colonial Experience in Malawi and Zambia* (New York, 1985); Feierman, *Peasant Intellectuals*; and many recent works, notably Jonathan Glassman, *Feasts and Riot Revelry, Rebellion, and Popular Consciousness on the Swahili Coast, 1856–1888* (Portsmouth, N.H., 1995). Historians have historicized continuity as uses that Africans make of remembered experience and inherited wisdom in trying to take advantage of their existential experience; see Vansina, *Paths in the Rainforests*.

57 For example, Jean and John Comaroff, eds., *Modernity and Its Malcontents: Ritual and Power in Postcolonial Africa* (Chicago, 1993); Rosalind Shaw, "The Production of Witchcraft/ Witchcraft as Production: Memory, Modernity, and the Slave Trade in Sierra Leone;" *American Ethnologist* 24 (1997): 856–67; Ralph Austen, "The Slave Trade as History and Memory: Mutual Confrontations of Slaving Voyage Documents and African/African-American Traditions" (unpublished paper, conference on "Transatlantic Slaving and the African Diaspora;" Omohundro Institute of Early American History and Culture, Williamsburg, Virginia, September 11–13, 1998); Elizabeth Isichei, *The Moral Imagination in Africa: A History and Ethnography; Or Explorations in the History of Popular Sensibility* (forthcoming). For a dramatic historical interpretation of a so-called "millenarian" anti-witchcraft movement in the Cape colony, see Jeffrey B, Peires, *The Dead Will Arise: Nongqawuse and the Great Xbosa Cattle-Killing Movement of 1856–7* (Bloomington, Ind., 1989). This understanding of witchcraft extends to the greed and accumulation of contemporary African politics: Peter Geschiere, *The Modernity of Witchcraft: Politics and the Occult in Postcolonial Africa* (Charlottesville, Va., 1997). Also see Luise White, "Vampire Priests of Central Africa: African Debates about Labor and Religion in Colonial Northern Rhodesia," *Comparative Studies in Society and History* 35 (1993): 744–70; or Tsetse Visions: Narratives of Blood and Bugs in Colonial Northern Rhodesia, 1931–9," *Journal of African History* 36 (1995): 219–45, among several other studies, for the historical sense of other African supernatural idioms.

58 And often as much through missionary and other European interests as by African ones. Leroy Vail, ed., *The Creation of Tribalism in Southern Africa* (London, 1989). For recent examples, see Thomas T. Spear and Richard Walter, eds., *Being Maasai: Ethnicity and Identity in East Africa* (London, 1993); Justin Willis, *Mombasa, the Swahili, and the Making of the Mijikenda* (Oxford, 1993).

59 Some recent names do in fact appear in the earliest European reports from the African coast: Paul Hair, "Ethnolinguistic Continuity on the Guinea Coast," *Journal of African History* 8 (1967): 247–68, but the contribution of Europeans to such apparently stable denomination has not been assessed. For the constantly updated contemporaneity of "tradition," see Vansina, *Paths in the Rainforests*.

60 Ed Wilmsen and James Denbow, "Paradigmatic History of San-Speaking Peoples and Current Attempts at Revision," *Current Anthropology* 31 (1990): 489–525; Richard B. Lee and Mathias Guenther, "Problems in Kalahari Historical Ethnography and the Tolerance of Error," *History in Africa* 20 (1993): 185–235. Also see Peter S. Garlake, *The Hunter's Vision: The Prehistoric Art of Zimbabwe* (London, 1995).

61 On the "pygmies": Vansina's emphasis on "autochthones" in *Paths in the Rainforests*, "New Linguistic Evidence," and elsewhere; most recently, Kairn A. Klieman. "Hunters and Farmers of the Western Equatorial Rainforest: Society and Economy from c. 3000 B.C. to 1880 A.D." (Ph.D. dissertation, University of California, Los Angeles, 1997).

62 The tone in African history of the 1960s that Wyatt MacGaffey once, acutely, character-
    ized as "the decathlon of social science"; in "African History, Anthropology, and the
    Rationality of Natives," *History in Africa* 5 (1978): 103.

63 Without slighting the steady, disciplined leadership of others rigorously trained in conven-
    tional fields of history.

64 With some justification, given styles of European history not then as profoundly engaged
    as they have since become with issues relevant to Africa or African history.

65 The journal *History in Africa* ("a journal of method" edited by David Henige at the University
    of Wisconsin and published by the African Studies Association) formalized this agenda in
    1974; it remains the starting point for systematic critical study of written as well as many
    other types of sources.

66 For the Muslim intellectual background of the Arabic-language documentation, see
    J. F. P. Hopkins and Nehemiah Levtzion, eds., *Corpus of Early Arabic Sources for West African
    History* (New York, 1981). John O. Hunwick's many initiatives have been critical to the
    historical contextualization of Arabic texts; see his newsletters and journals, including
    Sudanic Africa and Saharan Studies Newsletter, as well as numerous publications. And, recently,
    from the African context: Ralph A. Austen and Jan Jansen, "History, Oral Transmission
    and Structure in Ibn Khaldun's Chronology of Mali Rulers," *History in Africa* 23 (1996):
    17–28. Even this extensive list does not begin to mention the many project started in
    recent years to develop critical standards for written materials from Africa. David Robinson
    and several collaborators have edited publications of African materials of several sorts and
    are pursuing these efforts under the sponsorship of a West Africa Research Association.
    Critical editions form a central element in the strategy of the large "Nigerian Hinterland
    Project" directed by Paul E. Lovejoy. Ethiopian writings offer the same critical opportu-
    nity, which has been led in the United States by Harold G. Marcus as editor of *Northeast
    African Studies*; for a recent summary with emphasis on Ethiopian scholarship, see Donald
    Crummey, "Society, State and Nationality in the Recent Historiography of Ethiopia," *Journal
    of African History* 31 (1990): 103–19.

67 Where there must exist more productive parallels for specialists in both fields than either
    has yet exploited. An initial assertion of the point underlies John K. Thornton, *Africa and
    Africans in the Making of the Atlantic World, 1400–1800*, 2d edn., expanded (New York, 1998).

68 A cause sustained by Robin Law, Paul Hair, and others in *History in Africa*, and notably
    furthered by Adam Jones, *Raw, Medium, Well Done: A Critical Review of Editorial and Quasi-
    Editorial Work on Pre-1885 European Sources for Sub-Saharan Africa, 1960–1986* (Madison,
    Wis., 1987), and subsequent publications.

69 A key strategy of the enormously influential work on missionary engagement with southern
    African peoples in Jean and John L. Comaroff, *Of Revelation and Revolution*: Vol. 1, *Christian-
    ity, Colonialism, and Consciousness in South Africa* (Chicago, 1991): *Ethnography and the
    Historical Imagination* (Boulder, Colo., 1992); *Of Revelation and Revolution*: Vol, 2, *The
    Dialectics of Modernity on a South African Frontier* (Chicago, 1997).

70 For example, William H. McNeill, *The Rise of the Nest: A History of the Human Community*
    (Chicago, 1963).

71 A premise congruent with the unproductive interaction among the "tribal" groups recog-
    nized, which were not only static but also isolating and interacted with outsiders only as
    enemies, for example the "warring tribes" in international media coverage of Africa. The
    current premise that Africans constructed communal identities around interactive comple-
    mentarities (and also used them on occasion for competitive, hostile purposes) received
    early effective statements in John Iliffe, *A Modern History of Tanganyika* (Cambridge, 1979);
    and Richard Waller, "Ecology, Migration and Expansion in East Africa," *African Affairs* 84
    (1985): 347–70.

72 Immanuel Wallerstein theorizes only the European side of structured, unequal exchange
    among the elements of *The Modern World-System*, 3 vols. (New York, 1974, 1980, 1989)
    (through the 1840s), and thus excludes Africa for much of its history as beyond its
    "peripheries." Walter Rodney, *How Europe Underdeveloped Africa* (London, 1972; rev. edn.,
    Washington. D.C., 1982), attempted to reconcile external with internal differentiation in
    terms of political economy; Wolf, *Europe and the People without History*, extends this style
    of integration.

73 Robin Horton, "Stateless Societies in the History of West Africa," in J. F. A. Ajayi and Michael Crowder, eds., *History of West Africa*, 2d edn., 2 vols. (New York, 1976), 1: 72–113.

74 For example Claude Meillassoux, *Femmes, greniers et capitaux* (Paris 1975), and in English, *Maidens, Meal and Money: Capitalism and the Domestic Economy* (New York, 1981).

75 In a mature, fully theorized extension, Claude Meillassoux, *Anthropologie de l'esclavage: Le ventre de fer et d'argent* (Paris, 1986), trans. as *The Anthropology of Slavery: The Womb of Iron and Gold*, Alide Dasnois, trans. (Chicago, 1991). And extended again to issues of gender: Claire C. Robertson and Martin A. Klein, eds., *Women and Slavery in Africa* (Madison, Wis., 1983).

76 John Iliffe, *The African Poor: A History* (New York, 1987).

77 For example, the "big men" featured in Vansina's *Paths in the Rainforests.*

78 And in sometimes-heated opposition to "underdevelopment" theories that treated distinctions between the capitalist world and (implicitly noncapitalist) Africa in neo-Marxist language; the classic formulation is Rodney, *How Europe Underdeveloped Africa.*

79 Gender has not featured prominently in this discussion, since it has remained difficult to develop from the sources for earlier periods; one suspects that greater potential lies in linguistic reconstruction than has yet been exploited. For now, see Iris Berger " 'Beasts of Burden' Revisited: Interpretations of Women and Gender in Southern African Societies," in Harms, *et al.*, eds., *Paths toward the Past*, 123–41; Edna G. Bay, *Wives of the Leopard: Gender, Politics, and Culture in the Kingdom of Dahomey* (Charlottesville, Va., 1998); Herbert, *Iron, Gender, and Power.* Revealingly, but for a relatively recent period, see Helen Bradford, "Women, Gender and Colonialism: Rethinking the History of the British Cape Colony and Its Frontier Zone, ca. 1806–1870," *Journal of African History* 37 (1996): 351–70. For now-aging surveys on work on recent periods, and often from perspectives other than historical, see Claire C. Robertson. "Developing Economic Awareness: Changing Perspectives in Studies of African Women, 1976–1935," *Feminist Studies* 13 (1987): 96–135; Nancy Rose Hunt, "Placing African Women's History and Locating Gender," *Social History* 14 (1989): 359–79.

80 Among many other qualities illustrative of difference but marginal to advancing the central argument on historical epistemology.

81 I borrow this felicitous phrase from Austen, "Slave Trade as History and Memory."

82 For a promising exception, see Sutton, "African Lords of the Intercontinental Gold Trade:"

83 Two of the best documented people were women who attracted the attention of missionary writers in the Portuguese Catholic-influenced regions of Kongo and Angola. For the famous early seventeenth-century "Queen Nzinga," see Joseph C. Miller, "Nzinga of Matamba in a New Perspective," *Journal of African History* 16 (1975): 201–16; and John K. Thornton, "Legitimacy and Political Power: Queen Njinga, 1624–1653," *Journal of African History* 32 (1991): 25–40. For a Kongo prophetess at the turn of the eighteenth century, see Thornton, *The Kongolese Saint Anthony: Dona Beatriz Kimpa Vita and the Antonian Movement 1684–1706* (New York, 1998). Also for political women in eighteenth and nineteenth-century Dahomey, see Bay, *Wives of the Leopard.* The intricate interplay between a prominent, even dominant, personality, African constructions of it, and multiple European images deriving from those is elegantly evoked in Carolyn Hamilton, *Terrific Majesty: The Powers of Shaka Zulu and the Limits of Historical Invention* (Cambridge, Mass., 1998).

84 The reference here is to literacy as cognitive technique, not as a state of mind. Intensely diverse perspectives on the degree to which mnemonic and literate thinking reflected, or created, distinct mental styles, narrative genres, and much else have, as might be expected, emerged from the multiple disciplines that have sensed its importance, from the range of historical contexts where these distinctions have been applied around the world, and from confusion with various modern reformulations of the old distinction between "civilized" and "savage" minds. Jack Goody and Ian Watt initially combined the skills of a classicist with those of an anthropologist to emphasize literacy as mental technology in "The Consequences of Literacy," *Comparative Studies in Society and History* 5 (1962–63): 304–45; for a recent, clear summary of the thinking deriving from this seminal essay and its implications for African historiography, see Hofmeyr, *"We Spend Our Years as a Tale That Is Told,"* intro.

85   In Africa, structuralist anthropologists (or structural historians of several sorts) drew implicit support for their predilections toward static institutions from this African epistemology of similarly transformative, revolutionary change. A modern notion of historical change of this contrastive sort underlies the revolutionary transformations that are logically necessary in theoretical Marxism to move from one typologically contrasted "mode of production" to another, and more abstractly still in dialectical logic.

86   A cliché since the publication of Placide Tempels, *Bantu Philosophy* (Paris, 1952; orig. *Bantoe-filosofie, oorspronkelijke tekst* [Antwerp, 1946]), but recently rendered more historically in Emmanuel Akyeampong and Pashington Obeng, "Spirituality, Gender and Power in Asante History," *International Journal of African Historical Studies* 19 (1995): 481–508.

87   An insight developed, for example, in Randall M. Packard, *Chiefship and Cosmology: An Historical Study of Political Competition* (Bloomington, Ind., 1981); more recently, Herbert, *Iron, Gender, and Power.*

88   Although this commonsense observation should not be overstated: Jan Vansina, "The Doom of Early African History?" *History in Africa* 24 (1997): 337–43.

89   Examples that draw revealingly on historical context include Elias C. Mandala, *Work and Control in a Peasant Economy: A History of the Lower Tchiri Volley in Malawi, 1859–1960* (Madison, Wis., 1990); and B. Marie Perinbam, *Family Identity and the State in the Bamako Kafu, c. 1800–c. 1900* (Boulder, Colo., 1997).

90   J. F. Ade Ajayi put historical brackets around "Colonialism: An Episode in African History" (in Peter Duignan and Louis H. Gann, *Colonialism in Africa* [Cambridge, 1969], 497–509) to emphasize European rule as a superficial interlude in longer-term, deep-rooted African processes.

91   Most widely noted: Robert D. Kaplan, "The Coming Anarchy," *Atlantic Monthly* (February 1994): 44–76.

92   Also the major axis of change in Gomez, *Exchanging Our Country Marks* and Colin Palmer, *Passageways: An Interpretive History of Black America*: Vol. 1, 1619–1863 (Fort Worth, Tex., 1998).

93   Though not only in Africa, but also in the several other thriving regional fields outside Europe and North America: Steve J. Stern, "Africa, Latin America, and the Splintering of Historical Knowledge: From Fragmentation to Reverberation;" in Frederick Cooper, Allen F. Isaacman, Florencia E. Mallon, William Roseberry, and Steve J. Stern, *Confronting Historical Paradigms: Peasants, Labor, and the Capitalist World System in Africa and Latin America* (Madison, Wis., 1993), 3–20.

94   With grateful acknowledgment to Jan Vansina, who emphasized this aspect of history's logic in an elegant lecture, "The Unity of History" (unpublished, 1998), and an unpublished paper, "Historical Traditions Today" (also 1998), which helped focus the ruminations that preceded the present essay.

95   Closer to Hayden White, *Metahistory: The Historical Imagination in Nineteenth-Century Europe* (Baltimore, Md., 1973), as characterized by J. D. Y. Peel, "Two Pastors and Their *Histories*: Samuel Johnson and C. C. Reindorf," in Jenkins, *Recovery of the West African Past*, 69: "a historian's intention, formed from his experiences and his existing notions of what an account of the past might look like and be useful for, must always be prior to [my emphasis] his use of the evidence, even though it may be modified by working on it," than to Ranke's ordering of the balance, as quoted in Novick, *That Noble Dream*, 27–28: "*After* [my emphasis] the labor of criticism, intuition is required."

96   For a convenient collection of these perspectives (among others), see the internationally authored and edited UNESCO *General History of Africa*. Volumes 3 and 4 contain some of the few accessible syntheses from Islamic perspectives, vital for many parts of Africa.

97   As emphasized with a rich array of examples from recent African history and anthropology in Steven Feierman, "African Histories and the Dissolution of World History;" in Robert H. Bates, V. Y. Mudimbe, and Jean O'Barr, eds., *Africa and the Disciplines. The Contributions of Research in Africa to the Social Sciences and the Humanities* (Chicago, 1993), 167–212. In Feierman's phrase (p. 175), "tension between the new African evidence, showing autonomous processes, and the older vision of world history in which progress radiated from a few historical civilizations" also "changed our understanding of general history, and

of Europe's place, in the world in profound ways" (p. 182). For a rich contemplation of the challenges of decentering "World History in a Global Age," see Michael Geyer and Charles Bright under this title in the centennial volume of the *AHR* 100 (October 1995): 1034–60.

98   Whether centered on the northern Atlantic: Wallerstein, *Modern World-System*. Or the Indian Ocean: K. N. Chaudhuri, *Trade and Civilisation in the Indian Ocean: An Economic History from the Rise of Islam to 1750* (New York, 1985). Or southwestern Asia: Janet L. Abu-Lughod, *Before European Hegemony: The World System, A.D. 1250–1350* (New York, 1989).

99   A contemplation of the historical dynamics of "frontier" hypotheses; for theorization see Igor Kopytoff, ed., *The African Frontier: The Reproduction of Traditional African Societies* (Bloomington, Ind., 1987). The stimulating contacts among world civilizations across McNeill's "ecumene" in *The Rise of the West* utilize the underlying concept of confronted differences as energizing historical change but concentrate on effects at their centers rather than focusing on the process at the fringes. All, of course, realize the underlying Hegelian concept of dialectic in geographical metaphors.

100   And vice versa: as Feierman puts the complementing process, "The need for historians to hear African voices originates with the same impulse as the need to hear the voices that had been silent within European history"; "African Histories and the Dissolution of World History," 182.

101   The valuable sort of context that quantitative data set, and the questions they thereby raise; statistics cited by Ellis, Richardson, and Behrendt in various essays based on the Du Bois Institute database of slaving voyages.

102   As "Atlantic" historians are now exploring. From North America, Ira Berlin, "From Creole to African: Atlantic Creoles and the Origins of African-American Society in Mainland North America," *William and Mary Quarterly*, 3d ser., 53 (1996): 251–88; and *Many Thousand Gone: The First Two Centuries of Slavery in North America* (New York, 1998). From the African side, Thornton, *Africa and Africans in the Making of the Atlantic World*. Blending the two: Gomez, *Exchanging Our Country Marks*.

103   Bernard Bailyn, "The Idea of Atlantic History," *Itinerario* 20 (1996): 19–44. I anticipate the theme of the millennial program of the Organization of American Historians (to be offered in the year 2000): "The U.S. and the Wider World."

104   In its modern context, in a field familiar to me, see Robin Blackburn, *The Making of New World Slavery: From the Baroque to the Modern, 1492–1800* (London, 1997). For the year 2000, the theme of the conference of the American Society for Eighteenth-Century Studies is "The Eighteenth Century Seen around the World"; Harvard University's Program for the Study of German and Europe has announced a workshop (1999) on "Western Europe in an Age of Globalization."

105   For example, Curtin, "Depth, Span, and Relevance"; Frederic Wakeman, Jr., "Voyages," *AHR* 98 (February 1993): 1–17.

106   One of the AHA's most active affiliates, the World History Association, with its *Journal of World History*.

Chapter 35

Robin Law and Kristin Mann

WEST AFRICA IN THE ATLANTIC COMMUNITY
The case of the Slave Coast

THE SECTION OF THE WEST AFRICAN COAST known to Europeans as the "Slave Coast" was, as the name implies, a major source for the transatlantic slave trade between the seventeenth and nineteenth centuries. The two principal ports of embarkation for slaves in the region were Ouidah and Lagos.[1] The history of Slave Coast ports such as Ouidah and Lagos cannot be understood or adequately represented in isolation, since they were involved in wider regional and transatlantic networks. Within Africa, the operation of the slave trade linked the coastal ports not only to the countries in the interior that supplied slaves to the coast but also to one another, especially through the coastal lagoon system, along which slaves were commonly moved from port to port prior to embarkation.[2] Across the Atlantic, the commercial links established by the slave trade among ports in West Africa, America, and Europe are well known, but the trade also generated transatlantic social and cultural connections whose importance has been commonly underestimated. The scale and intensity of these bonds were such that the coastal communities of the Slave Coast, or at least their commercial and ruling elites, may be considered as participating in what can reasonably be termed an "Atlantic community." The degree of involvement in this wider community varied from case to case and from period to period. The wider Atlantic community itself was also subject to transformation, with the importance of links specifically to Brazil increasing over time.

The basis for this interpretation is primarily empirical, that is, it derives from the specific character of the evidence relating to the Slave Coast, which in turn reflects the exceptional scale of that region's integration into the Atlantic commercial system, and especially the intensity of its links with Brazil. In stressing the latter, we do not claim absolute originality but acknowledge in particular the late Pierre Verger's pioneering work on Afro-Brazilian interconnections.[3]

Beyond that, however, this article engages a growing body of literature concerned with the formation of Atlantic history and culture and, especially, the role of Africans and African Americans within it. Bernard Bailyn has recently drawn attention to the current popularity of the idea of "Atlantic history." He documents a growing trend toward studying the Atlantic world as a historical unit, as historians of Europe and of North and South America have broadened their focus to include "the entire Atlantic basin, not simply descriptively but conceptually." But, although Bailyn brings Africa into the discussion briefly through a treatment of the Atlantic slave trade, his references are primarily to works that equate Atlantic history with European civilization. In his conception, Africa has played a very limited role in shaping the history and culture of the Atlantic basin.[4]

In another recent contribution to this debate, Paul Gilroy has propounded the idea of a "black Atlantic" identity, which also treats the Atlantic as "one single, complex unit of analysis," but one in which blacks are "perceived as agents" equally with whites.[5] He conceives the Atlantic as "continually crisscrossed by the movements of black people—not only as commodities but engaged in various struggles towards emancipation, autonomy, and citizenship." Formally, our approach has similarities to Gilroy's, but the focus and content of our analysis are significantly different. These differences are partly chronological and geographical: whereas Gilroy deals with the period from the mid-nineteenth century onward and with the Anglophone world, we are concerned with the earlier period of the slave trade and, given the specific region of Africa on which we focus, with links to the Lusophone world. More critical, Gilroy approaches the Atlantic community from the perspective of the North Atlantic diaspora (and, more especially, of its intellectuals), in which Africa figures as an object of retrospective rediscovery, rather than as an active agent our starting point is in Africa itself, and our theme is the development and maintenance of continuous commercial, social, and cultural links across the Atlantic. Moreover, we conceive of the Atlantic community as transracial, rather than specifically "black."

More directly relevant to our own concerns is a recent article in this journal by Ira Berlin on the early stages of the creation of African-American societies in mainland North America that stresses the role played by "Atlantic Creoles," Africans who had acquired European languages and culture on the coast of West Africa and who crossed the Atlantic as freemen (in the service of European traders, for education, or as official emissaries of African rulers) as well as slaves. Berlin's analysis arguably exaggerates both the extent of cultural "creolization" in West African coastal communities in early times and the numerical significance of such "Creoles" among exported slaves. Even though the argument may be empirically problematic for the seventeenth century, the conceptual framework that Berlin develops, of a cosmopolitan culture linking seaports on all sides of the Atlantic littoral, can be fruitfully applied to later periods.[6]

Our perspective has been influenced, however, not only by modern scholarship but also by our understanding of the perceptions of history current among members of West African coastal communities themselves. A recently published history of the da Silva family of Bénin serves as an example. The earliest member of this family who can be unproblematically documented is Francisco Rodrigues da Silva (d. 1911), a trader at Ouidah in the 1870s, though he subsequently moved his residence east along the coast to Porto-Novo.[7] The family *History* as published is said to be based on a manuscript written circa 1940 by Francisco's son Deusdado da Silva (d. 1956)— then employed as a schoolteacher in the French colony of Senegal—that was intended to vindicate his claim to Portuguese nationality and thus (in the context of the times) to exemption from the disadvantageous status of "French subject." The work traces the family's ancestry to one Joaquim Rodrigues da Silva, who is credited with founding the Portuguese factory at Jakin, east of Ouidah, in the seventeenth century. Joaquim's son, José Rodrigues da Silva, served in the Portuguese factories

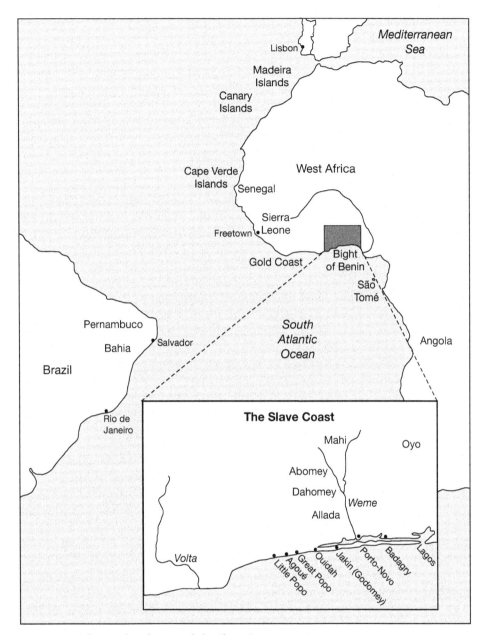

Map 35.1   The South Atlantic and the Slave Coast

at Jalcin and Ouidah in the 1730s and 1740s but subsequently set up as an independent trader. Although he returned to Portugal, where he died in 1791, he had previously married an African woman. The African da Silva family descends from this union. His son George da Silva (1758–1820) was educated at Bahia in Brazil, and George's son Firmiano da Silva (1815–1860) was seemingly born in Bahia, but both returned to live and die in Ovidah. Finniano's son Francisco Rodrigues da Silva (born at Ouidah 1844), the merchant of the 1870s, was educated successively in Brazil and Portugal—and, subsequently, in the 1860s, in the new British colony of Lagos, where he learned English. There are grounds for skepticism about this family history. None of the family's early generations is independently corroborated, except for José da Silva, who served in the Portuguese factories at Jakin and Ouidah in the eighteenth century, and the claiming of this man as an ancestor may be speculative, based on no more than finding the appropriate surname in Portuguese records.[8] But if the da Silva family history contains an element of literary contrivance, it is nevertheless significant that such a family chose to construct a specifically Atlantic identity. Although the da Silvas' transatlantic connections may have been in part invented, they in another sense accurately represent the historical milieu to which the family had belonged in the nineteenth century.

In a recent engagement with scholars seeking ways to understand Africa's contribution to the Atlantic world, Paul E. Lovejoy has developed a concept of the diaspora that begins in Africa during the era of the Atlantic slave trade and moves outward, tracing influences that have been situated in specific historical and cultural contexts from there to the Americas. He cites as an example the insurrection of Muslim slaves in Bahia in 1835, which Lovejoy links to the *jihad* (holy war) movement earlier in the nineteenth century in the hinterland of the Slave Coast from which these slaves had come.[9] By contrast, scholars have often conceptualized links between Brazil and West Africa in terms of a Brazilian diaspora to West Africa, as part of the "influence of Brazil on Africa," which is seen as a counterpoint to but distinct from the "influence of Africa on Brazil."[10] These two perspectives, however, represent different aspects of a single historical process that, to a considerable degree, involved the same persons. Thus, the links and reciprocal cultural influences between Brazil and Africa are better understood through the concept of an "Atlantic community": that is, through the study of the historical development of a community of people with shared relationships and cultural practices that bridged the Atlantic.

Theorizing about the appropriate conceptual framework for understanding both the incorporation of enslaved Africans into societies of the Americas and the historical relationship between Africa and its descendants abroad has proceeded to a point where much can be gained by submitting the questions under debate to regionally and historically specific investigation. We now know enough about the history of the parts of Africa involved in the slave trade, about the organization of the trade itself, and about the history of the societies in the Americas to which slaves were taken to make this sort of investigation possible. The goal of this article is to make a preliminary contribution to this endeavor by documenting the rise and transformation of a population on the Slave Coast during the era of the slave trade whose activities, interests, and outlook spanned the Atlantic.

The communities of the Slave Coast became part of a wider Atlantic world through their participation in the slave trade. David Eltis, David Richardson, and Stephen Behrendt have estimated that more than 1,900,000 slaves were shipped from the Bight of Benin (roughly coextensive with the Slave Coast) between 1662 and 1863. They suggest that between 1687 and 1811 departures from the Bight of Benin exceeded 10,000 slaves per year and that they probably continued at that level until 1830.[11]

Traders from a number of nations participated in the slave trade on the Slave Coast and shipped exports primarily to their own countries' settlements in the

Americas, but Portuguese, based mainly in Brazil, and native-born Brazilians dominated it. Eltis, Richardson, and Behrendt have estimated that six of every ten slaves that landed in the New World from the Bight of Benin between 1662 and 1863 went to Bahia, whereas two went to the French Americas—mainly Saint Domingue —and one went to the British Caribbean. Shifts occurred in the proportions of slaves sent to different destinations, with the English Americas taking the majority of slaves in the late seventeenth century, Bahia and the French Caribbean predominating until 1791, and Bahia alone absorbing 75 percent of the slaves between 1791 and 1830. In the final three decades of the trade, Spanish Cuba became a major market.

For most of the history of the trade, Ouidah was the principal shipper of slaves on the Slave Coast, but in the 1830s and 1840s Lagos replaced it as the dominant port. Other ports in the region—Little Popo (Aneho), Agoué and Great Popo to the west of Ouidah, and Jakin (Godomey), Porto-Novo, and Badagry, between Ouidah and Lagos—were of minor or intermittent significance. The principal supplier of slaves to the coastal ports in this region was initially the kingdom of Allada, but in the eighteenth century its place was taken by Dahomey, which conquered both Allada and Ouidah in the 1720s. The Slave Coast—especially the ports east of Ouidah—also drew slaves from the Yoruba area east of Dahomey, particularly from the kingdom of Oyo.[12]

The slave trade existed to move unfree labor from Africa to the Americas in exchange for textiles, tobacco, cheap liquor, and other commodities. It required regular transportation and communication between these two regions as well as with Europe. In the eighteenth century, for example, an average of eighteen ships sailed from Bahia to the Slave Coast each year, whereas in the first half of the nineteenth century the number increased to twenty-two.[13] Moreover, the slave trade required the construction and maintenance of effective commercial networks capable of buying and bulking a perishable and rebellious human trade good in Africa, transporting it across the Atlantic, and selling it in the Americas, with exchanges during the process commonly resting on credit. The regular communication around the Atlantic rim and particularly back and forth between the Slave Coast and Bahia that the slave trade required created opportunities for the relocation of traders and other free people as well as slaves. The need for efficient, reliable commercial networks drew those who established themselves on the Slave Coast into business and social relationships that spanned the Atlantic and linked political and commercial elites along the coast. These networks, moreover, facilitated the exchange of culture as well as trade. Just as slaves carried African religions and Islam as well as material culture and ritual practices into the Americas, so slave traders introduced literacy, numeracy, Christianity, European languages, new consumer goods, artisanal knowledge, and building styles to the Slave Coast.

Differences existed among the communities of the Slave Coast not only in the chronology and scale of their participation in the slave trade but also in the details of its local organization, which in turn shaped the character and development of the Atlantic community along the coast. At Ouidah and Lagos, strong African states existed whose officials participated directly in the trade and endeavored to regulate it, both opening opportunities for outsiders and constraining them. In the lesser ports west of Ouidah and between it and Lagos, the local polities were weaker and less centralized, which at times created opportunities for local big men to rise in trade and begin to concentrate power in their hands or for Europeans and Afro-Europeans, Brazilians and Afro-Brazilians to settle, trade, and found prominent families. In some places, European cumpanies or individuals maintained factories. Although these establishments were often ephemeral, at Ouidah the French, English, and Portuguese built factories between 1671 and 1721 (which were subsequently fortified) and maintained them throughout the eighteenth century. The Portuguese fort was administered from Bahia, rather than directly from metropolitan Portugal, and its officials were appointed from there. In Ouidah, these forts bulked slaves and organized services for visiting ships.[14] The personnel of the forts included not only Europeans (in the case of the French and Portuguese forts, there were Christian chaplains as well as traders and soldiers) but also African slaves and free employees, all of whom served as important agents in the dissemination of European languages and customs within the surrounding community. Some idea of the size of the local population that worked at the forts can be derived from the contemporary observation that the Portuguese fort, built in 1721, was located in a quarter of Ouidah where there were about three hundred houses, all the inhabitants of which were employed in the service of foreign nations trading in the town.[15]

The long and intensive trade in slaves on the Slave Coast led to the growth of a heterogeneous population involved in transatlantic commercial and social networks that played an active role in shaping Atlantic commerce and culture. Prior to legal abolition, links existed to England and France and, after it, to Cuba. But, throughout the era of the slave trade, connections with Bahia were closest and had the greatest social and cultural significance.

The two largest and most important groups that created the diaspora connecting the Slave Coast and Bahia were the slaves forcibly shipped across the Atlantic and the freed slaves who in the nineteenth century returned from Brazil. Both groups continued to look across the Atlantic to define their identity and way of life. Already by the late eighteenth century, the concentration of slaves from the Slave Coast in Brazil, together with the limited opportunities they enjoyed to earn income of their own (especially in urban Salvador), had created a market for products from West Africa, such as Yoruba cloth, which was "held . . . in much esteem by the black population" not only for its quality but also "because it is manufactured in a country which gave many of them, or their parents, birth." In the nineteenth century, if not earlier, the trade from West Africa to Brazil also included palm oil, kola nuts, black soap calabashes, and various spices. The growth of Yoruba cults among slaves and ex-slaves in Brazil further created a demand for religious and ritual objects made in West Africa.[16] Conversely, the Brazilians who settled in West Africa, including even ex-slaves of African origin or descent, continued to define themselves as such and to cultivate a distinctively "Brazilian" way of life. For example, former slaves living at Ouidah in the 1840s expressed nostalgia for their time in Bahia, which they claimed had been "their happiest days."[17]

When most Africanists speak of the Brazilian diaspora to the Slave Coast, they think of the freed slaves who returned to the coast in large numbers from the 1830s.[18] The freed slaves played a decisive role in the history of the diaspora because their return created a population of several thousands, permanently resident on the coast, that identified with Bahia, its language, religions, and cultures. Continuing commercial, cultural, and intellectual communication among the members of this group and family, friends, coreligionists, and business associates in Bahia kept the transatlantic community alive when it might otherwise have perished following the abolition of the slave trade. And yet, to understand fully the construction and character of the Atlantic community requires focusing on the *longue durée* and looking also at the period prior to the return of freed slaves in the mid-nineteenth century. For the diaspora has been created and re-created over a long period of time through the regular movement of people, goods, ideas, and culture back and forth between the Slave Coast and Bahia. Given that we know more about the mid-nineteenth century returned slaves and their contribution to the construction and maintenance of the Atlantic community, we will focus, in the first instance, on the earlier phases of this historical process.

The earliest surviving detailed account of European trade on the Slave Coast, relating to the kingdom of Allada in 1601, notes the presence of Portuguese residence. It might be assumed that these were merchants from metropolitan Portugal, but subsequent evidence suggests otherwise. In the 1650s and 1660s, a prominent figure in Allada, serving as one of the king's interpreters, was one Mattéo Lopes, a professed Christian, who is indeed described as "of Portuguese nationality" but was nevertheless black. Likewise, at Ouidah to the west, the king in 1694 had in his service a "Portuguese Negro," also a Christian, called João Fernandes, who served as his gunner and physician. It is not specified precisely where Lopes and Fernandes came from, but it was more likely the West African island of São Tomé, the local Portuguese headquarters in the region, than Brazil. The king of Allada reigning in 1670 is said to have been educated in a monastery on that island.[19]

Diplomatic contacts between African and European states initiated in the early modern era also helped create the Atlantic community, with emissaries traveling repeatedly between Africa, Europe, and America. On the Slave Coast, the earliest instance so far traced was in 1657, when the king of Allada sent an envoy named Bans to Spain (via Cartagena in South America) to request the sending of Christian missionaries. After baptism in Spain (as Don Phelipe Zapata), the ambassador returned to Allada with a party of Catholic priests in 1660; the mission also brought with it, as interpreter, an Allada man, presumably an ex-slave, who had resided in Spain for forty-four years and married there. Ten years later, in 1670, the royal interpreter Mattéo Lopes undertook a second mission for the king of Allada, accompanied by some of his wives and children, traveling via Martinique to France (and an audience with King Louis XIV) and returning safely to West Africa later in the same year.[20]

As far as the evidence goes, during the seventeenth century persons such as Lopes, Fernandes, and Zapata may have been isolated individuals, not sufficiently numerous to have had a major social and cultural impact. In the eighteenth century, however, the number of individuals settled on the Slave Coast who were not only engaged in the slave trade but also had social relations and cultural experience that crossed the Atlantic was much more substantial. These included not only returned former slaves and Africans who had traveled to Europe or America men but also Europeans who had settled and founded families in Africa.

In the eighteenth century, intermarriage between locally resident Europeans and African women was mainly associated with the permanently organized European forts at Ouidah. Although most of the European personnel of these forts died or returned home after brief periods, those who stayed longer often took local wives and fathered offspring. For example, João Basilio, who served as an official in the Portuguese fort for more than twenty years before being deported back to Bahia in 1743, fathered two mulatto children (by different African women), whom he took back with him to Brazil. One of the governors of the English fort, Lionel Abson, resided in the town for no less than thirty-six years, eventually dying there in 1803. He married a number of local women; with one he fathered several children. He sent his eldest son, George, to be educated in England, where he learned to read and write. George Abson was back in Ouidah by 1793, when a visiting English trader observed that his behavior "gave proof that his morals had derived no advantage from the imperfect education which he had received in England." George assisted his father in his dealings with ships trading at Ouidah; he was still alive and operating as a trader when his father died in 1803, but he left no descendants identifiable there today. [21]

One of Abson's contemporaries in command of the French fort at Ouidah. Joseph Ollivier de Montaguère 1775–1786), also married locally, taking as a wife a woman of mixed Afro-French ancestry called Sophia with whom he had two sons, Nicolas and Jean-Baptiste. Unlike Abson, Ollivier de Montaguère returned home to France, but his wife and sons remained behind; the wife, according to tradition, was entrusted to the care of King Kpengla of Dahomey and then to his successor Agonglo (r. 1789–1797), with both of whom she had children. Both Nicolas and Jean-Baptiste Ollivier, according to family tradition, were sent to be educated in France—though no corroboration of that has yet been traced in contemporary sources. [22] If they had been born earlier, the Ollivier brothers would presumably have been employed, like George Abson, in the service of the French fort at Ouidah. But the French fort was abandoned in 1797, and they instead set up as independent traders in Ouidah, founding a family and a quarter of the town that still exist today. The family name, however, is today given a Portuguese form, d'Oliveira, reflecting its absorption into the larger Portuguese-speaking community in the nineteenth century.

Outside Ouidah, foreign traders resident on the Slave Coast in this period were more commonly African ex-slaves (or descendants of slaves) who had returned from the Americas or Europe. An example was João de Oliveira, born in the interior of the Slave Coast and taken as a slave to Brazil. He left Bahia for the Slave Coast in 1733 and settled east of Ouidah. He was evidently still a slave when he returned to Africa, but he sent money back to Brazil to purchase his freedom. Oliveira was remembered in an official Portuguese source as having set himself up on the coast as the "greatest Portuguese protector, helping them to carry out trading negotiations speedily with the people or to protect them from suffering from the deterioration and losses to which tobacco is subject in this climate." The same source credited him with opening the slave trade at Porto-Novo in the 1750s and Lagos in the 1760s, "with his own labour and at his own expense." Despite his long residence in West Africa, Oliveira retained a close and continuing emotional and cultural association with Bahia, including a relationship with his former owner's family. While living on the coast, he heard that his former owner had died, leaving his widow destitute, and he is said to have "helped" the woman for as long as she lived. Having been converted to Christianity in Brazil, he also remitted money there for the building of a chapel and made "numerous donations of slaves" to religious fraternities. In 1770, after thirty-seven years' residence on the coast, Oliveira retired to Brazil, together with the slaves he had accumulated, because of his desire "to spend the rest of his life among a Catholic people, and to die having received all the sacraments of the Church." Ironically, on arrival in Bahia, he was initially arrested on suspicion of smuggling, but he was related after a month in prison, and his property was restored to him.[23]

In Porto-Novo a little later, the leading trader was one Pierre, whose African name was "Tammata." In origin a Hausa (from what is today northern Nigeria), he had been exported as a slave but was taken up by a French slaving captain, who had him educated in France, where he learned "reading, writing, and accounts." Pierre subsequently served his master on trading voyages to Africa, in reward for which he was not only freed but lent capital to set up as an independent trader, and he eventually resettled in Africa. He was established at Porto-Novo, and serving as secretary to the king, and continued in his capacity until at least 1788. Given the conjuncture of commercial links at this time, Pierre enjoyed the considerable advantage of "speaking the Housa, Eyeo [Oyo], and French languages." He described himself in 1787, writing to the authorities in France, as "raised in the French nation and attached to this respectable nation by gratitude and principle." In Porto-Novo, he dressed "as a European" and adopted various European fashions, including using silver cutlery and European-style furniture ("elegant sofas and chairs") and playing the French horn and billiards; his billiard room was adorned with "portraits of various members of the Bourbon family." He created a quarter of Porto-Novo that still exists today called after his name Fiekome ("Fie's [that is, Pierre's] Quarter").[24]

A contemporary and rival of Pierre in Porto-Novo was Antonio vaz Coelho, described as a "Free negro, born in Brazil, where he had been taught to read, write, and keep accounts." He had made "several voyages" to Porto-Novo as a trader, and he eventually settled there. He became "a very respectable trader" and married into "the first families" of the community, consequently acquiring "considerable influence . . . [and] a great ascendancy in the public councils" (though he did not, like Pierre, leave traceable descendants in the town). He was noted for arming his dependents with blunderbusses and is credited with the introduction of brass swivel guns on the war canoes employed on the coastal lagoon. His canoes, with their blunderbusses and cannon, played a prominent role in campaigns against neighboring coastal towns in the 1780s, reportedly saving the Porto-Novo forces from defeat on two occasions.[25]

In Ouidah, a prominent figure in the 1780s was another former slave from Brazil, Dom Jeronimo, whose African name was "Fruku," though the detailed circumstances of his return to Africa were rather different. He was by origin a prince of Dahomey, playmate to the future King Kpengla (r. 1774–1789), who had been sold into slavery in Brazil by Kpengla's father and predecessor Tegbesu (r. 1740–1774) but was then redeemed by Kpengla after his accession, following twenty-four years in slavery.[26] That an individual slave could be traced and identified in America is remarkable testimony to the effectiveness of transatlantic communication and cooperation. Unlike de Oliveira or Pierre, Jeronimo operated, not as an independent trader, but as a commercial official, part of the Dahomian ruling establishment. On Kpengla's death in 1789, he was even a contender for succession to the Dahomian throne.

Other members of Slave Coast communities acquired knowledge of European languages and culture through travel abroad as free men. In Little Pope, the founder of the Lawson family, Latévi Awoku, is said by tradition to have acquired the name Lawson from the captain of an English slaver, who took him to England to be educated. He is evidently to be identified with the man called "Lathe," met by the Danish trader Paul Erdmann Isert in 1784, who had risen from humble origins to the rank of "caboceer" (chief), having "served as a servant for the English" in his youth and learned Portuguese and Danish as well as English, Although not himself literate, in 1784 he had one son in England and one in Portugal who were learning literacy and numeracy. The son who was in England was presumably Akuété Zankli, alias George Lawson (d. 1857), who is said to have been educated in England and to have served as steward on a Liverpool slaver on a voyage to Jamaica before returning to Little Popo in 1812. Although George Lawson identified primarily with England, the family continued to maintain a range of overseas links and were described in 1850, for example, as "some living as Portuguese, others as Englishmen."[27]

Whereas the Lawson family acquired prominence in Little Popo through its overseas connections, in other cases members of existing ruling families went abroad for education. In Badagry, for example, the dominant chief in the later 1770s, the Jengen, had been educated in Brazil. When he was overthrown by his political rivals in 1782, he was deported back to Brazil. A few years later, in 1787, a son of this man returned from Brazil and was reportedly seeking assistance from Lagos and Porto-Novo to reinstate himself in Badagry. At Lagos, in 1789, a French slave ship delivered a passenger named "Lougué," said to be the thirteen-year-old nephew of the Oba (King) Ologun Kutere; although nothing more was said of the boy, he also might have been returning from education in Europe. Subsequently, King Adandozan of Dahomey (r. 1797–1818) sent two of his brothers to be educated in England. They were mistakenly sold into slavery in Demerara, but, through the intervention of some Liverpool traders, they were rescued and returned to Dahomey in 1803.[28]

With the expansion of the slave trade during the eighteenth century, diplomatic contacts between African states and their trading partners overseas became more frequent, as African rulers sought to encourage and regulate the commerce. In 1726, for example, King Agaja of Dahomey sent an English trader, Bulfinch Lambe, with a letter to the king of England. Lambe was accompanied by an African interpreter, Captain Tom (alias "Adomo Tomo"), formerly employed in the English factory at Jakin. Initially, instead of delivering the letter, Lambe sold Tom as a slave in Maryland; but, after a few years, he changed his mind, liberated Tom, and took him to England. There Tom had an audience with King George II, received instruction in the English language, and was baptized as a Christian. But after initial social success, the embassy proved a political failure when the letter delivered in King Agaja's name was officially judged to be a forgery. Tom, however, was safely delivered back to Dahomey, where his undoubtedly much improved linguistic ability and experience gained abroad were turned to official advantage through his appointment as assistant to the "English Chief," or the official charged with dealing with English traders at Ouidah.[29]

On the Slave Coast, such diplomatic contacts were especially regular with Brazil. Pierre Verger has compiled a register of no fewer than seven official embassies that arrived in Brazil from various states on the Slave Coast between 1750 and 1812 to discuss matters relating to commerce. In 1750. King Tegbesu of Dahomey sent an ambassador to Bahia, accompanied by "an interpreter from his nation who knew sufficient Portuguese," and two "noblemen"—the latter "so that they could be taught the language and be informed about the customs of the Portuguese." These envoys went back to West Africa the following year. In 1770, when João de Oliveira returned to Bahia, he had with him four "Caboceers of the King of Onim [that is, Lagos]," who had presumably been sent on diplomatic business. These envoys were seized on de Oliveira's arrest, apparently because they were believed to be his slaves, but they were later freed and repatriated to Lagos. In 1795, King Agonglo of Dahomey sent two ambassadors to, Bahia, accompanied by Luiz Caetano, a mulatto slave from the Portuguese fort at Ouidah who had deserted into his service, to act as interpreter. They were sent from Bahia to Portugal, where they arrived in 1796 and were baptized as Catholics. One of the ambassadors died in Portugal, but the other (now called João Carlos de Bragança) was dispatched to Brazil and then to Dahomey. Instructions were given to find the ambassador a wife in Brazil, "either . . . a black woman or . . . a light mulatress," but that did not take place, as the governor of Bahia explained, because of the ambassador's "choice of various slaves and other free persons whom I did not find qualified for this purpose." The ambassador returned to Dahomey in 1797, accompanied by two Catholic priests, but their attempt to convert King Agonglo was overtaken by the latter's assassination in a palace coup d'état.[30]

In 1805, the new King Adandozan of Dahomey in turn sent two ambassadors to Bahia accompanied by a Brazilian mulatto (a trader, taken prisoner in a recent attack on Porto-Novo) as interpreter. The embassy was again passed on to Portugal and then returned to Dahomey via Bahia. In 1807, "Prince Ajan" (later Oba Osinlokun) of Lagos sent an ambassador and a "secretary" to Bahia, with a letter to take to the king of Portugal. On this occasion, the governor of Bahia did not permit them to proceed to Portugal, however, and they were sent back to Lagos the following year. In 1810, the king of Porto-Novo sent an embassy to Bahia with a letter that was sent to the prince regent of Portugal, who was then at Rio de Janeiro; and, while they were still in Bahia, at the beginning of 1811, an embassy from Dahomey also arrived there. Both were sent back in 1811, and their leaders were presented with silver tea sets.

This history of regular diplomatic contacts with Brazil, together with the occasional instances of successful redemption of persons from slavery in the Americas noted earlier, lends credibility to the story told in Dahomian tradition that King Gezo, on his accession in 1818, sent an embassy to Brazil in an attempt to locate and redeem his mother Agotime, who had been sold into slavery by his predecessor Adandozan.[31] Given the duration and extent of diplomatic relations between the Slave Coast and Brazil as well as the importance of the slave trade to the economies of both regions, it seems entirely appropriate that the first recorded recognition of Brazilian independence by any foreign power, in 1924, was transmitted by a Portuguese claiming to serve as ambassador for the oba of Lagos, the "Emperor of Benin," and "other Kings of Africa."[32]

In the present state of the evidence, it is debatable whether the numerous persons residing on the Slave Coast who had links across the Atlantic in the eighteenth and early nineteenth centuries should be considered a single "community," rather than a range of individuals involved in diverse and distinct commercial and social networks. Links existed to England and France as well as to Brazil, though the connections with Brazil were clearly predominant. On the Slave Coast, Atlantic-oriented people seem likewise to have depended principally upon their individual links with local ruling families; how far persons with different overseas orientations also established commercial, social, and family relations among themselves within West Africa is unknown. The Atlantic community on the Slave Coast, however, acquired a greater coherence in the early nineteenth century, when it became more exclusively oriented toward Brazil and when its internal business, social, and family connections are more fully documented.

The involvement of the Slave Coast ports in the wider Atlantic world changed significantly in the first half of the nineteenth century, following the legal abolition of the slave trade. The most obvious effect of abolition was to accentuate even further the importance of links to Brazil. The abolition of colonial slavery by France in 1794 and of the slave trade by Britain in 1808 led quickly to the disappearance of French and British slavers from the coast and was soon followed by the abandonment of the two countries' forts at Ouidah.[33] But, although Portugal (in 1815) and subsequently independent Brazil (in 1826) also declared the prohibition of slaving in West Africa north of the equator, in practice the slave trade to Brazil expanded after the French and British departed and continued until 1850.[34] In consequence, the transatlantic links of the Slave Coast ports, which had been relatively multinational in the eighteenth century, now became much more heavily Brazilian, although links to other parts of the Lusophone world existed as well, and Spaniards, mostly from Cuba, also began to appear on the coast from the 1820s. Not until the rise of the palm oil trade with Europe from the 1840 would British and French influence again become significant.

This atrophying of French and British contacts can be seen clearly in Oaidah; when merchants of these nations reoccupied the former French and British forts in the 1840s, the French found that, although families descended from the former slaves of their fort were still in place, only one person among them could speak any French—and he only "very few words"—and the official interpreter for the British, Gnahoui, was found to speak Portuguese better than English.[35] At Lagos, which became a major post for the Atlantic slave trade at precisely the time when it was becoming overwhelmingly Brazilian, external contacts were primarily to Brazil before the middle of the nineteenth century.

Changes in the organization of the slave trade following legal abolition also contributed to the consolidation of the Brazilian diaspora on the Slave Coast. The higher risk and greater capital outlay per slave associated with the illegal trade led to concentration in the Bahia traffic. Three big merchants predominated in the 1820s—Antonio Pedrozo de Albuquerque, José de Cerqueira Lima, and Joaquim José de Oliveira. The first two continued into the 1830s and were joined by Joaquim Pereira Marinho and José Alvez da Cruz Rois and his son Joaquim, who went on to dominate the slave trade at Bahia in the 1840s.[36] This concentration was reflected on the West African coast, where at Lagos, for example, these same men owned many of the slaving voyages.[37]

At the same time, efforts to suppress the slave trade after 1815 increased the importance of resident agents in the Slave Coast ports. The conventions that Great

Britain signed with Portugal, Spain, and Brazil between 1817 and 1842 authorized the British naval squadron patrolling the West African waters to search ships flying the three countries' flags and seize those with slaves, and eventually slaving equipment, on board. Although these measures did little to end the slave trade, they dictated that slave ships should spend us little time as possible anchored off the coast of Africa with slaves, or later equipment, on board. That created a need for resident agents or independent traders who could buy and bulk slaves at factories on shore rather than on shipboard, as had usually occurred prior to abolition. To avoid capture by British cruisers, these people arranged rapid and clandestine embarkation of complete cargoes of slaves when the vessels sent to transport them arrived off the coast.[38]

At Ouidah, the effective abandonment of the Portuguese fort, whose contacts with Brazil lapsed from circa 1806, created an opportunity for a Brazilian, Francisco Felix de Souza (d. 1849), to establish himself as a big African-based slave trader. De Souza had originally come to Ouidah as a subordinate official in the Portuguese fort, and, when his superiors died, he became its acting director. In the face of official neglect of the fort, however, he set up as an independent trader, initially at Badagry and then at Little Popo rather than at Ouidah itself. Following a dispute with King Adandozan of Dahomey, de Souza supported the successful coup d'état that placed the king's brother, Gezo, on the throne in 1818. As a reward, he was appointed sole agent for the king's trade at Ouidah, with the title of "chacha," and he dominated the slave trade there until the 1840s.[39]

At Lagos, the big Bahian merchants stationed agents or entered partner ships with independent Brazilian traders already there. New private traders also began to arrive in the town and at some of the lesser ports on the coast, hoping to make their fortune in the booming slave trade. During the 1830s, at least twenty-two Portuguese, Brazilians, and Spaniards resided at Lagos and traded slaves.[40] Some either survived or elected to remain only a short time, but others built residences and storage facilities, forged alliances with the oba or prominent chiefs, entered domestic and commercial relationships with local women, and began employing domestic slaves and free laborers. Two such Brazilians were Manuel Joaquim d'Almeida and Joaquim de Brito Lima, both of whom had had earlier experience with the coast as captains of slave ships."[41] The leading locally based Brazilian slaver in the generation following de Souza, José Domingos Martins ("Domingo Martinez," d. 1864), also set up initially at Lagos in the 1830s; but, in 1846, he relocated to Porto-Novo, where he traded with King Gezo of Dahomey, and, after de Souza's death in 1849, established a second residence in Ouidah.[42] The arrival of such resident agents and new independent traders thus led to a growth in the size of the Brazilian population on the coast and its spread beyond Ouidah.

The "Brazilian" community on the Slave Coast was mixed—by race, class, and geographical origins.[43] The slave traders who settled on the Slave Coast included white Brazilians who married local women and fathered "Afro-Brazilian" families, such as Francisco Felix de Souza and Domingo Martinez.[44] But they also included persons who were themselves Afro-Brazilians, ex-slaves who re-emigrated to Africa as free persons. The most prominent of these was Joaquim d'Almeida (d. 1857), whose indigenous name was "Azata." He was by birth a Mahi (from the interior north of Dahomey) who had been owned in Bahia by Manoel Joaquim d'Almeida. Joaquim d'Almeida traveled back and forth between Bahia and the Slave Coast on slaving voyages and made some money trading on his own account. Ultimately, he freed himself and in 1845 settled at Agoué, where he worked both as an independent trader and as an agent for others, including his former owner M. J, d'Almeida. Others who came to form part of the Brazilian community were in fact Africans who had never been to Brazil but had assimilated Brazilian culture on the West African coast as slaves or clients of Brazilian settlers. For example, Pedro Felix d'Almeida of Ouidah came originally from Little Popo but was brought up in de Souza's household, where he learned to speak and write Portuguese.[45]

The growth of the commercial community on the Slave Coast created a demand for artisans to perform skilled work in the slave trade and to supply the taste of prosperous slave traders for Brazilian-style homes, goods, and services. Some of these early artisans may have been free, but many were slaves brought from Brazil or sent there for training. In 1841, for example, a Brazilian slave trader at Ouidah sent three slaves to Bahia to be trained as masons, and, in 1849, Oba Kosoko of Lagos was sufficiently impressed with the usefulness of what Brazilian carpenters and coopers could produce that he tried to buy slaves with these skills and export them to Lagos, reversing the direction of the transatlantic slave trade. Material evidence of the presence of some of these artisans may still survive in the buildings of the coast, although we know too little about the history of most of the Brazilian structures to date them. But few or no material remains of the work of others have survived because they performed services or produced perishable goods. José Paraiso, an ex-slave from Brazil who settled at Porto-Novo, worked originally as a barber, and, according to one account, he had been purchased from Brazil for this purpose by Domingo Martinez. José Francisco dos Santos, a free Brazilian settled in Ouidah, although later a slave trader, was originally a tailor in the service of the de Souza family (and kept the surname Alfaiate, "The Tailor," in later life).[46]

The social heterogeneity of the Brazilian community was further compounded by the more substantial return of free blacks to West Africa, most with no involvement in slave trading which began with the deportation of persons believed by the Brazilian authorities to have been implicated in the Bahia slave revolt of 1835. These immigrants included women and children as well as adult men, and, because Islam had been important in the revolt, they included Muslims as well as Catholics.[47] A group of 200 free blacks was deported to Ouidah immediately after the rebellion; they settled there, according to tradition, through the support or permission of de Souza. founding the quarter of the town called Maro. In 1847, Oba Kosoko of Lagos agreed to guarantee the safety of Brazilian repatriated slaves who settled in Lagos, and, during the following decade, his successor Akiroye granted land to a number of them, though both rulers imposed a tax on freed slaves immigrating to their territory. The British consul sent to Lagos in the 1850s to help suppress the slave trade and encourage the growth of commerce in other commodities also extended assistance to Brazilian repatriates and encouraged the settlement of more than 130 families.[48] Many of these freed slaves had worked as artisans in urban Salvador, and they found a ready market for their skills on the African coast. Others managed to save a little capital and make their living in small-scale trade. But few if any enjoyed the wealth of the successful slave traders.

Finally, the foreign commercial community on the Slave Coast was more variegated in its geographical origins than the use of the term "Brazilian" might suggest, including persons from Portuguese territories all around the Atlantic rim. This diversity became especially pronounced in the 1850s, as the last of the illegal slave traders shifted the location of their activities in an effort to escape pressures to end the commerce and to supply the continuing Cuban market. Samuel da Costa Soares, a leading figure in the slave trade to Cuba in the 1850s, who settled at Agoué and founded a family there, was from metropolitan Portugal and sent his children to be educated in Lisbon rather than Brazil. Francisco José de Medeiros (d. 1875), who settled at Agoué in the 1850s but moved to Ouidah in the 1860s, was from Madeira. Other, less prominent Ouidah families claim founders originating from the Island of São Tomé and from Angola.[49] The link to São Tomé was reinforced by the official reoccupation of the Portuguese fort at Ouidah in 1844 because the garrison and clergy for the fort chapel were supplied from that island.[50] There were also Spanish/Cuban as well as Portuguese/Brazilian slavers established on the coast. One such was Juan José Zangronis, or Sangron (d. 1843), son of a leading slave merchant of Havana, who settled at Ouidah in the 1830s, acting as consignee for cargoes shipped by his father. The Sastre family of Great Popo is descended from another Spanish trader, who came from the Canary Islands. There was also a less-well-known (and smaller) re-emigration to West Africa of ex-slaves from Cuba as well as from Brazil. In the long run, however, the "Brazilian" community absorbed such originally non-Lusophone settlers and, indeed, even some families of non-Iberian origin, such as the Afro-French Ollivier (d'Oliveira) family of Ouidah.[51]

This heterogeneity of origins poses a number of historical questions for which presently we can offer only partial answers. First, how and why did a Brazilian identity develop and become dominant in the first half of the nineteenth century among the Atlantic population on the coast? Second, how was a Brazilian community constituted and how were people incorporated into it? Answers to the first question must lie in part in the duration of ties to Brazil and the numerical preponderance of immigrants from that region among the coast's Atlantic settlers. However, Bahia's dominance of the region's external trade from 1808 into the 1840s must also have played a role. Most of the slave traders on the coast after 1808, even those who originated elsewhere, were part of a predominantly Brazilian commercial network. The great political power of two Brazilians residing on the coast—F. F. de Souza and Domingo Martinez—undoubtedly also contributed to the "Brazilianization" of its Atlantic population. Just as Brazil's leading role in the coast's external trade was ending, moreover, the infusion of more immigrants from Brazil in the form of freed slaves revitalized connections with that country.

The Brazilian community was defined above all by its use of the Portuguese language. The Roman Catholic religion was also an important, though not necessary, signifier of Brazilian identity and helped incorporate people into the community—though a significant minority of the returned ex-slaves were Muslims and continued to practice Islam.[52] Instances of the attachment of Brazilian settlers to Catholic Christianity can be found even before the establishment of an officially organized church. At Agoué, for example, a "Christian lady returned from Brazil" is said to have built a chapel in 1835; it burned down soon after, but a decade later Joaquim d'Almeida built a second, more lasting one equipped with "the necessary objects for saying mass." At Lagos a little later, another Brazilian ex-slave, "Padre" Antonio—not in fact an ordained priest, but a layman—built a chapel and began conducting services. In addition to worship and Catholic religious festivals,

Brazilian-style dress and cuisine also displayed identity and helped forge community.[53] Beyond this shared culture, critical integrative mechanisms were intermarriage and the incorporation of new arrivals into relationships of clientage with established families such as the de Souzas.[54] Much more research needs to be done on these questions, however, particularly on the evolving relationship between the early Brazilian community and the freed slaves who arrival from the 1830s. What is clear is that, in this period if not earlier, economic and social links operated not only between different families within each coastal community but also between different coastal communities. The business and social activities of the Brazilian community reinforced connections along the lagoon system as well as across the Atlantic, with Brazilian settlers commonly relocating from one community to another or maintaining residences in more than one community simultaneously.[55]

A further source of ambiguity in the external orientation and subjective identity of this community, though this is a matter whose implications are likewise as yet little researched, was the political secession of Brazil from Portugal in 1822. This secession had direct repercussions in West Africa, where the title to the Portuguese fort in Ouidah, although currently unoccupied, was disputed between the two countries but was confirmed to Portugal in the negotiations for the recognition of Brazilian independence in 1825. In the illegal slave trade across the Atlantic, national allegiances were fluid and opportunistic, with slave ships juggling among different national registrations, depending on which could offer the best protection against the attentions of the British naval squadron. In Ouidah, Francisco Felix de Souza notoriously flew the Portuguese and Brazilian flags alternately, according to the professed nationality of the ships he was dealing with. De Souza continued to assert his personal status as a Portuguese national and, indeed, his claim to have inherited command of the Portuguese fort at Ouidah; but this self-identification was probably as much for practical as for sentimental reasons, because Portuguese ships with no slaves on board were (until 1839) legally immune from arrest by the British antislaving squadron.[56] The connection to Portugal, however, acquired more practical significance with the reoccupation of the Portuguese fort at Ouidah from 1844, and, in the aftermath of the ending of the slave trade to Brazil in 1850, it offered the basis of an alternative role and identity, which became especially functional in a context of increasing imperialist pressure from Britain and France. Francisco Felix de Souza's eldest son and his successor in his title of "chacha," Isidoro Felix de Souza, in particular, contacted the Portuguese authorities on São Tomé to secure appointment as governor of the Portuguese fort in 1851, and the de Souzas continued to cultivate the Portuguese connection as a support for their position in Ouidah to the 1880s.[57]

From the 1830s, the evolution of the Brazilian community on the Slave Coast also interacted with a parallel movement of re-settlement by freed slaves and their descendants from the British colony of Freetown in Sierra Leone.[58] In certain contexts, Brazilians and Sierra Leoneans might see themselves as having common interests and a common identity, by distinction from the societies in which they had settled, through their shared allegiance to Christianity and European culture, and there was a certain amount of intermarriage between them.[59] But the two groups nevertheless remained essentially distinct, commonly occupying separate residential areas in coastal towns. They were divided not only by language but also by religious allegiance; the Sierra Leoneans were associated with the Anglophone Protestant missions, and the Brazilians, with the Roman Catholic Church.

The Brazilian community on the Slave Coast was forged, not through a process of one-way migration, but rather through the maintenance of continuous contacts across the Atlantic. That has been well documented among the repatriated ex-slaves, but it was also true among the earlier slave traders.[60] Several Brazilians and Afro-Brazilians traveled back and forth between America and Africa or (like João de Oliveira in the eighteenth century) returned to Brazil after periods of residence in Africa; and, even when such persons definitively settled in Africa, they commonly maintained family and other social ties with Brazil, often, for example, sending their children to be educated there. Some of these people, indeed, owned slaves and landed property and maintained households on both sides of the Atlantic.

The conduct of the slave trade required the construction and maintenance of dense, interlocking business relationships, often reinforced by social bonds. Slave traders on both sides of the Atlantic needed correspondents on the other who would serve as agents and creditors. Brazilians on the coast named their business associates as godparents and guardians of children sent to be reared and educated in Brazil and as executors of their wills. Legal abolition perhaps reinforced this dependence of business relationships on informal social ties, since the now-illegal slave trade no longer enjoyed an institutionalized framework for the enforcement of contracts. Such business and social relations sometimes existed even between former slaves and their former owners—as, for example, between Joaquim d'Almeida and M. J. d'Almeida.

The history of the de Souza family of Ouidah provides numerous illustrations of the continuing importance of such links with Bahia. The founder Francisco Felix de Souza evidently thought of returning to Brazil, for which he obtained a passport in 1821. His eldest son Isidoro Felix de Souza, although born in Africa (Ouidah, 1802), was sent back to Brazil to be educated and to perform military service before returning to West Africa, according to family tradition in 1822. A younger brother, Antonio Felix de Souza (surnamed "Kokou"), is said to have been sent to school in Portugal, where he learned horsemanship. Similar links were maintained in subsequent generations. Antonio Kokou in 1851 had sons being educated in Brazil, but they were called home in the insecurity following that country's final suppression of the slave trade.[61] When Isidoro died in 1858, the claim of one of his, brothers, another Antonio Felix de Souza (surnamed "Agbakoun"), to succeed to the family title of chacha was rejected by the Ouidah merchant community on the grounds that "he had never been in Brazil" and therefore "had no idea of the interests of most of them." The Family's personal connections with Brazil survived the ending of the slave trade: another brother, Julião, Felix de Souza (who ultimately became chacha, 1883–1887) traded palm oil to Brazil and is said to have traveled there "on several occasions" in connection with his commercial activities.[62]

The second leading Brazilian slave trader on the Slave Coast, Domingo Martinez, likewise returned briefly to Brazil, in 1844–1845. He evidently took with him (or perhaps had previously sent there) some of his children by African wives. By the time he made his will in 1845, prior to returning to Africa, he had five offspring (one son, four daughters), two born in Bahia in 1824–1825 and three in Africa in 1840–1841; all were then in Bahia, "entrusted to the care of my friends."

The daughters remained in Bahia and married there; but the son, Rafael Domingos Martins, eventually joined his father in Africa and was at Ouidah when Martinez died in 1864. In Africa, Martinez had meanwhile fathered more children; in 1857, when he was contemplating returning once more to Brazil, he tried to obtain passports to send six of his children there for education.[63]

The will of the ex-slave Joaquim d'Almeida, written in Bahia in 1844 before his departure to settle permanently in Africa, nicely illustrates the continuing transatlantic connections of another Brazilian slave trader on the coast. It began with provisions for masses to be said in Bahia for the repose of his soul. For alms to be given there to the poor, and for the interment of his body in the habit of the order of Saint Francis at the monastery in Bahia (but, in fact, he died and was buried in Agoué). He appointed his former owner and current business associate, M. J. d'Almcida, an executor of his will and also made a bequest to him. After declaring his Brazilian assets in the form of a house, nine slaves, shares of slaving voyages, and slaves in the hands of agents, he asked to have specific debts paid on the African coast and in Bahia. He made provision for various persons he was leaving behind in Bahia. He freed a "Nago" (Yoruba) slave woman who belonged to another man and made a bequest to her "to ease my conscience considering the good services she had given me." He also freed a creole girl Benedita and two slave women, a "Mina" (that is, from the Gold Coast) and a "Nago," whom he owned "as a reward for their good services to me." He named as his heirs a minor, Soteiro, son of the Mina woman he had freed, and the creole girl Benedita, presumably his children, though illegitimate, because the will later stated: "I have neither descendants nor forebearers who by right can inherit . . . my possessions." Intriguingly, d'Ahmeida named as second after Soreiro one Thomazia de Souza Paraiso, "a freed African woman, of the Gege nation [that is, from the Dahomey area], now living somewhere on the African coast," one of the people to whom he owed a debt. He named as second after Benedita his former owner, M. J. d'Almeida. As further evidence of the dense social connections spanning the Atlantic and linking slave traders and some former slaves, M. J. d'Almeída and Joaquim d'Almeida used the same business agent in Bahia, Caetano Alberto da França, and they both appointed this man executor of their wills. Da França was "a light skinned mulatto (*pardo*)," who had served on slaving voyages between 1818 and 1824. When he died in 1871, one of M. J. d'Almeida's sons paid for masses to be said for the repose of his soul.[64]

The correspondence of a Brazilian trader settled in Ouidah, José Francisco dos Santos ("Alfaiate"), further illustrates the involvement of West African coastal traders in transatlantic networks. The extant letters are from two distinct periods: 1844–1871, when dos Santos was engaged in the illegal slave trade, and 1862–1871, by which time he had shifted into legitimate trade in palm oil (and also kola nuts for the Brazil market). The correspondence documents the maintenance by dos Santos of social and cultural ties with the Brazilian homeland. In the 1840s, both his mother and his young son, Jacinto da Costa Santos, were in Bahia, and there are frequent references to arrangements for their maintenance and for his son's education and baptism. By the 1860s, the son was living with his father at Ouidah, and he remained there, founding a dos Santos family that still survives in the town. In 1863, Jacinto made a brief visit to his grandmother in Brazil—ironically, to dissuade her from joining her son and grandson in Africa. One of dos Santos's correspondents in the 1860s, who transmitted payments to his mother, was the same Caetano Alberto da França who had links to M. J. and Joacluim d'Almeida. The dos Santos correspondence also documents the supply of everyday goods and services across the Atlantic: in 1862, he sent his watch to Bahia for repair and his spectacles to be set in gold frames, and he subsequently placed orders for sundry tools, cigars, clothing, poison to kill termites, and calendars.[65]

As in the eighteenth century, the transatlantic network of business and social relations in this period sometimes incorporated, at least to some degree, members of indigenous coastal elites as well as foreigners and slaves or former slaves who came to work or settle on the Slave Coast. A second set of letters, found in Oba Kosoko's palace when the British attacked Lagos in 1851, shows his continuing connections with Bahian business associates and friends. The correspondence deals primarily with the sale of slaves shipped by the oba to commission agents in Brazil, but it also provides glimpses of a broader involvement. Like de Souza, Martinez, and dos Santos, Kosoko sent youths to be educated in Brazil, but they were slaves —Simplicio, Lorenzo, and Camilio—rather than sons, who returned to work as his clerks. And, like dos Santos, Kosoko looked to Brazil to satisfy his desire for certain consumer goods and services, ordering tiles, dyes, compasses, bells, cloth, and silver-handled knives and attempting to send muskets for repair. Moreover, the letters contain more than the formulaic expressions of friendship expected between business associates. In 1849, for example, one Colonia wrote to Kosoho: "Do me the favour to present my mother's compliments to all your wives and children; and do me the favour also to make my compliments to all your headmen, and accept yourself my assurances of friendship, as I am your friend."[66]

This article has explored the role of the Atlantic slave trade in the rise and transformation on West Africa's Slave Coast of a population that linked the region to the Americas and Europe as well as to Africa. This group existed first and foremost to move many thousands of slaves across the Atlantic each year. The creation of efficient commercial networks, however, also, fostered continuing demographic, social, and cultural exchanges that shaped not only the history of the community itself but also that of the regions of the world connected by it. Diverse actors helped create the Atlantic population on the Slave Coast—European and Brazilian traders and their African wives and mulatto offspring, African rulers and the emissaries they sent abroad to help attract slavers and other foreigners to the coast, former slaves who returned to West Africa as individuals to the 1830s and in groups thereafter. Prior to legal abolition, moreover, links existed to Britain and France and their settlements in the Americas as well as to Brazil and other parts of the Portuguese empire. After it, however, connections to Brazil predominated and became sufficiently dense and close that a Brazilian community developed on the Slave Coast, which both linked its towns and crossed the ocean to Bahia. This community was defined not only by common economic activities and interests but also by shared language, religion, and family and other social ties. The well-known return of the Brazilian repatriated ex-slaves to the region after 1835 built on a prior history of Brazilian settlement on the coast.

The Brazilian community on the Slave Coast was dynamic, as had been the earlier Atlantic population there. Although beyond the scope of this article, it is important to note in closing changes in the second half of the nineteenth century that further transformed this community. The long slave trade to Brazil finally ended in 1850, and, although the commerce to Cuba continued for a few years longer, it too was eliminated after 1863. The closing of the Brazilian slave trade coincided wilt British intervention in a succession dispute at Lagos, which led to the expulsion of all foreign slave traders from the town and, in 1861, to British annexation of the kingdom. A number of Brazilian slave traders expelled from Lagos resettled at Ouidah or lesser towns on the coast. The Sierra Leoneans on the Slave Coast believed, on the other hand, that the growing British presence at Lagos would create conditions conducive to the development of the palm oil trade and spread of Protestant Christianity in the town. A number of them relocated to Lagos in hopes of benefiting from these advantages and enjoying British protection. Thus, the ending of the slave trade to Brazil was accompanied by a shifting of the Brazilian and Sierra Leonean populations on the coast, although this was partially offset by the migration of Brazilian repatriated slaves to Lagos at this time. Henceforth, the origins of the Brazilian population at Ouidah, Porto-Novo, and elsewhere on the western Slave Coast were more heterogeneous than at Lagos, including many families founded by the early slave traders and their dependants as well as by repatriated free slaves.

With the end of the slave trade also came the rapid growth of a new Atlantic commerce—that in palm oil with Europe. A number of Brazilian slave traders and their families had difficulty adjusting to the commercial transition, which undermined their economic and political power on the coast: Francisco Felix de Souza was heavily in debt by the time of his death in 1849, and even Domingo Martinez, who engaged extensively in the oil as well as the slave trade, was rumored to be close to bankruptcy by the late 1850s. Among those who did make the change into palm oil, the new trade brought a shift in Atlantic orientation, since the main markets for oil lay in Europe rather than in Brazil. In the 1860s, the correspondence of dos Santos at Ouidah, for example, although still mainly to Brazil, also included letters to merchants in France and Britain. When dos Santos contemplated an overseas journey m 1863, it was to France, for medical treatment in Paris (with an excursion by train to Marseille, to visit a former trading partner), rather than to Brazil.[67]

The development of Lagos as the primary port in the region, accompanied as it was by the imposition of British colonial rule, the return of Sierra Leonean liberated slaves, and the arrival of northern European Protestant missionaries, led to the rapid development there of a complex, cosmopolitan colonial world in which the former slaves from Brazil were only one among a number of significant external influences. The Brazilian population there did not remain as powerful as at Ouidah and Porto-Novo, where even after the imposition of French colonial rule it continued to play a formative role in local politics and culture.[68]

The Atlantic community on the Slave Coast was not unique within western Africa, though it had a distinctive character, by comparison with similar groups elsewhere, because of its preponderant orientation toward Brazil and the prominence in it of repatriated free slaves. On the Gold Coast (modern Ghana) to the west, for example, transatlantic links were rather to Britain, the Netherlands, and Denmark (and to their American colonies), and the Atlantic commercial elite derived more commonly from intermarriage between European traders and African women.[69] On the Bight of Biafra to the east, links were (at least by the second half of the eighteenth century) overwhelmingly to Britain and took the form of indigenous merchants sending children to Europe for education—creating (at least in the case of Old Calabar) an unusual level of literacy in English among the coastal elite.[70] Even in other areas whose primary orientation was to the Portuguese-speaking world, their situation and experience were significantly different from that of the Slave Coast. In the Senegambia and on the Upper Guinea coast, small numbers of Portuguese known as *lançados* had settled in African coastal communities and intermarried with local women from the fifteenth century, giving rise to Luso-African populations connected to the Portuguese empire primarily through the Portuguese communities of the Cape Verde archipelago. Although these groups maintained a loose cultural orientation toward Portugal, as its economic and political power declined in the seventeenth century and French, British, and Dutch traders moved into the region the Luso-Africans' commercial ties were increasingly to other pares of Europe. In Angola, the long duration and vast scale of the slave trade produced a Lusophone community that was larger and wealthier than elsewhere, with commercial, social, and cultural ties stretching deep into the slave-gathering interior as well as across the Atlantic to Brazil—in this case, to Rio de Janeiro rather than to Bahia. The colonial status of Angola, however, gave this community a different character from elsewhere on the coast and neither there nor in Upper Guinea did returned freed slaves play the same role as on the Slave Coast.[71]

Notes

1 The "Slave Coast" was conventionally defined as extending from the River Volta to Lagos (or, sometimes, further east), corresponding roughly to the Bight of Benin (or, in terms of modern political geography, the coast of Togo, Bénin, and western Nigeria).
2 For connections along the lagoon, see Robin Law, "Trade and Politics behind the Slave Coast: The Lagoon Traffic and the Rise of Lagos, 1500–1800," *Journal of African History*, 24 (1983), 321–38; Law, "Between the Sea and the Lagoons: The Interaction of Maritime and Inland Navigation on the Precolonial Slave Coast," *Cahiers d'Études Africaines*, 29 (1989), 209–37.
3 See, especially, Pierre Verger, *Flux et reflux de la traite des nègres entre le Golfe de Bénin et Babia de todos os Santos, du XVIIe au XIX siècle* (Paris, 1968) (translated as *Trade Relations between the Bight of Bénin and Bahia from the Seventeenth to Nineteenth Century* [Ibadan, 1976]). Verger was not, of course, the first scholar to emphasize African-American links; we believe, however, that he was the first to conceive of these links in *interactive* terms, involving reciprocal rather than unidirectional (Africa to America) links.
4 Bernard Bailyn, "The Idea of Atlantic History," *Itinerario*, 20, no. 1 (1996), 38–44. Bailyn takes no account of the important revisionist work of John Thornton, *Africa and Africans in the Making of the Atlantic World, 1400–1680* (Cambridge, 1992).
5 Paul Gilroy, *The Black Atlantic: Modernity and Double Consciousness* (London, 1993), 6, 15–16.
6 Ira Berlin, "From Creole in African: Atlantic Creoles and the Origins of African-American Society in Mainland North America," *William and Mary Quarterly*, 3d Ser., 53 (1996). 251–88.
7 Rodrigues da Silva and Christophe da Silva, *Histoire de la famille Rodrigues da Silva sur la Côte du Bénin* (Cotonou, 1992). Francisco Rodrigues da Silva was among traders at Ouidah arrested by the local authorities after a British naval blockade of the port in 1876–1877 for alleged fraternization with the British: see Édouard Foà, *Le Dahomey* (Paris, 1895), 36.
8 Deusdado is said to have undertaken research in the archives of the Portuguese fort at Ouidah. Note that another man of the same surname Francisco Xavier Rodrigues da Silva, was an official of the Portuguese fort later (acting governor, 1805–1806); if the da Silva family of the 19th century was descended from an official of the fort, it might conceivably have been this man.

9   Paul E. Lovejoy, "Identifying Enslaved Africans: Methodological and Conceptual Considerations in Studying the African Diaspora" (paper presented at Social Sciences and Humanities Research Council of Canada and United Nations Educational, Scientific, and Cultural Organization Summer Institute, "Identifying Enslaved Africans: The Nigerian Hinterland and the Creation of the African Diaspora," York University, Ontario, July 1997). See also Robin Law and Paul Lovejoy, "The Changing Dimensions of African History: Reappropriating the Diaspora," in Simon McGrath et al., eds., *Rethinking African History* (Edinburgh, 1997), 181–200.

10 José Honório Rodrigues, "The Influence of Africa on Brazil and of Brazil on Africa," *Jour. of African Hist.*, 3 (1962), 49–67.

11 David Eltis and David Richardson, "West Africa and the Transatlantic Slave Trade: New Evidence of Long-Run Trends," *Slavery and Abolition*, 18 (1997), 16–35; Stephen Behrendt, Eltis, and Richardson, "The Bights in Comparative Perspective: The Economics of Long-Term Trends in Population Displacement from West and West-Central Africa to the Americas before 1850" (paper presented at SSHRCC and UNESCO Summer Institute, York University, July 1997).

12 For the history of Allada, Dahomey, and Oyo and their relations with the coastal ports, see, for example, Robin Law, *The Slave Coast of West Africa, 1550–1750* (Oxford, 1991); Law, *The Oyo Empire, c. 1600–c. 1836* (Oxford, 1977); I. A. Akinjogbin, *Dahomey and Its Neighbours, 1708–1818* (Cambridge, 1967); Colin W. Newbury, *The Western Slave Coast and Its Rulers* (Oxford, 1961).

13 These data are derived from a list of ships licensed to export tobacco to the area of the Slave Coast and, presumably, to return with slaves that was compiled by Verger, *Trade Relations*, 576–83. Third-grade tobacco was the primary Brazilian commodity traded for slaves in West Africa.

14 The only detailed study of the operation of one of these forts is Simone Berbain, *Le comptoir français de Juda (Ouidah) au XVIIIe siècle* (Paris, 1942).

15 Memoir, "Da Fortuleza Cezarea que o Capt José de Torries levantou na Costa da Mina as porto de Ajuda, no Vice Reinado de Visc Fernandez Cesar de Meneses," Colonial Minister of Portugal, vol. 1 (July–December 1917), 162, quoted in Verger, *Trade Relations*, 112.

16 John Adams, *Remarks on the Country Extending from Cape Palmas to the River Congo* (London, 1823), 97 (quotation); Pierre Verger, "Nigeria, Brazil, and Cuba," *Nigeria Magazine* (October 1960), 113–23; A. G. Hopkins, "An Economic History of Lagos, 1880–1914" (Ph.D. diss., University of London, 1964), 32; Manuela Carneiro da Cunha, *Negros, estrangeros: os escravos libertos e sua vola a Africa* (São Paulo, 1985), 119; Gilberto Freyre, *The Masters and the Slaves: A Study in the Development of Brazilian Civilization*, trans. Samuel Putnam (New York, 1946), 274.

17 John Duncan, *Travels in Western Africa* (London, 1847), i, 201. This benign view of the experience of slaves in Bahia is echoed in more recently recorded local tradition in Ouidah; see Casimir Agbo, *Histoire de Ouidah du XVIe au XXe siècle* ([Avignon], 1959), 52.

18 See the excellent work done on the subject by Verger, *Trade Relations;* Jerry Michael Turner, "Les Brésiliens: The Impact of Former Brazilian Slaves upon Dahomey" (Ph.D. diss., Boston University, 1975); da Cunha, *Negros;* Marianno Carneiro da Cunha, *From Slave Quarters to Town Houses: Brazilian Architecture in Nigeria and the People's Republic of Bénin* (São Paulo, 1985). See also, most recently, Lisa A. Lindsay, "'To Return to the Bosom of Their Fatherland': Brazilian Immigrants in Nineteenth-Century Lagos," *Slavery and Abolition*, 15 (1994), 22–50; Milton Roberto Monteiro Ribeiro, "Aguda—Les 'Brésiliens du Bénin: enquête anthropologique et photographique" (Thèse de Doctorat, École des Hautes Études en Sciences Sociales, Marseille, 1996); Bellarmin C. Codo, "Les afro-brésiliens de retour," in Doudou Diène, ed., *La chaîne et le lien: Une vision de la traite négrière* (Paris, 1998), 95–105.

19 Pieter de Marees, *Description and Historical Account of the Gold Kingdom of Guinea*, trans and ed. Albert van Dantzig and Adam Jones (London, 1987), 224–25; Robin Law, "Religion, Trade, and Politics on the Slave Coast: Roman Catholic Missions in Allada and Whydah in the Seventeenth Century," *Journal of Religion in Africa*, 21 (1991), 42–77 (quotations on 45, 46.

20 Law "Religion, Trade, and Politics on the Slave Coast," 42–77.

21   Verger, *Trade Relations*, 151, 177 n. 37; Adams, *Remarks*, 55; John M'Leod, *A Voyage to Africa* (London, 1820), 80.

22   Simon de Souza, *La famille de Souza du Bènin-Togo* (Cotonou, 1992). 18–19. Nicolas and Jean-Baptiste Ollivier are said to have been sent to Marseille; this detail, at least, looks anachronistic, since this town only became of major importance in Franch trade with West Africa in the period of legitimate trade in palm oil (from the 1840s).

23   Verger, *Trade Relations*, 477–78.

24   Adams, *Remarks*, 82–87; Verger, *Trade Relations*, 186; Adolphe Akindélé and Cyrille Aguessy, *Contribution à l'étude de l'histoire de l'ancien royaume de Porto-Novo* (Darkar, 1953), 73.

25   Archibald Dalzel, *The History of Dahomy* (London, 1793), 169n, 191, 197n.

26   Ibid., 222–23; Akinjogbin, *Dahomey and Its Neighbours*, 171, 178–79.

27   Fio Agbanon II, *Histoire du Petit-Popo et du royaume Guin*, ed. N. L. Gayibor (Lomé, 1991), 40, 42–43; Paul Erdmann Isert, *Letters on West Africa and the Slave Trade: Paul Erdmann Isert's "Journey to Guinea and the Caribbean Islands in Columbia,"* ed. and trans. Selena Axelrod Winsnes (Oxford, 1992), 62 (quotation), 90; F. E. Forbes, *Dahomey and the Dahomans* (London, 1851), i. 100.

28   Dalzel, *History of Dahomy*, 181; Verger, *Trade Relations*, 188; Jean Mettas, *Répertoire des expeditions négrières françaises au XVIIIe siècle* (Paris, 1978), 732; M'Leod, *Voyage to Africa*, 102–06

29   Robin Law, "King Agaja of Dahomey, the Slave Trade, and the Question of West African Plantations: The Mission of Bulfinch Lambe and Adomo Tomo to England, 1726–32," *Journal of Imperial and Commonwealth History*, 19 (1991), 137–63.

30   Verger, *Trade Relations*, 219, 224, 229, 231.

31   Edna G. Bay, "Dahomean Political Exile and the Atlantic Slave Trade" (paper presented at the SSHRCC and UNESCO Summer Institute, York University, July 1997). Whether Agotime was in fact recovered from Brazil is disputed.

32   Verger, *Trade Relations*, 241–42; Alberto da Costa e Silva, *As relações entre o Brasil e a Africa Negra, de 1822 a da Guerra Mondial* (Luanda, 1966), 7.

33   Robert Louis Stein, *The French Slave Trade in the Eighteenth Century: An Old Regime Business* (Madison, 1979), 43–47; Stephen D. Behrendt, "The Annual Volume and Regional Distribution of the British Slave Trade, 1780–1807," *Jour. of African Hist.*, 38 (1997), 205; Verger, *Trade Relations*, 209–12. Although the French slave trade was re-legalized between 1802 and 1818, French slaving at Ouidah did not significantly revive.

34   Leslie Bethell, *The Abolition of the Brazilian Slave Trade: Britain, Brazil, and the Slave Trade Question, 1807–1860* (Cambridge, 1970), chaps. 1–2.

35   Forbes, *Dahomy*, ii, 175; De Monleon, "Le Cap de Palmes, le Dahomey et l'Île du Prince en 1844," *Revue Coloniale*, 6 (1845), 5 (quotation). King Gezo of Dahomey (r. 1818–1858) is said to have sent his official interpreter for the French, Bokpe, to France to improve his proficiency—presumably, in the context of the reestablishment of French trade in the 1840s; see [Revnier], "Ouidah: organisation du commandement [1917]," *Mémoire du Bénin*, 2 (1993), 33.

36   David Eltis, *Economic Growth and the Ending of the Transatlantic Slave Trade* (New York, 1987), 148–63.

37   These data come from House of Commons Sessional Papers, 1821–1851, Class A. Correspondence with British Commissioners . . . relating to the Slave Trade.

38   Eltis, *Economic Growth*, 153.

39   David Ross, "The First Chacha of Whydah: Francisco Felix de Souza," *Odu*, 3d Ser., 2 (1969), 19–28. For de Souza family traditions, see Norberto de Souza, "Contribution à l'histoire de la famille de Souza," *Études Dahoméennes*, 13 (1955), 17–21; Simone de Souza, *La famille de Souza*.

40   House of Commons Sessional Papers, 1831–1839, Class A. Correspondence with British Commissioners . . . relating to the Slave Trade.

41   On M. J. d'Almeida's activities at Lagos and elsewhere, see Verger, *Trade Relations*, 365, 467; and House of Commons Sessional Papers, 1831, 1837–1838, 1841, Class A. Correspondence with British Commissioners . . . relating to the Slave Trade, Cases of the *Nossa Senhora da Guia, Lafayette, Fumega*, and *Agusto*. On J. J. de Brito Lima, see House of Commons Sessional Papers, 1826, 1841, Class A. Correspondence with British Commissioner . . .

relating to the Slave Trade, Cases of the *Bon Fim* and *Guiana*; House of Commons Sessional Papers, 1852, Papers Relative to the Reduction of Lagos, Commodore Wilmot to Commodore Bruce, Dec. 1, 1815, Enclosure in no. 76; Public Record Office, London, FO 84/950, Consul Campbell to the earl of Clarendon, Mar. 24, Dec. 1, 1854.

42   David A. Ross, "The Career of Domingo Martinez in the Bight of Benin, 1833–64," *Jour. of African Hist.*, 6 (1965), 79–90.

43   Bellarmin C. Codo, "Les 'Brésiliens' en Afrique de l'Ouest, hier et aujourd'hui" (paper presented at UNESCO and SSHRCC Summer Institute, York University, July 1997).

44   De Souza and Martinez were sometimes described in contemporary accounts as "mulattoes." "According to family traditions, the former's mother was Amerindian; see Turner, "Les Brésiliens," 89.

45   Verger, *Trade Relations*, 402–03, 418, 465–67; Turner, "Les Brésiliens." 102–05, 131.

46   Verger, *Trade Relations*, 538; Bello to Kosoko, Bewhia, Oct. 15, Nov. 8, 1849, House of Lords Sessional Papers, 1852–1853, Slave Trade Correspondence, XXII, 338–39; Turner, "Les Brésiliens," 102–05; de Souza, *La famille de Souza*, 53.

47   Turner, "Les Brésiliens," 29–54; Lindsay, "'To Return to the Bosom of Their Fatherland,'" 39–42. For the Brazilian Muslims on the Slave Coast, see Robin Law, "Islam in Dahomey: A Case Study of the Introduction and Influence of Islam in a Peripheral Area of West Africa," *Scottish Journal of Religious Studies*, 7 (1986), 108–09; T.G.O. Gbadamosi, *The Growth of Islam among the Yoruba, 1841–1908* (London, 1978), 28–29.

48   João José Reis, *Slave Rebellion in Brazil: The Muslim Uprising of 1855 in Bahia* (Baltimore, 1993), 220; "Note historique sur Ouidah par l'Administrateur Gavoy (1913)," *Études Dahoméennes*, 13 (1955), 69–70; [Reynier], "Ouidah," 44–45; Lindsay, "To Return to the Bosom of Their Fatherland,'" 26.

49   Turner, "Les Brésiliens," 125–27; [Reynier], "Ouidah," 40, 58.

50   The reoccupation was intermittent in 1844–1861 but continuous from 1865. Personnel supplied from São Tomé in some cases came ultimately from further afield. In the 1870s, the fort garrison consisted of "Congo" soldiers, recruited presumably from Angola, and the chaplain was "a Hindu priest from Goa"; see J. Alfred Skertchly, *Dahomey as It Is* (London, 1874), 174; Serval, "Report sur une mission au Dahomey," *Revue Maritime et Coloniale*, 59 (1878), 195.

51   House of Commons Sessional Papers, 1837, Class A. Correspondence with British Commissioners . . . relating to the Slave Trade, Case of the *Mosca*; Turner, "Les Brésiliens," 131; Rodolfo Sarracino, *Las que volvieron a África* (Havana, 1988). Today, local tradition describes the founder of the Sangron family of Ouidah as Brazilian; see de Souza, *La famille de Souza*, 71.

52   The role of Catholicism as an integrative factor was, however, complicated (at least in the case of Ouidah) by competition between the local branch of the Portuguese church, based in São Tomé, and the French Catholic Mission, which arrived in the 1860s; see Turner, "Les Brésiliens," 157–58, 191–96, 244–45.

53   Verger, *Trade Relations*, 533 (quotation), 549–50; da Cunha, *From Slave Quarters to Town Houses*, 24–30.

54   For example, de Souza, *La famille de Souza*, documents early marriage alliances with the Sangron, dos Santos, Martins, de Medeiros, and Sastre families (as well as with the indigenous royal family of Little Popo).

55   This coastwise dimension of Brazilian activities on the Slave Coast is well brought out in the historical novel by António Olinto, *A Casa do aqua* (Rio de Janeiro, 1969) (translated as *The Water House* [London, 1970]).

56   R[ichard] J. Hammond, *Portugal and Africa, 1815–1950: A Study in Uneconomic Imperialism* (Stanford. Calif., 1966), 69; Carlos Eugenio Corrêa da Silva, *Uma Viagem ao Establecimento Portuguez de S. João Baptista de Ajuda na Costa da Mina em 1865* (Lisboa, 1866), 59–60; House of Commons Sessional Papers, 1828, 1840, Class A. Correspondence with British Commissioners . . . relating to the Slave Trade, Cases of the *Trajano* and *Emprehendor*.

57   Corrêa da Silva, *Viagem*, 62, 81–82. The appointment was renewed for subsequent holders of the title of "chacha," younger brothers of Isidoro: Francisco Felix de Souza (surnamed "Chico"), in 1865, and Julião Felix de Souza, in 1884.

58 See, especially, Jean Herskovits Kopytoff, *A Preface to Modern Nigeria: The "Sierra Leonians" in Yoruba, 1830–1890* (Madison, Wis., 1965).

59 But to only a limited degree. In late-19th-century Lagos, Sierra Leonean elite males took 80% of their Christian wives from within the Sierra Leonean community; they took only 8% from Brazilian families; see Kristin Mann, *Marrying Well: Marriage, Status, and Social Change among the Educated Elite in Colonial Lagos* (Cambridge, 1985), 93.

60 Turner, "Les Brésiliens," 85–154; Lindsay, "'To Return to the Bosom of Their Father-land,'" 43–44; da Cunha, *From Slave Quarters to Town Houses* 20–40; J. Lorand Matory, "Return, 'Race,' and Religion in a Transatlantic Yoruba Nation" (paper presented at the Annual Meeting of the African Studies Association, San Francisco, November 1996).

61 Verger, *Trade Relations*, 408; de Souza, *La famille de Souza*, 42; Ross, "The Career of Domingo Martinez," 85.

62 Foà, *Le Dahomey*, 31; de Souza, *La famille de Souza*, 55.

63 Richard Burton, *A Minion to Gelele, King of Dahome* (London, 1864), i, 77–74. The text of the will is in Verger, *Trade Relations*, 425–27 (quotation); see also 414–15.

64 Will of Joaquim d'Almeida, in Verger, *Trade Relations*, 405, 475–77.

65 Correspondence of José Francisco dos Santos, in Pierre Verger, *Les afro-américians* (Dakar, 1952), 53–100.

66 Correspondence of Oba Kosoko, in House of Lords Sessional Papers, 1852–1853. Slave Trade correspondence, XXII, 340.

67 Ross, "The First Chacha," 25; Ross, "The Career of Domingo Martinez," 87; Jose Francisco dos Santos to Lartigue, July 6, 1863, in Verger, *Les afro-américains*, 91.

68 Jerry Michael Turner, "Democratic Instincts in Dahomey (Benin Republic), 1929–30 and 1989–96: Afro-Brazilian Political Behavior on the Benin Gulf" (paper presented at the Annual Meeting of the African Studies Association, San Francisco. November 1996): Elisée Soumonni, "Some Reflections on the Brazilian Legacy in Dahomey" (paper presented at the Symposium, "Rethinking the African Diaspora: The Making of a Black Atlantic World in the Bight of Benin and Brazil," Emory University, Atlanta. Ga., April 1998).

69 For an illustrative case, see the study of the family descended from the Irish trader Richard Brew (d. 1776), Margarer Priestly, *West African Trade and Coast Society: A Family Study* (London, 1969).

70 In the late 18th century, "many" of the inhabitants of Old Calabar were reported to be literate in English, and there were local schools "for the purpose of instructing in this art the youths belonging to families of consequence"; see Adams, *Remarks*, 144.

71 Walter Rodney, *A History of the Upper Guinea Coast, 1545–1800* (Oxford, 1970), 200–22; Philip D. Curtin, *Economic Change in Precolonial Africa: Senegambia in the Era of the Slave Trade* (Madison, Wis., 1975), 95–109; George E. Brooks, *Landlords and Strangers: Ecology, Society, and Trade in Western Africa, 1000–1630* (Boulder, Colo., 1993), 121–97; Joseph C. Miller, *Way of Death: Merchant Capitalism and the Angolan Slave Trade, 1730–1830* (Madison, Wis., 1988), 246–313.

Chapter 36

John Thornton

THE AFRICAN EXPERIENCE OF THE "20. AND ODD NEGROES" ARRIVING IN VIRGINIA IN 1619

NGEL SLUITER'S RECENT NOTE on the origins of the Africans brought to Virginia in 1619 to work as laborers in the emerging English colony serves as an opportunity to explore the background of the best known of the "founders" of African America.[1] Thanks to documentary records delivered by Sluiter, we now know that the "20. and odd Negroes" that arrived at Point Comfort in August had been taken on the high seas from the *São João Bautista*. This ship was a Portuguese slaver captained by Manuel Mundes da Cunha bound from Luanda, Angola, to Vera Cruz carrying slaves in uniformity with an *asiento*, a contract to deliver slaves to Spanish colonies. Sluiter thus establishes that they were not seasoned slaves of many origins brought from the Caribbean, as was previously accepted by most historians, but probably a much more ethnically coherent group just recently enslaved in Africa.[2] The information on the time and place of their enslavement in Africa allows us to present them in their own historic context and not simply that of their owners-to-be.

Knowing that these Africans came from Luanda, the recently established capital of the Portuguese colony of Angola, allows us to estimate their ethnic background and the likely conditions of their enslavement. In those days the colony of Angola was a sliver of land extending inland from Luanda and along the Kwanza River until its confluence with the Lukala River and not the larger country of the late twentieth century. Some of the cargo of the *São João Bautista* and the twenty-odd negroes may have been enslaved in the kingdom of Kongo, the Portuguese colony's northern neighbor, or by its eastern neighbors. Portugal had been exporting slaves from Kongo sources since the early sixteenth century, primarily through the port of Mpinda on the Zaire River. When the colony of Angola was founded, many traders shifted their export operations southward, and, by the end of the century Luanda-based merchants had developed a series of trading networks east across Kongo to the Maleba Pool area.[3] At the time, King Álvaro III of Kongo was involved in a complex dispute with his uncles, and, although this seems to have entailed little bloodshed, it had generated one major war against the duke of Nsundi sometime between 1616 and 1619 as well, perhaps, as some judicial enslavement.[4] Alternatively, the Africans may have come from beyond Kongo's eastern or northern frontier and been enslaved under circumstances that are beyond the reach of our documentation. It is quite possible, then, that among the slaves who boarded

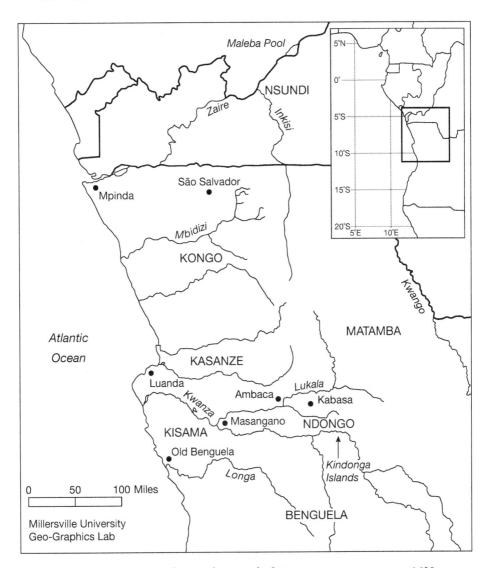

Map 36.1   Angola in West Africa in the period of Portuguese conquest, *circa* 1620

the *São João Bautista* in 1619 there were those who spoke the Kikongo language and were enslaved in Kongo's province of Nsundi or the land lying just beyond Kongo's eastern frontier.

It is also possible that some of those who left Luanda in 1619 were captured or otherwise enslaved in the lands south of the Portuguese colony across the Kwanza River. Since the late sixteenth century the Portuguese had been buying slaves there who probably spoke the Kimbundu and Umbundu languages and transporting them to Luanda for shipment abroad. Wars, especially those of a marauding group of mercenary soldiers known as Imbangala, had disrupted the region greatly. In 1618, the Imbangala had just left the region, and the area was so devastated that it is unlikely that any more captives could have come from those districts, at least for a time.

The most important military and enslavement operations in Angola, however, were the large and complex military campaigns waged in 1618–1620 under Portuguese leadership against the Kingdom of Ndongo, during which thousands of its Kimbundu-speaking subjects were captured and deported.[5] Given the significance and size of this war, most if not all of the slaves of the *São João Bautista* were very likely captured in these engagements. The Portuguese governor Luis Mendes de Vasconçeles, who arrived in the colony of Angola in 1617 and served as governor until 1621, led the campaigns. In the three years of his tenure, Angola exported about 50,000 salves, far more than were exported before or would be again for some decades.[6]

A self-confident man, Mender de Vasconçelos had served in Flanders as a soldier and had even written a treatise on the art of war.[7] He was sure that he could break through the military and diplomatic stalemate that had halted Portuguese advance in Angola since their decisive defeat at the Battle of Lukala on December 29, 1589, by a coalition of the Kingdoms of Matamba and Ndongo.[8] Indeed, he was so confident that, on receiving nomination as governor, he submitted a memorandum to the king announcing his intention to conquer the lands from one coast to the other and to join Angola with the equally new and uncertain Portuguese colony in what became Mozambique, thus opening a new route to India. In exchange, he proposed that he receive a variety of privileges and honors, including the title "Viceroy of Ethiopia" for his efforts.[9]

Mender de Vasconçelos suggested char he would achieve these goals by his own skill as a soldier (and some 1,000 additional infantry and 200 cavalry he thought the crown should give him from Portugal). Instead, he arrived with very few reinforcements and immediately became aware of the generally unfavorable military situation. Since the beginning of the "conquest" of Angola, the Portuguese had relied on an assortment of military assets: soldiers from metropolitan Portugal, a few more from the island colony of São Tomé in the Gulf of Guinea, and personal slaves of those people armed for war. But they mainly depended on the supply of soldiers provided by African rulers (*sobas*) who submitted to Portuguese authority. *Sobas* were petty local nobles whose domains, usually covered a few villages and who raised taxes and soldiers from among their subjects. Larger kingdoms such as Ndongo comprised dozens of these local vassals, who accepted the overlordship of larger powers while maintaining control in their local areas. The soldiers provided by the *sobas*, known as the "black army" or *guerra preta*, composed most of the troops in all Portuguese military efforts.[10]

Nevertheless, *guerra preta* had proven unreliable, for the *sobas* were playing a diplomatic game in which they balanced submission between one or other of the greater African powers. They might claim obedience to the Kingdom of Kongo to the north or the Kingdom of Ndongo to the east, or alternatively swear vassalage to Portugal, since 1580 under the rule of the king of Spain. Slight changes in the military balance might bring disastrous results, so when the Portuguese lost at the Lukala, there were massive defections of the *sabas*.[11] Likewise, *sobas* sometimes changed sides without informing the Portuguese also with catastrophic consequences for Portuguese policy.[12]

Portuguese inability in maintain an effective military force had compelled them to accept a status quo treaty (in 1599) with Ndongo, their principal African rival, after the Battle of Lukala. They had to content themselves with small-scale (and not always successful) raids against weaker polities to the north and south. The slave trade, which was the mainstay of Angola's international commerce, came to rely more on trading in the interior markets for people enslaved in surrounding countries than on direct capture in wars led by Portuguese officers. The Jesuit chronicler Pero Rodrigues wrote in 1594 that the numbers of "slaves taken in war are nothing compared to those bought at feiras [markets], at these feiras the kings and lords and all Ethiopia sell slaves," which were acquired in wars by the kings themselves or from among that portion of their population that was already enslaved.[13]

In the early years of the seventeenth century, help from an unexpected quarter allowed the Portuguese not only to break out of the military standoff but also to acquire thousands of slaves through direct capture. In those years, Portuguese merchants developing contacts south of their original colony, then known as the Kingdom of Benguela, first encountered the Imbangala, who would aid them and change the history of Angola fundamentally for the next half century.

The Imbangala are a mysterious group, and their origins have aroused much debate.[14] Although Portuguese officials of the time routinely called them "Jagas" and linked them vaguely with a group that had invaded the Kingdom of Kongo in the 1570s, modern historians deny that connection and place their immediate origins in the central highlands of Angola in the region containing the modern cities of Huambo and Lubango.[15] They are described for the first time in the historical record by Andrew Battell, a captured English sailor forced to serve the Portuguese. In an account of his sixteen-month stay with an Imbangala band led by Imbe Kalandula in about 1599 to 1601, Battell does not characterize the Imbangala as an ethnic or folk group (though some of their descendants became one in the late seventeenth century and persist today). Rather, the Imbangala were a company, or several independent companies, of soldiers and raiders who lived entirely by pillage.

The Imbangala seem to have been a quasi-religious cult dedicated to evil in the central African sense of violent greed and selfishness. They allowed no children in their camp, killing all newborn babies by burying them alive according to Battell, and reinforcing themselves and replacing their casualties by recruiting adolescent boys from among their captives. These boys were made to wear a distinctive collar until they had learned the art of war and had killed someone, when they were admitted to full membership in the group. Imbe Kalandulu's band had recruited so many of its people by this method that only the senior officers were said to be members of his original company; the rest had been recruited through capture.[16] Their penchant for cannibalism and human sacrifice was apparently rooted in beliefs about witchcraft. The Imbangala actively assumed the role of witches, whose fundamental characteristic was that they killed and ate their victims.[17] That they were viewed as fighting in the cause of profound evil is revealed by a folk belief recorded a half century later. According to this tale, the protective deities of the Gangela region were so terrified by the Imbangala that they went and hid in the lakes and rivers, only to reemerge when time had caused the Imbangala to soften their ways.[18] The Imbangala eschewed the cult of the protective deities (*kilundas*), who promoted peace and concord, in favour of their own ancestors, who were themselves selfish and bloody individuals and kept these characteristics in the Other World when they died.[19]

This radical devotion to evil was confirmed by their exploitative economy. Battell noted that "[they] doe reap thier Enemies Corne, and take their Cattell. For they will not sowe, nor plant, nor bring up any Cattell, more than they take by Warres." Their favorite pillage was palm wine taken from cultivated trees. Instead of tapping the trees and drawing small quantities of sap for oil or to ferment for wine, they cut down the whole tree. It gave no yield for ten days, then a small hole was drilled into the heart of the tree, which would yield about two quarts of sap a day for twenty-six days, when it dried up. By this method they destroyed all the palm trees in a region, and when all had been used up they moved on.[20]

The Portuguese from the colony of Angola took an interest in the Imbangala to their south largely because the marauders were prepared to sell their captives as slaves to Portuguese buyers. In the late 1590s, a group of Portuguese merchants had organized four voyages that included Bartell to the area for the express purpose of buying captives for export. These merchants assisted Imbe Kalandula in crossing the River Kuvo to attack the Kingdom of Benguela.[21]

The Imbangala generally made a large encampment in the country they intended to pillage, often arriving near harvest time. They forced the local authorities either to fight them outright or to withdraw into fortified locations, leaving the fields for the Imbangala to harvest. Once their enemies were weakened by fighting or lack of food, they could make a final assault on their lands and capture them. The presence of Portuguese slave buyers, who also provided firearms, made raiding people as profitable or even more profitable as raiding food and livestock had been before. Battell joined the group that entered the Kingdom of Benguela, and after their first successful battles they remained in that region for five months (during which time the Portuguese freighted three voyages with captives). Then, because they "wanted palm trees," they marched five days inland to an unidentifiable place named Kali Ka Nsamba, where they remained pillaging for another four months. This band, which valued Battell and his musket, traveled steadily eastward just north of the great highlands for sixteen months, almost as far as the southward bend of the Kwanza River. In general, they took about four to five months to waste completely each country in which they stayed.[22] Whether because of the large size of their fighting force (which Bartell estimated at 1600) or the terror they spread through rumors of their ruthless evil and cannibalism, they seemed to have been uniformly successful, overcoming the determined resistance of country after country.

The ruined Kingdom of Benguela was so stripped of people, cattle, and palm trees by the Imbangala whom Battell and his associates assisted that when Manuel Cerveira Pereira went to the country in 1617 to become governor of a new Portuguese colony of Benguela, which initially was planned to be built around the abandoned commercial settlement of Benguela, he was unable to find enough people and economic activity to justify his efforts and moved further south.[23] By the start of the second decade of the seventeenth century, much of the land south of the Kwanza River (more or less the southern border of Portuguese control) had been demolished and destroyed by Imbangala activity. For this reason, few people from this region probably found their way onto the *São Jaão Bautista* in 1619.

Portuguese private merchants, such as those whom Battell was forced to serve about 1598, hoped to continue what for them was a profitable enterprise in the north. At some point they began to introduce Imbangala bands north of the river into lands under Portuguese authority. Royal governors, especially Pereira (1615–1617) and Antonio Gonçalvez Pita (1617), made this unofficial practice official. They did so in large measure because governors could benefit more from leading military campaigns that took slaves directly than could benefit from their salaries, which derived from taxing exports at markets or the coast. The Portuguese crown, however, instructed its governors to promote peaceful trade and frowned on practices such as recruiting Imbangala raiders. Local Portuguese settlers, For their part, commonly preferred the crown's policy of staying clear of wars because they could acquire slaves by trade and conflict disrupted that trade.[24]

When Mendes de Vasconçelos arrived in Angola, then, despite his desire to conquer straight across Africa to Mozambique, he echoed the crown's concerns (and his own instructions), about the use of Imbangala by renouncing employment of those "who sustain themselves on human flesh and are enemies of all living things and thieves of the lands where they enter." Not only had they destroyed lands, but the government could no longer collect its tribute from the area, and even the markets were in ruins, thanks to Imbangala depredations. His predecessors' employment of them was a mistake, he argued, or even a crime, punishable by death and confiscation.[25] When Mendes de Vasconçelos took his first military action in the projected conquest of Ndongo, however, he quickly found he needed the Imbangala as allies.

An attack on Ndongo was inviting because the kingdom was undergoing a domestic political crisis. According to traditions collected about forty years later, the ruler of Ndongo, Mbandi Ngola Kiluanji, allowed the brothers of his wife to commit many crimes that outraged the nobility of the country, who, probably early in 1617, joined together, lured him into an ambush at the lands of a rebel *soba*, Kavulo ka Kabasa, near the Lukala, and overthrew him.[26]

Mbandi Ngola Kiluanji's son and successor, Ngola Mbandi, was nor yet secure on his throne, and, the coalition of *sabas* who had overthrown his father not yet fully loyal when Mendes de Vasconçelos arrived in August 1617. The new governor soon moved the Portuguese *presidio* of Hango eastward along the Lukala River to Ambaca, a point much closer to the court of Ndongo but the new fort, probably a simple palisade mounting a few pieces of artillery, was soon besieged by the local ruler, Kaita ka Balanga, "a favorite of the King of Angola."[27] In this predicament, Mendes found the Imbangala useful allies. Consequently, as Bishop Manuel Bautista Soares of Kongo wrote to Lisbon in 1619, "in place of leaving off with the Jagas, he embraced them, and he has gone to war with them for two years, killing with them and capturing innumerable innocent people, not only against the law of God but also against the expressed regulations of Your Majesty."[28]

To start his campaign Mendes de Vasconçelos brought three Imbangala bands across the Kwanza to assist him. He had two of them baptized as João Kasanje and João Kasa ka Ngola, although the third, Donga, apparently declined to be baptized.[29] Thanks to their assistance, in the campaign season of 1618 Mendes de Vasconçelos was able to defeat completely the forces of the *soba* Kaita ka Balanga and break out of the siege. His opponents were probably already mobilized at the start of the campaign.

Mobilization in Ndongo began, according to late sixteenth-century witnesses, by the sounding of the *ngongo*, a double clapperless bell used for war calls in all the settlements of the area, followed by the cry, in Kimbundu, "*Ita! Ita!*" (War!

War!). Old people, some women, and most children were ordered to retire to hills or other inaccessible places until the fighting was over, while the men prepared for battle. Some took up arms, mostly bows and arrows but also crescent-shaped axes and lances; others carried supplies. Some women accompanied the armies to cook for and comfort the soldiers. These militia soldiers were not expected to remain in position beyond the initial shock of battle, which progressed quickly. At some point the soldiers' nerves broke, and they retreated so rapidly that sometimes the front ranks hacked their way through the rearward soldiers who did not flee fast enough.[30] Although they might reform later, even within a few days, they left strategic positions undefended, and the remaining civilians who had not taken adequate shelter in hills or forests were vulnerable to enslavement.

The Portuguese–Imbangala forces capitalized on their victory by attacking the now undefended royal palace in the city of Kabasa, taking "many captives," who represented the real fruit of the war. The army "wintered" in the city but suffered a great deal from sicknesses common to the central African rainy season (September 1618 to March 1619). Falling ill himself, Mendes de Vasconçelos withdrew his forces to Hango and returned to Luanda, entrusting the new army to his nineteen-year-old son, João. In 1619, João returned to the field, defeated and killed the *soba* Kaita ka Balanga and ninety-four other nobles, attacked Kabasa, and drove out Ngola Mbandi, leaving his mother and wives, in the words of a contemporary Portuguese chronicler, "in our power, who with many prisoners and slaves were carried away as captives."[31] The bishop wrote in September 1619 that the dead from this campaign had infected the rivers, and "a great multitude of innocent people had been captured without cause."[32] The demographic impact of this war was starkly obvious that the campaign was resumed the next year; the army "met no resistance in any part of the back-country [*Sertão*], these provinces having become destitute of inhabitants."[33] Although many people had been killed or enslaved, others simply fled the region—either hiding in the hills or the bush or following the king to his new headquarters on the Kindonga Islands in the Kwanza River.

This stunning military success was largely the work of the Imbangala allies. As the bishop noted, "as he had Jagas [Imbangala], the wars were without any danger [to them] but with discredit to the Portuguese."[34] Although Mendes de Vasconçelos was a soldier experienced in European wars and thought himself capable of great achievements in Africa, his initial approach to warfare in Angola was flawed. According to later accounts, he endangered his troops in their first actions by mustering them into tight formations and only after suffering losses did he accept the wisdom of African methods of warfare, which included the use of Imbangala expertise and prowess.[35]

The military forces unleashed by Mender de Vasconçelos got far out of hand. The Imbangala hands broke free from Portuguese alliance and began a long campaign of freebooting in lands formerly under Ndongo's rule: one band, led by João Kasa ka Ngola, ended up entering the king of Ndongo's service against the Portuguese. The bishop maintained that some 4,000 baptized Christians from the Portuguese baggage train, some free, some enslaved, had been captured illegally by rampaging Imbangalas in the 1619 campaign.[36] Beyond that, the king of Kongo also protested on behalf of his own Kimbundu-speaking subordinates north of Ndongo who had also been attacked and closed the border to trade. A number of Portuguese settlers and the bishop protested vigorously as well, because they were all but ruined by the Imbangala raids on their lands and also saw their trade disrupted. But their protests were to no avail, for Mendes de Vasconçelos served out his three-year term and returned to Portugal, wealthier by far.[37]

So many people were captured and designated for sale abroad during this brief time that they overwhelmed the capacities of Luanda to manage them. During the confusion, thousands of slaves escaped to Kisama south of the city or to the swampy Kasanze region to the north, forming runaway communities that required an entire military campaign to round up two years later.[38] Shipping was probably inadequate to transport all the slaves captured in 1618 who remained imprisoned in the city in makeshift and not always secure pens, to be joined by the flood arriving from the more successful and devastating campaign of 1619. The *São João Bautista* was one of thirty-six slave ships that left Luanda for Brazil or ports of the Spanish Indies in 1619.[39]

The people enslaved by Mendes de Vasconçelos's army and his Imbangala allies were from the narrow corridor of land about thirty miles broad and some fifty miles deep between the Lutete Rivers, a cool plateau region mostly over 4,000-foot elevation. Within this larger region most of the enslaved came from the royal district of Ndongo, the target of both the 1618 and 1619 campaigns and the heartland of the area. As such, they were probably from urban backgrounds. Kabasa, the royal court, and nearby settlements formed a dense complex of towns in a thickly populated countryside. The royal district was not much different in 1618 than it had been in 1564 when it was first visited by Portuguese who described the nucleated town of Angoleme as being as large as the Portuguese city of Évora. Aligned along streets inside a stockade interwoven with grasses were 5,000–6,000 thatched dwellings that probably housed 20,000–30,000 people. There were several such enclosed towns in close proximity in the royal district as well as a rural population tightly settled between them. Central African cities were more rural than European ones, so there was a great deal of farming going on nearby, and many urban residents raised food crops and even domestic animals. Yet the rural areas formed a continuous landscape of settlement, so that when a fire broke out in Angoleme in 1564 the destruction of proximate houses spread for miles and was said to have displaced 100,000 people—clearly an exaggeration but suggestive of the size and density of the general region.[40]

The rural people of the district as well as many of the town dwellers raised millet and sorghum (American crops like manioc and maize had not yet become popular) to make into *funji*, a stiff porridge, that would be eaten along with *nicefo* (a banana) and a palm oil-based gravy. They also tended large herds of cattle and raised smaller stocks of goats, chicken, and guinea fowl in their fields and pastures. They dressed in cloth made locally from tree bark and cotton or imported from as far away as Kongo. They attended regular markets in their own district and regional markets to obtain what they did not produce—iron and steel from favored regions in an area famous for its steel production or salt from the region south of the Kwanza.[41]

The captives of Mendes de Vasconçelos's campaigns probably had a stronger sense of a common identity than was typical of single cargoes at other times or places, who might have come from diverse origins and have been acquired through wide-ranging trade routes, wars, or other means of enslavement. But because such a large number of captives in that year were taken from this single campaign, most of the people awaiting export in Luanda in 1619 must have come from a relatively small area.

People in seventeenth-century Ndongo had primary political loyalties connected to local territories, called *xi* in Kimbundu, which were ruled by the *sobas*. Within the area of the 1618–1619 campaigns, people in the royal district considered themselves "people of the court" (thus serving the king as a *soba),* which is more or less what Kahasa means, and subjects of Ndongo whereas those living farther away, in Kaita ka Balanga, for instance, might have taken their loyalty to that *soba* as equally important as their loyalty to the king.[42] In Kimbundu, *xi* represented geographically and juridicially defined communities such as the royal district or the lands of the *soba* Kaita ka Balanga. In the Kimbundu catechism of 1642, the primary text for the seventeenth-century language (probably first composed within five years of the great wars of 1618–1620), Jerusalem was defined as a *xi*, and Pontius Pilate was *"tandala ya xi imoxi ailûca 'Ierusalem"* or "governor of *xi* known as Jerusalem."[43] By contrast, in giving an example from local experience the Portuguese version of the catechism notes that "in the kingdom of Ndongo, when a vassal is a traitor," whereas the Kimbundu text simply reads *"o Ndongo"* ("in Ndongo") and omits any term for kingdom or territory. At another point, where the Portuguese refers to the "kings and lords who govern" the text produces *"o Michino, no gingâna ginêne jābata o xi gicalacalà,"* literally, "the kings, the great lords of villages and countries [*xi*] of all sorts.[44] These units were defined by clear boundaries (*mbande*), a term so widely used that it had entered Angolan Portuguese by the 1620s.[45]

These terms defined political loyalty, not necessarily ethnic sense. Although people surely had a parochial identification with their *xi*, in a region like that between the Lukala and Kwanza Rivers, which was integrated economically thanks to the presence of the court and its settlements and ruled politically by the king, they were likely to have a regional identity defined by the kingdom itself. Each person was, as the catechism notes, *mucu Ndongo* (a person from that place, that is, Ndongo).[46] In modern Kimbundu, the *mukwa-* prefix (plural *akwa-*) is the normal way to express membership in an ethnic group that combines the presonal class prefix with the locative prefix *ku-*; this is thus a second way of describing ethnic identity with a geographical place.[47] In the end, they also had a larger and vaguer identity as those who spoke Kinbundu. The "Amhundu language" (*lingua ambunda*) was a term for Kimbundu so widely used in Portuguese documents that Governor Fernão de Sousa, writing in 1626 told his subordinate to "make announcements in every *quilombo* [military camp] in Portuguese, and Ambundo."[48] Kimbundu speakers used this term when speaking of themselves, as the "Ambundu people."[49] Thus a certain ethnic identity extended beyond the barriers of an individual *soba*'s territories and provided even stronger ethnic glue to people from the area when their removal and transportation to America made political identities and loyalties irrelevant. In America, when Kimbundu-speaking people were able to communicate and visit each other, a sense of an "Angola Nation" emerged. It was certainly observable in Spanish America, if not yet at the very beginnings of English-speaking Virginia's reception of Africans.

The Mbundus of the capital region followed the local religion, but Portuguese law required all African slaves to be baptized and made Christian before their arrival in America. By 1619, a Kimbundu-speaking Christian community existed in Angola, with its own informal catechismal literature, delivered by the Jesuit priests who had accompanied the first conquerors in 1575. The basic catechism, for those captives awaiting embarkation or on board ship, probably followed the outlines set down in a late sixteenth-century text, though undoubtedly delivered in Kimbundu.[50] Such a rudimentary instruction was probably oriented to the syncretic practice of the Angolan church, which followed patterns already a century old from the Kongo church that had originally fertilized it.[51] Thus early seventeenth-century Spanish Jesuits, conducting an investigation of the state of knowledge of the Christian religion among newly arrived slaves, found that, for all the problems they noted, the Angolan slaves seemed to have adequate understanding of the faith by the time they arrived.[52] Quite possibly then those slaves who ended up in Virginia instead of Vera Cruz had at least been introduced to the Christian faith, though Virginia slave holders, with their fear that Christianity would make slaves free, would have been reluctant to admit it, had they known.

If the victims of Mendes de Vasconçelos's war were among the twenty slaves brought to Virginia in 1619, they did not conform to the stereotyped parochial image of Africans from precolonial villages. They were more likely from an urban or at least urbanized area (though they probably knew how to raise crops and domestic animals), and they had learned the rudiments of Christianity. It is probable that, in the decades that followed, those who survived the first year in Virginia eventually encountered more Angolans from their homeland or from the nearby Kongo, brought especially to New York by Dutch traders and resold to Virginia colonists.[53] They may even have met up with the slaves that one Captain Guy (or Gay) took from a ship off the Angolan coast and exchanged for tobacco in Virginia in 1628.[54] At that time, a series of wars in the region around the Kindonga Islands between Ndongo's new and vigorous Queen Njinga (ruled 1624–1663) and a Portuguese-assisted rival for her throne led to the enslavement of thousands.[55] These new captives perhaps gave a certain Angolan touch to the early Chesapeake. Significantly, the grandson of one of their contemporaries, who had arrived in 1621, in 1677 named his Pastern Shore estate "Angola."[56]

Notes

1   They were not the first, for the presence of some 32 Afro-Virginians was already noted 5 months earlier in a census; William Thorndale, "The Virginia Census of 1619," *Magazine of Virginia Genealogy*, 33 (1995) 155–70.

2   Sluiter, "New Light on the '20. and Odd Negroes' Arriving in Virginia, August 1619," *William and Mary Quarterly*. 3d Ser., 54 (1997), 396–98. I have changed the ship's and its captain's names to reflect Portuguese orthography rather than the Spanish of the documents.

3   A good survey of these routes and the merchants involved in the late 16th century can be found in Arquivo Nacional de Torre do Tombo, Lisbon, Inquisição de Lisboa, 159/7/877, "Visita a Angola," esp. fols. 23–23v, 28v, 54v–55v, 64–64v, 82–83, 102v–103v. These were traders denounced to the Inquisition, mostly for being secret Jews. For a fuller treatment of the Portugal–Kongo connection in this period see John Thornton, "Angola," in *O Império Africano*, vol. 9 of Joel Serrão and A. H. de Oliveira Marques, gen. eds., *Nova História de Expansão Portuguesa* (Lisbon, 1992–); on the life of these merchants see José da Silva Horta, "Africanos e Portugueses na Documentação Inquisitorial, de Luanda a Mbanza Kongo" (1596–1598), and Rosa Cruz e Silva, "As Feiras do Ndongo: A Outra Vertente

do Comércio no Século XVII," in Comissão Nacional para as Comemorações dos Descobrimentos Portugueses, *Actas do Seminário: Encontro de Povos e Culturas em Angola (Luanda, April 3–6, 1995)* (Lisbon, 1997), 301–22, 405–22.

4   Manuel Bautista Soares, "Relação," in António Brásio, ed., *Monumenta Missionaria Africana*, 1st Ser., 15 vols. (Lisbon, 1952–1988), 6:375.

5   For a general English-language overview of Angolan history see David Birmingham, *Trade and Conflict in Angola: The Mbunda and Their Neighbours under the Influence of the Portuguese, 1483–1790* (Oxford, 1966); for detailed chronology of this period the best work is Beatrix Heintze, "Das Ende des Unabhängigen Staats Ndongo (Angola): Neue Chronologie und Reinterpretation (1617–1630)," *Paideuma*, 27 (1981), 197–273; a revised version without full annotation is found in Heintze, *Studien zur Geschichte Angolas im 16. und 17. Jahrhundert Ein Lesebuch* (Cologne, 1996), 111–68.

6   On this interpretation see Heintze, "Ende des Unabhängigen Staars Ndango (*Paideuma* version, 206–09; *Studien zur Geschichte Augulas* version, 115, 119–20).

7   António de Oliveira de Cadornega. *História geral das guerras angolanas (1680–81)* (1940–1942), ed. José Matias Delgado and Manuel Alves da Cunha, 3 vols. (Lisbon, 1972), I:83. These notes were collected from recollections of contemporaries by the soldier-chronicler who arrived in Angola in 1639 and wrote his chronicle in 1680–1681. Although based on original materials, early portions of Cadornega's chronicle are sometimes garbled and contain errors of chronology. The treatise by Mendes de Vasconçelos, no longer extant, is cited in Cadornega.

8   The best account of the battle is in Pero Rodrigues. "História da residência dos Padres da Companhia de Jesus em Angola, e cousas tocantes ao reino, e Conquista" (May 1, 1594) in Brásio, ed., *Monumenta Missianaria Africana*, 4:574–76.

9   Mendes des Vasconçelos, "Adbierte de las cosas de que tiene falta el gouierna de Angola" (1616), in Brásio, ed., *Mouumenta Missionaria Africana*, 6:263–70.

10   On the miltiary situation see Thornton, "The Art of War in Angola, 1575–1680," *Comparative Studies in Society and History*, 30 (1988), 360–78.

11   Rodrigues, "História da residència dos Padres da companhia de Jesus em Angola," 570–71.

12   Ibid., 573–74; Baltasar Barteira, letter, May 14, 1586, in Brásio, ed., *Monumenta Missionaria Africana*, 3:328–30.

13   Rodrigues. "História da residência dos Padres da Companhia de Jesus em Angola" 561.

14   Although I use the word here (and previously) as an ethnonym, since it is so used today, its noun class suggests that it was not originally an ethnonym. Membership in this noun class (Bantu class 7/8, sing. *ki-*, plu. *i-* or *yi-*) is more likely to link it to a trait or characteristic than an ethnonym. Therefore, because in general I pluralize Kimbundu words by adding "s" to the singular and treat ethnonyms by ignoring class prefixes, I should make this term either "Kimbangalas" (a noun that is not an ethnonym) of "Mbangalas" (an ethnonym without a class marker). However, in my view the term Imbangala, used as an ethnonym, is too well fixed in the lexicon of central Africa to be handled this way, so I have retained what is now traditional image, treating the word as both singular and plural.

15   Earlier theories connected all the "Jagas" of 17th-century sources and linked them in turn with movements from the Lunda areas of modern-day Congo-Kinshasa. Joseph C. Miller, "The Imbangala in the Chronology of Early Central African History," *Journal of African History*, 13 (1972), 549–74, separates them from the Jagas who invaded Kongo. Miller initially thought that the Imbangala of Angola might have risen from a folk movement from Lunda, as he argued in *King and Kinsmen: Early Mbundu states in Angola* (Oxford, 1976), esp. 128–75. Thornton, "The Chronology and Causes of the Lunda Expansion to the West c. 1700 to 1852," *Zambia Journal of History*, 1 (1981), 1–5, attacked the folk movement idea in favor of a purely local origin in the central highlands. Miller has subsequently modified his argument, linking it to a movement of titles and ideas from the east (but not necessarily migrations from Lunda) in a local situation of ecological and political crisis; see Miller, "The Paradoxes of Impoverishment in the Atlantic Zone," in Birmingham and Phyllis M. Martin, eds., *History of Central Africa*, 2 vols. (London, 1983), 1139–43,

and seconded by Jan Vansina, "Population Movements and Emergence of New Socio-Political Forms in Africa," *UNESCO General History of Africa*, 8 vols. (Los Angeles, 1981–1993), 5:60–61.

16   Battell, "The Strange Adventures of Andrew Battel of Leigh in Essex," in Samuel Purchas *Purchas, His Pilgrimes* (London, 1625), vol, 6; mod. ed. E. G. Ravenstein, *The Strange Adventures of Andrew Battel, of Leigh, in Angola and the Adjoining Regions* (London, 1901; reprinted 1967), 21, 32–33. See also the "quixilla laws" that the founder of the Jagas gave her followers as reported in the 1660s by Giovanni Antonio Cavazzi da Montecuccolo, "Missione Evangelica al regno de Congo," MSS Araldi (ca. 1668), vol. A, bk. 26.

17   The most systematic later account is that of Cavazzi da Montecuccolo, an Indian Capuchin priest who spent more than a dozen years in the region and collected their traditions and observed their life. His original account is found in the "Missione Evangelica al regno de Congo," vol. A, bk. 1, pp. 1–44, much of which found its way into the published edition cited in note 16. For a modern interpretation see Miller, *Kings and Kinsmen*; for linkages with witchcraft and evil see Thornton, "Cannibals and Slave Traders in the Atlantic World," paper presented at the conference "More than Cool Reason: Black Responses to Enslavement, Exile, and Resettlement," Haifa, Israel, Jan, 18–20, 1998.

18   Cavazzi da Montecuccolo, "Missione Evangelica al regno de Congo," vol. A, bk. 1, 97.

19   Cadornega, *História geral das guerras angolas*, 3:223–35. I have pluralized all Kimbundu nouns according to English usage; the Kimbumdu plural of *kilunda* is *ilunda*.

20   Battell, in Ravensetin, ed., *Strange Adventures of Andrew Battel*, 30–31.

21   Ibid., 17–21.

22   Ibid., 21–28.

23   Pereira, according to Mendes de Vasconçelos to king of Portugal, Aug, 28, 1607, in Brásio, ed., *Monumenta Missionaria Africana*, 6:284.

24   For an overview and chronology see Heintze. "Ende des Unabhängigen Staats Ndonga 202–09 (*Paideuma*); 114–20 (*Studien zur Geschichte Angolas*).

25   Mendes de Vasconçelos to king of Portugal. Aug. 28, Sept. 9, 1617, in Brásin, ed. *Mounmenta Missionaria Africana*, 6:283–85, 286.

26   Cavazzi da Montecuccolo, "Missione Evangelica at regno de congo" (ca. 1665. updated to 1668), vol. A, bk. 2, 11–15; for the interpretation of these highly politicized and manipulated sources see Thornton, "Legitimacy and Political Power: Queen Njinga, 1624–1663." *J. African Hist.*, 32 (1991), 27–40.

27   The *presidio* was moved sometime before 1618, when Baltasar Rebelo de Aragão, one of the original conquerors of Angola, wrote his memoirs (a date established by Brásio as being 25 years after his arrival in 1593); Rebelo de Aragão to king of Portugal [?], 1618, in Brásio, ed., *Monumenta Missionaria Africana*, 6:334 (date on 343).

28   Soates, "Copia dos excessos que se cometem no gouerno de Angola que o bispo den a V. Megestade pedindo delles de presente, e de futuro," Sept. 7, 1619, in Brásio, ed., *Monumenta Missionaria Africana*, 6:368. If the "two years" in this statement is taken literally, Mendes de Vasconçelos would have begun the Imbangala alliance virtually on the same day as he wrote his letters to Lisbon denouncing their use by his predecessors, which strikes me as unlikely.

29   Fernão de Sousa, "Guerras do Reino de Angola," ca. 1630, fol. 217, in Heintze, ed., *Fontes para a História de Angola do século XVII*, 2 vols. (Stuttgart, 1985–1988), 1:212. This rather late source (de Sousa came to Angola only in 1624 but had access to official documents filed there) is the only one to name the Imbangala bands or to give details about their origins.

30   For military culture and the role of noncombatants see Thornton, "Art of War," and Rodrigues, "História da residência dos Padres da Companhia de Jesus em Angola," 562–64.

31   Manuel Severim da Faria, "História portugueza e de outras provinicias do occidente desde o anno de 1610 até o de 1640 . . .," Biblioteca Nacional de Lisboa, MS 241. fol. 163v, under date Mar. 1, 1619, to end of Feb. 1620, but related to material of a year earlier (1618–1619) quoted in Cadornega, *História geral das guerras angolas,* ed. Delgado, I:88–90 n. I. The formation of the Imbangala alliance and movement of the *presidio* is given as 1618 in Manuel Vogado Sotomaior, "Papel sobre as cousas de Angola" (undated, but probably around 1620), in Brásio, ed., *Monumenta Missionaria Africana*, 15:476 (date on 480).

32   Soares, "Copia dos excessos," Sept. 7, 1619, in Brásio, ed., *Monumenta Missionaria Africana*, 6:369–70. Vogado Sotomaior, then holdign the position of ouvidor geral de Angola noted that the city of Angola (Kabasa) was "sacked in such a way that many thousand souls were captured, eaten and killed" and all the palm trees were cut down (in Imbangala fashion) so that the area was effectively barren of them: "Papel," ibid., 15:476.

33   Manuel Severim da Faria. "História portugueza e de outras provincias," fol. 174v, Mar. 1621 to Feb. 1622, but relating to 1620–1621, quoted in Cadornega, *História geral des guerras angolas*, ed. Delgado, 1:90 n. 1.

34   Soares, "Copia dos excessos," Sept. 7, 1619, in Brásio, ed., *Monumenta Missionaria Africana*, 6:370.

35   Cadornega, *História geral das guerras angolas*, ed. Delgado, 1:83. For a fuller discussion of the art of war in Angola see Thornton, "Art of War in Angola," 360–78.

36   Soares, "Copia dos excessos," Sept. 7, 1619, in Brásio, ed., *Monumenta Missionaria Africana*, 6:370.

37   Ibid., 369–71; Vogado Sotomaior, "Papel sobre as cousas de Angola," ibid, 15:476–77.

38   On the general problem of slave flight see Heintze, "Gefährdetes Asyl. Chancen und Konzequenzen der Flucht angolanischer Skalven im 17. Jahrhundert," *Paideuma*, 39 (1993), 320–41, and revised but unannotated version of the same article in *Studien zur Geschichte Angolas*, 232–520. For details about the specific campaigns of 1621–1622 see Heintze, "Ende des Unabhängigen Staats Ndongo," 112–26 (*Studien zur Geschichte Angolas*).

39   Heintze, "Ende des Unabhängigen staats Ndongo," 115 (*Studien zur Geschichte Angolas*).

40   Francisco de Gouveia to Jesuit General, Nov. 1, 1564, in Brásio, ed., *Monumenta Missionaria Africana*, 15:230–31. This is the original version of a text printed from a copy ibid., 2:528. Although the text is from more than 50 years before, it is the only description of the capital of Ndongo available to us. For a description of Kongo's capital and central African cities in general see Thornton, "Mbanza Kongo/São Salvador: Kongo's Holy City," in Richard Rathbone and Andrew Roberts, eds., *Africa's Urban Past* (London, forthcoming).

41   Heintze, "Unbekanntes Angola: Der Staat Ndongo im 16. Jahrhundert," *Anthropos*, 72 (1977), 771–76: a revised but reduced version, "Der Staat Ndongo im 16. Jahrhundert," is in Heintze, *Studien zur Gechichte Angolas*, 74–75.

42   For detailed consideration of these elements of their identity see Virgílio Coelho, "En busca de Kábàsà: Uma tentativa de explicação da estrutura politico-administrativo do 'Reino de Ndongo in Commissão Nacional para as Comemorações dos Descobrimentos Portugueses, *Actas do Seminário: Encontro de Povos e Culturas em Angola (Luanda, Apr. 3–6, 1995)* (Lisbon, 1997), 443–78.

43   Francesco Paccoino, *Gentio de Angola sufficimente instruido* . . . ed. António do Couto (Lisbon, 1642), 4:2. The catechism was probably first composed by a native-speaking Kimbundo priest named Dionisio de Faria Barreto in the mid-1620s, though Paccoino, a long-serving Italian Jesuit, undoubtedly produced the finishing touches, returning with the text to Lisbon where he died in 1641 before bringing it to press. The final editor, do Couto, was from Kongo, born in its capital city São Salvador and probably a mulatto. Héli Chatelain, the Swiss Protestant missionary who did much to define modern Kimbundu with his grammar, collection of folklore, and other texts, praised this catechism for its rigor and fidelity to the language; see Chatelain, ed., *Folk-Tales of Angola* (New York, 1894). In this and following translations, I have made my translation directly from the Kimbundu and not from the accompanying Portuguese text.

44   Paccoino, *Gentio de Angola sufficimente instruido*, fol. 55v (Portuguese on facing page, 56).

45   See this usage in the Fernão de Sousa correspondence in Heintze, *Foutes para a História de Angola do século XVII.*

46   Paccoino, introduction, *Gentio de Angola sufficimente instruido*, ed. do Couto, unpaged.

47   Chatelain, *Grammatica Elementar do Kimbundu ou Lingua de Angola* (1888–1889), Ridgewood, N. J., 1964), xii.

48   Regimento of Fernão de Sousa to Bento Banha Cardoso, ca. Jan. 1626, ibid., 1:205.

49   The catechism, for instance, note that "Negroes of Angola who have not received baptism" (in the Portuguese text) were "*Ambundo carià mongoaùa Nzambi*" in Kimbundu or "Mbundus

who have not eaten the salt of God." Paccoino, *Gentio de Angola sufficimente instruido*, ed. do Couto, fol. 85. In this Kimbundu text, *Ambundu* is a plural form (hence my translation as *Mbundus*).

50 "Practica para bautizar as adultos de gentio dos R[ein]os de Angola" (undated but apparently late 16th or early 17th century). MS. Biblioreca Pública e Arquivo Distrial de Évora.

51 For more on the theology of these syncretic churches see Thornton, "Afro-Christian Syncretism in Central Africa," *Plantation Societies* (forthcoming).

52 Alonso de Sandoval, *Naturaleza, policia sagrada i profana, costumbres i risos . . . de todos Etiopes* (Seville, 1627); mod. ed Angel Valtierra, *De instauranda Aethiopum salute: el mundo de la esclavitud en America* (Bogotá, 1956), 372–77, 380.

53 T. H. Breen and Stephen Innes, *"Myne owne Ground": Race and Freedom on Virginia's Eastern Shore, 1640–1676* (New York, 1980), 70–71.

54 Alden T. Vaughan, "Blacks in Virginia: A Note on the First Decade," *WMQ*, 3d Ser, 29 (1992), 477.

55 Heintze, "Ende des Unabhängigen Staats Ndongo" (*Paideuma* version, 216–53; *Studien* version, 127–55).

56 Breen and Innes, *"Myne Owne Ground,"* 17.

Chapter 37

Daniel L. Schafer

FAMILY TIES THAT BIND
Anglo-African slave traders in Africa and Florida, John Fraser and his descendants

I N DECEMBER 1813 JOHN FRASER drowned in Spanish East Florida. A native of Scotland, Fraser was a slave trader who had migrated from South Carolina in 1809, a move prompted by the United States ban on the importation of African slaves in 1808. He had been in Charleston in 1807 and 1808, after migrating there from his home base at Bangalan on the Pongo River in West Africa where he purchased Africans captured in raids and wars in the interior. At the time of his death, Fraser was called the 'wealthiest and most extensive planter in Florida', the owner of two plantations and 375 slaves, in addition to other properties in South Carolina and Britain, and slaves in West Africa.[1] He bequeathed this entire estate to his African wife and five minor children, yet nearly 40 years would pass before the inheritance transactions were completed. Only his daughter Elizabeth would still be living. European-educated and a wealthy slave-owner, planter and merchant living on the Nunez River in coastal Guinea, Elizabeth would receive only a small portion of the original estate. A fortune had disappeared into the tangled web of Spanish, American and British courts and the avarice of executors, attorneys and kinfolk.

The story of John Fraser and his Anglo-African heirs is an important chapter in the history of the transatlantic slave trade. It reveals the complex multi-national and multi-racial nature of slavery and the slave trade as it existed on two frontiers of the Atlantic world: the St Johns and St Marys Rivers in Spanish East. Florida and the Nunez and Pongo Rivers of the Coast of Guinea.

Born in 1769 at Inverness, Scotland, Fraser became a maritime merchant with ties to Glasgow and Liverpool firms. Reliable witnesses placed him in West Africa by 1799, when he married an African woman named Phenda at Crawford's Island of the Isles de Los. Several Europeans attended the wedding of John and Phenda, the widow of another European trader, Thomas Hughes Jackson. They later testified that Fraser maintained a slave-trading establishment at Bangalan on the upper Pongo River (north of Conakry in today's Republic of Guinea). Five children were born of the marriage: James, Margaret, Mary Ann, Eleanor and Elizabeth.[2]

Fraser's move to Charleston in 1807 was not unusual for slave traders, several of whom alternated residences between England, West Africa and South Carolina. The reopening of slave imports to South Carolina in 1803 prompted several English traders to relocate there during the final years of the American trade. Thomas

Powell and William Lawson. Liverpool agents for John Fraser, alternated residences at Liverpool, Rio Pongo and Charleston, and employment as ship captains, super-cargoes and merchants. George Irving had an African family and a trading establishment at Rio Pongo, residences at Charleston and Liverpool, and captained British slave ships. This was a time of flux for slavers as Denmark, England and the United States moved to abolish the trade between 1803 and 1808. The American ban in 1808 prompted men like John McClure, Joseph Hibbenon, Henry and Philip R. Yonge, James Wilson, Daniel O'Hara, James and George Taylor, and James English to migrate to the port of Fernandina in Spain's East Florida colony where slave imports remained legal. The ban idled hundreds of slaving ships in American and English ports. Hibberson and Yonge, Arredondo and Son, and other East Florida firms purchased dozens of these ships and moved them to the Spanish ports of St Augustine and Fernandina.[3]

Fraser's schooners continued to bring slaves across the Atlantic Ocean after his move to Florida, but, his main project was acquiring labourers for his own plantations. Francis Richard, an overseer for Fraser, said his employer brought to Florida, 'one hundred thousand dollars in hand, in negroes and other effects'.[4] In April 1810 Captain Francisco Ferreyra brought 126 slaves to Fernandina from Africa aboard Fraser's ship the *Eagle of St. Augustine*. Eight months later, Captain Bartolome Mestre arrived from Africa with the frigate *Joana* carrying 140 Africans for Fraser.[5]

On 2 May 1810 Governor Henry White approved a grant to Fraser for a 500-acre tract on the St Marys River known as the 'Roundabout' for the circuitous path the stream cut around the 300-acre peninsula its previous owner had turned into a rice field. Fraser acquired intact dikes, drainage ditches and gates, along with a 200-acre corn field on the adjacent high ground. The following year, on 18 September 1811, Fraser purchased Greenfield Plantation, a 3,000-acre cotton and provisions estate located at the juncture of the St Johns and Pablo Rivers.[6]

The 375 labourers at the two plantations were called 'prime Africans' and 'picked young negroes by Florida planters who saw them at work. They also said it took two years for Africans new to America to 'become an equal worker to a country born slave', referring to the period necessary to regain their strength and health after the rigours of the ocean passage and the time needed to learn a new language and work routine. After subtracting for children and sick or injured workers who could not complete full daily tasks, approximately 270 full-working hands laboured at Roundabout and Greenfield. On 'first-rate hammock land' at Greenfield the workers tended 750 acres of Sea Island cotton, 400 acres of corn and peas (planted together), fields of sweet potatoes, as well as personal gardens, in both 1810 and 1811. The average annual yield was 150,000 pounds of cleaned cotton, 7,200 bushels of corn, 3,200 bushels of peas and 10,000 bushels of sweet potatoes, for a total value of $82,087. At Roundabout the 15,000 bushels of rice harvested in both 1810 and 1811, along with corn and potatoes, was worth $11,600 each year. The value of the aggregate yields would approximate $3,000,000 today.[7]

In August 1811, with his plantations established and the province's export economy booming, Fraser placed overseers in charge and made plans to leave Florida temporarily. Aware that life was 'at all times a precarious tenure, more so to those who commit it to the sea', Fraser had a Last Will and Testament witnessed before sailing for Africa.[8] Soon after his departure, however, East Florida experienced an insurrection known as the Patriot Rebellion which destroyed many of its largest plantations. Roundabout and Greenfield were burned and pillaged and slaves were abducted. Fraser returned in December 1813 at the height of widespread guerrilla skirmishing but drowned when his ship floundered at the entrance to the St Johns River.

By the time Fraser's estate was appraised, the assets had been significantly depleted. A sizeable fortune remained, but four decades would pass before the final assets would be delivered to Elizabeth Fraser Skelton, the sole surviving heir in Africa. It is a story complicated by the instability of the Spanish colony and its cession in 1821 to the United States, but also a tale of greed and avarice tempered by loyalty and courage.[9]

John Fraser's Last Will is a mixture of concern for his African children, loyalty to his siblings and an effort to untangle complex business interests involving dozens of people on three continents. Fraser had been away from Britain for so long that he had little knowledge of his family there, but he left generous bequests of $4,400 for his brother Archibald and the same for his sister Ann, whom he thought to be unmarried and unable to 'afford any protection to my orphan children'.[10] Fraser attributed his wealth to the 'God [who] has been pleased to reward me with the fruits of my industry in order of dispensing the same to my children'. He saw himself as a businessman engaged in legal trade who had genuine respect and affection for his African wife and mixed-race children. About his wife, Phenda, he wrote: 'She is a very sensible woman and of a clear mind, and as such would not meet with contempt in a country where little attention is paid to colour.' He bequeathed her ten slaves from 'my estates in that country [Rio Pongo], and these exclusively of such as she may have in her possession at the time of this legacy, leaving her the option or living in whatever place that may be most suitable to her together with her children'.[11]

Fraser also believed it 'incumbent on a Father to do his duty toward his children' and dedicated the majority of his estate for the entire use and benefit of my five mulatto children'.[12] His slaves and other properties in Florida and Africa were to be sold and the proceeds invested in US bonds with the interest that accrued used to educate his children. When the eldest child became 21, the executors were to divide the proceeds into five equal parts and give each heir a share at age 21. He also directed his executors to 'remove with all possible dispatch my children from Africa'. Fraser wanted his children well educated, his son to attend 'a good seminary' in the United States or England 'where no particular distinction is made as to colour, but to much more of good conduct and manners'. Fraser chose Andrew Charles and Thomas Napier, both long-term friends and Charleston merchants, to act as executors of his South Carolina properties and to become guardians of his five children.

Records of the children's lives are minimal, yet it is known that Margaret was sent to Liverpool at age four to be educated under the care of Thomas Powell. Executors of Fraser's Florida estate paid her school costs even though they were concerned that Margaret's fixation on inheritance was 'hardly conducive to her future happiness' and encouraged her to seek regular employment or to live with an aunt in Scotland. Margaret died in Liverpool in February 1818.[13]

James was attending school in Charleston when his father died, but by 1817 he had left that city. A Florida woman, Maria King, claimed that James Fraser (or Quail Fraser) was in Camden County, Georgia, on 7 August 1818, when her husband, Thomas King, paid $11,125 for James' inheritance rights. He was dead prior to 1824.[14] Mary Anne, Eleanor and Elizabeth, born 1804, 1806 and 1808, were baptized and educated at a school established in 1807 by the Church Missionary Society at Bashia on the Rio Pongo. The sisters were apparently at the Bashia school, and at its successor located at Canofee, between 1809 and 1816. Mary was described as having a 'haughty temper', Elena (Eleanor) a 'lovely temper', and Elizabeth a 'midling [sic] temper' in a 24 June 1814 comment by their teacher.[15] The sisters were accompanied at the school by a servant girl named Nancy Fraser. Among their schoolmates were other mixed-race sons and daughters of European slave traders and their African wives, and children of local Africans. After attending the CMS school, the sisters were sent to England for an additional four years of training. European traders who knew Mary Anne and Elizabeth in later years praised their fluency in English and French. One commented that Elizabeth toured Europe to add to her cultural refinement and social graces. Beyond the CMS records, little is known about Eleanor other than that she died aged 18 at Sunbauria, Rio Pongo, on 1 September 1824. Mary Ann died in 1846 at Deborea.[16]

In his Will, Fraser predicted his African properties at Bangalan on the Pongo River would 'amount to at least forty five thousand dollars', and requested they be traded for 'produce of the land'. Another 'factory' in this area of Guinea in West Africa was described by Joseph Hawkins us two storeys in height, built of sun-dried mud bricks, with outbuildings, a large courtyard to secure caravan properties, and it 'barracoon' (corral) where slaves were confined in chains. If Fraser's property resembled the one Hawkins described, his family would have lived on the second storey, with the first floor used for storage and conducting trade.[17] There is a description of life at Bangalan in 1826 by Theophilus Conneau, who claimed to have worked for John Ormond, the descendant of a Liverpool slave trader who settled at Rio Pongo and married an African woman. Conneau described a December 1826 commercial transaction with a caravan front Timbo in the Fula nation of Futa Jalon. Trading was conducted at Ormond's factory, 'a building 150 feet in front' which contained stores of tobacco, cloth, gunpowder, muskets and other items used to purchase slaves, ivory, gold, rice, hides, bullocks, goats and beeswax.[18]

Fraser also willed freedom for his 'trusty servant called Mamado Yonge residing at Rio Pongo as well as his wife called Susanna . . . for their good and long services. He also emancipated his 'faithful slave and interpreter . . . Charles together with the whole of his family'. Fraser's other slaves were not so fortunate; he directed that 'the rest of my negroes in those parts shall be disposed of to the greatest advantage possible according as the agents who shall have the management of this matter shall deem most expident'. His agents were European merchants residing at Rio Pongo, his 'respectable friends, Samuel Samo and Samuel Pall'.[19]

The majority of Fraser's assets were in Florida under the care of Zephaniah Kingsley and Philip Robert Yonge. Kingsley was one of Florida's leading slave-owner–planters who was in 1813 an African slave trader familiar with Rio Pongo.[20] Born in Bristol, England, and reared in Charleston, South Carolina, Kingsley also married an African woman, a Wolof from Senegal whom he purchased as a slave in Cuba and later emancipated in Florida. Yonge was a partner in a thriving Fernandina company with ships in the African trade.

The executors and Spanish officials appraised the value of property at Fraser's two Florida plantations at $56,744. Land was valued at $9,000, buildings, produce, livestock and miscellaneous at $4,036, gold and silver at $1,493, and a schooner, the *Floridano*, at $3,200. The remaining $39,015 represented the value of the slaves. Anglicized names predominate on the slave inventory, names like Sailor Jack, Paddy Jim, Tweed, Lucy, Patty and Yellow Mama, which provide few clues to ethnic homelands or African heritage of Fraser's slaves. Given the history of the Rio Pongo, however, it is probable the captives purchased at Bangalan were of Mandinka, Temne, Nalu or Landuman origin or were Sousou, Baga, Bulom, or other coastal people, although small numbers of Fula captives were also carried to the coast by Mandinka caravans. Traders familiar with the coast recognized that Africans possessed agricultural skills needed in the Americas, along with knowledge of construction techniques and architectural styles reflected in slave houses and other structures. It is likely there were carpenters and blacksmiths — even hunters who utilized the African quivers listed on the Greenfield inventory. Amidst the listing of flour, sugar, coffee and other household items is another intriguing entry: 27 pairs of gold earings valued at 60. Were the adornments brought to Greenfield by Black Cumba, Cook, Dolly, Coota, or Pinda, or by Fraser to use as incentives to influence the work and behaviour of his labourers? – the record is incomplete.[21]

Administration of Fraser's Florida estate was repeatedly beset by controversy, unpredictable problems and legal challenges. The immediate problem was the rigidity of Spanish law which lacked safeguards for non-citizen legatees. Kingsley and Yonge felt it mandatory to delay testamentary proceedings to prevent the governor from confiscating and selling the properties at auction and depositing the proceeds in the Spanish Treasury. Kingsley warned of 'dangers and vicissitudes' encountered daily in a province which had fallen into a 'total decay of commerce and agriculture [where] very frequently the slaves desert to the Indians who protect them and also to other vagabonds of the interior, and in this manner several inhabitants have lost the greater part of their slaves'.[22] Because only one in 20 enslaved men and women would bring two-thirds of true worth if sold in this period of depressed economy, Kingsley offered to purchase them at full value plus five percent annual interest. Governor Coppinger agreed. Mortgages to four of Kingsley's plantations worth $52,400 and a similar security from Yonge were exchanged for 158 slaves evaluated at $37,285.[23]

It is likely that news of Fraser's death and fortune was transmitted to his African heirs by Kingsley, who frequented the Rio Pongo area during his days as a slave trader. The children received funds from the executors for basic maintenance and for school fees at Rio Pongo and at Liverpool. Fraser's sister Ann may have met her African nieces when they attended schools in England or visited relatives in Scotland. Ann learned of her brother's fortune in 1817 when Philip Yonge delivered her legacy. Since her brother Archibald was dead by 1817, Ann also received his share, for a total of $8,800 (approximately $264,000 today). Within a year, she had married William Robertson, a draper, at Inverness, Scotland and moved to St Augustine to claim what remained of her brother's estate. A lawsuit initiated by the Robertson's in 1819 was still unresolved when East Florida became a Territory of the United States in 1821. Refiled in United States courts in 1823, the lawsuit charged that Phenda and her five children were slaves residing in a foreign country and ineligible to inherit in Florida. Ann Robertson asked the court to disallow her brother's will and award her the entire estate. Either by court order or litigant compromise – the record is incomplete – she was assigned eight slaves and a one-third interest in the estate. John Fraser had been careful to limit his sister and brother to a combined total of $8,800, yet Ann Robertson managed to garner a one-third share of a fortune intended exclusively for his African heirs.[24]

In the decade after Fraser's death, estate executors in South Carolina and East Florida conducted affairs promptly and with rectitude. Yonge travelled to England and Scotland in 1817 to pay legacies, and to Havana to collect $5,000 from Drake and Co. Wages paid to overseers, ship captains and mates, merchants and attorneys, and funds expended for expenses and commissions of the executors reduced estate funds by more than $25,000 during the decade. Yonge also withdrew an additional $12,000 to pay a claim presented by the Liverpool heirs of George Irving for slaves purchased in 1803 and 1804. In 1821 Yonge said he and Kingsley had consistently paid the annual interest on their slave mortgages and planned to pay off the mortgages when the legatees reached age 21. The executors disbursed proceeds of the estate for educational and other expenses of the heirs. Kingsley, one of Florida's major planters and maritime merchants, acted as on-site supervisor, advertising each year in local newspapers for a leaseholder for Greenfield Plantation. He also sought restitution when property worth $10,000 was damaged, suing the 1819–21 leaseholder, Benjamin Chaires, alleging he had 'girdled, deadened, injured and greatly damaged to wit two thousand live oak trees' and one thousand other trees at Greenfield.[25]

The executors also acted in concert with representatives of the African heirs. In January 1824 Eleanor, Mary Ann and Elizabeth Fraser appointed Stiles Edward Lightburn to act its their attorney. Lightburn was a Charleston native who married an African woman at Faringuia on the Pongo River and became one of the most prosperous slave traders on the Guinea Coast.[26] Elizabeth's husband, William Skelton, was authorized in 1826 to enter into any agreements he deemed necessary to secure the legacy. After 1826, Skelton authorized Kingsley and Yonge to act as attorneys on behalf of the legatees.[27] According to P.R. Yonge's records, Skelton collected at least $13,000 from the Florida executors between 1826 and 1834. In 1835 Mary Ann's husband, Thomas Gaffery Curtis arranged the sale of 1500 acres of Greenfield Plantation for $1,000.[28]

Between 1833 and 1836, Kingsley made three equal payments totalling $20,250 to clear the $18,000 debt he had incurred through acquisition of slaves from the Fraser estate. The sale of his White Oak Plantation, the largest in Nassau County, with provisions, sugar cane and cotton fields, a 500-acre rice field, and a rice pounding mill, apparently raised the money needed to redeem Kingsley's 1816 mortgage.[29] Fraser had been dead more than 20 years, his living heirs had all reached age of 21, the debts of the estate had been paid and the remaining assets distributed. In April 1836 Kingsley announced in the *Florida Herald* that he had 'adjusted his accounts with the heirs of and assigns of the Estate' and intended to ask the St. Johns County Judge of Probate for 'a full and final settlement and for discharge'.[30] There was, however, one asset still outstanding. P.R. Yonge, who lived in Georgia in 1836, had never redeemed his $18,000 mortgage for the 79 slaves he had acquired in 1816.

The infusion of $157,140 into the Fraser estate (worth at least $4,700,000 today) in 1842 created a flurry of activity that would lure several prominent attorneys to the St Augustine and Jacksonville courts. After a delay of nearly two decades, the US Treasury was in the 1840s making final payments on claims for losses suffered by East Florida residents during the 1812–14 'Patriot Rebellion'. The American government had agreed to honour legitimate claims under terms of the Adams–Onis Treaty of 1819 which gave sovereignty over Florida to the United States. For years, Judges Robert Raymond Reid, Joseph L. Smith, and Isaac Bronson presided over hearings and recommended settlements on dozens of East Florida Claims. In the Fraser claim, Judge Bronson recommended in 1841 a payment of $157,140 for losses at Greenfield and Roundabout Plantations.[31]

Zephaniah Kingsley resumed his involvement as executor of the Fraser estate in 1841. In September 1842 he sent an attorney, his nephew Kingsley Beatty Gibbs, to Georgia to meet Philip R. Yonge. Gibbs recorded the events of the journey in his diary:

> [3 September 1842] 'Father and I left for Darien – I had to go there to see P.R. Yonge about the claim of Fraser's Est. for Losses in 1812, so as to get his power as Ext. [executor] which he refuses to give – not desiring more to do with that Estate. [8 September] After quite a fatiguing trip, having on last night to sleep in the Boat, visited Darien but met Mr. Yonge at his residence on Doboy Isld. we came home in safety.[32]

News reached Gibbs on 9 November that the Secretary of the Treasury had confirmed Judge Bronson's decree, prompting hint to leave immediately for Washington. On 8 December he recorded:

> on this day I was very busy att the Treasury of the U.S. before the 1st comptroller in get thro' claim of Est Fraser – finally Mr Kingsley was paid $157,140 and at 5 p.m. Mr K [Kingsley] Genl Hernandez [Joseph M. Hernandez] & self left for New York – Mr K. had returned but a few days from Hayti – [12 December] We all got to New York in safety, and I was paid $5,000 for my services in the case.[33]

After deducting for attorney fees, commissions and expenses, Kingsley and Gibbs returned to Florida to divide the balance between Fraser's heirs in Africa and his sister in St Augustine. Gibbs' diary entries record the first stages of that division.

> [12 January 1843] Mr Kingsley and self now proceed to Augustine . . . to settle with Mrs Robertson, who owns 1/3d of the nett amount of the Fraser claim as his sister.
> [20 January] During all this time. Mr. K & self were in Augustine and very busy, [attorney Samuel L.] Burritt representing Mrs R. and we finally paid her $35,000 on Govt 6 pr ct: stock, redeemable in 1862 . . . We have a good deal of trouble, but the matter is now settled and the money paid, so far as Mrs R is concerned.

Kingsley then travelled back to New York City intent on delivering $70,000 to the Fraser heirs in Africa. After depositing $55,000 with the firm of Hussey and Mackey

— the security was clearly marked payable to Kingsley as executor to the Fraser estate — he began making arrangements for another Atlantic voyage. Kingsley would not make another trip to Africa. He died in September 1843 aged 78.

News of Kingsley's death prompted several attorneys to hurry to New York City. Philip Yonge arrived first to lay claim to the $55,000 security deposit. Samuel L. Burritt, the Florida attorney representing Ann Robertson, was not far behind. Kingsley B. Gibbs and Joseph M. Hernandez, attorneys for the Kingsley estate, also rushed to New York to contest for the money in Chancery Court. Yonge was given control, based on his prior appointment as executor. On 5 July 1844 he deducted a $3,300 commission and deposited $52,000 in City Bank of New York — in his own name, not as executor of the Fraser estate. Burritt, after filing a suit against Yonge in chancery Court, travelled to the Guinea Coast of Africa to secure powers of attorney from Elizabeth Skelton and Mary Ann Curtis, the surviving Fraser heirs. Gibbs returned to Florida and disbursed the last of the Fraser money Kingsley had retained, $15,000, to Elizabeth Skelton through her attorney Samuel L. Burritt, only recently returned from Africa.[34]

Although Yonge had been granted control of the $52,000 he deposited at City Bank of New York, he was never able to withdraw the money from the account. In the summer of 1842 a man motivated by loyalty and duty obtained a court injunction which froze funds in the account. Thomas Napier, one of the original South Carolina executors of Fraser's estate and a guardian of his infant children, had lost his eyesight and moved to Brooklyn to live with his daughter, Ann Theus Napier. When Napier heard of Yonge's bank deposit and Burritt's trip to Africa, however, he immediately petitioned the New York courts to seize the funds and to reappoint him executor of the Fraser estate. Assisted by his daughter as researcher and scribe, Napier accused Yonge of 'malfeasance' and initiated a major investigation of the estate's previous administrative activities. Eventually, Yonge was disqualified as executor, convicted of maladministration and fined $20,000.[35]

Yonge contested Napier's actions through the firm of Burr, Benedict, and Bisbee, which warned Napier he would 'be exposed to much danger' and filed counter motions intended to secure $30,000 for services their client previously provided to the estate.[36] Napier associated with Samuel M. Woodruff of Dana, Woodruff and Leonard, to handle motions before the Surrogate Court, and Elias B. Gould to assist in Florida. A settlement was signed 22 November 1851, requiring Yonge to surrender all claims against the estate along with his right to administer, while releasing him from the $20,000 judgment rendered by the Florida court. The agreement also released Yonge from the $18,000 mortgage he still owed to the estate.[37]

After the settlement, Napier, continued to guard the interests of Elizabeth Skelton. He routinely questioned Burritt's integrity and encouraged Skelton to find another attorney. He suspected the motivation for Burritt's trip to Africa in 1844 had been to deceive Elizabeth and Mary Ann about the amount of money involved in the US Treasury settlement and 'to purchase the interest of the heirs for a very small sum'.[38] In statements notarized in 1850 and 1851 at her home at Victoria on the Nunez River, Skelton acknowledged receiving a total of $14,000 from Burritt. Estate and court records, however, document that Burritt collected at least $40,000 in her name. After Napier informed Skelton that Burritt had become infected by the 'gold rush fever' and moved to California, she terminated his power of attorney in May 1851 and assigned it to Judge William W. Campbell of New York City. Judge Campbell had represented Elizabeth and her sister Mary Ann in a Florida indenture in 1833.[39]

Napier and Campbell were able to arrange a final settlement of the estate in December 1851. After deducting for court costs and related expenses, and only minimal charges for his own expenses and fees for Campbell, Napier sent to Skelton US Stock worth $33,360 (more than $1,000,000 today). Finally, 38 years after his death, John Fraser's fortune — or what remained of his fortune — was sent to his only surviving heir.

Significant conclusions emerge from the study of Fraser's life and the disposition of his fortune. The first is that it was of great benefit in the Florida courts to be white and a Florida resident. Ann Robertson's bequest was clearly capped at $8,800, yet she was able to pocket more than $50,000 (worth $1,500,000 today). Even Thomas Napier, the South Carolina executor, travelled to St Augustine in 1826 and 1832 to influence the compromise that assigned one-third of the Fraser estate to Ann Robertson. In 1848 Napier wrote: 'Providence is connected with it [legal delays] which . . . may be that more of that Estate may be designed for yourself and daughter.'[40] One year later, he described Ann as a 'very good old friend' and 'a woman of truth, Christian humility, and of pure piety'.[41] Perhaps they had known one another in their native Scotland years before, or in Charleston. It is never clearly stated, but the bond was a strong one.

Before Ann Robertson died in 1850, she assigned $33,000 to her daughter Margaret (Mrs Oliver Wood), and the same amount to religious and charitable organizations in Charleston, St Augustine and Philadelphia. Perhaps it was the memory of her nieces in Africa that influenced her decision to leave $5,000 for the Presbyterian Missionary Society of Philadelphia. Thus, Fraser's sister, and through her an orphanage, a church, a church school, a missionary society, and her daughter, received large portions of a fortune derived from the sale and labour of black slaves that Fraser had intended for his Anglo-African children. It was indeed of great benefit to be white in the Florida courts.[42]

It must also be noted that these same courts recognized rights of non-white and non-resident legatees when men of good conscience like Kingsley and Napier protected their interests. Several cases involving inheritance rights of mixed-race legatees were tried in north-cast Florida courts between 1821 and 1861, most notably the effort by Kingsley's sister, Martha McNeill to divest his African wife and children of rights to his estate. McNeill's effort failed because the Kingsleys were protected by terms of the treaty which ceded Florida to the United States, and because Kingsley's wife returned from Haiti to supervise family interests. The fact that her two daughters were married to wealthy and influential white residents of Duval County also contributed to her success.[43]

Mary Ann Curtis and Elizabeth Skelton lacked these advantages. From residences in Africa, they could only rely on white attorneys, distant strangers whose personal interests often prevailed over the welfare of legatees. It was Robertson, Yonge, Burritt and the other white attorneys and officers of the court who benefited most from John Fraser's fortune. However, between 1833 and 1836 Kingsley paid off his mortgage, with two-thirds of the payment intended for Fraser's daughters and one-third for Robertson.[44] Executors dutifully dispersed estate funds to educate Fraser's children and start them in business at Rio Pongo. Through the persistent and loyal services of Thomas Napier, Elizabeth Skelton inherited $33,360 in 1851. White guardians were needed to protect non-white legatees, but north-east Florida courts did on occasion recognize their inheritance rights.

The final conclusion is that slaving activities ran in parallels on opposite sides of the Atlantic Ocean. In the frontier regions of north-east Florida, planters used the same labour and export agriculture systems used in the Rio Pongo region of West Africa, where slaves living in separate villages cultivated rice, cotton, peanuts and other crops for the benefit of their owners. Planters in Florida and West Africa sometimes drew their labourers from the same sources; it is probable that some enslaved Africans who worked in fields near the Pongo River later worked at rice and other grain plantations in north-east Florida.[45] In 1788 an Englishman who had lived in the Sierra Leone and Guinea region for more than two years observed house slaves in the Rio Pongo region who were treated as family members and plantation slaves who lived in towns separate from their masters. Plantation slaves were permitted to marry and raise children and to cultivate plots of land for their own family's subsistence, but the rice, cotton and other crops raised for export were property of their owners. 'In tithes of scarcity', the English trader noted, 'many persons sell their slaves for salt.' Slaves sold to Europeans, however, came primarily from the interior: '[only] a small part are natives of the seacoast', the unfortunate victims of the limited wars between coastal peoples. Others were criminals condemned to be sold abroad as slaves, but the 'greatest part are war captives of the interior country, which is the Phoolieu [Fulu], who are Mahomatens [and] are perpetually warring against the pagans'.[46]

Captives purchased from the Fula caravans by the Rio Pongo merchants were 'employed in cultivating lands' until the annual rainy season brought such work to a halt, whereupon they were sold along with surplus rice to the European ship captains. In 1810, after Britain had abolished the Atlantic slave trade, a Fula leader wrote demanding the English 'give us orders for the selling of slaves,. . . We sell such as know not god, nor know any of the prophets, and they are the Kafirs [non-Muslims], they are like the cattle . . . Allow us to sell slaves' or we shall 'perish through poverty'.[47] Missionaries at the CMS school at Bashia, Rio Pongo, recorded visits to a local chief named William Fernandez, a slave trader at the town of Bramia. Fernandez, whose father was a Portuguese from Bissau, told a missionary in 1812 that 'he had 1,500 slaves and that the abolition act and its principles must not reach their ears'.[48]

Fraser operated in this milieu at Rio Pongo, owned slaves and other proper-ties there that he evaluated at $45,000 in 1813, and transported enslaved Africans to markets in South Carolina and Jamaica as well as his own plantations in Florida. The portion of Fraser's fortune inherited by Elizabeth Fraser Skelton was likely invested in slaving operations similar to those her father had managed decades earlier. In fact, nearly everyone involved in the Fraser estate, on both sides of the Atlantic, engaged in the slave trade or owned slaves and plantations.

The Fraser study also shows that many of the important trading firms along the Pongo and Nunez Rivers were controlled by descendants of Anglo-American men who settled on the African coast and married African women. George E. Brooks, Jr., and Bruce L. Mouser have identified dozens of foreign traders who formed liaisons with African women whose kinship ties to powerful African families permitted them to act as 'culture brokers', providing vital information in trade and political negotiations. Generally, the European 'stranger' negotiated with a local 'chief' for the right to use a specific site for a trade factory. The landlord became a middleman in subsequent trade with first access to imports. Children born of these unions were often educated in England, and, since death rates for Europeans in Africa were high, either the widows or the European-educated Anglo-African children were able to assume control of the businesses.[49]

Elizabeth Fraser's husband, William Skelton, Jr., was the son of an African woman and an Englishman who operated a slave factory at Kissing until his death in 1805. The younger Skelton attended English schools and worked in Liverpool. He also captained ships in the Liverpool trade and carried slaves to the Americas before returning to Rio Pongo to serve an apprenticeship under Samuel Samo, a native of the Netherlands. He eventually opened a business at Kissing in partnership with Mary Ann Fraser's husband. Thomas Gaffery Curtis, the son of an African woman and Benjamin Curtis, a slave trader from New England.[50] Curtis was also educated in Liverpool and worked in that city before returning to Africa to take over his father's business at Fallangia, where he and Mary Ann Fraser married in 1821. William Skelton and Elizabeth Fraser married in 1826 and moved to Victoria, on the Nunez River, a town Bruce Mouser has described as a 'conduit for slaves transported by canoe or overland from the Rio Pongo to Bissau in Portuguese Territory to the north'.[51] Skelton continued to work with his brother-in-law, Thomas G. Curtis, who had brothers at Kissing and an alliance with the ruling Kati family.[52]

Enoch R. Ware, an American trader, visited Elizabeth and William Skelton at Victoria on 15 January 1843 to deliver 'news of [a] fortune' which he could only have heard from Zephaniah Kingsley in December 1842. Ware wrote of Elizabeth:

> [She] looks very well and much younger than when I left here in 1841. She received the infortnation of their acquisitions with much dignity – more so than most white women. It is her inheritance from her father who married in the Rio Pongas, & this one & one sister are the only remaining children. The father was white and the property is the proceeds of an estate in Florida. Mrs. Skelton has never been in the United States & she tells me that it never was her wish to go there – probably on account of the prejudice against coloured people and low state they occupy in society there. She has passed four years in England where coloured persons are received almost or quite on an equality with whites. The daughters [Emma and Mary Ann] have grown very much in a year and a half, the eldest being about sixteen. Skelton has educated them himself [sic]: teaches them all the most useful branches of an English education, added to which is drawing, French, &c. They both write bold mercantile hands, which has been taught them by the father, who is fully competent, having passed a long time in a counting room in England after receiving an excellent education. Probably either of them are better instructed, both in the necessary branches and accomplishments, than many of the young wives among us who go into very good society. Nor has their religious instruction been neglected.[53]

After travelling to factories upriver, Ware returned to 'Mt. Pleasant, Mr. Skelton's Factory', to find him deathly ill. Ware helped Skelton write a will and attended his funeral, all 'Episcopal service for the dead', and witnessed documents for the widow. He met another mulatto slave trader, Benjamin Campbell, and wrote: 'Rather suspect he has designs on Betsy Skelton. Truly she is not an uncomely widow!'[54]

The deaths of Mary Ann and Thomas G. Curtis by 1846 left Elizabeth the only heir to an American fortune, which must have made her even more comely to the Nunez traders. In May 1848 Ware described her as 'about 40 or under' and 'a shrewd, cautious woman who understands her business [and] is respected among her class . . . She is possessed of property, has slaves, but owes as much as she owns or more.'[55] Eventually, Elizabeth married John Nelson Bicaise, a migrant from Trinidad of French and African parentage who became the leading trader on Nunez in the 1850s. It is not known when Elizabeth Fraser Bicaise and John N. Bicaise died, but John was still active as a trader on the Nunez and Pongo Rivers as late as 1880. During the late 1860s and the 1870s, as Victoria Bomba Coifman has established, Bicaise was the representative of French trading interests based at Goree Island.[56]

Abolition of the Atlantic slave trade and pressure from the British Royal Anti-Slavery Squadron drastically curtailed slave exports after 1820, yet slavery persisted on the Nunez and Pongo Rivers into the twentieth century. Caravans from Futa Jalon continued to bring thousands of captives to the Curtis brothers, Richard Wilkinson, John Ormond, Jr., and the Fabers, who put them to work on coffee, peanut, rubber and cotton plantations rather than aboard slave ships. With Elizabeth Fraser Bicaise as a congenial French-speaking hostess, the Bicaise factory attracted European merchants seeking 'legitimate' products raised by plantation slaves. Enoch Ware captured the ambiguity of this trade in 1844, writing that any product he sold 'sooner or later is used for purchasing slaves though it may go through half a dozen hands first . . . each time being carried farther into the interior . . . when finally slaves are bought with it'.[57]

Martin A. Klein concluded that as late as 1900 two-thirds of the residents of Rio Pongo were slaves. Guinea was then a French colony but the new rulers winked at the prevailing labour systems. The marriage alliances of the daughters of Elizabeth Fraser and William Skelton to scions of other trade families kept descendants of John Fraser in the centre of commercial activity. Mary Ann Skelton married Joseph Richmond Lightburn of Farranguia, where slavery stubbornly persisted. Emma Skelton married Nathaniel Isaacs, who purchased Matacong Island in 1844 and made a fortune in the peanut trade. Marie Curtis, reportedly a descendant of Mary Ann Fraser and Thomas G. Curtis, worked 236 slaves on the Nunez until 1908. By 1910 slavery along the Guinea Coast was over, banned by French officials after a mass exodus of slaves across the Sierra Leone border.[58]

By 1910 more than a century after John Fraser arrived on the Rio Pongo, his family's multigenerational participation in the slave trade and slave-operated plantations had ended. A study of Fraser's life and fortune shows that the history of human slavery is complex, multi-national and multi-racial, and that it thrived in Africa and America for a very long time.

Notes

1 Testimony of Francis Richard in File 54. Estate of John Fraser versus the United States government. Patriot War Papers and Patriot War Claims, 1812–1846. Manuscript Collection 31, St. Augustine Historical Society (hereafter PWC 31/54). Other major sources for this study are Robertson, William and Ann, versus Philip R. Yonge and Zephaniah Kingsley. Records of the Superior Court of East Florida, Box 156 File 59, SAHS (hereafter Superior Court 156/59); and the Thomas Napier Papers, South Caroliniana Library, University of South Carolina (hereafter Napier Papers). The only extant probate records of John Fraser's estate in Duval County Probate Records are copies made in 1846 by Judge William F. Crabtree, preserved in the Napier Papers.

2 Phenda was widowed in 1798. Works Progress Administration, *Spanish Land Grants in Florida* (Tallahassee, 1942), Unconfirmed Claims. Vol. I, 119 & Confirmed Claims, III, 141–45; and *American State Papers* IV, 280. Report I, No. 89. Original papers are at Florida State Archives, Tallahassee. Among the witness were Mathew Balthazar, a German native and Thomas Powell, then a resident of Crawford's Island and a partner of T.H. Jackson. Powell was a merchant in Liverpool on 20 Nov. 1826 when his statement was notarized.

   Bruce L. Mouser, in a private correspondence, suggested that Phenda was Baga or Susu, which would have given Fraser a stronger connection for local trade through her family. Using H.L. Macaulay's 1797 Journal (Huntington Library, San Marino, California), Mouser has identified Fraser as an African American who arrived in Sierra Leone in 1797. See 'Women Slavers of Guinea-Conakry', in Claire C. Robertson and Martin A. Klein, *Women and Slavery in Africa* (Madison: University of Wisconsin Press, 1983), p. 325. He was more likely the Caucasian male, 'late of Scotland', who applied for naturalization at Charleston in 1796, or the man who in 1807 gave his age as 38 and his birthplace as Inverness, Scotland. G-3, 129–30, (5 Feb 1796), Court of Common Pleas of Charleston, in Brent H. Holcomb (comp.), *South Carolina Naturalizations*, 1783–1850 (Baltimore: Genealogical Publishing Co. Inc., 1985). p. 93; and Court of Admiralty for the District of South Carolina, National Archives Microfilm 1183, Roll 1. p. 11 (Holcomb. p. 37).

   In a 25 Feb. 1998 private correspondence, Dr Mouser agreed with the identification of the John Fraser I present in this article, but provided evidence of other persons with the same dissertation has been for years the essential source for research on the region. See 'Trade and Politics in the Nunez and Pongo Rivers, 1790–1865' (Indiana University, 1972). See also Mouser, 'Trade, Coasters, and Conflict in the Rio Pongo from 1790 to 1808', *Journal of African History*, 14, 45–64; and 'Landlords-Strangers: A process of Accommodation and Assimilation', *International Journal of African Historical Studies*, 8, pp. 425–40.

3 Charleston merchant Paul Cross recorded purchases of slaves, ivory and gold in the Rio Pongo vicinity circa 1780. In three years he accumulated 60 'prime Negroes' while living 'in country surround with Mahomedians which' wanted 'to remit home'. See Cross, Paul (d. 1784) Papers, South Carolinina Library, University of South Carolina. Irving is mentioned often in the Napier Papers. Thomas Powell to Governor Zespedes, East Florida Papers, Reel 15 Bundle 37 K3 (EFP 15–36 K3 hereafter). EFP, documents from Spanish colonial archives, 1784–1821, preserved in the Library of Congress, abound in examples of imports, ship relocations and renamings, confiscations, and names of owners and captains (George Atkinson, Santiago Cashen, Carlos Hardy, Pablo Fontane, Zebulon Miller, William Scott, Vicente and Bernardino Sanchez, Daniel Hurlbert, Horatio S. Dexter, Luis Mattair, Thomas Backhouse, Enrique Wright, Antonio Sabulache, and Bartolome de Castro y Ferrer, for example). See EFP 58–143 M11: 59–145 B12; 60–146 C12, 61–147 D12; 80–190 H15; 98–233 I18; 98–234 M18: 131–297 P8; 133–299 P7. Reels 81, 133 and 134 are especially useful for ship 'naturalizations', which give names of owners, captains, and former ports, March 11, 1810. Benjamin Curtis, captain of the American frigate *Commodore Hubble*, and John Campbell, captain of the English frigate *William Heathcote*, were detained at Fernandina for lost papers. A Benjamin Curtis resided and traded at Rio Pongo. See EFP 60–146 C12; Christopher Fyfe, *A History of Sierra Leone* (Oxford University Press, 1962), pp. 61, 203, For the final months of slave imports at Charleston, see Michael E. Stevens, '"To get as many slaves as you can": an 1807 Slaving Voyage', *South Carolina*

Historical Magazine, 87 (July 1986), pp. 187–96, and advertisements in the *Charleston Courier*, 1803–1808.

4   Francis Richard. PWC 31/54. See EFP 149–325 R11 for (*Aguila de San Augustin* alias *Eagle of Charleston*, Capt. James Taylor). The *Floridano* alias *Eliza* was used by Hibberson and Yonge in 1813 and sold to Pedro Riser in 1814, EFP 149–326 R10, 9 April 1813, and 165/166–354 W6. EFP 48–198 C16 is List of Ship owners and Captains, 1808.

5   Fraser to Governor, EFP 133–300. 28 April 1810. Sixteen Africans belonged to Ferreyra and the crew. Ferando de la Mazay Arredondo to Governor, 20 Dec. 1810, EFP 173–385, See also Santiago Cashen to Governor White, 30 June 1810, EFP 60–146 C12 for a claim of John Fraser for Negroes sold to James English.

6   *Spanish Land Grants*, Unconfirmed I, p. 119; Confirmed, III, pp. 141–5. George Nightingale, the previous owner of Roundabout, returned with his slaves to his former home in Georgia. Greenfield was purchased from the estate of John McQueen.

7   PWC 31/54. There were 206 full-working hands at Greenfield and 70 at Roundabout. More than half the land of Greenfield was uncleared and heavily timbered with live oak, pine, cedar and cypress, between 1819 and 1825, 2,000 live oak trees of sufficient quality to produce ships for the navy, and 1,000 other valuable trees were felled at Greenfield. The site of Greenfield Plantation is Atlantic Blvd. and Pablo Creek in Jacksonville, Florida, now occupied by Queens Harbor, a luxury residential, yacht, and golf club resort. Roundabout, in rural Nassau County, retains to surface appearance of rice fields, Kingsley and Yonge vs Benjamin Chaires, Trespass Assumpsit 1819–21, Superior Court 121/17 SAHS.

    Pesos and dollars were then equal in value: for British Sterling multiply by 4.4. I converted to dollars throughout the essay. The comparison to contemporary values is based first on my study of newspapers and samples of commodity prices found in more than 100 northeast Florida estate inventories, excluding slaves and land values, from the 1780s to 1860. I concluded that $1 in 1815 is worth at least $30 today, probably closer to $35. The 'Composite Commodity Price Index', in Scott Derks (ed.), *The Value of A Dollar: Prices and Incomes in the United States, 1860–1989* (Detroit: A Manly, Inc., 1994) page 2, sets the value of $1 in 1860 at $30.838 in 1989. Throughout the essay, therefore, I have multiplied by 30 to obtain what is no doubt a conservative estimate of current value.

    Fraser's cotton yield averaged 200 pounds per acre and was valued at 50 cents a pound circa 1812. Rice was valued at seventy-five cents a bushel.

8   Will, Superior Court 156/59, Fraser was often absent from his plantations. See the 1811 militia roll in EFP 60–147 D12. The East Florida economy is explored in my ' "A Class of People Neither Freeman Nor Slaves": From Spanish to American Race Relations in Florida, 1821–1861', *Journal of Social History*, 26 (Spring 1993), pp. 587–609. In 1811 Fraser learned of mismanagement by his agent in Africa, Charles Hickson. For prosecution of Hickson and Samuel Samo of Isle de Los for illegal slaving, see Captain Maxwell to Earl of Liverpool, 1 June 1812, Sierra Leone, in Colonial Office 267/34, No. 15, Public Record Office of Great Britain.

9   The 'Patriot Rebellion' was a combination foreign invasion and internal rebellion covertly arranged by US President James Madison, and his secretary of State, James Monroe. Rembert Patrick's *Florida Fiasco: Rampant Rebels on the Florida-Georgia Border, 1810–1815* (Athens, GA. 1951) is the standard study.

10 Fraser's brother, Archibald, lived in China in the late 1790s. Dead by 1818, his bequest was added to the amount left to Ann. Yonge gave a legacy of $2,222 to 'Fraser of Tarralina', a cousin, in Glasgow. Fraser also bequeathed 'to Mrs. Elizabeth Maria Hughes . . . the sum of two hundred pounds sterling', Fraser also willed $2,200 to children of his uncle and aunt. See Exhibits A, B and J, Duval County, Florida, probate records in the Napier Papers.

11 Fraser's Will, I have been unable to find further information about Phendah's life.

12 The full quote reads 'although they have been born in African I value them as much as if they had been born in wedlock'. It is hard to understand what Fraser meant given the feelings for Phenda and the children found elsewhere in the will, and given the numerous European and American traders and African leaders who testified to the legality of his marriage to Phenda.

13 Philip R. Yonge to Napier, Charleston, SC 7 April 1822, in Superior Court 156/59. Yonge was an executor of Fraser's Florida estate.

14 Maria King, as executor of the estate of Thomas King, petitioned the judge of the Eastern Circuit Court of Florida on 9 February 1849. See P/1407, envelope 7, Napier Papers. The *Florida Republican* (Jacksonville) reported 17 Jan. 1850 that the suit was brought against Samuel L. Burritt, attorney and agent for Elizabeth Skelton and Mary Ann Curtis. Co-defendants were attorney A.M. Reed, Philip R. Yonge, and Thomas Napier. The court ruled the statute of limitations had expired. The Fraser daughters, in Power of Attorney, 1 Jan. 1824, Deed Book D, St Johns County, said James was dead.

15 [Reverend] Renner to Secretary, 24 June 1814, Reel 10 CA1/E4, Church Missionary Society Archives microfilm reels, University of Wisconsin Library (David Henige, Africa Bibliographer). Evidence for the Fraser daughters is in reels 1 through 3 for 1810 through 1816. Dr. Victoria Bomba Coifman kindly sent me copies of her personal notes. An entry received at CMS' London headquarters, 15 May 1815, indicates that a contribution was received at the Bashia school for the Fraser children. See C AI/E6. No. 2, The Society Account with the missionaries in Bashia Settlement. Received (London) 15 May by the [vessel] Mary Ann.

16 *American State Papers* IV, p. 280: also in John Fraser File, Spanish Lane Grants, Department of National Resources. Tallahassee. A document of 2 July 1826, witnessed by Rio Pongo chiefs and merchants dates Eleanor's death. Also, Mouser, 'Women Slavers', 327, and Enoch Richmond Ware, sworn testimony, 18 March 1848, Napier Papers. Ware recorded Mary Ann's death.

17 'Produce of the land' refers to either export slaves or grain or cotton textiles. The 'factory' description comes from Mouser, 'Women Slaves', p. 326, and from Joseph Hawkin, *A History of a Voyage to the Coast of Africa* (Troy NY, 1797), pp. 155–7. See a similar description by Mouser in 'Iles de Los as bulking center in the slave trade, 1750–1800', *Revue française d'historie d'outre-mer*, 83 (1996), p. 83.

18 Captain Theophilus Conneau, *A Slaver's Log Book or 20 Years' Residence in Africa: The Original [1853] Manuscript* (New York: Avon Books, 1976). The 1977 printing, with introduction by Marbel M. Smyth, was used here (pp. 75–82). I thank Svend E. Holsoe for reminding me of this source.

19 Fraser Will, Superior Court 156/59. Christopher Fyfe, *A History of Sierra Leone*, pp. 120–1, says Samuel Samo and Charles Hickson were seized in 1812 at Isles de Los and brought to Freetown to be tried under the Slave Felony Act of 1811. Samo, of Dutch ancestry and a 16-year resident of Isles de Los was found guilty and was later pardoned: Hickson was acquitted but found guilty on another charge in 1814. Hickson was John Fraser's agent circa 1810. Samo and Leigh are called 'unrepentant slavers residing on the Iles de Los' in George E. Brookes, *Yankee Traders Old Coasters, & African Middlemen: A History of American Legitimate Trade with West Africa in the Nineteenth Century* (Boston: Boston University Press, 1970), p. 171.

20 There is a reference to Kingsley at Rio Pongo in the 'Diary of Uncle Jack' in the New York Public Library. Sitiki was Uncle Jack's boyhood name in Africa. Sitiki, possibly a Maninka, captured when a boy in Futa Jallon and carried to the coast, possibly at a 'factory' on Rio Pongo. He became the slave of Buckingham Smith of St Augustine, in whose papers the 'Diary of Uncle Jack' is found. Dr Patricia C. Griffin is writing a biography of Sitiki/Uncle Jack. I thank her for this reference.

21 Inventory and Appraisement, Exhibits B, C, and D, Fernandina, 13 May 1815, Superior Court 156/59. Appraisers counted 79 males, 66 females, and 21 children. Six died subsequently, two were without value, thus the average value of the 158 slaves acquired by Kingsley and Yonge was $235. Evaluations of Florida estates in Duval County over seventy years under British, Spanish and American governments show consistency, human property was two to four times higher than the combined total of land, buildings, machinery, and livestock.

For evidence that the Gambia/Guinea/Sierra Leone coast continued to supply enslaved Africans for the Charleston market, look at the 1803–8 issues of the *Charleston Courier*, specifically at the ports of departure for slave ships arriving then. For African backgrounds see Daniel C. Littlefield, *Rice and Slaves: Ethnicity and the Slave Trade in Colonial South Carolina* (Baton Rouge: Louisiana State University Press, 1981), chapters 3 and 4; Judith A. Carney. 'From Hands to Tutors: African Expertise in the South Carolina Rice Economy', *Agricultural History*, 67 (Summer 1993), pp. 1–30; John Thornton, *Africa and Africans in the Making of the Atlantic World, 1400–1680* (Cambridge: Cambridge University Press. 1992); Philip D. Morgan. 'The Cultural Implications of the Atlantic Slave Trade: African Regional Origins, American Destinations and New World Developments', in David Eltis and David Richardson (eds.), *Routes to Slavery: Direction, Ethnicity and Mortality in the Atlantic Slave Trade* (London and Portland, OR: Frank Cass, 1997), pp. 123–45; and Eltis and Richardson, 'The Numbers Game' and Routes to Slavery' and 'West African and the Transatlantic Slave Trade: New Evidence of Long-Run Trends', in *Routes to Slavery*, pp. 1–15, 16–35.

22   Kingsley to Coppinger, 17 Jan. 1816, Testamentarios, EFP 165–16, 14 Feb. 1814.

23   Coppinger to Kingsley, St Augustine, 24 Jan 1816, in ibid. The exact number of slaves lost was not recorded. At least 20 escaped to a British naval vessel in 1814, for which the estate received $4,200. See Napier Papers and EFP 165/166–354 W6. On 10 June 1815 Kingsley submitted deeds for four plantations valued at more than $52,000; Yonge for three plantations and a house in St Augustine (EFP 168–364, Escrituras, 25 May 1820).

24   For the lawsuit under Spain see EFP 145–317 Q4 doc. 16; for the refiled lawsuit see Superior Court 156/59. The compromise is in Gould to Napier, 17 January 1843, 16 Nov. 1846, in P/1407 Box marked July 1804–Dec. 1857, Napier Papers.

25   See Superior Court 131/17 for theft of trees, and 156/59 for Yonge's administration; for interest payments see Napier Papers. The St Augustine *Florida Herald*, 5 Aug. 1829, advertised: 'To Rent. Plantation Greenfield, San Pablo, on St Johns River, belonging to the Estate of John Fraser. Dec., will be rented to the highest bidder at public auction on the Premises for the next ensuing year on Saturday, the fifth day of September next, between the hours of twelve and two o'clock, occupancy to prepare for crop may be had immediately and full possession for the year will be given on the first day of January 1830'.

26   St. Johns County Public Records, Deed Book D, 1 Jan. 1824. Twelve months before the sisters authorized Joseph Delespine, an East Florida planter, to recover their father's Negroes, lands, money and claims. For Lightburn see Mouser, Fyfe, and Brooks.

27   Skelton, acting also for his brother-in-law. Thomas Gaffery Curtis, signed the power of attorney in Liverpool on 10 Nov, 1826. See John Fraser file, original Spanish Land Grant papers. Florida State Archives, Tallahassee.

28   Duval County Public Records, Archibald Transcripts of Deed Records (11 Sept. 1835), 24–25, Greenfield became the property of Cyprian Cross in 1849, then Samuel Calvert, and in 1853 Sarah M. Vaught. Other owners prior to 1861 were Ephraim Harrison and James W. Bryant. See ibid., 36, 42, 51, 63–4, and 78–79. The 500-acre Roundabout sold for $500 in 1848 to Clements M. Caldwell by Elizabeth Skelton, and sole heir and legatee of Fraser, see Nassau County Public Records, Deed Book D (7 April 1848), 53–4. P.R. Yonge said that he transmitted the $13,000 to Skelton via Thomas Powell in Liverpool (Napier Papers).

29   Details of Kingsley's 21 Sept. 1833 indenture to William and Elizabeth Fraser Skelton, Thomas G. and Mary Ann Fraser Curtis, and Ann Robertson, are in deed Book A, 89–97, St. Johns County Courthouse. New York Attorney William W. Campbell represented the Fraser and Curtis families. Payment was in three equal payments, with a mortgage on White Oak Plantation as security. For its sale see Deed Book A, Nassau Country Public Records, 80–86. Kingsley previously announced plans to sell his properties and leave Florida. See *Florida Herald*, 9 Aug. 1832, placing Kingsley B. Gibbs and John S. Sammis, in charge of his affairs. See also my study of his African wife *Anna Kingsley* (St Augustine Historical Society, Rev. Ed., 1997), and 'From Spanish to American Race Relations in Florida, 1921–1861'.

30   25 March 1836. Elias B. Gould, a St Augustine attorney employed by Napier, sent details of Kingsley's payments to Ann Robertson. See Nov, 2, 1846, P/1407 Envelope 3, Napier Papers.

31   The Fraser claim is PWC 31/54, see part 11 of MS Collection MC 31, St. Augustine Historical Society, for a summary of procedures in the Patriot War Claims. The 1819

treaty is discussed in David J. Weber, *The Spanish Frontier in North America* (New Haven: Yale University Press, 1992), pp. 229–301.

32 See Gibbs' Journal entry for 3 and 8 Sept. 1842, in Jacqueline K. Fretwell (ed.), *Kingsley Beatty Gibbs and His Journal of 1840–1843* (St Augustine Historical Society, 1984), pp. 29–30.

33 Fretwell, *Kingsley Beatty Gibbs*, p. 31. It is not clear from the incomplete records whether Kingsley or Jose Mariano Hernandez, a wealthy planter and attorney with influence in Washington from his days as Territorial Delegate from Florida to the US Congress, collected the attorney fees of one-third of the settlement. See also Kingsley's probate file.

34 Yonge to Napier, 4 May 1818., Napier Papers. Gibbs stayed in New York for seven weeks, charging $479 for transportation and room and board. Hernandez demanded $10,000 plus expenses. Burritt acquired the power of attorney on 9 March 1844. Details are in Probate File of Zephaniah Kingsley, Duval County. For more on Burritt see my 'Freedom Was as Close as the River: African Americans and the Civil War in Northeast Florida'. David R. Colburn and Jane L. Landers, (ed.), *The African American Heritage of Florida* (Gainesville: University Press of Florida, 1995), pp. 157–84. See also Kingsley probate file.

35 Napier to Woodruff, 6 Sept. 1851, Napier Papers. Dozens of letters follow, including a summary written 6 Sept 1851.

36 Benedict to Napier, 2 Dec. 1846, Envelope 3, Napier Papers. The firm was at 70 Wall Street; Dana, Woodruff & Leonard at 56.

37 Woodruff to Napier, 23 Nov. 1851, Envelope 13, Napier Papers.

38 Napier to Woodruff, 8 Dec. 1846, Napier Papers.

39 See Note 28.

40 23 Aug. 1848, Envelope 6, Napier Papers.

41 Napier to Gould, 2 Oct. 1849, Envelope 8, Ibid.

42 Wills and Letters of Administration, St. Johns Co., 191, and Gould to Napier, 1 March 1850, Napier Papers.

43 For this challenge and some with different outcomes see *Anna Kingsley* and 'From Spanish to American Race Relations'.

44 Deed Book K. 89–97, St. Johns County Courthouse. Elizabeth and Mary Ann Fraser, and Robertson, divided $20,250 minus attorney fees.

45 Extracts of the Evidence of Mr. Matthews given to Committee of Inquiry Counsel, March 1788, Additional Manuscripts 18272, Long Papers, British Library. Especially valuable for evidence of gain production at slave plantations in the Rio Pongo area is Bruce Mouser's chapter in this volume.

46 Ibid.

47 Three Letters of Imam of Foota Jaloo of 1810, translated by J. Perronet Thomps, Capt of 17th Light Dragoons and formerly Governor of Sierra Leone, CO 268/8.

48 From CMS Archives (Victoria Bomba Coifman's notes): [Rev.] Butscher to Secretary, Sierra Leone, 22 October 1811 and 24 Oct. 1810; [Rev.] Renner to Secretary, 8 June 1812: all from Bashia. They also purchased large amounts of rice and 'Soosoo cloth . . . or country cloth to make trousers' from villages in the vicinity. For Fernandez, see also Mouser, 'Trader and Politics in the Nunez and Pongo Rivers', p. 310.

49 'Women Slavers', p. 321. Brooks has written extensively on 'landlord–stranger' relationships. Most relevant for this study are 'A Nhara of the Guinea-Bissau Region: Mae Aurelia Correia', in Robertson and Klein, *Women and Slavery in Africa*, pp. 295–319; 'The Signares of Saint-Louis and Goree: Women Entrepreneurs in Eighteenth-Century Senegal', in J.J. Hafkin and E.G. Bay, *Women in Africa: Studies in Social and Economic Change* (Stanford University Press, 1976); and *Yankee Traders*.

50 11 March 1810, an American frigate, the *Commodore Hubble*, Captain Benjamin Curtis, was detained at Fernandina for lack of registration and passport. EFP 60–146 C12. See Mediterranean Sea Passes, ADM 7/120. Public Record Office, for evidence of Skeleton captaining on African and American passages. Similar entries or 1804–1807 for George Irving, John McClure, Thomas Boyd (mentioned elsewhere in this essay) can be found.

51 Mouser, 'Women Salvers', p. 328.

52 Enoch Ware was with Thomas Curtis at Fallangia in Dec. 1840. He does not mention Mary Ann. Thomas is described as the eldest of three Curtises, one of whom, George, lived at another location on Rio Pongo. Norman R. Bennett and George E. Brooks, Jr., editors, *New England Merchants in Africa: A History Through Documents, 1802–1865* (Boston University Press: 1965), pp. 288–9. See also Victoria Bomba Coifman, 'The Western West African and European Frontier: Contributions from Former Archbishop of Conakry Raymond-Marie Tchidimbo's Autobiography for West African History, in Robert W. Harms *et al.*, *Path Toward the Past: African Historical Essays in Honor of Jan Vansina* (Atlanta, GA.: African Studies Association Press, 1994), pp. 273–92.

53 Bennett and Brooks, *New England Merchants in Africa*, pp. 303–4.

54 Ibid., pp. 304, 313–28. See also Napier Papers for depositions Ware gave in New York. Ware stopped often at Victoria. He first met Burritt on the African Coast, and refers to Thomas G. Curtis and the death of his wife, Mary Ann Fraser. Campbell, also a mulatto trader, had earlier lived at Farringuia with Styles Lightbourn's widow, Isabella, until a trade war broke out on Rio Pongo. I have seen no evidence to connect Judge William Campbell of New York and Benjamin Campbell of Rio Pongo as kin.

55 Testimony of Enoch Ware, 18 March 1848, Napier Papers. Ware criticized the two children of Mary Ann and Thomas G. Curtis, calling William, then age 25, 'weak' and a 'barbarian . . . below his class', and the unnamed daughter, then 19, 'uneducated' and immoral. See also Coifman, 'The Western West African and European Frontier': for Curtis and Skelton descent lines, based on Mouser, 'Trade and Politics in the Nunez and Pongo Rivers, 1790–1865', especially Appendix B 308–19. Two documents in the Spanish Land Grant files at Florida State Archives may add to that analysis; both dated 29 June 1826 and signed at 'Rio Pongas on the Coast of Africa' by Stiles Ed Lightbourn, Richard Wilkinson, Benjamin Curtis, Mongo Barky (Chief of Bashia Branch, Rio Pongas, signed on Arabic) and Mongo Besenty (Chief of Bahia Branch, in Arabic), Mary Ann Fraser at her home in Fallangia, William Skelton, and George Irving. On Bicaise, see Coifman. 'The Western West African and European Frontier', pp. 294–6, and Brooks, *Yankee Traders*, p. 203, and consider the 14 Dec. 1782, document in the Paul Cross Papers, cited earlier, which originated at Isles de Los, signed by John Ormond, Jan E. Colley, William Harrison, Elias Harrison and Thomas Bacaise (or Bicaise).

56 Coifman, 'West African and European Frontier', pp. 284–6.

57 Mouser, 'Trade and Politics in the Nunez and Pongo Rivers, 1790–1865', ch.4; Brooks, *Yankee Traders*, pp. 193–203, 205, and Fyfe, *A History of Sierra Leone*, pp. 255–7; W.E.F. Ward, *The Royal Navy and the Slavers* (New York: Pantheon Books, 1969).

58 Klein describes Marie Curtis as 'a member of an old Mulatto family' in 'Slave Resistance and Slave Emancipation in Coastal Guinea', Suzanne Miers and Richard Roberts, *The End of Slavery in African* (Madison, WI: University of Wisconsin Press, 1988), pp. 203–219. Fyfe, *A History of Sierra Leone*, 61, identifies Benjamin Curtis as a migrant from Boston. Also see Mouser, 'Women Slavers', p. 329, and Brooks, *Yankee Traders*, pp. 203, 206.

Index